# Contemporary
# Literary Criticism

# Guide to Gale Literary Criticism Series

| For criticism on | Consult these Gale series |
|---|---|
| Authors now living or who died after December 31, 1959 | *CONTEMPORARY LITERARY CRITICISM (CLC)* |
| Authors who died between 1900 and 1959 | *TWENTIETH-CENTURY LITERARY CRITICISM (TCLC)* |
| Authors who died between 1800 and 1899 | *NINETEENTH-CENTURY LITERATURE CRITICISM (NCLC)* |
| Authors who died between 1400 and 1799 | *LITERATURE CRITICISM FROM 1400 TO 1800 (LC)*<br><br>*SHAKESPEAREAN CRITICISM (SC)* |
| Authors who died before 1400 | *CLASSICAL AND MEDIEVAL LITERATURE CRITICISM (CMLC)* |
| Black writers of the past two hundred years | *BLACK LITERATURE CRITICISM (BLC)* |
| Authors of books for children and young adults | *CHILDREN'S LITERATURE REVIEW (CLR)* |
| Dramatists | *DRAMA CRITICISM (DC)* |
| Hispanic writers of the late nineteenth and twentieth centuries | *HISPANIC LITERATURE CRITICISM (HLC)* |
| Native North American writers and orators of the eighteenth, nineteenth, and twentieth centuries | *NATIVE NORTH AMERICAN LITERATURE (NNAL)* |
| Poets | *POETRY CRITICISM (PC)* |
| Short story writers | *SHORT STORY CRITICISM (SSC)* |
| Major authors from the Renaissance to the present | *WORLD LITERATURE CRITICISM, 1500 TO THE PRESENT (WLC)* |

ISSN 0091-3421

Volume 94

# Contemporary Literary Criticism

Excerpts from Criticism of the Works
of Today's Novelists, Poets, Playwrights,
Short Story Writers, Scriptwriters, and
Other Creative Writers

**Brigham Narins**
**Deborah A. Stanley**
EDITORS

**George H. Blair**
**Jeff Chapman**
**Pamela S. Dear**
**Daniel Jones**
**John D. Jorgenson**
**Aarti D. Stephens**
**Polly A. Vedder**
**Thomas Wiloch**
**Kathleen Wilson**
**Janet Witalec**
ASSOCIATE EDITORS

GALE

DETROIT · NEW YORK · TORONTO · LONDON

Library of Congress Catalog Card Number 76-46132
ISBN 0-7876-0768-1
ISSN 0091-3421

Printed in the United States of America
10  9  8  7  6  5  4  3  2  1

# Contents

Preface  vii

Acknowledgments  xi

# Preface

## A Comprehensive Information Source
## on Contemporary Literature

Named "one of the twenty-five most distinguished reference titles published during the past twenty-five years" by *Reference Quarterly,* the *Contemporary Literary Criticism (CLC)* series provides readers with critical commentary and general information on more than 2,000 authors now living or who died after December 31, 1959. Previous to the publication of the first volume of *CLC* in 1973, there was no ongoing digest monitoring scholarly and popular sources of critical opinion and explication of modern literature. *CLC,* therefore, has fulfilled an essential need, particularly since the complexity and variety of contemporary literature makes the function of criticism especially important to today's reader.

## Scope of the Series

*CLC* presents significant passages from published criticism of works by creative writers. Since many of the authors covered by *CLC* inspire continual critical commentary, writers are often represented in more than one volume. There is, of course, no duplication of reprinted criticism.

Authors are selected for inclusion for a variety of reasons, among them the publication or dramatic production of a critically acclaimed new work, the reception of a major literary award, revival of interest in past writings, or the adaptation of a literary work to film or television.

Attention is also given to several other groups of writers-authors of considerable public interest—about whose work criticism is often difficult to locate. These include mystery and science fiction writers, literary and social critics, foreign writers, and authors who represent particular ethnic groups within the United States.

## Format of the Book

Each *CLC* volume contains about 500 individual excerpts taken from hundreds of book review periodicals, general magazines, scholarly journals, monographs, and books. Entries include critical evaluations spanning from the beginning of an author's career to the most current commentary. Interviews, feature articles, and other published writings that offer insight into the author's works are also presented. Students, teachers, librarians, and researchers will find that the generous excerpts and supplementary material in *CLC* provide them with vital information required to write a term paper, analyze a poem, or lead a book discussion group. In addition, complete bibliographical citations note the original source and all of the information necessary for a term paper footnote or bibliography.

## Features

A *CLC* author entry consists of the following elements:

■ The **Author Heading** cites the author's name in the form under which the author has most commonly published, followed by birth date, and death date when applicable. Uncertainty as to a birth or death date is indicated by a question mark.

- A **Portrait** of the author is included when available.

- A brief **Biographical and Critical Introduction** to the author and his or her work precedes the excerpted criticism. The first line of the introduction provides the author's full name, pseudonyms (if applicable), nationality, and a listing of genres in which the author has written. To provide users with easier access to information, the biographical and critical essay included in each author entry is divided into four categories: "Introduction," "Biographical Information," "Major Works," and "Critical Reception." The introductions to single-work entries—entries that focus on well known and frequently studied books, short stories, and poems—are similarly organized to quickly provide readers with information on the plot and major characters of the work being discussed, its major themes, and its critical reception. Previous volumes of *CLC* in which the author has been featured are also listed in the introduction.

- A list of **Principal Works** notes the most important writings by the author. When foreign-language works have been translated into English, the English-language version of the title follows in brackets.

- The **Excerpted Criticism** represents various kinds of critical writing, ranging in form from the brief review to the scholarly exegesis. Essays are selected by the editors to reflect the spectrum of opinion about a specific work or about an author's literary career in general. The excerpts are presented chronologically, adding a useful perspective to the entry. All titles by the author featured in the entry are printed in boldface type, which enables the reader to easily identify the works being discussed. Publication information (such as publisher names and book prices) and parenthetical numerical references (such as footnotes or page and line references to specific editions of a work) have been deleted at the editor's discretion to provide smoother reading of the text.

- Critical essays are prefaced by **Explanatory Notes** as an additional aid to readers. These notes may provide several types of valuable information, including: the reputation of the critic, the importance of the work of criticism, the commentator's approach to the author's work, the purpose of the criticism, and changes in critical trends regarding the author.

- A complete **Bibliographical Citation** designed to help the user find the original essay or book precedes each excerpt.

- Whenever possible, a recent, previously unpublished **Author Interview** accompanies each entry.

- A concise **Further Reading** section appears at the end of entries on authors for whom a significant amount of criticism exists in addition to the pieces reprinted in *CLC*. Each citation in this section is accompanied by a descriptive annotation describing the content of that article. Materials included in this section are grouped under various headings (e.g., Biography, Bibliography, Criticism, and Interviews) to aid users in their search for additional information. Cross-references to other useful sources published by Gale Research in which the author has appeared are also included: *Authors in the News, Black Writers, Children's Literature Review, Contemporary Authors, Dictionary of Literary Biography, DISCovering Authors, Drama Criticism, Hispanic Literature Criticism, Hispanic Writers, Native North American Literature, Poetry Criticism, Something about the Author, Short Story Criticism, Contemporary Authors Autobiography Series,* and *Something about the Author Autobiography Series.*

## Other Features

*CLC* also includes the following features:

- An **Acknowledgments** section lists the copyright holders who have granted permission to reprint material in this volume of *CLC*. It does not, however, list every book or periodical reprinted or consulted during the preparation of the volume.

- Each new volume of *CLC* includes a **Cumulative Topic Index,** which lists all literary topics treated in *CLC, NCLC, TCLC,* and *LC 1400-1800.*

- A **Cumulative Author Index** lists all the authors who have appeared in the various literary criticism series published by Gale Research, with cross-references to Gale's biographical and autobiographical series. A full listing of the series referenced there appears on the first page of the indexes of this volume. Readers will welcome this cumulated author index as a useful tool for locating an author within the various series. The index, which lists birth and death dates when available, will be particularly valuable for those authors who are identified with a certain period but whose death dates cause them to be placed in another, or for those authors whose careers span two periods. For example, Ernest Hemingway is found in *CLC,* yet F. Scott Fitzgerald, a writer often associated with him, is found in *Twentieth-Century Literary Criticism.*

- A **Cumulative Nationality Index** alphabetically lists all authors featured in *CLC* by nationality, followed by numbers corresponding to the volumes in which the authors appear.

- An alphabetical **Title Index** accompanies each volume of *CLC*. Listings are followed by the author's name and the corresponding page numbers where the titles are discussed. English translations of foreign titles and variations of titles are cross-referenced to the title under which a work was originally published. Titles of novels, novellas, dramas, films, record albums, and poetry, short story, and essay collections are printed in italics, while all individual poems, short stories, essays, and songs are printed in roman type within quotation marks; when published separately (e.g., T. S. Eliot's poem *The Waste Land),* the titles of long poems are printed in italics.

- In response to numerous suggestions from librarians, Gale has also produced a **Special Paperbound Edition** of the *CLC* title index. This annual cumulation, which alphabetically lists all titles reviewed in the series, is available to all customers and is typically published with every fifth volume of *CLC*. Additional copies of the index are available upon request. Librarians and patrons will welcome this separate index: it saves shelf space, is easy to use, and is recyclable upon receipt of the next edition.

## Citing *Contemporary Literary Criticism*

When writing papers, students who quote directly from any volume in the Literary Criticism Series may use the following general forms to footnote reprinted criticism. The first example pertains to material drawn from periodicals, the second to material reprinted in books:

[1]Alfred Cismaru, "Making the Best of It," *The New Republic,* 207, No. 24, (December 7, 1992), 30, 32; excerpted and reprinted in *Contemporary Literary Criticism,* Vol. 85, ed. Christopher Giroux (Detroit: Gale Research, 1995), pp. 73-4.

[2]Yvor Winters, *The Post-Symbolist Methods* (Allen Swallow, 1967); excerpted and reprinted in *Contemporary Literary Criticism,* Vol. 85, ed. Christopher Giroux (Detroit: Gale Research, 1995), pp. 223-26.

# Suggestions Are Welcome

The editors hope that readers will find *CLC* a useful reference tool and welcome comments about the work. Send comments and suggestions to: Editors, *Contemporary Literary Criticism,* Gale Research, Penobscot Building, Detroit, MI 48226-4094.

# Acknowledgments

The editors wish to thank the copyright holders of the excerpted criticism included in this volume and the permissions managers of many book and magazine publishing companies for assisting us in securing reproduction rights. We are also grateful to the staffs of the Detroit Public Library, the Library of Congress, the University of Detroit Library, Wayne State University Purdy/Kresge Library Complex, and the University of Michigan Libraries for making their resources available to us. Following is a list of the copyright holders who have granted us permission to reproduce material in this volume of *CLC*. Every effort has been made to trace copyright, but if omissions have been made, please let us know.

## COPYRIGHTED EXCERPTS IN *CLC*, VOLUME 94, WERE REPRODUCED FROM THE FOLLOWING PERIODICALS:

*African American Review,* v. 27, Spring, 1993 for "Yusef Komunyakaa: The Unified Vision--Canonization and Humanity" by Alvin Aubert. Copyright © Indiana State University. Reproduced by permission of the author.—*The American Book Review,* v. 14, December, 1992-January, 1993. © 1993 by *The American Book Review*. Reproduced by permission of the publisher.—*American Indian Culture and Research Journal,* v. 4, 1980 for "The Uses of Oral Tradition in Six Contemporary Native American Poets" by James Ruppert. Copyright © 1980 James Ruppert. Reproduced by permission of the author.—*The Antigonish Review,* n. 61, Spring, 1985 for "Rereading Jacques Ferron" by Betty Bednarski. Copyright 1985 by the author. Reproduced by permission of the author.—*The Antioch Review,* v. 32, 1973. Copyright © 1973 by the Antioch Review Inc. Reproduced by permission of the Editors.—*Ariel: A Review of International English Literature,* v. 17, July, 1986 for "Holy Women and Unholy Men: Ruth Prawer Jhabvala Confronts the Non-rational" by H. Summerfield. Copyright © 1986 The Board of Governors, The University of Calgary. Reproduced by permission of the publisher and the author.—*Arizona Quarterly,* v. 25, 1969 for "The Prime of Miss Jean Brodie: Muriel Spark Bridges the Credibility Gap" by Ann B. Dobie. Copyright © 1969 by Arizona Quarterly. Reproduced by permission of the publisher and the author.—*Artforum,* v. XXXI, January, 1993 for "Left Hooks" by Beth Coleman. © 1993 Artforum International Magazine, Inc. Reproduced by permission of the publisher and the author.—*Belles Lettres: A Review of Books by Women,* v. 10, Fall, 1994; v. 10, Summer, 1995. Both reproduced by permission of the publisher.—*The Black Scholar,* v. 14, January-February, 1983. Copyright 1983 by *The Black Scholar*. Reproduced by permission of the publisher.—*The Bloomsbury Review,* v. 10, May-June, 1990 for "Retrieving the Melodies of the Heart" by Robert F. Gish; v. 10, May-June, 1990 for "The Poetry of Truth" by Samuel Maio; v. 12, September, 1992 for "Weaving the Line of the Spirit" by Carl L. Bankston III. Copyright © by Owaissa Communications Company, Inc., 1990, 1992. All reproduced by permission of the respective authors.—*Book World--The Washington Post,* May 14, 1995. © 1995, Washington Post Writers Group. Reproduced with permission.—*Booklist,* v. 80, March 15, 1984. Copyright © 1984 by the American Library Association. Reproduced by permission of the publisher.—*Books in Canada,* v. 17, January-February, 1988 for "La Conference Inachevee" by Betty Bednarski; v. 18, May, 1989 for "Rude Girls" by M. Nourbese Philip. Both reproduced by permission of the respective authors.—*The Boston Globe,* July 19, 1995. © 1995 Globe Newspaper Co. Reproduced courtesy of *The Boston Globe*.—*Brick: A Journal of Reviews,* n. 24, Spring, 1985. Reproduced by permission of the publisher.—*Callaloo,* v. 13, Spring, 1990. Copyright © 1990 by Charles H. Rowell. All rights reserved. Reproduced by permission of the publisher.—*The Canadian Forum,* v. LVI, October, 1976 for "Shared Concerns" by Paul Socken; v. LII, June, 1992 for a review of "Tales from the Uncertain Country" by Paul Socken. Both reproduced by permission of the author.—*Chicago Tribune--Books,* February 12, 1995. © copyrighted 1995, Chicago Tribune Company. All rights reserved. Used with permission.—*Choice,* v. 22, November, 1984; v. 25, September, 1987. Copyright © 1984, 1987 by the American Library Association. Both reproduced by permission of the publisher.—*Christianity and Crisis,* v. 49, October 9, 1989 for a review of "Talking Back: Thinking Feminist, Thinking Black" by Delores S. Williams. Reproduced by permission of the author.—*College Literature,* v. 18, October, 1971. Copyright © 1971 by West Chester University. Reproduced by permission of the publisher.—*The Commonweal,* v. 75, February 23, 1962. Copyright © 1962, renewed 1990

# Pat Barker

## 1943-

English novelist.

For further information on her life and works, see *CLC,* Volume 32.

## INTRODUCTION

Barker is one of the most highly acclaimed novelists of the last two decades. Her work is praised for its spare, direct prose, insightful depictions of working-class life, and sensitive evocation of historical figures and events. Barker's first works focused on the lives of working-class English women, earning her the label of feminist writer from several critics. Her later works—including the World War I trilogy comprised of *Regeneration* (1991), *The Eye in the Door* (1993), and the Booker Prize-winning *The Ghost Road* (1995)—refine and expand her thematic range. Critic Rob Nixon wrote: "Few novelists are so unsentimentally animated by people's ability to chalk up small, shaky, but estimable victories over remorseless circumstances. Readers come away from all her novels with an altered feeling for the boundaries and capacities of human courage."

### Biographical Information

Barker was born in Thornaby-on-Tees, England, to working-class parents. She attended the London School of Economics and Political Science, earning a B.S. degree in 1965 and going on to teach for several years afterward. Her initial, unpublished literary work dealt primarily with the middle-class environment that her education, profession, and marriage (to a professor of zoology) had provided her. After attending a writing class taught by English novelist and short story writer Angela Carter, Barker was inspired and encouraged to write about the milieu in which she was raised. Her literary career began at this point, and she has gone on to win numerous awards.

### Major Works

Barker's first novel, *Union Street* (1982), concerns seven neighboring women near a factory in northeast England. Life for them is trying and unrewarding: some are married to alcoholics; others are victims of spousal abuse. All of them, however, are resigned to suffering. Critics note that the bleakness of the portrait is offset by the strength of perseverance the women display—their refusal to succumb to the pain in their lives is depicted as a cause for hope. Like *Union Street, Blow Your House Down* (1984) details events in the lives of several women in working-class, industrial England. Unlike her previous characters, though, these women are prostitutes, and their problems include not only abuse and financial insecurity, but physical survival in a red-light district stalked by a vicious, Jack the Ripper-

like killer. *The Century's Daughter* (1986) offers further insights into the hardships of being a woman in industrialized England. The protagonist, an octogenarian named Liza Jarrett Wright, recounts her life to Steven, a homosexual social worker who befriends her while trying to move her out of her dangerous, decaying neighborhood. Liza tells Steven of her childhood spent in poverty and neglect. She also recalls her son, killed during World War II, and her promiscuous daughter, whose child Liza raised herself. Barker examines the male psyche in *The Man Who Wasn't There* (1989), a novel about Colin, a fatherless teenager who concocts fantasies about himself and his absent parent in an effort to alleviate the grief he feels. Barker's World War I trilogy is set primarily in England and centers on the historical figure of Dr. William H. R. Rivers, the anthropologist and neurologist who became famous for his work on the treatment of "shell shock"—the condition commonly referred to today as post-traumatic stress disorder. *Regeneration* is a fictionalized account of the relationship between Rivers and Siegfried Sassoon, the esteemed English poet who was also a hero in the Royal Army during the first world war. Sassoon was sent to the Craiglockhart War Hospital in Edinburgh in 1917 after writing a letter in which he denounced England's motives in the war and stated his refusal to suffer on behalf of an ungrateful nation. Rivers, then an army psychologist, takes his case and soon realizes the similarities between the stresses suffered by soldiers in the trenches and those experienced by poor women on the home front. *The Eye in the Door* continues Rivers's story, this time focusing on a bisexual lieutenant named Billy Prior (a purely fictional character) who has become mute and suffers from amnesia as a result of his wartime experiences. Prior returns to combat in *The Ghost Road*, the concluding volume of the trilogy. The narrative encompasses Rivers's therapeutic work, his musings on past experiences as an anthropologist among Melanesian head-hunters, and Prior's life on the frontlines as the war and the novel move toward their conclusion: the battle at Sambre-Oise Canal in November, 1918.

### Critical Reception

Barker's work has received unusually high and consistent praise. Her first four novels, those devoted to the lives of the dispossessed in English industrial centers, have been lauded for their realism, dialogue, and lack of sentimentality. *Union Street* was hailed by Eileen Fairweather as a "long over-due working-class masterpiece." The World War I trilogy, which many reviewers feel constitutes Barker's most accomplished work, is hailed by Peter Parker as "one of the richest and most rewarding works of fiction in recent times."

---

# PRINCIPAL WORKS

*Union Street*  (novel)  1982
*Blow Your House Down*  (novel)   1984
*The Century's Daughter*  (novel)   1986
*The Man Who Wasn't There*  (novel)   1989
*\*Regeneration*  (novel)  1991
*\*The Eye in the Door*  (novel)   1993
*\*The Ghost Road*  (novel)   1995

\*These novels constitute a trilogy focusing on World War I.

---

# CRITICISM

### Robert Christgau   (review date October 1986)

SOURCE: A review of *The Century's Daughter*, in *The Village Voice Literary Supplement,* No. 49, October, 1986, pp. 3-4.

[*In the following positive review of* The Century's Daughter, *Christgau argues that Barker's themes are well served by the novel's flashback structure.*]

As 84-year-old Liza Wright searched for her past in a bed of coals to begin Chapter 2 of Pat Barker's *The Century's*

*Daughter,* I felt annoyed if not betrayed. Just when I was all set to find out how Liza was going to get on with the social worker she'd met in Chapter 1, Barker was pulling a flashback on me. What a drag. But then I remembered that although Barker adheres skillfully and unquestioningly to realist convention, you don't read her for narrative momentum—she has no special gift for that particular illusion of coherence. The most formally satisfying of her three books—1982's *Union Street,* a collection of loosely interlocking stories whose ungainly overall shape suggests the chancy pattern of casual-to-intimate community that unfolds within it—doesn't pretend to be a novel, and 1984's *Blow Your House Down,* which does, regularly interrupts its whodunit conceit.

No, what makes Barker such a treat isn't plot. It's realism's other little secret: documentary value. Just as you read London to learn about the sea or Mann to learn about the German bourgeoisie or Mason to learn about K-Mart America, you read Barker to learn about England's justbarely-working class, especially the women of that class. While England's workingmen have their literary representatives (nothing of Barker's is up to Alan Sillitoe's *Saturday Night and Sunday Morning*), no male writer could approach the empathy with which Barker portrays her housewives, naive young things, prostitutes, factory workers, and scrabblers in the dirt, and no female writer has. Nobody else has fashioned such convincing, hard-edged accounts of the pain and occasional lucky pleasure of working-class marriage, the onerous joys of motherhood, or the killing details of menial labor.

*Union Street* takes place in 1973, *Blow Your House Down* in the present; neither departs from its uneducated characters for any outsider looking in. With *The Century's Daughter,* Barker clearly wants to stretch a bit. The flashbacks are for history, Liza's and the century's; the social worker, a turning-30 scholarship boy whose homosexuality gets just enough of the novel's space, is the first Barker character who represents her POV and also occasions a plunge into that great cliché of contemporary fiction, the death of a parent. Barker has a right to these indulgences, and she brings them off. No contemporary setting would permit her memorable realizations of pre-dole privation or pre-pill families, and Stephen's marginally more genteel circumstances enable Barker to demonstrate that oppression is hardly confined to the impoverished. But this stuff isn't what she's best at, and on the whole it transforms a compelling and original writer into a readable and worthwhile one.

What's made Barker's unromantic vision of working-class life so attractive is her refusal to abandon hope. Even the disturbing sexual descriptions—molested 11-year-old, blowjobs by the quid, Stephen's suddenly unemployed father's sudden obsession with little girls—aren't all she sees; there's a paid encounter between two over-sixties in *Union Street* that's as sweet as anything in *Fanny Hill.* But the new book doesn't find history encouraging. Yes, Barker tells us, the poor do have it easier now, but that doesn't mean that their capacity for community hasn't been sapped by everything from council flats to the cash nexus.

Fair enough, but after Liza was murdered by skinheads I felt annoyed if not betrayed. It's my guess that artistic renown has removed Barker slightly from whatever amalgam of experience and inspiration fired the sympathy—a sympathy almost indistinguishable from identification—on which that renown is based. Like her social worker, she's on the outside, a touch more skeptical than she once was. There's excellent reason for such skepticism, unfortunately, but since most writers are bourgeois outsiders, it comes cheap as a literary commodity. The identification is a rare thing.

## Kathleen Jamie   (review date 14-20 April 1989)

SOURCE: "Filling in the Blanks," in *The Times Literary Supplement,* No. 4489, April 14-20, 1989, p. 404.

[*Jamie is a Scottish poet, dramatist, and critic. In the following review of* The Man Who Wasn't There, *she applauds Barker's ability to draw interesting characters but suggests that the novel's plot is somewhat confusing.*]

The man who wasn't there is Colin's father. "Shot down", says Viv, his mum; "Buggered off", thinks Colin. He noticed on the first day at school his birth certificate was shorter than everyone else's. Now that he can read he's not going to wait till he's twenty-one to be told about his father, as Viv says he must. Next time Viv goes out to serve as waitress in a nightclub, he rifles the old handbag in the wardrobe till he finds the certificate. Against the space for his father's name is a blank.

Colin is twelve, smart, cheeky, always in trouble at school. Colin fills the vacuum left by the absence of his father by creating an ongoing B-movie, a ham adventure set halfway between *Boy's Own* and occupied France. Colin's film stars himself, alias Garçon: a twelve-year-old parachuted into France because of his uncanny fluency with the language. He is surrounded in the film by the people who inhabit his real life, only they're French, in cafés and stations. He tries out stories of espionage, betrayal, torture and confession. When Colin's friends say "My dad says", all that Colin has to counter with is images from films. His own film is funny, sometimes unwittingly; it is a retreat as well as an exploration.

Pat Barker's talent is for people, period and dialogue; and in Colin she perfectly creates the mind of a 1950s twelve-year-old, a latch-key kid. The war years, the time of Colin's birth, were the time of his mother's life. Her current boyfriend is the married owner of the nightclub where she works. To this romance Colin puts a quick and expert end. Pat Barker's community is made up of real people, tolerant and abrasive. It is they, and their dialogue, who make this book [*The Man Who Wasn't There*], with their matinées and outings, séances and beans-on-toast. The plot is slightly confusing: there is an uncertainty as to the identity of "the man in black"—a character from Colin's imagination who becomes real. Is he real? Is he Colin's father? A ghost? Is he Colin's future?

## Dinah Birch   (review date 20 April 1989)

SOURCE: "Growing Up," in *London Review of Books,* Vol. 11, No. 8, April 20, 1989, pp. 20-2.

[*In the following excerpt, Birch favorably assesses Barker's use of language and insights into her characters' lives in* The Man Who Wasn't There.]

[Pat Barker's] novels have all been versions of the same intense story: working-class families or, more specifically, the women of such families, contending with the inequities of poverty and ignorance. Men have always existed on the margins of her narratives. Etiolated and ineffective, they are seen only in relation to the lives of sturdier mothers, wives, sisters or daughters. As a rule they die or disappear, fading out of the story rather like the absent father in [Penelope] Lively's *Passing On.* Now Pat Barker has both confronted and reversed this attribute of her fiction. Her latest novel, ***The Man Who Wasn't There,*** focuses on a boy's relation with the father he has never known. What does it mean to mould your life on a man who isn't there?

Pat Barker answers this question in terms which will be familiar to readers of her earlier books, for one of the conclusions to emerge from this work is that to be a boy lost in a hostile and repressive world may not, after all, be wholly dissimilar from being a girl in the same world. The most unforgettable episode in her first book, ***Union Street*** (1982), deals with a girl led into disaster by the fantasy she constructs to fill the empty place of her absent father. Twelve-year-old Colin is the male reflection of this girl. Haunted by the same absence, he also creates an elaborate and consoling drama in his head. Creativity, for Pat Barker, always grows out of loneliness and loss. But such creativity may be a dangerous business. Colin's fantasy, shaped by comic books and adventure films, is set in a schoolboy's notion of Occupied France. Unfolding beside the squalors of a life that Colin rejects, this sustaining fiction, too, almost leads to catastrophe. The dark image of his father, a man in black, steps out of a scarcely controlled imagination and begins to dog his creator like a sinister ghost. Only when Colin is able to recognise what the man in black really represents is he able to rid himself of the self-pity and resentment which had given birth to a corrosive nightmare. Like Lively's middle-aged children, he frees himself by exorcising the ghost of a parent. Here, the parent is not dead but nameless. Recognising that he will never know his own father, Colin arrives at a matter-of-fact wisdom. 'So the blank space would remain blank, he thought. Well, he could live with that. People had survived far worse.'

[A] resigned book, then: but a hopeful one, too. Colin has broken out of an impasse. So, hearteningly, has Pat Barker. She has always written out of an almost uncanny sensitivity to the cadences of the people she has listened to all her life. Reminding us of what unlettered women working in the North of England have had to say, she has colonised a territory which remains unaccustomed ground for the novel. But the solidity of her identity as a writer has threatened to impose its own limitations. There were too many moments in the novels succeeding ***Union Street*** to give her readers the sense of *déjà lu.* ***The Man Who Wasn't***

***There*** proves her to be open to experiment. The solution she finds is a clever one, for since Colin's fantasy life in wartime France is fabricated out of parody and cliché, the inauthenticity of its language confirms its function in the novel. The point might have been made less strenuously, but it is worth making. Language is what separates the density of the life which surrounds Colin from the vacuously seductive scenes which he has constructed out of his daydreams. Fantasy has its uses. But it also has its own proper limits, and the resilience of Pat Barker's writing lies in knowing where they lie.

### Mark Wormald    (review date 24 May 1991)

SOURCE: "Treating War's Insanity," in *The Times Literary Supplement*, No. 4599, May 24, 1991, p. 20.

[*In the following highly positive review of* Regeneration, *Wormald praises Barker for the psychological insights into personality formation that make the book more than an excellent historical novel.*]

On April 12, 1917, Captain Siegfried Sassoon was wounded in action on the Hindenburg Line; ten days later, recovering at Denmark Hill Hospital in London, he wrote "The Rear-Guard", and later appended a note citing the poem's "strength" as a refutation of Edmund Gosse's idea that he "was suffering from severe shock". Readers of his *War Poems* are likely to side with Sassoon; they will also notice how his "Hindenburg Line Material" continued to blend, in that spring and early summer, with the experience of his convalescence, to produce a series of often savage but also revealingly consistent poetic oppositions. "The Hawthorn Tree", the sight of it blossoming in a lane the poem's persona visits daily, is "Not much to me"; but "my lad that's out in France / With fearsome things to see / Would give his eyes for just one glance" at it. And in "Supreme Sacrifice", another dialogue between the horror of the trenches and ordinary (though curiously shadowy) parental or sexual relations, it is his unidentified interlocutor whose, "tired eyes half-confessed she'd felt the shock / Of ugly war brought home".

Sassoon's next response to this shock is as much a matter of literary history as the poems themselves. In July 1917, he wrote and circulated more explicit evidence of his revulsion, as a sane and articulate man, from the insanity of the war and from the distended aims of the "warmongers" still conducting it. It is with a transcript of this cogent short prose piece, "Finished with the War: A Soldier's Declaration", that Pat Barker's fifth novel begins; and *Regeneration*'s chronology matches that of the subsequent, apparently surprising episode in Sassoon's life. Faced with the prospect of a Court Martial for his act of defiance, he was persuaded to appear before an Army Medical Board; from there—thanks to his friend Captain Robert Graves—he was sent for four months to Craiglockhart War Hospital near Edinburgh, before being finally discharged back to duty in France at the end of November.

Although Graves, Sassoon and another of the hospital's patients, Wilfred Owen, all appear in *Regeneration,* neither they nor their poetry dominate the novel. The central character is, instead, the immensely sympathetic figure of Sassoon's psychiatrist at Craiglockhart, Captain W. H. R. Rivers, before the war an eminent Cambridge anthropologist and, as Barker portrays him, an increasingly reluctant tool of army policy.

His discomfort is neither simply moral—though he does question the morality of sending young men back to hell again—nor is it strictly professional. Rivers did state his reservations on this score in a lecture delivered to the Royal Society of Medicine ten days or so after Sassoon's discharge from Craiglockhart; the poet's endorsement of Rivers's views and methods led him to retitle a poem drafted that July. "Repression of War Experience" was encouraged and even enforced in most institutions at that time, and not just the psychiatric ones: when Rivers insisted in the course of his gentle, gradualist, conversational treatment of war neuroses that "ugly" memories and feelings should be faced rather than denied, the psychiatrist, like the poet, was

> setting himself against the whole tenor of their upbringing. They'd been trained to identify emotional repression as the essence of manliness. Men who broke down, or cried, or admitted to feeling fear, were sissies, weaklings, failures. Not men. And yet he himself was the product of the same system, even perhaps a rather extreme product. Certainly the rigorous repression of emotion and desire had been the constant theme of his adult life. In advising his young patients to abandon the attempt at repression and to let themselves *feel* the pity and terror their war experience inevitably evoked, he was excavating the ground he stood on.

These are Barker's words, and they have to be. The rhythms are closer to the conversational, the colloquial, than Rivers allowed his own prose to become, either in his paper (well worth reading in *The Lancet* of February 2, 1918) or in what Barker gives us of his professional case notes.

The novelist's resources, by contrast, provide access to the contingent, unwritten world of speech and feelings in a manner quite beyond the scope of clipped medical records, of polished poetic performances, or even of the literary historian. Where poems appear they do so in manuscript forms, which vary tellingly from the final, "stronger" versions available in the standard texts; they are worried over in the course of dialogue the dynamics of which do far more to evoke and purge the experiences they skirt than any of the contemporary "treatments" to which the reader is also exposed. The (grimly documented) form of electric shock therapy practised in London by Dr Lewis Yealland is witnessed, in silence, by a horrified Rivers.

Barker pulls no punches in her depiction of these and other horrors. They aren't hers to pull. In a novel where, as she writes in a useful Author's Note, "Fact and fiction are so interwoven", it is a useful rule of thumb to assume that the more terrible the episode recounted, the more "historical" it is. Yet it is for its subtler, less extreme processes that *Regeneration* deserves our admiration. Barker's research is worn lightly; the deftness with which she integrates her historically remarkable characters, all of whom have "lost [their] chance of being ordinary", back into a reality marked by sufferings we can all too readily recognize, is the more outstanding for being so unobtrusive. Doctors as well as patients, a lover as well as her soldier-sweetheart who is finding his way back to speech, are united by a landscape and a web of images and colours. They also exhibit habits of speech and thought that we have inherited. They all grope for words, for the right phrase, they all split their "Ye-es"es and their "No-o"s. When connectives and prepositions and auxiliary verbs escalate unexpectedly in the middle of a spoken sentence, it often takes a moment to decide whether the effect is deliberate or not, rhetorical or unconscious.

> "What I can't understand is how somebody of Graves's intelligence can can can have such a shaky grasp of of *rhetoric*." [Sassoon complains to Rivers at one point.] "It suits him to attribute everything I've done to to to to . . . a state of mental breakdown, because then he doesn't have to ask himself any awkward questions."

It is because Pat Barker keeps such questions so convincingly before us, and so delicately explores their consequences for the cultural and psychological processes by which our personalities are formed, that **Regeneration** is so much more than the excellent historical novel other writers might have settled for. It is one of the most impressive novels to have appeared in recent years.

**Ann Ardis** (essay date October 1991)

SOURCE: "Political Attentiveness vs. Political Correctness: Teaching Pat Barker's *Blow Your House Down,*" in *College Literature,* Vol. 18, No. 3, October, 1991, pp. 44-54.

[*Ardis is an American critic and educator. In the following essay, she discusses the effect of Barker's* Blow Your House Down *on her college literature classes and examines the ways in which the novel addresses various feminist themes.*]

The author blurb on the inside back cover of the Ballantine paperback edition of Pat Barker's novel **Blow Your House Down** (1984) reads as follows: "Pat Barker was born in Thornaby-on-Tees in 1943. She was educated at the local grammar school and at the London School of Economics, where she studied economics, politics, and history. She is married to the Professor of Zoology at the University of Durham, and she has two children." Why, my students ask, did Barker write this book about working-class prostitutes trying to protect themselves from a serial killer? On what authority does an academic's wife, a mother of two, and a graduate of the London School of Economics describe the experience of working-class women in a decaying inner-city neighborhood who have only two means of employment open to them: walking the streets and working on the assembly line in a chicken slaughterhouse? On what authority, in other words, does Barker write about women who choose to *be* chickens (the English slang for prostitutes) rather than "sho[ve the birds'] legs up their arses"? And whom does she write this book for?

These are important questions, questions sustained by a tradition of Marxist criticism that values the authenticity of working-class writing—and that often, as Cora Kaplan has noted, alleviates the tension between the literary and the political in the Marxist critical project by advocating essentialism [Cora Kaplan, "Pandora's Box: Subjectivity, Class and Sexuality in Socialist Feminist Criticism," *Sea Changes: Essays on Culture and Feminism,* 1986]. Because I believe that questioning the authenticity of **Blow Your House Down** as working-class writing can be a defensive distraction on a reader's part, a means of avoiding Barker's very disturbing insights into the way "social divisions and ideologies [are] worked through psychic structures . . . [and] worked into sexual and social identity," I ask my students to bracket such questions temporarily in order to focus first on how this novel challenges us to confront the "powerful symbolic force of class and gender in ordering our social and political imagination" (Kaplan).

This essay is about what happens in the classroom when I teach **Blow Your House Down.** It is about teaching feminist theory and literature together: teaching literature *as* theory, teaching literary and theoretical texts that highlight the politics of the classroom. The charge of "political correctness" (read "academic fascism") is being levied more and more frequently against feminists, multiculturalists, and other advocates of curricular reform these days; particularly as this charge begins filtering down into the popular press, it serves to contain and curtail the debate on the curriculum by caricaturing one side of the argument. In other words, it is the latest and most effective excuse for not listening to feminists and multiculturalists. Through a discussion of classroom conversations about Barker's novel, I would like to suggest that there is an important distinction to be made between political correctness and political attentiveness. **Blow Your House Down** does invite students to reflect on how cultural categories such as class and gender reciprocally constitute each other—which might be termed a politically correct insight. But Barker's work also points up the radical instability of such categories. Hence it does not exemplify class-based paradigms of analysis. Nor does it fit neatly into feminist arguments about male violence against women. As I hope to show, it is too disturbing to be politically correct ("PC"). I teach it *because* it challenges my theoretical paradigms. I teach it because it teaches me as well as my students to be attentive to the ways we negotiate difference in the classroom and in the world at large.

### TEACHING CLASS AND GENDER

American culture does not have a highly developed discourse about class. Moreover, the discourse we do have is misleading, insofar as most Americans claim to be middle-class even though their incomes actually give them either a higher or a lower class standing. Which is all the more reason to ask students to read Barker's novel about a culture and a set of controversies that seem foreign to them. More than any other piece of literature I have taught, Barker's novel requires students to position themselves. It challenges them to acknowledge their own class allegiances as they try to talk about this text; it calls attention to all the differences in students' class background, economic status, and life experience that usually remain politely beyond the scope of classroom discussion, thanks to common assumptions about the classroom as an apolitical space and the educational process as a simple transmission of nonideological "Truths." Not more than five minutes into the first day's discussion of this novel in an "Introduction to the Novel" class last year, for example, one of my students stopped herself in mid-sentence when she realized that she was taking her own experience to be universal. She was assuming that this subject was equally exotic to all of her classmates, that this was everyone's first up-close-and-personal view of prostitution. Even as she was speaking, something someone else had just said finally registered with her, and when she realized that some of her classmates lived in neighborhoods where prostitutes hang out on street corners, she had to go back and qualify what she had just asserted about "normal" households and "normal" occupations.

That process itself—the process of putting quotation marks around such words as "normal," of destandardizing, de-naturalizing bourgeois experience—is something Barker's narrative demands of its readers from its opening pages. Consider the first scene of the novel:

> There were two beds and a wardrobe in the room. To get between them you had to stand sideways and shuffle your way along.
>
> Brenda was in a hurry to get out and grumbled as she bent down to tuck a blanket in. "I don't know, when I was your age I was making me own bed."
>
> Her daughters, getting ready for bed in the corner, turned and looked at her. Lindsey, the elder by two years, said, "I don't see why I have to go to bed the same time as our Sharon."
>
> "Because if I let you stop down you'd only have a carry-on and wake everybugger up. Besides, you'd start picking on your Uncle Norman, you know you would."
>
> "It's him picks on me."
>
> Brenda pulled back the sheets on the other bed and a powerful smell of urine filled the room. "Sharon, I wish you'd tell me when you're wet. I could've had this changed this morning if you'd told me."
>
> "God, what a stink," said Lindsey.
>
> Brenda rounded on her. "Shut your face, you. You want to think on, she's been ill."

As students are quick to note, this scene impresses us with its normality. Even if this bedroom is much smaller than those my middle-class and upper-middle-class students remember from their own childhoods, and even if the dialect takes some getting used to, the rituals are nonetheless familiar: an older child complains about having the same bedtime as her younger sister; a mother expresses her exasperation with her children's rivalry, but her rough scolding is well laced with affection.

In "Women on the Market," Luce Irigaray identifies three symbolic positions that women can occupy in a capitalist patriarchy: virgin, mother, and prostitute [see *This Sex*

*Which Is Not One,* translated by Catherine Porter, 1977]. Without necessarily requiring them to read Irigaray, I talk with my students about the way Barker collapses these three categories as she introduces her characters. The "respectable" lower-middle-class folks who live on the margins of this decaying inner-city neighborhood continue to assume that the categories are noncontiguous; they employ these classifications to construct reassuringly rigid distinctions between themselves and those who differ from them in various ways. In contrast, Barker's prostitutes are painfully aware of the contradictions fueling this ideological system.

As the entire first section of the novel—not just its opening paragraphs—stresses, Brenda is both a mother and a prostitute. Like Kath and Audrey, in fact, she is a prostitute because she is a mother. After her husband disappears, leaving her with the children and a sheaf of unpaid bills stashed under the seat cushions of the sofa, Brenda tries to make it on her own by applying for child support and then working full-time at the chicken factory. She quickly realizes several things. First, after she goes to the corner store for a pint of milk one evening and is accosted by a man looking for someone to give him a blow job, she is made to understand that in her neighborhood, a woman walking alone at night is assumed to be a prostitute whether she is one or not. In the symbolic economy of the bourgeois patriarchy, "working-class" equals "prostitute": a working-class woman, any working-class woman, is assumed to be sexually available to the middle-class man. As Kaplan writes, "Class discourse *is* gendered discourse"; again, "class is powerfully defined through sexual difference, and vice versa."

But if Brenda is upset by this encounter and others like it, she is even more upset by her social workers' visit, which starkly reveals to her the economic base subtending the bourgeois patriarchy's valorization of marriage:

> After they'd gone Brenda sat down and pressed her hands together to stop them shaking. What got her was the hypocrisy of it all. They went on about being married, but when you got right down to it, past the white weddings and the romance and all that, what they *really* thought was: if you're getting on your back for a fella, he ought to pay. *That* was what they really thought. And where did that leave you? You might just as well be standing on a street corner in bloody Northgate—at least it'd be honest.

In fact, that is exactly what Brenda does once she realizes that hooking will give her both more time and more money for her children than will the chicken factory.

If Brenda is alienated from her own body when she puts it on the market; if sexual desire is not a factor in the exchanges she makes with her customers; if, moreover, she cannot control the process of "switching off " (tuning out emotionally with her johns and "switching on" again when she is with her children), she recognizes nonetheless that a "respectable" life would be no different. For the women she worked with on the factory line are equally alienated from the products of their labor; they too switch off to get through the day. Moreover, while Edith, Brenda's mother-in-law, certainly claims both the respectability and the class status she refuses to grant Brenda, she is as alienated from her sexuality as are the prostitutes. As indicated by her single act of intimacy with her husband—dusting him off before he leaves the house for the day—desire simply is not part of the heterosexual economy of the patriarchy. Watching this strange daily ritual, Brenda notes that "it was just like scrubbing the front door step. It didn't matter what you thought about the bloke, it was just something you had to do."

Kaplan argues that "without the class and race perspectives that socialist feminist critics bring to the analysis both of literary texts and of their conditions of production, liberal feminist criticism, with its emphasis on the unified female subject, will unintentionally reproduce the ideological values of mass-market romance" because it "tends to represent sexual difference as natural and fixed—a constant, transhistorical femininity in libidinized struggle with an equally 'given' universal masculinity." She goes on to suggest that "a feminist literary criticism that privileges gender in isolation from other forms of social determination offers us a . . . partial reading of the role played by sexual difference in literary discourse, a reading bled dry of its most troubling and contradictory meaning." Thus it is striking that **Blow Your House Down** does not let readers isolate gender from other forms of social determination. You cannot bleed sexual difference dry of its "most troubling and contradictory meanings" in this narrative. Furthermore, there are no unified female subjects in this novel. For every encounter, every "speaking-to another person," in this novel is "fraught with the history of . . . sex and class," to borrow Minnie Bruce Pratt's phrasing [in "Identity: Skin Blood Heart," in *Yours in Struggle: Three Feminist Perspectives on Anti-Semitism and Racism*, edited by Elly Bulkin, Pratt, and Barbara Smith, 1984]. Every character experiences the kind of "vertigo" or "homelessness" that Pratt associates in "Identity: Skin Blood Heart" with an expanding consciousness of oppression.

### TEACHING THE "ZERO DEGREE OF SOCIAL CONCEPTUALIZATION"

"I'll never think about these ladies in quite the same way again." "I used to think that prostitutes were bad . . . that they were just sluts, dirty from the waist down or something like that. But they are mothers too and stuff." Such comments (the first from a senior in a feminist theory proseminar, the second from a freshman in an "Introduction to the Novel" class) suggest that the experience of reading Barker's novel "enlightens" students, introduces them to a world and a way of life that would otherwise remain foreign to them—and that therefore is the target of the negative stereotyping epitomized by the "dirty from the waist down" remark. But if this novel shows them how class and gender reciprocally constitute each other, I nonetheless consider responses like the above only the point of departure in class discussions.

Virginia Woolf writes in *Three Guineas:* "The number of books written by the educated about the working class would seem to show that the glamour of the working class and the emotional relief afforded by adopting its cause, are

today as irresistable to the middle class as the glamour of the aristocracy was twenty years ago." I teach Barker's novel regularly because it challenges students to deal with issues of class; more importantly, however, I teach it because it does not afford my middle-class students the kind of "emotional relief " Woolf discusses in *Three Guineas.* **Blow Your House Down** does not let us commend ourselves for the correctness of our politics. Instead it calls attention to the voyeurism involved in any reading experience, particularly when reading demands identification across lines of social classification. As her title might suggest, Barker refuses to let us sustain the self-congratulatory attitude reflected in my student's comment, "I'll never think about these ladies in quite the same way again." She refuses to let us construct either "the prostitute" or "the serial killer" as other to ourselves. (This is where students' reactions to the author blurb and the quotations from reviews featured on the back cover of the paperback edition become relevant again, as they can serve to introduce a discussion of the commodification of working-class experience for the "benefit" and pleasure of middle-class readers.)

Besides the title, several other aspects of the novel work to destabilize class and gender categorization by highlighting the psychological construction of otherness: the use of a first-person narrative in the third section of the novel; the final section's tangential relationship to the preceding three sections; and the narrator's direct addresses to the reader throughout. I want now to focus on students' reactions to these particular narrative strategies. What interests me here is students' resistance to the idea that they are implicated in the psychological dynamics Barker describes.

As I noted previously, **Blow Your House Down** has four chapters. The first focuses on Brenda, on her socialization as a prostitute, and on her relationship with Kath, an older woman who will be one of the serial killer's victims. The second chapter introduces us to the whole community of women who meet for drinks at a local pub before going out on their "beats." The third is about Jean, the only woman in the group who hooks because, as she herself notes, she likes the life—she enjoys the risk associated with the job. And the fourth deals with Maggie, a "respectable" chicken factory worker whom Brenda rescues after Maggie is knocked unconscious by an unidentified assailant on her way home from work one night.

Only Jean's story is narrated in the first person. It opens with the following observation: "You do a lot of walking in this job. More than you might think. In fact, when I get to the end of a busy Saturday night, it's me feet that ache. There, that surprised you, didn't it?" Interestingly enough, students are very uncomfortable with Jean's assumption of intimacy with her readers. "I can identify with Brenda, but I don't want to see the world from Jean's perspective," one of my students wrote last year; "I don't like the way she draws me into conversation." The victim of a client's violence, Jean too is capable of violence. And when she kills the man she thinks is one of her murdered lover's "regulars," when she perpetuates the cycle of violence rather than stopping it by solving the murder mystery, she violates two things: the reader's desire for narrative closure, for resolution of the central conflict in the novel; and the reader's assumption that he or she observes these characters without being observed by them—that reading is organized around a one-way mirror.

For very similar reasons, as Bauer notes [in Dale Bauer, "The Other 'F' Word: The Feminist in the Classroom," *College English,* Vol. 52, No. 4 (1990)], students are troubled by the fourth section. They want to dissociate Maggie's story from the rest of the novel. For example, even though Brenda is recognizable in this section (her name is not used, but her clothing and speech are familiar), students often do not identify her as the woman who calls the police and the ambulance after Maggie is attacked. "There's no connection between Maggie's story and the rest of the novel," they claim. "She's not a prostitute; why did she get attacked?"

If such misreadings are symptomatic, still more telling are students' responses to Barker's use of direct address in key scenes such as the murder of Kath. I quote at length from this scene in order to give you a sense of its impact. First, the murder itself, from the point at which her client's interaction with Kath escalates into violence:

> His cock felt small and worm-like inside her stretched arse. He pulled it out and examined it carefully. At first it looked much the same as usual, purple and glistening in the torchlight. But then a drop of gingery fluid gathered on the knob and dripped down onto her bum. He smelled the thin, sour smell of shit. And looked. Her cleft was full of it. He lashed out at her then, but she wriggled away from him and tried to stand up. She got as far as her knees.
>
> "There's no need for that," she said. "Look, you can have your money back."
>
> Those were the last words she spoke. He hit her again, full on the jaw, and she crumpled up on the floor and lay still. He dragged her back onto the mattress. Then reached into his pocket for the knife.
>
> It was almost soundless. There were only slight grunts of effort and the shadow of an upraised arm coming and going on the wall.
>
> At some point, unnoticed by him, Kath died.
>
> After a few minutes he was able to stop and look down. It wasn't enough that she was dead, he needed more. He gathered handfuls of feathers together and started shoving them inside her cunt. It wasn't easy: as fast as he pushed them inside they turned red. He had to practically stuff her with them, like stuffing a chicken, before he could get the effect he wanted: a ridiculous little white frill between her legs.

Five short paragraphs (less than a page of text) describing the murderer's rituals of self-distancing after he has finished follow the above. The last two paragraphs of the chapter, quoted below, are then set off from the preceding with a line of asterisks:

> The sleeping and the dead. Any resemblance be-

tween them is a contrivance of undertakers: they do not look alike. Kath's body seems to have shrunk inside its clothes. If you approached the mattress casually you would see nothing but a heap of old rags. You would tread on her before you realized a woman's body lay there.

> The window is boarded up, the room dark, except for five thin lines of moonlight that lie across the mattress like bars. One of them has just reached her eyes. They look so alive you wonder she can bear the light shining directly into them. Any moment now, you feel, her eyes will close.

Barker's use of the present tense and the second person in these last two paragraphs is as shocking as the detailed description that precedes them. My students often suggest that the graphic nature of Barker's descriptions makes this novel inappropriate for classroom discussion. (This point in itself constitutes an opportunity to talk about the institutionalization of literary study—both in terms of an English department's curricular commitments to a canon of high art and in terms of students' own expectations about the ways in which the texts they study should differ from the fiction they read on their own time, the language they hear in their own conversation, and the cultural forms they either produce or consume on Saturday nights.) They also note, rightly I think, that Kath's murder is pornographic, in the sense that Barker shows the murderer's association of sex and violence without reassuring us that we are being offered a critique of this behavior.

What they are much more reluctant to talk about, however, is the way Barker catches us peeping: turns the one-way mirror into a window, and then in effect breaks the glass and draws us into the scene of this horrific crime as she switches from past to present tense and describes our approach to Kath's body. As I noted earlier, this crime is never solved; there is no gratifying resolution to the whodunit plot. Instead the violence keeps spiraling outward, implicating not only this particular serial killer, not only Jean (who murders someone she thinks is the killer), but us as well.

This idea is reinforced in the final chapter through one of Maggie's most powerful meditations on evil. On one of her first forays back out into the world after being attacked, Maggie meets a neighbor in the grocery store. As she parries this woman's insinuations about her husband's having been her assailant, Maggie comes to the following realization:

> You thought evil was simple. No, more than that, you *made* it simple, you froze it into a single shape, the shape of a man waiting in the shadows. But it wasn't simple. This woman, this wheezy middle-aged woman, with her corrugated-iron hair and her glasses that flashed when she looked sideways to see how you were taking it, she knew what she was doing. And she was enjoying it. You couldn't put evil into a single, recognizable shape.

Passages like this one in Barker's novel, together with the other narrative strategies discussed above, challenge our attempts to classify human experience on the basis of binary oppositions. Neat, clean, simple distinctions of whatever sort—between "us" and "them," good and evil, middle and working class, male and female—are misleading, as Maggie acknowledges here. In this respect, ***Blow Your House Down*** invites us to confront what Hortense Spillers terms the "zero degree of social conceptualization" [see "Mama's Baby, Papa's Maybe: An American Grammar Book," *Diacritics,* Vol. 17, No. 2 (1987)].

In "Mama's Baby, Papa's Maybe," Spillers criticizes recent research in African American history for its reification of gender as a category of analysis—and for the erasure of certain chapters in American history that follows from this reification. Central to her argument is a distinction between "the body" and "the flesh." The "body" is gendered, marked by a "grammar" and an iconography of sexual difference; in contrast, "flesh" is the "zero degree of social conceptualization," "the primary narrative." Given this distinction, Spillers goes on to note what has been left out of revisionary "herstories" of American culture: female slaves were not only raped; they were beaten, lynched, and mutilated as well. That is to say, the violence against them wasn't gender-specific: their physical beings were not always treated as female. Instead they were treated as "flesh," flesh that could be "lacerated, wounded, torn, scarred [or] ruptured" by anyone who reduced a human being to a thing and denied that being subjectivity. What feminist revisionary historians have either wanted to forget or have failed to realize, according to Spillers, is that the African female subject has been "the topic of specifically *externalized* acts of torture and prostration that we imagine as the peculiar province of male brutality and torture inflicted by other males." Images of female bodies "strung from a tree limb, or bleeding from the breast on any given day of field work because the 'overseer,' standing the length of the whip [away], has popped her flesh open, ad[d a new] dimension to the narratives of women in culture and society," a "materialized scene of unprotected female flesh—of female flesh 'ungendered.' "

Perhaps I risk distracting you by this reference to Spillers's research, shocking you with visions of mutilated black bodies that now compete with Barker's description of Kath's murder for your attention. Certainly, as I write this, I feel anxious about being accused of appropriating a point that Spillers makes about black women's experience in order to focus exclusively once again on white women. The criticisms of white feminist theory that women of color voice in *This Bridge Called My Back* and elsewhere cannot be ignored. But perhaps Spillers also offers us a way to explore the relationships among systems of oppression, their interconnectedness—without, however, assuming that one system of oppression is exactly analogous to or subsumed within another. Spillers's distinction between body and flesh makes it possible, I think, to read the "grammar" of Kath's violated form.

As she lies on that pallet in an abandoned row house with her eyes still open, refusing to look like a sleeping body, Kath is "flesh." The crime that her murderer has committed is not merely an act of male violence against a woman. It is a crime against something more primary than a gendered body. For this reason, Barker's narrative does not fit neatly into feminist arguments about male violence against women. Nor does it exemplify class-based paradigms of analysis. As the safe spaces we usually construct to protect ourselves from otherness are blown down in this novel, as our modes of social analysis are exposed as secondary constructs (and inadequate ones at that), a primary narrative of domination becomes painfully, searingly visible in this text. This narrative is not always or necessarily played out along (race,) gender and class lines. Like the bodies of the black slave women who were lynched in nineteenth-century America, Kath's dead form and her still staring eyes can haunt us into awareness of our capacity to turn subjectivities into property, bodies into flesh. For this reason, I am not satisfied when my students offer politically correct pronouncements on class and gender oppression when we have finished discussing this novel. I want them to say, "This novel upset me." "This novel disturbed me." And, what is even harder, "This novel implicated me."

### Rob Nixon (review date 14 July 1992)

SOURCE: "Soldiers of Misfortune: In the Trenches with Pat Barker," in *The Village Voice,* Vol. XXXVII, No. 28, July 14, 1992, p. 91.

[*In the following highly positive review of* Regeneration, *Nixon discusses some of the major themes in Barker's work.*]

The cabbie who drove me the few miles from Durham to Pat Barker's home in Newton Hall announced that we were entering the largest housing estate in all of Europe. Newton Hall was also, he added and proved, Europe's easiest estate to get lost in: Some streets, Barker's among them, had not made it onto the map he thumbed with an air of practiced futility. Barker must be familiar with the sensation of being uncharted. Prior to ***Regeneration,*** she'd written mainly about the working-class women of England's industrial north: an unplaceable set of interests in terms of the expectations and prejudices of British publishing. Barker devoted much of her imaginative energy to establishing a literary resonance for what she calls the "voices that had not been listened to."

Her fifth and latest novel takes her work in an unpredictable direction. ***Regeneration,*** set in World War I Scotland, excavates the suspect foundations of a wartime masculinity which had to appear at all costs detached and commanding. It is a tribute to Barker's imaginative reach and the generosity of her feminism that she can produce such an affecting novel about the impact of war on men, and that she can do so without forfeiting the caliber of insight that distinguished *Union Street, Blow Your House Down,* and *The Century's Daughter*.

I asked her about her literary beginnings as we sat at the kitchen table, a gale battering the windows as if intent on blowing the house down—or at least testing its foundations. Barker explained that she had set out to write sedate middle-class novels, then decided that if her efforts were going to remain unpublished, she might as well attempt the book she had always dreamed of writing. The result, *Union Street,* became the first of three remarkable novels that draw on her memories of the working-class women of her childhood, their blunted dreams and bloody-minded heroism alike. These novels all testify to Barker's gift for perfectly pitched dialogue—a salutary antidote to that tradition of "committed" writing which embraces the working class with a bleeding heart and a cloth ear. By the late '80s, Barker had established a voice that was regional in the richest sense: dark, wry, sometimes outrageous, but never coy or merely dutiful.

Yet her success at depicting communities bypassed by the great motorways of Brit Lit brought its own dilemmas. That much became clear when I asked her why, with *Regeneration,* she chose to break so radically with her established haunts. What had prompted her to hazard a novel about people in every sense remote from her—young, male, upper-middle-class World War I officers in a Scottish mental hospital? Her grandfather, Barker told me, first ignited her curiosity about the war, plying her with tales of his military exploits while toying with his old bayonet wound. But the incentive to write *Regeneration* arose equally from her sensation of being boxed in, of finding her books held to standards of "authentic sociology" rather than fiction: "I had become strongly typecast as a northern, regional, working-class feminist . . . label, label, label. You get to the point where people are reading the label instead of the book."

For most of her career, Barker has found herself bereft of literary forerunners. D. H. Lawrence and David Storey wrote northern, working-class novels, but even they had proved of little use, as their female characters seemed alien or peripheral. In turning to World War I for her imaginative terrain, Barker faced the unfamiliar risk of smothering beneath a surfeit of precedents: "It takes a long time to have an original idea about something which has whole libraries devoted to it."

The originality of *Regeneration* flows largely from the unorthodox decision to set her war novel not on the battlefront but in a mental hospital. Craiglockhart, just outside Edinburgh, is a hospital crammed with war casualties, a "living museum of tics and twitches." By stationing the action away from the trenches, Barker can press beyond the point where most war novels are content to end. *Regeneration* asks not just "How does war feel?" but "What ideals of manhood make the conduct of war possible?" and "Why have these ideals failed?" Barker's protagonist, Dr. William Rivers, an army psychologist, inhabits the cusp between military and civilian life. This pioneering psychologist, neurologist, and anthropologist is ideally placed to grapple with the enormous issues the novel raises, most notably the crippling effects of emotional repression as a measure of manliness.

Barker reimagines the intense relationship that evolved at Craiglockhart between Rivers and his most renowned patient, the young poet Siegfried Sassoon. Decorated for "conspicuous gallantry," Sassoon arrives at the hospital in 1917 after stirring up a storm in Britain with a public indictment of the war. Sassoon's stand leaves the authorities two choices: to court-martial him or declare him psychologically unsound. His friends, particularly Robert Graves, intercede, eventually persuading him to avoid a court-martial by undergoing treatment at Craiglockhart, purportedly for shell shock. Sassoon faces a wracking dilemma. Either he accepts rejection by his troops as a traitor and pacifist or he submits to a plot to have his deepest principles swept away as "symptoms of mental collapse."

Rivers's quandary is no less tormenting. His morally, intellectually, and erotically intense exchanges with Sassoon sharpen his doubts about the ethics of his work. To Rivers has fallen the melancholy task of restoring disturbed officers to "sanity," but this simply means sending them back to the trenches that have undone them in the first place. Rivers believes the war-damaged men need to face and speak their fears. His colleague, Dr. Lewis Yealland, sees breakdown on the battlefront as a species of lapsed manliness. (Yealland remedies "weakness" like hysterical mutism by applying lit cigarettes to the patient's tongue and electric shock waves to his larynx.)

Rivers's great breakthrough was rejecting the conventional wisdom that officers broke down in the trenches because they were too feeble to cope with the bruising life of action. Instead, he saw analogies between the nervous disorders prevalent among men at war and the patterns of breakdown among women in peace-time. Young soldiers' training encouraged them to project the combat zone as a Great Adventure that would sort the men from the boys by testing their command of the virtues of courage, discipline, emotional control, and physical prowess. Yet the war offered anything but a life of action: "They'd been *mobilized* into holes in the ground so constricted they could hardly move," Barker writes. "The war that had promised so much in the way of 'manly' activity had actually delivered 'feminine' passivity, and on a scale that their mothers and sisters had scarcely known."

Paradoxically, women were more likely than men to experience the Great War as a Great Adventure. While male soldiers fought the demons of impotence in the trenches, war released tens of thousands of women from the confines of home. Work in the munitions factories allowed them to secure—at least for the duration of the war—new freedoms. War offered other forms of release to women whose domestic lives had degenerated into a state of war. In *Regeneration,* Lizzie, a survivor of battery, asks: "Do you know what happened on August 4th 1914? . . . *Peace* broke out. The only little bit of peace I've ever had. No, I don't want him back when it's over. As far as I'm concerned the Kaiser can keep him. . . . I'm going to get myself some false teeth, and I'm going to have a bloody good time." As Barker's other novels testify, for working-class women that "bloody good time" didn't last. The war ended, the men returned and reclaimed their jobs.

All of Barker's work reveals her singular gift for immersing readers in the atmospherics and pathologies of violence—whether rape, murder, trench warfare, torture, or unremitting confinement. Among the victims, she reserves her greatest sympathy for young people—19-year-old officers, 12-year-old rape survivors, 16-year-old prostitutes—whose early exposure to brutality plunges them into premature, bewildered versions of adulthood. Impatient with the official heroisms that crowd the bookshelves, Barker reiterates in *Regeneration* her attraction to the spectacular yet hidden braveries that sustain "unliterary" lives. (She's more impressed by Sassoon's inconspicuous than his public gallantry: His most impressive act of bravery, she suggests, is to deny his own need to be *seen* as hypermasculine.) Few novelists are so unsentimentally animated by people's ability to chalk up small, shaky, but estimable victories over remorseless circumstances. Readers come away from all her novels with an altered feeling for the boundaries and capacities of human courage.

But despite the rich continuities in her work, Barker has no doubts about which kind of writing taxed her talents more. Working on *Regeneration,* she was astonished at how much easier it was to infuse ideas into a novel populated by public school, Oxbridge men: "You can have all these bloody dons sitting around tables talking about the theme of the book. Frankly, I think it's a doddle compared to writing about semiliterate or illiterate people: you can have your character simply articulate what the book is about. It's money for old rope compared with what is required when your character cannot possibly do that."

During our conversation, Barker seemed, at times, justifiably worried that all the attention *Regeneration* has garnered might detract from the achievements of her earlier work. There's something all too predictable about the sequence of her success. The British press, after rationing praise for earlier books—American reviewers were less stinting—is suddenly all plaudits. And the BBC plans to screen a version of *Regeneration* next year to coincide with the 75th anniversary of the end of the war. Is the novel's success simply a repeat of the old story that a book about men's doings is more interesting to men—who constitute the majority of publishers, reviewers, critics, and prize-givers? Though *Regeneration* will probably go down in the annals of publishing history as the book that put Barker on the map, it's important to recognize that, with the exceptions of Angela Carter and Salman Rushdie, no British writer in the past 20 years has produced three novels to equal *Union Street, Blow Your House Down,* and *Regeneration*.

After the interview, we ventured outside. Beyond Barker's garden lay—and it seemed appropriate—a bewitching woodland on one flank, a military base on the other. She mentioned that she had long held two desires: to see one of the area's plentiful but elusive badgers, and to have a hedgehog take up residence in her garden. Both dreams were realized, though not quite in the way she'd imagined. A hedgehog came to stay and a badger devoured it. She told the anecdote lightly, with a storyteller's confidingness and a trace of that luminous melancholy which distinguishes all her tales about our halting efforts to stave off violence and despair.

**Claudia Roth Pierpont**    **(review date 10 August 1992)**

SOURCE: "English Lessons," in *The New Yorker*, Vol. LXVIII, No. 25, August 10, 1992, pp. 74-9.

[*In the following excerpt from a review in which she also discusses Caryl Phillips's novel* Cambridge *(1992), Pierpont favorably assesses* Regeneration.]

"My subject is War, and the pity of War. The Poetry is in the pity," Wilfred Owen wrote, in 1918, in an introduction he planned for his first collected volume. The lines eventually appeared in a slim edition of Owen's poems selected and published by friends in 1920, two years after his death, at age twenty-five, by German machine-gun fire during the week before the Armistice. Owen had begun his introduction with the warning "This book is not about heroes"—a hard-won lesson that, unthinkable in 1914, was largely taken for granted by 1920. From a writer, the lesson demanded the abandonment of England's long-ingrained pastoral-isle rhetoric. But the spareness and the irony with which Owen altered his work didn't come at once, in immediate response to the terror and squalor of the trenches. The disillusion found expression only afterward, under the tutelage of another poet-soldier, Siegfried Sassoon, in sessions of ardent reading and rewriting which took place during the brief months of their acquaintance, as fellow-patients at Craiglockhart War Hospital, a military psychiatric facility outside Edinburgh.

Craiglockhart, with a population of Royal Army officers consigned to it with the diverse symptoms of what was hesitantly and still suspiciously termed "shell shock," is the primary setting for Pat Barker's absorbing historical novel *Regeneration.* The story is taken up as Sassoon is admitted there, in mid-1917, with the war verging on the muddy destructions of Passchendaele, and with no one in command able to articulate the principles that separated one side from the other. Sassoon, an early volunteer, decorated for bravery, had issued a public declaration "of wilful defiance of military authority," in which he denounced his country's political motives and refused to return to service. Speaking as a soldier and for the sake of soldiers, he called for a clarification of England's war aims, and wrote that he hoped to destroy "the callous complacence with which the majority of those at home regard the continuance of agonies which they do not share, and which they have not sufficient imagination to realize."

Sassoon's statement, reproduced whole, leads off Barker's first page, and her novel is a tracing of its consequences, which were neither as public nor as clear as its valiant author had wished. Seeking to rescue Sassoon from himself ("I could see at once it wouldn't do any good, nobody would follow his example"), his friend Robert Graves had interfered with the Army Medical Board, providing evidence—true but irrelevant—that Sassoon was suffering from nervous exhaustion. Anticipating a court-martial and imprisonment, and a swelling of outrage and of support for his position, Sassoon was instead shipped off to the place he at once dubbed Dottyville. But there was never any doubt; his protest was his illness.

To label *Regeneration* an anti-war novel—which it is, in part—suggests a didacticism that figures no more than it should in this richly storied and peopled amplification of events. Nor is the book a dark journey into Bedlam, despite the evident pain and potential horror of the subject. The animated and diverting life of Craiglockhart—"that living museum of tics and twitches"—contains comedy as well as tragedy, and it is not the chill black comedy of the Joseph Heller tradition (or, indeed, of the Siegfried Sassoon tradition, which is its distant ancestor) but, rather, comedy flushed with warmth. For, as Sassoon discovers on passing through the hospital portals, he has entered into a carefully delimited arena of emotional exploration and nurturance which is not only the antithesis of his war experience but a reversal of all the mores of traditional English manhood. Shattered men may be rebuilt here, but not necessarily along the lines of their original construction.

Few historical novelists can have had such ample and minutely detailed sources to draw upon as Barker: Sassoon went on to publish six autobiographical volumes, chronicling his years up to and through the war, and, along with Graves and Edmund Blunden, he makes up a trio that Paul Fussell christened the war's "classic memoirists." Barker depends on all three, and more besides, and it is perhaps ironic, given the degree of self-confessed fiction present in the memoirs, that only in Barker's novel are the real names of all the principal figures restored. In episode and in observation, Barker adheres scrupulously to the facts: even the camaraderie of Owen and Sassoon conspiring over Owen's work derives, as Barker informs us in an endnote, from Sassoon's annotations on Owen's manuscript. But it may or may not be relevant that the novel is so factually secure, for Barker's whole creation breathes. "Real" characters rub shoulders in the long corridors with a host of equally tangible fictions, or with documented symptoms made flesh: Anderson, the Army surgeon, who breaks down at a drop of blood from a shaving cut; Prior, the "bad boy" from the North of England slums, who arrives unable to speak and makes the nurses wish at times that he'd never recovered; Fothersgill, who speaks only in mock medieval English: "lots of 'Yea Verilys' and 'forsooths'—as if his brief exposure to French horrors had frightened him into a sort of terminal facetiousness." But the steadying sympathy that holds the place together, and also presides over the book, is that of the good doctor whose task it is to cure these men, to mediate between the private violations of sanity which have sent them to his care and the public ones to which they must be returned.

That rarest thing in modern fiction (as, perhaps, in modern life), a man of utterly convincing higher moral instincts, Dr. W. H. R. Rivers was a figure as real (if not as well known) as Owen or Graves or Sassoon, and he is, historically, nearly as well delineated, by his words and by theirs. An anthropologist and a neurologist, and also a leading proponent of Freudian analysis in England (even before the pathologies produced by the war irrefutably demonstrated, as he saw, subterranean channels of pain and repression), Rivers was at this time over fifty and unmarried, entirely devoted to his work and to the men in his care, and he was in the midst of a crisis. As an official healer for the Royal Army Medical Corps, a physician in uniform, he had feared, in the words of his own memoir cum clinical record, "the situation that would arise if my task of converting a patient from his 'pacifist errors' to the conventional attitude should have as its result my own conversion to his point of view." This situation was not hypothetical. Sassoon was the patient to whom Rivers referred, and in Barker's book the two are paired as noble, loving antagonists—a mutually idealizing father and son

locked in a battle of words, even of dreams, for each other's souls. It is Rivers' duty to make the renegade understand and share his own sense of honor and obligation; it is Sassoon's nature to make Rivers understand, and, finally, share his.

Although *Regeneration* is essentially a moral drama, it is never static, never weighty. Barker is an energetic writer who achieves much of her purpose through swift and easy dialogue and the bold etching of personality—effects so apparently simple and forthright that the complications of feeling which arise seem to do so unbidden. The vivid immediacy of her style is perhaps better suited to situation and speech than to the processes of thought, however; the shifting interior lights by which doctor and patient gradually adjust their positions are a little too clearly outlined, too artificially legible. The author herself may have felt some unease about her ability to convey these sheerly intellectual developments: a scene of high melodrama placed late in the story, in which Rivers pursues his most desperately ill patient into a situation that, by chance, duplicates the conditions of a French battlefield—a beach at night, a wild storm, a watchtower, explosions—is contrived and murky, unlike anything else in the book. Rivers' on-the-spot revelation as he drags the stricken man to safety—*"Nothing justifies this. Nothing nothing nothing"*—seems a thought that this extraordinarily empathetic individual, trapped in a pointless war, should have come to long before. But, in a way, even this failure is a sign of Barker's exceptional gift for character: one rejects the scene in part because one knows the man so well.

It has been Pat Barker's accomplishment to enlarge the scope of the contemporary English novel. A woman of working-class background from the industrial North, she was educated in London but has kept to her roots. At its best—as in the sweetly raunchy scenes here between Lieutenant Prior and his munitions-worker girlfriend, or in the instantly compelling vignettes of the other women in the munitions factory—her work makes many of the currently efflorescent novels of manners, such as those by Anita Brookner and David Lodge, seem uncomfortably narcissistic or pert. The documentary realism of Barker's first novel, *Union Street,* a harshly elemental book about the interwoven lives of a group of extremely poor women, won from the British press the honorific—or the brand—of "working-class masterpiece." Set amid unemployment and scrimping and alcohol and pride in a Northern coal-mining city devastated by the policies of Thatcherism, *Union Street* is an unsparing book, and its scenes of the imperative biology of these women's lives—sex, childbirth, abortion—are fully as harrowing as the men's traumas of war recounted in *Regeneration.* Indeed, this seems to be part of Barker's point: the two subjects are counterparts. Rivers comes to understand of his patients' psychosomatic illnesses that "it was prolonged strain, immobility and helplessness that did the damage, and not the sudden shocks or bizarre horrors," and that "any explanation of war neurosis must account for the fact that this apparently intensely masculine life of war and danger and hardship produced in men the same disorders that women suffered from in peace." As for the "perpetually harried expression" on the faces of the young officers—boys who at twenty feel like fathers to the men they command—Rivers has seen that look in only one other place: "in the public wards of hospitals, on the faces of women who were bringing up large families on very low incomes, women who, in their early thirties, could easily be taken for fifty or more." He recognizes it as "the look of people who are totally responsible for lives they have no power to save." These are the people on whom Barker lavishes her precise and unsentimental care: deadbroke mothers, half-grown soldiers—those living outside the pale of societal comfort and illusion.

Barker's second novel, ***Blow Your House Down,*** was a deliberately blunt and even brutal work about a group of prostitutes stalked by a killer in an actual nineteen-seventies case in England. In an interview that followed its publication, Barker replied to a question about her evident concern with violence against women by suggesting that what was needed was for "gentle men" to become more involved in the upbringing of their sons, to release male children from the need "to find their maleness by rejecting what is feminine." The wise and saintly Rivers in ***Regeneration*** is certainly the quintessential "gentle" man, everybody's ideal father (the adoring reader's not least), and access to gentleness—permitting it, acknowledging it—is his lesson for the young and damaged patients who are his children. Accused by a particularly troubling patient of being not so much a father as a "male mother," Rivers bridles at "the implication that nurturing, even when done by a man, remains female, as if the ability were in some way borrowed, or even stolen, from women—a sort of moral equivalent of the *couvade,*" and reflects that "if that were true, then there was really very little hope."

It is perhaps to secure Rivers' point—which is also Barker's point, and more the thematic center of the book than any statement about war—and to retain the powerful example of male tenderness free from the stigma of effeminacy that Barker plays so lightly on the unmistakable erotic element here. There are allusions to the fact of Sassoon's having come to terms with his homosexuality during the course of his "cure" with Rivers (who, as a doctor, departed from Freud on the centrality and meaning of sexuality) and to Owen's attraction—he was also homosexual—to Sassoon. ("I knew about the hero-worship but I'm beginning to think it was rather more than that," Sassoon says, worrying over a letter from the younger poet.) There is some intimation, too, that Rivers, a generation older, may have once experienced what these men are going through, but this is so delicately imparted that it is almost impossible to hold on to—a matter of a book he once read, a cultural openness, a solitary resignation. Rivers seems at times a genteel and beardless Whitman nursing the wounded mind. And his lessons are not without risks, even to himself:

> In leading his patients to understand that breakdown was nothing to be ashamed of, that horror and fear were inevitable responses to the trauma of war and were better acknowledged than suppressed, that feelings of tenderness for other men were natural and right, that tears were an acceptable and helpful part of grieving, he was setting himself against the whole tenor of their up-

bringing. . . . And yet he himself was a product of the same system, even perhaps a rather extreme product. . . . In advising his young patients to abandon the attempt at repression and to let themselves *feel* the pity and terror their war experience inevitably evoked, he was excavating the ground he stood on.

There are many battles being fought in ***Regeneration,*** and the war, for some, may not always be the hardest to face. Preparing to return to his regiment, Sassoon feels cheerful: "Exactly the same feeling he had had on board ship going to France, watching England slide away into the mist. No doubts, no scruples, no agonizing, just a straightforward, headlong retreat towards the front." Barker does not follow her characters to their separate fates; it is the moment of mutual touch and transformation which concerns her. ***Regeneration*** is an inspiriting book that balances conscience and the vitality of change against a collapsing world—a book about voyages out.

## Julia O'Faolain    (review date 10 September 1993)

SOURCE: "The Suffering Classes," in *The Times Literary Supplement,* No. 4719, September 10, 1993, p 21.

[*O'Faolain is an English-born Irish novelist, short story writer, and critic. In the following favorable review of* The Eye in the Door, *she describes the novel as "an original and impressive achievement."*]

Pat Barker's sequel to her dazzling and disturbing ***Regeneration*** (1991) has as much scope as that book, greater buoyancy and an equally impressive ability to anchor major issues in the experience of her real and invented characters. Set in the spring of 1918, it shows the English psyche under pressure after four years of war. The first lines give the tone:

> In formal beds beside the Serpentine, early tulips stood in tight-lipped rows. Billy Prior spent . . . moments setting up an enfilade, then . . . seized an imaginary machine-gun and blasted the heads off the whole bloody lot of them.
>
> Myra stared in amazement. "You barmy bugger."

There is a bleak joke here for, while metaphors do lurk among the tulips, Myra, unknown to herself, has hit home. Prior has been close to insanity and has practised buggery, and public attitudes to both are threatening factors in ***The Eye in the Door,*** whose master theme is cracking-up.

Like the minds under scrutiny, the prose here is rarely innocent, so one stays alert and, sure enough, some lines further on, the sunlit twigs which glow like "live electric filament" recall the electrodes applied in ***Regeneration*** to the throats of shell-shocked soldiers suffering, as Prior did in that novel, from mutism. He was spared this treatment thanks [to] Dr William Rivers, who features here again, though the central role is now Prior's. Like Rivers in ***Regeneration,*** he is faced by a moral dilemma arising from the war.

Rivers's trouble was that when he cured officers who had

been driven mad by their experiences in the trenches—they were sent back to those trenches. Prior's quandary is more elusive. Of working-class origins, he is an officer and "temporary gentleman". He hates the war from which he was invalided home, but feels solidarity with the men at the front and works for the Ministry of Munitions Intelligence Unit. Discomfort sharpens when he is sent to visit Beattie, who looked after him as a child. She is a pacifist who has been imprisoned on a trumped-up charge of trying to kill Lloyd George, and Prior's superiors hope to use his old friendships to lead them to wanted pacifist leaders. Class is only one of the fault-lines along which his consciousness is liable to crack, so when Beattie asks if he even knows on whose side he is, he doesn't answer. Mutism again? Worse follows when he starts to experience fugue states during which he does things he cannot afterwards recall. Meanwhile, in nightmares, the eye painted on the spy-hole of Beattie's cell door fuses with the eyeball of a dead man which Prior remembers picking up when he was at the front. Noting the connection between eyes and spies, he begins to fear that his aberrant self may have betrayed him.

Homosexuality, so dangerously akin to soldierly comradeship, is the object of a witch-hunt which threatens other patients of Rivers, including Charles Manning, with whom Prior has a sexual encounter. What is intriguing about this scene is that its vibrancy comes as much from class antagonism as from sex. Englishness, so often dimmed or diluted by irony in English fiction, is here presented in all the vigour of its flayed, cocky virulence. Prior is a marvellous creation: familiar off the page and plausible on it. Pat Barker's triumph is that she makes us understand and therefore care about him, just as she makes us care about Rivers's other balky patient, Siegfried Sassoon. Painfully proud, Prior has suffered more, and his lively mind, riven by the cleavages afflicting society, embodies society's ordeal while remaining vividly particular.

Barker draws on a battery of skills: historical intelligence, a sense of how people from up and down the social scale feel and talk, a risky readiness to freight that talk with ideas, plus an anthropologist's eye for detail. Her narrative glints with graphic bits of social lore which lighten and enlighten our apprehension of the whole. Prior, finding a housemaid's uniform in the servant's quarters of Manning's bombed house, smells its armpits—"lavender and sweat, a sad smell"—and remembers his mother, who was a housemaid, "telling him that in the house where she'd worked, if a maid met a member of the family in the corridor she had to stand with her face turned to the wall". This bizarre memory gives edge to our suspicion that his fugues have led him away from his own kind. And to be sure, the fugues are allegorical. Half England must have had them.

Barker's final flourish—historically true, she tells us in a note—replays in farcical vein the bit of history for which her earlier novel was named. This was the devotion to duty of a colleague of Rivers who cut and sutured one of his own nerves so as to study the process of regeneration. The replay is an anecdote about Churchill, when Home Secretary, spending a dutiful afternoon with an aide testing a new sort of birch on each others' buttocks. Homophobes, getting wind of the incident, accuse both men of being dangerously open to German blackmail. Prior's laughter at this leakage of mild madness ends the novel on an optimistic note. It is exhilaratingly readable; an original and impressive achievement.

## Dinah Birch (review date 21 October 1993)

SOURCE: "Invalided Home," in *London Review of Books,* Vol. 15, No. 20, October 21, 1993, p. 22.

[*In the following positive review of* The Eye in the Door, *Birch describes the novel as "a continuation, and an enrichment, of* Regeneration."]

Working-class memory generated Pat Barker's writing. Her early fiction presented itself as a tribute to generations of suffering and survival in the industrial North-East of England. It seemed to fall into a ready-made tradition: 'the grit, the humour, the reality of working-class life', Virago burbled cheerfully about **Union Street** (1982). But there was more to Barker's work than that. Alongside the realism of her accounts of deprivation among the back streets was an intense imaginative inwardness. The lives she recounted were haunted, not only by the shared grind of poverty, but by private images of loss and love. There was a political edge to those novels, emerging as they did from the feminist Left, but what drove them was a long engagement with moments of vision, bleakly Wordsworthian spots of time that recur again and again in her fiction. Barker's first four books had a cumulative force, shaping histories of obsession out of the hardships of oppression. The people she spoke for had an intimate particularity that tested the limits of political analysis. Their fantasies had the insistence, and often the violence, of a lived nightmare. Images of the body imprint themselves remorselessly on the minds of her characters, and her readers: the sputum and blood erupting from a dying man, the putrescent body of the murdered prostitute, the aborted foetus of the unmarried teenager. 'She banished the image which always, in her rare moments of silence and solitude, returned to haunt her.' Much of Barker's fiction is involved with that attempted exorcism.

This self-reflectiveness carried with it the hazard of repetition, and **Regeneration,** published in 1991, consciously broke a compulsive pattern. It was a historical novel, based on the work of the Army psychologist W.H.R. Rivers, who treated Siegfried Sassoon and Wilfred Owen at Craiglockhart Hospital in 1917. The political burden of the fiction is explicit. This is the story of Sassoon's rebellion against the continuation of the war, and of the process which eventually persuaded him back to the trenches in France. But the change in direction was not as radical as this new choice of subject might suggest. Barker has consistently written about the inheritance of suffering and endurance, and the impact of war had already emerged as one of her central preoccupations. Rivers's mode of treatment for shell-shocked soldiers mirrors her method as a novelist: corrosive memories must be confronted if health is to be restored. The attempt to deny the trauma imposed by trench warfare is what pushes Rivers's patients into insanity. The culture that instigated the warfare also attempted to deny its consequences: madness was the result there, too. Rivers, rather than Sassoon, emerges as the moral pivot of *Regeneration,* as he feels his way towards a larger understanding of the reasons for his patients' misery. Unspoken but persistently present in the novel is the fact that Rivers was about to stand for Parliament as an independent Labour candidate at the time of his death shortly after the war.

*The Eye in the Door* is a continuation, and an enrichment, of *Regeneration.* It is a novel of formidable energy and integrity, and it confirms Barker's status as one of the most rewarding writers to have emerged in recent years. Impervious to literary fashion, Barker's fiction builds on its own solid achievements. Each succeeding novel absorbs and moves beyond what has gone before. Many characters from *Regeneration* reappear in *The Eye in the Door:* Rivers, Sassoon, Graves. Themes and images also return, brought into closer focus. The authority of the eye, what it sees and what it imagines, has always mattered to Barker. A single gazing eye has brooded over her fiction from the first. 'Her one naked eye staring out like the eye of God' is what we remember of Beattie, raddled prostitute in retirement, in *Blow Your House Down.* In *Regeneration,* the eye became an emblem of horror. Billy Prior, one of Rivers's patients, has buried the memory of picking up the eyeball of a dismembered soldier called Towers and holding it in the palm of his hand. 'He had very blue eyes, you know. Towers. We used to call him the Hun.' What is left of Towers, a bare blue gaze that is neither English nor German, reveals the fragility of the categories that supposedly regulate Prior's life. An officer but not a gentleman, intelligent, bitter and ambitious, Prior breaks down because the boundaries of what he has been taught to expect can't contain what he has seen.

Prior's slow regeneration is the dominant story of *The Eye in the Door.* As the novel begins he is simply looking for sex. Failing to induce his girl to provide it, he finds a more eager partner in a fellow officer called Charles Manning. The encounter is graphically described. Here, as in all her work, Barker insists that the intellectual and moral issues which she writes about are inescapably grounded in the life of the body—'because this mass of nerve and blood and muscle is what we are.' The body makes its own demands, oblivious of the cultural distinctions that hedge us in. Borders of class and gender constantly shift around Prior. The First World War exposed and often denied established patterns of social difference, and this is one reason for Barker's longstanding interest in its history. Traditional concepts of war assert the values of manliness, and of gentlemanliness, but the new experience of fighting in the trenches undermined both. It was the 'peculiarly passive, dependent and immobile nature of their experience' that led to trench soldiers' vulnerability to what was termed 'neurasthenia'. Their trapped helplessness was something that had been more usually experienced by women. As Rivers notes, it was one of the ironies of the war that the disordered minds of his patients would frequently display symptoms that had previously been identified as belonging to hysterical women. The officers' duties, too—disciplining and caring for their men, providing food

and comfort—were curiously domestic, like those of mothers rather than warriors. Meanwhile, the women at home were freeing themselves from the worst tyrannies of domestic service, often earning high wages in the munitions factories, and finding some degree of the freedom that the men at the front had lost.

The cultural anxieties provoked by the faltering definitions of gender pervade Barker's novel. Aberrant groups are ruthlessly watched, with consequences that are cruel and often grotesque. Pacifists and homosexuals are singled out. Ambivalent and divided, Prior hovers on the edge of both groups. He had been sheltered as a child by Beattie Roper (another Beattie—names, like images, constantly recur in Barker's fiction), a pacifist now imprisoned for an improbable plot to poison Lloyd George with curare. Her cell is under unremitting surveillance, and the spyhole in the door is surrounded by an elaborately painted eye. Increasingly convinced that she has been clumsily framed by the Intelligence Unit that employs him, Prior's loyalties are divided. He is pursued by nightmares about the eye in Beattie's door, and his life falls apart. Terrifying lapses of memory fragment his days. His recovery—partial and qualified—comes when he finally looks at the roots of his own duplicity. As Rivers guides Prior towards self-knowledge, Prior inverts the orthodox relation of power between doctor and patient. Rivers has no visual memory. Prior's evolving understanding of his own condition pushes Rivers into facing the reasons for this disability, and its effect on the institutional authority he assumes over his patients. Moved by Prior's abrasive affection, Rivers is compelled to realise that he is not as separate from his patients as he has chosen to believe. He, too, has been trying to submerge the pain of memory, and has diminished himself in the attempt.

Prior is barely sane; other seemingly respectable figures are still less so. One of the most bizarre stories here is that of the 'Black Book', said to contain the names of 47,000 homosexual men and women whose moral corruption laid them open to blackmail by German agents. This mysterious book had supposedly been discovered in the *cabinet noir* of 'a certain German Prince' by Captain Harold Spencer, who went on to claim that members of Asquith's War Cabinet were in the pay of Germany, and that many high-ranking British officers were in fact Germans. He was obsessed with the depravity of modern women, writing about what he called 'the Cult of the Clitoris' and suggesting that the list of subscribers to a private performance of Oscar Wilde's *Salome* would include many of the degenerate 47,000. Barker's point is that Spencer was clearly much crazier than many of Rivers's patients, yet he was taken seriously in many quarters. Maud Allen, the dancer who was to take the part of Salome, sued for libel. Spencer's evidence was admitted in court, and she lost her case.

Spencer's lunatic fabrications revealed, rather than caused, the anti-homosexual panic that prevailed in the final months of the war. The divided consciousness embodied in an extreme form by Prior was a pervasive consequence of a profoundly traumatic war, and was by no means confined to those who had seen active service. One of the strengths of *The Eye in the Door* is Barker's integration of historically documented events with the constructed imaginative lives of her characters. Charles Manning, invalided home from the trenches, has a dual existence, combining his homosexual activities with life as a loving husband and father. He is driven to breakdown by the fear of exposure triggered by Maud Allen's libel case. Manning, too, becomes Rivers's patient as fact and fiction weave patterns through the novel. In part, these designs are formed by the literary heritage left by the war. Barker, like the men and women she writes about, is working her way through memory, and books, like soldiers, leave ghosts behind them. The poetry of the war, often the creative product of homosexual doubleness, lingers in her prose. One function of the novel is the commemoration and celebration of Sassoon and Owen.

Robert Graves is a more equivocal spectre. The cadences of *Goodbye to All That* have sounded in Barker's work before. In a climactic moment towards the end of *The Century's Daughter* a social worker rescues the parrot belonging to the book's dead heroine. He recites a verse from Skelton:

> Parrot is a fair bird for a ladie.
> God of His goodness him frameéd and wrought.
> When parrot is dead he doth not putrify,
> Yea, all things mortal shall turn into nought
> Save mannés soul which Christ so dear bought,
> That never can die, nor never die shall.
> Make much of parrot, that popajay royál.

They are grand lines, but there is a touch of self-regarding evasion in the social worker's construction of an intellectual event out of the heroine's pitiless murder. The literary memory behind this moment is Graves's description of a wartime cricket match between officers and sergeants, in which a dead parrot in a cage serves as a wicket. Graves quotes the same passage from Skelton. The transposition is characteristic of Barker's writing, with its reflected and transformed image, brooding on memory and mortality. She has learned from Graves's engagingly direct style. But Graves had much to do with defusing Sassoon's politically inspired denunciation of the war, and his position betrays an element of arrogance. Describing his family background in the opening pages of *Goodbye to All That,* Graves mentions an inherited disposition to 'sudden and most disconcerting spells of complete amnesia. These fits, so far as I can discover, serve no useful purpose, and tend to produce in the victim the same sort of dishonesty that afflicts deaf people who miss the thread of conversation— they hate to be left behind and rely on intuition and bluff to get them through.' These blanks bear a close relation to the bouts of amnesia that afflict Prior, whose loss of memory also implies the loss of moral identity. The 'dishonesty', jovially dismissed by Graves, becomes a dark and fearful phenomenon in Barker's novel. Graves is no villain, but his literary presence hints at a kind of avoidance that runs counter to the rigorous confrontations with memory and the imagination that Barker imposes on her readers.

**Peter Parker    (review date 8 September 1995)**

SOURCE: "The War That Never Becomes the Past," in *The Times Literary Supplement,* No. 4823, September 8, 1995, pp. 4-5.

[*Parker is English nonfiction writer and biographer. In the following review of* The Ghost Road, *he remarks on the distinctive qualities of Barker's trilogy and praises her blending of fiction and historical fact.*]

As we approach the millennium, the pall cast across our century by the First World War shows no sign of lifting. In spite of later and bloodier conflicts, in spite of the gradual dilution of public ceremonies of remembrance, in spite of the fact that almost everyone who fought in the war has now died, the Great War for Civilization (as it was dubbed in a more innocent age) continues to haunt the collective imagination. A number of fine modern novels have been written about the war: Susan Hill's *Strange Meeting* (1971), Jennifer Johnston's *How Many Miles to Babylon* (1974), Timothy Findley's *The Wars* (1977) and William Boyd's *An Ice-Cream War* (1988); and the critical and popular success of Sebastian Faulks's lumbering *Birdsong* (1993) is evidence of a continuing—and undiscriminating—appetite for such fiction.

The insistence with which the war tugs at our consciousness is acknowledged by Pat Barker in her observation that: "The Somme is like the Holocaust. It revealed things we *cannot* come to terms with and cannot forget. It never becomes the past." There is an echo here of Siegfried Sassoon, whose entire life was haunted by his experiences in the war, and who—indulging his "queer craving to revisit the past and give the modern world the slip"—spent twenty years trying to come to terms with them in two autobiographical trilogies. It is appropriate, therefore, that Sassoon should occupy a central place in *Regeneration* (1991), the first volume of Barker's war trilogy, which opens in July 1917 with his arrival at Craiglockhart War Hospital after he had made his celebrated "Soldier's Declaration" against the conduct of the war. It was here that Sassoon was treated by W.H.R. Rivers, a neurologist and anthropologist who was serving with the RAMC. Rivers (1864-1922) is a fascinating figure whose influence extended far beyond medical circles and can be traced in the work of Robert Graves, who met him through Sassoon (and who makes a nicely judged cameo appearance in *Regeneration*), and W.H. Auden, whose doctor father admired Rivers and whose Berlin associate John Layard had been one of Rivers's anthropological colleagues. Rivers gradually emerges as the central historical figure in the trilogy, his experiences counterpointed by those of a fictional patient, Billy Prior.

It is Prior as much as Sassoon who challenges Rivers's beliefs and assumptions, and he does so without Sassoon's gentlemanly restraint. A young second lieutenant of northern, working class origins, Prior first appears in the trilogy as a mute, struck dumb by what Rivers would diagnose in a famous paper published in the *Lancet* in 1918 as "The Repression of War Experience". It was Rivers's contention that "neuraesthenia", a blanket term used to describe various sorts of battle trauma, might perhaps be triggered by some particularly dreadful incident, but that it was *caused* by prolonged exposure to what would sometimes become quite literally unspeakable conditions. The repression of such experiences led to mental breakdown, and Rivers's job was to get his patients to recall and confront what had happened to them.

One of the things that sets Barker's trilogy apart from most recent novels about the war is that it reaches beyond a meticulously researched account of life in the trenches, beyond the historical irony so well deployed by Sassoon and so frequently and crudely exploited since, right into the dark heart of the matter. In the preface to his classic novel of the Western Front, *The Middle Parts of Fortune* (1929), Frederic Manning wrote: "War is waged by men; not by beasts, or by gods. It is a peculiarly human activity." Barker's novels investigate what it is to be human, and what is demanded of those humans whom circumstances oblige to pursue that peculiar activity.

"Regeneration" may be defined as a process of "moral, spiritual, or physical renewal or invigoration", which is what many people thought the war represented for the nation. (Parallels with the Falklands War insistently present themselves here, as they do elsewhere in the trilogy.) Regeneration is also what the army expects Rivers to achieve with his traumatized patients. Rivers is acutely aware that, whereas a civilian doctor cures his patient in order to send him out into life again, he "cures" his in order to send them back into battle and probable death, and the book's title is cruelly ironic. Furthermore, this treatment goes against everything that society and the war has demanded of men, and is as hazardous for the doctor as it is for his patients:

> He was setting himself against the whole tenor of their upbringing. They'd been trained to identify emotional repression as the essence of manliness. Men who broke down, or cried, or admitted to feeling fear, were sissies, weaklings, failures. Not *men*. And yet he himself was part of that same system, even perhaps a rather extreme product. Certainly the rigorous repression of emotion and desire had been the constant theme of his adult life. In advising his young patients to abandon the attempt at repression and to let themselves *feel* the pity and terror their war experience inevitably evoked, he was excavating the ground he stood on.

The title also refers more specifically to an experiment to which Rivers's friend and colleague Henry Head subjected himself before the war. "The nerve supplying Head's forearm had been severed and sutured, and then over a period of five years they had traced the process of regeneration." Head's use of himself as a guinea-pig recalls *The Strange Case of Dr Jekyll and Mr Hyde,* a passage from which is used as the epigraph to the second volume in Barker's trilogy, *The Eye in the Door* (1993): "It was on the moral side, and in my own person, that I learned to recognize the thorough and primitive duality of man; I saw that, of the two natures that contended in the field of my consciousness, even if I could rightly be said to be either, it was only because I was radically both. . . ." This duality is one of the principal themes of Barker's trilogy, most notably embodied by Prior, who suffers from prolonged blackouts, during which the sadistic impulses he normally manages to suppress (except during dreams of battle, from which

he wakes ejaculating) come to the fore. Bisexual, a "temporary gentleman", now working in intelligence, supposedly against pacifist friends, Prior inhabits a sexual, social and moral no man's land. He is merely an extreme example of the "split personality", however; equally divided— between recklessly brave soldier and bitter, outspoken pacifist—is Sassoon; while the officers Rivers treats have been trained to suppress all human instincts in order to turn themselves into killing machines, but at the same time are expected to take on a paternal role in looking after the men under their command.

The doctors, too, are split between the compassion they feel for their patients as suffering humans and the objective interest in them as medical cases. It transpires that Rivers himself shares more with his patients than they might at first suppose. As a child, he suffered from a disabling stammer, which he has managed to control, and a stammer is one of the most prominent symptoms among the men at Craiglockhart. Having regained his speech, Prior insists that the demarcation between doctor and patients is not at all clear, and the trilogy is partly about Rivers's own attempts to reintegrate his fragmented personality.

---

**One of the things that sets Barker's trilogy apart from most recent novels about the war is that it reaches beyond a meticulously researched account of life in the trenches, beyond the historical irony so well deployed by Sassoon and so frequently and crudely exploited since, right into the dark heart of the matter.**

**—Peter Parker**

---

*The Ghost Road* amply fulfils the high expectations raised by its predecessors. The narrative is divided equally between Rivers, now at a hospital in London, and Prior, who is returning to the line with another Craiglockhart alumnus, Wilfred Owen. Drowsing through a bout of Spanish flu, Rivers recalls his earlier incarnation as an anthropologist doing field research among a community of former head-hunters on an island in the South Pacific. Gradually parallels arise between his encounters with these "savages", to whom "the language of introspection was simply not available", and his dealings with his "civilized" patients, in whom introspection has been ruthlessly suppressed by upbringing, education and military training. *"Look at us",* Prior writes in his diary. "We don't remember, we don't feel, we don't think—at least not beyond the confines of our job. By any proper civilized standard (but what does *that* mean *now*?) we are objects of horror." Rivers too comes to question the very notion of civilization, that intangible thing for which the war is purportedly being fought. Observing the behaviour of his principal native informant towards a man who is dying, he notes that: "Even Njiru who, within the framework of his culture, was a compassionate man (and we can none of us claim more, Rivers thought), seemed to feel, not indifference or contempt exactly, but that Mbuko had become merely a problem to be solved." This prefigures a terrible scene towards the end of the novel, just as the island's "stone ghosts . . . erected as memorials to men who died and whose bodies could not be brought home" inescapably suggest the row upon row of headstones that will spring up in the war cemeteries of the Western Front. The ghosts of dead warriors, which play an important part in the culture of the Melanesians, are linked to those which appear to the traumatized Sassoon. Rivers's terrifying experience in a cave thronged with bats makes him aware simultaneously of the common humanity he shares with the islanders and the sheer vulnerability—"the sense of being unshelled"—that is a principal feature of humanity, one which will be highlighted by the war. Holding a skull, Rivers thinks: "This blown eggshell had contained the only product of the forces of evolution capable of understanding its own origins"; but he also knows that this, "the object of highest value in the world", probably ended up in the island's skull house as the result of a murderous raid, and this too looks forward to the murderous raids of his own war and his attempts to repair the damage done to such fragile receptacles by bullets and high explosives. The trilogy's final, hallucinatory, page, on which these two apparently distant and disparate worlds come together, is quite extraordinarily moving.

Arnold Bennett wrote that one of Rivers's most striking qualities was a "gift of co-ordinating apparently unrelated facts". This is a gift Barker shares, and the historical framework of the trilogy, far from being constricting, allows her to make all sorts of connections between social, sexual and political dissent, particularly in *The Eye in the Door,* which features the notorious "Cult of the Clitoris" libel case of 1918 and a soldier with the suggestively Forsterian name of Scudder. Fact and fiction are so skillfully interwoven that one is never sure where one ends and the other begins. What seems at first a relatively straightforward and tightly controlled narrative gradually and spectacularly unfurls in the reader's mind.

The presentation of Sassoon and Rivers is wholly convincing, while Billy Prior, who carries with him a great deal of symbolic and representative freight, is never less than a fully realized character. Witty, alert and vibrantly alive, his sexuality uninhibited and unashamed, he is a positive life force amidst so much death and destruction, a point emphasized by graphic and extremely well-written descriptions of his couplings with both men and women. Prior is also valuable as a device for driving the narrative onwards. The difficulty with using historical figures is that the reader knows in advance how the story will end: as *The Ghost Road* moves towards its bloody conclusion at the Sambre-Oise Canal in November 1918, we are only too aware of what will happen to Owen—dispatched here in a sentence—but we do not know, though by now we genuinely care, what will happen to Prior.

*The Ghost Road* is a startlingly good novel in its own right. With the other two volumes of the trilogy, it forms one of the richest and most rewarding works of fiction of recent times. Intricately plotted, beautifully written, skill-fully assembled, tender, horrifying and funny, it lives on in the imagination, like the war it so imaginatively and so intelligently explores.

**Tony Gould   (review date 29 September 1995)**

SOURCE: "Undertones of War," in *New Statesman & Society,* Vol. 8, No. 372, September 29, 1995, p. 57.

[*In the review below, Gould remarks favorably on* The Ghost Road.]

[*The Ghost Road*] is the final volume in Pat Barker's impressive trilogy of novels about the first world war. The first, *Regeneration,* is set in Craiglockhart, the war hospital famous (in literary history, at least) as the place where Siegfried Sassoon and Wilfred Owen met, and centres on Sassoon's clinical relationship with the psychologist and anthropologist W H R Rivers. The second, *The Eye in the Door,* in which Rivers again plays a major role, also deals with historical events—the ill-treatment of pacifists and the hounding of homosexuals. *The Ghost Road* links Rivers' past, and his fieldwork in Melanesia, and his hospital work with victims of "shell-shock" as the war draws to a close.

But Rivers is not the only hero of the trilogy. There is also the entirely fictional Billy Prior, an infantry officer from a working-class background who provides the stroppy, gritty northern perspective familiar to readers of Barker's earlier novels. Where the bachelor Rivers' sexuality is a matter for delicate speculation, Prior is characterised by an aggressive bisexuality. What both men share is a damaged childhood. In Rivers' case, the damage seems trivial; in Prior's, it is extreme, the effect of a brutal father and an abusing priest. But this common thread establishes as wary affection between the two.

In *The Ghost Road,* Prior offers himself as a kind of test case for Rivers to see if the "cure" for neurasthenia achieved at Craiglockhart will hold under the renewed pressures of the front line. So his sensations and the events of the last weeks of the war, in which one of his companions is Wilfred Owen, are presented in diary form, giving them great immediacy. Rivers almost succumbs in the Spanish flu epidemic, and in his fever relives his time among Pacific headhunters.

The link between sex and both headhunting and war is emphasised. Rivers describes the headhunters, following the suppression of their favourite pastime by the British authorities, as "a people perishing from the absence of war". This may be ironic in the context of a war in which the peoples of Europe perished in their thousands. But that alone would hardly justify the juxtaposition of the two narratives. What really binds them is their common obsession with dying, death and ghosts. This subtle novel provides a worthy conclusion to a gripping series, which combines fact and fiction in an unusually satisfying manner.

**Charlotte Joll**　(review date 30 September 1995)

SOURCE: "Back to the Front," in *The Spectator,* Vol. 275, No. 8725, September 30, 1995, pp. 44-5.

[*In the following review, Joll remarks on Barker's treatment of shell shock and war in* The Ghost Road.]

*The Ghost Road* is the final volume of Pat Barker's trilogy about the first world war. It continues the story of a group of shell-shocked soldiers, some real (notably Siegfried Sassoon) and some fictional, who were lucky enough to be treated by the empathetic and dedicated neurologist William Rivers. Barker uses this framework to write about the lives of men who, for a time at least, were too ill to go on fighting, but while back in England felt guilty and at odds with all those who hadn't been in the trenches and, more importantly, were not going there in the future.

Shell shock or war neurasthenia, now termed 'post traumatic stress syndrome' was then often viewed as synonymous with shirking and funk, and the standard treatments of the day, including ECT, were both inappropriate and brutal. Rivers, first at Craiglockhart and then in London, was ahead of his time in using psychotherapy to get his patients to come to terms with what they had experienced in the trenches, the suppression of which resulted in a variety of different psychosomatic responses, including elective mutism, hysterical paralysis and olfactory hallucinations as well as the more run-of-the-mill nightmares, twitches and stammers.

While reading Sebastian Faulkes's *Birdsong* I made a mental note to find out what arrangements existed for collecting and disposing of the enormous number of corpses generated each day in the trenches. The answer, at least in part, lies in this trilogy; having to either clear up, or cohabit with, the dead and decaying bodies of their former comrades is the common denominator in precipitating the breakdown of many of Rivers's patients. 'Corpses were everywhere in the trenches. Used to strengthen parapets, to prop up sagging doorways, to fill in gaps in the duckboards'. It is no surprise that Sassoon hallucinates about bodies lying in piles in Piccadilly or that another of Rivers's patients develops anorexia having been thrown, head first, into the belly of a dead German soldier and getting a mouthful of decomposing flesh.

---

> In contrasting the practices and beliefs of a primitive tribe about war, superstition and death, with those of a civilised society, *The Ghost Road* illuminates the ironies of a world in which a single ritual murder is deemed unacceptable but the mass slaughter of millions is seen as heroic sacrifice.
>
> —*Charlotte Joll*

---

*The Ghost Road* follows the fortunes of Lieutenant Billy Prior, who first appears in *Regeneration* as one of Rivers's most difficult and prickly patients. His recovery begins when, having been hypnotised, he remembers deliberately picking up the eyeball of a friend he has witnessed being blown to bits. A spell in military intelligence, described in *The Eye in the Door,* reawakens a number of unresolved issues in his life. These include his transition from a working-class home to the officer corps and his opportunistic bi-sexuality at a time of hysterical homophobia, characterised by the Pemberton Billings case. His mental health deteriorates and he begins to experience long periods in a fugue state. Now, pronounced fit, he is eager to return to the front, the ultimate test case of the effectiveness of Rivers's régime.

In selecting Rivers as her hero Barker focuses on the contradictions involved in being a successful doctor, when success meant getting your patients well enough to be able to go back to France in order to be killed. In *The Ghost Road* Rivers's work with the damaged and the dying is interspersed with scenes from his previous existence, as an anthropologist, studying a Melanesian tribe on Eddystone Island. For these people, who have been forced to abandon their head-hunting tradition by the colonial authorities, the absence of war is destroying their raison d'être. In contrasting the practices and beliefs of a primitive tribe about war, superstition and death, with those of a civilised society, Barker illuminates the ironies of a world in which a single ritual murder is deemed unacceptable but the mass slaughter of millions is seen as heroic sacrifice. Are the skull houses of the islanders any more bizarre than the orderly cemeteries of the Flanders dead?

The description of Prior's experiences in the final months of the war is economical, authentic and emotionally intense, building to what seems to be an increasingly inevitable conclusion. We sense that Prior is becoming whole again. It is this regeneration that allows him to fulfil some form of destiny in rescuing a fellow officer who survives for long enough to be transferred back to London, to be looked after by Rivers during his long and painful death. Finally Prior, alongside Wilfred Owen, willingly, almost joyfully, takes part in the suicidal crossing of the Sambre-Oise canal, only days before the Armistice is finally signed.

This is a beautifully written book. It is ambitious in its subject matter, compelling in its content. The skilful blend of fact and fiction gives Pat Barker scope to write with authority and imagination and in doing so she has produced a trilogy which is right up there with the other classics of first world war literature. I could not recommend it more highly.

**Paul Levy**　(essay date 8 November 1995)

SOURCE: "Pat Barker Wins Booker Prize," in *The Wall Street Journal,* November 8, 1995, p. A20.

[*Below, Levy remarks on the awarding of the Booker Prize to* The Ghost Road *and criticizes the novel as anachronistic.*]

The Booker Prize jury has added insult to the ayatollahs' injury, cheating Salman Rushdie of the £20,000 ($31,600)

1995 Booker Prize for Fiction. In its 27th year, Britain's most celebrated (though no longer richest) award for a book has been given to Pat Barker for her *The Ghost Road,* which this year's Booker chairman, George Walden, praised faintly as "clear, hard prose." Following the heavily applauded announcement, several jubilant commentators said it was about time that a woman won again. . . .

Ms. Barker's *The Ghost Road* is the final part of her World War I trilogy, in which she successfully mixes fictional characters with historical ones such as W.H.R. Rivers, the army psychologist who pioneered the concept of shell shock, and the poet Wilfred Owen. She does this without meretriciousness, unlike, for example, E.L. Doctorow. But the book is full of anachronism—one of her characters calls the western front "a wanker's paradise" though this term for masturbation wasn't current until the next war or even later. And its *attitudes* are anachronistic, especially the author's toleration and even approval of homoeroticism. Is this on purpose—an enlightened present-day view of past events—or has Ms. Barker lost control of her material? The judges evidently gave her the benefit of the doubt and I am eager to read the first two volumes and be proved wrong.

---

## FURTHER READING

### Criticism

Caldwell, Gail. "Back to the Front: The Conclusion of Pat Barker's Extraordinary Trilogy of World War I, Winner of the Booker Prize." *Boston Globe* (3 December 1995): 72.
>   Comments favorably on *The Ghost Road,* praising Barker's grasp of World War I's effect on England.

Hoffman, Eva. "The Super Bowl of Fiction." *The New York Times Book Review* (26 November 1995): 35.
>   Comments on the awarding of the Booker Prize to Barker.

Pierpont, Claudia Roth. "Shell Shock." *The New York Times Book Review* (31 December 1995): 5.
>   Favorably reviews *The Ghost Road.*

Riding, Alan. "Testifying to the Ravages of Granddad's War." *The New York Times* (6 December 1995): C17, C18.
>   Remarks on Barker's portrayal of British society as dysfunctional in her World War I trilogy.

Rubin, Merle. "The Great War and All Its Scars." *The Wall Street Journal* (18 December 1995): A12.
>   Praises Barker's "gritty realism" and "imaginative use of symbols and leitmotifs," but contends that the novel's characters and themes lack depth.

---

**Additional coverage of Barker's life and career is contained in the following sources published by Gale Research:** *Contemporary Authors,* **Vols. 117, 122;** *Contemporary Authors New Revision Series,* **Vol. 50; and** *Contemporary Literary Criticism,* **Vol. 32.**

# A Clockwork Orange

## Anthony Burgess

(Born John Anthony Burgess Wilson; also wrote as John Burgess Wilson and under the pseudonym Joseph Kell) Born in 1917, Burgess was an English novelist, essayist, critic, playwright, translator, editor, scriptwriter, short story writer, poet, author of children's books, composer, and autobiographer. He died in 1993.

The following entry presents criticism on Burgess's novel *A Clockwork Orange* (1962). For further information on his life and works, see *CLC,* Volumes 1, 2, 4, 5, 8, 10, 13, 15, 22, 40, 62, and 81.

## INTRODUCTION

*A Clockwork Orange* is Burgess's best known and most controversial work. A kind of dystopian *bildungsroman* relating the "ultra-violent" life of Alex, a teenage hoodlum in a future English society, the novel is told in the first person and features Burgess's invented "nadsat" language, a patois comprised of distorted English and Russian words that is spoken by Alex and his cronies, or "droogs." The novel presents a bleak picture of society terrorized by street gangs and incompetently governed by hypocritical and self-serving officials. Through Alex's story, Burgess explores themes of free will, violence, and state-controlled behavior in a blackly humorous and subtly satirical style. Originally published in the United States in a truncated, twenty-chapter edition (which served as the basis for Stanley Kubrick's 1971 film), the complete novel ends with a twenty-first chapter in which a somewhat older Alex, grown bored with his violent lifestyle, dreams of beginning a family. Burgess later attempted to distance himself from *A Clockwork Orange,* believing that the novel—inflated by the popularity of the film—overshadowed his other works. In addition to the film version, *A Clockwork Orange* has served as the basis for three stage productions, two of which were written by Burgess.

### Plot and Major Characters

Alex and his "droogs," under the influence of hallucinogenic milk, engage in acts of extreme violence against innocent, randomly-selected citizens and other gangs. One night he and his gang steal a car and travel to the outskirts of town where they happen on a private residence called HOME. There they brutally beat and rape the wife of F. Alexander, a liberal intellectual writer and author of a book called *A Clockwork Orange.* The next day Alex feigns a headache and stays home from school. He goes to a record shop where he meets two young girls whom he leads to his house and rapes. Alex's starkly violent life is counterpointed by his startlingly inventive discourse and by his love for classical music, particularly Ludwig van Beethoven's Ninth Symphony. Later that evening, two of Alex's droogs, Dim and Georgie, challenge his

leadership of the gang. A fight ensues in which Alex reestablishes his authority by slashing the two with a razor. Later, however, while escaping the scene of a burglary during which Alex mercilessly beats an elderly woman to death, Dim hits his leader in the eyes with a metal chain and the gang abandons him to the police, or "millicents." Alex spends more than two years in the "Staja" (STAte JAil). In that time, the prison chaplin introduces Alex to the Bible, which he reads as though it were a lurid novel; Alex also kills a fellow inmate who made sexual advances toward him. He then accepts an opportunity to undergo the experimental "Ludovico Treatment," a form of behavior conditioning in which the subject endures drug-induced nausea while being forced to watch films of wildly violent acts. Alex is made incapable of considering violence without becoming physically ill and is released from prison. Lonely and bereft of vitality, Alex eventually runs into and is brutally beaten by Dim and Billyboy, his former droog and an old gang foe who have since become members of the police. Left for dead on the outskirts of town, Alex stumbles to the nearest house—F. Alexander's HOME—where he quickly becomes the pawn of a liberal political organization that attempts to use him as an example of the current government's sadistic and ineffective methods of dealing with crime. Alex then attempts suicide by jumping out of a window; the fall doesn't kill him, but it nullifies the effects of the Ludovico Treatment. After recovering from his injuries he considers himself "cured" and is again free to contemplate and commit acts of violence. In the novel's final chapter, the older Alex loses interest in his old way of life and dreams of being married and having a son. The novel ends with Alex melancholically imagining that his son will be much like himself: that, as a father, Alex will be no more successful controlling his son than his own father was at controlling him.

## Major Themes

A major theme of *A Clockwork Orange* is the ability of the individual to make moral choices. Burgess presents a society that experiments with radical behavior modification techniques on criminals to eliminate socially unwanted behavior; his argument is that it is morally and ethically preferable for the state to allow its citizens the choice between good and evil than it is for the state to destroy the capacity for choice. A side effect of Alex's conditioning is that, because classical music accompanied the films he watched during the Ludovico Treatment, he can no longer listen to Beethoven without getting sick. While this is a negligible by-product from the point of view of the government, it illustrates Burgess's point that destroying the ability to choose evil also destroys the capacity to choose good. The novel also juxtaposes the violence committed by Alex and his gangmembers with the violence committed by the state in the name of justice and security.

## Critical Reception

*A Clockwork Orange* has sparked controversy and debate since it was first published. Much of the critical commentary has focused on the novel's violent content. While some critics view it as titillating and gratuitous, others consider the severity of the violence committed by Alex as a thematic counterbalance to the extreme actions of the State. Debate has also focused on the function and interpretation of Burgess's ending. Some commentators argue that the twenty-first chapter detracts from the moral and ironic power of the novel; others find that the final chapter adds legitimacy to the notion of the novel as a *bildungsroman,* a story about Alex's moral and psychological growth. Views on the function and effect of the "nadsat" language also differ. Some critics see it as a "distancing" device that insulates the reader from the violence and thus makes it easier to identify with Alex. Others contend that the nadsat language reflects Alex's rebellion against his society's standardized and homogenized culture and see the use of nadsat as both parodic and heroic. Most critics agree, however, that the creation of the language itself is an impressive feat. Geoffrey Aggeler stated: "Both as satire and linguistic *tour de force, A Clockwork Orange* is one of Burgess' most brilliant achievements."

## PRINCIPAL WORKS

*\*Time for a Tiger*   (novel)   1956
*\*The Enemy in the Blanket*   (novel)   1958
*English Literature: A Survey for Students* [as John Burgess Wilson]   (criticism)   1958
*\*Beds in the East*   (novel)   1959
*The Doctor Is Sick*   (novel)   1960
*The Right to an Answer*   (novel)   1960
*Devil of a State*   (novel)   1961
*One Hand Clapping* [as Joseph Kell]   (novel)   1961
*The Worm and the Ring*   (novel)   1961
*A Clockwork Orange*   (novel)   1962
*The Wanting Seed*   (novel)   1962
*Honey for the Bears*   (novel)   1963
*†Inside Mr. Enderby* [as Joseph Kell]   (novel)   1963
*The Novel Today*   (criticism)   1963
*The Eve of St. Venus*   (novel)   1964
*Language Made Plain* [as John Burgess Wilson]   (nonfiction)   1964
*Nothing Like the Sun: A Story of Shakespeare's Love-Life*   (novel)   1964
*Here Comes Everybody: An Introduction to James Joyce for the Ordinary Reader*   (criticism)   1965; also published as *Re Joyce,* 1965
*A Vision of Battlements*   (novel)   1965
*Tremor of Intent*   (novel)   1966
*The Novel Now: A Student's Guide to Contemporary Fiction*   (criticism)   1967; revised edition, 1971
*†Enderby Outside*   (novel)   1968
*Urgent Copy: Literary Studies*   (criticism)   1968
*Shakespeare*   (biography)   1970
*MF*   (novel)   1971
*Morning in His Eyes* [translator and adaptor; from the drama *Oedipus Rex* by Sophocles]   (drama)   1972
*Cyrano* [translator and adaptor; from the drama *Cyrano de Bergerac* by Edmond Rostand]   (drama)   1973
*Joysprick: An Introduction to the Language of James Joyce*   (criticism)   1973
*‡The Clockwork Testament; or, Enderby's End*   (novel)   1974
*Napoleon Symphony*   (novel)   1974
*Beard's Roman Women*   (novel)   1976
*A Long Trip to Teatime*   (juvenilia)   1976
*Moses: A Narrative*   (poetry)   1976
*Abba Abba*   (novel)   1977
*A Christmas Recipe*   (poetry)   1977
*Ernest Hemingway and His World*   (biography)   1978
*1985*   (novel)   1978
*The Land Where Ice Cream Grows*   (juvenilia)   1979
*Man of Nazareth*   (novel)   1979
*Earthly Powers*   (novel)   1980
*§Quest for Fire* [with Gerard Brach and Jean-Jacques Annaud]   (screenplay)   1981
*The End of the World News*   (novel)   1983
*Enderby's Dark Lady; or, No End to Enderby*   (novel)   1984
*Flame into Being: The Life and Work of D. H. Lawrence*   (biography)   1985
*Homage to QWERT YUIOP: Selected Journalism 1978-1985*   (journalism)   1985; also published as *But Do Blondes Prefer Gentlemen?*, 1986

*The Kingdom of the Wicked*  (novel)  1985
*Little Wilson and Big God: Being the First Part of the Confessions of Burgess*  (autobiography)  1986
*The Pianoplayers*  (novel)  1986
*A Clockwork Orange*  (drama)  1987
*Any Old Iron*  (novel)  1989
*The Devil's Mode*  (short stories)  1989
*You've Had Your Time: Being the Second Part of the Confessions of Burgess*  (autobiography)  1990
*Mozart and the Wolf Gang*  (novel)  1991; also published as *On Mozart: A Paean for Wolfgang. Being a Celestial Colloquy, An Opera Libretto, a Film Script, a Schizophrenic Dialogue, a Bewildered Rumination, a Stendahlian Transcription, and a Heartfelt Homage upon the Bicentenary of the Death of Wolfgang Amadeus Mozart,* 1991
*A Mouthful of Air: Language and Languages, Especially English*  (nonfiction)  1992
*Chatsky; or, The Importance of Being Stupid* [translator; from the drama *Gore ot Uma* by Alexander Griboyedov]  (drama)  1993
*A Dead Man in Deptford*  (novel)  1993

---

*These works were published as *The Malayan Trilogy* in 1964 and as *The Long Day Wanes: The Malayan Trilogy* in 1965.

†These works were published as *Enderby* in 1968.

‡This work was published along with *Inside Mr. Enderby* and *Enderby Outside* as *Enderby* in 1982.

§Burgess devised the primitive language used by the characters in this film about prehistoric man.

---

# CRITICISM

**Julian Mitchell**   (review date 18 May 1962)

SOURCE: "Horrorshow on Amis Avenue," in *The Spectator,* Vol. 95, No. 6986, May 18, 1962, pp. 661-62.

[*Mitchell is an English novelist, playwright, and critic. In the following positive review, he lauds* A Clockwork Orange *as a brilliant mixture of horror and farce, calling Burgess's use of language an "extraordinary technical feat."*]

Anthony Burgess must have garnered some excellent reviews in his short, busy writing career (*A Clockwork Orange* is his eighth novel since 1956). No one can match his skill at anguished farce about the end of empire. His characters seem to be trapped in a tent whose pole has just been sawn in two by an over-enthusiastic administrator doing his part in a campaign to save wood. It is hilarious to watch their frantic heaving and humping beneath the spoiled canvas, to hear their absurd multilingual pidgin groans. But as we wipe away our tears of laughter, we notice that someone has just thrown petrol over the collapsed and writhing tent: frozen with horror, we see him strike a match.

If Mr. Burgess is, in some ways, a pupil of Mr. Waugh, he yet has an originality of manner and subject which

place him, to my mind, among the best writers in England. Yet he has never received the critical attention granted to Angus Wilson and Kingsley Amis, with whom at least he deserves to rank. Certainly his prose is more attractive than either's, and he is prepared to take risks which they are not. And if his novels seem rather hollow and heartless at times, from a tendency to move his characters about to illustrate his points instead of letting the characters find their own way to making them, the points are major ones about our times.

*A Clockwork Orange* is set in the future, in an England where the streets are called things like Amis Avenue. It is narrated by Alex, a beguiling adolescent gang-leader with ultra-violent tendencies and a passion for classical music, in a teenage slang which takes a few pages to grasp. A splendid slang it is, though, full of stuff like 'yarbles' and 'profound shooms of lip-music brrrrr' and 'droog.' The key praise-word is 'horrorshow,' for Alex's world is horrible and sadistic, and he is one of the toughest juvenile delinquents one could hope to meet. Very properly gaoled for killing a cat-loving old lady, Alex is subjected to a new cure for criminals, similar to that for alcoholics: he becomes sick and faint at the thought of violence or the sound of classic music (connected by him with violence). Released, he finds himself the victim of the entire world, at the mercy of policemen, old professors and politicians. His responses are no longer his own.

Mixing horror with farce in his inimitable manner, Mr. Burgess develops his theme brilliantly, though there is a certain arbitrariness about the plot which is slightly irritating and I find it difficult to accept the contention that being young is like being a clockwork toy—you walk into things all the time. But the language is an extraordinary technical feat, and the whole conception vigorously exhibits Mr. Burgess's great imaginative gifts. No doubt ignorant and anonymous reviewers will criticise him for 'experimenting' (as John Wain was recently and absurdly criticised): they will be merely exhibiting their ignorance and anonymity. Mr. Burgess is far too good and important a writer not to go in any direction he chooses.

**Stanley Edgar Hyman**   (review date 7 January 1963)

SOURCE: "Anthony Burgess' Clockwork Oranges," in *The New Leader,* Vol. XLVI, No. 1, January 7, 1963, pp. 22-3.

[*Hyman was an American critic and educator, long associated with the* New Yorker *magazine. In the following positive review, he praises Burgess as a satirist and calls* A Clockwork Orange *"an eloquent and shocking novel that is quite unique."*]

Anthony Burgess is one of the newest and most talented of the younger British writers. Although he is 45, he has devoted himself to writing only in the last few years. Before that he was a composer, and a civil servant in Malaya and Brunei. His first novel, *The Right to an Answer,* was published in England in 1960 and here in 1961. It was followed the next year by *Devil of a State,* and now by *A Clockwork Orange.* Burgess seems to me the ablest satirist to appear since Evelyn Waugh, and the word "satire" grows increasingly inadequate to his range.

***The Right to an Answer*** is a terribly funny, terribly bitter smack at English life in a provincial city (apparently the author's birthplace, Manchester). The principal activity of the townspeople seems to be the weekend exchange of wives, and their dispirited slogan is "Bit of fun" (prophetically heard by Mr. Raj, a visiting Ceylonese, as "bitter fun"). The book's ironic message is Love. It ends quoting Raj's unfinished manuscript on race relations: "Love seems inevitable, necessary, as normal and as easy a process as respiration, but unfortunately"—the manuscript breaks off. Raj's love has just led him to kill two people and blow his brains out. One thinks of *A Passage to India,* several decades more sour.

***Devil of a State*** is less bitter, more like early Waugh. Its comic target is the uranium-rich East African state of Dunia (obviously based on the oil-rich Borneo state of Brunei). In what there is of a plot, the miserable protagonist, Frank Lydgate, a civil servant, struggles with the rival claims of his wife and his native mistress, only to be snatched from both of them by his first wife, a formidable female spider. The humor derives mostly from incongruity: the staple food in Dunia is Chinese spaghetti; the headhunters upriver shrink a Belgian head with eyeglasses and put Brylcreem on its hair.

Neither book at all prepares one for the savagery of Burgess' new novel. *A Clockwork Orange* is a nightmarish fantasy of a future England where the hoodlums take over after dark. Its subject is the dubious redemption of one such hoodlum, Alex, told by himself. The society is a limp and listless socialism at some future time when men are on the moon. Hardly anyone still reads, although streets are named Amis Avenue and Priestley Place; Jonny Zhivago, a "Russky" pop singer, is a juke-box hit, and the teenage language sounds very Russian; everybody "not a child nor with child nor ill" must work; criminals have to be rehabilitated because all the prison space will soon be needed for politicals; there is an opposition and elections, but they re-elect the Government.

The endless sadistic violence in the book, unimaginably nasty, mindless and mind-hating, is described by Alex with eloquence and joy, at least until it turns on him. In the opening pages, we see 15-year-old Alex and the three other boys in his gang out for an evening of fun: They catch an old man carrying library books on the street, beat and kick him bloody, smash his false teeth and tear up his books; then, wearing masks (of Disraeli, Elvis Presley, Henry VIII and Shelley), they rob a shop, beating the middle-aged proprietor and his wife unconscious and undressing the woman for laughs; then they catch another gang raping a child and fight them, chaining one boy in the eyeballs and kicking him unconscious, carving another's face with a razor; they cap off the evening by stealing a car for the "real kick," "the old surprise visit," which consists of invading the suburban house of a writer, tearing up his manuscript, beating him bloody, holding him while they strip his wife and rape her in turn, then smashing up the furniture and urinating in the fireplace; finally they push the car into a filthy canal and go happily home to bed.

The next day Alex pleads a headache and stays home from school. He goes out, picks up two 10-year-old girls, gets them drunk on whisky, injects himself with dope, puts the last movement of Beethoven's Ninth on the phonograph, and rapes both girls, brutally and perversely. That night he fights two members of his gang for leadership and defeats them by cutting their wrists with his razor. It is his high point. The gang then does a burglary job, at which Alex beats an old lady to death. As he flees, with the police coming, one of the boys whose wrist he had cut blinds Alex by chaining him in the eyeballs, and the police catch him.

A streak of grotesque surrealism runs all through Burgess' books. By *A Clockwork Orange* it has become truly infernal. As the hoodlums drive to their "surprise visit," they run over a big snarling toothy thing that screams and squelches, and as they drive back they run over "odd squealing things" all the way.

Alex has no interest in women except as objects of violence and rape (the term for the sex act in his vocabulary is characteristically mechanical, "the old in-out-in-out"). No part of the female body is ever mentioned except the size of the breasts (it would also interest a Freudian to know that the hoodlums' drink is doped milk). Alex's only "aesthetic" interest is his passion for symphonic music. He lies naked on his bed, surrounded by his stereo speakers, listening to Mozart or Bach while he daydreams of grinding his boot into the faces of men, or raping ripped screaming girls, and at the music's climax he has an orgasm.

After his capture, Alex is treated as brutally by the police as he treats his victims. In jail, he kicks a cellmate to death, and his reward is being chosen as the first experiment in conditioned reflex rehabilitation. For two weeks he is injected daily with a drug and shown films of sadistic violence even more horrible than his own, accompanied by symphonic music. At the end of that time he is so conditioned that the thought of doing any violence makes him desperately ill, as does the sound of music. In a public display of his cure, he tries to lick the boots of a man hurting him, and he reacts to a beautiful underdressed girl by offering to be her true knight.

It is a moral fable, if a nasty one, and it proceeds with all the patness of moral fable. Eventually Alex tries to kill himself by jumping out a window, and as a result of his new injuries he recovers from the conditioning, and again loves violence and music. He is, he says, "cured."

A running lecture on free will, first from the prison chaplain, then from the writer, strongly suggests that the book's intention is Christian. Deprived of his capacity for moral choice by science, Burgess appears to be saying, Alex is only a "clockwork orange," something mechanical that appears organic. Free to will, even if he wills to sin, Alex is capable of salvation. But perhaps this is to confine Burgess' ironies and ambiguities within simple orthodoxy. Alex always *was* a clockwork orange, a machine for mechanical violence far below the level of choice, and his dreary socialist England is a giant clockwork orange.

Perhaps the most fascinating thing about the book is its language. Alex thinks and talks in the "nadsat" (teenage) vocabulary of the future, a remarkable invention by Burgess of several hundred words. It is not quite so hard to decipher as Cretan Linear B, and Alex translates some of it. I found that I could not read the book without compiling a glossary, although some of my translations are approximate. At first the vocabulary seems incomprehensible: "you could peet it with vellocet or synthemesc or drencrom or one or two other veshches." Then the reader discovers that some of it is clear from the context: "to tolchock some old veck in an alley and viddy him swim in his blood." Other words are intelligible after a second context: When Alex kicks an enemy on the "gulliver" it might be any part of the body, but when a glass of beer is served with a gulliver, "gulliver" is "head."

Some of the words are inevitable associations, like "cancer" for "cigarette" or "charlie" for "chapl[a]in," and may even be current English slang. Others are produced simply by schoolboy transformations: "appy polly loggy" (apology), "eggiweg" (egg), "interessovat" (to interest), "skolliwoll" (school). Still others are foreign words slightly distorted: Russian "baboochka" (old woman) and "bolshy" (enormous), Latin "biblio" (library), Chinese "chai" (tea), Italian "gazetta" (newspaper), German "forella" ("trout" as slang for a woman) and "knopka" (button), Yiddish "keeshkas" (guts) and "yahoodies" (Jews), French "sabog" (shoe) and "vaysay" (WC, watercloset).

Other words are onomatopoetic sound imitations: "collocoll" (bell), "razrez" (to tear), "toofles" (slippers). Still others are rhyming slang: "luscious glory" for "hair" (rhyming with "upper story"?) and "pretty polly" for "money" (rhyming with "lolly" of current slang). A few simply distort the word: "banda" (band), "gruppa" (group), "kot" (cat), "minoota" (minute). Others are amputations: "creech" (from "screech"; shout or scream), "domy" (domicile), "guff" (guffaw), "pee and em" (pater and mater), "sarky" (sarcastic), "sinny" (cinema). Some are portmanteau words: "chumble" (chatter-mumble), "mounch" (mouth-munch), "shive" (shiv-shave), "skriking" (scratching-striking).

The best of them are images and metaphors, some quite imaginative and poetic: "glazz" (eye), "horrorshow" (beautiful, beautifully), "lewdies" (squares), "pan-handle" (erection), "rabbit" (to work), "sammy" (generous, from "Uncle Sam"?), "soviet" (an order), "starry" (ancient), "viddy" (to see, from "video"), "yahzick" (tongue, from "say-*ah*-when-*zick*").

There are slight inconsistencies, when Burgess (or Alex) forgets his word and invents another or uses our word, but on the whole he handles his amazing vocabulary in a masterly fashion. It has a wonderful sound, particularly in abuse, when "grahzny bratchny" sounds infinitely better than "dirty bastard." Coming to literature by way of music, Burgess has a superb ear, and he shows an interest in the texture of language rare among current novelists. As a most promising writer of the '60s, Anthony Burgess has followed novels that remind us of Forster and Waugh with an eloquent and shocking novel that is quite unique.

---

**Anthony Burgess on *A Clockwork Orange*:**

I'm not particularly proud of *A Clockwork Orange,* because it has all the faults which I rail against in fiction. It's didactic. It tends to pornography. It's tricky. It's gimmicky. One may excuse any author for writing what he writes, because he's primarily earning a living, you see. He's turning out an artifact which will, he hopes, sell enough to pay the rent. It's Balzacian. It's almost, indeed, it's Shakespearean. Nothing wrong with it. But I do object very strongly to these theses that are written on the damn book. The book is not all that interesting or important.

*Anthony Burgess with Samuel Coale, in an interview in* Modern Fiction Studies, *Vol. 27, No. 3, Autumn, 1981, p. 448.*

---

**William H. Pritchard**   (essay date Summer 1966)

SOURCE: "The Novels of Anthony Burgess," in *The Massachusetts Review,* Vol. 7, No. 3, Summer, 1966, pp. 525-39.

[*Pritchard is an American critic and educator. In the following excerpt, he discusses the effect of Burgess's invented language, "nadsat," on the violent content of* A Clockwork Orange.]

*A Clockwork Orange, The Wanting Seed,* and **Honey for the Bears** are (at least the first and last) Burgess' most popular books and they ask to be considered together. All of them concern the individual and the modern state; all of them are felt to have a connection with the quality of life in the 1960's, but they approach life obliquely by creating fantasies or fables which appeal to us in odd and disturbing ways. As always with Burgess' work, and now to a splendidly bizarre degree, the creativity is a matter of style, of words combined in strange new shapes. Through the admiration these shapes raise, rather than through communication of specifiable political, philosophical or religious ideas about man or the state, is to be found the distinction of these novels; for this reason it is of limited use to invoke names like Huxley or Orwell as other novelists of imagined futurist societies.

*A Clockwork Orange,* most patently experimental of the novels, is written in a language created by combining Russian words with teenage *argot* into a hip croon that sounds both ecstatic and vaguely obscene. The hero, Alex, a teenage thug, takes his breakfast and morning paper this way:

> And there was a bolshy big article on Modern Youth (meaning me, so I gave the old bow, grinning like bezoomny) by some very clever bald chelloveck. I read this with care, my brothers, slurping away at the old chai, cup after tass after chasha, crunching my lomticks of black toast dipped in jammiwam and eggiweg. This learned veck said the usual veshches, about no parental discipline, as he called it, and the shortage of real horrorshow teachers who would lambast bloody

beggary out of their innocent poops and make them go boohoohoo for mercy. All this was gloopy and made me smeck, but it was nice to go on knowing one was making the news all the time, O my brothers.

Although the American paperback edition provides a glossary, one doesn't need it to get along very well after the first few pages. In fact such translation is a mistake for it short-circuits the unmistakable rhythms of speech by which the sentences almost insensibly assume meaning. Moreover, though the book is filled with the most awful violence—what in our glossary or newspaper would be called murder, assault, rape, perversion—it comes to us through an idiom that, while it does not deny the connection between what happens in the second chapter and what the newspaper calls a "brutal rape," nevertheless makes what happens an object of aesthetic interest in a way no rape can or should be. Life—a dreadful life to be sure—is insistently and joyously deflected into the rhythms of a personal style within which one eats lomticks, not pieces, of toast.

The novel is short and sharply plotted: Alex is betrayed by his fellow "droogs," imprisoned for murder, then by a lobotomizing technique is cured of his urges to violence; whereas music, Beethoven in particular, had inspired him to heights of blood-lusts, he now just feels sick. Caught between the rival parties for state power he tries suicide, but lives to recover his original identity, as listening to the scherzo of the Beethoven Ninth he sees himself "carving the whole litso of the creeching world with my cut-throat britva." The book concludes on this happy note, for oddly enough it *is* a happy note; we share the hero's sense of high relief and possibility, quite a trick for the novelist to have brought off. And without questioning it we have acceded to the book's "message," as radical and intransigent as the style through which it is expressed:

> More, badness is of the self, the one, the you or me on our oddy knockies, and that self is made by old Bog or God and is his great pride and radosty. But the not-self cannot have the bad, meaning they of the government and the judges and the schools cannot allow the bad because they cannot allow the self. And is not our modern history, my brothers, the story of brave malenky selves fighting these big machines. I am serious with you, brothers, over this. But what I do I do because I like to do.

Doing what you do because you like to do it is what the Burgess hero—Crabbe, Denham, others—has done and has been punished for doing by his creator. But the hero of *A Clockwork Orange* is rewarded and endorsed in a way more recognizably human characters in a more "realistic" atmosphere could not possibly be. In the world of creative fantasy we can admire hero and event as they are shaped by language; our response is akin to the old-fashioned "admiration" proper to the heroic poem. By the same token the defense of self, no matter how twisted it may be, and the condemnation of the state, no matter how benevolent it pretends to be, is absolute. Such a simple and radical meaning is not morally complex, but it must be taken as a serious aspect of fantasy. Within its odd but

carefully observed limits the book is entirely consistent, successful and even pleasing, Burgess' most eye and ear-catching performance.

### Robert K. Morris (essay date 1971)

SOURCE: "The Bitter Fruits of Freedom," in *The Consolations of Ambiguity: An Essay on the Novels of Anthony Burgess,* University of Missouri Press, 1971, pp. 55-75.

[*Morris is an American critic, educator, and biographer. In the following excerpt, he compares the structure and philosophic themes of Burgess's dystopian novels,* A Clockwork Orange *and* The Wanting Seed.]

What followed from Burgess' preoccupation with the transition and ultimate death rattle of colonialism abroad and the atrophy of "self-indulgent" England at home were his two dark visions of dystopia—*A Clockwork Orange* and *The Wanting Seed*. Even the parboiled paternalism of the Empire and the synthetic socialism of the welfare state had still apparently left room—though not much—for a dialogue between the individual and society and had kept alive discussions as to what was right and what was wrong with England (*The Right to an Answer,* for example, presumed some sort of question to begin with). The subsequent stasis—or worse, stagnation—setting in after reconstruction placed the mystery of understanding, as well as the burden of existence, on the individual alone. No longer of import were the questions of how to view, contain, serve, survive, or possibly love a state that clothed, fed, housed, and medicated. Now what had been the issue was exacted from the sensibilities of those who, glutted physically and socially, lived under what amounted to a deadening hedonism. It must have seemed only logical to Burgess, after exploring the dialectics of the single and collective mind, that the problem of the novelist was to probe its metaphysics—to see how the naked needs of his rebel anti-heroes (no longer even privileged to suffer the "consolation of ambiguity") could be met in a mad, lost, loveless, brutal, sterile world.

At first blush, *A Clockwork Orange* and *The Wanting Seed* may appear—one because of stylistic shockers, the other for its Gothicism and *grand guignol*—more like bizarre and fantastic companions to the Burgess canon than parts of it. Like the majority of sci-fi trading on metarealities, the novels risk having the parts dissolve in the whole, the vantage point become lost in the vision. Unless, that is, one grasps from the outset that they are actually extensions of present conditions rather than forecasts of future ones. Such terrors as perpetrated by teenage werewolves like Alex in *A Clockwork Orange* and the domination of gangs like Hell's Angels are near-mild "happenings" placed cheek by jowl with current youth revolutions. And if the prime target of *The Wanting Seed*—overpopulation—is not yet, technically, a *fait accompli,* its proliferating literature, written not by hysterical Cassandras but by sound demographers, attests less to its imminence than, failing a cracking good holocaust, its inevitability.

One, then, must zero in on the contemporaneity of Burgess' issues—something that the ingenious superstructures and novelistic devices often impede. Take as an example the style of both novels. The ferocious and coarse, partly archaic, partly mod, neologic "nadsat" of *A Clockwork Orange* captures perfectly the violence and pace of incidents, breaking down into standard English only when the hero is being brainwashed and stripped of individuality. Clearly, it is always an amazing feat to have the language of a novel not simply *match* the action, but *be* the action. Clearly, too, one quickly wearies of the innovative, especially in matters of an *outré* style that so dazzles readers as to its form that they are almost eager to overlook its content. The brevity of *A Clockwork Orange* probably accounts for the success of its linguistic excess. Burgess, at any rate, has more luck in overplaying his hand in language than in standing pat. Though he was undoubtedly after a much different effect in *The Wanting Seed,* the contrast between the scrupulous impersonality of a Defoe-like, third-person narrator and the nightmarish, surrealistic scenes never quite catches the tone of savagery that the satire seems to be striving for.

Again, there is the matter of structure. The triunal division of *A Clockwork Orange*—Alex damned, Alex purged, Alex resurrected—can be taken, depending on one's predilections at the start, as the falling-rising pattern of comedy or the rising-falling pattern of tragedy. That one may have it either way means, of course, there is a danger in having it neither. If the mode of a novel should say something about its meaning, or at least carry us forward so we may debate it, then we might have wished for a less open-ended conclusion, one that defined as well as disturbed. I find a similar falling off into diffuseness or blurriness in *The Wanting Seed,* in which Burgess, alternating the lives of Tristram and Beatrice-Joanna Foxe, attempts to match the "Pelagian-Augustinian" phases of ebb and flow that symbolize the arbitrary movement of historic cycles. Yet while the reunion of Tristram and Beatrice has been logically anticipated throughout, the pat, almost cliché ending of husband and wife rejoined, coerced no more by the forces of man and nature but rising above them—transfixed, as it were, in the still point of the ineluctable cycle—strikes me as an alogical apotheosis of the human spirit.

Yet both books conclude on notes of "joy": Alex fondling his "britva" as he anticipates the chorale of Beethoven's Ninth and more throat cutting; the Foxes (Adam and Eve and twin offspring?) standing in their Valéry-like "graveyard by the sea," facing the ocean out of which new life will come (*il faut tenter vivre*). The individual is thus endowed with regenerative powers never clearly woven into the fabric of the fiction, and Burgess barters even tentative answers for impressive technique. I feel, in short, that his adroit shock tactics with plot and language, expertise with satire, and partiality to apocalypse—all enviable attributes and potential pluses normally—come dangerously close here to outflanking the substantive ideas. Done as these novels are, with immense energy and cleverness, their sheer "physicalness" all but crushes their metaphysics.

That is a loss, for Burgess has much to tell us. However arbitrary the premises of these novels, however suspect their "political science," their speculations on freedom and free will are frighteningly pertinent. Violently opposing the sterile, mechanical life under totalitarianism, they point no less to the degeneration under anarchy and, further, offer no viable alternative. Freedom stifled is no less opprobrious than freedom unlicensed, but the middle ground—what every liberal imagines is the just and workable compromise—is accounted equally suspect. Burgess has given us in the earlier . . . novels a smug, self-satisfied, socialized England that has run down. Too much freedom creates the mess only stability can correct; of course, stability involves the surrender of freedom. Like those of Orwell and Huxley, Burgess' exaggerated portraits of the confrontation between individual and state will ever mystify—until too late—the addled sensibilities who, drugged by the present moment, will neither care about nor comprehend the moment beyond. Even more frightening, we have since Orwell and Huxley moved closer to the impasse where the problems at last overwhelm the solutions, and what we are left with for solution is perhaps only continual re-examination of the problem. Is it not, therefore, a trifle absurd to ponder tortuous issues of mind and soul when daily it grows impossible to cope with external realities like pollution, famine, and overpopulation? Can we even talk of freedom or free will to states that have written them off as mere philosophical aberrations? Yet what meaning can existence have without the continuing quest to define it?

On the one hand, Burgess answers these paradoxes through the nineteenth-century existentialism of writers like Dostoyevsky, Nietzsche, and Kierkegaard who dealt with freedom and free will, not in historic, but in metaphysical contexts. If revolution and the state initiated a new order of debate on freedom versus authority—from which arose the issue of free will—then the problems were quickly desocialized thereafter. Liberationism became as much the immovable force as necessitarianism the impenetrable object. Indeed, the best synthesis of the weird symbiosis between free will and freedom is still to be found in Ivan Karamazov's poem on the Grand Inquisitor, which, wrenched from its place in the novel, can satisfy radical and reactionary alike. Man, weak and imperfect as he is, can never bear the loneliness of living absolutely by free will and so surrenders the ideal of freedom to the *Realpolitik* of society. As Dostoyevsky realized all too sadly and well, most of us, lacking the superhuman inner strength necessary to do otherwise, submit our wills to Pilates and Inquisitors, rather than exercise them in an imitation of Christ.

Burgess' approach within this convention explains some of the broader outlines of both novels—especially since his hypothetical states dog the heels of totalitarian regimes. But clearly the Europe of a hundred years ago is not the "global village" of today. The revolutionary spirit abroad in the nineteenth century may have accounted in great part for its philosophy, but the trend of states toward a finer and fiercer repression (with no exit in sight) created an entirely new metaphysics on the older issues. Today, though man has more freedom to discuss his powers of freedom, the ugly fact is that the opportunities for demonstrating it have become more and more narrow. Striking out in acts of violence against the state that usurps freedom only binds our wills more rigorously to the state. Enigmatically, violence is not a display of free will at all, but an echo of historic determinism. For whether we like it or not, we cannot exercise free will in a vacuum; and though we like it less and less, the state is still the "objective correlative" for the freedom we seek. The true problem, in other words, is no longer how one learns to love Big Brother, nor what happens when one does not, but what results from not caring one way or the other about him.

What is chilling about *A Clockwork Orange* and *The Wanting Seed* is not so much Burgess' awareness of these philosophic questions, but the dead ends to which the empiricism of his answers leads. He achieves a partial perspective in *The Wanting Seed* in pirating from the Pelagian-Augustinian tussle over free will in order to superimpose metaphysics on history. His ENSPUN, a future conglomerate of English states, moves by fits and starts according to "theologico-mythical concepts" of two historic cycles that alternately place man in one phase or the other.

> "Pelagius [as Tristram Foxe tells his history class] denied the doctrine of Original Sin and said that man was capable of working out his own salvation . . . . All this suggests human perfectibility. Pelagianism was thus seen to be at the heart of liberalism and its derived doctrines, especially Socialism and Communism. . . . Augustine, on the other hand, had insisted on man's inherent sinfulness and the need for his redemption through divine grace. This was seen to be at the bottom of Conservatism and other *laissez-faire* and non-progressive political beliefs. . . . The opposed thesis, you see. . . . The whole thing is quite simple, really." [*The Wanting Seed*]

This exposition comes early on and *is* "quite simple"— that is, if one contents himself with surfaces. I mentioned above that this philosophic rationale provides the structure for the novel. It also supplies the several antipodal outlooks (the optimistic and pessimistic, borne respectively by Beatrice-Joanna and Tristram) and accounts for the crucial rationalistic and voluntaristic arguments over the individual and the state (the Pelagian would allow man freedom of choice to populate himself out of existence; the Augustinian would stifle his natural instincts and freedom in order to preserve the state). Finally, in the most clever of ways, the rationale parallels the lineal development of the protagonists as their lives crisscross in the alternating historic cycles.

But what is also "quite simple" to ignore are the modern ironies Burgess twists into the debate between the venerable bishop-saint and the heretic monk. Augustine and Pelagius clashed, one may remember, over the most fundamental issues relating to free will: original sin and divine grace. Augustine developed the theory that Adam's sin is transmitted from parents to children throughout all generations through the sexual act (which, inevitably accompanied by lust, is sinful), while Pelagius taught that sin originates in man's following the bad example of Adam and that it is continued in mankind by force of habit. Consequently, Augustine concluded that man's ultimate salva-

tion resided in the divine grace of God alone; Pelagius argued—with something approaching psychological insight—that divine grace is bestowed according to merit and that man, in the exercise of his free and morally responsible will, will take the determining initiative in matters of salvation.

This is very solemn stuff, and I hope the reader will not lose patience with me when I say that much of it is beside Burgess' main point, though very ingeniously tangential to it. As Tristram pedantically remarks, "The theology subsisting in our opposed doctrines of Pelagianism and Augustinianism has no longer any validity. We use these mythical symbols because they are peculiarly suited to our age, an age relying more and more on the perceptual, the pictorial, the pictographic." But translated into modern historic terminology, the theology has an added force, albeit an inverted one. The concept of original sin, the theory, is positively silly and insignificant when placed beside the desperate reality of overpopulation accruing from lust, fornication, and marriage. Birth is accountable for both the theological and historical problem as well as for the metaphysical bind of the protagonists. And, by the same token, one cannot even quixotically imagine that God's grace will clear up the population explosion; it is to God's modern counterpart, the state, that one looks for salvation. . . .

---

**Like all good satirists, Burgess lashes out with savage indignation at stupidity and blind error and lacerates our disastrous pretensions at solving human problems at the expense of human beings.**

**—Robert K. Morris**

---

Those skeptical of the chances governments afford us will find *A Clockwork Orange* sustaining to such skepticism. It is a book focusing on "the chance to be good" and proceeding from a single, significant existential dilemma: Is an evil human being with free choice preferable to a good zombie without it? Indeed, at two points in the novel Burgess spells out the dilemma for us. On one occasion, Alex, about to submit to conditioning, is admonished by the prison chaplain:

> "It may not be nice to be good, little 6655321. It may be horrible to be good. . . . Does God want goodness or the choice of goodness? Is a man who chooses the bad perhaps in some ways better than a man who has the good imposed upon him? . . . A terrible terrible thing to consider. And yet, in a sense, in choosing to be deprived of the ability to make an ethical choice, you have in a sense really chosen the good."

And on the other, the unwitting F. Alexander, with whom Alex finds sanctuary temporarily, similarly remarks:

> "You've sinned, I suppose, but your punishment

has been out of all proportion. They have turned you into something other than a human being. You have no power of choice any longer. You are committed to socially acceptable acts, a little machine capable only of good. . . . But the essential intention is the real sin. A man who cannot choose ceases to be a man."

Yet, were this all Burgess had to say on the matter, the impetus of the dilemma would lose substantially in force. Society at large has never troubled itself with the existential agony (unless to repress some manifestation of it), and judging from the preponderance of sentiment abroad today, it would undoubtedly applaud the conditioning process that champions stability over freedom. But Burgess has found inhering in the central dilemma considerations even more immediate. What distinctions between good and evil are possible in the contemporary world? As absolutes, have such distinctions not been totally perverted or obliterated? And as relative terms, depending for definition on what each negates or excludes, have they not become purely subjective? In a technically perfect society that has sapped our vitality for constructive choice, we are, whether choosing good or evil, zombies of one sort or another: Each of us is a little clockwork orange making up the whole of one great clockwork orange.

I am not suggesting that this spare masterpiece necessarily answers the questions it raises. Even a philosophic novel is fiction before philosophy, a fact too easily lost sight of in the heat of critical exuberance. If anything, Burgess sharpens our sensibilities, shapes our awareness of his main argument, by letting us see the extent to which the human quotient dwindles in the face of philosophic divisions. One must, therefore, reject equally any monistic or dualistic readings of the novel, not because the book, per se, is complex, but because the issues are. It is obviously impossible to resolve syllogistically which is the greater evil perpetrated in *A Clockwork Orange*: Alex's rape and murder or the state's conditioning of his mind and, as some would have it, soul. Passive goodness and dynamic evil are choices that in themselves may or may not be acceptable or unacceptable, but that in terms of the novel are neither. My own preference is to view the book pluralistically, to see it as a kind of varieties of existential experience, involving at every turn mixtures of both good and evil that move outward through widening concentric circles of choice from the esthetic (ugliness, beauty) to the moral (sin, redemption). And, as with *The Wanting Seed,* the experiences are empirically stated.

Let me start with the esthetic that is oddly integral to the novel—its language. *Vesch* and *tolchock* and *smeck* and about 250 other nadsat neologisms characterize Alex's era as distinctively as *phony* and *crap* do Holden Caulfield's. Whatever sources Burgess drew upon ([the character Dr. Branom describes Alex's language as] "Odd bits of old rhyming slang. . . . A bit of gypsy talk, too. But most of the roots are Slav. Propaganda. Subliminal penetration."), it has generally been the brutality, harshness, distortion, artificiality, and synthetic quality of the coinages that have fascinated those (myself included) who make the direct connection between the way Alex speaks and how he acts. The language is all of this—an "objective correlative"

with a vengeance—but it is something more. Burgess is also a musician, and any passage of sustained nadsat reflects certain rhythms and textures and syncopations. As the following:

> Oh, it was gorgeosity and yumyumyum. When it came to the Scherzo I could viddy myself very clear running and running on like very light and mysterious nogas, carving the whole litso of the creeching world with my cutthroat britva. And there was the slow movement and the lovely last singing movement still to come. I was cured all right.

In its simplicity and naturalness as well as its wholeness and continuity, this final paragraph of *A Clockwork Orange* sings to me much as those free-wheeling lapses in Molly Bloom's soliloquy. It is hardly coincidental that Alex's favorite piece of music is Beethoven's Ninth, rich in dissonances that only the professional ear can detect, but filled also with as many untapped, infinite (so it seems) harmonies. In a way it is easy to understand why musical conservatives of Beethoven's time could find the Ninth "ugly" by the then rigorous harmonic standards and why, as a matter of fact, more than one critic fled from the concert hall at the beginning of the "lovely last singing movement." Alex's language is, in its way, ugly, too; but place it alongside the bland and vapid professional or everyday language of the doctors and warders and chaplains and hear how hollow their language rings. Burgess was out to show how sterile and devitalized language could become without a continuing dynamics behind it; how, in fact, the juice had been squeezed from it; and how, contrarily, Alex emerges as something of a poet, singing dithyrambs to violence, but revealing through the terrifying beauty of his speech the naked beauty of an uninhibited psyche.

The choice of an esthetic substantiates the several existential modes without explaining how the maladjustment—itself an indication of social, psychological, and biological "evils"—came about. The causes are naturally grounded in current events, and Burgess has spelled them out in earlier writings. Alex, the gross product of welfare state overkill, is not "depraved because he is deprived" but because he is indulged. "Myself," he notes rather pathetically at the beginning of *A Clockwork Orange,* "I couldn't help a bit of disappointment at things as they were those days. Nothing to fight against really. Everything as easy as kiss-my-sharries." Alex's utopia is more than the result of suprapermissiveness and self-gratification; it is the consequence of the "original sin" inborn with every offspring of modern organizational leviathans. Having discovered that existence has always meant freedom, but never having been taught "goodness," Alex responds predictably and inevitably to the killing burden of choice.

Socially, he and his "droogs" parody the formless, shadowy, omnipotent political entity that sports with them as they with "lewdies." This Kafkaesque infinite regression is frightening enough, though I find even more so Burgess' repeated inferences that we are all, in some way or another, products of conditioning: tools to be manipulated and clockwork oranges whether we will or no. Alex, not unlike Meursault or K. or—as Burgess more slyly than reasonably lets us imagine—Christ, is the mere scapegoat. He is the one called upon to expiate for the existence of others because he has dared question—or (in this case) has been forced to question—his own.

I don't know that Burgess offers any clear-cut expansion of the psychological and biological evils of modern life, but he does dramatize with vitality the theory that we are by now—depending on our luck—either neurotic or paranoid. Alex's particular routine sado-masochism—nightly orgies of "tolchocking" and the old "in-out in-out," alternating between sabbaticals at the all-too-Freudian Korova Milkbar and withdrawals (onanistic and otherwise) into his multi-speakered stereo womb—may be the healthy neurosis standing between Alex and the paranoia of the populace, though it proves something of a disaster for those elected as outlets for his self-expression. Yet more insidious is the growing feeling one gets in reading *A Clockwork Orange* of governments encouraging violence in order to whip up and feed the paranoia that will ultimately engender allegiance through fear. Ironically, Alex, on the surface at least, is less psychologically distorted and biologically frustrated in his career of violence than those he terrorizes or those who seek to condition him. And, in a more significant way, his small-scale brutalities reflect no deeper abnormality than those of larger scale perfected by the engineers of power politics.

Alex, of course, does not intellectualize his *Non serviam*. For one thing, he wouldn't know how to; for another, there is no need to. The evils of intellect—ignorance and error—have brought the state to a point at which only the fruits of escalated intellectual achievement can check and contain (if that is now the sole function left the state!) the robots it has brought into being. Nothing is mystifying about our present disenchantment with intellectuals who, however motivated or why, have skillfully and near totally excised with their finely honed organizations, systems, and machines the last vestiges of our intuition. Burgess makes a case for the Alex-breed being one of the last, though obviously not impregnable, strongholds of intuition. Yet Alex is neither a purely feeling (if ignoble) savage nor a crusader warring against thought. He is a prototype of those who, muddling means and ends by lumping them together, rebel out of a studied defiance to intellect, rather than out of any untutored intuitive urge. Intellect having failed to show them the "truth that shall make men free," intuition alone must sustain the illusion of freedom and itself become accepted as the creative act or be confused with it. Such intuitional virtues seem to account for Alex's successful "dratsing" with Georgie and Dim:

> . . . when we got into the street I viddied that thinking is for the gloopy ones and that the oomny ones use like inspiration and what Bog sends. For now it was lovely music that came to my aid. There was an auto ittying by and it had its radio on, and I could just slooshy a bar or so of Ludwig van (it was the Violin Concerto, last movement), and I viddied right at once what to do.

What Alex does is carve up both of them a bit with his "britva," yet the episode is more significant in retrospect than in context. Alex's *natural* reflex of elation in the face of violence—inspired here by Beethoven—later becomes a *conditioned* reflex against violence after his bout with the "Ludovico technique," a name, I imagine, not chosen at random by Burgess. The distortion of intellect and intuition leads to an unresolvable Manicheanism: What are we, where are we when we can be programmed into calling evil what is so clearly the "good and beautiful?" In a clockwork-orange society we may as well surrender any pretense for distinguishing between good and evil; when we call them by the identical name we know we have been brainwashed past hope. In this respect, *A Clockwork Orange* shows refinements even beyond *1984*. Winston Smith, having undergone physical tortures on a par with primitive atrocities and unrelenting mental cruelties predicated on external fears, quite naturally betrays the woman he loves and learns to love Big Brother. But Alex, robbed of his will, reduced to an automaton, taught to be sickened by violence, is made "good" only by killing in him what was already *the* good.

Both Winston and Alex "die" when they can no longer love. Yet, if *1984* is grimly conclusive in showing the death of a mind and heart at the hands of the state, *A Clockwork Orange* is equally effective in questioning the finality of the death. Burgess brings in (not for shock tactics alone) one of the original archetypes through which Alex finds salvation: the fall, or in this case, the jump. His attempted suicide is, according to Christian dogma, a transgression against God's will, grace, and judgment, and, existentially, the inexcusable surrender of human freedom. Alex, in other words, has been half-dragged, half-propelled down paths of problematical and actual evil to arrive at the lethal nadir of moral evil: sin. And having plumbed the depths, he can only rise. He is a slave to fate rather than choice (the things that happen to him in the last third of the book recapitulate those he initiated in the first third), a victim (no longer victimizer) without refuge, unsuited for Christ-like martyrdom ("If that veck had stayed I might even have like presented the other cheek"), physically coming apart at the seams and mentally wracked. From this condition, his try at "snuffing it" becomes the last desperate exertion of a murdered will and, paradoxically, the means to its resurrection.

Despite the unanswerable paradoxes and dilemmas of *A Clockwork Orange,* which remain unaltered in the ambiguity of its conclusion, my own notions as to the book's ultimate intent are perhaps slightly more irreverent than ambivalent. I cannot escape the idea that Burgess has intended Alex's sickness—the *nausée* lodged in nonchoice—to symbolize a new concept of *Angst* neatly antithetical to Kierkegaard's "sickness unto death," the "fear and trembling" accruing from the infinite possibilities of choice. And, further, I suspect Alex's jump, the fall by which he is redeemed (the resulting concussion undoes his conditioning), in some way approximates the Kierkegaardian "leap into faith": the intuitive passage from doubt to faith after the cold logic of intellect fails. Alex has done wrong, been evil, sinned, but all as preparation for his redemption. The faith he finds is a specimen of love, joy, freedom. Ironically, he must leave HOME in order to reach it in the same way a man must "lose his life [before] he save it." And his cure is both of the body and soul. "It was," says Alex, "like as though to get better I had to get worse."

Burgess seems to be saying that, in a brutal, resigned, mechanical world—a world turned clockwork—love must come from hate, good from evil, peace from violence, and redemption from sin.

How? Unfortunately there are no panaceas for metaphysical or existential ills, and Burgess is not a prescriptive writer anyway. Human problems are inexhaustible so long as there are human beings; eradicate one and you eradicate the other. Short of that, one might find the answer to *A Clockwork Orange* in *The Wanting Seed*—and vice versa, but I very much doubt that either solution would serve for long. Give man unlimited choice? He will make a botch of it. Deprive him of all but the "right" choice? He is no longer a man. The seeds and fruits of freedom, both novels tell us, are bitter, but man is now harvesting only what he has sown.

### Robert O. Evans   (essay date March 1971)

SOURCE: "Nadsat: The Argot and Its Implications in Anthony Burgess' *A Clockwork Orange*," in *Journal of Modern Literature*, Vol. 1, No. 3, March, 1971, pp. 406-10.

[*Evans is an American critic and educator. In the following essay, he discusses the use of the "nadsat" slang in* A Clockwork Orange, *and its effect upon the novel as a dystopian vision.*]

The dustjacket of the Heinemann edition of Anthony Burgess's *A Clockwork Orange* (1962) promises that "it will take the reader no more than fifteen pages to master and revel in the expressive language of Nadsat." Perhaps that is what it will take to guess most of the meanings from context, but to master the argot of the teenage set with which the novel deals may be somewhat more difficult. It is indeed something like learning Russian vocabulary without the grammar. There are about a dozen words on every page of the novel that are non-English, and these words are almost entirely substantives. At a rough estimate about three per cent of the text is foreign or borrowed. That is a rather large amount of invasion, considering the nature of the non-English words. Were these words entirely symbolic, or imaginative, the novel might be as unintelligible as if it had been written in Esperanto. But in fact the roots are mostly Slavic. What the author has done is to inject a heavy element of Russian vocabulary into the speech of his characters.

There is one clear clue in the novel to the nature of this vocabulary. Somewhere beyond the middle of the book the protagonist, Alex, uses Nadsat words in conversation with two psychiatrists who are treating him. His language, Dr. Brodsky says, is "quaint." Then, he asks his partner, Dr. Branom, if he knows anything about its provenance. "Odd bits of rhyming slang," Dr. Branom answers, with "a bit of gipsy talk, too. But most of the roots are Slav. Propaganda. Subliminal penetration." All of these remarks quite exact, except perhaps the reference to gypsy talk. While there is plenty of slang, an odd German word or two, I can discover no gypsy words. Russian words are, however, ubiquitous.

Examine the first fifteen pages, that the dustjacket says will provide sufficient clue to meaning to enjoy the rest of the novel. We begin in the company of Alex and his three friends. They are called *droogs,* the Russian word for *friend* slightly Anglicized. They are making up their *rassodocks* (Russian *minds*) what to do that evening. The times are *skorry* (*sorry*). There is no law yet against some of the new *vesches* (*things*) they put into *moloko* (*milk*) to give one a *horrorshow* (*good*) feeling. Their pockets are full of *deng* (*money*). They decide to *tolchock* (*push, pound*) and old *veck* (*man*) in an alley. They *viddy* (*see*) him swim in his own blood. They consider doing violence to some *starry* (*old*) *ptitsas* (*birds,* feminine; *women*). They go away *smecking* (*laughing*) with the contents of a till.

Not all of the Russian words have to be guessed from context, for the author does not wish the novel to be totally unintelligible. Pete had a "rooker (hand, that is)" on the front of his tights. Georgie had a "clown's litso (face, that is)" in the same place. They wore built up shoulders "pletchoes we called them," as indeed every Russian calls them.

They met some *devotchkas* (*girls*)—the number of words for girls is remarkable—who wore little silver medals bearing the names of boys they had gone with (euphemism?) before they were fourteen on the *groody* (*bosomy*) part of their dresses. They considered spending the evening with a bit of *pol* (*sex*) but decided against it. There were only four *devotchkas,* which would mean *kuppeting* (*buying*) one of the unwholesome four enough to drink to keep him busy while the others enjoyed themselves.

The *chelloveck* (*man*) sitting next to them was already far gone on the drug. His *glazzies* (*eyes*) were glazed—a rather apparent pun. His *slovos* (*words*) were slurred. All this time in the background you can hear the *goloss* (*voice*) of the singer, crooning a real *starry* (*old*) oldie, You Blister My Paint, a more sophisticated play on words here. If we hadn't already guessed, the author would show us by such repetitions that here at least he was pulling our legs.

They go out into the winter *nochy* (*night*), searching for a *malenky* (*small, petty*) jest. They meet an old man, or at least an adult, coming from the Public Library. Pete holds his *rookers* (*arms*), while Dim yanks out his false *zoobies* (*teeth*). He makes *chumbling* (*dirty*) *shooms* (*noises*), so that George stops holding his *goobers* (*lips*) apart—exactly what he was doing is not especially clear even after translation. They pull off his *platties* (*trousers*) and read his private letters, which they consider to be filled with *chepooka* (*nonsense*). Their violence is punctuated with disgusting gestures. After a sentimental passage in a letter one of the four pretends to wipe his *yahma* (*hole*) with it.

They decide on a bit of shop-*crasting* (*stealing*), set up an alibi with three or four old *baboochkas* (*women*) in a bar, where the waiter has on a *grazzy* (*dirty*) apron, and spend all the money in their *carmans* (*pockets*). Dim is quiet for fear of being considered *gloopy* (*stupid*). They take pains to avoid the *millicents* (*policemen*) and *rozz* patrols. I take *rozz* to be a clipped reference to the Russian for *criminal investigation department*. Many of the English words in the novel, especially slang words, are clipped forms, and there is reason to believe the author employs the same practice with Russian words. For example, Pete keeps *chasso* (*sentry*—clipped) while they rob a smoke shop.

Before they get down to violence in the robbery, they are momentarily attracted by an advertisement for *cancers* (English coinage for *cigarettes*) in the form of a pretty girl showing off her *groodies* (*breasts*). The old woman in the shop is "all *nuking*" (*smelling*) of scent. After the robbery and violence they go back to the bar and ring the *collocoll* (*bell*) for the waiter. The *rozzes* (let us say, *cops*) come in wearing their *shlemmies* (*helmets*). But the cops have nothing on the young criminals. "Everything [was] as easy as kiss-my-sharries" (*balls*).

In the beginning of the next chapter they run into a "burbling old *pyahnitsa*" (*drunk*) whose words interest Alex. He likes to *slooshy* (*hear*) what some of these old *decreps* (clipped, *decrepit ones,* one supposes) have to say. An odd blurp rises from his *keeshkas* (perhaps Russian clipped for *intestines, guts*). Then they run across Billyboy and his five *droogs* (*friends*). Now there will be gang war. This is not the mean violence they commit on shopkeepers, drunks, and little girls but rather serious business with the *nozh* (*knife*), the *oozy* (this one escapes me), and the *britva* (*razor*). So the story progresses, but that takes us through the first fifteen pages which the dustjacket behooves us to master. The Russian vocabulary continues, but the introduction of new words is cut down—and many of those we subsequently meet are reasonably familiar, such as *chai* (*tea*) or *gavoreet* (*speak*). There is then some truth to the promise that if we master the first fifteen pages we can read the rest of the novel with little difficulty.

The fifty odd Russian borrowings we have been examining constitute a fair sampling of the vocabulary of the first fifteen pages of the novel, but they by no means exhaust the subject. There are a few borrowings from other languages; for example, *tashtook* for *handkerchief* (German) and *kartoffel* for *potato*. There are English coinages, some of them purely imaginative, as *vellocet, synthemesc, drencom* for LSD-type additives to the evil milk the boys drink, which puts knives in your stomach. Money can be *polly* or *cutter* as well as *deng,* and potatoes are also *spuds*. Heads are *gullivers,* and women are sometimes *sharps* or *lighters,* as well as *ptitsas, cheenas, baboochkas,* and *devotchkas*. Smokes are *cancers,* and a drink of whisky is a *Large Scotchman*. On the whole the language is as unusual and versatile as anyone might wish.

The novel is not, however, filled with linguistic pyrotechnics in the same way that Joyce's *Finnegans Wake* is. Joyce is attempting, however successfully, to delve beneath the conscious levels of speech; Burgess is playing with ordinary speech conventions. It is as if he were testing our ability to read. As we know, to read Shakespeare, say, requires coming to terms with the vocabulary, some of which is slang, some of which is simply out-of-date. To read *A Clockwork Orange* is to go through the same process artificially. Indeed it is even more difficult, for there is no apparatus with footnotes, and most readers will have too little Russian to provide the necessary clues.

It is fair to ask what is the purpose of this linguistic innovation? That is, what has the author accomplished with his unusual vocabulary? To do so is not quite the same as inquiring what the author intended by all this verbiage—clearly there are times when the words ran away with him and his intention, so far as one can ascertain, was simply to amuse the reader in the way that puns or nonsense verse amuse us. But *A Clockwork Orange* is not nonsense, nor is it simply "horror comedy," or sick humor, as the writer for Heinemann implies on the dustjacket. And it is certainly not "a fable of good and evil" demonstrating "the importance of human choice," the alternative suggested by the publisher.

It is, to begin with, a distopia related to the genre of Eugene Zamiatin's *We,* Huxley's *Brave New World,* Orwell's *1984,* Golding's *Lord of the Flies,* or even Edmund Wilson's unsuccessful play, *A Little Blue Light*. Like *We* and *Brave New World* and *1984* it presents a vision of society as it has developed at some future time, a vision that is not only unpleasant but is almost entirely unbearable. Unlike Zamiatin, Huxley, and Orwell (and there are of course others in the same category), Burgess holds no shred of hope for society. There are no important characters in *A Clockwork Orange* capable of seeing through the foibles and evils of the society created. There is no sign of hope for the future.

Like the characters in Golding's *Lord of the Flies,* those in *A Clockwork Orange* are all children—indeed the book is entirely the autobiography of Alex. The others hardly matter except as participants in events that illustrate Alex's total lack of moral values. But unlike Golding's novel this one is not about youngsters in order to clarify its moral purpose. Golding is discussing original sin; in order to do so without clouding the issues with sexual matters he makes all of his characters children below the age of puberty. Burgess's characters—or character—are not below the age of sexual experience. Indeed vicious rape is one of the attendant pleasures they enjoy as early as the second chapter of the novel.

That is not to say that the author is totally unconcerned with moral values. No doubt he deplores the actions of Alex as much as we do. What he is doing is creating a hopeless vision of a society taken over by youth. The youth do not share the values of their elders, nor do they admit any sort of normal associations with them. Parents are not to be obeyed, nor do they set examples. The best that can be hoped for in the world of Burgess is that the young will eventually grow up into copies of their parents. Physical and mental attrition will set in—it does for some of the gang. Dim and Billyboy, for example, end up as millicents (policemen).

But what has this to do with the special argot of youth, which incidentally—like the uniforms they wear—will inevitably change as new youths replace those who have passed into the ossifying adult world? Why should three per cent, or so, of the words be Anglicized Russian words instead of, say, Arabic or French? If most readers have to arrive at meaning from contextual repetition, Arabic would do for them quite as well. If the writer is merely trying to amuse with sounds and still wishes to communicate a large percentage of what his words say at once, surely

French would better serve English and American readers. It is interesting to speculate on what such a story might sound like written in Franglais. But in fact neither French nor Arabic would do. There is a real sense in the novel in which, to borrow Marshall McLuhan's terminology, the medium becomes the message. For the Anglo-American reader the Slavic words connote communist dictatorship, the society of *Darkness at Noon,* without moral value and without hope. How the young people in the novel learn the argot is never explained. It seems to come to them through the air somehow. Their parents, the police, the psychiatrists know about it, but they cannot speak it.

The writer is of course describing a common enough linguistic phenomenon. Those of us in our forties may understand "Cool it, man," but we cannot speak Beat. Where our children learned the argot, we do not know, nor do they. But Burgess is exaggerating beyond all reasonable bounds this sort of linguistic process. And he makes the argot Russian, as if to warn his readers of what society may become if it communizes itself along Soviet lines. The medium becomes the message in *A Clockwork Orange* with a vengeance, and the message is similar to that in other distopias that deal in visions of society in the future after it has become static, completely controlled, amoral, and heartless. The difference between *A Clockwork Orange* and, say, *We* or *Brave New World* lies in the fact that complete submission and total control in the latter novels, products of an earlier generation, lead to inaction or submission most of the time; whereas in Burgess the same destruction of moral values leads to absolute anarchy. The message is the same, but the specific warning of events to come is quite different.

Much of the appeal of works like *We, Brave New World, Lord of the Flies, Darkness at Noon* rests on what we consider to be the authenticity of the vision. It is on that count that Edmund Wilson's play, *A Little Blue Light,* particularly fails. Wilson was unable to convince us that his vision was clear, in the sense that Huxley's or Golding's is supposed to be. The test, after all, will come only with time. The problem, artistically speaking, is how the author goes about creating authenticity—in short the problem with works of this genre is the old one of verisimilitude.

On this score, I believe, *A Clockwork Orange* fails. Alex, the protagonist, is a totally amoral person—a thief, an arsonist, a rapist, though there are one or two qualities that tend to detract from Burgess's total version of a teenage fiend incarnate. For one thing, Alex likes serious music, though he uses it to encourage his nefarious escapades. When he is finally captured and incarcerated, he is given a chance to receive pardon and his freedom by submitting to a psychiatric experiment. Doubtless the author has his tongue in his cheek about psychiatrists while he describes this process. Alex is drugged, tied down, and subjected to very heavy doses of violence on film. It is suggested that by this method of vicarious participation in an extraordinary amount of violence, the violent part of his mind can be changed—or, more simply, the subject can be conditioned so that even the thought of violence can make him physically ill. It is as if he underwent a psychic frontal lobotomy, which altered his entire personality—not forever in the novel, however.

What Burgess suggests is that the spectacle of brutality can be used as a deterrent. Authors are not the only ones to think up such things. As Marshall McLuhan points out, the Santa Monica police offered (in 1962) a five dollar reduction in traffic fines to persons willing to watch the Ohio State Police movie *Signal 30*. But he also argues that the spectacle of brutality can itself brutalize. "Numbness," he says, "is the result of prolonged terror . . . The price of eternal vigilance is indifference." Whether a hot film, as McLuhan calls it, would cool off hot behavior is a psychologically moot point. Whether we accept media distinctions such as McLuhan makes does not really matter in attempting to weigh the success in terms of verisimilitude of the events depicted in a novel like *A Clockwork Orange*. We know, rationally and intuitively, if not from experience, that a hot book will not cool sexual ardor—or there would be no market for pornography. In short there is enough in question about the events of Burgess's novel to make its solution seem improbable rather than probable. If I am correct in that impression, the novel then is less than successful despite the attention it has attracted— that is, it is less than successful artistically. It breaks on the crux of verisimilitude. It fails to convince us because we do not believe in, as Mr. Branom called it, this kind of subliminal penetration. If that is so, it is certainly no moral fable of the importance of good and evil and human choice. It is a nightmare rather than a social satire.

There is admittedly always the possibility that the author intended to create a nightmare. Whether he wished to or not does not really matter, for we are left with what he gave us. The use of Nadsat as a device makes of the novel a sort of tour-de-force, and tour-de-force rates high with the English reading public these days. Witness Evelyn Waugh's *The Loved One* or Muriel Spark's *Memento Mori*. In that sense we have a literary work worthy of our attention. Beyond that, beyond the fire of the words, as a humanistic document and a vision of the future to make us sit back and think how we can mend ourselves to prevent its coming true—*A Clockwork Orange* is a failure, on artistic grounds probably and surely on moral grounds.

## A. A. DeVitis   (essay date 1972)

SOURCE: "England, Education, and the Future," in *Anthony Burgess,* Twayne, 1972, pp. 96-118.

[*DeVitis is an American critic and educator. In the following excerpt, he interprets* A Clockwork Orange *as a black comedy which illustrates the "horror of life without choice."*]

In a chapter entitled "Utopias and Dystopias" in *The Novel Now,* Anthony Burgess appraises the influence of H. G. Wells on the modern utopian novel:

> Many novelists set themselves the task—before and after the war—of exposing Wells's optimistic scientific liberalism as a sham. Science and education, said Wells, would outlaw war, poverty, squalor. All of us carry an image of the Wellsian future—rational buildings of steel and glass,

rational tunics, clean air, a diet of scientifically balanced vitamin-capsules, clean trips to the moon, perpetual world peace. It was a fine dream, and what nation could better realise it than the Germans? After all, their scientific and educational achievements seemed to put them in the vanguard of Utopia-builders. What, though, did they give to the world? A new dark age, a decade of misery.

After dreaming of a new race, Wells, as Burgess points out, died a disappointed liberal.

In 1962 Burgess himself published two "dystopian" novels, *A Clockwork Orange* and *The Wanting Seed,* both conceived and executed from the same philosophical orientation but quite different in content and development. Both are in many ways reminiscent of Aldous Huxley's and George Orwell's utopian novels, but both are, more importantly, advancements of the utopian genre and highly representative of the ideas and patterns that inform the majority of Burgess's works. *A Clockwork Orange,* written in the first half of 1961, is set in the near-future and, in many ways, borrows from Orwell's *1984; The Wanting Seed,* written between August and October, 1960, more elaborate and less polemical, is set in a further-distanced future and reminds the reader of *1984,* Huxley's *Brave New World,* Golding's *Lord of the Flies,* and Rex Warner's *The Wild Goose Chase* and *The Aerodrome.*

In terms of the loosely applied criteria of "black comedy," . . . Anthony Burgess's *A Clockwork Orange* concerns itself with a religious problem: the nature of human will and the importance of individual choice in a socialized and dehumanized world. A drunken prison chaplain says to Alex, the fifteen-year-old protagonist, before he is subjected to the Ludovico process which will force him to choose good at all times:

> It may not be nice to be good, little 6655321. It may be horrible to be good. And when I say that to you I realise how self-contradictory that sounds. I know that I shall have many sleepless nights about this. What does God want? Does God want goodness or the choice of goodness? Is a man who chooses the bad perhaps in some way better than the man who has the good imposed upon him. Deep and hard questions. . . .

Alex, the leader of a hoodlum gang and precocious in the ways of evil, can nevertheless appreciate the nature of the choice he makes for evil over good. Together with Georgie, Dim, and Pete, his "droogs," Alex's activities incorporate beatings, robberies, gang wars, rape, and finally murder. Betrayed by his gang after he has forced his way into the home of an old woman who cares for scores of cats and has killed her, Alex is placed in a progressive prison where his education in evil is advanced. His "brainwashing" and his subsequent return to society form the basic plot of the novel and afford Burgess the opportunity to comment hilariously and bitterly about the condition of man in a mechanized world.

Peculiar to the gangs that invade the London nights in the socialized state that Burgess fashions is the use of Nadsat (perhaps an anagram of "satan'd," for Burgess, like Joyce, is fond of puns and whimsies), which is described as "the language of the tribe": "odd bits of rhyming slang. . . . A bit of gypsy talk, too. But most of the roots are Slav. Propaganda. Subliminal penetration." A combination of Russian words and descriptive phrases, odd Cockney expressions, biblical locutions, and schoolboy humor talk, all of which suggest ironic overtones, Nadsat at first appears to the reader as a barrier to communication; but it actually becomes a device that enhances the narrative. The activities of Alex and his "droogs" become more terrifying, while, ironically, the language becomes more poetical. Phrases like "Being sore athirst, my brothers," "They know not what they do or say," and "mom gave me a tired little smech, to thee fruit of my womb my only son sort of," by their very incongruity with the activities being described, lend a note of poetic intensity to the narrative that contrasts with the nightmare horror of the action.

When Alex and his "droogs" speak Nadsat, the reader finds himself carried to the meaning by the very cadences of the words; and shortly he is conversant not only with the denotative meaning of the words but also with the witty, ironic connotations they convey. Conversely, when Alex speaks the conventional idiom, which he must do from time to time, his cadences are flat and unconvincing. By the end of the first chapter of the novel, the reader is intrigued by the language; and he is as conversant before long with Nadsat as Alex's "droogs" are. Burgess does not hesitate to play wittily with words as often as possible to suit his purpose. One needs to look only at such words as "lewdies" for people, "dama" for woman, "malchick" for boy, "horrorshow" for good, "slovo" for word, "Bog" for God, "bezoomy" for mad to appreciate the variety as well as the possibilities of Nadsat. What at first seems a device that calls more attention to itself than to the development of the novel's theme appears, upon reflection, more correctly a means to render the action more meaningful as it emphasizes the characterization and maintains the illusion of a dehumanized world at the same time.

Alex's world is not one of Roman Catholic good and evil, as is Graham Greene's Brighton. Yet there are both good and evil in Alex's cosmos, and freedom to choose evil over good becomes the chief consideration of the book. In Alex's words:

> If lewdies are good that's because they like it, and I wouldn't ever interfere with their pleasures, and so of the other shop. More, badness is of the self, the one, the you or me on our oddy knockies, and that self is made by old Bog or God and is his great pride and radosty. But the not-self cannot have the bad, meaning they of the government and the judges and the schools cannot allow the bad because they cannot allow the self. And is not our modern history, my brothers, the story of brave malenky selves fighting these big machines? I am serious with you, brothers, over this. But what I do I do because I like to do.

Alex's England is a socialized nightmare. People are forced by the government to live regimented lives in blocks of regimented apartments, all the same, all without individuality:

In the hallway was the good old municipal painting on the walls—vecks and ptitsas very well developed, stern in the dignity of labour, at workbench and machine with not one stitch of platties on their well-developed plotts. But of course some of the malchicks living in 18 A had, as was to be expected, embellished and decorated the said big painting with handy pencil and ballpoint, adding hair and stiff rods and dirty ballooning slovos out of the dignified rots of these nagoy (bare, that is) cheenas and vecks.

---

**Alex is punished by the system when his individuality, his love of music, can no longer be ignored by it. Alex is separated from the community not for his evil but because his individuality threatens the status quo.**

**—A. A. DeVitis**

---

Alex's only salvation is music, to which he responds emotionally, ecstatically. To Alex music is "gorgeousness and gorgeosity made flesh;" and his reaction to it at first appears mystical in its intensity as well as in its implications, eliciting as it does imagery of a religious nature. But, ironically, the music fails to raise the spirit; for Alex can react only in a physical way to the sounds of the orchestra. For Alex, a creation of the society in which he lives, there are no such things as love, affection, or duty; for only mechanical sex, compliance with the strong, and a display of power mean anything. In other words, Alex is the "clockwork orange" of the title: he is produced by a system, and he exemplifies in his actions the implications of it. He is punished by that same system when his individuality, his love of music, can no longer be ignored by it. Alex is separated from the community not for his evil but because his individuality threatens the status quo. The references to music are introduced to lend a comic as well as ironic perspective to the theme and to afford a unifying factor to the book.

Although Alex's taste in music seems eclectic—he admires modern composers (whose names are invented by Burgess for comic effect) and classical composers as well—it is Beethoven whom he most cherishes, and the *Ninth Symphony* is his favorite composition:

> Then I pulled the lovely Ninth out of its sleeve, so that Ludwig Van was not nagoy too, and I set the needle hissing on to the last movement, which was all bliss. There it was then, the bass strings like govoreeting away from under my bed at the rest of the orchestra, and then the male human goloss coming in and telling them all to be joyful, and the lovely blissful tune all about Joy being a glorious spark like of heaven, and then I felt the old tigers leap in me. . . .

Music arouses Alex sexually. At one point he goes into the street, into a record shop, picks up two little girls, gets them drunk on "moloko" (doped milk), and then rapes them, the old "in-out in-out." "Beast and hateful animal. Filthy horror," screams one of the children as she runs from Alex's room. His tigers no longer leaping in him, Alex falls asleep, "with the old Joy Joy Joy crashing and howling away."

In the funniest scene in the novel, Alex and his "droogs" attempt to terrorize the old woman who lives with scores of cats. As he lowers himself from a window into the room, Alex finds himself amidst the cats, their milk saucers, and the terrified old woman. To save himself, Alex, as he listens to the screeching symphony of cats and the solo of the old woman, grasps a statue of Beethoven.

Soon after this scene, deserted by his "droogs," Alex finds himself in prison for having caused the death of the "ptitsa." In order to remain near to music, the only relief that Alex has in his prison routine, Alex becomes assistant to the drunken chaplain; and his chief duty is to select and play the recordings used during religious services. When Alex finds himself confronted by evil in the form of a homosexual attack, Alex and his cellmates unite to destroy the pervert; Alex is blamed for the murder.

As a defensive measure designed to check the evil that is threatening the government and causing unrest in the state, Dr. Brodsky and the minister of the interior, or "Inferior" as Alex refers to him, have devised and sanctioned a process of conditioning human responses closely modeled on Pavlov's experiments with dogs. Alex volunteers for the brainwashing process, feeling that nothing worse can happen to him; but he is mistaken. The process of conditioning, referred to as the "Ludovico process," reminds the reader, of course, of Alex's passion for old Ludwig Van himself. The rehabilitation involves the showing of atrocity films and films of violence, horror, and terror of all kinds. A drug, injected into Alex's system immediately before he witnesses the films, induces nausea; and Alex soon begs to be released from the torment of witnessing the films. His pain becomes so intense that Alex soon discovers that he will do anything to avoid it—indeed, the evil that once had given him such passionate pleasure makes him ill. To do good, even to think good, is the only remedy for the discomfort that has been built into him by the Ludovico process.

Along with the conditioning films that Alex is forced to watch and "appreciate" there are, unfortunately, musical accompaniments; and frequently the music is Beethoven's. Thus the one factor that had set Alex apart from his "droogs," Dim and Georgie and Pete, becomes for him a new measure of pain. If before Alex was a "clockwork orange," subliminally conditioned by his society, now the irony is twofold. Before his brainwashing Alex had chosen, consciously as he thought, the evil action. As a result of his reintegration into a conventionalized society by means of Ludovico processing, Alex is denied choice itself. But, not fully comprehending the extent to which his psyche has been programmed, Alex seeks after his release the ecstasy of a musical binge. Pain and nausea result. To forestall the anguish that results from any confrontation with violence or terror, Alex, who had once reveled in evil, finds himself begging and pleading for everyone's pardon;

he has become one of the meek. But the earth is not his to inherit.

At this point the devices of melodrama serve Burgess well, for coincidence and chance unify the activities of the plot. Those very "lewdies" that Alex and his "droogs" had terrorized return to haunt and torment Alex in his newly discovered world of good action. A man who had been attacked while returning home with library books on crystallography sees Alex in the library where he has gone to escape the excruciating torment of piped-in music and exacts his measure of vengeance. When Alex begs for love and forgiveness, he receives instead a terrible beating. Rescued by the police, among whom is Dim, a former "droog," Alex is beaten and is left, covered with blood and half alive, in the country.

Perhaps the most obvious aspect of the melodramatic plotting concerns F. Alexander, the author of a novel entitled *A Clockwork Orange*. During an evening's escapade, Alex and his "droogs," wearing plastic masks, had forced their way into F. Alexander's house, a place significantly called "Home," where Alex had remarked the similarity of names. The gang had raped F. Alexander's wife, who had later died as a result of the outrage. It is to the house called "Home" that Alex once again finds his way. Left by the police, he finds himself befriended by F. Alexander himself. Aware of the irony, Alex for a time forestalls the author's awareness that he, Alex, now a famous personage because of his Ludovico processing, is the same Alex who had invaded the Alexander home earlier on.

Through F. Alexander, Alex is put in communication with the political party attempting to unseat the party that had determined that goodness could be forced upon people. Alex—who becomes a cause, then an issue, in the new political campaign—discovers that once again he is being used; for neither party is at all concerned with his moral emasculation. To serve party interests, Alex is programmed to commit suicide. Rather than endure the constant playing of music mysteriously coming into the locked apartment where he has been placed for his own "safety," Alex jumps from a window. "Friend," says one of the politicians who had coerced Alex, "friend, little friend, the people are on fire with indignation. You have killed those horrible villains' chances of reelection. They will go and will go for ever and ever. You have served Liberty well." But Alex is aware that he has been used; he also realizes that, had he died as a result of the jump, he would have served even better the cause of political expediency.

Either as a result of Alex's fall or as a result of reverse Ludovico processing—the point is never clarified—Alex returns to his old terror-loving, "bolshy" music ways. His final action in the American edition is to return to his "pee" and "em's" house, from which he had been dispossessed by an ersatz son, and to the music of Ludwig Van's *Ninth Symphony:* "Oh, it was gorgeosity and yum-yumyum," writes Alex at the novel's end. "When it came to the Scherzo I could viddy myself very clear running and running on like very light and mysterious nogas, carving the whole litso of the creeching world with my cutthroat britva. And there was the slow movement and the last

lovely singing movement still to come. I was cured all right."

The William Heinemann 1962 edition of *A Clockwork Orange* includes a chapter wisely omitted from the American editions. The last section of the English edition emphasizes a time perspective on the activities that Alex narrates to his "brothers" in the body of the novel, by pointing out quite simply that Alex had reached the ripe old age of nineteen. His luscious glory has been sacrificed to the current fashion of shaved heads, and Alex now wears wide trousers, a black leather belt, and shiny black leather jerkins. Only the heavy boots, fine for kicking, remain. Employed by the National Grasmodic Archives "on the music side," Alex earns good money; and he cherishes a desire "to keep all my pretty polly to myself." He also finds himself reluctant to participate in the horror-show activities he plans for his new gang of "droogs," preferring to listen to lieder and to study the picture of a baby "gurgling goo goo goo" which he has cut out of a newspaper. Alex is, indeed, bored; the only thoughts that interest him are of wife, son, and God. And these thoughts suggest a possible salvation for the antiheroic monster of the greater part of the novel; and the idea of possible salvation contradicts the rationale that animates the novel.

The final paragraphs of the 1962 edition attempt to reestablish the rationale but fail, for the idea of Alex as a father concerned with the future of the earth does not fulfill the characterization so brilliantly developed in the greater part of the novel:

> And so it would itty on to like the end of the world, round and round and round, like some bolshy gigantic like chelloveck, like old Bog himself . . . turning and turning a vonny grahzny orange in his gigantic rookers. . . . And to all others in this story profound shooms of lip music brrrrrr. And they can kiss my sharries. But you, O my brothers, remember sometimes thy little Alex that was. Amen. And all that cal.

In the course of *A Clockwork Orange*'s activities Burgess comments in "black comic" fashion on the horror of life without choice, whether for evil or for good. It is better, he says, to choose evil rather than to be denied the right of choice. Although the direct expression of an orthodox religious code does not figure dominantly within the narrative, the point that moral action and ethical rightness are essential to life in an ordered community is cogently made. Indeed, the final impression that the novel makes is that it is a parable. The point that is left undeveloped concerns the nature of government and the nature of individual responsibility. Burgess forces his reader to come to some logical conclusion, through his "creeching horror-show" scenes, about the choice for right and good action in a civilized community. Frighteningly enough, to choose evil is a privilege that cannot be denied the individual; for, when his choice for evil has been curtailed, his choice of or for good becomes meaningless.

That Alex is as much a "clockwork orange" before as after the Ludovico treatment is ironically and comically portrayed. The sociological implications of the theme are constantly emphasized; and the reader, mystified by the manner and seduced by the virtuosity of the language, at first fails to appreciate the simple homily that man is responsible to himself and to his fellow man.

Burgess, then, in *A Clockwork Orange,* succeeds in garbing a simple thesis in a startlingly telling and darkly humorous disguise. The violence and brutality—the slashing and rapings of the hoodlum gangs, the pack-hunting, the wanton killings—all that Alex represents, all can be found described in today's newspapers. The ultimate terror that Burgess suggests, and what best represents his concern for human beings is that what Alex and his "droogs" symbolize, governments too are involved in, and that depersonalization of family and community life produces "clockwork oranges," that regimentation of human animals into mechanized and orderly units of productive enterprise produces a world without meaning, a world without hope. Symbolically, the world that Alex lives in is one devoid of light and sun; and the majority of scenes take place at night. The people that he lives among are clearly "clockwork oranges," despite the fact that they have not been submitted directly to Ludovico processing.

## Anthony Burgess   (essay date 17 February 1972)

SOURCE: "Clockwork Marmalade," in *The Listener,* Vol. 87, No. 2238, February 17, 1972, pp. 197-99.

[*In the following essay, Burgess discusses the violence in* A Clockwork Orange *and reacts to criticism that both the novel and Stanley Kubrick's 1972 film version of it are gratuitous in their depictions of such content.*]

I went to see Stanley Kubrick's *A Clockwork Orange* in New York, fighting to get in like everybody else. It was worth the fight, I thought—very much a Kubrick movie, technically brilliant, thoughtful, relevant, poetic, mind-opening. It was possible for me to see the work as a radical remaking of my own novel, not as a mere interpretation, and this—the feeling that it was no impertinence to blazon it as *Stanley Kubrick's Clockwork Orange*—is the best tribute I can pay to the Kubrickian mastery. The fact remains, however, that the film sprang out of a book, and some of the controversy which has begun to attach to the film is controversy in which I, inevitably, feel myself involved. In terms of philosophy and even theology, the Kubrick *Orange* is a fruit from my tree.

I wrote *A Clockwork Orange* in 1961, which is a very remote year, and I experience some difficulty in empathising with that long-gone writer who, concerned with making a living, wrote as many as five novels in 14 months. The title is the least difficult thing to explain. In 1945, back from the army, I heard an 80-year-old Cockney in a London pub say that somebody was 'as queer as a clockwork orange'. The 'queer' did not mean homosexual: it meant mad. The phrase intrigued me with its unlikely fusion of demotic and surrealistic. For nearly twenty years I wanted to use it as the title of something. During those twenty years I heard it several times more—in Underground stations, in pubs, in television plays—but always from aged Cockneys, never from the young. It was a traditional trope, and it asked to entitle a work which combined a concern with tradition and a bizarre technique. The op-

portunity to use it came when I conceived the notion of writing a novel about brainwashing. Joyce's Stephen Dedalus (in *Ulysses*) refers to the world as an 'oblate orange'; man is a microcosm or little world; he is a growth as organic as a fruit, capable of colour, fragrance and sweetness; to meddle with him, condition him, is to turn him into a mechanical creation.

There had been some talk in the British press about the problems of growing criminality. The youth of the late Fifties were restless and naughty, dissatisfied with the post-war world, violent and destructive, and they—being more conspicuous than mere old-time crooks and hoods—were what many people meant when they talked about growing criminality. Looking back from a peak of violence, we can see that the British teddy-boys and mods and rockers were mere tyros in the craft of anti-social aggression: nevertheless, they were a portent, and the man in the street was right to be scared. How to deal with them? Prison or reform school made them worse: why not save the taxpayer's money by subjecting them to an easy course in conditioning, some kind of aversion therapy which should make them associate the act of violence with discomfort, nausea, or even intimations of mortality? Many heads nodded at this proposal (not, at the time, a governmental proposal, but one put out by private though influential theoreticians). Heads still nod at it. On *The Frost Show* it was suggested to me that it might have been a good thing if Adolf Hitler had been forced to undergo aversion therapy, so that the very thought of a new *putsch* or pogrom would make him sick up his cream cakes.

Hitler was, unfortunately, a human being, and if we could have countenanced the conditioning of one human being we would have to accept it for all. Hitler was a great nuisance, but history has known others disruptive enough to make the state's fingers itch—Christ, Luther, Bruno, even D. H. Lawrence. One has to be genuinely philosophical about this, however much one has suffered. I don't know how much free will man really possesses (Wagner's Hans Sachs said: *Wir sind ein wenig frei*—'we are a little free'), but I do know that what little he seems to have is too precious to encroach on, however good the intentions of the encroacher may be.

*A Clockwork Orange* was intended to be a sort of tract, even a sermon, on the importance of the power of choice. My hero or anti-hero, Alex, is very vicious, perhaps even impossibly so, but his viciousness is not the product of genetic or social conditioning: it is his own thing, embarked on in full awareness. Alex is evil, not merely misguided, and in a properly run society such evil as he enacts must be checked and punished. But his evil is a human evil, and we recognise in his deeds of aggression potentialities of our own—worked out for the non-criminal citizen in war, sectional injustice, domestic unkindness, armchair dreams. In three ways Alex is an exemplar of humanity: he is aggressive, he loves beauty, he is a language-user. Ironically, his name can be taken to mean 'wordless', though he has plenty of words of his own—invented, group-dialect. He has, though, no word to say in the running of his community or the managing of the state: he is, to the state, a mere object, something 'out there' like the Moon, though not so passive.

---

**Alex is evil, and in a properly run society such evil as he enacts must be checked and punished. But his evil is a human evil, and we recognise in his deeds of aggression potentialities of our own.**

*—Anthony Burgess*

---

Theologically, evil is not quantifiable. Yet I posit the notion that one act of evil may be greater than another, and that perhaps the ultimate act of evil is dehumanisation, the killing of the soul—which is as much as to say the capacity to choose between good and evil acts. Impose on an individual the capacity to be good and only good, and you kill his soul for, presumably, the sake of social stability. What my, and Kubrick's, parable tries to state is that it is preferable to have a world of violence undertaken in full awareness—violence chosen as an act of will—than a world conditioned to be good or harmless. I recognise that the lesson is already becoming an old-fashioned one. B. F. Skinner, with his ability to believe that there is something *beyond* freedom and dignity, wants to see the death of autonomous man. He may or may not be right, but in terms of the Judaeo-Christian ethic that *A Clockwork Orange* tries to express, he is perpetrating a gross heresy. It seems to me in accordance with the tradition that Western man is not yet ready to jettison, that the area in which human choice is a possibility should be extended, even if one comes up against new angels with swords and banners emblazoned *No*. The wish to diminish free will is, I should think, the sin against the Holy Ghost.

In both film and book, the evil that the state performs in brainwashing Alex is seen spectacularly in its own lack of self-awareness as regards non-ethical values. Alex is fond of Beethoven, and he has used the Ninth Symphony as a stimulus to dreams of violence. This has been his choice, but there has been nothing to prevent his choosing to use that music as a mere solace or image of divine order. That, by the time his conditioning starts, he has not yet made the better choice does not mean that he will never do it. But, with an aversion therapy which associates Beethoven and violence, that choice is taken away from him for ever. It is an unlooked-for punishment and it is tantamount to robbing a man—stupidly, casually—of his right to enjoy the divine vision. For there is a good beyond mere ethical good, which is always existential: there is the *essential* good, that aspect of God which we can prefigure more in the taste of an apple or the sound of music than in mere right action or even charity.

What hurts me, as also Kubrick, is the allegation made by some viewers and readers of *A Clockwork Orange* that there is a gratuitous indulgence in violence which turns an intended homiletic work into a pornographic one. It was

certainly no pleasure to me to describe acts of violence when writing the novel: I indulged in excess, in caricature, even in an invented dialect with the purpose of making the violence more symbolic than realistic, and Kubrick found remarkable cinematic equivalents for my own literary devices. It would have been pleasanter, and would have made more friends, if there had been no violence at all, but the story of Alex's reclamation would have lost force if we weren't permitted to see what he was being reclaimed from. For my own part, the depiction of violence was intended as both an act of catharsis and an act of charity, since my own wife was the subject of vicious and mindless violence in blacked-out London in 1942, when she was robbed and beaten by three GI deserters. Readers of my book may remember that the author whose wife is raped is the author of a work called *A Clockwork Orange*.

Viewers of the film have been disturbed by the fact that Alex, despite his viciousness, is quite likeable. It has required a deliberate self-administered act of aversion therapy on the part of some to dislike him, and to let righteous indignation get in the way of human charity. The point is that, if we are going to love mankind, we will have to love Alex as a not unrepresentative member of it. The place where Alex and his mirror-image F. Alexander are most guilty of hate and violence is called HOME, and it is here, we are told, that charity ought to begin. But towards that mechanism, the state, which, first, is concerned with self-perpetuation and, second, is happiest when human beings are predictable and controllable, we have no duty at all, certainly no duty of charity.

I have a final point to make, and this will not interest many who like to think of Kubrick's *Orange* rather than Burgess's. The language of both movie and book (called Nadsat—the Russian 'teen' suffix as in *pyatnadsat,* meaning fifteen) is no mere decoration, nor is it a sinister indication of the subliminal power that a Communist super-state may already be exerting on the young. It was meant to turn *A Clockwork Orange* into, among other things, a brainwashing primer. You read the book or see the film, and at the end you should find yourself in possession of a minimal Russian vocabulary—without effort, with surprise. This is the way brainwashing works. I chose Russian words because they blend better into English than those of French or even German (which is already a kind of English, not exotic enough). But the lesson of the *Orange* has nothing to do with the ideology or repressive techniques of Soviet Russia: it is wholly concerned with what can happen to any of us in the West, if we do not keep on our guard. If *Orange,* like *1984,* takes its place as one of the salutary literary warnings—or cinematic warnings—against flabbiness, sloppy thinking, and overmuch trust in the state, then it will have done something of value. For my part, I do not like the book as much as others I have written: I have kept it, till recently, in an unopened jar—marmalade, a preserve on a shelf, rather than an orange on a dish. What I would really like to see is a film of one of my other novels, all of which are singularly unaggressive, but I fear that this is too much to hope for. It looks as though I must go through life as the fountain and origin of a great film, and as a man who has to insist, against all opposition, that he is the most unviolent creature alive. Just like Stanley Kubrick.

## Anthony Burgess with Carol Dix (interview date Spring-Summer 1972)

SOURCE: An interview with Anthony Burgess, in *Transatlantic Review,* Nos. 42 and 43, Spring-Summer, 1972, pp. 183-91.

[*In the following excerpt, Burgess discusses the novel and film versions of* A Clockwork Orange.]

Anthony Burgess is one of England's most talented, scholarly and entertaining contemporary writers. He is 54 now, and has been writing for only twelve years. In that time he has published eighteen novels, six critical works, and one language primer; as well as a mountain of freelance journalism, reviewing, lecturing, TV scripting and screen playwrighting. In 1965, he left England to live in Malta, disgusted with tax laws that made it impossible for a writer to live by his trade.

Maybe something to do with the constant flow of his writing, but he has never become very popular in England (in fact it's impossible to find all his books in any one library and only two or three are in print in the bookshops). But in January, Stanley Kubrick's film of Burgess's novel *A Clockwork Orange* opened in London with an enormous amount of publicity, which may well bring Burgess into the universities and bookshops in England as he is in the States.

I met Burgess and his wife at Claridges, where they were staying in unaccustomed luxury at Warner Brothers' expense. His presence hardly caused a ripple in the tidal wave of publicity going on around *A Clockwork Orange* and its strange dialect 'Nadsat' which Burgess invented for the novel. He is not very impressed with public opinion in his own country, nor, as he sees it, their anti-intellectualism.

[*Dix*]: *Are you surprised that* **A Clockwork Orange** *is the first of all your novels to have been filmed?*

[Burgess]: No. The English have never liked it, but it has always been popular in America. It started off in the underground there, along with Tolkein's *Lord of the Rings* and has now been taken up in the universities. Things go like that. What begins in the underground ends up in the high school. They study it in literature courses along with *Catcher in the Rye.* **A Wanting Seed** is also popular in America; they often include that in sociology courses. Yet I went into a bookshop in London yesterday and I couldn't even buy a copy of **Clockwork Orange** for myself to read. It's even an underground book in Russia, you know. It's printed there on underground presses.

*You went to Russia in 1961. Did this have any connection with* **A Clockwork Orange?** *Did it influence the dialect at all? People have seen traces of Romany, rhyming slang and Russian in it.*

Ten years ago, I was writing it in England and trying to find the sort of dialect to use. It wasn't viable to use the existing dialect as it would soon be out of date. Then I went to Leningrad to gather material for **Honey for the Bears,** and I found they were having problems with teenagers too. So I combined the dialects.

*What about Kubrick's film version? How do you feel about it?*

I think it's a good film, and it's not often an author says that about an adaptation. Kubrick loves British authors and books. Look at the films he has done—*Dr. Strangelove,* and *Red Alert*—by British authors. He is immensely well read and a great chess player and interested in codes. He has a capacity for creating relationships without knowing it—like in *2001,* where the name of HAL was associated with IBM. He was totally unaware of it.

*Do you feel it's catching the public imagination now because teenage violence is becoming more commonplace?*

I was shocked last night when I read it again (the first time for ten years), to realise that when I wrote it in 1961, how very different the world was. Not even pop groups existed then. Top of the Pops for August 1961 was Lonnie Donnegan's *My Old Man's a Dustman.* There are some horrible prophecies in the book, but England was already on the way to becoming a police state. Youth violence isn't only a thing of today, you know, we'd already had the Teddy Boys in 1953, and the Mods and Rockers existed in 1961. The Beatles hadn't even come onto the scene though.

*Is that what the book is about, violence, its causes and effects?*

The violence in the book is really more to show what the State can do with it. I'm more scared of the possibility of the individual being cured under the State; of people being made to be good; of evil being rationalised out of existence.

*"You have no power of choice any longer. You are committed to socially acceptable acts; a little machine capable only of good"—as they say to Alex?*

Yes.

*Do you realise that Alex and his 'droogs' are very similar to today's skinheads? Is this direct prophecy on your part?*

In as much as Kubrick sticks to their manner of dress from the book, yes. But the film could be said to be a bit libellous in that sense, because it has been set in London today. It wasn't written like that, just something in the future. The policemen, for instance, look a bit too much like Belfast policemen, I think.

*Why does the film stop short and leave out the last chapter of the novel?*

That's because the American edition of the book is different from the British edition, which has the extra chapter. Now the new British edition also has the last chapter omitted. When I wrote it, originally, I put in a chapter at the end where Alex was maturing; he was growing up and seeing violence as part of adolescence. He wanted to be a married man and have a child. He sees the world going round like an orange. But when they were going to publish it in America, they said 'we're tougher over here' and thought the ending too soft for their readers. If it was me now, faced with the decision I'd say no. I still believe in my ending.

*Do you think the film will bring you the popular success in England that you've always missed out on as a writer?*

I doubt it. England is the funniest country in the world. It's a philistine country; the only country where a man of letters is actively looked down on; where it's a matter of pride that the Royal family love only horses and money. Still the stupidity of the English as a whole, has [been] and will be, I suppose, their salvation.

## John Cullinan    (essay date June 1972)

SOURCE: "Anthony Burgess' *A Clockwork Orange:* Two Versions," in *English Language Notes,* Vol. IX, No. 4, June, 1972, pp. 287-92.

[*In the following essay, Cullinan discusses the effect of the final, twenty-first, chapter of* A Clockwork Orange, *which was left out of the original American editions.*]

American readers of *A Clockwork Orange,* Anthony Burgess' best-known novel, are reading a truncated version of which the author does not approve. The Norton and Ballantine editions published in this country both omit the concluding twenty-first chapter which the English Heinemann edition contains. According to Mr. Burgess the discrepancy arose as a result of his negotiations with Norton for an American edition. Although he had published nine books in England by 1962, only *Devil of a State* and *The Right to an Answer* were available in American editions; and he was not well-known here. Evidently Norton insisted that the final chapter, in which the narrator-protagonist Alex shows signs of growing out of his adolescent viciousness, be excised, and that this lively rapist-murderer be left unregenerate at the end. Such insistence on a more bitterly ironic conclusion is the modern converse of Victorian periodical practice, whereby Thomas Hardy, for example, was forced to marry Angel Clare off to Tess Durbeyfield's sister to placate his readers for the heroine's death.

For Anthony Burgess the alteration has helped give an air of notoriety to *A Clockwork Orange,* a violent book he wishes readers would emphasize less than such later novels as *Tremor of Intent, Enderby,* and *MF.* The problem is intensified by the existence of a film version, directed by Stanley Kubrick and based on the shortened text. Burgess fears that the English edition may be shortened to conform to the American versions, though the fact that Heinemann reprinted the original edition as recently as 1970 seems to lessen the chances of that. He is also unhappy about the "Glossary of Nadsat Language"—the strange teenage slang in which the tale is told—appended to the Ballantine paperback edition by the late Stanley Edgar Hyman; this undercuts his purpose of teaching the reader a dialect by having him adjust to the context of each unfamiliar word or phrase. Such a glossary, as one critic has remarked, also allows the reader to avoid coming to grips actively with the novel's language [Christine Brooke-Rose, "Le Roman Experimentale en Angleterre," in *Les Langues Modernes,* March-April, 1969, pp. 158-68].

But Burgess seems to feel that nothing can be done about either distortion.

*A Clockwork Orange* is a dystopian novel of the near future in which an England of strongly socialist tendency is terrorized by teenage gangs dressed in the fashion of London's "Teddy boys" of the early 1960's. Alex, a gang leader of fifteen, delights in purely gratuitous acts of violence; when peer pressure drives him from the normalcy of assault, rape, and robbery to the rashness of murder, he is caught and sent to prison. Involved in the death of another convict, he is transferred to the new "State Institute for Reclamation of Criminal Types," where he is deprived of free-will—and thus, suggests Burgess, his humanity—through the application of drugs and electrical shocks while he watches atrocity films. Not only is Alex's taste for violence purged, but also his ability to defend himself from former victims and rivals seeking revenge after his release. Worse, his deep love for classical music has also been destroyed; for he has always associated Bach, Mozart, and Beethoven with the violence which now sickens him. Despair and the pressure of events drive Alex to attempt suicide; as a result, the therapeutic process is reversed by the authorities. The twentieth and concluding chapter of the American editions leaves Alex enjoying the scherzo movement of the Beethoven Ninth while dreaming of cutting the world's collective throat. "And there was the slow movement and the lovely last singing movement to come," he adds. "I was cured all right."

This ending reinforces one's sense of *A Clockwork Orange* as a dark, witty parable in which Alex's extreme license is opposed to the state's extreme tyranny, with no choice in between. As Bernard Bergonzi has noted, Burgess makes the problematical assumption with T. S. Eliot and Graham Greene that "it is better actively to do evil than to be spiritually dead" [*New York Review of Books,* May 20, 1965, p. 16]. One can assert freedom by willing the bad; but, as Alex says, the government and the schools "cannot allow the bad because they cannot allow the self." He adds unsentimentally, "But what I do I do because I like to do." Dreaming of violence at the end of this chapter, Alex is where he was at the start; yet he has not come full circle. A typical rogue-hero, Alex has survived a series of adventures; but he has not developed. What was done at the Institute destroyed him by eliminating his free will; his return to normalcy is a grotesque form of rebirth, and the reader is left shuddering at or delighting in his Augustinian incorrigibility.

The last chapter in the English edition presents Alex in a somewhat different light. Now eighteen and attired as a "Skinhead" with a new gang, he seems as ready for a night of violence as before; yet he is curiously bored by the prospect, and a baby's photograph he carries in his wallet indicates the onset of paternal feeling. With a flimsy excuse he goes off on his own, and a chance meeting with a former crony and his wife now safely ensconsced in minor office jobs makes him think of marriage. Alex reflects that youth resembles a mechanical wind-up toy, such as a clockwork orange, that moves "in a straight line and bangs straight into things bang bang and it cannot help what it is doing." This he will tell his unborn son, though aware he can't prevent the next generation's undergoing a similar adolescent phase. He concludes, "all it was was that I was young. But now as I end this story, brothers, I am not young, not no longer, oh no. Alex like groweth up, oh yes."

Burgess has said that he wrote the twenty-first chapter partly to symbolize the age of reason toward which Alex is moving; he is only eighteen at the end, so his insight is clearly only a first halting step toward maturity. [In a footnote, the critic adds: "This additional chapter, the seventh of Part Three in the Heinemann edition, also adds symmetry, since the first two parts are of seven chapters each. The American editions have section of seven, seven, and six chapters respectively."] Alex's development at this point also changes the emphasis of Burgess' fable, which emerges more clearly as a parodic *Bildungsroman* when one considers as well the many ironic references to the power of education which *A Clockwork Orange* contains. The author has no love for youth and its culture, as the devastating portrait of the rock singer Yod Crewsy in *Enderby* shows; and he was appalled to discover the slang in *A Clockwork Orange* picked up by London teenagers. What Burgess has said about small children applies as well to his general view of youth: "I don't see why I should be charmed by their slow lumbering along the road to rationality. It's the finished state I want; there's no substitute for adulthood" [*Spectator*, September 6, 1968, p. 322]. He has an avowed horror of violence as well, and he resents the implication of the American editions that the mixture of the violent and the musical which characterizes Alex is to be approved. Such reservations are understandable in view of Burgess' early career as composer and performer. As Dr. Brodsky, the Reclamation Institute's Director, remarks, "The sweetest and most heavenly of activities partake in some measure of violence." Anthony Burgess has a strong interest in the general conjunction of the daemonic and the aesthetic which stems in large measure from his reading of Mann's *Doctor Faustus,* as does the syphilitic Shakespeare he conjures up in *Nothing Like the Sun*.

One early reviewer was disturbed by the twenty-first chapter, which allegedly destroyed whatever credibility the rest of the novel contained by suggesting that Alex sheds his delinquency; since Alex is not Penrod it is nonsensical to treat his crimes as "adolescent awkwardnesses to be grown out of" [Diana Josselson, *Kenyon Review,* Summer, 1963, pp. 559-60]. This critique misses two fundamental points about the novel made in the final chapter. Burgess is indicating not simply that Alex has been a child, whose childish things must now be put aside, but also that the human propensity for violence is perversely childish—a form of the original sin that haunts most of Burgess' protagonists in a traditional Catholic way. Alex's extraordinary criminal history makes the swift onset of his paternal urges in the final chapter rather a jolt for the reader, however; the author is open to the charge of sentimentality at this point. In his defense one can say that Alex is not presented as morally "cured" at the end; the light has simply begun to dawn.

More important still is the cyclical view of history which this last chapter reveals; a classically pessimistic sense of recurrence is much stronger in *A Clockwork Orange* than

the tentatively progressive moral sense Alex is beginning to acquire at novel's end. The last chapter begins in exactly the same way as the first; Alex is at the Korova Milkbar with his current gang, and there are many recurrent phrases, e. g., the evening is "a flip dark chill winter bastard though dry." Apparently unchanged, Alex is seen to be bored with his role; and after reflecting briefly on youth and paternity, he realizes that he will be unable to persuade his own son to avoid the violence which has swallowed up his own life: "And nor would he be able to stop his own son, brothers. And so it would itty on to like the end of the world, round and round and round . . . like old Bog Himself . . . turning and turning and turning a vonny grahzny orange in his gigantic rookers." This picture of a malevolent or indifferent God playing with mankind as with mechanical toys or clockwork oranges is hardly sentimental, nor is Alex's perception that he is powerless to expunge violence from the future. In naming the Reclamation Treatment "Ludovico's Technique," Burgess, a noted Joyce scholar, seems to indicate that he is playing with the Viconian notion of cyclical recurrence, so central to *Finnegans Wake,* which figures prominently in *The Wanting Seed* as well.

The longer version of *A Clockwork Orange* thus makes clear Anthony Burgess' reservations about his protagonist, brings to the fore the idea of the cyclical nature of history, and outlines Alex's possibilities for growth. In the twenty-first chapter the theme of education emerges more fully as well, but one cannot draw utopian conclusions about the society for which Alex is to be educated. The young married couple Pete and Georgina whom he meets at the last are the type of *petit bourgeois* whose lives Burgess depicts as futile in *The Right to an Answer* and *One Hand Clapping;* besides, they live in a world moving rapidly toward brutal state tyranny. *A Clockwork Orange* thus contains its own critique of the author's essentially conser-

---

**Anthony Burgess on the twenty-first chapter of *A Clockwork Orange*:**

Yes—well, I was very dubious about the book itself. When I wrote the book my agent was not willing to present it to a publisher, which is rather unusual; and the sort of publishers in England were very dubious about the book. So when the American publisher made this objection to the final chapter, I didn't feel myself to be in a very strong position. I was a little hesitant to judge the book; I was a little too close to it. I thought: "Well, they may be right." Because authors do tend to be (especially after the completion of a book) very uncertain about the value of the book; and perhaps I gave in a little too weakly, but my concern was partly a financial one. I wanted it to be published in America, and I wanted some money out of it. So I said, "Yes." Whether I'd say "Yes" now I don't know; but I've been persuaded by so many critics that the book is better in its American form that I say, "All right, they know best."

*Anthony Burgess with John Cullinan, in* The Paris Review, *Vol. 14, No. 56, Spring, 1973, p. 137.*

vative assumption that it is society which makes the young savage civilized. A new complete edition would make these implications clear to Mr. Burgess' American readers.

**Wayne C. Connelly   (essay date December 1972)**

SOURCE: "Optimism in Burgess's *A Clockwork Orange,*" in *Extrapolation,* Vol. 14, No. 1, December, 1972, pp. 25-9.

*[In the following essay, Connelly argues that the untruncated version of* A Clockwork Orange *is a story of "life's movement, of growing up and of renewal."]*

Some ten years after its publication Anthony Burgess's *A Clockwork Orange* is finally beginning to receive justly deserved popular attention. It is unfortunate, however, that this attention is being given to a misleading and inferior version of the original novel. In both its British hardcover edition published by William Heinemann and its Pan paperback, the novel concludes with a seventh chapter to part three. This chapter is missing from the American Ballantine version as well as the recent Penguin edition. Furthermore, it is this incomplete version which Stanley Kubrick has so diligently followed in his successful filmscript. Why the original ending should be absent is a question best answered, of course, by Burgess; nonetheless, it seems safe to suggest that the consequences of its absence are regrettable. Without this concluding chapter *A Clockwork Orange* becomes totally distorted; the novel assumes the appearance of a satire lacking a moral centre, an unsatisfying shriek of violence remaining horrifyingly neutral.

In its longer form *A Clockwork Orange* is a tale of adolescence. It is a story of life's movement, of growing up and of renewal. Alex's literary "brothers" are truly Huck Finn and Holden Caufield, and like them he, too, must confront sinning humanity and emerge with a kind of loving. Before going on, though, it might be wise to give a brief account of the missing chapter.

The first significant point to note is that the opening of this final chapter parallels the novel's very beginning:

> 'What's it going to be then, eh?'
>
> There was me, Your Humble Narrator, and my three droogs, that is Len, Rick, and Bully, Bully being called Bully because of his bolshy big neck and very gromky goloss which was just like some bolshy great bull bellowing auuuuuuugh. We were sitting in the Korova Milkbar making up our rassodocks what to do with the evening, a flip dark chill winter bastard though dry . . . but I've told you all this before.

As Alex himself suggests, we have come full circle. He is once more the leader of a gang of droogs "tolchecking starry vecks" and buying "Scotchmen for baboochkas." Even the change in "nadsat" style is but a variation—"at this time it was the height of fashion to use the old britva on the gulliver, so that most of the gulliver was like bald and there was only hair on the sides."

Yet there is one remarkable difference. Alex himself is not the same. He is no longer "little Alex." In the preceding chapter, the ending for the American version and the Kubrick film, he had just returned to his old recidivist self, "slooshying the lovely music of the glorious Ninth" and dreaming of "carving the whole litso of the creeching world." In this chapter, however, his outlook and attitudes have undergone yet another dramatic change; only this time it has nothing to do with the Ludovico Technique. For example, he experiences ennui:

> But somehow, my brothers, I felt bored and a bit hopeless, and I had been feeling that a lot these days.

He has wholly un-nadsat feelings about money:

> There had come into my gulliver a like desire to keep all my pretty polly to myself, to like hoard it up for some reason.

Above all, though, his taste in music has altered. He is becoming sentimental:

> I was slooshying more like romantic songs, what they call *Lieder,* just a goloss and a piano, very quiet and like yearny.

In fact, Alex is no longer a schoolboy. He has a regular "lewdie" job with the National Gramodisc Archives.

Alex's new droogs are naturally quite shocked by this talk of not wanting to spend "hard earned pretty polly," but what truly bewilders them is a newspaper clipping that Alex accidentally lets drop from his wallet. It is a photograph:

> . . . of a baby gurgly goo goo goo with all like moloko dribbling from its rot and looking up and like smecking at everything, and it was all nagoy and its flesh was like in all folds with being a very fat baby.

Alex has no explanation for the picture, either for himself or for his droogs. He can only explain his odd behaviour as the effect of "a temporary illness."

Finally, unable to get into the mood for "a bit of the old dirty twenty-to-one," he leaves his new droogs to manage for themselves for the one night, and without knowing why, wanders into "a tea-and-coffee mesto full of dull lewdies." It is here that this final chapter achieves its ironic climax. For Alex encounters Pete, one of his former droogs, now dressed and talking like a lewdie and, worse, he has with him a "devotchka":

> 'Wife?' I like gaped. 'Wife wife wife?'
>
> Ah no, that cannot be. Too young art thou to be married, old droog. Impossible impossible.'

Alex's astonishment does not last long, however. In a moment, rather like an epiphany, he recognizes that Pete is old enough—and so indeed is he:

> Perhaps that was it, I kept thinking. Perhaps I was getting old for the sort of jeezny I had been leading, brothers. I was eighteen now, just gone. Eighteen was not a young age.

The final chapter of Burgess's novel ends, consequently, with Alex realizing that the time has arrived for him to begin looking for a wife, some devotchka to be the mother of his son. As he puts it, "a new chapter was beginning."

*A Clockwork Orange* is thus a story of adolescence. Without this final chapter, though, Alex never does grow up, and Burgess's statement remains grotesquely incomplete. Earlier, it was suggested that Alex's "brothers" were to be found in *Huckleberry Finn* and *Catcher in the Rye,* both classic tales of youth and coming-of-age. The narrative technique and style are unquestionably the same. That is, all three novels are presented ostensibly as first person vernacular narratives—or naive autobiographies. Compare, for example, these openings with that of the Burgess novel:

> You don't know me without you read a book by the name of *The Adventures of Tom Sawyer;* but that ain't no matter. That book was made by Mr. Mark Twain, and he told the truth mainly. There was things which he stretched, but mainly he told the truth. That is nothing. I never seen anybody but lied one time or another, without it was Aunt Polly, or the widow, or maybe Mary. Aunt Polly—Tom's Aunt Polly, she is—, and Mary, and the Widow Douglass is all told about in that book, which is mostly a true book, with some stretchers as I said before. [*The Adventures of Huckleberry Finn,* 1884]

> If you really want to hear about it, the first thing you'll probably want to know is where I was born, and what my lousy childhood was like, and how my parents were occupied and all before they had me, and all that David Copperfield kind of crap, but I don't feel like going into it, if you want to know the truth. In the first place, that stuff bores me, and in the second place, my parents would have about two hemorrhages apiece if I told anything pretty personal about them. [*Catcher in the Rye,* 1951]

In each instance, the narrator is an adolescent male; he appears to admit his readers to a special intimacy; and he addresses them in a peculiar spoken idiom. Alex's "nadsat" is simply a teenage slang, a patois or dialect not so unlike Huck's "Pike County" or Holden's "New York 1950's." Its real achievement and distinction lie in its being an altogether artificial construction. Fixed indefinitely in the future and based primarily on a mongrelizing of Russian and American, "nadsat" is able to suggest both the generality and the insularity of adolescence. It bridges those adult distinctions, time and place, and creates a private world of its own.

The humour of *A Clockwork Orange,* a somewhat surprising aspect of its art, likewise resembles the humour of *Huckleberry Finn* and *Catcher in the Rye.* It is a deceptively harmless surfacing that serves to undercut the pessimism. Even so, Alex's world often seems funny and always childishly pitiable precisely because it reflects, as do the worlds of Huck Finn and Holden Caufield, the condition which existentialists have described as "the Absurd." That is to say, there exists in all three novels a disparity between reality and the protagonist's vision.

It is the accommodation of reality and private vision, moreover, which constitutes the movement of the coming-of-age novel. Alex's nightmare world is a portrait of a dys-topian future, but the world of "twenty-to-one" and "the old in-out-in-out" is equally an adolescent fantasy—a youthful male living in his own private reality, a reality that only begins after dark, consisting exclusively of taverns and streets, of other youths and girls, and, of course—on the outside—of lewdies. When he determines it is time to grow up, Alex looks back on his old self and sees the limits of the "nadsat" vision:

> Yes yes yes, there it was. Youth must go, ah yes. But youth is only being in a way like it might be an animal. No, it is not just like being an animal so much as being like one of these malenky toys you viddy being sold in the streets, like little chellovecks made out of tin and with a soring inside and then a winding handle on the outside and you wind it up grrr grrr grrr and off it itties, like walking, O my brothers. But it itties in a straight line and bangs straight into things bang bang bang and it cannot help what it is doing. Being young is like being one of these malenky machines.

Nevertheless, Alex has no illusions about growing up. He knows that his own son will have to go through the same process—"yes perhaps even killing some poor forella surrounded with mewing kots and koshkas." Almost beyond-instinct in its determinism, Burgess's adolescence must be endured, not learnt from. Thus the ending of the novel does not arise from the preceding chapters; it is a new beginning.

In *The Wanting Seed,* another novel written in the same year and also having a future setting, Burgess describes human history as a cycle of Augustinian and Pelagian phases. It appears that in the individual movement of life, adolescence is correspondingly a period of inherent sinfulness, as well as a period of mechanism and anti-life. Accordingly, *A Clockwork Orange* can be characterized as Alex's personal "Augustinian night." Throughout all but the last chapter he shares in the existentialist pleasure in viewing life as innately evil. Still, for Burgess, Augustinian night is inevitably followed by Pelagian day. And so there exists in *A Clockwork Orange,* as in *The Wanting Seed,* a cosmic grace, a "mystery," that somehow moves Alex into his Pelagian phase, his own period of choice and life. Beatrice-Joanna decides for her "gurgling wooly rosy twins," and Alex, too, chooses the "gurgly goo goo goo" son of his news-clipping.

*A Clockwork Orange* is, finally, not a novel of paroxysm but of paradox, not of chaos but of dichotomy. There is a bright as well as a dark vision. However, without this last chapter the continuum of life (Burgess's moral centre) is absent, and we do not see the coming of day:

> . . . and so it would itty on to like the end of the world, round and round, like some bolshy gigantic like chelloveck, like old Bog Himself turning and turning a vonny grahzny orange in his gigantic rookers.

**Samuel McCracken　(essay date 1973)**

SOURCE: "Novel into Film; Novelist into Critic: *A*

*Clockwork Orange. . . Again,"* in *The Antioch Review,* Vol. 32, No. 3, 1973, pp. 427-36.

*[McCracken is an American critic and educator. In the following essay, he argues against interpreting* A Clockwork Orange *as a didactic novel concerning free will, taking issue specifically with Burgess's stated intentions for the book. He also notes some of the significant differences between the novel and the film.]*

Although *A Clockwork Orange* had a respectable little reputation before its visual enshrinement by Stanley Kubrick, it was not upon its publication widely or intensely reviewed. One of its champions, the late Stanley Edgar Hyman (whose discussion has recently been reprinted in a new edition of the novel), saw the work as a tract about free will, showing the unacceptable nature of the method by which the thug-hero Alex is turned from a free agent, however vicious still capable of salvation, into a state-produced "clockwork orange," however incapable of evil incapable also of good. Anthony Burgess himself, responding to recent criticism of both the novel and the film, has now told us that this is indeed what he (and Kubrick) had in mind [see *The Listener,* 17 February 1972]. While this interpretation is plausible enough as a schema for the film, for the novel it simply will not do.

Life in a post-intentional fallacy universe ought to have prepared us for a novelist who is a deficient critic of his own work; but since a careful reading of the novel leads to an interpretation very nearly opposite to that which he now provides, Burgess seems unusually unsure of what he was about. The essay in which he gives his analysis is an odd one, beginning as it does with an apparent plea of repentant hackery: ". . . I now experience some difficulty in empathizing with that long-gone writer who, concerned with making a living, wrote as many as five novels in fourteen months." Dropping the suggestion that the novel may be a bit of a potboiler, he proceeds to call it a tract, or sermon, the text of which is presumably somewhere in the Epistle to the Galatians. There is no chance of salvation without the choice of sin, and the brutal State, by brainwashing (Burgess' own word) Alex has deprived him of the choice and hence the chance. This is itself a serious sin, indeed: "The wish to diminish free will is, I should think, the sin against the Holy Ghost."

The belief that Alex has indeed been brainwashed and deprived of free will is possible only with the help of a careless reading of the crucial passage, during which he is subjected to what the State is pleased to call Reclamation Treatment; that this treatment is the sin against the Holy Ghost can be believed only by taking at face value the opinions of two characters, the writer F. Alexander (along with his late wife, one of Alex's principal victims), and the prison chaplain, the charlie, who has been trying his own more orthodox version of Reclamation Treatment. But as a careful reading of the novel will make quite clear, Alex is not deprived of free will and F. Alexander and the charlie are in any event consistently undercut as defenders of the view that he should not be deprived of what he has been, free choice.

Thus, The Treatment consists of no more than an unusual-ly efficacious form of aversion therapy: Alex is exposed to films of great violence and violent sex, to a background of the Beethoven which is his only love, while being kept in a state of extreme nausea. As a result, he can no longer wreak violence, experience sex, or hear Beethoven's Ninth, without getting very sick to his stomach. His new condition is demonstrated to an audience of those his regenerators wish to convince of his regeneration: taunted and knocked about by a bully, he falls to his knees and licks the bully's boots; confronted with a luscious girl, he can do no more than impotently worship her in the accents of *amour-courtois.* During this demonstration, an argument breaks out between Dr. Brodsky and the charlie. Brodsky describes the treatment:

> "Our subject, you see, is impelled towards the good by, paradoxically, being impelled towards evil. The intention to act violently is accompanied by strong feelings of physical distress. To counter these the subject has to switch to a diametrically opposed attitude. Any questions?"

> "Choice," rumbled a rich deep goloss. I viddied it belonged to the prison charlie. "He has no real choice, has he? Self-interest, fear of physical pain, drove him to that grotesque act of self-abasement. Its insincerity was clearly to be seen. He ceases to be a wrongdoer. He ceases also to be a creature capable of moral choice."

> "These are subtleties," like smiled Dr. Brodsky. "We are not concerned with motive, with the higher ethics. We are concerned only with cutting down crime. . . ."

At the very end of the demonstration Brodsky characterizes the new Alex: ". . . your true Christian." "Dr. Brodsky was creeching out, 'ready ever to turn the other cheek, ready to be crucified rather than to crucify, sick to the very heart even of killing a fly.' . . . 'Reclamation,' he creeched, 'Joy before the Angels of God.'

" 'The point is,' this Minister of the Inferior was saying real gromky, 'that it works.'

" 'Oh,' the prison charlie said, like sighing, 'it works all right, God help the lot of us.' "

Somewhat earlier, the charlie had put it this way to Alex, as he warned him against the Treatment: "You are to be made into a good boy, 6655321. Never again will you have the desire to commit acts of violence, or to offend in any way against the State's peace."

This characterization of what is done to Alex—common, so it seems, to F. Alexander, the charlie, and Burgess the critic, but not shared by Brodsky—is grotesquely inaccurate. First of all, it is not brainwashing as the term is commonly used. In life, the experience of certain Korean War prisoners shows what the process entails: they were provided with a new set of opinions and values by a relentless program of indoctrination masquerading as political education. One of the most famous fictional victims of the process, Raymond in *The Manchurian Candidate,* is turned into a puppet-gunman through processes he no longer remembers, becoming finally no more than an intermediate linkage between the finger of his masters and the trigger of the gun they have provided him.

Alex, in contrast, is not provided with new values. At no time after his conditioning, when he is offered an occasion of sin, is his reaction other than what it had been. During the demonstration, his first thought is that of the convict who tries to knife a cellmate before the guard can intervene: Alex wants to get his knife into his tormentor before the nausea can overwhelm him. What he *is* provided with, in supplement to his old drives, is a sort of internal injunction, the nausea which is always quicker than the knife. This resident injunctive power, far from depriving him of choice, merely offers him one: between eschewing violence and getting sick. And given the choice, he opts for the former. It is noteworthy that it is, as it were, a power of injunction and not of arrest. The latter could easily have been arranged by a technique which would paralyze him whenever the murderous rages well up. *Scene:* Alex, wired to the nausea-inducer, but free to move about; enter a tormenter; as long as Alex is absolutely motionless, neither nausea nor torment; as soon as he does, both. One might have thought that a novelist as inventive as Burgess should have had no difficulty in devising incidents thus more appropriate to his sermon.

Nor is Alex the victim of subliminal, even subtle, conditioning. He freely signs a release in order to undergo treatment, he is entirely conscious during the conditioning process, his memories of it are acute, and the mechanism itself, once installed, is entirely perceptible. In contrast, his restoration to his earlier state is accomplished through hypnopedia while he recovers from his suicide attempt; it is only those who wish him free to pursue the violent tenor of his ways who are willing, behind his back, to play about thus with his mind.

When the charlie early on warned Alex that he would never again have any desire to be bad, he was in error as to the fact, for Alex continues to have such desires. And when, later on, the charlie changes his tune, and argues the insincerity of the conversion, saying that Alex has no "real" choice, driven as he is by self-interest, he is in error as to the theory, for he equates freedom of choice with freedom *simpliciter,* believing that if society says Boo, it is repressive and fascist. One is almost embarrassed to draw so hackneyed a distinction, but the charlie has confused freedom and license. One can almost hear him saying: "But the law against murder, with its horrid penalties, deprives him of freedom. The insincerity of his not murdering is obvious, motivated by self-interest. He has no *real* choice." Real choice = absolute license.

The charlie is not the only commentator to be mistaken on this head. Burgess himself, it will be remembered, has described the State's treatment of Alex as having diminished his free will, an action he thinks to be no less than the sin against the Holy Ghost. However, he may see the matter these days, when he wrote the novel he made it abundantly clear that the Treatment left intact Alex's will towards the dreadful. What has been diminished is that which he enjoyed at the start of the narrative, uninhibited freedom for carrying out his will. Now, the State perennially tries to interfere with such freedom; the fact that it

failed to do so with Alex is a serious reproach of its competence. But it normally tries to bias the choice between behavior tolerable and that intolerable by entailing the latter with undesirable consequence. The charlie himself is part of a system of control which restricted Alex's choices, in the form of scope for action, far more narrowly than the Treatment. But neither the Treatment nor the prison diminish free will; this can be done only by a brainwashing which makes the having of certain desires either impossible or compulsory, a process to which Alex patently is not subjected. But free *choice* is diminished for everyone, by everyone; it is diminished whenever the State makes a law; whenever one man says No to another; whenever one man's desires outrun his own competence. None of which has anything to do with free will or salvation. If it did, the inhabitants of totalitarian societies, their capacity for evil made smaller by their limited opportunity to break the law (totalitarian law forbids much that is desirable to forbid, as well as much that is not) would attain an easier salvation than others. Burgess can hardly believe this, any more than he can believe that Alex is any less sinful because of the chains in which Brodsky binds him. The testimony of the novel is that Burgess once understood this all very well, for what he now says is the argument of the novel is presented there by two highly dubious spokesmen. The writer F. Alexander, himself the author of a flatulent treatise called *A Clockwork Orange* ("to attempt to impose upon man, a creature capable of growth and capable of sweetness . . . to attempt to impose, I say, laws and conditions appropriate to a mechanical creation, against this I raise my sword-pen. . . .") has enough sophistication to regard the reclaimed Alex, from the likes of whom he has suffered, as a pitiful victim. But when he finally realizes that he has suffered from Alex himself, his benevolence collapses into primitive feelings of revenge, and he must be put away in order to make the streets safe for Alex. For he will allow Alex free choice only on the condition that Alex foreswear the option of beating F. Alexander and raping his wife.

The charlie is never exposed to such a test of his benevolence. Living as he does in a fortress full of guards, one of the few places in the world he can live with Alex in safety, he can effort to luxuriate, arguing free choice. His Christianity (which Alex aptly calls 'Prison Religion') is protected by its maximum security environment, blurred by a continuous haze of alcohol. He is as much deluded by his safety and his drink as F. Alexander is by his prose and Alex by his slang.

### Language And Action

In this connection, commentators hitherto have been so dazzled by the cleverness of the language with which Burgess equips Alex that they have hardly wondered why he has done so. Burgess has recently provided an explanation which is more than a little difficult to take seriously: when the reader has finished the novel, he will have penetrated the vocabulary of the Russian-based Nadsat, and hence will have gotten, willy-nilly, a basic Russian lexicon. He will thus understand a little of what it means to be brainwashed. Although the process as Burgess describes it is perhaps more akin to brainwashing than anything which happens to Alex before his final "cure," it is so much like programmed instruction as to leave us in doubt just how seriously Burgess has violated our integrity. If we believe that this be the sin against the Holy Ghost, we will believe anything.

The more obvious effect of the Nadsat Burgess himself has pointed out: the reader, seeing the violence by means of a language he is yet learning, is insulated from it, and it becomes, as Burgess observes, largely symbolic. Symbolic certainly for the reader, but for Alex? Burgess describes his relation to language as a paradox: his name might be taken to mean *wordless,* yet he has plenty of words, and that he uses language is one of the criteria which mark him as a human being. But he uses it in a curious way. It seems clear that he *thinks* in Nadsat, and consequently he organizes reality by means of what is his second language. Whether or not he does this through choice (there are dark hints of subliminal penetration from the East) is beside the point. When describing the horrors which fill up his existence, he does so in something other than his mother tongue, in a jargon of limited, and (compared to English) syllabose, vocabulary. As we all know, for the practice of calling nasty things by other than their right names there is a perfectly good term. Whether or not we end up considering Alex's use of Nadsat as euphemistic, we must recognize that between reality and his perception of it he draws the veil of jargon. One is tempted to parody Orwell's famous metaphor: "the soft Slav roots fall upon the images like snow, gently blurring the outlines."

Thus the self-deluded members of the Free-Choice Party. In contrast is the cool, bureaucratic professionalism of its principal opponent. Although Brodsky carelessly and redundantly conditions Alex against sex, when a proper aversion to violence would have kept him from all rape but the statutory, and callously deprives him of his music, these are errors of technique, not of principle. What he does not do, as the charlie charges, is to try to make him good. Not only are all of Alex's bad intentions left untouched, but the extent of the areas in which he is enjoined from action is fairly modest. He is not provided with an aversion for theft, for bad language, for laying about idly, or any number of other behaviors which any sensible social engineer would wish to modify. *Scene:* Alex hooked up to the orgasm-inducer; on the screen, a time-clock; with every punch. . . . No, all that he desires to do is to keep Alex from committing a limited inventory of viciously antisocial acts by the simple expedient of a little deterrent in the form of nausea. It is no more than that will-o'-the wisp of law enforcement, the *certain* deterrent, levelled against the desire to act, rather than the act itself. No one would consider a law which prescribed thirty minutes' vomiting as the punishment for a life of murder and rape to have much deterrent effect. But when such a consequence is made absolutely certain, Brodsky shows us, that is all it takes.

Although Burgess seems to have the easy contempt for the State so familiar these days ("towards that mechanism, the State, which, first, is concerned with self-perpetuation, and second, is happiest when human beings are predictable and controllable, we have no duty at all, certainly no

duty of charity") Brodsky and the Minister of the Inferior, understanding that the State after all is responsible for maintaining society, realize that Alex, a creature who inflicts insensate violence on anything which gets in his way, cannot be allowed to run loose. The alternatives, life imprisonment or death, are restrictions on free choice far more severe than the Reclamation Treatment. Given the Alexes, who appear to be very numerous, perhaps all the teen-age males in England, and given the desire to maintain something a little better than the Hobbesian state of nature, the Treatment is the procedure of choice. The State's choice, and Alex's. Although Burgess the critic says that "such evil as Alex enacts must be checked and punished," in the novel this position is maintained only by the Prison Governor, who puts it in terms discordant with the Christianity which is supposed to inform the work: "An eye for an eye, I say. If someone hits you, you hit back, do you not? Why then should not the State, very severely hit by you brutal hooligans, not hit back also?" But Brodsky and the State, Alex concurring, reject the doctrine of punishment and opt for a combination of crude rehabilitation and deterrence.

---

**If I am to avoid instructing Burgess as to what his intentions were in *A Clockwork Orange,* I must accept his statement of them but reply that he has so spectacularly betrayed them as to have ended up on the side of his demons.**

**—Samuel McCracken**

---

F. Alexander and the charlie reject the positions of the Governor and the State alike, making a fatal substitution of theology for politics, quite as if Alex's free choice could never be exercised to the detriment of another's. Indeed, as the novel ends, the government, under pressure from the opposition party for which F. Alexander is a propagandist, coolly relieves Alex of his aversions and is about to turn him loose, a media-hero with a sinecure into the bargain. As the charlie said, God help us all. This appalling turn of events, most immediately the result of political expediency, has for its ideological justification thinking which confuses sin and crime so thoroughly as to treat all crimes as sins and leave their punishment to God, omitting any interest in preventing them as crimes; Brodsky, at least, does not make the symmetrical error of taking crimes for sins and punishing them, arrogating thus the function of God. He is entirely willing to concern himself, in his measured way, with a few of Alex's least permissible works, and to leave his faith to the charlies of the world; like Elizabeth I, he will not make windows into men's souls, willing as he may be to follow them about with an eternal process-server.

Now as it happens, I find social control by such a process-server nearly as repugnant as does Burgess the critic, if not for the same reasons. For one thing, Brodsky's real-life equivalents would never be so restrained. *Scene:* a group of six-year-olds attached to the nausea-inducer; on the screen, an angry mob chants "Down with the government!" And ever after, the slightest desire to criticize the State will put them into a state they will be at great pains to avoid. And the Reclamation Treatment has certain affinities with that regeneration through chemistry preached by the Learies and the Reiches, who tell us that certain drugs destroy the will to certain evils. But the Treatment is repellent most of all because it symbolizes the bankruptcy of a society which having bred an Alex cannot, try as it may, come up with any better solution to his problem than chaining him thus. But given the world of the novel, the State has pretty clearly opted for the best choice open to it; such is the most reasonable interpretation, and if I am to avoid instructing Burgess as to what his intentions were, I must accept his statement of them but reply that he has so spectacularly betrayed them as to have ended up on the side of his demons.

## Director and Directions

Those intentions are much better served by Kubrick's screenplay, which (although superficially faithful to the source) contrives through a complex shift of emphasis to present a considerably nicer Alex in a considerably nastier society.

Nothing very obvious has been done to the plot: little is excised, and nothing of importance, with the possible exception of an hallucinogenized milk-barfly of whom Alex sharply disapproves. The only interpolations of any duration are the long comic scene showing Alex's reception into prison, and the shorter one in which he unsuccessfully attempts to let pass his lips the drugged chalice offered him by F. Alexander. These do little beyond contributing a comedy of situation totally missing in the source.

But the minor alterations in plot and character are very much more important. Alex is given a pet snake, suggesting a capacity for affection entirely absent in his original. What is in the novel a particularly brutal rape of two teeny-boppers begins in the film as the invited seduction of two rather older girls, and ends, Marx Brothers-like as a real laff riot combining superspeeded action with the William Tell overture. In the novel, Alex's parents having had no warning of his reclamation and imminent return, their rejection is of someone they still assume to be a criminal lunatic; in the film, since they know about his treatment, their rejection reflects society's general unwillingness to begin afresh with Alex, an attitude which will keep him from living as one truly reclaimed. The cat-woman of the novel is a harmless eccentric, whose response to Alex's assault is a feeble blow with a stick; in the film, transformed into the proprietrix of a trendily erotic health-farm, she attempts to brain Alex with a bust of Ludwig van himself, in a scene in which Alex kills her as much in self-defense as by premeditation. The charlie of the novel is so utterly protected from the consequence of free choice by others that prisoners interrupting his sermon are beaten and hauled off to their cells; in the novel, such behavior warrants no more than a bellow from the guard. In the film, we see the Minister of the Inferior inspect Alex's cell and notice his Beethoviana, making less excusable the

careless deprivation of his music. The Treatment itself is more brutal in the film, Brodsky telling us that earlier patients have compared it to Hell itself. The scene in which Alex demonstrates his reclamation is touched up with a number of small strikes: Brodsky is put in the background, many of his lines being given to the Minister, whose motivations are a good deal more self-serving than Brodsky's. Confronted by the girl, Alex in the novel overcomes his nausea by playing courtly lover, thus developing a sort of sexual relation; in the film, he simply falls away retching. Most striking of all is the alteration of the final image: in the film, we know Alex has been "cured" when hearing Beethoven evokes a genteelly erotic scene in which two girls grapple in the dust as Edwardian toffs look on. This comparatively innocent entertainment replaces something vastly more sinister in the novel:

> . . . I could viddy myself very clear running and running on like very light and mysterious nogas, carving the whole litso of the creeching world with my cut-throat britva.

Even when sticking to the source, Kubrick goes easy on Alex. Violence done by him to others we see only through a tasteful veil of technique: it is shadowed, choreographed, speeded up, slowed down. But violence done by others to Alex is handled quite clinically, even emphasized: in the novel, he explicitly refuses to dwell on the details of the beating he gets from his former droogs, but the camera shows no such restraint. All this may be justified on the grounds that it shows us that Alex feels his own pain, but not that of others; even if we needed to be told this so clearly, the consequence is still that it is easier for us to feel his pain than that of others. The first time I saw the film, there was laughter during the raid on F. Alexander's home, but none as the droogs nearly drown Alex.

The larger effect of all these changes is to make it very much easier to see Alex as the victim of a vicious society; in the novel, it is hard to find anyone more cruel than Alex, in the film, very much less so. The shift in attitude is too detailed and consistent to be an inadvertence of translation from another medium; speculation into the rationale requires one to arraign the director's motives, something I am unsure to be in the proper province of criticism. But for one thing, the novel ends with Alex not only restored to his old brutal self, but with the State's protection; the millicents, we may be sure, will not bother little Alex again. If an audience is to accept this state of affairs as preferable to having Alex an unhappy, but harmless, clockwork orange, it will need to be more devoted to the principle of free choice than it is reasonable to expect. Hence, perhaps, the final vision of the film: sex a bit kinky, perhaps, but purged of the violence with which it up to this point has been invariably associated. More important, it seems likely enough that Kubrick recognized the Alex of the novel as a monster without a soul, no more suitable as the subject of a Christian parable than Richard III as a tragic protagonist. This recognized, I suspect he proceeded to give us not Richard, but Macbeth.

There is probably material here for a critical parable, on some such head as this: whenever a novelist presumes to tell the critic what his work is all about, he will offer the latter a troublesome choice. For if the critic finds himself differing with the novelist's interpretation, he is led to the impolite conclusion that the novelist must be insincere or incompetent as novelist or critic, possibly as both. This latter is unlikely, considering the high statistical association of ability in criticism with inability in fiction; of two things, then, probably one. Come to think of it (agreeing as I do with Pope that bad critics outnumber bad writers ten to one, and with Burgess that you pays your money and you takes your choice), the choice is not really so troublesome after all.

### Esther Petix   (essay date 1976)

SOURCE: "Linguistics, Mechanics, and Metaphysics: Anthony Burgess's *A Clockwork Orange* (1962)," in *Critical Essays on Anthony Burgess,* edited by Geoffrey Aggeler, G. K. Hall, 1986, pp. 121-31.

[*In the following essay, originally published in 1976, Petix discusses the philosophical underpinnings of Burgess's fiction and examines the ways in which they are manifested in* A Clockwork Orange.]

The second half of the twentieth century has passively acknowledged the emergence of its most controversial gadfly, John Anthony Burgess Wilson: philosopher, critic, theologian, linguist, musician, academician, and author. Yet the seemingly facile task of the Burgess critic is not so much a matter of ascribing priorities within Burgess's various spheres of expertise, but rather (and amazingly) in shouldering the onus of redressing the dearth of any critical attention. Serious and exhaustive research reveals that Burgess's tremendous energy and soaring imagination have netted only moderate acclaim, a modicum of intellectual authority, and a quasi-reputation as one of the century's comic artists. For too long Burgess's literary precision and satire have been obscured beneath labels of precocious, light wit. While his contemporaries moved to the heights of fame and fortune, garnering critical attention, esteem, and aggrandizement, the wealth of Burgess's knowledge and ingenuity within the form of the novel remained ignored.

Most certainly Burgess has his following, but his disciples' enthusiasm (at times almost hysteria) has not diverted attention to his themes, nor has it acquainted large numbers with the universality of his traditionalism and messages. Perhaps, then, he is in need of one fewer disciple and one more evangelist. For as any devotee of Burgess knows, this is an era that enjoys the dramatic sweep of technocracy. Today one must introduce status (of any sort) from the point of volume rather than quality or essence, and by contemporary standards, shibboleths, and axioms, Burgess's work is not established. In terms of sheer physical output, Burgess ranks high. Compared with the popularity of contemporaries, however, Burgess's sales offer only tepid comparison.

That Burgess is not a top seller has many implications. First, and obviously, there are distinct implications for Burgess himself. As a professional author, he is certainly aware of market returns to his own purse; aware, too, that what and how much he sells has a material effect upon his own life-style, if not his *raison d'être.* Unyieldingly, however, he tends toward remoteness and obscurity, holding out in effect for principle over capital. Ideally, Burgess's stand is consistent with his philosophy.

The implications for the reading public are another matter. Why, for example, is Burgess considered intellectually obscure? Why, after nearly thirty books, must one still introduce him as "the author of *A Clockwork Orange,*" and that reference only recognizable because of the barely recognizable film version (call it rather, perversion) of the novel? An obvious problem exists when an author who has so much to say and is possessed of such profundities is not widely read; is, in fact, dismissed as a perpetrator of violence or as a comic. But then, Burgess criticism is at best confused. It is further obfuscated by the fact that he holds sway over a devoted following (which includes some first-rate critics), yet does not hold commensurate stature among scholars. It is my contention that the major force of Burgess has been siphoned off into static frenetics rather than into direct qualitative evaluation. That a clouding of Burgess's fiction has occurred is patent; how and why it has occurred requires a deeper analysis of Burgess's fiction and mind, both of which are labyrinthine. The labyrinth, a symbol often invoked by Burgess himself, is charted with the aid of various threads and clues running through his fiction. And pursuing these leads, these seeming difficulties, these ambiguities, these strata and substrata brings the reader to the inner core of Burgess's central satire: the Minotaur's Cave.

As a maze-maker, Burgess challenges not only Dedalus in the manner of construction, but God in the act of creation—a device and theory he learned from Joyce. Yet such creations and constructs demand a more formal system, and often an elusive one. Like the protagonist, the reader is drawn through threads of the literal plot into the maze, formed often as not below the author's own hilarious crust of ego. Yet, concurrently, Burgess as readily hides himself in the center of his creation, sequestered and insulated by its vastness as well as its intricacies. Readers thus are invited, nay dared, to master the maze, to pick up the various threads and wander the labyrinth; but the same reader always comes to the mystical center—volitionally, and only after much effort.

Imperfectly read, Burgess is necessarily open to charges of philosophical bantering; misread he is often missed entirely. It remains, then, to follow those distinct, definitive threads designed by the architect himself which lead to the mind of the maze-builder, the "God-rival." For at the center the reader may discover an entire universe in which the author attempts to contain the human colony. As with all artists who attempt to match wits with God, Burgess provides only a scale model. Yet it is a model unique in many vital, identifiable ways. Stated as a more classical apostrophe, Burgess constructs his cosmogony to explain—there is no longer in the modern world any need to justify or vindicate—the ways of man to man: to see hope through failure; to set a course while adrift; to seek certainty in ambiguity. In following the threads leading into the center of the labyrinth, we are able to spin from Burgess's fictions something of our own identities.

Midway in Burgess's decade of authorship, and bleakest within his fictional cosmogony, are the years of the early sixties. It is a period marked by excessive concern with death (his own seeming imminent) and with protagonists only thinly disguised as alter-egos. Added to a medical diagnosis of (suspected) brain tumor were England's failures through socialism, her displacement as a world power in the aftermath of World War II, and her lack of character among the modern nations. All this greeted Burgess upon his return home from the Far East. In facing his own death, he also faced the demise of England. And the two-fold bitterness is reflected in a twin-bladed satire so lacerating and abrasive that it goes beyond satire into black comedy.

In 1962 Burgess published his two dystopian novels, *The Wanting Seed* and *A Clockwork Orange*. Both are horrible visions of the future, predicated upon the present. In essence what Burgess does in the two novels is to project socialism and the excesses of the Welfare State (*A Clockwork Orange*) and historical behaviorism (*The Wanting Seed*) into a future that is at once nebulous and contemporary. Through such an extension in time he contends that socialism leads to a loss of the will and behaviorism leads to a loss of the soul. These companion novels consider the impact of original sin, abortion, cannibalism, violence, and free will on human beings who daily grow more will-less and more soulless.

However bleak the authorial outlook, however black the comedy, Burgess in his dystopian mood is Burgess at his most lucid. No longer are the protagonists culled from Establishment posts: Ennis of *A Vision of Battlements* was a soldier; Crabbe of "the Malayan Trilogy" was a civil servant; Howarth, of *The Worm and the Ring,* was a schoolteacher. Now the anti-hero of Burgess has become a full-blown rebel, and the quiescent, or slightly recalcitrant Minotaur is savage and obvious. One must keep this in mind in turning to *A Clockwork Orange,* for it is not only Burgess's best-known novel; it is Burgess at his most exposed, and perhaps most vulnerable.

The central thematic and structural interrogative of the novel comes when the prison "charlie" (chaplain) laments: "Does God want goodness or the choice of goodness? Is a man who chooses the bad perhaps in some way better than a man who has the good imposed upon him?" Such a question, while it affords the concision necessary to a reviewer, is totally insufficient to the critic. For there is something at once delightful and horrible, dogged and elusive in *A Clockwork Orange* that even so profound a rhetorical question cannot contain. There is something about the novel so frightening that it demanded a new language, and something so immanent in the message of the novel that it refused to be separated from the language. Linguistics and metaphysics—the how and what of *A Clockwork Orange*—are the disparate, yet connected threads leading to the Minotaur.

*A Clockwork Orange is* in part a clockwork, not merely titularly, but essentially. Its cadence and regularity are a masterpiece of grotesque precision. The reader is as much a flailing victim of the author as he is a victim of time's finite presence. He is hurtled into a futuristic book of

twenty-one chapters and comes to acknowledge that he, as well as the protagonist-narrator, Alex, is coming of age; that he, too, is charged with advancement and growth. This "initiation" aspect of the novel is not gratuitous—of course. For the novel is further divided into three parts, reminiscent of the three ages of man; and each of these three parts begins with the question scanning the infinite and the indefinite: "What's it going to be then, eh?" Added to both of these devices is the haunting and vaguely familiar setting of the novel that teases the reader into an absurdly disquieting sense of regularity—as numbers have a way of doing—all the more unnerving because such regularity conveys a sense of rhythm about to be destroyed.

The novel's tempo, and its overwhelming linguistic accomplishment is to a great degree based upon the language Nadsat, coined for the book: the language of the droogs and of the night. It is the jargon of rape, plunder, and murder veiled in unfamiliarity, and as such it works highly successfully. Anthony De Vitis asserts that Nadsat may be an anagram for Satan'd [*Anthony Burgess,* 1972], but Burgess insists on the literal Russian translation of the word for "teen." The novel makes a fleeting reference to the origins of the language. "Odd bits of old rhyming slang . . . a bit of gipsy talk, too. But most of the roots are Slav. Propaganda. Subliminal penetration."

Close examination of the language reveals a variety of neologisms applied in countless ways. First, there is the overwhelming impact of a Russianate vocabulary that is concurrently soothing and unnerving to the reader. It most certainly softens the atrocities of the book. It is far simpler, for example, to read about a "krovvy-covered plot" or "tolchocking an old veck" than it is to settle into two hundred pages of "blood-covered bodies" or "beatings of old men." The author keeps his audience absorbed in the prolonged violence through the screen of another language. But the Russian has a cruelty of its own; and there are disquieting political undercurrents in Burgess's imposition of Slavic upon English, at least for the tutored ear.

Nadsat, like all of Burgess's conventional writing, harbors a number of skillful puns. People are referred to as "lewdies"; the "charlie/charles" is a chaplain; "cancers" are cigarettes, and the "sinny" is the cinema. There is, to be sure, little room for laughter in a novel as sobering as this, and Burgess's usual authorial grin is only suggested in this very bitter glimpse of tomorrow. Still, there is no absence of satire. In many ways Alex is still a youth, and the reader is repeatedly shocked by a profusion of infantilisms starkly juxtaposed with violence. Burgess flecks his dialogue of evil with endearing traces of childhood in words like "appy polly loggies," "skolliwoll," "purplewurple," "baddiwad," or "eggiwegg" for "apologies," "school," "purple," "bad," and "egg." It is necessary for Burgess to achieve an empathic response to Alex, and these infantilisms within Nadsat are reminiscent of Dickensian innocence—serving well as buffer zones (or are they iron curtains?) between the "good" reader and the "evil" protagonist.

Other clues to this grim future world are Burgess's truncated and mechanized synechdoches: The "sarky guff" is a "sarcastic guffaw." "Pee and em" are Alex's parents; the "old in-out-in-out" is sexual intercourse (generally rape!); a "twenty-to-one" (the number is scarcely fortuitous) is a gang beating; "6655321" is Alex's prison name, and "StaJa 84" (State Jail 84) is his prison address.

Closely linked with the mechanical hybrids used in Nadsat are certain words conspicuous by their absence. There are no words, for example, that give positive feelings of warmth or caring or love. When Alex wants to refer to goodness he has to do so by opting out of Nadsat and for English, or by calling evil "the other shop."

Yet the total effect of Nadsat is greater than the sum of its various parts. Alex, in the capacity of "Your Humble Narrator," uses the language to extrapolate a future both vague and too familiar. He sings of a time when all adults work, when very few read, and when society is middle class, middle-aged, and middle-bound. We are told only that 1960 is already history and that men are on the moon. The reader is offered no other assurances. And as the linguistic impact of Nadsat becomes more comprehensible, one is left to wonder if the world of clockwork oranges is so safely distant after all.

When one has truly and carefully followed the linguistic threads of Burgess's novel, the Minotaur guide can be heard arguing a matter deeply tragic in implications. By definition language, like its human author, man, has an essential right to reflect the fits and starts of a time-honed, familiar friend. There ought to be an ordered sense of choice, a spirit of chorus and harmony and solo. Jabberwocky is for fun; Nadsat is a very different construct and far more fearful. Though at times it can be beautiful, there is the lonely wail of tomorrow wrenched from the desperate sighs of today. In Nadsat one finds the Platonic form of mechanism: the cadence of a metronome and the ticking-tocking ramifications of humanity without its essence.

The deep and hard questions of *A Clockwork Orange,* however, are not veiled by the mechanical language. And standing richer when reviewed in light of the balance of Burgess's cosmogony, they stand even more specifically poignant when played against the panorama of all Burgess's writing. Through a reflective stage-setting, the reader is far more able to cope with the labyrinthine mind behind the dystopian clockwork.

Burgess is fond of envisioning himself as an exile. He has voluntarily absented himself from many situations with the voice of a vociferous (not a whimsical) outcast. He has politically removed his allegiances from Britain. He has removed himself from the aegis of the Catholic Church, voicing preference for a variety of heretical or mystical theologies. Burgess is truly a man of isolation, alone with his own thoughts and his fiction to espouse his maverick philosophy. The exclusive position that Burgess assumes lends his writing a metaphysically unique, if not philosophically original dimension.

Locked within that mind—that mental labyrinth—is a most clever approach to serious metaphysical questions. Burgess has fashioned and shaped a dualist system of eclectic, authentic origin and pitted it against the world of the past, the present, and the future. Burgess's theological contentions are amazingly astute from the point of authenticity, universality, and relevance.

Much of his metaphysics is genuine philosophy given a fresh approach. He has drawn upon Eastern and Western philosophies, concocting a novel brew of Eastern dualism, heretical Manichaeanism, Pelagian/Augustinianism, the cultural mythologies of ancient civilizations, the philosophy of Heraclitus, the implicit teachings of the Taoists, the Hegelian dialectic. The impact of Burgess's metaphysics, however, is not so much the clever jigsaw effect of a master eclectic; rather, it is that out of this syncretism Burgess has presented a serious allegory of the contemporary malaise, which has been diagnosed by all recent Existential and nihilistic thinking. He is answering through his writing the central paradoxes of life posed in Sartre's "nausea," Heidegger's "dread," and Kierkegaard's *Angst* and "fear and trembling."

Basically, twentieth-century man has come to live under the onerous speculations of recent philosophers. He has, in a sense, become a captive of his own (or what he used to feel was his own) universe. Ancient philosophers and artists were dedicated to the simple contention that the universe was a friendly home, divinely designed for mortal existence, and not incidentally mortal happiness. In varying degrees, yesterday's thinkers attempted to explain, rationalize, even challenge man's primacy upon earth; they seldom, however, questioned his right to be here or his natural relationship with the world in which he lived.

The last one hundred years saw the growing disaffiliation from the traditional acceptance of the world as benign. After thousands of years of philosophy dedicated to man's concentric sphere within the universe, nihilists and existentialists were now challenging not only man's place in the system but the entirety of the system itself. No longer was logic, or spirit, or mind, or even God the central force of the universe—these became only alternatives. The center of the universe was now existence; man's solitary life was enough just *in being.* Shockingly, this new paramount position of man left him not the conqueror of the universe but its victim. He was swamped by the very paradox that made his existence supreme. For in accepting and even reveling in the uniqueness of his own individuality, man was forced to accept that he was totally unnecessary. Adrift from the former Divine, or logical, or even scientific plan, adrift from Hegelian systems, humanity was presented with a position of supreme importance and, simultaneously, with the concept of its own total annihilation.

As the world more fully accepted that it was enough just to be, it became aware, too, that an individual existence, while central to that individual, was as nothing in the universe. With World War II and the prospect of total annihilation (not thousands, but millions of deaths and the promise of even greater debacle), the "nausea," "dread," and "fear" that had haunted the ivory towers of philosophers became a part of every living being.

Into this anxiety-ridden arena came the literature that chronicled, prescribed, and diagnosed a series of ways in which man could come to live with relative peace within himself. Yet always the paradox remained: each individual was a unique and single existence that had never been before and would never be again. Yet that same individual existence was nothing. It would die, never return, and the world would go on as before.

Burgess, for good or ill, has generally refused to enter the arena. Indeed, he has steered clear of the mainstream of the philosophical split alluded to above. He has removed himself as thoroughly and totally from this particular dialogue as he has from church and country. He is to be sure a chronicler of paradox. He, too, speaks and writes of polarity, ambiguity, juxtaposition. He does not, however, revile them; on the contrary—and this is perhaps what makes him unique among writers today—he seems to glory in them. Burgess's writing is dedicated to exposing the totality of the paradox and offering humanity an alternative to "fear and trembling." In a single shibboleth, Burgess demands that man first become aware of the paradoxes of life *and then accept them.* The injunction is neither so simplistic nor so naive as it may at first appear.

Burgess offers his readers a cosmogony spinning in exact parallel to their own world. Yet, rather than trembling in the face of paradox, Burgess's cosmogony is energized by it. One is not at all surprised to find living side by side in **The Wanting Seed** "Mr. Live Dog" and "Evil God." "God" and "Not God" thrive in **Tremor of Intent,** and the following references from **A Clockwork Orange** show how energetic such dualisms can become:

> Hell and blast you all, if all you bastards are on the side of the Good, then I'm glad I belong to the other shop.

> But, brothers, this biting of their toe-nails over what is the *cause* of badness is what turns me into a fine laughing malchick. They don't go into what is the cause of *goodness,* so why of the other shop? If lewdies are good that's because they like it, and I wouldn't ever interfere with their pleasures, and so of the other shop.

Burgess advocates a pure dualism, reflected variously on earth as "X and Y," "left and right," "black and white," or "lewdies good and lewdies not good." The names and terms change with each novel, but the concepts are serious, unswerving, and consistent—head-to-head combat between equal but opposite deities who are the forces behind creation.

Although Burgess does not shout innuendos from the novel's lectern, he does posit dualism as a means for explaining the unexplainable. Garnered from fiction itself—for Burgess has never formally outlined his philosophy—the dualistic system works something like this:

Each of the two divinities created a sphere. The "Good God" created an ascendant, ethereal sphere. It became a world of light, and summer, and warmth. Contrarily, the "Evil God" set his stage. His was a descendant sphere of darkness and winter and cold. Thus the spinning universe contained the dual divinity and a massive panoramic background. One, the "Bog of the Good," all "gorgeousness and gorgeosity made flesh," gave to man a spirit, while the "God of the other shop" gave man his flesh—

again, juxtaposition, ambiguity, paradox, and the need to choose.

The first and primary symbols of the Burgess cosmogony are the sun and moon. They are the mystical, mythical avatars that preside over the choosing upon the earth. Their qualities, both natural and allegorical, are the parameters of Burgess's fiction. Certain secondary symbols are, however, equally important for directing the protagonists' literal, as well as spiritual movement. From the partial list below, one can discern the two opposing spheres that directly relate to Burgess's dualistic universe, and the limbo sphere between them.

| *White* ("Good God") | *Gray* ("Man") | *Black* ("Evil God") |
| --- | --- | --- |
| sun | earth | moon |
| day | dawn/dusk | night |
| birth | life | death |
| creation | existence | destruction |
| grace | ambivalence | sin |
| past | present | future |
| soul | mind | body |
| summer | spring/fall | winter |

Burgess uses this highly Manichaean and dualistic world for most of his principal settings. His protagonists are allowed to live out their lives until the moment they are embodied in the novels. That moment becomes the moment of choice, and Burgess forces them to exercise the dualistic option. This aspect of choosing and "the choice" mark every plot and direct protagonists from **A Vision of Battlements** to **Napoleon Symphony**. A novel like **MF** is (if one might forgive Burgess's own pun) riddled with choices. **A Clockwork Orange,** however, is unique of aspect in that Burgess is not working on a multiplicity of levels but concentrating on the *nature* of choice which, by definition, must be *free.* To underscore his message, Burgess is far more translucent about his symbolism in **A Clockwork Orange** than in most of his other novels.

The moon and the night and the winter are Alex's arena. Burgess has always attached allegorical significance to the night and never more heavily than here: "The day was very different from the night. The night belonged to me and my droogs and all the rest of the nadsats, and the starry bourgeois lurked indoors drinking in the gloopy worldcasts; but the day was for the starry ones and there always seemed to be more rozzes or millicents about during the day."

Scattered throughout the first section of the novel are innumerable references to the night as the time of evil. ("The Luna was up" and "it was winter trees and dark.") On Alex's final night raid that ends in death, treachery, and incarceration, Burgess is continually outlining in black and white: "So we came nice and quiet to this domy called the Manse, and there were globe lights outside on iron stalks . . . and there was a light like dim on in one of the rooms on the ground level, and we went to a nice patch of street dark. . . . They [the droogs] nodded in the dark. . . . Then we waited again in darkness." Burgess continues the imagery—the black of the evening, the light from the windows, the white old woman, the pouring of white milk, the theft of a white statue of Beethoven. Nearly blinded by the most stupid of his droogs (significantly named Dim), Alex is captured by the police, brought through the black night to the white of the police station: "They dragged me into this very bright-lit whitewashed cantora. . . ."

Throughout the remainder of the novel Burgess employs a seemingly confused pattern of white and black. The white-jacketed doctors are evil, and as extreme versions of B. F. Skinner's behaviorists and advocates of "the Ludovico technique," understandably so. In their hands (or rather in their mechanical toils), Alex will become a clockwork orange: a piece of pulpless, juiceless flesh that acts upon command and not out of will. Conversely, the chaplain is a drunk garbed in black, yet he is the only character within the novel who honestly questions the morality of this application of behavioral science.

The white of the doctors, the black of the prison cell, the white of the technicians, the black of the chaplain, the white of the interrogation room, the black of Alex's reentry into society—all are carefully balanced inversions. The reader has often to unravel such inversions—to work, that is, in and out of the maze—particularly within scenes with institutional settings. The same sorts of inversion occur in *The Doctor Is Sick* and in the hospital scenes from *Honey for the Bears*. Burgess generally inverts his black-white imagery in situations where the morality and ethics are prescribed and not chosen. Schools, prisons, military installations, and hospitals—all places calling for Burgess's use of color imagery—underscore, through studied inversion, his perception of a morally inverted, indeed perverted world.

In *A Clockwork Orange* Burgess has crafted a childmachine, placed him in the pit of tomorrow, and "voiced" him with the lament of a world so mesmerized by technocracy that it has lost its essence. Alex chooses to sin and the world cannot live with his choice. Dystopia takes away neither his sin nor his existence, but does take away his right to choose, and thereby his soul: "Badness is of the self, the one, the you or me on our oddy knockies, and that self is made by old Bog or God and is his great pride and radosty. But the not-self cannot have the bad, meaning they of the government and the judges and the schools cannot allow the bad because they cannot allow the self. And is not our modern history, my brothers, the story of brave malenky selves fighting these big machines?" Alex does what he wants to do, so the world takes away his freedom to choose. He becomes a programmed good machine and no longer a person. Yet there has to be room for freedom, for by design this is a world of man. We are all "malenky selves on our oddy knockies" and the price of freedom runs high. We are a medial element, both desperate and sublime, with our *only* distinction being our right to choose. The paradox is one of enormity, for the stakes are enormous; the only alternative is a mechanized hell.

Oddly enough, Burgess, as man and as writer, is caught in the same paradox he espouses. The mind does not journey far from the body; the medial element, the victimized chooser of Burgess's fictions, is really Burgess himself. The spirit as well as the body yearns for a place, a time to belong. The Far East, England, Malta, are all bridges he has burned behind him. Burgess has, through his fic-

tion, his journalism, his determined stand, cut himself off in principle and in fact from much that he intellectually abhors yet emotionally loves. His church and his country go on, despite his verbal assaults. Like Gulliver, he might indeed be genuinely amazed that his satire of the human condition has not brought about immediate improvement

---

**An excerpt from *A Clockwork Orange***

'What's it going to be then, eh?'

There was me, that is Alex, and my three droogs, that is Pete, Georgie, and Dim, Dim being really dim, and we sat in the Korova Milkbar making up our rassoodocks what to do with the evening, a flip dark chill winter bastard though dry. The Korova Milkbar was a milk-plus mesto, and you may, O my brothers, have forgotten what these mestos were like, things changing so skorry these days and everybody very quick to forget, newspapers not being read much neither. Well, what they sold there was milk plus something else. They had no license for selling liquor, but there was no law yet against prodding some of the new veshches which they used to put into the old moloko, so you could peet it with vellocet or synthemesc or drencrom or one or two other veshches which would give you a nice quiet horrorshow fifteen minutes admiring Bog And All His Holy Angels And Saints in your left shoe with lights bursting all over your mozg. Or you could peet milk with knives in it, as we used to say, and this would sharpen you up and make you ready for a bit of dirty twenty-to-one, and that was what we were peeting this evening I'm starting off the story with.

Our pockets were full of deng, so there was no real need from the point of view of crasting any more pretty polly to tolchock some old veck in an alley and viddy him swim in his blood while we counted the takings and divided by four, nor to do the ultra-violent on some shivering starry grey-haired ptitsa in a shop and go smecking off with the till's guts. But, as they say, money isn't everything.

The four of us were dressed in the heighth of fashion, which in those days was a pair of black very tight tights with the old jelly mould, as we called it, fitting on the crutch underneath the tights, this being to protect and also a sort of a design you could viddy clear enough in a certain light, so that I had one in the shape of a spider, Pete had a rooker (a hand, that is), Georgie had a very fancy one of a flower, and poor old Dim had a very hound-and-horny one of a clown's litso (face, that is), Dim not ever having much of an idea of things and being, beyond all shadow of a doubting thomas, the dimmest of we four. Then we wore waisty jackets without lapels but with these very big built-up shoulders ('pletchoes' we called them) which were a kind of a mockery of having real shoulders like that. Then, my brothers, we had these off-white cravats which looked like whipped-up kartoffel or spud with a sort of a design made on it with a fork. We wore our hair not too long and we had flip horrorshow boots for kicking.

*Anthony Burgess, in his* A Clockwork Orange, *1962.*

---

of it. But then, like Swift—who, too, looks *down* to observe human nature, rather than *around*—he has been forced to pay for his olympian vision.

And, unfortunately, for his prophetic vision as well. Burgess's fiction is more alive today than even in the times it was written. One reads with amazement, if not indeed horror, that Burgess's prophesy has become fact. Zoroaster and Manes are dust now. Dualism is little more than an Eastern etiquette, permeating the life-style of Asia. Kierkegaard, Nietzsche, and Sartre are classics, venerable promulgators of the *Angst* and *nausée* that all of us have subliminally absorbed. But the dualistic paradox still continues to unwind itself, and we still throb in our gray cocoons, daring ourselves to opt for emergence into the day or into the night. Burgess would draw us out of ourselves and make us choose, would make us commit ourself to choice for choice's sake. Like Alex, we may become mere mechanism, or all will, incarnated in flesh and blood: a clockwork, or an orange. The responsibility is of course ours, and Burgess brilliantly instructs us how to shoulder the responsibility.

### Julie Carson　(essay date Spring 1976)

SOURCE: "Pronominalization in *A Clockwork Orange*," in *Papers on Language and Literature*, Vol. 12, No. 2, Spring, 1976, pp. 200-05.

[*In the following essay, Carson argues that pronoun usage in* A Clockwork Orange *is indicative of the power relationships between Alex and the other characters.*]

What discussion there has been of the language of *A Clockwork Orange* has dealt mainly with the gypsy talk of Alec, "nadsat," a hybrid of Russian and onomatopoetic words. Virtually no critic, however, has investigated a linguistic technique certainly as obvious as the nadsat lexicon: Alec's system of pronominalization. It is with the thou/you pronoun distinction, and not the nadsat vocabulary, that Burgess indicates the significant changes in the central character in the novel.

In "The Pronouns of Power and Solidarity," Roger Brown and Albert Gilman propose a "connection between social structure, group ideology, and the semantics of the pronoun." They base their conclusions on data from sixteen countries, whose native languages make distinction between familiar and formal pronouns [see *Style in Language,* edited by Thomas A. Sebeok, 1960]. Their findings are especially applicable to *A Clockwork Orange,* for Alec is the only character who deviates from the standard pronoun system. Burgess sets him off in two ways: from general society by giving him the nadsat vocabulary, and from his own group, with the pronoun distinction. The use of an argot to set a group apart is common enough. But a deviation from, yet within, an argot carries greater implications, revealing Alec's position of power relative to both society and to his droogs. Concerning power and pronouns, Brown and Gilman observe that "power is a relationship between at least two persons, and it is nonreciprocal in the sense that both cannot have power in the same area of behavior. The power semantic is similarly nonreciprocal; the superior says T and receives V." [In a foot-

note, Carson explains: "Gilman and Brown use the symbols T and V (from the Latin *tu* and *vos*) to designate familiar and polite pronouns in any language."]

Alec uses the formal "thou" in situations in which he is clearly in control, as in his dialogue with Dim, the least competent of his droogs: " 'Come, gloopy bastard as thou art. Think not on them.' " Later when his droogs are in rebellion, Alec draws a fine line in his respect among his droogs; Dim he continues to address "thou," but to the other two droogs he uses the conventional pronoun: " 'Oh now, don't, both of you malchicks. Droogs, aren't we?' " His droogs are not mollified, despite Alec's addressing them as "you," his equals, and they press their revolt. Alec then gets "more razdaz inside," frightened by the impending violence, and capitulates his position of power. After he agrees to go "bedways," in his acquiescent stance, Alec addresses Dim, the former object of physical abuse, as an equal: " 'You understand about that tolchock on the not, Dim. It was the music see.' "

There are three other important examples of the thou/you distinction early in the novel. One occurs when Alec and his droogs break into F. Alexander's HOME. As the bizarre scene begins to unfold, in the only line which calls for pronoun usage, Alec uses "thou"; " 'Never fear. If fear thou hast in thy heart, O brother, pray banish it forthwith." In the entire episode of destruction and rape, Alec dominates the situation. By telling Alexander not to fear, he clearly mocks Alexander, who indeed has a great deal to fear. Later in the novel, Alec uses "thou" when he deceives his father and asserts his ability to control situations: " 'Never worry about thine only son and heir, O my father,' I said. 'Fear not. He canst taketh care of himself, verily.' " The third significant use of "thou" occurs when Alec is verbally and then physically assaulting Billyboy: " 'Well, if it isn't fat stinking billygoat Billyboy in poison. How art thou, thou globby bottle of cheap stinking chipoil? Come and get one in the yarbles, if you have any yarbles, you eunuch jelly, thou.' " In the last example what appears to be ambivalence (the use of both pronoun forms) might be explained in either of two ways: first, the power relationship between Alec and Billyboy is not clear. They are rivals and peers. But in this scene, Alec is on the attack, not to Dim or to Alexander or to his father, whom he considers his subordinates-victims, but to a person he must hold in derision, yet whose power he respects. Billyboy is not so weak an adversary that he can be dismissed with the "thou" form; in fact, Alec does not win the encounter. It is broken up by police sirens. Interestingly, as the sirens wail, and the threat of a higher authority looms, Alec reverts to conventional usage: " 'Get you soon, fear not,' I called, 'stinking billygoat. I'll have your yarbles off lovely.' " The dialogue with Billyboy seems to reflect, then, what Brown and Gilman suggest: "the superior says T and receives V" in nonreciprocal power relationships.

When Alec and his droogs break into Alexander's HOME, the power relationship is clear: Alec is plainly in control. But in the next major crime they commit, a curious thing happens: although Alec seems to be dominating the situation (he has, afterall, only an old woman as his adversary) he uses the conventional pronoun form: " 'Hi hi hi. At last we meet. Our brief govoreet through the letter-hole was not, shall we say, satisfactory, yes? Let us admit not, oh verily not, you stinking starry old sharp.' " In no comparable situation had Alec lapsed into the conventional form "you"; Burgess offers here a linguistic clue to the imminent power change. Alec, of course, is caught in this crime and imprisoned. Perhaps most interesting of all is that from this episode until he is "cured" of the Ludovico technique, with one exception, Alec never says "thou" to anyone, no matter what his estimation of them. Clearly Burgess exploited the rare and subtle use of "thou" to indicate Alec's power position, thus affirming Brown and Gilman's observation that "a man's consistent pronoun style gives away his class status."

Alec perceives each of his relationships correctly: he knows, in other words, when he may use the "thou" form. As Brown and Gilman explain, "The general meaning of an unexpected pronoun choice is simply that the speaker, for the moment, views the relationship that calls for the pronoun used." Likewise, Alec knows when to use "you", as when the police brutally interrogate him and Deltoid spits in his face. Alec replies: " 'Thank you, sir, thank you very much, sir, that was very kind of you sir, thank you.' " With one exception Alec never uses any other second person pronominal form during his arrest, imprisonment, or hospitalization. [In a footnote, Carson elaborates: "The one time Alec does use 'thou' is to the hospital staff aide wheeling him back to his room after the first Ludovico session. The aide is described by Alec as an 'under-veck'; he is interpreted, in other words, as an inferior person. Alec's sensibilities (and therefore, his wrath) may have been especially aroused because the 'under-veck' was singing a 'hound and horny popsong.' Alec, with his sophisticated taste in music would have found then even greater reason to hold the aide in disdain."]

The Ludovico technique evokes a number of reactions in Alec: he becomes nonaggressive, nonviolent, and respectful to established societal codes. Accordingly, he also ceases to use "thou" in his dialogues. Perhaps the most significant example of the change effected in him occurs shortly after his release from the hospital. When he meets Dim, his pronominal style has altered considerably, revealing his apprehension of his new role in the power structure: " 'Read to you,' I said, a malenky bit nasty. 'You still too dim to read for yourself, O brother.' " After the beating that Dim and Billboy inflict on him, Alec ironically seeks help at Alexander's HOME, where he has earlier used the "thou" pronominal code. When he returns to seek help from Alexander (admittedly a subordinate position) he uses conventional pronouns, but later in the conversation after reading an attack on the government Alexander had written in his name, Alec comments: " 'Very good. . . . Real horrorshow. Written well thou hast, O sir.' And then he looked at me very narrow and said: 'What?' It was like he had not slooshied me before. 'Oh that,' I said, 'is what we call nadsat talk. All the teens use that, sir.' " Alexander's sudden close attention to Alec's speech could not have been evoked only by the obvious lexical deviance, "horrorshow." Earlier in their conversation Alec had defined "ptitsa" and "the charlie" for Alexander, or had used nadsat words which Alexander let pass by without questioning: "polly," "slooshy" and "jeezny." But after Alec revealed himself with the use of "thou" Alexander's suspicions about his identity were aroused.

There is some ambivalence in Alec's pronominal code in this episode at HOME. But it reflects Alec's uncertainty of his role there. The use of "thou" is an obvious slip on Alec's part. But later, when he asserts himself "I did not like that crack about zombyish, brothers, and so I said: 'What goes on, bratties? What dost thou in mind for thy little droog have?' " Alec allows himself to slip into the total nadsat argot of lexicon, syntax, and morphology because of his great fear. He is suddenly aware that Alexander and his group are acting in their own interests and not in his. He assesses the situation quickly and adopts nearly the proper linguistic posture for his power position, but he cannot restrain himself entirely; his language, after all, has been his greatest means of self-identification and self-assertion. Alexander's final torture of Alec consists of playing Beethoven, inducing him to commit suicide. As Alec prepares to jump to his death, he cries: " 'Goodbye, goodbye, my Bog forgive you for a ruined life.' " Again, in what appears to be his final role as victim, Alec uses the pronoun "you" appropriate to the situation, rather than the inappropriate power semantic "thou." Alec's suicide attempt is of course abortive, and his fall causes much of the Ludovico technique to be ineffective. Although Alec does not linguistically revert to his former self, as the story line might suggest, if one interprets only the action of the story during Alec's final hospitalization, it appears that he is indeed his former self. He relies heavily on the nadsat vocabulary; he exhibits his former usual extraordinary lust; he treats his parents with great disdain; he threatens physical violence to those who contradict him; and he insults the most overt symbol of the established order, the Minister of the Interior. But he does all these things with pronominal ambivalence. He addresses the nurse: " 'What gives, O my little sister? Come thou and have a nice lay-down with your malenky droog in this bed' "; his parents: " 'Well well well well well, what gives? What makes you think you are like welcome?' "; the Minister of the Interior: " 'Bolshy great yarblockos to thee and thine.' " To three of the four persons he speaks to in his final hospitalization, after he has been apparently cured of the Ludovico technique, he readopts his special pronominal code. He has reasserted himself to everyone but his parents, for their leaving him was on a tentative basis: " 'You'll have to make up your mind,' I said, 'who's to be boss.' " In Alec's final confrontation with the Minister of the Interior, he uses "thou" exclusively— " 'Bolshy great yarblockos to thee and thine' "—for he consistently interprets the Minister as inferior: "And in he came, and of course it was none other than the Minister of the Interior or Inferior. . . ." Other epithets he uses to refer to the Minister explicitly call attention to the inferior role he attributes to him: "int Inf Min" and "intinfmin."

Anthony Burgess thus draws subtle distinctions by developing a pronominal code within the nadsat argot which, in turn, gives explicit linguistic clues to the power structures in *A Clockwork Orange*. He reflects current findings of linguistic research which suggests that there is a power semantic which is clearly revealed in nonreciprocal power relationships. He has developed a linguistic technique both subtle and sophisticated and one that enhances the brilliance of *A Clockwork Orange*.

### Rubin Rabinovitz    (essay date Winter 1978-1979)

SOURCE: "Mechanism vs. Organism: Anthony Burgess' *A Clockwork Orange,*" in *Modern Fiction Studies,* Vol. 24, No. 4, Winter, 1978-1979, pp. 538-41.

[*Rabinovitz is an American critic and educator. In the following essay, he argues that the twenty-first chapter of* A Clockwork Orange *reveals a thematic synthesis of free will and determinism.*]

In his most famous novel, *A Clockwork Orange,* Anthony Burgess explores a number of interesting issues such as free will, the meaning of violence, and a cyclical theory of history. Resolving these issues, however, is complicated by an extraneous factor; the American editions of the novel lack Burgess' original conclusion and end with what is the penultimate chapter of the first English edition.

A good summary of the deleted section is provided by Burgess himself:

> In the final chapter of the British edition, Alex is already growing up. He has a new gang, but he's tired of leading it; what he really wants is to have a son of his own—the libido is being tamed and turned social—and the first thing he now has to do is to find a mate, which means sexual love, not the old in-and-out. [*Rolling Stone,* June 8, 1972]

The hero's abrupt decision to turn away from his old pattern of violence has caused some unrest among Burgess' critics. Shirley Chew, writing in *Encounter,* feels that with Alex's fantasy of domestic life "the novel loses its integrity and falls into the sentimental." The ending, Chew says, makes it appear that Burgess condones and even shares the hero's taste for violence [*Encounter,* June, 1972]. And A. A. DeVitis, author of a recent study of Burgess' fiction, says that the last chapter was "wisely omitted from the American edition" [*Anthony Burgess,* 1972].

The American publisher, like Shirley Chew, felt that the last chapter was too sentimental; but Burgess has defended the original conclusion:

> When they were going to publish it in America, they said "we're tougher over here" and thought the ending too soft for their readers. If it was me now, faced with the decision I'd say no. I still believe in my ending [Anthony Burgess with Carol Dix, *Transatlantic Review,* Spring-Summer, 1972]

On the face of it, publisher and critics seem right: the novel did enjoy better sales in America than in England, and Stanley Kubrick chose to use the shortened American edition for his film version of the book. But the original ending is not as sentimental as it first appears; there is truth, even poetic justice, in the idea of yesterday's reprobate changing diapers for his own neophyte reprobate.

If Alex remains violent, as he does in the American version, the reader's attitude towards him is mainly one of condemnation; but Burgess' inquiry into the origins of violence requires a hero who cannot be so easily condemned and dismissed. The original version in a sense provides the less sentimental ending if Alex is transformed from a monster into an ordinary human being with whom the reader can identify. Obdurate Alex is a threat to safety; Alex reformed threatens moral complacency, by suggesting that a love of violence is universal.

Regardless of which ending one prefers, Burgess wrote his novel assuming that it would appear intact, and it deserves to be considered in the complete version. As it turns out, many of his ideas are clarified when the last chapter is restored. An example is Burgess' treatment of the theme of freedom and determinism. Burgess appears in *A Clockwork Orange* to disapprove of the Ludovico technique (a scientific process for forcing criminals to reform); the loss of free will seems to be too great a price to pay. But if this is true, and if Burgess shares the point of view of the Chaplain and F. Alexander who oppose the Ludovico technique for similar reasons, it is unclear why Burgess portrays these characters in a sardonic fashion.

The novel's final statement about free will comes in the deleted chapter, when Alex says that in his youth he had not been free but determined. In his violent phase, he says, he had been

> like one of these malenky toys you viddy being sold in the streets, like little chellovecks made out of tin and with a spring inside and then a winding handle on the outside and you wind it up grrr grrr grrr and off it itties, like walking. O my brothers. But it itties in a straight line and bangs straight into things bang bang and it cannot help what it is doing. Being young is like being like one of these malenky machines.

The young are like clockwork men; their proclivity towards violence is built into them. His son, Alex says, will also go through a violent phase, and Alex "would not be able to really stop him. And nor would he be able to stop his own son, brothers."

Alex concludes that there is a cycle of recurring phases in which each young man undergoes a period of existence as a violent, mechanical man; then he matures, gets greater freedom of choice, and his violence subsides. The cycle, says Alex, will go on forever: "and so it would itty on to like the end of the world, round and round and round. . . ." The circularity of the repeating pattern leads Alex to compare the progress of generations to an image of God turning a dirty, smelly orange in his hands, "old Bog Himself (by courtesy of Korova Milkbar) turning and turning and turning a vonny grahzny orange in his gigantic rookers." The determined progress of the clockwork man, who must move in a straight line, is thus contrasted with the circular shape and movement of God's orange, symbol of life and organic growth. The "vonny grahzny" orange is also like the world, which on the same page is called "grahzny vonny." For Alex, life has aspects both of determinism and free will, line and circle, clockwork and orange.

Burgess used similar line-circle imagery in *The Wanting*

*Seed,* which was published in the same year as *A Clockwork Orange*. In both novels, determinism and mechanical progress are associated with lines, while freedom and organic growth are associated with circles. Reality for Burgess often emerges from the interaction of contrary principles like these; in *A Clockwork Orange* Alex's linear, determined youth is contrasted with his freedom in maturity when he decides to marry, have a child, and give up his violence. But the cycle continues, and paradoxically Alex's freedom will lead him to have a child who once more will be subjected to the deterministic phase of the process.

By the end of the novel, Alex is mature enough to deal with this paradox. Troubled as he is by the idea that his son will be violent, he remains resolute in his desire to have children. The growth of Burgess' heroes is often indicated by their willingness to accept life and the mixed bag of contradictory values it offers.

The sense that Alex has accepted life is enforced when he finally answers the question which introduces each part of the novel and which is repeated eleven times: "What's it going to be then, eh?" Initially the question seems only to be about what sort of drink to order, but as it recurs it acquires existential overtones. The answer finally comes towards the end of the deleted chapter:

> But first of all, brothers, there was this vesch of finding some devotchka or other who would be a mother to this son. I would have to start on that tomorrow, I kept thinking. That was something like new to do. That was something I would have to get started on, a new like chapter beginning.
>
> That's what it's going to be then, brothers. . . .

The question is answered just after Alex sees himself as a participant in the historical cycle and his life as a microcosmic version of the cycle. He has understood that history grows out of the struggle of opposing forces and has accepted a similar clash of contradictory urges in his own personality.

Alex's ideas suggest that Burgess has been influenced by Hegel's theory of history; and some of the characters in his other novels (like the history teacher who is the protagonist of *The Long Day Wanes*) actually discuss Hegel's theory. Burgess' system, however, differs in a number of respects from Hegel's. In the Hegelian dialectic, the opposition of thesis and antithesis produces a synthesis which resembles the stages that preceded it, but which is also different in some ways from these stages. The new element in the synthesis leads to the idea—very important in Hegelian thought—that progress comes with the dialectical historical cycle.

Burgess' theory denies this idea of progress. His system posits two antithetical, alternating stages; the third stage is actually only a repetition of the first. In this system, innovations are never permanent; the changes in one era are undone by a regressive process in the next, so there can be no true historical progress.

The idea that history repeats itself and the pessimistic outlook which it engenders may come from Toynbee or Spengler, whose cyclical theories of history were in vogue when Burgess was a student. Vico, whom Burgess mentions in his Joyce criticism, may also be a source. Burgess calls himself a Manichean, and he often takes a dualistic Manichean view of contending moral forces.

Another important source of Burgess' theory is the opposition of yin and yang principles in Chinese philosophy. Burgess refers to the yin-yang in his autobiographical first novel, *A Vision of Battlements,* and in a number of essays. According to Robert Morris, the yin-yang principles help to explain the historical dilemma of Crabbe, the hero of *The Long Day Wanes*:

> The East, as Burgess sees it, is both active and passive, containing the principles of yin-yang, humming at both poles of the dialectic at once. It is a phenomenon alien to the West, which, nurtured on Hegelian propositions, submits to the certainty of either cyclical or lineal progression. [*The Consolations of Ambiguity: An Essay on the Novels of Anthony Burgess,* 1971]

Morris' comment is useful for understanding how yin and yang are related to dichotomies in *A Clockwork Orange* such as line and circle, organism and mechanism, and determinism and free will.

Burgess feels that it is his work as an artist to portray conflicting elements which eventually blend into a single confluent entity. In *Urgent Copy,* a collection of reviews and essays, he gives an example: impressed by the juxtaposition of Spanish and British cultures in Gibralter, he composed a symphony in which disparate themes relating to these cultures clash initially but ultimately harmonize. The symphony was written before any of his novels, and this process of juxtaposing conflicting values provided him with a method he later used in his writing. A good discus-

---

**Anthony Burgess on free will vs. determinism:**

We are all both Pelagian and Augustinian, either in cyclical phases, or, through a kind of doublethink, at one and the same time. Orwell was Pelagian in that he was a Socialist, Augustinian in that he created Ingsoc. It sometimes seems that the political life of a free community moves in the following cycle: a Pelagian belief in progress produces a kind of liberal regime that wavers when men are seen not to be perfectible and fail to live up to the liberal image; the regime collapses and is succeeded by an authoritarianism in which men are made to be good; men are seen not to be so bad as the Augustinian philosophy teaches; the way is open for liberalism to return. We tend to Augustinianism when we are disgusted with our own selfishness, to Pelagianism when we seem to have behaved well. Free will is of the essence of Pelagianism; determinism (original sin makes us not altogether responsible for our actions) of Augustinianism. None of us are sure how free we really are.

*Anthony Burgess in* 1985, *Little, Brown, 1978.*

sion of how this principle works elsewhere in Burgess' *oeuvre* may be found in Thomas LeClair's study of his fiction [in *Critique: Studies in Modern Fiction,* Vol. 12, 1971, pp. 77-94].

Burgess, then, follows the yin-yang principles in understanding change as a clash and interaction of opposed values which can lead either to chaos or to harmony. In the concluding essay of *Urgent Copy,* he explains that, though one would like to live by a single set of values, reality is most often apprehended in sets of opposing values like good and evil, white and black, rich and poor. Politicians and theologians, who claim they can find unity in merging these values, actually offer either promises (a classless society, for example) or intangibles (God, metaphysical ideas). Only a work of art, says Burgess, can achieve a synthesis of opposites which presents an immediate vision of unity. Obviously, *A Clockwork Orange* is meant to serve as an example of the sort of work that can truly reconcile opposing values.

## Rubin Rabinovitz    (essay date Spring 1979)

SOURCE: "Ethical Values in Anthony Burgess's *Clockwork Orange,*" in *Studies in the Novel,* Vol. XI, No. 1, Spring, 1979, pp. 43-50.

[*In the following essay, Rabinovitz comments on Burgess's presentation in* A Clockwork Orange *of the notion of "social history as a cyclical alternation" of diametrically opposed views of human nature and morality.*]

In Anthony Burgess's most famous novel, *A Clockwork Orange* [1962 British edition, which includes the final, twenty-first chapter], the most obvious clash of values is between the lawless hero and a society that hopes to control him. This struggle obscures another conflict which is nevertheless very important: the opposing views of libertarians and authoritarians on how best to provide social controls. The theme of libertarian-authoritarian opposition recurs throughout Burgess's novels, often as a conflict between points of view Burgess has called Pelagian and Augustinian. The best exposition of this idea is given by Tristram Foxe, the protagonist of Burgess's novel *The Wanting Seed*.

Foxe (who is a history teacher) explains that Pelagianism is named for Pelagius, a monk whose teachings were condemned by the church. Pelagius argued against the doctrine of original sin and advocated the idea of human perfectibility; hence he is the patron of libertarian societies. St. Augustine, a contemporary of Pelagius, reaffirmed the doctrine of original sin; human perfectibility, he said, was possible only with God's grace. Because grace is not universally granted, there must always be sin, war, crime, and hence the need for social controls. Augustine therefore emerges as patron of the authoritarians.

Burgess often presents social history as a cyclical alternation of Pelagian and Augustinian parties which oppose one another like yin and yang. With the Augustinians in power there is a period of social stability which comes as the result of a rigidly enforced authoritarian moral code. Such controls make it appear that the populace is inherently ethical and encourage a growing faith in human perfectibility; eventually the strictness of the Augustinians seems superfluous. The populace begins to demand more freedom, libertarian arguments gain credibility, and finally there is a transition to a Pelagian form of government.

The Pelagians fare no better. Their libertarianism gives way to permissiveness and then to an anarchic period of crime, strikes, and deteriorating public services. After a transitional phase, the popular outcry for more law and order heralds the rise of a new Augustinian party and the beginning of another cycle.

This issue comes up in *The Clockwork Testament,* one of Burgess's more recent novels. Enderby, the hero, is obsessed with Augustine and Pelagius and decides to write about them. He finishes a dozen pages of a film script (included in Burgess's novel) which culminate in a debate between the two, Augustine arguing in favor of the doctrine of original sin and Pelagius disagreeing. The script is never completed and, fittingly, the dispute is never settled.

In *A Clockwork Orange,* the anarchic quality of the society portrayed early in the novel indicates that Pelagian liberals are in power. Upon Alex's release from prison he finds that a broken elevator has been repaired and that the police force has been enlarged; these are signs that a more authoritarian party has taken over. But the new regime is not as strong in its authoritarianism as, for example, the Augustinian society in *The Wanting Seed*. It avoids the extremes of Augustinianism—wars and religious fanaticism—because Burgess in portraying libertarian and authoritarian parties in a society committed to an underlying Pelagian dogma is satirizing the Labor and Conservative Parties of the English Welfare State.

The new government in *A Clockwork Orange* therefore is only in a subdued way Augustinian. Its leaders, however, do indicate their lack of faith in human perfectibility by utilizing the Ludovico technique and by getting their jails ready for great numbers of political offenders. The characters in the novel who most oppose this government are naturally those who are extreme libertarians.

A principal spokesman for the libertarians is the writer F. Alexander. His book proclaims his belief in human perfectibility and free will, but Alexander's histrionic prose style makes his Pelagian sentiments somewhat suspect. When a friend ascertains that it was young Alex who raped his wife, Alexander gives up his liberalism and agrees to collaborate in a plan to drive Alex to suicide. Another Pelagian character is P.R. Deltoid, Alex's rehabilitation officer. He epitomizes the libertarian belief that criminals should be reeducated and not punished; but despite Deltoid's efforts Alex remains incorrigible. "Is it some devil that crawls inside you?" Deltoid asks hardly the sort of question one would expect from a Pelagian. After learning that Alex has killed an old woman, Deltoid spits in his face: like F. Alexander, he has been reduced to a betrayal of his principles.

These failures of Pelagianism make it appear that Burgess, as some critics have maintained, favors an Augustinian point of view. But in *The Wanting Seed,* where he gives his most vivid portrayal of each type of society, Burgess seems to take the side of the Pelagians. In that novel the Pelagians undermine family life and encourage homosexuality as a form of population control; the Augustinians solve the population problem by staging pseudowars in which the participants are decimated and their flesh canned for human consumption. Even at their moral nadir, the Pelagians seem restrained when compared to the cannibalistic Augustinians.

In *Tremor of Intent* Burgess again seems to favor the Augustinian side when the views of a Pelagian scientist are satirized. Burgess's unsympathetic presentation of the scientist's views may, however, have another explanation. In *The Novel Now* he is critical of writers like H. G. Wells whose enthusiasm for technology leads them to rhapsodize over scientifically organized utopian societies. For Burgess, science deals only with external factors: it may improve living conditions, but it cannot alter the human condition. In *Tremor of Intent,* the shallowness of the scientist's arguments may be as much related to his profession as to his Pelagian beliefs.

It seems imprecise, then, to assume that Burgess consistently favors either an Augustinian or a Pelagian point of view. Similarly, those of Burgess's characters who are strongly committed to a single side in the Pelagian-Augustinian cycle fare badly. During one phase they are frustrated because they are out of power; during the next they are disappointed when their social theory fails to live up to its promise. Many of Burgess's heroes learn to change; like Alex, they begin to see how their old unilateral views fit into a cycle of interacting polar opposites. In *Tremor of Intent,* for example, the hero achieves this kind of understanding when he says, "Knowing God means also knowing his opposite. You can't get away from the great opposition."

An interaction of polar opposites in *A Clockwork Orange* emerges from Burgess's juxtaposition of the Augustinian views of Alex and the Pelagian views of F. Alexander. Many of Alex's characteristics are Augustinian: his dictatorial domination of his friends, his brutality, and his belief that criminals deserve punishment and not rehabilitation. Alex thinks that the world is wicked and does not believe in human perfectibility; F. Alexander, on the other hand, writes that man is "a creature of growth and capable of sweetness." Alexander's arguments in favor of free will indicate his Pelagianism; the connection Alex makes between evil and determined behavior recalls St. Augustine's concept of predestinarian grace. Like St. Augustine himself, Alex is redeemed after a sinful youth and, as an author, favors the confessional mode.

Many of the characteristics of Alex and F. Alexander may be resolved into examples of extremes that follow the pattern of polar antitheses: predator and victim; uncontrolled libido (rapist) and controlled libido (husband); youth and adult; man of action and man of ideas; destroyer and creator; conservative and liberal; alienated man and integrated man. The similarity of the names Alex and Alexander indicates an underlying kinship between the two which emerges if their opposing values are seen as the polar extremes of the same cycles. Alex (who comments on the similarity of the names) refers to his antagonist as "the great F. Alexander"; he himself is often called "little Alex."

The relativism resulting from this evenhanded treatment of contrasting values, however, sometimes leaves Burgess open to a charge of moral ambiguity. Burgess seems to be aware of this possibility, and in *Tremor of Intent* he tries to show that a belief in his cyclical system need not lead to a weakened moral stance. Here, an important ethical criterion is the degree of commitment to the cyclical system itself. Life and reality are expressed in polar oppositions which alternate cyclically; a commitment to the cyclical system, then, is tantamount to a commitment to life and reality. For Hillier, the hero of *Tremor of Intent,* an involvement with the cyclical system is the beginning of moral behavior. Those who ignore the cyclical system or attempt to disengage themselves from it—Hillier calls them "neutrals"—are guilty of immoral behavior which may be extremely destructive because, deceptively, it seems innocuous.

Hillier concludes that the neutrals are morally inferior to evildoers: the wicked are at least morally committed, albeit to a polar extreme which Hillier (recently ordained a priest) opposes. "If we're going to save the world," he says, "we shall have to use unorthodox methods. Don't you think we'd all rather see devil-worship than bland neutrality?"

The superiority of evildoers to neutrals is perhaps a reason for Alex's redemption in the original version of *A Clockwork Orange.* Alex is firmly committed to evil: he enjoys a sadistic fantasy in which he helps to crucify Christ, and, in a discussion of goodness, calls himself a patron of "the other shop." The neutrals are the scientists who destroy Alex's freedom of choice by administering the Ludovico technique. Dr. Brodsky, for example, cares little about the ethical questions raised by the treatment: "We are not concerned with motive, with the higher ethics. We are concerned only with cutting down crime." Alex—one would think he had little right to throw stones—calls Brodsky and his fellow scientists "an evil lot of bastards," and complains that their use of Beethoven's music in the treatment is "a filthy unforgivable sin."

Burgess apparently feels that science lends itself easily to the neutrality he detests; though Alex is often beaten in the novel and once driven to attempt suicide, this is the only place where he moralizes about his oppressors.

There are a number of reasons why Burgess considers the scientists who rob a man of his capacity for ethical choice morally inferior to the criminals they treat. In Christian terms, Alex as a sinner must be permitted to enhance the possibilities for his salvation by choosing good over evil. A man rendered incapable of moral choice can never attain salvation; but a sinner may choose to repent and win redemption.

In terms of Burgess's cyclical system, Alex in his youth may be predestined to do evil; but with maturity comes freedom, when his determined phase is transformed into its polar opposite. The Ludovico treatment, invented by ethical neutrals, forces its victims to become neutral; it removes them from the cyclical process and prevents their transition into a mature phase. The neutralizing treatment turns Alex into a perpetual victim whose weakness provokes violence in those who encounter him. But when Alex's ability to choose is restored he finally grows tired of violence, and reforms.

Burgess's moral point of view, however, still seems ambiguous. The neutrals, both in *Tremor of Intent* and in *A Clockwork Orange,* are given rather small roles; and in his zeal to condemn the neutrals Burgess seems to be condoning criminal behavior. It was perhaps with this problem in mind that Burgess made the following comment in an article entitled, appropriately enough, **"The Manicheans"**:

> The novelist's need to be adventurous, to pose problems, to shock into attention, is bound to lead him to ground perilous for the faithful. And there is something in the novelist's vocation which predisposes him to a kind of a Manicheeism. What the religious novelist often seems to be saying is that evil is a kind of good, since it is an aspect of Ultimate Reality; though what he is really saying is that evil is more interesting to write about than good. [*Times Literary Supplement,* March 3, 1966]

It may be that Burgess is speaking of himself; like Milton writing *Paradise Lost,* Burgess may occasionally be distracted by aesthetically interesting wickedness. But this hardly explains Hillier's enthusiasm for devil-worship, an endorsement which perhaps makes him unique among even the most liberal of modern clergymen. [In a footnote, Rabinovitz elaborates: "A friend of Hillier's says that his Manichean views are most unorthodox for a priest. It is then that Hillier makes his devil-worship remark (*Tremor of Intent*). But one of the original Manicheans would have been horrified by an implication that his religion tolerated devil-worship. The motivation for Manichean sexual abstinence and vegetarianism emerged from the religion's opposition to evil."]

The apparent inconsistencies in Burgess's dualistic moral views are sometimes seen as the result of his utilization of the Eastern yin-yang principles. Yin and yang may be expressed in morally relevant categories like good and evil, or in categories like hot and cold which have no moral connotations: such a view can lead to moral relativism. The Christian idea of an omnipotent, benevolent God, on the other hand, implies a belief in the superiority of good over evil and leads to moral absolutism.

In an attempt to make use of the Eastern yin-yang idea as well as elements of Christian belief from his background, Burgess has turned to Manicheeism, an eclectic religion which flourished both in the Orient and in the West. Manicheeism incorporates a number of Christian doctrines; moreover, one of its central ideas is a dualistic opposition both in nature (light and darkness) and in ethics (good and evil) which in some ways resembles the opposition of yin and yang. Very often, Burgess's use of Manichean dualism does work to reconcile differences in Eastern and Western thought; but problems arise when a choice must be made between relativism and absolutism. In Eastern terms, where a thing may be seen as both itself and its opposite, such a choice may not be necessary; but

to a Westerner, part-time absolutism is self-contradictory. Absolutism seems to demand absolute fidelity, and in this sense Burgess's moral point of view appears ambiguous or inconsistent.

In places Burgess seems to be an absolutist; in others, a relativist. *A Clockwork Orange,* for example, seems to be dominated by moral relativism when one examines the values of Alex and F. Alexander in the light of the yin-yang principles. But this apparent inconsistency is at times explained by another conflict, a struggle between the individual and the state. Here Burgess makes no attempt to maintain the balance of the yin-yang principles: he is vehemently on the side of the individual.

An emphasis on individualism becomes apparent after a series of symmetrical events in which many of the characters who have been abused by Alex find him helpless and avenge themselves. The revenge is no harsher than the act which provoked it, but an important difference does emerge: though the state condemns Alex's brutal crimes, it sanctions and encourages the avengers' brutality—even though it has already exacted its own vengeance in the form of a prison term. For Burgess, society's brutality is more threatening than the individual's; its power is inhuman, enormous, and unrestrained. Burgess, commenting on *A Clockwork Orange,* has indicated that he meant to encourage a comparison between Alex's brutality and society's: "The violence in the book is really more to show what the State can do with it." [Anthony Burgess with Carol Dix, *Transatlantic Review,* Spring-Summer, 1972].

Alex is an enemy of the state and, as he predicts early on, the state will attempt to destroy not only what is evil in him but also his individuality: "The not-self cannot have the bad, meaning they of the government and the judges and the schools cannot allow the bad because they cannot allow the self. And is not our modern history, my brothers, the story of brave malenky selves fighting these big machines?" Unlike Alex, whose violence is subdued when he outgrows the role of clockwork man, the state remains a machine, always inhuman and conscienceless in its violence.

The hero of *The Wanting Seed,* like Alex, learns that it is unwise to trust the state: "he that saw whatever government was in power he would always be against it." And Burgess himself takes the same stand: "My political views are mainly negative: I lean towards anarchy: I hate the State. I loathe and abominate that costly, crass, intolerant, inefficient, eventually tyrannical machine which seeks more and more to supplant the individual" [*Hudson Review,* Autumn, 1967]. Like Alex, Burgess sees the state as an evil mechanism against which individual humans must defend themselves.

It becomes clear, then, that Burgess's moral values are far less ambiguous than they first appear. When he is speaking in his own voice, Burgess reacts to youthful violence with a conventional sense of dismay. If this tone had been introduced in *A Clockwork Orange,* the novel could easily have become polemical. Without redeeming qualities, the morally repulsive Alex would be a cardboard villain; and similarly the ethically attractive qualities of F. Alexander must be balanced by a personality which is, like his prose style, devoid of grace. Nor is the effect of these characterizations unrealistic; a charming psychopath usually makes a better impression than a righteous neurotic. In this fashion Burgess's system leads to the creation of characters who are round in E.M. Forster's sense.

Burgess's cyclical system works best when it is applied to the subject which concerns him the most, human individuality. Here it becomes a useful metaphor for portraying psychological complexity, for delineating the unpredictability of human beings responding to conflicting urges.

Burgess has indicated that he feels these conflicts within himself just as he observes them in others. One might make a comparison between Burgess the young composer and Alex the music-lover, or between Burgess the middle-aged novelist and the writer F. Alexander. Like Anthony Burgess, F. Alexander has written a book called *A Clockwork Orange;* and Alex, who tells his own story, is in a sense also the author of a book with the same title. Burgess is hinting that he detects within his own personality elements of both characters, that they form a yin-yang opposition which he sees within himself. But if he indicts himself, Burgess also invites the reader to examine his own capacity for playing the roles of both Alex and F. Alexander.

### Philip E. Ray    (essay date Autumn 1981)

SOURCE: "Alex Before and After: A New Approach to Burgess' *A Clockwork Orange,*" in *Modern Fiction Studies,* Vol. 27, No. 3, Autumn, 1981, pp. 479-87.

[*In the following essay, Ray argues that the structure of* A Clockwork Orange *reflects the theme of inevitable human growth.*]

Most interpreters of Anthony Burgess' *A Clockwork Orange* have tended to follow the lead of such early commentators as Bernard Bergonzi, A. A. DeVitis, Carol M. Dix, and Robert K. Morris in defining the theme of the novel as the conflict between the natural and untainted Individual and the artificial and corrupt State. Bergonzi's observation that "in its emphasis on the nature of human freedom in a totalitarian society the book has philosophical as well as literary importance" is typical of the thinking that shaped the framework in which subsequent critical discussion has taken place. And this tendency has recently achieved a fitting culmination in the account of the novel that Burgess himself has published, an account which concludes with this dictum: "we may not be able to trust man—meaning ourselves—very far, but we must trust the State far less" [*1985,* 1978].

This essay attempts to present a different approach to both the content and the form of *A Clockwork Orange,* an approach which complements rather than contradicts the other. This essay will, however, focus on the relations of Alex, Burgess' hero and narrator, with characters frequently neglected or overlooked by the critics: the owner of the cottage named "HOME"; his wife; and the unnamed and unborn male child whom Alex mentions only in the final chapter. In other words, characters who are the willing or unwilling agents of the State—for example, the

prison chaplain, the prison governor, Dr. Brodsky, the Minister of the Interior—will receive less attention than they sometimes do. The specific thesis that this essay will argue for is twofold: that Burgess has the owner of HOME represent the person Alex will become, his future self, and the boy who does not yet exist represent the person he has already been, his past self, in order to express the view that human growth is inevitable; and that the tripartite structure of the novel directly mirrors this chronological sequence of Alex's identities.

The three parts of *A Clockwork Orange* are of equal length, each having seven chapters, but they otherwise fall into an ABA pattern. [In a footnote Ray explains: "To some readers, ABA may seem to be an abbreviation for 'Anthony Burgess Author.' Others, who are more familiar with Burgess' rapidly increasing canon, will recall the fact that the title of his 1977 novel *ABBA ABBA* refers to the rhyme scheme of the octave of the Petrarchan sonnet. But, as I will attempt to demonstrate below, the primary significance lies elsewhere."] Parts One and Three are set in the city streets and country lanes of a future England so paralyzed by violent crime that it has surrendered them to the very teenagers who commit the crimes. Part Two is set in a prison—"Staja (State Jail, that is) Number 84F"— where the government is attempting to regain the upper hand by checking within the mind of the particular criminal the impulse toward violence. Alex, who has his own gang despite his mere fifteen years, is sent to jail for murder at the close of Part One; in Part Two he successfully undergoes the State's experimental Reclamation Treatment only to reenter, in Part Three, a world that is unchanged. Thus Burgess has Alex's adventures in Part Three—especially his return to his parents' flat, his encounters with "the crystal veck" and with Dim and Billyboy, and his visit to the cottage named HOME—duplicate or parallel those in Part One with this significant difference: whereas he earlier victimized others in committing robbery, burglary, assault, rape, and even murder, he himself is now the victim. With his natural instincts and drives artificially blocked, Alex is the "clockwork orange" of the title. [In a footnote Ray elaborates: "It is important to realize that Alex does come to think of himself as 'a clockwork orange.' Significantly enough, when the State puts him on display, Alex protests to the audience: ' "Am I like just some animal or dog? . . . Am I just to be like a clockwork orange?" ' Thus Alex perceives that he has become something lower than an 'animal or dog' because part of him, and a crucial part at that, is now mechanical. On the phrase itself, Burgess again comments helpfully in *1985*: 'The book was called *A Clockwork Orange* for various reasons. I had always loved the Cockney phrase "queer as a clockwork orange," that being the queerest thing imaginable, and I had saved up the expression for years, hoping some day to use it as a title. When I began to write the book, I saw that this title would be appropriate for a story about the application of Pavlovian, or mechanical, laws to an organism which, like a fruit, was capable of colour and sweetness. But I had also served in Malaya, where the word for a human being is *orang.*' "] One part of the moral that Burgess wishes the reader to draw here is that, in attempting to transform the violent tough into the peaceful citizen, the State has succeeded in rendering Alex incapable of self-defense.

The other part of the moral is that the State has also rendered Alex incapable of enjoying the music of his adored "Ludwig van." To quote once again from Burgess' own account of the novel,

> I imagined an experimental institution in which a generic young delinquent, guilty of every crime from rape to murder, was given aversion therapy and rendered incapable of contemplating, let alone perpetrating, an antisocial act without a sensation of profound nausea. . . . A lover of music, he has responded to the music, used as a heightener of emotion, which has accompanied the violent films he has been made to see. A chemical substance injected into his blood induces nausea while he is watching the films, but the nausea is also associated with the music. It was not the intention of his State manipulators to induce this bonus or malus: it is purely an accident that, from now on, he will automatically react to Mozart or Beethoven as he will to rape or murder. The State has succeeded in its primary aim: to deny Alex free moral choice, which, to the State, means choice of evil. But it has added an unforeseen punishment: the gates of heaven are closed to the boy, since music is a figure of celestial bliss. The State has committed a double sin: it has destroyed a human being, since humanity is defined by freedom or moral choice; it has also destroyed an angel.

Thus the State has meddled destructively not only in the mundane area of morals but also in the higher realm of art.

But consider for a moment the notion that in figurative terms music is "celestial bliss" and Alex an angel. If this is so, then it is certainly logical to regard all of his utterances, the entire narrative related by him to the reader, as musical: if Alex is, in some sense, an angel, his story is, in that same sense, a song. And the question of what sort of song redirects our discussion to the matter of the novel's structure, for the ABA pattern in music is universally recognized as the distinguishing characteristic of the *da capo aria* in eighteenth-century Italian opera, a kind of aria which "consists of two sections followed by a repetition of the first, resulting in a tripartite structure ABA" [*The Harvard Dictionary of Music,* 1969]. [In a footnote, Ray comments: "The fact that Burgess first wanted to be a musician and continues to compose music is, I believe, so frequently mentioned as not to require documentation here. But a word is in order about Burgess' most ambitious and explicit use to date of musical structure in his literary work, the symphonic or four-part organization of his 1974 novel, *Napoleon Symphony*. The genesis of the novel he describes in a doggerel 'Epistle to the Reader,' which he appends to it:

> I was brought up on music and compose
> Bad music still, but ever since I chose
> The novelist's metier one mad idea
> Has haunted me, and I fulfill it here
> Or try to—it is this: somehow to give
> Symphonic shape to verbal narrative,
> Impose on life, though nerves scream and resist,

The abstract patterns of the symphonist.

It is possible to argue, then, that *A Clockwork Orange* anticipates *Napoleon Symphony* because, as he composed it, Burgess attempted to give the 'shape,' the 'abstract patterns' of the aria, to the narrative of Alex, whose single viewpoint stands in the same relation to the many viewpoints of *Napoleon Symphony* as the single voice of the aria singer to the many voices of the symphonic orchestra."] And it is perhaps no accident, then, that at one point in the story Alex listens with powerful emotion to what Burgess makes quite clear is an operatic aria:

> One of these devotchkas . . . suddenly came with a burst of singing, only a bar and a half and as though she was like giving an example of something they'd all been govoreeting about, and it was like for a moment, O my brothers, some great bird had flown into the milkbar, and I felt all the little malenky hairs on my plott standing endwise and the shivers crawling up like slow malenky lizards and then down again. Because I knew what she sang. It was from an opera by Friedrich Gitterfenster called *Das Bettzeug,* and it was the bit where she's snuffing it with her throat cut, and the slovos are "Better like this maybe." Anyway, I shivered.

One wishes that Burgess had provided more information about his imaginary composer of operas: when he lived, what kinds of operas he wrote, and so on. But he does provide enough so that certain parallels can be drawn later between Alex and the wretched heroine whose aria he now hears.

To return to the actual workings of the ABA pattern in the novel. Burgess reinforces the reader's sense of the pattern by opening each of the three parts with the question " 'What's it going to be then, eh?' " and by having Alex ask it in Parts One and Three and the prison chaplain ask it in Part Two. Thus, in the A Parts Alex is free to pose the question for himself, whereas in Part B someone else, significantly an employee of the State, must pose it for him. Similarly, the hero's name, which (as one would expect) remains constant in Parts One and Three, is replaced by a prison identification number in Part Two: "6655321." [In a footnote, the critic explains: "Burgess provides an illuminating gloss on the name in *1985*: 'The name of the antihero is Alex, short for Alexander, which means "defender of men." *Alex* has other connotations—a lex: a law (unto himself ); a lex(is): a vocabulary (of his own); a (Greek) lex: without a law. Novelists tend to give close attention to the names they attach to their characters. *Alex* is a rich and noble name, and I intended its possessor to be sympathetic, pitiable, and insidiously identifiable with us, as opposed to them.' "] In the A Parts Alex can call himself by whatever name he chooses (it is surely important that he never once uses his surname); in Part B he is called by a number, not even a name, chosen by the State. As Alex describes the change, "I was 6655321 and not your little droog Alex not no longer."

Alex's name is significant in another, even more essential way because it provides the chief clue to the thematic function of the owner of the cottage called HOME. When in Part One Alex and his "droogs" break into the cottage, they not only vandalize it but also beat the owner and rape his wife, who later dies as a result. When in Part Three Alex returns, he does so alone and, having just been beaten himself, stands utterly defenseless before the man he has wronged. The latter fails, however, to recognize Alex (primarily because he was wearing a mask on the night of the break-in) and provides him with aid and shelter instead of punishment or revenge. The owner of HOME even manages, in thinking aloud about his dead wife, to identify Alex with her when he says to Alex, " 'Poor poor boy, you must have had a terrible time. A victim of the modern age, just as she was. Poor poor poor girl.' " Alex, of course, does recognize the owner and, wishing to learn his name, searches for a copy of the book that he was writing, and that Alex read from, on that fateful night:

> It struck me that I ought to get to know the name of this kind protecting and like motherly veck, so I had a pad round in my nagoy nogas looking for *A Clockwork Orange,* which would be bound to have his eemya in, he being the author. . . . On the back of the book, like on the spine, was the author's eemya—F. Alexander. Good Bog, I thought, He is another Alex.

Having just been let out of prison, Alex has now ceased to be 6655321. He finds, however, that not only is he Alex again (with the addition of the "clockwork") but that someone else is Alex, too. He has somehow managed to encounter a second version of himself.

What, then, do Alex and F. Alexander have in common besides their names? Both, oddly enough, are authors of books entitled *A Clockwork Orange.* (Burgess keeps the reader aware of Alex's authorial role by having him frequently address his audience by means of the curious formula "O my brothers" and refer to himself as "Your Humble Narrator.") One important difference between the two authors is, of course, that, while F. Alexander is writing his book on the night of Alex's first visit to HOME and has a bound copy of it on his shelves during the second visit, Alex has not yet begun to write his. In the reader's eternal present, Alex is writing it now. But, precisely because he has already done what Alex will someday do, F. Alexander is being defined here as a future version of Alex's self.

At this point in the story, the second visit to HOME, Burgess hints at the theme of the inevitability of human growth, to which he returns in the final chapter. There he sounds it loudly by having Alex answer the oft-repeated question " 'What's it going to be then, eh?' " with the idea of getting married and having a son. As Alex himself puts it, "there was this veshch of finding some devotchka or other who would be a mother to this son. . . . That's what it's going to be then, brothers, as I come to the like end of this tale." Once he has found and wed his "devotchka," Alex will, of course, have come to resemble F. Alexander in his role as a married man. But here it is not yet apparent whether growth, which will be inevitable for everyone else, will be so for him. Having "clockwork" in his heart and brain may mean that Alex will be the same forever.

There is, however, one other obstacle in the way of Alex's growing up to possess a future, and that obstacle is, ironically enough, F. Alexander himself. When he learns that Alex is one of those responsible for the death of his wife, he tries to force Alex to commit suicide. The attempt fails when Alex, having thrown himself out of an upper-story window, receives medical care that not only saves his life but also reverses the effects of the Reclamation Treatment. Thus Burgess underscores his irony by having F. Alexander insure that Alex will possess a future through the former's effort to deny the latter a present. Trying to murder Alex has the indirect result of bringing him back to human life, for F. Alexander manages to kill only the "clockwork" inside his head.

F. Alexander is clearly, in some sense, a father to Alex, albeit a murderous one. Before the attempt on his life, Alex sees F. Alexander as treating him in a parental manner, although he gets the gender wrong: he calls his host and comforter "this kind protecting and like motherly veck." And perhaps, when he discovered the name on the back of the book, he ought to have considered the first initial as carefully as the surname. If, as seems almost certain, it stands for "Father," then Burgess has arranged this reunion as one between Son Alex and Father Alexander.

There is further evidence for this view of F. Alexander in the facts that he is the owner of HOME (that significantly named dwelling) to which Alex as a latter-day Prodigal Son returns and is not punished but rather welcomed and feasted; that, unlike Alex's actual father (whom Alex would never think of striking and to whom he always refers contemptuously as "pee"), F. Alexander arouses powerful feelings in Alex; and that he is married to the most important woman in the story and in Alex's life so far. Burgess follows here the Freudian model of family relations by placing the father and the son in competition for the mother and by having the son's path to manhood lead directly through the father's defeat or death. Alex the son succeeds not only in possessing the mother but also in taking her away from the father, an event which intensifies the latter's natural desire to triumph over his rival into a rage for murder and revenge. But, of course, that act of violence brings about the more rapid displacement of the father by the son when Alex finds that his suicidal leap has resulted in the removal of the "clockwork" and in no permanent injury to himself.

The actual fate of F. Alexander, Burgess leaves obscure until Alex's conversation with the Minister of the Interior in the novel's penultimate chapter. Visiting Alex in the hospital to assure him that all is now well and to exploit the favorable political publicity, the Minister informs him that

> "There is a man . . . called F. Alexander, a writer of subversive literature, who has been howling for your blood. He has been mad with desire to stick a knife in you. But you're safe from him now. We put him away."

The State now regards F. Alexander as it once regarded Alex. Certain phrases used by the Minister—"howling for your blood," "mad with desire"—would appear to be more appropriate if applied to a person both more animal-like and more physically violent than F. Alexander. But, in any case, he has been declared "a menace" just as though he were roaming the streets at night with a band of "droogs." Therefore F. Alexander gets, at the end of Part Three, precisely what Alex got at the end of Part One: imprisonment in a State Jail. This fate also makes sense, because he is Alex's double as well as his symbolic or mythic father: thus the career of F. Alexander not only anticipates but also repeats the career of Alex.

But this relationship also contributes to the working out of the ABA structure. In the first A section Alex is simply Alex; in the B section he becomes both 6655321 and the "clockwork" man; and in the second A section he resumes his public identity as Alex but is not truly or fully Alex because he still has the "clockwork" within him. When, however, he meets again the owner of HOME, he encounters a father figure, an older and wiser Alex, a future version of the self, who unwittingly assists him in the task of removing the "clockwork" and becoming himself once more. The ill effects of his prison stay cannot, in other words, be overcome until our hero wrestles with and defeats his own image invested with Age and Authority, until the son replaces the father. What could provide a more striking illustration of the process of human growth?

If the vision of his future granted him in the final chapter holds true, Alex will accomplish something in life that F. Alexander did not: the begetting and raising of a son. He describes his prophetic moment in the following passage:

> I kept viddying like visions, like these cartoons in the gazettas. There was Your Humble Narrator Alex coming home from work to a good hot plate of dinner, and there was this ptitsa all welcoming and greeting like loving. . . . I had this sudden very strong idea that if I walked into the room next to this room where the fire was burning away and my hot dinner laid on the table, there I should find what I really wanted. . . . For in that other room in a cot was laying gurgling goo goo goo my son. Yes yes yes, brothers, my son.

The place Alex describes is obviously an idealized version of home, which means that he has just paid, although in "vision," his third and final visit to HOME. The fire and the dinner are the comforts that Alex destroyed on his first visit but will soon require for himself; the "ptitsa all welcoming and greeting like loving" is the mother transformed into a wife who will in no way resist his advances; and the father, who earlier attempted to block his path, is now absent. To complete the circle, however, there is the baby boy, who, like F. Alexander, will be "another Alex" and bear Alex's other name, whatever that may be. This son will be F. Alexander's opposite in that he will represent Alex's past, whereas F. Alexander represented Alex's future. Alex perceives this even now, as he concedes in advance that he will be unable to prevent his son from making the very same mistakes that he made:

> My son, my son. When I had my son I would explain all that to him when he was starry enough to like understand. But then I knew he would not understand or would not want to understand at all and would do all the veshches I had done . . . and I would not be able to really stop him.

Knowing the "veshches" or things his son will do, Alex also knows that he will be unable to prevent him from doing them, both the good and the evil. As his son grows up, Alex will behold his past being repeated, just as F. Alexander beheld his. Everything human is inevitable, Burgess seems to say, both the good and the evil.

But Alex's tale is still a story of liberation: he has escaped from not only the literal prison of Staja 84F but also the figurative prisons of adolescent boyhood and "clockwork" humanity. And the reader who recalls that "music is a figure of celestial bliss" will want to translate "liberation" as "salvation." But it is the individual capable of growth— the " 'creature of growth and capable of sweetness,' " as F. Alexander puts it in his typescript—that has been liberated or saved, not the group, the tribe, or the species. When he is born, Alex's son will not be free or blissful. He will be doomed, rather, to live through the error of his father's ways. Here, then, is that final flowering of the logic of the novel's structure: after A, B; after B, A again. After the freedom of the mature Alex, the imprisonment of his son. Could Alex somehow liberate his son, the structure of *A Clockwork Orange* would surely have to be ABC, which would signify progress without repetition.

The *da capo aria* itself, if the reader chooses to think of either Alex or the heroine of *Das Bettzeug* as performing this sort of aria, represents the same lack of freedom: having sung A and B, the performer must sing A again. And it is precisely here that the meaning of this imaginary opera comes into clear focus. The surname of the composer, "Gitterfenster," is a German word best translated as "barred window," that is, the window of a prison. The heroine has sought presumably to escape this prison, whether literal or figurative, but, realizing that she can succeed only through suicide, has now taken that step: hence Alex's description, "it was the bit where she's snuffing it with her throat cut, and the slovos are 'Better like this maybe.' " She is, therefore, in the very same situation as Alex when F. Alexander's friends leave him in their locked flat with the music turned on: "I viddied what I had to do. . . . and that was to do myself in, to snuff it." The window in this prison is not barred, however, because F. Alexander and his friends want Alex to jump: "the window in the room where I laid down was open." And they have even left behind a helpful hint in the form of a "malenky booklet which had an open window on the cover," proclaiming: " 'Open the window to fresh air, fresh ideas, a new way of living.' " So Alex, saying in effect what the heroine said, goes to the window and jumps. And he succeeds, just as she may have, in achieving personal liberation—not through death, but rather through the return to life, or, to put the matter somewhat more accurately, by the return to normal life after the nonhuman existence of a "clockwork" man, which is merely another formulation of the sequence "freedom"-"imprisonment"-"freedom"; that is, ABA.

**Robert Bowie**    (essay date December 1981)

SOURCE: "Freedom and Art in *A Clockwork Orange:* Anthony Burgess and the Christian Premises of Dostoevsky," in *Thought,* Vol. LVI, No. 223, December, 1981, pp. 402-16.

[*In the following essay, Bowie compares the thematic treatment of freedom and beauty in* A Clockwork Orange *and in works by Fyodor Dostoevsky.*]

In 1961 Anthony Burgess interrupted his work on *A Clockwork Orange* and made a trip to the Soviet Union. Later he wrote a different novel, *Honey for the Bears,* based in part on his experiences in Leningrad, a novel that surely would never have been written if he had not made the trip. But there is also reason for asserting that without his knowledge of Russian language and literature Burgess would not have written *A Clockwork Orange* in the form it appeared. What comes to mind immediately is the "nadsat" language, based largely on Russian. But in this novel Burgess also develops a Christian theme that recalls one of the most important of nineteenth-century Russian philosophical writers, Fyodor Dostoevsky. Even certain scenes appear to be taken directly from *Crime and Punishment* or *The Brothers Karamazov.* Burgess does not choose to play upon Dostoevsky's style or attempt to draw exact parallels with numerous events in his works; but he does treat one of Dostoevsky's favorite themes, the theme of free choice, and he does use episodes that mirror important episodes in the great novels of the famous Russian. Burgess often suggests different answers to profound philosophical questions. While agreeing with Dostoevsky's Christian view of free choice, he seems also to be asking, "What is the standing of the Judaeo-Christian tradition in the modern world?" Indeed, Burgess has taken Dostoevsky's conclusions about the revolutionary possibilities of Christian doctrines and has submitted these conclusions to the test in a contemporary (or soon to be contemporary) society. My article attempts to explain Burgess' position on important moral, philosophical, and aesthetic issues by discussing what is simultaneously his agreement and disagreement with the most prominent Christian artist of nineteenth-century Russia.

## I. Freedom

God *is* precisely because there is evil and suffering on earth; the existence of evil is proof that God exists. If the world were exclusively good and beneficent, then God would not be necessary, the world itself would already be god. God is because evil is. That means that God is because freedom is.

—Nikolai Berdyaev
*The Weltanschauung of Dostoevsky*

Anthony Burgess has written that "ultimately, it is very doubtful whether any novel, however trivial, can possess any vitality without an implied set of values derived from religion" [*Times Literary Supplement,* March 3, 1966]. Although the author apparently has abandoned some of the beliefs of his Catholic upbringing, there is no doubt that at least one of the religious messages expressed in *A Clockwork Orange* is Christian, expressly the Christian insistence that if man is to retain his humanity, he must be allowed to choose good or evil:

. . . the central theme is one that is very impor-

tant, to me anyway. The idea of free will. This is not just half-baked existentialism, it's an old Catholic theme. Choice, choice is all that matters, and to impose the good is evil, to *act* evil is better than to have good imposed. [Anthony Burgess with Thomas Churchill, *The Malahat Review,* Vol. XVII, 1971].

Perhaps no writer in world literature has given a broader and more profound treatment to free will and its implications in regard to religion, crime, and social reform than Fyodor Dostoevsky. Beginning with *Notes from the Underground* and continuing throughout the famous novels of his mature period (*Crime and Punishment, The Devils, The Adolescent, The Idiot, The Brothers Karamazov*), he repeatedly emphasizes the necessity of choice. His argument refutes the most popular philosophical conceptions of his time (for the most part, ideas that still dominate our twentieth-century world)—positivism, utilitarianism, materialism, socialism. He argues with conviction that reliance on the scientific method leads nowhere since science depends on reason and people are perversely irrational creatures. He insists that the imposition of a supposedly rational order in which all men are to be made equal and to be brothers (socialism) is doomed to failure (because man will rebel against any artificial order that he has no choice in establishing) and is, in fact, the incarnation of the evil principle (since forcing man to be good rather than allowing him to choose good or evil leads to dehumanization). Above all, Dostoevsky sees the duality of the human spirit, the disturbing truth that man is good and evil simultaneously; he often dwells upon human perversity and irrationality:

. . . just what can one expect from man, a creature endowed with such strange qualities? . . . It's precisely his fantastical dreams, his horribly vulgar stupidity that he wishes to retain, simply to affirm to his very own self (as if that were so necessary) that people are still people, and not piano keys. . . . [*Notes from the Underground,* 1961; in a footnote, Bowie adds: "I have revised the MacAndrew translation based on examination of the Russian original."]

An examination of Burgess' philosophical position (as expressed in interviews, articles, works) reveals that his opinions are often identical to Dostoevsky's. Dostoevsky sees socialism and (rather unfairly, it seems) the Catholic Church as the greatest enemies of freedom—his Grand Inquisitor is a Catholic socialist. [In a footnote, Bowie adds: "Dostoevsky's hatred of Roman Catholicism is a complex issue, closely related to his nationalism, his veneration of Russian Orthodox Christianity, and his hatred and distrust of Western ideas. Attracted to ideals of utopian socialism in his youth, he rejected socialism completely after his prison experience; the great works of his mature years (beginning with *Notes from the Underground*) are full of vehement ridicule of all socialist principles."] While defending, in part, the spirit of Catholicism, Burgess suggests that the ancient heresy of Pelagius is the source of both gross materialism (represented by America) and a dehumanizing collectivism (represented by the Soviet Union). [In a footnote, Bowie elaborates: "The polemic carried on by St. Augustine against Pelagianism is at the heart of Burgess' literary art. It is an issue that he returns to almost obsessively in his treatment of human duality, free choice, and aesthetics."] The "ant-hill" or "Crystal Palace" (see *Notes from the Underground*) of socialism, so feared by Dostoevsky, is much closer to realization in the twentieth century. In his *Clockwork Orange* Burgess reveals that in the twenty-first century (or is it the late twentieth?) this ant-hill has spread to encompass all of the world. The only trace of the great Russian humanist tradition, of which Dostoevsky was a part, appears in the names of pop singers like "Jonny Zhivago" and "Goggly Gogol." The ideas against which much of Burgess' novel is aimed are, for the most part, the same ideas that Dostoevsky vehemently opposed a century ago. But perhaps the viewpoint expressed by the following question is even more pronounced in our time:

> Is it not . . . a trifle absurd to ponder tortuous issues of mind and soul when daily it grows impossible to cope with external realities like pollution, famine, and overpopulation? Can we even talk of freedom or free will to states that have written them off as mere philosophical aberrations? [Robert Morris, *The Consolations of Ambiguity*, 1971]

The critic who wrote the above concludes that we must, nonetheless, continue to speak of freedom and free will, but many behavioral psychologists think not. B. F. Skinner has stated convincingly that it is about time we started doing something about saving our world, and that since this means changing the behavior of human beings, it's about time we started changing it. Burgess disagrees:

> I recognize that the lesson is already becoming an old-fashioned one. B. F. Skinner, with his ability to believe that there is something *beyond* freedom and dignity, wants to see the death of autonomous man. He may or may not be right, but in terms of the Judaeo-Christian ethic that *A Clockwork Orange* tries to express, he is perpetrating a gross heresy. It seems to me in accordance with the tradition that Western man is not yet ready to jettison, that the area in which human choice is a possibility should be extended, even if one comes up against new angels with swords and banners emblazoned *No*. The wish to diminish free will is, I should think, the sin against the Holy Ghost. [*The Listener*, February 17, 1972]

Note the equivocation in the admission that Skinner "may or may not be right." In Burgess' *Clockwork Testament* (Ch. 7), however, all equivocation is absent in the portrayal of a behaviorist professor who is a travesty of Skinner. Here Burgess stands arms akimbo and spits in Skinner's direction (as Dostoevsky's Underground Man stands and spits in the direction of the Man of Reason). Just as the Underground Man compares man without free will to a piano key or organ stop, so Anthony Burgess considers man without free will a clockwork mechanism. But despite similarities in the viewpoints of Dostoevsky and Burgess, their conclusions are by no means identical; it is possible to interpret *Clockwork Orange* not only as a polemic with Skinner, but also as a polemic with Dostoevsky himself. As N. Berdyaev has written, there are two types of

freedom for Dostoevsky, initial freedom and ultimate freedom; this conception of *libertas minor* and *libertas major* was posited by St. Augustine in his struggle against Pelagianism. The lower order of freedom involves man's freedom of choice on earth; the higher is a freedom in God that is not irrational like the lower order of freedom—it represents the ultimate rational freedom that transcends earthly irrationality [Nikolai Berdyaev, *Mirosozertsanie Dostoevskogo*, 1923]. The difference seems to be that while Dostoevsky believes this ultimate freedom may be attained through Christ, Burgess has his doubts. Both men are aware of a split in the human psyche, but Dostoevsky believes man's duality may be overcome through Christianity. Burgess, on the other hand, has professed a kind of Manichaeism, a belief that the world is temporarily controlled by "the wrong god," who prohibits man from resolving his duality. In *The Wanting Seed* he posits a cyclic theory of history; Pelagianism alternates with Augustinism. But probably what is most important is that both the "Pelphase" and the "Gusphase" are Manichean—the basic split remains, and no matter which phase is ascendant in *The Wanting Seed*, people are still being killed and eaten.

What is most difficult for Burgess to accept in Dostoevsky is the conviction that Christianity is the answer to problems that Burgess sees as having no ultimate earthly answer. Since the issue of free will and crime is treated most extensively in *Crime and Punishment*, Burgess has written a crime novel that in many ways is a modern retelling of that novel; he adds touches from other Dostoevsky works and treats ideas that run through all of Dostoevsky's mature literary production. Throughout *A Clockwork Orange* subtle hints of Dostoevsky are provided. [In a footnote, Bowie adds: "There are similar hints in the book that is a kind of companion work or introduction to *Clockwork Orange*, *Honey for the Bears*. In this novel one of Burgess' Russian characters remarks: 'As for *Crime and Punishment*, it was a crime to write it and it is a punishment to read it.' "] For example, the Russian word for criminal (*prestupnik*) is used several times (spelled "prestoopnik" in "nadsat" language); this recalls the Russian title of *Crime and Punishment* (*Prestuplenie i nakazanie*). The title is also suggested in a phrase mouthed by the Minister of the Interior, a phrase that alludes to what is about to be done to Alex (the brainwashing): "crime in the midst of punishment." Alex meets his "Marmeladov" ("a burbling old pyahnitsa or drunkie") in Part I, Ch. 2 just as Raskolnikov comes upon the original Marmeladov in Part I, Ch. 2 of *Crime and Punishment*, but the old drunk in Burgess' novel has none of the faith in God and the radiant vision of Christ's forgiveness that the original Marmeladov preaches. Note also that Sonya, the glorious symbol of true Christianity, Raskolnikov's guardian angel and salvation, has no counterpart in *Clockwork Orange* (but one of the girls whom Alex rapes in Part I is called Sonietta). The heroes' responses to their Marmeladovs are also instructive. Guided by the idealistic, compassionate side of his split personality, Raskolnikov helps out a man in distress, while Alex responds to his "Marmeladov" in the same way that he responds to many of his earthly "brothers"—with malicious violence.

The murder of the old woman also suggests a famous scene from *Crime and Punishment*. Raskolnikov, who feels as if he is on the way to his own execution as he walks toward the scene of the crime, must ascend a long staircase before reaching the apartment of his victim. Paradoxically, his crime comes immediately after a kind of ascent since it is the first step in his long struggle for salvation (the decisive step is taken when he finally repents at the end of the novel). Alex, on the other hand, *descends* a staircase to reach his victim, possibly since the murder he commits represents the decisive step in his descent toward loss of free will. On the way downstairs he sees a painting of Christ, who for him is simply "the holy bearded veck all nagoy hanging on a cross." Christ means nothing to Alex, whose most important idol, Beethoven ("Ludvig van"), is represented by a bust in the old woman's room below. The murder weapon is not an ax, as in Dostoevsky's novel, but a small statue of a thin girl. [In a footnote, Bowie adds: "One could conjecture that this statue, like Dostoevsky's Sonya, represents a kind of eternal feminine divine principle; it, like the bust of Beethoven, is related to the theme of art and beauty in connection with baseness and perversity."] Of central importance is the reaction of each protagonist to the crime he has committed, a reaction predictable from the character of each. Raskolnikov is always good and bad simultaneously—one side of his inner nature (reinforced by Sonya) is always drawing him toward Christ and repentance; his other side (represented by Svidrigailov) draws him toward pride and willful self-assertion, which represents a kind of death-in-life for Dostoevsky. One must keep in mind that *Crime and Punishment,* above all, is a novel about crime and *contrition*—Raskolnikov seems to have begun repenting even before he has committed the murder (see the famous dream about the mare being beaten to death in Part I, Ch. 5), and the "punishment" of the title is primarily the result of his guilt, a punishment from within. Alex, however, is most notable in that he is absolutely *without guilt*—in his contemporary retelling of the famous work Burgess has chosen a Svidrigailov for his hero, a perverted human being who is almost inhuman since he is incapable of feeling pity for anyone but himself. In a way *Clockwork Orange* is a book about crime *without* punishment, at least without the kind of inner moral suffering that Dostoevsky considers a prerequisite for salvation.

Like Dostoevsky, Burgess criticizes (obliquely) some of the most fashionable sociological ideas of the nineteenth and twentieth centuries. Like Dostoevsky he believes that evil (and crime) is not the result of environment, of faulty social or political systems. Evil comes from within human beings, and blaming evil on society or on the inadequacies of politics simply furnishes rationalizations for criminals like Alex:

> ". . . it was the adult world that could take the responsibility for this with their wars and bombs and nonsense . . . So we young innocent malchicks could take no blame. Right right right."

Dostoevsky would agree with Burgess that "the self," the essential humanity of man contains both good and evil and that the self must not be destroyed by social engineering in an attempt to program out the evil. As Alex says:

> ". . . badness is of the self, the one, the you or me on our oddy knockies, and that self is made by old Bog or God and is his great pride and radosty."

Burgess' disagreement with Dostoevsky develops out of his belief that badness is inseparable from self—Dostoevsky spent his whole life forcing himself to believe that badness could be separated from self if human beings achieved *libertas major* through Christianity.

The triumph of evil is only potential in Dostoevsky since there are always characters like Sonya who demonstrate that people are capable of resisting evil. Dostoevsky sees reason as a delusion and advocates abandoning one's reason, as does Sonya, to accept the irrational truth of Christ. A century later Burgess reveals the triumph of evil in a world where human reason has been developed to such a degree that it has put men on the moon. Reason is ascendant but the human psyche is ruled by the beast, and Christianity no longer even seems relevant. A recurrent theme in Dostoevsky is what he saw as possibly life's most horrible perversity: torture of children, including sexual abuse of little girls. In *Clockwork Orange* this theme is given explicit treatment. Billyboy and his gang are raping a little girl when Alex appears, and Alex himself rapes two girls who "couldn't have been more than ten." Even more horrifying is the implication that episodes like these appear to be an everyday occurrence in the world of this novel. Christ might never have appeared on earth for all the evidence of his teachings in *A Clockwork Orange*. Raskolnikov ends up believing in Christ, but Alex's "Bog" is the God of wrath who appears, e.g., in the Old Testament book of Joshua. Raskolnikov finally accepts Christ; little Alex says he would have liked to have been in on the crucifixion ("I said I would like to have the old hammer and nails"). Nor is there any evidence of a Christian anywhere else in the book. Nearly everyone seems to live by the Old Testament aphorism "An eye for an eye" (the prison governor even quotes this aphorism). "You've made others suffer" [says Joe, the surrogate son, to Alex]. "It's only right you should suffer proper." The police are hardly distinguishable from criminals—they believe above all in punishment and vengeance, as do Alex's victims ("old Jack" and his consort, F. Alexander). No one turns the other cheek.

The principal spokesman for the Christian message of freedom is the prison chaplain ("charlie"):

> "Goodness comes from within, 6655321. Goodness is something chosen. When a man cannot choose he ceases to be a man."

> "What does God want? Does God want goodness or the choice of goodness? Is a man who chooses the bad perhaps in some way better than a man who has the good imposed upon him? Deep and hard questions, little 6655321."

But as the humor of the above passages suggests (i. e., the use of a number as the vocative for Alex), this is no Father Zossima of *The Brothers Karamazov,* no spiritual guide who leads his young disciple toward heavenly salvation. The prison charlie, who is usually under the influence of alcohol, says he would protest against the reclamation treatment "were it expedient" and rationalizes what is about to happen: "And yet, in a sense, in choosing to be deprived of the ability to make an ethical choice, you have in a sense really chosen the good." Other "defenders of freedom" (F. Alexander and his political allies) do not even pretend to uphold Judaeo-Christian ethics. They resemble the atheistic revolutionaries of Dostoevsky's *Devils* in that they are willing to crush freedom in the name of freedom. F. Alexander goes from lofty thoughts on liberty to repression of the individual in one paragraph:

> "There are great traditions of liberty to defend. I am no partisan man. Where I see the infamy I seek to erase it. Party names mean nothing. The tradition of liberty means all. The common people will let it go, oh yes. They will sell liberty for a quieter life. That is why they must be prodded, *prodded*—"

There is a pun here in the word "prod," which means "sell" in nadsat (from Russ. *prodat'*). The common people will sell liberty, but what F. Alexander is really doing is *selling out* the common man in the name of an abstract political freedom. Note that many different nationalities and ethnic groups seem to be represented in his political circle: Z. Dolin (Russian?), Something Something Rubenstein (Jewish?), D. B. da Silva (Italian or Portuguese?). This suggests that the suppression of real freedom in the name of freedom is in common practice throughout Western civilization.

The idea that most people will sell liberty for a quieter life recalls Ivan Karamazov's tale of the Grand Inquisitor in *The Brothers Karamazov* (Part II, Book 5, Ch. 5). The Grand Inquisitor has decided to correct the work of Christ, to relieve the masses of their freedom since most men cannot bear the responsibility that goes with freedom. Christ, who craved faith freely given, refused to attract believers through *miracle, mystery,* and *authority,* but the Grand Inquisitor asserts that the great majority of people are too weak and base to live by the horribly difficult teachings of Christ. They are glad to sell their freedom since it means so much suffering. All they really want is to be led like sheep. The Grand Inquisitor reveals that in correcting Christ's work he is working for Satan but that this is justified since he has relieved the great majority of people of the unbearable responsibility Christ's teachings entail and has brought them earthly happiness. F. Alexander, that "defender of men," is a kind of Grand Inquisitor himself. [In a footnote, Bowie notes that " 'Alexander' comes from the Greek *alexandros*—'defender of men,' " and adds: "The only defender of human freedom in *A Clockwork Orange* is, paradoxically, the perverted little Alex."] The other figure who may be based on Dostoevsky's Grand Inquisitor is the brainwasher Dr. Brodsky. Each of these men is interested in "correcting" the work of Christ in the name of the greater good for society. Therefore, neither the party of the government in power (for whom Brodsky works) nor the party of the opposition (for whom Alexander works) has any interest in preserving human freedom of choice, which Burgess and Dostoevsky consider paramount.

There are no true defenders of freedom or of Judaeo-Christian ethics in *Clockwork Orange,* and Burgess some-

times seems to be suggesting that there are few among the readers of his book. In his article on the film version Burgess challenges real Christians to observe the teachings of Christ by loving Alex, who is a human being like us all:

> . . . his evil is a human evil, and we recognise in his deeds of aggression potentialities of our own—worked out for the noncriminal citizen in war, sectional injustice, domestic unkindness, armchair dreams. In three ways Alex is an exemplar of humanity: he is aggressive, he loves beauty, he is a language-user. . . . The point is that, if we are going to love mankind, we will have to love Alex as a not unrepresentative member of it. [*The Listener,* February 17, 1972]

If one assumes (as does S. E. Hyman) that "Alex always *was* a clockwork orange, a machine for mechanical violence far below the level of choice," one makes quite a strong argument but underemphasizes the Judaeo-Christian message of the book. [Stanley Edgar Hyman, "Afterword," to *A Clockwork Orange,* 1963; in a footnote, Bowie adds: "Hyman's argument is strong especially since a subtle conditioning is demonstrated in the behavior of Alex and nearly everyone else in his society even before he becomes totally conditioned by the 'reclamation treatment.' Behind all of Burgess' insistence on allowing free choice there lurks constantly the question: How much free choice do we really have?"] Burgess would say that the true believer in the Judaeo-Christian tradition must love *even Dim.* [In a footnote, Bowie explains: "There are hints that even the beastly Dim retains traces of humanity. See, e.g., his attitude of wonder as he contemplates the stars and universe."] But how many of us are capable of loving and forgiving Alex and Dim? If we assume, in accord with Judaeo-Christian principles, that Alex is not below the level of choice, how many of us would prefer to leave him with his free choice when we know that there is a good possibility he would freely choose to smash our skulls? "Deep and hard questions," as the prison charlie would say. Burgess makes it much more difficult for us than Dostoevsky, who at least shows the possibility of a solution to the problem. Burgess presents the dilemma and says we must accept it if human beings are to remain human. If we deny Alex's humanity, we deny the humanity of all persons. Alex is our brother, as his incessant "O my brothers" (addressed to the readers of the book) implies.

But then there is the question of just how much free choice man really has. One cannot help noticing how events occur with almost a predetermined inevitability in a book emphasizing free will. In the second and third parts of the novel Alex is fated to repeat nearly all of the events of the first part (but as victim rather than victimizer). Even the rape at "HOME" is mirrored by the symbolic rape of Alex through the reclamation treatment. (Note that Alex says "Bog help us all" just before the rape, and the prison charlie says "God help us all" just before the treatment begins.) There is another replay of the rape scene (with Alex on the receiving end) in this forced inoculation:

> "What they did was to get four or five real bolshy white-coated bastards of under-vecks to hold me down on the bed, tolchocking me with grinny litsos close to mine, and then this nurse

ptitsa said: 'You wicked naughty little devil, you,' while she jabbed my rooker with another syringe and squirted this stuff in real brutal and nasty."

Alex is beaten by the police and vomits just as earlier his "Marmeladov" had been beaten and vomited. "Old Jack" and his friends at the liberty take their vengeance upon him, and almost inevitably he returns HOME near the end of the book. The same discrepancy is there in Dostoevsky's *Crime and Punishment*. Even before his crime it seems that Raskolnikov is almost destined to commit it *and to escape* so that he can spend the rest of the book on an inevitable path toward confession and redemption. (Note how one circumstance after another seems to be provided precisely so as to allow him to commit the murder and escape, despite a series of blunders that would normally mean the downfall of a criminal.) It seems paradoxical that God Himself could have a hand in murder, but events are arranged so as to suggest that the Spirit of the Universe leads Raskolnikov to commit the act as the first step toward suffering and eventual salvation. It is inevitable that the "free" Raskolnikov will confess—some transcendental force is guiding him in the right direction as he suffers through to expiation. It also seems as if Alex is destined to suffer the same pain that he has inflicted upon others—but his suffering, unlike Raskolnikov's, does not lead to contrition. It never occurs to Alex that perhaps he deserves what he is getting. Suffering does not lead to salvation; but maybe the charlie was right after all in his banal rationalization just before Alex's treatment began: "All may be well, who knows? God works in a mysterious way." It appears that the Deity may love little Alex in spite of his sins. At the height of his misery Alex calls out, "Oh, Bog in Heaven help me," and soon after this he recovers his ability to choose right or wrong. As God guides Raskolnikov to salvation so He guides little Alex back to free will.

If the artistic pattern of both these novels suggests an order that is too consistent to be anything but predetermined, where does this leave free will? Burgess would probably say that it leaves a free will that is limited, nonetheless extant. He is fond of quoting Hans Sachs from Wagner's *Die Meistersinger:* "Wir sind ein wenig frei" ("We are a little free"). Despite the difficulty of the whole question of free will vs. determinism, one must take a stand somewhere. Burgess decides that even if it is impossible to say exactly how much free will man possesses, "what little he seems to have is too precious to encroach on, however good the intentions of the encroacher may be" [*The Listener,* February 17, 1972]. Surely Dostoevsky would agree.

## II. Beauty

The notion of beauty not only does not coincide with goodness, but rather is contrary to it; for the good most often coincides with victory over the passions, while beauty is at the root of our passions.

—L. Tolstoy
*What Is Art?*

And what of the other god of Alex's life, "Ludvig van"?

Is Burgess suggesting that the quandary resulting from free choice may be transcended by an apotheosis of the beautiful, of art? He is, but the transcendence cannot be overrated since beauty as perceived by man is ultimately dualistic. In suggesting this apotheosis of art Burgess is arguing against a viewpoint long held in Western culture, against the idea that virtue and beauty can be equated, that upon contact with the beautiful (art) one is imbued with the proper ethical attitudes. A comparison with Dostoevsky's Christian views on aesthetic experience is instructive. [In a footnote, Bowie comments: "I do not mean to imply that treatment of this issue in **Clockwork Orange** amounts to a direct polemic with Dostoevsky. It is an issue long debated in Western culture (e.g., in the Germanic tradition of Schiller, Kant, Goethe, Mann), but treatment of all the sources for the philosophic debate lies beyond the scope of my article."] Dostoevsky is well aware of the profound implications that a dualistic view of beauty holds, but, unlike Burgess, he prefers to seek a solution to the problem by narrowing his own definition of beauty while letting a character such as Dmitry Karamazov express the dualistic view. In a famous passage from *The Brothers Karamazov* Dmitry says:

"Beauty! I cannot bear the thought that a man who possesses even loftiness of spirit and great intelligence begins with the ideal of the Madonna and ends up with the ideal of Sodom. What's still more terrible is that one with the ideal of Sodom already in his soul does not deny the ideal of the Madonna, and his heart is aflame with that ideal, verily, verily aflame, as in that time when he was young and innocent. No, man is broad, even too broad; I'd have him narrower. The devil himself doesn't even know what to make of it! What the mind sees as shameful is sheer beauty to the heart. Is it in Sodom that beauty is found? Believe me, Sodom is where it is found for the immense majority of people— did you know that secret or not? It's horrible that beauty is not only a terrible but also a mysterious thing. Satan and God are battling there and the field of battle is the hearts of men." [*The Brothers Karamazov;* in a footnote, Bowie notes that he has "revised the translation somewhat."]

In Dostoevsky's view the fact that man finds a kind of beauty in the ideal of Sodom (which is the ideal of sensuality) points to the tragic division between man's spiritual and carnal nature. For Dostoevsky there is only one true beauty, the absolute beauty of an ideal harmony to be found in acceptance of Christ: "to Dostoevsky it is not beauty that is ambivalent, but man who experiences two kinds of beauty"—not only the true, higher beauty, but also a low order of aesthetic sensation ('beauty in Sodom') which *he* calls beauty. Dostoevsky once viewed Hans Holbein's painting of the dead Christ and declared it devoid of beauty since it depicts an all-too-human corpse that looks as if it has already begun decomposing. Not only is it ugly, but it does not produce the right feelings in one who views it. "One's faith could be smashed by such a picture," he told his wife, but she also reports that the painting "so deeply impressed Fedya [Dostoevsky] that he pronounced Holbein a remarkable artist and poet" and was filled with "ecstasy" as he gazed at the painting [R. L.

Jackson, *Dostoevsky's Quest for Form,* 1966]. Surely the artist in Dostoevsky knew intuitively that the question of whether there could be beauty in ugliness, in the evil and the monstrous, could not be answered so easily. But he preferred to make art and beauty a concomitant to ethics as do most other Russian (and not only Russian) writers. While agreeing with Dostoevsky that it is not beauty (art) itself that is ambivalent, but the very nature of man, Burgess, in *A Clockwork Orange,* takes the issue farther.

Brahms is said to have remarked in regard to Alex's god "Ludvig van": "Beethoven would have been a master criminal had he not possessed his genius for composing." This calls into question the view that art has an inherent connection with lofty civilizing principles. Indeed, little Alex demolishes the argument of art as civilizer:

> "I had to have a smeck, though, thinking of what I've viddied once in one of these like articles on Modern Youth, about how Modern Youth would be better off if A Lively Appreciation Of The Arts could be like encouraged. Great Music, it said, and Great Poetry would like quieten Modern Youth down and make Modern Youth more Civilized. Civilized my syphilised yarbles. Music always sort of sharpened me up, O my brothers, and made me like feel like old Bog himself, ready to make with the old donner and blitzen and have vecks and ptitsas creeching away in my ha ha power."

Alex, a great lover of classical music, has nothing but contempt for the trashy pop music enjoyed by most of his peers. But the joy that beautiful music arouses in him is akin not to any lofty joy connected with love and brotherhood; it is the animal joy of primal chaos connected with mindless sensuality and violence. Alex uses Beethoven's Ninth as an accompaniment to rape; in a state of ecstasy inspired by music he has visions of "vecks and ptitsas, both young and starry, lying on the ground screaming for mercy" as he grinds his boot in their faces. Music is all "gorgeousness and gorgeosity made flesh," and surely that is the key word—"flesh." For in Burgess' Manichean vision our world is a world in which the beautiful is inextricably bound to the fleshy, the sensual, to the animal side of human nature. As interpreted by human beings, the very essence of music is linked to sensuality and violence, and as long as man's nature is dual it must remain so linked. As Dr. Brodsky says: "Delimitation is always difficult. The world is one, life is one. The sweetest and most heavenly of activities partake in some measure of violence—the act of love, for instance; music, for instance." Dostoevsky would say that "delimitation" is excruciatingly difficult, but possible if human beings choose the way of Christ.

Can there be art and grace in violence itself? Alex loves the beauty of flowing blood (not his own, of course, but that of others) and sees his razor almost as an object of art: ". . . I for my own part had a fine starry horrorshow cutthroat britva which, at that time, I could flash and shine artistic." Dostoevsky would hold that this is a perversion of true beauty, but Burgess takes the always dangerous step of divorcing beauty from ethics. Although he would not agree with Skinner that there is something of value

"beyond freedom and dignity," he seems close to agreeing with Nietzsche that there is something of value "beyond good and evil." Here is his Enderby's commentary on ethical and aesthetic good.

> "Well, there are some stupid bastards who can't understand how the commandant of a Nazi concentration camp could go home after torturing Jews all day and then weep tears of joy at a Schubert symphony on the radio. They say: here's a man dedicated to evil capable of enjoying the good. But what the imbecilic sods don't realize is that there are two kinds of good—one is neutral, outside ethics, purely aesthetic. You get it in music or in a sunset if you like that sort of thing or in a grilled steak or in an apple. If God's good, if God exists that is, God's probably good in that way." [*The Clockwork Testament*]

Like the Nazi commandant little Alex seems to have experienced that higher, aesthetic good while simultaneously violating moral law. This is a controversial position for an author to take, not any more likely to be accepted by most people than the implication that little Alex must be left with his free will despite the likelihood that he will freely choose to subject his society to mayhem. Burgess makes an amoral divinity of art itself since art can provide "the rarest and most desirable of all human experiences," "the sense of direct contact with God, or the Ground of All Being, or whatever we wish to call Ultimate Reality" [*Times Literary Supplement,* March 3, 1966]. He goes on to say in the article containing this quotation that "if we require some foretaste of Ultimate Reality, and if we are neither specially favoured of God nor given to asceticism or narcotics, we had better see what we can get out of art." These views are related to Burgess' Manichean premise, his idea of life's discordant concord, with good and evil inextricably intertwined:

> . . . there is something in the novelist's vocation which predisposes him to a kind of Manicheeism. What the religious novelist often seems to be saying is that *evil is a kind of good, since it is an aspect of Ultimate Reality;* though what he is really saying is that evil is more interesting to write about than good.

If one sees Alex's ecstasy through music as a prevision of Ultimate Reality, then the dubious triumph with which the American edition of the book ends is a double triumph—Alex is cured of the cure; he has regained not only his free will but also his ability to experience Ultimate Reality through art. But what about ethics? "Beethoven just wrote music," says Alex. "He did no harm to anyone." It is instructive to compare this statement to several lines from Burgess' "Epistle to the Reader," which concludes *Napoleon Symphony.* Alex, like Napoleon, "robs and rapes and lies and kills in fun," but the next line surely must be taken as grimly ironic: "And does no lasting harm to anyone." Behind both Alex and Napoleon "Another, bigger, hero is implied, Not comic and not tragic but divine, . . ." In both works the bigger hero is Beethoven, who represents a kind of artistic divinity, art as god. But does not his music do lasting harm if it inspires the violence of little Alex? Surely the sound similarity in the words "Ludvig van" and "Ludovico's Technique" is not coincidental—it suggests that Beethoven's music, which embodies lofty beauty, may also be the source of cruelty and suppression of freedom. Art, therefore, is dangerous; it inspires anti-social behavior and the most horrible perversity; it should be suppressed. Burgess answers this argument by burlesquing it in **The Clockwork Testament**. His Enderby denies obstreperously that art is to blame for any reprehensible human conduct. Original sin is the culprit, man's own duality. "You never take art for what it is," fulminates Enderby—"beauty, ultimate meaning, form for its own sake, self-subsisting, oh no. It's always got to be either sneered at or attacked as evil." It is difficult to argue with Enderby's position; but here, as in many of the controversial philosophical issues that Burgess treats, there seems to be some room for argument. Surely art is not to blame for evil, but if one begins by accepting original sin, by assuming that evil is inherent in at least one side of human nature, would it not be wise to suppress materials that *stimulate* the evil side? Of course the question is: After the suppression starts, where does it stop? Enderby is right in saying that once one assumes art leads to crime, nothing is safe. "Not even Shakespeare. Not even the Bible. Though the Bible's a lot of bloodthirsty balderdash that ought to be kept out of people's hands." With the humorous contradiction of the last line the matter becomes somewhat clouded again, and we are left with a dilemma.

This dilemma is, in fact, characteristic since the essence of Burgess' art consists of contradiction, dissonance. Like Nietzsche, whose re-evaluation of values and morals seems to have influenced his treatment of beauty, Burgess asks, What is man if not "an incarnation of dissonance"? [Friedrich Nietzsche, *The Birth of Tragedy*, 1872]. The dissonance is there again in the profound contradiction between philosophical ideas expressed in **A Clockwork Orange**. What appears to be a novel based on Christian premises (the defense of free will) simultaneously is a novel that (in its treatment of beauty) is thoroughly anti-Christian. When Beethoven is returned to Alex he not only begins enjoying once more his vision of Ultimate Reality—he also returns to his violent ways. Nothing is resolved. Unlike Dostoevsky, Burgess concludes that an irresolvable duality pervades human perception of the beautiful (art), but that, nonetheless, art, since it affords the only possible glimpse of Ultimate Reality, transcends earthly moral issues. The taint associated both with man's free choice and with his perception of the beautiful must be tolerated if we are to remain human and if we are to continue to seek ultimate answers. [In a final footnote, Bowie adds: "In this article I have confined myself to discussion of the American edition of **A Clockwork Orange**. The first British edition contains an extra chapter, never printed in any American edition. I prefer the book without this extra chapter, but a discussion of how the chapter changes the main focus of the novel would be the subject of a separate article."]

**Anthony Burgess    (essay date 26 March 1987)**

SOURCE: "Introduction: A Clockwork Orange Resucked," in *Rolling Stone,* No. 496, March 26, 1987, pp. 74, 76.

[*In the following essay, which appeared as an introduction to the first publication of the last chapter of* A Clockwork Orange *in America, Burgess discusses the publication history of the twenty-first chapter and how its inclusion changes the meaning of the novel.*]

I first published the novella **A Clockwork Orange** in 1962, which ought to be far enough in the past for it to be erased from the world's literary memory. It refuses to be erased, however, and for this the film version of the book, made by Stanley Kubrick, may be held chiefly responsible. I should myself be glad to disown it for various reasons, but this is not permitted. I receive mail from students who try to write theses about it and requests from Japanese dramaturges to turn it into a sort of *no* play. It seems likely to survive while other works of mine that I value more bite the dust. This is not an unusual experience for an artist. Rachmaninoff used to groan because he was known mainly for his Prelude in C-sharp Minor, which he wrote as a boy, while the works of his maturity never got into the programs. Kids cut their pianistic teeth on a minuet in G that Beethoven composed only so that he could detest it. I have to go on living with **A Clockwork Orange,** and this means I have a sort of authorial duty to it. I have a very special duty to it in the United States, and I had better now explain what this duty is.

Let me put the situation baldly. **A Clockwork Orange** has never been published entire in America. The book I wrote is divided into three sections of seven chapters each. Take out your pocket computer and you will find that these add up to a total of twenty-one chapters. The number twenty-one is the symbol of human maturity, or used to be, since at twenty-one you got the vote and assumed adult responsibility. Whatever its symbology, twenty-one was the number I started out with. Novelists of my stamp are interested in what is called arithmology, meaning that when they use a number, it has to mean something in human terms. The number of chapters is never entirely arbitrary. Just as a musical composer starts off with a vague image of bulk and duration, so a novelist beings with an image of length, and this image is expressed in the number of sections and the number of chapters into which the work will be disposed. Those twenty-one chapters were important to me.

But they were not important to my New York publisher. The book he brought out had only twenty chapters. He insisted on cutting out the twenty-first. I could, of course, have demurred at this and taken my book elsewhere, but it was considered that he was being charitable in accepting the work at all, and that all other New York, or Boston, publishers would kick out the manuscript on its dogear. I needed money back in 1961, even the pittance I was being offered as an advance, and if the condition of the book's acceptance was also its truncation—well, so be it. So there is a profound difference between **A Clockwork Orange** as Great Britain knows it and the somewhat slimmer volume that bears the same name in the United States of America.

Let us go further. The rest of the world was sold the book out of Great Britain, and so most versions—certainly the French, Italian, Spanish, Catalan, Russian, Hebrew, Rumanian and German translations—have the original twenty-one chapters. Now when Stanley Kubrick made his film—though he made it in England—he followed the American version and, so it seemed to his audiences outside America, ended the story somewhat prematurely. Audiences did not exactly clamor for their money back, but they wondered why Kubrick left out the denouement. People wrote to me about this—indeed much of my later life has been expended on Xeroxing statements of intention and the frustration of intention—while both Kubrick and my New York publisher coolly bask in the rewards of their misdemeanor. Life is, of course, terrible.

What happens in that twenty-first chapter? You now have the chance to find out. Briefly, my thuggish young protagonist grows up. He grows bored with violence and recognizes that human energy is better expended on creation than destruction. Senseless violence is a prerogative of youth, which has much energy but little talent for the constructive. Its dynamism has to find an outlet in smashing telephone kiosks, derailing trains, stealing cars and smashing them and, of course, in the much more satisfactory activity of destroying human beings. There comes a time, however, when violence is seen as juvenile and boring. It is the repartee of the stupid and ignorant. My young hoodlum comes to the revelation of the need to get something done in life: to marry, to beget children, to keep the orange of the world turning in the rookers of Bog, or hands of God, and perhaps even create something—music, say. After all, Mozart and Mendelssohn were composing deathless music in their teens, or nadsats, and all my hero was doing was razrezzing and giving the old in-out. It is with a kind of shame that this growing youth looks back on his devastating past. He wants a different kind of future.

There is no hint of this change of intention in the twentieth chapter. The boy is conditioned, then deconditioned, and he foresees with glee a resumption of the operation of free and violent will. "I was cured all right," he says, and so the American book ends. So the film ends too. The twenty-first chapter gives the novel the quality of genuine fiction, an art founded on the principle that human beings change. There is, in fact, not much point in writing a novel unless you can show the possibility of moral transformation, or an increase in wisdom, operating in your chief character or characters. Even trashy best sellers show people changing. When a fictional work fails to show change, when it merely indicates that human character is set, stony, unregenerable, then you are out of the field of the novel and into that of the fable or the allegory. The American or Kubrickian *Orange* is a fable; the British or international one is a novel.

But my New York publisher believed that my twenty-first chapter was a sellout. It was veddy veddy British, don't you know. It was bland and it showed a Pelagian unwillingness to accept that a human being could be a model of unregenerable evil. The Americans, he said in effect, were tougher than the British and could face up to reality. Soon they would be facing up to it in Vietnam. My book was Kennedyan and accepted the notion of moral progress. What was really wanted was a Nixonian book with no shred of optimism in it. Let us have evil prancing on the page and, up to the very last line, sneering in the face of all the inherited beliefs, Jewish, Christian, Moslem and Holy Roller, about people being able to make themselves better. Such a book would be sensational, and so it is. But I do not think it is a fair picture of human life.

I do not think so because, by definition, a human being is endowed with free will. He can use this to choose between good and evil. If he can only perform good or only perform evil, then he is a clockwork orange—meaning that he has the appearance of an organism lovely with color and juice but is in fact only a clockwork toy to be wound up by God or the Devil or (since this is increasingly replacing both) the Almighty State. It is as inhuman to be totally good as it is to be totally evil. The important thing is moral choice. Evil has to exist along with good, in order that moral choice may operate. Life is sustained by the grinding opposition of moral entities. This is what the television news is all about. Unfortunately there is so much original sin in us all that we find evil rather attractive. To devastate is easier and more spectacular than to create. We like to have the pants scared off us by visions of cosmic destruction. To sit down in a dull room and compose the Missa Solemnis or *The Anatomy of Melancholy* does not make headlines or news flashes. Unfortunately, my little squib of a book was found attractive to many because it was as odorous as a crateful of bad eggs with the miasma of original sin.

It seems priggish or Pollyannaish to deny that my intention in writing the work was to titillate the nastier propensities of my readers. My own healthy inheritance of original sin comes out in the book, and I enjoyed raping and ripping by proxy. It is the novelist's innate cowardice that makes him depute to imaginary personalities the sins that he is too cautious to commit for himself. But the book does also have a moral lesson, and it is the weary traditional one of the fundamental importance of moral choice. It is because this lesson sticks out like a sore thumb that I tend to disparage *A Clockwork Orange* as a work too didactic to be artistic. It is not the novelist's job to preach; it is his duty to show. I have shown enough, though the curtain of an invented lingo gets in the way—another aspect of my cowardice. Nadsat, a Russified version of English, was meant to muffle the raw response we expect from pornography. It turns the book into a linguistic adventure. People prefer the film because they are scared, rightly, of language.

I don't think I have to remind readers what the title means. Clockwork oranges don't exist, except in the speech of old Londoners. The image was a bizarre one, always used for a bizarre thing. "He's as queer as a clockwork orange" meant he was queer to the limit of queerness. It did not primarily denote homosexuality, though *queer* was the term used for a member of the inverted fraternity. Europeans who translated the title as *Arancia a Orologeria,* or *Orange Mécanique* could not understand its Cockney resonance, and they assumed that it meant a hand grenade, a cheaper kind of explosive pineapple. I mean it to stand for the application of a mechanistic morality to a living organism oozing with juice and sweetness.

Readers of the twenty-first chapter must decide for themselves whether it enhances the book they presumably know or is really a discardable limb. I meant the book to end in this way, but my aesthetic judgment may have been faulty. Writers are rarely their own best critics, nor are critics. "Quod scripsi scripsi," said Pontius Pilate when he made Jesus Christ the king of the Jews. "What I have written I have written." We can destroy what we have written but we cannot unwrite it. With what Dr. Johnson called frigid tranquillity, I leave what I wrote to the judgment of that .00000001 of the American population that cares about such things. Eat this sweetish segment or spit it out. You are free.

## Anthony Burgess    (essay date 31 May 1987)

SOURCE: "Alex on Today's Youth: Creeching Golosses and Filthy Toofles!," in *The New York Times Book Review,* May 31, 1987, pp. 7, 18.

[*In the following essay, which takes the form of an interview conducted by Burgess with Alex, the main character of* A Clockwork Orange, *Burgess examines Alex's personality by having him critique contemporary youth culture.*]

This month W. W. Norton & Company published a new edition of *A Clockwork Orange,* including the 21st chapter, which had appeared in the British edition in 1962 but was dropped from the first American version. In that chapter, the teen-age thug Alex, who is the narrator, tires of violence and resolves to turn to a new way of life. Anthony Burgess has had a running argument with the publisher ever since about that chapter, and has expressed strong feelings about Stanley Kubrick's film, which followed the American version of the book. Now, to mark the 25th anniversary of the novel's publication, *The Book Review* asked Mr. Burgess to interview the mature Alex about today's youth. The author has always insisted that a reader of the novel will quickly comprehend Alex's peculiar language, which includes a number of words adapted from Russian. Since the interview is rather brief, however, a small glossary is provided here of terms the meaning of which might not be obvious from the context in which they are first used.

### A 'Clockwork' Glossary

| | |
|---|---|
| applesins | oranges |
| bezoomny | crazy |
| britva | razor |
| chelloveck | man |
| doomat | think |
| dratsing | fighting |
| drencrom | a narcotic |
| golosses | noises |
| govoreet | talk |
| gromky | loud |
| jeezny | life |
| kneeg | book |
| koopat | buy |
| krovvy | blood |
| malchick | boy |
| mekansky | mechanical |
| mir | peace or the world |
| nagoy | naked, stripped |
| nogas | feet |
| nozh | knife |
| platties | clothes |
| plott | body |
| pomnit | understand |
| rookers | arms |
| sdach | change |
| sinny | movie |
| skaz | say |
| slooshy | hear |
| slovar | dictionary |
| slovo | word |
| smeck | laugh, ridicule |
| toofles | sneakers |
| vellocet | a narcotic |
| veshch | thing |
| voina | war |
| yahzick | tongue, language |

[*Burgess*]: *Alex—if I may call you that—there's always been some doubt about your surname.*

[*Alex*]: Never gave it, brother, to no manner of chelloveck. The gloopy shoot that put me in the sinny—Lubric or Public or some such like naz—he gave me like two, Alex Burgess and Alex Delarge. That's because of me govoreeting about being Alexander the Big. Then he forgets. Bad like editing. Call me Alex.

*In 1962, when the book about you was published, you were a nadsat, teen-ager that is. Now you must be about 42 or 3 or 4. Settled down, finished with the ultraviolence. Raising a family. Pillar of society.*

For you, little bratty, I am what I was. I am in a book and I do not sdacha. Fixed like, ah yes, forever and never, allmen.

*Sdacha?*

Pick up the old slovar some time, my brother. Shonary, Angleruss.

*Fixed forever and never, allmen, as you skaz. Eternal type of molodoy aggression. And yet there are changes. The youth, or molodoy, of the space age is not what it was in 1962.*

That old kneeg was in the space age. In it there are chellovecks on the old Luna. It was like pathetic.

*Prophetic?*

And pathetic too. The jeezny of all chellovecks is like pathetic and very pathetic. Because they are always the same. Because they are mekansky applesins. That being the Russ like naz of the kneeg written by Burgess or F. Alexander or whatever his naz is or was. And you would know what?

*To put it plain, your opinion of youth today.*

They are not like what I was. No, verily not. Because they have not one veshch in their gullivers. To Ludwig van and his like they give shooms of lipmusic prrrr. It is all with them guitars and creeching golosses. And their platties. It is all jeans and filthy toofles. And tisshuts.

*What are tisshuts?*

They are like worn on the upper plott and there is writing on them like HARVARD and CALIFORNIA and GIVE IT ME I WANT IT. Very gloopy. And they do not have one missal in their gullivers.

*Meaning not one thought in their heads?*

That is what I skazzed.

*But they have many. They are against war and all for universal peace and banning nuclear missiles. They speak of love and human equality.*

What they want they will not get. There will always be voina and no mir, like old Lion Trotsky or it may be Tolstoy was always govoreeting about. Chellovecks are all like very aggressive and do not sdach. The Russkies have a slovo for it, two really, and it is prirozhdyonnuiy grekh.

*Let me consult my ah Angleruss slovar. Odna minuta—it says here original sin.*

Real dobby. Original sin is good and very good.

*The young say their elders have ruined the world, and when they are not trying to rebuild that ruined world with love and fellowship they withdraw from it with hallucinogens.*

That is a hard slovo, O my brother.

*I mean that they take drugs and are transported to heavenly regions of the inner mind.*

Meaning that they are in touch with Bog and all his holy angels and the other veshches?

*Not God, in whom most no longer believe. Though some of them follow the one you would call the bearded nagoy chelloveck who died on the Cross. Indeed, they grow beards and try to look like Him.*

What I skaz is that these veshches, like drencrom and vellocet, are not good for a malchick. To doomat about Bog and to itty off into the land and burble about lubbilubbing every chelloveck has to sap all the goodness and strength out of a malchick.

*Do you consider the youth of today to be more violent than the generation to which you belong?*

Not more. Those that want deng or cutter to koopat their teeny malenky sniffs and snorts and jabs in the rooker must use the old ultraviolence to take and like grab. But such are not seelny, strong that is. The ultraviolence is less now of the molodoy than of terror by air and land, O my brother. Bombs and guns, they were not ever my own veshch. Very cowardly, for it is ultraviolence from a long long long like way off. Dratsing is not what it was. It was better in what they call like the Dark Ages before they put on the like lights. The old britva and the nozh. Rooker to rooker. Your own red red krovvy as well as the krovvy of the chelloveck you are dratsing. And then there was another veshch I do not pomnit the slovo of all that good.

*Style, you mean style?*

Style and again style. Style we had. And the red krovvy did not get onto your platties if you had style. For it was style of the nogas and the rookers and the plott, as it might be tansivatting.

*Dancing?*

That is the slovo that would not like come into my gulliver. The yahzick of the kvadrats I could never get my yahzick round.

*Kvadrat means quadratic, doesn't it? And that means square. By using such terminology you give away your age. But let us return to this business of the music preferred by the young.*

It is not music. It is gromky and bezoomny and like for little children. There is no music like Ludwig van and Benjy Britt and Felix M. and Wolfgang Amadeus. And what the molodoy of now slooshy is not music. And the slovos are like pathetic. What I say to these molodoy chellovecks is that they must like grow up. They must not smeck at what is gone behind. Because that is all we have.

*You seem to me to be ah govoreeting about the preservation of the past. You seem to me also to be ah skazzing that artistic creation is a great good. And yet you ah jeezny was dedicated to destruction.*

It was the bolshy great force of the jeezny that was in myself. I was molodoy, and none had taught me to make. So break was the veshch I had to do. But I get over it.

*You get over it? Meaning you grow up?*

There is no kneeg about me growing up. That is not writ by no matter of writing chelloveck. They viddy me as a very ultraviolent malchick and not more, ah no. To be young is to be nothing. That is why I skaz to the molodoy of now that they must not be as they are. What they have to do is to like grow up.

*Can you transport yourself to the future, or rather your part in the future—which has not been written about and, I speak with some authority, never will be—and deliver a final message to the world?*

In the yahzick of the mir at like large?

*Yesli bi mozhno.*

Your Russian is deplorable, but I take it you mean "if possible." Very well. I speak as a taxpaying adult. And I say that the only thing that counts is the human capacity for moral choice. No, I will not speak. I will sing. I will take Beethoven's setting of Schiller's "Ode to Joy" in the final movement of the glorious Ninth, and I will put my own slovos, I mean words, to it:

> Being young's sort of sickness,
> Measles, mumps or chicken pox.
> Gather all your toys together,
> Lock them in a wooden box.
> That means tolchocks, crasting and dratsing,
> All of the things that suit a boy.
> When you build instead of busting,
> You can start your Ode to Joy.

*Thank you, Mr. ah——*

Bog blast you, I haven't finished.

> Do not be a clockwork orange,
> Freedom has a lovely voice.
> Here is good and there is badness,

Look on both, then take your choice.
Sweet in juice and hue and aroma,
Let's not be changed to fruit machines.
Choice is free but seldom easy—
That's what human freedom means.

Gloopy sort of slovos, really. Grahzny sort of world. May I now, O my brother, return to the pages of my book?

*You never left them.*

## Jean-Pierre Barricelli   (essay date 1988)

SOURCE: "Beethovenian Overlays by Carpentier and Burgess: The Ninth in Grotesque Juxtapositions," in *Melopoiesis: Approaches to the Study of Literature and Music,* New York University Press, 1988, pp. 140-54.

[*Barricelli is an American fiction writer, critic, and educator. In the following excerpt, he argues that the use of Beethoven's Ninth Symphony in* A Clockwork Orange *is arbitrary and inappropriate, "overlay[ing] with negative associations one of the supreme compositions in the musical repertory."*]

[The] Ninth Symphony, with its lofty reputation, is not *ipso facto* always an object of celebration, and it continues to appear in grotesque contexts. With the author of *A Clockwork Orange,* Anthony Burgess, it is once more de-mythicized and overlayed with negative associations. Here again, the Ninth is treated, not as a work of art, but as a device in the novel whose dystopian vision centers around politics (the authoritarian socialism of future society), the media (thought control through technology), and morality (actually the immorality of the curtailment of freedom of choice). Carpentier's narrator thought he had found goodness in the jungle; Burgess, who replaces contrast with irony and seeming allegory with whimsical reality, sticks to the urban setting. At the end of *The Wanting Seed,* the question is asked: "Do you think people are fundamentally good?" The reply is grim: "Well . . . they now have a chance to ge good"—grim in light of *A Clockwork Orange,* where a conditioning process assures stability by eliminating freedom, and where the impossibility of distinguishing good from evil anymore in a totally mechanical environment results in "good" human zombies assembled like a clockwork. Like Carpentier, Burgess critiques the West, though less for its spiritual bankruptcy than for its idealistic faith in natural goodness. Free choice provokes anarchy, conditioning establishes control.

Carpentier's intellectually sophisticated language gives way to what has been called a Technico-Russo-Anglo "slanguage" called Nadsat, replete with neologisms to fit the society portrayed but also pleasantly rhythmical, indeed musical. The narrator Alex, after all, is a hoodlum who loves classical music, especially Beethoven, and his jargoned idiom, where neologisms act as dissonances, betrays a musical affinity. In the words of one critic, "It is hardly coincidental that Alex's favorite piece of music is Beethoven's Ninth, rich in dissonances that only the professional ear can detect, but filled also with as many untapped, infinite (so it seems) harmonies" [Robert K. Morris, *The Consolations of Ambiguity,* 1971]. As an example,

I might single out one passage; after a successful "drasting" with his buddies, Alex writes:

> When we got into the street I viddied that thinking is for the gloopy ones and that the oomny ones use like inspiration and what Bog sends. For now it was lovely music that came to my aid. There was an auto ittying by and it had its radio on, and I could just slooshy a bar or so of Ludwig van (it was the Violin Concerto, last movement), and I viddied at once what to do.

Alex, a lad of fifteen, is "ultra-violent," and the music he loves primarily is German, a preference that combines artistic greatness with the naked horrors of two world wars. Carpentier would agree. His motto is antiestablishmentarian: *Non serviam,* or "Kiss-my-sharries." He and his gang of three masked "droogs" commit all kinds of atrocities, "drasting" and "tolchocking": more than robbery and theft, they beat up an old professor and a drunkard to a pulp, attack another gang with razors and chains, savagely kick a pair of lovers, invade a writer's "HOME" and rape his wife. After breaking into an elderly, cat-loving woman's house and knocking her unconscious, Alex is arrested; sent to jail, where he is number 6655321 and accidentally kills a homosexual inmate; and is turned over to Dr. Brodsky for a reclamation treatment called Ludovico's Technique: brainwashing through films and drug injections that cause Alex to become violently ill the moment he starts experiencing pleasure at violent thoughts. The chaplain has reservations about the treatment: "The question is whether such a technique can really make a man good. Goodness comes from within, 6655321. Goodness is something chosen. When a man cannot choose he ceases to be a man. . . . It may be horrible to be good." But Alex sees this as the only way out of prison. He undergoes the cure and is declared cured, "ready to be crucified rather than crucify," by the doctors and state officials. Released, he is rejected by his parents; attacked by the old professor; rescued by his former "droogs" (now policemen), who beat him mercilessly for having previously beat up one of them during an argument; revisits "HOME", where the writer, a liberal out to "dislodge this overbearing government," at first recognizes him as a victim of that freedom-choking Ludovico Technique, later as the rapist who violated his wife—at which point he metes such excruciating punishment on the narrator through music that Alex attempts suicide by jumping out of a window. In the hospital he is restored to his former "ultra-violent" sexmaniacal self (the state is under pressure over its methods) and the Minister of the Interior makes a deal for his support in order to discredit the writer's political party. In one version of the novel, a final chapter (Chapter 21) [in an endnote about the significance of this number, Barricelli adds that Burgess places "Symbolic meaning in the number 7—the seven days of creation— . . . through his narrator's three sections, each of seven days"] has him mature to realize that "ultraviolence is a bit of a bore, and it's time he had a wife and a malensky googoogooing malchickiwick to call him dadada" [Anthony Burgess, quoted in Richard Matthews, *The Clockwork Universe of Anthony Burgess,* 1978].

In this gruesome fantasy, Beethoven plays a telling role,

with a helping hand from Johann Sebastian Bach and George Frideric Handel. For Alex, music is a salvation, "gorgeousness and gorgeosity made flesh," producing "a cage of silk around my bed," resembling "silvery wine flowing in a spaceship, gravity all nonsense now": "Great Music . . . and Great Poetry would like quieten Modern Youth down to make Modern Youth more Civilized. Civilized my syphilised yarbles. Music always sort of sharpened me up, O my brothers, and made me feel like old Bog himself." Therefore Alex, who strikes his friend for simply ridiculing a woman singing opera at the Korova Milkbar, retires to his room afterward and masturbates while listening to Beethoven. After beating and bloodying the writer's wife, and with feelings of violence racing through him in bed, he again experiences an orgasm listening to classical music:

> I wanted something starry and strong and very firm, so it was J. S. Bach I had, the Brandenburg Concerto. . . . Listening to the Bach, I began to pony better what that meant now, and I thought, slooshying away to the brown gorgeousness of the starry German master, that I would like to have tolchoked them both harder and ripped them to ribbons on their own floor.

And in prison he is allowed to listen to the "holy music by J. S. Bach and G. F. Handel," even while reading the Bible: "While the stereo played bits of lovely Bach I closed my glazzies and viddied myself helping in and even taking charge of the tolchocking and the nailing in" [In an endnote, the critic adds: "The allusion is to Christ. Critics have brought out the sin–penance–resurrection analogy relating to the three parts of this complex novel"]. But his favorite composition is Beethoven's Ninth. He picks up two ten-year-old girls at the bar and rapes them, incited by the symphony:

> Then I pulled the lovely Ninth out of its sleeve, so that Ludwig van was not nagoy too, and I set the needle hissing on to the last movement, which was all bliss. There it was then, the bass strings like govoreeting away from under my bed at the rest of the orchestra, and then the male human goloss coming in and telling them all to be joyful, and the lovely blissful tune all about Joy being a glorious spark like of heaven, and then I felt the old tigers leap in me and then I leapt on these two young ptitsas.

Alone later he falls asleep "with the old Joy Joy Joy crashing and howling away." Indeed, there is black humor as well as grotesque irony attached to this type of Beethovenian overlay, like that of the cat-loving woman who tries to protect herself against the invader wielding a bust of the master from Bonn, or like that of the dream he has of Beethoven, during which he hears a violence-ridden parody of the ode:

> Boy, thou uproarious shark of heaven,
>   Slaughter of Elysium,
> Hearts on fire, aroused, enraptured,
>   We will tolchock you on the rot and
> kick
>       your grahzny vonny bum.

It dawns upon us at one point that in the name "Ludovi-co's Technique" Ludovico is really Ludwig, "Ludwig van" in Alex's parlance. When the narrator is subjected to the horrid state-sponsored rehabilitation process, complete with wires, drug, and film ("a very good like professional piece of sinny"), the background music turns out to be Beethoven's Fifth Symphony, which then produces such an abhorrence for this music which up to now has aroused his sexual violence (the old "in-out in-out"), that the revengeful writer conceives of locking him up in a room and having symphonic music piped in, a diabolical punishment of hypercruelty. Even Alex, now sixteen, begins to realize the degrading nature of what is taking place:

> I don't mind about the ultra-violence and all that cal. I can put up with that. But it's not fair on the music. It's not fair I should feel ill when I'm slooshying lovely Ludwig van and G. F. Handel and others. All that shows you're an evil lot of bastards and I shall never forgive you, sods.

At the end, as part of the deal with the Minister of the "Inferior" and to make sure he has been returned to his original self with his "bloshy" musical ways, he asks to hear the Ninth Symphony (end of Chapter 20), and he is convinced in a manner Beethoven might not have appreciated:

> Oh, it was gorgeosity and yumyumyum. When it came to the Scherzo I could viddy myself very clear running and running on like very light and mysterious nogas, carving the whole litso of the creeching world with my cutthroat britva. And there was the slow movement and the lovely last singing movement still to come. I was cured all right.

As in Carpentier, this network of musical references may well provide a unifying factor in the novel, identifying the protagonist's individuality throughout, an individuality that in *A Clockwork Orange* threatens and in *Los pasos perdidos* opposes the status quo. But here, too, one must wonder about the suggestion, in the former work, that the mathematical music of Bach or, more pervasively, the lyrical and jubilant music of Beethoven, sparks even more violence than the hoodlum had in him originally. Similarly, one must wonder about the appropriateness, in the latter work, of associating the Ninth Symphony with violence after a token tribute to childhood memories. It is not enough to say that we are merely dealing with a whimsical selection, a convenient image, or an interesting device. For some reason, something about Beethoven—his titanic stature or what he represents in the cultural patrimony of the West—activates a devil's advocate's adrenalin in the authors of *Los pasos perdidos* and *A Clockwork Orange*. Grass reacted similarly toward St. Paul. To be sure, other works by Carpentier and Burgess, like *El acoso* and *Napoleon Symphony*, pay homage to the master, at least to the extent of their structural transpositions of the Third Symphony. But then again, look in passing at Richard Ennis in Burgess's *A Vision of Battlements*, who incites an anti-aircraft unit to combative violence with words about this same master: "Beethoven was a musician. . . . He had absolutely no respect for authority. . . . He was independent, fearless, alone, no base crawler." We cannot overlook Dr. Brodsky's remark, either: the "sweetness and most heavenly of activities partake in some measure of violence— . . . music, for instance." Hence Alex's unwittingly profound observation: "It was like as though to get better I had to get worse." Is it that in a clockwork, mechanical world good derives from bad like peace from violence—a restatement of Charles Baudelaire's *Les Fleurs du mal* or Giovanni Papini's *Un uomo finito?* Or that man has reached a hopeless impasse in his savage quest for improvement? But the existential messages of Kierkegaard, Nietzsche, Dostoievsky, Pirandello, and Kafka have already been recorded. Carpentier's narrator hurts spiritually under authority; Burgess's challenges it physically. One feels like a Prometheus for a moment in the jungle but knows he is too weak to be one and that he will get worse before getting better; the other feels like a "fruit" who ultimately *is* that clockwork orange and that, if he has been made better for society, it is actually worse for society. Thus, we are left with paradoxes in the throes of a Manichaean dialectic: the Apollonian or the Dionysian, freedom of choice or submissive choicelessness, the authentic or the synthetic? More troublesome still, is either side of the equation possible today? If the culture of the Western city has not found fulfillment, is the alternative the primitive jungle? And if the promise of social governance has not matured, is lawless instinct the only avenue left? Answers to these questions are never clearly suggested. The ends of both novels are open-ended—indeed, unhealthy in light of their inconclusiveness. And it is the Ninth Symphony, incongruously, that shapes the contexts.

Yet the language of Beethoven's composition rings too lucidly with vitality and conviction to provide backdrops for such ambiguities and paradoxical modes. The overlays obfuscate the truth. As one critic has commented, "if the mode of a novel should say something about its meaning, or at least carry us forward so we may debate it, then we might have wished for a less open-ended conclusion, one that defined as well as disturbed" [Morris]. Without the definition, Beethoven is merely "used." In "Beethoven's Ninth Symphony and the King Cobra," the poet Edgar Lee Masters sounds more convincing:

> Beethoven's soul stepped from darkness to brilliant light,
> From despair to the rapture of strength
> Overcoming the world.

### John J. Stinson    (essay date 1991)

SOURCE: "Dystopias and Cacotopias," in *Anthony Burgess Revisited,* Twayne, 1991, pp. 47-63.

[*Stinson is an educator and critic specializing in modern British literature who has spent many years studying the work of Burgess. In the following excerpt, he discusses themes and stylistic aspects of* A Clockwork Orange, *and comments on the history of the major critical issues involved with the novel.*]

Any reasonably informed discussion of utopian and antiutopian fiction in our own century must soon involve the

---

> **Anthony Burgess on "goodness" in art:**
>
> The goodness of a piece of music and the goodness of a beneficent action have one thing in common—disinterestedness. The so-called good citizen merely obeys the laws, accepting what the State tells him is right or wrong. Goodness has little to do with citizenship. It is not enacted out of obedience to law, to gain praise or avoid punishment. The good act is the altruistic act. It is not blazoned and it seeks no reward. One can see how it is possible to glimpse a fancied connection between the goodness of Beethoven's Ninth Symphony—composed in deafness, disease, squalor and poverty—and that of the saint who gives his cloak to the naked, embraces the leper, dies to save others. But Beethoven's goodness is outside the field of action, to which the saint is so committed. Art is a vision of heaven gratuitously given. Being quasi-divine, it is beyond human concerns. Unlike the heaven of Christian doctrine, it is as freely available to the morally evil as to the morally good: the equivalent of Saint Augustine's God's grace, impartially bestowed. This, to the narrower moralist, renders it suspect.
>
> *Anthony Burgess in* 1985, *Little, Brown, 1978.*

---

names of H. G. Wells and George Orwell. Wells, the cheerful apostle of rationalism, scientism, and technology, believed that the world's people, all basically benevolent by innate disposition, could, at some sufficient point of general enlightenment, produce a New Jerusalem on this earth. Wells believed, as Burgess writes in *The Novel Now,* that "there was no such thing as Original Sin; man was born free to build good—not to earn it or inherit it by divine grace. Wells believed that a Utopia was possible; he called himself a Utopiographer" [*The Novel Now,* 1967]. Burgess, of course, would call him a Pelagian. Burgess notes, correctly it would seem, that Wells "died a disappointed liberal." When we think of Orwell, we are apt to think of him as the exact antithesis of Wells: we remember the starkly brutal admonitory parable that is *Nineteen Eighty-four.* But Burgess is right again when, in an essay titled **"After Ford,"** he notes that "Orwell exhibits the sickness of a disillusioned liberal." [*But Do Blondes Prefer Gentleman?,* 1986]. In *The Novel Now,* Burgess gravely delivers his own oft-repeated warning: "Liberalism breeds disappointment . . . Accept that man is imperfect, that good and evil exist, and you will not, like Wells, expect too much from him." . . .

The sheer memorability of *A Clockwork Orange* points to its successful achievement of the mythic dimension. Burgess, however, has frequently expressed slight chagrin that this is his best-known book, indicating his feeling that it is a didactic little book, and, elsewhere, that it "was very much a *jeu de spleen* when I wrote it" [Anthony Burgess with Thomas Churchill, *Malahat Review,* January, 1971]. He has grown wearied, and become annoyed, by questioners who, having in mind mostly the near notorious film version of Stanley Kubrick, seek to elicit his thoughts on the pornography of violence and his own presumed abdication of the artist's social responsibility. Discussions of the comparative merits of the British and American versions (the latter appearing, until 1987, without the last chapter) have also long ceased to hold any real interest for him. Burgess's ostensible disinterest (which is perhaps, genuine embarrassment) occurs despite, or maybe because of, the fact that this is the book that altered his career and profoundly affected his life.

The British (or, possibly, North American) society to which the reader is introduced at the beginning of the novel is dull, grey, and oppressive. Although the terms Pelagianism/Augustinianism are not used, it is apparent, employing Foxe's lesson in *The Wanting Seed,* that the society depicted is in a late Pelagian phase, like the one in the opening of that novel. All citizens not children, nor with child, nor ill, are compelled by state law to work. People live in "municipal flatblocks"; this night they have been instructed to tune into a "worldcast" on their tellies. The sought-after homogeneity of this engineered, perhaps one-world society, is thwarted only by the presence of teenage rebels who rule the night streets. The protagonist and our "humble narrator," fifteen-year-old Alex, is the foremost rebel of those we meet. The *nadsat* (teenage) language of Alex and his *droogs* (gang members) is one sharp indicator of their effort (a product, it would seem, of both instinct and will) to resist mindless standardization. In nadsat, in fact, "to rabbit" is to work, to do as Alex's pee and em (father and mother) do every day because they are like timid animals who run in circles and live in hutches, or, noting the probable Slavic (here Czech) etymology, they are robots. Animals or automatons, they are in either case dehumanized. Alex, seemingly depraved, is very human. On the axis of paradoxes like this, the novel turns.

Alex, killer, rapist, sadist, and maker of general mayhem at age fifteen, is, in fact, one of the mouthpieces for Burgess's own ideas. Addressing the reader about people's shocked dismay when confronted with manifestations of evil, he expresses a rather amazingly sophisticated anti-Pelagian view:

> this biting of their toe-nails over what is the *cause* of badness is what turns me into a fine laughing malchick. They don't go into what is the cause of *goodness,* so why of the other shop? If lewdies are good that's because they like it, and I wouldn't ever interfere with their pleasures, and so of the other shop. And I was patronizing the other shop. More, badness is of the self, the one, the you or me on our oddy knockies and that self is made by old Bog or God and is his great pride and radosty. But the not-self cannot have the bad, meaning they of the government and the judges and the schools cannot allow the bad because they cannot allow the self. And is not our modern history my brothers, the story of brave malensky selves fighting these big machines? I am serious with you, brothers, over this. But what I do I do because I like to do.

Burgess insists that Alex's actions, atrocious assaults and all, proceed from deliberate choices of his own free will. The question, "What's it going to be then, eh?," which opens all three parts of the novel and the last chapter as

well, reinforces the idea that people are free to choose their own actions. Some readers have felt that Burgess has to shout this point at them because it goes against the evidence. Alex is, in their view, something very much like a robot programmed for violence, or if not quite that, a young man who acts out in disturbed fashion a universal need to assert life and independence in a tyrannously dull society. Their point is that whether he likes it or not, Alex's life has been heavily molded by his environment. If the environment were not so oppressively constrictive, Alex would not have the need to act out his rebellion so outrageously. Thus, environment has made Alex what he is, and it is the job of the behavioral psychologist to prescribe the means whereby emotional imbalances may be redressed. In insisting that Alex acts out of free choice, these readers maintain, Burgess has disregarded his own evidence. These are the readers, then, more inclined to accept the claims of Drs. Brodski, Branom, and cohorts to the effect that they are not doing something that goes against nature by conditioning Alex toward the good; rather, they are removing the "error" of some past conditioning that inclined Alex so heavily toward "the old ultra-violence." Actually, the freewill/determinism conflict in the work of Burgess, as in that of most writers, takes the reader down a dark, tricky, winding road.

Thematically, the behaviorists in the novel are portrayed as not particularly intelligent villains. Burgess's antibehaviorist stance in the novel is so pronounced that the print media have felt that Burgess cast himself as the bête noir of B. F. Skinner, thus virtually announcing himself as available on call to refute any proclamations of the renowned behaviorist about necessary abridgments of freedom and dignity. Burgess very unfairly stacks the deck against the behaviorists, say many who regard *A Clockwork Orange* as a thesis or philosophical novel. In the novel the behaviorists are pliant tools of a totalitarian state. They employ Ludovico's technique on Alex because the authorities need to get his type out of the prisons to accommodate hordes of political prisoners (the Interphase obviously having begun, liberal belief in basic goodness has apparently given way to sore disappointment because of the likes of Alex). The behavioral psychologists are seen as two-dimensional, uncultured shrinkers of the soul, clumsy in the application of procedures they themselves have devised. Dr. Brodsky says of music, "I know nothing about it myself. It's a useful emotional heightener, that's all I know." He is unconcerned that the radical aversive conditioning process—Ludovico's technique—has destroyed Alex's enjoyment of Beethoven along with his ability to carry out violence.

Burgess's short novel inclines toward the fable, and it is unreasonable to expect that its sociophilosophical ideas are argued with the concentrated weight and scrupulous fairness with which they would be argued in an academic treatise. Burgess's novel did, though, so memorably strike some decidedly contemporary chords that it provided a ready reference point for certain social issues that were seriously, and heatedly, debated in the real world. By the mid-1970s aversive conditioning was making headway in the U.S. penal system: some inmates were given shots of apomorphine, inducing violent vomiting and dry retching;

others were given Anectine, which produces agonizing sensations of suffocation and drowning; sex offenders were given electric shocks to the groin. Such practices were generally successfully opposed by the American Civil Liberties Union and other groups as "cruel and unusual punishment"; *A Clockwork Orange* was almost always at least mentioned in media reports about litigation connected with this troubling but ethically complex issue.

*A Clockwork Orange* stayed in the news because of the currency and vigor of its ideas, but it is a significant work of literature for other reasons. Burgess employs black humor and the grotesque—two highly favored forms of the late sixties—more integrally, and therefore more successfully, than any other writer of the period with the possible exceptions of Joseph Heller and Günter Grass. What might be referred to as the "violent grotesque" is employed at the very outset as the demonically engaging Alex recounts for us, his "brothers," with relish and a delicious savoring of detail, how he and his "droogies" (gangmates) perpetrated various nightly horrors: an old man returning from the library is insulted and assaulted; his false teeth are ripped from his mouth and crunched by the stomps of the teens' heavy boots; heavy-ringed knuckles slam into the old man's bared gums until his mouth is a riot of red; he is stripped and kicked for good measure. This is only the very beginning of violence that exceeds that of de Sade in intensity if not imaginativeness. Storekeepers, husband and wife, are brutally beaten and robbed; a writer's wife (Mrs. F. Alexander) is savagely gang raped in her home and her husband is forced to watch helplessly; two barely pubescent girls of ten are raped; an old woman (the Cat Lady), a well-to-do recluse, meets her death trying to defend herself and her valuables during a robbery. All this—and more—is accomplished by Alex, Dim, Pete, and George on the two consecutive days that comprise part 1, eighty-four pages of the novel.

The high level of Burgess's black comic craft is testified to by his ability to make us approach the vicious assault of an old lady with something very much like mirth and excitement. Burgess writes in his introduction to the New American Edition that his "intention in writing the work was to titillate the nastier propensities of my readers." He might be thought almost to prove his theological (Augustinian) point by the success with which he carries out his intention. Readers come to have ambivalent feelings only when their moral reactions, linguistically stupefied into unwatchfulness, suddenly rouse themselves and come panting up indignantly. By the near-miracle of his craft, particularly by his linguistic inventiveness, Burgess has succeeded in temporarily making his readers one with the wantonly brutal young assaulters:

> He [the old man returning from the library] looked a malenky bit poogly when he viddied the four of us . . . coming up so quiet and polite and smiling, but he said: "Yes? What is it?" in a very loud teacher-type goloss, as if he was trying to show us he wasn't poogly. . . . "You naughty old veck, you," I said, and then we began to filly about with him. Pete held his rookers and George sort of hooked his rot open for him and Dim yanked out his false zoobies, upper and

lower. He threw these down on the pavement and then I treated them to the old boot-crush, though they were hard bastards like, being made of some new horrorshow plastic stuff. The old veck began to make sort of shumbling shooms— "wuf waf wof"—so Georgie let go of holding his goobers apart and just let him have one in the toothless rot with his ringy fist, and that made the old veck start moaning a lot then, then out comes the blood, my brothers, real beautiful. So all we did then was to pull his outer platties off, stripping him down to his vest and long underpants (very starry; Dim smecked his lead off near), and then Pete kicks him lovely in his pot, and we let him go.

What forestalls reader revulsion at this basically realistic scene of violence is distancing through the use of invented language. "It is as if we were trying to read about violence in a foreign language and finding its near-incomprehensibility getting in the way of a clear image," Burgess says in a *New York Times* piece [April 20, 1975]. The distinct teenage language serves also to reawaken the reader's awareness of the anarchic impulse of the teenager and the instinct to be one with the herd, to regard other groups just as "other," utterly alien, in no way like the self. The original (British; now "New American") ending emphasizes that Alex and his droogs should be seen first as teenagers before they are seen as all men. These teenagers have their own language, *nadsat* (the Russian word for teen), a language that the reader, seeing the words repeatedly in context, will soon assimilate. In the novel Dr. Branom explains to Dr. Brodsky its provenance: "Odd bits of rhyming slang . . . , a bit of gipsy talk, too. But most of the roots are Slav. Propaganda. Subliminal penetration." Actually, gypsy elements are virtually indiscernible; Cockney influences are quite noticeable, but not too important; words of Russian origin are heavily present and Burgess adapts them, with marvelous felicity, to various purposes. A few of the Burgess words convey a sharp sensory vividness through onomatopoeic effect. For example, in gang warfare, Dim's most skillfully employed weapon is his "oozy," his "real horrorshow length of chain," twice round about his waist. As Geoffrey Aggeler remarks, a "bicycle chain . . . , its shiny coils shaken out along a sidewalk or whizzing through the night air, is so much more like an 'oozy' than a 'chain' " [*Anthony Burgess: The Artist as Novelist,* 1979]. Or, we might take the word "horrorshow" from the same sentence. A believable anglicization of the Russian word *khorosho* (good, well, excellent), it conforms to Alex's propensities exactly, for to him nothing is more excellent than "a bit of the old ultra-violence," his personally choreographed "horror shows" that he puts on nearly every night. The most important function of the language is the softening of the otherwise unbearably repulsive violence, but the violence itself is thematically integral. Not at all pornographic, the grotesque violence is the means by which Burgess attacks the failures of rationalism. While it has proved difficult to define the grotesque precisely, many commentators seem to agree that it frequently involves the sudden subversion of the apparent world of order and form by the shocking appearance of the absurd, purely irrational, or primally chaotic. Naïve liberals and rationalists willfully shut their eyes to primal discords, but they are forced open by the "horror shows" staged by a Hitler or an Alex. Frequently used as a means of exposing the naïveté of excessive rationalism, the grotesque is associated with Conrad's Kurtz, the liberal humanist who, in quick descent, comes to preside over "unspeakable rites"; and Golding's Piggy, the bespectacled emissary of rationalism whose precious brain is spilled grotesquely out on a rock. Alex is a producer of the grotesque, but Alex is in all of us, which is the point that Burgess most cleverly gets across as he disorients his readers just enough by the language to cause them vicariously to share the thrill of cruelty.

Alex (his name seemingly suggesting "without law") is more an extraordinary teenage rebel than he is Satan or even Dionysus (as Burgess's own ending makes clear), but he has a winsome effect on the reader because, in a world of pale neutrals, he has energy and commitment. (By contrast, Alex's parents "rabbit" every day at mindless jobs, stare vacuously each evening at insipid programs on the telly, and retire to bed, sleeping pills in their bloodstreams, lest they be awakened by the blast of Alex's stereo.) From the beginning we sympathize with Alex because he is, in his own words, "our faithful narrator" and "brother." This is an old novelistic trick, readers tending to sympathize with anyone, save a total monster, who continually tells them about his life and makes them vicariously share it. Then, too, Alex has wit, some intelligence, a love of classical music, his gift of pungent language, and a kind of artistry in his violence. We react with sympathy and pathos when Alex falls into the clutches of the state, particularly when it attempts "rehabilitation" by reducing him to a "clockwork orange." This term is explained by F. Alexander, Burgess's mock double and another ironic mouthpiece, a pompous sort who has just completed a flatulently styled tome titled *A Clockwork Orange:* "The attempt to impose upon man, a creature of growth and capable of sweetness, to ooze juicily at the last round the bearded lips of God, to attempt to impose, I say, laws and conditions appropriate to a mechanical creation, against this I raise my sword-pen."

Alex does become a clockwork orange temporarily when, in order to gain a much speedier release from prison, he assents to Ludovico's technique. The "therapy" consists of showing Alex atrocity films after he has been given a drug to induce pain and nausea. The association of violence and nausea incapacitates Alex from further violent action, any attempt instantaneously provoking literal wretchedness. Released, Alex finds himself quickly at the mercy of all those whom he had previously victimized. In a schematic plot framework almost parodically designed to show retributive justice in action, each of these victims pays back the now defenseless Alex. One of those who gets the satisfaction of a payback is F. Alexander, reputedly—and, in his own mind—an idealist and bastion of liberal values. His view of man had gone untested, however. An unsuspected part of himself powerfully leaps out when he discovers that Alex was one of the rapists responsible for his wife's death. Very much human, he is not above the philosophy of an eye for an eye. This is one of Burgess's "proofs" that evil is endemic in man, that it has always been there and always will be. Another proof is found in

Alex's prison reading: the "big book," the Bible, in which he "read of these starry yahoodies tolchocking each other and then peeting their Hebrew vino and getting on to the bed with their wives' like handmaidens, real horrorshow."

Alex suffers greatly—emotionally, mentally, and even physically—as a result of the Ludovico "therapy." Burgess's point is clear, since, in fact, it is presented somewhat didactically through a third spokesman in the novel, the prison Charlie; but Burgess's expression of it outside the novel is even clearer: "What my and Kubrick's parable tries to state is that it is preferable to have a world of violence undertaken in full awareness—violence chosen as an act of will—than a world conditioned to be good or harmless" [*New York Review of Books,* April 16, 1972]. Not to be able to choose is not to be human. If evil were somehow to be eradicated, its opposite—goodness—would, having no meaning, cease to exist. "Life is sustained by the grinding opposition of moral entities," Burgess writes in the introduction to the New American Edition. In most discussions that the book has generated this prime thematic point has generally been agreed with. The expostulations of B. F. Skinner have, though, given some listeners serious pause. Basically (most notably in *Beyond Freedom and Dignity*), Skinner argues that the very survival of the race depends upon the surrender of some freedom, as that term has been historically understood. No Augustinian, Skinner also pleads that we examine carefully the operant conditioning that underlies people's choices to behave poorly. He has made clear that his strong preference is always for positive reinforcement rather than aversive techniques to correct maladaptive behavior. Burgess likes to make the point that evil exists, and must exist, as a part of the human self; he is fond of pointing out that "live" is "evil" spelled backwards.

The novel's ending has always been problematic. Burgess's last chapter, the twenty-first, was deleted from the first American edition (Norton, 1963) and all subsequent American editions until 1987, although this chapter appeared in the British (Heinemann) edition and most foreign translations from the very first (1962). Burgess maintains that Norton insisted on the excision; Norton maintains it was only suggested as an artistic improvement. Kubrick's boldly imaginative film version (1971), which spiralled the novel to far greater fame, ended as the American version did. Persuasive arguments can be made for the superiority of either version. The twentieth chapter (chapter 6 of part 3) ends as the government authorities, under strong pressure from politically aroused public opinion, reverse the effects of the aversive therapy by deep "hypnopaedia," restoring Alex to his old self—he "viddies" himself "carving the whole litso of the creeching world with my cut-throat britva." Chapter 21—the famous deleted chapter—presents a mellowing, increasingly reflective, eighteen-year-old Alex who is coming to see that this previous violent behavior was childishly perverse. He thinks of marriage, stability, and the son he one day hopes to have. He contemplates explaining to his son all his own past crimes as an admonition, but then thinks that he "would not really be able to stop him [prevent his son from enacting similar crimes]. And nor would he be able to stop his own son."

The truncated ending, which leaves the reader with a stark presentation of unregenerate evil, surely carries more impact. Burgess's own ending, besides having just a whiff of sentimentality about it, is easily exposed to ridicule. Detractors might say that it reduces the novel to a spectacular but largely meaningless comment on those oh-so-difficult teenagers and their problems of adjustment. Burgess prefers his own ending, with his own worldview, his own "theology." The truncated version, closing with a view of unregenerate human evil, would be a more fitting conclusion for a William Golding novel. With his own ending, Burgess implies a more nearly equal tug from the Pelagian and Augustinian poles, proving once again that he is not quite an Augustinian, and that he is a believer in eternally recurrent cycles. He writes that the Norton editors believed in 1962 that the last chapter "was bland" and "showed a Pelagian unwillingness to accept that a human being could be a model of unregenerable evil." The truncated ("Augustinian") version, he says was "sensational," but not a "fair picture of human life." No matter what the reader's perspective, *A Clockwork Orange* provides a picture that remains painted on the walls of the mind near the place where the conscious and subconscious meet.

## William Hutchings   (essay date March 1991)

SOURCE: " 'What's It Going to Be Then, Eh?': The Stage Odyssey of Anthony Burgess's *A Clockwork Orange,*" in *Modern Drama*, Vol. XXXIV, No. 1, March, 1991, pp. 35-48.

[*In the following essay, Hutchings discusses the stage adaptations of* A Clockwork Orange, *focusing on the two written by Burgess.*]

Since its publication in 1962, *A Clockwork Orange* has remained Anthony Burgess's best-known and most controversial work, distinguished not only by his stylistic virtuosity in creating the polyglot, pun-riddled teenage slang in which the novel is written but also by the vividness of the violence-wracked dystopian society within which Alex, the book's narrator and protagonist, thrives. Yet even within the tradition of disaffected adolescent narrator/protagonist/anti-heroes—ranging from Huckleberry Finn to Holden Caulfield to Smith in Alan Sillitoe's *The Loneliness of the Long-Distance Runner*—Alex is decidedly an extreme and appalling case: the leader of a teenage gang, he is a thief, a mugger, a convicted murderer and rapist, who frankly and unrepentently describes even his most heinous deeds and dares to assert the essential humanity that he shares with the readers, whom he addresses repeatedly as "my brothers." Rife with theological implications about the Christian doctrine of free will, filled with anti-authoritarian and anti-behaviorist satire, and prophetically accurate about the urban violence that would ever-increasingly characterize subsequent decades, Burgess's novel is among the most prescient works of the postmodern era—and one of its most outrageous. With its clear *agons,* its moral conundrums, and the added advantage of its numerous and notorious scenes of sex and violence—which would particularly help to assure its box-office appeal—*A Clockwork Orange* was soon recognized

as eminently adaptable for the screen and/or for the stage. Controversy has accompanied every version of the work that has been presented, and the various strategies used in the course of its transformations from page to screen to stage raise issues that are germane to all studies of such adaptations.

### I

Anthony Burgess has long been dissatisfied with the truncated text of *A Clockwork Orange* that was published in the United States, which omitted the novel's final chapter and added an unauthorized and unnecessary glossary; the untruncated text remained unavailable in the United States until 1987. Stanley Kubrick's much-acclaimed 1971 film (with which Burgess was also highly displeased) was based on the American edition of the novel; Burgess did not write the screenplay, which was also separately published in 1971. Several years earlier, however, a quite different film of the novel had been planned, for which he was to prepare the script, as he recently disclosed:

> . . . In . . . 1965 . . . the rock-group known as the Rolling Stones expressed an interest in the buying of the property and acting participation in a film version which I myself should write. There was not much money in the project, because the permissive age in which crude sex and cruder violence could be frankly presented had not yet begun. . . . The film . . . was not made. [*A Clockwork Orange: A Play with Music,* 1987]

Surely, Mick Jagger's portrayal of Alex with the other band members as the droogs must rank alongside the Beatles's unproduced film of *Up Against It* (from the script written by Joe Orton) as one of the most intriguing unmade films of the 1960s.

The first known stage adaptation of *A Clockwork Orange* was created by John Godber, produced at the Edinburgh Festival in 1980, and revived in "pub theatre" productions in 1982 and 1984; since Godber's unauthorized version has not been published, however, details of his adaptation must be gleaned from reviews. His most startling innovation is the use of a wheelchair-bound narrator, identified as Alex II, who observes the action from atop a black-box set of walls and raked floors, while another actor, playing Alex I, reenacts events from his earlier, violent life—though these were, in reviewer Christopher Hudson's view, "mimed too discreetly to be threatening" [*Evening Standard,* March 2, 1984]. At the end of the play, Alex II leaves his wheelchair, becoming an even more menacing presence; as reviewer Barney Bardsley remarks, "he swishes his truncheon in idle remembrance of those bruising, battering days"—an indication that Godber's adaptation, like Kubrick's, presented the truncated "American" ending of the novel rather than Burgess's own. "My unease with this production, [which is] so beautifully directed and executed," continued Bardsley, "is that it made of Alex not a despicable little shit—which he surely is—but a rather appealing folk hero" [*City Lights,* March 9, 1984].

In order to "stem the flow of amateur adaptations that [he had] heard about but never seen" (*Play*), Burgess completely reworked the novel into his own "authorized" dramatization, first published in 1987 as *A Clockwork Orange: A Play With Music*. While retaining many of the book's now-famous scenes and its invented "nadsat" teenage slang, Burgess's adaptation is surely no less controversial than Kubrick's own, since it not only restores the novel's "original" ending but adds a surprising final confrontation between Alex and a character resembling Kubrick himself. Designed as "a little play which any group may perform," Burgess's stage version requires only minimal props and offers few specifics about costume design; "this is not grand opera," he wryly remarked in its preface (*Play*).

In February 1990, a *second*, greatly expanded, and radically different "authorized" adaptation, known as *A Clockwork Orange 2004*, was produced by the Royal Shakespeare Company at the Barbican Theatre in London; although Burgess is credited as the sole author in the published version, in a prefatory note he acknowledges that the play's director, Ron Daniels, gave "invaluable help with the adaptation" and may be presumed to have been responsible for many of the changes made between the two versions. With music provided by Bono and the Edge, *A Clockwork Orange* became—if not "grand opera"—at least what reviewer John Heilpern termed "a cryptomusical designed as a commercial blockbuster" [*Vogue*, June, 1990, p. 132], as the English-language adaptation of *Les Misérables* had become since its production by the Royal Shakespeare Company in 1985. It was, however, far less enthusiastically received.

## II

Since the novel is divided into three parts containing seven chapters each, *A Clockwork Orange* would seem to be readily adaptable into a three-act play—depicting, respectively, Alex's experiences before, during, and after the prison incarceration during which he is subjected to the "Ludovico Technique," the behavioristic therapy that is designed to inculcate in him a pathological aversion to violence and/or evil. However, in each of Burgess's stage versions there are only two acts; the first ends with Alex's initial subjection to the mind-altering regimen, and the second begins as he completes his final session under the doctors' supervision. By thus eliding most of Alex's treatment, both stage versions avoid subjecting the audience to prolonged, basically repetitive depiction of the treatment whereby Alex is exposed to what one of his doctors describes as "a real show of horrors" (*2004*); at the director's discretion, a montage of scenes (or stills) from the brutal films that Alex is forced to watch may or may not be projected for viewing by the audience as they are described aloud by his doctors. Although their methodology is amply demonstrated in the first such session, and although the change in Alex's personality is apparent at the beginning of Act Two, the dramatic elision of his treatment by placing it between the acts may unintentionally undercut the fact that it constitutes no less a form of violence than the heinous acts that Alex perpetrates before being apprehended. Indeed, in terms of the novel's thematic structure, the acts of violence that are sanctioned, sponsored, and administered by the collective power of the state are inherently more ominous than Alex's *individual* acts of vio-

lence; the former are also no less dehumanizing for their victim, and, when considered dispassionately and objectively, no less horrifying.

The portrayal of the book's more violent scenes has long been a central issue in all adaptations of *A Clockwork Orange*, since an on-stage or on-screen enactment of a beating, murder, or rape is inherently different from its novelistic description in language, particularly Alex's "nadsat" slang which provides a certain distancing (and often comic) effect in the book. Stung by criticism that the book's violence is excessive and might incite such behavior among impressionable readers—fears that were even more widely (and loudly) voiced after the release of Kubrick's film—Burgess sought to minimalize the violence in his initial stage adaptation, wherein stage directions are reduced to a minimum. Thus, for example, in the confrontation between Alex's droogs and the rival gang headed by Billyboy, the stage direction indicates only that

> The knives and bicycle chains come out. . . .
> There is now a fight, very exactly choreographed
> to music. DIM is the most vigorous but least
> stylish of the four droogs. The gang of BILLY-
> BOY limps off, slashed, bloody. (*Play*)

With appropriate choreography, such a scene could easily become as balletic as that between the Sharks and the Jets in *West Side Story* (1957), on which it may in fact have been modeled; although much is left to the director's discretion, the scene's stylization and the presence of the music (as in the film) mitigate its realism. In the 1990 version, however, the music is removed, the stage directions are more specific, and the violence is more graphic:

> The knives and bicycle chains come out. . . .
> There is now a fight. . . . DIM is the most vigor-
> ous but least stylish of the four droogs. Dancing
> about with his razor, ALEX slashes. Blood
> pours down either side of BILLYBOY'S face,
> while LEO, his number one, blinded by DIM's
> chain, howls and crawls about like an animal.
> Police sirens are heard. The droogs scatter.
> (*2004*)

Even when portrayed this directly, however, such violence seems tame in comparison to that in other contemporary plays (e. g., those of Edward Bond) or in modern productions of *Macbeth* or *Titus Andronicus* (among many others), and in countless films that have been marketed primarily on the basis of their state-of-the-art special effects and ever-more-graphic mayhem, cruelty, mutilation, and gore.

Whereas such depictions of violence have long since surpassed anything in any version of *A Clockwork Orange*, the film's notorious scene in which the writer F. Alexander is accosted, beaten, bound, and forced to watch while his wife is raped has retained its notoriety as a landmark in cinematic sadism; in the film, notoriously, the scene is choreographed to the tune of "Singin' in the Rain." Each of the three stage adaptations adopts a different strategy in depicting this crucial scene, however. In Godber's work, presumably, it was among the incidents from Alex's past that were (however unconvincingly) mimed; in Burgess's 1987 version, the scene was moved off-stage entirely, and the initial assault occurred in the street rather than in their home (where it takes place in the novel, the film, and the subsequently revised version). With surprising coyness, Burgess demurs even at using the word "rape" in his stage directions in his 1987 text and intends to have the action conveyed solely through music: after "having their mouths stuffed by the balled-up manuscript . . . the man is left for near-dead on the ground while the wife is, God help her, prepared for—" [sic], an act so unspeakable that its name is unspoken even in the playwright's stage directions. The "preparation" (the nature of which is also unspecified) is to be accompanied by "the melody of the second movement of Beethoven's Sonata Pathétique" as the droogs sing about loving "the old in-out"; as "the lights dim as they take the struggling girl off," the music becomes more "manic" before it post-coitally "dies away" (**Play**). Yet, however much Kubrick's rendition of the scene exploits its violence and prurience (particularly in its use of close-ups as Alex cuts to shreds the woman's red jumpsuit before the rape itself occurs), Burgess's 1987 version seems too drastic in its remedy, undercutting the incident's inherent horror by reducing it to an unseen act in an unspecified off-stage elsewhere. Although ample precedents for off-stage violence abound from classical times onward, and although musical alarums can denote scenes of struggle of whatever kind, the omission of such scenes from *A Clockwork Orange* would seem inevitably to mitigate a work to which violence is literally (and physically) integral.

Accordingly, in the 1990 version, the rape scene was returned both to the stage and to the home of F. Alexander, where it occurred in the novel. Wearing a Disraeli mask (while his droogs sport masks of P.B. Shelley, Elvis Presley, and Henry VIII), Alex orders Dim to "grab hold of this veck here [F. Alexander] so that he can viddy all"; then, following a gratuitous "Bog [God] help us all," Alex/Disraeli "untrusses and plunges" as F. Alexander "howls in rage." However, the stage directions then specify that, "suddenly unmasking," Alex resumes his role as on-stage narrator, directly addressing the audience:

> Then after me it was right old Dim should have his turn, then Pete and Georgie had theirs. Then there was like quiet, and we were full of like hate, so we smashed what there was left to be smashed. The writer veck and his zheena were not really there, bloody and torn and making noises. But they'd live. (**2004**)

In "suddenly" removing the mask and resuming his role as narrator (surely a unique redefinition of *coitus interruptus*), Alex in effect distances himself from the action by mediating it through language, reliably but briefly reporting events that remain unseen, though their nature has been unmistakably demonstrated on stage. In so doing, he maintains the distinction between the minacious, antisocial Alex-who-acts (Alex I in Godber's version) and the forthright, confiding, post-reformation Alex-who-narrates (Godber's Alex II).

The fact that Alex's narrative voice pervades the novel provides an inevitable problem for all of the various adapters of *A Clockwork Orange*—and one that they have attempted to resolve in a variety of ways. Because it is imme-

diately recognizable with its pervasive nadsat slang, it is perhaps the most distinctive "voice-print" in modern literature—the unique and idiosyncratic product of his particular sensibility, cunning but confiding, minacious but oddly meliorative, inherently asking the reader to understand if not condone; he addresses the reader repeatedly as "brother," with the fervor and insidiously affective intent of a reformed sinner at a religious revival meeting, while remaining wholly and sincerely unrepentent. Paradoxically, it creates within the novel a sort of "alienation effect," distancing the reader from even his most horrific exploits, rendering them less "alienating" than a realistic (i.e., ostensibly objective) third-person description of the same events would be. Most importantly, however, it is both adolescent and postadolescent at the same time. Alex's bravado and *brio* epitomize the hormone-charged sensibility of many fifteen-year-old males: aggressive, heedless, headstrong, and combative but occasionally physically awkward in the presence of his elders (slipping and sliding in saucers of milk while assaulting the cat-owning elderly lady), unconcerned about the consequences and implications of his rash but immediately gratifying actions, and insensitive to whatever discomfort he causes others, whether inadvertently or by design. Yet, notwithstanding its narrative immediacy, Alex's *apologia pro vita sua* is in fact a retrospective account of events; it is recounted by a postcorrective, reconditioned and deconditioned Alex who uses the past tense throughout in describing his former self (or, more precisely, selves). In the twenty-first chapter, he has not only assumed all the postadolescent respectability that lawfully gained income from a worthwhile job can convey, but he also looks forward to assuming the domestic (and ostensibly domesticating) responsibilities of a home, a wife, and a child. The dual narrative perspective of adolescent and postadolescent sensibilities, both of which are integral to the novel, has been notoriously difficult for the various adapters to sustain.

Whereas Godber presented Alex-who-acts and Alex-who-narrates as two separate characters, with the latter being inexplicably wheelchair-bound, and whereas Kubrick utilized a voiceover in the film, Burgess attempted to dispense with Alex's narrative function almost entirely in the 1987 version of the play. Apart from a song in which the phrase "my brothers" may be addressed either to the audience or his droogs (**Play**), Alex speaks directly to the audience only twice in this adaptation: immediately before jumping out the window in his suicide attempt ("Goodbye. May Bog forgive you for a ruined jeezny" [**Play**]) and at the very end of the play, in a speech that is taken from the novel's final paragraph. The remainder of Alex's lines are skillfully reworked into dialogue with other characters, though this version of the play reduces the novel to a too-small number of vignettes. The number of scenes from the novel has been greatly increased in the 1990 version, however, and Alex's narrative function has been restored, beginning with the play's opening lines. Whereas Burgess's previous adaptation had begun with a droog's aria "freely adapting the Scherzo of Beethoven's Ninth Symphony" (**Play**), the later stage version omits the novel's famous opening line, " 'What's it going to be then, eh?' " and begins instead with the book's second sentence,

"That ['There' in the novel] was me, that is Alex, and my three droogs, that is Pete, Georgie and Dim . . ." (*2004*). While the 1990 version is thus the most faithful to the book in sustaining Alex's narrative tone and function, its retention led the critic for *Sight and Sound* to charge that the book had been "incompletely dramatised" [Philip French, Spring, 1990].

Another significant change between the 1987 and 1990 stage adaptations involves the play's use of the theatrical space, which is more flexible in the earlier version—particularly as it is suddenly redefined in the scene in which the Chaplain's sermon is addressed directly to the audience, "which we must imagine is a group of prisoners in the prison chapel" as wardens watch carefully over them, occasionally "shout[ing] threats and objurgations into the audience" (*Play*). In the 1990 version, however, the sermon is presented to an on-stage audience of prisoners and not directed at the theatregoers (*2004*).

A more remarkable change between the two stage adaptations involves the on-stage depiction of a second murder for which Alex gets blamed—the death of one of his prison cellmates. Given the name Pedofil in the play, he is one of the unnamed characters referred to in the novel as "two like queer ones who both took a fancy to me, and one of them made a jump on to my back, and I had a real nasty bit of drasting with him," though he is not murdered as Pedofil is in both of Burgess's stage adaptations. Surprisingly, however, in the 1987 version Alex is almost an innocent bystander: during the fatal beating that Pedofil receives, Alex is "comparatively unviolent," according to the stage directions (*Play*), though the other inmates subsequently blame him rather than the actual perpetrator, Jojohn. In the 1990 version, however, as in the novel, Alex is in fact guilty, reacting violently against being sexually assaulted by his fellow prisoner in the middle of the night; the stage directions indicate that he "joyously cracks at" Pedofil, "fists him all over," and "gives him a final kick" (*2004*)—all of which, of course, Alex's own victim was prevented from doing when he raped her. Nevertheless, Burgess's purpose in twice reworking this relatively brief and minor scene from the novel and increasingly developing this second murder remains unclear; whether or not Alex is an active participant, the violent deeds that he has already perpetrated have surely established those aspects of his personality, and the scene (which Kubrick omitted from the film) seems not only expendable but stereotypical, even if it does provide a certain role reversal in which Alex the sexual victimizer is himself victimized (though he seems to learn nothing from the new perspective). The stereotyping is particularly evident in Burgess's depiction of a character identified only as "the Big Jew," a lisping felon whom Pedofil refers to as "yid" and whose dialect—e.g., "Yeth, yeth, boyth, that'th fair" (*2004*)—pointlessly resurrects the sort of deplorable caricatures whose popularity should presumably have waned several generations ago.

A particular problem in devising the stage adaptations has been how to create the visual images of a future dystopian state without reduplicating the images from the film that Burgess deplores—images that are among the most widely known and readily recognizable in modern cinema. Probably as a result of budgetary constraints and the circumstances of its production in pub theatres, Godber's version used a minimalist black set, allowing the audience members' imaginations to fill in the details however they liked; similarly, Burgess's 1987 adaptation gives few details about the set. Thus, like both the novel and the film, Burgess's play opens in the Korova Milk Bar—though its interior is as undescribed in his script as it is in the novel. Only a neon-lit window-sign, featuring the word MOLOKO written backwards in Cyrillic letters, designates the locale in the play. The startling decor that Kubrick devised for the film—with its nude female bodies contorted into tables and adapted into mechanical beverage dispensers with drug-laden milk squirting from their nipples on demand—is conspicuously absent from the stage, if not from the viewers' minds. For the Royal Shakespeare Company's production, designer Richard Hudson created a basic set that the reviewer for *Plays and Players* described as "similar to a red-painted interior of a gasometer" which, in the Korova Milk Bar scene, was

> augmented by a huge white milk bottle protruding through the wall, and adorned with various frenetic dancers and glazed weirdos stoned on spiked milk. . . . The milk bottle is the first of a series of outsize white objects, somehow clinical as well as phallic, which project through the main set. They act as symbols for the brutality of this future world and also the unremitting male focus of the play. [Nick Curtis, April, 1990]

Other familiar scenes from the film and the novel have been similarly modified in Burgess's adaptations for the stage. The scene in which Alex intrudes into the home of the woman whom he inadvertently murders lacks the enormous phallic *objet d'art* that he wields against her in the film, and the cats (missing in the 1987 version) were restored to the scene in 1990. In the earlier adaptation, P.R. Deltoid, Alex's probation officer, encounters and counsels him in the Milk Bar rather than in the home of his parents, and there is none of the gratuitous homosexual groping that was added in the film. Even the costume design in the play countervenes that of the film: Alex and the droogs dress primarily in black in the Royal Shakespeare Company's production, whereas they wear white jumpsuits in the film. [In an endnote, Hutchings comments: "Although Burgess clearly wishes to distance himself as much as possible from Kubrick's film, the publishers of his stage adaptations clearly have no such interest; the virtually identical graphic design used on the covers of both books is clearly derived from the film logo. Each features a drawing of a rather sinister face that is remarkably like Malcolm McDowell's [Kubrick's Alex], adorned with one false eyelash (a detail from the film that is not mentioned in the novel). The plays' covers show Alex's face within a white triangle with its point downward; in the film logo McDowell is seen within (or emerging from) a black triangle with its point upward."]

Alex's self-justification in the stage version includes a plea that his misbehavior is an expression of a Blakean Orc-like adolescent energy that is allowed no other means of release in the society of his day:

> Energy's something built into a boy,
> But neither the church nor the state
> Has taught us how to create,
> So we've got to use energy to destroy.
> Destruction's our ode to joy.
>
>                            (*Play; 2004*)

Emphatically, Burgess asserts in the 1987 preface that "Alex the hero speaks for me when he says in effect that destruction is a substitute for creation, and that the energy of youth has to be expressed through aggression because it has not yet been able to subdue itself through creation" (*Play*).

As the second act begins, Alex is in the final stages of his treatment, still strapped into the chair but screaming in protest against the desecration of Beethoven's music, which is to the scientists "a convenient heightener of emotion, no more" (*Play*). As in Kubrick's film, the extent of Alex's rehabilitation is demonstrated in a series of confrontations, first with a comedian whose boots he is made to lick, and then with "a most beautiful GIRL, near nude"—toward whom his lust is so suppressed that he can offer only the worship of a "true knight" seeking to be her "helper and protector from the wicked like world" (*Play*), to which he is himself subsequently returned. Repudiated by his parents, displaced in their affections by Joe the lodger, Alex is left alone and unable to commit suicide, the impulse towards which sickens him as yet another violent act. He soon encounters his former droogs, finding that *all three* have become policemen who beat him "balletically, to the Scherzo of [Beethoven's] Ninth," though "the lights dim before we can see the worst of it" (*Play*)—unlike the film's brutally explicit scene at an outdoor water trough. The lights rise on the interior of the writer F. Alexander's apartment where, on the morning after an initially cordial welcome, Alex is tormented from his sleep by the music of the Ninth Symphony and leaps out the window. In the next scene, as Alex sleeps in a hospital bed, a doctor discloses that the physical trauma of the fall may have undone his earlier conditioning—a fact that is soon confirmed through psychological free-association tests. His cure is announced by the government's Minister of the Interior, who presents him with a large stereo system—and Alex agrees that, in the last words of the final chapter of the truncated American edition of the novel, he is "cured all right" (*Play, 2004*).

"The scene ends, but not the play," Burgess remarks at this point in the stage directions of the 1987 version (*Play*); there follows a scene which recapitulates the final chapter of the novel in its British edition, made available in the U.S. for the first time in *Rolling Stone* in March 1987 and subsequently in an unexpurgated edition of the novel for the American audience. In this final scene and chapter, a "visibly older" Alex finds the company of his three new droogs unsatisfying, his taste for the old ultraviolence having simply been outgrown. More conservatively dressed, rather than at the height of nadsat fashion that he wore before (and, in the novel, sentimentally carrying a newspaper photo of an infant in his wallet),

Alex takes a job at the State Music Archives cataloguing recordings of classical music. He looks forward to marriage, a happy home life, and a son of his own—a prototypical respectability that is carried even further in the novel when he encounters Pete, one of his former droogs, who has recently married and settled down to a life of "little parties . . . mostly wine-cup[s] and word-games . . . very nice, very pleasant," becoming in effect a proto-yuppie in a work written two decades before the word was coined. Alex's former life of "crasting and tolchocking" was, it seems, simply to be outgrown, since "Being young's a sort of sickness/[Like] Measles, mumps or chicken pox" (*Play*).

The 1987 version also contains a surprisingly personal coda that was cut from the 1990 adaptation. In Burgess's initial script, he specifies that at the end of the play the entire cast should reassemble on stage, "friendly as at a party while ALEX comes downstage and speaks to the audience" before joining the entire company in delivering the blatantly (and banally) didactic moral-to-the-story, sung to the tune of the "Ode to Joy" from Beethoven's Ninth:

> Do not be a clockwork orange,
> Freedom has a lovely voice,
> Here is good, and there is evil—
> Look on both, then take your choice.

The stage directions specify that during this song the cast is to be joined by "a man bearded like Stanley Kubrick [who] comes on playing, in exquisite counterpoint, 'Singin' in the Rain' on a trumpet. He is kicked off the stage" as the play ends (*Play*). Apart from its final fillip of violence, this scene exactly recapitulates the closing moments of Lindsay Anderson's film *O Lucky Man!* (1973)—which, like Kubrick's version of *A Clockwork Orange,* starred Malcolm McDowell. In Anderson's final sequence, the entire cast is shown joyously dancing at the cast party, joined in celebration by Anderson himself. Burgess's final scene is not only a final rebuke to Kubrick but a deft homage, perhaps, to Anderson's densely intertextual film, which was based on an original idea by Malcolm McDowell and is partly autobiographical. In the most obvious of the scenes that allude to *A Clockwork Orange,* an "old drunk tramp" and his derelict cohorts (i. e., geriatric droogs) take revenge on McDowell's character Mick Travis when he is himself "down and out" in London and attempts to appeal to the downtrodden using Alex's favorite term, "brothers." [In an endnote, Hutchings continues: "In *The Clockwork Testament, Or Enderby's End* (1974) Burgess makes similarly intertextual allusions in assessing the problems—and the disastrous consequences—of adapting a linguistically innovative text into cinematic form; obviously, he is satirizing the problems by which he found himself beset after the release of Kubrick's film. In this novel, the dyspeptic writer Enderby finds himself beleaguered by members of the public who were outraged over a film version of Gerard Manley Hopkins's *The Wreck of the Deutschland* which he had once suggested to a Hollywood producer but for which he did not write the final script. Apart from the title, very little of Hopkins's work survived after having been given the typical 'Hollywood treatment': its religious and intellectual content was decimated (since such arcane concerns lack appeal to the 'mass' audience), its historical period was changed for more 'historical relevance,' and the dramatic action of the shipwreck was 'enhanced' with a number of erotic flashbacks, in one of which the nuns were raped by a gang of four teenaged Nazi storm troopers—a scene which has supposedly prompted viewers to commit a series of such attacks on actual nuns, for all of which the film-maker and (especially) Enderby himself receive the blame. Yet, as outrageous as Burgess's comic invention of this filmed travesty is, it is also a deftly satirical confluence of Kubrick's *A Clockwork Orange* and Ken Russell's *The Devils*, both of which were released in 1971. The latter, which was based on John Whiting's 1961 stage adaptation of Aldous Huxley's 1936 *The Devils of Loudun*, featured several then-shocking scenes of convent carnality. Such a film, like the one based on his own novel, is a product of what Burgess has more recently termed 'the dawn of the age of candid pornography that enabled Stanley Kubrick to exploit, to a serious artistic end, those elements of the story that were meant to shock morally rather than merely titillate' (*Play*)."]

Although the concluding scene of the play—and the now-restored concluding chapter of the novel—clearly establishes the author's intent, he concedes in the introduction to the chapter as published in *Rolling Stone* that "my aesthetic judgment may have been faulty." As his American editors contended from the outset, Burgess's still vigorously defended preference for an ending showing "the capacity of regeneration in even the most depraved soul" (*Play*) does indeed seem to undermine the effectiveness of the work, particularly by undercutting its theological complexity. Though Burgess cites an intended epigraph from *The Winter's Tale* in which the shepherd remarks that "I would there were no age between ten and three-and-twenty, or that youth would sleep out the rest; for there is nothing in the between but getting wenches with child, wronging the ancientry, stealing, fighting," the necessity of the *choice* between good and evil is *not* simply to be outgrown with adolescence, as the author's preferred final scene and chapter so strongly contend. In effect, such a facile solution—like the astonishingly trite verse that expresses it—reduces the complex moral issues of free choice and personal responsibility to the uncomplicated moral strictures of James Russell Lowell's "The Present Crisis" of 1844 (whose cadence makes it no less suitable than Burgess's banal lyric to be sung to the "Ode to Joy"): "Once to every man and nation, comes the moment to decide/In the strife of Truth with Falsehood, for the good or evil side." In the modern (or postmodern) world, however, the choice of Truth and "the good . . . side" is infinitely more complex, far more ambiguous, and much less certain than Lowell would so reassuringly have us believe: the "decision" seldom if ever comes but "once," clearly drawn in black-and-white absolutes—and it is certainly not to be "outgrown" with adolescence.

During an interview with Samuel Coale in 1981, Burgess remarked that it had become "a damn nuisance" to have become associated so much with only *A Clockwork Orange,* and he added that

> I'm not particularly proud of *A Clockwork Orange,* because it has all the faults which I rail

against in fiction. It's didactic. It tends toward pornography. It's tricky. It's gimmicky. . . . The damn book . . . is not all that interesting or important. It's had a mythical impact of some kind. [*Modern Fiction Studies,* Vol. 27, No 3, 1981]

Yet, in providing still more versions of the story, Burgess has assured the continuation of both the controversy and the choice that have surrounded the novel since its appearance over a quarter of a century ago; indeed, on the opening night of the Royal Shakespeare Company's production, he reportedly denounced the play's rock score as "Neo-wallpaper"; it replaced unpublished music that Burgess himself had composed for the 1987 version (subtitled *A Play with Music*), so yet another controversy has begun. In effect, those who want to see and/or read *A Clockwork Orange* now have more choices than ever before: two different versions of the novel (one with twenty chapters, one with twenty-one), Kubrick's film, his published screenplay, and two Burgess stage adaptations are now available, with no two versions being the same. The story of Alex and his droogs has, in fact, taken on an essential mythic quality, as Joseph Campbell defined it—the ability to be transformed variously through time, while retaining much of its underlying, valuable, and original content.

## Deanna Madden   (essay date 1992)

SOURCE: "Women In Dystopia: Misogyny in *Brave New World, 1984,* and *A Clockwork Orange,*" in *Misogyny in Literature: An Essay Collection,* edited by Katherine Anne Ackley, Garland Publishing, 1992, pp. 289-313.

[*In the following excerpt, Madden discusses elements of misogyny in* A Clockwork Orange.]

The future society of *A Clockwork Orange* is a violent world in which the weak are at the mercy of the strong. Like *Brave New World* and *1984, A Clockwork Orange* portrays a patriarchal culture in which women are subordinated and peripheral. Women are perceived through the male gaze, in this case that of a fifteen-year-old delinquent, Alex. While Alex's views may reflect his immaturity, they are also a reflection of the culture in which he lives. In the Russianized teenage slang, or "nadsat," there are many words for females: "devotchka" (girl), "sharp," "cheena," "ptitsa" (a vulgar-sounding word which seems to stress their bodies, or "tits"), "baboochka," "lighter," and "forella" (the last three used only for old women). To Alex females are sexual objects perceived mainly in terms of their "groodies" (breasts). The three girls at the Milkbar in the first chapter are typical teenaged females of their society: the silver badges they wear announcing the names of boys they have slept with before age fourteen suggest their promiscuity. It is a society in which females are initiated into sexuality at a tender age and often violently: the two girls whom Alex picks up at the "disc bootick" and then rapes are only ten years old, as is the girl menaced by Billyboy and his droogs.

Alex regards females primarily as objects to rape. His attitude toward women is one aspect of his violent rebellion against society. Destructive and anti-social, he is a criminal who robs, assaults, and rapes, a sociopath who takes pleasure in venting his aggression and inflicting pain. Women are vulnerable to the violence Alex represents because he is stronger and they weaker. He demonstrates these violent sexual politics when he and his droogs rob a convenience store by assaulting the owner's wife and ripping her clothes. Later the same evening, still seeking thrills, they break into a house and brutally gang rape another woman as the culmination of their night of violence.

Old women, doubly vulnerable because of age and gender, are also victims in the novel. Alex's mother is a passive woman who tries not to aggravate her dangerous son. He perceives her as one of the "pitiable" old. She is powerless to influence him: to make him attend school, to keep him from his street violence, or even to persuade him to turn down the volume of his loud music. The old women at the Duke of New York pub are also intimidated by Alex. They are easily bullied and bribed by Alex's gang to provide the young delinquents with alibis during their crime sprees. An old woman who lives alone with a houseful of cats is Alex's last female victim. Although he is apprehended by the police during this break-in, he manages first to kill the old woman with a fatal blow.

Alex's violence toward women (and the elderly) in the early chapters of the novel make of him a sort of monster from whom the reader tends to recoil. [In an endnote Madden adds: "The technique of first person narrative plus the distancing effect of the inventive language tend to mitigate this impression, as many critics have observed. A female reader may recoil more than a male since she will find it difficult to identify with Alex's male violence directed against females and probably identify to a certain extent with the female victims."] However, when Alex becomes in turn the victim of the police, who brutally beat him, and of Dr. Brodsky and Dr. Branom, who make him the guinea pig in their diabolic experiment with the Ludovico technique (behavior modification designed to turn him into a model citizen), Alex becomes a more sympathetic character. Forced to watch horrifying films of rape, assaults, and war crimes, he is made nauseous with injections until he comes to associate violence with nausea. Alex begins to seem like a naif compared to the corrupt State which has him at its mercy. Burgess suggests that, compared to the State's crimes, Alex's crimes are small. Burgess is more alarmed by the power of the State to eradicate the individual's free choice and turn him into a machine. By using the Ludovico technique, the State plays God and interferes with the most important aspect of man—his free will. Worse yet, if the State can control Alex with this behavior modification technique, it can control others and by this means become all-powerful.

Thus, Burgess wishes the reader to view the violence which Alex and his droogs have committed as a form of choice. The reader is expected to perform the mental gymnastics of seeing that, viewed from a certain angle, violence is good, that Alex the rapist is preferable to Alex the clockwork orange. When the conditioning is reversed and Alex is returned to his old violent self, it is a victory for free will.

While this message is difficult for many readers to accept

since it appears to condone violence and in particular violence against women, another disturbing aspect of the novel is its tendency to equate rape and eroticism. Throughout most of the novel Alex's first and only impulse toward women is to rape them. He appears unable to relate to them in any other way or to feel sexually attracted without the urge to be violent. The result is to offer only two extremes of male sexual behavior. This becomes clear in Alex's appearance before a live audience after he has successfully undergone the Ludovico technique. When a nubile young woman is presented to him, he must suppress his urge to rape her to avoid the nausea it triggers. Instead he responds to her platonically, as if he is the knight and she the damsel on the pedestal. The ridiculousness of this response is made clear by the titters of laughter it elicits from the audience. Dr. Brodsky also suggests there is an obvious connection between violence and eroticism: "The sweetest and most heavenly of activities partake in some measure of violence—the act of love, for instance; music, for instance." Curing Alex's aggression amounts to emasculation. After his cure, he cannot defend himself, enjoy Beethoven (the violent classical music he prefers), or experience erotic desire. Released from prison, he is a mere shell, anxious to lose himself in drugs, depressed, and suicidal.

When *A Clockwork Orange* was first published in the United States in 1963, it omitted a final chapter that had appeared in the British edition. The difference in endings makes a considerable difference in the impression left with the reader by the novel, as Burgess notes in his Introduction to the revised American edition (1988), which includes the missing chapter. The first ending leaves the impression that Burgess endorses the violence of the clockwork orange society, for Alex's return to his old violent self is a victory for the individual. He has won out against the State which would control him. Burgess explains that he wanted instead to show that his "young thuggish protagonist grows up. He grows bored with violence and recognizes that human energy is better expended on creation than destruction. Senseless violence is a prerogative of youth. . . ."

In the restored final chapter Alex, now age eighteen, feels vaguely dissatisfied with his life. The teenaged girls at the Milkbar no longer attract him. In his wallet he carries a picture of a baby clipped from a newspaper. When he encounters his old droog Pete, now married to a pretty young woman, he is envious and begins to fantasize, in Burgess's words, "a different kind of future." In his fantasy he imagines "coming home from work to a good hot plate of dinner" prepared by a "ptitsa all welcoming and greeting like loving." But in his vision this "ptitsa" is vague, a faceless female whose main attributes are her ability to cook a hot meal, to have a fire burning on the hearth, and to welcome him home with open arms. She is less important than the child she will bear him—the baby in the next room. In true patriarchal fashion, Alex envisions the baby as a boy. The idea that he might father a daughter apparently never occurs to him. At this point in his reverie he forgets the woman, as if once she has borne his son, she is no longer important, and contemplates at length his relationship with his imaginary future son. But obviously there will be no son until first there is a mate, so he tells himself that what he must do next is find "some devotchka or other who would be a mother to this son." She is, it seems, just a necessary next step in achieving his ultimate goal—an heir. Thus, while the final chapter shows Alex turning away from rape and violence, his image of women merely changes from targets of rape to useful breeders. He never sees them as human beings equal to himself.

It might be argued that Alex's attitude toward women reflects his own warped mentality and the violence of his clockwork orange culture, not Burgess's views, but the salient feature of violence remains, especially violence against women. Then there is the disturbing linking of eroticism and rape. Alex's final attitude toward women as breeders of sons also calls into consideration Burgess's own attitudes toward women, since this is where he ultimately wishes to lead the reader. The focus is not only on a male protagonist who has failed to figure out any way of relating to females except to rape them, beat them, impregnate them, or, as in the case of his mother and his future wife, to be served by them, but on a male who ultimately only relates to another male, his mirror image, his son.

Critics have suggested that the misogyny to be found in Burgess's work may have its roots in his personal life. His mother died when he was two years old, his stepmother did not love him, and his first wife, to whom he was married for twenty-six years, was repeatedly unfaithful to him. In his autobiography *Little Wilson and Big God,* Burgess describes this marriage as marked by many infidelities on both sides. The curiously neutral manner in which he relates his wife's infidelities conceals how he felt about them, but the reader infers he must have been hurt by her refusal from the beginning of their relationship to be exclusive. Burgess implies that since she chose to be unfaithful, he saw no reason why he too should not be. In spite of the adulteries, he claims to have loved her. The issue of female promiscuity arises in *A Clockwork Orange* in the form of the devotchkas in the Milkbar with their silver medals and the ten-year-old girls who wear padded bras and lipstick.

Another influence on Burgess's attitude toward women was no doubt his Roman Catholicism. While Burgess now considers himself a lapsed Catholic, his work is permeated by ideas drawn from the Catholic Church, such as the doctrine of original sin. Burgess is a highly moral writer, interested in man's spiritual dimension and his relation to God (or "Bog" in *A Clockwork Orange*). According to his autobiography, the early influence of Catholicism caused him to regard sex as sinful and instilled in him feelings of guilt.

One of the most brutal scenes involving a female in *A Clockwork Orange* is the gang rape of F. Alexander's wife. Burgess has confessed that this incident had its origins in an assault on his wife in 1944 by four men. While the assault was brutal (Burgess's wife Lynne was kicked unconscious and subsequently suffered a miscarriage), it was not a rape. Burgess, who was stationed in Gibraltar at the time, felt anger at the American GI deserters who had attacked her and at his commanding officers for refusing him leave to rush to her. Both in his wife's promiscuity

and in her assault, Burgess must have felt a lack of control over her body. By rewriting the incident as a rape which the husband is forced to watch helplessly, he includes his own feelings of anger, frustration, and guilt.

Elsewhere Burgess's comments on the subject of rape, however, must strike a female reader as remarkably callous. He admits in his Introduction to *A Clockwork Orange* that in writing the novel he "enjoyed raping and ripping by proxy." These are not emotions that the typical female reader would share. When he dismisses Alex's acts of violence, including rape, as a sort of phase that Alex will outgrow, the female reader may balk. Does Burgess really expect us to agree that "senseless violence is a prerogative of youth"? Is it simply a part of growing up that young males should rape? And when Alex observes that his son will probably do all the things he has done, should we feel no shiver of horror?

Kate Millett in *Sexual Politics* points out that the threat of rape in a patriarchal society can be an "instrument of intimidation." It is a way of keeping women subordinate. She also notes that "patriarchal societies typically link feelings of cruelty with sexuality, the latter often equated with evil and power." Perhaps this helps to explain why rape is linked to eroticism in Burgess's novel. But clearly rape is an act of aggression in which the chief motive is to inflict hurt and thereby assert the rapist's power. As Millett explains, "In rape, the emotions of aggression, hatred, contempt, and the desire to break or violate personality take a form consummately appropriate to sexual politics."

The world of *A Clockwork Orange* is a distorted mirror world of London in the early 1960's and also of Russia. [In an endnote, the critic comments that "Burgess travelled to Russia shortly before writing *A Clockwork Orange* and noted the phenomenon of youth gangs there."] Many of its images are identifiable reflections of a contemporary society which regards young women as sex objects and exploits them. In the convenience store which Alex and his droogs rob stands "a big cut-out showing a sharp [female] with all her zoobies [teeth] going flash at the customers and her groodies [breasts] near hanging out to advertise some new brand of cancers [cigarettes]." The novel also reflects contemporary society's devaluation of the older woman, who having lost her youth and attractiveness, finds herself powerless and despised.

---

## FURTHER READING

### Bibliography

Coale, Samuel. *Anthony Burgess.* New York: Frederick Ungar, 1981, pp. 209-15.
> Listing of secondary sources, including doctoral dissertations on Burgess.

————. "Criticism of Anthony Burgess: A Selected Checklist." *Modern Fiction Studies* 27, No. 3 (Autumn 1981): 533-36.

Listing of secondary sources, including general essays, interviews, and discussions of specific works.

## Criticism

Dix, Carol M. *Anthony Burgess.* Burnt Mill, Harlow, Essex, England: Longman, 1971, 31 p.

General overview of Burgess' life and works through 1971.

Evans, Robert O. "The *Nouveau Roman,* Russian Dystopias, and Anthony Burgess." In *British Novelists Since 1900,* pp. 253-66. New York: AMS Press, 1987.

Discusses the place of Burgess's works within the genre of the dystopian novel.

Hammer, Stephanie Barbé. "Conclusion: Resistance, Metaphysics, and the Aesthetics of Failure in Modern Criminal Literature." In *The Sublime Crime: Fascination, Failure, and Form in Literature of the Enlightenment,* pp. 154-74. Carbondale and Edwardsville, IL: Southern Illinois University Press, 1994.

Discusses *A Clockwork Orange* as an example of "criminal literature."

LeClair, Thomas. "Essential Opposition: The Novels of Anthony Burgess." *Critique* XII, No. 3 (1971): 77-94.

Argues that there is a "dialectic of opposites" that structures meaning in Burgess's novels.

Nehring, Neil. "The Shifting Relations of Literature and Popular Music in Postwar England." *Discourse* 12, No. 1 (Fall-Winter 1989-1990): 78-103.

Discussion of literature and music in relation to youth subculture in England.

## Interviews

Coale, Samuel. "An Interview with Anthony Burgess." *Modern Fiction Studies* 27, No. 3 (Autumn 1981): 429-52.

Discussion of Burgess's personal life and his views on religion and modernism in literature.

Cullinan, John, "Anthony Burgess." *The Paris Review* 14, No. 56 (Spring 1973): 119-63.

Discussion of Burgess's writing techniques, influences, and his views on music, Catholicism, and politics.

---

**Additional coverage of Burgess' life and career is contained in the following sources published by Gale Research:** *Authors in the News,* **Vol. 1;** *Concise Dictionary of British Literary Biography, 1960 to Present; Contemporary Authors,* **Vols. 1-4, rev. ed., 143 [obituary];** *Contemporary Authors New Revision Series,* **Vols. 2, 46;** *Contemporary Literary Criticism,* **Vols. 1, 2, 4, 5, 8, 10, 13, 15, 22, 40, 62, 81;** *Dictionary of Literary Biography,* **Vol. 14;** *DISCovering Authors: British Edition; DISCovering Authors Modules: Novelists* **and** *Major 20th-Century Writers.*

# Edwidge Danticat

## 1969-

Haitian-born American novelist and short story writer.

## INTRODUCTION

Winner of a Pushcart Short Story Prize and a finalist for a National Book Award in 1995, Danticat has received positive critical attention for her first novel, *Breath, Eyes, Memory* (1994), and her short story collection *Krik? Krak!* (1995).

### Biographical Information

Born in Haiti, Danticat was separated from her parents at the age of four when they emigrated to the United States. In 1981 she joined her family in Brooklyn, New York. Recognized for her depictions of the Haitian experience both in Haiti and the United States, Danticat has been described by Margaria Fichtner as a writer whose work "has much to say about what it is like to be young, black, Haitian and female wandering in a world too often eager to regard all of those conditions as less than worthwhile."

### Major Works

*Breath, Eyes, Memory,* told through the eyes of Sophie Caco, details the lives of four generations of Haitian women as they struggle against poverty, violence, and prejudice in Haiti and the United States. Encompassing contemporary Haitian history, the novel portrays the country's recent upheavals at the hands of the Duvalier regime and its brutal secret police, the Tonton Macoutes. While the stories in *Krik? Krak!*—the title refers to a Haitian storytelling game in which one person's story is exchanged for another—employ a wide range of plot types and characters, each story is, as Ellen Kanner has explained, "part of the same tale. Women lose who and what they love to poverty, to violence, to politics, to ideals."

### Critical Reception

Most commentators have found Danticat's works to be powerful fictions conveyed with sure-handed style. *Breath, Eyes, Memory* has been praised by many critics for its lyric language, which off-sets and counterpoints the novel's at times dire subject matter. Some reviewers of the novel suggested that Danticat did not display complete control of her material in this book, lavishing detailed descriptive passages on things and events that did not warrant them. But most point out that this is a flaw common to many first novels. Critics have lauded *Krik? Krak!* for the diversity of narrative voices and literary styles presented in the stories. Danticat is again praised for making potentially downbeat material readable and enjoyable through her skillful, lyrical use of language. Critics have

noted that some of the stories reveal a too self-conscious manipulation of form and structure, a false note of "preciousness" that detracts from their realism. Most critics agree with Richard Eder, however, that the "best of [the stories], using the island tradition of a semi-magical folktale, or the witty, between-two-worlds voices of modern urban immigrants, are pure beguiling transformation."

## PRINCIPAL WORKS

*Breath, Eyes, Memory* (novel) 1994
*Krik? Krak!* (short stories) 1995

# CRITICISM

### Mary Mackay  (review date Fall 1994)

SOURCE: "Living, Seeing, Remembering," in *Belles Lettres: A Review of Books by Women,* Vol. 10, No. 1, Fall, 1994, pp. 36, 38.

[*In the following positive review of* Breath, Eyes, Memory, *Mackay praises Danticat for her "extraordinary optimism," "vivid characterization," and "allusive language."*]

Edwidge Danticat dedicates her powerful first novel [**Breath, Eyes, Memory**] to "The brave women of Haiti . . . on this shore and other shores. We have stumbled but we will not fall." Such optimism is extraordinary, given the everyday adversity faced by the women whose stories are interwoven with that of Sophie, the narrator.

Grandmother Ifé, mother Martine, aunt Atie, and daughter Sophie (and later Sophie's daughter, Brigitte) are rooted as firmly in their native Haitian soil as they are bound to one another, despite the ocean, experiences, and years that separate them. The ties to Haiti, the women's certainty of meeting there at the "very end of each of our journeys," affords their only apparent security. "Somehow, early on, our song makers and tale weavers had decided that we were all daughters of this land," Danticat writes. Structurally, the book reflects the centrality of Haiti: the longest of its four sections takes place there, although covering only a few days in a novel that covers years.

The story begins in Haiti. Through Sophie's 12-year-old eyes, the island seems a paradise of bougainvillea, poincianas, and the unconditional love of Tante Atie. Then Martine, the mother Sophie knew only as a photograph, sends for her from New York City. It seems a mean place that has worn out her mother: "It was as though she had never stopped working in the cane fields after all." Sophie is haunted by the hardships of immigrant life, together with the ghosts from the past and the burdens of womanhood in a hostile world. She describes herself as a frightened insomniac, but somehow survives the test. Her older, jazz-musician husband, Joseph, one of the novel's few male characters and certainly the most loyal and gentle, gives her some strength. She copes through a resilient mélange of love, ties to home, and therapy. And when she returns to Haiti as an adult, she senses a sinister edge to the place, represented by the Tonton Macoutes (militiamen), the boat people, and her Tante Atie's bitterness.

"There is always a place where nightmares are passed on through generations like heirlooms," writes Danticat. In this book, one of those places is "testing," part of a "virginity cult, our mothers' obsession with keeping us pure and chaste," in which the mother probes her daughter's vagina (sometime violently) to see if she is still *whole.* She also listens to her daughter peeing to see if the sound suggests a deflowered, widened passage. Even rape has one positive result: the end of "testing" by an otherwise trusted mother. The invasiveness, pain, and humiliation turn daughter against mother generation after generation, Atie against Ifé, Sophie against Martine.

But there is reconciliation, too. As mothers and daughters, the women are bound in love as in hate. A mother may inflict on her daughter the same pain that drove her from her own mother. Why? "I did it because my mother had done it to me. I have no greater excuse." The book is a plea to end these divisive rituals. Mothers indeed long to break the cycle of pain, asking pointedly from beyond the grave, " 'Ou libéré?' Are you free, my daughter?"

Suffering inflicted by a well-intentioned mother is all the more treacherous in a world where the birth of a girl child is marked by "no lamps, no candles, no more light." Danticat leaves the reader with no illusions as to why the welcome is so dark. As well as "testing," the women in this family endure rape, unwanted pregnancy, and violence that lead to mental illness, nightmares, sexual phobias, bulimia, and self-mutilation. Breast cancer seems almost benign in this context; being unmarried and childless does not.

---

In a personal essay, Danticat calls Haiti a "rich landscape of memory." But she is afraid that female storytellers like herself may be Haiti's last surviving breath, eyes, and memory. In this compelling novel, the reader experiences the Haiti that Danticat fears will be lost.

—*Mary Mackay*

---

Sophie wants and seems to be the hope for breaking with painful tradition. Returning to Haiti with her mother's body for burial, she reaches an important understanding: the testing was painful for Martine, too. Doing what she had to do as a Haitian woman, "My mother was as brave as stars at dawn." Sophie breaks free as she madly attacks the sugar cane in the midst of which her father had raped and impregnated her mother. We sense that Sophie—and Brigitte—are finally safe.

Despite all the suffering (" 'Can one really die of chagrin?' I asked Tante Atie."), Danticat writes with a light and lyrical touch. Her characterization is vivid, her allusive language richly unembellished. Color (literal as well as linguistic) carries the reader from the daffodil yellow associated with Haiti and Sophie's early days in New York, to the more ominous red with which her mother surrounds herself in interior decoration as in death.

Occasionally Danticat devotes too many details to a banal incident or action, but this is a minor criticism for a first novel.

In a personal essay, Danticat calls Haiti a "rich landscape of memory." But she is afraid that female storytellers like herself may be Haiti's last surviving breath, eyes, and memory. In this compelling novel, the reader experiences the Haiti that Danticat fears will be lost.

**Garry Pierre-Pierre   (essay date 26 January 1995)**

SOURCE: "Haitian Tales, Flatbush Scenes," in *The New York Times,* January 26, 1995, pp. C1, C8.

[*In the following essay, based on discussions with Danticat, Pierre-Pierre examines her past in Haiti and her present life as a Haitian-American living in Brooklyn.*]

It was the kind of dark, cold New York winter day that sundrenched people from the Caribbean dread. But Edwidge Danticat, a 25-year-old Haitian-American novelist who immigrated to Brooklyn a little more than a dozen years ago, would not let it dampen her spirits.

"You want some coffee, tea?" she said in a soft melodic voice, as if the liquids would warm the day. "The tea is cannelle."

So Ms. Danticat (her name is pronounced ed-WEEDJ dahn-tee-CAH), the author of **Breath, Eyes, Memory,** her first novel, which was published by Soho Press last spring and received respectful reviews, set small flowered, ceramic cups on a coffee table. She settled into a plastic-covered velour chair in the beige-carpeted living room of her parents' attached brick home in East Flatbush and explained that the cannelles, or cinnamon sticks, had been bought just blocks away, from Haitian street vendors.

"It's wonderful," she said, pouring the steamy light brown liquid into the cup. "It's like 'infusion' tea. Haitians think of tea as a cure-all."

While much is written about the troubled, mountainous island nation, Ms. Danticat's debut novel is probably the first to chronicle the Haitian-American experience. In the last decade, the number of Haitian-Americans has grown to more than a million; their communities are centered in New York and Miami.

The book is about four generations of Haitian women who struggle to overcome poverty, powerlessness and abuse. The story is told through the point of view of Sophie Caco, a teen-ager who, after spending years with her aunt in rural Haiti, is reunited with her mother in Brooklyn. Sophie feels compelled to return to Haiti after she learns that her birth resulted from her mother's rape there.

Critics have praised Ms. Danticat's vivid sense of place and her images of fear and pain, which have been compared to Alice Walker's.

The *New York Times Book Review* said the book "achieves an emotional complexity that lifts it out of the realm of the potboiler and into that of poetry."

Ms. Danticat has dared to probe into some of the most painful and hidden Haitian traditions, including "testing," a mostly rural practice in which a mother inserts her fingers in her daughter's vagina to ascertain that she is still a virgin.

"Haitian men, they insist that their women are virgins and have their 10 fingers," Sophie's aunt says after Sophie is tested, explaining to her the virtues of virginity and the reasons for testing.

Sitting in her living room, Ms. Danticat said that among Haitian-American women, "there is a great deal of rage toward the book." At readings across the country, she said, some of the strongest opposition comes from middle-class Haitian-American women who consider themselves modern and liberated. They are ashamed of things like testing, she said, and some, raised in cities, are shocked to learn that it is exists.

"I think a lot of people see Haiti as the good guys against the bad guys," she said. "It is so much more complex than that."

Ms. Danticat insisted that the story is not about herself, although she too was raised for several years by an aunt in Port-au-Prince after her parents—her father, André, is a cabdriver, and her mother, Rose, is a factory worker—left for Brooklyn in search of a new and better life. She said the most autobiographical aspect of the book is the heroine's emotional reaction to coming to America. Like Sophie, Ms. Danticat said it left her feeling severed from her roots.

"The first time was when my mother left, when I was 4," Ms. Danticat said. "I remember vividly being yanked from her as she was getting on the plane. The second time was coming here. My uncle had a laryngectomy. At that time I was the only person who could read his lips and understand what he was saying. Without me he would have had no voice."

Ms. Danticat began working on what became her first novel soon after she arrived in Brooklyn, in 1981. Taunted at school for her Creole lilt and her not-so-hip wardrobe and coiffure, she found solace in her writing. Even her dimpled and expansive smile faded as she recalled the painful memories of those early years in New York.

"It was very hard," she said, shifting in her chair as if to dispel an intense feeling that was still with her. " 'Haitian' was like a curse. People were calling you, 'Frenchy, go back to the banana boat,' and a lot of the kids would lie about where they came from. They would say anything but Haitian."

It was a time when the bodies of Haitian boat people routinely washed up on the beaches of South Florida. The early 1980's was also a time when Haitians were officially classified as a high-risk group for AIDS by the Centers for Disease Control in Atlanta.

Her love for Haiti and things Haitian, of which she spoke again and again in the course of a day's visit, was deepened by memories of neighbors in her first building who helped her through the tough years.

On Sundays, they shared pumpkin soups, as people do in Haiti. They looked after each other.

"It was a . . . la cour," she said, referring to a Haitian courtyard, where almost communal living is commonplace among the poor, especially in the countryside. "It was a shelter in a storm."

The ambiance at that building, in Flatbush, was not too different from that in Bel Air, the teeming Port-au-Prince slum where Ms. Danticat spent 12 years before coming to America.

"This friend of mine kept saying that in Haiti his mother had a maid, but here his mother *is* a maid," she said. "I can be friends with women that, if we lived in Haiti, our paths would never cross. People where I was from were the maids."

Ms. Danticat, however, has become a quintessential Haitian-American, living in both worlds and speaking flawless American English interrupted with an occasional Creole word.

She dresses smartly and conservatively. On this day she was wearing an ankle-length black skirt, a black sweater and moccasins; her hair was in long, narrow braids. She looked every bit the Barnard College and Brown University graduate that she is.

She has blended her two worlds, and when she talks about her beloved East Flatbush, her delight shows through.

She relishes the sounds of calypso, compa and reggae that thunder from the assorted shops along Avenue D in the East 40's, a stone's throw from her parents' home. The conversations on the streets are enlivened by hints of the Caribbean, peppered with a Haitian Creole clip here and a Spanish intonation there.

In fact, after living in Providence, R.I., where she earned a Master of Fine Arts degree at Brown, she craved the familiarity of East Flatbush and rushed back to Brooklyn and her family, which includes three brothers—Eliab, 24, a teacher in the Bronx, and Kelly, 20, and Carl, 18, both college students.

"To me, Brooklyn is the world," she says, adding that she tells people she is from Brooklyn by way of Haiti. "I can eat Haitian food or any food I want. You just can't get that anywhere."

In the tradition of Haitian families, where art and literature are seen more as pastimes that vocations, her parents still think of her as unemployed.

But she is very much at work.

A tiny room on the second floor, decorated with her Alpha Kappa Alpha relics and African tarot stickers, serves as her bedroom and office.

She writes on a Macintosh that is perched on a desk under a loft bed. It is there she completed a second book, *Krik? Krak!,* a collection of short stories to be published by Soho in April. She is doing research on another novel about Haitian sugar-cane cutters in the Dominican Republic.

When she rejoined her family in New York in 1981, Ms. Danticat told her father of her aspiration to become a writer. But he had other ideas. He told her she could write on weekends. A more respectable profession like medicine would be more suitable, he thought.

"My parents think that it's a hobby that ended up well," she said of her writing. "The only time that my work seemed honorable was when they came to the book party. That's when they finally grasped the importance of it."

During her high school years, Ms. Danticat said, she barely spoke above a whisper because she was embarrassed by her accent, which has now faded to almost nothing.

Having published her novel, she has to wear the mantle of being "the voice" of Haitian-Americans. It is a responsibility that she has accepted hesitantly.

"I think I have been assigned that role, but I don't really see myself as the voice for the Haitian-American experience," she said. "There are many. I'm just one."

---

**An excerpt from *Breath, Eyes, Memory***

The streets along Flatbush Avenue reminded me of home. My mother took me to Haiti Express, so I could see the place where she sent our money orders and cassettes from.

It was a small room packed with Haitians. People stood on line patiently waiting their turn. My mother slipped Tante Atie's cassette into a padded envelope. As we waited on line, an old fan circled a spider's web above our heads.

A chubby lady greeted my mother politely when we got to the window.

"This is Sophie," my mother said through the holes in the thick glass. "She is the one who has given you so much business over the years."

The lady smiled as she took my mother's money and the package. I kept feeling like there was more I wanted to send to Tante Atie. If I had the power then to shrink myself and slip into the envelope, I would have done it.

I watched as the lady stamped our package and dropped it on top of a larger pile. Around us were dozens of other people trying to squeeze all their love into small packets to send back home.

After we left, my mother stopped at a Haitian beauty salon to buy some castor oil for her hair. Then we went to a small boutique and bought some long skirts and blouses for me to wear to school. My mother said it was important that I learn English quickly. Otherwise, the American students would make fun of me or, even worse, beat me. A lot of other mothers from the nursing home where she worked had told her that their children were getting into fights in school because they were accused of having HBO—Haitian Body Odor. Many of the American kids even accused Haitians of having AIDS because they had heard on television that only the "Four Hs" got AIDS—Heroin addicts, Hemophiliacs, Homosexuals, and Haitians.

I wanted to tell my mother that I didn't want to go to school. Frankly, I was afraid. I tried to think of something to keep me from having to go. Sickness or death were probably the only two things that my mother would accept as excuses.

*Edwidge Danticat, in* Breath, Eyes, Memory, *Soho Press, 1994.*

**Richard Eder   (review date 30 March 1995)**

SOURCE: "A Haitian Fantasy and Exile," in *Newsday,* March 30, 1995, pp. B2, B25.

*[In the following favorable review of* Krik? Krak!, *Eder describes some of Danticat's stories as "pure beguiling transformation."]*

"Beyond the mountains there are mountains" goes one of the Haitian proverbs that work their tutelary spirit through Edwidge Danticat's stories. The Creole sayings of that misfortunate island keep it in one particular sense from being utterly bereft. For Haitians to hurl those six laconic words at the harshness that forbids them passage is to acknowledge it and lift it at the same time. Haiti's proverbs, like Chekhov's plays, light up what rises when men and women are borne down.

So do the best of these pieces by a young and beautifully voiced Haitian-American writer. When Guy falls to his death from the balloon he has stolen, or Celiane jumps after the dead baby she has hurled from the raft in which she is fleeing Haiti, or an old immigrant woman turns to laugh and be reconciled with her bitter past, Danticat's words go the opposite way from the terrible things she writes so truly about.

Can words redeem starvation? If they could anywhere it would be in Haiti, one of whose greatest proverbs mocks hunger with a sudden expulsion of the breath: "If you cannot eat from a plate of soup you can always spit in it."

Of the stories in ***Krik? Krak!***—the traditional spoken invocation to a Creole folktale—one or two beautify their pathos with a little too much arranging. The best of them, using the island tradition of a semi-magical folk-tale, or the witty, between-two-worlds voices of modern urban immigrants, are pure beguiling transformation.

**"A Wall of Fire Rising"** uses a man's dream of freedom and the frail sanctuary of a family home that can neither keep out the dream nor survive it. It is told wonderfully well, in the voice of a little boy whose father, Guy, struggles desperately for an occasional meager job at the sugar mill, and whose mother, Lili, walks two miles each morning to fetch water.

The child lives in the sweetness that his parents fight to maintain. To Lili, though, Guy speaks of his despair at living in the same wretchedness that enslaved their parents; and of his dream of flying in a balloon that belongs to the mill's owners. God would have given men wings had He meant them to fly, she says. No, Guy replies, what He has given them is a reason to fly: "the air, the birds, our son."

Like millennia of women whose men's longings have made windows of them, Lili is tragically skeptical. But when Guy takes the balloon and falls to his death she refuses the foreman's request that she close his eyes: "My husband, he likes to look at the sky."

That is moving but not quite finished. In another story we hear that Lili killed herself years later when her son moved to Miami. Irony cuts the uplift; curiously, it lifts it higher. In a powerful, ghastly story, a Port au Prince maid, unable to bear a child, finds a dead baby, names it Rose and hides

it for days, washing it frequently to dispel the odor. Finally she tries to bury it at night beside the swimming pool. Though he has been her lover, the gardener calls the police. (However far the poor are from the rich, they are even farther from each other.) Again, the lofty gothic horror gets a twist of Haitian irony. "We made a pretty picture standing there," the maid remarks. "Rose, me, him. Between the pool and the gardenias, waiting for the law."

**"Caroline's Wedding"** is set in New York where two sisters who teach in the city schools live with their mother. They are mainly American; Gracina is about to get her U.S. passport and Caroline will marry her Bahamian fiancé, Eric. The prospect scandalizes Ma, who maintains her Haitian ways and longs for the formalities of a village engagement.

For Ma, America is exile. When one daughter dons a T-shirt for a softball game, Ma sews on a lace collar. It is a perpetual duel with Eric, who goes to the trouble of cooking Ma a dinner only to be snubbed because it doesn't taste Haitian. There are layers of comedy and, interleaved, of loss and bitterness. The deepest bitterness is a memory. Her husband, who drove a New York taxi to provide for them until he died, had divorced her in Haiti to marry a woman in America so he could immigrate; then he divorced the woman and remarried Ma. It was done out of extremity and love, but it killed love between them. They were never intimate again.

Danticat tells of Ma's gradual reconciliation; at the end, she accepts Eric and brings herself to tell her late husband's favorite joke. In a way **"Caroline's Wedding"** is a variation on other tragicomedies of two generations of immigrants—Italian, Jewish, Chinese. But that does not make it less precious or original. In our literary ecology each species is treasured: The finch is no less a miracle because there are warblers, wrens and thrushes.


**Joanne Omang   (review date 14 May 1995)**

SOURCE: A review of *Krik? Krak!* in *Book World-The Washington Post,* May 14, 1995, p. 4.

*[In the following review of* Krik? Krak!, *Omang observes that "Danticat seems to be overflowing with the strength and insight of generations of Haitian women."]*

In Haitian-American Edwidge Danticat, modern Haiti may have found its voice. "When you write," she says in an epilogue, "it's like braiding your hair," and into these nine short stories she has woven the sad with the funny, the unspeakable with the glorious, the wild horror and deep love that is Haiti today.

Only 26, Danticat seems to be overflowing with the strength and insight of generations of Haitian women. In the past under Papa Doc, in New York now and on the leaky rafts in between, she speaks through the dead and through the living and the walking wounded alike, her tone changing without apparent effort to be as various as the need.

**"Children of the Sea"** is virtually flawless, a heartbreaking exchange of letters never sent, never received, between a young woman and her lover as his leaky boat full of people drifts toward Miami. All the island's troubles are braided seamlessly into these letters.

Trying not to think about their prospects, the refugees tell stories: "Someone says, Krik? You answer, Krak! And they say, I have many stories I could tell you, and then they go on and tell these stories to you, but mostly to themselves." A woman who gives birth on that boat to a baby who doesn't cry reappears four stories later in **"Between the Pool and the Gardenias."** Her barren goddaughter, a rich family's maid half-crazed from loneliness, finds an abandoned baby on the street, another child who doesn't cry.

---

**Only 26, Danticat seems to be overflowing with the strength and insight of generations of Haitian women.**

*—Joanne Omang*

---

And the maid's grandmother is the subject of **"1937,"** in which she is imprisoned for witchcraft, her head shaved, starving, but still able to make a statue of the Madonna cry. In **"Night Women,"** a hard-working mother watches her son sleep and thinks of "women who sit up through the night and undo patches of cloth that they have spent the whole day weaving . . . so that they will always have more to do." The image of Penelope, waiting for a man, is breathtaking.

Danticat's longest tales appear to be autobiographical portraits of her family, and we can only be grateful for them. If the news from Haiti is too painful to read, read this book instead and understand the place far more deeply than you ever thought possible.

**Paul Moses** (essay date 21 May 1995)

SOURCE: "Haitian Dream, Brooklyn Memory," in *Newsday,* May 21, 1995, p. A52.

[*In the following essay, Moses provides an overview of Danticat's life and career.*]

Novelist Edwidge Danticat remembers that when she went to junior high school in Crown Heights, it was hard to be proud of being Haitian.

The newcomers took separate classes taught in Creole. When they gathered with other students, they were met with taunts that Haitians had AIDS. "There were a lot of fights with blood, because when teased, the students would react," Danticat remembers.

But childhood memories have served Danticat well, helping to inspire her in writing two books that have won her national attention at the age of 26. Her work has brought the Haitian immigrant experience to the American literary world and introduced a new chapter in the literature of Brooklyn.

In an interview last month in the living room of her East Flatbush home, she was serene but full of anticipation. She sat straight up in an easy chair and said she looked forward to a national book tour.

Her 1994 novel, **Breath, Eyes, Memory,** had just been issued by Vintage Books in paperback; a collection of short stories, **Krik? Krak!,** was released that day by Soho Press.

"It's hard to imagine it all started last year," she said as she described her plans to travel to Atlanta, Washington, D.C., Seattle, Los Angeles, San Francisco, Chicago and Minneapolis to promote her books.

They were new places for Danticat, who moved to Brooklyn at the age of 12.

Like the people she writes about, her life has been detoured by the politics and hardships of her homeland. Her father, Andre, a taxi driver, left Haiti when she was a toddler. Her mother, Rose, a factory worker, followed when she was 4. She remained behind to be raised by an aunt.

In her novel, she writes about Sophie Caco, who took a similar path.

"It's something we're always trying to define, what it means for our children, when they lead half their lives in one place and half their lives in another," Danticat said.

Sophie loves the yellow daffodils, the smell of cinnamon rice pudding, the plantains, the yams, the magical stories and games of childhood in Haiti. And she loves her Tante Atie, who raised her.

"You kind of know more the wonderfulness of it as a child," Danticat said of her homeland.

But Haiti's troubled politics also intrude on Sophie's life. As she heads for Port-au-Prince to catch a flight to New York, her aunt hurries her away as soldiers shoot and beat demonstrators.

When Sophie arrives in Brooklyn, there are fights over "HBO"—Haitian body odor. "Many of the American kids even accused Haitians of having AIDS because they heard on television that only the 'Four H's' got AIDS—heroin addicts, hemophiliacs, homosexuals and Haitians," Danticat wrote.

That detail comes from her years at Jackie Robinson Intermediate School in Crown Heights. "The most autobiographical part involves my childhood because my story is very similar," Danticat said.

She went on to Clara Barton High School in Prospect Heights, where she wrote about her experiences for New Youth Connections, the citywide newspaper for high school students.

"When she was a ninth grader, she was in my writing class. I really was very impressed with her," said teacher Fay Thomas. "She was very creative and wrote well. The thing that I really remember about her is that she was very quiet in class, very conscientious."

Guidance counselor Marianne Finn recalled Danticat, who graduated in 1986, as a very quiet and family-oriented young lady.

"She pretty much stood in the background, very shy, extremely reticent about speaking up," she said. Then she saw Danticat on the "MacNeil-Lehrer Newshour," outspoken on immigration issues. "I said this is not the Edwidge I knew, by no means."

Danticat got her bachelor's degree from Barnard College and then a master of fine arts degree from Brown University—the novel was her thesis—before returning home to live with her parents and three brothers.

Today, home is a quiet side street off Avenue D. with spacious, one-family brick-and-frame detached houses, a block association, friendly neighbors and birds chirping in the trees.

"For a long time, Brooklyn was America. It's a place that has made a big impression on me," she said. She enjoys watching how people of many national origins adapt to life here.

"People are re-creating home all over Brooklyn," she said. "The way I see Brooklyn, it's like a country, a world with all its neighborhoods. There's a lot here, especially for immigrants. For Haitian immigrants, it's often a first stop."

This theme of adapting to change appears in the longest story in her new collection.

The story, **"Caroline's Wedding,"** focuses on two Haitian-American sisters and their mother. One sister has just become a U.S. citizen, the other is about to marry an American man despite her mother's uneasiness.

"I kind of pictured it happening in this house," she said.

The scene is indeed East Flatbush, right down to the B-8 bus.

Danticat's work "has been extremely well received in the Caribbean community, especially in the Haitian community," said Règine Latortue, chairwoman of the Africana Studies Department and professor of comparative black literature at Brooklyn College.

Her first book, Latortue added, "is the first novel we know of entirely in English by a Haitian woman. . . . In many ways, she is a pioneer."

"Naturally there are some reservations," continued Latortue, an immigrant from Haiti. "Particularly about her depiction of the family practice that she describes."

She was referring to passages in the novel about "testing," a practice in which mothers physically examine their daughters to check whether they are virgins. In the novel, it is seen as contributing to sexual dysfunction.

"Almost virtually everybody says that has not been done in their families," Latortue said. ". . . But other than that, and that really has riled people up, people are happy."

"We don't really talk comfortably about these things in our culture," said Danticat. She said people have told her:

"There's so many things negative [that] people say about us. Why would you want to write about this?"

But for the most part, "I think people in the community in general are very kind," she said. "Women will say, 'Thank you for telling our story.'"

### Kimberly Hébert    (review date June 1995)

SOURCE: "A Testament to Survival," in *Quarterly Black Review,* June, 1995, p. 6.

[*In the following review, Hébert applauds* Krik? Krak! *for its stories about Haitians and their lives in Haiti, but notes that Danticat never fully examines the complicated relationship between Haitian-Americans and America.*]

And over the years when you have needed us, you have always cried "Krik?" and we have answered "Krak!" and it has shown us that you have not forgotten us.

Edwidge Danticat's powerful collection of short stories, **Krik? Krak!** is a complicated, yet connected, chorus of Haitian voices affirming survival. Each one explores how memories of Haiti are passed on from one generation to the next—how Haiti will live on in the children of exiles in the United States, in the children of those who survived.

We know people by their stories.

Born in 1969 during the dictatorial regime of Papa Doc Duvalier, Danticat, author of the novel **Breath, Eyes, Memory,** was 4 years old when her parents emigrated to the United States and left her behind. She would not be able to join them until she was 12. The stories she tells—filled with such horrible details of rape, incest, extreme poverty, violent death—make you wonder what happened during those eight years of her development. But the awful-ness of the pain and the tragedy of Haitian poverty are not all Danticat has to tell. She weaves a rich web of remembered rituals and dream fragments that connects the first story to the last. As the stories progress from one to the next, we realize that Danticat is tracing a family lineage, a history of people related by circumstance.

They say behind the mountain are more mountains. Now I know it's true.

**"Children of the Sea"** is the first and most powerful story in the collection. A 20-year-old radio show host is hunted down by the military because he has spoken against its overthrow of the government. He (we never know his name) escapes the island, along with 36 others who are also fleeing political persecution and certain death, leaving behind the young woman he wants to marry. The story is told through their "letters": hers, from the midst of turmoil and violence in Haiti's cities and countryside; his from a makeshift raft in the middle of the Caribbean Sea. The cruel irony is that, of course, neither knows if the other is still alive. In the midst of such tragedy, the tale that sustains the young exile adrift at sea is of "the children of the deep blue sea, those who have escaped the chains of slavery to form a world beneath the heavens and the blood-drenched earth where you live."

Life is never lost, another one always comes up to replace the last.

In **"Nineteen Thirty-Seven,"** Danticat takes us inside the walls of a Haitian prison. Images of shaven heads, torture and the burning of bodies are reminiscent of the Jewish holocaust. Told from the viewpoint of a daughter whose mother, a suspected witch, is imprisoned to keep her from "flying," we learn of ritual passed down from mother to daughter to protect them from the horrors of the present, the future, and most of all the past. Stories about the women's power became accusations of infanticide: "They were said to have been seen at night rising from the ground like birds on fire. . . . *Lougarou*, witch, criminal!" Danticat's stories often examine this fear of the female principle and its power of passing on stories, and consequently, culture.

What kind of legends will your daughters be told? What kind of charms will you give them to ward off evil?

Like the maternal power she invokes, Danticat's Haiti has a power to destroy and to create. Its people are caught between a place they want to be and the place they have to be. In her other stories set in Haiti, there are suicides, prostitution, miscarriages, murders. The sun shines while the people suffer. Her characters are individuals, not the indistinguishable masses of suffering Haitians featured in the Western media. Through her lens we hear the screaming, we see the blood, we smell the burning of human flesh. Danticat tells these stories as an act of recovery, to prevent the dis-membering of the Haitian spirit for those who would have to leave Haiti and cross over to another side—the United States.

The last two stories in *Krik? Krak!* tell of Haitians who have made Brooklyn, New York, their home. In **"New York Day Women,"** a young woman who works for a Madison Avenue advertising agency spots her mother on Fifth Avenue during her lunch break and observes her on her way to take care of rich white folks' children. **"Caroline's Wedding"** represents the last "crossing over": The American-born daughter of Haitian refugees chooses to marry someone who is not Haitian.

You have lived this long in this strange world, so far from home, because you remember.

Danticat's stories strongly reflect her desire to re-member and re-tell stories that have kept her Haitian spirit alive in the disjointed American landscape. She chronicles a people's spiritual resistance to oppression without exploring in any depth America's complicated and contradictory connection to it. Unlike her representations of Haitians under military rule and their conflicting desires to both stay and flee, Danticat's Haitian-American characters—those like herself who have been educated in the United States, who either have very remote memories of Haiti or none at all—have uncomplicated relationships to their "American" identity. Are there no "stories" to tell of America's reluctance to allow Haitians to enter Miami during the "AIDS scare"? Are there no "stories" of America leaving thousands of Haitians to drown in the Caribbean sea rather than give them political asylum? Are there no "stories" of the horror of America's earlier brutal

occupation? These and other "stories" would surely problematize a second-generation Haitian-American's "American"-ness.

The stories that Edwidge Danticat has chosen to tell are deeply spiritual and ultimately disturbing. They are a powerful synthesis of the old with the new; the past with the present; a looking backward to go forward; a loud and powerful Krak! to her ancestors' spirit-giving Krik?

### Jordana Hart    (review date 19 July 1995)

SOURCE: "Danticat's Stories Pulse with Haitian Heartbeat," in *The Boston Globe*, July 19, 1995, p. 70.

[*In the following review, Hart commends Danticat for providing "honest and loving portraits of Haitian people, both on the island and in the United States."*]

More than anything else, the storytelling of the young Haitian-American writer Edwidge Danticat has given the world honest and loving portraits of Haitian people, both on the island and in the United States. She has smashed the numbing stereotypes created by a barrage of media accounts of Haitian poverty, misery and death.

Danticat's debut novel, **Breath, Eyes, Memory,** garnered international acclaim last year. In her new book, a collection of nine short stories called **Krik? Krak!,** she draws on her experience growing up in dictatorial Haiti as well as stories of Creole culture and myth.

Danticat, 26, a teller of stories in the truest sense, takes us heart-pounding into a breathtaking Haiti, whose culture and people are so often diminished, even disfigured, in the writings of those who do not know and love the island.

Of course, Danticat cannot avoid placing her tales within the brutal world of the *tonton macoutes*, Haiti's former thuggish soldiers, and the oppressive political system that until recently pushed tens of thousands of Haitians to flee the island by vessel—often only to meet their death or internment in a Florida camp.

It is the details of everyday life, however, the depth of her characters and Danticat's own love and respect for her culture that make her stories at once disturbing yet beguiling.

Like her first novel, these stories are mostly told from the perspective of women: her mother, whom she follows unseen along a New York City street only to find out she is a 'day woman,' a nanny caring for a white child; a young wife deeply in love with her husband, who kills himself by jumping out of a hot-air balloon because he's despondent that he cannot raise his family out of poverty.

Danticat tells a couple of her best stories in two voices. The first one, **"Children of the Sea,"** is told by a young woman and also by a politically active young man, her would-be lover, who is fleeing Haiti with 36 other "deserting souls" in a rickety boat. He writes to her about the experience in a journal:

> Once you have been at sea a couple of days, it
> smells like every fish you have ever eaten, every

crab you have ever caught, every jelly fish that has ever bitten your leg. I am so tired of the smell. I am also tired of the way people on this boat are starting to stink. The pregnant girl, Celianne, I don't know how she takes it. She stares into space all the time and rubs her stomach.

With such detail, Danticat manages to place us in the midst of this terrifying voyage—the middle passage to the United States we have read about so often in news accounts—as the boat takes on water and the people are forced to throw even their most cherished belongings overboard to lighten the load. Celianne clutches her still-born infant to her chest, he says, refusing to give her up to the sea god, Agwe.

In **"New York Day Women,"** Danticat recounts with humor the intergenerational and cultural gaps that have developed between the older Haitian mother and her Americanized daughter, Suzette. The account is set off in unusual paragraphs, some only a sentence and statement long, as Suzette recalls her mother's quirks.

---

**It is the details of everyday life, the depth of her characters and Danticat's own love and respect for her culture that make her stories at once disturbing yet beguiling.**

*—Jordana Hart*

---

"My mother . . . sews lace collars on my company softball T-shirts when she does my laundry," Suzette recounts.

"Why, you can't look like a lady when you play softball?" —obviously a retort from her mother.

In **"Nineteen Thirty-Seven,"** a story wrapped in haunting folklore about winged women who escape a Dominican massacre, a girl visits her mother in a Port-au-Prince prison, jailed for life for being a *"lougarou,* witch, criminal." The mother has been wrongly accused of killing a child with witchcraft.

Before the prisoners go to sleep, the guards force them to throw cups of cold water on one another so that their bodies cannot generate enough heat to grow "those wings of flames, fly away in the middle of the night, slip into the slumber of innocent children and steal their breath."

In the storytelling tradition of Haiti, the children ask "Krik?" urging the stories to begin, and the elders reply "Krak!" and tell the fables "so that the young ones will know what came before them." This is very much what Danticat, as a child and now as a writer, has done.

**Edwidge Danticat with Renée H. Shea**　(interview date Summer 1995)

SOURCE: An interview in *Belles Lettres: A Review of Books by Women,* Vol. 10, No. 3, Summer, 1995, pp. 12-15.

[*In the following interview, Danticat discusses the stories included in* Krik? Krak!]

This epigraph sets the stage and tone for the nine stories of the heart by Haitian-born Edwidge Danticat in her recent collection entitled **Krik? Krak!** In these tales of the politics and people of Haiti, past and present, on their island home and in newly formed immigrant communities, she lures us not simply to read but to participate in the tradition of Krik? Krak! that she remembers from childhood:

"Krik? Krak! is call-response but also it's this feeling that you're not merely an observer—you're part of the story. Someone says, 'Krik?' and as loud as you can you say, 'Krak!' You urge the person to tell the story by your enthusiasm to hear it."

So compelling are these stories, filled with the myth and poetry of Haiti, that as one ends, it is hard not to call out a resounding, "Krak!" to keep the momentum of Danticat's storytelling going.

Taken individually, several stories are stunning in the power of both the tale and language. **"Children of the Sea"** is told as a dialogue between two young lovers—one on a boat bound for Miami, the other reporting from Haiti on the horrors wrought by the TonTon Macoutes. The young man reports the desperate life of himself and the "thirty-six other deserting souls on this little boat" and the story-within-the-story of Celianne. Pregnant after a gang rape by the TonTon Macoutes, Celianne fled her accusing family, and when she gives birth aboard the boat to a still-born child, she refuses to give it up. Finally forced to throw the baby overboard, she follows by jumping into the sea. The young woman's story of her family's struggle in Haiti, the increasing violence, and the lengths her father finally goes to protect her are counterpoint. The nightmarish reality of the TonTon Macoutes is challenged by the fierce love of the two young people; the unnamed he wonders, "Maybe the sea is endless. Like my love for you," and she exclaims, "i love you until my hair shivers at the thought of anything happening to you." The vividness of their "letters" belies the reality that only we can hear both voices. Will he survive? Will she? Will their written records?

What will survive is memory, a collective spirit that the young man speculates may be "life eternal, among the children of the deep blue sea, those who have escaped the chains of slavery to form a world beneath the heavens and the blood-drenched earth where you live." Danticat changed the original title of this story, "From the Ocean Floor," to **"Children of the Sea"** to emphasize the link to the Middle Passage:

"It's a very powerful image—from the ocean floor. No one knows how many people were lost on The Middle Passage. There are no records or graves—and the ocean floor is where our fossils are. That journey from Haiti in the 1980s is like a new middle passage. Not to romanticize it, but the comforting thing about death is that somehow all these people will meet. I often think that if my ancestors are at the bottom of the sea, then I too am part of that. So we are all children of the sea. There are no museums, no graves, really no place to visit—there's a timelessness about it."

The passion of the two young people in **"Children of the Sea"** reappears, though in a horrific form, in **"Between the Pool and the Gardenias,"** a sublimely written story of a maid in Port-au-Prince whose childlessness drives her finally to claim a dead baby she finds "on the dusty curb, wrapped in a small pink blanket, a few inches away from a sewer." Naming the baby Rose, the woman nurtures her, gives into "a sudden desire to explain to her my life," and keeps Rose in her room until the baby "began to smell like the intestines after they hadn't sold for a few days." Before the woman can bury her beloved Rose in order to free her spirit, her lover, assuming she has killed the child with some voodoo-related purpose, calls the authorities. This stark story combines a plot of almost Gothic horror and a lyrical simplicity that is chilling, perhaps never more so than during a public reading of this story when a baby in the audience cried and cried—"an eerie coincidence," muses Danticat, who describes the story's origin:

"The woman in this story is so many different women. It began as a story about someone who wants something so badly that she'll go to any length, but then I started thinking, 'what if?' and 'what if . . .'—taking it further and further. In some ways, it's the story of a woman who wants a child very badly and then finds one. That should be a happy ending, but then you ask, "What if it is a child that she doesn't have in mind?" It pushes reality further and forces you to realize the depths of the person's wanting to have a child. As long as it's possible to overlook the reality, she can have the child briefly. But then she ends up paying a very high price."

*Krik? Krak!* is populated with stories of mothers and daughters, several of them about searches for connections between generations that grew up in different countries. In **"New York Day Women,"** a daughter watches in surprise as her mother makes her way from her home in Brooklyn to Madison Avenue, where in Central Park she cares for a young child while his Yuppie mother does her hour-long jog. The imagined dialogue between mother and daughter underscores the different worlds they inhabit, though the tone is playful: The mother sews lace collars on her daughter's company softball T-shirts because she wants her to "look like a lady playing softball." In **"Caroline's Wedding,"** the twin occasion of one daughter's new American citizenship and her older sister's wedding prompt the sisters and their mother to forge new relationships while preserving ways and means of the old. In **"The Missing Peace,"** Lamort, so named because her mother died giving birth to her, helps an American who has come to Haiti in search of her journalist mother, an "old regime journalist. For a newspaper called Liberté in Port-au-Prince." The connection between the two grows as the older recognizes the futility of her search, and the younger claims her mother's legacy by taking her name, Mary Magdalene.

Mothers and daughters are familiar terrain to Danticat, whose first novel, **Breath, Eyes, Memory,** centered on Martine and her daughter, Sophie. That novel, however, extended the central ties to a sustaining web of women that includes grandmothers, aunts, cousins, and other members of the female community. Danticat dedicates *Krik? Krak!* to her aunts Josephine and Marie Rose— "And to Paule Marshall, the greatest kitchen poet of all."

"It's so important for people to read things that somehow mirror their own experience. I remember when I was in junior high school and read Paule Marshall. *Brown Girl, Brownstones* was the first book that was similar to what we were going through. My father always had a desire to own property. He wanted to buy a house. We had to have something concrete, a piece of the country, a piece of the land—like the people in this novel: they wanted to have a brownstone. I had three brothers, and I'm the only girl. In most of my adolescence, that was okay, but I had to be in the kitchen with my mother, learning how to cook. Marshall's essay on 'kitchen poets' describes something very similar to when my mother's sisters would come over—their talking, the way they said things, their faces. It was so beautiful! I used to resent being in the kitchen with them because I wanted to be with the boys, but then I read Marshall's essay. She talks about doing her homework on the kitchen table while the women were talking about home, what was happening there, what they're doing—and just sort of soaking it in. She called it 'kitchen poetry.' After reading that, I didn't resent so much being in the kitchen. I felt like part of a sisterhood, and I remember feeling then that I didn't necessarily have to rebel."

To read Danticat is to learn about Haiti—the folklore and myth, the traditions, and the history. Two of the stories in *Krik? Krak!* involve actual historical events, one of these, **"Wall of Fire Rising,"** indirectly. Two very poor parents proudly listen to their young son recite his part in the school play of Boukman, the legendary runaway slave who in 1791 organized a revolt in Haiti. Guy, the father, trapped in a janitor's job at the sugar mill, dreams of piloting the hot air balloon owned by the mill's owner. Lili, the mother, dreams of her son. The tension between the parents' views of their child's future is symbolized in their view of the balloon: When Lili points out, "If God wanted people to fly, he would have given us wings on our backs," Guy replies, "But look what he gave us instead. He gave us reasons to fly. He gave us the air, the birds, our son."

In this story, which Danticat began as an undergraduate, language both reflects and defies the history of imperialism. As the young boy's speech opens, "A wall of fire is rising and in the ashes, I see the bones of my people," and the parents "felt as though for a moment they had been given the rare pleasure of hearing the voice of one of the forefathers of Haitian independence in the forced baritone of their only child." The narrator comments, however, that "It was obvious that this was a speech written by a European man, who gave to the slave revolutionary Boukman the kind of European phrasing that might have sent the real Boukman turning in his grave." Such subtle evidence of the profound impact of Haiti's colonial past is characteristic of Danticat, who explains:

"You can see the Creole texts of what Boukman was saying, but I've read it in books where it sounds like Shakespeare. In plays, it's 'frenchized'—kind of washed of the anger. [The young character] and his family are living it. They're bringing the revolutionary sense back."

The revolutionary spirit returns, too, in **"1937,"** a story centering on the Dominican Republic's dictator Rafael Leonard Trujillo Molina's massacre of Haitians at the river separating Haiti from the Dominican Republic. Written as a kind of history told through magical realism, **"1937"** opens: "My Madonna cried. A miniature teardrop traveled down her white porcelain face, like dew on the tip of early morning grass. When I saw the tear, I thought, surely that my mother had died." The narrator of this story visits her mother, imprisoned like many others on suspicion of being a "lougarou" or witch: "They were said to have been seen at night rising from the ground like birds on fire." Learning of her mother's death from a prescient old woman, the daughter returns to the prison where she asks, "What would be the use" of watching when the body is burned. The old woman replies that the prison officials "will make these women watch, and we can keep them company." As the narrator agrees, she "remembers" the story of 1937 and her mother flying: "Weighted down by my body inside hers, she leaped from Dominican soil into the water, and out again on the Haitian side of the river. She glowed red when she came out, blood clinging to her skin, which at that moment looked as though it were in flames." She understands her connections and her place in time and history, both through the bonds of women.

This story previews Danticat's next novel, which centers on the massacre of 1937:

"Right now, I'm talking about it more than working on it. It's going to stay in the 1930s, and it's one woman's survival story. I've been researching this for a very long time, but the narrative way of telling the story didn't present itself until very recently. I was thinking about the ending: I write first and last chapters to give myself perimeters. At the end, there is an old woman telling the story, like a woman who is still alive today looking back at the '30s on the massacre and how she survived. I'll do more research by going to that place in Haiti, but first, I wanted to have the character.

"When I mentioned in one reading that I was working on a novel about the 1937 massacre, people called me with information, books, articles. I often think I'm in a communal endeavor. People are investing in what I'm doing. I've gotten tons of books about the massacre. Writers often feel as though they're writing alone, but I feel a sense of solidarity. I have a lot of collaborators! This is a part of history that's not in the history books; it's not something we talk about. But it's about survivors, and we're children of survivors."

Taken together, the stories in *Krik? Krak!* have a continuity derived from recurrent themes and motifs, yet they are more profoundly bound by a spiritual vision where "the warm sea air" and "the laughter of children" coexist with the painful history of slavery and more recent violence:

"My idea was to have a progression. The first story would

be **'1937'** and the last, historically, **'Caroline's Wedding.'** We also go from Haiti to the New York stories. My editor and I chose them with that idea in mind. Just naturally from writing the stories over several years, some of the characters recurred, so that came together too. But we ended up with a different order because my editor thought that **'Children of the Sea'** is a story that's easy to get into; also, it has 'krik? krak!' in it, which introduces the idea of why to write the stories. The book was put together with the idea of the stories flowing together and complementing one another."

Such interconnections, resonances, echoes, and blending are best described by Danticat's own image of braids in the final selection, **"Epilogue: Women Like Us,"** a poetic coda to the nine stories:

"When you write, it's like braiding your hair. Taking a handful of coarse unruly strands and attempting to bring them unity. Your fingers have still not perfected the task. Some of the braids are long, others are short. Some are thick, others are thin. Some are heavy. Others are light. Like the diverse women in your family. Those whose fables and metaphors, whose similes and soliloquies, whose diction and *je ne sais quoi* daily slip into your survival soup, by way of their fingers."

Recurring characters are one connection: the main character of **"Between the Pool and the Gardenias"** is the goddaughter of Lili from **"A Wall of Fire Rising"** and the granddaughter of Defile, the alleged lougarou in **"1937."** When asked if not knowing Haitian myths and folklore makes it difficult to appreciate her work, Danticat calls on yet another connection in response:

"I think more of the depths of emotion. The stories deal with humanity and what we all go through. Different people will walk away learning different things; there'll be differences even among people from Haiti."

Generations of women strengthen these connections. Even death cannot break the line, as she writes in the Epilogue: "The women in your family have never lost touch with one another. Death is a path we all take to meet on the other side. What goddesses have joined, let no one cast asunder. With every step you take, there is an army of women watching over you. We are never any farther than the sweat on your brows or the dust on your toes."

---

**So compelling are these stories, filled with the myth and poetry of Haiti, that as one ends, it is hard not to call out a resounding, "Krak!" to keep the momentum of Danticat's storytelling going.**

**—*Renée H. Shea***

---

An image that recurs throughout Danticat's work is the butterfly as symbol of both continuing life and transformation. In **"Dream of the Butterflies,"** a poetic vignette published in *The Caribbean Writer* in 1991, violence is juxtaposed with tenderness, danger with safety, and, finally, sheer hatred with pure love. She sees the redemptive butterfly as suggesting that hope triumphs even in the face of terrible loss:

"There aren't that many legends in Haiti about butterflies, but I'm fascinated by the idea of transformation. I think in some ways we all think we could go from a caterpillar to a butterfly—that whole metamorphosis is a metaphor for life, especially a life of poverty or struggle because you hope that this is temporary and that one way or another, you'll get wings. It's the Christian ideal we grew up with that people are willing to suffer very much if that means one day they'll get their wings and fly. Haiti has such beautiful butterflies in all different colors."

The most uncanny connections seem to assert themselves in the life of this author who bears witness:

"The year I wrote **'Children of the Sea'** there were so many boating accidents; whole families would be wiped out. One woman I had read about was Marie Micheline, whose mother and daughter were on the boat with her. They all died."

Danticat dedicated the original publication of this story as follows: "In ancestral kinship, I offer this piece to Marie Micheline Marole, her daughters, and her granddaughters—three generations of women lost at sea." Coincidentally—or maybe not—another "Marie Micheline" played a key role in Danticat's life:

"My cousin Marie Micheline taught me to read. I started school when I was three, and she would read to me when I came home. In 1987, when I was in France, there was a shooting outside her house—where her children were. She had a seizure and died. Since I was away from her, my parents didn't tell me right away. They were afraid I might have a reaction. But around that same time, I was having nightmares; somehow I knew.

"Marie Micheline was very dear to me. When I read about this woman who drowned, I was so struck that they had the same name."

In *Krik? Krak!,* Danticat serves a "survival soup" of characters struggling to find a place of peace, a sliver of happiness, a glimmer of a brighter future amid terrorism and political chaos. Ultimately, it is in these stories that they find a moment of grace, stories that Danticat believes give people "a sense of the things that I have inherited." It's a rich inheritance—and one, we can be thankful, she generously shares.

# Jacques Ferron

## 1921-1985

French-Canadian novelist, short story writer, novella writer, playwright, and essayist.

The following entry presents an overview of Ferron's career.

## INTRODUCTION

Known for his medical accomplishments and political activities as well as his literary works, Ferron was a vocal supporter of Quebec separatism and the author of novels and short stories that combine the fantastic with the mundane in celebration of Quebec's cultural heritage. He received a Governor General's Award in 1963 for his short story collection *Contes du pays incertain* (1962) and was selected by the Front de Libération du Québec (FLQ) to act as mediator during the 1970 October Crisis, during which the FLQ kidnapped a British official and the Canadian minister of labor. Remarking on the author's career, Paul Matthew St. Pierre has written that "Ferron's contributions to Quebecois literature [not only] point to his admirable involvements in medicine and politics but they also manage to reflect the cultural development of Quebec over the past forty years."

### Biographical Information

Ferron was born on January 20, 1921, in Louisville, Quebec, and received his early education at Trois-Rivières before attending the Collège Jean-de-Brébeuf in Montreal. His mother died from tuberculosis when Ferron was ten, and critics have traced his literary fascination with death to this event. Two of Ferron's sisters also became artists: Madeleine, a novelist, and Marcelle, an Automatiste painter. During his time at Collège Jean-de-Brébeuf, Ferron developed an interest in Quebec's cultural heritage and was also introduced to socialism. In 1943, while studying medicine at Université Laval in Quebec City, he married a communist, Madeleine Therrien, whom he later divorced. After graduating in 1945, Ferron entered the Canadian army, serving as a doctor in camps in Quebec and New Brunswick. In 1946 he established a private practice in Rivière Madeleine on the Gaspé Peninsula; two years later he set up practice in the working-class Montreal suburb of Ville Jacques-Cartier, which later became known as Longueuil. Ferron published his first play *L'ogre* in 1949 and followed it with several more dramas and a collection of poetry before achieving widespread success with *Contes du pays incertain*. Beginning in 1951 and continuing for the next thirty years, Ferron became a regular contributor of literary, medical, philosophical, and political essays to the journal *L'information medicale et paramedicale*. In 1952 he married Madelaine Lavallée. Aside from his many essays published in various periodicals and newspapers, his political activities included

founding the Rhinoceros Party—a satirical political organization—in 1963; acting as mediator between the FLQ and the Canadian government following the kidnapping of Pierre Laporte during the 1970 October Crisis; and co-founding in 1980 the Regroupement des Ecrivains pour le OUI—an organization of writers who favored Quebec separatism. Despite Ferron's success with *Contes du pays incertain* and the numerous novels, novellas, and short story collections which followed, his reputation outside Quebec has developed slowly. He died of a heart attack on April 22, 1985, leaving behind a collection of short stories and an autobiographical essay which were published together as *La conference inachevée* in 1988.

### Major Works

Ferron's interest in medicine and politics pervades much of his literary work, and the image of Quebec as an exiled country—suggested in the title of his first short story collection *Contes du pays incertain* ("Tales of the Uncertain Country")—is employed throughout his writing. The major themes in Ferron's stories and novels include death, sanity versus madness, and the complex relationship between Quebec and English Canada. A pervasive theme throughout his fiction, death is the principal subject for two of his novels—*Cotnoir* (1962, *Dr. Cotnoir*) and *La charette* (1968, *The Cart*)—and is often linked with salvation and redemption. In *The Cart,* which centers on a doctor who dies and then experiences a journey through the underworld, Ferron satirizes the pomp and solemnity associated with death and examines the subject from a first-person perspective that changes to third person after the character's demise. The dual themes of madness and sanity are most evident in the novel *Les roses sauvages* (1971; *Wild Roses*). The novel centers on the Baron, a highly-successful businessman whose wife committed suicide after going insane, and Rose-Aimée, the Baron's daughter who resists her father's attempts to circumscribe her life. Characterized as a sell-out, the Baron is isolated from his culture and, like his wife, eventually goes insane and commits suicide. Numerous critics have linked the theme of insanity in *Wild Roses* to Quebec's cultural destiny, arguing that collective alienation is a form of insanity and is comparable to a patient locked in an isolation ward who becomes servile and dependent. In "L'exécution de Maski" ("The Execution of Maski"), Ferron examines another psychological theme, the divided self. Here, Notary, the writer within Dr. Maski, attempts to kill the doctor but finds that the doctor's destruction heralds his own. The relationship between Anglophones and Francophones in Ferron's oeuvre is, according to critics, complex. In his tales Ferron often pokes fun at the English, portraying them as foreign and quaint. However, his longer works, though concerned with Quebec's self-affirmation, argue the necessity of considering the English "other" in any definition of Quebec. In *Les grands soleils* (1968, *The Flowering Suns*), for instance, it is an English woman who is cast as a potential Joan of Arc for Quebec. In *La nuit* (1965, *Quince Jam*), the English character Frank Archibald Campbell, also known as Frank Anacharsis Scott, acts as an alter ego to a Quebecois narrator, while in a later novel, *Le ciel de Québec* (1969, *The Penniless Redeemer*), Frank achieves redemption on becoming "Québeckized." Remarking on the role of Ann Higgit, an English-speaking character from *Wild Roses,* Betty Bednarski states that Quebec's reality is "sympathetically translated by an English outside mind, and it is this characteristic projection of one's own reality into the mind of another that constitutes the most interesting aspect of Ferron's attitude to the English. To truly exist, and ultimately, to be truly saved, Québec, it would seem, has to be perceived and have substance, individually and collectively, in the English mind."

### Critical Reception

Ferron's dramas, written early in his career, are commonly considered unremarkable, and his works did not begin to receive serious critical attention until *Contes du pays incertain* won the Governor General's Award. Commentators have noted his use of fantasy, his frequent attempts to demythologize Quebec's historical figures by placing them in fictional situations, and his persistent concern with the fate of Canada's French-speaking population. With the publication of several translations, Ferron's writing has gained recognition beyond French-speaking Cana-

da. However, his work is still met with ambivalence by many English-speaking Canadians.

---

## PRINCIPAL WORKS

*L'ogre* (drama) [first publication] 1949

*La barbe de Francois Hertel; Le licou* (dramas) [first publication] 1951

*Tante Elise; ou, le prix de l'amour* (drama) [first publication] 1956

*Le cheval de Don Juan* (drama) [first publication] 1957; also published as *Le Don Juan chrétien* in *Théâtre* [revised edition], 1968

*Le Dodu; ou, le prix de bonheur* (drama) 1958

*Le licou* (drama) 1958

*Les grands soleils* [*The Flowering Suns*] (drama) 1968

*Corolles* (poetry) 1961

*Contes du pays incertain* (short stories) 1962

*Cotnoir* [*Dr. Cotnoir*] (novel) 1962

*Cazou; ou, le prix de la virginite* (drama) [first publication] 1963

*La tête du roi* (drama) [first publication] 1963

*Contes anglais et autres* (short stories) 1964

*La Nuit* (novella) 1965; also published as *Les confitures de coings* [*Quince Jam*] [revised edition], 1972

*Papa Boss* (novella) 1966; revised edition, 1972

*La Charrette* [*The Cart*] (novel) 1968

*Contes—edition intégrale: Contes anglais, contes du pays incertain, contes inédits* (short stories) 1968

*Théâtre.* 2 vols. (dramas) 1968-75

*Le ciel de Québec* [*The Penniless Redeemer*] (novel) 1969

*Historiettes* (essays) 1969

*L'Amélanchier* [*The Juneberry Tree*] (novel) 1970

*Le salut de l'Irlande* (novel) 1970

*\*Les Confitures de coings et autres textes* [*Quince Jam*] (novels and short stories) 1972; also published as *Les Confitures de coings et autres textes, suivi de le journal des confitures de coings* [revised and enlarged edition], 1977

*Les Roses sauvages; Petit roman suivi d'une lettre d'amour soigneusement présentée* [*Wild Roses: A Story Followed by a Love Letter*] (novel) 1971

*La chaise du maréchal-ferrant* (novel) 1972

*Le Saint-Elias* [*The Saint-Elias*] (novel) 1972

*Tales from the Uncertain Country* (short stories) 1972; also published as *Selected Tales of Jacques Ferron* [expanded edition], 1984

*Du fond de mon arrière-cuisine* (essays) 1973

*Escarmouches: La longue passe.* 2 vols. (essays) 1975

*Gaspé-Mattempa* (novella) 1980

*Rosaire précédé de l'exécution de Maski* (novellas) 1981

*Le choix de Jacques Ferron dans l'oeuvre de Jacques Ferron* (selections) 1985

*La conférence inachevée* (short stories) 1988

---

\*This book and its translation contain the following works: *Papa Boss, Quince Jam,* "La créance" ["Credit Due"], and "L'appendice aux confitures de coing" ["Appendix to Quince Jam, or, The Sacking of Frank Archibald Campbell"].

---

# CRITICISM

**Paul Socken   (review date June 1972)**

SOURCE: A review of *Tales from the Uncertain Country,* in *The Canadian Forum,* Vol. LII, No. 617, June, 1972, pp. 41-2.

[*In the following review, Socken remarks on the style and themes of the stories collected in* Tales from the Uncertain Country.]

Jacques Ferron is one of Quebec's most highly acclaimed writers, and a translation of some of his short stories by Betty Bednarski makes his writing accessible to an English-speaking audience for the first time.

In **Tales from the Uncertain Country,** a collection of eighteen short stories, the reader can acquire a representative glimpse of Ferron's very unusual world. Ferron is concerned with people's origins, and their quest to determine who they are and where they belong. His is a study of people's roots, and the relationships people establish with those around them. Ferron's only enemy is complacency and unfounded pride, as we see them ridiculed in **'Tiresome Company'**, a story in which a young doctor's pride is quickly deflated in very picturesque terms.

Ferron's creative approach, the reader should be forewarned, is not commonplace. He is the only writer writing today, anywhere, who uses the fable, the legend, what the French call the 'conte', as his literary vehicle. He does not simply make allusions to Greek myth or tales like 'Little Red Riding Hood', he actually uses the framework of the legend itself, preserving certain elements of the story, discarding others. The language and style is a mixture of the ancient, the modern, and what Bednarski calls 'Ferronesque'. This unusual literary device places Ferron's works in an historical context of didactic or 'message-oriented' writing, and there are indeed many lessons to be learned from these little stories. What one gains is a new perspective, a new way of seeing our familiar world, but any reader tempted to look for simplistic solutions is mocked in tales like **'The Buddhist'**. In that story, the smug, self-satisfied statement at the end serves to caution the reader against facile interpretations and sententious judgements. The 'conte' framework also gives Ferron a flexibility that he uses to great advantage. As narrator, he is able to distance himself from the scene he is presenting, sometimes for ironic effect (**'Ulysses'**), sometimes allowing him to comment on what has taken place (**'The Archangel of the Suburb'**). One is not accustomed to reading this kind of story, and in the end the reader finds himself very much involved, participating actively in the story and its meaning.

---

> **Ferron is the only writer writing today, anywhere, who uses the fable, the legend, what the French call the 'conte', as his literary vehicle.**
>
> **—Paul Socken**

---

Ferron treats a wide range of subjects that include love, marriage and death, but his focus is always on people trying to make sense of their relationships with others and trying to reconcile themselves to the world they live in. In **'Cadieu'**, a boy who has succeeded in the world beyond his home tries to rediscover his home and his past and cannot as his family fails to recognize him on his return. In **'Black Cargo Ships of War'**, a woman waits for her son to return to her after he has gone to war, and they are united again only in death. In **'The Sirens'**, a modern-day Ulysses finds that the world of legend is incomprehensible to his neighbours and that he himself is cut off from his heroic past. People in Ferron's world are often isolated from the ones they love and from a sense of their own fulfilment.

Ferron views the stuff of human relationships very cynically. In **'Back to Val d'Or'**, a woman's unbounded love becomes an obstacle to her relations with the world, and in **'How the Old Man Died'** and in **'The Child'** the sterility of the husband-wife relationship is vividly portrayed. But for all his cynicism, Ferron's very real sympathy and concern come through most emphatically in such stories as **'The Bridge'** and **'Les Méchins'**.

Ferron's very deep concern that people be able to relate to one another is felt in these stories. He uses the fable, where distinctions between the animal world and the human world, between reality and fantasy are blurred, in order to build a new world and a new reality. In the original version of **'Little Red Riding Hood'**, the wolf succeeds in its plot to eat the little girl. In this new world, however, Little Red Riding Hood laughs with her grandmother as the wolf is outsmarted. The uncertain country Ferron writes about is the land of the imagination where the artist restructures reality and dispenses justice according to his own concepts.

There is no doubt that Ferron himself feels the isolation that we find in his characters and that is so characteristic of Quebec writers. As Ferron says in **'Back to Kentucky'**, 'Montreal is only a stop on the way from Belgium to Kentucky.' The feeling of being a minority, a colonized people, lends an interesting insight into Ferron's fascinating world. The political and social reality cannot be ignored. It adds a profound dimension to Ferron's work, and anyone interested in Quebec culture and society will read Ferron with interest. But there is so much more to Ferron's work that overemphasizing the political aspect of it would be an injustice to the work as a whole.

Betty Bednarski has given us both a good translation and

a good selection of Ferron's short stories, one that will be welcomed by English-speaking Canadians.

## Len Early  (review date Spring 1976)

SOURCE: "Fine-Rooted Blossomer," in *Essays on Canadian Writing,* No. 4, Spring, 1976, pp. 76-7.

[*In the following excerpt, Early criticizes Ferron's* The Juneberry Tree *for containing too many details, but states that "it has beauties enough."*]

"I am called Tinamer de Portanqueu. I am not the daughter of nomads or gypsies." So begins Jacques Ferron's brief novel of childhood and childhood's end. First published in French in 1970, it now appears in the "French Writers of Canada" series undertaken by Harvest House to make more Quebec fiction available in English translation. *The Juneberry Tree* is not self-consciously a story of Quebec: there are no priests, revolutionaries, swarming mulots or families of emaciated urchins, though there is a burning cathedral, attesting perhaps to the vitality of cultural archetypes. The novel is a curious hybrid of fable, dream and monograph.

While Tinamer is no Ishmael, she does survive terrors and voids which threaten to whelm her under. From the viewpoint of her twentieth year she evokes and analyzes her experience as a six-year-old when the wood behind her home was an enchanted world presided over by a benign thaumaturge, her father, Leon de Portanqueu. Their relationship is the heart of the tale. Their wonderland, "the good side of things" according to the myth they cherish, is set over against "the bad side of things," the mundane world of asphalt streets as yet unexplored by Tinamer, into which her father ventures daily to maintain his wife and child. The fairy-tale richness of Tinamer's earliest vision of life is conveyed with unsentimental delicacy:

> When night had fallen and my father had set up his telescope in the yard, he said to me, "Tinamer, do you see the moon?" It was emerging fully round from behind the leaves, amazed to be larger than the sun. Certainly I saw it. It was rising noiselessly in the sky before our eyes. I said nothing. Why would I have answered such a question? The higher it rose the smaller it grew. My father said to me, "When the moon is full, can you believe that you only see half of it?" I remained silent. He had finished adjusting his lens and was now looking at the Sea of Tranquility, the wood, the yard, and at his side, his little daughter standing quietly with dew on her feet.

For the child, the wood is inhabited by marvellous presences—a phantom, a compass, a Juneberry tree—which glide in and out of the tale, glowing with a mysterious significance destined to vanish as childhood passes. While Ferron reworks the familiar story of the Little Girl Lost, with its echoes of Goldilocks, Alice and others, he generally avoids triteness. Upon "the bad side of things," the fabulous shapes of centaurs and villains are superimposed by the father's words and the child's imagination. Ferron's theme is the value of our parents' love in our gropings for

identity, and he stresses the ambiguous nature of our human minds, to which we become both heirs and victims.

The greater part of *The Juneberry Tree* proceeds with verve and a prodigality of incidental detail which distinguishes it from Ferron's fine collection, *Tales from the Uncertain Country,* where economy and precision impart tension and point to his narration. Nevertheless, the episodic development in the novel recalls his virtuosity in the shorter form, and at times it seems to me that Ferron includes fragments which should be more effectively burnished, and published elsewhere. A whole chapter on the Portanqueu lineage remains flat and vaguely rendered, even if intended as a parody of earnest genealogy or of mythmaking. Ferron's verbal wit may be enough to sustain the French version, but as the translator's footnotes indicate, this quality is diminished in the English text.

Toward the end of the novel, Ferron suddenly brings in a bitter indictment of the soul-wrecking machinery established by society for orphans and cast-off children. We learn that Tinamer's father works as a "jailer" at Mont-Thabor, a psychiatric hospital where his compassion is especially focussed on a youth whose potential has been devastated by confinement to institutions since infancy. This revelation of Leon as an entrenched idealist perpetually saddened by contemporary life, coincides with the inevitable rupture of Tinamer's enchanted world and her disillusionment with her father when she begins school and acquires a first-hand impression of "the bad side of things." A few pages report the deaths of her father and mother, and at the very end we return to Tinamer at twenty, studying "psycho-pedagogy" and summarizing for herself and for us the meaning of her Proustian reveries. Here the language becomes clotted and pretentious, an irritation even if intended as a measure of her exile from the magic realms.

Jacques Ferron obviously shares the revulsion of the Portanqueus, father and daughter, from the atrocities wrought and impending among us. *The Juneberry Tree,* like *Tales from the Uncertain Country,* is in some ways a pessimistic book, but its pessimism is limited. Tinamer's final recognition is of the incalculable value of her fortunate childhood to her perplexed humanity and her personal equilibrium. The art of the story is similarly mixed. Ferron seeks to graft upon the fragile perspectives of tale and fable the ponderous formulations of theoretical prose. Though *The Juneberry Tree* splinters under this weight, it has beauties enough.

## Paul Socken  (review date October 1976)

SOURCE: "Shared Concerns," in *The Canadian Forum,* Vol. LVI, No. 665, October, 1976, pp. 33-4.

[*In the following excerpt, Socken examines the major themes in* Wild Roses.]

In *Wild Roses,* Jacques Ferron explores the topography of the land inhabited by the sane and the mad and raises questions about some of our society's most fundamental assumptions about those two states. The result is a novel which implies that no map can be drawn to distinguish the two areas, no clearly-defined borders can be established, for they are part of the same country, the uncertain country of the human mind.

The story centres on the Baron, a man whose wife bears him a daughter, goes mad shortly thereafter and commits suicide. Totally devoted to the daughter, Rose-Aimée, the Baron decides to leave her with a good Acadian family and to visit her every spare moment. He is described as a "tall, handsome, impeccably dressed young man, who was courteous and considerate in spite of his exuberance. . . ." This, and similar descriptions of him, repeatedly occur and serve as a refrain which explains everyone's admiration for him. He appears to be the best society can produce, the very epitome of success. The tone of the descriptions is mocking, however, and alludes to the Baron's complacency and superficiality. As the Baron becomes more and more devoted to rising in the company hierarchy and his daughter grows increasingly attached to her Acadian adoptive family, he realizes that they are becoming irrevocably estranged. He makes a last desperate attempt to reclaim her affections by taking her home to live with him and Sister Agnes who will care for them.

Sister Agnes has retired from a lifetime devoted to caring for the mentally ill and feels out of place in her new environment. She "did not like this world, which unlike an asylum, did not declare its insane." Her unique experience of having witnessed life among the "sane" and the "insane" lends a profound insight to the novel:

> Sister Agnes had seen misery and some horrible suffering in her long years at Saint-Jean-de-Dieu. She had shown compassion and implored heaven's mercy. She had been on the side of misery and suffering then. Now she had broadened her scope, she was in the midst of life, life which must go on, must find a way round misery and suffering . . . she knew it was her duty to keep life's tragedy locked in her heart, that the beauty of each day might be spared.

This comment reveals much of what is at the heart of the novel. Life, inside and outside the walls of the asylum, is seen to be fundamentally the same. It is tragic and full of suffering, yet without any obvious meaning or justification to alleviate the misery. Life, in this absurdist sense, is thus insane. Yet life outside the asylum is different in one crucial sense—it must contain and surpass suffering so that it may "go on." This involves a certain pretense ("life's tragedy locked in her heart") which is necessary to continuing the struggle. Pretense gives one the illusion that life is rational and under some control. Why this accent on persevering? Because, as expressed in the preceding quotation, there is "beauty" in living life for the moment ("each day") and it is one's obligation ("duty") to preserve it. Sanity, this passage and the novel seem to be saying, is ultimately recognizing the fundamental insanity inherent in life and working dutifully to salvage what is beautiful.

The wild roses symbolize the paradox of the novel, the value of beauty and its threat. For centuries roses have been celebrated as the most perfect, the most beautiful of flowers. The Baron plants some around his home, but becomes so enamored of them that each summer he lets them almost overrun the house. Their wild nature (in French, "sauvage"), which is paradoxically inseparable from their magnificence, constantly threatens to displace him. Beauty must be restrained, but the Baron cannot establish this control. He too goes mad. The roses are, in fact, uprooted at the end of the novel when the Baron is dead and Rose-Aimée and her husband move into the house:

> They never knew that Sister Agnes had cut down the rose-bush and torn up its roots, and that in its place she had planted some very ordinary flowers, gloriosas, poppies, and petunias.

The use of the word "ordinary" describing the other flowers implies that the roses were extraordinary, that their exceptional beauty and intoxicating fragrance could no longer have a place there. With the death of the Baron and the removal of the roses we have the end both of beauty and of the threat beauty poses and in its place come the ordinary, the mundane, that which can be managed and subdued.

---

**Sanity, *The Wild Roses* seems to be saying, is ultimately recognizing the fundamental insanity inherent in life and working dutifully to salvage what is beautiful.**

**—Paul Socken**

---

It is interesting that it is Sister Agnes who cuts down the roses. Her choice signals a conscious desire, perhaps a need, for constancy after contact with so much instability. Her action suggests that in the final analysis she values the manageable (sane) over the potentially chaotic (insane), even if the latter yields beauty and the former does not. Perhaps her action speaks for all of society. We uproot wild roses and lock away "exceptional" people since both pose a threat to our mediocrity. Neither roses nor humans can be allowed to grow wild. Our need for order and constancy is stronger than our ability to cope with the challenge of the exceptional.

Society, in Ferron's works, is responsible for the disorientation it produces. It is portrayed as stiff, rigid, and totally unaccommodating. Even expressing emotion must be authorized: "to a man people in the firm seemed to have decided to feel sorry for him" (when the Baron's wife died). Francophones in particular are alienated from society and from their own culture. As the narrator comments: the graduates of the University of Moncton "work harder and end up third in line for jobs, after the graduates of Dalhousie and Fredericton. It will take them ten or twenty generations to become Anglophones." In the process they are set adrift and float rudderless, culture-less, and alienated from themselves as much as from everything around them.

Ultimate responsibility, Ferron states explicitly, rests with the British "conquerors," the Americans who have displaced them, and the society both have imposed: "The victor (Britain) has felt the need to perpetuate his racist instincts, extending his policy of ethnocide to European immigrants, Quebecois, Acadians, little suspecting that in so doing he is creating in their place Americans more monstrous than himself." It is at this point that one perceives Ferron either as a writer expounding profound truths about the nature of modern Quebec and Acadian society or as a radical voicing ill-founded platitudes. It is up to the reader to choose, depending on his own bias. But let us not lose sight of the fact that we do not have to agree with Ferron's view of Francophone turmoil in order to appreciate his insights. Whatever the historical causes, Francophone Canadians share a sense of apprehension about their future and Ferron gives their fears eloquent and imaginative expression. Confused and uncertain in a turbulent society, they represent modern man; in this way their concerns are ours.

## Linda Sandler    (review date November 1976)

SOURCE: "Ferron's Fairy Tale about a Corporate Madman," in *Saturday Night,* Vol. 91, No. 8, November, 1976, pp. 58-61.

*[In the following excerpt, Sandler remarks on the underlying political message in* Wild Roses.*]*

No one takes much notice of a Quiet Revolution, but who can ignore an "apprehended insurrection"? We know instinctively that people who are capable of writing their history with blood are bound to write interesting books, so it's no accident that translations of Québec literature have proliferated since October, 1970. And it's not surprising that English Canadians are interested in Jacques Ferron, the man who interceded between Pierre Trudeau and Paul Rose of the FLQ.

Jacques Ferron, physician and man of letters, has been quietly influencing Québec politics and literature for twenty years. He was known as a playwright when his first book of fiction, *Contes du pays incertain,* established his reputation as a brilliant, ironic story-teller. It wasn't until 1972 that a selection of his fables, *Tales from the Uncertain Country,* appeared in English, but there are now six of his novels in translation: *Dr. Cotnoir, The Saint Elias, The Juneberry Tree, Papa Boss, Quince Jam,* and *Wild Roses,* which has been elegantly translated by Betty Bednarski.

Writing, for Ferron, is not unlike practising medicine—it's a way of humanizing the world. Ferron complains that his reputation as a humorist prevents people from taking him seriously, but in fact he's something of a national saint. When he was a young doctor in Montréal's Ville Jacques-Cartier (where he still lives and works without growing rich), Ferron's dedication made a strong impression on a boy called Pierre Vallières. In 1968, when Vallières was formulating his terrorist programme, Ferron, characteristically, was using parody to undermine the federal elections; he founded the Rhinoceros Party, whose clownish plan was to unite Canada under one "polyethnic, rhinoceroid, and papist" government.

The comedian and the terrorist might seem to have little in common, but they're both involved in diagnosing a social disease and proposing a cure—Québec, of course, is the patient. Ferron's professional acquaintance with Saint-Jean-de-Dieu, Montréal's infamous madhouse, is the source of one of his central metaphors for Québec—the isolation ward.

The world evolves but the inmate is locked into a timeless world of fantasy; he's less and less capable of acting in the real world. If you lock him up long enough he becomes a child, dependent on those who have authority. And a people which doesn't govern itself, Ferron believes, remains servile and dependent in the same way. Ferron's books are all parables about the national psyche; even *The Juneberry Tree,* a seemingly innocent tale, asks disturbing questions about the hermetic Wonderland a father devises for his daughter. Fathers and figures of authority, as we know, have a stake in prolonging childhood innocence. And *Wild Roses,* which has all the features of a bourgeois fairy tale, turns into a life-and-death struggle between a father and his daughter—and that, for Ferron, is what coming of age is all about. For the nation and for the individual, adulthood implies self-direction.

*Wild Roses* is the story of a very modern epic hero, a man of corporate business. The Baron, so named because of his lordly elegance, is one of Ferron's sell-outs. His company prescribes a way of life and a view of the world, and he conforms—he becomes a successful American. He's cut off from his heritage and his language, and is therefore a nonperson, a madman. *Wild Roses* has a long documentary interlude about Moncton, which Ferron uses to project an image of cultural neurosis. Moncton is a besieged city—it recalls Montréal under the War Measures Act. Everyone is furtive, and the French conceal their identity like a guilty secret. The Baron isn't given to reflection, but he seems to see his own face in the mirror.

When the Baron and his wife move into Montréal's suburban kingdom, they plant wild roses outside their bedroom window. The roses are white and luminous, and they have a strange hold on the Baron's imagination; when his daughter is born he names her Rose-Aimée. There's something demonic about the child; from the first day she demands an exclusive relationship with her father. Her mother's suicide follows, and Rose-Aimée goes to live with an Acadian family in Moncton. In the Baron's imagination she becomes his dead wife, who will eventually return to him.

Ferron works by superb indirection, and various meanings attach themselves to his symbols and events. But the Baron's plan for Rose-Aimée is clear: a rural childhood, a convent education. He's trying to ensure her innocence, to insulate her from reality; he's trying to resurrect his dead wife and replay his own past. That can't be done. Rose-Aimée defies her jealous father and goes off to find her Acadian psychiatrist-lover. She belongs to the future and her marriage stands for an ideal union of paganism and science. That's the fairy-tale ending, but I'm not sure that Ferron believes it. (**"Love Letter,"** a story which appears in the same book with **"Wild Roses,"** is less impressive artistically, but more convincing on the subject of incest.)

History hasn't been gentle with irrelevant social classes, but the judgment of history is no match for the retributive justice devised by writers and terrorists. The Baron is one of the Québecois who made it to "the top" by selling his soul. Ferron turns this against him with masterful irony: the Baron dies by leaping from the top of the water tower at Saint-Jean-de-Dieu. *Wild Roses* is a novel of symbolic execution.

## Betty Bednarski    (essay date 1976)

SOURCE: An afterword to *Wild Roses: A Story Followed by a Love Letter,* McClelland & Stewart Limited, 1976, pp. 120-23.

[*Bednarski is an educator and critic who has translated several of Ferron's works into English, including* Wild Roses. *In the following essay, she remarks on the theme of insanity in* Wild Roses *and examines the novel's distinctive qualities.*]

By now Jacques Ferron needs little introduction to English Canadian readers. Acclaimed for over a decade in Quebec, he is rapidly gaining the recognition he deserves in the rest of the country. But as a writer he is many-sided, elusive, and *Wild Roses* may well come as a surprise to those who feel they already know his work. Disconcerting in its simplicity, almost Victorian in tone, it lacks the fantasy, the baroque complexity of his other books. Readers accustomed to Ferron's mordant wit and black humour will find this novel unexpectedly sober. There are few winks here, few barbs, and he permits himself only the gentlest of irony. While there is much that is familiar—the theme of the salvation of one human being through the death of another, the preoccupation with mental illness and institution life, the concern for the fate of Canada's French speaking minorities—the perspective is new. And this perspective, unique so far in Ferron's work, is of particular significance in the context of an English translation.

In *Wild Roses,* as in *The Juneberry Tree, Dr. Cotnoir,* and several of his short stories, Ferron views mental illness from his own highly personal standpoint, drawing on his experience as a doctor at Saint-Jean-de-Dieu psychiatric hospital, yet searching beyond the limits of psychiatry for some deeper meaning in the lives of the insane. The barely fictionalized case history told in **"Love Letter"** reflects his dissatisfaction with professional terminology, and in the novel itself he accounts for the failing of individual minds in terms which are not those of medical orthodoxy, nor indeed of medicine itself, seeking not so much to negate psychiatric interpretation as to complement it. There is the haunting symbolism of the roses and a spell that can be likened to a curse. There are allusions to wrathful deities and to tragic destiny. And *Wild Roses,* with its grandiose perspective, is above all a novel of destinies.

Individual destinies, but also collective ones. For the lives of the characters are linked irrevocably to the historic destinies of three Canadian peoples: the French in Quebec, the Acadians, and the English-speaking Maritimers.

For Ferron, who writes, as he says, to help his "uncertain country" towards certainty, Quebec's struggle to attain dignity and autonomy has been a major preoccupation. In this novel it is more an implicit than an explicit theme. Baron, the Montrealer, is a businessman whose only loyalty is to his company and in whom political consciousness is all but stifled by personal ambition. His daughter, however, is independent, outspoken, and the new era of happiness heralded at the end is perhaps an era of collective fulfilment, for with Baron's death and the uprooting of the roses, a young generation is freed from the harmful influences of the past. But in *Wild Roses* this concern for Quebec, central to Ferron's work, is eclipsed by his affection for Acadia and a people even more uncertain than his own.

Ferron's vision of Acadia is first an idyllic one, and reflects his nostalgia for simple values and a way of life fast disappearing from Quebec. The gentleness of *Wild Roses* is, in part, his hommage to the gentleness of Acadia. *Le pays chiac* has inspired some of the book's most lyrical passages. It is also the pretext for its most clear-sighted political comment. Like Pierre Perrault, another sympathetic Quebecker, whose film, *L'Acadie, L'Acadie,* first brought the plight of New Brunswick's French-speaking minority to the attention of the Canadian public, Ferron has registered the complex and often elusive reality Acadian writers are now beginning to express for themselves. He himself has walked the streets of Moncton, he tells us—was it in 1966 or 1967? He is familiar with other parts of Acadia—north-eastern New Brunswick in particular—has often written articles about it, but never before a book. In Acadia Ferron is no crusader, no revolutionary, no prophet. He is a mere observer. He is not out to provoke. His remarks are deliberately low-key and lack the violence of much of his comment on Quebec. Yet in spite of the restraint one can sense his emotion, the indignation at past and present injustices, reluctant pessimism with regard to the future, and the sad conviction that Acadia's destiny is indeed a tragic one. It is Ferron's position as a concerned Quebecker which gives his vision of Acadia its particular intensity. And at the same time to discover Acadia, its landscape, its history, its mythology, is, for the Quebecker, to discover a unique vantage point from which to view himself and his people. Baron's Moncton idyll provides him with much food for thought and the occasion for some rather disquieting self-assessment.

Baron discovers Acadia in the company of an English-speaking Maritimer, the dignified young descendant of a race of conquerors, on whose territory he finds himself in Moncton. This people is in search of its destiny and, if we are to judge by Ann Higgit, every bit as uncertain as the other two. After being symbolically rejected by the people her ancestors conquered, she goes to spend her life in England, more at home there than in Ontario or her native Newfoundland. Much has been said and much remains to be said about Ferron's anglophilia. The English, great at the expense of others, proud yet ill at ease in their role as conquerors, have won his sympathy and admiration, though they may often be the targets of his scorn. English-ness—one kind of Englishness—exerts a great fascination for him. He is drawn in particular to qualities he considers British: simplicity, candour, restraint, and a kind of sober dignity, all lacking, he feels, in the brasher world of Upper Canada and the United States, but present still in the Maritimes, where Victorian England has left its indelible mark. On to this very personal vision of the English Maritimes he has projected something of the stark grandeur of the puritan New England he knows from the novels of Nathaniel Hawthorne. These, then, are the qualities embodied in the young woman from Newfoundland. They are also the most striking qualities of the book itself, the very qualities that make it stand out as unique among Ferron's works.

For Ann Higgit is more than the representative of the English Maritimes. Here is the central mind of the novel. It is in her consciousness that meanings crystallize. It is through her comments, and in particular through her reflections on the life and work of Louis Hemon, that the reader reaches a deeper understanding of the tragic significance of Baron's life. And while she is not the narrator, it is in her somewhat grandiose yet simple terms that events are conveyed to us. To her particular qualities of Englishness correspond qualities of Ferron's style, which, while they are not absent from his other works, are nevertheless present here to the exclusion of all else. Indeed, in *Wild Roses* Ferron has shed so much that he risks disconcerting his reader. He has done so in order to explore to the full a fascination, a temptation, one side of his nature perhaps, one element in his Canada. Call it what we will, Victorianness, Englishness, puritan innocence, the result is a narrative voice unheard in his work before *Wild Roses*, and unrepeated since.

This voice, for all its Englishness, speaks French. To translate it into English has, ironically, not always been an easy task. But I feel it has been an important one. There is great wisdom in this deceptively simple little book. And English Canadian readers will recognize in Ferron a Canadian writer whose deep concern for reality beyond the borders of Quebec sets him apart from other writers of his province.

---

**Ferron on *The Cart*:**

*La Charrette* is a rather interesting book from the point of view of the politics of language. Campbell has lost his language. English (which has become the language of everybody and nobody) will never give him back his gaelic. I think he'd really like to be a true *québécois,* but that's not easy. . . . In *La Charrette* he doesn't succeed and remains a kind of disinherited witness, but at the end of *Le Ciel de Québec* he does succeed. Of course, after that, the October crisis came along and spoiled everything.

*Jacques Ferron, in a letter to Ray Ellenwood, in* The Cart: A Novel by Jacques Ferron, *translated by Ray Ellenwood, Exile Editions, 1980.*

---

## Donald Smith    (essay date 1983)

SOURCE: "Jacques Ferron: The Marvellous Folly of Writing," in *Voices of Deliverance: Interviews with Quebec & Acadian Writers,* translated by Larry Shouldice, Anansi, 1986, pp. 83-103.

[*In the following essay, based on correspondence and an interview, Ferron discusses his British literary influences, symbolism, character, and the place of Quebec history and legend in his works.*]

Interviewing Jacques Ferron seemed at first to be something of a Mission Impossible. I had been told several times that Ferron almost never granted interviews and that, although he was not a complete recluse like Réjean Ducharme, the good doctor was not very fond of talking about his writing. However, I was not about to let myself become discouraged. I had just spent five years working on a doctoral dissertation dealing with Ferron, and my head was teeming with his work: 16 plays, 12 novels, two collections of short stories, two books of fictionalized biography, two volumes of polemical writings and a book of historical tales. So I sat down with a blank piece of paper and wrote as follows:

> Cher Monsieur Ferron,
>
> I am not Scott Ewen in your play *La tête du roi,* a paternalistic Englishman if ever there was one; nor am I that enemy of the Québécois, Frank Archibald Campbell, whom you poison in *La nuit*. And I'm certainly not one of those Englishmen from Ontario in *Les contes anglais,* fanatics for the Red Ensign and that belligerent anthem "The Maple Leaf Forever." On the other hand, I must admit to being rather kindly disposed towards Frank-Anacharcis Scot in your novel *Le ciel de Québec*. [In an endnote, the critic adds: " 'The name Anacharcis comes from one of my patients who was called that because his father spoke Greek.' '(note from Jacques Ferron).''] Frank, a poor Scot who sold his soul to the imperialist English, finally came to his senses and turned into François Sicotte. This is what you refer to as Jaxonization, in memory of Henry Jackson, Louis Riel's secretary from Toronto, who quite naturally spoke French when he took up the cause of the Métis. All that to say I'd be delighted if you would grant me an interview.

A few weeks later, Monsieur Ferron replied:

> Your request for a meeting has been lying here in front of me for several weeks now, and I haven't been able to reply. I found you terribly naive. I had nothing to say to you. I could only disappoint you and I had no wish to do that, being incapable of acting like Msgr Savard in your interview with him. And also, I liked what you had to say about *La tête du roi* in your article in *Études françaises*. It's a play I wrote with affection and I still have a soft spot for it; it's my "Riel," my reality, at least indirectly . . . It seems to me I could manage to see you.

Before going off to meet Monsieur Ferron, I mentioned in a letter what a unique and unforgettable pleasure it had been for me to read *Le ciel de Québec*. I said in particular that I'd been fascinated by the Frenchman, Monseigneur Turquetil, a character based on Arsène Turquetil, a former Superior of the Oblate missions in the Hudson Bay area, an imperious miracle-worker on the great ice-floes of the North, author of one of the first grammar books of the Eskimo language and a friend of the canonical visitor to the missions in the north of Saskatchewan, Gabriel Breynat, who was known as the flying bishop, the bishop of wind (he travelled by plane, since skidoos didn't exist at the time) and occasionally the lousy bishop (an appellation the reader can interpret as he/she wishes). Obviously Jacques Ferron is not the historian of the Oblate Fathers, but he does have a gift for satire, changing his "Borgia prelates" into strutting pigeons, into "turtle-preachers" with three wisps of hair on their skulls. In any case, it is thanks to Jacques Ferron that, in my mind, an Oblate is no longer an Oblate. I wanted Monsieur Ferron to know just how powerfully evocative his words are, and also to thank him for creating all those images that keep constantly recurring in my mind. The best way to do this, it seemed to me, was to describe the Ferronesque scene that lay before me that day as I looked through my living-room window. After all, it was Jacques Ferron who had taught me about the metaphorical possibilities inherent in our surroundings. Thus I wrote as follows:

> Your Turquetil from the Land of Aurélie reminds me of the Mennonite neighbours of my sister June who, far from your amélanchiers/Juneberry trees, lives in typical Ontario—or in other words Mennonite territory. Everything there is tinged with black: the car-hearses, the buggies, the clothes, even the bread. June, who happens to be an excellent painter although in no way similar to your overly theoretical Borduas, does marvellous sketches of the Ontario landscape.
>
> As for me, although my ancestors came from the Far-Ouest where they were familiar with the amélanchier/saskatoon berry, I myself live on Nelson Street in Ottawa. Often when I close my eyes I imagine I live on the same street as your famous patriot, Wolfred Nelson, but that must be an illusion, since this is quite clearly Bytown, where Viscount Horatio Nelson lives on.
>
> Also, just across from my place, at 305 Nelson, there are 168 air conditioners sticking out from the windows of the Oblate Monastery; 168 black suits—I haven't actually counted them—eat, sleep and distribute their pamphlet about the beatification of their founder, Monsignor de Mazenod, a friend of the second bishop of Montreal, Ignace Bourget. At 307 Nelson there are 17 white-robed Sisters of the Holy Family who cook in the cafeteria. The black suits are always crossing through the tunnel that connects 305 to 307. The trap-door opens and closes. The scandal-mongers say that the mouse-trap is getting emptier and emptier.
>
> What fascinates me the most about this scene, however, is the majestic, black, skeletal oak tree on which someone has written in large white letters: PQ. The tree is located on the left side of 305 and is thus at the half-way point between the middle of the Oblate Monastery and the entranceway of the white nuns.
>
> There's nothing literary about this description. I see the same scene every day and I'm only a simple spectator. You, however, living in the Land of Longueuil, must be able to contemplate scenes of equal significance at the Nunnery of the Sisters of the Holy Names of Jesus and Mary.

Several days later Monsieur Ferron sent me the following reply:

> One of my distant Oblate cousins, who is a supply teacher and thus always travelling, came to see me one day and spoke about the Mennonites with some envy and a great deal of respect. At the end of his career, it was almost as if he'd found a new vocation.
>
> On the other hand, I know a fellow named Schneider who was banished from the Mennonite community because he wanted to get an education. The first time I saw him he was hoping to get back into the good graces of his father. The last time, he was sad and a lot less sure.
>
> Those Mennonites are one of our fascinating minorities in the West. The French spoken outside Quebec reminds me of the Flemish dialect that the Belgian missionaries wanted to impose on the Congo.

I thought to myself ahead of time that Jacques Ferron, whose letters are written as metaphorically as his books, would certainly not enjoy playing the traditional analytic game of interviewer-interviewee. And so it occurred to me that I would probably end up having to reconstruct a good part of the interview and fill in the gaps between certain sentences myself.

Jacques Ferron is a medical doctor; however, he's not the sort of doctor for whom a *portuna* (as a doctor's bag is called in the Gaspé) and an office are a sign of prestige, a barrier that sets him apart from the rest of society. Ferron is a "misbeliever," in the sense that he does not possess the ordinary "faith" in medicine, writing or the Quebec nation. And although he does not follow the beaten paths, he has beaten some very strange ones of his own in his creative writing. The path of medicine, for example, leads him to asylums, those lugubrious prisons for the insane, where Coco the Misunderstood in *L'amélanchier* waits blindly for death and where the doctors, locked into their individual worlds, avoid any thought of social considerations and hold fast to the established rules—which Ferron suggests is the cause of most illnesses. As for the various pathways the nation has taken or will take, Ferron claims that these get dangerously muddled and lost in the "Labyrinth of Progress," whereas the nation's people, suffering all too often from a lack of hereditary memory, perish in the wastelands of unconsciousness and anonymity. The literary language Ferron uses is like a living tree that grows in every little corner of the land of Quebec. According to Ferron, the reader learns in his own "Bible" that "The space that surrounds us plays a good joke on time by constantly replanting itself like wheat." As a writer, his references constantly move in the direction of local reality, whether that be Longueuil, Trois-Rivières, Louisville, the Gaspé, Quebec City or Montreal. Ferron interiorizes the landscapes of his country so that by recreating them, he can foster a deeper sense of belonging.

Jacques Ferron had little use for what he called the "parasites of literary criticism"—critics with their graphs in hand, ready to tear works of literature apart and deform their meaning. I wondered whether he'd see me as yet another academic, a discipline of Bachelard and Freud or member of some literary "coterie."

Before setting off to meet him, I finally decided that I would take Jacques Ferron for what he is: a doctor who cares for the working-class people in Longueuil, a man who clearly sets out his own positions in life, and above all a writer with a tremendous gift for storytelling. I was prepared to react to what he said, since I suspected he would talk more or less as he wrote, using images as anecdotes. This was certainly the case; blessed with an extraordinarily fine memory, Ferron sometimes unconsciously repeated complete sentences from his published work.

I finally got into the taxi which was to take me to Dr. Ferron's office. "1285 Chambly Road, please," I said to the driver; "1285, oh yeah, that's close to the shopping centre," he replied, flicking on the metre. Deep in Ferron's home territory, which had become almost mythological in my mind, I discovered that the phrase "shopping centre" recalled for me the marvellous passages Ferron had written about Longueuil—especially about Old Longueuil, when there were still animals and fields and swamps. And I realized that Old Longueuil had definitely been taken over by what Ferron in his novels calls the "terrible sameness of urban, suburban, gas-station, American banality." We drove by an immense and appropriately filthy grain elevator, which paradoxically looked like a gigantic castle. A few minutes later Ferron would refer to the elevator as an "urban castle," and at that point I realized the same elevator must be the source, in *La nuit,* of the malevolent castle of Montreal. After almost running into a young man who was no doubt suffering from a hangover and whose car was stopped in the middle of the road, the taxi driver yelled out "maudit flo!" ("damned kid"), and there I was again, right back in the middle of Ferron's work, since it was in his *Contes du pays incertain* that I had first discovered the Quebec word *flo*—apparently derived in the Gaspé region from the English "fellow." I got out of the taxi and found myself in front of an ordinary little red-brick house, which reminded me of *Papa Boss* and the "nice red-brick row houses, the achievement of a lifetime" for low-income workers and the unemployed. I entered the house. Monsieur Ferron, wearing a dark-blue suit and powder-blue turtleneck, greeted me warmly in an office filled with a curious mixture of books, paintings and bottles of medicine. We chatted for a few minutes about *flos* and grain elevators and gradually our conversation turned into an interview.

My first question dealt with the act of writing. Some writers build up a collection of filing cards and construct their books brick by brick, letting themselves go only occasionally, when inspiration strikes. If Ferron had worked in this

way, I could have asked him precise questions about such and such a theme or the development of a particular symbol. However, this is how he explained the way he writes:

> Sometimes after seeing something that has caught my attention, I put it into a book without even being aware of it. That's what happened with the nighthawks, those poor insect-eating birds that have trouble walking and that hovered over Montreal. They symbolize the City, but they've disappeared since then, I think, since the City doesn't even tolerate insects any more.

> In the act of writing, images simply emerge. You don't actually know what you're doing. Just inventing things gives you pleasure. It's an accomplishment. You reveal yourself. When I have my historical character Chénier drink rubbing alcohol in *Les grands soleils,* for example, I added an unexpected dimension to the character, turning him into a beggar for a moment or two. This was a surprise. Writing makes time stand still. The hours go by and you're not even aware of it.

> I did my apprenticeship as a writer with my plays. I learned how to create places, how to provide a setting. It appears that Jean-Marie Lemieux is going to produce *Les grands soleils* this fall, which will be sort of like taking up nationalism where Louis Fréchette left off in the 19th century with his *La légende d'un peuple,* I wanted to write a play entitled *Riel* but I wasn't able to do it. The situation around the character was utterly crazy! There was nothing crazy about Riel himself, proudly declaring that the Métis nation existed: "Here we are, established as a nation!" He was brilliant in both his words and his intelligence.

In *La nuit,* Ferron states that "reality is hidden behind reality." The critic Jean Marcel has previously underlined the importance of this phrase. Ferron, however, tells me that it is simply the "phrase of a madman," and since I know that madness in his work is often a sign of profundity, fantasy and illumination, I conclude that literary madness and the symbolic dimension hidden behind external reality are equivalents. From this perspective a nighthawk is not a nighthawk, but the macabre bird of Ferron's urban castle. In a similar way the magnificent canvas "Le bout du monde" ("The World's End"), painted by Ferron's mother, Adrienne Caron, is not simply a landscape of Maskinongé County; through the reality of a sinuous, black river and leafless trees in an autumnal evocation of the end of the world, it expresses a certain anguish caused by the dying natural world. Hung directly opposite Dr Ferron's desk, "Le bout du monde," because of its sinister atmosphere, seems to have strange connections to the novels and short stories—and to the sad, dull suburbs "flattened out so they spread wider, and spreading wider so they can drink more oil, the new blood of Christ and the milk of the new civilization" (*La nuit*).

I've always been fascinated by rivers in Ferron's work. I remember a passage from *La nuit*:

> My own childhood was a river, and all along this river there was a succession of little compart-

mentalized countries marked off from one another by the bends in the river. After each bend comes another, and in this way my childhood reaches back into the past—at least a century or two, and perhaps more. My childhood includes a beginning of the world and an end of the world. It is my Genesis.

I had imagined Ferron's river of childhood to be sunny and surrounded by vegetation. I was mistaken, at least as far as the maternal river of "Le bout du monde" is concerned.

If a river isn't a river in Ferron's novel, then an animal is rarely an animal, but rather the incarnation of an individual or group of human beings. Cows, horses, pigs and wild boars, dogs, nighthawks and martins—all these are used as images through which Ferron speaks to us. When he was a young child in Louiseville, he told me, he often used to go to look at the cows that belonged to a neighbouring farmer, and *"every cow had its own name."*

Jacques Ferron has published almost nothing recently and this silence troubles him a great deal:

> I wanted to do a book about madness, based on my experiences as a doctor, but I botched it . . . I had writer's block. Not being able to write any more has taken away my power.

> Madness interests me. The insane are often more serene than the rest of us. All this goes back to my childhood. In Louiseville people talked about the ones who had escaped from the asylum in Beauport. They also used to say someone "was ready for Mastaï," for the Saint-Michel Archange Hospital named after Pius IX, Cardinal of Mastaï. Mastaï was a "very classy" place to be locked away, like Shakespeare's "Bedlam," a corruption of Bethlehem. Speaking of Shakespeare, British novels are among my favourite books. I really liked Dickens' *Hard Times*, and *The Mill on the Floss* and *Silas Marner* by George Eliot. The British countryside resembles our own more than France does. The French countryside is foreign to me.

Jacques Ferron's "English readings" seem to me rather significant. Dickens' *Oliver Twist*, with its elements of the traditional British "tale" and a sense of fantasy both light-hearted and nightmarish, is not unlike Ferron's own stories or tales. Like Ferron's young character Tinamer, Oliver Twist struggles against social injustice, "hard times," corrupt police officers and the evil personified in Fagin, who in turn is not unlike Ferron's Bélial, a *gripette* or devil in Quebec French. Furthermore, in *L'amélanchier,* the marvellous story of Hubert Robson of Tingwick in Arthabaska County is reminiscent of Mr Pickwick in *The Pickwick Papers,* although this would appear to be simply a coincidence since Ferron took the episode almost word-for-word from *Les bois-francs* by Abbé Mailhot. In any case Mr Pickwick shares Ferron's revolt against the inhumanity of our institutions. With regard to George Eliot, it was through her realistic nineteenth-century novels that Ferron first made acquaintance with the English countryside. Also, in Eliot's *Silas Marner* as in the works of Ferron, childhood serves as a "humanitarian orientation." As far

as the reference to Shakespeare's Bedlam is concerned, the insane asylum Saint Mary of Bethlehem, founded in 1247 by a group of nuns in London and infamous for its "Bedlam Beggars," is in much the same league as Ferron's "madmen's prisons"; his Mont-Thabor, Mont-Providence and Saint-Jean-de-Dieu, all sanctioned by the Church, are described as mediaeval "institutions of torture." [In an endnote, the critic adds: "Regarding his readings in Quebec literature, Ferron confesses to being particularly fond of the writings of Hubert Aquin."]

Jacques Ferron attaches a great deal of importance to Quebec's history. He demythifies almost the entire group of Quebec heroes glorified in the schoolbooks published by the Christian Brothers and the Clercs de Saint-Viateur. Jacques Cartier, for example, is transformed into an apostle of free enterprise, coming to America in the name of "extraction" and "plunder." The "handsome but good-for-nothing Dollard de Zoro" (Dollard des Ormeaux) becomes the "bandit of the Long Sault" and not the pious hero depicted by the Church. For Jacques Ferron, however, the *historiette* (historical tale) is a good deal more than simply a collection of anecdotes. Here is what the author has to say on the subject:

> The *historiette* is true history without any window-dressing or prettifying. Too many of our historians have glorified men who were in fact bandits. Those who falsified our national history had to be silenced.

> The title *historiette* occurred to me because of the *Historiettes* written by Tallemant des Réaux. In his work, as in the witty memoirs of Hamilton, history becomes a series of picturesque and racy military escapades. One of my Polish friends said that the *historiette* is a "madman's paper."

The expression "a madman's paper" strikes me as being a very appropriate description of the way Ferron approaches history. He sets out to dispel certain myths and it is only in that sense that he sees himself as an historian. Moving from history to the historical tale, he "disenhaloes" events or characters that have been falsely acclaimed in the past and then moves on to the "picturesque," the colourful and the comic (satire, irony, puns and off-colour jokes). Emile Nelligan is a case in point. Ferron does not agree with the nebulous fame of the poet described by some literary critics as condemned, insane, castrated, mother-repressed, father-repressed or even martyred:

> Nelligan couldn't do any better than he did. He wrote some remarkable poems in a very short period of time, but then he started pounding his head against the wall and he was declared insane, which was normal at Saint-Jean-de-Dieu. That was it for Nelligan. I met his nephew recently. He told me that Nelligan's father, an Irishman who repudiated his country of origin in the name of the civil service, was earning $8,000 a year, which was a considerable amount for the time.

In the case of the poet Saint-Denys Garneau, Dr Ferron diagnoses a "swelling of celebrity" and he assigns this first of Quebec's modern poets, changed into Orpheus for the occasion, to the hell of those Québécois who can't make up their minds. Orpheus, the aristocratic "little brown-haired boy" in *Le ciel de Québec* is condemned for having disavowed his patriotic ancestor, François-Xavier Garneau, and for having written "intimist poetry" based on a rejection of the space, colour and games of his native land. According to Ferron, the critic Jean Lemoyne also lacks a "collective memory" and an "internal river." Lonesome for the "track of Confederation" and carrying a C.N. lantern, Ferron's "Pope" of the magazine *La relève,* a veritable choir-boy "hung up" on the Jesuits, accompanies Orpheus to hell.

Monsieur de La Barre is another example of an actual historical figure viewed through the deforming lens of the historical tale. After being sent out to Ville-Marie by Anne of Austria, La Barre took command of a group of 60 men fighting the "wicked Iroquois." In Ferron's view La Barre is another of those historical bandits who need to be given a "picturesque" and "racy" metamorphosis in the historical tale. Thus Ferron's version has Monsieur de La Barre, an extremely devout man with a crucifix hanging from his belt, being discovered by Maisonneuve stretched out in the underbrush beside a pregnant Indian woman. Ferron's achievement is to be able to take various historical realities and blend them into an original concoction of fact and fiction.

Ferron talked to me about the *Mémoires du Comte de Gramont* by Anthony Hamilton, an Irishman who wrote in French. Hamilton too was a writer of historical tales who always managed to find just the right combination of "picturesque" images and significant abbreviations to describe the vices and virtues of England at the time of the Restoration. The "francization" of Hamilton reminds me of all the Irishmen in Ferron's work, including his novel *Le salut de l'Irlande* (literally *The Salvation of Ireland*), who are "in the process of Quebecification" and thus contributing to the "Salvation of Quebec" in French-speaking North America. In Ferron's writings there are a certain number of English-speaking characters who break free of their minority/majority attitudes. Such was the case, in *Le ciel de Québec,* with Frank-Anacharsis Scot, who Ferron assured me "may one day become François-Anacharsis Sicotte, nicknamed Pit." In *Le salut de l'Irlande,* Connie Haffigan sets out on the same rocky road to "Quebecification" when he sympathizes with certain aspirations of the F.L.Q. As Ferron put it:

> English people who have been assimilated make the best Québécois. At the beginning some of them were only here for industry. But there are always a few who come to understand that money is less important than identity. They start seeing themselves as an oppressive minority, they're ashamed of it, and they become nationalized. In Louiseville (the village Ferron grew up in) I had my first contacts with assimilated English people, Hamiltons and Lindsays. Later, in the Gaspé, I knew a British woman who became as Gaspesian as you can get.

In Ferron's writings names and nicknames are extremely significant. The author, like country people generally, is a "nominalist" (the term is defined in the *Appendice aux confitures de coings ou le congédiement de Frank Archibald Campbell*). He likes the way names sound, the senses and images they evoke. The character Papa Boss, who represents the "bonus value" and net profit of the American Way of Life, as the Commanding General of all the G.I. Joes, the new Eternal Father and the principal director of "Asshold Finance," was, Ferron explained, originally based on the Haitian dictator Papa Doc Duvalier. The "nominalist" power of the key words in Ferron's work is so great and so fascinating that, for me, one night in Montreal, Papa Boss took on the altogether different nominal form of a unilingual English-speaking waitress in a restaurant called Papa Joe's. That night Papa Boss or Papa Joe became my own "reality behind reality."

The same family names frequently recur in a variety of forms in Ferron's writings, often in connection with Quebec history. These historical references are not always easily identifiable, however, and the reader may take a great deal of pleasure in discovering their origins. Perhaps the most flagrant example is that of "Frank Scott." Ferron's Frank Scot (not to mention George Scott, who goes hunting for Acadians in *Les roses sauvages,* the paternalistic Scott Ewen character in *La tete du roi,* and the Métis Henry Scott, who becomes Henri Sicotte) points the reader towards a whole family of Canadian and Quebec Scotts, some of whom, Ferron pointed out, were not terribly sympathetic to the Quebec cause. There is, to be sure, the English-Canadian poet Frank Scott, translator of Anne Hébert and son of an Anglican Bishop of Quebec City. That particular Frank is a social-democrat, a staunch federalist and a champion of bilingualism—in short, as "Hughmaclennenesque as they come," in Ferron's opinion. A rapid glance through the country's history, however, reveals a number of other important Scotts who have become part of Ferron's mythology: Thomas Scott, a young Ontario Orangeman who was executed by the Riel tribunal in 1870; Alfred H. Scott, representative of the English settlers in the official Métis delegation sent to Ottawa in 1870 to negotiate Manitoba's entry into Confederation, whom Ferron depicts quite positively; William Henry Scott, the patriot elected in Deux-Montagnes, a friend of Chénier and Girod and a supporter of Papineau, although he was in league with the Curé Paquin and thus opposed to the use of arms; and William Henry Scott's brother, the merchant Neil Scott from Sainte-Thérèse, who was also a peace-seeking patriot. Ferron's Scotts and Scots oscillate between the Quebecified Sicottes and the Scots along the line of the Anglican Bishop of Quebec City, who stands admiring the monument to Wolfe. It might be noted that even the name Sicotte is taken from Quebec history, since a farmer from Mascouche named Toussaint Sicotte was a minister in the Union government and a patriot charged with high treason in 1837. Jacques Ferron has an obsession with names. The same name or nickname may pop up in a number of different works, with or without changes in spelling. And in the course of our conversation that Sunday morning in the month of March, he spontaneously referred to a number of names that appear in his writings. At first these names may seem somewhat random, but it gradually emerges that they inevitably refer to four major thematic thrusts in Ferron's work: political, social, medical or religious betrayals and injustices. In *L'amélanchier,* Mr Northrop, for example, is an Englishman by birth and by choice, his compass firmly pointed in the direction of London. In this case the reference is obviously to the English-Canadian critic Northrop Frye, ironically described to me by Ferron as "a former Quebecker who prefers the anatomy of criticism and of the University of Toronto to the anatomy of Quebec." This is followed by one of Ferron's wry little smiles, an endearing gesture that manages to be almost childlike and at the same time reminiscent of the fox in *Le salut de l'Irlande.*

---

**Jacques Ferron has an obsession with names. The same name or nickname may pop up in a number of different works, with or without changes in spelling. At first these names may seem somewhat random, but it gradually emerges that they inevitably refer to four major thematic thrusts in Ferron's work: political, social, medical or religious betrayals and injustices.**

**—Donald Smith**

---

Ferron then goes on to explain that his character Rédempteur Fauché, the son of Papa Boss and a Québécoise virgin in *Papa Boss,* is somewhat closer to the criminal of the same name, who settled his accounts by setting fire to a house (although he got the wrong house by mistake), than to any real Redeemer (*Rédempteur*). "With my Rédempteur," Ferron continues, "I intended to make some annunciations. That wasn't what happened. Young Rédempteur, the little bum, became a sacrilege." Sacrilege does not seem too strong an expression, in fact, since in the world of Rédempteur Fauché, the Almighty Dollar replaces the sacristy, soldiers replace the Messiah, and "Asshold Finance" replaces church collections and tithes. "I use names to conquer, to nationalize," says Ferron. I ask him if Abbé Surprenant in *Le ciel de Québec,* a pleasant local ethnologist, a "pilgrim" who is more interested in the unemployed than in holy places, who admires the communists, actually existed. "Not at all," laughs Ferron, happy at having led me down the garden path. The Abbé is a fictional character who is *surprenant* (surprising) in comparison to the prestigious, plutocratic clergy of the establishment in the novel. He is at the bottom end of the Catholic hierarchy, close to the people. Ferron himself was once a communist, but he left the movement because he found it too theoretical, full of contradictions and corrupted by "that strange talent so many reformed communists have for property speculation," (*La charrette*). Still, in *Le ciel de Québec* Abbé Surprenant can claim, like Ferron, that communism

> takes account of historical reality and gives people in distress something that will save them quicker than bread and board—I mean an un-

derstanding of their situation . . . In [the Church's] abstract philosophy, we've bet our money on the absolute; in the concrete world we offer nothing but cheap escape, such as pilgrimages to fight unemployment; bowls of soup to people starved for justice.

(trans. Ray Ellenwood, *The Penniless Redeemer*)

For anyone who plunges into the nominalist world of Jacques Ferron, it is clearly interesting and perhaps even useful to know whether such-and-such character actually existed, but it is not essential. I had understood the significance of Abbé Surprenant, and that's what really matters. Nominalist that he is, however, and whatever the degree of consciousness or unconsciousness involved, Ferron's Surprenant reminded me of the Lorenzo Surprenant in *Maria Chapdelaine,* a character who was much more a man than his eunuch-like rival, Gagnon. Jacques Ferron is fascinated by the religious history of nineteenth-century Quebec:

> The most baroque and flamboyant manner of preaching was taught to us by Msgr Forbin-Janson, the Bishop-Prince of Nancy. His two-week retreat, as reported in *Les mélanges religieux,* was very useful for me in *Le ciel de Québec;* I only had to arrange his sermons and put them into the mouth of Msgr Cyrille Gagnon. I don't believe Msgr Bourget was one of our great religious tenors, who like Chiniquy were all students of Forbin-Janson; nor was Msgr Lartigue, who must have preached in the serious, sober style of the Sulpicians.

> The Sulpicians of Montreal, in close collaboration with their counterparts in Paris, sent the first Bishop of Montreal, Msgr Lartigue, into retirement in Longueuil. In actual fact the first Bishop was the second, Msgr Bourget, who came from Quebec City. Without going so far into the past, I can quote from my own experience: in Louiseville, my first teachers, the Frères de l'Instruction chrétienne, were Canadians at the bottom of the ladder, Bretons in the hierarchy. But an even stranger thing was that in the kindergarten in Trois-Rivières, the Filles de Jésus, who were referred to as the French Nuns, were under the authority of two British ladies, who were in fact remarkable creatures.

> Forbin-Janson had been an Ultra and it was after the Revolution in 1830 that he went into exile in America.

Brother Marie-Victorin is another religious "tenor" in whom Ferron shows an interest. Marie-Victorin is famous for identifying the plant-life of the Laurentian shield, and in his own way Jacques Ferron has identified the places and families of Quebec. The "family history" of Quebec, Ferron affirms, has its roots in the legend of the three brothers (which is told in *L'amélanchier* and in an article published in *La revue de l'Universite de Moncton,* vol. 8, no 2, May 1975).

> My father used to talk about the three brothers. People with other family names have also told me the same story. At the very beginning, there

were three brothers. There's always one who turns out badly, a famous rascal named, in my case, Jean Ferron. When I went to Shippigan in New Brunswick, the Acadian Ferrons were amazed to learn there were Ferrons in Quebec.

In Acadian mythology it's the women who dominate: they dream of Evangeline, they know about Ave Maris Stella, they have their great Saint Anne. For us, the woman is an element of reunion and confidence who comes after the three brothers. The Acadians and the Québécois have different archetypes.

Popular legends are scattered throughout Ferron's writings. Their authenticity is less important than their unifying effect and their amusing, liberating qualities. Léon de Portanqueu in *L'amélanchier* claims that every family should "make itself into the stuff of tales so as to give new vitality to an old heritage and revive the tales and songs that are part of life's necessities." The cart, which Ferron uses as a symbol of capitalist corruption, human stupidity and the hard labour of the working people, has its origins in the legendary past of the Ferron family:

> "La charrette" ("The Cart") was my father's favourite song. It's a song about a peasant farmer who runs into trouble with the middlemen. The Devil picks up the whole lot of them, except him. At the end he's a free man.

Jacques Ferron has a reputation for being deeply involved in nationalist causes. He tells me that he hasn't always been a nationalist and that when he was at classical college, even Pierre Laporte, who wore the little green beret of the Action francaise, was more nationalistic than he. "The situation was pretty well reversed in October, 1970," he remarks thoughtfully, perhaps recalling his role as intermediary between the police and the F.L.Q. after Laporte had been kidnapped and killed. It was well before the Quiet Revolution that Ferron first began to regard himself as Québécois and not French Canadian. This is already apparent in *La barbe de Francois Hertel,* written in 1947. The nationalist orientation began to take hold when Ferron thought back to his childhood, especially to that distant night the village church burned down (Ferron assures one that the fire Léon de Portanqueu talks about really did take place); this revealed to Ferron that, even without a church, the village could still exist. Quite independently from his father, who was somewhat infatuated with his own success as a lawyer, and his mother, an artistic woman who had a nationalistic streak but who died of tuberculosis, Ferron started thinking on his own about the problems of existence and the splendours and miseries of Quebec. From that time on he became his own saviour and considered any other messiah as "worthless."

Jacques Ferron's earliest memory of his childhood in Louiseville contains, in capsule form, the basic structure of his future work as a writer:

> In Louiseville the overall structure was completely Manichean: lower and upper, good and evil, the big village of the important people, and the little village of the proletariat. Don't forget that today's Lachine used to be the little village of Montreal. The "little villages," no doubt of

Indian origin, only had paths for streets. I saw the same thing in 1946 in the Micmac village in New Brunswick—an Indian reservation where there were Chinese men and Black women working. Micmac and Fredericton: little village and big village. Sydney and Montreal: little village and big village. The Black women in Sydney and the French Canadians: two little villages.

This obsession with villages should in no way be construed to mean, as the critic Gilles Marcotte has claimed, that Ferron, true to the old "agriculturalist" complex of French Canadians, is advocating a return to the land. The little village compared to the big village is simply one way of representing the small versus the large, Quebec versus the United States and Canada, the working man versus the boss. Ferron is, of course, fascinated by the parish structure, but this is how he explains it:

> What more did the French settlers do than set up parishes? That's where the meaning of those little communities comes from—little communities in a larger community. That's why the main subject of *Le ciel de Québec* is the founding of a parish. In the old days they used to put a curse on the grasshoppers to drive them into other parishes, which were considered "foreign."

In an article entitled "Jacques Ferron et l'histoire de la formation sociale québécoise" (*Etudes francaises,* 12/3-4), Robert Mignier takes issue with Ferron, who sees the beginnings of Quebec's national history as emerging about 1837. Mignier claims that Ferron confuses history with nationalism, and that after the conquest, the French-Canadian people, contrary to what the author of the *Historiettes* states, did have a sense of patriotism, which came mainly from the fact that they were populating the country. Ferron objects to this, as follows:

> There were barely 60,000 French Canadians after the Conquest. There weren't enough people to develop any real national awareness until the 1830's. A nation's history has a starting point. It's important to establish when it was.

In the writings of Jacques Ferron, the leading figures in the emergence of a national spirit are Papineau, the patriots Chénier and Bonaventure "le Beau" Viger, and the historian Francois-Xavier Garneau. The author confides to me that the episode in *Les grands soleils,* where Chénier collapses in a cemetery, was taken from a tale called "Petite scène d'un grand drame" by Pamphile Le May. In the case of Viger, a number of historians have told the story of the patriots' first encounter with the British soldiers on Chambly Road at the corner of Coteau-Rouge. Ferron was able to point out the exact spot to me: three blocks from his office, where a traffic light flashes anonymously at a busy highway intersection. The beautiful fields of Longueuil are gone forever.

They were there on November 17, 1837, however, when Bonaventure Viger, a farmer from Longueuil and captain of the militia, captured the colours from Colborne, Dr Davignon and the notary Demaray. I point out to Ferron that the man nicknamed "le beau Viger" was not Bonaventure, but rather Louis-Michel Viger, a lawyer, first cousin to Papineau, and founder of the People's Bank, a sort of precurser to today's Caisses populaires. I add, however, that in my opinion an "error" of this sort is not really an error, since Ferron's "beau Viger" and the historical "beau Viger" do not necessarily have to be the same person. For Ferron the expression "le beau Viger" acts as a leitmotif. And through a marvellous "coincidence," "le beau Viger" who is missing part of his thumb is related to the good-for-nothing brother in the legend of the three brothers: a strange beggar who also lost the end of his thumb, in this case in a battle against the English at Fort Maskinongé. In Ferron's world the history of the nation and the history of the family are never entirely distinct.

It was already the noon-hour and Monsieur Ferron and I had been chatting back and forth for three hours. Not wanting to impose upon him, I glanced at my watch and Monsieur Ferron offered to drive me to the Métro station. Since we were driving in a yellow Renault, I remarked that Dr Ferron, unlike some of the more pretentious characters in his work, didn't drive the black "hearse" favoured by his doctors, prelates and incompetent honourable ministers. We drove past the house that formerly belonged to the Ferron family. "It was a lot more shaded by trees when we sold it two years ago," Ferron sighed. Behind the house I was amazed to see how far the woods extended; here was the origin of the "airy, chattering and enchanted" second-growth forest where the Ferrons' little girl, named Tinamer in *L'amélanchier,* used to spend her afternoons. There was no Minotaur stalking down Bellerive Street, as in Ferron's supernatural tale, but the street was as subdivided and asphalt-covered as I had imagined. The Juneberry tree (*l'amélanchier*) that young Tinamer refers to as "rakish and mocking, in league with the birds," is enormous for a shrub of that species. "It's the size of a small tree," Ferron remarks, "but it doesn't flower every spring." What does matter, I thought, is that it flowers and acquires new meaning in the minds of Ferron's readers.

The Renault drove past a shopping centre. I looked out at the huge parking lot with horror and heard Ferron remark:

> I once saw Marie-Victorin give a lecture at the College in Longueuil. Did you know that in one of his tales ("Ne vends pas la terre") he tells the story of a proud and admirable farmer who refused to sell his land to the speculators swarming over here after the Jacques-Cartier Bridge was built? He sold it a few years ago, for a higher price.

Does the lust for money always win out in the end? How is it possible to resist the "urban sprawl" that Ferron depicts so effectively in his writings? These were the questions I was asking myself, and I couldn't help thinking of *Le salut de l'Irlande* and Major Bellow, a former land speculator in Quebec now living in Victoria, a city Ferron amusingly transforms into "a plastic English place" of retired "golden-agers" and American tourists from Seattle. If the Major "bellows," it must be out of contentment, although "sneer" might be a more appropriate expression, considering how he exploited the people of Quebec. As for the shopping centre, the only thing left grazing there is the Steinberg supermarket. I left Monsieur Ferron with a firm handshake and thanked him for the images he had awakened in me. A few minutes later the Métro was whisking me under the St. Lawrence, under what Tinamer refers to so marvellously and so "anachronistically"—after all, writing does make time stand still—as the "majestic St. Lawrence, filled with greasy dishwater," the most impressive "of all the sewers of Upper and Lower Canada."

### Ray Ellenwood (essay date 1984)

SOURCE: "Translator's Afterword," in *The Penniless Redeemer,* translated by Ray Ellenwood, Exile Editions, 1984, pp. 339-42.

[*In the following essay, Ellenwood discusses Ferron's mixture of the mundane and the fantastic in* The Penniless Redeemer.]

'In the beginning is *Le Ciel de Québec,* our great and only novel of initiation,' writes Philippe Haeck [in *Voix & Images,* Vol. VIII, No. 3 (1983)]. And he calls the book 'our Bible.' Why? Maybe because it is so inclusive, the most complete account of his uncertain country by a man who seems to know more about it than anyone. It functions almost as a Book of Numbers, but also as gossip, stories told over the kitchen table, carefully detailed little jokes about priests, politicians, public figures of all kinds. Myth has that side to it as well, telling who did what to whom, taking plenty of time to focus on homely details, even though the characters (with names like Apollo, Orpheus, Calliope) may be larger than life.

I don't know how anyone could not enjoy this book on the level of pure irreverent tale-telling, for the fun it has at the expense of half-crazed clerics and other notables. To do so is not to forget the important observations it makes about social and cultural relations, language, compassion and power. Gradually, the broad themes impose their order on apparent chaos.

The story begins *in medias res,* like a true epic. Msgr. Camille is on his way to say Mass, Eurydice and Cotnoir are dead, Frank has left home, Orpheus is emerging from the Underground and the creation of the Parish of Sainte-Eulalie is yet to be completed. The next chapters move backward in time, setting the stage, introducing us to characters and places, many of them 'real' in the sense that they could be found in a chronicle or atlas of Québec in the thirties. These portraits, I understand, are tremendously evocative for anyone who can remember the time and place. But the narrative contains such a mixture of real and fictional characters they are hard to distinguish. History is dead, long live the novel. We move freely in time and space, especially after the middle of the book, and the effect is a kind of disorientation.

If we step back for a moment, however, we soon notice how deliberate is the structure. We are reminded more than once that the year is 1937, which was significant not only for the publication of Saint-Denys-Garneau's *Regards et jeux dans l'espace* and the first article on Paul-Emile Borduas, but also marked a heating up in the Spanish Civil War (involving a genuine hero for Ferron: Norman Bethune), the early stages of the Moscow Trials, and an important political event in Québec: the imposition of Maurice Duplessis' Padlock Law, designed to discourage the spread of Communism. Exactly one hundred years earlier came the Patriot Rebellion in Québec and the extermination of the Mandans in the West. Threads in the carpet connect.

All this confusion of historical and fantastic events, the whole action, is enveloped by a very significant movement. The story begins and ends with Msgr. Camille making his way down from the *Grand Séminaire* of Québec City into Lower Town, past the brothels on Rue Saint-Vallier and eventually to the Convent of the Precious Blood. That motif of movement from high to low is repeated over and over in the novel. Frank moves from his home to the Hôtel des Voyageurs and eventually to Chiquetteville, making his way, as he says in the Conclusion, 'down from the absurd, pompous and rickety ladder of a society built in air.' Frank's father is in a lighthouse, or up a ladder or a tree and must also come down to make any human contact. A Cardinal falls to his knees in front of a child. The moral and political significance of all this descent is explained in Chapter 28 when Msgr. Camille and François-Anacharcis discuss the need to identify with, and protect, those who are not eminent, those who are low and have no power. That is the organizing thematic principle of the book. Although almost everyone we see is a figure of fun, the sympathetic characters are all trying, in one way or another, to bridge a Manichean gulf between high and low, good and evil, strong and weak, in order to reduce as much as possible man's inhumanity to man. Sometimes that involves trying to tame virtuous fanatics, or even whole parishes. Its most comic expression, of course, is in François-Anacharcis Scot's attempts to become a Québécois, about which Dr. Ferron had this to say, in a letter of 1976:

> An elderly gentleman, a retired RCMP officer, was reading *Le ciel de Québec* for news of Frank Scott. He accused me of making Scott do slightly off-color things, if not indecent things, near the end. I could only congratulate the gentleman because he was the first reader I've ever met who actually got that far in the book. As for the slightly off-color things he mentioned, I had to explain I had no choice. We in Québec don't have any recognized procedure for conferring nationality on a dear friend, and so I was forced to give François a dose of the clap.

Fine enough, but what do Saint-Denys-Garneau and Borduas have to do with that? For an answer, perhaps we could look at what Msgr. Camille might call the Westmount point of view.

The late John Glassco, talking about Saint-Denys-Garneau [in his introduction to *Complete Poems of Saint-Denys-Garneau*, (1975)], says, 'his minor vanities—satirized by Jacques Ferron in *Le ciel de Québec* with typical horseplay and venom—his uneventful life and casual death, are now of little importance.' What matters for Glassco is the quality in Garneau's poetry which can be seen as universal:

> It is even doubtful if he saw himself as a French-Canadian poet at all, if indeed he did not hold himself superior to the very spirit of French-Canadian poetry, or at least aloof from it . . . His attitude was in this respect characteristically exclusive and fastidious; more important, his anguish was not localized in any sense of a vulgar *dépaysement,* as in a Hertel or a Miron, but in that of the universal human being.

Glassco argues that Garneau's 'rejection of parochialism—one might call it *québécisme*—is what situates [him] in the mainstream of poetry, not as [a poet] of Québec but of the world.' For Ferron, of course, Saint-Denys-Garneau's 'universalism' is alienation, and his life, far from being unimportant, is a shining negative example to be compared unfavorably with that of François-Xavier Garneau. It only makes things worse, from Ferron's point of view, that Saint-Denys-Garneau should be made a cultural hero and martyr through the machinations of academics and intellectuals such as Jean Le Moyne, who are alienated themselves. More than art is involved here; it is a political and moral question. That is surely why Ferron goes to so much pains to situate Saint-Denys-Garneau and the *Relève* group in the context of the Depression. Paul-Émile Borduas and Claude Gauvreau are implicated because, though their hearts may have been closer to the right place, they also formed a group with certain elitist qualities and a universalist philosophy. Ferron clearly suggests that art and the artist must relate to an immediate social context or be in limbo.

This, of course, is one of the great subjects of debate in twentieth century art and literature. I have quoted Glassco because he expresses so well the point of view under attack by Ferron. It has been the dominant point of view in English-speaking Canada, which may explain why Anne Hébert and Saint-Denys-Garneau were translated so much before Gaston Miron, and indeed before Ferron. But our author can speak for himself. What I want to emphasize is the fact that the debate is woven into the thematic and fictional structure of this novel. Garneau and Borduas are both purists in their own way, and each has his own descent. We watch them deflate one another; we see Orpheus, stunned by the loss of Eurydice (his muse?), comforted and encouraged by Msgr. Camille who, though no saint in Ferron's heaven, was at least an important spokesman for local cultural nationalism. Perhaps the pathetic story of Cotnoir and Eurydice is there to remind us that more is involved than pure aesthetics, and surely the whole cultural and mythological context of Henry Sicotte provides a contrast to, and comment on, the Québec and Montréal points of view.

But, along with the polemic, what a marvelous world this book offers, moving with such grace between the mundane and the fantastic. Just to give one example: if you were so inclined, you could follow Monsignor Camille out of the Seminary to the corner of Rue Saint-Jean and Côte du Palais. There would be too many cars and a new McDonald's hamburger palace very near the spot where he met Martial O'Farrell, but otherwise everything would be quite vividly as the prelate saw it. While going down the hill past the Hôtel-Dieu, you would notice the train station ahead of you. As you proceeded, however, the landscape would become more and more unfaithful to fiction, the streets would not quite correspond, the houses on Rue

Saint-Vallier would not be tall enough, and you would never find the Convent of the Precious Blood, any more than you would have found it in 1937. All of this is mere fact, of course, and not very interesting. Perhaps you should have stayed in the book, where you could have seen a state-of-the-art hell, or a talking rat, or legendary horses and devils incarnate, not to mention fascinating historical personages. Some might liken this to the magic realist world of Latin-American writers such as Gabriel Garcia Marquez, but the closest analogy I can find is with the *Haywain Triptych* of Heironymus Bosch, center panel, where insouciant lovers are flanked by angels and devils, where high and low mingle in pomp and scurrility, where hell-holes gape, allowing devils and mortals to pass. Perhaps Ferron really is, as Philippe Haeck suggests, Québec's great Catholic writer.

## Betty Bednarski    (essay date Spring 1985)

SOURCE: "Rereading Jacques Ferron," in *The Antigonish Review,* No. 61, Spring, 1985, pp. 43-9.

[*In the following essay, Bednarski comments on the relationship between life and literature in Ferron's works.*]

When Jacques Ferron died this spring, I began immediately rereading books of his, some of which had remained unopened on my shelf for several years. It must be a natural reaction to seek to re-establish contact in this way and to re-affirm a bond with a writer who has died. Especially if we have known and loved the man. For me Jacques Ferron the writer had always been inseparable from the man. And I no doubt brought to this most recent reading the particular intensity of my loss and, in spite of long held critical convictions and academic habits of mind, the desire, unconscious, perhaps, but no less intense, to rediscover in the texts a life which was no more, and which, in some compelling way, had touched and engaged my own. I also brought a recent and quite conscious preoccupation with the nature of the reading/writing process and curiosity about the subtle interplay between literature and life.

And so I read, following no particular order, heeding I know not what unconscious promptings, letting each book itself call forth the next. The Jacques Ferron I rediscovered was himself a reader, a voracious reader of other writers, great and small—writers as different as Lewis Carroll and Nathaniel Hawthorne, Louis Hémon and Claude Gauvreau, Samuel Butler and Paul Valéry—as if reading were a precondition of writing, a complement and accompaniment to that act. And not only did Ferron interpret and gloss the work of others, commenting, quoting, even stealing unabashedly, as if all literature were his to absorb, to draw on, to recycle and rework, but he read his own works too, and what is more, in texts that were to become increasingly and, in the end, almost exclusively, autobiographical, his own life. Not only did he offer a view of literature where boundaries of time and culture and individual *oeuvres* became indistinct and insignificant, but a view of reality in which boundaries between life and fiction also blurred, and where not only books but lives could be read.

I found Ferron the reader in the appendix to **Quince Jam,** elaborating on his own novel, linking the two protagonists

of his fiction—the Québecois, Francois Ménard, and the English Canadian, Frank Archibald Campbell—to their counterparts in real life—Ferron himself for Francois ("You don't have to be very clever to guess that it's me behind this character whose humility and principle of humility I admire."), and for Frank, Montrealer, F.R. Scott ("politiciser from McGill, son of a bishop or archdeacon, self-deluding idealist who thought he was a reformer, ahead of his time, when in fact he could only be, as a member of a dominant minority, a well-intentioned Rhodesian, more pernicious than anything."). I found him moving back and forth with ease and grace between fiction and life, weaving together memory, fantasy, supposition and fact, creating a text of uncommon richness and density. And in the novel itself I found two fictional lives so closely bound together as to seem almost to form one. Frank not only embodies for Francois all that is admirable and despicable in the English Canadian, he is an *alter ego,* not an enemy—or not just an enemy—but a veritable other self. At once the same and different, hated and loved, the English "other" is a vital point of reference in Francois' search for himself. Frank is a medium and an obstacle. To come to terms with him, to deal with him, is absolutely essential if the Québécois narrator is to recover his soul—his own and, by implication, Québec's. I knew that for close to a decade little of consequence, and certainly neither death nor redemption, could come about in Ferron's fictional universe without reference to this same Frank, identified clearly in **Quince Jam's** appendix, recognizable always, in his various guises, as the one and only F.R. Scott. In **Quince Jam** (a second version of **La Nuit,** an earlier novel), Francois and Frank meet in the Montreal morgue, and Francois is instrumental in bringing about the only slightly ambiguous poisoning of Frank. In **The Cart** it is Frank who summons the Québécois narrator and doctor to his death, and who, as the Devil's henchman, the Blarneyman—Bailiff of the Night, presides over the nocturnal rituals surrounding the demise. Finally, in the **Penniless Redeemer,** he even achieves the status of first person narrator. He takes part in the momentous events leading up to the birth of the Redeemer who is to bring about the salvation of the Québec people, and is himself redeemed, after a fashion, becoming indisputably, if somewhat unceremoniously, *Quebeckized*. Later, after the events of the October Crisis, he would be just as unceremoniously "sacked" . . . ("I was sorry that **La Nuit** was only fiction. It will remain fiction, but I am changing the title to stress the poison.")

I knew that Ferron and Scott had known each other, that they had had the C.C.F. and literature in common and had disagreed over the question of independence for Québec, but it seemed that they had not been associated in any regular or lasting way. The fictional association, however, was so long, and so intense, that I found it not at all surprising, indeed strangely logical, that Ferron's death should have followed so closely after Scott's, in spite of the more than twenty years of age that separated the two men. Already, to the reader-observer I was at the time, the first death (Scott's) had seemed to call up the second and to make it imminent, necessary. Now, in the light of my rereading, I had no trouble accepting that the close connection between two inhabitants of a fictional universe should be reflected, after the fiction, so to speak, in *real life*. Not only was life in this case as strange as fiction, fiction almost seemed to exert an influence on life, or at least to extend its logic beyond the confines of the printed page. It seemed impossible to speak of accident or coincidence. The closeness of the two deaths signified in some vaster sense the inextricable nature of the lives. In the logic of a total universe every detail was meaningful.

There were, I discovered, other circumstances of Ferron's death that were so like those described in this books as to make the latter appear almost prophetic. And it even seemed to me, as I reread them, that he had over the years written primarily of this, his own death, now facing it front on, now obliquely, jokingly, predicting even the time of day, the time of year. Could one, I wondered, write a life to bring it into line with fiction? Indisputable master of his fictional world, had Ferron managed, in some comparable way, to order, to author life? Or was he merely reading, seeing with heightened vision, the shape and sense of things to come?

There was no question in my mind that my comportment as Ferron's reader was governed, at least in part, by my relationship with the man, and by the fact that he had been as real to me as his books. With Ferron I would be drawn, as with no other writer, to abandon my normal critical stance and to re-integrate fiction and life. But I was equally sure that the work itself authorized, indeed invited, readings such as mine.

Not only does Ferron provide us with a fascinating example of author-reader, but there are in his books fictional readers, too, characters whose most significant activity is to read and interpret books. One of them caught my attention for the particular quality of her insights. She was Ann Higgit, the young English-speaking Maritimer of *Wild Roses*. Ann studies the works of French writer Louis Hémon, the author of *Maria Chapdelaine,* and discovers in them hidden messages, ciphers almost, cries for help directed to his sister who has stayed in France, while he, Hémon, has travelled to England and Canada. And the pleas remind her of those, unspoken, of her Québécois friend, Baron, with whom she has spent a few days in Moncton. Baron's wife, like Hémon's has gone mad, leaving him alone with a little daughter, who, like Hémon's child before her, must now be saved. Ann Higgit has read Hémon's fiction and made the connection between his life and work. She has interpreted his messages just as his sister did, and what is more, through this reading she has found new meaning in the life of Baron. But that is not all. Ann is well-read. In the course of her studies she has acquired some notion of mythology and a sense of tragic destiny. When she learns more about the biography of Louis Hémon and the circumstances of his tragic death, she fears for Baron and sees Hémon's fate as a kind of foreshadowing of Baron's end. She sees and understands, but she can do nothing to help Baron and knows she must abandon him to his cruel fate. In this case, strange though it may seem, conclusions are being drawn, on the basis of one man's life, about another's. Here, clearly, life itself is being read, with the same interpretive skills that are normally applied to literature. All this happens so easily and

so naturally that Ferron seems to be inviting us, through the intervention of Ann Higgit, to make the same kind of connection between his life and work, and, what is more, to apply directly to life, to his, to our own, the processes we have refined for the reading of literature.

I realized in retrospect that this was in fact what I had always done. Attentive to the laws of Ferron's universe, I had always read his books in conjunction with his life, finding in both signs, patterns, messages and a coherence I liked to call meaning. It was not surprising that ultimately I had come to read his death. If Ann Higgit was so important to me it was because she authorized and confirmed conclusions that, intuitively, I had reached, and because, as a reader, she resembled me.

Ann knew Hémon, the writer, and Baron, the man—two separate lives, which, in the perspective of the book, mirror each other and finally merge. Ferron himself identifies as surely with Baron as he does with Hémon, for each represents different possibilities of the same self. (Interestingly enough, while Baron/Hémon can be seen as a composite, the theme of the writer as split self is explored fully in the moving *Execution of Maski,* Ferron's most recent work, where the writer, Notary, conspires to be rid of Maski, the intrusive man.) Like Ann, I am a special kind of reader, because I knew both the writer and the man. But what does such a reader do with her insights? Can her reading be of significance to anyone but her? Ann Higgit taught literature. One can teach, though there are insights that would seem to have little place in the lecture room. One can teach . . . and one can also write.

In the appendix to *Quince Jam,* Ferron says of writing, "I consider it a right more than a profession, and I've often tried to convince others to do the same." And he adds jokingly that if his uncle, already a fine storyteller, were to take up writing, perhaps he himself might feel free to divert some of his own creative energies elsewhere ("Maybe if you'd write, then I'd feel more free to go chasing skirts.") . . . implying, albeit frivolously (the uncle in question was a devoted womanizer), that by exercising his right, the writer is at the same time performing a kind of duty, a function vital to the well-being of those around him. Writing is an activity that goes on in the name of all.

I found in *Dr. Cotnoir,* Ferron's first novel, where there is also, incidentally, an uncanny description of a doctor's April death, a passage on the power of writing, which summed up for me the writer's role as I had experienced it in my life. And I mean by that not just any writer's role (like mostly anyone, I have dozens of writers who are important to me), but that of the one great writer it was my privilege to know as a man.

In this novel there is a character who writes, not books, but a humble diary. She is the doctor's wife, and in the eyes of her husband she is creating an ark in which all whom she describes find salvation, for she elevates them, through the act of writing, to a kind of blessed state. The doctor has never looked inside the diary, and he wonders if he will recognize himself when he finally comes to read what she has written over the years. Transformed he will most likely be, but saved in some miraculous sense, too, he is sure. This doctor talks to his wife at the end of each day, offering up his experiences to her, and he tells us, "I've gotten a good many people aboard that ark and all the animals I've met in my twenty years in the suburb." Ferron himself has left us with a formidable ark, some forty years in the making, upwards of thirty volumes, a monument to his unbounded curiosity, his tolerance and his humanity. Inside, a multitude of individuals, an astonishing assortment of lives, extraordinary in their diversity, moving in their contradictions. And on them all he has bestowed dignity and the miracle of meaning. Like Cotnoir, some of us who knew Ferron must have sensed what he was building, for we would often bring to him treasures for safekeeping—people, thoughts, insights, disconnected fragments of our incoherent lives—convinced that to present them to him, to entrust him with them, was to somehow ensure their significance and their integration into a larger and coherent whole. And for this they did not need to find their way, transformed or otherwise, onto the printed page of an actual book. It was enough, we felt, to share them with him and so expose them to the meaning-seeking process we are all involved in, but in which writers overtly and systematically engage. It is writers who provide us with the strongest assurances that meaning can be found in life, or, if it is not already there, that it can at least be made to exist. Writers are, by their very existence, living models for a double activity which is fundamental to us all.

We are all readers and writers. I am Ferron's reader, and beyond that I am the reader of my own life, of which he is forever a part. But I am also, by natural extension, the virtual writer of that life. We are all of us virtual writers, carrying our texts around inside us, like the picture Jeremiah, the simple-minded "landscape painter" of Ferron's short story, saw, but never produced. ("No one recognized it. The artist had forgotten to sign.") We all tell, shape and order, just as we record the patterns, signs and meanings we have perceived. But very few of us ever become actual writers, giving to our texts a tangible and resonant form. Ferron's uncle the storyteller came very close. Ferron himself, in spite of his achievements, recognized inside him a virtual creation, which remained as real and compelling as any of his finished books—those *débris*—to quote his beloved Paul Valéry—those mere fragments of a vaster, more glorious whole. And, sensing the virtual all around him, he could encourage others to write. As for me, the only words I ever wrote that were of lasting significance to me were addressed to Jacques Ferron. And I see my letters to him, not as true writing, but as humble jottings, *notes de lecture,* notes written by a reader in the margins of her life . . .

As reader/writer of my life, I cherish my association with Jacques Ferron, the writer and the man. I consider myself enriched by him, immeasurably, more than I could possibly put into words. As a reader of literature, I have gained insights I am still unsure how to share. Ann Higgit did talk to her students of Hémon (Baron), but when she spoke they noticed there were tears in her eyes.

## Ray Ellenwood    (essay date Spring 1985)

SOURCE: "Death and Dr. Ferron," in *Brick: A Journal of Reviews,* No. 24, Spring, 1985, pp. 6-9.

[*In the essay below, Ellenwood discusses Ferron's treatment of death in his stories and novels.*]

He was obsessed with it; defied it and courted it virtually all his life. His mother died young of tuberculosis, his father committed suicide a few years later, he was tubercular himself and was sent to a sanitarium just after the war. Deciding he wasn't ready for a slow, passive demise, he went over the wall and continued working twenty hours a day, smoking like a chimney, conducting pharmacological experiments on himself, even trying, unsuccessfully, Mithridates' silken escape ladder until death finally caught him napping on the morning of April 22, 1985. *Neveurmagne,* he'll have the last word. No writer I'm aware of has ever said so much, so wisely, humorously, mordantly, compassionately about death.

In the tales, most of which were written in the fifties and early sixties, death is handled ironically and coolly, with the narrator as a more-or-less detached spectator. The event takes place in a clear social context. Its banality and ego-centricity often contrast with the conventional actions and basic impatience of the survivors. Sometimes the moment of death gives us an image of an entire life, as in **"How the Old Man Died,"** where we witness a quiet struggle between a moribund but stubborn old man and his wife, who would like him to show a little dignity for once:

> Short waves shook the old man. This lasted an hour or more; then after the final wave came the final hour; the old man was at peace at last in his bed; the bone pained him no more; he was healed; he was about to die. The women had returned to his side, smothering seagull cries in their handkerchiefs. The priest was saying the prayer. It was too good, too good; it was too good to last.
>
> "The pot," cried the dying man.
>
> The priest stopped. The chamber pot was brought, but the old man pushed it away:
>
> "Too late; I'll go on the other side."
>
> And he died.
>
> When they had put him in the coffin, clean-shaven and smartly dressed, he looked very distinguished. The old woman could not stop gazing at him, and tearfully she told him:
>
> "Oh, old man, my old man, if only you'd always been like this, sensible, clean, quiet, how I'd have loved you, how happy we'd have been!"
>
> She could talk all she liked, poor woman! The old man was not listening to her: he was in the kitchen laughing with his boys, laughing as much as one dare laugh at a wake.

In **"The Child,"** a husband "who was playing games with death, . . . not taking dying seriously," rises to the surface of consciousness and then sinks again like a seal until he suddenly floats up, breaks a bubble and sees his wife dreaming of the child they could never have. "Then he found the strength to raise himself up, put out the candle, and die." In **"The Lady From Ferme-Neuve"** the narrator is a doctor whose patient falls on her face almost immediately after opening the door for him, an embarrassing and messy predicament which finds his silent wish (that she should die and stop bleeding) quickly granted. To the priest, his amicable competition, he explains that they have established some kind of record: death, extreme unction and official certification have all been completed within twenty minutes after the patient opened her door.

> A gull flew very low. Right above our heads, it let out its cry. The Canon asked me: "Does that remind you of anything?" We sometimes talked about the past. I remembered I was in a hurry. I shrugged my shoulders. He did the same. And we went our separate ways.

I should mention that Ferron was also capable of writing very effective sentimental passages on the subject, as in Chapter Eight of **The Saint Elias,** when Canon Tourigny performs a marvellous, theatrical, pagan funeral for his friend, Dr. Fauteux, whose suicide note has prevented him from being buried in consecrated ground. It is one of the very few scenes in literature which can still move my jaundiced eyes to tears. But Ferron's more usual tone, by far, is the darkly humorous one, often used to describe the deaths of various doctors who seem to be alter-egos for the author, as if he were imagining over and over again, from different sardonic angles, his own agony. One of the best examples is the death of the rather pathetic, lonely, alcoholic (and yet quite admirable) Dr. Cotnoir, in [**Dr. Cotnoir**]. Here is the moment of truth:

> In the middle of the night, hearing a rattle in his throat, he asked himself, "Am I drunk or sick?" Having asked the question, he suddenly realized he only had a second to answer, which is what decided his fate. For years he'd been finding it difficult to stay alive and he would have given up long ago if not for his wife. And so here he was, now, completely unprepared, faced with the simple act of dying, which, besides being involuntary (that's its weakness) is really nobody else's business. It becomes especially personal when you take it all on yourself. He had enough dignity not to cry out. He just went, "ouf!" and sank down, but there was time enough beforehand to imagine how his staggering death would confound everybody and how they would come too late to his rescue. He was not at leisure to be amused, however. Dying men are humourless, anyway. They see, they are aware, nothing more. The instant is so quick they can't savour or appreciate it in any depth. The cameraman falls over, the film keeps rolling, a last bit of footage that will never be projected. The heart stops, the hair keeps growing. It's all just part of the leftovers. Nobody's interested.

A mythological figure who appeared in some of Ferron's major writings around this time (including the tale **"Cadieu"** and the play **The Flowering Suns**) allowed him to combine his fascination with mortality and his political preoccupations. Ferron's Mithridates is an old wino who hangs around parks philosophizing, but he is very clear about his antecedents. The original Mithridates was the king of Pontus who, in the first century B.C., was successful in defeating the Romans. Knowing his days were numbered, fearing assassination by poison, he immunized himself with small doses. He was attractive to Ferron, of course, because he had embarrassed the Romans and therefore held out some hopes for the Quebeçois. But there was also his formula for survival. The old wino in **"Cadieu"** says:

> As for me, my name is Mithridates, I am the King of the Bridge [a pun, in French, on "pont" and Pontus]. Water is of no interest to me. I pass above the canal, I drink wine. To live it is necessary to feel oneself die, to poison oneself drop by drop.

Ferron made no secret about identifying with the ancient king. In **"Purple Loosestrife,"** he quotes him as saying, ". . . when I'm surrounded, when my back is to the wall, I'll still have death behind me, like a silken ladder, to allow Mithridates to save Mithridates." He represented not only the possibility of survival against great odds, but also of choosing one's own death—suicide as an expression of liberty. Of course, such a happy notion could not hold out for long against the ironies of life and Ferron's own wit. His sister died suddenly in 1968 and he himself almost ended "stupidly" with a heart attack. The result was **The Cart,** surely one of the most outrageous mockeries ever written of the solemnity and pomp of death. The narration of this strange tale begins in the first person but the narrator is forced to change his status, grammatically as well as biologically, when he drops dead on rue Saint-Denis just across from the entrance of what is now the Université du Québec à Montréal:

> From the grammatical point of view, his slip was absolutely correct, which is to say, it was decidedly unlike the walk he was doing previously. He'd passed too quickly to consider the consequences from the first person singular to the third (which is the only one used in this kind of acrobatics). And yet the sidewalk was clean and dry, the best of all sidewalks, just poured last year, a Catholic sidewalk in front of the Maison de la Providence, a few feet from Saint-Jacques church. Montreal Public Works were innocent. If our citizen stumbled, it was because he had the banana peel in his soul. And he fell with all his weight, like a packet. Just lucky he was dead, otherwise he would have hurt himself.

> A poor corpse blocking the sidewalk, curled in on himself, not stiffening yet, but concentrating. You can talk all you want, he won't listen, he's thinking. About what? Maybe about the love he won't be making any more or about chances he let slip by. Dead men with their wet underwear seldom have elevated thoughts. They're more often obscene, I suppose . . .

So it goes on, with appropriate observations from the many onlookers, until a rag-and-bone man comes with his tip-cart and throws the corpse aboard, taking him on a fantastic journey to the gates of Hell (in downtown Montreal) and back, accompanied by some of his recently deceased patients and neighbours. A brush with death may have changed Ferron's view of it slightly, but not his tone. Thus, he could say, about two years later in an interview published by Jean Marcel, *Jacques Ferron malgré lui,* 1970:

> The ego is a hateful thing, said the gentleman; but most of all, it can smother you. Hell is easy enough to imagine: you're left all alone in a tomb: Well, they won't catch me in one of those. If I can't have the Huron rites, I'll get myself cremated. Add a little itching powder to my ashes and my oldest daughter will make the rounds of my friends: I'll be dead, but you'll be scratching.

At about the same time he was saying these jovially macabre words, however, Ferron was experiencing the first signs of a debilitating depression and fatigue which he describes in **"Purple Loosestrife,"** referring to himself impersonally as "you."

> You never worried about your faithful old carcass, assuming you could do whatever you wanted with it. Of course you knew it couldn't last forever and that finally the thread of time would have to snap. But meanwhile you had nothing to lose by living, getting to know the world, feeling freer and more understanding of things, even while you became more of a recluse. Death was the triumphal arch of your salvation at the terminus of this progressive enrichment. It didn't frighten you. The disappearance of you as an individual would put the finishing touches on your achievements; because you counted on leaving the world more beautiful than you'd found it. On the other side of the triumphal arch you would cease to be anything, having become everything, melted into a whole as vast as God. But does the tenuous thread always snap suddenly? You'd forgotten that a person can die while still living, surviving himself on earth as well as in hell. . . .

> And then you felt this fatigue of living and lost your illusions. It happened before death, before nightfall, when the still blazing sun had scarcely begun to ease off and was hatching with its heat a beautiful July afternoon. You'd just turned fifty, you were rich with wise and decisive years hidden behind your back, and you counted heavily on them for work, for study, for reflection. The years ahead were about as important to you as your dog. You'd had your share of inconsequential pleasures. . . . This unexpected fatigue mortified you more than death, because death can't be lived and you had living to do, driven by your occupations: full-time doctoring at Saint-Jean-de-Dieu, evening consultations at Longueuil in the office you kept as a precautionary measure so as to hold your own with your colleagues at the hospital, besides having to write enough to publish at least one book per year. Had you pushed yourself too hard? Was it age, was it work that suddenly wore you out? Had you caught something contagious from your patients? Was it the effects of the chlorpromazine you were testing on yourself?

A few years later, fatigue and depression would express themselves in an attempted suicide which Ferron alluded to in **The Execution of Maski,** one of two short pieces in the last full book he ever published. This most peculiar autobiographical fantasy is narrated by an "I" called The Notary, representing Ferron the writer, who describes his plot to get rid of Maski, representing Ferron the doctor.

> After the October Crisis (which, in Maski's mind, was worse than a crime; it was an affront to a people and an outrage to the integrity of speech), Maski started pretending that he'd had more than his share of life and was sick to death of it. But nothing stopped just because of that. Life kept rolling along like a creaky machine, piling one day on the next. Maski didn't go to bed at night to sleep any more, but hoping he might die. Next day he'd get up disappointed, tired out already by the new day waiting for him. . . .

> Maski kept me posted on everything, in other words on nothing because the machine was barely ticking over. Strangely enough, the more he became an encumbrance to himself, the more I realized how he'd been one to me. I'd been living in his shadow from the very beginning and the thought of his death made me so minimally gloomy that I actually felt I should give him a hand. He was considering the possibility himself. After all, what could be easier than doing away with yourself when you're a doctor?

But the Notary was no more efficient than Maski, and Ferron had a few years left. As far as I know, his last journalistic polemic was an astonishing little essay called **"The Alias of the 'NO' and Nothingness"** in which he commented, at the invitation of *Le Devoir* (April 19, 1980), on the up-coming referendum on "sovereignty-association." The statement begins with an evocation of his own state of mind:

> Nearing sixty, I no longer profit from life. I'm not what I'm to be any more, I'm what I've been, which is considerably less. Seeking, I've reached an impasse, and I stand before the wall of darkness. What is behind it? Nothingness? Before being in this impasse, I tended to think so but didn't let it upset me. Now I revolt against the notion. "Nothingness" appears to me to be an alias, the supreme, the perfect alias. Not only would I be completely bereft of myself—of my body, certainly, but also of my children and country—moreover, I would be so reduced it would be as though I had never lived—and that strikes me as sheer madness. So, it's not death I fear but a conclusive and decisive inconsistency, my disavowal.

Soon this possibility of personal annihilation is expanded to include the dead in general—the dead of an entire people, the dead who may, paradoxically, live on under certain circumstances:

> Oh, I know that the dead have a hard time of it! Struggling to keep their identity while being eaten away on all sides, they manage to hold out for a while before they themselves eventually die. But then, instead of disintegrating without colour or contour into immateriality, whether it

be the Godhead or empty nothingness, they could do so more simply in their own country provided that country really had become one, was no longer merely a country in fact but a country by law, a country recognized as such, a country with an inner and an outer side. This would be a country we would no longer have to preach to all our lives, generation after generation, a country where the living wouldn't need to wave flags and make proclamations, where the dead might rest in peace and remain as they were, their identity intact. This is the country I'm thinking of, dreaming of in 1980.

This sense of survival after death is also applied to Ferron as a writer, because he does not want to be stuck in Purgatory, like Paul-Emile Borduas in Ferron's *The Penniless Redeemer,* waiting until his country is no longer uncertain before he can be declared a great painter and admitted into Quebec's Heaven.

> Moving from the Gaspé, a land of colourful and spirited language, to Montreal, an outpost just as Lowell had once been, where two languages defile each other, where French decomposes the better to be digested by English—in consternation, I wondered. "What's the use of writing for a people who just might give me the slip someday?" But more than the loss of readers, I feared that my colourful language, indispensable to a writer, might wither away.

By the end of the article, we have come full circle and the threat of an individual's death is totally bound up with a threat of national and cultural annihilation:

> Perhaps I have already entered the Kingdom of the Dead. Thus it is that the idea of nothingness came to me, the idea that it was an alias, a fraud perpetrated on oneself, an abandoning of those nearest to one-self, the loss of all honour.

A vote of NO on the famous referendum of May 20, 1980, thus becomes a wilful vote for the alias of nothingness—vote for collective death.

The negative vote, as we know, eventually carried the day. Ferron dropped more and more from public view. When asked if he was writing, he said he found it very difficult, but was making some progress on a posthumous work. Even his letters became short and rare. One in March, 1984, announced that he had found a buyer for the Rhinoceros Party, "and the sale should make it clear that it was a private political party." A few weeks later, he wrote, "When we sold the Rhinoceros, we didn't sell the titles of Eminence. We'll need those as our permit for entering Quebec's Heaven through the great gates. And if you want to run away from your Ontario Limbo and come join us there, all you have to do is wear this insignia." Enclosed was a Rhinoceros button.

About six weeks before his death, he sent a small book by William Henry Drummond, including a poem entitled "Phil-o-Rum's Canoe." This was in response to a question involving images of the Quebeçois in North-American (English-speaking) minds. Of course, Drummond is famous for his patronizing view of French-Canadians. Ferron had turned the tables and quebecized him in *The Pen-*

*niless Redeemer,* making him the inventor of *joual,* and a man "whose ambition (not unlike James Joyce's) was to make English incomprehensible." In any case, this loan of Drummond's book seemed to be nothing but an ironic smile at the expense of true poetic "camp". And yet, something more *may* have been intended, because Phil-O-Rum complains to his canoe that she is not as lively as she used to be:

> "O ma ole canoe! Wat's matter wit' you, an' w'y was you be so slow? Don't I work hard enough on de paddle, an' still you don't seem to go. . . ."

And the canoe replies that she's just tired out:

> "Don't do any good feex me up agen, no matter how moche you try, For w'en we come ole an' our work she's done, bot' man an' canoe mus' die."

Phil-O-Rum eventually decides, "dat's smart canoe" and his meditations eventually lead him to a conclusion that seems very pertinent, under the circumstances:

> . . . I know I was comin' closer on place w'ere I mus' tak' care W'ere de mos' worse current's de las' wan too, de current of Dead Rivière.

> You can only steer, an' if rock be near, wit' wave dashin' all aroun', Better mak' leetle prayer, for on Dead Rivière, some very smart man get drown . . . .

## Betty Bednarski   (essay date 1985)

SOURCE: An introduction to *Selected Tales of Jacques Ferron,* translated by Betty Bednarski, Anansi, 1985, pp. 11-6.

[*In the following essay, Bednarski remarks on the central place of the tale in Ferron's work.*]

Jacques Ferron, winner of the Governor-General's Prize for literature, the *Prix France-Québec,* the *Prix Duvernay* and the *Prix David,* has long been recognized as one of Quebec's foremost writers. Novelist, essayist, playwright, polemicist and, above all, master storyteller, he has begun in recent years to achieve the recognition he deserves outside Quebec, in France and in the rest of Canada.

In spite of his literary fame, many people in Quebec still know Ferron only as a doctor. He completed his medical training in 1945 at Laval University and shortly afterwards went to work as a country doctor in a remote fishing village in the Gaspé. Since 1948 he has lived and practised in Longueuil (formerly Ville Jacques-Cartier), which lies opposite Montreal on the south shore of the St. Lawrence River. In *White Niggers of America* Pierre Vallières has paid tribute to Ferron's contribution to the lives of his working class patients there, and the doctor has shown a similar commitment to the mentally ill, working first with disturbed children at Montreal's Mont Providence and later with women patients at Saint-Jean-de-Dieu Psychiatric Hospital. To many others, Ferron is a political figure, whose name has been associated for some time with the struggle for an independent Quebec. In 1966 he ran as a candidate for the separatist R.I.N. During the 1970 October Crisis he was chosen as a mediator between the government and the Laporte kidnappers. And he is famous above all as founder of the Rhinoceros Party, which came into being in 1963 as a kind of political practical joke aimed at pointing out the futility of federal elections. In that party's pranks and antics can be seen the fantasy, the humour and the sense of the absurd so apparent in the work of Jacques Ferron, the writer.

Even though the writer concerns us most, it is difficult to separate him from the doctor and the political figure. From his contact with the poor rural classes in the Gaspé and with his patients in Ville Jacques Cartier and Saint-Jean-de-Dieu, Ferron has gained insight into the lives of ordinary people and deep sympathy for the quirks and foibles of humankind. Death and insanity have become familiar to him, and are themes which haunt his work. As for his political involvement, it springs first and foremost from a desire to write in a land no longer uncertain. Ferron believes, and his work reflects this belief, that a writer must above all else be true to himself and to his origins, that a work must explore to the full the particular before it can lay claim to any universality. In his writing, the doubt and ambiguity surrounding the lives of his fellow Québécois find expression, yet arc at thc same time transcended. For Ferron believes too that art, in its way, can change the world, taking reality as its point of departure, then transforming it. His works, while depicting real situations, bathe them in a fresh new light, sharpening their significance and establishing a new order, a new reality.

Many critics are tempted to talk of Ferron's realism. There is in his work a down-to-earth quality, a gallic impudence, which is realism of a kind. There is realism too in the blunt frankness with which he faces death, and, above all, there is that exactness of setting in which he often seems to delight, noting, with care and a kind of loving insistence, names and place names, and names of streets, mountains, rivers. And having identified the setting, he goes on to examine many of the perplexities of modern Quebec: those of a society caught in the painful transition from rural to urban life; those of sons exiled from home, forced off the land and into "foreign" surroundings—outside of Quebec or within its cities; those of a search for identity which often ends in tragic failure, as in the case of the wretched Cadieu, who renounces his ancestral name and ends up not only without a past, but also with no hope of progeny, no future. Yet despite the semblance of realism, Ferron transports us to another world—a world of fantasy, where archangels walk the streets, where hens and dogs converse with people and even trees are capable of thought—the fabulous world of the tale.

The tale is an art we have tended to forget, relegating it as often as not to the nursery. But it has been kept alive for centuries in Quebec, where, in the guise of the folktale, its earliest and perhaps most vital form, it has been handed down by word of mouth, independent of the printed page, from father to son, from one generation of *conteurs* (storytellers) to another. These folktales fulfilled a salutary social function in the emptiness of the New World, bringing

people together and providing, with the folksong and the dance, the surest rampart against the rigours and uncertainties of life in a hostile land. They were at the same time the vehicle of popular wisdom and the perfect expression of human aspirations in that rural society. For through them the inaccessible was brought near, the impossible became possible, as, momentarily, in the atmosphere of complicity generated by the tale, the *conteur* and his listeners transferred their allegiance to another world. More recently the move to the cities has resulted in a weakening of the structures of traditional rural society. In Quebec, as in the rest of Canada, the society which has taken its place is a society in transition, confused and uncertain, a society in search of itself. The folktale ritual has all but disappeared.

Ferron picks up where the folktale left off. He transforms it from a spoken into a written art and broadens its relevance and its appeal. His are tales for the present, providing at the same time continuity with the past. Fantasy spreads from the country into the urban environment. The subject matter is resolutely up to date, though Ferron occasionally offers a bizarre blend of old and new, as in **"Ulysses"** or **"Little Red Riding Hood,"** where he juxtaposes time-honoured traditional and legendary sequences and elements both inventive and modern, or **"Mélie and the Bull"** which, in spite of its contemporary setting, draws its inspiration from a folktale of international renown. For the most part his material is anecdotal, often relating personal experiences; but in his treatment of it he remains true to the spirit and atmosphere of the tale. He retains many of the formal features of the oral tale: the often enigmatic opening sentence, the stereotype endings, and above all, the recurring lines, the almost ballad-like refrains, which give rhythm to the text and remind us that this is an art still close to its spoken source. However, it is no naive art; it is a highly sophisticated one, often precious, and even, at times, obscure. Ferron delights in the nuance of the written word and explores its every subtle possibility, taking us far beyond the simplicity of the popular tradition. He is conscious of his debt to the folktale, examples of which he heard as a child and during those years he spent in the Gaspé; but he shows great independence in his handling of it. It is a vital part of his cultural heritage and as such he has assimilated it and made it quite his own. I know of no other Quebec writer who has achieved such masterful autonomy in this form, while remaining at the same time in such close harmony with its origins. He is a *conteur* in his own right—the last, as he says, of an oral tradition, the first of the written one.

Ferron has published two collections of tales—the first, ***Contes du pays incertain,*** which won him the Governor-General's Prize in 1962, the second, ***Contes anglais et autres,*** which dates from 1964. These were grouped together in 1968, along with several hitherto unpublished stories *(Contes inédits),* under the general title ***Contes.*** ***Tales from the Uncertain Country,*** published by Anansi in 1972, was the first selection of Ferron's stories to be translated into English, and while it took its title from the first French collection, it contained stories drawn from both. The present selection includes all of the eighteen translations in the original Anansi volume as well as nineteen new ones. *Contes du pays incertain* is translated here in its entirety for the first time. To it is added an array of the most memorable *Contes anglais* and the haunting "Chronicle of Anse Saint-Roch" from the *Contes inédits*. Thus, with more than twice the material included in the 1972 volume, *Selected Tales of Jacques Ferron* gives the English reader access to a wider range of stories than has ever been available before and a fine base from which to review Ferron's other, longer works, more and more of which are appearing in translation.

*Dr. Cotnoir, The Saint Elias, The Juneberry Tree, Wild Roses, Quince Jam, The Cart*—all of these long works contain themes and motifs already clearly visible in the tales. The tales themselves often point the way to novels. A story like "The Bridge" marks the earliest notation, the first attempt at fusion of elements later to come together so movingly in *The Cart*. In the tales narrative voices abound: there are those that speak with the humour, the fantasy and the timeless authority of the traditional *conteur,* those that adopt the urgency of the polemicist, and those, especially in the first person stories with a contemporary setting, that announce the more personal narrator, disabused yet compassionate, who asserts himself in many of the novel-length texts. Characters, too, first come to life in the tales—doctors and derelicts, clergymen and countryfolk, men and women of the urban sprawl, the simple-minded and the mentally disturbed, and the much-loved, much-railed-at Englishman. Indeed, everything is present in the tales. All Ferron is there. They form a veritable microcosm of his work.

It has often been suggested that Ferron's works spring from the same source, that they conform to the laws of a single genre. And the significance of the tales stems above all from the importance of this genre. Critics maintain, for example, that the longer texts, the so-called novels, are in fact simply longer and more complex *contes*. The *conte* is clearly Ferron's most personal form of expression, privileged in his work as it has been in the culture of Quebec. And, what is more, rich and moving though the longer works may be, there is in the smaller units—the tales here present—a sustained magic, a perfection seldom achieved elsewhere. It is fitting that the first book to reach the English speaking public should have been a selection of these tales. In the new, expanded edition the reader will once again discover Ferron at his finest. The stories that follow contain the very essence of his art.

**Betty Bednarski    (essay date 1986)**

SOURCE: "Jacques Ferron," in *Profiles in Canadian Literature*, Volume 5, edited by Jeffrey M. Heath, Dundurn, 1986, pp. 121-28.

[*In the essay below, Bednarski surveys Ferron's works, focusing on such themes as Quebec-English relations, death, insanity, and alienation.*]

There is one title which more than any other sums up the literary universe of Jacques Ferron. It is *Contes du pays incertain* (*Tales from the Uncertain Country*), that of the Québec doctor's first book of short stories, which won the Governor General's Prize for 1962 and gained him his

first true recognition as a writer. [In an endnote, the critic explains that "[*Tales from the Uncertain Country*] was the English title of a collection published in 1972 by Anansi, but of the eighteen stories translated, only ten were from *Contes du pays incertain*. The French collection is translated for the first time in its entirely in *Selected Tales of Jacques Ferron*."] This title evokes, first of all, the social, political and ideological uncertainty of a Québec caught in the painful transition from rural to urban life and grappling with the ambiguities inherent in its status within the Canadian confederation. It also suggests the equivocal atmosphere of a literary landscape where nothing is clear-cut, where the seemingly contradictory elements of pathos and humour, polemics, and pure fun, blunt down-to-earthness and unrestrained fantasy combine to disconcert and to delight. And it evokes the tale, heir to the folktale, that fabulous genre of the magical and the commonplace, privileged in Ferron's work as it has been in the culture of Québec.

An author of rare compassion, one of the subtlest, most original minds Canada has ever known, Ferron reflected on the human condition from his own distinctly Québécois vantage-point. He embarked on his career in the last dark years of the Duplessis era and matured as a writer during the Quiet Revolution, at a time when poets, novelists and playwrights were seeking to give expression to Québec's new national consciousness. For Ferron, as for writers like Hubert Aquin or Gaston Miron, literature would never be truly universal unless it first reflected the concerns of its particular time and place. Nor could it be a wholly private undertaking: there could be no self-expression, no individual soul-searching, which was not at the same time the exploration of collective truths. Ferron himself attempted to retell a collective experience, or, as he put it, a *pays* (or country) that had hitherto been *mal dit* (that is, badly or inadequately told), translating it into terms that were adequate and acceptable. His work has been an example and an inspiration to a whole generation of young writers, who see him as the great chronicler of Québec's recent and not-so-recent past, as a kind of prophet, too, and a builder of the future. For his writing not only reflects a people's doubts and perplexities; it seeks at the same time to redefine an identity, providing Qaébécois readers with a new image of themselves, firing their imaginations with the elements of a new mythology.

In his best known play, *The Flowering Suns,* Ferron recreates some of the events of the 1837 rebellion and reinstates a national hero, the patriote Dr. Jean-Olivier Chénier, in his eyes far more worthy of veneration than many of the fake figures promoted by the Catholic Church. In the novel, *The Saint Elias,* he elaborates myths of rebirth and renewal symbolized by a nineteenth century Québécois sailing ship, the pride of the Batiscanais ship-builders, which sails out of the Gulf of St. Lawrence to make contact with the wide world. *The Penniless Redeemer,* Ferron's only lengthy novel, is a veritable Bible of the beginnings of contemporary Québec. In it he gathers together an astonishing array of characters from Québec's recent past—poet Saint-Denys Garneau, painter Paul-Emile Borduas, cleric and literary critic Camille Roy, and many, many more—according them myth-like status and postulating the existence of a Québec Heaven (*Le ciel de Québec*) for the dead of that uncertain land.

Though there are many characters in Ferron's books who, through their recurring intervention, contribute to the redefining of Québec reality, English readers will be quick to note the continued presence of the *Anglais*, who has in this enterprise a special role to play. English Canadians are not new to Québec literature. But no writer has portrayed the Québécois' complex relations with this group with such insistence or with such obvious hope for understanding and reconciliation as Jacques Ferron.

It is at the expense of the English that Ferron achieves much of his most memorable humour. In the *contes*, or tales, the *Anglais* makes brief, comic appearances. Sometimes British, like the Reverend and Mrs. Andicotte and their three red-headed daughters in **"Chronicle of Anse Saint-Roch"**, sometimes Upper Canadian, like the frustrated Ulysses of **"Ulysses"** and **"The Sirens"**, and sometimes not clearly one or the other, like the kilt-clad, hairy-legged Sergeant-Major in **"The Buddhist"**, he is a foreign being and somewhat quaint, viewed with surprise and a kind of amused respect. Ferron gently mocks these lanky *rousseaux*. He pokes fun, tickles, deflates, absorbing them lovingly but cheekily, into a Québécois reality of which they are only a part. The English are acknowledged, but rendered merely amusing and therefore harmless, their real power momentarily deactivated by the humour.

This same good-humoured fun is had at the expense of the English in Ferron's novels and plays. But it is impossible to ignore that there is something far more serious going on here. In these longer works, the broader context of Québécois self-affirmation is relentlessly explored, and little of significance can be achieved without reference to the English "other". For Ferron, the notion of "two solitudes" had, by the 1960s, become hopelessly out of date, and some more dynamic rendering of French-English relations was necessary. Like the nationalist prosecutor in his play *La tête du roi*, who has one anglophile and one anglophobe son to embody his own warring tendencies, Ferron himself is ambivalent. His is the kind of ambivalence one can feel towards an authority figure, or even towards one's own self.

It is the English of Québec whom Ferron most assiduously harries and courts. Throughout his work can be found examples of worthy English residents "Québeckized" or aspiring to be "Québeckized", many of them active on behalf of French Québec. Among the most notable is Elizabeth Smith of *The Flowering Suns*, seen as a potential Joan of Arc inciting patriotic fervour in the hearts of Québécois men. Equally active and far more complex is the function performed by a certain Frank (Frank Archibald Campbell, alias Frank Anacharsis Scot) whose "real life" counterpart was the late Montréal poet and legal reformer F.R. Scott. Frank appears in several novels as an *alter ego* with whom a Québécois narrator must come to terms. In *La nuit* (an early novel, later reworked in the light of the October Crisis and renamed *Quince Jam*) he dies, poisoned, enabling the narrator, François, to recover his soul—his own and, by implication, Québec's. In *The Cart*, he returns as the devil's henchman, this time summoning

the narrator to his death and presiding over the Faustian rituals of a Montréal night. It is in *The Penniless Redeemer* that Frank receives his most sympathetic treatment. He takes part in the momentous events leading up to the birth of the Redeemer who is to bring about the salvation of the Québec people, and is himself redeemed, after a fashion, becoming at last indisputably, if somewhat unceremoniously "Québeckized". And by the end of the book he has even achieved the status of first-person narrator. Later, after the events of October 1970, an embittered Ferron would have him just as unceremoniously "sacked". "I was sorry *La nuit* was only fiction", he wrote in his **"Appendix to Quince Jam"** (subtitled "The Sacking of Frank Archibald Campbell"). "It will remain fiction, but I am changing the title to stress the poison" (contained, of course, in the jar of quince jam). . . .

Frank, having achieved the highest status possible in a fictional universe (for what greater authority can a novelist confer on a character than that of first-person narrator?), would thus be banished from Ferron's work, never to return. This banishment reveals how deep and bitter was Ferron's disillusionment at the imposition of the War Measures Act, just as Frank's prior attainment in *The Penniless Redeemer* (1969) indicates how great had been the trust placed by the author in English Canadians like F.R. Scott. By relating events that have to do with the coming of Québec's saviour, Frank Anacharsis Scot becomes implicated in these events in a manner at once acquiescent and powerful. Some might see in this handing over of the narration to Scot a mark of Québécois alienation. It is true that the first person *je* to which most Québec narrative tends in the 1960s and 1970s is an authentically Québecois *je*. But before Frank can achieve a discourse of his own (and it must not be forgotten that this discourse is in French), he must go through the somewhat undignified but no less serious ritual of "Québeckization". He has to have his Québec "night" just as François, in search of his soul in *La nuit* (and *Quince Jam*), had to have his. When we marvel at the authority vested in him, we must remember that it can come only after he has been symbolically assimilated and, so to speak, taken possession of by Québec.

No English voice would ever again achieve this authority in Ferron's universe. Frank having fallen from favour, his successor, Ann Higgit, the young English-speaking Maritimer of *Wild Roses*, is not permitted to narrate. But she, in her own way, is active too. She is a most perceptive observer, a reader of literature, and through literature, of life. She interprets and reads, as no one else can, the destiny of the Québécois, Baron. Once again Québécois reality is being sympathetically translated by an English outside mind, and it is this characteristic projection of one's own reality into the mind of another that constitutes the most interesting aspect of Ferron's attitude to the English. To truly exist, and ultimately, to be truly saved, Québec, it would seem, has to be perceived and have substance, individually and collectively, in the English mind.

Ferron's attempt to come to terms with the English is not the only significant element in his portrayal of his uncertain country, although, since it will be of special interest to English readers, I have chosen to stress it here. Much could be said about his attitude to politicians and to the immensely influential Catholic Church, to what he perceives as a rigid and moribund rural world and to the urban sprawl of North American "petroleum civilization" and the reign of the money-god, Papa Boss. This one illustration will have helped to show, I hope, that Ferron's work does not give simply a reflection of an existing situation, nor even a reaction to it, it is essentially an acting on and a reworking of reality, an attempt to shape and order, and its prime motivation is the need to improve.

Not surprisingly, perhaps, in a doctor's work, another of the most persistent themes is death. In many of the tales, Ferron deals with the subject in a tone that is familiar, joking, almost cynical. There is little sense of awe or mystery. And in the longer texts, although he is occasionally quite lyrical, he seems to delight, as in his first novel, *Dr. Cotnoir,* in mocking the solemnity surrounding the event. But he is at the same time seeking in death seriousness of another kind. Death is associated with notions of salvation and redemption. In *Dr. Cotnoir,* a doctor dies, but his simple-minded charge is "saved". So, too, is Rose-Aimée of *Wild Roses,* when her father, Baron, commits suicide. In *The Cart,* Ferron explores the death of a first-person narrator, which necessitates a sudden change in grammatical person, the first person "I", once dead, giving way to the third person "he". Ferron wrote *The Cart* after the death of his younger sister, Thérèse, at a time when memories of his mother's premature passing were particularly vivid and when he himself had narrowly escaped death from a first heart attack. The first-person method allows him to explore more intimately and, for all the macabre sense of fun, more seriously, this theme of death, which was to haunt him more and more.

By the early 1970s, overworked and disillusioned, Ferron had begun to experience the weariness and depression that would characterize his last decade. Not surprisingly, the death he contemplated now seemed almost exclusively to be his own, for even other deaths—like those of poets Claude Gauvreau and Yves Sauvageau—awakened in him a painful awareness of his own unworthiness to live. "Who should commit suicide, Sauvageau or yourself?" he asks himself in "Purple Loosestrife." As his own death came to haunt him more and more, so, too, did a vision of his country's imminent demise, of the fading away of a whole people into nothingness. Québec's disappearance would signify the loss of all that could give meaning and substance to his own brief life, dignity to his death and lasting value to his literary work. And that loss, imagined in adulthood, is contemplated with a lyrical intensity equalled only in the evocations of the childhood loss of his mother, found in *La Nuit* and *Quince Jam* (especially in its "Appendix" and "Credit Due") and in *The Cart.*

Like death, insanity is a theme that haunts Ferron's work. He returns again and again to the subject of mental illness, which he views from his own highly personal standpoint, drawing on his experiences as a family doctor and on his work, with patients in psychiatric hospitals. The barely fictionalized case histories we find in *Rosaire* and "A Love Letter" (a text appended to *Wild Roses*) reveal his impatience and dissatisfaction with professional terminology and his desire to account for the failing of individual minds in terms other than those of medical orthodoxy. Here, as elsewhere, he stresses the importance of the wider social fabric of which any individual is a part and insists that no mind should be diagnosed without reference to this context. Rosaire teeters in the first place on the brink of insanity because he is trained in a trade which modern technology has made obsolete. Aline Dupire of "A Love Letter" has been uprooted from her close-knit family unit.

Because of the vital relationship that binds an individual to his group, Ferron is also concerned about the confinement and isolation of patients. The theme of the doctor as "jailer" returns constantly, as does that of callous families willingly imprisoning undesirable "loved ones" behind institution walls. In the tales, treatment is generally light (though who could fail to be haunted by the underground journey of discovery, the devastating *descente aux enfers* made by the "Jailer's Son"?) and at times veers towards the grotesque (as in "The Parrot", the story of the prim little old lady who follows the obscene example of a parrot and exposes herself to passersby). But in the novels (*Dr. Cotnoir, The Juneberry Tree, Wild Roses*) and essays like "Claude Gauvreau" or "Purple Loosestrife" or the medical *Escarmouches,* it is dealt with in a profoundly serious vein. Ferron's polemics against the medical profession in general and psychiatrists in particular are as fierce at times an any of his celebrated attacks in the realm of politics. [In a endnote, the critic adds: "Ferron's political jibes, delivered mainly in letters to newspapers and *historiettes,* gained him much notoriety. His targets were occasionally English Canadians, but more often Québec provincial politicians and, predictably, federalists like Trudeau."]

Though Ferron himself does not make the connection explicitly, the subject of insanity is not unrelated to the theme of country and collective well-being. His conclusions on the subject of an individual's sense of identity and belonging and the vital guarantees of language, place, and name, lead inevitably to the discovery of the roots of collective alienation. And there is another connection he makes often and quite explicitly—that between the writing process and the natural reactions of a beleaguered mind.

There is, Ferron seems to be saying, something extraordinary going on inside the mind of a writer, which is in some way related to certain kinds of creative delusion apparent in the insane. Rose-Aimée of *Wild Roses* reads her mad father's letters: "She found them beautiful, well-written, almost literary. And it occurred to her that literature might well be madness that has been transcended and seeks its own cure." Of Aline Dupire in "A Love Letter", Ferron writes: "If [she] has kept her sense of fun and gives the impression of being happy, it is because in her confinement she has discovered the power of words, and with the grade five she never completed they have taught her the art of self-enchantment." And in the "Appendix to 'Quince Jam'", written around the same time as *Wild Roses* and "A Love Letter", he makes a startling connection between the first person narrator of *La Nuit* and *Quince Jam,* with whom he clearly identifies, and this woman patient who has fascinated him so: "Who then is this François Ménard . . . ? Perhaps he's a metamorphosis of Aline Dupire who went mad at Sorel, far from the indispensable company of her own people."

As time went on, Ferron would explore what he saw as the split in his own mind, creating doubles for himself, doubles who converse, collaborate, vie with each other and, finally, conflict. **"The Execution of Maski"**, his last published text, is autobiography transposed, the highly fantastic account of a failed suicide. Notary, the scribe or writer in Ferron, conspires to rid himself of Maski, the doctor, an intrusive other self, whose life has until now provided him with his inspiration, but whose continued presence has become a burden and an embarrassment to him. However, once Maski is gone, the scribe is powerless, and attempts in turn to destroy himself: "Maski's execution announced my own."

Jacques Ferron's work is rich in observations and insights on writing—the origin and the nature of the process, the writer's role in society, the relationship of the writing self to other selves, and the subtle interactions between fiction and life. Ferron does not, like so many Québécois writers of his generation, present us with a narrative which is, totally or in part, an account of or comment on a text being written. Yet his work, while not genuinely self-reflexive, is still self-conscious in every sense of the word, and writing is itself a major theme.

---

**The tale is the form that Ferron has made most clearly his own, and the most significant elements of the tale, apart from its relative brevity, is its association with a strong cultural heritage, its remembered link with an important past. For Ferron's is a style that consciously remembers.**

**—Betty Bednarski**

---

There is, for example, the doctor-writer in *The Saint Elias* who remakes his country according to his own desires. There is the vagabond *conteur* in the story **"Martine"**, whose tales (the oral predecessors of Ferron's own written ones) give style and substance to his land, and who, each time he takes leave of his audience, is content in the knowledge that his art has made the world a better place. The picture of the writer that emerges from Ferron's work is first and foremost that of an individual obsessed with correcting and improving, whose function is to recreate the world, presenting to his readers, individually and as a group, a picture not only of what they were and are, but of what they one day might be. And through writing comes, always, a kind of salvation. In *The Juneberry Tree,* Tinamer is confused and adrift and writes to save herself. In *Wild Roses,* Louis Hémon, celebrated author of *Maria Chapdelaine,* is seen as having brought about, through his writing, the salvation of his tiny daughter, and this salva-

tion is mirrored and confirmed by the saving of Baron's child, Rose-Aimée. Mme. Cotnoir, the doctor's wife, in *Dr. Cotnoir,* saves everyone she writes about in her diary, which becomes a kind of ark, and this is reaffirmed in the saving of the simpleminded Emmanuel. There is, then, in Ferron's work, a whole system of affirmations and assumptions about the nature of writing, and from most of what he wrote there emanates a kind of faith. But there are, undeniably, toward the end, questionings and doubts. The writer's experience belies his earlier belief that he would leave the world more beautiful than he had found it. The "prototype" writer, the vagabond of **"Martine"**, is interrupted in his activities when something in the outside world (social and technological change) disturbs his function. One could say that it is the writer who succeeds, him, but ultimately the writer, too, is vulnerable—vulnerable to his disillusionment with society and the intractability of the world, vulnerable to his own weariness as a man.

In Ferron's work, just as all themes, however personal, are linked to the all-embracing theme of *le pays,* so too this lifelong preoccupation with a country's destiny translates into a theory of literature and significant elements of form and style. For Ferron's concept of writing grows out of a deep attachment to language—language as it is shared by a community—language made up of "words used by everybody", which gives to an individual his first sense of belonging. It was the precariousness of that language in Québec which first brought Ferron to political consciousness. Moving to Montréal in the late 1940s, he soon diagnosed his country's uncertainty, observing the contamination of the language of the masses with the concern of a physician and the vested interest of a writer already embarked on his career and disconcerted to find his medium perverted and his readership threatened with extinction.

Ferron recognized that responsibility for linguistic health rested squarely with provincial governments, who until the 1960s had refused consistently to act in the interests of "public hygiene". But he himself sought in his own way to consolidate his people's language, writing in a style of great elegance, whose structures recalled those of the classical writers of seventeenth and eighteenth-century France. He felt no need to integrate into his texts elements of urban popular speech and avoided the political protest-cum-linguistic regionalism of the *joual* movement. The only reflection of the country' linguistic situation to be found in his work is his treatment of isolated English words for which he invents highly imaginative and, to the French eye, extremely humorous gallicized spellings, taking possession of them for Québec with a sly wink (for example, "cuique lounche", "ouiquène", "brecquefeste", "ouhonnedeurfoule-dé"). He thus attempts to assimilate the English language in playful vengeance, much as he does the mind and person of Frank Anacharsis Scot, in *The Penniless Redeemer*.

Nor could he follow the example of writers like Claude Gauvreau, whose work and suicide were nevertheless to haunt him. Gauvreau, a poet and playwright associated with painter Paul-Emile Borduas' *Refus global,* explored language in *Automatiste* terms, risking the coherence of the common tongue in the name of a private liberation.

Ferron saw Gauvreau as a writer for whom language had become independent of dictionaries, whereas he himself once admitted feeling an urgent need for the reassurances and discipline they and grammars could provide. For not only was Québec French undermined by English; it was itself particularly vulnerable, having survived as part of a primarily oral culture, without the reinforcement a long written tradition can give. To young writers of Québec's avant-garde who chastised him in 1967 for not being more innovative, he replied: "At the point I'm at, in *rang des Ambroises* in Saint-Léon de Maskinongé, how do you expect me to shake the bridle? I've never known that bridle and, if anything I'm anxious for discipline, for glossaries and for dictionaries. I'm the last of an oral tradition and first of the written transposition" [*Escarmouches,* Volume 2].

Here Ferron is referring not only to his language but also to his transformation of the folktale, a form he became familiar with in his childhood in Maskinongé County and during his years as a doctor in the Gaspé. He had profound admiration for the oral storytellers of rural Québec, and even went so far as to affirm in 1970 in an interview with Jean Marcel: "The most interesting literature here [in Québec] is still the oral literature" [*Jacques Ferron malgré lui*]. Indeed, one of the most striking characteristics of this style is his wedding of this oral tradition, from which he borrows freely, and his own inventive and highly sophisticated written art.

Ferron has published some thirty books, covering almost every conceivable genre, from the political broadside to the most precious one-act play, with a preference, always, for those shorter forms which best accommodated the limitations imposed upon him by medical practice. But the tale is the form that he has made most clearly his own, and the most significant element of the tale, apart from its relative brevity, is its association with a strong cultural heritage, its remembered link with an important past. For Ferron's is a style that consciously remembers. Memory constitutes for him one of the most fundamental moral, psychological, and aesthetic necessities. And along with memory, fantasy. In 1948, at a time when he was embarking on his first stories, and in particular **"Martine"**, he wrote to his friend and fellow writer, Pierre Baillargeon: "I've made a discovery: *The Thousand and One Nights,* or the salvation of the world through fantasy. It's match for the other Bible any day" [*Escarmouches,* Volume 1]. This deep-seated faith in what Bettelheim would call "the uses of enchantment", this commitment to fantasy, so evident in the tales, also extends to many of Ferron's longer, equally fabulous works, and it is for that reason—that and the fact that the long works are often composed of smaller, detachable units—that many critics have seen in these other writings just so many variations on the form of the tale. The tale is a form that also happily accommodates irony and the strong didactic strain present throughout Ferron's work. A piece like **"The Dead Cow in the Canyon"** draws heavily on the tradition of the Voltairian *conte philosophique.*

Ferron saw literature as a means of bringing his troubled and uncertain country to some kind of certainty. He felt obliged to expose and to denounce, and his work is at times highly political, highly polemical. However much he may have longed to be free of that obligation and "to write in peace, without thought for [Québec], as writers can in normal countries" [*Jacques Ferron malgré lui*], he was unable to dissociate himself from the collective plight. By the end of his life he had come to see himself as an unfulfilled writer, his finest ambitions unrealized and the destiny of his literary work bound up inevitably with the destiny of his "unfinished" country. Yet Ferron transcends the immediately political. He achieves in his finest pages a fusion of the personal and the collective, which is intensely lyrical and profoundly moving. Defiant, precarious, at times despairing, like his Québec, his work bears poignant witness to a country's struggle to be. It points, too, beyond Québec, beyond Canada even, to the precariousness of a whole civilization and, ultimately, to ambiguities inherent in every individual mind.

**Betty Bednarski**   (review date January-February 1988)

SOURCE: "Unfinished Business," in *Books in Canada,* Vol. 17, No. 1, January-February, 1988, pp. 21-2.

[*In the review below, Bednarski remarks on the sense of loss and despair in* La conférence inachevée.]

At the time of Jacques Ferron's death in 1985 no major new book by him had been published in Quebec for many years. The silence was troubling and eloquent in the case of a writer whose voice had been resonant throughout the 1960s and '70s. The old books—the fantastical novels, the essays, and the *contes,* by now living classics—were consistently reprinted, but there was nothing from the present, nothing to indicate that the great work could be continued or renewed.

Most readers knew that Ferron was going through a period of painful personal crisis and that he had effectively withdrawn from public life. But he had not given up writing, and before he died he had prepared a collection of texts that now have been published under the title **La Conférence inachevée.** They are, for the most part, short pieces. Fifteen are stories—*contes* or *historiettes*—originally published in periodicals, and there is a long autobiographical essay on the subject of madness, segments of which had been printed in the late '70s and early '80s in *L'Information médicale et paramédicale,* where over the years some of Ferron's finest writing had first appeared. Together they comprise a literary testament that in Quebec has been hailed as *"un texte sacré"*—a sacred text.

*Inachevée*—unfinished. The title of the collection, which is Ferron's own (as is the ordering of the individual parts), contains an admission of incompleteness. It implies a project unrealized, a literary work whose ambitions for itself have remained unfulfilled. This, toward the end of his life, is how Ferron had come to regard the whole of his work. But in the latest book one text in particular—the personal account of experiences inside the walls of a mental hospital—represents the impossibility of realizing a specific dream.

The dream for Ferron in the last 10 years or so of his life was to create a work on madness and literary creation that would express all of his intuitions and perceptions, a great book, a kind of culmination, a coming together of thoughts and themes that had found their way with increasing obstinacy into almost everything he had written. The 70 pages of **"Le pas de Gamelin"**—final but unfinished—bear witness to the virtuality of that other book which had at once haunted and eluded him.

Gamelin is another name for Saint-Jean-de-Dieu hospital, where, in 1970 and 1971, Ferron, a general practitioner, ministered to the mentally ill, often defying medical orthodoxy and the institutional authority he was answerable to. He recounts successes and failures with humility and humanity and a profound respect for the patients—all women—whose individual stories he has told. In the presence of the most abject cases he reaffirms human dignity, denouncing psychiatry's brutal assaults on minds and bodies and, in a broader sense, the institutionalization of medicine and the ensuing degradation of modern woman and man.

It is recognizably Ferron the polemicist writing here. But while there is sharpness of focus and unflinching condemnation, there is none of the violence so apparent in the celebrated written "skirmishes" of the 1960s and early 1970s. There is anger but, above all, sadness—sadness at his own failure to do more to help—and one wonders in the end if Ferron is not hardest of all on himself. **"Le pas de Gamelin,"** for all its disquieting revelations, is a gentle, humble and infinitely compassionate text. And it is moving in a way the purely polemical writings can never be. It is not just a system that is being called into question here, but Ferron himself, the doctor, the writer . . . the lifetime's work.

The incompleteness suggested by Ferron's title no doubt signals his regret. But it does not rule out continuation. If all is not said, it may still be said—presumably by someone else. We know that Ferron saw his work not as a purely individual endeavour but as part of an ongoing process of collective creation. By 1980 he had abandoned all hope of writing the great book of his ambition, announcing humbly but confidently that other writers younger than he would come along and fulfil his dream. But for him that dream was political as well as literary, and his ambitions as a writer were bound up inevitably with his aspirations for his unfinished country.

On the eve of the Quebec referendum, in a short but powerful text titled **"L'Alias du 'Non' et du neant,"** Ferron had equated the denial of collective identity (*le "Non"*) with the collapse of all meaning (*le neant*). The no vote, he implied, would usher in the reign of nothingness. Later, in preparing his last manuscript, he would consider several titles. One of those suggested and subsequently rejected was *Contes du pays perdu.* In 1962, *le pays incertain* or uncertain country, now *le pays perdu*—a country lost.

In one of the most beautiful pieces in the book, **"Les deux lys,"** Ferron confronts the two lilies of his childhood: the white one, rare, delicate and sweetly perfumed, with its biblical and patriotic connotations; the orange one, hardy and prolific, symbol of a persistent domination. The white lily, tended lovingly by his mother before her premature death, has lived on in his mind with the memory of her—the focus of all his hopes for his country.

> The winters are long and the frosts deep. Of the two lilies, only hers is miraculous. And faith may waver and one of these years my mother's life in me may fail to bloom again. I will die then a second time. . . . Could it be that I have lived uselessly in an obsession for a country that was lost? O Lord, if it be so, I say to you now, let the Devil take me.

Another title considered at the manuscript stage was *Contes d'adieu.* The three possible titles translate three preoccupations, separate but related. Nothing could sum up more eloquently than they do the spirit that has presided over the writing of Ferron's book: **La Conférence inachevée,** the notion of a project incomplete; the *adieu,* his personal farewell, his own bowing out of a life he senses will soon be over; the *pays perdu,* the bitter realization that he will not live to see his country free. If there is something open, something less irrevocable about the title of Ferron's choice, with its stress on the virtual and allowances for continuation, the texts that make up this book are nevertheless all tinged with despair. They are texts written in the shadow of death, and they have, without exception, taken shape in a mind grown accustomed to the contemplation of loss.

---

# FURTHER READING

## Criticism

Allen, Antonia. "A Master Storyteller Emerges from Quebec." *Saturday Night* 87, No. 8 (August 1972): 37.
    Laudatory review of *Tales from the Uncertain Country.*

——. "Living in the Midst of Death." *Saturday Night* 89, No. 2 (February 1974): 32.
    Argues that in *Dr. Cotnoir* Ferron "furnishes us with the essence of Quebec. It is an experience at once scintillating and depressing."

Bednarski, Betty. "Jacques Ferron (1921-1985)." *Canadian Literature,* No. 107 (Winter 1985): 193-95.
    Tribute to Ferron in which Bednarski remarks on Ferron's reputation and the links between his works and politics.

*Brick,* No. 16 (Fall 1982): 4-47.
    Special issue on Ferron containing a brief introductory note, translations of several stories, and a bibliography of other works available in translation.

Ellenwood, Ray. "Morley Callaghan, Jacques Ferron, and the Dialectic of Good and Evil." In *The Callaghan Symposium,* edited by David Staines, pp. 37-46. Ottawa, Canada: University of Ottawa Press, 1981.
    Compares Callaghan and Ferron, focusing on Ferron's *The Penniless Redeemer.* Ellenwood concludes that both authors evoke a world "where sin and redemption have meaning, where manifestations of good and evil walk

abroad, where . . . the word ceases to be an abstraction and is made flesh."

Stuewe, Paul. Review of *Selected Tales of Jacques Ferron,* by Jacques Ferron. *Books in Canada* 13, No. 10 (December 1984): 28.

> Favorable review in which Stuewe states that in *Selected Tales* "one will find everything from surreal farces to slice-of-life vignettes to fabulist myths."

---

**Additional coverage of Ferron's life and career is contained in the following sources published by Gale Research: *Contemporary Authors,* Vols. 117, 129; *Dictionary of Literary Biography,* Vol. 60; and *DISCovering Authors: Canadian Edition 2.0.***

# bell hooks
## 1952-

(Born Gloria Watkins) American essayist.

## INTRODUCTION

Known as one of the new African American intellectuals along with Cornel West, Michael Eric Dyson, and Derrick Bell, hooks reaches a wider audience than most essayists because of her dismissal of academic convention and her inclusion of personal reflection in her scholarly work. Hooks, who addresses such subjects as feminism, civil rights, and black womanhood, raises important questions about the tension between black women and white women in the feminist movement and analyzes how the media and popular culture portray African Americans.

### Biographical Information

Born Gloria Watkins in Hopkinsville, Kentucky, hooks chose to write under the name of her great-grandmother to honor her foremothers; she often refers to a household full of strong black women as one of her greatest influences. Hooks received her bachelor of arts degree from Stanford University in 1973 and her Ph.D. in English from the University of California at Santa Cruz in 1983. Throughout her years of study, hooks had difficulty reconciling her small-town Southern roots with her academic life. This disparity would later become a subject in her essays. In the mid-1980's, hooks became an assistant professor of Afro-American Studies and English at Yale University. Later she became a professor of English and Women's Studies at Oberlin College and then moved to City College in New York as a professor of English. Hooks had always been interested in expressing herself through writing, and a friend finally convinced her to write her first collection *Ain't I a Woman* (1981). In 1991 hooks was presented the Before Columbus Foundation's American Book Award for *Yearning* (1990).

### Major Works

The major theme of hooks's first two works, *Ain't I a Woman* and *Feminist Theory* (1984), is that of black women finding a place in mainstream feminism. She explores this issue by tracing the oppression under which African American women have suffered since slavery. Arguing that domination is at the root of racism, classism, and sexism, and that black women are at the bottom of the hierarchical struggle in this country, hooks asserts that mainstream feminism is interested in raising only white women up to the level of white men. According to hooks, real equality can only be gained by overturning the whole hierarchical system. In *Talking Back* (1988), hooks begins

to infuse more of her personal life into her work. In this collection she combines her personal experience as an African American woman with theory and analysis to show that feminist perspectives can be useful to assess the position of African American women in American society. In several of her works hooks discusses how portrayals of African Americans in the media have hurt African American women. *Breaking Bread* (1991) is a dialogue with African American social critic Cornel West in which hooks and West discuss the crises many black communities face, and how the media has contributed to these problems. Hooks also asserts in *Black Looks* (1992) that the mass media has denied the existence of a critical black female subjectivity. In addition to criticizing the media's complicity in racism and sexism, hooks attacks the educational system in *Teaching to Transgress* (1994) for its role in perpetuating the hierarchical system in this country. She asserts that true freedom can only be obtained when our education system is free. The focus of all of hooks's work, including her most recent book, *Killing Rage* (1995), is to heal the divisions in American society by creating a dialogue that respects all people and leads the way to rebuilding a new society.

## Critical Reception

Hooks has received varied critical response throughout her career. Many reviewers praise her for her insight and boldness. However, while most agree that her arguments are strong and challenging, many disagree with her opinions. The flaw most often noted by critics is her flouting of academic style. Many are uncomfortable with hooks's lack of footnotes and scholarly references and her reliance on self-help rhetoric and pop psychology. They also argue that she shows contempt toward black men and what they have suffered, and that she appears to be homophobic. Many of her reviewers, however, praise her for bringing a balance to feminist theory by including nonwhite, poor, and working class women into feminist discussions. Patricia Bell-Scott has observed that "we must keep in mind [hooks's] goal, to enrich feminist discourse and 'to share in the work of making a liberatory ideology,' as we struggle with the uncomfortable issues she raises."

# PRINCIPAL WORKS

*Ain't I a Woman: Black Women and Feminism* (essays) 1981
*Feminist Theory: From Margin to Center* (essays) 1984
*Talking Back: Thinking Feminist, Thinking Black* (essays) 1988
*Yearning: Race, Gender, and Cultural Politics* (essays) 1990
*Breaking Bread: Insurgent Black Intellectual Life* [with Cornell West] (essays) 1991
*Black Looks: Race and Representation* (essays) 1992
*A Woman's Mourning Song* (essays) 1992
*Sisters of the Yam: Black Women and Self Recovery* (essays) 1993
*Outlaw Culture: Resisting Representations* (essays) 1994
*Teaching to Transgress: Education as the Practice of Freedom* (essays) 1994
*Art on My Mind: Visual Politics* (essays) 1995
*Killing Rage: Ending Racism* (essays) 1995

# CRITICISM

**Barbara Smith** (essay date January-February 1983)

SOURCE: "Black Feminism Divorced from Black Feminist Organizing," in *The Black Scholar*, Vol. 14, No. 1, January-February, 1983, pp. 38-45.

[*Smith is an American editor. In the following essay, she criticizes hooks's antagonism toward black men and white women as well as her apparent homophobia in* Ain't I a Woman: Black Women and Feminism.]

In 1973, when I began to identify as a black feminist and

to do black feminist organizing, there was barely a word in print that spoke about black women from a feminist perspective or which even admitted that sexism was a daily factor in our lives. In women's movement literature there was a stray sentence here or there. And in writings by black women and men black women were occasionally discussed without, miraculously, ever breathing a word about male privilege or women's lack of it. The best source for those of us who were dying to read something about ourselves that made sense was black women's creative writing. Hurston, Lorde, Petry, and Walker at least told the truth. perhaps theory would have to wait until we got our movement off the ground.

In 1982 there are more things to read that supposedly address the sexual politics of black women's lives, but too often the writing seems peculiarly untouched by a Third World feminist movement that is now at least ten years strong. Such disconnectedness is not surprising in books from trade and academic publishers. Unfortunately, Bell Hooks' *Ain't I A Woman; Black Women and Feminism* from South End Press, an alternative, left publisher, is also full of the contradictions that result when one attempts to talk about black feminism divorced from black feminist organizing.

Before going any further, I have to admit that this book has worried me nearly to death and reviewing it is no easy task. I wanted *Ain't I A Woman* to be good, incisive, and, most of all, useful. The fact that Hooks provides information about black women's historical oppression and asks some significant questions about sexism and racism raised my hopes. But from the very beginning I found myself questioning the conclusions she draws from the factual material she presents and being constantly surprised by her answers to the questions she poses. It soon became clear that despite its subject I was in profound disagreement with the assumptions of this book.

The book is divided into five chapters which potentially address pivotal black and feminist issues: "Sexism and the Black Female Slave Experience"; "Continued Devaluation of Black Womanhood"; "The Imperialism of Patriarchy"; "Racism and Feminism"; and "Black Women and Feminism." The first two chapters contain interesting documentation of black women's continuously inferior status in the U.S. I was mystified, however, to see that in these first chapters, as throughout the book, there are numerous quotations, but no footnote references and at times not even references to the author or book from which the quotations are taken. These omissions make *Ain't I A Woman* much less useful for research. Such an oversight is not merely the author's responsibility, but her publisher's, and is just one indication that this book was editorially handled in such a way that was a disservice to all.

The book's analytical difficulties are apparent in the first chapter. In order to disprove the familiar argument that slavery and racism were worse for black men than for women, simply because men are inherently more valuable beings, Hooks attempts to show not only that black women suffered more in slavery, but that black men suffered less than is commonly believed. This is tricky territory that scholars continue to debate: what was slavery actually like and what was the typical slave experience? I basically agree with Hooks that because of sexual oppression, systematized rape, forced breeding, and responsibility for domestic tasks, black women suffered in more ways than black men. What I find so upsetting is the contempt that Hooks shows for black men in the process. For example, in refuting the concept that black men suffered from a loss of masculinity in slavery, she writes:

> Enslaved black men were stripped of the patriarchal status that had characterized their social situation in Africa but they were not stripped of their masculinity. Despite all popular arguments that claim black men were figuratively castrated, throughout the history of slavery in America black men were allowed to maintain some semblance of their societally defined masculine role. In colonial times as in contemporary times, masculinity denoted possessing the attributes of strength, virility, vigor, and physical prowess . . . That white people recognized the "masculinity" of the black male is evident by the tasks assigned the majority of black male slaves.

Of course Hooks conveniently ignores power and autonomy as essential components of masculinity and male privilege. Being an unpaid and terrorized beast of burden has never had much to do with exercising power. Hooks continues:

> The sexism of colonial white male patriarchs spared black male slaves the humiliation of homosexual rape and other forms of sexual assault. While institutionalized sexism was a social system that protected black male sexuality, it [socially] legitimized sexual exploitation of black females.

If the system protected Black male sexuality so thoroughly, what in the world is the history of lynching all about? This statement is disturbing on a number of levels. One is that it's not clear what is humiliating—the rape or the homosexuality. If the word homophobia had been used instead of sexism to explain why black men were not victimized in this way, it would be obvious that the author is critical of negative attitudes toward male homosexuality and lesbianism. But as I will discuss in more detail subsequently, she is not.

It isn't necessary to prove that slavery wasn't so bad for black men in order to prove how very bad it was for black women. It is obvious, however, that Hooks' conclusions are affected by her animosity toward black men which surfaces repeatedly throughout the work. It is perfectly legitimate to criticize, even castigate, black men for their oppression of black women, but I found the author's unveiled hostility shocking.

Hooks obviously has an ax to grind with black men and to an even greater extent with white women. There's nothing inherently wrong with that, but it does not make for sound theory. Why do I constantly get the impression that Hooks sees *Ain't I A Woman* as an opportunity to finally put black men and white women in their place? Certainly her tone is a factor. Another is the major and minor inconsistencies of the book, the way that Hooks in building her case reshapes logic and history. According to the author

even black women are culpable for perpetuating their own oppression.

At the conclusion of the first chapter Hooks states:

> The fact that enslaved black women were forced to labor as "men" and to exist independently of male protection did not lead to the development of a feminist consciousness.

Her evidence for this assertion is that black women wanted the "considerations and privileges given white women" and that as soon as slavery ended many black women "refused to work in the fields." Hooks seemingly does not consider that "forced" equality under the horrors of the slave system, which she has just vividly described, might not automatically lead to higher consciousness, but merely to a desire for some relief. The ex-slave women probably did not want to *be* Miss Ann as much as she wanted to *stop being* sexual and economic chattel. Hooks also does not consider that a desire to leave the fields might have been a desire to have only one full-time job—childrearing and housework—instead of two. Ignoring these realities, she concludes the chapter:

> By completely accepting the female role as defined by patriarchy, enslaved black women embraced and upheld an oppressive sexist social order and became (along with their white sisters) both accomplices in the crimes perpetrated against women and victims of these crimes.

Who are these black women who "completely accept[ed] the female role" and who are their descendants? I haven't met them. What I always find so heartening about black women, no matter how nonfeminist they might be in their pronouncements, is how seldom they unthinkingly conform to conventional feminine behavior. We've always had too much sense for that. Nevertheless, in the book's introduction Hooks states unequivocally:

> Twentieth century black women had learned to accept sexism as natural, a given, a fact of life. Had surveys been taken among black women in the thirties and forties and had they been asked to name the most oppressive force in their lives, racism and not sexism would have headed the list.

To cite just one piece of evidence to the contrary which indicates that black women were indeed concerned about sexual discrimination in the 1940s, I refer readers to an article by novelist Ann Petry, published in March 1947, entitled "What's Wrong With Negro Men?" Petry's article appeared in *Negro Digest,* a widely distributed publication, and attacked head-on black men's bad attitudes about women, including sexual harassment on the street and unfair division of labor at home. For further evidence of black women's criticism and resistance to male dominance, as well as commentary on a host of other social problems, I refer everyone to the blues.

Hooks' interpretation of events to suit her purposes is most blatant in her discussion of the women's movement. She describes a movement I find barely recognizable. Hooks collapses the totality of feminism into its most conservative manifestations: bourgeois, reformist, professional, and self-aggrandizing. It is the equating of the women's movement with its least progressive elements (long a tactic of the slick media and certain varieties of anti-feminists) which I think most distorts the impact of the book. Hooks describes the women's movement and white feminists in such derogatory terms that it is hard to imagine why any black woman reading this would want any part of it or why any white woman would be inspired to change. Yet ostensibly it is Hooks' purpose to encourage feminist opposition to sexual oppression in the black community and racial accountability among white women. It is necessary to examine how this fundamental contradiction in the book came about.

First, I want to validate Hooks' perception that the women's movement has indeed been and continues to be racist. And since being racist in this country is thoroughly interlocked with being white, this racism has affected all sectors of the movement, from conservative to revolutionary. What Hooks does not acknowledge is that the differing *politics* of white feminists have resulted in many differing responses to the issues of racism and cultural difference, ranging from merely cosmetic to absolutely serious. Hooks never admits that there are parts of the women's movement, especially in the last five years, that define taking responsibility for racism as a top priority. Instead she makes the following statement:

> Few, if any, white women liberationists are willing to acknowledge that the women's movement was *consciously and deliberately* structured to exclude black and other non-white women and to serve primarily the interests of middle and upper class college-educated white women seeking social equality with middle and upper class white men. While they may agree that white women involved with women's liberationist groups are racist and classist *they tend to feel that this in no way undermines the movement.*

> [Italics added by Smith]

There are countless statements like this in the chapter "Racism and Feminism" which combine partial truth with opinion so as to undermine understanding of this crucial issue.

One of Hooks' cherished beliefs which reinforces her negative view of the movement is that all white women are better off than all black women dating from slavery. Not surprisingly she also believes that: "No other group in America has so had their identity socialized out of existence as have black women," thus completely erasing the existence and struggles of Native American, Asian-American, and Latin women. Hooks makes no effort to examine parallels in the experiences of all women of color, which, at the very least, would have strengthened the work analytically. Instead she puts all her energy into emphasizing the gulfs between women, black and white. She writes:

> Prior to slavery, patriarchal law decreed white women were lowly inferior beings, the subordinate group in society. The subjugation of black people allowed them to vacate their despised position and assume the role of a superior.

Consequently, it can be easily argued that even

though white men institutionalized slavery, white women were its most immediate beneficiaries.

As in her previous statements about black men's masculinity, the factors of autonomy and power are completely ignored. Hooks firmly believes that:

> In America, the social status of black and white women has never been the same. In 19th and early 20th century America, few if any similarities could be found between the life experiences of the two female groups. . . . In fact, white racial imperialism granted all white women, however victimized by sexist oppression they might be, the right to assume the role of oppressor in relationship to black women and black men.

The first sentence in this statement is absolutely accurate. The second sentence overlooks the reality of obligatory child-bearing, rape, and battering, to name only a few common female life experiences. Both the second and third sentences astonishingly do not take into account class as a factor in white women's oppression. Class oppression is certainly something poor and working class women of all races have in common, no matter how much the system tries to obscure this fact. In the period Hooks refers to there were poor white women on farms south and north, white women working in unspeakable conditions in factories, white women domestic servants and prostitutes, and millions of women immigrants from Europe who came here with nothing. Yes, they had white skin privilege and were no doubt racist, but why doesn't Hooks examine the complexities of being white combined with being economically *and* sexually exploited instead of acting as if no such women exist? For one thing, integrating an analysis of class would not support her opinion that white women are not oppressed.

---

**The problems with *Ain't I A Woman* lead me to ask what is theory and what comprises good analytical writing? Theory and analysis are not merely the listing of opinions, but this is generally Hooks' method.**

**—Barbara Smith**

---

The lack of a realistic perspective on class is one of the book's major theoretical flaws. It's not that class isn't mentioned at all in the work, and this is what makes Hooks' mode deceptive, it's that it is never integrated into her analysis, but only invoked to prove that white women have it over black women. So much of *Ain't I A Woman* is based upon a "pitting against" mentality, black women against white women and black men, which simply would not hold up if class oppression was taken into account. Hooks writes:

> In fact, the contemporary women's movement

was extremely class bound. As a group, white participants did not denounce capitalism. They chose to define liberation using the terms of white capitalist patriarchy, equating liberation with gaining economic status and money power. Like all good capitalists, they proclaimed work as the key to liberation. This emphasis on work was yet another indication of the extent to which the white female liberationists' perception of reality was totally narcissistic, classist, and racist.

How does socialist feminist analysis and practice, campaigns to organize clerical workers, other unionizing efforts, the exposing of sexual harassment at the work place, and a general desire to equalize women's salaries, working conditions, and job opportunities fit in with "total narcissism, classism, and racism"?

But Hooks does not seem to know anything about these aspects of the movement. Her examples are overwhelmingly drawn from "women's studies classes", "conferences," "books," and "groups" whose purposes are never identified. I have often been frustrated when talking with black women about feminism that they have little knowledge of the activist women's movement with which I am most familiar. *Ain't I A Woman,* which could have provided such information, perpetuates this problem. Even in relying on printed matter, Hooks could have drawn from a vast array of feminist periodicals and books from feminist presses. Of the more than one hundred sources she lists in her bibliography, however, only one could be considered a women's movement publication. Almost all of the works cited in the bibliography also appeared before 1975, the very point at which Third World women's organizing began to take hold.

According to Hooks, however, even black feminist organizing is neither positive nor important. I found her criticism of autonomous black women's groups absolutely heartstopping. She writes:

> Some black women who were interested in women's liberation responded to the racism of white female participants by forming separate "black feminist" groups. *This response was reactionary.* By creating segregated feminist groups, they both endorsed and perpetuated the very "racism" they were supposedly attacking. They did not provide a critical evaluation of the women's movement and offer to all women a feminist ideology uncorrupted by racism or the opportunistic desires of individual groups. Instead, as colonized people have done for centuries, they accepted the terms imposed upon them by the dominant group (in this instance white women liberationists) *and structured their groups on a racist platform identical to that of the white-dominated groups they were reacting against.* White women were actively excluded from black groups. In fact, the distinguishing characteristic of the black "feminist" group was its focus on issues relating specifically to black women. The emphasis on black women was made public in the writings of black participants. The Combahee River Collective published "A Black Feminist Statement" to explain their group's focus.

> [Italics added by Smith]

Hooks then quotes from the opening paragraph of the Statement which affirms a commitment to coalition politics and a multi-issued approach. She then comments: "The emergence of black feminist groups led to a greater polarization of black and white liberationists."

Obviously she does not comprehend the meaning of the word coalition. As a founding member of the Combahee River Collective, I can verify that this particular organization was never racially separatist, that it always considered itself a part of the women's movement, and that it practiced coalition building in countless ways.

Why is Hooks so scathingly critical of contemporary black feminist organizations, accusing them of "anti-white racism," yet quite supportive of nineteenth century independent black feminist efforts? Of these groups she writes:

> In fact, black female reform organizations were solidly rooted in the women's movement. It was in reaction to the racism of white women and to the fact that the U.S. remained a society with an apartheid social structure that compelled black women to focus on themselves rather than all women.

There may be other reasons for this inconsistency, but one I suspect is that those early black women organizers were ostensibly heterosexual while many contemporary black feminists are also lesbians. In a book of over two-hundred pages Hooks does not mention the word lesbian once. This is the other crucial key to the author's perspective on feminism, her overriding homophobia. Her constant attacks on the women's movement are no doubt tacitly motivated by her anti-lesbianism, although her position of course is never clearly stated.

Why is it when a black woman dismisses lesbianism, she acts as if she is not attacking a single black woman? There are hundreds of thousands of black lesbians and hundreds of thousands more black gay men for that matter alive and well in the U.S. at this very moment, not to mention the millions of us that cover the globe wherever people of African descent live. To attack lesbianism is not merely to slap the wrist of the "white" women's movement, it is to eviscerate *us.*

By ignoring lesbianism and lesbian-feminism, Hooks conveniently ignores some of the most vital and radical work of the movement. Because of my involvement with Third World and white lesbians who are radical activists, I can, despite all its failings, feel positive about the movement we've created. In 1981, Hooks, on the other hand, writes in her conclusion:

> Right now, women in the U.S. are witnessing the demise of yet another women's rights movement. The future of collective feminist struggle is bleak. The women who appropriated feminism to advance their own opportunistic causes have achieved their desired ends and are no longer interested in feminism as a political ideology.

Hooks' homophobia not only eliminates essential theory and facts, it totally distorts the history of contemporary feminism. For instance, it allows her to avoid mentioning an organization like D.A.R.E. (Dykes Against Racism Everywhere), the kind of racially mixed antiracist group she implies does not exist, or citing Elly Bulkin's important article, "Racism in Writing: Some Implications for White Lesbian Critics." Homophobia also results in a narrowly heterosexist perspective on the issues she does address, leading to yet another level of distortion. Heterosexist solipsism results in the following statement:

> White and black women have been socialized to accept . . . fierce competition between the two groups; a competition that has always been centered in the arena of sexual politics, with white and black women competing against one another for male favor. This competition is part of an overall battle between various groups of women to be the chosen female group.

What does it mean for lesbians that all racial conflict between women can be reduced to vying for male favor?

The closest Hooks comes to suggesting that lesbians exist is not surprisingly in a general put-down of the women's movement. She writes:

> Attacking heterosexuality does little to strengthen the self-concept of the masses of women who desire to be with men. . . . The women's movement has become a kind of *ghetto or concentration camp* for women who are seeking to attain the kind of power they feel men have. It provides a forum for the expression of their feelings of anger, jealousy, rage, and disappointment with men. It provides an atmosphere where women who have little in common, who may resent or even feel indifferent to one another can bond on the basis of shared negative feelings toward men.

> [Italics added by Smith]

So feminists and lesbians are nothing but man-haters who make life difficult for women with heterosexual privilege. Haven't I heard this somewhere before? This comment seems particularly ludicrous in the context of a book which itself evidences so much negative feeling toward men. I also find Hooks' image of the women's movement as "a kind of ghetto or concentration camp" appalling because she completely trivializes the suffering of the Jews and the experience of every group that has been forcibly segregated, at the same time she uses the image to attack another group. Didn't anyone read this manuscript and react to the devastating implications of these words?

This brings me finally to the issue of the publisher's role in the problems with this book. Why did South End Press, a publisher known for its high-level primarily white-male theory, demand so little from a book on feminism by a black woman? The answers are no doubt themselves lessons in the racism and anti-feminism that pervade white-male-left establishments. Some left/socialist groupings have made sincere efforts to integrate an understanding of sexual and racial politics into their theory and practice. In this case, however, South End's desire to appear "politically correct" with minimal effort is transparent. Clearly an insidious double-standard was operating that led the editors-publishers to overlook the book's grave analytical and ideological problems, which would never have been permitted in another work—for example, not requiring footnotes or a concise approach to class. I despise the kind of racism that says, "black people are just different. We can't ever understand them and it's not our place to question or challenge them." This attitude no doubt explains why the book's homophobia was allowed to stand and why such a blatant deficiency did not lead to a serious questioning of the politics of the work as a whole, *before* it was published. But how better to disavow the significance of the women's movement than through the words of a black woman who is supposed to be a feminist? The fact that there are countless women who need a good book about black feminism was clearly of little concern. From all accounts *Ain't I A Woman* is selling well and spreading confusion and division in its wake.

The problems with *Ain't I A Woman* lead me to ask what is theory and what comprises good analytical writing? Theory and analysis are not merely the listing of opinions, but this is generally Hooks' method. She never says what kind of organizing is to be done, what kinds of political issues are crucial, how black women might be brought together around feminism, or what issues and organizing she herself has been involved in that have contributed to the formation of her analysis. Ultimately, I find this and similar books so worrisome, because they make the real work of black feminist organizing so much more difficult than it needs to be.

### Dorothy Randall-Tsuruta (essay date January-February 1983)

SOURCE: "Sojourner Rhetorically Declares; Hooks Asks; Kizzy Spits in the Glass," in *The Black Scholar*, Vol. 14, No. 1, January-February, 1983, pp. 46-52.

[*Randall-Tsuruta is an American writer and educator. In the following essay, she expresses disappointment with the lack of documentation and the abundance of unsubstantiated opinions in* Ain't I a Woman, *stating "the book is a disgrace to American publishing."*]

A startling foretelling of Bell Hooks' *Ain't I a Woman* comes in the Acknowledgements and Introduction. She begins by sharing how when out to dinner she discussed with companions the subject of the book in question and "one person in a big booming voice, choking with laughter exclaimed, 'What is there to say about black women!' Others joined in the laughter." The author does not tell us if these were friends or strangers, but the liberties they take, and the fact that she dines with this sort is an indication of what she can stomach.

The excellent thing about Hooks' book is that it pinpoints annoyances over which many black American women daily sigh, yet repress, in an attempt to get through the work day without flying off the handle. Then just as we begin to vent our rage through Hooks', she confounds us by drawing conclusions, to her experience, which are either damaging to black women or unsupported by black experience in America.

Point in fact. In the introduction Hooks' own chagrin

belts to crescendo her "white sisters" for among other things feeling:

> . . . comfortable writing books or articles on the 'woman question' in which they drew analogies between 'women' and blacks. . . . By continuously making this analogy, they *unwittingly* suggest that to them the term 'woman' is synonymous with 'white women'
>
> [Italics added by Randall-Tsuruta]

Any black woman who has ever had to deal with white women in an organizational setting, or neighborhood, or friendship, knows that whites—women and men—do not "unwittingly" assert a racial complex. However cathartic Hooks' anger is at times, she nonetheless reasons wildly—thus the troubled complexion of her study.

Hooks is so mad at her white sisters that she cannot sit still; yet prefers them to black feminist thinkers who "responded to the racism of white female[s] . . . by creating segregated feminist groups . . . and structured their groups on racist platform." Hooks expounds:

> White women were actively excluded from black groups. In fact the distinguishing characteristic of the black 'feminist' group was its focus on issues relating specifically to black women.

Besides being flabbergasted that Hooks should think it wrong for black feminists to organize independently, I find it scandalous that Hooks places in quotes the word "feminists" referring to black women. Is this a slip of tongue, a scoff of sorts, a denigration translated, "if you ain't white (nor under white umbrella), you sho ain't no feminist?" But most incredible is Hooks' wording which singles black feminists out, for "creating segregated feminist groups." This despite her own words denouncing white feminists as "reactionary." Half the time while reading this book I kept asking the author if she was for real—and not rhetorically either.

According to Hooks, slavery was worse for black women than for black men because while black men may have had their testicles cut off this was not as frequent as rape, nor were they forced to perform homosexual acts. (Hooks' way of knowing this last suggests she is reincarnated with a clear memory and omnipresent.)

*Ain't I a Woman* contains five chapters: 1—Sexism and the Black Female Slave Experience; 2—Continued Devaluation of Black Womanhood; 3—The Imperialism of Patriarchy; 4—Racism and Feminism: The Issue of Accountability; and 5—Black Women and Feminism.

The historical data on slavery provided in chapter one is bereft of documentation, and is further reduced by argumentation which begs the question; specifically whether slavery was worse for women or men. The author plays down the suffering of black male slaves saying, that "individual black men were castrated by their owners or by mobs" for the purpose of setting "an example for other male slaves so that they would not resist authority." But she contends that white "women and men" were not "obsessed by the ideal of destroying black masculinity" for they did not force "black men to assume 'feminine' attire or perform so-called 'feminine' tasks." And she argues, comparatively, that they were obsessed with destroying black femininity for they forced "black women [to] perform the same tasks as black men," plowing, planting, and harvesting crops. When I was approaching graduate school, the noted scholar St. Clair Drake counseled a gathering of black students, saying when it comes time for dissertation, don't waste your time researching where slavery was worse—Brazil or the United States: it was horrible in both to the extent that figuring the degree is ludicrous.

In this chapter Hooks also criticizes black parents for their failure to "warn their daughters about the possibility of rape or help them to prepare for such situations." On and on she controverts. She concludes:

> The slave parents' unwillingness to openly concern themselves with the reality of sexual exploitation reflects the general colonial American attitude regarding sexuality.

Hooks has the galling habit of allowing enslaved ancestors choices of action no master allowed them. Further she demeans her ancestors, without benefit of documented evidence. Who told her this about slave parents?

Hooks singles out slave men for chiding, reasoning they did not move to protect female slaves from rape because in Africa they were socialized to aid only the women of their own tribe. No mention of how in America they were restrained. Alas, more global reductionism for Western anthropologists out to prove the heathen's halo is an Afro. Hooks thus aptly reads down the white sister's ancestor for her role in all this.

Chapter three plunges into "The Imperialism of Patriarchy." Here Hooks wins my applause for taking on Baraka and Jim Brown for their rationalizations bereft of admission that the white woman fills their dreams. Hooks submits for review, almost as an effigy, Baraka's response to the question concerning militant black men and white women:

> Jim Brown put it pretty straight and this is really quite true. He says that there are black men and white men, then there are women. So you can indeed be going through a black militant thing and have yourself a woman. The fact that she happens to be black or white is no longer impressive to anybody, but a man who gets himself a woman is what's impressive. The battle is really between white men and black men whether we like to admit it that is the battlefield at this time.

While no footnote is provided, the bibliography implies that Baraka's quote is taken from *Black World,* 1970. Seeing as how this is dated material, its purpose is limited, but does attest to what yet pains black women.

In chapter four, "Racism and Feminism," the author returns to her overriding contention with white feminists, taking on black feminists as well. Here the book succeeds in painting a graphic, and in this informative, sketch of her coming to grips with her "white sisters" as well as black feminist sisters who split off into race related groups—she calls the latter "Others." Considering the chapter—indeed the entire book—reads in large like an angry cry to white feminists, it smacks of a letter from an unrequited love. The reader feels at times like an eavesdropper, seeing the author seated miserably amongst "white sisters" whom she depicts as coolly indifferent to truths with which she confronts them. She exclaims they are just apt to turn on such as herself, snorting, "We won't be guilt tripped."

Yet Hooks bad raps black women who, "to express their anger and rage at white women" evoke "the negative stereotypical image of the white woman as passive, parasitic, privileged being living off the labor of others as a way to mock and ridicule the white women liberationists [sic]". In this chapter poet Lorraine Bethel is singled out for chastisement because of her poem "What Chous Mean We White Girl? Or, The Cullud Lesbian Feminist Declaration of Independence." (No reference given for this work.)

Interestingly here, Hooks suggests that hostilities between blacks and whites involved in the women's liberation movement, were not only due to disagreements over racism, but were also due to "jealousy, envy, competition, and anger, which took root during slavery." She explains how, as she sees it, slavery provided white women with creatures who were more denigrated by white men than they themselves. She seems to be saying this drove white women to sadistic acts, resorting "to brutal punishment to assert authority," which yet "could not change the fact that black women were not inclined to regard the white female with the awe and respect they showed the white male." She seems to be saying black slave women preferred their male torturers to their female torturers—you remember, those men who brutally raped them, beat them harder than they did men, hung their babies upside down until dead if they did not eat their food, and made them harvest the ground along with the men to the loss of their femininity. The point here is Hooks' penchant for arguing the degree of difference in the face of unmentionable horrors.

Hooks romanticizes slave owners much as Capote does criminals in *In Cold Blood*. Pretty soon these sadists start to emerge as personalities. If they were alive they might be able to turn a pretty profit from their crimes as did the John Deans and Richard Nixons, and presently the Dan Whites (George Wallace convinced a needed black votership of having changed for the better).

Finally in chapter five, "Black Women and Feminism" Hooks returns to the theme begun in her introduction, that black women passively stand outside the women's movement because they lack sexual esteem. She also returns to her witness of what whites "unwittingly" do, this time rendering the white man who yelled at Sojourner, 'I don't believe you really are a woman.' Hooks reasons he "unwittingly voiced America's contempt and disrespect for black womanhood." Since Hooks again offers no documentation for this quote, one can only assume it is hearsay across generations. But in what context and at what event was Sojourner being thus read down? Hooks' book would be better if such documentation were supplied. It leaves one wondering at the publishing motive which dumps on the public such poor black scholarship.

Besides not documenting evidence, Hooks, throughout the book, works quotes which do not even serve her intent—like a puzzle piece forced into a pattern. For instance, referring back to her discussion of white women flaunting a "women and blacks" analogy, in her introduction, Hooks asserts that:

> When black people are talked about sexism militates against the acknowledgment of the interests of black women; when women are talked about racism militates against a recognition of black female interests. When black people are talked about the focus tends to be on black men; and when women are talked about the focus tends to be on white women.

But then for proof she offers (from William O'Neill's book *Everyone Was Brave*):

> Their shocked disbelief that men would so humiliate them by supporting votes for Negroes but not for women demonstrated the limits of their sympathy for black men, even as it drove these former allies further apart.

Whatever the point she was trying to make becomes lost in the scathing "humiliate" (in this reference) incites.

But Hooks has some interesting things to say about black women's organizations—how they changed over the course of history from being concerned with social *services* to focus instead on social *affairs* like debutante balls and fundraisers. In this she is instructive, and given a second attempt might even embed this information in a book more carefully organized, researched and edited. Yet, even as she sounds promising, in chapter five, she also reduces Angela Davis to "a poster pinup" who Hooks says was not admired for her intelligence but for her beauty. Again Hooks shows herself not contained by her own opinion, but wallowing in the stew whites would make of blacks. She offers further antagonism toward black women who dared deem themselves free, criticizing now black sociologist Joyce Ladner, and essayists Ida Lewis and Linda LaRue. Even charging this she insists that black women today are afraid to "openly confront white feminists with their racism." Deaf and dumb to her own conflicting charges, priding herself on being able to turn the other cheek, Hooks closes the book on the hope that black women everywhere will take courage from her pioneering in feminist ideology and follow suit.

While the book straddles five chapters, it is the essence grasped in the Introduction that essence recalls its passion long after the book is closed. For it is here that the author springs an admirable spirit let down by a sputtering intellect. The section also alerts the reader to Hooks' summation of blacks, that lack of racial esteem which so intrigues social scientists rent with wicked purpose. If the black reader approaches the book with the understanding it is addressed to Hooks' "white sisters," she or he may only wince seeing red when coming across such fabricated confidences as:

> Contemporary black women could not join together to fight for women's rights because we did not see 'womanhood' as an important aspect of our identity.

and further along:

> When white men supported giving black men the vote while leaving all women disenfranchised, Horace Greeley and Wendell Phillips called it 'the Negro's finest hour' but in actuality what was spoken of as a black suffrage was black male suffrage. By supporting black male suffrage and denouncing white women's rights activists, white men revealed the depths of their sexism—a sexism that was at that brief moment in American history greater than their racism.

Is Hooks serious? Is she really so naive as to believe white men ever embraced the needs of black men in preference to those of white women, suffragette or not? And could this mean she actually believes white men neglected to build into the system control of black men—vote or no vote?

What emerges here is the embarrassing probability that Hooks derives hope for a united women's movement by drawing analogy from white males' support of black males which she contends for a brief moment relegated sexism more important than racism: thus if white men can do this perhaps their womenfolk can as well.

This glimmer of hope lurks in the shadow of her voice, when vicariously reliving the words of toxic pig Elizabeth Cady Stanton whom she quotes cringing aghast that " 'niggers' should be granted the vote while 'superior' white women remained disenfranchised." Though purporting to be alerting her sisters to racism, her voice betrays something akin to despising what the enemy despises, a condition sadistic biographers report gave strut to Hitler's walk, and entertained him in idle moments.

Concluding observations turn first to Hooks' title. As the words are Sojourner Truth's, taken from her famous speech it does us well to review them in context:

> That man over there say that woman needs to be helped into carriages, and lifted over ditches, and to have the best place everywhere. Nobody ever helped me into carriages, or over mud puddles, or gives me a best place . . . And ain't I a woman? Look at me. Look at my arm! I have plowed and planted and gathered into barns, and no man could head me . . . And ain't I a woman? I could . . . eat as much as a man when I could get it, and bear the lash as well . . . And ain't I a woman? I have borned thirteen children and seen them most all sold off into slavery. And when I cried out with a mother's grief, none but Jesus heard . . . And ain't I a woman?

Speaking this, Sojourner stepped into the limelight asserting the will of a visionary disgusted with the charade before her eyes. Clearly in her phrasing "ain't I a woman?" she is not asking a question but asserting indeed I am! Here we are presented with a wonderfully proud woman. She was no tail along feminist-hopeful, but a leader who as Hooks admits "could refer to her own life as evidence of woman's ability." Her patience, desire for certain comforts, sturdy arms firmed by plowing, equal footing with men, motherhood, and sufferings which none but Jesus heard are strengths she claimed. Sojourner delivered this

speech in 1852 before a group of white women who Hooks informs, "deemed it unfitting that a black woman should speak on a platform in their presence screamed: 'Don't let her speak! Don't let her speak! Don't let her speak!' " Seeing as how that was 131 years ago, yet the picture Hooks paints of white feminists reveals them significantly unchanged today, it seems this would suggest something to her—other than that her patience is meritorious.

For many black women Sojourner's message has been instructive as they grew keen on living embraced by a compassion which yet never undermines that spirit of fight Sojourner resounds. You see these black women everywhere; some grouped for action in clubs or organizations which bear witness to our having come a long way since the only organization addressing female concerns was a band of white women. My early years as a teacher in a community college in Northern California saw my coming into a newly built school and helping to form a women's organization concerned with directions for black women, though open to other Third World women and working class women of all races who joined us from time to time in a common cause. Our group served the entire campus and community, providing model to middle class whites who that first year were enlightened at our conference, and the second year started a women's program of their own—then commenced to fret because we were separate. But we yawned perplexed by their behavior, continuing purposefully and intact until their tactics debilitated those in our ranks who believed "white folks water wetter and their ice cooler." A reading of Hooks' book leaves the impression she knows only of black women organizing in reaction to negative treatment from white women. The group I helped form, typical of many in this nation, came together quite naturally as a first impulse.

In contrast to the firm declaration Sojourner's "ain't I a woman?" sounds, Hooks' adaptation is marked by uncertainty. In the latter's delivery neither contextual clues, nor content reveal a sense of self. Indeed it is a sob in her mouth, revealing one painfully in doubt which could be eased if only her white sisters would mend their ways.

Hooks defines feminism, then goes on, ignoring the connotation, to label so many of our black female ancestors "feminist." While a fine title for contemporary women who self proclaim this attuned to problematic aspects, it is not fair to those dead who cannot be consulted. She goes on and on about "black feminist Mary Church Terrell," when here I sat holding that woman's autobiography aptly titled, *A Colored Woman in a White World*. The pervasive theme of the work is injustice endured, fought, and survived by blacks, with much focus on the black family. Here and there is constructive analysis of purposeful uses of suffragette agitation, but in no way does she paint her life as one given to feminist impulse. Black women have long been organized in the silent manor of prisoners of war—signaling when conversation meant death, and passing on to daughters ideas and remembered models that kept them from going mad; from standing on the corners burning bras. Much of what black women have long known about how to raise a family while holding down a job, white women are presently celebrating as some new discovery. In her introduction Terrell states, "this is the story of a colored woman living in a white world." Note she does not qualify it solely a white male world. In fact the first paragraph suggests an analogy of "women and whites." The second sentence reads, "It cannot possibly be like a story written by a white woman."

Terrell continues the paragraph with:

> A white woman has only one handicap to over-come—that of sex. I have two—both sex and race. I belong to the only group in this country which has two such huge obstacles to surmount. Colored men have only one—that of race.

Since Terrell speaks posthumously telling the group to which she belongs—black women—her example serves better black feminist groups (which Hooks decries) than white feminist groups (though Hooks ignores history insisting otherwise). In the page before the last of *Colored Woman in a White World* Terrell boasts being made an honorary member of the black sorority Delta Sigma Theta, and how she happily complied with that organization's request for her to write their creed. Thus further proof of the racial group with which she identified, and felt significant impact on her womanhood. The final thought Terrell leaves us with, however, in her autobiography focusses not on sex but race. The final paragraph reads:

> While I am grateful for the blessings which have been bestowed upon me and for the opportunities which have been offered, I cannot help wondering sometimes what I might have become and might have done if I had lived in a country which had not circumscribed and handicapped me on account of my race, but had allowed me to reach any height I was able to attain.

When referring to contemporary black feminists, as shown, Hooks is not very kind. She is particularly competitive with Michelle Wallace (*Black Macho and the Myth of the Superwoman*), saying of Wallace's book:

> While the book is an interesting provocative account of Wallace's personal life that includes a very sharp and witty analysis of the patriarchal impulses of black male activists, it is neither [sic] an important feminist work nor an important work about black women.

To this condescending assessment of Wallace and her work, Hooks adds (inadvertently perhaps), "All too often in our society it is assumed that one can know all there is about black people by merely hearing the life story and opinions of one black person." Yet in her acknowledgement she admits *Ain't I a Woman* is about her own "lived experiences."

Of Wallace's book "sister" Steinem has praise. Hooks, however, is miffed that Steinem could value Wallace's book comparable to Kate Millett's *Sexual Politics*. (Seems ole Steinem makes out the report cards.)

As stated in the outset *Ain't I a Woman* gives vent to much that is daily suppressed by black women who look askance on white feminists, while accepting of black feminists as exercising their right to join the movement which best attends their needs. Given time to rethink some of her con-clusions, to add documentation, to have edited, and to re-confront her identity, Hooks might just write a book we all can be proud of. As is the book is a disgrace to American publishing. One wonders the motive backing its release.

**Patricia Bell-Scott** (review date February 1985)

SOURCE: "The Centrality of Marginality," in *The Women's Review of Books*, Vol. II, No. 5, February, 1985, p. 3.

[*In the following review, Bell-Scott praises* Feminist Theory: From Margin to Center *because of its critique of American feminism and its vision of the future of the feminist movement.*]

Four years ago, I was introduced to Bell Hooks 'with the publication of *Ain't I A Woman: Black Women and Feminism*. This "first book" by a courageous, young, talented social critic generated a great deal of controversy and debate—some substantive, some unmerited. Hooks was charged with being ahistorical, unscholarly (there were many complaints about the absence of footnotes), and homophobic. Whether or not one agrees with any of these charges, *Ain't I A Woman* was an important book for at least three reasons: it provoked discussion between and among black and white women about the issue of racism and American feminism; it represented one of few efforts at Black feminist analysis; and it was accessible to (readable by) people outside of academe. *Feminist Theory: From Margin to Center,* the latest book by Bell Hooks, is a continuation of what was begun in 1981. It reflects the maturing of a brilliant writer and is certain to have a lasting impact on feminist theory and praxis.

"To be in the margin is to be part of the whole but outside of the main body." This, the first sentence in the book, summarizes the basic theme—that the masses of poor and minority women are marginal to feminist activism and theory-building. Though some readers might find Hooks to be repetitive in her emphasis on this theme, her analysis of how racial, sexual and class oppressions are inextricably intermingled proves to be powerfully illuminating.

In twelve chapters, she provides a comprehensive, well-documented (there are footnotes for each chapter and a bibliography) critique of contemporary American feminism. Most issues considered to be central to a feminist agenda are addressed: female sexual oppression, sisterhood as political solidarity, the role of men in feminist struggle, the devaluation of women's paid and unpaid labor, the design of educational curricula, the restructuring of parenting and family life, the redefinition of power, the American culture of violence, and revolution versus reform as social change. In a discussion of these issues, Hooks offers a vision of what feminism is not and should be.

For example, she warns that contemporary feminism has taken a "dangerous direction" toward cooptation, equivalent in significant ways to the "competitive, atomistic liberal individualism" characteristic of traditional American thinking. To illustrate this point, she quotes from an essay by Carol Ehrlich, which outlines major contradictions in feminist theory and praxis:

> Women need to know (and are increasingly prevented from finding out) that feminism is *not* about dressing for success, or becoming a corporate executive, or gaining elective office; it is *not* being able to share a two career marriage and take skiing vacations and spend huge amounts of time with your husband and two lovely children because you have a domestic worker who makes all this possible for you, but who hasn't the time or money to do it for herself; it is *not* opening a Women's Bank, or spending a weekend in an expensive workshop that guarantees to teach you how to become assertive (but not aggressive); it is most emphatically *not* about becoming a police detective or CIA agent or marine corps general.

Of what feminism should be, Hooks writes:

> Feminism is the struggle to end sexist oppression. Its aim is not to benefit solely any specific group of women, any particular race or class of women. It does not privilege women over men. It has the power to transform in a meaningful way all our lives. Most importantly, feminism is neither a lifestyle nor a ready-made identity or role one can step into.

Of the book's twelve chapters, I found chapters Four, "Sisterhood: Political Solidarity Between Women," and Six, "Changing Perspectives on Power," to be especially noteworthy. Not since *Common Differences: Conflicts in Black and White Feminist Perspectives* by Gloria I. Joseph and Jill Lewis have I read such an affirming and poignant account of the barriers between black and white women. Major obstacles to women's political solidarity include a general distrust of women among women; exclusionary social bonding among women along racial and class lines; the use of the notion of women's "common oppression" as a strategy for avoiding the reality of women's varied experiences; the perpetuation of negative social stereotypes about women who are non-white and/or economically disadvantaged; internalized oppression among poor women and women of color; and intolerance for women's right to make choices about their own sexuality.

Hooks admonishes those of us who flaunt the banner of sisterhood and solidarity but practice something else:

> The bourgeois woman who takes a less privileged "sister" to lunch or dinner at a fancy restaurant may be acknowledging class but she is not repudiating class privilege—she is exercising it. Wearing second hand clothing and living in low-cost housing in a poor neighborhood while buying stock is not a gesture of solidarity with those who are deprived or under-privileged.

She also explains why black women and other women of color remain alienated from the feminist movement. The reasons include a general unfamiliarity with the language and traditions of feminism, the media misrepresentation of feminists, the portrayal of all men as enemies and attacks on motherhood and family by some feminists, as well as recognition of white women's racism.

Hooks accurately points out that the elimination of the barriers among women of color, poor women and white women will be particularly difficult in light of the fact that consciousness-raising groups, once a forum for addressing such issues, are no longer popular or commonplace. Because few strategies for bridging the schisms among women exist, building solidarity is perhaps the greatest challenge facing modern-day feminism.

In Chapter Six, she calls for a redefinition of the concept of power. No longer can feminist theorists and activists accept and use patterns of human interaction characterized by control, manipulation and domination. Despite the obvious distinctions between decision-making processes which are consensual/collectivist as opposed to authoritarian/bureaucratic, many feminists find it difficult to break with traditional patterns of dominance. As an example of the way these practices undermine feminist efforts, Hooks excerpts a letter by Theresa Funiciello published in the July 1983 issue of *In These Times*:

> Prior to a conference some time ago on the Urban Woman sponsored by the New York City chapter of NOW, I received a phone call from a NOW representative (whose name I have forgotten) asking for a welfare speaker with special qualifications. I was asked that she not be white—she might be "too articulate—(i.e. not me), that she not be black, she might be too angry. Perhaps she could be Puerto Rican? She should not say anything political or analytical but confine herself to the subject of what the women's movement has done for me."

Funiciello's account is not unlike the numerous conversations I have had with people soliciting advice about women of color who might speak on women's issues. I am often asked (in not so subtle ways) to suggest women who are articulate and congenial (the implications being that women of color—including those who are academics—have difficult personalities and poor interpersonal skills). I am especially annoyed by the carefully phrased requests to speak on black women's issues, which suggest that neither I nor any woman of color is capable of speaking about women's issues generally and that black women's experiences are outside of, marginal to, women's issues proper.

---

***Feminist Theory: From Margin to Center*** **is a readable, comprehensive, analytical critique of American feminist theory which should be widely used in women's studies courses and read by both scholars and activists.**

**—*Patricia Bell-Scott***

---

It is unfortunate that authoritarian practices as well as race and class biases continue to shape the development of feminist theory and praxis. Many of my feminist colleagues are unable to see that the exclusion of perspectives from poor women and women of color makes women's studies, feminist theory and feminist praxis less whole and therefore invalid. This means that those of us who have any measure of race and class privilege must resist the old ways of behaving and relating; we must redefine power. Though consensual/collectivistic practices are time-consuming (and difficult for some of us), the result will be a broadening of the feminist constituency base and development of inclusive theory.

Though I found *Feminist Theory* to be challenging and affirming, it was not an "easy read." In fact, it was unsettling: Hooks raises questions that most of us would prefer to avoid. Some readers will take issue with the chapters on men as comrades, female sexual oppression, and the feminist movement to end violence, as Hooks takes positions contrary, on the whole, to the popular feminist viewpoint. Others may be irritated by her phraseology; there is a Marxist flavor. Some readers may even react defensively to some arguments, as I did sometimes. However, we must keep in mind the author's goal, to enrich feminist discourse and "to share in the work of making a liberatory ideology," as we struggle with the uncomfortable issues she raises.

The book could have been strengthened by extended discussion of strategies for activists. Translating theory into action is a difficult task—even for the well-educated. For this reason, more discussion of how feminist education for men and women might be designed and how barriers between women of color might be eliminated, for example, would have been useful.

But in spite of these shortcomings, *Feminist Theory: From Margin to Center* is an important book. It is a readable, comprehensive, analytical critique of American feminist theory which should be widely used in women's studies courses and read by both scholars and activists. We should all be encouraged by the author's vision of a theory and praxis, wherein

> Women do not need to eradicate difference to feel solidarity. We do not need to share common oppression to fight equally to end oppression. We do not need anti-male sentiments to bond us together. . . . We can be . . . united by shared interests and beliefs, united in our appreciation for diversity, united in our struggle to end sexist oppression, united in political solidarity.

**Joyce Pettis** (review date Summer 1986)

SOURCE: A review of *Feminist Theory: From Margin to Center,* in *Signs: Journal of Women in Culture and Society,* Vol. 11, No. 4, Summer, 1986, pp. 788-89.

[*In the following review, Pettis praises* Feminist Theory: From Margin to Center *for the balance it brings to feminist theory and the feminist movement.*]

Bell Hooks's second book [*Feminist Theory: From Margin to Center*] is distinguished from other texts on feminist theory by her Black feminist stance. Hooks's perspective, as one who understands not only the meaning of being on the margin but also the workings of the center, informs her

merciless dissection of conceptual blunders in the ideology of feminist theory that excludes nonwhite and poor white women or masses of American women.

Chapter by chapter, Hooks points out how the articulators of feminist theory have excluded nonwhite and working-class women primarily by disregarding "white supremacy as a racial politic," and by ignoring "the psychological impact of class, of their political status within a racist, sexist, capitalist state." Through these lenses, Hooks scrutinizes the shaping of feminist theory, the definition of feminism, the meaning of sisterhood, what feminist struggle can mean to men, and power, work, violence, education of women, and revolution as legitimate subjects of feminist theory.

Pointing out successive biases and omissions in a systematic critique of feminist theory accounts only for a portion of Hooks's text. Equally important are her ideas for altering the current direction of feminist theory so that it reflects and includes the lives of masses of nonwhite, poor, and working-class women.

A number of strengths are apparent in the text. Hooks's methodical and straightforward exposure and analysis of basic but ignored problems—capitalism, patriarchy, classism, racism, sexism—in the formulation of feminist theory is commendable. Her explanations of how these systems interact with each other and her discussion of their effects on the formulators of feminist theory are cogent, forceful, and objective. The prose conveys her impassioned convictions. Additionally, the text does not deviate from the thesis explicit in the title: the need to bring women who have existed only marginally in the feminist movement into the center of it. Hooks's text, rather than being antimale, suggests that men should be a part of feminist efforts to end oppression since they, too, will become beneficiaries of the ultimate freedom.

Hooks's argument that the feminist movement, as originally conceived and executed, was for the benefit of middle-class white women is consistent with Paula Giddings's research as revealed in "The Woman's Movement and Black Discontent," in *When and Where I Enter* and in agreement with Black feminist Gloria Joseph's conclusions in "The Incompatible Menage À Trois: Marxism, Feminism and Racism" in Lydia Sargent, ed., *Women and Revolution: The Unhappy Marriage of Marxism and Feminism.* Hooks and Joseph also agree that the ideology of patriarchy, capitalism, and racism is inextricably connected to the sexual oppression of Black women.

In spite of Hooks's unorthodox way of listing references (she lists them by chapter and page number at the end of the text, and neither publication information nor the names of editors for anthology pieces is listed in the notes), her text is a useful one that brings a needed balance to the steady proliferation of books on feminist theory and the feminist movement.

**Marlene Nourbese Philip** (review date May 1989)

"Rude Girls," in *Books in Canada,* Vol. 18, No. 4, May, 1989, pp. 25-6.

[*In the following review, Philip discusses the major themes in* Talking Back, *stating "one of the strongest themes . . . is the need to talk back or come to voice, as an act of resistance for individuals and groups that have traditionally been oppressed or silenced."*]

Where I come from, talking back to adults meant you were rude. It was proof that you weren't well brought up; this in turn was a reflection on your parents and their ability to raise clean, quiet, tidy children. In the Caribbean (which is where I am from), this tradition was a hangover from Victorian times; it was also an essential part of the baggage our parents carried with them from the time of slavery, when the ultimate sin was talking back to massa. It could result in severe punishment, if not death. And so, if they were able to keep their children quiet, and could successfully instill in them the taboo against talking back, African parents were, in fact, carrying out that oldest and most fundamental of parental duties—keeping their offspring safe.

Talking back as a metaphor for the empowerment of the oppressed is, therefore, a powerful one, and like all good metaphors resonates with a multiplicity of meanings. Talking back means the breaking of proscriptions and taboos against coming to speech, against coming to voice, against, in many respects, coming to life. One of the strongest themes running through bell hooks's *Talking Back,* a collection of 25 essays, is the need to talk back, or come to voice, as an act of resistance for individuals and groups that have traditionally been oppressed or silenced.

An equally strong theme in this work, and one that is closely related to the process of coming to voice, is "education as the practice of freedom" as Paolo Freire articulates it in his *Pedagogy of the Oppressed,* a work from which hooks quotes frequently. She argues persuasively that unless and until education at all levels becomes the practice of freedom, it remains yet another system of domination.

*Talking Back* covers a multitude of important topics. Suffice it to mention a few: the need to dismantle all systems of domination; the need for dialogue between black and white feminists; the need for theory written by black women; racism in academe; changing class as a consequence of education; white supremacy; and homophobia in black communities. Hooks engages virtually every issue of concern to individuals interested in profound and revolutionary change within society. *Talking Back* ought to be read.

Of particular interest to me, in the light of a current debate among writers in Toronto, was an essay entitled **"feminist scholarship: ethical questions."** In this essay hooks concerns herself with what she describes as the abdication of responsibility by white women "for responding [analytically and critically] to work by 'different others.'" Hooks considers this failure to respond to such work to be a retreat to a passive position, and states that she would like to hear what white women have to say *as white women.*

> Such a position would allow white women scholars to share their ideas about black women's writing (or any group of women's writing) without assuming that their thoughts would be seen

as "definitive" or that they would be trying to be "the authority."

While I agree with hooks's position, I would add that white writers, academics, and scholars have always had the privilege of engaging with all aspects of any culture; this has certainly not been the case with their black counterparts. Often the only time a black writer has an opportunity to do reviews is on work by other black writers. While this is a welcome change from having only whites review work by blacks, this practice, of blacks writing only about blacks, could serve, as hooks points out, to shore up differences and even, in some instances, racism.

Hooks admits she had difficulty putting this work together: in her introductory essay she describes her problems in trying to bring together idea, theory, and personal experience in one essay or article. When they came together, she writes, that "was the moment when the abstract became concrete, tangible, something people could hold and carry away with them." She found that she could be open about "personal stuff" in her speeches but not in her writing; her struggle was to bring the personal into her writing, to achieve in writing what she did in orality. And herein lies the problem I have with this collection of essays: they often read like speeches, but without all that goes to enliven a talk. This impression is further borne out by the repetition of the same quotations in many of the essays. There is, however, no acknowledgement that these are speeches, beyond what hooks writes in the introduction:

> Often I stopped myself from editing, from working to construct the politically correct feminist thinker with my words, so that I would just be there vulnerable, as I feel I am at times.

"Translation" from orality to the page has not, in my opinion, been completely successful in *Talking Back.* In talk we are "allowed" to be far more expansive and anecdotal than we can successfully be in writing. This, of course, raises the very issue hooks talks about in her introduction—that what is acceptable in one forum is inappropriate or unacceptable in another. While each essay yields some valuable nugget of information or some new idea, I found that individual essays often lacked a centre or appeared to change focus midway. The collection as a whole has a rambling quality, and while the overall usefulness of the work may not be lessened, the reader's enjoyment certainly is. The repetition of quotations, for instance, becomes somewhat irritating and encourages the reader to skip in a work that ought to be read closely.

Hooks's desire to marry form and content has been, to my mind, best fulfilled in **"writing autobiography"** and **"to gloria, who is she: on using a pseudonym."** Less rambling and more focused, these two essays deal less with theory and more with personal experience and ideas. Content and form are less at odds with each other than in many of the other pieces. If hooks intended us to think about how and why we accept information, and how important a part form or the manner of delivery plays in this process, she has, however, succeeded.

## Delores S. Williams (review date 9 October 1989)

SOURCE: A review of *Talking Back: Thinking Feminist, Thinking Black,* in *Christianity and Crisis,* Vol. 49, No. 14, October 9, 1989, pp. 317-18.

[*In the following review, Williams praises* Talking Back: Thinking Feminist, Thinking Black *for putting forth a new model for the relationship between black women and feminism.*]

With her usual polemicism and honesty, Bell Hooks peppers her latest book [*Talking Back*] with observations that are sure to unsettle just about everybody. Take her characterization of the academy: "The academic setting . . . is not a known site for truthtelling." Or her thoughts on a "revolutionary feminist pedagogy":

> My classroom style is very confrontational. . . . Unlike the stereotypical feminist model that suggests women best come to voice in an atmosphere of safety (one in which we are all going to be kind and nurturing), I encourage students to work at coming to voice in an atmosphere where they may be afraid or see themselves at risk. The goal is to enable all students, not just an assertive few, to feel empowered in a rigorous critical discussion. Many students find this pedagogy difficult, frightening and very demanding. . . .

Herself a feminist, Hooks is careful to indicate why such a pedagogy is needed: " . . . to overcome the estrangement and alienation that have become so much the norm in the contemporary university."

*Talking Back* contains 25 essays on a variety of subjects—from Hooks' experience as a black female graduate student, to homophobia in black communities, to Spike Lee's exploitation of black female sexuality in *She's Gotta Have It.* Along the way Hooks reflects on violence in intimate relationships, militarism, men, scholarship, black women and feminism, and feminism as a transformational political practice.

One of the most interesting efforts in this assortment is Hooks' essay on the links between her black working-class background in small-town Kentucky, her experiences in a white college and graduate school (Stanford University), and her professional life as a teacher at Yale. Hooks' ability to think about her suffering in a way that leads to new insight gives profound meaning to her journey.

> One of the jokes we used to have about the "got everything" white people is how they just tell all their business, just put their stuff right out there. One point of blackness then became—like how you keep your stuff to yourself, how private you could be about your business. That's been a place where I've been hurt by family, by black folks outside family, by friends who say, "Girl, you shouldn't even be talking about that!" And then it seemed all through graduate school, and when my first book was published, white folks were saying the same thing: "Do we want to hear what you are saying?" . . . It has been a political struggle for me to hold to the belief that there is much which we—black people—must speak

about, much that is private that must be openly shared, if we are to heal our wounds (hurts caused by domination and exploitation and oppression), if we are to recover and realize ourselves.

As Hooks sees it, healing for black people (especially black women) involves an openness—but an openness related more to survival than to "the luxury of 'will I choose to share this or tell that?'" Openness is about how to be well. It is about truth telling that has to do with putting " . . . the broken bits and pieces of the heart back together again. It is about being whole—being wholehearted."

While she points to some limitations in feminism as far as black women are concerned, Hooks believes adamantly that gender analysis is one of the best tools black women have for assessing the forces of domination in their lives—both within and beyond the black community. In discussing blacks' reaction to Alice Walker's novel *The Color Purple* ("**Black Women and Feminism**"), Hooks is especially critical of folks who argued "that sexism in black communities has not promoted the abuse and subjugation of black women by black men." She advises black women that they "must separate feminism as a political agenda from white women or we will never be able to focus on the issue of sexism as it affects black communities."

Hooks is also critical of the tendency among some black women to use the term "womanist" as against "feminist." She reminds us that Alice Walker, who coined the word *womanist,* did not mean to " . . . deflect from feminist commitment." Rather, Walker defined a womanist as also a feminist. Hooks' reservation about *womanist* is that it is not connected with a tradition of "radical political commitment to struggle and change." Her final advice to black women: " . . . the most basic task confronting black feminists (irrespective of the terms we use to identify ourselves) is to educate one another and black people about sexism, about the ways resisting sexism can empower black women, a process which makes sharing feminist vision more difficult."

*Talking Back* (like Hooks' two earlier works, *Ain't I a Woman* and [*Feminist Theory:*] *From Margin to Center*) is an effort to resist the forces that have historically dominated black women's lives. Feminist insights inform her method; she uses them to show her intended audience (apparently women—especially black women) instances of the domination of black women in North America. At the same time she insists that feminists cannot separate racism and sexism. She criticizes the tendency among some black women to identify racism as the major force oppressing them while ignoring or subordinating sexism; and she also faults white feminists for subordinating racism in their analysis of sexism.

Hooks' essay on "**Keeping Close to Home**" is especially meaningful to many black women who have, like Hooks, journeyed from black southern working-class roots through graduate school into teaching positions. Here Hooks shows clearly the tensions and anxieties that emerge for both black parents and their college-bound woman-child. The parents fear " . . . what college education might do to their children's minds even as they [parents] unenthusiastically acknowledge its importance." Alluding to her own experience, she says: "They [her parents] did not understand why I could not attend a college nearby, an all-black college. To them, any college would do. I would graduate, become a school teacher, make a decent living and a good marriage."

Even greater tensions and anxieties emerged as she tried to make sense of her working-class values in an upperclass white environment:

> I was profoundly shocked and disturbed when peers would talk about their parents without respect or would say . . . they hated their parents. This was especially troubling to me when it seemed that these parents were caring and concerned. To my white, middle-class California roommate, I explained the way we were taught to value our parents and their care, to understand that they were not obligated to give us care. She would always shake her head, laughing all the while and say, "Missy, you will learn it's different here, that we think differently."

By the time Hooks landed her position at Yale, she saw the class hiatus between professional blacks and black workers. "When I first came to Yale," she says, "I was truly surprised by the marked class divisions between black folks—students and professors—who identify with Yale and those black folks who work at Yale or in surrounding communities." "I soon learned that the black folks who spoke on the street were likely to be part of the black community and those who carefully shifted their glance were likely to be associated with Yale." In order for educated black people to deal with this class division, Hooks advises, they must fully understand and appreciate the "richness, beauty, and primacy of [their] familial and community backgrounds." She defines education as "the practice of freedom" to suggest that the function of education is not to fragment or separate. Rather, education as the practice of freedom ". . . brings us closer, expanding our definitions of home and community."

*Talking Back* combines personal experience with theory and analysis to demonstrate that feminist insights are indeed useful for assessing black women's predicament in North America. Obviously Hooks' goal is to foster the kind of transformation that leads to new models for thought, action, and relationship. I can only hope that women take her efforts seriously.

### Rebecca Walker　(review date January-February 1991)

SOURCE: "A Political Homeplace," in *Ms.*, Vol. 1, No. 4, January-February, 1991, pp. 62-3.

[*In the following review, Walker asserts that "Yearning is about wanting to find health in an ailing community, and doing so through coming to voice, sharing ideas, and healing the whole community."*]

In these times of increased division and coalition, based on ideology and political consciousness, it is helpful to find a writer who wants to put us all together, but who does not want us to be the same. bell hooks, in her fourth collection of essays, *Yearning: Race, Gender, and Cultural Politics,* writes about the need for those of us engaged in what her publishers call "the politics of radical social change," to speak with true voices to one another in order to forge a healthy and spiritually dynamic community.

She proposes that criticism be used as a means for diversity and integration; she suggests that we not hate or cut out what does not exactly jibe with our agenda, but instead engage it, unearth its fallacies or hegemonic tendencies, and bring that interpretation back to the group. Setting an example, she enjoins us to follow her interpretations of popular culture, and as we allow her words to form new spaces in social political theory, we begin to envision new forms of counter-hegemonic togetherness.

In this book, hooks applies her "critical yet supportive" model to a myriad of relationships and situations, many of which engage some of today's most dynamic issues. In the essay **"Postmodern Blackness"** she looks at what it means to be black and interested in elitist, usually white-male-dominated postmodern theory. In **"Counter-Hegemonic Art: Do the Right Thing"** she writes about Spike Lee's *Do the Right Thing* in terms of what it doesn't do to relieve oppression. In **"A Call for Militant Resistance"** she fearlessly connects the words of Lorraine Hansberry with Euzhan Palcy's film *A Dry White Season,* in recognition of the much maligned power of militancy.

A self-avowed African American feminist, hooks tackles many of the "detrimental to the community" pitfalls often found in relationships among black women, between black women and Euro-American women, and between black women and men. Her insights into perceived power relations and nonproductive assumptions are uncanny and enlightening.

Many of these problems are addressed in essays about black cultural reclamation, as in the especially powerful piece, **"Homeplace."** Here, hooks remembers the homes of her own black community as safe places of humanization, created by women as acts of resistance against the brutality that raged outside. She identifies the homeplace as a traditional site of resistance, and reveals how the current patriarchal order has corrupted this space. Not only has violence against women made the home physically unsafe, but also, hooks argues, we live in a society that fails to recognize—and value—the political work that women have put into the creation of the homeplace.

While there is something here for everyone, some may feel the book is a bit academic, somehow inaccessible to those not versed in "the academic discourse." Others may find fault with just the opposite, the personal, not-strictly-academic tone. This ambiguity of style that blends prose with literary theory, and popular culture with deconstruction, embodies the message: interdisciplinary, intercultural, international discussion. In demystified terms, please.

*Yearning* is about wanting to find health in an ailing community, and doing so through coming to voice, sharing ideas, and healing the whole community. It is about knowing how to read the nihilist, sexist attitudes that permeate our community, from Ice Cube and the new radical chic to Harvard seniors and "third world diva girls." It is about using that reading, that piece of cultural criticism, to forge a sustainable community. This equalized community unites peoples from all fronts, and is a space for inclusive and progressive politics rather than exclusive and reactionary ones.

This is not, I repeat, not a community in which the critics bond in the process of criticizing the Other. hooks calls for a space in which criticism is understood as a necessary act of love and respect, and a base upon which revolutionary struggle can be built.

## Natalie Alexander (review date Spring 1992)

SOURCE: "Piecings from a Second Reader," in *Hypatia,* Vol. 7, No. 2, Spring, 1992, pp. 177-87.

[*In the following review, Alexander discusses the themes and postmodernist techniques in* Yearning: Race, Gender, and Cultural Politics.]

In *Yearning* (1990), her fourth book, bell hooks writes across disciplines of a variety of longings and desires: for beauty, for artistic freedom, for complexity, for spiritual awakening, for community and a home place, for renewed political partnership between black women and men, and—on a more ominous side—for a nostalgic, romanticized past, for erotic playgrounds, for support from academic institutions (at whatever cost), for commodities and material goods, for liberal individualistic success, for addictive substances—for all the postmodern ways of dying.

Yet all of these yearnings—some liberatory, others destructive—are woven together as enactments or displacements of the yearning that most concerns her:

> . . . as I looked for common passions, sentiments shared by folks across race, class, gender, and sexual practice, I was struck by the depths of longing in many of us.

> . . . the yearning that wells in the hearts and minds of those whom such ["master"] narratives have silenced is the longing for a critical voice.

In one of two interviews in which she, as Gloria Watkins, interviews herself, as bell hooks, she asks herself why she makes this split in her identity: "Funny to say 'split in two'—when for me these are two parts of a whole self that is composed of many parts." In the second interview, she speaks of her desire "to write in multiple voices, and not to privilege one voice over another."

She speaks/writes in this text with many different voices, acutely aware also of the different groups among her listeners/readers. Let me write briefly about the position from which I read and respond, about my own voice as reviewer. I am a white woman, a scholar and feminist, raised in a small midwestern city. *Yearning* is peppered with excellent warnings to readers like me. For example, hooks notes

> how often contemporary white scholars writing about black people assume positions of familiarity, as though their work were not coming into being in a cultural context of white supremacy, as though it were in no way shaped and informed by that context.

Earlier, she observes that "even the most progressive" sometimes assume that "the first people we must always be addressing are privileged white readers."

Reading this text, I find it impossible to assume that I am being addressed as a "first" reader. Her "we" rarely includes me; usually, "we" means black women or black women and men or black radical women and men, occasionally radical people of many colors, including white—never black and white women. On the other hand, I read without any sense of intruding or eavesdropping; such is hooks's skill that I feel invited to read along—welcomed openly, even warmly—but always as a second reader.

In one of the pieces on aesthetics, hooks writes of her grandmother's practice of quilting and especially of the everyday quilts, crazy quilts pieced together out of worn-out clothing and other scraps:

> Together we would examine this work and she would tell me about the particulars, about what my mother and her sisters were doing when they wore a particular dress. . . . To her mind these quilts were maps charting the course of our lives. They were history as life lived.

Her grandmother, Sarah Hooks Oldham, learned quilting from her own mother, Bell Blair Hooks, to calm her "renegade nature"; bell hooks, resolved upon the naming of these women's names, writes about quilting as a ritual, even meditative, practice of surrender, of coming back to oneself, of making space for stillness. The quilts themselves were both beautiful and warm, combining style and utility, aesthetics and practicality.

*Yearning* itself is a collection of twenty-three short pieces, commenting on popular films and current literature, discussing tensions between black academics, developing new black aesthetics, and critically reshaping resistance to racism. Critical discussions of relations between black women and men form one of the recurring patterns, punctuated by critique of white academic—especially white feminist—misappropriation of black people's work. She engages with insight and freshness in postmodern discourses on the nature of subjectivity, on identity politics and essentialism, on the nature and value of marginal spaces.

Like her grandmother's quilts, *Yearning* is made up of separate scraps, each piece a site of yearning, each potentially a site of resistance. hooks writes of the book's multiplicity that "there are so many different locations in this book, such journeying." Through this journeying among sites of yearning, she stitches together a diverse batch of short pieces to create a harmonious whole that is at once aesthetic, political, and spiritual. I look briefly at the piece with which she opens the book, then examine a pattern of opposition emerging from a sequence of four essays found near the end, and finally, give a reading of one of the many pervasive patterns that give harmony to the whole work—hooks's developing conception of postmodern black subjectivities.

hooks opens by discussing Hansberry's *A Raisin in the Sun* (1959) as a counterhegemonic production, in which Mama pits the survival value of blacks' "oppositional ways of thinking" against Walter Lee's assimilationist desire to buy a liquor store; Hansberry prophetically suggests the linkage of "consumer capitalism with the production of a world of addiction." hooks argues that *A Raisin in the Sun* interrogates the desire in black communities for white-controlled commodities.

The recent film version, on the other hand, portrays Walter Lee as an "isolated black male terrorist," an image commodified to fit "with popular racist stereotypes of black masculinity." This image no longer allows an interrogation of longings for material commodities; it is itself a commodity. hooks's analysis turns on this displacement; commodification is not interrogated, but enacted.

How does this displacement alter Mama's message? hooks does not discuss it, but it seems to me that, stripped of its oppositional, anti-assimilationist character by the displacement of Walter Lee, her message becomes "reassuring" to the dominant white audience for which it was packaged. It becomes a conservative warning that blacks must stay in their own place, a warning that hooks analyzes elsewhere as conforming too neatly to—quoting Mark Miller—whites' "lunatic fantasies of containment."

Against the desire to evaluate representations of blacks simplistically in terms of good versus bad images, hooks repeatedly pits a cool, balanced, and complex vision. She evokes the active, critical, "oppositional" viewing of films and television as recalled from her childhood; she evokes also the politics of representation, "crucial for colonized groups globally in the struggle for self-determination" but as yet underdeveloped here.

This complex vision, this oppositional gaze, is nowhere more apparent than in the pattern made by the stitching together of four consecutive pieces about films. The outer pair of "movie reviews" places this gaze within a context of erotic desire, but the inner pair, which I discuss here, forms the lips of her desire for a voice linking aesthetics and politics. At the center of this pattern, she juxtaposes her discussion of Spike Lee's popular *Do the Right Thing,* marketed and commodified as radical, to that of Euzan Palcy's antiapartheid film *A Dry White Season,* often criticized for focusing on the radicalization of whites.

While recognizing Lee's courageous attempt to critique racism and his own sensitivity to class and gender as well as race issues, hooks provides a scathing indictment of *Do The Right Thing*:

> Privileged elite white folks can be reassured that they are not "racist" since they do not espouse the crude racism expressed by Sal and his sons. . . . Bourgeois black folks can . . . be reassured that they have made it. . . . Underclass urban black people . . . may feel momentarily empowered . . . [blotting] out the way that experience is appropriated and used.

The stereotypic characters and the separatism (containment?) "assuages" white audiences' fears. White viewers identify with Mookie, an individualist making free, rational, considered responses, even throwing the garbage can, a gesture provoking violence. For black viewers too "this gesture sets him apart from the other black folks in the neighborhood," who are portrayed as powerless and lack-

ing agency. Mookie's individualism conveys a simplistic notion of "freedom" based on individualistic concerns, a concept hooks analyzes in an earlier piece as feeding a "new racism" against black solidarity.

In contrast, hooks finds a complex portrayal of a spirit of militancy in *A Dry White Season.* It offers a "complex representation of 'whiteness,' " from the white father and son who become radicalized to the "privileged phallocentric white women," whose representations "do not allow the viewer to overlook race and class and see these characters as 'just women.' "

The calm, black militant—Stanley—is "the *rational* revolutionary strategist"; yet in contrast to the individualistic Mookie, he needs "collective support." Yet the blacks in this film have different understandings of their common plight: "Palcy shows radical critical consciousness to be a learned standpoint emerging from awareness of the nature of power and domination that is confirmed experientially." hooks poignantly describes a scene that "may have had little impact on viewers in this society who pay no attention to the affairs of little black girls"; a child faces the police who just shot her sister, "saying 'You killed my sister, kill me too!' " Crucial to this account is the girl's courage, her seeing, her remembering, her speaking. hooks's account of this film is juxtaposed to that of *Do The Right Thing* precisely in order to contrast their counterhegemonic power of representation, the power (expressed here but so lacking in the other film) to represent the spirit of militant resistance.

Let us turn to one of the many pervasive patterns that reach across the whole expanse of **Yearning,** stitching the diverse pieces into a harmonious whole. I refer here to the pattern of hooks's engagement with postmodern discourses, through which she envisions postmodern black subjectivities as standpoints, sources of insight, strategies, constructed grounds of struggle. She hopes that such a radical postmodernism may help other groups also to foster empathy, solidarity, and coalition.

But do such concepts—"radical," "struggle," "subjectivity," "solidarity"—belong in the postmodern lexicon? hooks plays with this tension, in various guises, gazes, sights, and sites, throughout this text. Here I will convey the harmony of this quilted pattern, interpreted through my own gaze, keeping wary for the dangers of any overly facile familiarity.

To establish a motif through which to display these patterned tensions, I re-ask a question hooks has asked herself:

> GW. . . . I'm dying to know if you think that **Yearning,** despite its critique of postmodernism, is a postmodern work?
> . . . . To some extent the book could be seen as postmodern in that the very polyphonic vocality we are talking about emerges from a postmodern social context.

Not only does she place herself in that social context, but she also engages in the critiques of essentialism that have become standard postmodern fare. Three such critiques that I find particularly fascinating are her analyses of black aesthetics, black power movements, and patriarchal black social structures.

She recognizes that the Black Arts Movement "provided useful critique based on radical questioning of the place and meaning of aesthetics for black artistic production." Yet she criticizes its essentialism, which led it eventually to subordinate art to politics:

> [It] was fundamentally essentialist. Character-ized by an inversion of the "us" and "them" di-chotomy, it inverted conventional ways of think-ing about otherness. . . . Ironically, even though the Black Arts Movement insisted that it represented a break from white western tradi-tions much of its philosophical underpinnings re-inscribed prevailing notions about the rela-tionship between art and mass culture.

Specifically, this movement assumed that an art for the masses must not be "complex, abstract, or diverse"; its paradigms became "restrictive and disempowering," throwing "many Afro-American artists . . . into a retro-gressive posture where they suggested there were no links between art and politics."

She frames this discourse in ways familiar to her readers but not common in the white postmodern academy. She tells stories about her grandmother's house and her prac-tice of quilting. She calls neither for a dismantling of the Black Arts Movement—in many ways that has already been done—nor for an anti-aesthetic. She calls for a new "aesthetic of blackness—strange and oppositional."

Using a similar pattern, hooks discusses the black power movement of the sixties, acknowledging its accomplish-ments while noting how it "conformed to a modernist un-iversalizing agenda." In particular, she critiques again and again the narrow politics of identity that would deny black diversity. Yet she never wholly repudiates the politics of identity, nor does she concur with the postmodern criti-cism of subjectivity that often follows such critiques. She wishes not to discard subjectivity but to multiply black subjectivities in a way that still somehow encourages unifi-cation. In this pattern, she frames her discussions with narratives—stories that she characterizes as nostalgic and even sentimental—about her segregated Southern up-bringing, about the sense of black community from a cir-cumscribed past to which she cannot and should not re-turn.

Using a slightly altered pattern, hooks criticizes contem-porary black cultures for misogyny, for essentialist accep-tance of a patriarchy modeled on white America:

> Let's talk about why we see the struggle to assert agency—that is, the ability to act in one's best interest—as a male thing. . . . Since the culture we live in continues to equate blackness with maleness, black awareness of the extent to which our survival depends on mutual partnership be-tween women and men is undermined.

Yet the patriarchal model that harms both black women and men is supported not only by white racist mythologies but also by the very terms in which blacks have envisioned liberation.

This piece of the pattern also belongs to hooks's criticisms of white feminist racism. Many white feminists have held that male commitment to patriarchy erases racial differ-ence. hooks carefully agrees that "oppressed black men and their white male oppressors . . . shared the patriar-chal belief that revolutionary struggle was really about the erect phallus." Yet she argues repeatedly against the sim-plistic thinking that blinds many of us and insists on inter-rogating these interlocking systems of domination and on resisting "either/or ways of thinking that are the philo-sophical underpinning of systems of domination."

She gives a lucid and poignant analysis of the origins and historical permutations of the "overlapping discourses" of race and sex. "That discourse began in slavery. . . . Then, black women's bodies were the discursive terrain . . . . rape was a gesture of symbolic castration." Yet that story "was long ago supplanted" by the myth, "invented by white men," of the black male rapist.

Much of the history of race in this country has been played out in the tension between these narratives:

> The discourse of black resistance has almost al-ways equated freedom with manhood, the eco-nomic and material domination of black men with castration, emasculation.

These discourses are hinged together on the pivot point of women's bodies. When black revolutionaries brag of rape, seeking to appropriate patriarchal power, they reinscribe the racist myth. In a less horrific but no less bitter exam-ple, when black men see themselves solely as victims they recognize neither their accomplishments nor their sexist dominance; both failures of vision harm them.

It happened that I was reading *Yearning* as the media-shaped confrontations between Clarence Thomas and Anita Hill were broadcast. hooks's discussions of these is-sues offered keys for reading these proceedings. (Note her references to prior political exploitations of race and sex.) Let me briefly explore some interlocking insights, ques-tions, wonderings shaped by my reading of *Yearning.*

Reading hooks's analyses of the "either/or ways of think-ing," I began to understand why media reactions focused on questions of either race or sex, rarely both. Newscasters lacked a language for discussing interlocking systems of domination, which they usually analyze "so well" sepa-rately; how could a "victim" be a "harasser?" They fell back on a more retrogressive, more simplistic pattern, ask-ing the essentialist question of which story was "the whole truth."

I wondered about the impact of these televised images: ar-ticulate, suave, upper-middleclass, educated, conservative, and black. I wondered especially about their impact on young black viewers. Surely, here were exemplars of mul-tiplicity within black subjectivity; here were blacks on TV who did not mirror the usual televised stereotypes. On the other hand, the very sharpness of the contrast might throw the impact back to dangerous, simplistic questions of good and bad images.

I tried to interpret Thomas's claim that Hill was evoking stereotypes about black male sexuality. Whatever the "truth" of this accusation, I found it fascinating for many reasons: it contrasted starkly with the nonstereotypic images of Thomas and Hill themselves; Thomas's own political ideology would seem to deny that such stereotypes ever hinder a black man from receiving employment; many Senators evinced such naive outrage, purporting never to have heard of such stereotypes.

hooks's interpretation of the overlapping discourses of race and sex made sense of Thomas's claim. He employed a slight shift of strategy: from representing himself as a victim who is not quite sure what all the fuss is about, a strategic blindness to sexism, to representing himself as a victim who is able to explain the fuss in terms of racism alone. Evoking racism reinforces the blindness to sexism.

I wondered too about the intersection of race and sex for Hill. Did the fact that both are black diminish or erase race as a factor? hooks's criticisms of such assumptions among white feminists point toward a different understanding. Both the context of the hearings and the "stereotype" accusation kept Thomas's blackness at the forefront. How did Hill's blackness shape the hearings?

Her accusation evoked in many a sense of betrayal. Some felt that, quite separate from the question of "truth," she shouldn't have told. If liberation is "the right to participate fully within patriarchy," then "black women who are not willing to assist black men in their efforts to become patriarchs are 'the enemy' " and "black women who succeed are taking something away from black men." Could these myths have exacerbated reactions to Hill's accusations into the claims that she must be a crass publicity hound, an insanely jealous scorned woman, or a pathological liar? *Yearning* reveals insight but also warns me when to stand back from assuming that I know what's at stake.

Let me return to examining one of the pervasive patterns shaping *Yearning,* hooks's engagement with postmodernism. I've shown how her criticisms of black modernist essentialisms—aesthetic, political, sexual—are never offered in isolation from stories of her childhood or from visionary, sometimes utopian, descriptions of new, nonessentialist black aesthetics and communities.

Her critique of the racism of white feminists has already figured in this pattern. Postmodern academic discourses have exacerbated the erasure of women of color: "White feminists could now centralize themselves by engaging in a discourse on race, 'the Other,' in a manner which further marginalized women of color." Furthermore, why do white feminists willing to overlook racism or sexism in "important" writers such as Derrida or Said, cite misogynism when they refuse to read, for example, Ismael Reed?

hooks also discusses racism "in interactions between powerful Third World elites and black Americans in predominantly white settings," in which, for example, they act as interpreters between black and white Americans:

> The current popularity of post-colonial discourse that implicates solely the West often obscures the colonizing relationship of the East in relation to Africa and other parts of the Third World.

I am ashamed of the relief with which I fell upon these passages, reassured not to be the sole oppressor—let somebody else take the heat. Yet hooks teaches her readers to mistrust reassurance as reinscribing paradigms of oppression.

She criticizes any "solidly institutionalized and commodified" cultural studies, divorced from radical political strategies; postmodern buzz words like *difference* and *the Other* "are taking the place of commonly known words deemed uncool or too simplistic, words like *oppression, exploitation.* . . ." What anti-essentialist, deconstructive, postmodern slippage is achieved here? None. This language serves to divorce talk of race from recognition of racism, masking the absence of Afro-American voices and allowing the reinscription of racist paradigms.

Insofar as she is addressing white readers, hooks must use a "counter-tongue" to the exclusionary voices discussing multiplicity, which erase the concern with racism when talking of race, which employ a deconstructive rhetoric, but reinscribe essentialist paradigms, old hierarchies. Those of us who have sometimes spoken with that voice are only second readers here; she is waiting for us to stop talking. She asks herself: "Dare I speak to oppressed and oppressor in the same voice?"

What reinscribing essentialism grips her first readers? It is not black modernism; she finds white appropriation far more frustrating. Indeed, the modernist "elements were soon rendered irrelevant as militant protest was stifled by a powerful, repressive, postmodern state." What, then, is the pervasive essentialism confronting her first readers? Hopelessness plays out everywhere: in drug and alcohol addiction; in violent crime; in erotic longings inexorably tied to despair; in feelings of apathy, indifference, and powerlessness, coming from "the real concrete circumstances of exploitation" that feel inevitable in the televised light of colonizing values; in feelings of nostalgia for inaccessible modes of experience. Privileged blacks no longer feel connected, accountable to poor and underclass blacks but are subject to a "compulsive consumerism," what West called "commodified stimulation."

"Nihilism is everywhere." Against the deadening weight of this negative essentialism, this metaphysics of absence, this reification of despair, hooks envisions a postmodern blackness, a pluralistic, historicized solidarity, epitomized by the powerful space of her aesthetics, her sense of black identity, her thoughts about community, margin, home.

The aesthetic hooks envisions and practices develops aspects of her grandmother's way of seeing: "Aesthetics is a way of inhabiting space . . . of looking and becoming . . . of a sense of history." Linked to this sense of history is the conception of art as bearing witness, as intrinsically political; her aesthetic "explores and celebrates the connection between our capacity to engage in critical resistance and our ability to experience pleasure and beauty."

This aesthetic-erotic-political space is a place of testimony, of sounds and silences: "Language is also a place of struggle." She recognizes identity politics as one stage in a process of liberation, and she uses the postmodern critique of essential identity to call forth a multiplicity of black voices:

> This critique should not be made synonymous with a dismissal of the struggle of oppressed and exploited peoples to make ourselves subjects. Nor should it deny that in certain circumstances this experience affords us a privileged critical location from which to speak.

As shown in her discussion of *A Dry White Season,* this standpoint emerges from specific historical experiences, informed by collective struggle, historically and culturally bound.

So, her space is also a place of community. Crucial to the development of such communities is a radical reworking of relationships between diverse groups of blacks, in particular between black women and men. She envisions a spiritual sense of community moved by love and joy of struggle yet unifying diverse and polyphonic voices.

She identifies this space as the margin, a place of both deprivation and resistance. From this space, she transforms the meaning of memory, calling for

> a politicization of memory that distinguishes nostalgia, that longing for something to be as once it was, a kind of useless act, from that remembering that serves to illuminate and transform the present.

She transforms the meaning of "home" to name this space as a site that makes possible new ways of seeing. The language with which she writes is quasi-religious, inspirational, perhaps madly utopian. But when set against the gravity of pervasive, essentialist nihilism, it is strangely moving.

Just as her grandmother spoke to her of the spiritual work of quilting, hooks writes to us of her work:

> I choose familiar politicized language, old codes . . . no longer popular or "cool"—hold onto them and the political legacies they evoke and affirm, even as I work to change what they say, to give them renewed and different meaning.

From the remnants of modernist political theories and from "that lived-in segregated world of my past and present," hooks stitches together the old words she takes up like scraps for a crazy quilt, transforming this quilted space, this complex landscape, this site of erotic, spiritual, political, aesthetic yearning.

### bell hooks with Lisa Jones   (interview date October 1992)

SOURCE: "Rebel Without a Pause," in *VLS,* No. 109, October 1992, p. 10.

[*In the following interview, Jones and hooks discuss how contemporary media portray black men and women.*]

It began, as it often does, with a photograph. Cultural critic/feminist poobah bell hooks received a postcard of a 19th century black Indian woman. The photograph bewitched hooks: how direct the woman's gaze was, how contemporary she looked. Every detail of her visual persona challenged simplistic constructions of black identity. To hooks, the photo underscores how representations of race in mass media, though *très chic,* still fail to envelop the complexity of black lives and viewpoints. When we see black images, on screen, in advertising, and in fashion magazines, what are we looking at, hooks asks, and what's missing from the frame? This meditation hatched *Black Looks,* hooks's latest, and what may be her most slyly provocative, collection of essays. Gracing the book's cover is the black Indian woman of the photograph—gilded, silent, but many moons from complacent.

A sought-after lecturer and popular professor (at Oberlin, her courses on black women's fiction and the politics of sexuality are booked solid), hooks has journeyed in the last 10 years from unsung women's-studies scholar to internationally known critical thinker. Her six books include *Yearning,* 1990, which solidified her reputation as an interrogator of postmodernism and cinema, and last year's *Breaking Bread,* a compilation of spirited dialogues with Cornel West. *Publishers Weekly* called hooks "one of the foremost black intellectuals in America today." She even made a recent roundup of "who's hot" in *Essence* magazine, sharing company with Wesley Snipes, George Wolfe, and Ice Cube. Media junkies, academics, diversity mavens, and 9-to-5 sisters looking for womanist affirmation—hooks groupies are a varied bunch.

*Black Looks* is cultural criticism at its sexiest for the essay titles alone. "Eating the Other" picks the bone of mass media's appetite for racial difference. The long-awaited manifesto on Madonna comes with the subtitle "Plantation Mistress or Soul Sister?" An exploration of black female sexuality in the marketplace of images is packaged as "Selling Hot Pussy."

The new collection further installs hooks as an important American film critic. "Ivory-tower film criticism," she says, is not her design; she's after your white supremacist, patriarchal jugular, and is not stopping to observe any parlor games of this trade. There's no such pretense as entertainment in the hooks camp; film is just fodder for a larger ideological work horse. So, bring your 3-D glasses, and be warned: if you don't have those critical lenses on, you're likely to become what you consume.

[*Jones*]: *In* "Eating the Other," *the anchor essay of* Black Looks, *you argue that fashionable tropes of cultural difference in popular culture do little to challenge racism. But still you see hope.*

[hooks]: I hold on to the idea of pleasure as a site of resistance. Not just pleasure (in exploring cultural difference) as an end in itself, but that pleasure might be the beginning of something else: of real subversion.

In writing the essay, I was trying to break through a sense of despair about it all. We just have so much commodification of blackness right now. Take a film like *White Men Can't Jump.* To me it's the quintessential expression of commodification that doesn't seek to change things, but to reestablish black people as territory for white people to invade. I saw an old James Bond movie, *Live and Let Die,* about a lone white man who defeats black people in every country in the world. I thought *White Men Can't Jump* was the 1990s version of that. Look what it did with Rosie Perez's character. What a plantation sexual relationship between Rosie's character and the white leading man! It was as if she was confined to this shack and the white man visited her.

There's a suggestion that white supremacist imperialism is more elastic these days, that it can actually open up to multiculturalism. But in many ways that's a power move. There's a little change, enough to appear like a progression, but not enough to institutionalize systems of liberatory racial and sexual justice.

I continue to be fascinated, though, and I feel that the jury is still out about whether these types of images can lead to changes in how people think about race. Many of the consumers of black commodification are young people. I'm acquainted with little white boys whose model for selfhood and identity is black masculinity in popular culture. Does this mean that there will be a new generation of white men who will respect the dignity and lives of black males? Or will they be positioned to become Mel Gibson in *Lethal Weapon*—a generation of white folks who aren't afraid of black folks, and who can use them more effectively to serve their ends?

*Why is film so crucial to representations of race right now?*

When we talk about the commodification of blackness, we aren't just talking about how white people consume these images, but how black people and other people of color consume them, and how these images become our way of knowing ourselves. Black kids aren't going to see a film like *White Men Can't Jump* and consume it passively. They're also learning their ideas about how to be black.

A recent film that absolutely bugs me in its use of black people is *Fried Green Tomatoes*. Films that try to transgress one boundary often pacify us by reinforcing other status quos. I feel this about Spike Lee's movies. In *Fried Green Tomatoes,* we may be transgressing a boundary about how lesbianism is pictured, but the images of black people in that film fit every sort of stereotype. It was sad to see Cicely Tyson, a distinguished actor, assigned once again to the role of darkie on the plantation; the film was simply a modern plantation story with a white-lesbian twist.

*You argue that black female spectators often experience the pleasure of cinema through denial, given the scarcity and one-dimensionality of representations of black women. How did you emerge as a critic through this wasteland of images?*

Growing up in the Jim Crow period, one was always positioned as a critic, because without a critique of what you saw, you had no possibility of a redeeming image. No matter how educated black folks were, there was this recognition that one had to have some kind of critical gaze.

Watching TV shows like *Amos 'n' Andy,* my older siblings and I were very conscious of how representations of black people were being manipulated. My youngest sister, who grew up in the age of integration, is less able to accept that there are manipulative forces behind what she sees. It occurred to me how black people at this point in history are more deeply American than ever before. We're much more collectively taken in. That's why, to some extent, integration was necessary for the continuation of white supremacy.

---

**It's disturbing me that practically every black woman I know, from every social class, from all walks of life, can talk about the stereotypes of black womanhood. But when I ask these same women to name what types of images they'd like to see, they can't answer that question. That's scary.**

**—bell hooks**

---

*So, in a sense, representations of black people work to pacify us?*

Absolutely. I ask myself, what does it mean that 20 years ago black people could not have imagined sitting in movie theaters and laughing at the kinds of degrading images of blackness that we see in the mass media today? And it's important to note that these representations aren't just made by white people. Many assume that if a film is made by a black person, the representations will automatically have integrity beyond anything a white person can produce. But what we're seeing is black people reproducing the prevailing "exploitative" images to create work that sells. And because these films are solely judged by their representation of narrow ideas of blackness, they can get away with having anything-goes standards of production.

*Many of us are counting on black female filmmakers to provide more complex visions of African American life. But judging from your critique of contemporary fiction by black women and its failure to imagine new identities, should we have any reason to be hopeful?*

It's disturbing me that practically every black woman I know, from every social class, from all walks of life, can talk about the stereotypes of black womanhood. But when I ask these same women to name what types of images they'd like to see, they can't answer that question. That's scary.

I had a sad feeling after reading Terry McMillan's new book, *Waiting To Exhale,* and Alice Walker's *Possessing the Secret of Joy.* Sometimes it seems we are offered only two messages around black female representation. One says: become the "expected" image, but work it, like the bitchified, take-no-prisoners black women we see in *Waiting To Exhale.* Or the other option is to be the tragic black women we see so much of in contemporary fiction. The prototype for this is Toni Morrison's character Sula, and Tashi in *Possessing the Secret of Joy* follows suit. How can we move away from casting ourselves as trapped in those two images—the tragic figure, or the tough, sexualized survivor? What disturbs me about the Walker book is that she has the resisting black woman character, who follows the same path as Sophia in *The Color Purple.* But once again, this resisting woman, who tries to define herself completely outside the realm of fixed roles, is punished. Part of what I want to turn my life into is a testimony to the fact that we don't have to be punished. That we don't have to sacrifice our lives when we invent and realize our complex selves.

As I approach 40, sometimes I ask myself, will I see in my lifetime diversified representations of black womanness?

*Do you see these coming from any quarters?*

Camille Billops's latest film, *Finding Christa,* has many provocative images. We meet, in the film, the woman who becomes Christa's adoptive mother. When I say there are subversive images, I felt this is one. This is a black woman—heavy-set, dark-skinned—who never enters Hollywood except as mammy, except as someone who is subjugated. Billops shot that image with the kind of beauty and power it's rarely shot with.

---

**I believe much is going to come from the world of theory-making, as more black cultural critics enter the dialogue. As theory and criticism call for artists and audiences to shift their paradigms of how they see, we'll see the freeing up of possibilities.**

**—*bell hooks***

---

Some of the most arresting images of black women I've ever seen were gathered in the film Julie Dash did for PBS's *Alive From Off-Center* of the dance group Urban Bushwomen. These images are about black women struggling to find space to exercise creativity, and that's what made them so powerful for me.

In my bedroom I have that famous photograph that I mention in *Black Looks* of Billie Holiday taken by Monetta Sleet. It was given to me by the curator Deborah Willis, who does much of the work on black photographers. I am always thankful that there was significant visual documentation done of Holiday's generation of black artists and thinkers. It's been crucial to my generation to see pictures of those black artists and thinkers in their studies and their spaces. The posture Holiday has in that photo is like that of Rodin's *The Thinker.* Every morning when I wake up and see this picture, I feel an affirmation from her of the space that I have claimed in my life, as a black female, to be a contemplative person.

I believe much is going to come from the world of theory-making, as more black cultural critics enter the dialogue. As theory and criticism call for artists and audiences to shift their paradigms of how they see, we'll see the freeing up of possibilities. It's my hope. That's one of the reasons so much of my new work is focusing on looking rela-

tions—in a sense, on seeing. I think it's the main source of intervention right now.

**Beth Coleman** (review date January 1993)

SOURCE: "Left Hooks," in *Art Forum,* Vol. XXXI, No. 5, January, 1993, pp. 10-11.

[*In the following review, Coleman discusses hooks's attempt to "decolonize" the minds of African Americans in* Black Looks: Race and Representation.]

> We have to change our own mind. . . . We've got to change our own minds about each other. We have to see each other with new eyes. We have to come together with warmth.
>
> —Malcolm X

> Loving blackness as political resistance transforms our ways of looking and being, and thus creates the conditions necessary for us to move against the forces of domination and death and reclaim black life.
>
> —bell hooks

A call to action is different in 1992: the tactic is a privately owned liberation theology, the faith Blackness, the patron saint Vision. In her latest book of essays [*Black Looks*], cultural critic bell hooks gives up the quotidian for the spooky no-man's-land of mass-media representation, her site of excavation "images of black people that reinforce and reinscribe white supremacy." The dig takes her across, rather than down, the broad face of American film, advertisement, and literature, in an effort to "decolonize" the mind and locate "Revolutionary Attitude."

The argument includes a feminist reconstruction of black masculinity, a discussion of "hot pussy" in the marketplace, and a conjuring of the renegade alliance between blacks and Native Americans. In **"A Feminist Challenge"** (subtitle: "Must We Call Every Woman Sister?"), hooks asks not whether Anita Hill is a black feminist hero—her answer is no—but what justice Hill expected from the Senate Judiciary Committee when she brought her naive albeit poised testimony to their table. Though Hill might have lost her case faster had she enlisted an explicit feminist agenda, hooks argues that she would have gained ground as a speaking, public person, and would have given the viewing audience—the black female and every other viewer—something more to sink our teeth into than despair. Madonna, **"Plantation Mistress or Soul Sister?,"** is hooks' other woman, in a surprisingly dry analysis after such a fabulous title. "Though I often admire and, yes at times, even envy Madonna because she has created a cultural space where she can invent and reinvent herself and receive public affirmation and material reward, I do not consider myself a Madonna fan." Too high to go over, too low to go under: must we all position ourselves in relation to la M?

Despite the interest of these analyses, it's the three essays on film that moor the book, and where hooks hits stride. **"Is Paris Burning?,"** a very rough read of white consumption, presses the question of whether a film is de facto radical because its subject matter is. In **"Micheaux's Films,"** hooks gingerly unfolds Oscar Micheaux's celebration of a complex image of blackness in his movies of the '20s. The tour de force is **"The Oppositional Gaze,"** which locates black female spectatorship beyond the pain of the offensive black images that Hollywood is so good at, to include pleasure. In perhaps the most subversive maneuver of the book, hooks looks for pleasure in every situation—for recovery of a private, personal joy that a lot of living in America can take away.

When hooks writes as film critic, working within the relative safety zone of a subject contained by the screen, her arguments stand thorough and coherent. When actual black people enter the picture, things get irksome. There is a flavor of being Saved to the writing, a degree of: "If you don't see it this way then you are in denial." And in this jihad for the souls of black folks, denial is tantamount to conspiring with the enemy. Hooks portrays herself as a decolonized person in a position of righteousness . . . because she is decolonized. Fine, but for those who might still be in the loop of oppression, a leap of faith needs to happen. Hooks does not explain this leap.

Something of a tender tyrant is hooks, teaching the politics of self-liberation as bound by a rather rigid authorial presence that overwhelms equally as it withholds. In **"Loving Blackness as Political Resistance,"** for example, she writes in the aphoristic style of the manifesto, which either speaks to those who already understand what it is to love blackness, becoming an exercise in flaunting, defiance, or else wants detail, more explanation. What it is we are talking about when we say "blackness"? Hooks utilizes the many slipping meanings of "black"—cultural/historical construct, true fact in the eyes of God, transcendent state of grace and pain—without owning the slippage.

To be sure, revolution doesn't come with a directive (Buy bread at Muslim bakery!) anymore. Compare Malcolm X's easily quoted call to love black, which hooks uses to introduce her essay on the subject, to hooks' own. One is a paragon of self-containment and practicability; the other poses more questions than answers. The purpose of comparison here is not to decide "worth" but rather to acknowledge history and, well, yes, difference. Recognizing our post-civil rights, post-Modern moment—the public oratory and soapbox gone—hooks calls for the revolution to begin at home, privately, with reflection and introspection, then clangs the phone down hard in your ear. Now, is that ringing noise the sound of a specious identity politics or a strategy to disrupt?

**D. Soyini Madison** (review date 28 February 1993)

SOURCE: "Seeing is Believing," in *The New York Times Book Review,* February 28, 1993, p. 23.

[*Madison is an American writer. In the following review, she discusses hooks's attempt to delineate the "connections between race, representation, and domination" in the media in* Black Looks: Race and Representation.]

How we are represented by others shapes how we represent ourselves, what is real to us and the worlds we imagine; and images and representations are a formidable cultural force. An urban street gang logo, a painting, a flag, Rodney King, Malcolm X or Anita Hill—each can become a sacred icon, a taboo and something worth fighting for.

For victims of what Bell Hooks calls "white supremacist culture"—and for those who 'resist it—representation becomes more provocative and complex. Precisely because representation is so important a force in self-identification, particularly for people of color, **Black Looks: Race and Representation,** the sixth book of essays by Bell Hooks (the pseudonym of a feminist and cultural critic who teaches at Oberlin College), is an important work.

In 12 essays, she lays out the connections between race, representation and domination in literature, popular music, television, advertising, historical narrative and film. Forcefully stating that controlling the images of a people is central to dominating them, she moves her argument forward in two ways: through a discussion of the pain these representations can cause people of color seeking to create a sense of self, and through her stress on the need for progressive thinkers to intervene to combat the destructive consequences of that pain.

"If we, black people, have learned to cherish hateful images of ourselves," Bell Hooks asks, "then what process of looking allows us to counter the seduction of images that threatens to dehumanize and colonize?" Her answer: "Clearly, it is that way of seeing which makes possible an integrity of being that can subvert the power of the colonizing image. It is only as we collectively change the way we look at ourselves and the world that we can change how we are seen."

Engaging her readers in a discussion of the power of "looking," she argues that recognizing the influence of domination is the first step to change. Bell Hooks contends that sexism and racism overlie the way we see, and she holds up an oppositional gaze as a counter, declaring that one must look a certain way in order to resist. Deploying a range of selected contemporary images, Bell Hooks helps the readers do precisely that, with a critical, oppositional and interventionist gaze.

Her most striking illuminations come in her essays on the Clarence Thomas hearings, the documentary film *Paris Is Burning,* and Madonna. In her analysis of Judge Thomas's cry that he was being subjected to a "high-tech lynching," she forcefully asserts that Anita Hill needed a more developed strategy, one that went beyond "daring to name publicly that she had been sexually harassed" to explicitly challenging the system that made the Thomas choice inevitable. Her discussion of *Paris Is Burning,* a documentary about black and Hispanic cross-dressers, raises important questions about the way black life can be appropriated as spectacle and turned into a commodity. In her critique of Madonna, she extends this argument, contending that even as Madonna, mocks the idea of " 'natural' white girl beauty," she strives to embody it. Seen through Ms. Hooks's oppositional eye, the black characters in the Madonna video "Like a Prayer" are no different from the early Hollywood images of singing black slaves in the plantation movies or the Shirley Temple films, where "Bojangles was trotted out to dance with Miss Shirley and spice up her act. Audiences were not supposed to be enamored of Bojangles, they were supposed to see just what a special little old white girl Shirley really was."

The 12 essays are uneven in their analytical complexity and originality of thought, but such nuggets overall provide insight into race, representation and dominance.

**bell hooks with Desiree Cooper (interview date 24-30 August 1994)**

SOURCE: " 'I Think White Women Are Really Happy When Black Women Abandon Feminism': Bell Hooks on Being a Black Woman in Middle America," in *Metro Times*, Vol. XIV, No. 47, August 24-30, 1994, p. 14.

[*In the following interview, hooks and Cooper discuss feminism and African American men.*]

Since ***Ain't I A Woman,*** published in 1981 and recently named one of the 20 most influential women's books of the last 20 years by Publisher's Weekly, Bell Hooks has been a trailblazer and guide in the nebulous territory that belongs to the contemporary black American woman. A professor at Oberlin College in the English and Women's Studies departments, Hooks has received numerous literary awards. Her most recent book, ***Sisters of the Yam: Black Women and Self-Recovery,*** is a call for reunification among a diverse, and increasingly divergent, segment of society.

In this edited interview, Hooks talks about white feminism, black men and where to go from here.

[*Cooper*]: *What do you think of the much-publicized schism between the traditional feminist movement and African-American women?*

[Hooks]: I think this is really a fiction. Part of that fiction arises from the tremendous ignorance people have about feminism, about where it began. Individual African-American women were always part of feminist movement. We were not there in large numbers; we tended to be in the minority. So what ends up happening is our presence gets erased altogether. People forget that Shirley Chisholm was one of the first politicians in this country to really champion abortion rights in the interests of young black females and older black females who were suffering repeated, undesired pregnancies.

That history gets lost, because white women weren't interested in it and didn't call attention to it. When younger black women like myself came on the scene in the '70s and began to critique that racism of white women, many people took that critique to mean (we were critiquing) the absence of black women. But our absence is very different from erasure on the part of those who are ignorant.

*What you're describing is, perhaps, the conflict that black women feel choosing between racism vs. sexism, and often being forced to make that choice if they're going to be called a feminist.*

I think that you said it, that we're often forced by others. I think white women are really happy when black women abandon feminism and act like our needs are not the same as theirs, because then they get to really dominate. It's really clear that white women have been that group which has most benefited from affirmative action in this society. And bourgeois, mainstream, white-dominated feminism was very crucial to putting that into place. So, of course, that group loves it when black women say, "Oh, this has nothing to do with us."

And, I think, of course, black men and white men love it when black women say feminism has nothing to do with us. Because it continues this age-old competition between women for male favor.

I think that a lot of black women realize that black men often are very threatened by the term feminism, and threatened by some sense that we are uniting past race.

Have we ever heard any black men, intellectual, from W.E.B. Dubois on to Cornel West, have any of them been told, "You must choose between being black and being on the left? Are you a Marxist first or black?" We won't see those questions asked of contemporary black male intellectuals on the left.

Twenty years ago, when I first became involved with feminism, the question I was most asked was, "Are you black first or a woman?" Twenty years later, that's still the question I'm most asked, particularly by other black people.

*And what is your response?*

My response is that it's precisely that kind of dualistic split that is at the heart of racist, sexist thinking around domination, this either/or. The thing is, what most black women say is, "We do not have a choice; we are both black and women."

*In taking what you're saying as a given, then how does a black woman who wants to tackle the politics of dominance fit herself into the traditional feminist movement?*

First of all, I think we don't try to fit into the mainstream feminist movement, because that movement is narrow-minded in its vision for all women. I think that what we have done in such a grand and revolutionary manner that's so threatening to mainstream white women is that we've said, "This movement isn't really useful for the masses of people." We need to re-vision it. We need to make it more inclusive. If you look at the work of contemporary black feminists—Audre Lorde, who's passed away—you see such a call for a more expansive feminist vision. We don't just call for expanding that vision for blacks, we call for expanding it because it's really not very helpful for masses of men and women.

I also think that you get powerful black women revolting, calling this out, establishing the terrain for ourselves, for black people, and for the public as a whole to say, "Wait a minute. We're not going to just walk away from feminism. We're going to challenge this. We're going to demand change, and we're going to be at the forefront of creating theory that revolutionizes our thinking. Black women's demands that white women cut through their denial and face the reality of racism created a revolution in feminist thinking.

I think that part of the myth of white bourgeois feminism was that there isn't any price to be paid. You can have it all. You can have your beautiful yuppie home, you can have your beautiful yuppie children, your beautiful cars, your house in the Hamptons, you can have everything.

But the fact is there are not the structures in place to allow black women who are moving from the underclass and the working class into whole new spheres of class power to "have everything" in a kind of neat, simplistic way. And I'm not saying that we can't have everything. I'm saying that the mechanisms by which we grow into having everything may be very, very different from those that white women who are from more privileged classes, because I think white women who are not privileged suffer the same kinds of things we're talking about in terms of black women.

*Let me ask you a more personal question. Your given name is Gloria Watkins, and you now prefer to be called Bell Hooks. Who is Bell Hooks and why is she different from Gloria Watkins?*

I chose that name to honor my grandmother, my mother's mother, because I wanted to say, black women come from generations of powerful women who had given us something.

For me, Bell Hooks is a constant reminder of the fact that, as a black woman, I am not alone. And I think that's important for us, because while I might be the only black woman distinguished professor, and I could sit around being paranoid about what my colleagues are thinking about me, it's so much better for me to sit around and be thinking about how proud Bell Hooks would be of me, that I have not compromised myself.

Shirley Chisholm is so important to me. Girlfriend wrote that book *Unbought and Unbossed,* and when I read it, I thought, God, I want to grow up to be like this black woman, who can look at the world and say, "I am unbought and unbossed." That is what Bell Hooks means to me: fundamentally, that constant reminder of our creativity, our choice, the fact that I can choose this name, that I can play with words, that I can be as funky as a I want to be. All of those things are a source of empowerment for me.

*There is such a large rift, it seems, between black women and black men. I've always said there's been a women's movement and no men's movement. The question is how to move for there to be real healing, I think.*

I feel like I want to do more books like *The Sisters of the Yam.* I can't tell you how many black men come up to me and say, "I loved *Sisters of the Yam.* Why don't we have something like this?" Partially, we won't have things like this for black men until more black men dare to challenge their sexism.

I think this is absolutely true, and I think it's on the horizon. And that's exciting.

**Jerome Karabel    (review date 18 December 1994)**

SOURCE: "Fighting Words," in *The New York Times Book Review,* December 18, 1994, p. 27.

*[Karabel is an American educator and sociologist. In the following review, he discusses* Teaching to Transgress: Educating as the Practice of Freedom *and* Outlaw Culture: Resisting Representations. *Although he complains of hooks's occasional excess of language, he states that "hers is a voice that forces us to confront the political undercurrents of life in America."]*

Like her friend Cornel West, with whom she wrote an absorbing book of dialogue, **Breaking Bread: Insurgent Black Intellectual Life,** Bell Hooks (nee Gloria Watkins) is an unconventional scholar, constantly crossing the boundaries separating the academic disciplines as well as the division between scholarship and politics. Ms. Hooks has produced a formidable body of work, including more than a half-dozen books on topics ranging from feminist theory to representations of blacks in popular culture.

Now Ms. Hooks, who is a Distinguished Professor of English at City College in New York, has published two new collections of essays, both bearing her distinctive combination of autobiographical narrative and cultural critique.

The first, **Teaching to Transgress: Educating as the Practice of Freedom** is inspired by the work of Paulo Freire, a radical Brazilian educator known worldwide for his advocacy of education for "critical consciousness." Ms. Hooks attempts to put Mr. Freire's pedagogy of liberation, which holds that students should be active participants and not passive consumers, into practice in America's multicultural context. Situating "identity politics" based on race or sex, which has become so pervasive on American campuses, as emerging "out of the struggles of oppressed or exploited groups to have a standpoint on which to critique dominant structures," she nevertheless acknowledges that the militant assertion of group identities can itself become "a strategy for exclusion or domination." A genuine pedagogy of liberation, Ms. Hooks suggests, will honor the need of marginalized groups to assert positive identities while rigorously challenging their own myths about themselves and the sources of their oppression.

As in much of Ms. Hooks's work, the strength of **Teaching to Transgress** resides in the jarring character of its insights. She evokes a shock of recognition for me, for example, in reminiscing about her days as a Stanford undergraduate, when she attended classes taught by "white male professors who wore the same tweed jacket and rumpled shirt." The real message of such professors, she says, is that they are in the classroom "to be a mind and not a body." Only the powerful, she notes acidly, have "the privilege of denying their body."

Unfortunately, the collection is often marred by a disconcerting reliance on pop psychology. A truly liberatory education, Ms. Hooks insists, will do more than stimulate critical consciousness; it will also be an experience in which "healing" and "recovery" can replace the "pain" and "abuse" of childhood. By forcing the radical third-world pedagogy of Mr. Freire into a troubled and unlikely marriage with the quintessentially American language of self-help, Ms. Hooks ends up at times sounding more like Norman Vincent Peale than Nelson Mandela.

*Outlaw Culture: Resisting Representations* ranges widely over the American cultural landscape, as Ms. Hooks looks at contemporary cinema, rap music, feminist thought and the racial politics of beauty. She brings to the task of cultural criticism an astute eye and a courageous spirit, and her judgments—as in her essays on the art of Jean-Michel Basquiat and the writings of Camille Paglia ("sensational sound bites that often appear radical and transgressive of the status quo") and Katie Roiphe ("Roiphe completely ignores the connection between maintaining patriarchy and condoning male violence against women")—are frequently discerning.

Perhaps the best essay here is a penetrating discussion of censorship. Drawing on her own experience, Ms. Hooks notes that censorship is not simply a matter of state repression (though her book *Black Looks: Race and Representation* was seized for a time by Canadian authorities as "hate literature"). Candidly describing her fears of publicly criticizing an essay on the Op-Ed page of this newspaper by the prominent black writer Henry Louis Gates Jr., Ms. Hooks acknowledges that repression can take the form of self-censorship, especially when what one wishes to say seems likely to elicit disapproval and even reprisals from one's peers. Particularly among members of marginalized groups, pressure to conform can be overwhelming because of the fear that dissent will undermine group solidarity. Yet in the end, Ms. Hooks argues, even oppositional movements must find space for their own dissenters and "the courage to fully embrace free speech."

Though often evocative, Bell Hooks's prose suffers from lapses into academic obscurantism. One passage in *Outlaw Culture* speaks of feminists who "experience our most intense sexual pleasure in the oppositional space outside the patriarchal phallic imaginary." Yet to dwell on excesses in Ms. Hooks's language would be to miss her considerable power as a writer. For hers is a voice that forces us to confront the political undercurrents of life in America.

### Shelley P. Haley   (review date March 1995)

SOURCE: "Practicing Freedom," in *The Women's Review of Books,* Vol. XII, No. 6, March, 1995, pp. 10-11.

[*In the following review, Haley provides a detailed analysis of* Teaching to Transgress *and* Outlaw Culture.]

Have you ever read a book and felt that it was written about you? This usually happens to me only with novels, so I was especially startled to read bell hooks' latest collection of essays, *Teaching to Transgress*. Like hooks, I have been teaching in a college or university setting for twenty years. Like hooks, I am a Black woman who advocates feminism; like hooks, my degree is in a traditional Eurocentric field—Classics for me, English literature for her. We share a passion for curricular transformation and critical thinking.

As I read *Teaching to Transgress,* I found myself sighing

with relief many times; here, for all to read, was *my* experience of teaching, pedagogy and classroom dynamics. Here, clearly articulated, was a Black feminist critique of a hierarchical system of higher education that promotes research over teaching and service. I can't help emphasizing how important it is to have the voice of this Black feminist activist/teacher as a counterpoint to books like *The Bell Curve:* Hooks—always an academic outlaw—sharply criticizes its "liberals-are-taking-over-the-ivy-tower" mentality.

The main message of *Teaching to Transgress* is that the teacher is also a student and the student is also a teacher. In **"Embracing Change,"** hooks writes:

> To teach effectively a diverse student body, I have to learn these [cultural] codes. And so do students. This act alone transforms the classroom. . . . Often professors and students have to learn to accept different ways of knowing, new epistemologies, in the multicultural setting.

One of the most striking aspects of *Teaching to Transgress* is the way it echoes the works of early Black women educators like Fanny Jackson Coppin, principal of the Institute for Colored Youth in Philadelphia from 1869 to 1906, who emphasizes in her 1913 *Reminiscences of School Life, and Hints on Teaching* the importance of the reciprocity of respect between teacher and student. The personal anecdotes hooks interweaves with scholarly sources demonstrate the respect she has for both her students and colleagues. She offers a touching tribute to a student, O'Neal LaRone Clark, to whom the book is dedicated: ". . . we danced our way into the future as comrades and friends bound by all we had learned in class together."

For hooks, education is the practice of freedom—especially as crystallized in Paolo Freire's liberation pedagogy, which she also espouses. My own experience with the excitement of education mirrors hooks' engagement with Freire's work. I was educated in upstate New York schools that were overwhelmingly white; the facilities were quite good, but my self-esteem and independence of thought were established at home by my mother, grandmothers and aunts. The women in my family showed me how to use education to rise above the bigotry of my teachers: reading, writing and learning other languages became safe spaces where I expanded my mind.

In **"Paulo Freire"** hooks uses the dialogue form to convey the impact of his work on her. In recent years, she has increasingly constructed dialogues as a way to represent different voices and positions. In **"Building a Teaching Community,"** she notes:

> To engage in dialogue is one of the simplest ways we can begin as teachers, scholars, and critical thinkers to cross boundaries, the barriers that may or may not be erected by race, gender, class, professional standing, and a host of other differences.

Hooks' first dialogue was with Cornel West in her 1991 book *Breaking Bread: Insurgent Black Intellectual Life.* What makes the dialogue in **"Paulo Freire"** different is that she holds it with herself as Gloria Watkins (her given name), and through it we find out as much about hooks/Watkins as we do about Freire. (We learn, for example, that Freire reinforces her deep convictions about the importance of social and political activism.) This dialogue also reveals how hooks copes with the male orientation and sexism of Freire's language in his early works: "There is no need to apologize for the sexism. Freire's own model of critical pedagogy invites a critical interrogation of this flaw in the work. But critical interrogation is not the same as dismissal."

Hooks, in everything she writes, strives to make her work accessible to a broad and diverse audience. This has meant rethinking academic format and eliminating obstacles to understanding, whether footnotes or jargon. She often draws on the whole range of human knowledge and doesn't concern herself with petty questions of scholarly appropriateness. The Vietnamese Buddhist monk Thich Nhat Nanh is quoted alongside Paulo Freire; articles from *The Village Voice* are given as much weight as those by feminist scholars Mimi Orner or Chandra Mohanty; and a collection of essays edited by Marianne Hirsch and Evelyn Fox Keller, *Conflicts in Feminism,* shares the spotlight with *The Black Man's Guide to Understanding the Black Woman.*

In **"Theory as Liberatory Practice,"** hooks explains why she has adopted this format: "my decisions about writing style, about not using conventional academic formats are political decisions motivated by the desire to be inclusive, to reach as many readers as possible in as many different locations." However, my reaction to this subversion of academic format is split. My inner rebel says "You go, girl!" At the same time my prim classicist self says "It would facilitate the location of articles and books cited if there were a bibliography. I mean, really, who is going to read this except academics?"

As much as I admire *Teaching to Transgress*—and I do plan to use it in a seminar on Black feminist thought and practice—I was annoyed by some of hooks' assumptions. I have always been sensitive about class. I am a middle-class Black from the North; my "Black" vernacular is the vernacular of central New York; yet I have known poverty, racism and sexism. As a radical in the sixties, I always resented the notion that only Southern, working-class Black folks are authentic Blacks.

Hooks is from a Southern working-class background and she rightly focuses on this, but her negative attitude toward the middle but her negative attitude toward the middle class puts me on the defensive. In **"Language,"** she claims that by using Black vernacular "we take the oppressor's language and turn it against itself. We make our words a counter-hegemonic speech, liberating ourselves in language." But "we" are not all from Southern, rural, working-class backgrounds. "We" all don't speak Black vernacular, though we still strive to liberate ourselves in language, in theory and in teaching.

In fact, hooks is quite aware of problems with essentialism. In **"Essentialism and Experience"** she criticizes Diana Fuss, author of *Essentially Speaking*: "I am disturbed that she [Fuss] never acknowledges that racism, sexism, and class elitism shape the structure of classrooms, creating a lived reality of insider versus outsider that is predetermined, often in place before any class discussion begins." But while hooks emphasizes the importance of experience here, I worry that when it comes to social class, she falls into the same essentializing trap that she so very persuasively criticizes.

Nevertheless, hooks raises important questions throughout *Teaching to Transgress*. For instance, how can we teach with our bodies as well as our voices? In **"Building a Teaching Community,"** a dialogue with Ron Scapp, a philosophy professor at Queens College in New York, she discusses the body in the classroom. Questions of movement, body language, placement of teacher and students are closely tied to the level of intellectual risk-taking with which both teachers and students are comfortable. **"Eros, Eroticism, and the Pedagogical Process"** and **"Ecstasy"** are extensions of this discussion. In the former, hooks recalls an occasion when she had to use the restroom partway through a class in order to examine how we teachers are forced to deny our bodies and become disembodied voices of expertise. She then critically questions whether that approach is fruitful for anyone involved in a truly liberatory pedagogy.

*Outlaw Culture* takes on another contested subject: recent representations of Blacks in popular culture. My reaction to these essays was more mixed. Part of the reason is that when it comes to popular culture, we are all experts. While reading *Outlaw Culture,* I had to restrain myself from dissing hooks' interpretations merely because they disagreed with my own. Often I wished she and I were sitting at my kitchen table so we could talk through our differences. As in *Teaching to Transgress,* the language is accessible, but I did get tired of reading polysyllabic phrases like "white supremacist capitalist patriarchy" and "stimulate voyeuristic masturbatory pleasure."

The essay titles grab your attention—who can resist **"Power to the Pussy"**? Despite the catchy, colloquial title, this discussion of Madonna's coffee-table book *Sex* is informed by both feminist and queer theory. Hooks analyzes how Madonna has moved away from her former "transgressive female artistry" and toward "cultural hedonism." The non-revolutionary, homophobic and racist representations are what rightly disturb hooks: "Throughout *Sex,* Madonna appears as the white imperialist wielding patriarchal power to assert control over the realm of sexual difference."

*Outlaw Culture* was an exhilarating read when hooks and I were in sync—and we were most of the time. I was happy that she agrees with my assessment of *Mama, There Is a Man in Your Bed.* This 1989 French film is a collage of folktale themes, primarily based on Cinderella and Romeo and Juliet (in fact, the main characters are named Romauld and Juliette). Romauld is the CEO of a yogurt company in Paris; Juliette is the office cleaner for his building. Greed and marital infidelity combine to ruin Romauld's reputation. Soon he is fired from his position and is in need of an avenger: Juliette comes to the rescue. As a Black domestic, Juliette is invisible and able to gather evidence of wrongdoing the other executives leave behind. She carries through a plan to reinstate Romauld and clear his name.

My summary doesn't do justice to the intersection of race, class and sexuality in this film, but it is one of the most important recent films about Black women. (I've seen it five times!) Juliette is smart, perceptive, observant; she has good business sense; she is a loving mother, a proud, independent and absolutely gorgeous woman. It's also true this film could only have been made in France. Applying all these character traits to a woman of African descent is so foreign to Hollywood that here we are, five years after the French release of *Mama,* and there's still no American remake.

Hooks also echoes my own concerns about *The Crying Game.* In **"Seduction and Betrayal,"** she analyzes the significance of gender roles inverted, supposedly, by terrorism. The white woman, Jude, is not a nurturing mother figure but an IRA terrorist; the nurturing role is taken on by Fergus, the reluctant terrorist—and the reluctant lover of the Black transvestite Dil. Hooks makes a crucial observation:

> Most critical reviews of *The Crying Game* did not discuss race, and those that did suggested that the power of this film lies in its willingness to insist that race and gender finally do not matter: it's what's inside that counts. Yet this message is undermined by the fact that all the people who are subordinated to white power are black.

I only wish hooks had added that the movie billboard (which shows an elongated Jude dressed all in black and holding a smoking gun) contributes a demonic twist to the only biological female in the film.

Yet even given her interesting interpretation of these movies and Madonna, I had serious reservations about some of the essays in *Outlaw Culture.* For example, in **"Ice Cube Culture: A Shared Passion for Speaking Truth: bell hooks and Ice Cube in Dialogue,"** I was surprised and deeply distressed that hooks doesn't acknowledge the misogyny and mother-blaming of the recent movie *Boyz N the 'Hood.* The movie tracks the everyday violence of South Central LA through the lives of three friends: Tre, the boy who goes to college through the support of a strong father; Doughboy, out on parole as a teenager (and played by Ice Cube); and Ricky, Doughboy's more successful brother, bound for college football until he is brutally murdered. In hooks' dialogue, Ice Cube says, "and I think Doughboy would a been just like him [Tre] if he had the right guidance, the right father." Bell—call him on his sexism, please! As the mother of a black man-child of sixteen (who, by the way, identified more with Tre than Doughboy), I'm worried about the backlash against single Black mothers in the community and in the media. Audre Lorde's inspirational piece, "Man-child: A Black Lesbian Feminist's Response," has clearly grappled with these issues. If only hooks had suggested this to Ice Cube, instead of validating his patriarchal, macho pronouncement that "a woman can't raise a boy to be a man."

A more satisfying essay is **"Malcolm X: the Longed-for-Feminist-Manhood."** I was intrigued by hooks' assertion

that before his death Malcolm X was moving toward a new and transformed view of sexism and gender issues. She highlights two anecdotes from his life, both involving Fannie Lou Hamer, the civil rights activist. In the first, early in his career, hooks notes: "Malcolm castigated black men for their failure to protect black women and children from racist brutality." She analyzes his patriarchal socialization and how that still informs Black Muslim thought. The break with the Nation of Islam gave Malcolm X an opportunity to rethink his position on gender, hooks argues, pointing out that "it was again in the company of Fanny Lou Hamer, shortly before his death that Malcolm made one of his most powerful declarations on the issue of gender. . . . Malcolm declared: 'You don't have to be a man to fight for freedom. All you have to do is be an intelligent human being.' "

Hooks challenges us to look at Malcolm X through a feminist lens, not just to condemn the sexism of his early work. But for me, Malcolm X was never a mentor; what hooks reads as passion, I read as aggression. I remember the painful reaction of my family members whenever Malcolm referred to Blacks like us as "so-called Negroes." I wondered then what good could come from such divisiveness. Now with the reclaiming of Malcolm, I wonder why no one, neither Spike Lee nor bell hooks, remembers the pain that this divisiveness caused our community.

As hooks herself writes in *Teaching to Transgress,*

> Again and again, black women find our efforts to speak, to break silence and engage in radical progressive political debates, opposed. There is a link between the silencing we experience, the censoring, the anti-intellectualism in predominantly black settings that are supposedly supportive (like all-black woman space), and that silencing that takes place in institutions wherein black women and women of color are told we cannot be fully heard or listened to because our work is not theoretical enough.

In *Outlaw Culture*'s **"Censorship From Left and Right"** she targets censorship by the Black intellectual elite:

> What cultural conditions enable black male thinkers to be critical of black women without being seen as giving expression to sexist or misogynist opinions? And what critical climate will allow black women a space to critique one another without fear that all ties will be disrupted and severed?

I will always be grateful to hooks for her articulation of Black women's need for a space where we can constructively criticize each other's work. In *Outlaw Culture* she acknowledges that "critique causes some pain and discomfort." Truth be told, no one likes negative criticism, but, as hooks points out, dialogue is the key and not dismissal. It takes courage to hold a dialogue with a hostile or patronizing critic. In fact, all the dialogues hooks has held so far are with folks she respects and fundamentally agrees with: Cornel West, Ron Scapp and Marie France Alderman. I'd love to see a dialogue between bell and Madonna or Diana Fuss—I have no doubt she is up to the task. Thank you, bell/Gloria, for making feminism the location for an exciting discussion of education, popular culture and life.

## Michele Wallace   (essay date November 1995)

SOURCE: "For Whom the Bell Tolls: Why America Can't Deal With Black Feminist Intellectuals," in *VLS,* No. 140, November, 1995, pp. 19-24.

[*In the following excerpt, Wallace complains that hooks's work has become increasingly "self-centered, narcissistic, and even hostile to the idea of countervailing perspectives."*]

It's interesting to visit different bookstores in Manhattan just to see how they handle the dilemma posed by the existence of a black female author, who is not a novelist or a poet, who has 10 books in print. At the Barnes & Noble superstore uptown, they are getting perilously close to having to devote an entire shelf to hooks studies, in the manner that there are presently multiple shelves on MLK and Malcolm X.

And yet she might prefer it if instead I compared her to the white male Olympians of critical theory—Barthes, Foucault, Freud, and Marx—and that it was only conformity to what she likes to call "white supremacist thinking" that prevents me from classing her with the founding fathers.

In the past 14 years, as the author of 10 books on black feminism, bell hooks has managed to corner the multicultural feminist advice market almost singlehandedly, bell hooks is the alias of Gloria Watkins, who is now Distinguished Professor of English at the City College of New York. Raised in the rural South of Hopkinsville, Kentucky, Watkins collected her B.A. at Stanford, going on to finish her Ph.D. in English at UC Santa Cruz over a decade ago. We've been hearing from hooks regularly ever since.

Much like her previous work, *Killing Rage: Ending Racism,* consists of a collection of unconnected essays, some of them recycled from earlier books. As usual, the writing is leftist dogmatic, repetitive, and dated. For instance, in the book's penultimate chapter, called **"Moving From Pain to Power: Black Self-Determination,"** Watkins offers the following turgid explanation of the failure of black struggle in the '60s:

> Revolutionary black liberation struggle in the United States was undermined by outmoded patriarchal emphasis on nationhood and masculine rule, the absence of a strategy for coalition building that would keep a place for non-black allies in struggle, and the lack of sustained programs for education for critical consciousness that would continually engage black folks of all classes in a process of radical politicization.

But then it was never in the expectation of beautiful writing, or subtly nuanced analysis, that we turned to bell hooks. With chapters bearing titles like **"Healing Our Wounds: Liberatory Mental Health Care," "Where Is the Love?"** and **"Overcoming White Supremacy,"** we are being offered, simultaneously, a series of potentially contradictory solutions to what ails us.

Hooks suggests that a black feminist analysis of "race and racism in America" is the essential missing component in current mainstream perspectives on race, at the same time that she offers a defense of black rage, in all its masculinist appeal, as inherently liberatory. "I understand rage to be a necessary aspect of resistance struggle," she writes. Meanwhile, interspersed with the rage and the feminist analysis, she is also slipping us a kind of hit-or-miss guide to self-healing, self-recovery, and self-actualization.

The new hooks began to emerge, like a butterfly from a chrysalis, about a year or two ago when Watkins abandoned the leftist rigors of the South End Collective in Boston and her post as associate professor at Oberlin College, more or less at the same time, moved to New York and CCNY, published *Outlaw Culture* and *Teaching to Transgress* with Routledge, and *Art on My Mind* with the nonprofit New Press, only to turn around a few months later to publish *Killing Rage* with Holt, her first major mainstream publisher, this fall.

Using cultural analysis of popular culture, film, visual art, and pedagogy, with occasional outbursts of self-help rhetoric (to which hooks had already devoted an entire book— *Sisters of the Yam*), *Teaching to Transgress, Outlaw Culture,* and *Art on My Mind* all continue in the direction hooks's work has taken the past few years, as amply demonstrated in *Black Looks, Yearning: Race, Gender, and Cultural Politics,* and *Talking Back: Thinking Feminist, Thinking Black.* However, with *Killing Rage,* hooks is clearly trying to drive a wedge into the current white market for books on race and the recent upsurge in the black market for books on spirituality and self-recovery.

Given this onslaught of publication, accompanied by an alarming dearth of explanatory or analytic criticism about her work, either in mainstream or alternative venues, perhaps it should come as no surprise that the poorly researched cover story in *The Chronicle of Higher Education* (the *New York Times* of academics) on the hooks/Watkins phenomenon considers her not only the most viable voice of black feminism, but also the only acceptable black female candidate for inclusion in the roster of the "new black intellectuals," whose emergence has been repeatedly announced in the pages of *The Atlantic Monthly, The New Republic, The New York Times, The New Yorker* and even the *VLS.*

"When black feminism needed a voice, bell hooks was born," *The Chronicle* proclaimed a few months ago. Which makes her a candidate for the only black feminist that matters? Not. Perhaps the dominant discourse is given to these lapses of amnesia because some ideas are so repugnant to Western culture that they are forced to emerge, again and again, as if new.

There hasn't been much resistance lately to the idea of a mainstream feminist discourse or even to a left-wing alternative and/or academic feminism. But what continues to boggle the minds of the powers that be is that black feminism has been around for a long time. . . .

All of this black feminist activity preceded the publication of bell hooks's first book, *Ain't I a Woman: Black Women and Feminism,* in 1981, as Gloria Watkins well knows. Indeed, Watkins begins the book she now claims to have actually written years before by chastising Gloria Steinem for her blurb on the jacket of *Black Macho*.

> Steinem makes a such narrowminded, and racist, assumption when she suggests that Wallace's book has a similar scope as Kate Millet's *Sexual Politics* . . . One can only assume that Steinem believes that the American public can be informed about the sexual politics of black people by merely reading a discussion of the 60's black movement, a cursory examination of the role of black women during slavery, and Michele Wallace's life.

I wouldn't go so far as to suggest that hooks is deliberately and maliciously attempting to obliterate the vast and subversive history of black feminist discourse. In *Ain't I a Woman* hooks does a fine job of providing the historical overview of black feminist thought. But progressively her analysis has become more and more self-centered, narcissistic, and even hostile to the idea of countervailing perspectives. Given more to the passive-aggressive approach in dealing with black women, she is never direct.

For instance, in an essay called "Black Intellectuals" in *Killing Rage,* while she claims for herself an exemplary humility, simplicity, open-mindedness, and commitment to revolutionary struggle, she also distances herself from the rank and file of black intellectuals with comments like "Most academics (like their white and non-white counterparts) are not intellectuals" and "Empowered to be hostile towards and policing of one another, black female academics and/or intellectuals often work to censor and silence one another."

In *Black Looks,* hooks repeatedly rails against those pseudo-progressive whites who would "eat the other" in their perpetual attempt to appropriate the transgressive energies of artists, writers, and theorists of color. But then hooks is also capable of writing. "When patriarchal support of competition between women is coupled with competitive academic longing for status and influence, black women are not empowered to bond on the basis of shared commitment to intellectual life or open-minded exchange of ideas. . . . Since many women in the academy are conservative or liberal in their politics, tensions arise between those groups and individuals like myself, who advocate revolutionary politics."

What hooks is doing here is what I call eating the other. Yes, people of color can eat each other, too.

Those of us who first became black feminists in the early '70s knew so little about the black women—the artists, intellectuals, and feminist activists—who had come before us. It took a long time to find the record they had left. However, this wasn't because the record didn't exist. Rather, the documentation was either destroyed or mouldering in dusty attics and rare-book collections, and it was no simple matter to retrieve them. It no longer surprises me that Zora Neale Hurston, Nella Larsen, and Jessie Fauset all had to be rediscovered.

And it should come as no surprise to anyone that, not only was there a black feminism before bell hooks, there was a black feminism long before most of us were born. There were black feminist abolitionists before the Civil War and there were black women suffragettes, whose works are now preserved and annotated by the Schomburg Collection of 19th-century black women writers, as well as by other publishing efforts such as Florence Howe's Feminist Press.

But when I was a kid, the only one I knew was Sojourner, and I didn't know much about her.

The black feminist historian Nell Painter, professor of history at Princeton, is currently working on a biography of Sojourner Truth and has already published several excerpts from her research in which he suggests that the famous "Ain't I a Woman" which so many feminists have clung to over the years, might have been a historical conflation of a number of different events and speeches, none of them anything like the speech we've come to know and love.

Since Truth was illiterate, not an intellectual but a charismatic itinerant preacher who wandered about the countryside expecting strangers to provide her next meal and her next place to sleep, she wasn't exactly into knowledge production.

Moreover, Painter suggests that part of the legacy of the racisms of the period comes down to us in the iconography of Sojourner Truth. All of her portraits were carefully posed to confirm the myth of her unlettered, inborn, commonsensical strength, and as such, to confirm, as well, the peculiar and essential otherness then considered characteristic of the black woman—an "otherness," not coincidentally, that also served to highlight the beauty, delicacy, and intelligence of the women of the "superior race."

Meanwhile, Truth's "Ain't I a Woman" speech has been institutionalized as the originary moment of black feminist discourse. Many works—hooks's first book, as well as Deborah Gray White's history of slave women, *Ar'n't I a Woman,* and even *Black Macho*—bear witness to her presumed power as a black feminist foremother. But suppose Painter has uncovered a nasty little paradigmatic secret about black feminism: that the iconic status of Truth is much like the iconic status of Hurston, or indeed any single black female figure, in that it is meant to stand in for the whole. Its primary function is to distract us from the actual debate and dilemma with which black feminist intellectuals, artists, and activists are really engaged.

In fact, I would even go so far as to say that the media success of *Black Macho* placed me in possible danger of the same instant iconic status. But I was 27, naive, inexperienced, and had no concept of the big picture that Painter is outlining. Whereas hooks has had a long, steady climb, from the publication of her first book to her present position, poised to enter the mainstream. Is she being manipulated by the structural racism and misogyny of the mainstream media or is she an opportunist trying to turn a fast buck? I think perhaps a little of both. Frankly, she can't begin to make a dent in this structural thing by herself. As for the opportunism, how do you suppose revolutionaries will occupy themselves in these reactionary times? And the timing is perfect.

In case you hadn't noticed, there's a black book boom. It has many dimensions, from the apartheid of the publishing industry itself, to the phenomenon of the black public intellectual, to *Time* magazine's construction (with Henry Louis Gates Jr.'s help) of a new black cultural renaissance. But one aspect of the boom that is grossly underreported is the accelerating interest in a New Age kind of spiritualism and the rhetoric of self-recovery. When this tendency is combined with a public black intellectual component— such as in the case of the works of bell hooks, Cornel West, and a host of others—it can be unfortunate indeed.

Watkins is openly and proudly religious, or what she would call spiritual, which is a euphemism for religious. Nobody has ever accused black folk of not being religious enough. But it may be precisely this religiosity that not only serves to fuel the overreported anti-Semitism but also the much more prevalent anti-intellectualism that is fast becoming the only thing that most dark peoples splattered around the tristate area have in common.

Watkins's **Killing Rage** suggests that we bury the racial hatchet in places like New York through spiritual growth. But in the title essay, hooks still has a long way to go. Her story begins with the words, "I am writing this essay sitting beside an anonymous white male that I long to murder." She and her traveling companion had sought first-class upgrades in exchange for their coach airline seats at a New York airport, but when they got on the plane, there was a white man sitting in the friend's first-class seat. Watkins immediately reads this situation as deliberate racist sabotage on the part of the airline representative at the counter.

A stewardess was called to clear up the dilemma of whose seat it was, but anybody who flies on airplanes with any regularity knows who won. If there are two people with the same seat assignment, the butt in the seat has the right of way.

But not without Watkins going ballistic. "I stared him down with rage," she writes, "tell him that I do not want to hear his liberal apologies . . . In no uncertain terms I let him know that he had an opportunity to not be complicit with the racism and sexism that is so all-pervasive in this society" by voluntarily giving up his cushy seat in first class to her black friend now condemned to the cramped conditions of coach.

I guess I'm just hard-hearted Hannah, but somehow I'm not weeping for Watkins here. I can remember the insanity that began to grip me in the midst of the whirlwind of publicity around *Black Macho* when, all of sudden, it became desperately important to me whether or not I traveled first class or coach. I am quite familiar with this illness. I call it first-class-itis, or, more simply, celebrity-itis. Given the symptoms, you shouldn't be surprised at all that there is no hint in Watkins's narrative of the seemingly obvious antibourgeois alternative of joining her friend, in solidarity, in coach.

Black feminist intellectuals generally kowtow to hooks and dutifully quote her numerous books, but they don't like her and they don't trust her. She doesn't represent the views of black feminist academics (most of whom she would dismiss, in any case, as privileged members of the bourgeois academic elite), and yet we go on mumbling under our breath.

Released in her last books from the rigor of the South End Press collective—where editorial decisions are made jointly—what was once merely typically bad leftist writing has become self-indulgent and undigested drivel that careens madly from outrageous self-pity, poetic and elliptical, to playful exhibitionism, to dogmatic righteous sermonizing. Sometimes as I read some of this stuff, I can't believe that I am reading what I'm reading.

For instance, in **Outlaw Culture** hooks sets an *Esquire* reporter straight about the notion that the women's movement was prudish in the '70s. "We had all girl parties, grownup sleepovers," she told him. "We slept together. We had sex. We did it with girls and boys. We did it across race, class, nationality. We did it in groups. We watched each other doing it."

Or, hooks will say, "the vast majority of black women in *academe* are *not* in revolt—they seem to be as conservative as the other conservatizing forces there! . . . I've been re-reading Simon Watney's *Policing Desire,* and thinking a lot about how I often feel more policed by other black women who say to me: 'How can you be out there on the edge? How can you *do* certain things, like be wild, inappropriate? You're making it harder for the rest of us.' "

Watkins knocks everybody. She has done everything and known everything, long before it was fashionable to do so. Yet she is rarely specific or precise about her experiences or her references.

She can also be a chameleon, taking on camouflage colors in different environments, as in her interview with the rapper Ice Cube. In talking with him about *Boyz'n the Hood,* she says of the lead character, Tre, falling into the vernacular.

> You don't want to be him 'cause he didn't have no humor hardly, he didn't have much. Part of what I try to do as a teacher, a professor, is to show people just 'cause you're a professor and you got a Ph.D., you don't have to be all tired, with no style and with no presence.

Constantly citing her experience of child abuse at the hands of her family, physical abuse by her former lover, as well as the "racist" and/or "sexist" reaction of the "white feminist" and/or "black male" and/or "white supremacist patriarchal" establishment, she epitomizes the cult of victimization that Shelby Steele, Stanley Crouch, and Jerry Watts have written about so persuasively.

While I have no desire to play into the hands of the right, everybody knows that p.c. rhetoric has become a problem, and hooks has made herself queen of p.c. rhetoric. Without the unlovely code phrases, "white supremacy," "patriarchal domination," and "self-recovery," hooks couldn't write a sentence.

Hooks reminds me of the young people in my youth who would come from the suburbs, dress up like hobos, and hang around in the Village for the weekend. You just sprinkle these words around and you're an automatic academic leftist.

In *Manufacturing Consent,* Noam Chomsky reminds us that the principal function of mass culture is to distract most Americans, perhaps as many as 80 per cent, from issues of real power, domination, and control. The other 20 per cent, whom Chomsky identifies as the educational/intellectual elite, votes, runs the media and academic, and, as such, is actively, although probably not consciously, engaged in manufacturing consent. Although it's not all that important how the 80 per cent chooses its poison, the predilections of the 20 per cent elite can be crucial.

According to Chomsky's vision, the correct information is almost always out there, but it is literally buried under the continuous and overwhelming flow and bombardment of mass cultural noise and distraction.

---

**For the most part, hooks grossly underestimates the willingness of her reader to comprehend her particular journey.**

—*Michele Wallace*

---

In an imperceptible shift from automatic leftism to Cultural Studies, most of what hooks chooses to write about—Madonna, *The Crying Game, The Body Guard,* Camille Paglia, shooping, and so forth—is noise. Part of the distraction of mass culture, and now the most popular mass cultural commentary (sometimes called cultural critique or cultural studies) as well, is that its function is increasingly continuous with that of its object of study. At best, it is becoming mind-fuck candy for the intellectually overendowed. In other words, much of it has become just high-falutin noise.

As for what there ever was to value about hooks's work, I am not the ideal person to say since I have never felt comfortable with the world according to bell hooks. Yet it should be said that hooks/Watkins has a saucy, mischievous, and playful side, which is fascinating. It emerges occasionally in her affect and intonation as a public speaker, but rarely makes it to the page. Although that edge peeks out in some of the riskier moments in *Outlaw Culture*— when she is dissing Camille Paglia, or in some of her speculations about rap—for the most part, hooks grossly underestimates the willingness of her reader to comprehend her particular journey.

In black feminism, two clearly divergent paths are emerging: Either one travels the high road, the intellectual-creative route, out of which such women as Walker, Morrison, and Bambara have carved their path—every step earned and copiously contextualized so that you know exactly where you are all the time; or one travels the low road, the gospel according to bell hooks firmly in hand, the path etched in the vertiginous stone of rhetoric, hyperbole, generalizations, platitudes, bad faith, phony prophetism, and blanket condemnation.

Inspired though we may be by the Morrisons, the Walkers, the Fannie Lou Hamers, the June Jordans, most of us don't have it in us to be them. And you can't really follow them because they're not leaders. I don't mean this as criticism. They don't present themselves as leaders. Whereas hooks is all too happy to present herself as your leader, if you just have to have one.

But, in fact, black feminists don't have any leaders, if you mean by leaders people who will stand up and say that they are leading black women down one independent and autonomous path because black women—whether they are lesbian, intellectual, married to white men, or considered atypical in any other way—have no desire to put more distance between themselves and black men, either individually or collectively. It has to do not only with romance, but with a political commitment to black identity, black struggle, and the painful lessons of black history.

On the other hand, if one stops looking for leaders who claim to know the direction black women should follow and looks instead for black female role models, for lack of a better term, who know their stuff and who have spent their lives conquering a particular field, there are tons of potential "leaders" all over the place.

If you think of an ideology as a religion, then the church of black feminists is not one that you have to attend or even declare yourself a member of. In fact, it is better if you don't. Like the Quakers, black feminists don't proselytize or seek converts, and they hold very few meetings. The history of organized women's movements and their symbiotic relationship to the dominant discourse is nasty indeed: see the work of Davis, Giddings, or any feminist historian worth her salt for details.

Also, it is precisely the point of black feminism, or any feminism on behalf of the dispossessed, to empower the disenfranchised—both women and men—what Gayatri Spivak has called the subaltern. Subalterns are not necessarily defined by race (although their skins are usually dark), gender, sexuality, or geography (although they are concentrated in certain parts of the world), but by their relationship to global issues of class, poverty, and power.

Their problem is their lack of symbolic power and agency in the dominant discourse. The subaltern speaks but it doesn't speak to us. hooks is not the link. The subaltern doesn't write books. As for whether or not Ice Cube can speak for the subaltern, I'll leave it to you to figure that out.

---

## FURTHER READING

### Criticism

Berube, Michael. "Public Academy." *The New Yorker* LXX, No. 49 (13 February 1995): 73-80.
    Discusses the new generation of black thinkers, including Cornel West, bell hooks, Michael Eric Dyson, and Derrick Bell, and their public following.

Giddings, Paula. "Black Feminism Takes Its Rightful Place." *Ms.* XIV, No. 4 (October 1985): 25-6, 30.

>Criticizes hooks's *Feminist Theory: From Margin to Center* and Jacqueline Jones's *Labor of Love, Labor of Sorrow: Black Women, Work, and the Family from Slavery to Present* for measuring black women's commitment to feminism by their participation in predominantly white organizations.

Willis, Ellen. "Sisters Under the Skin?" *Village Voice Literary Supplement,* No. 8 (June 1982): 1, 10-12.

>Discusses the issue of antagonism between black women and white women, especially in the feminist movement, and how hooks and other authors deal with this issue in their writing.

**Interview**

hooks, bell, Gloria Steinem, Naomi Wolf, and Urvashi Vaid. "Let's Get Real About Feminism." *Ms.* IV, No. 2 (September-October 1993): 34-43.

>Four activists debate why so many women hesitate to call themselves feminists.

---

**Additional coverage of hooks's life and career is contained in the following sources published by Gale Research: *Black Writers,* Vol. 2; and *Contemporary Authors,* Vol. 143.**

---

# Ruth Prawer Jhabvala

## 1927-

German-born English novelist, screenwriter, and short story writer.

The following entry provides an overview of Jhabvala's career through 1995. For further information on her life and works, see *CLC,* Volumes 4, 8, 29.

## INTRODUCTION

Born in Germany to Jewish Polish parents and raised in England after her family fled the Nazis in 1939, Jhabvala began writing fiction after relocating with her husband to his native India in 1951. She frequently utilizes her vantage point as an outsider among India's bourgeoisie, and her characters, both Indian and European, often have an uneasy relationship with their cultural heritage. Critics have compared Jhabvala's novels to those of Jane Austen, citing her propensity for middle-class characters overly concerned with social status and tradition—thematic points that have given the author the reputation, like Austen, for being a social satirist. Jhabvala has also written many screenplays, adapting both her own novels as well as others' into elaborate costume dramas and comedies of manners for the filmmaking team of Ismail Merchant and James Ivory. Her screenplay for *A Room with a View* (1986), adapted from E. M. Forster's novel, won her an Academy Award in 1986 as well as wider recognition in the United States.

### Biographical Information

Jhabvala was born in Cologne, Germany. With Hitler's seizure of power in 1933, members of Jhabvala's extended family moved to various countries in Europe; her parents escaped to England in 1939. Jhabvala's family first lived in Conventry and later moved to a Jewish suburb of London. She earned a master's degree in English literature from Queen Mary College at London University in 1951. Upon her graduation, she married Cyrus S. H. Jhabvala, a Parsi architect whom she had met on a houseboat in London, and moved with him to Delhi, India, to raise their three daughters. In India she began writing novels and had little trouble getting published; her first work, *To Whom She Will* (1955), was accepted by the fourth publisher she queried. Independent filmmakers Merchant and Ivory approached her following the publication of *The Householder* (1960) to ask if she would write the screenplay for their film adaptation, thus beginning a long and prosperous, as well as exclusive, partnership.

### Major Works

Jhabvala's novels frequently examine the social milieu of middle-class Indians who have profited from India's increasing urbanization and industrialization, and on Euro-

pean expatriates who have married into Indian families. *The Householder,* for example, concerns the comic adventures of Prem, a young, recently married man facing the second in the four traditional Hindu stages of human life: the householder stage. Prem becomes enamored of the life of the swami, Hindu religious teachers whom he sees as free of the stresses of being husbands, providers, and fathers. In Hans, a young, carefree German travelling through India in search of a teacher, Prem finds a role model. Eventually, Prem capitulates to his traditional role and returns to his exotic, sybaritic wife, Indu, realizing that his desire to be a holy man was driven by his avoidance of responsibility. In *Esmond in India* (1957), the title character is a womanizing British civil servant with an Indian wife and an English mistress. On assignment in India, Esmond befriends a number of social-climbing, middle-class Indian women, all of whom are beguiled by his charm and cultural sophistication and overlook his boorish nature. As the characters engage in social and political intercourse, Esmond's long-suffering wife deserts him, and he considers fleeing back to England with Betty, thereby leaving his new mistress, Shankutala, a woman he brought to ruin, behind in the country he loathes. *A Backward Place* (1965) concerns the plights of several expatriate European women whose reasons for remaining in India vary. Etta, a Hungarian women whose marriage to an Indian crumbled years ago, lives as the mistress of a hotel tycoon whose dalliance with his "niece" and their impending departure for Europe causes Etta to attempt suicide. In contrast, Judy, a British woman, admires her extended Hindi family whose laughter and closeness is a stark contrast to her strict English upbringing. *Heat and Dust* (1975), for which Jhabvala won the Booker Prize, tells two stories: that of Olivia, a young English bride taken to live in India in the 1920s, whose seduction by an Indian prince ends in disgrace; and that of her granddaughter, who, guided by the elder woman's diary, traces Olivia's path through India and ultimately meets the same unfortunate fate. *In Search of Love and Beauty* (1983), written after Jhabvala left India for New York, is her first novel to take place primarily in the United States, though the main character—a guru—entices women to ruin just as in her previous works. Jhabvala's most popular screenplays are adaptations of other writers' works. With *The Europeans* (1979) and *The Bostonians* (1984), both adapted from novels by Henry James, Jhabvala gained a reputation for scripting witty period dialogue. Her recognition among moviegoers increased with *A Room with a View, The Remains of the Day* (1993), and *Jefferson in Paris* (1995). She has also published several collections of short stories, including *How I Became a Holy Mother, and Other Stories* (1975) and *Out of India: Selected Stories* (1986).

### Critical Reception

Critical reaction to Jhabvala's works has been mixed. While reviewers have praised her screenplays, some have found her novels and short stories uneven and thematically limited. Often lauded for her depictions of India from a detached viewpoint, her use of irony and satire, and her explorations of such themes as isolation, rebellion, and cultural assimilation, Jhabvala is nonetheless occasionally faulted for her continuing focus on middle-class Indian life and what some critics have called her simple plots and unconvincing characterizations. Some critics have also disparaged Jhabvala's seeming lack of concern over the extreme poverty and wretched conditions under which millions of India's lower classes live. Jhabvala, however, has readily acknowledged that living in India is to live "on the back of this great animal of poverty and backwardness. It is not possible to pretend otherwise." Critics frequently remark on the literary nature of Jhabvala's screenplays, particularly *Howards End* (1992) and *A Room with a View,* and note how her cinematic works have influenced her novels. Others compliment the tone and mood evoked by her filmic renditions of Edwardian life. Vincent Canby has called the screenplay for *A Room with a View,* for example, a "faithful, ebullient screen equivalent to a literary work that lesser talents would embalm" and observes that the film's voice is "not unlike that of Forster, who tells the story . . . with as much genuine concern as astonished amusement." Concerning Jhabvala's literary accomplishments as a whole, Francine du Plessix Gray has observed: "With the exception of E. M. Forster, no 20th-century writer has more eloquently described Westerners' at-

tempts to grasp the ambiguities of Indian culture than [Jhabvala]."

## PRINCIPAL WORKS

*To Whom She Will*  (novel)  1955; also published as *Amrita*, 1956
*The Nature of Passion*  (novel)  1956
*Esmond in India*  (novel)  1957
*The Householder*  (novel)  1960
*Get Ready for Battle*  (novel)  1962
*\*The Householder*  (screenplay)  1963
*Like Birds, Like Fishes, and Other Stories*  (short stories) 1963
*A Backward Place*  (novel)  1965
*\*Shakespeare Wallah*  (screenplay)  1965
*\*The Guru* [with James Ivory]  (screenplay)  1968
*A Stronger Climate: Nine Stories*  (short stories)  1968
*\*Bombay Talkie*  (screenplay)  1970
*An Experience of India*  (short stories)  1971
*A New Dominion*  (novel)  1971; also published as *Travelers*, 1973
*Autobiography of a Princess*  (novel)  1975
*\*Autobiography of a Princess*  (screenplay)  1975
*Heat and Dust*  (novel)  1975
*How I Became a Holy Mother, and Other Stories*  (short stories)  1975
*\*Roseland*  (screenplay)  1977
*\*Hullabaloo over Georgie and Bonnie's Pictures*  (screenplay)  1978
*\*The Europeans* [adaptor, with Ivory; from the novel by Henry James]  (screenplay)  1979
*\*Jane Austen in Manhattan*  (screenplay)  1980
*\*Quartet* [adaptor, with Ivory; from the novel by Jean Rhys]  (screenplay)  1981
*\*Heat and Dust*  (screenplay)  1983
*In Search of Love and Beauty*  (novel)  1983
*\*The Bostonians* [adaptor; from the novel by Henry James]  (screenplay)  1984
*†The Courtesans of Bombay*  (screenplay)  1985
*Out of India: Selected Stories*  (short stories)  1986
*\*A Room with a View* [adaptor; from the novel by E. M. Forster]  (screenplay)  1986
*Three Continents*  (novel)  1987
*‡Madame Sousatzka* [with John Schlesinger]  (screenplay)  1988
*\*Mr. and Mrs. Bridge* [adaptor; from the novels *Mr. Bridge* and *Mrs. Bridge* by Evan S. Connell]  (screenplay)  1990
*\*Howards End* [adaptor; from the novel by E. M. Forster]  (screenplay)  1992
*Poet and Dancer*  (novel)  1993
*\*The Remains of the Day* [adaptor; from the novel by Kazuo Ishiguro]  (screenplay)  1993
*\*Jefferson in Paris*  (screenplay)  1995
*Shards of Memory*  (novel)  1995

\*These films were directed by James Ivory and produced by Ismail Merchant.

†This film, made for British television, was jointly directed by Jhabvala, Ivory, and Merchant.

‡This film was directed by John Schlesinger.

# CRITICISM

### Haydn Moore Williams    (essay date June 1971)

SOURCE: "Strangers in a Backward Place: Modern India in the Fiction of Ruth Prawer Jhabvala," in *Journal of Commonwealth Literature,* Vol. VI, No. 1, June, 1971, pp. 53-64.

[*In the following essay, Williams discusses several of Jhabvala's novels, focusing on her sense of satire and irony and illustrating how her depiction of middle-class life subtly addresses various social and religious issues in India.*]

The novels and short stories of Ruth Prawer Jhabvala stand in a unique relationship to Indian literature in English. Though she lives in India and is married to an Indian, she is European by origin, and her work belongs in some ways to the literature about India written by foreigners with close connections with India, the tradition to which P. Meadows Taylor, Kipling, and John Masters belong. Yet her close personal, experience of Indian life and her exclusive interest in it as a novelist as well as her ability to identify very closely with Indians, notably Indian women, take her nearer to indigenous Indian writers like R. K. Narayan and Raja Rao. Khushwant Singh cites her, together with Narayan, as a fine interpreter of contemporary India in fiction and as one who is free from the political alignments and extreme nationalism of other Indian writers. Such recognition was overdue in 1961. Perhaps, at least in a technical sense, she is the best fiction writer now writing in India and about India. She shows a mastery of English style and considerable skill in dialogue and plot. Jhabvala is a very able comic novelist of India, though her comedy is quite different from that of Narayan, who relies on the absurdity that comes from deviation from accepted Indian customs, and on a poetry of the grotesque. Jhabvala's strengths are irony, satire, and detachment; her comedy depends much on detached and critical observation of real life. The strength comes from Jhabvala's European origin which makes her still see with the eyes of the artist-outsider the Indian life she has come to know and share. One reason, perhaps, why her work has not received much critical attention is that critics tend to judge Jhabvala more harshly than they do native Indian writers who use English. Perversely her popularity with the non-literary public (her books are always off the shelves of public libraries) tells against her. It is too easy to write her off as a middle- brow author. That her narratives read well and easily and appear to yield their meaning quickly, does not mean, as I hope to show, that she lacks subtlety and depth.

I hope to demonstrate the cohesion and unity of her work, to explore the ironies in her treatment of recent Indian life, and to show how the central subject of her novels is the theme of isolation, rebellion, and reconciliation, and the problems of expatriation and adaptation to a foreign culture.

Broadly speaking, Jhabvala's novels descend from the novel of social behaviour, the novel which sets out specifically to explore such institutions and 'feelings' as the family, marriage, romantic love, expatriation, love of power and money, and pursuit of them, youth's desire for liberation, snobbery. She does not, in her novels at least, step outside these chiefly social concerns to explore ideologies. It would be wrong however, to see no ideological conflicts behind the confrontation and clash of fathers and children, men and women, husbands and wives, mothers and sons, in the Indian world she creates. Behind all marriages lies the idea or ideal of marriage sanctified by many centuries of Indian custom. Behind the large family of a modern middle-class business-man like Lalaji (*The Nature of Passion*), and behind the broken marriage of Gulzari Lal (*Get Ready for Battle*), lies the Indian undivided family as a tradition and an ideal. Behind the decision of characters like Sarla Devi (*Get Ready for Battle*) and Sudhir (*A Backward Place*) to lead a life of disinterested virtuous action, lies the idea of the *sannyasi* stage of life and the teachings of the *Bhagavad Gita*. Yet Jhabvala does not parade or discuss these ideologies. They are accepted or rejected by her characters in the various circumstances they find themselves in. There is, of course, an important cultural difference between 'East' and 'West' which Jhabvala is careful never to conceal; it is that Indian life is much more subject to tradition and that the power of religious and social institutions and attitudes is much stronger (especially if the comparison is between New Delhi and New York rather than between South India and Southern Italy where the cultural situations are closer). In Raja Rao's *The Serpent and the Rope* ideas are paramount. A comic realist like R. K. Narayan depends considerably on brilliant caricature and on the 'humours' of men like Mr Sampath behaving like characters out of Ben Jonson or Dickens. Ideas of men and life are therefore highly significant for both Rao and Narayan. Jhabvala seems less bothered by them. To create her novels she takes subjects and characters from ordinary, middle-class Indian life. Narayan's art, especially in his later novels (*Mr Sampath, The Man-Eater of Malgudi*), takes as its *point de départ* the disturbing of an eccentric but peaceful society by characters and events from outside. Disorder is created and then order restored after a suitable purgatorial period. This is not Jhabvala's way at all. Her natural world is not eccentric and the disturbances do not come from outside but from inside the society; they are in a way self-generating. Narayan's problems are 'comic-epic'—the invasion of the hero's private world and the repelling of the invasion, and this pattern is reminiscent of fairy-tale, romance, and heroic literature. Jhabvala's problems by contrast are small-scale, more usual and expected, almost tritely realistic, though with many opportunities for satire, irony, and surprise well-exploited. Her novels point to no worlds of significance outside her ostensible subject-matter, the bourgeoisie of modern India. She has little symbolism and draws no parallels between her stories and those of the great Indian epics and the *Puranas*. Yet, unlike Narayan, she is fond of using quotations from Hindu scriptures as titles for her books. Both *The Nature of Passion* and *Get Ready for Battle* are taken from the *Gita,* and another title, *The Householder,* suggests one of the traditional stages or *ashramas* of Hindu life. The title of *To Whom She Will* comes from the *Panchatantra.* But the titles are intended, partly at least, to be ironical.

Her novels are set in Delhi, and the community of which she writes is mainly the educated, westernized middle-class and the vulgar, but powerful and influential, *nouveaux riches* profiting from Indian urban expansion and industrialization. She usually takes one family, perhaps a large sprawling 'joint family' living in a huge house, and explores the problems that would inevitably arise—the conflict between the 'liberated' younger people and the older orthodox members, the arrangement of marriages, business life, the search for power, influence, wealth. The plots and counter-plots of Jhabvala's stories always arise within this narrow, intensely in-bred family context. *The Nature of Passion* is one of the best examples. The 'hero' is a 'raja', Lala Narayan Dass Verma, or Lalaji as he is called, a corrupt financial tycoon from the Punjab who has fought his way to the top of Delhi society, securing wealth and power for his family. He is a powerful, earthy, oddly attractive villain with infectious vitality and a determination to do his best for his family, come what may. Jhabvala cleverly shows him early in the book in his most attractive and sympathetic role, as benefactor, paterfamilias, and simple lover of his grandchildren. In his indulgence of his own children he has encouraged the rebellion of his son (Viddi) and his daughter (Nimmi). Both threaten to break away completely from the tyranny of the family. Viddi modishly disclaims the world of money and is contemptuous of the bourgeois conformist exemplified by his elder brother Om—the only one of Lalaji's children who shares his simplicity, his love of wealth, and his fascination with finance. Viddi, a prodigal son, spends his time in cafés with literary bohemians who flatter, exploit, and secretly deride him. Nimmi has demanded emancipation, which for a girl in India is difficult. Her father overcomes the opposition of the women and sends her to college. She falls in love with a Parsee playboy, a frequenter of Delhi nightspots, and rebels romantically against the marriage which is being arranged for her with the son of another millionaire.

In his family life Lalaji is shown to the best advantage, combining a pleasant affection for old-fashioned ways with sentimentality towards the young rebels, shielding them from the wrath of the older members of the family. In business life however, Lalaji shows the ruthlessness and cunning of a predatory beast. He has not got where he is without resorting to corruption; and he has at last gone too far. Evidence of bribery to obtain government contracts now lies waiting to be examined. His own son Chandra, a civil servant highly educated in England at Lalaji's expense, is the only one who can save him by destroying the evidence. But Chandra is alienated from his father. He has become an ultra-modern Indian, living in sophisticated circles where Lalaji would not be welcome; and he has married a snobbish wife who is ashamed of his father's crude manners and old-fashioned ways.

The novel ends, as a comic novel should, with Lalaji the hero free of his difficulties. Jhabvala does it without seriously punishing the old capitalist, although he has to suffer a purgatory of suspense and narrow squeaks before he is clear of danger. Lalaji triumphs by a mixture of cunning and good luck. He wins back Viddi by giving him such a generous allowance that the would-be artist is fired with a consciousness of the power of money and of the influence of his family, and turns his back on his fellow-artists who have been bleeding him white. Luck and time bring answers to his problem with Nimmi. Her boy-friend turns out to be fickle; but she accidentally falls in love with another member of the gay cocktail party circuit, one Kuku, who turns out to be the very boy chosen for her by her family. Lalaji thus wins a new fortune and a rich son-in-law, and retains the affection of his favourite Nimmi. Luckily also for Lalaji and Om, the snobbery and social-climbing of Chandra and his wife overcome their scruples. Rather than suffer from the exposure of his father's crookedness, Chandra destroys the vital evidence and saves him. Lalaji ends with a united family again, more wealth on the way and freedom from fear of prosecution for corruption. Crime does pay.

The outcome appears cynical, but Jhabvala's tone is deliberately and satirically ambiguous. Lalaji is a crook, it is true, an exploiter, a ruthless businessman. Yet he is in so many ways shown as morally superior to the rest of the family. The young rebels, Nimmi and Viddi, are selfish, easily led, foolish and vain. There is an amusing episode at the Kutub Minar at night when Nimmi is clumsily kissed by Pheroze. She feels romantic, but the only lines of poetry that come into her head are Browning's 'I galloped, Dirk galloped, we galloped all three,' from her College Browning Selection. As for Viddi, he believes, until he is disillusioned, that the so-called artists he consorts with are free from the greed of his father and Om, whereas it is obvious that they only tolerate Viddi because he is the son of a very rich man. It comes home to Viddi when they hold a party in his honour, buy vast amounts of food and drink, invite scores of guests, and then send him the bill. Chandra and his wife are worshippers of etiquette books, lacking the warmth and generosity of the great family-man Lalaji. They soon surrender their precious principles from fear of social ostracism and the dashing of Chandra's hopes of promotion to a higher grade, should Lalaji be disgraced. Even Om, nearest to Lalaji in character and interests, in his dislike of the modern and the western, in his single-minded devotion to business, is Lalaji's inferior. Though he is loyal to the family, he finds the atmosphere of the house dominated by women, including his wife, too stuffy to endure and takes occasional time off to visit prostitutes. Lalaji emerges victorious only because he genuinely loves his family and has luck on his side. His behaviour is justified, somewhat satirically, by reference to the *Gita* and to Radhakrishnan's comments on it: '. . . the rajasa nature wishes to be always active . . . and its activities are tainted by selfish desires.'

Jhabvala employs gentler irony in *The Householder.* Here the threat to the very small family of Prem, a Hindi teacher, comes from that oldest of all family jokes, the mother-in-law. Prem saves his marriage in the end when he comes to love his wife. But not before he has to fight the demon of his mother who would smother him and drive his wife away, and the demons within himself, his longing for his old bachelor days and his excited wonder before the life of the *sannyasi,* the holy man. The story therefore revolves at one level round the demands of the four *ashramas.* Prem having passed the stage of bachelor-student (*brahmacharya*) is not yet ready for the stage of *sannyasi* (the laughing swami) until he has learnt to live in the stage of the householder (hence the significant title of the novel) and in this, he is far from successful. With ironical charm Jhabvala shows Prem's fumbling, self-conscious attempts to become an efficient professor, householder, and husband. Love helps him to get rid of his mother and learn to become a mature and competent husband, while Indu blossoms from a shy, embarrassed schoolgirl into a first-rate (and pregnant) wife and cook. Yet in his other ambitions Prem fails. He fails to get his salary raised; on the contrary, his principal, the odious Khanna, threatens him with the sack unless his discipline improves; and his landlord puts off with all too convincing excuses his pleas to have his rent lowered. Yet in the last scene of the book the monsoon breaks over North India, bringing relief to Prem and Indu. They invite Raj and his wife round to a meal and 'Prem felt really proud' when Raj complimented Indu on her cooking. The gentle Chekhovian ending is tinged with irony, for Prem has solved none of the practical financial problems of the householder and Indu's baby will increase the need for money. There is no villainy in this book on the scale of Lalaji's corrupt tycoonery. The nearest to it are the Dickensian grotesques, Mr Khadda and Mr and Mrs Khanna:

> Mr and Mrs Khanna were having their midday meal. They ate in English style, sitting facing one another at a table and using fork and spoon. Mrs Khanna had just speared a piece of cauliflower pickle on to the point of her fork and she was holding it like a trident while she looked furiously at Prem.

*The Householder* is nearly all pure humour, rather than satire.

An interesting subordinate feature of *The Householder,* in view of subsequent novels, is the exploration of the holy life exemplified by the swami and Hans. The claims of spirituality against materialism provide the major theme of one novel, *Get Ready for Battle.* The heroine is an old woman, Sarla Devi, a dedicated idealist devoted to the ideals of the *Gita* and Mahatma Gandhi, and the words of the title (taken again from the *Gita*) sum up her policy of disinterested action in the pursuit of her vocation—to help the poor and oppressed. In the *Gita,* Krishna quells Arjuna's scruples about engaging in warfare by expounding the virtue of disinterestedly acting in accordance with one's vocation (Arjuna's is that of a warrior and ruler). It is Sarla Devi's vocation to serve the poor and needy. She has ceased to live with her rich husband, Gulzari Lal, because he does not share her ideals; on the contrary he is an unscrupulous materialist. Disapproving of his life, she refuses him a divorce. As Jhabvala portrays her, somewhat ironically, she is a complex character who unwittingly produces results which are the opposite of what she in-

tends. The novel charts the failure of her holy and charitable life. She wants her son, Vishnu, whom she loves, to give up his life as a business executive in her husband's company and to follow her vocation of working among the toiling masses. But Vishnu is pulled both ways, by his father's money and by his mother's idealism; his will is weakened by sensuality and longing for change and the 'sweet life' of the fast-livers: Toto and Gogo and his uncle, Brij Mohan, a decrepit Casanova living off Sarla Devi's money. Completely muddled and repelled by his mother's possessiveness and over-earnestness, Vishnu throws himself into a scheme for manufacturing fountain-pens and turns his back on everything his mother stands for. Sarla Devi is equally unsuccessful in a wider context. She champions the rights of refugee squatters in a malodorous slum, Bundi Busti. They are in danger of being evicted to make room for a big industrial development of her husband's, backed paradoxically by the 'socialistic' Congress government in the interests of progress and hygiene. Following in the footsteps of the Mahatma, Sarla defends the rights of the wretched squatters to remain housed where they are. Her efforts are frustrated; the leader of the squatters is bribed to sell out the cause to Gulzari Lal. As a final blow, even her dissolute but dependent brother, Brij Mohan, is disloyal and intrigues with Gulzari Lal's tenacious mistress Kusum, in order to get Sarla to give Lal a divorce. As the novel ends, Sarla compromises with her principles so far as to allow the divorce to go through, but she clings to her ideals in general. We last see her setting off for the red-light district of Old Delhi intent on reclaiming from prostitution her brother's discarded mistress. She is, no doubt, a failure by ordinary pragmatic standards. Yet the *Gita* urges those who would be good to struggle on and do their duty without worrying about the consequences. Here lies Sarla Devi's only consolation, and it gives her character dignity. In some ways her good works are seen as a meddling with human relationships that she little understands; thus she drives Vishnu from her for ever. She gravely underestimates the pursuit of wealth, power, and the sensual (in her brother Brij, in Vishnu's infatuation with women, in her husband's enslavement to money and his mistress). Nevertheless, this ' . . . skinny ageing woman, with her skin wrinkled and darkened by the sun and her short hair almost quite grey', who has withdrawn from the new India in revulsion against its materialism, its money-making, its corruption and its neglect of the great ethical teachings of the *Gita* and the Mahatma, is much nobler and finer than the men and women who circle about her—Mrs Bhatnagar, the rich 'do-gooder' who hypocritically supports the eviction of the squatters in the name of progress, the young and old sensualists, the grasping tycoon, and the would-be tycoons (Joginder, Vishnu). The picture of contemporary Delhi is as satirical as in *The Nature of Passion* and much more pessimistic, since the capitalist of *Get Ready for Battle* lacks the benevolent charm of Lalaji. The essence of the book is the dramatic conflict between heroic virtue and selfish sensuality and materialism. Though its implications for contemporary India are depressing, the novel keeps coming back to personal rather than national problems; it begins and ends with the activities of two remarkable women, Kusum and Sarla Devi.

Indeed the problems of women in marriage, in love, in personal relationships, are always prominent in Jhabvala's novels and no more so than when combined, as in *A Backward Place,* with the problems of expatriation in India. Twice expatriated herself (from Germany to England and from England to India), Jhabvala is obviously fascinated by the problems of expatriates. *A Backward Place* is the only one of her novels so far which can be said to dwell exclusively on the subject. It is also, I believe, Jhabvala's finest and most sophisticated novel. In the same Delhi setting of her other books, it deals less with Indian characters and more with Europeans, and some of its power springs from the interaction of European consciousness and life in India. It is the nearest that Jhabvala has yet come to such novels of East-West confrontation as Forster's *A Passage to India* and Raja Rao's *The Serpent and the Rope.* She rigidly excludes the political, racial, metaphysical, and poetic approaches of Forster and Rao, and sticks firmly to her 'forte' of exploring the private lives of a few women in middle-class Delhi. The three women are all expatriates, and their common problem is coming to terms with the 'backward place' which is modern India. The title is again ironical. India's 'backwardness' is constantly assailed by Etta, a Hungarian, who, after the failure of her marriage to an Indian student, has had a succession of love-affairs and is trying desperately to retain the affections of a business man more powerfully attracted by the charms of a younger woman. Etta's view of India is bound to be emotional. 'Backwardness' takes on a different irony when India is viewed by Clarissa, the English eccentric who wears sarees, imitates Indian customs, and raves about the spirituality of the East. India is her ideal, her holy land, the land of Vivekenanda and Ramakrishna she has read about in dingy old England. She has found to her bitter cost that a great gulf lies between holy India and the India of reality. Her life, which was to have been the pursuit of metaphysical wisdom, has turned out to be a struggle with the climate, predatory landlords, and the need to make ends meet; when the novel opens she is exclusively concerned with finding a new flat. The third girl, Judy, also English, is in no danger of falling in love with metaphysics, or of regarding India as anything more than the country she has chosen to live in by marrying an Indian, Bal. Unlike the passionate, violent and possessive Etta and the scatter-brained Clarissa, Judy is the very embodiment of common sense and Anglo-Saxon coolness. She finds Bal's large united Hindu family a tremendous relief after her small miserable family in England with its history of depression and suicide. Her problem is not a nostalgia for England but a dread of moving from Delhi and a constant fear of the fecklessness of her unemployed actor-husband Bal. Expatriation is examined tragi-comically in Etta, humorously and satirically in Clarissa. Etta hates India and longs for the idealized Europe of her girlhood. Only the love and protection of her lovers can atone a little for her misery. When 'Guppy' deserts her for a young Indian charmer with 'lushly prominent' breasts and 'large round buttocks', she is only too painfully aware of her own complexion ageing and cracking in the Indian sun, and attempts suicide. Clarissa's eccentricity has been increased by the effect of expatriation. Moving from one flat to another, forever searching for a good place, she is mocked by beggars who tear at her saree, and she explodes in anger and physical violence at the India she has so sublimely and sadly idealized. (For these outbursts she suffers cruel remorse.) Attracted to women rather than men she pursues Etta with the zeal of a lover, and her jealousy precipitates Guppy's final break with Etta. At the end of the novel, as she slowly recovers from the hideous climax of her misery, Etta allows Clarissa to move into her flat with her. Both have to come to terms with their fate as expatriates in the 'backward place'. Jhabvala treats Etta with sympathy mixed characteristically with some irony aimed at her pretentiousness. She is seen strolling down a street in Old Delhi as if it were the *Champs Elyseés,* and her longing for Europe and scorn for India cannot hide the fact that she lives by bartering her sexual favours for security and status. It is Guppy's defection which makes her realize that she is at the end of the road, though she snatches hope from a meeting with a potential admirer at the Cultural Dais where Judy works as an assistant secretary. There is some satire in the treatment of Clarissa and the Germans, Herr and Frau Hochstadt. The Hochstadts on a short visit to India are mad about Indian culture and 'spirituality' and cannot understand the problems of either Etta or Judy who look to them for help and advice. They prefer to talk about Sanscrit drama. They fail to see that living in India has driven Etta to despair. Clarissa has come to India to worship at the shrine of Vedantism and has been bogged down in mundane searches for a flat and a lesbian lover. Etta shrewdly comments that the Hochstadts would not be so enthusiastic about India if they had to stay there permanently.

The sharper edge of Jhabvala's satire is reserved for Mrs Kaul, the rich Indian director of the Cultural Dais, an intellectual snob and hypocrite who pays lip-service to the highest ideals of service and benevolence, but, for a trivial offence, cruelly dismisses an Indian girl-employee who badly needs the job. Mrs Kaul is the most odious of the series of rich, fat, middle-class Indian women in Jhabvala's novels, including Mrs Bhatnagar (*Get Ready for Battle*) and Lady Ram Prashad Khanna (*To Whom She Will*). Much gentler satire is directed at Judy, with her intense conservatism that leads her to condemn the old Indian woman Bhuaji for falling in so readily with what Judy regards as Bal's idiotic plans to move to Bombay. The young English 'humanist' is seen as less enterprising than the old, orthodox, religious Indian woman. Judy's foolish husband Bal is more roughly satirized. He is vain, aimless, completely dominated by the oily, glamorous film-actor Kishin Kumar. Jhabvala's satire is therefore directed equally at the Indians and the expatriates. The 'backwardness' of India is a concept rejected by Clarissa, the Hochstadts, and Mrs Kaul. It is bitterly affirmed by Etta, accepted gratefully by Judy in her search for peace (she is greatly attracted to Bhuaji's piety for this reason only), and by Sudhir, the discontented secretary of the Cultural Dais in his realization of India's need for dedicated service.

Expatriation and the mixed ('East-West') marriage are also the themes of an earlier novel, *Esmond in India.* The expatriates are both English, Esmond and his mistress Betty. Esmond is perhaps the only completely unattractive villain among all Jhabvala's characters. He hates India but makes a living by teaching Hindi and 'Indian culture' to rich Indian women and English and American tourists. He is also a gigolo. Another writer might have made a comic study of such a character, but as the novel develops the lines deepen and Esmond shows the devil's hoof. He has (mysteriously) married a fat, pretty, but brainless Indian girl called Gulab, who is satirically presented as spending all her time at home stuffing herself and her little boy with rich sweets and spicy foods—a fine comic tableau. When Esmond returns from his mercenary philandering expeditions he descends to pinching, slapping, abusing, and threatening the wretched woman and her child, both of whom dread him. The climax of his villainy is his heartless seduction of a young, educated, beautiful, but foolish Indian girl, Shakuntala, who falls deeply in love with him. Her eventual fate illustrates the lines from the *Panchatantra,* from which the title of *To Whom She Will* is taken:

> For if she bides a maiden still
> She gives herself to whom she will . . .

Gulab returns to her mother's house with her son, while the sadistic Esmond abandons both her and Shakuntala when his old mistress Betty offers to pay for their joint return to England. Both Esmond and Betty, like Etta in *A Backward Place,* loathe India and are glad to be leaving it.

It is clear from this brief exposition that Jhabvala shows considerable understanding of, and sympathy with, such institutions as the Hindu united family, the pursuit of holiness by the *sannyasi,* and the concept of the *ashramas.* At the same time she points out the serious defects and weaknesses of contemporary Indian life, ready prey for a satirist and ironist. She presents a remarkably sympathetic interpretation of a corrupt capitalist in Lalaji of *The Nature of Passion,* but does not spare the snobs or the pretentious members of Lalaji's family and the hypocritical self-styled 'artists'. Corruption runs deep in this society, as is shown by Gulzari Lal's success in *Get Ready For Battle* in finding government support to evict a wretchedly poor community of refugees, in order to make more money for himself. Pretentiousness and hypocrisy afflict young and old in the new India; both Shakuntala and her father are affected by this disease in *Esmond in India;* she loses her virginity, her father his self-respect. Jhabvala's vision is unclouded by romanticism or poetry. It is severely realistic for the most part. There is, of course, some sentimentality in Jhabvala's novels. *To Whom She Will,* her first and rather immature novel, has been passed over in this article. It contains an interesting, but occasionally sentimental, narrative of the love-affair of Amrita and Hari, who are in collision with their families. Amrita is an emancipated young woman in revolt against traditional arranged marriages, and therefore is an early sketch for Shakuntala of *Esmond in India.* Amrita's rash and bossy behaviour certainly invite punishment as much as Shakuntala's silliness. The sudden switch at the end of the book, when Amrita falls in love with Krishna Sen Gupta, is both sentimental and incredible. To my taste there is some sentimentality in the end of *The Householder,* when Indu proves herself to be such a good wife. The cynicism of Jhabvala's

blackest book, *Esmond in India,* comes as a relief after *To Whom She Will,* and the satire of *A Backward Place* is exhilarating after *The Householder.*

Jhabvala constantly stresses the universality of India's problems. Though institutions like the arranged marriage are traditionally Indian, many of the problems of the characters of Jhabvala's New Delhi could also be set in New York or London. This universality juxtaposed against the slightly exotic Indian settings gives a special flavour, a combination of nearness and distance, of familiarity and unfamiliarity, to her novels. She gains this universality the more easily by concentrating on personal, amorous and marital, themes within an acutely vivid observation of urban Indian society in the second half of the twentieth century.

---

**Ramlal G. Agarwal on Jhabvala's India:**

In a broader perspective, Jhabvala belongs to the tradition of the nineteenth-century comic English novelists like Dickens, Thackeray and Trollope. The post-Independence India resembles, in some ways, the nineteenth-century England. When Jhabvala came over to India, the country was passing through a period of unusual buoyancy. The longings of the people, which had been suppressed by centuries of subjection, had suddenly taken wings and started soaring high. The democratic faith that Indians had adopted had enkindled a sense of release and freedom among all sections of society. In the sudden momentum the country had gathered, the old and the new, the rich and the poor, the good and the bad made common cause and marched hand in hand.

*Ramlal G. Agarwal, in his* Ruth Prawer Jhabvala: A Story of Her Fiction, *Sterling Publishers, 1990.*

---

**Ruth Prawer Jhabvala    (essay date 18 November 1983)**

SOURCE: "Writers and the Cinema—A Symposium," in *The Times Literary Supplement,* No. 4267, November 18, 1983, p. 1287.

[*In the following essay, Jhabvala comments on the reciprocal relationship between writing novels and screenplays.*]

I suppose my experience with films has been different from that of most other writers because I've always worked with the same team, the director James Ivory and the producer Ismail Merchant. This has protected me in so far as they have stood between me and what I would have found terribly unpleasant: a collaborative effort at what is called the script level; the dreaded story conference. The only sort of story conference we ever seem to have is when Jim says "Oh that's terrible, awful, can't you do better than that", thereby usually echoing my own thoughts.

But besides protecting me from the real world of films, they have also brought it close, in the sense of home, to me. I know what they go through every time they have to raise money for a film—that is, I know about the financiers who draw up solemn contracts and then disappear when cast and crew are already on location and the producer is desperate for money. Once Ismail found a shipping magnate who wanted to be involved in films but one of whose ships sank every time Ismail needed money; another time a rich widow (actually, this happened several times with several rich widows) was already planning her outfit for the première and the village she was going to rent for the festival at Cannes when her accountant advised her against the investment. Then there are the actor's agents who always seem to be more important (or do I mean self-important?) than their clients; and everybody's lawyers whose fees take such a major bite out of a film's budget; and the actors—stars—surely the most comprehensive amalgam of human qualities any writer could hope to meet. All these people have enlarged my world and my landscape; and so have the locations we have used, admitting me into houses, palaces, whole strange cities—what an opportunity for a shy writer who would otherwise be restricted to peering through people's windows at night when the lights are on.

Another kind of advantage that I have gained through films has been in the editing room, where I have learned a whole new method of narration by watching scenes being moved to and fro in various juxtapositions, and time-schemes manipulated through flashbacks and flash-forwards. It has been a two-way traffic for me—what I have learned in films I have put back into my books, and what I have learned about characterization, relationships, happenings, and everything else that goes into writing fiction I've put to use in writing films. I can't think what it would have been like for me to have had one and not the other. I've needed both to keep going—I mean imaginatively as well as financially.

### Yasmine Gooneratne (essay date April 1984)

SOURCE: "Apollo, Krishna, Superman: The Image of India in Ruth Prawer Jhabvala's Ninth Novel," in *Ariel: A Review of International English Literature*, Vol. 15, No. 2, April, 1984, pp. 109-17.

[*Gooneratne is a Ceylonese-born critic, poet, and educator. In the following essay, she examines Jhabvala's novel* In Search of Love and Beauty, *which she contends concerns itself more with Western culture than Jhabvala's previous novels.*]

> *Q. Is there one thing you might just like to do which you have not done before?*
>
> A. Something I would like to do is combine my three backgrounds: my European background because it was Continental; and then I had an English education. Then I had a 5-year immersion into India and now I am beginning an immersion into America. So if I can bring all these elements together, well, that's just fine by me. (*Newsweek*, October 31, 1977)

With *In Search of Love and Beauty*, Ruth Prawer Jhabvala's ninth novel, and the first to be published since she won the Booker Prize for *Heat and Dust* in 1975, she brings off with conspicuous success her stated intention to

combine her "three backgrounds" if she can. There have been other, earlier, attempts. In *Hullabaloo Over Georgie and Bonnie's Pictures* (1978), a film directed by James Ivory for which she wrote the screen-play, a young American art-collector and the representative of a British museum of fine art struggle for the possession of a Maharaja's famous collection of Indian miniature paintings. In "A Summer by the Sea," a short story, the young American narrator speculates about the origins of Hamid, an Indian visitor to the United States:

> . . . I guess Hamid had a stronger personality than the rest of us, including Boy. Or maybe it was because he is a foreigner, an Oriental—someone different in an exotic way—and we kept looking at him in a fascinated way to see what he would do next.
>
> At first we thought that he must be some kind of prince, on account of his looks, but he was too poor for that, really. He never had any money at all. Not that it bothered him, because there were plenty of people eager to pay for anything he needed. Boy said that maybe he came from one of those very ancient royal lines that were extinct now, except maybe for a few last descendants working as coolies in Calcutta. Or maybe, Boy said—he has plenty of imagination and also quite a bit of Oriental background, thanks to his study of art history—Hamid was a descendant of a line of famous saints, dating back to the thirteenth century and handing down their sainthood from generation to generation.

The satire directed here at a handsome Indian tramp who lives like a parasite on the goodwill and generosity of his gullible American friends blends, almost imperceptibly, with the tone of innocent wonder natural to Susie, the perplexed young American narrator. Susie, clear-sighted enough to note that it is not sainthood but eroticism that dwells in Hamid's beautiful eyes, is one of the latter's victims. Another is her husband Boy, whose elaborate theories spring not only from a lively imagination and a smattering of "Oriental background," but from willing self-deception: Boy, a homosexual, is infatuated with Hamid. A third victim is Susie's mother, whom Hamid calls "Golden Oldie" behind her back but flirts with outrageously in order to infuriate and distress Boy.

The emphasis in "A Summer by the Sea" is not, however, on Hamid and his mysterious Indian background, but on the Americans whose psychological weaknesses he exposes and pitilessly exploits. Boy's romantic speculations regarding Hamid's "sainthood" link Hamid with Swamiji, the religious rogue of Jhabvala's *A New Dominion*, while his spectacular good looks and callous heart link him with Gopi in the same novel. Boy, Susie, and Susie's mother find their lives laid waste by Hamid in much the same way that Raymond, Lee, and Asha are reduced to despair by Swamiji and Gopi in *A New Dominion*; and they too are willing victims, who joyfully open their hearts and homes to the predator. That the predators in question happen to be Indian is entirely by the way: it seems only too clear that exploitation would have come from one source or another, so obvious and inviting are the weaknesses displayed by the "victims" in both **"A Summer by the Sea"** and *A New Dominion.*

This impression is reinforced by a reading of *In Search of Love and Beauty,* a novel which has among its characters a large number of victims and predators, but in which the image of India seems at first sight to be unimportant and peripheral. Instead, it is the "Continental" background Ruth Jhabvala wished to explore in her American fiction that seems best represented in the private lives and secret longings of the Sonnenblick family and their friends, German-Jewish refugees who are building a new life for themselves in the United States. The novel focuses in particular on Bruno and Louise Sonnenblick, their daughter Marietta, their grandson Mark and adopted granddaughter Natasha, and Louise's childhood friend Regi; also on Leo Kellermann, a charismatic "genius" with whom both Louise and Regi are deeply and inescapably in love. As these European refugees recreate their pre-War lives amidst New York's "unending vista of towering buildings" with the help of their own imported furniture, cosy reunions in restaurants like the Old Vienna, and pastries from Blauberg's, Ruth Jhabvala makes contact for the first time in her published fiction with the obliterated world of her German childhood. Louise, she notes, "had grown up in a suburb of the town of D— in Germany". Whether or not D— stands for Dresden which (like Cologne, Ruth Jhabvala's birthplace) was bombed out of existence during the Second World War, we read for the first time in any of her novels and stories of a schoolgirl who lived in "a villa with a garden in which grew apple and plum trees," and travelled by tram every day to school.

India "officially" enters this European-American world only on page 22 when the restless Marietta, prototype of the Western self-seekers in Ruth Jhabvala's later Indian fiction, discovers at a dance recital in New York an Indian sarod player named Ahmed "and with him India and the particular brand of fulfilment to be discovered there." Unlike the European expatriates in their West Side and Central Park apartments, Ahmed has no intention of settling down in the United States. He "liked life in the West," and takes happily to Scotch, cigarettes, late-night TV and Marietta, but his life and his music cannot be uprooted from the Indian soil. When Marietta follows him to India, Ruth Jhabvala summarizes through Marietta's responses to India an aspect of her own relationship with the land in which she lived for twenty-five years.

Marietta's initial enthusiasm for all things Indian places her at first in Stage One of the cycle of Indian experience that Ruth Jhabvala has described in her essay **"Myself in India"**:

> How she exclaimed! And at what he considered such common, everyday things, one was almost ashamed of them. She adored, simply adored, the bazaars and the merchants . . . copper pans, or silver ornaments, textiles fluttering in the wind, gaudy sweetmeats—such colours, she had never seen, never dreamed such colours! She liked the smells, too, of incense and clarified butter, and even the denser ones of rotting vegetables and more sinister rotting things—even those didn't bother her, for she regarded them as part

of everything: as the beggars were part of it all, and the corpses on the pyres, and the diseased people healing themselves in the sacred river, and the very fat priests . . . She wondered and wondered at everything and exclaimed and shone with joy so that there was absolutely no language barrier—feeling streamed out of her [see *An Experience of India*].

Despite this early enthusiasm, however, Marietta does not surrender her Western sensibility: "She wanted to see everything but as herself." She is saved, therefore, from the disillusionment and revulsion Ruth Jhabvala associates with later stages of her cycle, and while heavy German furniture and upholstery darken her mother's West Side apartment, the Indian influence lights up Marietta's flat in Central Park West. Her oriental rugs "bloom" with "delicate floral motifs," while raw silk upholstery, "a shining gold Buddha," and exquisite Indian miniatures in golden frames illuminate her stylish, if unsettled, way of life.

While Marietta represents in the novel what is essentially a sensitive Westerner's enthusiasm for India, a hint of deeper and more serious concerns is conveyed through Ahmed: he, unlike Marietta, is "restful," "impassive," "imperturbable." He is a disciplined musician who achieves his moments of most intense joy when he is either making or listening to music. He refrains from making personal or moral judgments about the astonishing people and experiences he encounters in the West, but his own personality and his outlook on life and art combine in an implicit statement that is not lost on those about him who have eyes to see and wit to understand it:

> When Leo asked Ahmed about his music: "Is it of the senses or of the spirit?" then Ahmed understood him less than ever. He had no conception of any division between the two, and if he had thought about it, he would have said, surely the one is there to express the other? That was what his music was for—he knew this so deeply that he had absolutely no thought or words for it.

In view of the chasm that exists between Ahmed's unspoken philosophy of life and art and the worldliness and sensuality of voluble, "pot-bellied and short-breathed" Leo Kellermann, it is ironic that "Ahmed's music opened up Leo's Tantric period," providing inspiration and starting-point for a new variation on the pseudo-philosophical theories Kellermann expounds to the impressionable members of his Academy of Potential Development. The "Tantric period" is one of a variety of stages through which Kellermann's philosophy passes before it reaches its culmination in what he terms "The Point," and it is on his journey toward "The Point"—at which, hopefully, man's highest spiritual and physical experiences intersect—that we have our last glimpse of Kellermann driving blindly into snow and a mist that is partly real, partly a confusion of the spirit.

In her characterization of Leo Kellermann, Ruth Jhabvala achieves her aim of inclusiveness, combining her "three backgrounds" at a very ambitious level that takes in *In Search of Love and Beauty* far beyond the comparatively easy satiric strokes of *Hullabaloo* and **"A Summer**

**by the Sea.**" Until he encounters Ahmed in New York, there seems to be nothing "Indian" in either Kellermann's genesis or his personality. On the contrary, he is very "European" indeed, has arrived in New York from Europe in the 1930's as a penniless refugee, and makes his first appearance on page one of the novel among a group of German and Austrian women expatriates whom he manages from the very start to delight with his charm and fascinate with his ideas. But as things turn out, Kellermann's impact on American life as depicted in the novel is not human in any narrowly national sense but superhuman. He enters the novel on a note of divinity: "An Apollo! —A god," cries Regi to her friend Louise, describing this new and superb acquisition, and as his extraordinary influence spreads together with his fame, Kellermann becomes the "reigning deity of the Old Vienna" and the "beneficent deity" of the massive Gothic house in the Hudson Valley that houses his Academy of Potential Development. Described at various times in the novel as a "pagan god" possessed of a "great Olympian laugh," and admirers who are at once his "followers" and "disciples," Kellermann has the "wonderful gift of making each (woman) feel that he was in intimate contact with her, on the deepest and most thrilling level; and moreover, that he had absolutely no difficulty in understanding as well as condoning whatever secret, or secret longing, she might be harbouring."

To Louise Sonnenblick, whose lover he becomes, he is nothing less than "a *tornado,*" and even in the most unlikely circumstances retains his divine aspect: for example, while taking a bath and demanding that his back be scrubbed, he holds out a loofah as if it were a trident. The lives of Regi and Louise are changed by his theories. Religious symbolism thickens about Kellermann, whose very hair resembles a "burning bush" and "a prophet's halo," whose garments include a "robe like a monk's," and who cultivates in later life "an air of benign blessing." But such associations are counteracted, if not entirely given the lie, by symbolism of a very different, indeed sinister kind. Suggestions of the bestial and of a rank and mysterious underworld combine in the very name of this European adventurer who, like Hamid in **"A Summer by the Sea,"** "never really had any difficulty in getting people to look after him"; and cluster about the "den," the "lair," the "escape hatch" to which Kellermann flees in order to avoid his disciples and be himself. His classes in physical expression culminate in a **"Day of Wrath"** in the description of which animal references proliferate: "roaring as of lions, such bellowings of bulls, chatterings of monkeys, shrieks of hyenas." To Regi, forty years after he first enchanted her, he becomes—still larger than life—an "old monster." Mark sees him as a "stranded whale," and as "some superannuated circus animal." These divine and bestial images are brought together skilfully in the "Dionysian figure" of a tramp who resembles Kellermann, and whose appearance wins from little Natasha (the character who, above all others, seems to be her creator's persona in the novel) tears of "overwhelmed pity for all the hungers of humanity":

> Natasha led (her grandmother) to the corner:
> the awful vision was still there. He sat enthroned
> on the dustbin, like a god wafted up from its
> depths. He was enormous and red in the face and

wore a hat without a crown on his wild hair; a pair of stiff black trousers encased one massive leg but was ripped open on the other, exposing a surprisingly soft, lily-white expanse of thigh. His trident, or escutcheon, was an empty bottle held aloft in one hand, and he was alternately shouting and singing to passers-by.

It is Natasha, perceptive beyond her years, who draws her disgusted grandmother's attention to the fact that the derelict tramp resembles Leo Kellermann. The scene, which ends with Louise thrusting coins and reproaches simultaneously on the tramp, permits the reader an oblique insight into the mixture of sensual and spiritual elements in Kellermann's character, and foreshadows the novel's penultimate scene in which the founder of the Academy of Potential Development, crazed with the despair of an ordinary unrequited love, drives (evidently to his death) with Natasha beside him, "glad to be there with him: not that she could do anything as, blinded with tears, he drove them further into snow and mist, but at least so he wasn't alone."

It is inevitable that the blending of spiritual and bestial associations in Ruth Jhabvala's characterization of Leo Kellermann should remind readers of her novels of a somewhat similar technique used by her in building up the personality of another seeming charlatan, Swamiji in her earlier work, *A New Dominion:* particularly striking there were Lee's recollection of her sexual encounter with her *guru* in bestial terms, and the scene in which Swamiji runs "a broad, pale tongue swiftly round his lips" as he tells Raymond of his (overtly spiritual) desire that Lee should return to him. The similarities do not end there. Swamiji's ashram parallels Kellermann's Academy, and the conversation of both men ambiguously combine spiritual and sexual elements: for example, Swamiji's statement that "the old Lee must be broken before the new Lee can be formed, and we are now only at the first stage of our task" has a parallel in Kellermann's pursuit of Marietta:

> Leo . . . issued many invitations to her—which
> she ignored as she did her best to ignore every-
> thing to do with him. But Leo had never given
> up. He loved it when people resisted him, noth-
> ing pleased him more. "It's like fishing," he
> said—"It's no fun unless the fish resists; unless
> it struggles—flaps and fights and wriggles for its
> life until—yupp! you've got it: up in the air
> where you want it, dangling there, with all your
> hook, line and sinker inside it." He tended to use
> this image for both his sexual and his spiritual
> conquests.

But in Kellermann's ability to communicate intimately and secretly with each of the women who make up the adoring circle that surrounds him, we see not only a reflection of Swamiji's easy fascination of a roomful of admiring Western tourists, there is here a skilfully hidden allusion to the god Krishna's ability to manifest himself before Radha and her fellow milkmaids individually and collectively.

Here, then, so cunningly woven into the stuff of her novel as to be unobtrusive and almost invisible, and yet undoubtedly at the very centre of it, is Ruth Prawer Jhabvala's image of India, larger than life, containing within it intimations of divine joy and intense disgust, of god and beast, of Heaven and Hell. The ironic presentation of the character of Swamiji had made it possible for two contradictory, yet perfectly consistent, interpretations of his personality to run throughout *A New Dominion:* spirituality on the one hand, opportunism on the other. Although there is no Natasha to weep for him, it is not possible for the careful reader to dismiss Swamiji as a mere sensualist and charlatan. And so it is with Leo Kellermann, in Ruth Jhabvala's latest and most complex work of fiction: with the added advantage in his case that Natasha's pity for him, which impels her to what is presumably her final, fatal, act of "self-immolation," helps us to see him with the compassionate eyes of his creator as more pitiable in his final, dreadful, banal despair than any of his helpless victims.

"Having assimilated all this Indian experience I don't want to forget it or cast it off; what I want to do is to take it out again as a Westerner, enriched by what I have learnt there." *In Search of Love and Beauty,* while confronting "life's disenchantments with alert and humorous resilience," unobtrusively achieves this personal authorial aim through a plot that brings together characters convincingly representative of its author's "three backgrounds" to work out a universal theme; but most triumphantly through the chief of those characters, the novel's anti-hero Leo Kellermann—Apollo, Krishna, and Superman.

### David Rubin   (essay date Winter 1984)

SOURCE: "Ruth Jhabvala in India," in *Modern Fiction Studies,* Vol. 30, No. 4, Winter, 1984, pp. 669-83.

[*In the following essay, Rubin categorizes Jhabvala not as an Indian novelist, but as an "Indo-Anglian" novelist in the tradition of R. K. Narayan and Raja Rao.*]

> Although the Major was so sympathetic to India, his piece sounds like a warning. He said that one has to be very determined to withstand—to stand up to—India. And the most vulnerable, he said, are always those who love her best. There are many ways of loving India, many things to love her for—the scenery, the history, the poetry, the music, and indeed the physical beauty of her men and women—but all, said the Major, are dangerous for the European who allows himself to love too much. India always, he said, finds out the weak spot and presses on it.
> —Ruth Jhabvala [*Heat and Dust,* 1975]

From Flora Annie Steel to Paul Scott the English novelists who have written about India—and they are so numerous that a complete bibliography would fill a small volume— have virtually all reached certain conclusions, whether expressed or implicit: first, that successful communication (and still more, successful fusion) between India and the West is always imperfect when not absolutely disastrous; second, that Indians are somehow deficient in the more admirable qualities of character as understood by the West (which may make them more perilously seductive to Europeans); and third, that India is a source of disillusion, disgust, and corruption for the naive Western pilgrims

who flock to her for illumination. It is also characteristic of most of these novels that there is little humor (Scott's *Staying On* is one happy exception) and, even more surprising, no sense of wonder or delight at the obvious beauties of India and the pleasures and excitements of daily life there—inevitable, one imagines, at least occasionally even for the most disaffected visitor. It would seem that filth and poverty, "heat and dust," have annihilated the first and bureaucratic entanglements the second, leaving behind only ill temper and bitterness.

A great many of the Indian novelists who write in English are also preoccupied with the confrontation of East and West (for example, Raja Rao, B. Rajan, Kamala Markandaya), and although their conclusions are not identical they tend to concur with their English counterparts on one essential point, namely, that relations between representatives of the two cultures are certain to be difficult, dangerous, and often tragic in their consequences.

Considering the consistently negative nature of the British novelists' response to India one may well be surprised that they continue to be fascinated by the subcontinent and cannot leave it alone. For some, India may provide only a backdrop for a tale that has fundamentally nothing to do with the country. Others may employ India as a springboard for a ruthlessly objective look at Victorian ideals and bungling, as in James Farrell's *The Siege of Krishnapur,* a fictional recreation of the siege of Lucknow in 1857. Less intellectual writers have seen in Indian history the opportunity for the nostalgic review of a romantic and to some extent chimerical English heroic past, as in the novels of John Masters and M. M. Kaye. Or India itself may emerge as the inexhaustibly spellbinding protagonist—such is the case, I believe, with Paul Scott's *Raj Quartet,* although even here the central symbolic actions of rape, indiscriminate irrational violence, and the frustration of almost every attempt to bridge the cultural and psychological chasm between the two worlds all reveal a fundamental acceptance of the late Victorian image of India.

Of these recent novelists Ruth Prawer Jhabvala, because of the special nature of her case, seems to me the most interesting, whatever the limitations of her work. When I speak of her "case" I mean the question of how she is to be classified by the literary historian, a point not merely of technical interest but one of fundamental importance. Ruth Jhabvala was born in 1927 in Frankfurt, Germany, of Polish-Jewish parents, who in 1939 took her to England. She lived there until 1951, when she married a Parsi architect and went with him to Delhi, where she lived for the next twenty-five years and brought up three daughters. During this time she wrote all but the last of her nine novels, as well as four volumes of short stories and various screenplays, including the prize-winning *Shakespeare Wallah.* In 1975 she left India and settled in America, which has become the subject both of her most recent novel, *In Search of Love and Beauty,* and of her screenplay *Roseland.* Most Indian and Western critics regard her as an Indian writer, one of the "Indo-Anglian" school that includes such diverse novelists as Raja Rao, Mulk Raj Anand, Anita Desai, R. K. Narayan, and Kamala Markandaya. I believe, however, that not only should she not be viewed as an Indian writer but that she is actually in the mainstream of the English novelists cited above, and that not to see this seriously compromises the possibility of a genuine comprehension of the significance of her work.

Let us consider first the grounds for regarding Jhabvala as an authentic Indian voice. Are her marriage and residence sufficient to justify classifying her as Indian? If so, then by the same standards Kamala Markandaya (married to an Englishman and living in London) must be judged British. If we consider the problem from the viewpoint of her material, which is mostly Indian in setting with a fair mix of Indian and Western characters, Markandaya for her part could again just as fairly be called British. The question is further complicated by Jhabvala's recent abandonment of India for the United States. The solution to this puzzle of national identification is not idly speculative for on it hangs the far more complex mystery of Jhabvala's sense of her own identity and its relation to the world she has created, and ultimately of the real value and meaning of her fiction.

Speaking of Indo-Anglian writers in general, Klaus Steinvorth writes:

> The position of Indo-English novelists is on the periphery of their own society, they are partly even separated from it by emigration or expatriation, which does not mean they are sufficiently integrated in their new society. . . . Almost every one of them feels, or is considered, an outsider standing between India and the West, often led to believe that these two complex and abstract ideas can be reduced to a pair of simple opposites. [*The Indo-English Novel: The Impact of the West on Literature in a Developing Country*, 1975]

The curious thing about Jhabvala, of course, is that, unlike the other novelists Steinvorth considers, her exile is not from but to India. Her position as a kind of permanent refugee has, I am convinced, the greatest significance for an understanding of her work, and I shall return to this point later. Steinvorth also maintains that Jhabvala's fiction is strongly moulded by Hinduism, to an extent even greater than one finds in a Hindu writer such as, say, Manohar Malgonkar. The unlikelihood of this thesis should become clear in what follows.

Here it will be useful to see what Jhabvala herself has said about this question:

> The central fact of all my work, as I see it, is that I am a European living permanently in India. I have lived here for most of my adult life and have an Indian family. This makes me not quite an insider but it does not leave me entirely an outsider either. I feel my position to be at a point in space where I have quite a good view of both

> sides but am myself left stranded in the middle. My work is an attempt to charter this unchartered territory for myself. . . . My books may appear to be objective but really I think they are the opposite; for I describe the Indian scene not for its own sake but for mine. . . . My work is only one individual European's attempt to compound the puzzling process of living in India. [*Contemporary Novelists*, 1976]

This straightforward and candid statement, made in 1972, offers useful clues for the interpretation of Jhabvala's fiction, some of which I shall return to later. Here I will point out only the somewhat enigmatic use of the word "compound" where one might have expected the less ambiguous "understand."

From Jhabvala's point of view there is, of course, a considerable advantage in being thought of as Indian. It allows her to be ruthlessly critical of both traditional and "modern" India without incurring the odium of a hostile and uninformed outsider. She also need not anticipate banning (unlike John Masters, to take one example) on the grounds of offensiveness to a particular community or tradition. In writing of the India that she knows from her own experience she has the advantage, as she suggests, of being as it were both of it and out of it. To her observation of Indian city life she brings both a European irony that can come only with a certain detachment and an insider's knowledge of detail and nuance that few other non-Indians could hope to command. At moments (and I believe they are her best) she writes with a finely controlled irony that is neither necessarily Indian nor European but more her own individual manner—an accomplishment few genuine Indo-Anglian writers can claim, with the notable exception of R. K. Narayan.

Apart from its exotic interest as a reflection of Indian experience, it is as a triumphant example of comedic art that Jhabvala's work has been most consistently praised. The comparison of her work to Chekhov's has become a reviewer's cliche. Her novels have been called comedies of manners in the tradition of Austen and James. To cite only one instance, V. S. Pritchett finds her "an ironical observor of what Chekhov called the false emotions, the comedy (in the sternest sense) of self-delusion without drastic condemnation of the deluded." This conception of Jhabvala strike me as inaccurate as the view of her as Indian and derives in part from it, as I hope to demonstrate.

In reevaluating Jhabvala's work at this stage, which may be said to mark the definitive finale to her career as an "Indian" writer, it would be impossible in an essay of this scope to examine her complete oeuvre. I propose instead, after some preliminary remarks about her early work, to discuss her three most recent novels with Indian settings, in all of which problems of East-West understanding assume ever greater prominence, and her extraordinarily revealing autobiographical essay, **"Myself in India,"** which more clearly and explicitly than any other of her writings calls into question her status both as an Indian writer and a comic novelist of manners.

> To her observation of Indian city life she brings both a European irony that can come only with a certain detachment and an insider's knowledge of detail and nuance that few other non-Indians could hope to command.
>
> —*David Rubin*

Jhabvala's first five novels may be said to constitute the first phase of her work. With the exception of *Esmond in India* they are not particularly involved with Europeans but portray, rather, Indian family life and its constant preoccupation with finding suitable husbands for younger daughters. Although the tone darkens after the relatively sunny first novel, *Amrita,* the principal characters are viewed in general with some compassion and their eccentricities as usually endearing. The third novel, *Esmond in India,* the first to take up what may be called Jhabvala's international theme, is noticeably sourer and more bitter in tone. It seems as though a European presence automatically calls up tension, anxiety, and disappointment. The novel that followed, *The Householder,* is again a mostly Indian story, one in which Jhabvala achieves her most sympathetic insight into middle-class domestic life with nuances both tender and melancholy—her most genuinely Chekhovian work; its only defect comes from the occasional intrusion of minor European characters—unbelievable caricatures that anticipate the hippies and other questers who flocked to India in the Sixties and who were to become almost an obsessive preoccupation in Jhabvala's later work.

*A Backward Place* (1965) may be taken as the novel that initiates Jhabvala's second phase, in which the international theme becomes all-important. As in all of Jhabvala's fiction the focus here is on women—there are no memorable male characters in her work. In this case the central figures are three European women who represent in varying degrees the East-West malaise exemplified in the recurrent subjects and themes of Jhabvala's work: the troubled marriages and love affairs between Indians and Europeans; the romantic, vaguely questing Westerner; the adventures and fight for survival of bored, superficial, and Indophobic drifters, mirrored by their egomaniacal, mindless, and predatory Indian counterparts. In *A Backward Place* the Indian characters (with two minor exceptions, Shanti and Bhuaji) are characterized by shallowness and mediocrity, combined in individual cases with infantile selfishness, cupidity, stupidity, and extravagant vanity. They are, in short, caricatures, occasionally amusing and generally predictable. The Western characters show only slightly more realistic individuality.

The action of the novel is of the simplest nature. Judy, married to Bal ("child"), unemployed and unemployable, works in the office of the Cultural Dais until finally she gives in to her husband's harebrained scheme of going to Bombay to look for work in films. Clarissa, an adumbra-

tion of the later hippies, is a painter, an expert sponger, and wildly in love with the elemental India of nature and villages, about which she knows nothing. She says that Romain Rolland's *Life of Vivekananda* inspired her to come to India, and she has "rejected all Western values." Etta, a Hungarian refugee, is a fading blond who survives by having affairs with Indian businessmen. Unlike Clarissa she clings to everything Western. This limited material is sufficient for Jhabvala to present a cutting satire of the way foreigners live in New Delhi. Her fiercest scorn is reserved for a German exchange economist at the university and his wife, victims of the reverse Indian myth—a gushy uninformed Indophilia sustained by the good life guaranteed by their government grant ("Even the furniture was provided by the government. . . ."):

> [the Hochstadts] saw in it a reflection of the spirit of India as a whole—of that new India, which strove to bring itself in line with the most highly developed technical achievements of the twentieth century and yet retain its own culture: its art, its religion, its philosophy (and where in India, as Dr. Hochstadt so aptly remarked to his wife, can one draw a dividing line between these three manifestations of the human spirit?) which had ever been and would ever be, an inspiration to the world.
>
> Another few months and Dr. Hochstadt's assignment would be at an end, and it would be time to return to the normal course of their duties. In a way they were not sorry: all good things must come to an end, and they were beginning to miss the cosy flat in St. John's Wood . . . and several other features of their normal settled lives. [Jhabvala, *A Backward Place,* 1965]

The Indian characters are just as cruelly satirized. Mrs. Kaul, the rich patroness of the ineffectual Cultural Dais (which presents a farcically inept performance of Ibsen's *A Doll's House*), is a modern variation on Dickens' Veneerings:

> Then some of her own friends came, and they were very much more acceptable. They were all dressed, spoke good English and had been abroad; in short, they were cultured people.
>
> "Last year we were in Berlin where Mr. Kaul was head of the economic mission at the International Conference of Civil Servants. We were shown many interesting cultural events such as the State Opera and the Berliner Theatre. From there we went to U.K. and saw *Rosenkavalier* at the Covent Garden Opera House. This too was a beautiful experience. In Moscow we saw the Bolshoi Ballet—oh my own dear Bolshoi Ballet!" she cried and clapped her hands and shut her eyes for joy.

Jhabvala's most delicate satire is aimed at Mrs. Kaul. This lady would like to fire Judy to oblige some influential friends by hiring their daughter.

> He pointed out that it was hardly possible to slide one person out of a job for no better reason than that you wished to slide another person into it; but here she could not follow him, for as far as she was concerned it was entirely possible.

Most of the other Indian characters are even less attractive: Guppy, the grossly self-indulgent businessman; Kishan Kumar, a mindless, narcissistic film star; snobbish, Europe-mongering Mr. Jumperwala; the pompous Doctor; and so on. Jaykar, the editor, feels some indignation at the idleness and silliness of the young Indians who crowd the coffeehouses, but he expresses it only in editorials composed in a desolatingly trite style. "Now is the time it behoves our Youth to leave their cushioned chairs, gird up their loins and stride out into those areas of our vast land where the trumpet of Progress has not yet sounded its first triumphant notes". Sudhir, who has decent instincts, is, like the majority of Jhabvala's characters throughout her work, passive, ineffectual, and ultimately aimless.

Judy, the most (almost the only) sympathetically drawn of all the characters, seems to promise the possibility of a sane middle path between Etta's Indophobia and Clarissa's gush. She is happy to work to support her husband and children, content in the society of her sister-in-law and husband's aunt (a conventional religious old Hindu woman). But Judy herself is without any strong motivation or discrimination and seems indeed to be almost simple-minded; her capitulation to her husband at the end of the novel, in a kind of irrational, euphoric surrender, is difficult to credit. (In *Esmond in India* [1958] Jhabvala had told a more convincing story of an Englishman and Indian woman whose marriage ends in divorce, to the relief of all concerned.)

Despite their flatness and predictability, the European characters in *A Backward Place* have a little more individuality than the Indians. As for the Indians, Jhabvala's estimation is not far from that of V. S. Naipaul as expressed in *India: A Wounded Civilization.*

Considered in itself this novel is a deft and entertaining satire of the way some Europeans live in Delhi. But it is not genuine comedy. The classical conception of comedy—a literary process in which illusions and confusions are dispelled and true identities at both symbolic and literal levels reestablished with the protagonists given, as it were, a second chance (the point at which comedy diverges from tragedy) so that their lives are clarified, sweetened, and, in short, redeemed—cannot be applied to *A Backward Place.* The outcome of each character's conflicts and quests is too sour, too negative, to be called comic. As in so much of Jhabvala's work there is a persistent, one might say dogged, concentration on the perverse, the mediocre, and the disappointing that is actually not the correction of the exaggeratedly romantic but merely its opposite extreme and too unbalanced to be considered realistic—a facile cynicism of the kind that an unhappy Indian experience can breed so effectively. This is the world of Evelyn Waugh's early novels successfully transplanted to India.

The cynicism and emotional deadness are reinforced by the prose style. It is self-consciously flat. There are hardly ever any conjunctions except for "and" and "but"; consequently, there is scarcely ever any subordination of clauses, which in turn means a heavy restriction on affective highlighting, indignation, or other moral implications. Superficially this may seem like Hemingway, but in Hemingway—at least in the earlier novels and stories—the coolness and evenness of style are used to communicate and enhance extraordinary events, intense emotional shocks, and a definite moral viewpoint. In *A Backward Place* the affectation of indifference does not serve any such purpose. Instead of lending conviction to passionately felt experiences and hard-won stoicism in the face of tragic losses, the style merely confirms the obvious mediocrity of the novel's characters and their reaction to experience. Almost any paragraph chosen at random illustrates this.

> Bal had a brilliant idea. He woke up with it one morning and couldn't wait to tell Judy. Unfortunately she had already left for work—he was always the last to get up, for he got home late at night and liked to make up for it in the morning—so he had to lie there and think about it by himself. He lay for quite a long time, but in the end jumped out of bed for he had got so excited about his idea that he felt he had to share it with someone, even if it was only Bhuaji who wouldn't understand properly. But she had gone out too, and the children were at school, and the servant in the bazaar.

Even at a moment that is charged with some emotion, the writer downplays it to rob it deliberately of serious impact.

> "She has insulted me!" he suddenly shouted. With a vehement gesture he flung away his chicken leg (Mrs. Hochstadt, who hated to see litter, had to check an impulse to run after it and pick it up and put it in her special disposal box). He shouted again, "I have been insulted!"

This is farce rather than comedy and it depends not on insights but rather on facile generalizations and accurate observation only of the surface of things. Chekhovian comedy depends on a ready recognition of what is typical and expected, but its effectiveness derives from the way this is set off by what is neither typical nor expected. The apparently placid surface conceals and gradually reveals a depth and tension, a sympathetically conceived human personality, not a clinically sound diagnosis. In Chekhov the sadness of life is constantly counterpointed by flashes of recognition of a current of joy in living; laughter and tears are natural partners in his stories and dramas. In *A Backward Place* one finds only a dry and occasionally humorous chronicling of the bleak totality of Indian experience; India is used as an instrument to diminish and denigrate the characters.

The limitations of one particular novel become far more significant when we see that the flatness of tone, the cynical attitude, and the pervasive desolation are characteristic of Jhabvala's work in general. One finds no particular evolution in the style, no increase in depth or richness of response to India, almost no expansion of the subject matter—the restricted world of middle- and upper-class Delhi and Bombay, with the exception that in the succeeding novels the hippies become significant. Jhabvala's special interest has always been the refugee. "What I am interested in now is myself in India," she writes in the essay **"Myself in India."** Herself a refugee, she is fascinated by the various kinds of emotional and philosophical escape artists who have gravitated to India, some of whom may represent projections of her sense of her own identity. "My books may appear to be objective but really I think they are the opposite."

The novel that follows *A Backward Place, Travelers* (1973, titled *A New Dominion* in England), might well have been called "Refugees." The two central Indian characters—Asha, a middle-aged Rani, and Gopi, a young sponger—drift from one place to the other as their affair progresses. Raymond, a young middle-class Englishman in love with Gopi, follows them around despite his disillusionment with Gopi's superficiality and rapacity. Lee, an American girl, one of several spiritual questers, floats sometimes with them, sometimes away, drawing them after her, amid a group of other ashram-dwellers and foreign pilgrims whose apathy, which they apparently mistake for illumination, is so great that even when one of them dies of the diseases that torment all of them, it causes no great stir. At the end of the novel a weary Raymond sets out for home and the family business. Lee, who has been seduced, almost raped, by a swami, is apparently on her way back to his ashram. The swami, a particularly nasty Dickensian caricature, is a monster of ambition, greed, and lust. "Dickensian" is perhaps inaccurate: he appalls but does not amuse. The element of caricature extends to all the major characters. The three parts of the novel (their titles—"Delhi," "The Holy City," "Maupur"—sounding vaguely Forsterian echoes) are coldly and wryly critical portraits of the capital, an ashram in Varanasi, and a Raja's broken down provincial palaces that are the stock in trade of Jhabvala's novels and filmplays. To emphasize the author's distance from the material, the novel is further subdivided into mostly brief scenes, each with its title, for example, "Gopi Is Displeased with Raymond," "Lee and Gopi Eat Kebabs," "Asha Feels Old."

V. S. Pritchett writes, "A large number of these passages are perfect as short stories in which the light changes from the bizarre to the poetic, from the comic to the horrifying, from the thoughtful to the mischievous—all with an allusiveness, a susceptibility to mood, a tenderness of which Chekhov was the exemplar." Again I find it difficult to see much that is Chekhovian in this work, where the style and technique appear calculated to dispel any suspicion of sympathy on the author's part by reducing events to something like the panels of a comic strip.

Pritchett finds the Western characters less successful than the Indian. "The Hindus are Mrs. Jhabvala's complete characterizations—above all, the ancient Princess Asha and the impossible young Gopi." But Asha (who may be fading but is hardly "ancient") and Gopi, far from being complete characterizations, are scarcely even recognizable as Hindus. (Perhaps Pritchett means "Indians.") As certain Indian types, yes, types made familiar by Hindi-language films of unquestioned, unashamed triviality. The only element that distinguishes Asha and Gopi (like the swami) from the Europeans in the story is their capacity to exercise their willpower, their relentless and sometimes crafty grasping. The Westerners for their part are once

again apathetic, passive, and vague; and once again the novel's narrative style serves mainly to diminish them. What we have is a series of vignettes, virtual cartoons, in which nobody is more important than anyone else, nothing much has value, and nothing much matters: the depressed world of voluntary displaced persons who somehow fail even as refugees.

If we return to the question of whether to consider Ruth Jhabvala an Indian novelist, it is worthwhile to call attention here to the kind of characterizations found in the fiction of her Indo-Anglian contemporaries, where characters are endowed with clearly defined, rounded, and heightened individuality. Although it is outside the scope of this essay to discuss them in detail, let me cite the novels of writers such as Kamala Markandaya, Anita Desai, and even that most Brahmanical of writers in English, R. K. Narayan. The same can be said of those novelists who write in Hindi: for example, Rakesh, Vatsyayan, Ashk, and Sobti. The contrast of all these writers' approach to characterization with Jhabvala's is striking and serves to emphasize how much of an outsider after all (like all the English who have written fiction about India) she has remained.

The nature of Jhabvala's relationship to India and the effect that country has had upon her work may be clarified by her essay **"Myself in India."** In these fourteen pages Jhabvala describes with the cool precision we expect from her and a raw intensity we do not her own private anguish over her Delhi life and the unsettling ambivalences, familiar to so many who have lived a long time in India, of being unable to live with the country or without it, a special kind of *odi-et-amo,* or as she candidly terms it, a disease. Even the most commonplace social pleasures are fraught with malaise. Of a Delhi hostess she writes:

> In her one may see the best of East and West combined. She is interested in a great variety of topics and can hold her own in any discussion. She loves to exercise her emancipated mind, and whatever the subject of conversation—economics, or politics, or literature, or film—she has a well-formulated opinion on it and knows how to express herself. How lucky for me if I could have such a person for a friend! What enjoyable; lively times we two could have together!
>
> In fact, my teeth are set on edge if I have to listen to her for more than five minutes. . . .

Out of context the point may seem trivial, but it has emblematic importance for Jhabvala. If one does not enjoy the limited and artificial society of the Civil Lines or the rich new colonies and if, on the other hand, one is not a "strong person who plunges in and does what he can, a doctor, or a social worker," as she puts it, what is left? Extraordinarily, she can summon up only a handful of isolated images to express her sense of all the rest of the subcontinent—a smiling leper, the carcass of a dog, a human sacrifice, Shiva on Mt. Kailash sporting his necklace of skulls, outlaws with the hearts of wild beasts, the naive and touching devotion to the cow—none of which ever appears in her fiction. One cannot suppress a decided disappointment that this acute observer should feel obliged to evoke the shade of Katherine Mayo, no matter how superior the style. Her Delhi life is haunted by the knowledge that she is "on the back of this great animal of poverty and backwardness. It is not possible to pretend otherwise. Even if one never rolls up the blinds and never turns off the airconditioner, something is bound to go wrong. People are not meant to shut themselves up in rooms and pretend there is nothing outside."

So we are back again in India as experienced by all the earlier British novelists who have tried to come to grips with it: Europeans are not meant to live there (perhaps nobody is, as N. C. Chaudhuri contends), with the possible exception of pathologically passive, egoless drifters like Lee; the country somehow accentuates sexual craving and offers easy gratification, but the sexual adventures are always disappointing and corrupting; the spiritual values of Indian thought are an illusion; and Europeans and Indians are doomed not to understand one another.

In *Heat and Dust* (1975), the last of Jhabvala's Indian novels to date, there is some attenuation of the attitudes prevalent in the preceding books. At first glance it seems to be an apologia for, almost a refutation of, the earlier novels. Although caricature and stereotyping are still in evidence, the major characters are more fully delineated, and for a change there is at least some ambiguity (allowing a note of affirmation, albeit a feeble one) in the conclusion. The unnamed narrator comes to India in part to unravel the story of Olivia, her grandfather's first wife, who had caused a scandal by becoming the mistress of a navab and renouncing England forever—whether happily or not we are never permitted to know. In the process, the narrator herself is fascinated with India, becomes pregnant by her Indian landlord, and, unlike Olivia, resolves to have her baby. We last see her awaiting its birth in the lower Himalayas and planning vaguely to go eventually to a mountain ashram.

An unwonted element of allegory is discernible in this novel. The navab's palace is near a village called Khatm ("finished") and Olivia and the narrator resides in Satipur, the city of the faithful wife—Jhabvala's penchant for irony once again evident here. Satipur is notable for its English cemetery, like Paul Scott's Pankot in *Staying On*. This cemetery, with its graves of British soldiers, their wives, and children, overgrown with weeds and its tombstones and statues broken, is all that remains of the Raj in Satipur. The only English in evidence today, including the narrator (herself the representative of a British colonial family), are partially Indianized vagrants. Olivia aborts her half-Indian baby but remains ever faithful to its Indian father, whereas the narrator, in a more enlightened age, or perhaps merely one more decadent, though she discards her Indian lover, after unsuccessfully trying to abort her child finds a rapture in the idea of having it. Although Pritchett had found *Travelers* Forsterian rather than Chekhovian, the adjective is more applicable to *Heat and Dust.* The concern with "bridging" is treated more seriously than anywhere else in Jhabvala; the possibility of a positive value in at least some Hindu holy men and women is suggested; and even Forster's tendency to sententious

and intrusive observations of a moral nature can be found, as exemplified by this essay's epigraph.

It is difficult to assess how much of a development in Jhabvala's sense of India *Heat and Dust* represents. As so often in her work, the author has remained elusive, difficult to pin down. Unlike Forster, for instance, who expresses his moral viewpoint in his fiction in his own person, Jhabvala never does. What Etta or Raymond or the narrator thinks may or may not coincide with her personal ideas. We must try to draw conclusions only through a process of inference by examining the consistency of story patterns, the fate of each of the characters, and the dominant elements of the narrative style. In all these respects, *Heat and Dust* has after all not gone so far beyond the world of *A Backward Place.* The irony of the later book may be deliberately blunted, the value of Indian experience for Europeans less defined (and therefore at least potentially positive), the attitude toward India's victims (including the indispensable hippies) a trifle more sympathetic. But the fundamental modality is still flatness of presentation and the major characters still passive, almost without either will or awareness. In both her sexual adventures (they can hardly be called love affairs) the narrator is virtually inert. By the very nature of the novel's structure—present-day events recorded in the narrator's matter-of-fact diary and the distant past, reconstructed from Olivia's letters, retold by the same narrator—we are excluded from an opportunity to confront characters and situations with either intensity or certainty. Once again the technique provides a skillful screen that allows the writer to remain uncommitted to any position that might hint at the sentimental, the emotional, or even the genuinely compassionate. Just as in the later Hemingway the controlled concealment of emotion leads to a suspicion that there is little feeling to conceal, so here we are troubled by the unrelenting deadpan and the steady letdown from what at best is only ground level.

In all these novels no Indian and no European experiences a moment of fulfillment or even of pleasure. In **"Myself in India"** Jhabvala herself records no agreeable Indian experience apart from the enjoyment of *bhajan,* traditional devotional songs. In the same essay she writes:

> However, I must admit that I am no longer interested in India. What I am interested in now is myself in India—which sometimes, in moments of despondency, I tend to think of as my survival in India. I had better say straightaway that the reason I live in India is because my strongest human ties are here. If I hadn't married an Indian, I don't think I would ever have come here for I am not attracted—or used not to be attracted—to the things that usually bring people to India. I know I am the wrong type of person to live here. To stay and endure, one should have a mission and a cause, to be patient, cheerful, unselfish, strong. I am a central European with an English education and a deplorable tendency to constant self-analysis. I am irritable and have weak nerves.

She concludes the essay by saying that she gets bored after a time in Europe and finds it difficult to stand the European climate. "I have got used to intense heat and seem to need it". Nevertheless, in 1981, she writes [in *Contemporary Novelists*], "In 1975 I left India and am now living in and writing about America—but not for long enough to be able to make any kind of comment about either of these activities." It is obviously too early to say whether without that country's "intense heat" her inspiration will wither or whether, after a respite, she will return to India as her subject with a new perspective and greater depth. Until the present her Indian fiction has constituted a clever and disarming set of variations on the long tradition of the Anglo-Indian novelists. Although her earlier novels, like those of any genuine Indian writer, tend to deal with Indians as people first and only secondarily as Indians, in her later ones this is reversed as the East-West theme comes to obsess her. Her characters become increasingly emblematic and less human, the impoverishment and triviality of the Indian life she knows is presented more and more bitterly, and in consequence the alleged comic nature of these books appears ever more dubious. Their relation to her "constant self-analysis" can only be speculated upon in the light of her abandonment of India, but it seems likely that she can no longer allow herself to be regarded as an Indian novelist. The third phase—the American—has only begun, bringing with it, it is safe to assume, ever greater contradictions and complexities.

## H. Summerfield   (essay date July 1986)

SOURCE: "Holy Women and Unholy Men: Ruth Prawer Jhabvala Confronts the Non-rational," in *Ariel: A Review of International English Literature,* Vol. 17, No. 3, July, 1986, pp. 85-101.

[*In the following essay, Summerfield discusses critics' frequent comparisons of Jhabvala to Jane Austen and Anton Chekhov, concentrating on her frequent depictions of swamis and their relationships to their female followers.*]

Any woman who writes witty novels in English about courtship and family life faces the occupational hazard of being compared to Jane Austen. Despite the exotic character (to Western readers) of her Indian settings, this has frequently been the privilege and the fate of Ruth Prawer Jhabvala. It does not often happen, however, that the novelist who is compared to Jane Austen for wit is also compared to Anton Chekhov for humour tinged with melancholy. The fact that Jhabvala is the subject of both comparisons suggests that the atmosphere of her books is richly varied, but the affinity of her work with Austen's novels and Chekhov's stories is more than a matter of surfaces. Austen carried the values of the Age of Reason into the Romantic period, Chekhov opposed the anti-scientific outlook of the Russian Slavophiles and of Tolstoy, and Jhabvala attacks the proliferation of mystical cults. All three writers base their judgements of people and actions on experience and reason; they share a deeply rooted suspicion of the non-rational without being rigidly narrow in their outlook.

As an heir of the eighteenth century—Johnson, Cowper, and Crabbe were her favourite authors—Jane Austen measured people and their feelings by the standard of rea-

sonableness, and, like so many of the Augustans, she accepted a kind of Christianity which stressed rational morality far more than belief in the supernatural. (Even the devout Dr. Johnson, reacting to Boswell's anxiety about the strength of Hume's argument against miracles, warned his friend "that the great difficulty of proving miracles should make us very cautious in believing them.") Characteristically, Austen feared imagination or emotion that could carry people beyond the control of reason. Christians might legitimately be Evangelicals, she thought, if they were so "from Reason and Feeling," and she considered that a powerful imagination would corrode judgement unless it was guided by "Religious Principle."

The outlook of the Age of Reason was expressed in the empirical philosophy, according to which reality is to be apprehended by applying reason to the data acquired through sensory experience. This philosophy underlies the tradition of natural science, which was a central element in the life of Chekhov, a physician as well as an author. His biographer Ronald Hingley observes [in *A New Life of Anton Chekhov,* 1976] that his allegiance to medicine "reinforced his pragmatical, down-to-earth view of life," helping to keep him from reaching "conclusions based on combined instinct and ignorance" and to remain "scrupulous in his respect for evidence throughout his writing career." Scientific objectivity was accompanied in Chekhov by abundant compassion and ready humour but was not modified by religion, for Chekhov was a non-believer. As a pragmatist he rejected the Slavophiles' devotion to autocracy, church, and peasantry seen as noble expressions of the essence of Russia as firmly as he rejected Tolstoy's contempt for medical science and absolute commitment to the Sermon on the Mount. "I have peasant blood flowing in my veins," he wrote, "and I'm not the one to be impressed with peasant virtues. I acquired my belief in progress when still a child . . . Prudence and justice tell me there is more love for mankind in electricity and steam than in chastity and abstention from meat." Beverly Hahn observes [in *Chekhov: A Study of the Major Stories and Plays,* 1977] that "Chekhov's work belongs to that European tradition of humanist literature, classical in spirit and often centring in comic modes of perception, which links Pope and Swift with Jane Austen, Henry James and James Joyce."

Ruth Prawer Jhabvala was born in Germany, educated in England, and for twenty-four years domiciled in India, where her first published fiction and most of her subsequent work are set. Her first three novels—***To Whom She Will*** (1955; U.S. title: ***Amrita*** [1956]), ***The Nature of Passion*** (1956), and ***Esmond in India*** (1958)—focus on courtship, marriage, and social status and expose their characters' pretensions and unreasonableness in ways that make comparison with Jane Austen easy and natural. The aspect of Indian civilization furthest removed from the rational empiricist outlook, however, is the country's rich religious life, with its artistic, philosophical, and devotional components. In recent years certain lightweight gurus, very different from the great figures of Hindu philosophy and holiness, have attracted numerous Western disciples, and since the mid-sixties scathing portraits of such men have enriched Mrs. Jhabvala's works along with a comic and pitiable parade of their gullible European and American disciples.

The figure of the swami first appears prominently in her fourth novel, *The Householder* (1960), where he has only Indian disciples and is neither lauded nor damned. At one time, Mrs. Jhabvala recalled in a lecture,

> I wanted to believe in such a man too. Whenever opportunity came to visit a swami, I did so. I loved to think I was near someone holy, within the range of such wonderful vibrations. (**"Disinheritance"**)

In *The Householder* there is a hint that for all his good will the swami may be ineffective in a harsh world: "With the swami," thinks the downtrodden hero at a time of stress, "there would be an escape, for however brief a time, from his sense of the world's oppression." (Similarly the swami glimpsed in *Esmond in India* would talk comfortingly "in the abstract, in large philosophical terms," but could give little help with specific problems.) In *The Householder* it is not, however, the swami who is mocked but English-speaking ladies and a German youth who are grotesquely naïve in their search for an Indian guru.

Mrs. Jhabvala's fifth novel, *Get Ready for Battle* (1962), shows that her attitude is beginning to change. A friend of the hero suggests that female devotees sometimes unconsciously fall in love with the younger swamis, but the book implies that a number of these teachers have an influence for good: the only upper-class character who associates with them is also the only one who has genuine compassion for the miserable shanty-dwellers. Yasmine Gooneratne, Jhabvala's foremost critic, considers that both *The Householder* and *Get Ready for Battle* portray swamis favourably. In the sixth novel, *A Backward Place* (1965), there is a passing reference to two fraudulent men of this class—one claims that God, feeling a sudden craving, steals sweets through him—and by 1966, when, in the short story **"A Spiritual Call,"** she paints her second portrait of a swami, she is unambiguously hostile to him. The guru in this story exploits his young English disciple Daphne as an unpaid literary secretary and editor to help him shape his trite and incoherent thoughts for international marketing. Called to consult with him at night while his other followers sleep, Daphne observes him eat with gusto and, as the light falls on his face, she sees for the first time "something disagreeable" on his "short, blunt, and common" features—something which gives way to his usual "wise, calm, and beautiful" expression when he raises his head back into the shadows. This swami, who loves to travel and has plans for an ashram with air-conditioned rooms, is as grotesque as Molière's Tartuffe, with his hair shirt and his valet. Daphne—the author especially regrets this—surrenders to him her rational, university-trained mind, and only slowly and incompletely realizes that she became a disciple because she fell in love with him.

When Mrs. Jhabvala returns to the subject of the self-seeking guru five years later in her story **"An Experience of India"** (1971), she describes a large, robust swami of singularly unspiritual appearance who reaches a new level of viciousness, for he forces himself sexually on a woman disciple in what is almost a rape. Elements of **"A Spiritual Call"** and **"An Experience of India"** are much further developed in the subtle and complex novel *A New Dominion* (1972; U.S. title: *Travelers*). This book tells the story of Lee, an American girl deceived by a swami; of Raymond, an English visitor, and Gopi, the Indian youth with whom he falls in love; and of Asha, an Indian princess who seduces Gopi to console herself for the onset of middle age. The novel is divided into short sections, some narrated by the author in the third person, others written in the first person and ascribed to Lee or Raymond.

Jhabvala makes it clear that Lee's swami, a hypocrite who enjoys meat and alcohol, is driven primarily by a craving for power. To a Hindu, his teachings, though good and true, are commonplace—Gopi, who respects religion despite his low moral standards, does not have to read through the man's pamphlets, for he knows what is in them. Combining characteristics of his forerunners in the short stories, the swami intends to travel widely, plans an air-conditioned ashram, uses a young girl to help him write a book, subdues his disciples with his hypnotic eyes, and, in an horrendous scene, rapes Lee. He seeks to obliterate the personal identities of his followers, and in his lust to dominate causes the death of Lee's friend Margaret by manoeuvring her into rejecting modern medical treatment for her hepatitis. When Lee, who is probably, as Asha suggests, in love with him, continues to assert herself—at first, for example, she cannot bring herself to touch his feet—he breaks her spirit by conspicuously ignoring her and ultimately rapes her while yelling loathsome insults. Though she flees the ashram, he feels that he can draw her back—and then, he assures a mutual friend, "I will take her far, very far, right to the end if need be—and this time, Raymond, this time there will be no running away." Yet the swami is such a skilful actor that Raymond, even when he knows why Lee fled, continues to enjoy his company—"sometimes," the author observes, "in spite of himself."

The swami, whose capacity for evil recalls Rasputin's, perverts the traditional doctrine that by obliterating the ego a person can make way for the emergence of the soul or divine self in a mystical rebirth. This belief is Western as well as Eastern: *The Book of Privy Counselling,* a fourteenth-century English treatise, speaks of the soul's "noughting of it-self," and when Blake in his later prophetic books advocates "self-annihilation" he is employing a Christian term of respectable antiquity. The principle was expressed within an institutional framework in the monastic vows of poverty, chastity, and obedience. The Western disciples in *A New Dominion,* however, encounter a crude form of this doctrine, for while the aspirant must renounce worldly self-assertion and attachment to the pleasures of the senses, he is not required to surrender all judgement and discrimination. When the nineteenth-century teacher Sri Ramakrishna found that his disciple Jogindra had purchased a cracked vessel, he exclaimed, "What—you bought a pot and didn't examine it first? . . . Just because you're a devotee, that's no reason to be a fool." When Jogindra spied on him at night, afraid that he was going to his wife (as an ascetic, Ramakrishna did not consummate his marriage), he commended the young man saying, ". . . before you accept anyone as your guru, you should watch him by day and by night" [in Christopher Isherwood, *Ramakrishna and His Disciples,* 1965]. But Lee and her friends come to India without any knowledge of mystical traditions and are dazzled by unfamiliar ideas and romantic swamis that they are ill-equipped to judge.

---

**Jhabvala does not explicitly mention the ignorance of the Western disciples she portrays, probably because she not only deplores swamis but distrusts the mystical doctrine itself in spite of her desire that holy men might really exist.**

*—H. Summerfield*

---

Jhabvala does not explicitly mention the ignorance of the Western disciples she portrays, probably because she not only deplores swamis but distrusts the mystical doctrine itself in spite of her desire that holy men might really exist. Characters as different as Raymond and Lee recoil from the swami's cruel attempt to obliterate the egos of his disciples. For all his enjoyment of the swami's company, Raymond cannot accept his failure to acknowledge that his disciple Evie is present with them. When Raymond offered her a beverage,

> she put up one frail hand as if to say please don't bother about me. I'm not here, or if I am, I am as nothing. But—unlike Swamiji, who did so without effort—Raymond could not regard her as nothing . . .

Lee, finding herself beside two fellow disciples one of whom is in a coma and the other meditating, discovers that it is "like being with two people who were not there," and when she describes the pain and degradation of being raped by the swami she tells how "I didn't feel as if I were a person any more . . . *He* was the only person there." The author's view becomes particularly clear when Raymond tempts Lee to disclose the misery that engulfs her on the ashram while her guru ignores her: "his voice," she realized, "was also full of concern—*personal* concern—caring for me. At that moment I was ready to open my heart."

As one counterweight to the contemplative life of the fraudulent swami, Jhabvala describes the good works of the elderly English missionary Miss Charlotte, who busies herself with the sick and the aged. She paints an attractive picture of Miss Charlotte, but, although she herself is Jewish, she does not raise the question of whether missionaries are detaching non-Christians from their spiritual and cultural heritage. Miss Charlotte, however, is not narrow-minded: her favourite authors are the unbelievers George Eliot and Thomas Hardy, and she is touched by celebrations commemorating the Moslem saint Salim Chisthi.

Ruth Prawer Jhabvala's writings show that she would in general agree with George Orwell's humanist rejection of Mahatma Gandhi's values: according to Orwell, "our job is to make life worth living on this earth, which is the only earth we have," and "sainthood . . . is a thing that human beings must avoid." Nevertheless, when Jhabvala explained how she had once delighted in swamis but had now come to loathe them, she admitted that she was "at the same time always wishing: if only it could be. . . ." She observed young women like Evie:

> they got jaundice and became very pale and worn away physically and as people, in their personalities. They had given up their personalities (as tough, thinking, fighting European or, more often, American girls). Their eyes and thoughts and souls were only for their guru. I deplored them . . . I laughed at, even despised, them; but also envied them—for thinking they had found, or maybe—who am I to judge? —they had found, what I had longed to find and never could and I guess never would now. (**"Disinheritance"**)

Ruth Prawer Jhabvala's hope that "it could be"—that "a man so good he was holy" (**"Disinheritance"**) might exist—seems not to have completely died. Her later work contains portraits of three women who are reputed to be holy and whose remarkable qualities are not easily explained. The first is a shrivelled old woman whose ecstatic storytelling, singing, and dancing, which are certainly innocent and perhaps inspired, lead the jaded American heroine of **"An Experience of India"** to seek a teacher who can bring her to what this person has found. The old woman is holy in other people's eyes, not her own. The second such figure of wisdom—Banubai in *A New Dominion*—is small, old, toothless, wrinkled, and joyful, like her forerunner in the short story, and she is described as "a prophetess" in the list of characters which introduces the novel. Gooneratne sees Banubai as a bogus saint, but she does not deserve this condemnation. She is not, indeed, perfect—none of this novelist's characters are: she is fond of sweets and handsome men, she considers that Raymond is unable to love, she exaggerates the perniciousness of Western materialism, and she claims—clearly in contradiction to the author's views—that suffering is good when it draws people's attention from this world to the next. Superficially, indeed, Banubai has some resemblance to the swami: in particular, Lee and Raymond feel that both of them have eyes that gaze into people's very thoughts. Banubai, however, not only has exceptional insight into her visitors' minds but uses it to give them what help she can. When Lee, having fled the swami, comes to her, she is glad of the girl's escape from an evil master but sees that her emotions are not detached from him. With comparable insight, she recognizes that the homosexual Raymond has corrupted Gopi, luring him away from his widowed mother and sisters and his college studies into a life of unfamiliar luxury and smoothing the way for the rich and aging Asha to make him her lover or kept man. For a time Raymond even encourages their relationship, though when Gopi's family want to arrange his marriage he tries in vain to undo the mischief that he has done. Banubai, for her part, attempts to transmute Asha's passion into maternal love, but her apparent success proves only temporary. Trying to redeem Asha, too, she has to struggle against the latter's old woman-servant Bulbul, who is descended from a long line of unmarried singing and dancing girls and whose delight it is to minister to her mistress's illicit pleasures.

In portraying Banubai, Jhabvala tries to give as rational an explanation of her powers as possible: "she had always," says the author herself,

> been an unusual person with unusual gifts. She could look deep into other people's personalities, and it enabled her to have so immediate an intuition of what activated them that it was often possible for her to tell them something about their past and make a guess at their future. She gained quite a reputation that way, and people began to come to her for guidance. . . .
>
> . . . She even had a number of sophisticated, highly westernized visitors, and if most of them came in the first place to see her as a curiosity, some of them were truly impressed by her powers.

We are given an opportunity to see how rational Banubai's counselling can be when a family distraught at the mysterious disappearance of one of its members comes to her for help. She astutely describes just the thoughts and feelings which would afflict the near relatives of a missing person, and gives them the best advice that she can offer fellow believers: whatever happens will be God's will, and they must submit. Asha notices that they depart "somewhat lightened" (though this does not happen with all of Banubai's troubled visitors), and Banubai is left exhausted by her effort to give comfort. In spite of the predominating rational element in such counselling, there is also a vein of strangeness, even of mystery in Banubai's proceedings. As long as Gopi visits her, she dotes on him, caresses him affectionately, and claims that he has been her son in many previous lives; as soon as she hears of his betrothal, she seems to detach her emotions from him—when the news comes, it hardly causes a pause in her joyful singing to Lord Krishna. Indeed, as the author herself says, "Banubai was an extraordinary woman".

The narrator of Mrs. Jhabvala's next novel, *Heat and Dust* (1975), is a contemporary young woman who tells how she comes to India to investigate the experience of her grandfather's first wife, Olivia. Half a century before, Olivia deserted her husband for a minor Muslim prince. Though this novel contains less humour than the earlier books, it portrays a bizarre English youth who, under the name Chidananda, has become an initiated Hindu sadhu or holy man—a sadhu with a saffron robe, a shaven head, a Midlands accent, and a voracious appetite for food and sex. What most disturbs the narrator—and here she seems to be the author's mouthpiece—is his flight from reason: his chanting of his mantra, she complains,

> seems somehow so *mindless* that it drives me crazy. It is as if all reason and common sense are being drained out of the air.

As Lee's swami is contrasted with Banubai, Chidananda is contrasted with a coarse, elderly peasant widow known as Maji and regarded by others as a holy woman. The sober-minded narrator admits

it always seems to me that she has powers that others don't. Once I had a headache and she put her hand on my forehead and I can't describe the strange sensations transmitted to me.

The narrator becomes pregnant by a married Indian, and Maji massages her, ostensibly to cause an abortion. The massage, however, seems to infuse a radiance into her that makes her instantly decide to keep the child. The author clearly respects Maji, for she is the only person the narrator can find to tend to a destitute and dying beggarwoman. Chidananda, by contrast, remains indifferent to the agony of a young wife being burned with red-hot irons as a cure for fits. Maji recommends a pilgrimage as a better form of therapy—and as a beneficial activity for Chidananda. Both go, and while we are not told whether the wife is cured, Chidananda sloughs off his assumed identity and reverts to Christianity. Like Banubai, Maji combines strange insights with good sense.

In her most recent novel, *In Search of Love and Beauty* (1983), Mrs. Jhabvala turns from the aberrations of Indians and their Western visitors to the domestic follies of Americans. The North American counterpart of her swamis is the gluttonous, philandering Leo Kellerman, who shares their knack of making each member of a group feel that he is looking into his or her soul as well as their skill in attracting wealthy female admirers and their ambition to found an institution with many branches. He bases his community—the Academy of Potential Development—on a blend of theatre, psychiatry, and Eastern religion, but his only true gift is an exceptional insight into people. Despite Leo's affinity with the swamis, the book contains no counterpart to the prophetesses. The one major character who is not culpably self-centred is the plain, ungifted but exceptionally compassionate Natasha. She is self-sacrificing, and unacquisitive, cares deeply about people without being possessive, and has the good sense not to believe in Leo's work. Her unsatisfied longing for a settled and traditional way of life underlines the author's penetrating satire on the fads and philandering of contemporary Americans; similarly Leo's posturings reflect her uneasiness about the cultivation of prolonged introspection—an uneasiness that may spring from what she refers to in **"Myself in India"** as her "deplorable tendency to constant self-analysis" (*How I Became*).

To a considerable extent, Ruth Prawer Jhabvala identifies the outlook she regards as non-European with the predominance of emotion over reason, an imbalance which she associates with a turning away from reality and a passive acceptance of evil and suffering. As she tells us in **"Myself in India,"** she loves India's devotional songs, which can make her temporarily feel that everything that distresses her "is of no importance at all because all that matters is this promise of eternal bliss," but she asks "whether religion is such a potent force in India because life is so terrible, or . . . is life so terrible because, with the eyes of the spirit turned elsewhere, there is no incentive to improve its quality?" (*How I Became*). In *A New Dominion,* she can treat the theme lightly through the innocently naïve founder of the University of Universal Synthesis, who wishes to bring together scholars from the rational West and the feeling East "to educate the mind in the language of the heart and the heart in the language of the mind." Jhabvala probably regards this ideal as unattainable and agrees—as she partly confirms in an interview—with Major Minnies in *Heat and Dust,* who believes that the Western mind should guard itself against becoming Indian. A British political officer so devoted to India that he spends his retirement there after independence, Minnies holds that a Westerner who loves that country should love her "with a virile, measured, *European* feeling," and that "One should never . . . become softened (like Indians) by an excess of feeling"—no doubt the kind of feeling that allows the dishonest businessman in **"How I Became a Holy Mother"** (1976) to be filled with rapture by a holy man's blessing (*How I Became*) or Chidananda to ignore the tortured wife's agony. A particularly striking example of such an aberration occurs in *A New Dominion,* where the disciple Evie, her face suffused with a look "so gentle, so good, so full of kindness for all created beings," ignores the needs of the mortally sick Margaret to gaze with adoration on the swami, who has recently insisted that an injured dog must be left to howl in anguish until it died. Yet in *Heat and Dust* the charitable Maji passes through religious trances without moral injury, perhaps even with advantage, suggesting that Mrs. Jhabvala, despite profound misgivings, is not prepared to condemn categorically all mystical practices and their accompanying emotions.

The predominance of feeling over reason is a common object of Jane Austen's satire. In *Pride and Prejudice,* Elizabeth Bennet observes that her sister Jane, who is rapidly falling in love with a new acquaintance, "cannot even be certain of the degree of her own regard, nor of its reasonableness." Subsequently Elizabeth's own experience confirms the superiority of rational love, which grows slowly and is based on esteem, over the love which "is so often described as arising on a first interview with its object, and even before two words have been exchanged." It is a lesson that Jhabvala's Gulab, an Indian girl who does not "form decisions" but follows "her instinct" and who impetuously marries an entirely unsuitable Englishman—"an unredeemable cad and sadist," Haydn Moore Williams calls him—badly needs to learn (*Esmond in India*). Similar irrational emotions drive Jhabvala's spiritual seekers: the German youth in *The Householder* comes to India because he has seen a holy man in a dream, and Daphne in **"A Spiritual Call"**—like the Countess in **"How I Became a Holy Mother"**—conceives an instantaneous devotion to a swami she meets in the West. Lee's experience, though not so sudden, is of a comparable nature; her and her companions' disastrous misjudgement of their guru has a comic counterpart in Jane Austen in Catherine Morland's misjudgement of General Tilney under the influence of Gothic novels—novels that have so excited her that an invitation to a residence with the romantic name of Northanger Abbey can work up her emotions "to the highest point of extasy." Nevertheless, as has been shown, Austen's devotion to rationality does not prevent her from being a pious Christian and from believing that feeling as well as reason has a place in religion.

Chekhov, too, exposes delusions that spring from limitations of character, but the quality that Jhabvala most obviously shares with him is a combination of insight into the nuances of joy and sorrow with the humour of a detached observer, a combination that is responsible for the characteristic Chekhovian atmosphere. Thus the young girl Shakuntala in *Esmond in India,* with her partly assumed sensibility and her imaginary idealism, has a likeness to the less self-conscious Irina in Chekhov's play *Three Sisters,* and such Jhabvala characters as the idle, effeminate young husband of **"The Interview"** (1957), the elderly widow of **"The Man with the Dog"** (1966) with her Dutch lover, and the neglected wife of **"Rose Petals"** (1971) have a notably Chekhovian flavour. That Chekhov's values resemble Jhabvala's can be seen especially clearly in one of his most famous stories—"Ward Number 6." As Jhabvala's devotees ignore the suffering around them in their pursuit of personal holiness, so Chekhov's provincial physician, Dr. Ragin, asks himself

> why pain *should* be relieved. Firstly, suffering is said to bring man nearer to perfection. And, secondly, if mankind should really learn to relieve its sufferings with pills and drops it would completely turn its back on religion and philosophy which have hitherto furnished a bulwark against all manner of ills, and have even brought happiness too.

In defiance of reality, Ragin maintains that despite the discoveries of modern medicine

> the essence of things has not changed a bit, sickness and mortality still remain. . . . between the best Viennese clinic and my hospital there is no real difference at all

and that

> You can find consolation inside yourself in any surroundings. . . . Diogenes lived in a barrel, but was happier than all the emperors of this world.

Not until he is forcibly confined in his own mental ward does he recognize the truth of his patient Gromov's argument that it is only because his own life has been so comfortable that he has been able to hold such a theory. Gromov, like the author, judges theories on the basis of experience and reason, but Chekhov is no blinkered materialist. In his story "On Official Business" the coroner Lyzhin—a character who, as Ronald Hingley notes [in *Oxford Chekhov, IX: Stories 1898-1904,* 1975], serves as a spokesman for Chekhov—comes to perceive all human beings as part of the one entity which is life, "a single miraculous and rational organism," so that a prosperous person cannot without guilt condone the suffering of a single one of the masses whose poverty sustains the rich. However, it is only through "the gift of penetrating life's essence," a gift transcending reason, that Lyzhin comes to see the rational essence of human life, and his mode of perception is comparable to those of Banubai and Maji.

Superficially, Jhabvala resembles Austen in her witty portrayal of snobbery and self-deception, and Chekhov in her delicate, humorous evocations of mood and feeling. On a deeper level, she shares Austen's and Chekhov's conviction that the dictates of reason and experience should prevail over emotion and provide a guard against irrationality. Jhabvala regards submission to a guru as a form of extreme emotionalism accompanied by indifference to others' suffering and by a failure of the respect due to the uniqueness of each individual. Even Banubai, Asha notices, is "like the sun and wind that play on all alike" (*A New Dominion*). Most of the swamis, in addition to promulgating a false theory, are the very opposite of the ego-free persons they pretend to be. But although in **"Myself in India"** Jhabvala writes sadly of "ashrams full of little old half-starved widows who skip and dance about, . . . giggle and play hide and seek because they are Krishna's milkmaids" (*How I Became*), her fiction contains portraits of three very different aged female devotees. Her characterization of the Krishna-worshipper in **"An Experience of India,"** of Banubai, and of Maji shows that Ruth Prawer Jhabvala, like Chekhov, is open to the possibility that there may be non-rational, non-sensory modes of perception which can contribute to the betterment of human life.

---

**How could I be considered an Indian writer? I'm not, am I? There's no getting away from that fact. I write differently from Indian writers because my birth, background, ancestry, and traditions are different. If I must be considered anything, then let it be as one of those European writers who have written about India.**

***—Ruth Prawer Jhabvala, in an interview with Ramlal Agarwal, in* Quest, *September/October, 1994.***

---

## Ruth Prawer Jhabvala with Michael McDonough (interview date 1986)

SOURCE: An interview with Ruth Prawer Jhabvala, in *San Francisco Review of Books,* Vol. 11, No. 4, Spring, 1987, pp. 5-6.

[*In the following interview, which was conducted in New York in 1986, Jhabvala discusses her screenplays and her novel* In Search of Love and Beauty, *which she considers her first American novel, having written it after moving to New York City.*]

Ruth Prawer Jhabvala was born to Jewish parents in Cologne, Germany on May 7, 1927. Her father, Marcus Prawer, came to Germany to escape military conscription in Poland; he met and married Eleanor (Cohn) Prawer in Cologne. Ruth Prawer's grandfather was the cantor of the largest synagogue in that city and prided himself on his friendship with Christian pastors; her grandmother studied at the Berlin Conservatory of Music and played the piano. Her family identified with Germany and celebrated all national, civic and Jewish festivals and holidays. She was raised in this solid, well-integrated, civilized atmo-

sphere, surrounded by life-loving aunts and uncles, and the fragrance of her grandmother's tea cakes.

Ruth Prawer started school when Hitler came to power in 1933; then, one by one, all her relatives emigrated—to France, Holland, Palestine, and America. In April 1939, she and her immediate family became refugees and moved to England. She studied at Stoke Park Elementary School, Coventry; Hendon County School; and Queen Mary College, London University, where she majored in English literature and earned her Master's degree in 1951. She married the Parsi architect CSH Jhabvala that same year and moved with him to Delhi, India. While there, Mrs. Jhabvala wrote eight novels and four volumes of short stories.

American film director James Ivory and Indian producer Ismail Merchant met Ruth Jhabvala in Delhi in 1962 and asked her to script their version of her novel *The Householder.* Their next work, *Shakespeare Wallah* (1965), was based on her original screenplay. Other Jhabvala-scripted films followed, the most popular being *Heat And Dust* (1983), and, most recently E.M. Forster's *A Room With A View.* Her adaptations of Henry James' include *The Europeans* (1979) and *The Bostonians* (1984).

Ruth Jhabvala left India and came to live in New York City in 1976. Her ninth novel, *In Search Of Love And Beauty* appeared in 1983. Mrs. Jhabvala winters in Delhi where her husband runs an architectural firm and teaches; her brother Siegbert Salomon is professor of German literature at Oxford; her three daughters are grown and have independent careers.

In March of this year, Ruth Prawer Jhabvala won an Academy Award for screenwriting. The following conversation took place in 1986 at Mrs. Jhabvala's upper East Side apartment.

[*McDonough*]: *Your writing is not novelistic in the sense that most stories simply put up the machinery of setting; your characters seem more intuitively related to the setting—*

[Jhabvala]: I'd like it to be that way. I'm not writing a literary exercise. If something doesn't matter, if it isn't real, then I want nothing to do with it. I'm not interested in anything made up.

*But then the stories themselves, though they feel real, don't appear to be autobiographical.*

No, they're not autobiographical, but on the other hand I like to make the situation personally authentic, as though it could have happened to me, if my responses had been those of the character in the story, like a sort of vicarious living, I suppose. I want it to be almost like nonfiction, fake biographical, fake autobiographical, but on the other hand I also want it to have form and a kind of beauty.

*Intuitive structure seems important in your work. The scenes and episodes flow into each other as in* **Heat And Dust** (1975), *though my first experience was with* **Travelers** (1973), *where you had these little panel-like stories which seemed to interrupt and form a larger picture at the same* *time, yet you weren't aware of the structure except that it fit and was natural.*

All this is, as you say, intuitive, because I can't think it out, if it doesn't happen it doesn't happen—I set up the situation and follow along slowly and see what happens.

*How did* **Travelers** *start?*

**Travelers** was at a time when I started meeting girls who were traveling all over India in buses and trains, everything that I must say that I myself have not done. I used to look at them quite enviously for traveling this way in India which is a difficult place that they had chosen to travel in.

*Did you meet them in passing or were they introduced to you?*

They were introduced to me. They were friends of friends—someone would say, "when you're in Delhi you must look for Ruth," so they would write me, and I was eager to meet them. And then at one point I lived next door to one of those American programs that bring people to India for a year and that was very interesting and had a lot to do with it. One of those girls got involved with some guru and there was a sort of secret report that I managed to have a look at which concerned this girl and how she got involved with this guru and got very sick, and then her family tried to get her back, and then they tried to hush it up, and that spurred me on and crystallized everything that I saw happening there in the mid-to-late '60s.

*The theme of search on a very basic level seems to be a common thread in your work.*

Yes, that started off quite unconsciously but now it's more conscious. Usually it's a search for something higher and better. There are so many frauds who really want to take advantage of this really rather noble streak, I mean there were these girls who had come to India and were very open and wanted to make themselves better and then there were those frauds who took the most horrible advantage of them in every way. I've seen that happen again and again, not only in India but everywhere. So many people seem to get trapped by the ignoble. So that's becoming a quite conscious theme also connected, I suppose, to obsessive passions for unworthy characters. I see something noble and beautiful in that search that's dragged down to a workaday level.

*People seem to be looking for something beyond the material world, especially Americans.*

I don't think Americans are particularly materialistic, I mean look how they came here in search of religious freedom. That sort of thing always seems to be with them, but in the meantime they made so much money that the society became materialistic. There seems to be this split between the altruistic soul and the desire to increase their wealth.

*This search becomes explicit in* **In Search of Love and Beauty** *(1983) in which a fraudulent guru who has been donning and shedding guises for years uses his charm to start a spiritual community.*

I think the guru there is more worked-out and interesting than the one in **Travelers.**

*He's had more transformations within the world than Swamiji—*

transforming himself into what a particular generation wants.

*In* **Heat** *Anne is looking for her great-aunt Olivia—*

and also "looking for herself," as people do nowadays or did then.

*I read the character as trying to escape a materialistic world—*

but most people come to India not only to escape a materialistic world but their boring English background too.

*The characters in your novels seem both physically and socially displaced.*

The European characters do: that's why they came to India in the first place.

*There isn't that mystical tradition in Europe and America that there is in India with all the religions, the sense of rebirth and transformation, because things are in a way more set.*

That's part of the boringness—religions are set because so many of them are no longer alive and people can no longer find the living fountain, they're so sealed up that they can't get anything out of them. I'm writing a new novel which is concerned with search more than ever; the working title is **Three Continents**: it's about two 19-year-old American twins who are very rich heirs in search of something nobler and higher and who get caught up in a world political movement which is also partly financed by smuggling drugs, paintings and art objects.

*Events in your writings are framed and presented so clearly that the reader can discern how the characters relate to one another.*

I go along completely ignorant of what's going to happen.

*Do you re-write much?*

I have to polish, and if a thing isn't working well I feel it's a kind of warning to stop and try something else, but I can't change the direction or the meaning except on the more superficial stylistic level of how to present the scene such as maybe someone else should be talking here. But on the deepest level you can't force a meaning into or out of a story or force a character into something that they're not naturally growing into. The same with a situation—if it's not developing along then, too bad. For one successful story you have to write a lot that don't work.

*Are you a strict critic of your work?*

I'm a bad judge and can't tell for a long time—I have to distance myself—but when the writing's really going well then I know.

*Does a story ever write itself in the sense that something you've thrown away comes back and finally happens?*

Something I've thrown away sometimes comes back in a different form as if it had been a practice work.

*Some of the stories in* **Out Of India** *seem to be studies for your novels.*

**Heat** was almost a companion piece to the film **Autobiography Of A Princess**—both had the same sort of themes—and all the guru stories went finally into **Travellers; How I Became A Holy Mother** (1976) was after that but I've been going back again and again.

*How did you go about adapting* **Heat** *with James Ivory?*

I had to do something I hate doing—I had to re-read the book which was published in '75; and in '81 or '82 I wrote the script. So I re-read the book and did what I always do—I put the book aside and tried to find a completely new form to present the story—of Anne coming to see the only survivor. I had to find a way to tell the two-level story—that was the major problem. And the novel itself was written in a very strange way. It wasn't laid-out sequentially because I wrote big chunks of 1923 and big chunks of present time and then afterwards I cut it all up and thought what scenes of present and past would best set each other off, complement or contrast with each other, so I juxtaposed them—edited them in relation to each other—more like a film. I didn't do that much juggling in **In Search.**

*That's a sort of Central European-American novel. Did you feel you were getting back in touch with your roots with that?*

Absolutely. New York would have been the place you'd logically come to from Europe, so when I came here it was what should have happened in 1939. The first time I came to New York was in 1966 when I was here for ten days and I liked it because it was like a cosmopolitan European city, so when the question came of leaving India I came here. I was also keen to write something not about India, something closer to my own background and this was the background I could write about so that's how **In Search** came about; I consider it my first American novel.

*It's remarkable.*

I'm glad you liked it because all that time I was writing in India no one was taking any notice. The reviews of **In Search** said my Indian work was better and I should go back and write about that and this after twenty years when nobody cared a damn about what I was writing in India. My first American thing was my script about the New York dancehall, Roseland, for the film with the same name which we did in 1977, and then there was **The Europeans** in 1979.

*How did that come about?*

I always thought that Henry James would be good for James Ivory because they had a lot of things in common—the way James viewed the world, and the characters he admired was a lot like Jim himself—so I thought they ought to get together. But the film we really wanted to make was *The Portrait Of A Lady* though that would be very expensive whereas **The Europeans** was much simpler—a smaller cast of characters, more restricted American locations,

and easier to get financing for. Then **The Bostonians** (1984) was actually started by WGBH who wanted to do a whole series on the James family and one American-set feature film but the funding for our part of the project fell through so we got our own funding for **The Bostonians.**

*Ivory was quoted in* The New York Times *as saying that your new project,* **Three Continents,** *would be similar to* Portrait.

There's something very peculiar about that. Somebody said he would finance a film for us and he said what do you want to do and we vaguely had an idea about a modern *Portrait*—what would a modern American lady do—she wouldn't go to Europe but maybe to India on a quest in search of herself, but somehow I had the idea of nineteen-year-old twins, and so the man said OK, go ahead, but Jim said why don't you think of it as a novel and work it out in detail before you present the finished script. So I worked it out into a novel which moves from America to England to India and I'm so glad to have written what I suppose is my second American novel which is a sort of stepchild to my other work. Now after all these years the Indian novels are getting more attention, but **In Search Of Love And Beauty,** the new path I've turned onto seems not to have been recognized so I suppose it just does take twenty years for the work to be known and then it's there and you go on to something else. I think the film **Roseland** and some stories I wrote then were the beginning of a move away from India, but I hesitate to call these in any way American novels because I'm not an American though America's a mixture, as I am.

**Bruce Bawer   (essay date December 1987)**

SOURCE: "Passage to India: The Career of Ruth Prawer Jhabvala," in *The New Criterion,* Vol. VI, No. 4, December, 1987, pp. 5-19.

[*Bawer is an American literary critic. In the following essay, he analyzes several of Jhabvala's novels, including* The Householder, Travelers, *and* Heat and Dust, *commending her more recent works for including American characters, while criticizing them for their preoccupation with Westerners who try to become Indians.*]

Probably most Americans who recognize the name of Ruth Prawer Jhabvala know her mainly as a screenwriter, one third of the celebrated international movie-making team whose other members are the Indian producer Ismail Merchant and the American director James Ivory. In this country, at least, Jhabvala and her partners are known almost exclusively for three recent films that were based upon major modern novels: **The Europeans** (1978) and **The Bostonians** (1984) both derived from works by Henry James, and **A Room with a View** was an adaptation of one of E.M. Forster's less familiar novels. Though many reviewers carped about the casting and the slow pace (among other things) of the first two films, even the harshest critics almost invariably praised the filmmakers for their seriousness, for their wonderful attention to period detail, and for their manifest effort to be as faithful as possible not only to the word of the text but to James's tone and sensibility. The word "literate" was widely invoked—

and, at a time when films often seem to be more illiterate than ever, the literateness of the Ivory-Merchant-Jhabvala productions was more than enough to inspire fervent expectations, on the part of many critics who were unhappy with the two James adaptations, that in time a truly magnificent film would be forthcoming from the team. These expectations, in most instances, seem to have been satisfied with the release of *A Room with a View.* This splendid film received better notices than either of its two immediate predecessors; it was nominated for the Academy Award for best picture and earned Jhabvala the award for best screenplay adaptation. When she appeared on the awards telecast last spring to accept her statuette, it was doubtless the first time most Americans had heard her name.

Despite her relative obscurity in this country, however, Jhabvala's writing career has been a long and distinguished one. Her motion-picture partnership with Ivory and Merchant dates back to the early Sixties; prior to the films I have mentioned, the team collaborated on a number of productions, none of which was shown widely in the United States. In addition, Jhabvala has written ten novels—the most celebrated of them being the Booker Prize-winning *Heat and Dust*—and several collections of short stories. Most of these books, if obtainable at all in this country, have hitherto been available only in British editions; but, largely as a result (one assumes) of the success of *A Room with a View,* that situation has lately begun to change. Both *Heat and Dust* and the 1973 novel *Travelers,* as well as the short-story collection *Out of India,* have recently been issued by the Fireside division of Simon and Schuster in handsome, well-distributed paperback editions. Alongside them on the bookstore shelves is Jhabvala's newly published novel, *Three Continents.* As if this were not enough compensation for years of stateside neglect, during the months of September and October the Asia Society in New York held screenings of a number of Ivory-Merchant films—six of them scripted by Jhabvala—as part of a twenty-fifth anniversary tribute to the team. Though she has been writing fiction and movies for more than a quarter of a century, then, it is not much of an exaggeration to say that Jhabvala is only now being introduced to a broad American public. There could hardly be a more appropriate occasion to examine some of the highlights of this most interesting—and, on these shores, largely neglected—career.

Probably one important reason for America's neglect of Jhabvala's novels is that most of them—as well as the majority of her pre-Henry James screenplays—are set in the country where she has lived, whether full- or part-time, for decades: India. Though she still spends several months of the year on the subcontinent, her principal residence is currently in New York. The problematical question, however, is whether Jhabvala herself—born in Germany of Polish parents, and educated in England—can be considered Indian. Her own answer to this question, given in an essay entitled **"Myself in India"** (which serves as the introduction to her recent story collection *Out of India*), is no. "I have lived in India for most of my adult life," she declares at the beginning of the essay. "My husband is Indian and so are my children. I am not, and less so every

year." India, she goes on to say, is a country that one either loves or hates; it offers "a special problem of adjustment for the sort of people who come today, who tend to be liberal in outlook and have been educated to be sensitive and receptive to other cultures. But it is not always easy to be sensitive and receptive to India: there comes a point where you have to close up in order to protect yourself." Her reason for living in India, she tells us—and I quote this at length because I think it helps to explain some of the distinctive qualities of her fiction—is that

> my strongest human ties are here. If I hadn't married an Indian, I don't think I would ever have come here for I am not attracted—or used not to be attracted—to the things that usually bring people to India. I know I am the wrong type of person to live here. To stay and endure, one should have a mission and a cause, to be patient, cheerful, unselfish, strong. I am a central European with an English education and a deplorable tendency to constant self-analysis. I am irritable and have weak nerves.

She is not, in other words, the type who has come to this land of desperate poverty—a poverty of which she, in her very nice air-conditioned house, is nonetheless always vividly aware—to be of service as a doctor or social worker. "I often think," she writes, "that perhaps this is the only condition under which Europeans have any right to be here." (According to a recent article by Dinitia Smith in *New York* magazine, Jhabvala's reason for living part of the year in New York is that "by 1976, she had grown overwhelmed by the subcontinent.") If her fiction is predominantly about "modern, well-off, cultured Westernized Indians," it is because her way of adjusting to life in India is to do her best to ignore the backward and hungry multitudes (which she refers to continually as a "great animal" on whose back she rides). Yet she doesn't associate with many Westernized Indians, either, for she believes that their social lives are synthetic, their conversation empty ("Everything they say . . . is not prompted by anything they really feel strongly about but by what they think they ought to feel strongly about"), their perspective on India's poverty and backwardness thoroughly detached. They talk about India "as if it were some *other* place—as if it were a subject for debate—an abstract subject—and not a live animal actually moving under their feet." Her problem, then, is essentially one of cultural adaptation: "To live in India and be at peace, one must to a very considerable extent become Indian and adopt Indian attitudes, habits, beliefs, assume if possible an Indian personality. But how is this possible? Should one want to try to become something other than what one is?"

This question, in a sense, is at the center of Jhabvala's fiction. Many of the prominent characters in her novels and stories are either Indians who try to be Westerners, or Westerners who try to be Indians. Jhabvala's tone, when she writes about such people, invariably combines affection with irony—affection, because she knows that it is only human to be attracted to that which one is not, to long for that which one does not possess; irony, because she recognizes how delusory most such attractions are, how fruitless most such longings. Jhabvala is a humorist as well as a humanist: she laughs at man's moral and intellectual imperfections even as she laments his inability to transcend those imperfections. For she does perceive (it is the central perception of her fiction) that the human animal craves transcendence—transcendence of uncertainty, of mortality, of the banality of day-to-day life. Characteristically, Jhabvala sees this craving as both beautiful and foolish. Or, more precisely, she sees it as a beautiful longing that people—not knowing where they can go to find satiation—try to satisfy in foolish ways. In her novels, characters are always seeking, travelling, roaming the world in search of a *locus amenis,* making fools of themselves by reaching out for the impermanent, the inappropriate, the unnatural, the impossible.

The longing for transcendence often takes the form, in Jhabvala's work, of a passionate attachment (and *passion* is a word that she does not hesitate to use) to someone grand, exotic, forbidden, even evil—usually someone of a different race. In her novel *Esmond in India,* for instance, the sheltered young Indian woman Shakuntala is smitten with the haughty, married, extremely European Esmond; in *Heat and Dust* Olivia, the wife of a British officer, falls for the Nawab, a rich, shady local prince; and in *Three Continents* the naïve American girl Harriet adores the mendacious, mysterious Crishi. The narrator of *Heat and Dust* speaks of reaching "a higher plane of consciousness through the powers of sex."

Another form taken by the longing for transcendence is the reverence of movie stars and swamis. (Yes, movie stars and swamis.) Jhabvala recognizes that however different they may seem—the movie star an embodiment of modern Western popular culture at its trashiest, the swami a symbol of ancient Indian religion at its most sublime—they are really very closely related, in that they both represent for the common man a type of transcendence; if swamis (embodying as they do the mysteries of India) hold a special fascination for certain Westerners, so movie stars (embodying the affluence and glamour of the West) hold a special fascination for Indians. Nothing, by the way, is more characteristic of Jhabvala's unique vision and perspective than her recognition of such a bizarre cross-cultural affinity. Movie stars and swamis thus pop up frequently in her work. (One of her films—probably her most unsuccessful, in fact—was *The Guru,* a 1968 character portrait starring Michael York.) Though she pokes fun at both movie stars and swamis, however, she does not make them out to be thoroughgoing fools and rascals; in Jhabvala's fiction, even they have their moments of goodness and wisdom. This is one of the things that make Jhabvala special: she perceives that man is neither basically good nor basically evil, that neither pure materialism nor pure idealism—the struggle between which she often depicts—makes very much sense as a philosophy of life. She knows that we all have in us both good and evil, that we consist of both body and spirit; we are, in short, holy but imperfect creatures, and she writes about us with an empathy that stays well clear of bathos and a cynicism that only occasionally descends into bitterness.

Her career can be divided into two periods. Between 1955 and 1971 Jhabvala published six novels. Typical of these early books are *Esmond in India* and *The Householder,* in which Jhabvala is very much a novelist of manners in the tradition of Jane Austen, as well as a natural storyteller *à la* Chekhov. These novels also bring to mind the Indian novelist R. K. Narayan, though her characters are generally more well-to-do than his, and her novels more obviously aimed at a Western audience. Conventional in style and structure, they are strong on character development and social detail; they lie squarely in the realistic tradition of the English novel, and, among twentieth-century English novels, belong in the camp of Evelyn Waugh, Joyce Cary, and Kingsley Amis rather than with such foursquare modernists as Woolf and Conrad.

Take, for instance, her third novel, *Esmond in India* (1958), which is set in the years immediately following India's independence from Britain. The title notwithstanding, the character who is really most prominent in the novel is a young woman named Shakuntala, who has just earned her B.A. and returned home to New Delhi to live with her family. They are a wealthy clan who pride themselves on their Westernization: Shakuntala's father, Har Dayal, a Cambridge-educated government minister, spices his conversation with quotations from Keats, Wordsworth, and Matthew Arnold; her fair-skinned mother, Madhuri, remembers proudly the time a friend told her that in Europe she'd "be taken for Italian or Spanish"; her married older brother, Amrit, a businessman (and a subscriber to *Reader's Digest*), has moved up quickly because his British-owned firm is following a "policy of gradually replacing British executives by Indian ones," and he is "very suitable for this purpose, as he had attended an English university and was also very English in all other respects, except in his complexion"; Shakuntala herself is a fan of Sibelius and Liszt.

Shakuntala considers herself and her father, though, to be different from the other members of her family, especially Amrit. Her brother is a materialist, she complains, whereas she and her father are "idealists" and know that "art and culture are the only important things in life." From the outset, it is clear that Shakuntala's and Har Dayal's culture is superficial and their idealism pragmatic. The truth is that Har Dayal enjoys art and culture less than he enjoys his image of himself as a friend of art and culture.

The novel's other New Delhi family is strikingly different. Its patriarch, Ram Nath—once Har Dayal's friend and mentor and a respected leader of the struggle for Indian independence—has lately gone down in the world as steadily as Har Dayal has gone up. So traditionally Indian is Ram Nath's clan, moreover, that his niece Golub, to the disgust of her despicable English husband, Esmond, cannot even make conversation with his European friends. When this family enters Shakuntala's life it is because Ram Nath wants her to marry his son, Narayan—a brilliant young doctor who has rejected a lucrative practice to care for the rural poor. Unbeknownst to everyone, however, Shakuntala has fallen in love with the superficial Esmond, who represents to her everything Western, and who doesn't care for her in the slightest. Esmond or no Esmond, though, one never has any question about the outcome of Ram Nath's proposal. One knows that Har

Dayal, for all his supposed devotion to Ram Nath, will manage to argue slickly against the marriage. And one knows that the idealistic Shakuntala will decide that "my ideals are different than [Narayan's]. . . . I love Art and Beauty and Poetry, how can I give these things up as I shall have to if I go and live with Narayan in a village to do good to the poor?"

It should be said that some of the characters in *Esmond* are less credible than others, their motivations more dubious and their fatuities too strongly exaggerated. It is hard to believe, for instance, that the pathetically meek Golub could ever have worked up the nerve to marry Esmond against her family's wishes—especially since she cannot now summon up the same nerve to leave him, though she and her whole family realize that the marriage is a lost cause. Equally difficult to swallow is that a rich, sheltered young Indian woman of the 1950s would have opened her chaste treasure, especially to a married man, as readily as Shakuntala opens hers to Esmond. In any event, one sometimes wishes, while reading *Esmond,* that Jhabvala would let up a bit on the irony, particularly when she is writing about Shakuntala. Quite often the girl is just too foolish to be believed. When her mother asks her, on one occasion, what she is doing, Shakuntala replies, with a child's solemnity, "I am thinking quite hard"; at the end of the novel, when she has a marketplace rendezvous with Esmond, she is absurdly deluded and happy, and Jhabvala, who wants to indicate that life is nowhere near as wonderful as Shakuntala thinks, makes her point with less subtlety than might have been desirable: "She knew now that life was more wonderful, a hundred times more wonderful, than even she had suspected. It was not the moment nor was she the person, to hide such a sentiment, so she told him, 'Life is wonderful—wonderful!' letting her hand slide from his arm down to his hand which she firmly and fearlessly held as they made their way through the crowd." Though Jhabvala's affectionate attention, then, to the little details of human relations, attitudes, and customs is very charming, she is at times so ironic in this novel that she comes off as downright misanthropic.

*The Householder* (1960) might be read as something of a companion piece to *Esmond in India.* Instead of concerning herself with a rich young lady who has returned to her father's house after being graduated from college, Jhabvala gives us a middle-class boy named Prem who, as the novel opens, has recently earned a second-class B.A., has undergone an arranged marriage with a girl named Indu, has taken up residence with her in a seedy little flat in Delhi, and has entered upon a low-paying teaching job at a seedy little private college. He is, then, a brand-new "householder"—which is, according to the ancient writings, the third (after child and student) of the four stages of a man's life. The novel is concerned with describing his period of adjustment to this role. For this timid, unambitious, and only moderately intelligent young man is not quite ready for the responsibilities of manhood. Though Indu is with child, he does not find her attractive, and considers her pregnancy a "terrible embarrassment," for "[n]ow everybody would know what he did with her at night in the dark." He tries to behave in a manner befitting a proper Indian husband, but is not very good at it; Indu

blithely ignores his orders. At the college, too, his attempts at discipline are ineffectual. Though he spends much of the book, moreover, trying to work up the nerve to ask Mr. Khanna for a raise in salary and his landlord for a lower rent, one knows from the start that when he finally manages to choke out these requests, they will be brushed aside breezily: one knows this as surely as one knows that Shakuntala will never marry Narayan. (One reads Jhabvala novels like *Esmond in India* and *The Householder* not to discover what will happen—one knows pretty much what will happen—but to delight in, among other things, the perceptiveness with which Jhabvala depicts self-important, self-deceiving people like Har Dayal and Mr. Khanna in the act of justifying their ignoble actions.) But one also knows that eventually—and very gradually—things will improve for Prem. Perhaps he will not come to enjoy his new life, but he will grow used to it; it will come to seem less of a burden, and at times even pleasurable.

About Prem: although he is a believable and pitiable character, he is not an extremely likable one. Like Shakuntala, he seems abnormally puerile for a college graduate, buying candy on the way home and eating it quickly so he will not have to share it with Indu. As in the case of Shakuntala, the irony Jhabvala brings to his characterization is sometimes excessive; on occasion he is so passive and ineffectual that one feels as if one is being invited not to sympathize with him but to feel superior to him. This is true not only of Prem, to be sure, but of many of the characters in the book, whose banality is of grotesque dimensions. Prem's fellow teachers, for example, speak almost entirely in clichés. Since they are minor characters, however, this is not a crucial failing, and the results are admittedly very funny; the inane pretentiousness displayed at Mr. Khanna's tea party, for example, is reminiscent of Dickens:

> "As I was saying," said Mr. Khanna; he took up his position in the centre again and replaced his thumb in his armpit. "It is very pleasant to have the ladies with us. Very agreeable." The ladies all stared straight in front of them, without any change of expression. Only Mrs. Khanna said, "I think the tea-water is nearly boiling."
>
> Mr. Chaddha said, "The society of ladies is said to have a very softening effect." He was wearing a cream-coloured silk suit which seemed to have been washed quite a number of times, and he sat with his arms and his little bird legs crossed in an attitude of ease suitable to a tea-party.
>
> "It is not for nothing," suggested Mr. Khanna, "that they are known as the gentle sex." Led by Mr. Chaddha, the gentlemen politely laughed. "It is good sometimes to break off in the midst of toil," Mr. Khanna continued, "and enjoy an hour's leisure and ease in their charming company."
>
> "As our heroes of old," said Mr. Chaddha, "withdrew for respite from their battles to have their wounds dressed and their brows soothed by the hands of their consorts." He seemed pleased by this remark; he cleared his throat and crossed his legs the other way. The other teachers looked

at the Principal, and when they saw him smile in appreciation, they too smiled in appreciation.

Outlandish as they are, furthermore, the teachers are a lot easier to take than Hans Loewe, a German boy who befriends Prem. Hans has come to India from "materialistic" Europe because he thinks this is "the country where people renounce the flesh and think only of the Spirit!" Nothing, apparently, can make him see things any differently. (He is as obtuse about the real nature of India as Shakuntala is about Esmond's lack of affection toward her.) He says to Prem,

> "Only think—in this country where everything is beautiful, the sunset and the fruit and the women, here you call it all Illusion! How do you say—Maya?"

> Prem said, "Yes, Maya," though he was not quite sure.

"How I love your India!" Hans tells Prem, but *his* India is not at all the same as Prem's; when Prem begins to speak of India's independence and its economic progress, Hans seems not even to hear him: "Everything is so spiritual—we can wash off our dirty materialism when we come here to your India!" At first these speeches are somewhat amusing, and this Westerner's admiration of India's supposed spiritual *richesse* is certainly deliciously ironic in light of post-revolutionary India's desperate longing for a Western-style material affluence. But though Hans appears several times in the book, Jhabvala never develops him any further than this; he remains incredibly obtuse and deaf to Prem's practical-minded conversation. To Hans, indeed, Prem is little more than a symbol of India. Of course, Jhabvala finds Hans ridiculous for taking this simplistic, condescending attitude. But Hans is such a blatant, uncomplicated stereotype of the European in India that it could be argued that Jhabvala herself, in creating such a character, is as guilty of gross simplification and condescension as he is.

The most peculiar episode of *The Householder* is one in which Prem spends part of an evening with a swami and his followers. Nobody says anything profound during this encounter, but the mere fact that the swami and his followers speak—even in the vaguest terms—of God and of the heart's longings and of "what is valuable in the world and what is not" makes the experience overwhelming for Prem; the "unaccustomed purity" of the meeting goes to his head, and causes him to laugh and feel drunk and experience, like Shakuntala at the marketplace, a brief sense of transcendence:

> He thought yes, this is how one must live—with love and laughter and song and thoughts of God. All his former worries about his rent, his rise in salary, his lack of authority as teacher and husband, were nothing but a thin scum floating on top of a deep well of happiness and satisfaction. Nothing, he thought, would ever trouble him again. From now on he would live in contemplation only of spiritual things. Indu would be like a sister to him—he would love her as a sister and both would sit at the feet of the swami and think of God and indulge in happy, innocent play.

But of course the pressing circumstances of daily life make Prem's determination to live such an existence fade quickly away. Though this episode is well done, Prem seems in it to be rather out of character; one feels as if he has been led to the swami less by the longings of his soul than by Jhabvala's desire to work a swami into the novel, and to have somebody speak of transcendent things.

The strength of *The Householder*—and a great strength it is—is that Jhabvala manages to make an unremarkable phase of an unremarkable life very touching and compelling. Like many contemporary English novelists—the late Barbara Pym comes to mind—she seems deliberately, in these early novels, to cultivate a certain smallness; in size, style, setting, scope, intentions, ideas, and range of feeling, *The Householder* is a modest book. Jhabvala concerns herself with a protagonist who we know from the start will not change dramatically, will not do anything admirable, will never amount to much. Jhabvala's restraint is remarkable, as is her understanding of character. She captures with great skill Prem's feelings of fear, uncertainty, deprivation, and hopelessness. (In fact, she makes the life of these middle-class Indians seem so barren and banal—which I don't doubt for a moment it is—that one can only be grateful she doesn't take on the life of the abject poor.) She has extraliterary goals, of course: here—as throughout her fiction—she is out to destroy the sentimental views that Western readers may have of India. Furthermore, her attention to homely details seems to be designed, in part anyway, to ridicule the grandiose pretensions of characters like Mr. Khanna. Whatever the case may be, *The Householder* is wonderfully attentive to the details of Indian life—the jarring of pickle, the making of poori and chapati, the conservations about the desirability of government jobs, the entreaties of beggars ("You are my mother and my father"). As for the novel's prose, it is even more lucid and luminous than that of *Esmond in India.* Compared to that novel, *The Householder* is shorter, simpler, more focused, more austere in its manner, and more concerned with conveying a sense of everyday Indian life; in the latter regard, in fact, it is, despite its drawbacks, a veritable *tour de force.*

Aside from the swami, the one thing in Prem's life that seems to transcend everyday reality is the cinema. Jhabvala's novels poke merciless fun at the film world—at the shoddiness of most of its products, at the large role it plays in most Indians' lives (and imaginations), and at the preoccupation of many Indians with the romances and scandals described in movie magazines. (In *The Householder* a paper-man passes by Prem's mother's train, shouting, "*Film-Fun, Film-Fare, Film-Frolic!*") It seems ironic, then, that Jhabvala has herself made such a large contribution to Indian film. The first motion picture on which she collaborated with Merchant and Ivory was a charming black-and-white adaptation of *The Householder* (1963), starring Shashi Kapoor as Prem. Though the film has the same story, and much the same grim, claustrophobic atmosphere, as the book, there are a few notable differences: several episodes are shuffled around; Prem is not quite as spineless as in the book, and is rather more talkative; and Hans from Germany—who probably should have been an

American in the first place—is transformed into Ernest from Philadelphia.

The film of *The Householder* was succeeded by two good films about India, the West, and the decline of culture. *Shakespeare Wallah* (1965) concerns a small travelling company of English Shakespearean actors who have spent years in India but who, thanks to the growing popularity of movies, have had increasing trouble finding employment, and are thus beginning to feel as if there's nothing left for them in India. "We should've gone home in '47 when they all went," complains the company's lead actor, Mr. Buckingham. But his wife (and leading lady) observes that "We always used to think *this* was our home." Indeed, the Buckinghams' teenage daughter, Lizzie, has never even been to England. Nor, in spite of her family's wishes, does she want to go there to be educated—especially after she meets, falls in love with, and begins an affair with a rich, handsome young man named Sanju (Shashi Kapoor). The affair is doomed from the start, of course. For one thing, Sanju's values and way of life contrast sharply with those of the Buckingham family; for another, Sanju already has a woman in his life, the glamorous film star Manjula, who is as wily and superficial as Lizzie is sincere and sensitive. *Shakespeare Wallah* may be the best of Jhabvala's early films: it is a gentle comedy with the audacity (and the good sense) to imply that certain products of a foreign culture—that is, Shakespeare's plays—might be better for Indians than certain products (i.e., tacky films) of their own culture.

After *Shakespeare Wallah* came *Bombay Talkie* (1970), yet another Jhabvala movie whose primary concern is to deplore the influence of movies. The heroine is Lucia Lane (Jennifer Kendal), a restless, superficial, several-times-married hack writer from England who has come to India hoping to change her luck. On a Bombay soundstage—where a musical number featuring a giant typewriter is being filmed—she meets two men who are attracted to her. One of them is a good-hearted bachelor screenwriter named Harry; the other is the dashing movie actor Vikram (Shashi Kapoor again), who is as superficial as she is. Though Vikram is married, Lucia has an affair with him; so insensitive is she that even when his meek little Indian wife walks in on the two of them in the couple's bedroom, it doesn't occur to Lucia to feel guilty or uncomfortable. Vikram is one of many men in Jhabvala's work (Esmond is another) who blithely cheat on their Indian wives with Western women; to these husbands, their wives represent tradition and permanence, where as Western women—who need not be taken seriously anyway, because they are prostitutes by nature—represent adventure, sophistication, modernity. Of course, no Jhabvala story about restless Westerners in India would be complete without a swami, and so Lucia spends some time in an ashram, trying (without much success) to adapt herself—and her very healthy sex drive—to a disciple's ascetic life. *Bombay Talkie* is a good movie; if it is less satisfying than *Shakespeare Wallah,* it's because the principal characters are less sympathetic, the theme more familiar (with only a few changes, the story might have been set in Rome or London), and certain development (notably, the stabbing at the end) downright corny.

Beginning with *Travelers* (1973), Jhabvala's novels represent quite a different sort of accomplishment from their predecessors. If the early novels tend to depict India from Indian points of view, in these later novels the subcontinent is more usually seen through the eyes of Westerners. In these books the country seems more exotic, somewhat less a geographical entity, a way of life, and somewhat more a state of mind; her view of the country, that is to say, is less down-to-earth, more cosmic—more symbolic. Whereas in the early novels the story is paramount, and narrative coherence a priority, the later novels are more fragmented; Jhabvala is less interested, in these books, in telling a story than in painting a single broad canvas; she seeks to give us India, it seems, not by offering us a series of discrete connected images but by depicting one image, as it were, from a multiplicity of angles. These later Jhabvala novels are more sensual, experimental, modern; though the later Jhabvala, like her earlier incarnation, has affinities to Waugh and Cary, say, she is closer than the early Jhabvala to the camp of Virginia Woolf, Conrad, Lawrence, and Joyce.

*Travelers* reads like a sort of trial run for the new Jhabvala. In it she moves back and forth between the points of view of four characters whose paths cross in India. Raymond, a pleasant young Englishman, is a Cambridge graduate who lives in New Delhi and is in love with Gopi, a college student; Asha is a rich middle-aged woman who also becomes smitten with Gopi, and Lee is a young Englishwoman who has come to India "to lose herself in order . . . to find herself," and who spends time in an ashram as a swami's disciple and lover. The stories of these characters' lives, as they develop over a period of several months, are told in brief chapters, many of them no longer than a page or two, some of them in epistolary form; they carry flat, descriptive titles such as "Raymond and Gopi Meet Lee," "Lee Writes to Asha," and "Raymond Arrives in the Ashram."

There is much talk about India and what it means, and in this connection many characters and settings take on symbolic dimensions. Raymond grows very fond of Indian music because it has become for him "a distillation of everything he loved in Gopi and everything he loved in India. These two were now inextricable." Lee notes that her friend Margaret looks down on Miss Charlotte, an elderly English missionary, because

> she can't sympathize with her *attitude,* which she says is old-fashioned and patronizing. She says people just don't come any more to India to do good, those days are over. What they come for now is—well, to do good to themselves, to learn, to *take* from India. That's what Margaret's here for. Above all she wants to be pure—to have a pure heart untainted by modern materialism. Margaret hates modern materialism. Of course, so do I; that's why we're both here.

It is this hatred of "modern materialism" that leads Lee to the swami, who plans to develop his following into the Universal Society for Spiritual Regeneration in the Modern World, "a worldwide religion uniting men of all creeds and all colors into one family and so bringing peace and harmony into the world." It is Lee's naïve faith in the swami that provides Jhabvala with her biggest opportunities, in this novel, for irony. "[H]e's so *phenomenal,*" Lee exults, "I mean it's so fantastic the way his mind is always alert. . . . [H]e has this power of knowing people before he's actually physically met them." Contrasted with the swami and his thriving ashram are Miss Charlotte and her mission—an institution that has actually done a great deal of good, but which is closed by the Indian government because "philanthropy is a form of charity that the government of India, indeed I may say the people of India, can no longer allow themselves to accept."

The travellers of this novel are in search not only of a number of great abstractions—truth, enlightenment, spiritual regeneration—but of one thing that is very concrete: family. If Lee is so easily taken in by the swami, it is because he has made it possible, at his ashram, for her to be part of something that resembles a family; likewise, Gopi becomes attached to an old swami-like woman named Banubai of whom he says, "She is my mother. She is everyone's mother." Appropriately, the novel ends with two of its protagonists making travelling plans: Raymond arranges to return to his only real family, his mother in England; Lee—who has left the ashram—decides to return to it, because it is the only real home she has.

*Travelers* is an odd book. The writing is crisp and vivid throughout, and some of the episodes are wittily done. At a high-toned dinner, for instance, the English host and an Indian minister get into a friendly argument over whether there is a "special relationship" between England and India; it's an absurd argument, because the Indian—who denies the existence of such a relationship—sounds as English as the Englishman. But after the smoothness, concision, and focus of *Esmond in India* and (even more so) *The Householder, Travelers* seems choppy, sprawling, meandering. Yes, the directionlessness of its characters and plot is part of the point; this is a book about four confused people meandering through life—and, to an extent, across the landscape of India—in search of something. Such a book can certainly work, but more than anything else it needs particularly appealing and sympathetic characters in order to do so; and the fact is that the characters in *Travelers* simply are not all that engaging. Even at the end of the book, one does not feel as if one knows them very well or cares strongly about any of them. Interestingly, the words of praise quoted on the back cover of the Fireside paperback edition point directly to the book's cardinal weakness. The quotation from *The New York Times Book Review* describes *Travelers* as a "distinguished psychological survey"; Ved Mehta observes that the "central character in *Travelers* . . . is India, which for [Jhabvala] is not so much a country as an experience, after which no one is ever the same." Both Mehta and the *Times* critic are correct. But to refer to the novel as a "psychological survey" is to suggest—with justification, I think—that Jhabvala's characters seem more like case studies of personality types than they do like distinctive individuals; and to say that India is the novel's central character is plainly to admit that the human characters in the book are overwhelmed by the setting.

Jhabvala's most celebrated work of fiction, *Heat and Dust*

(1975), has several affinities with *Travelers,* the most important being that it, too, is concerned with Anglo-Indian relations and cross-cultural romances; as with the earlier novel, moreover, it might be said of *Heat and Dust* that one of its central characters is India itself. Here, too, Jhabvala presents us with more than one protagonist—with a pair of them, in fact—but, unlike the foursome in *Travelers,* they never meet each other. They are, as it happens, two women who are divided from each other by time, but who belong to the same family and have a great deal in common. One of them, Olivia—whose story is set in 1923, in the Indian town of Satipur and its environs—is the bored young wife of Douglas Rivers, a British officer; she loves him, yet gradually finds herself becoming fascinated by the Nawab, a charming but dissolute (and married) prince whose palace is in the nearby town of Khatm and whose income appears to derive largely from the petty crimes of various sordid hirelings. The attraction is mutual, and in the end Olivia runs off with the Nawab, lives out her days in his house in the remote town of X, and is never seen again. The other protagonist is a young lady—Douglas's granddaughter by his second wife—who, fifty years later, having read through a trove of Olivia's old letters, journeys to India in an attempt to understand this woman whose story is now a skeleton in the family closet. The novel alternates between a straightforward recounting of Olivia's story—as revealed, we are to understand, by the letters—and the granddaughter's successive entries in the journal she keeps of her several months' visit to Satipur, during which time she has her own affair with an Indian.

As is to be expected in a Jhabvala novel, however, the narrator's reasons for coming to India are not entirely related to Olivia. She explains that "many of us are tired of the materialism of the West, and even if we have no particular attraction towards the spiritual message of the East, we come here in the hope of finding a simpler and more natural way of life." Inder Lal, her lover, considers this attitude a mockery; he is as acutely and painfully aware of his material poverty, as compared with the lot of the typical European, as she is aware of what she considers her spiritual poverty, *vis-a-vis* the average Indian: "He says, why should people who have everything—motor cars, refrigerators—come here to such a place where there is nothing?"

*Esmond in India* and *The Householder* have strong story lines that develop clearly and fluently, and characters that blossom rapidly into life; *Heat and Dust* is a more elliptical work, its characters more enigmatic, their motives less readily apprehended. Its feel—the tone peculiarly dry, the episodes often crabbed and unyielding, the chronological leaps disorienting, even jerky—is similar to that of *Travelers,* but it is far more surefooted, almost as if *Travelers* were the rough draft and *Heat and Dust* the finished work; there is a symbolic force to the latter book that *Travelers* doesn't quite achieve. If in *Travelers* the landscape of India seems to dwarf the characters, in *Heat and Dust* the characters partake of the country's vastness; the simple, elliptical stories of Olivia and the narrator have an archetypal, a legendary, quality that the muddled, prosaic case histories in *Travelers* don't.

The stories of Olivia and the narrator are at once similar and different; in this they reflect the similarities and differences between the British India of Olivia's day and the independent India that the narrator visits—connections which Jhabvala draws with a fine subtlety and elegance. Of course it is the differences—especially those between the nature of Anglo-Indian relations in 1923 and in the 1970s—that are most dramatically apparent. The house in which Olivia and Douglas lived now contains Indian government offices; there is a chumminess now between Englishmen and Indians that would have been rare in Olivia's time. But in all essential things the India that the narrator becomes familiar with is the same India that Olivia knew. The heat and dust, for instance, persist. India is the same intolerably hot and dry land that it was half a century ago—or, for that matter, half a millennium ago. India is still a land that "always changes people." Though, in comparison to Jhabvala's other novels, it seems to have received somewhat more than its share of critical attention and praise, *Heat and Dust* most assuredly represents a high point of Jhabvala's art.

In the same year that this most substantial novel (which became a film in 1982) was published, there appeared a surprisingly slight Merchant-Ivory-Jhabvala movie entitled *The Autobiography of a Princess.* It is of interest, though, for its thematic similarity to *Heat and Dust.* Far from the sweeping spectacle that the title might lead one to expect, this film takes place in a modest London house where, one afternoon, a middle-aged Indian princess (Madhur Jaffrey) has an elderly English bachelor (James Mason) to tea. This is, one gathers, an annual ritual; her guest—who was once right-hand man to her late father, a maharajah—has come to celebrate with her the birthday of her father by watching home movies and sharing memories. During most of the film, the princess talks incessantly of Papa, whom she remembers as a great and cultured man, but who—one gradually realizes—was actually very much like the Nawab in *Heat and Dust*: a tyrant, a criminal, and an adulterer, who romanced a film star and lost his throne as the result of a scandalous affair with a lower-class Englishwoman. It is not till the last minutes of the film that the guest speaks at length of his relationship with the maharajah, which sounds exactly like that between the Nawab and his homosexual English friend Harry (who, in turn, rather reminds one, with his endless letters home to mother and his quiet worship of his Adored One, of Raymond in *Travelers*). So ends the film.

It is a baffling piece of work: barely an hour long, set in one room in "real time," it has no plot, no action, no dramatic conflict, and consists mostly of one rambling, interminable speech. As for the home-movie-within-a-movie, it is a bizarre compilation containing, among other things, a *60 Minutes*-style interview with disenfranchised Indian nobles, grainy scenes of elephants on parade, and truly repulsive footage showing the beheading of goats. Its only apparent points are that daughters often have highly selective memories of their fathers, and that for many high-born Indians who now live in reduced circumstances, British India is a glorious memory and independent India a nightmare. At best, the film is an *outré* footnote to *Heat and Dust*—a drastically less effective variation, that is, on the theme of family memories of British India.

The novel that directly preceded Jhabvala's new novel is of interest for several reasons. For one thing, it is the first of her novels written during her residency in New York. For another, it has many similarities to *Three Continents.* Interestingly, *In Search of Love and Beauty* (1983) is set mostly in America—in Manhattan, to be specific—and takes place over several decades of the mid-twentieth century. At its center are three generations of a well-heeled West Side family: Louise (whose husband Bruno dies young), her businesswoman daughter Marianne (who calls herself Marietta), and the grandchildren, the world-travelling real-estate entrepreneur Mark and the otiose, idealistic homebody Natasha. The family is surprisingly close-knit—more like an Indian family, one cannot help but think, than a typical New York family; Marietta's fulfillment, we are told, lies in Mark, and for the utterly friendless Natasha, her grandmother, mother, and brother are "her home, her life, everything she knew and cherished." Yet family attachments are not enough to sustain and satisfy them. All four—aside from Natasha, who never even has a boyfriend—share a history of unorthodox, intense, and impermanent romantic entanglements, as well as a vague but persistent dedication to spiritual realization. They also share a fascination with a man named Leo Kellerman, whom Louise first meets in the 1930s, recognizes as "a yet undefined genius," and remains enthralled by for the next several decades. Leo is a swami in everything but name: he gives lectures and workshops, has a group of followers, and seeks to establish an Academy of Potential Development—a goal that Louise's family, of which he becomes something of an associate member, helps him to achieve.

Here, as in *Heat and Dust,* Jhabvala eschews a straightforward chronological structure. Instead, she leaps back and forth through the history of Louise's family, favoring us now with an episode set in the 1970s, now with one set in the 1940s. This practice of skipping around in time has a striking effect: it makes the family's life seem like a *fait accompli* rather than like something that mysteriously unfolds from moment to moment and can be changed by the characters' actions. This, in turn, makes the characters' incessant spiritual searching seem particularly pathetic and useless: we already know, after all, that they will never find transcendence. (Alas, Jhabvala doesn't get Americans quite right. She has them speak of "laundrettes" instead of "laundromats," of "blocks" instead of apartment houses; she has them drink too much tea and use British colloquialisms.)

This being a Jhabvala novel, there must be at least one Indian in the cast. That quota is filled in part by Ahmed, a musician whose recital at a converted New York porno theater Marietta attends. She is attracted not so much to Ahmed, she insists, as to "his sarod [a sort of Indian lute], his music; and not even that but the world it opened—the world beyond worlds—the promise of peace and fulfillment that was like a hand laid on her restless heart." Marietta hires Ahmed to give her sarod lessons, and she thereafter invites him (as Raymond does Gopi in *Travelers*) to move in with her. He does so, only to return eventually to India, which Marietta thereafter visits yearly, often passing through ashrams in the course of her travels; on one of her trips she forms an intense friendship with a woman musician named Sujata who represents her "most meaningful encounter there, or her deepest immersion and enchantment." (Like Asha, by the way, Sujata is in love with a boy who is young enough to be her son; she asks Marietta "if it was so wrong to have these feelings, then why were they sent?") Mark, for his part, devotes his life to a series of homosexual affairs. In a conflict over a mutual lover named Kent, an older man stops just short of stabbing Mark with a carving knife: Mark handles the crisis well, but the object of their affections breaks down in tears. Jhabvala explains:

> He was still very young, only at the beginning of his career, and knew nothing of what could sometimes happen among people with very strong feelings.

> About these feelings: Leo had once likened them to the voices of the great *castrati,* in which a man's vigour was made to give body to a woman's nervous delicacy. Unhuman voices, Leo called them; unnatural hybrids. "All the same," Mark had replied, "no one ever said they weren't beautiful."

This is what *In Search of Love and Beauty* is about: the way that unnatural, strong, and beautiful longings can lead people into foolish acts and harmless liaisons. For the truth about Louise, Marietta, and Mark seems to be that, though they cherish the family bond, each of them still hopes for some more transcendent form of human connection than that which they have. Leo, Ahmed, Kent are all ways of trying to build a new kind of family, a more nearly perfect union of souls. But one never really understands why one generation after another of this family should be so restless, so dedicated to the intercontinental search for "inner fulfillment," so devoted to the Leo Kellermans and Ahmeds of the world. Indeed, though one wants very much to believe in these extremely interesting people, one doesn't.

Jhabvala's new novel, ***Three Continents,*** is in many respects very similar to *In Search of Love and Beauty.* For one thing, the new novel—which in style and structure is Jhabvala's most conventional in over a decade—centers upon three generations of an affluent American family. The narrator is a young woman named Harriet Wishwell, who begins with a capsule family history: she and her twin brother, Michael, are the product of a broken marriage between a spoiled father, Manton, who has spent his life drawing on a trust fund, and a mother, Lindsay, who lives on the family ranch with a woman named Jean; since neither parent has very strong parental instincts, both Harriet and her brother were brought up largely by their paternal grandparents, a diplomat and his wife, in a number of Asian capitals. This upbringing bred in the children a "restlessness, or dissatisfaction with what was supposed to be our heritage—that is, with America." Neither lasted in college more than a year; both always "wanted something other—better—than we had. Of course people would say

that what we had was pretty good, and from a materialistic point of view that would be true."

---

> **This is what *In Search of Love and Beauty* is about: the way that unnatural, strong, and beautiful longings can lead people into foolish acts and harmless liaisons.**
>
> **—Bruce Bawer**

---

But, needless to say, theirs is an idealistic rather than a materialistic point of view. And it is not until their twentieth year—when Michael shows up at Lindsay's ranch house, fresh from yet another restless swing through Asia, with a swami and several disciples in tow—that things start looking up for them, idealistically speaking. The Rawul (for so the swami calls himself) is "as idealistic as Michael," the founder of something he calls the Fourth World movement. He has, as Harriet puts it, "this simple but forceful idea of constituting himself the savior of world civilization." In the new world—the Fourth World—"all that was best in the other three would come to fruition." Sharing this goal with him are the Rani, his consort, and Crishi, whom Harriet takes to be their adopted son. Michael himself declares, "This is it, Harriet. *Om,* the real thing." It is, in other words, what the two of them have been seeking all their lives. Harriet explains:

> While our parents were having marital squabbles and adulterous love affairs and our grandparents were giving diplomatic cocktail parties, [Michael] and I were struggling with the concepts of Maya and Nirvana, and how to transcend our own egos. Anything smaller than that, anything on a lower plane, disgusted us. I was used to following Michael's lead, so when he said that the Rawul and Rani and Crishi operated on the highest level possible, I didn't contradict him, although it seemed to me at that time that they were very worldly people.

This impression would seem to be confirmed by the reaction of Manton's girlfriend, Barbara, the daughter of a famous movie actress: the atmosphere around the Rawul, she says, reminds her of the atmosphere around her mother. (Like previous swamis in Jhabvala's work, in short, the Rawul seems to be to idealism what movie stars are to materialism.)

Before long, however, Harriet has become not only the Rawul's disciple but Crishi's wife. It is plain to the reader—though not at all to Harriet—that Crishi's main reason for marrying her is his desire to control the ranch, which the twins will inherit on their twenty-first birthday, and which Michael wants to donate to the movement. And little by little the Rawul's people do take control of the ranch. The gradually increasing sense of domination, as communicated by Jhabvala between the lines of Harriet's placid narrative, is chillingly reminiscent of *Animal*

*Farm*; these sections of the book represent an impressive accomplishment in *mise en scène*. But the characterizations give one pause. For why in heaven's name does almost nobody at the ranch notice how chilling these developments are? What is it about Harriet, Michael, and Lindsay that causes them to succumb so readily to the Rawul's empty rhetoric? Why is the only voice of common-sense reality that of Jean, who pleads with Harriet: "How could you allow these people—these strangers—to take over your house? Our house? It's like a nightmare." How is it that Harriet is able to recognize momentarily the truth of Jean's remark, only to drift back into mindless passivity? In short, why has Jhabvala chosen to create a family all of whose members are capable of being swallowed up by a cult in record time? Surely we are meant to understand that the Wishwells have been deprived of a strong sense of family and, like the clan at the center of *In Search of Love and Beauty,* yearn for a feeling of spiritual transcendence and for something larger than themselves to belong to; in a way, obviously, we are meant to see them as representative of the contemporary decay of the Western family and of family values. But the Wishwells are so grotesque a family that it is impossible to see them as representative of anything in the real world. Though it would be difficult enough to believe in any of them in isolation, to expect a reader to accept them all as members of a single family seems rather too much to ask.

And of all of them, the hardest to believe in is Harriet. She reminds one less of any real individual than of Alice Mellings, the obtuse protagonist of Doris Lessing's *The Good Terrorist,* who, desperate for a family of her own, falls for a third-rate terrorist group even more readily than Harriet falls for Crishi and the Rawul's cult. In Harriet, Jhabvala has created a textbook example of an unreliable narrator. Things are quite clearly not the way Harriet would have us think they are—or, indeed, the way she herself perceives them to be. Take her marriage, for instance. When the Rawul and his cohorts relocate to London, Harriet and Michael go with them; there Harriet meets Rupert, an art gallery owner who turns out to be the Rani's husband. Though Harriet doesn't realize it at all, the circumstances strongly suggest that the Rani married Rupert for his money, his government connections (which she used to straighten out her visa problems), and his family's seventeenth-century house (which the Rani liquidated soon after the marriage). Just as the Rani has used Rupert, so it is clear that Crishi, in marrying Harriet, is out to use her; indeed, as the party moves (in the book's second section) from America to London, and then (in section three) from London to India, everyone seems to await her twenty-first birthday as if it were the coming of the Messiah.

What's more, Harriet never faces squarely the facts about the Rawul's cash flow: like the Nawab's wealth in *Heat and Dust,* the movement's money appears to derive largely from crime. And Harriet knows this. She sees Crishi and Michael beat people up: she sees the Rawul's followers being trained in the use of weapons; she hears stories about Crishi's criminal past; and she speaks in passing of the arrest of some of the Rawul's followers "at certain borders," with each arrest representing "a considerable financial setback with the impounding of whatever it was that was being carried from one place to another." But she only mentions these things en passant. What is it that is being carried from one place to another? If Harriet knows, it's apparently not important enough to her to deserve mention. She seems incapable of adding it all up—the violence, the guns, the smuggling—and seeing the Rawul's movement for the sleazy enterprise that it really is. Why doesn't it occur to her to address the movement's blatant criminality as a moral issue? Why can't she see the utter divergence between the brutal reality of the movement and her image of it as a force for peace and love and brotherhood? The answer is, simply, that though her mother refers to her and Michael as the family "intellectuals," actual ratiocination is alien to her; it is not in her nature to think about her experiences. Although she considers herself a devotee of the movement, her understanding of it never progresses beyond the public-relations level; she fails to notice that the "ideas" in the Rawul's "program" are nothing but fuzzy platitudes.

To write a long novel—and this is one of Jhabvala's longest—in the voice of such a character seems an inordinately challenging task, and that Jhabvala does it as well as she does is a tribute to her gifts. This is a very smoothly written book—stately, lucid, and balanced. But the character of Harriet weakens it enormously. Like Shakuntala, Harriet is a heroine created expressly to be looked down upon; her unmitigated stupidity, and Jhabvala's incessant irony, eventually become too much to take. What's more, for all her sarcasm about people who are drawn to swamis, *Three Continents* seems to me to demonstrate—as if any more demonstration were necessary—that Jhabvala herself is in the grip of an inordinate fascination with them. To read the first few pages of this novel, with its multi-generational swami madness, is to get the mistaken impression that it is set somewhere around 1970, at the height of many Americans' love affair with gurus, mystics, and Ravi Shankar. So narrowly limited is Jhabvala here by her long-time theme of Indians who try to be Westerners and Westerners who try to be Indians that *Three Continents* comes off as stale and anachronistic, a recycling of dated and familiar motifs. It is encouraging, to be sure, that here, as in her preceding novel, Jhabvala's principal characters are Americans; both novels suggest that she is determined to bring new settings and concerns into her work, to move beyond her usual material. But just as her American protagonists, in these most recent novels, are pulled, as if by some force beyond themselves, to India, so for Jhabvala herself India remains unwaveringly the final destination, the figure in the carpet. In a very real sense, India has made Jhabvala; let us hope now that her preoccupation with the subcontinent is not her undoing as well.

### Ramlal Agarwal   (essay date 1987)

SOURCE: "A Critical Study of *Heat and Dust*," in *Studies in Indian Fiction in English,* edited by G. S. Balarama Gupta, Jiwe Publications, 1987, pp. 53-60.

[*In the following essay, Agarwal discusses the stories of Olivia and her granddaughter in* Heat and Dust, *proposing that their tragic fates in India are due to their "liberalism and sensitivity."*]

When the Booker Prize for 1975 was given to *Heat and Dust* the literati in India refused to be impressed. They thought that Jhabvala was awarded the prize for her ruthless damning of India, the country in which she had lived for over a quarter of a century. Naturally they hit back by damning the book. In an article called "Cross-cultural Encounter in Literature," published in *The Indian P.E.N.* [November-December, 1977] Nissim Ezekiel observed:

> I found *Heat and Dust* worthless as literature, contrived in its narrative structure, obtrusive in its authorial point of view, weak in style, stereotyped in its characters and viciously prejudiced in its vision of the Indian scene. To the distinguished English novelist who was the Chairman of the Jury for the Booker Prize, and to his colleagues, this judgement would no doubt be quite inexplicable, though it was widely shared in India. Indian reviewers dwelt on the India of *Heat and Dust* on the character of the Indian Nawab or Prince who has an affair with the wife of a British Civil Servant stationed in his town, and on the explicit and implicit commentary on Indian mores as well as the Indian setting, things Indian generally. For them, there could be no separation between these and the quality of the novel, its authenticity, its literary substance. English reviewers seemed to ask only how such matters were used within the novel's pattern of events, what light they threw on the writer's perceptions of character and conduct. The intercultural encounter was secondary, minor, interesting but not in any sense disturbing. *Heat and Dust* did not generate any heat or raise any dust in England. It did both in India, partly because of the Booker Prize which put on the novel the stamp of British approval, naturally without any concern for Indian sensibilities. The gulf between the two viewpoints seems unbridgeable.

Obviously Ezekiel found *Heat and Dust* worthless, contrived, etc. because of Jhabvala's explicit and implicit commentary on Indian mores as well as the Indian setting. One can understand Ezekiel's righteous indignation at what he considers an attempt to ridicule India, but one wonders whether it can stand as literary criticism. Jhabvala's explicit and implicit commentary on Indian mores and Indian setting is not extraneous but an integral part of the novel itself. It surfaces by itself though the two heroines of the novel try their best to turn a blind eye to it. The two heroines of *Heat and Dust* love India perhaps more than Ezekiel does. They give themselves over to it unreservedly. In the end they come to grief because they overlook the fact that it is disastrous to get mixed up with an alien culture however rich or ancient it may be. This is the theme of the novel and once this is clear one can see the reasons for which it was received so enthusiastically in the West.

*Heat and Dust* tells two stories instead of one. One of them deals with an English woman called Olivia and the other deals with her granddaughter. Olivia is in India because her husband Douglas is a District Officer at Satipur. She loves her husband but he is too busy to keep her company all the time. Soon Olivia finds herself oppressed with loneliness. When she meets the Nawab of Khatm, a small princely state, she finds herself attracted to him. She is impressed by his opulence, his authority, his unfailing hospitality, and above all, by his courteous attention to her. At the first meeting itself, Olivia realizes that "here at last was one person in India to be interested in her the way she was used to." Olivia does not like the English community at Satipur and remains shut up all day. She develops an intimate friendship with Harry, an Englishman living with the Nawab in an undefined position and this leads to a friendship with the Nawab himself. Olivia's assessment of the Nawab's personality agrees in many respects with Harry's:

> He is a very strong person. Very manly and strong. When he wants something, nothing must stand in his way. Never, ever. He's been the Nawab since he was fifteen (his father died suddenly of a stroke). So he's always ruled, you see; always been the ruler.

She finds that the English at Satipur do not approve of the Nawab and avoid discussing him in her presence. They do however, make sly remarks about his marriage and about his being connected with dacoits, which displeases and shocks Olivia. Her sympathy for the Nawab is part of her attitude to the Natives which is radically different from that of the others in her community. This sympathy is partly a result of her innate goodness and partly a consequence of her ignorance of the people and customs of India. She develops a critical attitude to her community and to her husband. Douglas' complacency and Olivia's mistrust of it are beautifully illustrated in the following passage:

> 'Oh goodness, darling, you have seen it hundreds of times . . . Why were they laughing? What did you say?'
>
> 'I just told them, in a roundabout way that they were a pack of rogues.'
>
> 'And they like being told that?'
>
> 'If you say it in Hindustani, yes.'
>
> 'I must learn!'
>
> 'Yes, you must,' he said without enthusiasm.
>
> 'It's the only language in which you can deliver deadly insults with the most flowery courtesy . . . I don't mean you, of course.' He laughed at the idea. 'What a shock they'd have!' Why? Mrs. Crawford speaks Hindustani; and Mrs. Minnies. 'Yes, but not with men. And they don't deliver deadly insults. It's man's game, strictly,' 'What isn't it?'
>
> Olivia said. He sucked at his pipe in rather a pleased way which made her cry out sharply:
>
> 'Don't do that!' He took it out of his mouth and stared in surprise. 'I hate you with that thing. Douglas,' she explained.

Her refusal to accompany the other Englishwomen, Beth Crawford and Mary Minnies, to the mountains in summer is a characteristic act of rebellion, though it is subtly camouflaged by an exhibition of love and concern for Douglas.

On many issues she takes up positions which are repulsive to the other members of her set. For example, she defends *Sati,* a savage Hindu custom in the eyes of the English people:

> 'It's part of their religion, is not it? I thought one wasn't supposed to meddle with that.' Now she looked down into her Windsor soup and not at all at Douglas; but she went on stubbornly; 'And quite apart from religion, it is their culture and who are we to interfere with anyone's culture especially an ancient one like theirs. . . . I know,' Olivia said miserably. She had no desire to recommend widow-burning but it was everyone else being so sure—tolerant and smiling but sure—that made her want to take another stand. 'But in theory it is really, isn't it, a noble idea. In theory,' she pleaded. Without daring to glance in Douglas' direction, she knew him to be sitting very upright with his thin lips held in tight and his eyes cold. She went on rather desperately, 'I mean, to want to go with the person you care for most in the world. Not to want to be alive any more if he wasn't.'

Olivia, unlike the others in her set, treats the Nawab as a friend. She does not believe, in her innocence, that the Nawab is associated with dacoits though it makes no difference to her relationship with him when later she discovers that he had dealings with them.

It is her interest in him as a human being which draws her closer to him, but in the end she is totally captivated by him and her surrender to him is complete. The Nawab's approach to the relationship is different. He finds Olivia attractive and sympathetic to him and deliberately sets out to win her. His talk about his daring ancestors and past glory is calculated to impress her. The tale of his present difficulties draws out Olivia's sympathy. The conquest of Olivia is for him, as for his ancestor Amanullah Khan, a subtle way of avenging himself on the English community. Even as the Nawab is closing in on Olivia, he recounts a story of how Amanullah Khan took revenge on a Marwar prince:

> "Listen," he said. Once it happened that a Marwar prince did something to displease him. I think he did not offer opium out of the correct silver chalice—it was only a small thing, but Amanullah Khan was not the man to sit quiet when insulted. . . . He invited this Marwar Prince and all his retainers to a feast. A ceremonial tent was put up and all preparations made and the guests came ready to eat and drink. Amanullah Khan greeted his enemy at the door of the tent and folded him to his heart. But when they were all inside he gave a secret sign and his men cut the ropes of the tent and the Marwar prince and his party were entangled within the canvas. When they were trapped they were like animals, Amanullah Khan and his men took their daggers and stabbed with them through the canvas again and again till there was not one enemy left alive. We still have that tent and the blood is so fresh and new, Olivia, it is as if it had happened yesterday.

What the Nawab does to Olivia is not very different from what Amanullah Khan did to his guest. Olivia becomes pregnant by the Nawab, undergoes a painful abortion because she comes to know that the baby might show the signs of its origin. The primitive method of abortion used by the local maids makes her sick and she is finally treated by the English doctor who sees through everything. Naturally Olivia quits the English camp. From this point onwards, she recedes to the background of the Nawab's *zanankhana.* What happens to her there is only a matter for guess. She spends her last days somewhere in the Himalayas.

Douglas' granddaughter by his second wife is fascinated by Olivia's story, which she gets from old relations and letters, and comes out to India to reconstruct Olivia's story. What happens to her in India has a close parallel in what happens to Olivia.

By the time the young woman arrives in India, the palace in which the Nawab lived has become a derelict place. All its splendour has gone. Its riches have found their way to Europe. But the township of Satipur has grown, though in an amorphous manner. The places where the English lived have been converted into government offices. She rents a small room from Inder Lal, a government official. Inder Lal also acts as her guide to the places around Satipur. The young English woman keeps a diary in India. She meets a trio of Westerners, a young man and his girl and another youth. The diarist asks the girl why she is in India. The girl laughs grimly and says: "To find peace. But all I found was dysentery." One of the two men had taken the Indian name of Chidananda. After a few days, the diarist finds Chid lying in an old tomb, dying of diseases and hunger. She takes him home, in spite of Inder Lal's protests. In the course of her research tours, the diarist goes to the shrine of Baba Firdaus. The shrine is famous because it is said that there the peoples' wishes are heard. At the shrine the diarist and Inder Lal, very much like Olivia and the Nawab in the past, develop physical intimacy which results in the diarist becoming pregnant. But unlike Olivia, she does not terminate her pregnancy. She accepts responsibility for her action and wants to have the child. In the end she too, like Olivia, goes to the Himalayas, which are to her a symbol of the spiritual mystery that India offers to the seeker beyond the heat and dust, the spiritual presence of India's mystery:

> Mountain peaks higher than any I have dreamed of, the snow on them also is whiter than all other snow—so white it is luminous and shines against a sky which is of deeper blue than any known to me. That is what I expect to see. Perhaps it is also what Olivia saw: the view—or vision that filled her eyes all those years and suffused her soul.

The ending of *Heat and Dust,* in terms of the careers of both the heroines, Olivia and the Diarist, is full of ambivalence.

*Heat and Dust* is remarkable for its structural innovations. Though the two stories are very much like each other, the manner of telling them is different. The first one is dramatic. It tells itself. One episode follows another. The author just brings characters with different attitudes and backgrounds together and leaves them to depict them-selves by their behaviour and by the way they interact upon one another. Psychology is telescoped or taken for granted. So little of what goes on inside the characters is ever mentioned that they seem empty or flat. But this is a deliberate fictional strategy on the part of the novelist. Olivia's story presents a cool reconstruction of bygone days with multiple points of view. The novel derives its au-thenticity from the truthfulness of their points of view and not from the objective reality of the Indian scene or char-acter. Douglas, for example, represents the typical view held by British officials that they were here to rule the country and that they could not rule it unless they learnt to discriminate between the rulers and the ruled. Douglas, like his colleagues, wants to preserve the identity of the English in India. Harry represents the Englishmen who had been closer to the Indian Maharajas and Nawabs. Harry is an extension of Raymond in *A New Dominion* but he is not detached as Raymond was and he is not in tune with the Englishmen in India. He belongs to the Nawab's camp and is, therefore, hated by his compatriots. Harry, like Raymond, goes back to England and starts hating his Indian experience. When he meets the Nawab in England he gets the shock of his life:

> Harry said that he had a shock when he saw him again in London. Fifteen years had passed, the Nawab was fifty years old and so fat that there was something womanly about him. And the way he embraced Harry was womanly too: he held him against his plump chest with both arms and kept him there for a long time. And then all the old feelings came back to Harry. But after-wards he found that his feelings towards the Nawab had changed—probably because the Nawab himself had changed so much. He seemed softer and milder, and with many trou-bles of a domestic nature.

Major Minnies represents a more balanced view based on an understanding of Indian climate and Indian character. If Douglas represents one extreme view, Olivia and her granddaughter represent the other. They are too sympa-thetic and liberal in their outlook. If Douglas and others like him show a sneering attitude to India, Olivia and her granddaughter show an understanding one. Olivia knows that religion and culture are not to be mocked at. The sec-ond story uses the first person narrative. The narrator-heroine records what she sees or what happens to her in the most matter-of-fact style. Here too psychology is tele-scoped. Naturally the story is pictorial. It presents the pic-ture of India in which the English are no longer the ruling class and if they are there, they are there as visitors or seekers, very different from their predecessors, and very much at the mercy of their Indian hosts or Gurus. The story presents the picture of India seen through a single subjective point of view. The stories dealing with the ob-jective and the subjective points of view are so structured as to reinforce each other. They are also brilliantly inter-locked. One offers a distant perspective, the other a close view. As such, the novel moves on two levels in time. It shuttles between the past and the present. Though the two heroines are separated by half a century, they are not un-like each other in their sensitivity and receptiveness to

India and both of them go through identical experiences. The novel moves backward and forward. This is because time is assumed and the action is a static pattern continu-ously redistributed and reshuffled in space. Jhabvala fol-lows this device to show the timeless aspects of the coun-try. The spatial reality of India is conveyed through the descriptions of the dry, parched up land, smouldering rub-bish, mud-thatched houses, lying beggars, over-crowded hospitals and hysterical people. This spatial reality is, as she sees it, still operative even though the temporal reality has changed inevitably. The India of princes and palaces has made room for the India of petty government servants and overcrowded huts and hospitals, but the heat and the dust are still there, and they still affect people as they af-fected people fifty years ago.

'The novel,' says Trilling, 'is a perpetual quest for reality, the field of its research being always manners as the indi-cation of the direction of man's soul' [*The Liberal Imagi-nation,* 1970]. The quest for reality through the study of manners has been Jhabvala's preoccupation. We know the Nawab through his preoccupation with his ancestor, and the old legend of the British community. What is true of the Nawab is also true of Inder Lal and other characters. We know Inder Lal through his preoccupation with his of-fice work, his relationship with his mother and wife and with the diarist. Jhabvala's characters are set in a crowded country where the pressures of its climate and complicat-ed tradition of manners are great. To say that those who are not born in such a country find it overwhelming is not to malign India.

In *Heat and Dust* Jhabvala shows that the two English heroines of the novel lack moral realism. They become vic-tims of illusions generated by their liberalism and their sensitivity. They are carried away by their generosity. Therefore, they do not perceive the dangers of excess of feeling for a country they love but do not understand. Olivia admits that she does not understand India but she is not deterred from responding to the country unreserv-edly:

> I enjoy being here. I enjoy your company. We have a good time. Don't look like that, Harry. You're being like everyone else now: making me feel I don't understand. That I don't know India. It's true I don't, but what's that got to do with it? People can still be friends, can't they, even if it is India.

*Heat and Dust* is Jhabvala's last novel with Indian setting. Naturally it sums up her experience of India, an experi-ence reinforced and refined over the years. Small wonder if the novel has a pure gem-like quality about it.

### Charmazel Dudt    (essay date 1988)

SOURCE: "Jhabvala's Fiction: The Passage from India," in *Faith of a (Woman) Writer,* edited by Alice Kessler-Harris and William McBrien, Greenwood Press, 1988, pp. 159-64.

[*In the following essay, Dudt examines four of Jhabvala's novels—*Amrita, Esmond in India, Travelers, *and* Heat and Dust—*and discusses the ways in which her views of India have changed over the course of her writing.*]

It is a truism that woman today is caught between old strictures and new possibilities. She is well aware of her historical role and, therefore, struggles to establish a consistent, reliable identity as a member of a world which has not yet absorbed her as an integral part. When this struggle with temporal change is compounded with spatial and cultural challenges, what is written must be considered carefully for what it reveals of the struggle itself, and for the end it prophesies. The novels of Ruth Prawer Jhabvala, thus, have an immediate poignancy, for they reflect her personal journey from illusory myth to dusty reality.

Born of Polish parents in Germany in 1927, she went to England as a refugee at the age of twelve, achieving an easy transition from writing in German to composing stories in English about the lower-middle classes in England. She met an Indian architect while she was studying English Literature at Queen Mary College, London University, and married him. They moved to Delhi, where she has lived from 1951. "I have lived here for most of my adult life," she says [in *Contemporary Novelists,* 2nd edition, 1976], "and have an Indian family. This makes me not quite an insider but it does not leave me entirely an outsider either. I feel my position to be at a point in space where I have quite a good view of both sides but am myself left stranded in the middle."

According to Jhabvala, her books are an attempt "to present India to myself in the hope of giving myself some kind of foothold. My books may appear objective, but really I think they are the opposite: for I describe the Indian scene not for its own sake but for mine. . . . My work can never claim to be a balanced or authoritative view of India but is only one individual European's attempt to compound the puzzling process of living in it." A survey of four of her novels, written over nearly twenty years, from 1956 to 1975, reveals through her reaction to India, the difficulty in establishing a personhood and the price one has to pay for it.

When she first went to India, she wrote easily about the country and its people: "I did this quite instinctively. . . . It never struck me at that time that there was anything strange in my writing in this way about Indians as if I were an Indian" [in *World Authors, 1950-1970,* 1975]. In her first book, *Amrita,* the central character is the new woman who clashes directly with the old world. She is fiercely determined to keep her job at the radio station despite her mother's desperate attempts to arrange for her marriage within her pseudo-European circle of friends; Amrita, however, is in love with Hari, a fellow-worker from a different caste. Yet she is neither a Nora nor a Hedda. Amrita delights in shocking her elders, but hesitates to go to a local restaurant in the company of two men. When compelled to go, she "kept her eyes lowered, and listlessly crumbled a small cream cake on her plate." The boys enjoyed themselves thoroughly. One cannot avoid the impression that the westernized characters in the book are so only superficially. Her grandfather lives in a musty house surrounded by a litter of tastelessly chosen *objets d'art,* and dreams of the good old days when he was a bar-

rister. One aunt has a wealthy husband who does nothing but affect boredom, while another aunt can only indulge her appetite for clothes and sweets. Both women are incapable of action, exactly like the grandfather's music box from Baden-Baden in Germany whose insides have long since ceased to move.

Hari's family, on the other hand, is life itself; simple and unspoiled, their ways are traditional. They are boisterous Punjabis who live in the center of town, and they are determined to marry their son to a "good" girl. Sushila Anand is their choice, for she knows how to cook and sew, and has wisely chosen to marry instead of developing her voice for the record market. The contrast between the feverish activity connected with the wedding and the languid humidity of Amrita's house where the servants do nothing but count and recount the silver cutlery, is almost too obvious for comment. The bias of the author towards the ancient and ritualistic seems undeniable in the last sentence of the novel: "It was all over, a high pitched voice sang a hymn . . . ; he had led her round the fire seven times and now she was his; and though he still could not see her . . . he was suddenly so happy, he felt he had/never been so happy in his life."

In 1958, seven years after her own marriage, Jhabvala introduced into an increasingly bitter portrait of India, the theme of an East-West marriage. Each of the characters in *Esmond in India* is led by dreams towards destruction, and the conflict arising from Western influences is given strong statement. Ram Nath, the center of an admiring Cambridge crowd long ago, has sacrificed his life as a lawyer for the emergence of new India. His wife, prepared to live in a large house with many relatives and servants, does not understand the cause for which he forfeited his property and subjected himself to prison. He is no longer the bright, sharp little flame that conveyed a sense of urgency; instead, he has grown old, and his sister notices that life itself seems to have withdrawn from him. The degree of his present ineffectiveness is emphasized in his inability even to arrange a marriage between his only son and the daughter of his once-best friend. "His past had been so full; and his present was nothing. He had lost contact, not with the world of affairs, of politics, meetings; he did not mean that, because that he had relinquished deliberately—but with all the world, all life."

If Ram Nath represents the old world, then it is an unsatisfying one. Adherence to the classical prescription for Indian behavior that demands a retreat from things of this world has not brought an enlargement of the mind, but rather a narrow isolation. Can we then assume that those who throw themselves into the affairs of life have any sense of satisfaction? The answer again is "No." Har Dayal, the successful politician-litterateur is devoted to the Public Cause. He presides over never-ending meetings, advises Ministers, and allows himself to be garlanded at public functions. Surrounded as he is by adoration from friends and family, and busy as he may be with lectures and meetings and "many things to be arranged" he is, nevertheless, aware of the absence of spiritual satisfaction within. There is an ever-present sense of futility, and as he walks away from a successful lecture, he reminds himself of Shelley's Ozymandias.

That which has once served to inspire man, now appears to Har Dayal illusory and leaves him with little consolation. Even the central character, Esmond, is enticed into marrying India only to be trapped by her reality. His wife, whose eyes he had once thought "full of all the wisdom and sorrow of the East" was merely a dumb animal who did not even react to his brutality. "His senses revolted at the thought of her, of her greed and smell and languour, her passion for meat and for spices and strong perfumes. She was everywhere; everywhere he felt her—in the heat saturating the air which clung to him and enveloped him as in a sheath of perspiration . . . in the faint but penetrating smell of over-ripe fruit; everywhere, she was everywhere, and he felt himself stifling in her softness and her warmth." His only recourse is to escape, not into himself as Ram Nath has done, nor into frenetic activity as does Har Dayal; for Esmond the only escape is from India herself—furtively and secretly.

In 1959, Ruth Jhabvala, too, returned to England for the first time since her marriage. The impact of the visit was profound: "I saw people eating in London. Everyone had clothes. Everything in India was so different—you know, the way people have to live like that, from birth to death. . . . So after that visit to England I felt more and more alien in India [in *The New York Times,* May 15, 1976]. It is, therefore, not surprising that her next novel, written in 1973, is entitled **Travelers.** She is increasingly interested in those who seek enlightenment in India, for the country seems to have become a stronger and stronger adversary and travelers in it seem to get nowhere. The novel is an account of the journeys made in search of that spiritual core which seems to elude modern man. Some characters, like the Englishman Raymond, are prevented by their own Stoic background from ever becoming a part of India. That he should return to England disappointed, even frustrated by the realities of caste and dirt and bigotry is not surprising. What affects us is what happens to those who surrender to the demands of Indian life.

Asha, the spoiled sister of a successful politician, seems only to wish to indulge in the satisfactions of the flesh; surrounded by silk and lace negligés, swathed in foreign perfume, and gratified by a young boy, she seems too obviously in need of guidance. She flees to an old friend who has gained the reputation of a seer, only to feel uncomfortable if left alone with her, and to witness the indifferent advice given to those who suffer. To parents whose son has mysteriously disappeared, Banubai says: "If He [the One who has willed that it should happen so] wills it, He will bring him back; if not, then not." Perhaps this detachment is commendable, for classical texts enjoin disinterest in action, yet one is compelled to question the fatalistic attitude recommended. Though it is one traditionally associated with India, it is empty of promise.

The other characters meet with similar discouragement. Lee, a young American, is free to travel in any direction, to stop at any station, and walk down any street. She allows herself to be taken to an ashram headed by a Swami of supposedly limitless power and knowledge. Here, Jhab-vala succeeds brilliantly in creating the embodiment of brute power. The Swami compels his disciples to lose themselves in singing hymns to God—an action normally innocent, but here carefully controlled to create unusual excitement. Each of his devotees thinks he speaks only to him, looks only at her. One is literally mesmerized into his being for he will not brook any individuality. He is a loathsome character who demands abject surrender, and when questioned about its necessity, replies in a strange passionate way: "I want her [Lee] to be mine. She must be mine completely in heart and soul and . . . in body also, if I think it necessary." When the surrender occurs, we feel only vile pain, and hear Lee's whimpering sounds against his animal breathing.

It is significant that though India is a country romantically associated with light and truth, travelers seeking those find neither. It is not as if the country identifies a wrong or a right path—what is devastating is that no path, no alternative proves satisfying. The soul, seeking itself, succumbs, eventually to futility. Jhabvala's novel, written in 1975, is delineated in its very title: the dominant image in **Heat and Dust** is that of disease, its smell is of decay. The spirit is whirled around in the duststorms of late March and succumbs to the heat of midsummer. Early in the novel we are warned, "India always changes people," but they are not transformed into Shakespearean objects strange and new, but seem to be stripped of everything that is their identity and left to die, as if life itself is indifferent to their destiny. The cruelty of India seems more terrible, because it is inhuman. In this novel, most of all, we are reminded of the horrible aspect of Kali who dances on the bodies of her victims, who devours their very entrails in a macabre vision of the life cycle.

"Nothing human means anything here. Not a thing." A young English couple seem merely to repeat a never-changing experience: they came to find peace and all they get is dysentery. "They had been robbed of their watches in a house of devotion in Amritsar; cheated by a man they had met on the train to Kashmir who had promised them a cheap house-boat and had disappeared with their advance; . . . in Fatehpur Sikri the girl had been molested by a party of Sikh youths; the young man's pocket was picked on the way to Goa . . ." If this seems a pathetically amusing account of naïve tourists, we are soon assured that similar "robberies" have taken place before, and the victims have been those who know India.

The very structure of the novel reminds us that history is, indeed, repeated. The narrator comes to India in search of the truth about her grandfather's first wife who ran away with an Indian prince in 1923. Clutching the journals she has inherited, she relives in fact and memory, the earlier journey. The English characters in the earlier story are puppets pulled by the strings of duty, stiff-upper-lipped propriety, and all the other shocks Empire was heir to. Amongst this sober lot of petty officials, Olivia seeks to "feel" India. She cannot understand how, surrounded by the exciting life outside, her circle can be satisfied discussing this year's trek to the hills or the washerman who ruins a crepe-de-chine blouse. She is gradually wooed away from this lifelessness by the Nawab who seems to promise her the excitement she craves. He is the charming sensualist who, in order to maintain his lifestyle, relies on thugs to plunder neighboring states. Olivia will not admit to this, and succumbs to him, even to the demand that her pregnancy be terminated in a primitive abortion. Ultimately, all that is left of her is a forlorn house in the hills containing an out-of-tune piano, and some tattered yellow cushions and curtains.

The story of her granddaughter is similarly disillusioning. As she retraces Olivia's journey, she is caught up in the charm of prayer-threads tied for fertility, and gets involved in the delicate problems of caste and personal relationships. Finally, she escapes to the mountainous village where Olivia spent her last days, but here there is no consolation or source of strength. As she looks out of the window of the old house, she can see nothing for it is raining heavily; "it might have made a difference to know that," she murmurs, "I'm impatient for it to stop raining because I want to move on, go higher up. I keep looking up all the time, but everything remains hidden."

If she has attained a solemn peace instead of a grand fulfillment, it may be because she has attained the only degree of contentment offered by contemporary India, and has acquired this only by a stark confrontation with, recognition, and rejection of the old. Is the Doctor's analysis correct that India is only for Indians? Does the Mother Goddess destroy any other who trespasses on her territory? Or does she enjoy a challenge? In a memoir written after his retirement, the English advisor to the Nawab warns, "The most vulnerable are those who love her best . . . India always finds out the weak spot and presses on it . . . Yes, it is all very well to love and admire India but one should never, be warned, allow oneself to become softened by an excess of feeling; because the moment that happens—the moment one exceeds one's measure—one is in danger of being dragged over to the other side. . . . She always remained for him an opponent, even sometimes an enemy, to be guarded and if necessary fought against from without and, especially, from within; from within one's own being."

This last sums up the journey made not only by Jhabvala's characters, but by the author herself. "India will exhaust physically and morally, any Westerner that tries to stay . . . the squalor, heat, indifference, smells and poverty will destroy those not born in the place." In self-defense, Mrs. Jhabvala left the country in 1976 and settled in New York. Significantly, she did not return to her home in England but chose the New World, not because of its promise, but because she feels it is a home for displaced persons. This sense of "immigrant awareness" is her inheritance—an absence of any nostalgia for what is left behind; she feels no ties to any particular country. Those who study her novels cannot avoid their lesson—the individual is left to shift for himself, for the old world provides little strength and the new mutters few words of consolation.

---

**An excerpt from *Heat and Dust***

Everyone considers it a privilege for me to have him in my room. It seems I have been presented with an excellent opportunity to acquire merit by serving a holy man in charity. The question as to whether Chid is holy may remain open, but as far as the town is concerned, he has made a promising first step in shaving his head and throwing away his clothes. For this they seem ready to give him the benefit of many doubts. I've seen them do the same with Indian holy men who often pass through the town with their ochre robes and beads and begging bowls. On the whole they look a sturdy set of rascals to me—some of them heavily drugged, others randy as can be, all it seems to me with shrewd and greedy faces. But as they pass through the streets, some half naked, some fully so, rapping their pilgrim staffs and shouting out the name of God as peddlers shout their wares, people come running out of their houses to lay offerings into the ready begging bowls. Chid also has a begging bowl and often people put something in it—a banana or a guava—which he eats by himself in a corner of my room, afterwards leaving the peel on the floor. When I tell him to pick it up, he does so quite meekly.

Inder Lal is much impressed with Chid. As soon as he comes home from the office, he climbs up to my room and sits there for hours listening to Chid. Chid tells him about the centres of energy within the body and the methods to be employed in order to release them. He points now to his skull and now contorts himself so as to dig himself in the base of his spine; and then he weaves his hands about in the air as if drawing down spiritual forces to be found there. I get very bored with all this. It seems to me that Chid has picked up scraps of spiritual and religious lore here and there, and as he is neither an intelligent nor very educated boy, it has all sort of fermented inside him and makes him sound a bit mad at times. Perhaps he is a bit mad.

*Ruth Prawer Jhabvala, in her* Heat and Dust, *Harper and Row, 1975.*

---

**Penelope Fitzgerald   (review date 25 March 1993)**

SOURCE: "Family Life," in *London Review of Books,* Vol. 15, No. 6, March 25, 1993, pp. 22-3.

[*Fitzgerald is a British novelist and biographer. In the following review of* Poet and Dancer, *which she calls "the saddest of Jhabvala's books," Fitzgerald discusses the strained relationship between the two main characters, Lara and Angel.*]

The poet is not a poet in Ruth Prawer Jhabvala's new novel [***Poet and Dancer***], and the dancer is not a dancer.

> 'Although her movements were always the same—she waved her arms above her head, she ran now to the right of the room, now to the left—her audience obligingly saw what she wanted them to see. She was pleased, she ran faster, she attempted to spin round; her tread

was not light, and she was flustered and breathing hard.'

The dancer aims to impress, but she is also self-deluded. The poet is not.

> 'When she came upstairs she sat at this table and tried to write poetry. It came very hard. When she was small, words had flown out of her like birds; now they fell back into her like stones. Their hardness seemed to lacerate her, and often she had to rest her head on the table to recover before she could go on.'

These two girls, Lara and Angel, are first cousins. Angel's grandparents, Anna and Siegfried Manarr, arrived from Germany in the Twenties to run the New York branch of the family business. 'Every day Siegfried left for an office and Anna saw him off, helping him into his coat.' There is an exact shade of meaning in 'an'; they were not really interested in the business, they were interested in each other. 'They were two separate, large, plump bodies, but in everything else they were one. Music was their principal interest,' and though Jhabvala, with characteristic dryness, tells us that Siegfried was unable to sing a note in tune, we recognise something beautiful, a lifetime of soothing courtship of which later generations will lose the secret.

The Manarrs have two children, Helena and Hugo. Helena marries Peter Koenig, son of the formidable Grandmother Koenig, who lives enshrined with her ancient German maid among massive furniture. Angel is Helena and Peter's only child, a bespectacled little girl who has to endure the ordeal of solitary luncheons with her grandmother, perched opposite her at a table which once seated 20. Hugo's wife, on the other hand, always seems to be away. His daughter, Lara, left more or less to his care, is very pretty, and 'knew the attendant obligation to be charming. She fully accepted it. She kissed her relatives with her lips thrust far forward to show the pleasure this gave her.' If Jhabvala, the wisest and sanest of writers, ever allows herself to show dislike, it is for young women like Lara Manarr.

The relationship between the cousins is obsessive from the first time they meet, when Lara invites the plain and serious-minded Angel into bed with her and teaches her to masturbate. After Peter deserts the family, Angel lives with her mother and helps her to run her boutique. Like Anita Brookner's dutiful daughters, she seems to have the disposition to obedience. She is prepared for slavery, but she becomes a slave not to Helena but to Lara, forgiving her everything, or rather feeling there is nothing to forgive. Lara, in fact, needs to be needed as much as her cousin does. She is promiscuous, magpie-like in her greed for jewellery, monstrous in her insecurity which takes refuge in a battery of drugs and pills, equally monstrous in her demands on Angel. She gets the expected response. 'I'm never going to leave you alone, ever again. Wherever you are, I'll be with you.'

Very effectively, Jhabvala shows that Angel does have some times of happiness, and even of peace, with Lara. One aimless Sunday evening they go out to the riverside suburbs to see where Peter now lives. He is out, and in the end they do nothing but drive about with a kindly young taxi-man and catch the last crowded train back to Grand Central. 'After a while Angel and Lara were too tired to stand and they slid to the floor. Lara fell asleep, and she, too, was smiling like the other sleeping passengers.' In this eventless interlude the dangerous friendship becomes, for a while, intelligible.

The background of *Poet and Dancer* is the Manhattan of the recent past, still almost as pastoral as Scott Fitzgerald makes it in *The Great Gatsby*. Angel gets her early vision of the city from the attic of her grandparents' brownstone, 'looking down into the little paved garden with the brilliant new towers rising above and round her'. All through the first part of the book she catches glimpses of mysterious points of light, the streetlights and the stars together, forming a 'fabulously shifting panorama' whose reflection shimmers in the depths of the East River. It is only towards the end that she perceives the city as oppressive.

For forty years Jhabvala has been respected as an interpreter of cultures and of human beings stranded or transplanted; in particular, of course, of the European in India. In 1975 she left India for America. In *In Search of Love and Beauty* (1983) she considered the German and Austrian refugees in New York, along with her own heritage and identity. In *Poet and Dancer* the Germanness of the Manarrs and the Koenigs is not the most important element, but it is a very distinctive one. As she first did in *A Backward Place* (1965), she contrasts, or at least brings close together, the German and the Indian understanding of life in exile. Both Helena and Angel find consolation—which, it's suggested, might have been something like salvation— in their friendship with Mrs Arora and her son Rohit. The Aroras, whose tiny apartment seems always full of visiting relations, have the insistent, engaging charm which Jhabvala has always known so well how to express. Mrs Arora, who goes into business partnership with Helena, importing Indian convent embroideries for the boutique, is sympathetic and caressing. 'Gliding in her sari, she seemed not so much to enter a room as to insinuate herself into it; the same was true of her manner of establishing relationships, which slid subtly over the dividing line between acquaintance and intimacy.' She makes little presents of spicy food covered with lace mats, sprinkles rosewater, withdraws instantly at the slightest hint of rebuff. Rohit, who works in an airline office, is a good boy, a devoted son, and, when she has time for him, a loyal friend to Angel. But in the Aroras' recent memory there is a cruel scar. The elder son Vikram, a delinquent, was stabbed to death in jail while still awaiting his sentence. For that reason Mrs Arora has felt it necessary to emigrate. When Rohit at last tells the whole story of the family disgrace to Angel, sitting beside her in a crosstown bus, she feels an impulse not to go back to Lara, but to give way to 'an opposite desire' and to get off and walk away with him. However, the 'moment of friendship' passes and comes to nothing. This is the unemphatic way in which Jhabvala prefers to record tragedy.

She has suggested herself that her success as a screenwriter has had its effect on her work as a novelist, and certainly the structure of her stories, since *Heat and Dust,* has become more complex. *Poet and Dancer* begins with a detached narrator, a woman patient of Hugo Manarr's (he is a psychiatrist). She gets to know Helena, now an eccentric old woman living in a musty apartment on the West Side—living alone, for Angel, it seems, is dead. The narrator, who is a novelist, is asked to write the truth—that is, the story of Angel's life. It is to be (Helena insists) the life of a poet, but there are no poems to be found, except for childish verses, only a collection of Angel's old books, in one of which she has underlined the words:

> 'And this truly is what a perfect lover must always do, utterly and entirely despoiling himself of himself for the sake of the thing he loves, and that not only for a time but everlastingly. This is the exercise of love, which no one can know except he who feels it.'

This is a passage which might describe not only Angel, but Mrs Arora and her passion for her criminal son. But, the narrator reminds us, she herself has never written anything but fiction, and 'it is not for me to ascribe an epigraph to someone else's life-story.'

Love hasn't much in common with other emotions—fear, anger, pride—because the question of justification hardly arises. Love for the unlovable, as we know, transforms the object from a toad into a prince. But there is no miracle for Angel. Her fate is a wretched one, and there is an overwhelming sense of waste which makes this the saddest of Jhabvala's books. At the very end

> 'her principal feeling was that a great promise had been made and broken, although it was not clear whether she herself had made and broken it, or whether this had been done to her.' . . .

### Francine du Plessix Gray   (review date 28 March 1993)

SOURCE: "The Cult of the Cousin," in *The New York Times Book Review,* March 28, 1993, pp. 13-14.

[*Gray is a Polish-born American journalist, novelist, and critic. In the following negative review of* Poet and Dancer, *she laments the absence of the "talismanic force of the subcontinent" that energized her previous novels.*]

With the exception of E. M. Forster, no 20th-century writer has more eloquently described Westerners' attempts to grasp the ambiguities of Indian culture than Ruth Prawer Jhabvala. In novels like *Travelers* and *Heat and Dust,* Ms. Jhabvala's portrayals of the subcontinent's *Zeitgeist*—its puzzling composite of emotional prodigality and glaring inequalities, mysticism and materialistic greed—were deft and firm. Critics began to note that her India had become as rich a metaphor for universal experience as Faulkner's Yoknapatawpha County or the czarist Russia of Chekhov's fiction.

Ms. Jhabvala's insights into India have been based on an acquaintanceship far more extensive than Forster's. A Central European Jew whose family fled to Britain just before the outbreak of World War II, she married a Parsi Indian in 1951 and moved to New Delhi. There she brought up three daughters, wrote her first 13 books of fiction and

began her fruitful collaboration with the film makers Ismail Merchant and James Ivory. She continued to live on the subcontinent until 1975, when she felt she could no longer struggle, as she put it, with "the tide of poverty, disease and squalor rising all around . . . the alien, often inexplicable Indian character." She settled permanently in New York City, where she has lived ever since, returning to India every year for a few months in the winter.

Such a relocation is bound to have a deep effect on any writer's work. The first two novels Ms. Jhabvala published after leaving India—*In Search of Love and Beauty* and *Three Continents*—were predominantly set in the United States. Albeit far more minimally, Indian themes and locales continued to inform both these works, which featured Westerners who travel to the subcontinent to seek meaning and redemption with bogus swamis.

This is where *Poet and Dancer* makes a radical break with all of Ms. Jhabvala's earlier fictions: India as place is totally absent from it; and even India as spirit makes but a brief cameo appearance, in the form of a mother-and-son duo who are merely accessory to the narrative. Indeed, the only perceptible link between *Poet and Dancer* and her preceding works is that theme of transcendence-through-submission that incited Ms. Jhabvala's previous cult seekers, a motif that this novel's saintly heroine, Angel, exemplifies in her submissive love for her diabolical first cousin, Lara.

Angel is a homely, gauche, introverted girl who early abandoned the precocious, wondrous gift for poetry she possessed as a child. She is plagued by a need (read it as either pathological or angelic, as her name implies) to sacrifice herself to others, to experience that perfect love in which the lover "utterly and entirely [despoils] himself of himself for the sake of the thing he loves" (a quote from a medieval text Angel scribbles in her journals as an adolescent).

In her youth Angel found such blissful subservience in her passion for her mother, the prosperous divorced businesswoman Helena, and for her maternal grandparents, German Jewish émigrés settled in Manhattan's Upper West Side. Patterns of bonding in *Poet and Dancer* are all matriarchal or Amazonian; the novel's principal male characters—Angel's father, Peter, a feckless country-club suburbanite who divorced Helena shortly after Angel's birth, and her mother's brother, Hugo Manarr, a philandering psycho-spiritual guru who wishes to "fashion a new humanity"—are strikingly shadowy and ineffectual.

After the death of her parents, Helena goes into a sorrowful decline and Angel dedicates herself to taking care of her mother, so elated by her selfless devotion that she goes through school and college "waiting for the moment when she could return home." Helena is also brought out of her doldrums by benevolent Indian émigrés, Mrs. Arora and her son, Rohit, who not only revive her spirits but also rebuild her business and ultimately move into her house. In her early 20's Angel finds a new medium of self-negation in her infatuation for her beautiful cousin, Lara, an erstwhile dancer. The young women met just once, when they were 8 years old, and indulged then, at Lara's instigation, in some memorable genital foreplay.

From the moment the monstrously narcissistic, self-indulgent Lara enters the scene, we know that Angel has found the self-immolating love she has sought since childhood. Angel moves in with her cousin and, blinded by passion, becomes mere putty in Lara's invidious hands, abetting all her lies, condoning her most violent tantrums, admiring her lavish shopping sprees, overlooking her demonic egotism, even sanctioning Lara's tempestuous affair with Angel's own father.

As Lara gets increasingly stoned on her pill binges, wounds Angel by throwing a laser disk at her face and brings home innumerable male strangers into their flat, Angel's infatuation with her cousin (a lesbian relationship is implied) only grows more masochistic and obsessive. Angel's mother, Helena, Helena's Indian companions (the only likable and benevolent figures in this grim narrative) and Lara's own hapless psychotherapist father vainly warn Angel of Lara's destructiveness. And when Lara's family decides to hospitalize her, Angel, true to her promise of never leaving Lara's side, must bring the novel to its unspecified but clearly implied and tragic end.

What are we to make of this fable, in which a symbol of absolute evil—the satanically manipulative and egotistical Lara—is pitted against an emblem of absolute good—the self-immolating, saintly Angel? The clearest clue to the author's moral intent is given by one of Lara's victimized lovers, who says years later: "She wasn't mad. Just bad. People are, believe it or not. You can call it by all the fancy names you please."

But the lusterless predictability of this novel's allegorical figures, and their monotonously described Manhattan setting, make it all the harder to take that platitude to heart. Angel and Lara's wooden supporting cast—devoid of any vivid characters like the buffooning guru and picturesque dowagers of *In Search of Love and Beauty*—brings no respite or relief. The prose of *Poet and Dancer* is as pristinely sparse and finely honed as that of Ms. Jhabvala's earlier fictions, but one misses her wry humor and her rapier eye for detail.

It is significant that the only characters in *Poet and Dancer* who begin to come to life are Helena's Indian helpmates; deprived of the mythic undertow and talismanic force of the subcontinent, the damaged creatures who populate Ms. Jhabvala's bleakly two-dimensional Manhattan can be viewed only with horrified detachment. Given the splendor of her previous work, one can only hope that she will eventually re-endow her American terrain with a vigor analogous to that of her Indian novels.

### Claire Messud　(review date 16 April 1993)

SOURCE: "Tainted by Misery," in *The Times Literary Supplement*, No. 4698, April 16, 1993, p. 20.

[*In the following review of* Poet and Dancer, *Messud claims that Jhabvala's depiction of New York City is less compelling than her portrayals of India in her previous works, and ultimately regards the novel as a failure for its inability to persuade the reader to care about its tragic characters.*]

Unlike her past fictional triumphs, such as *Heat and Dust* or *The Householder,* Ruth Prawer Jhabvala's first novel for six years, *Poet and Dancer,* is not set amid the beautifully conjured complexities of India. It is, rather, a New York novel, but one in which location is important only in so far as its protagonists—Angel, the poet of the title, and Lara, her cousin, the dancer—refuse to engage with it.

New York appears a disordered place, where "there were Japanese businessmen moving in shoals, and stout blond Israelis who ran around on short legs with speed and purpose"; but it is a city where (as in the actual New York) characters glide between apartments or brownstones or restaurants, indoor oases of significance where the world outside does not enter or matter. This is a novel about people rather than about a place—about people's existence despite a place rather than because of it. There is no better setting for such a novel than New York.

Angel and Lara are first cousins. Angel, who has always lived with her mother Helena in a cosy brownstone belonging to her grandparents, the Manarrs, is contented, reclusive, plain and adored by her family. Lara, the daughter of Helena's brother Hugo, spends her childhood being taken round the globe; when she surfaces in New York, she is glamorous, dazzling, beautiful and mysteriously tainted by misery.

Jhabvala captures Lara's nature perfectly when she writes of her as a child visiting the Manarrs in New York:

> "She threw herself into her performance. To help the audience, she called out 'Now I am a flower!' 'Now a princess!' 'See the deer!' Although her movements were always the same . . . her audience obligingly saw what they wanted them to see. She was pleased, she ran faster, she attempted to spin around; her tread was not light and she was flustered and breathing hard . . .".

As the reader might expect, Angel, to whom Lara appears an exotic and precious butterfly, devotes herself adoringly to her cousin; but Lara proves dangerous and ultimately mad, and the result of their closeness is their mutual destruction. Up to a point it is a familiar scenario—the intimacy between doomed creatures of beauty and devoted observers is a powerful literary convention, from *Brideshead Revisited* or *The Great Gatsby* to Donna Tartt's *The Secret History*—although in most cases side-kicks do not perish alongside the objects of their affection.

Angel, sadly, is not as fortunate as most, and though an observer, she does not survive to narrate the novel (had she done so, it would presumably be called simply "Dancer"). Rather, the narrative is framed by a prologue, in which an unnamed writer explains how she has pieced together the tale that follows from the outpourings of Angel's grief-stricken but now deceased mother, Helena, and from snippets told by Roland, a former bellhop in a hotel Lara inhabited, and her sometime lover.

The prologue's failure is, ultimately, the failure at the

heart of the novel; despite Jhabvala's precise and often lovely prose, the premiss does not persuade the reader. Helena is too murky a figure for us to comprehend the narrator's obsession with her story. The dispassionate tone (for example: "Unfortunately it was impossible to tell whether the daughter ever developed as a poet, for there was nothing beyond the juvenilia I had seen on the park bench") does not bring any urgency to Angel and Lara's bond.

That the relationship at the book's core does not come alive is all the more disappointing because of the emotion and skill with which Jhabvala draws the surrounding figures: the Aroras, an Indian mother and son who befriend Helena and Angel, overflow with intriguing detail; the book follows Grandmother Koenig, Angel's paternal grandmother, through a decline into senility (which parallels Lara's descent into madness, but is more affecting); and Rose, the maid who tends her, is rendered charming in her slovenliness. Even the thumbnail sketches of Hugo, Lara's father; of Peter, Angel's father and Lara's lover; of his wife Lilian; and of Roland, the bellhop, suggest more complexity and animation than do the poet and dancer themselves.

It is, on one level, inevitable that this should be so; the bond between any couple is unknowable from the outside, and as long as it is imagined from a distance rather than told from within, it must lose focus and immediacy. It is not mere coincidence that *Brideshead Revisited, The Great Gatsby* and *The Secret History* are first-person narratives. Perhaps Ruth Prawer Jhabvala intended to convey the mystery, puzzlement and dissatisfaction about Lara and Angel's relationship with which those characters around them were left. But she seems unaware that her readers are likely to share those sentiments.

### Judie Newman    (essay date Spring 1994)

SOURCE: "Postcolonial Gothic: Ruth Prawer Jhabvala and the Sobhraj Case," in *Modern Fiction Studies,* Vol. 40, No. 1, Spring, 1994, pp. 85- 100.

[*Newman is a British educator, editor, and critic. In the following essay, she discusses the Gothic elements of* Three Continents *and its main character, the multi-national murderer Crishi, who resembles the real-life serial killer Charles Sobhraj.*]

Gothic motifs are exceptionally prevalent in postcolonial fiction, even from very different locations. Classic postcolonial transformations of Gothic emanate from the Caribbean (Jean Rhys's *Wide Sargasso Sea*), Africa (Bessie Head's *A Question of Power*) and India (Ruth Prawer Jhabvala's *Heat and Dust*). In Canada, Gothic is almost the norm, whether in Margaret Atwood's comic *Lady Oracle,* or Anne Hébert's *Héloïse* (the Québecois tale of a vampire who haunts the Paris Metro), or Bharati Mukherjee's Asian-Canadian *Jasmine.* Not surprisingly, when the heroine of Alice Munro's *Lives of Girls and Women* thinks of writing about Jubilee, Ontario, she promptly chooses to begin a Gothic novel. Nearer home, ghosts wander the pages of Paul Scott's *Raj Quartet,* and J. G. Farrell begins his *Empire Trilogy* in a decaying Great House, complete

with mysteriously fading heroine, demonic cats, and an ever-widening crack in the external wall. Further afield, what is Isak Dinesen doing on a coffee farm in Kenya in 1931 but writing *Seven Gothic Tales?*

It is Dinesen's activity which first raises the question of the ideological consequences of the transfer of a European genre to a colonial environment. Gothic does not always travel well. As Eric O. Johannesson was swift to note, Dinesen creates a fictional Africa which is the counterpart of the eighteenth-century European feudal world of her tales. Setting out into an African forest, she writes: "You ride out into the depths of an old tapestry, in places faded and in others darkened with age, but marvelously rich in green shades" [*Out of Africa,* 1937]. One suspects the Kikuyu did not share her view of a leopard as "a tapestry animal." Dinesen exemplifies here the tendency of the West to textualize the colonial, to transform the Other into a set of codes and discourses which can be recuperated into its own system of recognition, as hegemonic discourse accomplishes its project of endlessly replicating itself. The consequences of generic transfer suggest, then, the difficulty implicit in any counter-discourse—the danger of reinscribing the norms of the dominant discourse within its own apparent contestation, as (to quote Richard Terdiman), "the contesters discover that the authority they sought to undermine is reinforced by the very fact of its having been chosen, as dominant discourse, for opposition" [in *Discourse/Counter-Discourse: The Theory and Practice of Symbolic Resistance in Nineteenth Century France,* 1985].

Rewritings, counter-texts, run the risk of slippage from oppositional to surreptitiously collusive positions. Postcolonial Gothic is therefore Janus-faced. At its heart lies the unresolved conflict between the imperial power and the former colony, which the mystery at the center of its plot both figures and conceals. Its discourse therefore establishes a dynamic between the unspoken and the "spoken for"—on the one hand the silenced colonial subject rendered inadmissible to discourse, on the other that discourse itself which keeps telling the story again and again on its own terms. As a European genre, Gothic cannot unbind all its historical ties to the West. Conversely, its ability to retrace the unseen and unsaid of culture renders it peculiarly well-adapted to articulating the untold stories of the colonial experience. Eve Kosofsky Sedgwick has analyzed the Gothic emphasis on the "unspeakable," both in the intensificatory sense of "nameless horrors," and in the play of the narrative structure itself, with its illegible manuscripts, stories within stories, secret confessions, and general difficulty in getting the story told at all. As Sedgwick puts it, Gothic novels are "like Watergate transcripts. The story does get through, but in a muffled form, with a distorted time sense, and accompanied by a kind of despair about any direct use of language" [in *The Coherence of Gothic Conventions,* 1986].

In her analysis a central privation of Gothic is that of language. When the linguistic safety valve between inside and outside is closed off, all knowledge becomes solitary, furtive and explosive. As a result dire knowledge may be shared, but it cannot be acknowledged to be shared, and is therefore "shared separately," as the barrier of unspeakableness separates those who know the same thing. This Gothic apartheid is almost a classic definition of Imperialism's hidden discourse—the collaboration in a surreptitious relationship, never openly articulated, which is that of colonizer and colonized.

It is possible, however, for a novel to exploit both strategies—to politicize Gothic by overcoming the taboo on speaking, without slipping into the dominant discourse. A symptomatic reading of Ruth Prawer Jhabvala's *Three Continents* is instructive. *Three Continents* is situated at the sharp end of the Gothic generic transfer, both because of its Indian subject matter, and because of its relation to one of the West's more recent horror stories: the Sobhraj case. Jhabvala indicates the relationship of the "unspoken" of Gothic with the activity of "speaking for" of culture by firmly connecting the "unspeakable" nature of events (dark hints, half-told stories) to a story which has already been told so often as to be recognizably a product of Western hegemonic discourse. In modeling her central protagonist, Crishi, upon Charles Sobhraj, the Asian serial killer, Jhabvala contests a dominant cultural narrative while she avoids buying into the cultural stereotype of the exotic Gothic villain. Rather than shifting the problem of violence onto universal grounds (Gothic evil), Jhabvala emphasizes the mutual implication of literary, cultural and political texts in its production. Social dislocation and socioeconomic dispossession in the wake of the end of Empire become determining factors in the representation of the Gothic protagonist.

---

**A strong strain of Gothic has been identified in the works of Jhabvala, which feature demon lovers, mysterious Indian palaces with intricately concealed secrets, ruined forts, poison, willing victims, and the eroticization of spirituality, with gurus standing in for sinister monks and ashrams for convents.**

**—*Judie Newman***

---

A strong strain of Gothic has been identified in the works of Jhabvala, which feature demon lovers, mysterious Indian palaces with intricately concealed secrets, ruined forts, poison, willing victims, and the eroticization of spirituality, with gurus standing in for sinister monks and ashrams for convents. Jhabvala is, of course, influenced by eighteenth-century European literature. Her London University M.A. thesis concerned **"The Short-Story in England 1700-1753,"** and among other topics discussed are the Oriental tale and the falseness of its "East," which was based on preconceived literary notions. Jhabvala also lamented the prevalence of the tale of the "unfortunate maiden fallen into the hands of a dusky seducer." This is nonetheless precisely the plot of *Three Continents,* in which Harriet Wishwell, the scion of a wealthy, if now declining, Ameri-

can clan, stands to inherit a fortune with her twin, Michael, on their twenty-first birthday. When the pair fall under the spell of the mysterious Rawul, one of Jhabvala's ambivalent guru figures, the possibility looms that their legacy will pass swiftly through his hands and into those of his charismatic second-in-command, Crishi, Harriet's husband, whose sexual favors she shares with homosexual Michael and the Rawul's mistress, Rani. In the novel Jhabvala conflates historical Gothic with the plot of modern Gothic. As defined by Joanna Russ [in *The Female Gothic,* edited by Juliann, E. Fleenor, 1983], the latter involves a young, shy, passive heroine, with absent or ineffectual parents and a friend or ally in the pale, bloodless "Shadow Male." She travels to an exotic setting, forms a connection with a dark, magnetic "Supermale," finds herself up against "Another Woman," and has to solve a "Buried Ominous Secret," usually in modern Gothic a criminal activity centered on money. The plot generally ends in attempted murder. In *Three Continents* the exotic area is India; the persecuted Harriet is totally passive and after an initial ambivalence towards dark, super-phallic Crishi, becomes his sexual slave, disregarding sinister rumors. (There was, of course, a first wife with a nameless fate.) Rani features as the other woman. Harriet's family includes a conventionally vapid mother and a pathologically spendthrift father, neither of whom is much help to her. The pallid Michael fulfills the textbook role of the Shadow Male, apparently representing the security of childhood, but actually inducting Harriet into the Rawul's "Sixth World" movement. The Buried Ominous Secret turns out to be an international smuggling ring, masterminded by Crishi who transports jewels and *objects d'art* across borders under cover of the movement. Throughout the novel the reader is afforded glimpses of the real situation, with recurrent dark hints and a veritable anthology of half-told stories and half-heard conversations in the wings, creating an atmosphere of sustained menace. Elements of historical Gothic are self-consciously introduced, often in a fashion which suggests the conditioning force of the literary genre on Harriet. Her first encounter with Crishi in her brother's room is presented as an erotic shock, "as of a live wire suddenly coming in contact with an innermost part of one's being," though the demon-lover has appeared only to borrow some shaving cream. Later he succeeds in binding Harriet to him, forcing her body to move in unison with his "as if my body obeyed him more than it did me" until she makes good her escape and flees, in true Gothic heroine mode: "I didn't stop running till I was in the house." The scene is somewhat undercut by the fact that what Crishi was enjoying was a three-legged race at a Fourth of July party. Nonetheless, Harriet soon awakens in the night "suddenly as if someone had called me." As a matter of fact, somebody has—Crishi—who is standing by her bed (no Jane Eyre long-distance telepathy here). The couple repair to the emblematic locale of the ruined Linton house, where, after peering through the windows at its ruined splendors (Cathy and Heathcliff), Crishi seduces Harriet. Later, exulting in passion, Harriet describes herself as "a woman savage running to her mate" when in fact she has been dispatched to fetch Crishi's trousers. Quite clearly Jhabvala is consciously exploiting Gothic conventions while underlining the distinction between the conditioning force of literary genre and the resistant fact of Crishi. A group of "bhais," the Rawul's henchmen, rival any eighteenth-century group of banditti, and Rani takes to haunting Harriet's bedroom by night, "her reflection ghostlike in the mirror", like some madwoman in the attic. After a journey through "uncharted regions" sealed in a small chamber lit by a ghostly blue light (the sleeping coupe of an Indian train—an interesting variation on the Gothic image of live burial), the novel ends with the ascent of a winding stair to a crenellated roof terrace, reminiscent of Thornfield Hall, where all is revealed by the villain. The twist in the tale lies in Harriet's transition from victimhood to complicity. At the close, Harriet joins with her demon-lover to conceal Michael's murder and to forge the suicide note which will ensure that his fortune passes to them.

As a smuggler of art objects, Crishi is explicitly connected to the cynical and exploitative transfer of art from one culture to another, in his case via the plundering of the East to the benefit of the West. The questions raised by generic transfer are therefore thematized within the action itself. Artistic transfer is nonetheless a two-way traffic, as Jhabvala's exploitation of European conventions in a postcolonial environment demonstrates. Is this use of "Asian Gothic" merely a Eurocentric, Orientalist strategy, to adopt Edward Said's terminology? Or does it offer the postcolonial writer opportunities to criticize European textual and ideological practices by strategies unavailable to the realist novel? Does it merely contribute to the already abundant literature of India as horror story? Or can it illuminate the roots of violence in the postcolonial situation?

The answer to these questions depends upon an informed awareness of the other story within the novel. Sobhraj's early life stands as emblematic of all those who have been displaced, whether by war, the redrawing of territorial boundaries, changes in cultural sovereignty, political oppression or economic dispossession: all are factors which interact in the production of his story. As the illegitimate offspring of a Vietnamese mother and an Indian father, born in Saigon when it was under Japanese occupation administered by the Vichy French regime, Sobhraj's early experiences included capture by the Vietminh, rescue by the British, abandonment by his mother who married a French lieutenant, and life on the streets of Saigon. When French defensive activity reintensified and the lieutenant returned, his mother reclaimed him, only to move to Dhakar, French West Africa, then France. Sobhraj ran away by ship to Saigon, only to be promptly sent to Bombay by his father in a vain attempt to gain Indian citizenship. Stateless, institutionalized at various points, Sobhraj shuttled between countries until adulthood, excluded from the dream of nationality, economic security or family identity.

In the 1970s Sobhraj left a trail of bodies across India, Thailand and Nepal; he specialized in smuggling gems for which he needed a constant supply of fresh passports, bought or stolen from overlanders on the hippie trail. He then graduated to the *modus operandi* of a "drug and rob" man, first surreptitiously administering laxatives and other drugs, then "medicines" which reduced his victims

to helplessness. Many of his targets, like Harriet and Michael, were seeking mystic enlightenment in the East. While planning to rob the jewelry store in Delhi's Imperial Hotel in 1976, Sobhraj was finally caught when he drugged an entire package tour of sixty French graduate engineers, whose instantaneous and simultaneous collapses in their hotel lobby finally aroused suspicion. Sobhraj was at various points arrested and jailed in Kabul, Teheran, Greece and Paris, and made several daring escapes, notably following an unnecessary appendectomy, from which he bore identifying scars. A man of considerable charisma, he often gained the sympathy of his victims and accomplices by tales of his awful youth (as Crishi does with Harriet). His main female accomplice, a young Canadian, appears to have been kept in total sexual thrall to him. Other parallels with the fictitious Crishi are legion. Both men spend part of their youth in Bombay, live by jewel smuggling and participate in murder. The hotel jewelry shop is the locus of mystery in *Three Continents.* Crishi goes in for martial exercises (for Sobhraj, it was karate), has abdominal scars, prison sentences in Teheran and elsewhere and has carried out jailbreaks. Both Sobhraj and Crishi relish media exposure, the former after his arrest, the latter in connection with the "Sixth World" movement. For both, mobility is all. Harriet tends to assume that Crishi is somewhere around the house, only to receive phone calls from New York or Zurich. (Sobhraj once walked out saying that he would be back in an hour, then sent a telegram from Iran.) At the close, when Harriet is looking for Michael, she encounters Paul, one of the Westerners, who is clearly very unwell. Like others in the group, he has given Crishi his passport and is begging for its return. It is an exact replication of the means by which Sobhraj surrounded himself with couriers, targets and accomplices. Paul came to India "to get away from home, from his family, from himself . . . not to be bound by anything." Boundless freedom has left him, however, without the means to move on, in a position of statelessness.

Charles Sobhraj's story has already been told several times, in two works of "faction," one since revised and updated, in a T. V. mini-series, and in various newspapers and magazines, quite sufficient to suggest that the Sobhraj case is one of those "Orientalist" horror stories which the West likes to repeat. From the first, the story served ideological purposes. In India it broke at an opportune moment during the Emergency Rule powers of Indira Gandhi, when the Maintenance of Internal Security Act meant that anyone suspected of "subversion" could be jailed indefinitely. In India the international dimension of the story was insisted upon: "India's newspapers, subdued and fearful under Indira Gandhi's dictatorial powers, relished a story that had no political overtones. The 'notorious gang' and 'international killers' were profiled endlessly, mug shots decorating Sunday feature pages" [Thomas Thompson, *Serpentine,* 1980].

In the West the evolution of the story was classically hegemonic, its political complexities steadily watered down in favor of a stereotypically Orientalist tale. One of the first in the field, Thomas Thompson, in his "faction," *Serpentine,* drew explicit parallels between the events of Sobhraj's life and the dismantling of the French colonial Empire. Thompson's portrayal of him as a casualty of colonialism, lacking roots, security and identity, ends on a note that appears to have offered Jhabvala the cue for the American opening of her novel. In jail in India Sobhraj was apparently considering his future:

> He required a country in which he was neither known nor wanted by police, one in which riches abounded, one whose boundaries were easy to traverse illegally, one whose residents were generous with attention and applause. At last report, the serpentine roads of destiny—he believed—would lead him to the United States.

Thompson's implicit recourse, here, to the "invasion scare" model of Gothic is very much the emphasis of other works, which have tended to minimize the post-colonial background. In *Bad Blood* Richard Neville and Julie Clarke read Sobhraj in terms of a paradigm of early deprivation. Neville went to Delhi to interview Sobhraj with a theory "of Charles as a child of colonialism, revenging himself on the counterculture" [in *Shadow of the Cabra: The Life and Crimes of Charles Sobhraj*]. He concluded, however, that Sobhraj's claims to anti-lmperialist motivation were groundless, and read his story in terms of individual psychological rejection. Updating the book ten years later for a television mini-series, Neville revealed that his relationship with his co-author had been severely threatened by his involvement in the case, and that the pair had come close to being polarized into victim and accomplice. Julie Clarke's sympathies had remained with the killer's victims; Neville however admitted that when interviewing Sobhraj he came to feel "like a conspirator." The mini-series, *Shadow of the Cobra,* developed the hint, focusing its plot on the threat to one romantic relationship (two young journalists) and transforming Sobhraj from child of colonialism to diabolical villain. In an artistic trajectory which says much for the extent to which the rage for the Raj has been transformed into the redemonization of the East, the role of Sobhraj was taken by Art Malik, veteran of *The Jewel in the Crown, The Far Pavillions* and *Passage to India.* The blurb to the reissued tie-in said it all: "An audience with psychopathic mass murderer Charles Sobhraj. It was like having supper with the devil." Reviewers concurred that Sobhraj was a "plausible, Bruce Lee style, Asian fiend" operating in the "dangerous jungle" of Asia. There, this "diabolically charismatic" villain took his victim on a "descent into hell." The evolution of the various accounts shows the West writing and rewriting Sobhraj into the norms of the snaky Oriental villain, with socio-economic readings excised in favor of (at best) popular psychoanalysis, and (at worst) elements of *Vathek,* Milton's Satan and Fu Man Chu.

In contrast, Jhabvala's understanding of the socio-economic dimension of the story is already evident in her first attempt at the theme. In her short story **"Expiation,"** the plot centers upon a nouveau riche Indian family who have made a fortune in textiles, and their son's fatal involvement with Sachu, a criminal from a deprived background. Sachu's target for kidnap, ransom and murder is the child of an Indian military family, described as light-skinned educated gentry who speak Hindi with an accent "like Sahibs." Arrested, Sachu boasts of his philosophy to

the press, much as Sobhraj did. In **"Expiation,"** the crime is less the product of a fiendish Oriental torturer than a revenge across both class and race, against the preceding Imperial norms (the Sahibs) and their replication in a newly industrialized India.

The account chimes with recent research on the serial killer, which contextualizes his motivation in socio-economic terms. Anthropologist Elliott Leyton has argued that serial killers are intensely class conscious and obsessed with status [in *Hunting Humans: The Rise of the Modern Multiple Murderer,* 1986]. The majority are adopted, illegitimate or institutionalized in youth, and seek a sense of identity in international celebrity. Typically their victims are drawn from a social category above that of the killer, and the prime mission is to wreak revenge on the established order. (Ted Bundy, for example, took the most valuable "possessions" of the American middle class, their beautiful and talented university women.) In **"Expiation"** the fictitious Sachu wreaks revenge simultaneously on the Eurocentric army officers *and* the new entrepreneurial class via the deaths of both their offspring. For Layton, as for Jhabvala, serial killers are the dark consequences of the social and economic formations that pattern our lives. Killings of this nature are a protest against a perceived exclusion from social discourse, and constitute a form of utterance on the part of those who have looked at their lives and pronounced them unlivable:

> The killings are thus also a form of suicide note (literally so with most mass murderers, who expect to die before the day or week is out; metaphorically so for most serial murderers, who sacrifice the remainder of their lives to the "cause"), in which the killer states clearly which social category has excluded him.

The act itself is therefore the "note," an unspeakable crime which is nonetheless a message that society must learn to read. Unlike mass murderers, serial killers tend to want to live to tell their stories and bask in fame. Once society has read the message, the story will be retold by press and media, and become a means to identity. Two other factors cited by Leyton in the formation of the serial killer have a bearing on *Three Continents:* firstly the inculcation of a dream or ambition which society betrays, and secondly the necessary existence of cultural forms that can mediate killer and victim in a special sense, ridding victims of humanity and killer of responsibility. (Leyton cites the social validation of violent identity in modern films, television and fiction. Jhabvala employs a totalitarian political movement.)

In recasting events in the Gothic mold Jhabvala is able to re-politicize the story, revealing its horrors without stereotypical demonization by insisting on the interrelationship of the Gothic "unspeakable" and the "spoken for" of culture, the discourse from which the postcolonial is excluded, the discourse into which the Other can break only by violence.

Where the Sobhraj case was used in India as a diversion from the increasingly dictatorial nature of the political settlement, Jhabvala supplies a public political dimension by the introduction of the Rawul's militaristic "Sixth World" movement, which dehumanizes its followers and legitimizes brutality on the basis of a vaguely transcendental cult. Ostensibly devoted to the unification of the globe by "Transcendental Internationalism," the Rawul plans its transformation into a "stateless, casteless, countryless" world by transcending not so much spiritual as national and political bounds, and with them "the tiny concepts, geographical or other, of an earlier humanity." Linda Bayer-Berenbaum has connected the resurgence of twentieth-century Gothic with the waning of Sixties cults, arguing that both movements were motivated by the search for an expanded and intensified consciousness. She therefore likened the Gothic revival to "a variety of religious cults that have grown in popularity, be they Christian fundamentalist, Hari Krishna, the Sufis, or most recently, the Moonies. Unlike these movements though, Gothicism asserts that transcendence is primarily evil."

In *Three Continents* the Gothic "secret" provides an ironic revelation of the real import of the Rawul's transcendental activities in the political world and the extent to which they operate as a legitimizing cover for Crishi, the excluded. Natural and political boundaries *are* crossed, but for criminal reasons. The movement towards being citizens of the world depends heavily for its day to day activities upon stolen passports. The plan to unite the best of all civilizations translates into the pillaging of material artifacts. Harriet and Michael throw off Western materialism, only for it to come back to haunt them from the Third World. Mobility is the mark of both the Western truth-seeker—and the serial killer. Just as the latter links the culturally spoken and the unspeakable, so Crishi reveals in his actions the revenge of the excluded. Sobhraj, the stateless exile, killed those whose willful deracination parodied his own state, just as Crishi, who has had disinheritance forced upon him, sees to it that his condition is shared.

In addition to reflecting the Rawul's project in a dark mirror, so the Gothic structure dramatizes Harriet's surreptitious slippage from a countercultural to a collusive position, from victim to accomplice, and implicitly from a readerly to a writerly role. At the beginning of the novel Harriet's stunned silence as the Rawul takes over is such as to make her almost a voyeur, watching her story unfold and guessing its outcome from the same hints available to the reader. Again and again the text tells us that Harriet can get no explanations from the men: "What was it all about? Who were they, and why had they come? I waited for Michael to tell me, but he had no time to tell me anything. 'You'll find out,' was all he said." The reader is thus brought into close affective proximity to events, while being simultaneously warned off from any uncritical suspension of disbelief. Originally Harriet and Michael communicate wordlessly, the one often completing the other's thoughts. Crishi, however, appropriates their private language (specifically the term "neti" meaning "phony") and deprives them of it. Though each is enjoying Crishi's sexual favors, neither feels able to discuss the matter, converting their former spiritual communion into a shared secret, separately held. When Harriet shares her bed with Rani as well as Crishi, she feels Michael "willing me not to speak" so that the act remains "unmentioned, rather than

unmentionable." The prohibition on speech even extends to Crishi's marriage proposal. He manages to propose by proxy, through Rani, so that Harriet becomes "spoken for" without ever being spoken to.

The secret engagement and muffling of events is in strong contrast to the ever more publicity conscious Movement, which develops to the point at which "interviews became the central activity of the house." The Rawul has a tendency to convert all his utterances into speeches for public consumption, even those delivered to his small daughters. Linguistic and political structures evolve together. A chat with the Rawul becomes "more in the nature of an audience. Everything around the Rawul was taking on more formality." The movement to transcend all boundaries begins to use security guards and checkpoints and to beat up intruders. Even Michael's speech patterns change so that instead of groping for thoughts he becomes brisk and unreflective: "he no longer had to think. . . . It was all there, all formulated." Where Gothic mystery preserves the possibility of unvoiced stories, the Sixth World movement accretes everything to one public formulation, assisted by Anna Sultan, a journalist who provides their first "major media exposure." Harriet's difficulty in getting at her story contrasts with Anna's ease. Harriet notes that "Everything I had only guessed at Anna seemed to know for sure." Anna's account nonetheless includes a highly fanciful tale of the Rawul's initial encounter with Crishi, first in his dreams, then promptly discovered asleep in a poet's tomb. Over the others' protests, Rani and Crishi endorse the story: " '[I]t's what the common reader wants,' Crishi said. 'Ask Harriet. . . . Harriet liked it and she's a very common reader. You have to give them these sort of stories.' " The incident provides an explicit comment on the way in which cultural formations function to legitimize exploitation. Anna Sultan herself turns the personal into the public, making her reputation with a daring profile of a Lebanese leader: "daring because she had recorded his private along with his public activities, and had not drawn back from chronicling her own affair with him."

For Anna any assignment involves a love affair, which is speedily terminated when her story is finished. In Crishi, however, she meets her match, as the postcolonial subject refuses textualization except on his own terms. Crishi's only interest is the book which will publicize, authenticate and create his identity, whereas Anna becomes personally attached and exploited in her turn—the fate which threatened Richard Neville at Sobhraj's hands. It is a telling image of the revenge of the excluded subject, who turns his own exploitation against his exploiters to write his own social message.

It is not for nothing that the group is compared to a movie company; their lives are being swallowed up by public performance. The Rawul even stages appropriate public ceremonies to authenticate the movement. Harriet's wedding is briskly converted into a symbol of the synthesis of East and West, so symbolic that Crishi spends the wedding night with Rani. From perceiving herself with Michael as "blank pages no one had ever written on," Harriet is being steadily scripted into a public role. A second ceremony which involves the public weighing of the Rawul against a pile of books, supposedly representing the wisdom of the ages, reveals both the totalizing project of the movement, and its amorality. Like Crishi, the Rawul intends to textualize himself on his own terms. Michael had wanted to buy bound sets of volumes as counterweights, but Crishi exercises a financial veto so that the Rawul is actually outweighed by a motley collection of tattered secondhand copies of the Bible, Plato, *The Tibetan Book of the Dead,* Carlos Castaneda and Kierkegaard. The form of this attempt to appropriate all cultures to one universal meaning is ludicrously parodic; several volumes have to be removed from the scales to balance the Rawul. Significantly "it was at Kierkegaard that the Rawul started to swing up"—appropriately, given Kierkegaard's separation of the religious and the ethical spheres. The twins, however, react uncritically. For Michael the event is a summation of "everything he had thought and read and experienced. . . . It was all summed up for him in the pile of books on the one hand . . . and the Rawul on the other." Meanwhile Harriet uses the mythologizing process in order to put a high gloss on Crishi's activities, reflecting that "it doesn't seem to matter that sometimes these gods don't behave too well, Venus running off with Mars, Krishna cheating on Radha—they still remain gods."

Once on Indian soil however, Crishi lives up to Krishna, his trickily elusive namesake, and naked power emerges from behind the myths and legends as the Rawul's movement swiftly modulates into a conventional political party. Harriet and Michael are now linguistically isolated—they speak no Indian languages. Michael's death is the direct result of the clash between the spoken and the unspoken. Impatiently he demands that the Rawul make a religious oration, rather than merely entertaining influential politicos: " 'When's he going to speak? He's got to speak,' he insists." Michael is slow to realize that: "everyone knows that real power, whether political, economic, social, psychological or even mystical, functions silently and has no need of the semblance of speech, even though it never ceases to use that semblance to persuade that we participate" [in *A Rhetoric of the Unreal: Studies in Narrative and Structure, Especially of the Fantastic,* by Christine Brooke-Rose, 1983]. Secure in his power base, the Rawul dispenses with the mediating forms which had previously legitimized him. Instead, his wife speaks, giving secret instructions in her own language to her henchmen who promptly remove Michael. The power to which Michael contributed by his rhetorical formulations is unleashed to silence him, and to consign him to the unspoken of Gothic.

In contrast, Harriet's movement into collusion with crime is rendered as a progression from the unspoken to the fully discursive, as Jhabvala demonstrates that the final horror is equally located in the process of "speaking for." Harriet's collusion is dramatized at the close in the suicide note which she co-authors with the presumed killer. Harriet knows very well that Crishi's account of Michael's suicide is a lie (the supposed suicide note is too badly spelled to be his). She collaborates nonetheless in rewriting the note in more convincing fashion, revising a visibly false story to make it more believable. Revision becomes replication-as-falsity. Harriet would have been truer to the facts of

murder if she had allowed the gaps and absences in the original to speak for themselves. No longer a common reader, Harriet has progressed to writing as complicity and betrayal. She writes "with ease," almost with enjoyment, as if becoming Michael, speaking for him, constructing a fiction of defeated dreams as his motive:

> I said that I—that is, I, Michael—was going away because there was nothing in this world that was good enough for me. . . . I said that if once you have these expectations—that is, of Beauty, Truth, and Justice—then you feel cheated by everything that falls short of them; and everything here—that is, here, in this world—does fall short of them. It is all neti, neti.

As that last word indicates, Harriet uses their private language to authenticate a public document. Spiritual communion has become the unspeakable. Framed to meet legal requirements, the note is multiply authored—ostensibly by Michael, actually by Harriet, partly at Crishi's dictation. It is the product of multiple silencing: that of the postcolonial subject, of the woman excluded from knowledge and, fatally, of the representative of the society which excluded them. At the close Crishi has carried out the action which communicates a social message of defeated hopes, while Harriet, writing as a male and at the same time "writing off " a male, has produced a socially legitimizing text. The note therefore conceals—and sanctions—an act of violence.

This essay began with a question—whether the Gothic novel is an accomplice in the process of Eurocentric textualization of the East, or whether it may serve to reveal the sources of violence in the colonial encounter. In countercultural Harriet, who slips into the position of accomplice, Jhabvala provides a searching investigation of the psychopathology of power, the process of domination and its relation to mediating cultural forms. The complicity of the writer in generic manipulation and transfer may indeed amount to collusion in violence and exploitation, but may also reveal the bases of such violence in silencing and exclusion. The duplicity of Gothic—its propensity for crossing boundaries, violating taboos, transgressing limits, together with its sense of blockage, privation and prohibition against utterance—makes it the perfect means to dramatize the horrors of the relationship between the social group which sanctions its actions by cultural forms, and the excluded from discourse who speak by deeds. The Gothic undermines the Rawul's pretensions to one-ness and totalization at the same time as it preserves the unspeakable quality of the killer's actions. By its intertextual nature, its ability to translate from one text to another and back, it prevents the univocal from holding sway. At the close, therefore, Jhabvala offers a multiple text, a piece of writing which conceals a secret and reveals a silenced story, which demonstrates the writer's complicity and—by highlighting issues of fictionality—separates the reader from affective collusion. As the original suicide note showed, truth for the postcolonial writer may be measured as much by its failure to represent itself as by its social production. What the Gothic does not say, its half-told stories, constitute the evidence of a contrary project undermining public formulations. By preserving the unspoken within the text, Jhabvala remains true to the events of both political and social history.

## Molly E. Rauch    (review date 11 September 1995)

SOURCE: "Other Voices, Other Rooms," in *The Nation,* New York, Vol. 261, No. 7, September 11, 1995, pp. 244-5.

[*In the following mixed review of* Shards of Memory, *Rauch calls the complex relationships of the novel part of a "paradox that . . . lacks depth."*]

In her twelfth novel, Ruth Prawer Jhabvala once again addresses the themes of family and history through the premise of a set of old papers. It's a method she cultivated many books and screenplays ago in her Booker Prize-winning **Heat and Dust** (1975), in which a woman discovers her late step-grandmother's scandalous letters and goes to India to investigate. As in Bharati Mukherjee's more recent *Holder of the World* (1993), the double-time plot can make for a refreshing reclamation of the past.

But not always. From a cache of scraps and scrawlings, **Shards of Memory** traces the lives of an American/British/Indian clan with Jhabvala's familiar multicultural ease. A pianist-turned-devotee travels from her lavish New York home to London, where she meets a young Bombay native reciting sticky poetry. They both want to sit at the feet of the Master, their spiritual teacher, who, typically, never shows up. No matter: The disciples marry and have a child, Baby. Baby becomes a wise woman who routinely flies to London to rescue needy relatives. In time, her grandson Henry, crippled by a near-fatal car accident, inherits several trunks stuffed with the Master's polyglot scribblings. His parentage uncertain—the Master may have been his father—Henry delves into the documents in search of this elusive, mango-loving charismatic.

In bits and pieces—shards, of course—Henry learns not only about the Master but also about his family. True to her title, Jhabvala manages to leave out whole chapters of crucial information. Take the Master. Strange thing this: His teachings and preachings are practically absent from the book. For instance, Henry sums them up: "Overcome your self." And Henry's mother, Renata, wanders for so much of her life and this novel in a "vague mist" that we never know what she's thinking, or even if she can.

With gaps such as these, Jhabvala is waving an impatient hand at us. Shoo, she may be saying, I have three more generations to go. And it's true, she occasionally guns the engine of her saga: Three main characters die, one is crippled for life and ten years pass all in the space of three pages. But she also means the gaps.

Her shrewd satire implicates her characters—if not her skill—in the allowance of such holes. Kavi, for example, the patriarch of the family, is a "shriveled sage in white muslin." After he sinks into his "final darkness," his progeny trek to the Hudson River and scatter his ashes, which "seemed to disappear not into the water but into the blaze of light reflected on its surface." Compare this holy departure with the death of the Master, who gorges himself on a decadent feast and drinks bottle after bottle of liquor until, bulging and sweating, he chokes on a piece of meat. "He clutched in his agony at the tablecloth, bringing all the plates, dishes, glasses, bottles, and decanters crashing down with him. . . . He heaved and retched and swelled till, unable to explode, he imploded." Ugh. His devotees hardly blink at this debauched ending. They are desperate for spiritual fulfillment, and their blind attraction to the Master requires a disregard for details and reasons that mirrors Jhabvala's own disregard for such particulars.

The devotees nevertheless persist in their quest for enlightenment, thwarted by their ambitious dreams of masterhood and their stubborn resistance to change. So many male centerpieces: Besides the spiritual Master, there is Kavi, the florid poet, as the literary master; Henry, the leader of the future, as the intellectual master; and stodgy Graeme, Baby's husband and a rather cloistral Brit, as a patriarchal master.

Women? Well, yes, and women of extraordinary strength. But they all have their masters, spiritual or nuptial, and their masters are men. Even the most tenacious and determined of them all, Baby, speaks her first words in self-deprecating subservience: "I'm not really the right person to tell you anything because my thoughts—if I have any at all, my husband would have said—are not very orderly." That she then goes on to explain immensely complex relationships in a lucid and amusing manner is a paradox, but a paradox that, like much of the novel, lacks depth. If Jhabvala were remarking on such patterns, or exploring their implications, there might be provocative insights borne of this male-centeredness. Instead, themes such as Baby's self-effacement are made to seem inevitable. Thus Jhabvala's fictional family ends up, four generations later, where it started: still crossing signals, still passive in the face of disappointment, still befuddled by missed opportunities. How unmasterly of them all—except the one winking mischievously, waving her hand at us, shooing us on our way.

## C. K. Stead    (review date 30 November 1995)

SOURCE: "The Master," in *The London Review of Books,* Vol. 17, No. 23, November 30, 1995, p. 12.

[*Stead is a poet, fiction writer, and critic from New Zealand. In the following review of* Shards of Memory, *he suggests that when Jhabvala does not attempt "to represent India truthfully, accurately, in all its complexity," her novels, like this one, lack energy and focus.*]

Henry James's injunction to the novelist was 'Dramatise! Dramatise!' Ezra Pound advocated 'the presentative method'. A dozen lesser but important voices have urged that modern fiction must enact, not tell. The strongest intellectual pressures on the serious novelist in this century have all been, that is to say, in the direction—the ultimate direction—of the playscript or the screenplay and away from the elaboration of prose as prose. But what does the writer do in her novels who finds herself engaged outside them in writing screenplays? Does her fiction push back in the opposite direction, against the flow of history? Does the novel become a space for the kinds of writing which screenplays forbid—a large loose bag into which she can pop odd pieces of narrative embroidery?

Such questions may help to explain the unsatisfactoriness of Ruth Prawer Jhabvala's recent novels. Or simpler explanations may be more pertinent: waning energy, for example, and the loss, or abandonment, of her real—her serious—subject.

Polish-born, English-educated, married to an Indian, and living, at least until the Eighties, most of her adult life in India, Jhabvala has been a writer with a subject. She has been able to put India into Western drawing-rooms in a way that made it almost intelligible. She has belonged to India, but not entirely. In an essay she once described the three stages of a Westerner's reaction to that country: 'first stage, tremendous enthusiasm—everything Indian is marvellous; second stage, everything Indian not so marvellous; third stage, everything Indian abominable.' For some people, she says, the cycle goes on: 'I have been through it so many times that now I think of myself as strapped to the wheel.'

The result has been a special kind of detachment. All her views of India are provisional. She can present its manners and people comically without mocking or demeaning them; she can present them tragically, while preserving a few grains of irony. And there has been a gradual sense of deeper understanding. The view from the outside has become (especially, perhaps, in the short stories) a view not just from within Indian society but almost from within the Indian temperament and sensibility.

Her subject has been, of course, not so much India as India in Westerners' perceptions of it; and there are certain things which she will not let us forget. It is 'a backward place' (the title of one of her novels) where poverty, violence and injustice exist on a scale too huge to be corrected, are impossible to escape from and depressing to the sensitive soul, not least because in time they come to be accepted. It is also a place of great physical discomfort, especially of 'heat and dust' (another title). It is a society which baffles the Western mind, combining a terrible passivity with a mysterious and even dangerous power. It is a place of contrasts—ugliness and beauty, sensuality and spirituality.

I suppose it was inevitable that as Jhabvala's life changed (she now divides her time, the blurb tells us, between New York and Delhi), the fiction would change too; and *Three Continents,* the novel before the last, signalled that it was to be a change entirely for the worse. *Shards of Memory* continues along the same lines. What is lost, I suspect, is the discipline of trying to represent India truthfully, accurately, in all its complexity. Without that effort, Jhabvala's imagination appears to have few clear reference points and little ballast. The Indian novels impressed because they were real, truthful, observant, conscientious, witty and plausible. *Three Continents* and *Shards of Memory* seem by comparison like a child's game of 'let's pretend'.

The new novel is set mostly in New York with some scenes in London and a few flashbacks to Delhi. It covers an ill-defined but considerable timespan which, given the generations passed through, ought to be even greater than the novel's few defining points allow. American Elsa, daughter of Dorothy Kopf, while visiting London in search of a guru known as the Master, meets and marries an Indian poet, Hormusji Bilimoria, known as Kavi. Their child, known throughout the novel, even in her old age, as Baby (she has a name but unlike her father's it is not divulged), tells the opening 40 pages of the story, after which it continues in the third person. Elsa leaves Baby with her mother in New York and returns to London to live in a warring lesbian relationship with Cynthia Howard, another devotee of the Master. So there are two households: in New York, Kavi with his mother-in-law and daughter; in London, Elsa and Cynthia.

In the flip of not many pages (with sections beginning, 'Several more years passed . . .') Baby has grown up and married English diplomat Graeme, a nephew, as it happens, of Cynthia. These two stay together only long enough to engender a daughter, Renata, after which Graeme goes on his philandering way, and Baby on hers. In not too many more pages Renata has grown up and gone to London to stay with her grandmother Elsa and great-aunt Cynthia. There she meets and is almost imperceptibly (in the sense that neither he nor she seems to notice) impregnated by Carl, a young German who carries about with him a manuscript entitled 'Education as Elevation', attempting to interest people he meets in the street in its ideas. This he will continue to do without success for the novel's next 20 years and 40 pages—long enough for Henry, his child to Renata, to grow up in New York, receive terrible injuries in a car crash in London while visiting his great-grandmother Elsa and great-great-aunt Cynthia, and learn that he is the spiritual child of the Master. This is so, it seems, because it was the Master who, while idly touching Renata's breasts and belly during her first visit to him, perceived that she was pregnant—something she had not guessed; and also because the Master's death (he chokes on a piece of meat) and Henry's birth are more or less simultaneous.

Parallel to this blood-line, which passes through five generations in 100 pages while losing only great-great-grandmother Dorothy, there is another, that of Madame Richter, a Russian immigrant piano teacher in New York, and her female descendants. Madame Richter lives with her daughter in one room in a rundown house on the West Side; and with the appalling and implausible stasis which afflicts the characters in this novel, 'she lived there for years, her granddaughter was born and brought up there.'

By page 47 the granddaughter is giving the piano lessons, but Madame Richter is still present, making sure it is done right. The old lady 'seemed not to have changed, except that she had only a few strands of her white hair left and almost no teeth. Even her black coat looked the same, green with age and threadbare.' Here one must feel sympathy with the novelist labouring under contradictory pressures. Madame Richter is 'hardly changed' because she has only been around for forty pages; but the passage of time, which is considerable, has robbed her of hair and teeth. This seems to me only just short of saying someone was hardly changed except that she was dead.

Much further on in the novel, in a retrospect on this female line, we learn that Madame Richter's daughter Sonia was almost certainly fathered by the Master. Sonia's daughter Irina was in turn fathered by Madame Richter's landlady's son, who then went to jail and was not seen again. And Irina's daughter Vera was fathered by an itinerant Irishman beside whom Irina carelessly came to rest one afternoon in Central Park. Thus when Henry inherits the Master's papers and takes Vera as his assistant to work on them, there is an appropriateness in that she is the great-granddaughter and he the spiritual son of the papers' author.

What is in these papers? Not much, it seems, since the Master gave little away, and perhaps had little to give. In any case such esoteric truths as gurus deal in are difficult for the novelist to invent—they have to be suggested rather than presented. But we have to accept that there is enough to make it necessary for Henry to need an assistant—this, of course, because the plot needs Vera—and enough to keep Henry and Vera occupied while Jhabvala jams into the bag, or tacks onto the patchwork, one or two fictions that she perhaps had no other place for. One of these, in two parts, is extraordinary; and not surprisingly it takes us back to her old subject, India.

Cynthia's nephew Graeme appears first on page 35, marries Baby on page 39, fathers Renata on page 42, and having done the service which is the males' sole, or chief, function in this novel, disappears until page 92, by which time he is already retired: 'Now, fifty years later and at the end of his career, Graeme came [to Cynthia's and Elsa's house] every Sunday for the traditional roast beef lunch.'

But a hundred or so pages further on Jhabvala decides to bring him back into the story. He suffers a heart attack and is returned to Baby, who looks after him until the final page. By this device he is made the source and revealer of information and reminiscences, some of which concern the Master and are thus part of the story, others of which are there simply for their own sake.

Two of these are from Graeme's varied love life. One concerns a single sexual encounter with a woman in a poor quarter of Delhi; the other is a prolonged affair of the mind with the niece of an Indian leader who herself rises to fame and leadership in later years, and is assassinated. Coming close to the end of a novel in which the sense of real life, real human character, is so thin, these fifteen or so pages are a fatal mistake. They leap out and take one by the scruff of the neck, and become the measure by which all the rest is found wanting. They confirm for the self-doubting reader that it is not he but the novelist whose batteries have needed recharging.

Stories are commonly designed to make us hope for a particular ending; sometimes our wish is granted, sometimes not—either outcome, the happy or the sad, is equally conventional. In this novel the conventional hope is that Vera and disabled Henry will declare their deep but secret feeling for one another. The hope is disappointed on the final page. But if you care to reread, you will be rewarded with (more or less) the hoped-for ending, which will have meant nothing when you first encountered it—a brief jump into the future on page 40. 'Henry checked with ev-

eryone else still alive—his parents, and also Vera (Mme Richter's great-granddaughter), though that was not until several years had passed, after Vera's marriage broke down and she more or less came back to him.'

---

# FURTHER READING

## Bibliography

Crane, Ralph J. "Ruth Prawer Jhabvala: A Checklist of Primary and Secondary Sources." *The Journal of Commonwealth Literature* XX, No. 1 (1985): 171-203.
> Bibliography of Jhabvala's books, articles, screenplays, and short stories, as well as annotated list of reviews and essays on her work.

## Biography

Lassell, Michael. "The Passionate Observer." *The Los Angeles Times Magazine* (28 November 1993): 30-4, 62.
> Recounts Jhabvala's youth, mentioning her family's flight from the Nazis, her unpopular reputation in India, her film career, and sense of cultural rootlessness.

Streitfeld, David. "Cool Candidate." *Book World—The Washington Post* (28 March 1993): 15.
> Brief overview of Jhabvala's career following the release of the Merchant-Ivory film *Howards End* and the publication of *Poet and Dancer*.

## Criticism

Agarwal, Ramlal G. *Ruth Prawer Jhabvala: A Study of Her Fiction.* New Delhi: Sterling Publishers, 1990, 126 p.
> Discusses eight of Jhabvala's novels at length, as well as many of her short stories. Includes a bibliography.

Atlas, James. "A Cinematic Sensibility." *Vogue* 183 (March 1993): 248, 254.
> Article based on an interview with Jhabvala in which she discusses moving to New York. Atlas criticizes her books and screenplays as a world "faintly unreal."

Belliappa, Meena. "A Study of Jhabvala's Fiction." *The Miscellany,* No. 43 (January-February 1971): 24-40.
> Analysis of several of Jhabvala's books, including *The Householder, Of Whom She Will,* and *The Nature of Passion,* concentrating on how the characters conduct themselves in society.

Craig, Patricia. "Those for Whom India Proves too Strong." *The London Review of Books* 10, No. 31 (31 March 1988): 27.
> Positive review of *Three Continents,* which Craig summarizes as being about "the dangers inherent in not adopting a properly sceptical attitude to strangers who come proclaiming unity and amity."

Cronin, Richard. "*The Hill of Devi* and *Heat and Dust.*" *Essays in Criticism* XXXVI, No. 2 (April 1986): 142-59.
> Comparative essay focusing on E. M. Forster's *The Hill of Devi,* an account of the author's relationship with the Maharajah of Kohlapur in the 1920s, and Jhabvala's novel *Heat and Dust,* parts of which take place in the same period.

Dudar, Helen. "In the Beginning, the Word; at the End, the Movie." *The New York Times* (8 March 1992): H15, 20-1.

Discusses the making of *Howards End* with Jhabvala and James Ivory. Jhabvala states that "the first rule [of screenwriting] is not to be reverent. The only thing is to be disrespectful."

Freeman, Judith. "Cousine, Cousine." *The Los Angeles Times Book Review* (14 March 1993): 3, 9.

Positive review of *Poet and Dancer,* which calls the relationship between cousins Angel and Lara a "guru-disciple relationship run amok."

Gooneratne, Yasmine. " 'Traditional' Elements in the Fiction of Kamala Markandaya, R. K. Narayan and Ruth Prawer Jhabvala." *World Literature Written in English* 15, No. 1 (April 1976): 121-34.

Comparison of several contemporary writers of Indian fiction, whose writing Gooneratne contends is influenced by English fiction as a result of colonialism.

------. "The Expatriate Experience: The Novels of Ruth Prawer Jhabvala and Paul Scott." In *The British and Irish Novel Since 1960,* edited by James Acheson, pp. 48-61. London: Macmillan, 1991.

Comparative analysis.

Gray, Paul. "Tribute of Empathy and Grace." *Time* 127, No. 19 (12 May 1986): 90.

Reviews Jhabvala's short story collection *Out of India.*

Harrison, Barbara Grizzuti. "Eastward Ho!" *The New York Times Book Review* (17 September 1995): 12.

Mixed review of *Shards of Memory.*

Jenkins, Victoria. "Two Obsessed Girls Observed." *Chicago Tribune—Books* (28 February 1993): 3.

Positive review of *Poet and Dancer,* comparing Angel's and Lara's unhealthy relationship to a psychological case study.

Lenta, Margaret. "Narrators and Readers: 1902 and 1975." *Ariel* 20, No. 3 (July 1989): 19-36.

Comparative essay which relates the similarities and differences of Joseph Conrad's *Heart of Darkness,* published in 1902 and intended for a primarily European audience, with Jhabvala's *Heat and Dust,* published in 1975 and geared towards a more cross-cultural readership.

Pym, John. *The Wandering Company: Twenty-One Years of Merchant Ivory Films.* New York: The Museum of Modern Art, 1983, 102 p.

Chronicles the collaborative film efforts of Merchant, Ivory, and Jhabvala, from *The Householder* through *The Courtesans of Bombay.*

Sastry, L. S. R. Krishna. "The Alien Consciousness in Jhabvala's Short Stories." *The Two-Fold Voice: Essays on Indian Writing in English,* edited by D. V. K. Raghavacharyulu, pp. 164-73. Guntur: Navodaya, 1971.

Discusses stories from *Like Birds, Like Fishes* and *A Stronger Climate.*

Towers, Robert. "Breaking the Spell." *The New York Review of Books* (8 October 1987): 45-6.

Review of *Three Continents,* stating that though the novel takes place in the United States and England, Jhabvala has infused it with an Indian theme, that of "the relationship of a circle of needy and demanding disciples to the authoritarian guru at their center," though he complains that the novel contains too many stereotypical characters and complicated events.

**Interviews**

Agarwal, Ramlal G. "An Interview with Ruth Prawer Jhabvala." *Quest* 91 (September/October 1994): 33-6.

Discusses critics' comparisons of Jhabvala with Jane Austen, as well as complaints that her novels deal only with a small slice of Indian life.

Freedland, Jonathan. "The Books of Ruth." *The Washington Post* (7 November 1993): G4-5.

Discusses her 32-year association with Merchant and Ivory.

Fuller, Graham. An interview with James Ivory and Ruth Prawer Jhabvala. *Interview* XX, No. 11 (November 1990): 130-5.

Discussion of the making of *Mr. and Mrs. Bridge.*

May, Yolanta. An interview with Ruth Prawer Jhabvala. *The New Review,* No. 21 (1975): 53-7.

Discusses the awarding of the Booker Prize to *Heat and Dust.* The author comments on her insights into Indian community life from the perspective of a European.

---

**Additional coverage of Jhabvala's life and career is contained in the following sources published by Gale Research:** *Contemporary Authors,* Vols. 1-4, rev. ed; *Contemporary Authors New Revision Series,* Vols. 2, 29, 51; *Contemporary Literary Criticism,* Vols. 4, 8, 28; *Dictionary of Literary Biography,* Vol. 139; *Discovering Authors: British; Discovering Authors Modules: Novelists;* and *Major 20th-Century Writers.*

# Yusef Komunyakaa

## 1947-

American poet and editor.

The following entry provides an overview of Komunyakaa's career through 1994. For further information on his life and works, see *CLC*, Volume 86.

## INTRODUCTION

Best known for *Neon Vernacular* (1993), which won the Pulitzer Prize in Poetry in 1994, Komunyakaa is noted for verse in which he uses surrealistic imagery, montage techniques, and folk idiom to focus on his identity as an African American, his upbringing in the small community of Bogalusa, Louisiana, and his experiences as a soldier during the Vietnam War. Incorporating violence, death, racism, and poverty, his poems are often infused with rage and exhibit a pessimistic outlook on life while invoking feelings of tenderness and hope. Toi Derricotte has observed: "Komunyakaa takes on the most complex moral issues, the most harrowing ugly subjects of our American life. His voice, whether it embodies the specific experiences of a black man, a soldier in Vietnam, or a child in Bogalusa, Louisiana, is universal. It shows us in ever deeper ways what it is to be human."

### Biographical Information

Komunyakaa was born in Bogalusa, Louisiana. After graduating from high school, he enlisted in the U.S. Army in 1969; he served in Vietnam as a front-lines correspondent and editor for the *Southern Cross,* eventually earning a Bronze Star. Komunyakaa attended the University of Colorado, graduating with a B.A. in 1975, and began writing poetry and publishing in small presses. He later earned an M.A. at Colorado State University and an M.F.A. in 1980 at the University of California at Irvine. After his early poems appeared in such journals as *Black American Literature Forum* and *Beloit Poetry Journal,* Komunyakaa published his first collection, *Dedications and Other Darkhorses*, in 1977. Komunyakaa has held fellowships and teaching positions in New England and New Orleans and has been a professor of English at Indiana University at Bloomington. He has been the winner of many awards for poetic achievement, including Creative Writing Fellowships from the National Endowment for the Arts in 1981 and 1987, and—in addition to the Pulitzer—the Kingsley Tufts Poetry Award for *Neon Vernacular.*

### Major Works

*Lost in the Bonewheel Factory* (1979), Komunyakaa's second collection of verse, is comprised of six sequences addressing a wide variety of themes, including beauty, pathos, and moral degradation. *Copacetic* (1984), the first of his works to gain the attention of reviewers, is a collection

of blues and jazz poems in which Komunyakaa focuses on his childhood and youth. In "Jumping Bad Blues," for example, Komunyakaa writes: "I've played cool, / hung out with the hardest / bargains, but never copped a plea." In *I Apologize for the Eyes in My Head* (1986), Komunyakaa examines the effect of the past on the present, invoking lost loves, scenes of Bogalusa, his experiences in the Vietnam War, and past generations. In "Go Down Death," considered one of the most powerful poems in the collection, Komunyakaa states: "The dead / stumble home like the swamp fog, / our lost uncles and granddaddies / come back to us almost healed." The poems about Vietnam in *Dien cai dau* (1988) were not started until 1983—fourteen years after his tour of duty—but as Komunyakaa told critic Bruce Weber in a 1994 interview, beginning them "was as if I had uncapped some hidden place in me. . . . Poem after poem came spilling out." Focusing on the mental horrors of the war, Komunyakaa uses surrealistic imagery, a variety of personas, and the present tense to describe his experiences. Komunyakaa followed *Dien cai dau* with *February in Sydney* (1989) and *Magic City* (1992)—the latter a highly autobiographical examination of childhood and rites of passage. *Neon Vernacular* reflects Komunyakaa's penchant for travel and his passion for jazz, blues, and classical European music. Komunyakaa has also edited *The Jazz Poetry Anthology* (1991) with Sascha Feinstein.

## Critical Reception

Komunyakaa's reputation as a poet has grown steadily over the years, with original charges of obscurity or superficial treatment of subjects and themes giving way to praise for both surrealistic juxtaposition of images and compelling storytelling. Critics especially laud Komunyakaa's examination of such complex themes as identity, war, and the paradoxes of art; his ability to transcend moral, social, and mental boundaries; and what Vince F. Gotera has called Komunyakaa's "counterbalancing of seeming oppositions and incongruities." As Kirkland C. Jones has stated, "Komunyakaa has come of age, not only as a Southern-American or African-American bard, but as a world-class poet who is careful to restrain the emotions and moods he creates, without overdoing ethnicity of any kind."

# PRINCIPAL WORKS

*Dedications and Other Darkhorses*  (poetry)  1977
*Lost in the Bonewheel Factory*  (poetry)  1979
*Copacetic*  (poetry)  1984
*I Apologize for the Eyes in My Head*  (poetry)  1986
*Toys in a Field*  (poetry)  1986
*Dien cai dau*  (poetry)  1988
*February in Sydney*  (poetry)  1989
*The Jazz Poetry Anthology*  [editor, with Sascha Feinstein]  (poetry)  1991
*Magic City*  (poetry)  1992
*Neon Vernacular: New and Selected Poems*  (poetry) 1993

# CRITICISM

## Joseph Parisi    (review date 15 March 1984)

SOURCE: A review of *Copacetic,* in *Booklist,* Vol. 80, No. 14, March 15, 1984, p. 1024.

[*Below, Parisi offers a mixed assessment of* Copacetic.]

Born in Bogalusa, Louisiana, but bred all over the place, Komunyakaa once edited a magazine called *Gumbo.* His own verse is rather a spicy concoction, too, mixing the scents, sights, and sounds of "cottonmouth country" with the patois of the bayous and the blues joints of Bourbon Street. Sometimes this heady brew [in ***Copacetic***] conjures up authentic images of those southern climes and eccentricities, especially in several vignettes of jazz stars (among them Thelonious Monk and Charles Mingus) and lesser known New Orleans "characters." When the poet's tran-

scripts drift further from these deeply felt, personal experiences, the results are less satisfying. Perhaps it's the sophistication of his further education (especially those advanced arts degrees) that puts the somewhat off-putting "processed" and professionally jived up tone into others of these verses. Still, in the bluesy lyrics and elegies, there's a good deal of the steamy high spirits, as well as the sadness, of real life.

## J. A. Miller    (review date November 1984)

SOURCE: A review of *Copacetic,* in *Choice,* Vol. 22, No. 3, November, 1984, p. 425.

[*In the following review, Miller highly recommends* Copacetic, *stating that the work reflects a "wry, hard-won wisdom."*]

***Copacetic,*** Yusef Komunyakaa's first collection of poetry, signals the emergence of a fresh and distinctive Afro-American voice. Like that of many of his contemporaries, Komunyakaa's work is deeply influenced by the blues, but his poetry draws upon both the idiom and the philosophical core of the blues with a facility that is striking for a young poet. Komunyakaa associates the term "copacetic" with ". . . jazz musicians and street philosophers who have been educated by some real hard falls," and the voices he creates in his poetry often reflect this wry, hard-won wisdom. Komunyakaa has a fine command of language and rhythm. He is definitely a poet worth watching—and reading.

## Yusef Komunyakaa with Vince F. Gotera    (interview date 21 February 1986)

SOURCE: " 'Lines of Tempered Steel': An Interview with Yusef Komunyakaa," in *Callaloo,* Vol. 13, No. 2, Spring, 1990, pp. 215-29.

[*In the following interview, which took place on February 21, 1986, in Bloomington, Indiana, Komunyakaa discusses such subjects as his upbringing, his poetic influences, and the nature of poetry.*]

[*Gotera*]: *Why don't we start with your background, biographical stuff, books you've written, and so on?*

[Komunyakaa]: Okay. I grew up in a place called Bogalusa. That's in Louisiana, about 70 miles out of New Orleans. It's a rural kind of environment, and I think a great deal of the bucolic feeling gets into my work. If not directly, then indirectly so.

I started writing in the military. It was a different kind of writing, of course—it was journalism. That was in Vietnam, between '69 and '70. I started writing poetry in '73 in Colorado, where I lived for seven and a half years—in Boulder, Colorado Springs, and Fort Collins.

Actually, I had been reading poetry for many years; in fact, that's one of the things that kept me in contact with my innermost feelings when I was in Vietnam, because I would very systematically go through anthologies such as Donald Hall's *Contemporary American Poetry,* Dudley Randall's *Broadside Press* editions, and the *New Directions* annuals. But I didn't attempt to write poetry then; I just enjoyed reading it.

*Were you writing any creative stuff at all, at the time? Fiction, perhaps?*

I had started experimenting with short stories, in an attempt to emulate James Baldwin and Richard Wright, but I never really stayed with short fiction long enough to develop it in any significant way. Perhaps I'll return to that genre in the near future. I admire and love Baldwin, especially his *Go Tell It on the Mountain* and *Another Country.* And as an essayist, he can be meticulous and almost heartless with the truth. That is what keeps me returning to his *Nobody Knows My Name* and *The Fire Next Time.* As a matter of fact, I remember first checking out *Nobody Knows My Name* at the black library in Bogalusa that was really a bedroom-size building in the late '50s. I read that book about twenty-five times.

Anyway, it took some time for me to actually start writing for myself. At the University of Colorado in '73, I took a workshop in creative writing, and that was my introduction, really, to imaginative writing as such.

In '77 I came out with a limited edition—a few poems—called **Dedications and Other Darkhorses,** published by *Rocky Mountain Creative Arts Journal,* which was edited by Paul Dilsaver. In '79, I had another limited kind of edition, called **Lost in the Bonewheel Factory,** published by Lynx House Press.

Of course, I kept writing, and I went into the graduate program in writing at Colorado State in '76 with Bill Tremblay. Bill is certainly one of the most underrated poets in America—check out his book *Crying in the Cheap Seats.*

Well, okay, and from there, I went on to the University of California at Irvine, studied with Charles Wright, C. K. Williams, Howard Moss, Robert Peters, and James McMichaels. There were also some wonderful student writers there: Garrett Hongo, Deborah Woodard, Vic Coccimiglio, Debra Thomas, and Virginia Campbell.

Then I went to the Provincetown Fine Arts Work Center—I was there in '80. That was an interesting time: a kind of semi-isolation in which I could very methodically deal with my writing. It was a close community of artists where I could get feedback; but mainly it was a place to develop one's own voice, I suppose. Well, in essence, really, one's voice is already inside, but a sort of unearthing has to take place; sometimes one has to remove layers of facades and superficialities. The writer has to get down to the guts of the thing and rediscover the basic timbre of his or her existence.

*Where does your first book,* **Copacetic,** *fall into this process of unearthing and rediscovery?*

**Copacetic** falls into, or better yet, accumulates from many places, because it has some of my very first poems in it. The book covers a time when I had traveled around a whole lot: I lived in Panama for a year, also Puerto Rico, Japan for a while, too. Along with all that, I had spent seven years in Colorado. **Copacetic,** however, was finished

in Louisiana; I went back to Bogalusa in '81, after being away for many years. It was almost like going back to a hometown inside my head, to my own psychological territory, but in a different way, from a different perspective—hopefully a more creative, objective point of view. And also it was an opportunity to relive, to rethink some things.

Bogalusa definitely has its problems, and some of those are racial problems. At one time, it was the heart of Ku Klux Klan activity, and consequently a lot of civil rights work went on. The Deacons of Defense worked in that particular area.

*And now, in Indiana, you're almost in the heart of that again. Just twenty miles down the road is a town, as you know, with the dubious fame of being the residence of a one-time Grand Dragon of the Klan.*

I realize that; I see it around me [laughing]. I can deal with it. I've learned to deal with it. Some of those things—some of the racial problems—surface in **Copacetic.**

*But, a lot of that in* **Copacetic** *seems to be focused on South Africa.*

Right, right. There are parallels—definitely parallels. Even though we might not see those parallels on the surface, they do exist, I think. People are people, I suppose, wherever you are, and they definitely have their problems, things to work through.

And that's true for many writers; a good example would be Galway Kinnell. He worked near where I grew up, I think, in the late '60s and early '70s. He was a field director for CORE. I remember some photograph—you might have seen it—on the cover of *Life* or maybe *Look:* it was Galway Kinnell with a bloody face.

*Etheridge Knight addressed a poem to Galway Kinnell.*

Okay, that makes sense. I know that the two appeared together at the Great Mother Earth Festivals with Robert Bly.

*What are you working on now?*

I'm working on some performance pieces, theater pieces. Which I've been writing since I've been here [in Bloomington, Indiana] . . . able to have a distant, disembodied kind of voice at times. You need that to work on certain kinds of monologues and soliloquys.

I'm also working on a book called *Beaucoup Dien Cai Dau;* these are Vietnam-related poems. Also, a book called **Magic City,** about growing up in Louisiana: childhood experiences, observations. Trying to throw myself back into the emotional situation of the time, and at the same time bring a psychological overlay that juxtaposes new experiences alongside the ones forming the old landscape inside my head. Trying to work things through, still; I suppose writers constantly do that.

*What about the book that's upcoming?*

Well, it will be published in September by Wesleyan. It's called **I Apologize for the Eyes in My Head.** Actually, it's not really an apology, of course. [Laughing.] It's the opposite of that, in an ironic, satirical way. Once you look at the book, you'll see that I'm not really apologizing for anything.

*Have you found that living in Indiana has affected your work? Do you find that Indiana—the place itself, or the people you've met here, perhaps their speech—is that impinging at all on your work?*

No, not really. There's a sort of Southern tinge to speech here, perhaps even more than in Louisiana, particularly near New Orleans. Of course, Louisiana is a mixture of things—a mixture of people, of cultures. A different psychological terrain, an interesting place. Yet I don't know if I could really live there, especially since I'm on my way now to Australia, you know? The other side of the world. . . . But, anyway, Indiana has been a part of a growth process of sorts. Both in my personal life and in my writing—poetry and drama.

One effect Indiana *has* had is that I've had more time here to work on certain things. For some reason, I had been thinking of certain poems, certain monologues and soliloquys in New Orleans, but they never really got down on the page. Now I have the space, I suppose; it's not really a physical space but more of a psychological space to actually deal with certain things and put them down on paper. A space for me to go back to my early childhood. At one time, I saw all of my experiences in a negative context; that's probably true of most of us. But I see those now in more of a positive framework, and that's good for me. It's liberating, necessary for growth.

*Actually, you've had a similar effect on my work. For many years, I had been resisting certain memories, resisting my Filipino-American identity as a poetic subject. When you introduced me to Garrett Hongo's book,* Yellow Light, *many things came together for me.*

It's interesting, the way Garrett is able to work those things through, you know, and I think he influenced me, especially in *Magic City,* to return to my childhood experiences and respect them for what they are.

*Let's talk about some larger, more universal issues. What is your definition of poetry? How do you go about writing it?*

My definition of poetry is, I suppose, grounded in everyday speech patterns. I really think the poem begins with a central image; it's not tied down in any way, not pre-defined. When an image, a line, develops into a poem, if it has an emotional thread running through it, when it can link two people together, reader and poet, then it's working.

I don't necessarily disagree with Wallace Stevens when he says that "a poem is a pheasant," but I think I feel closer to Coleridge's statement: "What is poetry?—is so nearly the same question with, what is a poet?—that the answer to the one is involved in the solution of the other." In essence, poetry equals the spiritual and emotional dimension of the human animal.

Poetry is so difficult to define, I think, because it's constantly changing, growing. It's becoming something else

in order to become itself—amorphous and cumulative until it forms a vision.

---

> **My definition of poetry is, I suppose, grounded in everyday speech patterns. I really think the poem begins with a central image; it's not tied down in any way, not pre-defined.**
>
> **—*Yusef Komunyakaa***

---

*When you say that an image or a line occurs and develops, does that mean you keep a notebook, and let jottings or ideas percolate?*

I keep a mental notebook. I realize that I might write an image down that has recurred for four, five or six years. And so I know where it came from. A good example is my Vietnam poems, where it's taken me about fourteen years to start getting those down. But some of the images go back to a time when I was writing more journalistic kinds of articles.

It's difficult to define what poetry is, and yet numerous people have tried to define poetry as such. I think it ties into the oral tradition for me, because I grew up with some strange characters around me. You know, storytellers and sorcerers. One of my first *Magic City* poems was about a gentleman who used to tell me ghost stories—it's about how he was able to pull me into those stories and create a kind of near-agonizing mystery. I'm definitely attracted to that.

*In much of your work, probably more so in* **Lost in the Bonewheel Factory** *than in* **Copacetic,** *it seems to me that you strive for a tension between levels of diction. I see you yoking, for example, Latinate words with everyday ones.*

That's probably who I am. Fluctuating between this point over here and another strain over there: the things I've read that come into my work, and also the things I've experienced that affect my work at the same time. And both of these work side by side. I don't draw any distinctions between those two, because after all that's the totality of the individual.

It goes back to a statement by Aimé Césaire: essentially, he says that we are a composite of all our experiences— love, hatred, understanding, misunderstanding—and consequently we rise out of those things like—to use a cliché—a phoenix. We survive the baptism by fire, only to grow more complete and stronger. The way we are, perhaps today, might be entirely different tomorrow.

*It's interesting that you bring up the word cliché. In your Vietnam poems, I see you doing something different from what you do in* **Copacetic** *and* **Lost in the Bonewheel Factory.** *You thread in clichés and then deflate them.*

Right, the kind of intellectual wrestling that moves and weaves us through human language.

*And that strikes me as something that's very hard to do.*

That's interesting, because, especially with soldiers, for some reason—individuals coming from so many backgrounds: the deep South, the North, different educational levels—clichés are used many times as efforts to communicate, as bridges perhaps. And soldiers often speak in clichés—at least this is what I've found.

I've been using quotations a whole lot, as I remember them. Certain things in a poem will surface, and I can hear a certain person saying those things. And I can see his face, even when I cannot put a name to the face.

*That really rings true for me. I've been thinking about an Army poem and trying to hear those voices, you know? And I hear, "No brass, no ammo" and "Smoke 'em if you got' em."*

Yeah, right. [Laughing.] Those *are* clichés, but they work in poems, mainly because there are real people connected with those words. I've been going through faces in writing these Vietnam poems, and I'm surprised at how few of the names I remember. I suppose that's all part of the forgetting process, in striving to forget particular situations that were pretty traumatic for me. Not when I was there as much as in retrospect. When you're there in such a situation, you're thinking about where the nearest safest place is to run, in case of an incoming rocket. You don't have time to even think about the moral implications.

*Does that mean that you find yourself psychologically resisting some of those memories?*

Yes, I did at one time. Now, it's more or less a process of recall. I had pushed many of those images aside, or at least attempted to. It's amazing what the mind can do; the mind does work like a computer, storing information.

And that's how poetry works as well: in **Magic City,** I'm recalling images from when I was four or five years old. I've always been fascinated by certain plants, Venus's-flytraps, for example, their ability to digest insects. Of course, you know, something like that would fascinate a kid at four years old. Going back to that time . . . I was able to do that only a few years ago.

*Is poetry then some sort of need fulfillment?*

It's a way of working things out; it's a way of dealing with all the information taken in. I write every day. I'm probably writing when I'm not sitting down at the typewriter or scribbling the first draft of a poem on a pad. I think all writers probably do that.

*Yeah, I would agree. It's interesting that you talk about "working things out." Not all readers may see your poems in that light; in one review of* **Copacetic,** *the reviewer complains that you can tell a good story, but you're trying too hard for effects, and your poems are "too hip."*

Too hip? [Laughing.] I think, perhaps, he's talking about diction. And that's a similar thing: someone else accused those poems of being "too sophisticated," which is ridiculous. Going back to that whole thing of New Orleans as a composite of influences, the word "copacetic" for me conjures up a certain jazz-blues feeling. And many times,

for the speakers in those poems, that's their psychic domain: a blues environment.

That was especially the case for me when I was in New Orleans, because there are so many layers to everything there. You have the traditional and the modern side by side; there's a xenophobia among New Orleanians, and it's all grounded in what the blues are made of. An existential melancholy based on an acute awareness. Those are some pretty hip characters, right? [Laughing.]

I admire that to an extent, because linked to it is a kind of psychological survival. How one deals with life: to be on this plane one moment and the next moment, a different plane—the ability to speak to many different people. For example, I can more or less rap with my colleagues, but I have to be able as well to talk with my grandmothers, whom I'm very close to. They're not educated, and yet we can communicate some very heartfelt emotions. I'm still learning a whole lot from them.

We were talking earlier about Etheridge Knight; he, of course, belongs to a long line of poets, starting with Phillis Wheatley, the abolitionist poets Frances Harper and James Whitfield, and, later on, Paul Lawrence Dunbar. Poetry for blacks, for the most part, has functioned as a "service literature." What I mean is that there has been a systematic need to define just what the essence of being black in America is about. But in a certain sense, it has moved beyond that service-literature category, especially within the 1980s, where there has been more of an introspective poetry, a voyage inward, and my belief is that you have to have both: the odyssey outward as well as inward to have any kind of constructive, informative bridges to vision and expression.

*How does this double journey surface in your own work?*

Basically, it's a recognition of history. It's almost like having one foot in history and the other in a progressive vision. The future as well as the past inform one another in possibility. A good example of this in action is Robert Hayden: in a work like "The Middle Passage," or an earlier poem called "The Diver," we find intense images which conjure up a journey *on* the ocean as well as *in* the ocean to a certain depth, touching the tangible—the slave ship—as well as the unconscious in various symbolic ways.

*How have you been influenced by other black poets?*

Melvin Tolson is one poet who achieves an interesting play on language: he brings together the street as well as the highly literary into a single poetic context in ways where the two don't even seem to exhibit a division—it's all one and the same. Langston Hughes is another important poet because he celebrates the common folk—the true strength of black America—and his work clearly rises out of a folk tradition. Another poet who comes to mind is Sterling Brown, again a poet who celebrates the blues tradition. One of the most important voices is Gwendolyn Brooks, mainly because of her concern for language, forms, and content—all three of these come together to create a unique poetic synthesis.

Other contemporaries of Hughes also come to mind: Countee Cullen and Claude McKay, especially the poem

"If We Must Die"—which is a challenge more than anything else. McKay also has a number of protest sonnets which display so much strength and control at the same time. Of course, we are again in the period of "service literature." During the same period as Cullen and McKay, Helen Johnson was also an important poet—there are a number of women, in fact, who are not often acknowledged as writers of the Harlem Renaissance, although they were an intricate, important part of that movement.

After the Harlem Renaissance, of course, comes the time in which we see women as vivid presences: Margaret Walker and, of course, Gwendolyn Brooks. A later important poet is Nikki Giovanni, whose work arises out of the '60s and is really grounded in oral tradition. Her poems are quite effective but, let's face it, she is a popular poet. And we may wonder how popular poets will endure in terms of literary history. Gwendolyn Brooks is clearly an example of a poet whose reputation will continue to endure. And there are other significant black voices—I've already mentioned Etheridge Knight—also we have Ishmael Reed, Imamu Amiri Baraka, Michael Harper, Sonia Sanchez, June Jordan, Alice Walker, Rita Dove, Colleen McElroy, Quincy Troupe, Lucille Clifton, and many others.

*Etheridge Knight has clearly been influenced by the blues, in the same way that a poet like Michael Harper or Sonia Sanchez has been influenced by jazz. Do you find that the rhythms of blues and jazz influence your work?*

Yes, yes. I think we internalize a kind of life rhythm. The music I was listening to when I was seven or eight years old and the music I listen to today are not that different. Because I listen mainly to jazz and blues, and some of the same artists are still around: B. B. King, Ray Charles, Nina Simone, Bobby Blue Bland, Aretha [Franklin], and so on.

I listen to a lot of classical jazz, as well as European classical music. I think you do all those things side by side, and it's not a kind of disparate incongruity. You need an ability to accept different things and not feel them to be in absolute conflict.

*Does teaching poetry as opposed to writing poetry involve that sort of resolution for you? What do you consciously try to do when you teach poetry?*

I like to listen to what different people are doing. I try to point out a poet's strongest points. Some may produce a baroque kind of poetry, while others may produce a "down-home" sort. Usually I can detect what the poet is trying to do and when that individual succeeds or when he or she falls short. What you have to do is look at the poem in its overall context, so you see when the diction strays, when it's off the mark. The poem has to be believable.

What I look for is conciseness of language. Yet, you can probably relate a given scene in a hundred different ways, and to an extent those hundred ways might work. I like to have an open-endedness in a class situation, and yet still have a structure there. That's the space where people can grow; that's where I found myself growing. A relaxed kind of space.

*When you revise your own work, do you go about it in the way I see you approaching poems in a workshop: cutting words, superfluous language?*

That's what I do, yes. For the most part, I cut. I believe that we all over-write. As a matter of fact, in my own work, I find that I will go back to poems as they were originally typed, with fewer linear connections. I might have ten versions of a poem, and midway through, the fifth version may work better than the ninth or tenth.

Some poems I write just off the top of my head, and I realize that I don't really have to revise those poems that much. But the writing of them has been a continuous process inside my head. I can pretty well see the poem in lines, and I can go back to it day in and day out, without putting it on paper. Usually, I'm working on five or six such poems at once.

*That brings up a question I've had about the way you break up your lines. When I have heard you read, it has seemed to me that the spoken chunks are quite different from the lines on the page.*

Many times that's the case, yes. I find myself doing that. For the simple reason that, when I first write a poem, I will confine it to its initial line breaks, but when I'm reading, I read basically according to how I'm feeling.

*Some people view the line break as a clue to the reader about how to read a poem aloud. Does what you say mean that for you lineation doesn't have the purpose?*

That can be bent. It's got to be flexible. I might have more of an improvisational kind of feeling about me on a particular night. When I'm reading, I'm not always looking at the page, but I remember the words.

*Even if you read the lines as markedly different from the way they might have been published, do the line breaks nevertheless remain for you as entities in themselves?*

Yes, they still exist. I probably couldn't go back and change a line break on paper. That's definitely the line break for me, that's the way the end word falls, and there's no possibility I could break it any other way. There's a completeness about a line, a completeness and yet a continuation. It's the whole thing of enjambment, what I like to call "extended possibilities." The line grows. It's not a linguistic labyrinth; it's in logical segments, and yet it grows. It's the whole process of becoming; that's how we are as humans. There's a kind of fluid life about us, and that's how poetry should be. Say you're down to line three—sometimes, I will cut a line. I would like to write poems that are just single lines. That is, a continuing line that doesn't run out of space because of the margin. I would like to write poems like that.

**There's a sameness about American poetry that I don't think represents the whole people. It represents a poetry of the moment, a poetry of evasion, and I have problems with this. I believe poetry has always been political, long before poets had to deal with the page and white space.**

**—*Yusef Komunyakaa***

*In some ways, a prose poem may be described in that way. Do you see the prose poem as a different creature?*

Yeah. Incidentally, I was looking at Michael Benedikt's anthology of prose poems from years ago, and I was really surprised not to find Jean Toomer, especially excerpts from *Cane.* Essentially, it's a novel composed of prose poems. The chapter "Karintha" is a very beautiful, compassionate prose poem.

But, yeah, the prose poem is different. What I mean by a continuing line is . . . well, it's the same way that Marquez can write a thirty-five-page sentence, linking things without having strict categories. Where feeling becomes the connective. I see things as blending into each other, as a painter would do, blending colors to make a single emotional landscape. A kind of spatial elasticity. Lines should be able to work that way.

*Okay. You don't mean linearity as such, not just a string of words that extends only horizontally. But that there are vertical relations happening as well.*

Right.

*Samuel Delany suggests in his criticism on science fiction that each word, as you add words, affects all the other words, so that even he contends that the beginning "the" in a sentence is already a picture, and for Delany that's something like a gray ellipsoid about a yard off the ground, if I'm remembering this correctly. And that an "a" or "an" may be pink. And then of course the first content word affects the overall picture in its own way. So there's a cloud of meaning, a valence, around each word that affects each other word, including spaces, or in poetry, line breaks.*

Okay, yeah. Definitely. Language is color. All the tinges and strokes equal the whole picture; it is what converges within the frame of reference. The same as music and silence. And one doesn't need psychotropic drugs to see and feel the intensity of expression. After all, language is what can liberate or imprison the human psyche. Yes, all the parts are important; in that sense, language is like an organism. It's interesting what Delany says about "the" and "a," because I tend often to leave out articles. I feel that they're excessive baggage for the image and the line. Creeley and Ginsberg use a similar approach.

*Speaking of other poets, what would you say the state of poetry is in America, by any definition? Where do you see poetry going? And where do you think it should go?*

I've been kicking around the phrase "neo-fugitives" inside my head. What I mean by that is that there tends to be a fugitive sentiment which can be compared to John Crowe Ransom and Allen Tate. The creed states that basically the poet shouldn't get social or political. That he or she would do better to stick with the impressionistic and ethereal to the extent that true feeling evaporates off the page. That's much safer, and too often it insures a poet's empty endurance and superficial reverence in the literary world.

There's a sameness about American poetry that I don't think represents the whole people. It represents a poetry of the moment, a poetry of evasion, and I have problems with this. I believe poetry has always been political, long before poets had to deal with the page and white space . . . it's natural. Probably before Socrates, in Plato's *Republic,* banished poets from his ideal state—long before South Africa, Chile, Mississippi, and Marcos in the Philippines suppressing Mila Aguilar and others. There seems to be always some human landscape that creates a Paul Celan. Too many contemporary American poets would love to dismiss this fact. Of course, there are exceptions to the rule: Michael Harper, June Jordan, Forché, Rich, C. K. Williams, and Baraka. But still, if you were to take many magazines and cut the names off poems, you would have a single collection which could be by any given poet; you could put one name on it, as if they were all by one person. True, a writer can say almost anything in America and have it completely overlooked, yet I think we should have more individual voices.

*Would you say that this situation—a milieu that fosters a "poetry of the moment" or, we might further coin, a "poetry of fashion"—is attributable to the writing-workshop system that's developed in academe, the MFA industry?*

That brings up another point: for the first time, there is also a rather healthy community of readers and poets. There are probably more poets writing today than [laughing] . . . there are more poets writing than reading. We can look at the amount of books written and the number which are sold, for example, and see that.

Anyway, on one hand the poetry community is healthy, and on the other hand it is unhealthy. There are very few individualistic kinds of voices. We tend to emulate each other and also imitate success. You might have someone writing in a unique voice, and before you know it, you have twenty, thirty, or forty clones. I think we are so easily influenced without realizing that we have a unique voice that we can improve, each of us. That is, if we're willing to take risks and reach deep enough into ourselves and touch the true passion. Yes, there's a vacuum that our waste economy has created that reaches into the arts . . . a cultural hedonism that touches everything.

What workshops do many times is they will get rid of, or at least downgrade, that which is different. Consequently there's a kind of threat: if it's different, people ask "do I really understand that?" or "shouldn't I have some kind of objection?" There's often a censorship against so-called taboo or inviolable topics and uniqueness, creating a kind of taciturnity.

*Do you think this fosters a kind of "missionary" mindset? That there's a "correct" way to write poetry?*

Correct, yes. But without realizing that what is considered wrong today is often right tomorrow. That's happened to certain writers. Ginsberg is a good example; in the '50s, the literary world said "no" to him, and now it's "Ginsberg, yeah, we know exactly what you were doing, and we agree with it." It probably has something to do with endurance and tenacity as well. If the risk-taker and innovator survives, he is then accepted in the academic realm.

*Who would you classify these days as having that sort of individualistic voice you're talking about?*

I admire all of Alan Dugan's work. Also Michael Harper. I think C. K. Williams is another. If you look at Williams's work, in his recent books *With Ignorance* and *Tar*, he has these long lines. His images and phrases are strung together with commas. He was doing something like that in his earlier two books, *Lies* and *I Am the Bitter Name:* short lines with slash marks. A continuous kind of voice.

Who else? Ai has a unique voice. A sense of hard reality. At times, however, I wonder if it has really been earned. I don't know how long she can carry on that kind of voice. Let's see. There's something different in Denis Johnson: a straightforwardness in some of his work. I think Garrett Hongo is different; he's able to weave things together in a unique way, and his sense of history is almost flawless. There are also a number of high-energy poets I like a lot: Jayne Cortez, Larry Neal, Wanda Coleman, Shirley Ann Williams, Anne Waldman, Dionisio Martinez, the Japanese poet Kazuko Shiraishi, and others.

*What about the place of rhyme, meter, form? There's clearly more and more of a movement towards that kind of formality.*

There's one poet who does that quite well, I think, and that's Marilyn Hacker. It's not obvious that she's using rhyme because she does it in such an off-handed, very effective way. You don't know you're reading a sonnet or a villanelle even if she puts "villanelle" or "sonnet" in the title. And I admire that in her work. I also love her political breadth and depth in formalized structures. She has some of the same surprises and playfulness as Brooks and Roethke, especially in her earlier works.

As a matter of fact, there's a book that I've been slowly working on called *Black Orpheus and Other Love Poems*. The book is made up of poems with traditional structures, and it's something that's going to take me a long time to write, partly because of the forms dictating the tone indirectly. I think form does that, and a poem does not really fly off the page like it's supposed to . . . it doesn't stay with the reader.

*What you say about inherited form not staying with the reader, at least in a contemporary context, reminds me of Hayden Carruth's Asphalt Georgics. In that book, he's taken enjambment to even further lengths. He achieves his rhymes by hyphenation—quite a tour de force. But it's the other direction from Hacker, where you think of her rhymes as being natural and subtle; instead, Carruth's rhymes are broken . . .*

Automatically drawing attention . . .

*It's like Hopkins taken to the furthest extreme. But it is technically interesting, perhaps even significant.*

Carruth has done so much—he's really prolific. I think he probably started with a formalized structure. I also like what he's done with jazz and blues. I've been working on an anthology off and on for a number of years now—a jazz poetry anthology. You'd be surprised at the number of poets who have been influenced by jazz. There are some wonderful poems by Hayden Carruth on jazz musicians— and of course, there are some important poems by William Matthews, Al Young, lots of people.

I'm interested in all the things a poet can do in a single poem. Tolson comes to mind; if you look at his book *Harlem Gallery*, you'd be surprised at what he can accomplish, as I said earlier. I partly agree with Allen Tate's statement that "Tolson out-Pounds Pound." If you want to really see things coming together from so many places and points of view without clashing, look at Tolson.

*Well, speaking of Pound, what about experimentation today in American poetry? You mentioned Robert Peters as one of your teachers, and I'm reminded of his books on single people, like* Kane *and* Hawker.

Robert Peters is very prolific and inventive. He has an amazing talent which, I think, is often underestimated. I admire especially "Gauguin's Chair" and what he did with the Shakers. Which I understand is an impromptu rendering, where he's actually taken over by voices and things of that sort. I admire that capacity, especially since he was trained as a Victorian scholar, and yet he's able to go on these voyages and imaginative *tour-de-forces*, using different kinds of voices.

What's happening in experimentation. . . . Well, the language poets like Michael Palmer and Ron Silliman and others on the West Coast, mainly in San Francisco, and of course the people associated with Colorado's Naropa Institute, the Jack Kerouac School of Disembodied Poetics. I think Anne Waldman and Laurie Anderson and Tom Waits are others. . . . And yet there is a resistance in the academic community when you bring up these names. Perhaps that resistance is what we should look at: why? I've been asking myself that question.

*I recently read an article written by a photographer which addresses the issue of conflict of interest in the world of art—how any single person may be asked simultaneously to be artist, critic, curator, collector, and so on. One wonders how that affects the objectivity and ethics of the artist.*

Yes, the artist can be easily forced into the position of demigod . . . catering to a number of factors that have little to do with artistic merit and talent . . . controlled by others and divided against himself or herself. That can take the passion and need out of the artist, who can become Faust overnight. Yet, I would like to believe that such multifarious persons often meet the challenge in maintaining objectivity and ethics, but I know that too often that isn't the case. What we lose is art, and what we get is only a ghost of true possibility.

In rejecting Walter Benjamin's stern analysis and contempt for Baudelaire, Ernst Fischer [in *The Necessity of Art,* 1963] says this: "For the vulgar hypocrite and the anaemic aesthete, beauty is an escape from reality, a cloying holy picture, a cheap sedative: but the beauty which arises out of Baudelaire's poetry . . . is like the angel of wrath holding the flaming sword. Its eye strips and condemns a world in which the ugly, the banal, and the inhuman are triumphant. Dressed-up poverty, hidden disease, and secret vice lie revealed before its radiant nakedness. It is as though capitalist civilization had been brought before a kind of revolutionary tribunal: beauty holds judgment and pronounces its verdict in lines of tempered steel."

## Fred Muratori   (review date December 1986)

SOURCE: A review of *I Apologize for the Eyes in My Head,* in *Library Journal,* Vol. 111, No. 20, December, 1986, pp. 115-16.

[*Below, Muratori notes that* I Apologize for the Eyes in My Head *"showcases a talented surrealist."*]

Komunyakaa's poems [in *I Apologize for the Eyes in My Head*] create and populate a world in which the linchpins of common sense and everyday appearances come loose, "where simple / answers fall like ashes / through an iron grate." Photographers airbrush the truth, Cinderella wakes up in a California pleasure dome. Even individual poems take on phantasmagoric dimensions akin to Bosch's busy but fascinating paintings as the poet reels off catalogs of apocalyptic events: "A white goat / is staring into windows again. / Bats clog the chimney like rags. / An angel in the attic / mends a torn wing." The invention is considerable, and though the accretion of wild images and preposterous characters eventually wears thin, this volume showcases a talented surrealist whose future work will warrant close attention.

## J. A. Miller   (review date September 1987)

SOURCE: A review of *I Apologize for the Eyes in My Head,* in *Choice,* Vol. 25, No. 1, September, 1987, p. 125.

[*In the following positive review of* I Apologize for the Eyes in My Head, *Miller calls Komunyakaa "one of the important poets of his generation."*]

[*I Apologize for the Eyes in My Head* extends] and deepens the terrain Yusef Komunyakaa explored so effectively in his first collection of poems, *Copacetic.* Komunyakaa is a poet of the night and of the streets, and in this collection his narrator roams through the dark alleys and side streets of the American landscape—a world populated by hustlers, prostitutes, angels, and ghosts—witnessing and participating in the world he records. Ordinary experience is often transformed into allegory and everyday people appear as mythic figures: The Thorn Merchant, Mr. Magnifico, The Thorn Merchant's Wife. And the "I" that records these poems is also the eye that perceives them, seeking in the process to restore the vital connection between the heart and the brain, the mind and the senses. Komunyakaa's poems are works of impressive verbal dexteri-

ty and striking images and rhythms, and this collection should consolidate his place as one of the important poets of his generation.

## Matthew Flamm   (review date 4 October 1987)

SOURCE: "Facing Up to the Deadly Ordinary," in *The New York Times Book Review,* October 4, 1987, p. 24.

[*Flamm is an American journalist. In the following excerpt, he characterizes* I Apologize for the Eyes in My Head *as "fierce yet mysterious," though he also notes some "poetic posturing."*]

Yusef Komunyakaa's first book of poems was called *Copacetic,* a description it lived up to with its street-rhythmic, impromptu style. His new collection, *I Apologize for the Eyes in My Head* (the book is better than the title), continues his explorations of local history, private experience and the charged, semi-surreal language that can dig out the difficult truths in either one. Mr. Komunyakaa works intuitively, with an intense distrust of any sort of conventional knowledge. "The audacity of the lower gods— / whatever we name we own," he says.

> I'd rather let the flowers
> keep doing what they do best.
> Unblessing each petal,
> letting go a year's worth of white
> death notes, busily unnaming themselves.

Born and raised in Bogalusa, La., Mr. Komunyakaa in his poems is pain's constant witness, often speaking for the historically dispossessed, but with the assumption that he does so only on his own idiosyncratic terms. Truthfulness is the supreme virtue in his world; lying, like the touch-up man "airbrushing away the corpses," is the worst evil. But since Mr. Komunyakaa deliberately chooses instinct over reason as his guide, the path to reality can be as lush, thick and hard to fathom as the backwoods. In **"How I See Things"** (a poem in which Mr. Komunyakaa does not apologize for the eyes in his head), he reminds a former freedom marcher about the civil rights days, the poet's impressions having an eerie feel to them. "Negatives of nightriders / develop in the brain," he says. Ghosts haunt the landscape, injustice continues—all you have to do is look:

> You're home in New York.
> I'm back here in Bogalusa
> with one foot in pinewoods.
> The mockingbird's blue note
> sounds to me like *please,*
>
> *please.* A beaten song
> threaded through the skull
> by cross hairs.
> Black hands still turn blood red
> working the strawberry fields.

That is Mr. Komunyakaa at his best—fierce yet mysterious. But the poems are not always so clear, and sometimes their obscurity seems no more than hip poetic posturing:

> Like some lost part of a model kit
> for Sir Dogma's cracked armor
> an armadillo merges with night.

Fortunately, Mr. Komunyakaa is more often worth the effort he requires.

**Wayne Koestenbaum** (review date 24 September 1989)

SOURCE: "Distortions in the Glass," in *The New York Times Book Review,* Vol. XCIV, No. 39, September 24, 1989, pp. 50-1.

[*Koestenbaum is an American educator and critic. In the following excerpt, he examines Komunyakaa's use of literary conventions in* Dien cai dau.]

Yusef Komunyakaa's third volume, *Dien Cai Dau* (Vietnamese for "crazy" and "American soldier"), renders a kind of experience so extreme it seems to forbid a merely esthetic response. These poems record Mr. Komunyakaa's service in the Vietnam War, for which he received a Bronze Star. Though his tersely-phrased chronicles, like documentary photographs, give us the illusion that we are facing unmediated reality, they rely on a predictable though powerful set of literary conventions.

First, the poems depend on orchestrated, theatrical juxta-positions—in particular, between scarifying war and suc-coring nature. Sometimes the vegetation or planets that frame the combat are amoral or demonic: "The moon cuts through / night trees like a circular saw / white hot." At other moments, nature offers camouflage, and soldiers blur into what surrounds them: "The five men breathe like a wave / of cicadas." When he portrays war as a part of nature, he makes it seem natural—foretold, justified. In such images as "Smoke-colored / Viet Cong / move under our eyelids," Mr. Komunyakaa turns combat into art; and yet he also describes piercingly how extremity heightens the senses. Like nature, sex provides an ironic foil to war: "silhouettes of jets / ease over nude bodies on straw mats." Whether through the consoling presence of land-scape or of flesh, his poems affirm some imagined whole that war only temporarily ruptures, as if nature were able to repair itself around the soldiers' ravages: "Spiders mend webs we marched into." I doubt nature so easily mends itself.

Mr. Komunyakaa's preferred tool is the simile or meta-phor; his brief fables proceed through—and climax in—such sharp images as "he merely rocked on his good leg / like a bleak & soundless bell." One poem, **"You and I Are Disappearing,"** is simply a list of similes—repeated, futile attempts to find an image sufficient to describe a Vietnamese girl in flames:

> She burns like oil on water.
> She burns like a cattail torch
> dipped in gasoline.
> She glows like the fat tip
> of a banker's cigar.

Simile, here, is a kind of theodicy, an effort to explain something morally incoherent. Imagery may pose as reasonably accurate reportage, but it also subtly editorializes. Figurative language varnishes the incident, gives it a luster, a permanence—as if beneath museum glass. Mr. Komunyakaa thus maintains a double relationship to his material—using images that raise *and* beg questions.

The book works through accretion, not argument, the poems are all in the present tense, which furthers the illusion that we are receiving tokens of a reality untroubled by language. However, because Vietnam's aftershock still shapes the poet's life, it is logical, and touching, that he renders war as if it were still present:

> Again, thanks for the dud
> hand grenade tossed at my feet
> outside Chu Lai. I'm still
> falling through its silence.

Of the Vietnam Veterans Memorial, he writes: "I touch the name Andrew Johnson: / I see the booby trap's white flash." The leap from engraved name to explosion occurs, as in a Pound ideogram, without transition. Mr. Komunyakaa, almost echoing Pound's "Cathay," writes, "Peasants outside Pakse City / insist the wildflowers / have changed colors." The ostensibly photographic technique of imagism is not, in fact, morally neutral; because Pound honed his imagistic method by imitating Chinese poetry, that oblique style—which Mr. Komunyakaa borrows—comes burdened with the values of Orientalism, the appropriate attempt to describe Asian experience through Western perspectives.

Though I regret the absence of a poem in this volume that exceeds in form, length or ambition the scope of individual, atomized narratives, the book's implications are richer than the poems separately betray. Issues of race and gender, in particular, complicate the collection's more straightforward preoccupation with warfare. Mr. Komunyakaa writes sensitively about the difficulties and ironies of being a black American soldier fighting along-side white men, and of American servicemen's sexual relations with Vietnamese women. In two lines, he sketches an encounter with the Vietnamese girlfriend of his sergeant major: "Once I asked her about family. / 'Not important, GI,' she said." *Dien Cai Dau* is filled with such unsentimental cameos, powerful because foreshortened. But foreshortening itself is an ambiguous, murky process. It distorts or disguises point of view, and mystifies the events it seems to describe so lucidly.

**Alvin Aubert** (review date 1989)

SOURCE: "Rare Instances of Reconciliation," in *Epoch,* Vol. 38, No. 1, 1989, pp. 67-72.

[*Aubert is an American educator, critic, and writer who specializes in African-American studies. In the following review, he discusses the major themes in* Dien cai dau, *including war, nature, and home.*]

Yusef Komunyakaa, a Black American poet and Vietnam vet, achieves striking surrealistic effects in his poetic renditions of the horrors of Vietnam. He is careful, however, not to overdo it. We find him equally cautious in dealing with his ethnicity, apparently apprehensive of some of the aesthetic risks involved on both counts. In incorporating his African-Americaness into his poems he maintains a balanced general European- and African-American perspective of Vietnam combat experiences while keeping his readers sufficiently aware of the extent to which the Black

American soldier still has to contend with the differential burden of racial, oftime racist, inequities.

Thus, ironically, Komunyakaa's Vietnam experiences and perceptions and the poems in which he so aptly inscribes them are simultaneously distressed and relieved, both in their ideological or socio-political concerns, by the strain of Vietnam wartime conditions, relief stemming from the peculiar camaraderie and ceremonies of survival the two groups of GIs—Blacks and whites—must devise for confronting a relentless foe in a nightmarish, absurdist warscape that acknowledges no racial, ethnic or sociopolitical distinctions and would as soon mangle the flesh of a Black American GI as that of a white.

> **Komunyakaa has succeeded as few artists ever have in depicting the artistic sensibility struggling to come to terms with experiences as harsh as those encountered in Vietnam.**
>
> *—Alvin Aubert*

Perhaps the most significant theme in *Dien Cai Dau*—as suited to a literary rendition of absurdist wartime experiences as it is to their surrealistic representation—is that of the relationship between war and nature; specifically, warfare's subversion of nature. In the poem **"Somewhere Near Phu Bai"** for example, instead of casting nature in its familiar signifying role of proffering alternatives to war, Komunyakaa employs apt surrealistic conceits to portray certain natural elements as in complicity with the ravishes of war and as totally unresponsive to human appeal: there being no recourse, for example, in a moon that "cuts through / night trees like a circular saw," or in "blue-steel stars." The moon image recurs in **"Phu Bai,"** typifying the poet's persistent rendition of normally benevolent natural manifestations as systematically devalued by the accidents of war, equating them reductively with such *man*ufactured objects of destructiveness as anti-personnel mines. The allusion to nature we get in connection with the mines in **"Phu Bai,"** more complex than space allows dealing with here, is that of bestial predation, involving the natural image of the identifying ear markings of prey-stalking tigers viewed from the rear: "The white-painted back / of Clamore mines / like quarter-moons," the explosive fronts of which Vietcong soldiers mark with identical quartermoon images and turn deceptively and destructively in the direction of their American foe.

The idea of nature as perpetrator of violence appears again in the poem **"Prisoners,"** in the surrealistic rendition of "Sunlight [that] throws / scythes against the afternoon." Also, in its closure (quoted below), **"Prisoners"** exemplifies the sprung lyrical stylistics generated by the surrealistic effects in Komunyakaa's poems in textual support of their absurdist strategies. The subjects of **"Prisoners"** are a group of recalcitrant Vietcong captives, perceived by the

poem's isolated poet-observer as shrouded in the aura of an enviable ancient alien culture, evoked in the poem in distancing, ne'er the twain shall meet surrealistic terms that are deftly intermingled with typically Komunyakaaian grounding images of earthbound concreteness: the reference to the Cobra combat helicopter and to the no-nonsense stare of the corporal in charge that stand in stark contrast to the attenuating visionary glance of the poet-observer. The overall effect is an intensification of the poet's sense of otherworldliness about the place, a perception that is at once elusive and productive of a somewhat apocalyptically epiphanic moment that typifies the recurring war-induced epistemological dead-ends the speaker experiences in poem after poem:

> Everything's a heat mirage; a river
> tugs at their slow feet.
> I stand alone & amazed,
> with a pill-happy door gunner
> signaling for me to board the Cobra.
> I remember how one day
> I almost bowed to such figures
> walking toward me, under
> a corporal's ironclad stare.
> I can't say why.
> From a half-mile away
> trees huddle together,
> & the prisoners look like
> marionettes hooked to strings of light.

The poem **"Hanoi Hannah"** employs even more telling sprung stylistics. In its depiction of the Vietcong's propagandistic efforts to demoralize the black American GIs, it focuses the racial issue in the book. "Soul Brothers," Hannah's alluring female broadcast voice inquires, "what are you dying for?" The "Brothers" respond with a volley of small arms automatic weapons fire in the direction of the elusive voice, precipitating a surrealistic display rendered in words that allude thematically to the biblical Genesis, World War II's Tokio Rose and the Virgin Mary, among other things. The effect is an amplified confirmation rather than a silencing of the seductress's taunting words:

> We lay down a white-klieg
> trail of tracers. Phantom jets
> fan out over the trees.
> Artillery fire zeros in.
> Her voice grows flesh
> & we can see her falling
> into the words, a bleeding flower
> no one knows the true name for.
> "You're lousy shots, GIs."
> Her laughter floats up
> as though the airways are
> buried under our feet.

A related thematic concern of Komunyakaa's lies in bridging the experiential gap between the Nam and back-home scenes, coordinating the experiences of GI and vet, backhome usually being associated with the figure of the woman imbued with redemptive potentialities. **"Sun Threnody,"** the ironically titled **"Combat Pay,"** and **"Facing It,"** the closing poem of the book, are three such pieces. The first of the three typifies Komunyakaa's myth-making propensity as he locates the poem in a field of African-American folk and popular culture with allusions particularly to the various forms of expressive behavior issuing therefrom. In black folk/popular parlance dating back at least to World War II, the name Jody is short for the black homefront folk figure trickster Joe the Grinder (usually a military rejectee or deferee or even, adding insult to injury, an older man) who seduces the wives and lovers left behind. The conclusive incident in the poem, which is scenically split between incidents occurring in Vietnam and backhome, is after the fact; the speaker, now a vet or a black GI on post-Vietnam leave of absence, recalls his first wartime experiences and the love letters he received from his fiancée and the sustaining memories and images of her they evoked. The experience is rendered in a surrealistic comingling of images of violence and sex:

> & it took closing a dead man's eyes
> to bring the war's real smell
> into my head. The quick fire
> danced with her nude reflection,
> & I licked an envelope each month
> to send blood money,
> kissing her lipstick mouth-prints
> clustering the perfumed paper,
> as men's voices collected
> in the gray weather I inhaled.
> Her lies saved me that year.
> I rushed to the word
> *Love* at the bottom of a page.

His tour of duty over, the speaker finds himself in a backhome bar sitting across a table from the Jody of his case who provides, somewhat ritualistically, the specific terms of the young warrior's cuckoldry:

> I asked her used-to-be
> if it was just my imagination,
> since I'd heard a man
> could be boiled down to his deeds.
> He smiled over his wine glass
> & said, "It's more, man.
> Your money bought my new Chevy."

**"Sun Threnody"** is one of the most interesting of Komunyakaa's poems. The opening statement ("She's here again.") might refer to the lost lover of the Jody poem or it may evoke memories of the elusive "night Muse" of an earlier poem in the book who "shows up in every war." Like these other women, she is something of the *femme fatale*, for like them (she is an army nurse, ironically) and the other women of Komunyakaa's poems, in addition to her role of redemptress she is closely associated with the masculine allurements of war. When the speaker of the poem sees her she is "Shaking the ice in her glass / to beckon the waitress / for another Tom Collins," a gesture which simultaneously beckons him. He recalls the brushes he has with death and finds himself futilely resisting her charms as he is transported back to Vietnam:

> & I'm a man fighting
> with myself. Yes, no,
> yes. I'm crouched there
> in that same grassy gully
> watching medevac choppers
> glide along the edge
> of the South China Sea . . .

But as he moves toward her, the all-in-all in his life for the moment, we perceive that he moves simultaneously into a combat zone:

> I'm still
> there (in Vietnam) & halfway to her
> table where she sits
> holding the sun
> in her icy glass.

**"Facing It,"** too—the last poem in the book—ranks among Komunyakaa's finest. The "It" of the title is literally the Vietnam Veterans [Memorial] in Washington, D.C. but the reflective wall functions metaphorically as an enter-Lewis Carrollian "black mirror," signifying the speaker's multidimensional confrontation of his past. Entrance or enterableness is multidimensional, also, temporarily; the black Vietnam vet speaker in the poem apprehends the reflective wall's present and future as well as its past, the war itself, and all three definitely in terms of the speaker's blackness, a commensurable, undeniable fact of his existence, past, present, and future. On first facing the wall the vet experiences the urge to cry, which he suppresses partly by allowing his face to be absorbed into the wall: "My black face fades, / hiding inside the black granite." Suppressing the urge to cry, he gains release from the stone only to be absorbed into it again, at which time he finally begins the memorial ritual he has come to perform:

> I go down the 58,022 names,
> half-expecting to find
> my own in letters like smoke.
> I touch the name Andrew Johnson;
> I see the booby trap's white flash.

The potentially redemptive woman is introduced:

> Names shimmer on a woman's blouse
> but when she walks away
> the names stay on the wall

but the closure of the poem posits redemption only as a future possibility. It briefly calls forth the irrepressible human urge to revoke the past, to expunge the names from the wall, but the poem and with it the book ends, albeit on a note of hope in the interaction between the woman, presumably a war widow, and her young son, in gestures suggestive that life must go on. Before perceiving this, however, the black vet seems to sense the need to make peace with his white counterpart. Seems to, because the reconciliation—perhaps more of a balancing of opposites for the moment—is ambiguous at best and may simply mean that once back home from the impelling wartime camaraderie of Vietnam, the old familiar racial attitudes take hold, the old backhome racist conflict resumes for, after all, the white vet's "pale eyes" are perceived as looking uncommunicatively *through* and not *into* those of his black counterpart:

> A white vet's image floats
> closer to me, then his pale eyes
> look through mine . . .
>
> . . . In the black mirror
> a woman's trying to erase names:
> No, she's brushing a boy's hair.

Komunyakaa has succeeded as few artists ever have in depicting the artistic sensibility struggling to come to terms with experiences as harsh as those encountered in Vietnam. The poems in *Dien Cai Dau* are works of heroic confrontation and, though they achieve only rare instances of reconciliation, such is to be expected. Very little has been resolved, the experiences have by no means been totally lived down, but in these very fine poems Komunyakaa has shown how the artist might proceed in quest of such an ideal.

## Steven Cramer   (review date May 1990)

SOURCE: A review of *Dien Cai Dau*, in *Poetry*, Vol. CLVI, No. 2, May, 1990, pp. 102-05.

[*In the following positive review, Cramer examines Komunyakaa's depiction of the Vietnam War in* Dien cai dau.]

*Dien Cai Dau* (the title, meaning "crazy," is Vietnamese slang for "American soldier") strives for total immersion in the visceral horrors of America's most unpopular war, the book's forty-four poems assembled without the intervention of section dividers or the mediation of an epigraph. It's as if Komunyakaa wanted nothing to palliate the blinding immediacy of combat.

Komunyakaa served in Vietnam as a correspondent, and as a number of his titles signal—"Camouflaging the Chimera," "Somewhere Near Phu Bai," "Starlight Scope Myopia," "We Never Know"—he seeks to depict the sheer confusion of war, the infantryman's chronic sense of dislocation. Sometimes the soldier's survival depends upon this absence of distinct outlines: "when will we learn / to move like trees move?" asks a GI who has unwittingly crossed paths with the Viet Cong; elsewhere the image of camouflage epitomizes how quickly the landscape can swallow its infiltrators, who "move like a platoon of silhouettes / balancing sledge hammers on our heads, / unaware our shadows have united / from us, wandered off / & gotten lost."

To convey the ordinary soldier's edgy watchfulness—the helpless awareness that mortal threat looms on the periphery—Komunyakaa deploys his present-tense, declarative sentences over a gridwork of enjambed free verse, coupling syntactical nervousness with a method of detailing that suggests the darting glance of a jittery sentry:

> The moon cuts through
> night trees like a circular saw
> white hot. In the guard shack
> I lean on the sandbags,
> taking aim at whatever.
> Hundreds of blue-steel stars
> cut a path, fanning out
> silver for a second. If anyone's
> there, don't blame me.
>                       ["Somewhere Near Phu Bai"]

If visual murkiness is Komunyakaa's metonym for the blurred moral outlines of all wars, *Dien Cai Dau* is also charged with the Vietnam veteran's peculiarly anguished knowledge of *this* war's moral ambiguities. In naming his book after a Vietnamese phrase for the American occupier, Komunyakaa articulates a deeply divided allegiance,

his ambivalence reinforced by his status as a black GI, who experiences recurrent inklings of solidarity with his nonwhite antagonists: *"VC didn't kill / Dr. Martin Luther King,"* claims one propaganda leaflet Komunyakaa encounters. In "Starlight Scope Myopia," Viet Cong stacking a cart with supplies and ammunition are "brought into killing range" through an infrared lens. The longer the poem spies on these enemies, however, the more individuated *and* representatively human they become:

> Are they talking about women
> or calling the Americans
>
> *beaucoup dien cai dau?*
> One of them is laughing,
> You want to place a finger
>
> to his lips & say "shhhh."
> You try reading ghost talk
>
> on their lips. They say
> "up-up we go," lifting as one.

This epiphanic recognition of mortal enemy as fellow mortal—as Whitman put it, "my enemy is dead, a man divine as myself is dead"—forms one of the thematic centers of war literature. Komunyakaa renders that tragic identification most indelibly in the terse "We Never Know." The poem recalls the famous trench scene from *All Quiet on the Western Front,* but in its collision of images drawn from the sacred and the technological, the sexual and the murderous—in short, from the chimerical paradoxes of modern combat—it derives unmistakably from that war we televised but never declared:

> He danced with tall grass
> for a moment, like he was swaying
> with a woman. Our gun barrels
> glowed white-hot.
> When I got to him,
> a blue halo
> of flies had already claimed him.
> I pulled the crumbled photograph
> from his fingers.
> There's no other way
> to say this: I fell in love.
> The morning cleared again,
> except for the distant mortar
> & somewhere choppers taking off.
> I slid the wallet into his pocket
> & turned him over, so he wouldn't be
> kissing the ground.

The last ten or so poems of *Dien Cai Dau* depict the war's aftermath—the panicked efforts of the South Vietnamese to camouflage their collaboration, the GI's alienating reentry into American society, the legacy of MIA's and Amerasian children, the cathartic reunion with the dead at the Vietnam Veterans Memorial. Lacking the immediacy of the combat lyrics, these poems sometimes rely on a kind of editorializing by juxtaposed details—"using gun mounts / for monkey bars, / Vietnamese children / play skin-the-cat"—and even, occasionally, on banality: "I'm a man fighting / with myself." Not so much implausible as overmanaged, these poems seem to fabricate paradoxes for effect; they're reductively theatrical. But in the poems growing directly out of combat, Komunyakaa makes a major contribution to the body of literature grappling with Vietnam—a poetry that pierces the artificial border between moral and aesthetic engagement.

## Samuel Maio   (review date May-June 1990)

SOURCE: "The Poetry of Truth," in *The Bloomsbury Review,* Vol. 10, No. 3, May-June, 1990, p. 27.

[*Maio is an American educator and critic. In the following excerpt from a comparative review of* Dien cai dau *and Lowell Jaeger's* War on War *(1988), he discusses Komunyakaa's examination of the psychological effects of the Vietnam War in* Dien cai dau.]

Of the many recent books of poetry concerned with the Vietnam War, *Dien Cai Dau* by Yusef Komunyakaa and *War on War* by Lowell Jaeger share the most in common, each resembling the other in thematic focus: the mental anguish of this war, for combatants, observers, participants, and objectors, which Komunyakaa calls "the psychological terrain that makes us all victims." This peculiar aspect of Vietnam continues to rage "behind the eyes" (Komunyakaa's phrase) of all those affected by the war, those who fought in it, as did Komunyakaa, and those who refused, choosing instead to fight against it while remaining, then fleeing home, as did Jaeger.

Many of the opening poems in Komunyakaa's book (his third full-length collection, yet first taking his Vietnam experience as subject matter) allude to, if not address directly, the most singular aspect of this war: that American soldiers carried on mental battles as dangerous as the physical war surrounding them. The guerilla attacks, the booby traps, the lethal snipers, the unseen enemy in their tunnel network, all loomed in mythical proportions to the average soldier, leaving him bewildered, frightened, unsure of his ability. And bored, finally, having too much time between maneuvers or skirmishes. This "down time" grew contemplative, causing horrific fantasies to fester, compounding the confusion, turning thoughts to the homelife and lover left behind. Other poems depict scenes in which the speaker is involved directly with sudden death, half-expected and accepted as imminent, that quick end to life germane to war (even one called merely a "conflict").

In **"Camouflaging the Chimera,"** the book's opening poem, we are alerted to the strangeness of the GIs' commingling with nature, of their heightened sensory perception rendering the natural to the surreal, the physical world to a spiritual, ghosted darkness—which becomes the metaphor for Komunyakaa's war. The "chimera" in mythology, of course, is a she-monster, one vomiting flames, a disfigured being composed of a goat's head and lion's body. Another, ancillary, definition is that of an illusion or one's intellectual fabrication. Both uses of "chimera" function significantly in this poem, which serves as a prelude to the book's principal themes. The GIs literally camouflage themselves as they lie waiting to spring an ambush, curiously entwining with nature yet acutely aware of their separateness from it:

> We wove
> ourselves into the terrain,

content to be a hummingbird's target.

> . . . Chameleons
> crawled our spines, changing from day
> to night: green to gold,
> gold to black. But we waited
> till the moon touched metal . . .

The reality of this eerie, nightmarish circumstance—forcing concentration in darkness, blending with nature towards a deceptive end—assumes a mythical quality, a surreal flavor. The chimera that the ambushers are yields to the chimera in each GI's mind:

> We hugged bamboo & leaned
> against a breeze off the river,
> slow-dragging with ghosts
> from Saigon to Bangkok,
> with women left in doorways
> reaching in from America.

The frightful baggage behind each man's eyes (as the poem suggests)—apparitions of the past and of future promise—is the chimera which cannot be camouflaged, but only brought to the forefront of one's thoughts in this quiet moment just before a surprise attack so characteristic of Vietnam.

Ghosts—imaginations—the dark of night, the past growing more unreal each day, the present undefined, the future as unclear as a distant dream which cannot quite be recalled except for the doubt and fear it left behind—these combine to create the atmosphere surrounding Komunyakaa's representation of the war. The mania of a *dien cai dau* (meaning "crazy," but taken as the Vietnamese term for an American soldier) suggests the imbalance of perspective engendered in an absurd situation such as the Vietnam War, in which the biggest battle for the GI was psychological, the struggle for reason and comprehension.

The spiritual dimension, or that particular sensitivity the speaker of **"Night Muse & Mortar Round"** attributes to his metaphysical conditioning generated by this war, is depicted as a protective (rather than prohibitive) force. Invoking the traditional folkloric motif of an angelic—if momentary—savior, this poem recounts such an "extrasensory" experience, nearly divine, which saved his life. A "night muse," or spirit, who "shows up in every war," according to folklore, tries to flag down the jeep driven by the speaker, who stops suddenly upon seeing his vision of the muse, then he continues:

> When you finally drive back
> she's gone, just a feeling
> left in the night air.
> Then you hear the blast
> rock the trees & stars
> where you would've been that moment.

The vision of the night muse saves this soldier/speaker's life—then his C.O., riding shotgun, threatens him with court-martial for stopping the jeep for no apparent reason and without an order to do so.

These mysteries, real and imagined, and the losses incumbent upon war—lovers left at home, the sight of best friends dead in the jungle, faith left in the barracks—comprise the mental terrain the anguished GI occupies.

His only solace, ironically, is to surrender to the inherent sterility ("**Seeing in the Dark**") or to prostitution ("**The Edge**") or, finally, to the jungle itself ("**Jungle Surrender**"), its covered terror, hiding an enemy known for torturing prisoners. But conquering the war of the mind—as difficult as "winning" the Vietnam conflict—only to return home unwelcomed and misunderstood remains the last, continuing challenge the soldier confronts ("**Facing It**").

Komunyakaa, through his simple and vernacular diction, his evocative images and chronicled experiences, successfully provides us with glimpses into the mind of a *dien cai dau*, often quite aptly named, the insanity of Vietnam measuring against (and similarly affecting) its principles, as these terrifying poems—drawn by the precise hand of an unerring craftsman—make so strikingly clear.

### Vince F. Gotera   (essay date 1990)

SOURCE: "Depending on the Light: Yusef Komunyakaa's *Dien Cai Dau*," in *America Rediscovered: Critical Essays on Literature and Film of the Vietnam War,* edited by Owen W. Gilman, Jr., and Lorrie Smith, Garland Publishing, 1990, pp. 282-300.

[*In the following excerpt from a comparative study of Vietnam War poets, Gotera discusses Komunyakaa's use of surrealism, language, and imagery in* Dien cai dau.]

***Dien Cai Dau*** is Komunyakaa's fourth book of poems. In his earlier three books, he has not included a single poem on Vietnam, because he has been waiting for emotional distance—objective and journalistic—from his 1969-70 Army tour there. George Garrett, in his introduction to [D. C.] Berry's *saigon cemetery,* proposes that "ordinary judgment [of Berry's poems] must be suspended. We are too close, and the wounds and scars, literal and metaphorical, are too fresh." It is just such a suspension of judgment that Komunyakaa does *not* want; he wishes his work to be tested with the full rigor applied to all serious poetry.

The fact that Komunyakaa has waited almost two decades to publish poems on Vietnam differentiates his work significantly from that of other veteran poets, especially those who published in the early '70s. The difference is not so much that he has achieved a distance from his Vietnam experience but rather that the development of his craft has not been inextricably bound up with Vietnam. . . . Komunyakaa comes to the material with an academic grounding in modernist and contemporary poetics as well as classic surrealism, and his work registers an esthetic advance not only of poetry about the Vietnam War but also of war literature in general.

From his first chapbook, ***Dedications and Other Darkhorses***, (1977), through his most recent book, ***I Apologize for the Eyes in My Head*** (1986), Komunyakaa's forte has been the counterbalancing of seeming oppositions and incongruities. Critics of Surrealism have pointed to "The poet Isidore Ducasse, the 'comte de Lautréamont,' who . . . had provided the classic example in writing of 'the chance encounter of a sewing machine and an umbrella on a dissection table' " [William S. Rubin in *Dada, Sur-*

*realism, and Their Heritage,* 1968], a serendipitous yoking in whose interstices an immanent, wholly startling signification can well. Komunyakaa has inherited this mode of juxtaposition from the Surrealists, specifically through the poet Aimé Césaire. A typical example is "**2527th Birthday of the Buddha**":

> When the motorcade rolled to a halt, Quang Duc
> climbed out & sat down in the street.
> He crossed his legs,
> & the other monks & nuns grew around him like petals.
> He challenged the morning sun,
> debating with the air
> he leafed through-visions brought down to earth.
> Could his eyes burn the devil out of men?
> A breath of peppermint oil
> soothed someone's cry. Beyond terror made flesh-
> he burned like a bundle of black joss sticks.
> A high wind that started in California
> fanned flames, turned each blue page,
> leaving only his heart intact.
> Waves of saffron robes bowed to the gasoline can.

This poem takes as its base a kind of journalistic language, and of course the seed of the piece is the rumor that the heart of a self-immolated monk literally had not burned, a rumor perhaps gleaned from an actual news story. But the poem quickly moves into the contrapuntal surrealistic plane with "the other monks & nuns . . . like petals," setting up a group of images: petals, leaves, and finally pages, reminding us of Holy Writ. (And the phrase "terror made flesh" of course vibrates for Christian readers.) But the Komunyakaa wrinkle here is how the political situation is mystically manifested—American collusion made evident by the "high wind that started in California." The astonishing final image juxtaposes "saffron robes" with "the gasoline can," succinctly summing up the Vietnam War which arises from this volatile situation: "the gasoline can," a harbinger of technology which emblemizes violence and death, becomes a new deity, and all the saffron robes will be ultimately consumed.

Komunyakaa's surrealism varies from that of the other veteran poets because he does not depict Vietnam itself or the Vietnam experience as *literally* surreal, as do many of the other poets. Surrealism has been defined as "the attempt to actualize *le merveilleux,* the wonderland of revelation and dream, and by so doing to permit chance to run rampant in a wasteland of bleak reality" [Herbert S. Gershman, in *The Surrealist Revolution in France,* 1969]; in other words, the exploration of the strange, through fortuitous juxtaposition, allows revelation to occur in the midst of the real. Through surrealism, Komunyakaa *discovers*—or perhaps more appropriately, *reveals*—Vietnam and does not only document its apparent surreality for an incredulous audience. "**Camouflaging the Chimera**" enacts this process of revelation:

> We tied branches to our helmets.
> We painted our faces & rifles

with mud from a riverbank,

blades of grass hung from the pockets
of our tiger suits. We wove
ourselves into the terrain,
content to be a hummingbird's target.

We hugged grass & leaned
against a breeze off the river,
slowdragging with ghosts

from Saigon to Bangkok,
with women left in doorways
reaching in from America.
We aimed at dark-hearted songbirds.
In our way station of shadows
rock apes tried to blow our cover,
throwing stones at the sunset. Chameleons

crawled our spines, changing from day
to night: green to gold,
gold to black. But we waited
till the moon touched metal,

till something almost broke
inside us. VC struggled
with the hillside, like black silk

wrestling iron through grass.
We weren't there. The river ran
through our bones. Small animals took refuge
against our bodies: we held our breath,

ready to spring the L-shaped
ambush, as a world revolved
under each man's eyelid.

Surrealism in this poem does not function to present Vietnam to the reader as exotica, but rather to underline the existential reality of ambush: the internal psychic state of each combatant. The wish-fulfillment of camouflage involves *becoming* the landscape, abdicating one's memories and anything else which might disrupt the illusion. The angst of the situation, the impending firefight, is focused by "a world revolved / under each man's eyelid," a revamping of the cliché "my life passed before my eyes." Of course, the phrase also refers to "the world" or everything not Vietnam, delineating each soldier's acute realization that he does not *belong* in this place, that his death here would be literally senseless. The dramatic situation of this poem also acts certainly as a signifier for the entire war, and thus the word "Chimera" in the title serves as a political statement.

The poem " 'You and I Are Disappearing' " (a quote from Björn Håkansson) is a bravura performance highlighting Komunyakaa's technique of juxtaposed images:

The cry I bring down from the hills
belongs to a girl still burning
inside my head. At daybreak
    she burns like a piece of paper.
She burns like foxfire
in a thigh-shaped valley.
A skirt of flames
dances around her
at dusk.
            We stand with our hands
hanging at our sides,
while she burns

like a sack of dry ice.
She burns like oil on water.
She burns like a cattail torch
dipped in gasoline.
She glows like the fat tip
of a banker's cigar,
        silent as quicksilver.
A tiger under a rainbow
    at nightfall.
She burns like a shot glass of vodka.
She burns like a field of poppies
at the edge of a rain forest.
She rises like dragonsmoke
    to my nostrils.
She burns like a burning bush
driven by a godawful wind.

In this poem, Komunyakaa is performing "the kind of intellectual wrestling that moves and weaves us through human language," as he told me in an interview. According to Komunyakaa, "language is what can liberate or imprison the human psyche," and this poem dramatizes a speaker who is simultaneously liberated and imprisoned. The speaker here is at a loss to describe this scene fittingly. The charged language grapples with a view that is both unimaginably beautiful and incredibly horrible, all at the same time. The speaker, again and again, tries to find a metaphor that will convey both the beauty and the horror—the dilemma of speaking the Sublime, in Edmund Burke's terms. And the speaker comes enticingly, asymptotically close without finding the ideal phrase. Finally, he simply has to stop. And the final image points a biblical finger: the girl will always burn in the speaker's mind in the same way that the burning bush could have burned forever unconsumed. What really nails this image is the phrase "godawful wind" which puns on "awful God," straight out of the Old Testament, while it resurrects the root meaning full of awe, or more properly here, filling with awe.

" 'You and I Are Disappearing' " also demonstrates Komunyakaa's poetic ancestry in English, specifically William Carlos Williams and his use of the image. . . . [According to critic Marjorie Perloff], Williams' recurrent images—wind, flower, star, white, dark—are perfectly ordinary, but it is their *relationships* that matter." If we ignore for a moment that the signified is "she"—a human being—Komunyakaa's images here are similarly ordinary: "a piece of paper," "oil on water," a "cigar," "a shot glass of vodka," "a field of poppies"; others are lexically more interesting but still reasonably innocent: "foxfire," "a sack of dry ice," "a rainbow," "dragonsmoke." What drives this poem is the anaphoric repetition of "she burns"—the accretion of which underlines the intrinsic horror of the poem and, by extension, the war itself. The ultimate focus is on humanity and on humaneness.

Many of the poems in **Dien Cai Dau** deal with human response and connection in combat. **"Nude Pictures"** begins at the end, only implying the story which comes before:

I slapped him a third time.
The song caught in his throat
for a second, & the morning
came back together like after
a stone has been dropped

through a man's reflection
hiding in a river. I slapped him
again, but he wouldn't stop

laughing. As we searched
for the squad, he drew us
to him like a marsh loon
tied to its half-gone song
echoing over rice fields
& through wet elephant grass
smelling of gunpowder & fear.
I slapped him once more.
Booby-trapped pages floated
through dust. His laughter
broke off into a silence
early insects touched
with a tinge of lost music.
He grabbed my hand & wouldn't
let go. Lifted by a breeze,
a face danced in the treetops.

In **"2527th Birthday of the Buddha,"** the typical Komunyakaa opposition is the documentary vs. the figurative; here the conflict is between nature and human intrusion. The morning shattered by a firefight "came back together like after / a stone has been dropped through a man's reflection / hiding in a river." The "stone," a semaphore for gunfire, intrudes upon the harmony between humans and nature—here, the squad and the morning. Now the hysterical soldier intrudes upon the reassembled morning, "like a marsh loon / tied to its half-gone song" (i.e., nature gone mad).

The final human intrusion occurs in the arresting close: "Lifted by a breeze, / a face danced in the treetops." Literally, of course, this is a wafting scrap of girlie magazine, with the face coincidentally framed. On a figurative level, however, the image finally rescues humanity: the lexical territory of "Lifted" and "danced" argues for an upbeat ending here. Just as the speaker and the sole surviving soldier hold hands . . . so too are humans and nature harmoniously reunited, if only metaphorically.

Komunyakaa's devotion to a highly textured language is clearly evident in the poems already discussed. There are arresting turns of phrase throughout *Dien Cai Dau:* a tunnel rat moves "Through silver / lice, shit, maggots, & vapor of pestilence"; the Viet Cong are "lords over loneliness / winding like coralvine through / sandalwood & lotus"; conspirators plan a fragging, "their bowed heads / filled with splintered starlight"; an armored personnel carrier is "droning like a constellation / of locusts eating through bamboo." For the most part, however, the language of *Dien Cai Dau* is a spoken language, in the Wordsworthian sense—it is the extraordinary way in which these everyday words are combined which makes the poems significant. . . .

[Komunyakaa] uses the "grunt's" language and speech for credibility. In **"Hanoi Hannah,"** however, he places the argot in the mouth of the enemy, to demonstrate the ambivalent ambience of Vietnam:

*Ray Charles!* His voice
calls from waist-high grass,
& we duck behind gray sandbags.
"Hello, Soul Brothers. Yeah,

Georgia's also on my mind."
Flares bloom over the trees.
"Here's Hannah again.
Let's see if we can't
light her goddamn fuse
this time." Artillery
shells carve a white arc
against dusk. Her voice rises
from a hedgerow on our left.
"It's Saturday night in the States.
Guess what your woman's doing tonight.
I think I'll let Tina Turner
tell you, you homesick GIs."
Howitzers buck like a herd
of horses behind concertina.
"You know you're dead men
don't you? You're dead
as King today in Memphis.
Boys, you're surrounded by
General Tran Do's division."
Her knife-edge song cuts
deep as a sniper's bullet.
"Soul Brothers, what you dying for?"
We lay down a white-klieg
trail of tracers. Phantom jets
fan out over the trees.
Artillery fire zeros in.
Her voice grows flesh
& we can see her falling
into words, a bleeding flower
no one knows the true name for.
"You're lousy shots, GIs."
Her laughter floats up
as though the airways are
buried under our feet.

It is interesting to note here that Hannah speaks not just colloquial English, but fluent black English; her speech is so well tuned as to be virtually indistinguishable from the American voice who says "Let's see if we can't / light her goddamn fuse / this time." That Komunyakaa is black generally makes no difference in many of the poems in *Dien Cai Dau,* but here it is significant because blacks (and hence the poet) are being directly addressed here by the Viet Cong; Hannah plays Ray Charles and Tina Turner, speaks to "Soul Brothers," and taunts them with Martin Luther King's assassination—it may well be the speaker's first realization of that event. As this poem shuttles between reported speech and narrative passages, it displays a seamlessness of diction, unlike that of earlier Vietnam—veteran poets like Paquet, who deliberately embattles one set of connotations against another for tension. Here, the everyday diction—"duck behind," "light her . . . fuse," "buck like a herd / of horses"—is allowed to rest easy with slightly more elevated phrases—"carve a white arc," "knife-edge song," "white-klieg / trail of tracers." But the salient point here is Hannah's intimate command of English and the social nuances conveyed by language.

The plight of the "grunt" home from the war is handled by Komunyakaa differently from other veteran poets, and this variance arises partly from questions of race. The black soldier remembers a different Vietnam: Viet Cong leaflets saying, *VC didn't kill / Dr. Martin Luther King*"; the white bars and the black bars on "Tu Do Street" in Saigon, the black POW remembering "those rednecks" in

Georgia, "Bama," and Mississippi to help him through VC torture. But other poems focus more universally on the generic returnee. The poem **"Combat Pay for Jody"** focuses on a soldier and his inevitable encounter with Jody, the folkloric figure back home who steals every combat soldier's wife or girlfriend:

> I counted tripflares
> the first night at Cam Ranh Bay,
> & the molten whistle of a rocket
> made me sing her name into my hands.
> I needed to forget the sea
> between us, the other men.
> Her perfume still crawled
> my brain like a fire moth,
> & it took closing a dead man's eyes
> to bring the war's real smell
> into my head. The quick fire
> danced with her nude reflection,
> & I licked an envelope each month
> to send blood money,
> kissing her lipstick mouthprints
> clustering the perfumed paper,
> as men's voices collected
> in the gray weather I inhaled.
> Her lies saved me that year.
> I rushed to the word
> *Love* at the bottom of a page.
> One day, knowing a letter waited,
> I took the last chopper back to Chu Lai,
> an hour before the firebase was overrun
> by NVA. Satchel charges
> blew away the commander's bunker,
> & his men tried to swim the air.
> A week later when I returned
> to Phoenix, the city hid her
> shadow & I couldn't face myself
> in the mirror. I asked her used-to-be
> if it was just my imagination,
> since I'd heard a man
> could be boiled down to his deeds.
> He smiled over his wine glass
> & said, "It's more, man.
> Your money bought my new Chevy."

This poem literally brings clichés to life. The testimony of a "grunt" for whom the thought of his lover functioned as a chivalric favor preserving him from harm is so common that it becomes apocryphal. Ditto for the stories of Jody's legendary exploits. In **"Combat Pay for Jody,"** Komunyakaa has composed a vividly lyrical narrative which encompasses the thousand days of the speaker's Vietnam tour and his eventual return to "the world." More importantly, he has created a realistic voice which re-enlivens the overworked clichés of military life and which points up the returning soldier's inability to navigate in what used to be his personal landscape.

The Vietnam Veterans Memorial has become an emblem of the difficulties of the Vietnam veteran, and Komunyakaa's poem **"Facing It"** (the closing poem in the book) does exactly what its title says—face the monument and what it signifies:

> My black face fades,
> hiding inside the black granite.
> I said I wouldn't,
> dammit: No tears.

> I'm stone. I'm flesh.
> My clouded reflection eyes me
> like a bird of prey, the profile of night
> slanted against morning. I turn
> this way—the stone lets me go.
> I turn this way—I'm inside
> the Vietnam Veterans Memorial
> again, depending on the light
> to make a difference.
> I go down the 58,022 names,
> half-expecting to find
> my own in letters like smoke.
> I touch the name Andrew Johnson;
> I see the booby trap's white flash.
> Names shimmer on a woman's blouse
> but when she walks away
> the names stay on the wall.
> Brushstrokes flash, a red bird's
> wings cutting across my stare.
> The sky. A plane in the sky.
> A white vet's image floats
> closer to me, then his pale eyes
> look through mine. I'm a window.
> He's lost his right arm
> inside the stone. In the black mirror
> a woman's trying to erase names:
> No, she's brushing a boy's hair.

This poem is literally a reflection about reflections; it is a "facing" of the dualities that govern this everyday life: there and here, America and Vietnam, living and dead, night and day, old and young, white and black (i.e., Caucasian and Negro). Komunyakaa does not declaim, does not decry; instead he presents, practically unmediated, a series of images. Like the speaker of " **'You and I Are Disappearing'** "—the poem about the burning girl—the poet here is faced with an ineffable scene, but instead of searching for apt metaphors to voice his feeling, he reverts to a reportorial mode. Everything ultimately is point of view, and we are always "depending on the light / to make a difference." This is what Vietnam poetry (and all poetry in essence) *must* do—enlighten, give light, illuminate, the better for all to see and see well.

*Dien Cai Dau* is a breathtakingly original work of art because of the believable, down-to-earth language which speaks the thoughts and feelings of authentic characters, filtered through Komunyakaa's atypical vision. In the last line of *Dien Cai Dau*—a book whose title, after all, means "crazy"—a woman is "brushing a boy's hair," an action which affirms sanity and life in the face of the insanity of the war: the love between a mother and child, between two human beings. Writing about [Bruce] Weigl's *The Monkey Wars,* Smith proposes the potential of a "salvific poetic vision which might unify past and present, anguish and affirmation" [Lorrie Smith, in "A Sense-Making Perspective in Recent Poetry by Vietnam Veterans," *American Poetry Review* (November-December) 1986]; Komunyakaa fulfills this promise in *Dien Cai Dau.*

Komunyakaa's achievement points to the possibility and actuality of self-renewal and solace in poetry by Vietnam veterans. As the body of poetry by veterans moves from mere documentary to self-discovery and personal commitment, from a gratuitous surrealism to a conscientious use of French surrealistic technique, future work by Vietnam-veteran poets becomes increasingly able to transcend the paralyzing horror of the Vietnam War. . . . The transcendental possibilities in poetry by Vietnam veterans, therefore, can make possible a more accurate national vision of the Vietnam War—both in documentary and spiritual terms—allowing us, as a nation, to confront fully the moral consequences of our presence in Vietnam. Perhaps, in some near future, it may not be too optimistic to wish, with [W. D.] Ehrhart, that "the soul of the nation might somehow be cleansed" by poetry.

### Eileen Myles    (review date 12 January 1993)

SOURCE: "Lost City" in *The Village Voice,* Vol. XXXVIII, No. 2, January 12, 1993, pp. 80-1.

[*In the following review, Myles states that while* Magic City *"starts off a little sticky," its "information is unforgettable."*]

Yusef Komunyakaa, an African American poet whose last book, *Dien Cai Dau,* drove a shaft of light into the inarticulate spectacle of the Vietnam War, has now taken on a story easy to mistell: childhood. *Magic City* is the name of this foray. It starts off a little sticky, in my opinion. I don't think Komunyakaa feels confident with the first person—certainly not a re-assembled first person, like that of the speaker in the first poem: **"Venus's-flytraps":**

> The tall flowers in my dreams
>     are
> Big as the First State Bank,
> & they eat all the people
> Except the ones I love.
> They have women's names,
> With mouths like where
> Babies come from. I am five.

Komunyakaa has said of this work that he was "trying to throw myself back into the emotional situation of the time, and at the same time bring a psychological overlay that juxtaposes new experiences alongside the ones forming the old landscape inside my head." This is an elaborate construction, but to my mind a "child voice" is almost no voice at all. It lives in the description of one's memories. And what's stellar about these poems are lines like "flesh-colored stones along a riverbed." Whose flesh? The ambiguity asks nothing and everything of the reader. Komunyakaa's physical descriptions of things are bursting with matter-of-factness, a sublime flatness that delivers the unconscious unscathed, because it's a participant rather than an invited guest.

Mostly, he lets the information speak. Quiet rage informs the telling of **"History Lessons,"** which in one of three stanzas describes the former site of a lynching—"No, I couldn't see the piece of blonde rope . . . the / Flayed tassel of wind-whipped hemp knotted around a limb / Like a hank of hair." Later, Komunyakaa gives an account of the murder of a young black boxer who was "running & punching the air at sunrise / how they tarred and feathered him & dragged the corpse / Behind a Model T . . . / How they dumped the prizefighter on his mother's doorstep . . . two days later three boys / Found a white man dead . . . in blackface." The overt content of this poem,

and much of the work in this book, is about living under a system of racism, but what's astonishing about Komunyakaa's handling of racism is that every hair of the poem (when he's on) is about that, too. The blondness of the hanging rope tells more about the perpetrators and their victim than any blow-by-blow. In its shorthand, it humanizes the revulsion, making this white reader see the horror of the world in the hues it really comes in.

In the course of Komunyakaa's telling, the ante is raised word by word—the "young boxer" becomes a "prizefighter" who is then rendered lifeless and placed, empty of future meaning, on his mother's doorstep. What could be worse? By the time we get to the man in blackface whose head is tenderly resting "on a clump of sedge," we're simply numbed. Komunyakaa's system of signs and codes is as strongly installed in his work as racism is in society at large; one can't help but share in his fascination with the stray mysteries the system of black / white, male / female yields. These objects of his gaze are delivered point-blank: **"Boys in Dresses"** is an almost ceremonial poem about just what the title says. "We felt the last kisses / Our mothers would give us / On the mouth . . ." In **"Fleshing-out the Season,"** a man has two wives: one black, one white. The women are friends and the three live in peace and he sends their children to college and they divide his body when he dies: "One sprinkled him / Over the Gulf of Mexico, / & the other put him under roots / of pigweed beside the back gate—/ Purple, amaranthine petals, / She wore in her hair on Sundays." Such oddities glisten like myth rather than having any moral purpose. Which is another aspect of his collection I adore. The title keys it too: *Magic City* is more than a bit of an amusement park, with an almost Angela Carter perspective on a southern Black youth. Thereby glints its horror and its power and the information is unforgettable.

### Alvin Aubert    (essay date Spring 1993)

SOURCE: "Yusef Komunyakaa: The Unified Vision—Canonization and Humanity," in *African American Review,* Vol. 27, No. 1, Spring, 1993, pp. 119-23.

[*In the following essay, Aubert discusses Komunyakaa's "quest for a unified vision, his bid for literary canonization, and his push for the completion of his humanity."*]

In an interview in the journal *Callaloo,* Yusef Komunyakaa, author of seven collections of poems, expresses his admiration for poets whom he considers to have achieved a "unified vision" in their poetry, an achievement he apparently strives for in his own work. A closely associated, if not identical, goal and a source of tension in Komunyakaa's poetry is his desire to gain admittance into the American literary canon, but not at the expense of surrendering his African American cultural identity.

At the core of Komunyakaa's pursuit of a unified vision and literary canonization is his stern resistance, textualized formalistically as well as thematically in his poems, to those forces in the hegemonous counterculture aimed at excluding him as an African American from the ranks of humanity. Indeed, in the singularity of his perseverance and in both the high quality and quantity of his poetic output, Komunyakaa approaches the intensity of no less a figure than prototypical canonization quester Ralph Ellison in his bid for mainstream American literary status. Komunyakaa, however, lacks the irritability Ellison sometimes displays in his attitude toward other African American writers, in particular the young black writers of the culturally insurrectionary 1970s.

The unified vision Komunyakaa seeks involves the integration and aesthetic instillation in his poetry of cultural material from both his African American and his European American sources. A useful sampling of Komunyakaa's artistry at work—including his quest for a unified vision, his bid for literary canonization, and his push for the completion of his humanity—can be found in two poems from his ironically titled fourth collection, *I Apologize for the Eyes in My Head* (1986): **"When in Rome—Apologia,"** the last two lines of which supply the title of the book, and **"I Apologize."** I will also refer briefly to **"The Music That Hurts."**

A particularly illustrative passage appears in **"I Apologize,"** a dramatic monologue that intertextualizes Robert Browning's prototypical dramatic monologue "My Last Duchess": "I'm just like the rest of the world: / No comment; no way, Jose . . ." After staking his claim for unqualified status in the human race and issuing his somewhat tongue-in-cheek declaration of no comment (ironically noting the extent to which further comment might implicate him in the negatives as well as the positives of the humanity he holds in common with his white auditor), the persona comments anyway. Addressing the person designated as "sir," who occupies the position of the implicit, silent auditor of the traditional dramatic monologue, the persona observes that he "want[s] spring always / dancing with the pepper trees," etc.

Like most of Komunyakaa's poems, **"I Apologize"** is markedly obscure. On first reading, the persona might be the typical, racially or ethnically unspecified, Peeping Tom, but we soon realize that he is the archetypal reckless eyeballer, the fated African American male in the U.S. South of not too many years ago who is accused of looking too long, and by implication with sexual intent, at some white woman, a tabooistic infringement for which he is likely to be lynched. The accused's only defense, his only recourse in such a predicament, is a desperate and futile excuse. This is typified in the poem's opening lines, which also encapsulate the kind of redemptive humor black people engage in among themselves: "My mind wasn't even there / Mirage, sir I didn't see / what I thought I saw. / . . . I was miles away, I saw nothing!" Then there is the sheer desperation of the poem's concluding line and a half—"This morning / I can't even remember who I am"—an apparent plea of insanity.

**"When in Rome—Apologia"** aptly intertextualizes Browning's monologue as well. Both of Komunyakaa's poems allude to the fate of the wife of Browning's jealous persona, the Duke who had his spouse killed for smiling excessively at other men. In Komunyakaa's poems, however, an ironic readjustment of roles takes place, for it is the would-be suitor whose life is at stake, prompting his desperate plea:

Please forgive me, sir,
for getting involved

in the music—
it's my innate weakness
for the cello: so human.
Please forgive me
for the attention

I've given your wife
tonight, sir.

We note the gap posited by the interstanzaic enjambment between "involved" and its complement "in the music," suggesting a deliberate, playful withholding of the right information from the "sir" of the poem—the sense being *I won't say it but it's not music I'm talking about, it's life: Excuse me, just a dumb nigger, for insisting on being involved on an equal basis with you in life.* Ironically, the speaker's "innate weakness" is the humanity he has in common with his auditor, as expressed in the phrase "so human." And the use of a highly prized wife to epitomize the cultural exclusion that diminishes the persona's human status is an appropriate choice in view of the idea that enjoys considerable currency among African American artists and intellectuals that, not only are women co-creators with men of culture, they are singularly carriers and dispensers of it as well. Furthermore, the irony informing the speaker's plea borders on sarcasm, thus implying that irony may be too exalted a sentiment to spend on the insensitive "sirs" of this world.

The petitioner's final, desperate plea evidences a loss of control which is due to intoxication: "I don't know / what came over me, sir. / After three Jack Daniel's / you must overlook / my candor, my lack of / sequitur." In a statement that engenders the title of the book, the poem concludes: "I apologize for / the eyes in my head," an ambiguously metonymical reference to the outer (physical) and inner (intuitive) facilities of sight that interact in the process of creating poems. *Forgive me,* the implication goes, *not only for insisting on seeing all that there is humanly possible to see in the world but also for being so presumptuous in my reputed inhumanity as a person of African descent to aspire to write poetry of a quality and comprehensiveness equal to your own.*

Who is the forbidden woman in these poems? Is she the same as the "white wife" of the surrealistic poem **"The Music That Hurts,"** personified there as "Silence"? Although Komunyakaa's poems incline toward non-referentiality, they are not characterized by the nonfigurativeness nonreferential poetry reputedly strives for. Thus, viewed in the context of Komunyakaa's work as a whole, music in these three poems is metaphorical of life; its opposite, "Silence," signifies outsiderness, comprehending an absence of humanity. Add to this the act of seeing as literally and figuratively a means for fulfilling one's humanity, and Komunyakaa's ironic apology may be stated as *Sorry, but have I not eyes to see all that there is to be seen in the world, which accords with my right as an American citizen and, preeminently, as a human being?* In the very act of laying claim to and pursuing canonical status in his poems, Komunyakaa demonstrates his "qualification" for it in rhetorical and aesthetic maneuvers that include a repudiation of racial or ethnically based limitations or boundaries. He comes across as a person who is well-versed in the poetic traditions of Anglo-Europe and Anglo-America, and who is also aware of the abundant technical and material properties that are available for the advancement of the art of poetry in America, especially the rich resources that abound in African American life and culture.

Not all of Komunyakaa's poems contain African American cultural material, and in some of those that do, the material is not always easily recognizable, possibly identifying these poems as exemplary achievements of Komunyakaa's unified vision. These are among the numerous poems by Komunyakaa that occupy the right end of an accessibility continuum that ranges from obscure on the right to clear on the left, and they provide a unique glimpse into Komunyakaa's artistry, especially in the extraordinary challenge the poems present to the reader who must work to discover, process, and integrate the works' African American cultural material into the fabric of meaning of the poems. The poem, **"I Apologize"** is a case in point, with its subtle inscription of the persona's African Americanness in a poem not easily identifiable as the work of an African American author. Clues to the persona's identity appear in one of a sequence of desperate alibis he concocts in his apologetic response to the person he addresses as "sir," who implicitly has accused him of reckless eyeballing. "I was in my woman's bedroom / removing her red shoes & dress," he pleads, adding in cadences reminiscent of Browning's poem and in mildly contradictory terms as he attempts to extricate himself, that he could not have committed the "crime" because

> I was miles away, I saw nothing!
> Did I say their diamond rings
> blinded me & I nearly lost my head?
> I think it was how the North
> Star fell through plate glass.
> I don't remember what they wore.

The "sir," as indicated earlier, is a white man; the "they" of the last line quoted above are white women, the reputed objects of the defensively comedic African American male persona's reckless eyeballing. The white women, whom he denies having seen at all, yet whose attire he contradictorily indicates he cannot "remember," are identified with diamonds and refined attire, in contrast with the "red shoes & dress" worn by the person whom we justifiably assume to be the persona's African American woman, with whom he was supposedly, and perhaps actually, too preoccupied in her bedroom to be paying attention to anyone else. The red shoes and dress allude ironically to the reputed fondness of black women for the color red and to the disparagement to which they were subjected in white society's stereotyping of them as sexually promiscuous, as scarlet women.

Another, possibly less obscure, allusion is to the North Star, a symbol of freedom derived from its use as a guide by fugitive slaves on their journeys out of slavery. The persona claims he was more concerned with the star than the white women's diamond rings. Throughout the poem the persona is portrayed as a ludicrously bumbling trickster figure, offering one lame excuse after another in his effort to escape the lynching he is likely to receive for his reckless eyeballing. For all its comedic trappings, however, **"I Apologize"** is a serious dramatization of the obstacles confronting the African American poet who wants his humanity acknowledged—and a rightful place in the American literary canon.

---

**At the core of Komunyakaa's pursuit of a unified vision and literary canonization is his stern resistance, textualized formalistically as well as thematically in his poems, to those forces in the hegemonous counterculture aimed at excluding him as an African American from the ranks of humanity.**

**—Alvin Aubert**

---

Also of particular interest are some of Komunyakaa's Vietnam war poems, which appear in the chapbook *Toys in a Field* (1987) and the full-length *Dien Cai Dau* (1988). In my review of the latter work for *Epoch* magazine [Vol. 38, No. 1 (1989)], I noted the appropriateness of Komunyakaa's use of surrealism for depicting the absurdity of Vietnam combat experiences, especially as they involved black and white American GIs together in situations where, despite the combat survival value of camaraderie, the African American soldier had to contend with the differential burden of racial, and ofttimes racist, inequities (which is not to say that one should overlook the absurdity that frequently surfaces in relations between whites and blacks generally).

Especially relevant to the present discussion is the poem **"Tu Do Street,"** from *Dien Cai Dau,* with its titular punning on "two door." The persona is an African American GI and is immediately identifiable as such, but he also has a penchant for invisibility. He is a quester of sorts for whom invisibility, or at least a certain neutrality, is prerequisite, since he is intent on testing out the waters of racial interfacing along a Saigon bar strip frequented by black and white GIs who enter the area, as it were, through separate doors as they seek relief from the stress and strain of combat among the mama-sans and their attendant bar girls.

An implicit distinction is drawn in the poem between the GIs' quest for sexless or pre-sexual socialization in the bars and their quest for sex in other rooms, for although the black GIs are shunned by the mama-sans and bar girls in the bars frequented by the white GIs, "deeper into alleys," in off-limits areas, the black soldiers have access to prostitutes whose services are available on a nondiscriminatory basis. These assignations take place in "rooms" that invoke a transformational combat landscape: They "run into each other like tunnels / leading to the underworld." Implicit in these conduits is a common humanity, linked to a common death, figuratively in sex and literally in war, for black and white GIs alike:

> There's more than a nation
> inside us, as black & white
> soldiers touch the same lovers
> minutes apart, tasting
> each other's breath . . .

What's "more than a nation / inside" the GIs, black and white, is of course their shared humanity.

The persona knows about the two doors, but impelled by purposes of the persona behind the persona—the poet in quest of a poem and, consequently, of his equalization and literary canonization—he goes in through the opposite door anyway, purposefully and perhaps ritualistically subjecting himself to the rejection on racial grounds he knows he is sure to get. When he enters the bar frequented by the white GIs, where the music is different from that in the bars where the black GIs go, the bar girls "fade like tropical birds" in their evasiveness. The experience triggers a memory involving an ironic representation of music that separates rather than unites by virtue of its inherent harmony:

> Music divides the evening.
> I close my eyes & can see
> men drawing lines in the dust.
> America pushes through the membrane
> of mist & smoke, & I'm a small boy
> again in Bogalusa. *White Only*
> signs & Hank Snow.

The impulse that motivated Komunyakaa as a small boy in his Louisiana hometown of Bogalusa impels him now as a GI in Vietnam, both personae laying claim to their humanity. And as it was at home, so it is on the war front—at least in the rear echelon in Saigon where the soldiers go for rest and recuperation. In the combat zone, where "only machine gun fire brings us / together," where interracial camaraderie has immediate survival value, a different code of behavior prevails:

> Back in the bush at Dak To
> & Khe Sanh, we fought
> the brothers of these women
> we now run to hold in our arms.

The surface implications of the last two lines quoted are apparent, but just as we should not miss their function in expressing the common humanity that is the object of the persona's quest, we should not overlook the note of respect the passage affords women in its emphasis on the humanistic aspect of the embrace, virtually annulling the sexual import of the situation and betokening the generally humanistic portrayal of women we find in Komunyakaa's work as a whole.

The bar girls and prostitutes of Saigon are metonymically depicted in **"Tu Do Street"** as victims, their "voices / wounded by their beauty and war." These women are also a part of the "nation / inside us" quoted and commented on above, for it is they—"the same lovers" touched by black GIs and white GIs alike, implicitly by virtue of their capacity for motherhood, for bringing life into the world, and as the primary sources of nurturing—who are the

conferers and common denominators of the universal, of the common humanity that populates Komunyakaa's projected socio-literary commonwealth and makes material his "unified vision."

**Marilyn Nelson Waniek**   (essay date Spring 1993)

SOURCE: "The Gender of Grief," in *The Southern Review,* Vol. 29, No. 2, Spring, 1993, pp. 405-19.

[*Waniek is an American educator, poet, and critic. In the following excerpt, she examines* Magic City, *stating Komunyakaa "makes a great contribution to one of the newest genres in the canon: the black male epic of self."*]

*Magic City,* Yusef Komunyakaa's eighth book of poems, is punctuated by dramatic encounters, most of them racial. The thrust of the book is clearly autobiographical, yet its subject remains for the most part a point of view, clear-eyed and loving, yet rarely differentiated from the communal "we." Partly a *Bildungsroman* and partly an album of snapshots by which a neighborhood can remember its history, the book is rooted in family, community, and place. In **"Glory,"** Komunyakaa remembers baseball games played by

> . . . married teenagers
> Working knockout shifts daybreak
> To sunset six days a week—
> Already old men playing ball
> In a field between a row of shotgun houses
> & the Magazine Lumber Company.

He remembers the cheering children and wives, the daring, impossible catches, how "The old deacons & raconteurs / Who umpired made an *Out* or *Safe* / Into a song & dance routine." And he understands that "A stolen base or homerun / Would help another man / Survive the new week."

In several such clearly realized poems the community comes to life and takes on meaning. In **"Slam, Dunk, & Hook"** a group of boys—"Bug-eyed, lanky, / All hands & feet . . . sprung rhythm"—plays basketball:

> . . . Nothing but a hot
> Swish of strings like silk
> Ten feet out. In the roundhouse
> Labyrinth our bodies
> created, we could almost
> Last forever, poised in midair . . .

They play because

> . . . Trouble
> Was there slapping a blackjack
> Against an open palm.
> Dribble, drive to the inside, feint,
> & glide like a sparrow hawk.

While retrospectively understanding their poverty and the unspecified but palpable threat of racism with which they live, Komunyakaa at the same time fully enters the memory and the community of boys:

> Lay ups. Fast breaks.
> We had moves we didn't know
> We had. Our bodies spun

On swivels of bone & faith,
Through a lyric slipknot
Of joy, & we knew we were
Beautiful & dangerous.

The poems in which the young Komunyakaa appears as a character are quiet and introspective, their grief caused by something larger than poverty or racism. They mourn the passage of time, "the struggle underneath," inexplicability, love's mystery and that of sex, the pain we inflict, death. In **"The Smokehouse"** the child prowls through a smokehouse:

I was a wizard
In that hazy world,
& knew I could cut
Slivers of meat till my heart
Grew more human & flawed.

In **"My Father's Love Letters"** the boy writes weekly letters for his illiterate father to his mother, who has run away from her husband's beatings:

Words rolled from under the pressure
Of my ballpoint: Love,
Baby, Honey, Please.

Komunyakaa confesses he

. . . sometimes wanted
to slip in a reminder, how Mary Lou
Williams' "Polka Dots & Moonbeams"
Never made the swelling go down.

But finally he stands humbled by his father's inarticulate love:

. . . This man,
Who stole roses & hyacinth
For his yard, would stand there
With eyes closed & fists balled,
Laboring over a simple word, almost
Redeemed by what he tried to say.

There is in Komunyakaa's work a tendency to let figurative language grow unpruned. This tendency flaws several poems with overwriting. In one poem a disemboweled pig carcass is described as "opened like love / From snout to tail." Excuse me, but "like love"? Another poem, **"The Millpond,"** describes time's passing:

Till April oozed sap
Like a boy beside a girl
Squeezing honeycomb in his fists.

But would honey squeeze out of a boy's fists any differently because he is "beside a girl"? Sometimes one simple sentence contains as many as three unrelated metaphors and one simile. Occasionally he resorts to the paint-box trick: thinking colors named "fulvous," "molybdate," and "titanous" more poetic than yellow, orange, and white, for example. I'm sorry to say that he often allows himself to be both coy and what Etheridge Knight used to call "fancy-schmancy." Several important stories—most painfully the one about the grandfather whose "true name" Komunyakaa has chosen to carry, are left in misty innuendo. About this grandfather we learn in a poem called **"Mismatched Shoes"** that "He wore a boy's shoe / & a girl's

shoe." There must be an interesting story there. Enquiring minds want to know.

Despite this criticism, I applaud the courage with which Komunyakaa has confronted his childhood and youth. With his sensitive evocations of the child's sense of the natural world, the driving curiosity of adolescent sexuality, and the slow transformation of the dreamer-child into the poet, he makes a great contribution to one of the newest genres in the canon: the black male epic of self.

### Robyn Selman    (review date June 1993)

SOURCE: A review of *Neon Vernacular: New and Selected Poems*, in *VLS*, No. 116, June, 1993, pp. 6-7.

[*In the review below, Selman examines stylistic features of Komunyakaa's poetry, noting in particular his focus on music in* Neon Vernacular.]

An old anger drips into my throat,
& I try thinking something good,
letting the precious bad
settle to the salty bottom.
Another scene keeps repeating itself:
I emerge from the dark theatre,
passing a woman who grabs her red purse
& hugs it to her like a heart attack.

Most of Yusef Komunyakaa's poems rise to a crescendo, like that moment in songs one or two beats before the bridge, when everything is hooked-up, full-blown. Over the course of Komunyakaa's seven books, much has been made of the recurring themes in his work: autobiography, African American experience in the South and in Vietnam. Much has also been said about the music in his poetry, the song lyrics and musicians' names.

Dexter Gordon's tenor sax
plays "April in Paris"
inside my head all the way back
on the bus from Double Bay.
*Round Midnight,* the 50's,
cool cobblestone streets
resound footsteps of Bebop
musicians with whiskey-laced voices
from a boundless dream in French.
Bud, Prez, Webster, & the Hawk,
their names run together riffs.

While many critics have remarked on the musical names (Coltrane, Billie Holiday, Leadbelly) that crop up in Komunyakaa's work and the work of other African American poets such as Cornelius Eady, they often regard these ghostly appearances as emblems or elegies, an African American musicians' museum. But while building such a gallery might be worthwhile, there's more to these ghosts than that. In Komunyakaa's poems, they're clanking the very chains of language.

Pinetop's boogiewoogie
keys stack against each other like syllables
in tongue-tripped elegies for Lady Day
& Duke.
Don't try to make any sense
out of this; just let it take you
like Pres's tenor & keep you human.

Komunyakaa is an innovator; his language plays on the infinite nature of vocabulary. In scads of borrowed lyrics, from the upbeat "Ta-ra-ra-boom-de-ay" down the druggy slope of "Purple Haze," the lexicons of jazz and blues supply him with a raw, articulate alter ego: "The tongue labors, / a victrola in the mad African-American mouth-hole / of 3 A.M. sorrow." Like a brother less self-conscious than the poet, music as Komunyakaa hears it is not merely a celebration or even a culmination of heritage and culture, but an entire alternate linguistic anatomy.

Music appears when and where traditional vocabulary falters. When, for example, a hot day triggers a black man's lust for a white woman, the poet segues to Johnny Mathis's "Beside Her Like a Whisper"; when a black farmer works his stubborn land and turns up nothing but rocks, he hums "Amazing Grace." Each song comes with scores of connotations. The light-skinned Mathis and the prayer "Amazing Grace" become evocative synonyms for more familiar and flatter words like *impossibility, forbidden, coaxing,* and even *goddammit.*

Komunyakaa speaks out of more than one side of his mouth—there's the narrator, his musical partner, the language we're used to, and the edges of something newer. *Neon Vernacular,* Komunyakaa's eighth collection, pushes the layered dialogue further. It contains about 30 pages of new poems, followed by generous selections from previous books. One of the longer new poems is **"Songs for My Father,"** a piece in minute-long, verselike sections caused by sounds the poet hears—a hyenalike laugh, a meditative quiet, the noises of lovemaking—each of which remind him of his father.

> You were a quiet man
> Who'd laugh like a hyena
> On a hill, with your head
> Thrown back, gazing up at the sky
> But most times you just worked
> Hard, rooted in the day's anger
> Till you'd explode. We always
> Walked circles around
> You, wider each year . . .

The 170 long-playing pages amplify Komunyakaa's tonal range. He says, "The beast & the burden lock-step & waltz," and they do. *Neon Vernacular* gives rise to the hope that Coltrane, Duke, and Gordon will materialize as synonyms for *sinewy* or *lugubrious, dimensional* or *heard* in the turn-of-the-century thesaurus.

> Tremolo. Dexter comes back to rest
> behind my eyelids. A loneliness
> lingers like a silver needle
> under my black skin,
> as I try to feel how it is
> to scream for help through a horn.

**Toi Derricotte    (essay date Fall 1993)**

SOURCE: "The Tension between Memory and Forgetting in the Poetry of Yusef Komunyakaa," in *The Kenyon Review,* Vol. XV, No. 4, Fall, 1993, pp. 217-22.

[*In the essay below, Derricotte surveys Komunyakaa's works, focusing on his major themes.*]

The publication of Yusef Komunyakaa's *Magic City* and his new and selected poems, *Neon Vernacular,* provide an opportunity for a detailed examination of the body of his work. Nine collections have been published since his first, *Dedications & Other Darkhorses,* in 1977. All the poems discussed here can be found in *Neon Vernacular,* except those from *Magic City*. Quite simply, Komunyakaa is one of the most extraordinary poets writing today. This review will consider the characteristics of the voice in four of his books, its style, intent, and the possible reasons for changes in that voice.

"It's truth we're after," Komunyakaa says in **"Safe Subjects,"** a poem from his third book, *Copacetic*. But it won't be an easy truth:

> Redemptive as a straight razor
> against the jugular vein—
> unacknowledged & unforgiven.
> It's truth we're after here,
> hurting for, out in the streets
> where my brothers kill each other . . .

In his earlier work, that truth is not a matter of conveying literal or narrative subjects. In fact, his earlier poems retreat from language in terms of these functions—not retreat in the sense of giving up but retreat as an act of resistance, as one retreats in military strategy. In a world where African-American identity—in particular, African-American male identity—is constantly threatened, language and the poem itself become a last defense, the ultimate weapon of the ego against dissolution. Poetry avenges pain, brings back what is lost, masks suffering, denies and heals it. For Komunyakaa, poetry is the expression of an embattled ego determined by whatever means necessary to survive.

In the first poem in *Copacetic,* **"False Leads,"** the speaker warns "Mister Bloodhound Boss" that a worker he is looking for, "Slick Sam," is extremely dangerous. "They say Slick Sam's a mind reader: / he knows what you gonna do / before you think it. / He can lead you into quicksand / under a veil of swamp gas." He assures the man of his own sincerity: "Now you know me, Uncle T, / I wouldn't tell you no lie." Though the tone is playful, as John Wideman has said of black speech such as "the dozens" and so-called "street language," words are a deadly serious game. Here, they intend to turn the tables in favor of the underdog—as they did in the Brer Rabbit folktales—to obfuscate the reality of the one who is seemingly in charge at the same time they clarify the speaker's cleverness and control.

Rarely is the word *I* used in his earlier poems. The title, **"False Leads,"** may suggest that the poems themselves lead us away from a personal narrator. The recent poems are led by memory, but the earlier poems are controlled by focused shots of brilliant imagery that capture an emotional constellation. "Believe this, brother, / we're dice in a hard time hustle. / No more than handfuls of meat," the poet says in **"Letter to Bob Kaufman."** The disappearance of the poet is often signaled by his taking on the persona of another person or entering another state of being. "I am this space / my body believes in," he says in **"Unnatural State of the Unicorn,"** a poem from *I Apologize for the Eyes in My Head,* his fifth collection.

In *I Apologize for the Eyes in My Head* Komunyakaa deepens and extends themes expressed in his earlier work. Images of war appear over and over again in poems that evidently were written before *Dien Cai Dau,* Komunyakaa's haunting book about his experience in Vietnam. "I am a man. I've scuffled / in mudholes, broken teeth in a grinning skull / like the moon behind bars," he says in **"Unnatural State of the Unicorn."** In **"Touch-up Man,"** he says, "I lean over the enlarger, / in the light table's chromatic glare / where I'm king, doctoring photographs, / airbrushing away the corpses." In **"Landscape for the Disappeared,"** in a grotesque and macabre procession, "The dead / stumble home like swamp fog, / our lost uncles & granddaddies / come back to us almost healed." At the end of the poem, in one of the most beautiful passages in this—or any—book, suddenly one face becomes clear and singular:

> Here's this lovely face so black
> with marsh salt. Her smile,
> a place where minnows swim.
> All the full presence
> shiny as a skull under the skin.
> Say it again—we are
> spared nothing.

It may be a particular girl he remembers, perhaps a girl he saw in Vietnam. In saying, "We are spared nothing," Komunyakaa refers to the fact that we cannot escape memory, that, in this case, his own poetry has led him back to his buried past. Has she come to accuse or forgive the speaker? "Her smile, / a place where minnows swim. / All the full presence / shiny . . ." suggests a redemptive transformation.

The poems in *Dien Cai Dau,* Komunyakaa's sixth book, published in 1988, are held together by the excruciating tension between memory and forgetting. In **"Camouflaging the Chimera,"** the first poem in the book, soldiers prepare themselves for combat. "We tied branches to our helmets. / We painted our faces & rifles / with mud from a riverbank." Their union with nature—their disappearance—suggests both death and transcendence. Later in the poem he says, "We aimed at dark-hearted songbirds." This reference to the gentleness of the adversaries and to their darkness shows the mixed feelings he faces in this conflict against people of color, the sense that he is doing the dirty work of the oppressor of them both. The soldiers are faceless, anonymous. They are so still "The river ran through [their] bones." Are they already dead? Are they ghosts? While they wait to ambush the enemy, each man is lost in his own private vision; "we held our breath, / . . . as a world revolved / under each man's eyelid." Is the war a dream? Is the poem itself a dream? The title of the book, *Dien Cai Dau,* is a Vietnamese expression that American GI's picked up and used a great deal during the war meaning "crazy in the head." So we are introduced to the states of depersonalization and denial that war wreaks on the psyche. This is a book about seeing and not seeing, about not being there in order to be there. It pres-

ents the paradoxes of a psyche, of an art that is compelled to examine itself, and yet is determined to control reality in a way that makes it able to be endured.

---

**Komunyakaa takes on the most complex moral issues, the most harrowing ugly subjects of our American life. His voice, whether it embodies the specific experiences of a black man, a soldier in Vietnam, or a child in Bogalusa, Louisiana, is universal. It shows us in ever deeper ways what it is to be human.**

**—Toi Derricotte**

---

In **"Starlight Scope Myopia,"** the soldiers are given a scope for their guns that makes them able to see at night. The title of the device, "Starlight Scope," like other military terms—for example, "friendly fire,"—masks the horror of what is really happening—that it brings men into killing range. The use of the word "Myopia" suggests that the poet is writing not about what can be seen with the scope, but about what can't be seen—the human toll of the war and, in particular, the toll of a war that seems unjustified. Dream and memory mix so that the "Viet Cong / move under our eyelids / . . . years after this scene ends." The last lines of the poem are emblazoned on the mind with an image that, paradoxically, owes a debt to the language and evocative imagery of Eastern poetry, "You / peer down the sights of your M-16, / seeing the full moon / loaded on an oxcart." In a sense the horrors of Vietnam become a metaphor for the psychic threat in his earlier poems, a state in which insanity protects sanity. This inner conflict illuminates the nature of forces that operate within the minds of individuals and in communities threatened by mental and/or physical extermination—what one may term as pathological is, in fact, a necessary and healthy response to an untenable reality.

Komunyakaa understands fire and has articulated its destructiveness as few poets ever have. "A girl still burning / inside my head," he says in **" 'You and I are Disappearing' "** (the title is a phrase from Björn Hakansson), "She glows like the fat tip / of a banker's cigar" and "She burns like a burning bush / driven by a godawful wind." It is most appropriate that fire—that god of transcendence and changing states—is so present in these poems.

The new poems in *Magic City* are among Komunyakaa's most beautiful. They have a straightforward lyricism, as if the terrible confrontation with the self in *Dien Cai Dau* has brought about an expansiveness, accessibility, and narrative directness:

> At noon, Daddy would walk
> Across the field of goldenrod
> & mustard weed, the pollen
> Bright & sullen on his overalls.
> He'd eat on our screened-in

Back porch—red beans & rice
With ham hocks & cornbread.
Lemonade & peach Jello.

("The Whistle")

The new poems contain images of great sensuality and beauty—metaphors to die for! "An orgasm of golden dust / clung to the wooden floor" (**"Gristmill"**), and "Her breasts / Rose like swamp orchids" (**"Salome"**), and "as if the tongue was a latch / Holding down a grace note" (**"Albino"**). There is great love for the people in the community in which he grew up, Bogalusa, Louisiana. He writes about his childhood among people in a rural, black, southern community isolated by racism, driven by compelling economic, physical, and spiritual needs, "Unable to divide love from hunger", he says in **"Banking Potatoes."**

The time frame for these poems is from about the age of five to fourteen or fifteen, from boyhood to sexual initiation, that protected period when a boy learns to be a man. The period of so-called sexual latency provides a wonderful vantage from which to examine the community in which he grew up. "Soon we'd be / Responsible for the chambered / Rapture honeycombed in flesh," he says in **"Boys in Dresses."** In a wonderful way, the poet combines a child's vision and passion, an adult's compassion and wisdom, and a poet's language in these poems. "Don't mess with me / 'Cause I have my Lone Ranger / Six-shooter. I can hurt / You with questions" (**"Venus's-flytraps"**). There is always a driving question: What is the nature of good and evil? Martin Luther King distinguished the difference between primary evil and secondary evil by saying that primary evil is the evil that causes other evils to happen. If so, certainly the community Komunyakaa evokes in these poems—even in their acts of violence—are innocent.

No matter how grim the nature of the event, no matter how bloody—for example, the slaughter and butchering of a pig—there is always the coolness and exactness of one who must become used to hard things. "They smile as she passed / Through their hands," the poet says in **"Immolatus."** "Next day / I tracked blood in a circle / Across dead grass, while fat / Boiled down to lye soap." In **"Yellowjackets,"** when a plowblade strikes an old stump, the bees swarm all over the horse:

He shivered, but not
The way women shook their heads
Before mirrors at the five
& dime—a deeper connection
To the low field's evening star.
He stood there, in tracechains,
Lathered in froth, just
Stopped by a great, goofy
Calmness. He whinnied
Once, & then the whole
Beautiful, blue-black sky
Fell on his back.

In **"Glory,"** the poet talks about a baseball game played "In a field between a row of shotgun houses / & the Magazine Lumber Company." He speaks of the hard life of the players, "Most were married teenagers / Working knockout shifts daybreak / To sunset six days a week—/ Al-ready old men playing ball. . . . They were all Jackie Robinson / & Willie Mays, a touch of Josh Gibson & Satchell Paige / In each stance & swing, a promise / Like a hesitation pitch always / At the edge of their lives." He shows the saving grace of ritual, how "A stolen base or homerun / Would help another man / Survive the new week."

In the end, Komunyakaa's poetry is about art, about how it alters reality, how it can change the past, how it is both a desperate and a redemptive act. In **"My Father's Love Letters,"** the father, who can't write, asks the speaker to write a letter to his mother begging her to come home: "He would beg, / Promising to never beat her / Again." The speaker remembers "how Mary Lou / Williams' 'Polka Dots & Moonbeams' / Never made the swelling go down." The words of the letters "rolled from under the pressure / Of my ballpoint: Love, / Baby, Honey, Please." The poet recognizes his father's culpability, yet, at the same time, sees his reasons. "My father could only sign / His name, but he'd look at blueprints / & say how many bricks / Formed each wall." In a final image of resolution, Komunyakaa speaks about the healing work of language, "Laboring over a simple word, almost / Redeemed by what he tried to say." Like life, art must be equal to the brutalization from which it has emerged. Its beauty and meaning must balance horror and give the ego a reason to survive.

In *Magic City* Komunyakaa revisits his childhood. Perhaps the real magic is that he can come back with the compassion of a man who himself has had to do terrible things. In **"Blackberries,"** Komunyakaa says, "I ate the mythology & dreamt / Of pies & cobbler, almost / Needful as forgiveness." It is as if the new poetry has found a vantage for forgiveness—and, first, of the self!

I am reminded of Romare Bearden who said: "Art celebrates a victory. And that victory is twofold. In general, it involves capturing and redeeming both the beauty and the sullenness of the past. In particular, it proclaims that black people have survived." Komunyakaa takes on the most complex moral issues, the most harrowing ugly subjects of our American life. His voice, whether it embodies the specific experiences of a black man, a soldier in Vietnam, or a child in Bogalusa, Louisiana, is universal. It shows us in ever deeper ways what it is to be human.

**Michael Collins**    (essay date 1993-94)

SOURCE: "Staying Human," in *Parnassus,* Vol. 18, No. 2, 1993-94, pp. 126-50.

[*In the following essay, Collins provides an overview of Komunyakaa's career.*]

"I went to Vietnam as a basic naive young man of eighteen. Before I reached my nineteenth birthday, I was an animal. . . . They prepared us for Vietnam as a group of individuals who worked together as a unit to annihilate whatever enemy we came upon . . . There was this saying: 'Yeah though I walk through the valley of death, I shall fear no evil, 'cause I'm the baddest motherfucker in the valley' . . . I collected about 14 ears and fingers. With them strung on a piece of leather around my neck, I would go downtown, and you would get free drugs, free booze, free pussy because they wouldn't wanna bother you 'cause this man's a killer. It symbolized that I'm a killer. And it was, so to speak, a symbol of combat-type manhood."

—Specialist 4 Arthur E. "Gene" Woodley, Jr. (aka Cyclops and Montagnard)

" . . . There seems to be always some human landscape that creates a Paul Celan. . . ."

—Yusef Komunyakaa

Reading the Vietnam poems of Yusef Komunyakaa, one is reminded that culture is made as often on battlefields as it is in the thinker's notebook, or in the schoolroom; that heroes, those bloody-handed fellows, are the originals of our great men. There are days when the sun seems to rise for no other purpose than to illuminate some killer of genius: to make his uniform glow like a nation's stained glass windows on Sunday. True, Michelangelo is the equal of Napoleon in fame, but it is Napoleon's example that is most often followed: More men aspire to populate tombs than to carve them.

Komunyakaa is more the Michelangelesque carver than the populator of tombs. Yet though his *Neon Vernacular: New and Selected Poems* ranges far and wide in its subject matter, it turns willy-nilly round his battlefield epiphanies and traumas, round the question of survival when that question is, in Emily Dickinson's phrase, "at the white heat." **"At the Screen Door,"** for instance, one of the "new" poems in *Neon Vernacular,* chronicles Komunyakaa's return after many years to his Louisiana home town; yet its true subject is the question of survival and survival's cost in coins of madness. In this poem, Komunyakaa, at what appears to be his mother's door—at the fountainhead of his life—wonders, as any bemused prodigal son would, "Is it her?" But in the next clause war rears its head: "will she know / What I've seen & done, / How my boots leave little grave-stone / Shapes in the wet dirt . . . ?" At that door he recalls a buddy who ended up in "a padded cell . . . After all the men he'd killed in Korea / & on his first tour in Vietnam, / Someone tracked him down. / That Spec 4 he ordered / Into a tunnel in Cu Chi / Now waited for him behind / The screen door, a sunset / in his eyes, / a dead man / Wearing his teenage son's face. . . ." In the poem **"Please,"** Komunyakaa reports an occasion when he gave a similar order—an order that so haunts him that in the midst of lovemaking he cries out, "Hit the dirt!" This arduous journey into the self recalls the climbs in the Tour de France that, too difficult to rate, are called "beyond category."

As both **"Please"** and **"At the Screen Door"** demonstrate, Komunyakaa often chooses as his subject experiences painful enough to destroy the personality, not so much to exorcise them as to connect them to insights that, like certain icons and kings of the old religions, might heal the halt and the sick. The bridges he strives to build between pain and insight are those of the jazz musician—that improviser's leaping among epiphanies on which, Komunyakaa has said, his consciousness, was nurtured: "I

think we internalize a kind of life rhythm," he told an interviewer [Vince F. Gotera]: "The music I was listening to when I was seven or eight years old and the music I listen to today are not that different. . . . I listen to a lot of classical jazz, as well as European classical music. I think you do all those things side by side" [*Callaloo,* 1990]. Discovering rhythms that tie two moments or two traditions of music together, Komunyakaa pulls the one thread of pleasure in the valley of death and unravels, one poem at a time, that dour place woven from suffering. This unraveling can disorient and blind those grown accustomed to the Valley of the Shadow, and it is something like the disorientation and still earthly rage that salvation brings that one finds in the last image of **"At the Screen Door,"** where Komunyakaa writes of "Watching a new day stumble / Through a whiplash of grass / Like a man drunk on the rage / Of being alive."

The "rage" of being alive but limited—whether by society, by the other army's bullets, by your bloodguilt, or by the borders of the human itself—can make even the dawn's light harsh, as if not a new day, but flakes of brimstone were sifting down upon all human effort. The rage to live beyond limitation is nowhere more compelling than in the heart of a warrior. From Alexander and Hannibal to Powell and Schwarzkopf, the man who spills blood has been loved, looked upon as a shaman who knows death by heart, who can recite it or swallow it like a secret code. Not without reason, people assume that the man of blood is the best protector: General de Gaulle and General Eisenhower led their nations after World War II. America's last President reached the heights of public approval as a warlord; its current Vice President is a Vietnam veteran, and President Clinton's Achilles heel is his ignorance of warfare. The generals can talk back to him, and their talk carries weight.

The talk of the man of action *always* carries weight. It fascinates, for who doesn't want to know the workings of the mind of war, from whose every detail spring whole trees of language and metaphor? General Schwarzkopf's memoirs conquered the best seller list. Homosexuals and many women have begun to clamor for their right to validate themselves in battle: In modern (and ancient) culture, it often seems that killing is the one royal route to proving oneself human and noble. All this makes the best poetry of Yusef Komunyakaa—the poetry in which he directly describes his Vietnam experiences, and the poetry for which that experience acts as a kind of antimatter power source—an invaluable resource. It gives even some of Komunyakaa's lesser work and apprentice efforts the patina of the man of action's recollections of his formative kneescrapes and triumphs. For Komunyakaa is the real deal twice over—a brilliant poet in his best work and a hero who came back from Vietnam not only with a Bronze Star like a piece of the firmament on his chest, but with a knowledge of what it is to live without vanity, without any tradition but the Darwinian one that says: first survive, *then* return to history and its haze of manners and names. He told Vincente F. Gotera [in *Callaloo*] that when he began to write the Vietnam poems he remembered many faces from his tour of duty, but few names:

I suppose that's all part of the forgetting process, in striving to forget particular situations that were pretty traumatic for me. Not when I was there as much as in retrospect. When you're there in such a situation, you're thinking about where the nearest safest place is to run, in case of an incoming rocket. You don't even have time to think about the moral implications. . . .

The poems he produced about Vietnam are a deliberate and painful reconstruction of those missing—one might say vaporized—implications. Komunyakaa has said it took him "about fourteen years to start getting" the poems down on paper. One of the most moving of the group is **"We Never Know,"** in which Komunyakaa recalls how a man he shoots

> . . . danced with tall grass
> for a moment, like he was swaying
> with a woman. Our gun barrels
> glowed white-hot.
> When I got to him,
> a blue halo
> of flies had already claimed him.
> I pulled the crumpled photograph
> from his fingers.
> There's no other way
> to say this: I fell in love.
> The morning cleared again,
> except for a distant mortar
> & somewhere choppers taking off.
> I slid the wallet into his pocket
> & turned him over, so he wouldn't be
> kissing the ground.

The portrait of tenderness in reverse, of understanding in reverse—indeed, of *time* in reverse, for the whole is remembered, like that past-backwards solo Jimi Hendrix devises for "Are You Experienced?"—drives home the irreversibility of violence and understanding. Its great poignance and power derives from the fact that it shows us the moral wilderness of the Vietnam war and the way out, inaccessible in this poem, but not forever. It shows also one of the characteristic sonic patterns of Komunyakaa's free verse, which sometimes, as in this poem, looks to the eye like a thousand magazine poems. This formal signature has to do with the way the end words communicate with each other: not so much through rhyme or slant rhyme as through the more mysterious language of echoes—the reincarnation of vowels which, unlike men, do return. Thus the "a" in "grass" alters slightly, but changes its spots in "barrels," whose "e" surfaces, cropped but visible, a ghost of itself, in the hyphenated incandescence of "white-hot." "Hot" of course rhymes with "got," and that uncloseable "o," like the mouth of a man hit by gunshot, draws its circle in the dead man's nightmare halo of flies. Komunyakaa has fashioned from the banqueting flies the ancient sign of the blest, and he sees, too late, that the man he has killed is a blessed thing—a human, deserving of the company of whatever angels he believed in when alive, and, even in death, commanding love.

That same sonic pattern is at play on a larger scale in the gorgeous **"Starlight Scope Myopia,"** which, unlike **"We Never Know,"** approaches strict formality and manages a virtuoso incorporation of rhyme and slant rhyme:

> Gray-blue shadows lift
> shadows onto an oxcart.
>
> Making night work for us,
> the starlight scope brings
> men into killing range.
>
> The river under Vi Bridge
> takes the heart away
>
> like the Water God
> riding his dragon.
> Smoke-colored
>
> Viet Cong
> move under our eyelids,
>
> lords over loneliness
> winding like coral vine through
> sandalwood & lotus,
>
> inside our lowered heads
> years after this scene
>
> ends. The brain closes
> down. What looks like
> one step into the trees,
>
> they're lifting crates of ammo
> & sacks of rice, swaying
>
> under their shared weight.
> Caught in the infrared,
> what are they saying?
>
> Are they talking about women
> or calling the Americans
>
> *beaucoup dien cai dau?*
> One of them is laughing.
> You want to place a finger
>
> to his lips & say "shhhh."
> You try reading ghost talk
>
> on their lips. They say
> "up-up we go," lifting as one.
> This one, old, bowlegged,
>
> you feel you could reach out
> & take him into your arms. You
>
> peer down the sights of your M-16,
> seeing the full moon
> loaded on an oxcart.

In this poem Komunyakaa achieves his chronic ambition to be a jazz poet with a lineage as traceable to Louis Armstrong's trumpet as a Roman centurion's would have been to the sea foam from which Aphrodite rose. The alternating two- and three-line stanzas, with a pattern of three beats that Komunyakaa now and then expands to four or telescopes to two, combines with the end-word pattern of slant rhyme, assonance, and consonance that chimes throughout the poem to mime the magnifying powers of a starlight scope. The poem itself is a kind of starlight scope to which the reader presses his eye and sees ordinary words and terms under extreme magnification, like genetic proteins brought to light by some unblinking microscope: The Vietcong, appearing all alone in their two-beat line (#11), are scarier, larger, more vulnerable than life.

The "myopia" facet of the starlight scope makes itself felt in the fact that the Vietcong, technologically cut off from space and time and fixed to astral coordinates "inside our lowered heads / years after this scene / ends," are easier to shoot; having been transformed into creatures of the starlight scope, gathered at the wrong end of the technological rainbow, they are already dead:

> Are they talking about women
> or calling Americans
>
> *beaucoup dien cai dau?*
> One of them is laughing.
> You want to place a finger
>
> to his lips & say "shhhh."
> You try reading host talk
>
> on their lips. They say
> "up-up we go," lifting as one.

Mao Tse-tung wrote that the theory that " 'weapons decide everything,' which is a mechanist theory of war, [is] a subjective and one-sided view," since in war there are "not only weapons but also human beings" and "the contest of strength is not only a contest of military and economic power but also of human power and morale." Mao, a strong influence on Communist Vietnam's General Vo Nguyen Giap, according to the historian-general Philip B. Davidson, would seem to have been proven right by the decades of military success during which Giap drove first France and then the United States out of his small country. **"Starlight Scope Myopia"** exposes both the power and the myopia of the "mechanistic" view, while suggesting a third view: that "human power"—the power of being "lords over loneliness," of *speaking* ("Caught in the infrared, / what are they saying?" Komunyakaa asks in the poem)—may be incompatible with weaponry, which is designed to expand the empire of silence. Writing his poems, Komunyakaa tries to steer clear of the world's starlight scopes, to correct their imposed myopias, to reinfuse them with what he says poetry is: "in essence . . . the spiritual and emotional dimension of the human animal," a source of spontaneous communication that "can link two people together, reader and poet. . . ."

The two- and three-line stanzas, with their haiku terseness, provokes a kind of double vision through their invocation of the Water God—from a *believer's* point of view—and the paradox of traditional Vietnamese reverence for the old man at the moment he is killed ("you feel you could reach out / & take him in your arms."). They enact the deep cultural exchange that might have gone on between the American soldiers and the Vietcong under other circumstances. (Such exchanges did and do occur, even in the midst of war, despite the propaganda on both sides thick as wax dripped in the ears.) Yet they suggest that when the chips are down, such exchanges make no difference. What the American soldiers know of the Vietnamese does not foster mercy. It "takes the heart away." Mercy and humor ("One of them is laughing") are foolhardy in a combat zone. In fact, with the help of high-tech weapons they can be twisted to detach a soldier from his actions. In the heat of battle or the cover of ambush, such feelings are best kept locked up in a mind patrolled by fear

mounted on anger. The Vietnamese, after all, are loading ammunition meant to kill Americans along with their rice. The flickering identification with them—before, during, and after their deaths—must contend with the fingers of history moving to snuff it out.

In **"Starlight Scope Myopia,"** this unexpected empathy is best expressed by the words Komunyakaa puts into the mouths of the Vietnamese who may be "calling the Americans / *beaucoup dien cai dau*" (very crazy). This multicultural insult begins with a word the Vietnamese took from the French, whom they defeated, then switches for exactitude into Vietnamese to characterize the Americans, whom they are in the process of defeating. (The ironic phrase spans all the relevant cultures in the long Vietnam nightmare. That an American is wondering whether the Vietcong are using this phrase demonstrates both discomfort and a certain muted triumph at having them in his sights. Even a battlefield is a society with rules and language games.)

It also crystallizes a point Komunyakaa suggests in his interviews with Gotera, that societies of strangers, or even of traditional enemies, can be ever so delicately held together by infinitely recycled bits of language, by clichés:

> [Among American] soldiers, for some reason—
> individuals coming from so many backgrounds:
> the deep South, the North, different educational
> levels—clichés are used many times as efforts to
> communicate, as bridges perhaps. And soldiers
> often speak in clichés. . . .

Clichés, like tatoos on the bodies of languages, are useful decorations of places where a common vision is hidden, or being brought to light. The cliché *"Beaucoup dien cai dau"* is Komunyakaa's assessment of the war itself and perhaps of America's role in it. True, his Vietnam lyrics display none of the sense of outrage, of being pierced by betrayal, so evident in the testimony of some black Vietnam veterans. Gene Woodley, who gives this essay its first epigraph, told journalist Wallace Terry of being transformed into an "animal" by his boot camp training and by the brutality of Vietnam and insisted that in shipping him and other "bloods" off to its rice paddy war, America

> befell upon us one big atrocity. It lied. They had
> us naive, young, dumb-ass niggers believin' that
> this war was for democracy and independence.
> It was fought for money. All those big corpora-
> tions made billions on the war, and then Ameri-
> ca left.

On the other hand, Komunyakaa is no indestructible patriot like the blood Terry interviewed who narrated the following anecdotes about his experience as a prisoner of war in Vietnam:

> They would read things in their behalf about the
> Communist way and downgrading the United
> States, blah, blah, blah, all the time. . . . When
> Dr. King was assassinated, they called me in for
> interrogation to see if I would make a statement
> critical of the United States. I said no, I don't
> know enough about it . . . . My personal feeling
> is that black people have problems and still have
> problems in America. But I never told them

that, because I had no intention of helping them to defeat us. We deal with our problems within our own country. Some people just do not live up to the great ideals our country stands for. . . .

Komunyakaa's poetry conveys the pain and grace involved in maintaining not so much the middle ground *between* these two positions as the shifting ground of possibilities that lies under them both. He illuminates these and other positions in part by creating a "tension between levels of diction," as Gotera has said, by deploying what he himself calls a "neon vernacular" in which argots and forms of life blink on and off like those neon signs with which a cityscape expands and contracts, caressing and reshaping the night. Consider the masterful **"Hanoi Hannah"**:

> *Ray Charles!* His voice
> calls from waist-high grass,
> & we duck behind gray sandbags.
> "Hello, Soul Brothers. Yeah,
> Georgia's also on my mind."
> Flares bloom over the trees.
> "Here's Hannah again.
> Let's see if we can't
> light her goddamn fuse
> this time." Artillery
> shells carve a white arc
> against dusk. Her voice rises
> from a hedgerow on our left.
> "It's Saturday night in the States.
> Guess what your woman's doing tonight.
> I think I'll let Tina Turner
> tell you, you homesick GIs."
> . . . . "You know you're dead men,
> don't you? You're dead
> as King today in Memphis.
> Boys, you're surrounded by
> General Tran Do's division."
> Her knife-edge song cuts
> deep as a sniper's bullet.
> "Soul Brothers, what you dying for?" . . .

One of the many heartbreaking nuances of this poem is its suggestion that when people at last learn each other's language, they will do so the better to hook and destroy each other with narcotics of commiseration, gossip, trust, half-truth, or, unkindest cut of all, some inaccessible sweetness, some Tina Turner dancing in the mind's high grass. Hannah's questions are, as she well knows, also the questions asked by the bloods and, by the time of Komunyakaa's 1969-1970 tour, by most Americans: "what you dying for?" She also suggests to the "soul brothers" that they are fighting on the wrong side—*against* a people of color that has suffered colonial oppression. Her grains of truth, for all the soldiers' resistance to them ("Let's see if we can't / light her goddamn fuse / this time"), must sooner or later call up those emotions dangerous to bring to the battlefield. One of the veterans quoted above spoke of joining the Black Panthers after the war because they were a semi-military group ready to prolong what General Giap would have called the "armed struggle."

Komunyakaa, who served as a correspondent and editor for *The Southern Cross* in Vietnam, illustrates the black soldier's agonized dilemma in **"Report from the Skull's Diorama."** Here he writes of

> . . . . a platoon of black GIs
> back from night patrol
>
> with five dead. . . .
>
> These men have lost their tongues,
>
> but the red-bordered
> leaflets tell us
> *VC didn't kill*
> *Dr. Martin Luther King.*
> The silence etched into their skin
>
> is also mine. . . .

What can be more unnerving than to find your lost voice coming back to you through the leaflets of an enemy? As General Giap knew, no weapon is more powerful than the weapon that cuts the mind. Thus Hanoi Hannah uses the "moonlight-through-the-pines" beauty of Ray Charles' voice to kindle, amid the gun barrels and starlight scopes and killing, "the spiritual and emotional dimension of the human animal" at exactly the time that soldiers most strive to remain machines. The healing voice is thus made into its opposite: a kind of psychological napalm that sets fires in the ganglia and carries out General Giap's "strategy of revolutionary war [which] totally integrated two principal forms of force: armed force and political force . . . , military *dau tranh* (struggle) and political *dau tranh*." According to Philip B. Davidson [in *Vietnam at War: The History 1946-1975,* 1988],

> their combined use created a kind of war unseen before: a single war waged simultaneously on several fronts—not geographical fronts, but programmatical fronts—all conducted by one and the same authority, all carefully meshed. It was a war in which military campaigns were waged for political and diplomatic reasons; economic measures . . . were adopted to further political ends; political and diplomatic losses were accepted to forward military campaigns; and psychological campaigns were launched to lower enemy military effectiveness.

By showing how all this works in his poetry, Komunyakaa engages in an equal and opposite *dau tranh*. With poetry as his weapon and tool, he seeks to rebuild the psyche that war and other social traumas disorder. He recalls reading poetry avidly in Vietnam, before he himself became a poet, in order to keep "in contact with [his] innermost feelings" and not be mummified by the starlight scopes or caught on the hook of some perfectly-baited propaganda broadcast: in other words, to keep thinking, to keep being human, to keep humming the rhythm of life. "The real interrogator," he writes in **"Jungle Surrender,"**

> . . . . is the voice within.
> I would have told them about my daughter
>
> in Phoenix, how young she was,
> about my first woman, anything
>
> but how I helped ambush two Viet Cong
> while plugged into the Grateful Dead.
>
> For some, a soft windy voice makes them

snap. Blues & purples. Some place between

central Georgia & Tay Ninh Province—
the vision of a knot of blood unravels

& parts of us we dared put into the picture
come together. . . .

This daring to put the unbearable first into memory, then into the poem, reconstructs the war-broken rhythms losing track of which, as a Thelonious Monk sideman once said of Monk's asymmetries, would mean plunging down a kind of elevator shaft away from sanity, but even more from the ability to speak, to play. Climbing the precipice of memory, the soldier-poet proves his mettle in peace. He is like an amputee who feels his missing hand and looks down to find that it is there.

Not only Komunyakaa's war poems, but also his peacetime poetry is obsessed with recovering what is lost, with scope and possibility and with jazz, the music of possibility—the noise freedom makes when it moves through the nerves. The peacetime poems in *Neon Vernacular* and *Magic City* display the conceptual and emotional range that is available only to a man who has been to the lip of the abyss and looked around. High-school football, horniness, warfare, sex, torture, rape, racism, loneliness, yellow-jackets, history—Komunyakaa probes them all. In a *Magic City* ballad about prepubescent interracial hijinks called **"Albino,"** Komunyakaa milks everyday incidents for their drops of revelation:

> . . . Some summer days
>   We shot marbles with ball bearings
> For hours before the first punch
>   & the namecalling
>
> Erupted. But by dusk
>   We were back to quick kisses,
> Hollering *You're It & Home*
>   As we played hide & seek.
>
>       . . . . .
>
> She led me to their clubhouse
>   Beside the creek, a betrayal
>
> Of the genes . . . . .
>
>       . . . . .
>
> An odor in the air made its own
> Laws, as if the tongue was a latch
>   Holding down a grace note.

If Komunyakaa finds his way to the kingdom of things past in such *Magic City* reveries, it is because he put in his hours of dusty apprenticeship. The early books excerpted in *Neon Vernacular* are certainly uneven, and some of the poems, such as **"Light on the Subject"** from *Lost in the Bonewheel Factory,* would have been better left unselected. *That* poem dates from a period when Komunyakaa was struggling to find his "own voice." He began writing poetry in a University of Colorado workshop in 1973 and continued taking workshops throughout the seventies, studying under such luminaries as Charles Wright, C. K. Williams, and Howard Moss before landing a fellowship in 1980 at the Provincetown Fine Arts Work

Center. "Well, in essence," Komunyakaa admitted to Gotera,

> one's voice is already inside, but a sort of unearthing has to take place; sometimes one has to remove layers of facades and superficialities. The writer has to get down to the guts of the thing and rediscover the basic timbre of his or her existence.

This unearthing is what must be done in the writing of *every* poem. Like ditch digging or distance running, it builds up a poet's strength. Komunyakaa's "basic timbre" is not so much a "voice" as the meter-making arguments that Emerson espoused, where the heart beats out time on the brainstem.

In Komunyakaa's weak poems, he is simply "not in form," as the athletes say. **"Light on the Subject"** finds Komunyakaa pumped up, like a blood doper, with an exaggeration of a "voice": "Hello, Mister Jack / The Ripper, come on in / make yourself at home." Most of Komunyakaa's poorer efforts follow the glib workshop technique in which tones of voice clash together to make brassy ironies, and verb phrases are paired with nouns not to make meaning, but to startle, like the marriage of the three-foot midget and the 1000-pound giantess in a circus. Komunyakaa writes, "In this gray station of wood / our hearts are wet rags, / & we turn to ourselves, / holding our own hands / as the scaffolds / sway." Despite their authenticity of feeling, these lines betray a paint-by-numbers imagery.

None of this criticism is meant to deprecate Komunyakaa's "pre-war" volumes. Even when most weighed down by ill-considered borrowings, the early poems rarely fail to display flashes of Olympian form. **"Chair Gallows,"** from his first book, *Dedications & Other Darknesses,* is a fine elegy for the folksinger Phil Ochs, only mildly flawed by its soft-focus Bob Dylan ending and the somewhat forced imagery of its fourth line:

> Beating wind with a stick.
> Riding herd on the human spirit.
>
> It's how a man slips his head into a noose
> & watches the easy weight of gods pull down
>
> on his legs. I hope this is just another lie,
> just another typo in a newspaper headline.
>
> But I know war criminals
> live longer than men lost between railroad tracks
>
> & crossroad blues, with twelve strings
> two days out of hock.
>
> I've seen in women's eyes
> men who swallow themselves in mirrors.

The poems in *Copacetic* (1984), Komunyakaa's strongest pre-war "set," have their flaws, like bumpy light aircraft, but they do sooner or later lift off. In **"Back Then,"** Komunyakaa, like one of his acknowledged literary fathers, Aimé Césaire, manages to give surrealism a political backbone:

> I've eaten handfuls of fire
> back to the bright sea

of my first breath
riding the hipbone of memory
& saw a wheel of birds
a bridge into the morning
but that was when gold
didn't burn out a man's eyes
before auction blocks
groaned in courtyards
& nearly got the best of me
that was when the spine,
of every ebony tree wasn't
a pale woman's easy chair. . . .

. . . . .

at the pottery wheel
of each dawn
an antelope leaps
in the heartbeat
of the talking drum

Here the collective memory of an entire people is caught in the poem's talking drum. Komunyakaa makes all that history contemporaneous. He boldly casts his rhythmical net from the "the bright sea / of my first breath" to the slave trade (the "auction block") to the results of age-old economic apartheids ("the spine / of every ebony tree [is] / a pale woman's easy chair"). Like a jazz musician playing a standard such as "When the Saints Come Marching In," he composes a talking poem out of the major chords (sea, slavery, economic injustice). The escape from history that Stephen Daedalus could not achieve is managed on the page: The antelope on whose skin—the poem's "drumskin"—the enjambed rhythms are beaten out suddenly lives again, leaping. Even more than the enjambments in **"Starlight Scope Myopia,"** the ones here resist death by burning its endstops. "There's a completeness about a line," Komunyakaa told Gotera,

a completeness and yet a continuation. It's the whole thing of enjambment, what I like to call "extended possibilities." The line grows. It's not a linguistic labyrinth; it's in logical segments, and yet it grows. It's the whole process of becoming; that's how we are as humans. There's a kind of fluid life about us, and it's how poetry should be. . . . I would like to write poems that are just single lines. That is, a continuing line that doesn't run out of space because of the margin. . . .

This sort of perpetual motion, the ability to play notes that orbit forever in the mind's outer spaces, is clearly what Komunyakaa is after in **"Back Then."** This is what he admires in the jazzmen—Thelonious Monk, Louis Armstrong, Duke Ellington, Ray Charles, and Charles Mingus—about whom he writes. Strangely, poems or passages tendered as tributes to his musical fathers—an elegy for Thelonious Monk, for instance—are among his weakest riffs; sprung from the will, or a sense of filial duty, they give the impression that the poet is intimidated, like a piano student auditioning before some severe master. Komunyakaa seems to feel, too, the long shadow of Auden's twentieth-century elegies. In the backsliding Monk elegy, Komunyakaa writes what he thinks his readers want to hear: an impersonation of angry grief. "Damn the snow. / Its senseless beauty / pours hard light / through the hemlock. / Thelonious is dead." These lines work against the anguish they seek to express.

---

**Not only Komunyakaa's war poems, but also his peacetime poetry is obsessed with recovering what is lost, with scope and possibility and with jazz, the music of possibility—the noise freedom makes when it moves through the nerves.**

**—*Michael Collins***

---

More successful are the poems in which jazz appears like an angel that wanders into the lines and breaks into song. In its blues feeling, **"Audacity of the Lower Gods"** (from the 1986 collection *I Apologize for the Eyes in My Head*) is a jazz ballad. The pronoun "I" is not a site of anxiety or drama, but a place where the reader can rest without discomfort, a leaping off point for the ride down the long, vowel-extended, mostly iambic beats:

I know salt marshes that move along like one big
trembling wing. I've noticed insects
shiny as gold in a blues singer's teeth
& more keenly calibrated than a railroad watch,
but at heart I'm another breed.

The audacity of the lower gods—
whatever we name we own.

. . . . .

I'd rather let the flowers
keep doing what they do best.
Unblessing each petal,
letting go a year's worth of white
death notes, busily unnaming themselves.

In a volume as cynical as *I Apologize for the Eyes in My Head,* the fat tone of these drawling iambs offers a seemingly anti-poetic paradox: that the happiest world may be a world left alone, untroubled by so much as a curse or a blessing or a name, all of which limit possibility, Komunyakaa's muse and first love.

That such a world is not for humans, but for angels and flowers in their haze of death notes, means that the search for possibility, and the eternal rediscovery of it, goes on, as it does in **"Copacetic Mingus"** (from *Copacetic)* and **"Changes; or, Reveries at a Window Overlooking a Country Road, with Two Women Talking Blues in the Kitchen"** (a "new" poem in *New and Selected*.) These poems are proof that pleasure, as much as any dour wargod, can dominate and set its stamp on a life. **"Copacetic Mingus"** is made from two- to four-beat lines that hover like notes under Mingus' fat fingers and from punctuation that comes in now a little ahead, now a little behind the movable beat (made not from stresses so much as from whole words and phrases: whole notes of "hard love . . . hard love"):

Heartstring. Blessed wood

& every moment the thing's made of:
ball of fatback
licked by fingers of fire.
Hard love, it's hard love.
Running big hands down
the upright's wide hips,
rocking his moon-eyed mistress
with gold in her teeth.
Art & life bleed
into each other
as he works the bow.

. . . . .

. . . Here in New Orleans
years below sea level,
I listen to *Pithecanthropus.*
*Erectus:* Up & down, under
& over, every which way—
thump, thump, dada—ah, yes.
Wood heavy with tenderness,
Mingus fingers the loom
gone on Segovia,
dogging the raw strings
unwaxed with rosin.
Hyperbolic bass line. Oh no!
Hard love, it's hard love.

Here the jazzman's and the poet's vision of time meet, like the two sides of some fantastic commemorative medal. This is possible because there is so much delight and devotion in Komunyakaa's portrait, so much diamond-hard love. If the poem has a flaw, it is that it lacks the metaphysical edge—the at times stark terror—of the grand war poems that begin two volumes later.

The question arises whether the peacetime poems can achieve the intensity that their "mighty subject" gives the wartime ones. The answer, inevitable for a poet of Komunyakaa's gifts, is yes. In the new poems with which **Neon Vernacular** begins and in the poems that evoke the neighborhoods of **Magic City,** Komunyakaa taps a seam of memory deep into his childhood in Bogalusa, Louisiana—at the time a complicated spot roamed by both the Ku Klux Klan and anti-Klan civil rights organizers—and up into the untappable future.

In **"Changes,"** Komunyakaa sets two columns of text parallel on the pages, just as one might place two old friends and one stranger between two mirrored walls and then sit back to be instructed by the infinite series of reflections on either side. In the mostly three-beat lines of the left hand column Komunyakaa writes a conversation between two women whose subject is the losses, like some dyslexia of the fates, that make life unreadable. In the right hand column, Komunyakaa sets down what appear to be his own historical reveries, his own rearrangement and orchestration of the unreadable. The effect he achieves is that of a vast conceptual rhyme, the written equivalent of harmonics in music. Possibility is extended and made equal to what Komunyakaa calls the "psychic domain" of his speakers:

> a blues environment. . . . [like that] in New Orleans . . . [where] there are so many layers of everything. . . . [where] you have the traditional and the modern side by side. . . . [to create]

an existential melancholy based on an acute awareness . . . I admire that to an extent, because linked to it is a kind of psychological survival. How one deals with life: to be on this plane one moment and the next moment, a different plane. . . .

In the same interview Komunyakaa speaks of the necessity of keeping "one foot in history, and the other in a progressive vision." Thus, in **"Changes,"** the country women, one's voice italicized, the other's voice in plain text, speak of death while the poet, in a smaller typeface to indicate the unspoken stream of consciousness, probes like Miles playing with his back to the audience and muses on beginnings:

| | |
|---|---|
| *Joe, Gus, Sham* | Heat lightning jumpstarts the slow |
| *Even George Edward* | afternoon & syncopated rainfall |
| *Done gone. Done* | peppers the tinroof like Philly Joe |
| *Gone to Jesus, honey.* | Jones' brushes reaching for a dusky |
| Doncha mean the devil, | backbeat across the high hat. Rhythm |
| Mary? Those Johnson boys | like cells multiplying . . . language & |
| Were only sweet talkers | notes made flesh. Accents & stress |
| & long, tall bootleggers. | almost sexual. Pleasure's knot; to wrestle |
| Child, now you can count | the mind down to unrelenting white space, |
| The men we usedta know | to fill each room with spring's contagious |
| On one hand. They done | changes. Words & music. "Ruby, My Dear," |
| Dropped like mayflies— | turned down on the cassette player. . . . . |

A full analysis of this fabulous poem would require another long essay, but even in this short excerpt one can see Komunyakaa achieving some of that jagged grandeur that the old man of strangeness, Thelonious Sphere Monk, set down in tunes such as "Ruby, My Dear," which Komunyakaa here conjures up like a familiar spirit. The poem is clearly an *ars poetica* of sorts: an ode to Komunyakaa's beloved possibility and poetry's enacting of it. Again, Komunyakaa finagles his way around death and destruction:

| | |
|---|---|
| *It's a fast world* | dragging up moans from shark-infested |
| *Out there, honey* | seas as a blood moon rises. A shock |
| *They go all kinda ways.* | of sunlight breaks the mood & I hear |
| *Just buried John Henry* | my father's voice growing young again, |
| *With that old guitar.* | as he says, "The devil's beating |
| *Cradled in his arms.* | his wife": One side of the road's rainy |
| *Over on Fourth Street* | & the other side's sunny. Imagination— |
| *Singing 'bout hell hounds* | driftwood from a spring flood, stockpiled |
| *When he dropped dead.* | by Furies. Changes. Pinetop's boogiewoogie |
| *You heard 'bout Jack* | keys stacked against each other like syllables |
| *Right? He just tilted over* | in tongue-tripped elegies for Lady Day |
| *in prayer meeting.* | & Duke. Don't try to make any sense |
| *The good & the bad go* | out of this; just let it take you |
| *Into the same song.* | like Pres's tenor & keep you human. . . . . |

If an ex-warrior's meditations on death are always of interest, his meditations on life are specially revelatory. To have the two meditations joined together in this tour-de-force arrangement makes for the "extended possibility—what falls on either side of a word—" that Komunyakaa explicates later in the poem. The columns are like two numbers multiplied together, generating something larger. Like that ferocious Max Roach-Cecil Taylor encounter in which the drummer and the pianist go to war on their instruments, aurally sprouting extra arms like a pair of Shivas, all the while creating spontaneous and phantasmagorical harmonies, Komunyakaa in his two columns reaches the goal he proclaims at the end of the poem. He gets "beyond the tragedy / of always knowing [as in the starlight scope poem] what the right hand / will do." As is only feasible from a poet whose right hand really does know what his left hand is doing, we can read straight across the page ("Right? He just tilted over     in tongue-tripped elegies for Lady Day" or "The good & the bad go     out of this; just let it take you"). The crossover lines enact little resurrections: The man who tilts over comes up singing. The good and the bad slip out of ordinary ethical perception, as if they found a world of pure beauty on the other side, where evil is as unthinkable as the violation of the laws of physical symmetry. Death, as some scientists like to tell us, is nothing to be afraid of. It is only change. It is on death as change that Komunyakaa rings his **"Changes."** The columns of the poem end up wrapping suggestively around each other, like strands of DNA: strands of hope, of humanity. Don't let your fear of death lock you up in hurt and bloodshed, they seem to say: "just let it take you / like Press tenor & keep you human."

In our day Hamlet's question is "Shall we be human, or not be human?" Technology and foolishness have ordained this choice. Komunyakaa's Bogalusa memories, collected in **Magic City** and at the beginning of **Neon Vernacular,** include a double portrait of the town's Ku Klux Klansmen and their African American opponents, the "Deacons of Defense." In the first stanza of the poem, entitled **"Knights of the White Camellia & Deacons of Defense,"** the dragons and all the Klansmen gather "in a big circle / Beside Mitch Creek, as it murmured / Like a murderer tossing in his sleep. . . ." Shrouded in their robes and hoods, like small tepees possessed by the ghosts of lunatics, the Klansmen choose to become a color: to *not* be human. The conscience of the river is deeper and faster-flowing than theirs. As the poem progresses, Komunyakaa manages the considerable feat of teaching the reader about politics without resorting to diatribe. The Ku Klux Klan as an evil institution is remarkable mainly for what it shares with many a "mainstream" organization:

> The sacrament. A gallon
> Jug of bootleg passed from hand to hand . . .
>
>             . . . . .
>
> Bibles, icons, & old lies. Names

Dead in their mouths like broken
Treaties. . . .

In the poem's second stanza, describing the nonviolent resistance of the "Deacons" on the day after the Klan assembly, Komunyakaa sips the mead of troubled warriors: "a radiance / Not borrowed from the gleam / of gun barrels. . . ." Radiance, after all, has always been a great teacher. It was the study of radiance that led Copernicus to conclude that the earth was not the center of the universe. The Deacons and the other freedom marchers prove among humans what Copernicus' observations proved among the stars; and all those mythical beings—shining knights and dragons and thoroughbred whites to whom the bursting wood of burning crosses speaks—cannot get used to the idea that they no longer exist. And ghosts walk the earth.

---

# FURTHER READING

## Criticism

Collins, Michael. "The Metamorphoses: Jazz and Poetry." *Parnassus: Poetry in Review* 19, No. 2 (1994): 49-80.
> Negative review of *The Jazz Poetry Anthology* in which Collins states Feinstein and Komunyakaa "lose the way to the bridge between poetry and jazz."

Ratner, Rochelle. Review of *The Jazz Poetry Anthology,* by Yusef Komunyakaa and Sascha Feinstein. *Library Journal* 116, No. 4 (1 March 1991): 94.
> Brief mixed review of *The Jazz Poetry Anthology.*

## Interview

Kelly, Robert; Matthews, William; and Komunyakaa, Yusef. "Jazz and Poetry: A Conversation." *The Georgia Review* XLVI, No. 4 (Winter 1992): 645-61.
> Conversation in which Kelly, Matthews, and Komunyakaa discuss the roots of jazz and the effect of jazz on poetry.

---

**Additional coverage of Komunyakaa's life and career is contained in the following sources published by Gale Research:** *Contemporary Authors,* Vol. 147; *Contemporary Literary Criticism,* Vol. 86; and *Dictionary of Literary Biography,* Vol. 120.

# Doris Lessing

## 1919-

(Born Doris May Tayler; has also written under the pseudonym Jane Somers) Persian-born English novelist, short story writer, essayist, dramatist, poet, nonfiction writer, journalist, and autobiographer.

The following entry provides an overview of Lessing's career from 1988 through 1995. For further information on her life and works, see *CLC,* Volumes 1, 2, 3, 6, 10, 15, 22, and 40.

## INTRODUCTION

Considered among the most significant writers of the postwar generation, Lessing has explored many of the most important ideas, ideologies, and social issues of the twentieth century. Her works display a broad range of interests and concerns, including racism, communism, feminism, psychology, and mysticism. The major unifying theme of her work is the need for individuals to confront their most fundamental assumptions about life as a way of avoiding preconceived belief systems and achieving psychic and emotional wholeness.

### Biographical Information

Lessing was born in Persia (now Iran) to English parents who moved their family to Rhodesia (now Zimbabwe) when she was still very young. She was educated in a convent school and then a government-run school for girls before her formal education ended at the age of thirteen. Always a precocious reader, Lessing had excelled at school and continued her education on her own through the wealth of books her mother ordered from London. By age eighteen, Lessing had written two drafts for novels and was selling stories to South African magazines, although she would not publish her first novel, the autobiographical *The Grass Is Singing*—which centers on an unhappy woman living on an impoverished, isolated farm in Rhodesia—until 1950. In 1939 she married Frank Wisdom, a much older man, with whom she had two children that she neglected and left in the care of relatives. The marriage, which lasted only four years, inspired *A Proper Marriage* (1954), considered one of her most autobiographical novels. Lessing joined the Communist Party in the early 1940s—she severed her ties to the party during the early 1950s—and subsequently met and married Gottfried Lessing, a Jewish German with whom she had a son, Peter. The marriage was short-lived, however: Gottfried went to East Germany and Lessing and Peter moved to England. She has lived in London since 1949.

### Major Works

Lessing's first novel, *The Grass Is Singing,* was one of the first books to confront the issue of apartheid. In this story

of an impoverished white couple's farm life, the wife vents her hatred of her social and political situation on a black man, whom she eventually provokes into killing her. The novel established two of Lessing's early major concerns: racism, or "the colour bar," and the way that historical and political circumstances can determine the course of a person's life. Lessing also established a strong reputation as a short story writer early in her career. Among her most acclaimed volumes of short fiction are *Five: Short Novels* (1953), *The Habit of Loving* (1957), and *African Stories* (1964), all of which deal with racial concerns in African settings and with the emancipation of modern women. Her growing reputation was secured with the highly acclaimed "Children of Violence" series, in which she traces the intellectual development of Martha Quest, a fictional heroine who resembles Lessing in several ways. Martha, like Lessing, is a "child of violence" born at the end of World War I, raised in the bleak postwar era of social struggle, and faced with the tragedies of World War II. In the course of the series, as Martha progresses from personal, self-centered concerns to a larger awareness of others and the world around her, she pursues various beliefs to gain psychic wholeness. *Martha Quest* (1952) is a *bildungsroman* in which Martha attempts to escape her restricted upbringing and her domineering mother. *A Proper Marriage* and *A Ripple from the Storm* (1958) recount Martha's two unsuccessful marriages to politically oriented men and her involvement in left-wing, anti-apartheid, and communist activities. *Landlocked* (1966), a novel considered by many to be an abrupt departure from the realistic concerns of the series, reflects Lessing's emerging interest in telepathy, extrasensory perception, and Sufism, an offshoot of Islam that proposes that mystical intuition should replace rationalism as a means of alleviating world problems. In this novel, which focuses on Martha's mother, May, Martha travels to England and experiences an apocalyptic vision. Britain, and then the world, are destroyed in *The Four-Gated City* (1969), a novel in which Martha comes to realize the limitations of rational thought and seeks to embrace and understand the higher truth of her intuition. Although faulted for its radical ideas, this novel was praised for its skillful evocation of apocalyptic and psychic elements. *The Golden Notebook* (1962) is widely considered Lessing's masterpiece. This complex novel centers on Anna Freeman Wulf, various aspects of whose life are collected in four notebooks, each of a symbolic color, and are viewed from numerous perspectives. Parts of a novel Wulf is writing are juxtaposed with sections from the four notebooks; the sections can be read in many ways to assume different levels of significance. The "golden notebook" of the title is Anna's desperate attempt through art to integrate her fragmented experiences and to become whole in the process. *The Summer before the Dark* (1973), one of Lessing's most popular novels, centers on a middle-aged woman who has a brief affair with a younger man as a means of rediscovering her identity. During the 1970s, Lessing began writing what she called "inner space fiction." These works reveal the influence of Carl Jung and particularly R. D. Laing, a well-known radical psychologist who proposed that insanity is merely a convenient label imposed by society on those who do not conform to its standards of behavior. In *Briefing for a Descent into Hell* (1971), two psychiatrists attempt to restore a delirious Cambridge professor to their idea of sanity. The professor undergoes an odyssey through the space/time warp of his own psyche, envisioning the oneness of creation and a future apocalypse. This novel hinges on the question of whether his vision is valid or the product of hallucination. *The Memoirs of a Survivor* (1974) expands upon a similar idea. In this novel, Lessing suggests that humanity, given a choice between extinction or a radical change of values and behavior, must reject rationalism and develop a more intuitive approach to existence and survival. In the late 1970s, Lessing dismissed her acclaimed realist work as trivial and began a "space fiction" series, "Canopus in Argos: Archives." In these volumes, three competing galactic empires—the benign Canopeans, self-centered Sirians, and evil Shammat—are revealed to have manipulated earth history to retain a gene pool for their own immortality. These forces continue to influence events on earth through the intervention of immortal beings. *Shikasta* (1979), the first volume of the series, is a collection of records accumulated by Johor, a Canopean agent whose mission is to divert humanity from the destructive course set by the Shammat. *The Marriages between Zones Three, Four, and Five* (1980) is an allegory that centers on an enforced marriage between rulers of two seemingly antithetical regions in the hope of adapting a peaceful coexistence. *The Sirian Experiments* (1981) consists of a series of documents in the manner of *Shikasta* narrated by a female member of an insensitive colonial administration. *The Making of the Representative for Planet 8* (1982) evidences Lessing's interest in dystopian themes in its story of a slowly freezing planet whose inhabitants expire while awaiting a promised transport to a warmer environment. *Documents Relating to the Sentimental Agents in the Volyen Empire* (1983) is a satire on language in which rhetoric is used as a tool for social enslavement. Writing under the pseudonym of Jane Somers, Lessing published two novels, *The Diary of a Good Neighbor* (1983) and *If the Old Could . . .* (1984), to dramatize the problems faced by unknown writers and to receive unbiased critical appraisal. Ten publishers rejected the first novel, and when it appeared in a limited, hardcover edition, many literary magazines ignored it altogether. The major concerns of the Somers books are similar to those of Lessing's feminist works: love, loneliness, and the problems of women. Both novels feature the diaries of Janna, whom critics presume represents Somers/Lessing. Following Lessing's exposure of the pseudonym, both works were collected under Lessing's name and published as *The Diaries of Jane Somers* (1984). In the novel *The Good Terrorist* (1985), a middle-class woman's extreme liberal idealism leads her to organize a group of would-be counterculture revolutionaries who commit an act of terrorism. Here Lessing examines the role of such rhetorical devices as political slogans in contemporary life. Somewhat similarly, *The Fifth Child* (1988) concerns a violent, antisocial child who wreaks havoc on his family and society. The first volume of Lessing's autobiography, *Under My Skin* (1994), covers the first thirty years of her life in Persia and Rhodesia, up to her departure for London in 1949. The first half of the book examines her unhappy childhood on a Rhodesian farm with her parents and younger brother. In the second half of the book, Lessing focuses on her early writing and her two failed marriages.

## Critical Reception

Lessing is generally recognized as one of the most important writers of the twentieth century. Using detailed, realistic descriptions, symbolism, and imagery to evoke a wide range of environments and moods, Lessing achieves what Edward J. Fitzgerald termed "tension and immediacy" in her work. Critics argue that her enlightened portrayal of marriage and motherhood, her anti-apartheid stance, and her experimentation with genre and form have made her an exciting—and often controversial—literary figure. Although many critics have not thought highly of her science fiction and mystical works, contending that her abandonment of realism entailed neglecting the social analysis that made her earlier works so valuable, Jeannette King argues that even "in her most experimental fantasies, Lessing has consistently explored the relationship between the individual psyche and the political, sexual, and religious ideologies that structure it. . . . For if Lessing's work has a single 'message,' it is probably this: only by distancing ourselves from our own most deeply held assumptions and beliefs can we ensure individual or social growth."

---

# PRINCIPAL WORKS

*The Grass Is Singing*  (novel)  1950
*\*Martha Quest*  (novel)  1952
*This Was the Old Chief's Country*  (short stories)  1952
*Before the Deluge*  (drama)  1953
*Five: Short Novels*  (novellas)  1953
*\*A Proper Marriage*  (novel)  1954
*No Witchcraft for Sale*  (short stories)  1956
*Retreat to Innocence*  (novel)  1956
*Going Home*  (essays)  1957
*The Habit of Loving*  (short stories)  1957
*Each His Own Wilderness*  (drama)  1958
*Mr. Dollinger*  (drama)  1958
*\*A Ripple from the Storm*  (novel)  1958
*Fourteen Poems*  (poetry)  1959
*In Pursuit of the English: A Documentary*  (novel)  1960
*The Truth about Billy Newton*  (drama)  1960
*The Golden Notebook*  (novel)  1962
*Play with a Tiger*  (drama)  1962
*A Man and Two Women*  (short stories)  1963
*African Stories*  (short stories)  1964
*\*Landlocked*  (novel)  1966
*The Storm*  [adaptor; from a drama by Alexander Ostrovsky]  (drama)  1966
*Winter in July*  (short stories)  1966
*Particularly Cats*  (autobiographical essay)  1967; revised edition entitled *Particularly Cats . . . and Rufus,* 1991
*Nine African Stories*  (short stories)  1968
*\*The Four-Gated City*  (novel)  1969
*Briefing for a Descent into Hell*  (novel)  1971
*The Story of a Non-Marrying Man, and Other Stories*  (short stories)  1972; also published as *The Temptation of Jack Orkney, and Other Stories,* 1972
*The Singing Door*  (drama)  [first publication]  1973
*The Summer before the Dark*  (novel)  1973
*The Memoirs of a Survivor*  (novel)  1974
*A Small Personal Voice: Essays, Reviews, and Interviews*  (essays, reviews, and interviews)  1974
*Collected Stories.* 2 vols.  (short stories)  1978; also published as *Stories,* 1978
†*Shikasta*  (novel)  1979
†*The Marriages between Zones Three, Four, and Five*  (novel)  1980
†*The Sirian Experiments*  (novel)  1981
†*The Making of the Representative for Planet 8*  (novel)  1982
*The Diary of a Good Neighbour*  [as Jane Somers]  (novel)  1983
†*Documents Relating to the Sentimental Agents in the Volyen Empire*  (novel)  1983
‡*The Diaries of Jane Somers*  (novel)  1984
*If the Old Could . . .*  [as Jane Somers]  (novel)  1984
*The Good Terrorist*  (novel)  1985
*Prisons We Choose to Live Inside*  (essays)  1987
*The Wind Blows Away Our Words*  (nonfiction)  1987

*The Fifth Child*  (novella)  1988
*African Laughter: Four Visits to Zimbabwe*  (nonfiction)  1992
*The Real Thing*  (short stories)  1992
*Under My Skin: Volume One of My Autobiography, to 1949*  (autobiography)  1994
*Playing the Game*  (graphic novel)  1995
*Love, Again*  (novel)  1996
*The Pit*  (short stories)  1996

\*These novels are collectively referred to as the "Children of Violence" series and the "Martha Quest" novels.

†These novels were published together under the title *Canopus in Argos: Archives* in 1992.

‡This work comprises two earlier novels, *The Diary of a Good Neighbour* and *If the Old Could . . . ,* that Lessing published under the pseudonym Jane Somers.

---

# CRITICISM

**Katherine Fishburn   (essay date Summer 1988)**

SOURCE: "Wor(l)ds within Words: Doris Lessing as Meta-Fictionist and Meta-Physician," in *Studies in the Novel,* Vol. 20, No. 2, Summer, 1988, pp. 186-205.

[*In the following essay, Fishburn contends that Lessing's novels are highly complex, subtly self-conscious "metafictions" and that "Lessing has never truly been the realist (we) critics thought her . . . [she] only masqueraded as one."*]

—A book which does not contain its counter-book is considered incomplete.

Jorge Luis Borges

Although Doris Lessing is probably best known as the author of ***The Golden Notebook,*** I think it is safe to say that most critics would not characterize the bulk of her fiction as formally experimental or even up-to-date. In fact, with the possible exception of ***Canopus in Argos,*** they would probably consign her fiction to the venerable but old-fashioned school of expressive realism. Widespread as this perception of Lessing has been, I would argue that it has had the unforeseen consequence of deflecting critical attention away from those very qualities of her fiction that serve to undermine and de(con)struct realistic texts. Quite ironically it is a perception that Lessing herself has fostered—and one that helps to explain why she has enjoyed such popularity with her readers. It was in her own 1957 manifesto, **"The Small Personal Voice,"** after all, that Lessing claimed the aesthetic principles of nineteenth-century realism as her own, thus helping to confirm what her readers had already discovered: Doris Lessing was a novelist of the old school who could give shape and meaning to their lives—an old-fashioned novelist with a contemporary point of view. Lest it appear that I think Lessing's work has only appealed to an unsophisticated band of readers who were incapable of reading her correctly, let me hasten to add that I count myself among those who originally saw her as a realist. I also recognize that she has been read for a variety of reasons. But I still think the initial appeal of her fiction lay in its abundance of likable, intelligent, and perceptive heroines. Unlike the bitches, witches, vacuous virgins, and man-eating troglo/dykes of far too much contemporary men's fiction, the characters Lessing has created have been both realistically portrayed and easy to identify with. Sometimes, as in the case of Martha Quest, the shock of recognition was almost too much to bear, but in the main readers loved seeing themselves in print—and loved this nervy new novelist who allowed them this unaccustomed privilege. Given these reasons, which are as much emotional as intellectual, was it any wonder her readers missed all the other things she was up to?

Because most readers saw her as the realist she claimed to be, they remained blind to all the subversive (fictional) activity she was engaged in. In short, she had created a fiction of herself as writer that was in direct conflict with the kind of fiction she was writing. So compelling was the fiction "Lessing-as-realist," most readers missed the point of *The Golden Notebook* when it was first published in 1962. Although there were narrative hints aplenty that something extraordinary was afoot, most critics regarded the text as yet another portrait of contemporary women—a convoluted portrait, perhaps, but one that still lent itself to New Critical interpretations. Finally, in despair at being so gratuitously misunderstood, Lessing appended the now famous 1971 "Preface" to her novel, in which she tells us that her "major aim was to shape a book which would make its own comment, a wordless statement: to talk through the way it was shaped." But even then readers refused to relinquish their original perception of her as a realist par excellence. So when she published *Briefing for a Descent into Hell* in 1969, the critics tried to ignore it; and when she announced that *The Memoirs of a Survivor* (1974) was her "attempt at autobiography," the critics pretended they had not heard her. Still clinging to their original view of Lessing, readers were shocked to the very core when their beloved realist announced with the publication of *Re: Colonised Planet 5, Shikasta* in 1979 that she had embarked on what would become an entire series of science fiction novels. *How could she do this to us?* readers and critics alike asked rhetorically. Where was the Lessing they had known and loved all these years? The answer, of course, as Martha Quest discovered near the end of *The Four-Gated City,* was "Here, where else, you fool, you poor fool, where else has [she] been, ever."

For, as I intend to argue in this paper, Doris Lessing has never truly been the realist (we) critics thought her. She has only masqueraded as one, an authorial *Wulf* in sheep's clothing. Behind the mask, she has always been a metafictionist, a writer of self-conscious fiction. As Patricia Waugh describes it, metafiction is fundamentally "the construction of a fictional illusion . . . and the laying bare of that illusion" [*Metafiction: The Theory and Practice of Self-Conscious Fiction,* 1984]. "Metafiction sets up an opposition, not to ostensibly 'objective' facts in the 'real' world, but to the language of the realistic novel which has sustained and endorsed such a view of reality" (Waugh). In showing us how literary fiction creates its imaginary worlds, Waugh explains, "metafiction helps us to understand how the reality we live day by day is similarly constructed, similarly 'written.' " In short, it reminds us that

both history and reality are "provisional"—that we no longer inhabit "a world of eternal verities but a series of constructions, artifices, impermanent structures" (Waugh). The "formal self-consciousness" characteristic of metafiction can range anywhere from the limited (like that of Muriel Spark) to the all-embracing (like that of Raymond Federman), with many steps in between. The chronology of Lessing's earlier writing roughly reflects this range, moving from the limited metafictional aspects of *The Grass is Singing* to the all-embracing metafiction of *The Golden Notebook*. Although it is true that her first few novels display only a minimal self-consciousness, the metafiction has always been there. As far back as the 1950s, for example, she was already trying to communicate the essential fictionality of reality itself by calling attention to the power and the provisionality of our language systems, be they political, social, or mythic. But readers have been so enchanted by the fact that this fiction mirrors their own reality, they have failed to see that—all along—the narrative mirror has been also held up to itself.

In *The Grass is Singing* (1950), for example, the story of Mary Turner's breakdown and the unkind behavior of her neighbors is so emotionally charged that it is easy to overlook the book's metafictional qualities. But contrary to the reviews it got, this novel is more than a riveting account of a woman's tragic deterioration. And, contrary to what an earlier critic has suggested, it is also something more than "a little novel about the emotions" seen through a Marxist lens. [In an endnote, Fishburn continues: "My observation is not meant to fault this essay, which argues its point quite effectively. By showing the dialectical tension between Mary and her society, in fact, it helps to prepare the critical ground for my own argument. Zak argues that Mary Turner, like other modernist figures, 'suffers [from] schizophrenic impoverishment'; but unlike most modernist texts 'the novel itself keeps before us . . . the nature of the world from which Mary is compelled to withdraw.' I take Zak's ideas one step further by arguing that the dialectic is portrayed with a degree of formal self-consciousness that calls attention to the fictionality of the world Mary withdraws from."] As textually innocent as it might appear, *The Grass is Singing* is a self-conscious novel that de(con)structs the two-storied edifice of apartheid and domestic bliss. It is not insignificant to Lessing's purpose here that the heroine is destroyed by a combination of racial mythologies and domestic fictions (what Betty Friedan calls the "feminine mystique" in her 1963 book of that name). For both, to one degree or another, dehumanize their participants by forcing them to function less as individuals than as ideas. Thus it is central to the twisted mythology of apartheid that blacks are racially and incorrigibly inferior to whites, an assumption that inspires all sorts of neurotic vigilance among the whites who must constantly monitor one another to maintain the myth of their own superiority. And it is central to the feminine mystique that women find happiness and identity only in marriage, where they subordinate themselves to their husbands. As a classic example of metafiction, Lessing's text simultaneously invokes and de(con)structs these two social myths that bring her heroine not the status they promise but only grief and pain.

As long as Mary is relatively young, she is relatively safe from social pressures, allowed to play the role of social butterfly while she fills her days with parties, dances, and other forms of impersonal socializing. But as she ages it soon becomes clear that she needs to be brought into line, because she is "not *playing her part,* for she did not get married" (emphasis added). In other words, she is not living up to the idea(l)s of what a woman should do with her life. Once her friends notice this failure, they gossip endlessly about what kind of a person she is, finally driving her to look for a husband to prove that they are wrong in thinking "Something missing somewhere." This effort to silence her friends forces her into a marriage she really does not want and ruins her "casual friendship" with other people. In short, after overhearing her friends' unkind gossip, "Mary's *idea of herself* was destroyed and she was not fitted to re-create herself" (emphasis added). Faced with the bleak reality of living on the veld with a hopelessly inept farmer, Mary tries valiantly to make a go of it. But there is no happy ending for this marriage. For various complex reasons, Mary cannot endure married life with Dick Turner. At one point, she tries to escape by returning to town; like other unhappy wives before her, "she dressed, packed a suitcase, and left a note for him, quite in the *traditional way*" (emphasis added). But escape is not in the script. So Dick brings her back to the farm—to loneliness, despair, and death.

Once she is back, her psychological problems become so severe that she no longer acts like a white person is "supposed" to act in racist South Africa. At this point her society's defense mechanism automatically clicks into place, leaving her lost and vulnerable. Under the circumstances, the only person left for her to turn to is Moses, her black houseservant, with whom she develops a forbidden, latently sexual friendship. Bizarre as the relationship becomes, it does involve some expression of simple human kindness. But because the fiction of apartheid is nothing if not perverse, Mary is not allowed to seek comfort from her black servant—even after all the whites have deserted her. Having broken the rules, she must be punished. And the punishment is death—at her servant's hands. Although it is true that Mary suffers from severe mental disorders and Moses's motives are never spelled out, her death is a direct result of their forbidden friendship. In short, Mary is acceptable to her society for only as long as she is willing to inhabit the political fictions of apartheid and maintain the appearance of marital happiness. When she rejects these fictions by preferring the company of her black houseboy to that of her husband, Mary *sentences* herself to death. Her murder, therefore, serves the double purpose of vindicating her society's fear of black violence and silencing a dangerous nonconformist. As far as Mary is concerned, the victory of her white society is unconditional, sealed by her death. But as far as Lessing's readers are concerned, it is an empty victory. Although all of Mary's neighbors, near and far, rally round in their common fears, we as readers do not share their condemnation of the poor woman. Instead, we join Lessing in condemning Mary's society. In so doing we join her in de(con)structing the institution of apartheid and the myths that would sustain it. For in a striking example of narrative economy, Lessing has exposed the absolute corruption central to the fiction

of apartheid by using the black servant to enforce the white code. And by placing the events in the context of a domestic tragedy, she has also de(con)structed the myth of happy endings—the myth of the romance—for it is this myth that lies behind Mary's own destruction.

The clues to this book's metafictionality and the source of much of its bitter irony lie in the way Lessing describes how her heroine chooses to live by the social script when she could have chosen to remain single and "become a person on her own account." But theoretically free as Mary Turner is to reject the conventional script, in reality she does not appear to have either the strength or the imagination to write her own. So even though she eventually behaves in a rebellious fashion, she does so less out of a sense of purpose than out of a sense of hopelessness and desperation. It is not her behavior we should model ourselves after, therefore, but the text itself as it successfully challenges two of the Western world's most cherished fictions. As a story, in other words, it disappoints our desire for a happy ending. But as a text, it explains why happy endings do not work.

The critical context provided by Rachel Blau DuPlessis's *Writing Beyond the Ending: Narrative Strategies of Twentieth-Century Women Writers* (1985) is helpful here. DuPlessis works from the premise that "narrative structures and subjects are like working apparatuses of ideology, factories for the 'natural' and 'fantastic' meanings by which we live." As this statement suggests, DuPlessis finds the relationship between fiction and reality to be a two-way street. Narrative is informed by ideology, and social conventions act "like a 'script,' which suggests sequences of action and choice." In searching for evidence of ideology in eighteenth- and nineteenth-century fiction about women, DuPlessis found a telling pattern to its endings. For the most part, these novels ended either in the heroine's marriage or in her death. In other words, the fiction warned women to abide by social expectations of the time. If the heroine married, all well and good, she could have a happy ending. But if the heroine refused to marry for whatever reason, the novel (and thus society) "punished" her by killing her off or portraying her as insane. But scripts can be rewritten and what has been constructed by language can also be de(con)structed by it. Thus DuPlessis finds in much twentieth-century women's fiction the "invention of strategies that sever the narrative from formerly conventional strategies of fiction and consciousness"; this is what she calls "writing beyond the ending." These strategies range anywhere from the "rupture of story" (such as that found in Olive Schreiner's 1883 *The Story of an African Farm*) to the creation of "collective protagonists" (such as those found in women's speculative fiction). As this range suggests, some of the strategies are more successful than others in liberating women from old scripts. In Lessing's novel, for example, as in Charlotte Perkins Gilman's 1892 "The Yellow Wall-Paper," the de(con)struction of restrictive narratives occurs at the heroine's expense. In fact, in some respects, the fate of Lessing's heroine is worse than that of eighteenth- and nineteenth-century heroines. For, unlike the pattern DuPlessis found in earlier novels where the heroine is subjected to *either* marriage *or* death *or* insanity, this novel subjects its heroine to all three fates. As we have seen, even though *The Grass is Singing* does not technically end with marriage, nonetheless it is the heroine's decision to marry that destroys her.

The bitter irony in Lessing's story is just this: Mary goes insane and is murdered precisely because she abided by social conventions. It is true, of course, that she does break her racist culture's code of behavior for whites. For this, she can expect to be punished and is. But because breaking the code means treating a black person like the human being he is, the irony of Mary's situation is intensified. In effect, she is punished both for honoring and breaking illusions. She cannot win. Thus the book reveals itself as metafiction, reminding us of the punishment in store for those who violate society's fondest fictions of racial superiority. And in its tragic conclusion, when Moses murders Mary, the book effectively lays bare the illusion of marital happiness and the fictions that would maintain it. For it is as clear as anything that Mary welcomes this release from bondage.

A similar metafictional critique of marriage can be seen in Lessing's story, **"To Room Nineteen."** Here both Susan and Matthew Rawlings construct a kind of blueprint marriage for themselves, a "marriage that was grounded in intelligence." For a while everything goes swimmingly. They both have good jobs; for two years they spend their time "giving parties and going to them, being a popular young married couple, and then Susan became pregnant, she gave up her job, and they bought a house in Richmond." "And so they lived with their four children in their gardened house in Richmond and were happy. They had everything they had wanted and had planned for. *And yet . . .*". (Lessing's ellipsis). Suddenly the text begins to question what their reason for living rests on. Their children? Matthew's job? Their love? "Yes, it was around this point, their love, that the whole extraordinary structure revolved . . . And if one felt that it simply was not strong enough, important enough, to support it all, well whose fault was that?" Even with this sense of their love's inadequacy, they muddle along, trying desperately not to make the same mistakes they see their friends making. But try as they will to preserve the form, as soon as the children leave home, this perfect marriage begins finally to take its toll on Susan. No longer able to avoid the consequences of participating in a conventional marriage, Susan slowly goes mad and eventually kills herself—demonstrating once again that abiding by the social scripts can drive a woman crazy.

In her second novel, **Martha Quest** (1952), Lessing continues her criticism of social conventions and institutions, reminding us that they are but fictions—powerful but provisional. And here she more obviously uses the novel to comment on itself. In the very title she chose, she violates the traditional quest narrative by naming a woman as hero. As Joanna Russ's oft-cited essay reminds us, male plots don't work for women. In "What Can a Heroine Do? or Why Women Can't Write" [in *Images of Women in Fiction: Feminist Perspectives,* edited by Susan Koppelman Cornillon, 1972], Russ effectively defamiliarizes old plots by reversing the roles of heroines and heroes. Her revi-

sions are quite amusing and very instructive; for example: "Two strong women battle for supremacy in the early West." "A young man who unwisely puts success in business before his personal fulfillment loses his masculinity and ends up as a neurotic, lonely eunuch." Is it any wonder, then, that Martha cannot get on with her life? What is a heroine to do? According to Rachel Brownstein, the answer is simple: the heroine gets married. In *Becoming a Heroine: Reading about Women in Novels,* Brownstein argues that the heroine's "quest is to be recognized in all her significance, to have her worth made real by being approved. When, at the end, this is done, she is transformed . . ." In short, she becomes a bride: "the *very image of a heroine.* For a heroine is just that, *an image;* novel heroines, like novel readers, are often women who want to become heroines" (Brownstein, emphasis added). But because Martha simultaneously desires and dreads the role, becoming a heroine is not quite so simple for her. She is romantic enough to long for dissolution in love, yet she is sensible and skeptical enough to realize that a marriage like her mother's will not bring her the wholeness, happiness, and recognition promised by romantic fiction. In short, she is a modern girl caught in a traditional script: becoming a bride may be her fate as heroine, but there is no guarantee she will like it. When the novel ends in Martha's marriage to Douglas Knowell, therefore, it is most assuredly not a happy ending. But it is *the* conventional happy ending, one she seems almost doomed to accept. For the "main thing about the heroine," writes Brownstein, "is that hers is always the same old story." In sum, the "idea of becoming a heroine marries the female protagonist to the marriage plot, and it *marries the woman who reads to fiction*" (Brownstein, emphasis added).

The relationship between "novel heroines" and "novel readers" that Brownstein discusses is nowhere made clearer than in **Martha Quest** where Lessing continually demonstrates that her heroine has been (de)formed by fiction—by all her reading. Among the authors Martha reads are Havelock Ellis, Engels, Dickens, Dostoyevsky, Hugo, Whitman, and Thoreau, taking from them a fragmentary romantic view of life that has no practical connection to the world around her. Not only do these "authorities" (as she sees them) fail to help her make sense of her world, they have failed to give her suitable role models to pattern her life after. And even when she and her husband try to abide by "the book," their sexual experiments are mechanical and unfulfilling. Martha's perceptions of reality are both correct and incorrect. On the one hand, she knows intuitively that external reality is a kind of fiction (a metafictional concept). But the fiction she tries to impose on it is a literary fiction, one based almost entirely on her reading. Thus, according to the novels she has read, a farm should be "orderly, compact, cultivated." When she looks at her parents' farm, what she sees is the wild, encroaching bush, against which the "fields were a timid intrusion." Is she to believe what she had read or what she sees? Is she to do what she is told or what she wants? Unfortunately for her, she believes what she reads and does what she is told. Instead of fulfilling the heroic promise of her name, by the end of the novel Martha has been trapped by a system she despises and fears. She is a knight-errant who has gone nowhere. She is a quester without a grail, married to a know-all who knows nothing. She is, in short, a heroine.

In the ironically titled *A Proper Marriage* (1954), Lessing continues to de(con)struct the fiction of wedded bliss that has managed to seduce even the skeptical and uncooperative Martha Quest. As she did in *The Grass is Singing,* here too Lessing shows the interaction between the social and the political fictions that are operative in her heroine's life, highlighting the emptiness of Martha's marriage against the apparently more meaningful political activities of her leftist friends. In this novel also, Martha turns to books for aid in understanding her life. Unhappily married to the callow and rather insensitive Douggie Knowell, she relies on various "handbooks" to explain the situation, taking considerable comfort in the fact that her problems are the universal problems of women. After she and Douglas make love without contraceptives, for example, she angrily quotes the *"book of words"* to him that it is now too late to stop "those little dragons" of his (emphasis added). Hoping to make sense of her life and her marriage, she kneels by the bookcase: "Books. Words. There must surely be some *pattern of words* which would neatly and safely cage what she felt—isolate her emotions so that she could look at them from outside" (emphasis added).

As dependent as she is on books to help her, when she thinks it is likely she will at some point become her mother all over again, she *"had no words* to express this sense of appalling fatality which menaced everyone, her mother as well as herself" (emphasis added). One reason she has no words could lie in Martha's "half-formulated though that *the novelists had not caught up with life;* for there was no doubt that the sort of things she or Stella or Alice talked about found no reflection in literature." This surely is a broad textual hint that Lessing herself is in the process of creating a new kind of literature—a new fiction where women like Martha (and presumably like Lessing herself) can find themselves. Not only does Martha continually make reference to fiction and books, so does the narrator (speaking, one presumes, for the author herself). In a paragraph that describes how Martha is deeply affected by "an unsympathetic description of a character similar to her own in a novel," the narrator remarks that "it is of no use for artists to insist . . . that their productions are only 'a divine play' or 'a reflection from the creative fires of irony,' etc., etc." Later, describing Martha's revulsion to Douglas, the narrator states: "There is a type of woman—although whether she is a modern phenomenon or has always existed is *not a question for novelists*—who cannot bear to be found wanting physically" (emphasis added). Remarking on some of these scenes, DuPlessis notes that these early novels "undertake the discrediting of the conventional life of women—in romance, marriages, affairs, motherhood, the nuclear family, and other family ties." But she apparently does not see that this discrediting amounts to a metafictional attack on the fictions of romance, marriage, affairs, etc. Yet the attack permeates the entire series—slyly but unremittingly undermining the authority of all fictions.

One way it consistently undermines fictional constructs is by showing how inadequate they are in helping Martha complete her quest for meaning and selfhood. For whichever way she turns, be it to the myths of romance or those of politics, she is doomed to disappointment—as we see in *A Ripple from the Storm* (1958), where Lessing invokes the familiar (and by now self-parodic) metalanguage of Marxism to make it even more abundantly clear how language systems seduce and isolate her heroine. In this novel, Lessing returns more openly to the thematic concerns of *The Grass is Singing,* where she juxtaposed the failures of marriage to those of politics. But here the politics under attack are the politics of the Left, those of the communist sympathizers. Just as *Martha Quest* fairly shimmers with allusions to romantic love, *A Ripple from the Storm* reeks with Marxist jargon, as various "comrades" try to impose their vision of the future on a basically indifferent society. Thus we are treated to such gems of rhetoric as Anton's claim that he and his comrades have "the responsibility to be living in a time when mankind takes the first great step forward from the barbarity and chaos of unplanned production to the sunlight of socialism." Or his statement, repeated so often as to become a parodic motif, " 'Comrades, it seems clear that we must analyze the situation.' " It is not insignificant that Martha marries this communist orator—thus merging the two themes. For Anton proves to be as inept a husband and lover as he is a communist, leaving Martha once more longing for "that man who must surely be somewhere close and who would allow her to be herself."

Although it is our major socio-political language systems that bear the brunt of Lessing's attack in these first four novels, literary fiction itself does not escape unscathed. By suggesting that her heroines have been formed by the books they read, for example, Lessing demonstrates in no uncertain terms exactly how conventional novels work to entrap and subdue women—thus helping to reinforce Rachel Blau DuPlessis's premise that "ideology is coiled . . . in narrative structure." But what can be used to defend an ideology can also be used to attack it. When Lessing uses narrative to discredit and dismantle socio-political fictions, therefore, she is in effect uncoiling the narrative—discrediting and dismantling the traditional literary fictions of realism itself, turning a former ally of social reality into its enemy.

If I am correct in reading these books as metafiction, why have we missed it before? I think because Lessing herself still claimed as late as 1957 [in **"The Small Personal Voice"**] that realism was the "highest form of prose writing" an author could choose and because she virtually buried her metafiction in such conventional looking novels. Why would she do this? In part, because her models were the nineteenth-century realists she so esteemed. And as a self-taught writer, it was only reasonable that she should at least try to emulate them. But I think even as she tried to model her writing after them, she knew intuitively it would never work. After all, how could nineteenth-century European realism begin to accommodate the ideas of an unrepentantly rebellious twentieth-century South African woman? It boggles the mind even to consider the possibility of confining Lessing to the restrictive codes of traditional realism. Although she herself might not have been able to articulate the problems she was having with realism in the 1950s, I think on some level she knew precisely what they were and why she had them. What she wrote, therefore, was a kind of reluctant or pseudo-realism, a realism that contained the seeds of its own destruction. In short, what she wrote was metafiction—but metafiction of a fairly limited kind, not the fullblown metafiction of her later years. One rebels, after all, as best one can. So Lessing rebelled first of all against what she knew best: the fictions of marriage and apartheid. And, ironically enough, it was probably the ideas she gleaned from European realism that helped her make this initial break with her country's socio-political systems.

Lessing's early dissatisfaction with form can be seen in a quick comparison between *Martha Quest* and *Emma* (1816). When Jane Austen ends *Emma* with her heroine's marriage to the appropriately named Mr. Knightley, the irony is only situational, a reflection of Emma's youthful self-deception. Given her time and circumstances, it is probably best for Emma to marry Knightley; it is, therefore, a marriage we can all take pleasure in. But when Martha *Quest* marries the falsely named Douggie *Knowell,* the irony is both situational and generic: a reflection of Martha's failed rebellion and an implicit commentary on happy endings and the comic mode itself. It is not delightful that Martha is hoisted by her own petard; it is dreadful. It is most assuredly not a marriage for any of us to take pleasure in. In this novel Lessing merely implies metafictional contradiction. She could not yet see her way clear to "write beyond the ending," to use Rachel Blau DuPlessis's felicitous phrase. She could only indicate the inadequacy of traditional endings. She was limited in what she could do with Martha at the end, I would suggest, because old stories maintain a terrible grip on the imagination. Just as Martha was haunted in life by what she calls "the nightmare *repetition*" [*A Proper Marriage*] of women's fate, Lessing herself was still haunted by traditional realism. If Martha had refused to marry, what would she have done instead? It was a question Lessing could not yet answer.

It was only later, when she had fully mastered her craft, that she could rebel openly against the same fictions she had tried at first to model herself after. It was only then that she could invent her own tradition—providing firm support for Jorge Luis Borges's contention that "every writer *creates* his own precursors. His work modifies our conception of the past, as it will modify the future." [In an endnote, Fishburn cites Jorge Luis Borges, "Kafka and His Precursors," in *Labyrinths: Selected Stories and Other Writings,* ed. Donald A. Yates and James E. Irby, 1964. "Borges prefaces this remark with the following assertion: 'If I am not mistaken, the heterogeneous pieces I have enumerated resemble Kafka; if I am not mistaken, not all of them resemble each other. This second fact is the more significant. In each of these texts we find Kafka's idiosyncrasy to a greater or lesser degree, but if Kafka had never written a line, we would not perceive this quality; in other words, it would not exist.' "] Just as Kafka is seen in Borges's story to have invented his own precursors, revealing each of them in a striking new light, so too has Lessing invented hers. It has been a tradition that Borges himself would have appreciated, moving as it does both backward and forward in time, backward to the subversive women writers of the eighteenth and nineteenth centuries (only just now being revealed to us) and forward to those of the late twentieth. [In an endnote, Fishburn continues: "How many rereadings of early women's fiction have been made possible by the fact of Lessing's work? We shall never know, of course, but the literary criticism that has made these rereadings possible did not emerge in a vacuum, and I suspect that Lessing herself can be given some of the credit for freeing her critics from some of the traditional thought patterns we inherited from our instructors and their texts."] But it is also the case, I believe, that Lessing has created her own private tradition, limited to her own works. That is, the more she writes, the more we see in what she has already written. To be specific, once Lessing began to write beyond the ending, we suddenly realized she had been challenging it all along. And how did Lessing finally rupture the story? She turned her heroine into an author. In effect, she turned her into an updated version of herself. Finding in her own life an unconventional, unencumbered model for her fiction, she could finally free herself from Dickens and Tolstoy. It may be ironic, but it is hardly unexpected, that the writers who helped Lessing escape South Africa would become the second intellectual prison she had to break out of. For no fiction could contain her—not even her own.

Because of the political independence she had tenaciously maintained for herself in her earlier novels, by the time she came to write *The Golden Notebook* (1962), Lessing had established an intellectual base from which to critique all language systems. She says in the preface and elsewhere that writing this novel changed her, but she never spells out exactly how. One way it surely changed her was to liberate her once and for all from "the highest form of prose writing" and all those antediluvian literary ancestors she had been shackled with from birth. After several preliminary skirmishes in her first four novels, suddenly she could declare all-out guerrilla war: fully armed with craft and a newly defined purpose, she was finally in a position to subvert literary fiction in the same way she had been subverting social fictions all her life. But *The Golden Notebook* not only openly overthrows realistic fiction, it also implicitly undermines the status of everyday reality itself—a covert narrative action that would become a fullfledged assault in just a few years. But before Lessing could grapple directly with epistemological questions, she had to free an earlier heroine from the fictional prison she had constructed for her. Having completed *The Golden Notebook,* it was time to prepare Martha's escape from South Africa by naming and demolishing the social and political fictions that for too long had kept her heroine feeling "landlocked," a feeling which Lessing describes in the novel of that name. Once she got Martha out of Africa, it was easy; for she had made the break herself. Having herself left two husbands, two children, and an entire continent, it was getting easier all the time to write new plots for her own life. The least she could do for Martha was to bring her along. In *The Four-Gated City* (1969), she did just this. She broke the hold South Africa had on her fiction and transported her heroine to new shores and new adventures. In London Martha was free to explore new kinds of reality and so was the novel she lived in. As evidence of Martha's new status as free agent, Lessing unleashed a veritable Babel of language systems—including character sketches, Dorothy's lists, Martha's notes about madness and visionary insights—and let them, in Waugh's terms, "compete for privilege." Topping it all off was an apocalyptic science-fiction ending that catapulted her so-called "realistic" novel into the future.

Completely free from the restrictive fictions of historical realism and political systems, Lessing could then forthrightly challenge the fiction of reality itself—as she does in *Briefing for a Descent into Hell* (1971), a text that refuses to account for its competing fictional worlds. By presenting one of these realities exclusively through the narrative eye/I of one character, she reminds us that reality is what we "say" it is. By portraying two competing co-equal realities, which both depend on language for their existence, she reminds us that fiction and reality have the same provisional ontological status. Then in *The Summer Before the Dark* (1973) Lessing reminds us again of the failed fictions of domesticity. Like Lessing's earlier heroines, Kate Brown too has been seduced and abandoned by marital happiness. The novel is replete with hints of its metafictionality. The language systems here consist of the "blueprints" for marriage Kate and her husband draw up, the "false" language of memory, and the symbolic language of dreams. And Kate's expertise is, after all, as a translator; to the people who hire her "she *was* language." Using her new status and job as a way to break the stultifying pattern of her marriage, Kate learns to live beyond the ending by heeding the message of her dreams, thus replacing one language system with another more meaningful one. A similar but more profound doubling of realities takes place in *The Memoirs of a Survivor* (1974). Here Lessing describes the life of an anonymous woman who is able to live in two alternate worlds, one a rough sketch of the near future, another a combination of the recent past and a dream world. As strange and incomprehensible as some of this book is, Lessing nonetheless continues to identify it as her "attempt at autobiography." By identifying it as such, she invites us to read it metafictionally as a commentary on the form itself—strongly implying that anyone's life story is (merely) fiction. But the book is also a commentary on the fictionality of reality itself—which, as Waugh reminds us, is the ultimate message inherent in all metafiction.

It probably goes without saying that the entire *Canopus in Argos* (1979-1983) series is metafictional, focusing as it does on chroniclers, editors, and narrators, as well as a myriad of competing language systems (reports, histories, letters, diaries, political rhetoric, propaganda, songs, etc.). This series, as I argue in *The Unexpected Universe of Doris Lessing* (1985), is written in such a way that it calls attention to its own rhetorical devices, making self-conscious readers of us. At the same time, Lessing challenges the assumptions and principles of some of our most powerful language systems—the institutions of religion, politics, and science. Her purpose in these five novels, as in *Briefing for a Descent into Hell* and *The Memoirs of a Survivor,* is to question the fabric of reality itself. Drawing on the principles of Eastern mysticism and those of particle physics, Lessing uses her fiction to challenge the Cartesian dualities that inform the Western world's concept of reali-

ty. In short, these books remind us that what we take for reality is only fiction—a familiar but entirely provisional construct—and what we take for "realism" is only an attempt to shore up the fiction of reality. In short, they are metafiction at its best. And it is precisely because these seven novels are all so clearly metafictional that we have finally been able to see the less obvious metafiction in Lessing's other novels.

Having established the metafictional aspects of Lessing's earlier novels, this leaves three later books to account for. The first two, *The Diary of a Good Neighbor* (1983) and *If the Old Could . . .* (1984)—republished together under the title *The Diaries of Jane Somers* (1984)—consist of novels that are disguised as diaries, written by a novelist disguised as a journalist disguised as an editor and author of romantic fiction, who quite self-consciously writes the diaries we read as novels. By writing these novels under the pseudonym "Jane Somers" Lessing has managed to turn herself into a fiction; as she says in the introduction to the single volume, "as Jane Somers I wrote in ways that Doris Lessing cannot." The third book is another metafictional novel craftily disguised as realism. But just as *Briefing* and *Memoirs* contain their own internal contradictory texts, so too does *The Good Terrorist* (1985). Its heroine, having identified herself as a terrorist by repudiating her parents' bourgeois life, nonetheless still speaks in their voice—complaining after one political demonstration, for example, that she hadn't got "her money's worth." Her combination of double-vision and double-speak occurs in another scene, when she sees a group of blue-collar workers in a restaurant. At first she feels warmly toward them, thinking "The salt of the earth!" Then she notices their greasy food and thinks "Cholesterol." Seeing what they are reading, she finally dismisses them with the phrase "Only lumpens." At another point, she characterizes the middle class as "Bloody, filthy accumulating . . . creeps"—only to reflect shortly afterwards that one of her co-tenants "hasn't got the expertise of the middle class."

Although she tries very hard to become a terrorist like her friends, she is the one who phones in a warning about the bomb they are about to set off. And the same world that her co-conspirators would destroy without thought or remorse, Alice tries valiantly to resurrect in the guise of the house they live in. In so doing, she symbolizes the "good terrorist" in Lessing herself. For as we have seen, throughout her writing career, Lessing has engaged in political terrorism of a literary kind by using the conventions of fiction against themselves. Unlike poor Alice's somewhat feeble efforts, Lessing's terrorism has also been epistemological, a direct challenge to our sense of reality. As drastic as her purpose has been, however, she has often housed her ideas in very domestic-looking fiction. In fact, she has frequently used a house itself as the symbol of psychological or ontological change. So what might appear in this novel to be a fairly innocent account of a misguided terrorist is another in a long line of books with a revolutionary purpose. Seen in the context of Lessing's other fiction, the house that Alice brings back to life/repairs/renovates/renews is the house of fiction/politics/society/reality that Lessing herself brings back to life/repairs/renovates/renews.

In her efforts to heal, Alice is also symbolic of Lessing. Although Alice does not succeed in healing society at large, she does save her suicidal comrade from death. And she also saves the house they have been living in; for, after she renovates it, the Council decides to convert it to flats rather than demolishing it as once planned. The house really symbolizes Alice's function in the story. For without being fully aware of the significance of her acts, she is trying to do some good in saving this lovely old building. But in doing so, she gets little help or encouragement from either friends or Council in trying to get it repaired. In short, to borrow a phrase from Stanley Fish, she is a character equivalent of the kind of author he calls the "good physician." As Fish uses the term in *Self-Consuming Artifacts,* the "metaphor of the good physician" describes an author who has the intention of telling "patients what they *don't* want to hear in the hope that by forcing them to see themselves clearly, they may be moved to change the selves they see." It is clearly a term that is applicable to Lessing's purpose in this novel. As she has done so often before, in this account of failed terrorism Lessing illuminates our faults—trying as so often to heal the body politic by telling us what we do not want to hear.

But Lessing is not just the "good physician" in this novel; she is also, as elsewhere, the good meta-physician: one who deals with questions of ultimate reality and the nature of knowledge itself. As a good meta-fictionist, from her first novel to her latest, she continues to tantalize us with the thought that all reality is but fiction—from our fondest dreams to our greatest fears. And in *The Diaries of Jane Somers* she reminds us that even Doris Lessing is a fiction—as is the Lessing of this paper. The paradox that she has so loved to play with is that she has been forced to use fiction to de(con)struct the fictions we live in. It is only fitting, therefore, that she free us from her own fictional constructs by de(con)structing them. Thus she has simultaneously held a fictional mirror to her readers' lives and broken that mirror in an effort to free us from its frame. Rather than looking to her early fiction only for self-portraits we would do well, therefore, to look to it for *narrative instruction* on how to break the codes that would constrain us—be they social, political, or literary. Mary Turner, Martha Quest, and Susan Rawlings might have been seduced by the script, but their author was not. Instead of repeating the old pre-*script*ive and pro-*script*ive conventions found in realistic fiction, Lessing has invented her own narrative strategies for subverting them. In so doing, she has given readers invaluable de-*script*ions of how to rewrite fiction to suit ourselves. Readers and writers alike—men and women both—would all do well to embrace Doris Lessing not as "their realist" but as "their metafictionist"—a code-breaker par excellence.

But is she doing something that is all that different from other women writers today?

I think not. For, after all, much contemporary women's fiction is quite overtly metafictional. Maureen Howard's elegant *Expensive Habits* (1986) is metafictional in much the way E. L. Doctorow's *The Book of Daniel* (1971) is. Dyan Sheldon wittily challenges myths of love and romance in *Victim of Love* (1982), which also contains a story within a story that is written by the protagonist's husband—himself a would-be novelist. In *The Life and Loves of a She-Devil* (1983), Fay Weldon gives a brutally amusing twist to the story of how a wronged wife prevails over the "other woman" by quite literally becoming her. Alice Walker clearly "writes beyond the ending" in *Meridian* (1976), where she rejects both the old storylines and the old myths about being female and black. Angela Carter reconstructs old fairy tales from a feminist perspective in *The Bloody Chamber and Other Adult Tales* (1979). Joanna Russ does the same thing for science fiction in her classic novel *The Female Man* (1975). Maxine Hong Kingston reinvents the autobiography in *The Woman Warrior* (1976) by focusing less on herself than on her female ancestors, making stories up when history is incomplete. Monique Wittig throws out the basis of most realistic fiction, including plot and character, in her feminist utopian novel *Les Guérillères* (1969). Iris Murdoch warns us of the dangers of seeing other people's lives as fiction in *The Unicorn* (1963), where two of the main characters both believe they are participating in a modern-day fairy tale—as, of course they are! And Anita Brookner invites the smudging of distinctions between fiction and reality in *Look at Me* (1983), where we watch the narrator give novelistic form to the events of her "real" life.

But as clearly as these books are metafictional, there are others, like some of Lessing's work, that are less clearly so. One problem in identifying them, as Molly Hite suggests in a recent [unpublished] paper on Lessing, has been that critics haven't known quite what to look for. Trapped by the tradition of male metafictional writers, we have not yet seen what constitutes women's metafiction. The problem is compounded by the fact that critics haven't always known what women's realistic fiction amounts to either, trapped as we have been by what Roland Barthes calls the *doxa*. In "Emphasis Added: Plots and Plausibilities in Women's Fiction," Nancy K. Miller reviews the way women's novels have been dismissed when they did not conform to the requirements of the *doxa* or the principle of *vraisemblance,* which she translates as "plausibility" ["Emphasis Added" is in *The New Feminist Criticism: Essays on Women, Literature, and Theory,* edited by Elaine Showalter, 1985]. Defining the term as "an effect of reading through a grid of concordance," she suggests: "If no maxim is available to account for a particular piece of behavior, that behavior is read as unmotivated and unconvincing." Fiction that dares to violate the maxim, therefore, runs the risk of being dismissed as implausible and unworthy of serious critical attention. She concludes by arguing that "the plots of women's literature are not about 'life' and solutions in any therapeutic sense, nor should they be. They are about the plots of literature itself, about the constraints the maxim places on rendering a female life in fiction." In short, she implies that all women's writing is metafictional, because it all, in one respect or another, comments on the fictions we read or the fictions we live by. This view finds support in Joanna Russ's previously mentioned essay in which she reminds us that most of our traditional plots are male plots and thus not available to women. It also finds support in Rachel Blau DuPlessis's idea that twentieth-century women writers are breaking out of the old scripts and writing beyond the ending. In telling their own stories—inventing their own plots—could not all women, then, be writing metafiction?

I suggest they are. I propose, therefore, that we work from the premise that all women's fiction, until proven otherwise, is metafictional.

It is true that some feminist critics have expressed serious reservations about adopting the term. Molly Hite, for example, cautions feminist critics to adopt it only after they have carefully considered whether it is indeed one they want to appropriate from a "male and masculinist tradition." Although her reservations are valid ones, I have two reasons for urging the immediate adoption of the term. The first reason is the political one described by Nina Auerbach in "Engorging the Patriarchy," where she urges women to "absorb the patriarchy before it embraces—and abandons—us into invisibility" [see *Feminist Issues in Literary Scholarship,* edited by Shari Benstock, 1987]. By appropriating the concept of "metafiction" in the way I have suggested, feminist criticism would have the opportunity, in effect, to regard "male metafiction" as a subspecies of "women's fiction"—or, to borrow the French term, one example of the many subversive, disruptive discourses known as *l'écriture féminine.* [In an endnote, Fishburn states that the phrase comes from Julia Kristeva; Fishburn also cites significant essays on the subject: Ann Rosalind Jones, "Writing the Body: Toward an Understanding of *l'Écriture féminine,*" in *The New Feminist Criticism: Essays on Women, Literature, and Theory,* ed. Elaine Showalter (1985); Toril Moi, "Marginality and Subversion: Julia Kristeva," in her *Sexual/Textual Politics: Feminist Literary Theory* (1985); and Julia Kristeva, *Desire in Language: A Semiotic Approach to Literature and Art,* ed. Leon S. Roudiez, trans. Thomas Gora et al. (1980).] The second reason I would urge us to adopt the term is that it is so well suited to describe the de(con)structive activity of women's fiction, especially because it helps to draw theory and practice together. For, ultimately, metafiction is a liberating concept, empowering us to rewrite all the fictions of our lives—even the *doxa.* [In an endnote, Fishburn continues: "In *Roland Barthes by Roland Barthes* (trans. Richard Howard [New York: Hill and Wang, 1977]), Barthes defines the *Doxa* as 'Public Opinion, the mind of the majority, petit bourgeois Consensus, the Voice of Nature, the Violence of Prejudice.' What he says of the 'two monstrous modes of rhetorical domination: *Reign* and *Triumph*' is also suggestive for the project of women's metafiction. The *Doxa* he describes as being 'content to reign; it diffuses, blurs; it is a legal, a natural dominance.' In contrast, 'militant language, whether revolutionary or religious . . . is a triumphant language: each action of the discourse is a triumph *à l'antique:* the victors and the defeated enemies are made to parade past.' Although he is speaking of social discourses here, it would appear that women's metafiction could be described as a kind of 'militant language,' a discourse that parades its victory over its defeated enemies by rupturing the very texts that would silence it."] Like Lessing's early novels, models are everywhere waiting to be unmasked. Once we give them our attention, we will see that hidden in even the most innocent seeming texts are more than paper tigers. Behind the mask of women's realism we will find texts that contain their

countertexts, fictions that contain their anti-fictions, wor(l)ds within words without end.

### Virginia Tiger   (essay date Autumn 1990)

SOURCE: " 'Taking Hands and Dancing in (Dis)Unity': Story to Storied in Doris Lessing's 'To Room Nineteen' and 'A Room,' " in *Modern Fiction Studies,* Vol. 36, No. 3, Autumn, 1990, pp. 421-33.

[*Tiger is a Canadian critic and educator. In the following essay, she focuses on Lessing's short stories "To Room Nineteen" and "A Room" in her discussion of the author's use of narrative voice and realistic literary techniques. Tiger also examines the ways in which these two stories relate to the novels Lessing constructed from them,* The Summer Before the Dark *and* The Memoirs of a Survivor, *respectively.*]

> "To see" is the dominant verb in the realist text "à la gastronomie de l'oeil" as Balzac expressed it—and realist fiction is preeminently concerned with seeing, with a seeing in detail.
>
> —Mark Seltzer [*"The Princess Casamassima: Realism and the Fantasy of Surveillance,"* Nineteenth-Century Fiction 35 (1981)]

To view Doris Lessing's short fiction in relation to "the coercive network of seeing, power and surveillance" (Seltzer) that characterizes the literature of the realist enterprise invites triply the hazardous. Of first concern is the author's well-known opposition to theoretics. On principle, Lessing dismisses critical terms like realism (and its contemporary companion, feminism) as prescriptive about rather than descriptive of her project. Her position (itself prescriptive, especially as polemicized in the 1971 Introduction to **The Golden Notebook,** the 1979 Remarks upon **Shikasta,** and the 1984 Preface to **The Diaries of Jane Somers**) would seem to suggest hostility as much to the realist readings as to those of the feminist. Of second concern—although this has yet to be critiqued—Lessing aligns herself with those critics and readers who take as axiomatic that the authoring of texts represents an unassailable authoritative act. Hers becomes the claim that intertextual contexts can be ignored. Third—and finally in this article's critical speculations—there are the problematics of the shorter fiction. To speak of short and long fiction is to make the assumption that distinguishing between one kind of text and the other is defensible, a distinction encouraged by the practice of such writers as James Joyce, Virginia Woolf, William Faulkner, and the later Nabokov. Like them, Lessing has extrapolated from and transformed several of her short stories, reembedding them in longer narratives. Forming an enriching—although not so very rigorously examined—part of her work, the sixty or more short stories raise intertextual matters about the shorter fiction's relation to the longer works as well as intriguing questions about the overall production of text.

The stories seem to have been written during periods especially crucial to the author's development, as has been observed in a discussion of Lessing's first decade in England [see Claire Sprague and Virginia Tiger, "Introduction," *Critical Essays on Doris Lessing,* 1986]. These turbulent, prolific years—the 1950s—saw a political novel, two reportorial works, plays, poems, essays, and reviews as well as a regiment of short stories. Appearing first in such magazines as the *New Statesman and Nation, Encounter,* the *Partisan Review,* and the *Kenyon Review,* the stories "contain[ed] most of the themes of her major novels, including concerns that did not clearly emerge till later" [Jean Pickering, "The English Short Story in the Sixties," *The English Short Story: 1945-1980,* edited by Dennis Vannatta, 1985]. More than several of the stories from this period anticipated what in the 1970s appeared to be new dimensions in Lessing's fiction. Their marking of shifts in ideology and narrative strategies amounted to the laying of foundations for what Betsy Draine has since identified as the competing attitudes and warring styles upon which the later work was constructed [*Substance Under Pressure: Artistic Coherence and Evolving Form in the Novels of Doris Lessing,* 1983]. As Lessing's longer fiction has moved away from the realism and materialism of the first series, *Children of Violence* 1952-1969, toward the speculative fantasy and mysticism of the second series, *Canopus in Argos* 1979-1983, the English stories (in Britain collected in 1978 under the titles *To Room Nineteen,* Volume One and *The Temptation of Jack Orkney,* Volume Two) observed—sometimes, with a piercing malice—prevailing social arrangements. At the same time flickering across these canvases and diffusing overt meaning in the manner Jacques Derrida terms dissemination were incursions of the unreal, dream intimations, the unlocking of buried visions.

That there is an insistent continuity between the short fiction and the longer works seems incontrovertible. Several of the stories republished in the 1978 collection are related directly to later novels: *Shikasta*'s (1979) intergalacticism earlier appeared as fictional landscape in **"Report on the Threatened City"** and the first Jane Somers novel, *The Diary of a Good Neighbour* (1983), derives inspiration and theme from **"An Old Woman and Her Cat,"** a short story about an eccentric and ancient woman who outwits the agents of Social Welfare by hiding, like a crafty wild cat, in the crevices of London. These reweavings are tempered reimaginings, their strategy like Joyce's first play with *Ulysses* in a *Dubliners'* story to have been called "Mr. Hunter's Day." In contrast to such modified reimaginings, three stories by Lessing, **"The Temptation of Jack Orkney," "A Room,"** and **"To Room Nineteen"** are substantially recast, finding their encodings in *Briefing for a Descent into Hell* (1971), *The Summer Before the Dark* (1973), and *The Memoirs of a Survivor* (1974). And importantly, these three novels (ones so solidly linked to and developing amply from the shorter fictions' initial explorations) mark an interlude between Lessing's two major narrative series. *Briefing for a Descent into Hell, The Summer Before the Dark,* and *The Memoirs of a Survivor* appear in the years between the realism of *Children of Violence* and the speculation of *Canopus in Argos.* To argue from story to storied, one could make a sound case for Lessing's success in and need to test fictive limits in her interrogation of fiction's capacity to represent what she takes to be reality.

It is less the continuity between the story and its storied

encoding and more the problematics of the short story that will here be attended. More precisely, I want to explore two questions. First, does the foreshortened discourse in the short story result in texts of singularity: that is, texts not evidencing plurality. Second, do Lessing's short fiction rehearsals reveal an early impatience with the realist project and its impulse to document, control, and supervise "things as they are." To engage these questions, I will examine in some detail **"To Room Nineteen"** and **"A Room,"** both of which appeared in *A Man and Two Women* (1958). In these two stories, Lessing offers exemplary models of writing in the neutral discourse of the realist mode. Nevertheless, by means of their ruptured narrative surfaces, the two stories make eruptive what usually remains *under* control in a realist text: the operations of the libidinal, the anarchic. And the thematics of opposition between the intelligible and the irrational, the everyday and the aberrant becomes apparent by the calculated strategy of disfiguring the world of the realist project so as to refigure its significance.

More than many others **"To Room Nineteen,"** Lessing's much anthologized short fiction, demonstrates how problematic is the conventional notion that short stories thrive on unitary schema. For in this single text competes a diversity of narrative codes; indeed, the text seems at first to embarrass its own ruling system, showing contradictions that its novel counterpart, *The Summer Before the Dark,* does not embrace in its limpidly straightforward structure. Assessed significant enough in the production of the Lessing canon to lend its title to Volume One of the 1978 edition of her collected non-African stories—thus privileging by inference that period and narrative modality in subsequent discussions of Lessing's work—**"To Room Nineteen"** first appeared as the nineteenth as well as final story in the most self-reflexive of Lessing's collections, the anthology, *A Man and Two Women.* Rather more variegated, indeed uncertain, than the African collection *This Was the Old Chief's Country* (1951) in terms of thematic consistency, these British texts heralded what was then still the colonial marginality of their author by their persistent tone of deflected detachment. Observing with clinical condescension the troubled attachments of the sophisticated, liberal bourgeoisie, the stories judged and found wanting conventional social creatures—publicists, journalists, set designers, professional layabouts working on the edges of the arts in the London of the late fifties.

In these texts, the author demands authority. So insistently does omniscient point of view control that ironical distance seems more authorial performance than narratorial stance. The "panoptic" eye/I of the narration conveys impatience with social codes and roles, its tone sometimes even that of the spiritual sneer. As **"To Room Nineteen"** 's first sentence commands: "This is a story, I suppose, about a failure in intelligence: the Rawlings' marriage was grounded in intelligence."

Readers and critics alike have been seized by **"To Room Nineteen,"** celebrated by one Lessing scholar as "one of Lessing's most moving . . . texts" [see Mona Knapp, *Doris Lessing,* 1984]. Introduced by way of summary and sketch is a middle-class English woman, a commercial artist sensibly married and sensibly attentive to her "handsome, blond, attractive" husband, a sub-editor on a large London newspaper. "And this is what happened," pronounces the narrative, its parodic discourse flat, dry:

> Susan became pregnant, she gave up her job, and they bought a house in Richmond. It was typical of this couple that they had a son first, then a daughter, then twins, son and daughter. Everything right, appropriate, and what everyone would wish for if they could choose. But people did feel these two had chosen; this balanced and sensible family was no more than what was due to them because of their infallible sense for choosing right.

The effect of the discourse (what in another context has been described as Lessing's "exaggerated use of a particular linguistic register") is to undercut "the characters [so as] to make us feel that they are no more than puppets, creatures of convention" [Clare Hanson "Free Stories: The Shorter Fiction of Doris Lessing," *Doris Lessing Newsletter* 9, No. 1 (1985)]. The assertive commentary delivered by the narrator—who interrupts, interrogates, and then retires—intensifies the intended readerly perception that character is culturally scripted and behavior socially constricted:

> And so they lived with their four children in their gardened house in Richmond and were happy. They had everything they had wanted and had planned for. *And yet* . . .
>
> Well, even this was expected, that there must be a certain flatness . . .
>
> Yes, yes, of course it was natural they sometimes felt like this. Like what?
>
> Their life seemed to be like a snake biting its tail. Matthew's job for the sake of Susan, children, house, and garden—which caravanserai needed a well-paid job to maintain it. And Susan's practical intelligence for the sake of Matthew, the children, the house and the garden—which unit would have collapsed in a week without her.

What happens? Were this a text conforming to prescriptive definitions of the short story genre, Susan Rawlings would undergo change as a result of conflict, a change to which all elements in the narrative had contributed harmoniously and economically. However, so flattened is the portrayal of character that **"To Room Nineteen"** subverts conventional expectations, endorsing—it would first appear—the very typicality it has exposed through parody.

> So what did it matter if they felt dry, flat? People like themselves, fed on a hundred books (psychological, anthropological, sociological), could scarcely be unprepared for the dry, controlled wistfulness which is the distinguishing mark of the intelligent marriage. Two people, endowed with education, with discrimination, with judgement, linked together voluntarily from their will to be happy together . . . *one sees them everywhere, one knows them, one even is that thing oneself.* (italics mine)

By means of the pronominal shift from first-person to third, an intertextual conspiracy is set up between the narrator's construction and that of the reader. The "I"/eye of the first line ("This is a story, I suppose, about a failure in intelligence" shortly becomes the "one"/[unitary] one where effected is the merging of reader and narrator into one unit. As the text quoted above insists "*one* sees them everywhere, *one* knows them, *one* even is that thing oneself " (italics mine).

And what happens? Having negotiated a sensible, intelligent marital détente at the age of forty or so, sensible, intelligent Susan Rawlings—her husband (although dallying in thin affairs) still very much a good husband, a good father, her four children off at school, her Richmond house managed by an agreeable housekeeper—goes mad. And the text too goes berserk, its surface coherence being, as Lessing remarked of *The Golden Notebook,* "shot to hell."

Like her counterpart, Kate Brown in *The Summer Before the Dark,* Susan Rawlings is that "well-documented and much-studied phenomenon, the woman with grown-children and not enough to do." Unlike Kate Brown, Susan Rawlings is not permitted a summer of solitude— the text's foreshortening strategies forbidding the integrative psychic voyage the longer fiction (with its obligatory longer-leashed development) allows. Invaded, like Kate, by restlessness, irritation, resentment, "emotions that were utterly ridiculous, that she despised," Susan tries to confront them calmly, intelligently: "She spoke to herself severely, thus: All this is quite natural. First, I spent twelve years of my adult life working, *living my own life.* Then I married . . . I signed myself over, so to speak, to other people. To the children. Not for one moment . . . have I been alone, had time to myself. So now I have to learn to be myself again. That's all."

By this point in the narrative's progression, the gesturing narrator has withdrawn from commentary, judgment being conveyed largely through the protagonist's stream of thought. To a degree, the strategy permits the individuation of what was first presented as a merely typical character. More important, it extends the identification of narrator/reader (earlier valorized in the pronominal "one") to include a now valorized protagonist. The reader observes from a centered vantage point of empathetic identification (the text's authorial sneer having vanished along with its posturing narrator) as Susan Rawlings—craving "a room or a place, anywhere, where she could go and sit, by herself "—takes steps away from her big, beautiful Richmond house in order to begin to reinhabit herself. The room nineteen of the story's title is the seedy Paddington hotel cell Susan hires and visits daily.

That this room of her own should be expropriated by a concerned, proprietary husband sending detectives contributes in overt ways to the text's dénouement as well as the context of its reception by readers. The "easing hours of solitude" are invaded, as the text implores: "Several times she returned to the room, to look for herself there, but instead she found the unnamed spirit of restlessness, a pricking fevered hunger for movement, an irritable self-consciousness that made her brain feel as if it had coloured lights going on and off " inside it. Like her nineteenth-century counterpart, *The Awakening*'s Edna Pontellier, Susan returns a final time to the place of her awakening and—turning on the gas—swims into that ultimate anonymity: death.

As with Edna's self-immolation, Susan's suicide is unassimilable: a negation. "Why did she kill herself?" undergraduate and graduate students alike have exploded, "she should have gone back to work." "Or told her husband she was hurt by his infidelities," they expostulate, using the same pragmatic "intelligence" the story is intent on subverting. Graduate students have tempered their sense of the text's displacement by arguing from the context of received feminism. Both responses amount to a production of text resembling one given in, for example, a 1984 reductive reading—twenty odd years after the story's publication and two decades after the construction of the contemporary Anglo-American feminist critique: "The story clearly implies that without the colossal middle-class apparatus to tie her down, and without a patriarchal system to require that she cheerfully welcome her bondage, her personality would never have been eroded to the point of breakdown and suicide" (Knapp). As pedantic [as] this interpretation seems, it indicates how strenuously the voice of the nominally detached narrator commands and controls, how effectively the pronominal shift from "I" to "one" implicates the reader.

An alternate narrative code, submerged yet vital, calls into question any reading of the text as solely a realistic representation of contemporary women's estate. **"To Room Nineteen"** 's surface design conceals a less accessible narrative code in which the author, Doris Lessing, is exploring spiritual possibilities, mysteries on the other side of the given, the typical, the representatively real. Here the text insists that crises of the spirit are resolvable through meditative modalities, that fluid motility should be associated with libidinal desire. As in Kate Chopin's *The Awakening*, the ending of **"To Room Nineteen"** undercuts its primary text: in both, death is vital, fructifying, caressing. Forces bathe each heroine in solipsistic pleasure, giving truth to Freud's insight in *Beyond the Pleasure Principle* that death is the ultimate object of desire.

Susan Rawlings and her husband plan everything "intelligently," a word which appears in the text fifteen times, although its sense is carried, by my count, some fourteen additional times. Numerically the word allies itself with the cognate term "sensible" while warring with the libidinally evocative "garden," a word appearing sixteen times and whose metaphoric sense is carried through seven scenes in which the protagonist visits the oceanic, heterogeneous, and haunting realm beyond her big, mortgaged, and beautiful white Richmond house. "She went to the very end of the garden, by herself, and looked at the slow-moving brown river; she looked at the river and closed her eyes and breathed slow and deep, taking it into her being, into her veins." In this undergrowth with its "wild sullied river" she begins to prowl, a wild cat, "howling with rage." She is terrorized by an image of her spirit: a demon she imagines invading her, the devil of "reddish complexion and ginger hair" wearing "a reddish hairy jacket, un-

pleasant to the touch." Shortly, she will give this haunting hallucination form. "Well, one day she saw him. She was standing at the bottom of the garden, watching the river ebb past, when she . . . saw this person. . . . He was looking at her, and grinning . . . out of an absent-minded or freakish impulse of spite . . . ." The wild cat who prowls through the thickened garden appears in another libidinal image: the "intelligent" Susan Rawlings standing before a mirror, brushing back near-electric hair, its Medusa energy crackling. Glancing at her own image, she "thought: Yet that's the reflection of a madwoman. . . . Much more to the point if what looked back at me was the gingery green-eyed demon with his dry meagre smile."

Eruptive narrative codes like these recall doubling strategies deployed by nineteenth-century female gothic modes. As the example of Jane Eyre in the red room instructs, women and mirrors are intimately linked. In Lessing the motif of the mirrored mad double registers (and dislodges) competing modes of consciousness as well as competing codes of narration. To shatter the glass is to set free the mirror's enclosed prisoner *and* the realist text's supervised captive: the mystery below fact's surface. Put another way, Susan Rawlings' voyage through the looking glass will take the wayfarer-soul to room nineteen, there to remake interiority by unmaking intelligence. The "dark creative trance" in which the protagonist is submerged by her author is an unsilencing of the irrational, libidinal pulse "intelligence" contrived to mute. Thus as disquieting as is the submerged/emergent text, its last sentence affirms the human spirit in all its heterogeneity: "She was quite content lying there, listening to the faint soft hiss of the gas that poured into the room, into her lungs, into her brain, as she drifted off into the dark river."

In this tale of narratorial making, unmaking, and remaking there are unearthed the powerful workings of desire, the story having traced those stages of release that allow its protagonist to be free at last. Yet it is at the greatest of expenses, this freedom. For authorial homicide has occurred; Susan Rawlings is dead, however gently the text swims round her. The second short story under examination—one sharing with **"To Room Nineteen"** as privileged symbol the room—offers a redeeming rather than promissory note. It represents as well a very different modality of short fiction, hardly a story at all but rather a mediation, a sketch, a sojourn in (rather than voyage to) consciousness—titled, tellingly, **"A Room."**

The title—invoking in feminist terms a now irreversible metaphor for physical, psychological, social, and gendered entrapment—recalls what the story will come to revoke. At the text's inauspicious beginning, an unnamed narrator observes: "When I first came into this flat of four small boxlike rooms, the bedroom was painted pale pink, except for the fireplace wall, which had a fanciful pink-and-blue paper." The opening sentence announces the realist project, its uninflected tone being buttressed by other familiar strategies of realism. Factual detail abounds: for example, information as incidental as the commercial name for a dark purple paint that covers a fireplace's obtrusive bulk, its presence thereby appealing to the readerly wish for stable, predictable fictional worlds.

There is as well the presumed unproblematic matter of narratorial veracity. The narrator's stance as a visual observer and authorial recorder—an eye and an "I"—augments the reader's sense of the room as particular, substantial, real. Made memorable by the recording scrutiny of the narrator are the room's ugly iron fire grate, the grainy lumpy wall beside a bed, blue curtains, plum-colored woodwork, the square solid bronze gas fire that strikes discordant notes. "So the whole wall doesn't work, it fails to come off," the disinterested narrator informs. Discursive commentary continues as the observing "I" annotates the flat's previous inhabitants and describes other occupants of the apartment building. For example, there is the Swedish woman in an identical flat one floor above. "Sometimes, when I sleep in the afternoons, which I do because afternoon sleep is more interesting than night sleep, she takes a nap too. I think of her and of myself lying horizontally above each other, as if we were on two shelves." Recorded are the blended sounds of footsteps, quarrelsome voices and rattling cups that drift from the apartment house through the flat's walls; interrogating the room's stillness, they soon become (like Susan Rawlings' green-eyed double) its spectral tenants.

Here, the realist's scrutiny—its fascination with seeing, reporting, supervising, and controlling significant detail—represents not compliance with convention but a witty narrative ploy. Essentially, the subversive strategy furthers the text's intent to have its readers collude in constructing the credible in order to reinforce a jettisoning of realist/materialistic assumptions. Thus the non-naming of the unnamed narrator in the context of a story characterized by reliance on detail dislodges another realist mainstay. Un-named the narrator is not named. Divesting the narrator of all but the first person pronominal identification implies she has neither proprietary nor proprietory name—from the perspective of property as a species of the material order.

Yet the text also proposes that the "I"/eye narrator is an autobiographical projection of the author, the not unnamed Doris Lessing: author in/of **"A Room"** by way of her performance before readers in the character of a writer. "I always drift off to sleep in the afternoons with the interest due to a long journey into the unknown," records the dream-intent author:

> with the interest due to a long journey into the unknown, and the sleep is thin and extraordinary and takes me into regions hard to describe in a waking state. But one afternoon there was no strange journey, nor was there useful information about my work. The sleep was so different from usual that for some time I thought I was awake.

In the text's voyage through thresholds—another journey through the looking glass—is a crossing over into unfamiliar regions whose "facts" are to be placed beside the constraining certitude of the physical world.

As so often in Lessing's longer fiction, the dream state here in **"A Room"** announces the locus for transpersonal metamorphosis. Brooding on the hideous black iron grate, the writer/narrator experiences herself as a child sitting be-

fore a smoking fire; the walls are now unpainted, the room mean with poverty. It is a time of war, and she is desolate with loneliness, the smoke tearing the back of her throat. Just as evanescently as it has appeared, the dream ("or memory—*whose?*" wonders the writer) recedes. Left is the conviction that the other room exists, "under this room, or beside it, or in it." Frontiers distant from the apparent certitudes of representational scrutiny with which it began, the text settles back into stasis, closing with two questions: "*what?* And why?"

"To hear," not "to see," is the dominant prepositional verb in **"A Room,"** despite the text's seductive use of the realist project. The frequency with which hearing is used on a level of description and act (by my count seventeen times as compared to seven references to sight) suggests the significance of the attentive listener, not the documenting scrutinizer. Privileged is the passive soft receiver, the "soft dark intelligence" so favored as heroic material in Lessing's novel, *The Memoirs of a Survivor*. And if **"A Room"** marks an early critique of the idea of personality as fixed, *Memoirs'* recasting of the shorter fiction represents a conclusive rebuttal of the realist assumptions in favor of impersonal psychic economies. In the longer fiction another unnamed narrator journeys through dissolving walls to rooms; as these merge and separate, the anonymous voyager overlaps with other selves, merging and separating. Like the land visited by **"A Room"**'s narrator, the one entered by *Memoirs'* protagonist hides behind the face of the factual world. Some visited spaces, the benevolent ones, remain empty "impersonal" images of desire while a recurrent "personal" nightmare grows to compelling shape in one overheated, overstuffed Edwardian setting. Entering one room to reshape the past by soothing a miserable child, the narrator instead finds herself experiencing the mother's emotions. The child she finally reaches is not the sad daughter but the oppressive mother, shifted back in time to her own frustrated infancy.

What emerges from the longer fiction is a text that threatens to dismantle itself, so "warring [are its] codes" (Draine). Nevertheless, *Memoirs* (like its germinal story, **"A Room"**) provokes without pomposity. This cannot be said of *Briefing for a Descent into Hell,* the many layered novel whose "collage technique of . . . diary, letter, news report, science fiction speculation, medical dialogue, poetry, stream of consciousness, popular song, interpolated short story and afterward" (Sprague and Tiger) orchestrates bombastically a simple theme, one developed economically in what was the novel's donné, **"The Temptation of Jack Orkney."** The shorter fiction is a singular example of a capacious plot being foreshortened and a steadfast theme—the temptation to get religion—being relentlessly foregrounded. A conventional chronological narrative marks the slow process undergone by the eponymous protagonist following his father's death, a death which disturbs the middle-aged liberal into questioning all his beliefs. The action culminates in Orkney's awareness of the possibility of an invisible world; the landscape he inhabits at the story's end is analogous to the one visited by the unnamed narrator of **"A Room."** Nightly, Orkney enters behind "the face of the sceptical world"; his world of dreams is "another country, lying just behind his daytime one."

Nightly, Orkney voyages through walls and past partitions, and navigates dream-realms as promissory in their libidinal energy as the dark river Susan Rawlings was designated to drift down.

In bringing these three stories to their conclusions, Lessing expands the range of her subversive discourse. Disorderings are not confined to the narrative conventions of the short story. For Lessing also appropriates and reformulates the more massive conventions that have structured Western mythologies for three centuries: the tropes and typologies of realism. Michel Foucault, we recall, suggests that the realistic fiction "forms part of that great system of constraint by which the West compelled the everyday to bring itself into discourse" ["The Life of In Famous Man," *Michel Foucault: Power, Truth, Strategy,* edited by Meagham Morris and Paul Pallon, 1979]. His is a claim that Doris Lessing—with her loathing of labels, her distrust of orthodox Western thinking, her increased impatience with the realist enterprise—might well applaud.

## John Bemrose   (review date 24 August 1992)

SOURCE: "London Calling," in *Maclean's,* Vol. 106, No. 34, August 24, 1992, p. 62.

[*In the following positive review of* The Real Thing, *Bemrose singles out "The Pit" as "the collection's finest story."*]

In 1777, the English writer and wit Samuel Johnson remarked, "When a man is tired of London, he is tired of life." By that standard, British novelist Doris Lessing, 72, has a good deal of vitality left. She first arrived in London in 1949, a young, unpublished novelist from Rhodesia (now Zimbabwe) intent on winning her literary spurs in the imperial capital. More than 40 years and almost 40 books later, she still makes London her home. The city appears in the background of many of her works, including her ground-breaking 1962 novel about the lives of women, *The Golden Notebook*. But only in her latest collection of short stories and sketches, *The Real Thing,* does her beloved adopted home seem like a character in its own right. London "was like a great theatre," she writes in the sketch **"Storms."** "You could watch what went on all day, and sometimes I did. You could sit for hours in a café or on a bench and just watch."

In *The Real Thing,* Lessing's London-watching has unearthed a variety of human types and predicaments of the sort that would surely have delighted Dr. Johnson. Some of the entries are only a few pages long, yet they are remarkable at distilling the essence of people Lessing has observed. In the sketch **"Sparrows,"** the narrator eavesdrops on a middle-aged couple in a restaurant garden. It soon becomes clear that their relationship has grown stale. But when the woman coaxes a timid fledgling sparrow to take the crumbs that she offers, her joy at her success strikes the scales from her husband's eyes. "For the first time since they had sat down there," Lessing writes, "he was outside his selfish prison and really seeing her."

Such pieces hover between journalism and fiction. They appear to be based on real-life incidents, but Lessing is too much the novelist to refrain from interjecting her favorite themes. Her career-long concern with the awkward dance between the sexes dominates **"Her,"** a description of a London party in which a group of male politicians unwittingly exclude and demean a female colleague. As so often happens in Lessing's work, the woman seems more mature and resourceful than the boyish men around her. Lessing does not portray men as well as she does women, but in such stories as **"D.H.S.S."** and **"The Mother of the Child in Question"** she at least lends them a certain besieged dignity.

Besides the shorter observation pieces, *The Real Thing* also contains a handful of short stories in which Lessing's imagination is working at full throttle. The title story concerns two middle-class couples, Sebastian and Angela, and Henry and Jody. The four Londoners, all friends, are spending a weekend together at a country cottage. What complicates matters is that Henry and Angela used to be married to each other. The American Jody, Henry's girlfriend, is deeply troubled by the fond, talkative intimacy between the two former spouses. Indeed, they spend much of the weekend away together, attending to their sick daughter, who is staying at a nearby farm. That leaves Jody and Sebastian alone for hours on end. Inevitably, they fall into a long discussion of the situation, allowing Lessing to offer a fascinating meditation on the nature of maturity and emotional honesty.

The collection's finest story is **"The Pit."** Sarah, a woman who enjoys her life alone, is suddenly confronted by her ex-husband. James had left her years earlier for a beautiful woman named Rose. Now, Rose is having an affair with someone else. Crushed, James has come limping back to ask Sarah if she will have an affair with *him.* Sarah is tempted because James is still attractive, and the pain of his desertion has long since modulated into something more mellow. The tension in the story flows from Sarah's indecisiveness as she reviews her options and remembers her marriage.

One of the great achievements of **"The Pit"** is its portrait of Rose, who never actually appears in the story. Detail by detail, she comes to life in Sarah's perceptive mind, until the profoundly insecure, manipulative and theatrical Rose seems ready to walk off the page.

Like most of Lessing's best fiction, **"The Pit"** is an exploratory work that tests the limits of conscience and behavior. London is not mentioned: indeed, it is the sort of story that could happen almost anywhere. Yet London seems to hover in the background, the matrix of the fertile, unpredictable human mystery that Lessing loves.

## K. Anthony Appiah   (review date 28 June 1993)

SOURCE: "The Art of Sympathy," in *The New Republic,* Vol. 208, No. 26, June 28, 1993, pp. 30-4, 36-7.

[*Appiah is an English-born American critic and educator who has written extensively on philosophy, literature, and African culture. In the following largely positive review of* African Laughter, *he discusses some of the major themes of Lessing's work, namely her depiction of "the moral intricacy of human life."*]

Early in *African Laughter,* Doris Lessing recalls a childhood visit to her brother's colonial school:

> Everything was clean and tidy and there were green English lawns. I felt alien to the place. This was because I was alien to the English middle class, playing out its rituals here, as if on a stage. I knew even then they were anachronistic, absurd and, of course, admirable in their tenacity.

It is the last phrase, the sting in the tail, that alerts you that this is Lessing, not some moralizing theorist. Absurd people, of course, have admirable traits: that is one of the ways in which moral life, even the most passive moral judgment, is intricate. In the face of the glaring injustices of racial domination in Southern Rhodesia, it is a moral achievement to keep such complexities in mind; and to do so requires a clear-eyed attention to the everyday details of human life.

It is unfashionable in the literary academy to discuss such worn-out themes as the moral vision of novelists, the sort of thing that Lionel Trilling did those long years ago; and it is correspondingly de rigueur to expatiate upon their politics, and to complain about them. Since Lessing has often been weighed in a "progressive" political scale—that is, according to her views on racism, communism and feminism—there has been an especially strong pressure to neglect those aspects of her moral imagination that cannot be reduced to politics. And this is a disaster, since distinguishing between morality and politics is especially important with a writer like Lessing, whose moral intuitions so strongly resist implementation as a social program.

Lessing's first and last lesson—a lesson that has been announced by theorists but can only be grasped, it seems, through narrative—is precisely the moral intricacy of human life. She seems to have come out of Africa already aware of this complexity. You might have thought she had learned it from the circumstances of her upbringing, were it not a secret that many with histories like hers have not known.

Her circumstances were extraordinary enough. Though she was born in Iran, in 1919, to British parents, Lessing was raised in Southern Rhodesia. Her father, Alfred Cook Tayler, invalided (like so many) in the First World War, married (like so many) the woman who had nursed him back to health. After his wartime experiences, Tayler "could not face being a bank clerk in England," as Lessing once wrote, and so he took a job with the Imperial Bank of Persia. On leave in England in 1925, he saw a Southern Rhodesian display at one of the empire exhibitions, discovered that he could buy 3,000 acres at 10 shillings an acre and emigrated "on an impulse" with his wife and two children, Doris and her younger brother, Harry.

The land on which they lived had been alienated, like most of Rhodesia, by the colonial government, which had crowded the Africans into what were called "Native Reserves." Her father grazed cattle. In an autobiographical essay, his daughter reports that he

> . . . cultivated about 300 acres of his land; the rest was left unused. He employed between 50 and 100 black men, and their wages were 12s. and 6d. a month, with rations of maize meal, beans and a little meat. The laborers came from the Reserves, Nyasaland [Malawi], Portuguese territory [Mozambique]. They built themselves a mud hut in the "compound." They were given a day to do this. . . . They worked from six in the morning till six at night with an hour off at midday, seven days a week in the busy season. These were the conditions of the whole country: my father was a better, more humane employer than most. But no one can be more humane than an economic framework allows one to be.

The nearest white neighbors were several miles off, and Rhodesian racial etiquette kept the Tayler children from real friendship with black children. Her brother was away at boarding school. So Lessing grew up with books and with the African landscape. Though she was sent to a convent school in Salisbury (now Harare), she was allowed to stop her formal education at 14, staying on in the city to work for a couple of years as a nanny, before returning to the family farm, convinced of her calling as a writer. At home and after school she educated herself, reading "the best—the classics of European and American literature." Two years later, having written and destroyed some "bad novels," she returned to Salisbury to work. Then, on the brink of the Second World War, she married a Rhodesian civil servant, with whom she had two children.

In 1942, in her early 20s, after the failure of her first marriage, she joined the local Communist Party and became, as she says, a "rackety 'revolutionary,' " "interested in the possibilities of black resistance." She had learned, as she grew up, that she did not want to belong to the master race in a society of white masters and black servants. Now the party gave to her conviction a theoretical framework and helped to complete her shapeless education. The party also provided the introduction to Gottfried Lessing, her second husband, a German Communist, whom she married in 1945. In 1949 she left Lessing and made her way to London, bearing his name, their young son and the manuscript of her first novel. "Let us put it this way: I do not think marriage is one of my talents," she told Roy Newquist in the early '60's.

But if marriage was not one of her talents, writing was. The novel in her baggage, *The Grass is Singing* (1950), brought her immediate acclaim. There were seven reprints within five months; reviewers pronounced her the finest new novelist since the war. A year later she published her first short stories in *This Was the Old Chief's Country*. In the next few years she published novels and short stories regularly, mainly set in Africa; and in 1956 she made a return visit to the country of her youth (which she described in *Going Home,* her first travel book). Lessing was not to return to that country for more than a quarter century, though she continued to write about Africa into the late '60s. She was declared a "prohibited immigrant" by the prime minister of Southern Rhodesia, who once sharply told her: "I wasn't going to have you upsetting our natives."

Though Lessing learned that she did not want to live as a white settler, she also discovered that white Rhodesia—

for all its middle-class British snobbisms, its provincialism and tedium and its even more appalling blindness to the black lives that made possible its standard of living—was not without its virtues. This sense for the intricate has made Lessing impatient with politics and parties. The Rhodesian Communist Party, which was the creation of servicemen and various war exiles, was "so pure," she felt, that "if we had been in any other part of the world . . . the beautiful purity of the ideas we were trying to operate couldn't have worked." Faced with the considerably less pure British Communist Party, with its deference to Stalin and its odious political correctness (the term in those days had rather more meaning than it does today), Lessing rebelled, leaving the Party in 1956, and not simply, she has insisted, out of disgust with the Russian invasion of Hungary. Her entrance into the Rhodesian Communist Party reflected the seriousness of her moral engagement with the evils of racial domination, and her departure from the British Communist Party reflected the same moral seriousness.

That Lessing would not stay long with the Party should have been obvious to anyone who had read *The Grass is Singing*. The novel begins with a newspaper report of the death, apparently at the hands of her "houseboy" Moses, of Mary Turner, a white woman on a remote Rhodesian farm. As the book unfolds, we live through the events that have led up to this unlikely murder, following always the life of its victim.

Mary Turner is a strange, sad woman, suffering under the burden of obligations imposed upon her as a white woman by the sad, strange conventions of a colonial settler society. The novel is intensely humane in its attentiveness to the minutest details of the mental life of this central character: her small-mindedness and her ambitions, her silent rage at her uncomprehending husband, her longing for the life of the small town where she had worked as a secretary before her marriage. As her mind goes and her husband becomes more and more distant, she begins a sexual dalliance—its true scope only hinted at, never quite clear—with Moses. And when, near the end, caught in a moment of intimacy with him by a white neighbor, she dismisses this black man disrespectfully, we understand—we know it is not our business to forgive—this betrayal of the only human meaning in the withered landscape of her existence.

Throughout her career Lessing has been able to enter sympathetically into the lives of ordinary, morally fallible people, living in circumstances that make nobility impossible. The capacity of her unloveliest characters to engage the human in each other—even when they have inherited a racism that blinds and separates, even when the physical burdens of old age have made their lives tedious to them— is one of the finest achievements of Lessing's fiction. Nothing could be further in spirit from the mechanics of socialist realism.

The fact that Lessing combines compassion with nuance is important to appreciating *African Laughter,* her ruminations on four visits that she made back to the country of her youth after it finally achieved its independence as Zimbabwe in 1980. Her strictures carry so much weight because they flow from a clear and sympathetic appreciation of the humanity of those whom she observes, and especially because she is able to turn the same beady eye on those she admires, and even, surprisingly often, on herself.

On the first of these visits, for example, in 1982, Lessing found herself talking to the "garden 'boy'—the old word still used, quite unself-consciously"—of a white family with whom she was staying. Once the gardener's employers were out of earshot, he asked her

> . . . if he could come and work for me, he needed to better himself. . . . He said he had seen rich black people on television and in films, and he wanted to be like them. This took me back thirty odd years, to when I used to sell Communist newspapers around a certain "Coloured" (that was the correct word politically then for people of mixed race) suburb in old Salisbury. While I preached informed opposition to white domination, I was being stopped on every street corner by aspiring young men who wanted to go to America where everyone was rich. I used to give them gentle lectures on the need to think of the welfare of All before self-advancement. What a prig. What an idiot. I can see myself, an attractive but above all self-assured young woman . . . with revolution as a cure for everything.

In our mistrustful times it will no doubt occur ungenerously to some that moments such as these are rhetorical ploys, designed to put careless readers off their guard: "See, I can criticize myself! You can have faith in my objectivity. You can rely on my criticisms of others." But this suspicious reading of such passages misses what is, I think, their moral thrust: they are meant to exemplify the balanced assessment of all sides, even one's own. Clearly Lessing believes that such balance is the only way to heal Zimbabwe's racial and ethnic wounds. Lessing, in short, is practicing what she preaches.

Another kind of skeptic will see in Lessing only another ex-lefty, banging on about the moral blindness of those who left the Party later than she did. This suspicion, too, is misplaced. Lessing is able to recognize the decent impulses that lie behind political rhetorics—on the left and the right—and that recognition does not weaken her loathing for oppression. The result is a kind of judicious human accounting, a credit here, a debit there, that is reflected in the episodic character of the book. Just when we have had too much of the bad news—corruption in high places, despair among the poor—Lessing reminds us of the splendid new energies released by the end of Rhodesian apartheid.

At least as important as this moral good sense is the clear-sighted human understanding that makes it possible. One is oneself fixed in the beam of Lessing's penetrating gaze from the first moments of the book. The opening chapter begins:

> Southern Rhodesia was a shield-shaped country in the middle of the map of Southern Africa, and it was bright pink because Cecil Rhodes had said the map of Africa should be painted red from Cape to Cairo, as an outward sign of its happy

allegiance to the British Empire. The hearts of innumerable men and women responded with idealistic fervor to his clarion, because it went without saying that it would be good for Africa, or for anywhere else, to be made British. At this point it might be useful to wonder which of the idealisms that make our hearts beast faster will seem wrongheaded to people a hundred years from now.

At the start of this passage it might seem that we are being asked simply to mock Rhodes's ambitions or to condemn imperialism. But once Lessing has tempted us to this simple response (the irony of "happy allegiance" cheerfully baiting the trap) she deprives us of the confidence of our moral superiority. The British in Rhodesia, she points out soon, did not engage in genocide; they did build hospitals for "natives"; they banned alcohol out of paternalism, not out of spite. "If it is asked, How did these people, no more or less intelligent than ourselves, manage to accommodate so many incompatibles in their minds at the same time, then this belongs to a wider query: How and why do we all do it . . . ?" Indeed, Lessing often suggests that our contemporary openness to these earlier sins of the fathers conceals from us our own new sins, among them the destruction of the natural world.

The book is pervaded with a kind of ecological gloom. When she is speaking on the first of her visits, in 1982, with three black men to whom she has offered a ride in her car, Lessing reflects:

> I wanted to talk about the emptying and thinning of the bush, how the animals had gone, and the birds and the insects, how this meant everything had changed; how myriads of small balances, hundreds in every small patch of bush, necessary for water, soil, foliage, climate, had been disturbed. I had already begun to suspect that these changes were more important than, even, the War, and the overthrow of the whites, the coming of the black government. Now, years later, I am sure of it. But I could not talk like this to these people then, at that time. It would have sounded like an irrelevance: at best, like one of the eccentricities the whites go in for.

This death of the bush is one of her themes, a theme that connects her with her own childhood in Southern Rhodesia and her own memories of what the bush meant to her as a child. She writes of long-ago trips with her family through this landscape she loves; of lying in their encampment, surrounded by an enclosure of cut branches to keep out the leopards, sleeping on a platform of fresh grass under the stars. ("Being in the bush was to be with animals, one of them.") But the disappearance of the bush is more than the subjective loss of childhood, it is also the real end of the dawn chorus that woke the Taylers from those nights of wonder.

This concern for nature is something that binds Lessing to the world of her childhood *and* to the whites whom she visits in the present. Sometimes she suggests, as in some of her short stories, that the blacks, too, some of them, love this land, but she never quite puts her finger on their feelings. She cannot chart their sense of the landscape as she can map out the nature-worship of the strange white settler culture she grew up in.

This reticence about black sentiments is part of a long-standing pattern. In her work of the '50s, when Lessing was writing about Africa, it was almost never from an African point of view. The one exception is instructive. It is the short novel *Hunger,* a piece of socialist realism, which almost all her critics (the predictable exception being the Soviets) agree with Lessing in regarding as a failure. Lessing reports the origins of this story in her ruminations after a gathering of writers in Moscow in 1952, where the British contingent, united in little else, agreed that "writing had to be a product of the individual conscience, or soul." The Russians, of course, did not agree. Then, one hot day, after leaving the rest of the party on a tour of "a building full of presents for Stalin," Lessing sat down by herself and began to ruminate. Were they, the British writers, really right?

> . . . after all, there was Dickens, and such a short time ago, and his characters were all good or bad—unbelievably Good, monstrously Bad, but that didn't stop him from being a great writer. Well, there I was, with my years in Southern Africa behind me, a society as startlingly unjust as Dickens's England. Why, then, could I not write a story of simple good and bad, with clear-cut choices, set in Africa? . . .
>
> I tried, but it failed. It wasn't true. Sometimes one writes things that don't come off, and feels more affectionate towards them than towards those that worked.

One wonders, at first, if it is in reaction to this single conspicuous failure that Lessing settled on the most striking strategy of *African Laughter*: namely, its silence about the interior lives of black Zimbabweans.

This restraint sometimes disappoints. One longs for speculation about what some of the characters she meets are "really thinking." And yet, in the end, her reticence is another expression of her good sense. I think, by contrast, of Naipaul, with his confident epistemology, his perpetual certainty that he has penetrated the true meaning of the "native," even in lands he barely knows. And immediately I prefer Lessing, who, even in this land where she grew up, is willing (and then, after so many years' absence, only carefully) to speak just for the part of it she really knows.

That these two writers are, in this way, so different, is a reflection of the depths to which the culture that we share with them—this culture of the West—is committed to an epistemology of the skin. Because Naipaul is not white, he has been encouraged to believe that he knows where he is going in the nonwhite world; and he must distance himself from that world, or risk being identified with its failings. Because she is white, Lessing has been brought up to an equal certainty that she does not know her way among the black and the brown; and she can be confident that whatever these people do, and despite her upbringing among them, she will never be held responsible for their doings.

In truth, color has very little to do with it; but the reticence of color that seems to underlie Lessing's position leads to the right judgment. She does not know much of how life looks to the peasants and workers of Zimbabwe; and she knows, too, that the reason is not their color but their experience. Lessing shows us only the exterior of the black Zimbabweans, but still we are in her debt for what that view teaches us about what is happening in Zimbabwe.

And we owe Lessing an even more substantial debt for her interior portrait of the white community in its transition out of the trauma of losing the war. On the first of her visits, soon after the war's end, Lessing goes to visit her brother Harry, a staunch supporter of white minority rule who fought in the war in the bush. On their first evening together, they begin by avoiding the subject that divides them: his sister's "funny ideas" about black equality. An angry exchange almost ensues when Harry says, "I suppose you do still have those funny ideas about—well, about everything," and Lessing replies:

> "You could say that I have my funny ideas. You could say they've turned out not to be so funny in the end."
>
> At this he goes red, he is really angry. This is the moment when we could explode into argument. I say hastily, "Today, when I came past Marandellas, I remembered how we used to camp out there, near the school."
>
> He smiles, and nods, meaning, Yes, you're right, let's not . . .

But as he is going off to bed, Harry stands in the doorway, a glass of brandy in his hand.

> He couldn't bear to put off what had been at the back of his mind while we talked, just as it had at mine, and now he delivered a monologue, in a hot, angry, frustrated bitter voice, and it was exactly the same as the one I had listened to only last night, on the plane, from the race-horse breeder.
>
> "Your precious Africans . . ."

This diatribe becomes so familiar that Lessing quietly dubs it "The Monologue." In its canonical form, The Monologue refers not to "Your precious Africans" but to "The Affs"; dilates upon the absurdity of the name of Canaan Banana, the first president of Zimbabwe; observes that "they" don't know how to make anything—television, democracy, anything—work; talks of leaving for "The Republic" of South Africa (this is before the release of Mandela); and ends, as Harry does, with: "They're inferior to us, and that's all there is to it."

In response to problems in his business—lost white customers, newly empowered black workers—Harry has decided to do what many white Rhodesians did both before and after independence: he is going to "Take the Gap." ("White people," Lessing explains, "who left Southern Rhodesia, and then Zimbabwe, for The Republic, 'Took the Gap.'" She does not know where the phrase came from.) Lessing says that "looked at impersonally, and I certainly had been forced to do that, my brother was interesting from a cultural point of view." But it is also clear

that, in 1982, his psyche was, like many white Rhodesian psyches, deeply wounded.

The historical processes that led to Zimbabwean independence—and which therefore allowed her to return—included an extremely bloody civil war in which the government's black armies, led by whites, fought against the freedom fighters of Robert Mugabe's ZANU and Joshua Nkomo's ZAPU. It is unsurprising, therefore, that the whites who lost so recently were, in 1982, still resentful and unhappy. What is slightly more surprising is that the blacks, whose frank oppression was the aim of the war, and who lost friends and families to its brutality, seem largely to have been released by victory from the necessity of resentment.

The recognition of how damaging the war has been to the white psyche comes upon Lessing suddenly. She is talking to her brother about his conversion to a form of fundamentalism preached by his son, a young man who fought during the war against the freedom fighters (or "terrs," short for terrorists, as the whites tend to call them in their abbreviating patois). "Suddenly I understood something: . . . What my brother and my father had in common was not genes: at least, genes were not why both were slow, hesitant, cautious, dream-logged men who seemed always to be listening to some fateful voice only they could hear: they were both men hurt by war." The war in the bush was for Harry what the First World War had been for his father.

Harry, like Doris, mourns the loss of the bush, the death of the old ecology. As he talks of Taking the Gap, he tells his sister that "at least" he "won't have to watch" the bush "being destroyed here." The genuine love for the bush—and for farming with the land, not against it—is clearly something that Lessing understands very well, even if she is not "the right kind of Rhodie." She records, again and again, the conversations of white people truly in love with the land:

> If The Monologue in its various forms was boring, and you wished only to be somewhere else as it started up again—again, again—when these people talked about farming techniques, it was a very different thing. These reformed pirates and landgrabbers know about inventions and discoveries from every part of the world. They experiment, they innovate, they wonder if tree-planting in Scotland or the thousands-of-years-old tricks used to wring water from deserts being used by Israel could be applied to Zimbabwe. They discuss wind power, solar power, water-screws from the Middle East and Egypt, new ways of building dams, the introduction of drought-resistant plants from semi-deserts, the control of pests by other pests or helpful plants, the farming of eland instead of cattle.

Indeed, Lessing's first rebuke to the new African government is that, in spreading rumors, during the war, that "making contour ridges to stop erosion" and "compulsory dipping of cattle" were sinister plots by whites "to undo the blacks," Mugabe, and his "Comrades in the bush," said "things that were less than intelligent." In taking up, for herself, this theme, Lessing is explicitly borrowing an element of The Monologue.

> . . . I sat in cars, being driven through areas crowded with every kind of shack, hut, shanty, each surrounded by straggling mealies and a few pumpkins. The earth was eroding into gullies, the trees were being cut for fuel. Who drove me? Explosive, splenetic whites.
>
> "Just look at that, look at it, there won't be any soil left . . ."

Lessing is willing to be seen agreeing with these splenetic bigots because she is convinced that, about this, they are right. Complexity rules.

Lessing second trip since independence was six years later, in 1988. Much had changed. For a start, the two black parties in the Zimbabwean parliament had amalgamated. At the same time, Lessing says, political corruption had spread everywhere. She quotes a U.N. official: "It is not exactly unknown for the victorious side in a civil war to line their pockets, but Zimbabwe is unusual in creating a boss class in less than ten years and to the accompaniment of Marxist rhetoric." You can tell this is Lessing, however, because the next paragraph goes on: "But reading newspapers from Zimbabwe, listening to travelers' tales, what came across was not the flat dreary hopelessness of Zambia, the misery of Mozambique, but vitality, exuberance, optimism, enjoyment."

In the 1980s Zimbabwe did create a class of bosses—or "Chefs," as they were called in contrast to the "Povos," or the poor (a word from the Portuguese picked up by the guerrillas when they were hiding out in Mozambique during the civil war). But in those first few years after independence, the Marxist rhetoric went with a real sense of nationalist excitement. As Lessing tells it, this feeling was shared by many, black and white.

On the verandas, where a few years earlier she had listened to the "explosive, splenetic whites," she now listens to a group of Zimbabweans (black or white, she does not say), some of them supporters, during the bush war, of Mugabe, some of Nkomo, some of Bishop Muzorewa. "Every conversation at once turns to the Unity Accord, between ZAPU and ZANU, Matabeleland and Mashonaland, Mugabe and Nkomo, the Accord which has transformed the atmosphere, everyone optimistic, everyone saying, 'At last Zimbabwe is one country.' " These people talk of Mugabe with "idealism, of a kind frightening to people"—like Lessing—"who remember similar talk about despotic leaders." They ask, "Why doesn't President Mugabe stop the corruption?" They say, "Mugabe says . . ." and tell Mugabe stories. "I swear this isn't far off being in love."

Because this is like love, they will not listen to Lessing when she points out that eight years is not long after a destructive war; that corruption is to be found everywhere. The particular form this love took in Zimbabwe was "the naivest, most untutored enthusiasm for communism. The newspapers printed nothing critical of Communist countries. The Gorbachev revolution was hardly mentioned."

In 1971, long before Zimbabwean independence, Lessing had written in *Briefing for a Descent into Hell*: "I had an old thought . . . that no matter what changes of government or what names were given to a nation's system of organization, there was always the same flavor or reality that remained in that place." Now she notices the continuities between the old Rhodesia and the new Zimbabwe, and the same Herodotean environmentalism suggests itself:

> Sometimes one is tempted to believe that the mental attitudes of a country have something to do with its sun and soil. Old Southern Rhodesia was the same, complacently indifferent to the outside world. Leaving it was like leaving a stunned or a drugged country. The only comparable places are in certain midwestern states in America, where curiosity about the world ends at, let's say, the borders of Iowa or Nebraska. A university audience will hardly know where Afghanistan is—or Sri Lanka, or Pakistan. In California, sun-drugged youngsters will stare at the mention of Gorbachev.
>
> Similarly, Zimbabwe. You may spend an evening with a professor of history, or of literature, whose attitudes toward the Soviet Union or China are identical with those of thirty years ago.

This strange blindness—rooted in the soil of Rhodesia-Zimbabwe—produces from Lessing her own Monologue. She "grew up when 'everyone' was a Communist"; she can recognize, as a result, in the Communist politicos the "scarcely concealed glitter of mendacity, the pride at cleverness that knows how to outwit opponents with election rigging, or the fixing of statistics, character assassinations, the whole 'bag of tricks.' "

In the records of Lessing's later trips, in 1989 and 1992, we see the decline of Zimbabwe. The enthusiasm of the mid-'80s is eaten away by corruption and economic decline. By the end even she is finding it hard to keep a balanced view. "During a game of Epitaphs, it was decided there was only one possible epitaph for Robert Mugabe: 'A good man fallen among thieves.' " Perhaps Lessing is right. I have not been to Zimbabwe since the mid-'80s. Then I saw what she saw: the excitement of a bustling new nationalism. It seems to me that I still hear some of that excitement from Zimbabwe. Things may not have been going well, but this is still a country that believes, in its new multiracial incarnation as in its old racialist one, in its own election. Robert Mugabe and the Chefs may have settled into the depressing rituals of a one-party state; cynicism may have seeped into more of the increasingly impoverished crevices of Zimbabwean life: but here and there remain these strange—perhaps even dangerous—pockets of faith.

Because she has so little taste for politics, I do not quite trust Lessing's political judgment. Indeed, it is her overwhelming hostility to politics that accounts for many of the moments when her touch seems not quite certain. "So bullied are we all by ideologues," Lessing complains at one point, "it is hard to say the Africans have anything whites do not, or that we have anything they do not, but the fact is, up and down Africa, as travelers have always averred, they enjoy themselves." The trouble with this notion (which provides her book's title) is not that it is politically incorrect, but that it is sentimental and fatuous. (They have, after all, been known to enjoy themselves "up and down" Europe, too.) Similarly, many of Lessing's complaints about Zimbabwean political rhetoric seem utterly oblivious to the task of politics: to the problems of building national solidarity in the fragile landscape left by civil war.

What we learn from this book, then, is not so much the political history of Zimbabwe in its first dozen years, but the psychic history of Southern Rhodesia, the inner history of the white settlers and what has become of them: the best of this book is the white man's story. And none the worse for that. But there is a different story to be told; and the people who tell it will be writers like Tsitsi Dangarembga, author of *Nervous Conditions,* as fine a novel as the subcontinent has produced in recent years, a novel for which Lessing herself declares her admiration. Dangarembga began life in a peasant family; and one need hardly add that she is black. There is no question that she could tell the story of black Zimbabwe from the inside. She has already begun to do so.

In 1982 at the Harare show—the big trade fair and, in the past, like the Salisbury Show, a great event for white society—Harry meets an elderly white woman who has been to visit South Africa. "I've been in The Republic to have a look. But I'm sticking it out here. They're a nice lot compared with there. You can always have a good laugh with our Affs." This, Lessing's book suggests, is what most white Zimbabweans were like back then, when they were feeling well-disposed toward their black fellow citizens: condescending, bluff, complaining. Not a pretty picture. But on their verandas, with their dogs and their children and their immense hospitality toward each other, they have their attractions—if, that is, you can forget, for a moment, about the black men and women who serve their vast meals and work in the landscape beyond the lawn. Anachronistic and absurd, to be sure; but also, in their sense of community, admirable.

### Harriet Ritvo    (review date 13 January 1994)

SOURCE: "A Dog's Life," in *The New York Review of Books,* Vol. XLI, Nos. 1-2, January 13, 1994, pp. 3-4, 6.

[*Ritvo is an American critic and educator whose works include* The Animal Estate: The English and Other Creatures in the Victorian Age *(1987). In the following excerpt from a review in which she also discusses the books* The Hidden Life of Dogs *(1994) by Elizabeth Marshall Thomas and* Cats: Ancient and Modern *(1993) by Juliet Clutton-Brock, she examines the revised version of* Particularly Cats . . . and Rufus, *arguing that Lessing implicitly criticizes "many of those who study animal behavior [and] automatically treat anthropomorphism as a weakness that distinguishes the soft-headed and the simple-minded among humans."*]

Although they may not always be aware of it, pet animals are caught between worlds—members of the family, in an emotional sense, but only in very rare cases having any of the responsibilities or rights of their human companions. However comfortable, or even privileged, their lives may seem, they are always vulnerable—not only to the caprice of their owners, but, if they are allowed to spend part of their time at liberty out of doors, to the random cruelty, spite, and greed of other people. If sold or abandoned, they may find relations with humankind abruptly altered, so that they end their days in a laboratory or a cage in a pound, not on a sofa. And their status is often equivocal. An accountant once advised me (incorrectly, as it turned out) that although the costs of moving books, furniture, and close relatives were tax deductible, the cost of moving cats was not.

Conversely, if pet cats and dogs are not quite human, they are not quite animals either. They have lost their wildness, and the reciprocal intensity of their relationships with people distinguishes them from most farmyard beasts. Of course some pets turn out to be capable of independent lives if their human support system disappears, and both cats and dogs can still interbreed with their nearest wild relatives. But many thousands of years of adaptation to the exigencies and opportunities of human companionship have produced psychological alterations perhaps as profound, if not as striking, as the physical differences between the chihuahua and the wolf.

Few people would bar a labrador retriever or a siamese cat from their homes, at least on grounds of temperamental unsuitability; and even fewer would admit a wolf or a European wild cat to similar intimacy. But this obvious reaction begs several more difficult questions. Domestic cats and dogs are complicated organisms, and their actions are far from merely instinctive or automatic. What qualities of temperament or personality account for their relatively accommodating dispositions? What explains the reciprocity of the relationships that many people enjoy with their cats and dogs? Has their protracted and intense experience of domestication made pets more intelligent and adaptive than their wild relatives, or less so? Do they have minds, and, if so, what is on them? . . .

Like most pet owners, Doris Lessing shares [Elizabeth Marshall] Thomas's conviction of mutual understanding and reciprocal communication taking place between humans and their animals [see Thomas's *The Hidden Life of Dogs,* 1994]. In ***Particularly Cats . . . and Rufus*** (reissued, after a quarter of a century, with the addition of one chapter and many fine illustrations by James McMullan) this conviction constantly informs [Lessing's] moving, sympathetic, and shrewdly observed descriptions of her life with cats. Thus she says of one animal she nursed through an unpleasant illness: "No, of course cats are not human; humans are not cats; but all the same, I couldn't believe that such a fastidious little beast as black cat was not suffering from the knowledge of how dirty and smelly she was." And she describes the way that another cat accepted her explanation for inadvertently threatening him, after he had let her know, by fleeing, that he feared raised sticks: "I picked him up, brought him back, showed him the harmless broom handle, apologised, petted him. He understood it was a mistake."

Lessing's experience with domestic cats has been unusually broad. Before she moved to Londoner, she had lived on a Rhodesian farm where the family's many cats had to deal with the special dangers and opportunities of nearby wilderness, as well as the ordinary ambiguities of agricultural life—whether one was a barn cat or a house cat, for example. Yet despite the alarming presence of snakes and eagles and other exotic predators, the greatest threat to these rural African cats, as to the housecats of Europe and North America, was posed by human beings. Lessing makes this point by means of a very sobering anecdote. Controlling the numbers of various animals, domestic and wild, was the responsibility of Lessing's mother, and she routinely drowned superfluous kittens. But after years of slaughter, she wearied of these duties and refused to perform them, ultimately leaving Lessing and her father alone with an exploding feline population. In what Lessing describes as "the holocaust of cats," they shot as many as they could find.

Despite this strong language and the quietly conveyed horror of the experience, Lessing claims that she did not grieve for the dead animals. An earlier trauma—abandoning a cherished kitten when her family had moved from Persia to southern Africa—had forced her to harden her heart against the emotional claims of cats. Thus she begins a memoir of typically urban experiences with pampered pets, thoroughly integrated into a human household, by recalling the poignant paradox that underlies all human relationships with cats and dogs. As much as their similarity to us may be acknowledged by the intimacy with which they share family life, the consideration accorded their wishes and demands, and the time and money devoted to their maintenance, their difference is constantly made clear. Although particular animals may be valued, even extravagantly, cat and dog life is cheap. Even the strongest bonds between human and pet can be violated with ease, and for reasons that would, in an exclusively human setting, be considered trivial or even criminal.

Lessing displays this paradox in her own sensibility and experience. Capable as a teen-ager of shooting cats without flinching and as an adult of killing excess kittens (she does not say how), she participates in the lives of her pets with deep empathy, shares vicariously in their triumphs and disappointments, tries to cure their illnesses, and mourns their aging and death. She exercises her controlling influence gingerly, trying to balance their needs and desires with her own. She is, for example, particularly uneasy about depriving her cats of their sexuality, because she feels that with it they lose some of their looks and their personality. Thus she describes the transformation in a favorite cat that had been spayed. "Her confidence had been struck. The tyrannical beauty of the household had vanished. . . . A strident note entered her character. . . . In short, she had turned into a spinster cat. It is a dreadful thing we do to these beasts. But I suppose we have to do it." And she continues to do it when she feels she has to.

Although *Particularly Cats* is hedged around by the tragedies of feline existence, it is memorable as an account of the depth and the pleasures of the relationship between humans and cats, in which Lessing describes a series of feline companions, each distinct, each admired, and each beloved. Her account is intensely personal and particular. She makes no claims to objectivity or to any authority besides that of the eyewitness. She portrays herself simply as a committed cat lover, and even offers occasional, slightly uncomfortable, specimens of the language in which she addresses her pets: for example, "beee*ooo*tiful, de*lici*ous puss." Nevertheless, Lessing presents as powerful an argument in her way as Thomas does in hers, and to much the same effect. For both a degree of identification with animal feelings—anthropomorphism—offers direct insight into the minds and characters of domestic animals, an enlightenment not available by any other means. And both therefore raise the question—Thomas explicitly and Lessing implicitly—of why many of those who study animal behavior should automatically treat anthropomorphism as a weakness that distinguishes the soft-headed and the simple-minded among humans. Perhaps the people who minimize the possibility of communication and understanding between humans and other animals are the ones who should have to defend their assumptions.

**Lisa Tyler    (essay date Spring 1994)**

SOURCE: "Our Mothers' Gardens: Doris Lessing's 'Among the Roses,' " in *Studies in Short Fiction,* Vol. 31, No. 2, Spring, 1994, pp. 163-73.

[*In the following essay, Tyler examines Lessing's short story "Among the Roses" from a feminist perspective, elucidating its mother-daughter theme in relation to the ancient Greek myth of Demeter and Persephone.*]

Doris Lessing has long demonstrated in her work a love-hate relationship with women's magazines, which she seems to regard as contemporary equivalents of conduct books: repressive, didactic works that stress conformity to tired gender roles and celebrate frivolity at the expense of thought. Ella, the fictional figure that Anna creates in *The Golden Notebook,* works for *Home and Hearth;* its parodically conventional name perhaps suggests a certain disdain on Anna's part, and quite possibly Lessing's. Lessing is more openly scornful in *Play with a Tiger*. When Harry taunts Tom with the prospect that his new job will entail "administering to the spiritual needs of the women of the nation through the 'Ladies Own' [sic]," Tom responds, "I'm only going to be on the business side. I won't be responsible for the rubbish they—" and "stops, annoyed with himself. Harry and Mary laugh at him." Clearly, women's magazines epitomize the establishment, and writing for them amounts to selling out.

Lessing modifies her stance slightly in *The Diaries of Jane Somers,* in which Janna edits a women's magazine named *Lilith;* here, Lessing recognizes the work that goes into such publications, although not exactly endorsing their contents. Nonetheless, the publication of a Lessing short story [**"Among the Roses"**] in the April 1989 issue of *Ladies' Home Journal* came as something of a surprise. Given the story's content, however, its publication there is not altogether inappropriate. [In a footnote, Tyler adds: "'**Among the Roses'** has since been published in *The Real Thing,* a collection of Lessing's sketches and short stories."]

As the magazine puts it, in **"Among the Roses,"** "The renowned British writer examines the most complicated relationship of all: the one between a mother and her daughter." [In a footnote, Tyler adds: "In taking my title from Alice Walker's essay, 'In Search of Our Mothers' Gardens,' I am perhaps taking a dubious liberty. The myth of Demeter and Persephone may be decidedly more problematic for black women writers, for whom mother-daughter repetition may be a decidedly less desirable goal. African-American mothers are more likely to face poverty, exploitation, discrimination, and oppression, experiences that they would prefer that their daughters not have to face. In Toni Morrison's novel *Beloved,* for example, the mother kills her daughter precisely to save her from repeating her mother's life—in this case, a life of slavery. For a less extreme example, see Walker's essay, in which she laments that her mother's artistry was 'muzzled'—a fate Walker herself has resisted, not repeated."] In the story, Myra, the mother, visits a rose garden in Regent's Park and unexpectedly encounters her daughter, Shirley, whom she has not seen since they quarreled in Myra's garden three years earlier. Shirley had earlier made clear her disdain for her mother's hobby: "Shirley not only hated plants and gardens, but the country as well. . . . [S]he thought people who gardened were stupid and boring. Yet here she was." Spotting her daughter, Myra thinks to herself, "What was she doing here? The last place! Flower gardens were not her style at all, let alone being by herself. Shirley was never alone, she hated it." Myra watches her daughter take a cutting from one of the roses on display and marvels, "Shirley into gardening! Was it likely?" Myra only gradually realizes why Shirley is there at all: "Suddenly it occurred to [Myra]: Perhaps she came here hoping to run into me? She knows I come here a lot." Myra's suspicions are confirmed when she moves away, only to hear Shirley's "noisy feet running after her."

Every event in the story takes place in the context of one garden or another. The imagery of roses, birds, and fountains suggests traditional Marian imagery, and Myra's name is an anagram of Mary; the garden is at one point identified as "Queen Mary's Rose Garden," in reference, of course, to the former Queen of England, but perhaps suggesting the Queen of Heaven as well. The ubiquity of gardens in the work further suggests the idyllic meadow of flowers from which the young Kore was abducted in the ancient Greek myth of Demeter and Persephone, and the rebirth of vegetation when mythological mother and daughter were reunited in the *Homeric Hymn to Demeter,* the oldest known version of the myth. In the myth, Persephone or Kore is abducted by Hades and taken to the underworld. Her mother, Demeter, seeks her in vain; grieved by her loss of her daughter, Demeter, goddess of vegetation, refuses to let seeds sprout or plants grow and thus causes a famine on earth. Zeus orders that Persephone be returned to her mother, but because she had eaten a pomegranate seed in the underworld, she must return to the underworld for a part of each year. When mother and daughter are reunited, Demeter restores fruitfulness to the planet (Athanassakis 1-15).

Like Persephone, Shirley, too, suffers during her exile to the underworld—in this case, marriage to a physically abusive man who roughly parallels Hades. Myra notes that Shirley looks "discontent," "sad," "alone and lone-ly." Shirley later, uncharacteristically, tells her mother, "I'd just like to see you, I've been missing you, believe it or not." The separation has hurt Myra as well. When she first spots her daughter, "Myra at once felt a much too familiar anguish, which she *chose to ascribe* to the tactlessness that permitted that dress on that body" (emphasis added). She is later more honest with herself: "Soon Shirley came in, and Myra's heart hurt at the sight of that face. . . ." Clearly their separation has grieved them both.

If they need each other so desperately, why, then, have they spent three years avoiding each other? Shirley ostensibly broke off the relationship over her mother's nosiness. Myra had gone over to Shirley's house on a visit: "No answer from the front door, so she went to the back and there, through the window of the kitchen, saw Shirley having it off with some man certainly not her husband." Not surprisingly, a quarrel follows this inverted primal scene. As Shirley then indicates, it's not her mother's "spying" that bothers her, but the prospect of her mother's life: "If she, Shirley, thought she was going to end up like her mother, then . . . It went on and on . . ." (first ellipses Lessing's). Shirley doesn't want to "end up like her mother," to *be* like her mother, to *become* her mother.

Timid and conventional, Myra abhors conflict and much prefers the peace of rose gardens to the *sturm und drang* of human relationship. In her passage through the gardens, she considers that what she most enjoys is her sense of control and choice: "There was no greater pleasure than this, wandering through roses and deciding, I'll have you . . . no, you . . . no, perhaps. . . ." In her role as a mother, she lacks such control and choice, and clearly this lack disturbs her. Two years earlier, she had chosen a rose called "Just Joey"; "joey" is a slang term used to refer to a young animal or child (*OED*). "This charmer had done well," Myra recalls, not unlike her elder daughter, Lynda. As this year's choice, she prefers a rose called "L'Oreal Trophy" to the one Shirley chooses, "Troika": "Myra was not going to buy that, it lacked subtlety, did not have that unearthly shimmer to it." Unfortunately, Myra cannot so easily reject her daughter, who is also, in her opinion, "bold, highly colored" and lacking in subtlety.

What seems to disturb Myra most about her problem child is Shirley's physicality: "The dress was too tight and emphasized a body that managed to be thin and lumpy at the same time, because of big buttocks and prominent shoulders." During the confrontation that results in their three-year separation, ". . . Myra stood listening to Shirley standing there with her hands on her round hips, her big knees showing under a short ugly dress, her face scarlet with rage—and thought how common she looked." The version of the story published in *The Real Thing* offers an even harsher statement from Myra: "[She] thought she looked like the common little bitch she was." Myra later observes Shirley, "her big shoulders hunched forward, her shining black hair making licks down her red cheeks, her short gaudy skirt showing big knees" and paradoxically notes immediately following this extraordinarily uncharitable description, "This ugly woman was attractive to men, always had been, even as a small girl. Men were looking at her now." Myra's description of Shirley is obviously distorted by Myra's own biases. She is, perhaps, a little jealous of (and even threatened by) her daughter's strength and physical attractiveness, qualities she herself lacks. She is especially uncomfortable with Shirley's sexuality, perhaps because she has so thoroughly repressed her own. Ironically, this daughter is more "earthy" than Demeter.

Like Shirley, Myra is dismayed by the differences between herself and her daughter. Greatly disturbed by their quarrel, "Myra had not bothered to get in touch after that. The truth was, she was glad of the excuse not to see her." She prefers the more congenial Lynda, whom she thinks of as "her other (her real!) daughter" to the troublesome Shirley:

> Lynda, the elder daughter . . . now lived the same kind of life her mother did, with two children, a boy and a girl. When the two women were together, Myra and Lynda—ample, slow, calm-eyed—people knew at once they were mother and daughter, but no one had ever at once thought Shirley was Myra's daughter or Lynda's sister. Where had Shirley come from?

Myra apparently sees Shirley as a kind of changeling, a daughter so foreign to herself that any relationship is certain to be complex at best. Yet ironically, the two are more alike than they are different.

For example, Shirley pauses before "a rose Myra herself rather fancied," and Myra thinks to herself, "By this time next year the plant would be in Myra's garden. And in Shirley's?" Similarly, Myra is described as "adjusting her pace to her daughter's."

Later, in a less peaceful moment, Shirley shrieks that her mother "always put up with everything" and angrily demands to know why her mother has never stood up to "Dad"—yet paradoxically, she herself admits of her former husband, "He beat me, Mum!," and Myra detects a tone of admiration in Shirley's voice. As Adrienne Rich writes:

> Many daughters live in rage at their mothers for having accepted, too readily and passively, "whatever comes." A mother's victimization does not merely humiliate her, it mutilates the daughter who watches her for clues as to what it means to be a woman. (*Of Woman Born: Motherhood as Experience and Institution,* 1986)

Rich later goes on to point out that "a daughter can feel rage at her mother's powerlessness or lack of struggle—because of her intense identification and because in order to fight for herself she needs first to have been both loved and fought for." Thus even Shirley's anger grows from her sense of unity with her mother.

Moreover, throughout the story, both Myra and Shirley consciously make reciprocal gestures of identification with each other: Shirley begins by taking up her mother's hobby of gardening; Myra responds by inviting Shirley to see her roses. Myra mentions that Dad is "off fishing this weekend," and Shirley in turn confides that the man she

lives with "goes on nature rambles . . . every bloody weekend." Myra notes the similarity of their situations: "'Then I'll be a fishing widow and you'll be a nature-ramble widow,' dared Myra, smiling—as she knew—with nervousness."

It is this final gesture of identification that very nearly sets Shirley off once again. These tentative gestures of identification further echo the Demeter-Kore myth, in which the mother and daughter are doubles for each other [see C. Kerenyi, *Eleusis: Archetypal Image of Mother and Daughter,* translated by Ralph Manheim, 1977]. The myth centers on "the achievement of a successful identification with the mother," which works in the myth as a "form of female solidarity . . . whose basis is the special and particular comfort, affection, and general gratification which women are able to offer one another." She emphasizes that this mother-daughter bond, which is central to the myth, is "a female solidarity which is discovered in the context of a patriarchal world."

The *Homeric Hymn* and Lessing's short story resemble each other structurally, as well as thematically. Male family members are conspicuous by their absence; the reader knows next to nothing of Myra's husband, and Shirley's husband and lovers are only slightly more present. Christine Downing's remark about the hymn pertains equally well to Lessing's story: "Clearly this representation of a primal dyad between mother and daughter, not intruded upon by a father or siblings, could fairly be called 'a family romance.'" Moreover, in both the *Homeric Hymn to Demeter* and Lessing's short story, "the attempt to re-establish the mother child unity is related . . . from the mother's point of view" [Marilyn Arthur, "Politics and Pomegranates: An Interpretation of the Homeric Hymn to Demeter," *Arethusa* 10 (1977)].

At least in part the breach between mother and daughter suggests a division between two not-quite-reconcilable worlds—one of female community and another of heterosexuality. When Shirley initially rejects her mother's gardening as a hobby, "She claimed she loathed Nature except (wink, wink) for a little of what you fancy"—thus making explicit this choice between two alternatives. It is, after all, her mother's (literal) glimpse of her active sexuality that causes the breach between them in the first place. Others have noted such divided allegiances in Lessing's *oeuvre,* most notably, perhaps, in *The Marriages Between Zones Three, Four, and Five,* the second volume in her space fiction series. [In a footnote, Tyler adds: "See for example Kaplan:

> The avatar of this triangle may be Doris Lessing herself, the Outsider, Everywoman on the veld, with the wise, omnipotent, unattainable, remote British Empire on one side, and the warm, human, emotional, impoverished, culturally inferior (in the eyes of white settlers), ignorant, black population on the other. Or perhaps the paradigm is even more personal: Doris Lessing torn between the remote, aloof father and the emotional, irrational, less admirable mother of the *Children of Violence* novels." [Carey Kaplan, "Britain's Imperialist Past in Doris Lessing's Futurist Fiction," *Doris Lessing: The Al-*

*chemy of Survival,* edited by Carey Kaplan and Ellen Cronan Rose, 1988]

This pattern, which Marianne Hirsch describes as one of "oscillation" [*The Mother/Daughter Plot: Narrative, Psychoanalysis, Feminism,* 1989], can be life-affirming: " . . . the life cycle itself arises from alternation between the world of women and that of men" [Carol Gilligan, *In a Different Voice: Psychological Theory and Women's Development,* 1982]. Lessing affirms this pattern in **Marriages,** in which only the marriage of a man and a woman who come from alien worlds can restore fruitfulness to both their planets.

Certainly, as a number of her critics have noted, Lessing favors dialectic both as a mode of thought and as a narrative strategy. She implies in **"Among the Roses"** that this relationship may be a dialectical one, that mother and daughter will once again quarrel—and once again return to each other, that they will endlessly repeat the cycle. As in the myth, "Even in their reunion there is still a portion of bitterness . . . The mother never quite succeeds in getting her daughter back again" [C. Kerenyi, "Kore," *Essays on a Science of Mythology,* C. G. Jung and Kerenyi, translated by R. E. C. Hull, 1969]. Before Shirley approaches her, "Myra decided for the hundredth time she didn't want any more of Shirley." Later, Shirley, perhaps a little frightened when her mother uses the word "widow" to refer to them both, very nearly explodes in a fit of temper: "She stopped, evidently remembering that she had just made up with her mother and did not want to quarrel again. At least, not yet." Even the story's final sentence suggests repetition; Myra sighs: "But she changed the sigh into a cough, for fear it would set Shirley off again." As Marianne Hirsch writes of the myth, "Loss is presented as inevitable, part of the natural sequence of growth, but, since time is cyclical, mother-daughter reunion forms a natural part of the cycle."

Lessing's story, then, emphasizes cycle as well as dialectic. Myra apparently returns to the rose garden annually, and her route is a "circuit" that brings her back "to where she had started." She and her daughter repeatedly meet in rose gardens, and a rose garden will be the site of their next meeting.

Adrienne Rich has publicly criticized Lessing for what she calls "a real failure to envisage . . . any kind of really powerful central bonding of women, even though individual women get together in her novels and go through intense things together" ["An Interview with Adrienne Rich," by Elly Bulkin, *Conditions,* 60 (April 1977)]. But Lessing seems, in this story at least, to be showing women attempting to create such a bond, although admittedly with great difficulty and some reluctance. Shirley's anger at her mother is extreme, out of proportion. Her response perhaps suggests that there is something fishy about her father's fishing trip; marriages in Lessing's fiction are rarely portrayed positively, and she generally implies that extramarital affairs are almost inevitable. But Shirley's "furious black resentment that positively scorched her mother" may also be displaced anger, anger at the men and the society that place both her mother and herself in such a weak, dependent position that they must "put up with *ev-*

*erything"* and never stand up to their husbands. As in the Demeter-Persephone myth, then, "The grievous separation of mother and maiden implies that in a patriarchal society women are divided from each other and from themselves" [Susan Gubar, "Mother, Maiden and the Marriage of Death: Women Writers and an Ancient Myth," *Women's Studies* 6 (1979)].

Contrary to Rich's argument, Lessing's women do not see each other as inadequate substitutes for heterosexual relationships; on the contrary, men are merely inadequate, unsatisfactory substitutes for that unattained and unattainable first love of Lessing's female protagonists:

> Increasingly in her later fiction, Lessing indicates that women's future is with each other. In several of her novels in the 1970s and 1980s, women thrive better with one another than with men so that her women's needs to fuse and suffer in heterosexual relationships look like neurotic distortions of their unhealed needs for mother love. [Judith Kegan Gardiner, *Rhys, Stead, Lessing and the Politics of Empathy,* 1989]

Lessing's own jealousy of her sibling and her use of the word "Troika" in this story suggest a possible family love triangle in which the father (so crucial to Freud's Oedipal stage) is never involved.

In **"Among the Roses,"** Lessing posits a complex relationship between a mother and her daughter, a relationship that avoids both the symbiotic unity of infancy (which, as Nancy Friday rather graphically points out, becomes grotesque in adulthood) and the matrophobia that characterizes so many women's works, and particularly the works of feminist daughters with conventional, traditionalist mothers. Their relationship is not assured; on the contrary, Lessing stresses how stormy and difficult fashioning such a relationship is likely to be. But both women are clearly trying, and the story ends rather comically (especially for the sometimes dour Lessing, whose sense of humor rarely appears in her work) on a note of mutual tolerance and agreement:

> "Oh, *God,*" said Shirley. "I can't believe. I simply *cannot* believe . . . ." She stopped, evidently remembering that she had just made up with her mother and did not want to quarrel again. At least, not yet. "Oh, well, it takes all sorts," she conceded, as agreeably as was possible to her.

> "Yes, it certainly does," said Myra with a sigh. But she changed the sigh into a cough, for fear it would set Shirley off again.

This story perhaps constitutes Lessing's most optimistic examination of the mother-daughter relationship; certainly it is one of her most tightly focused. Her novels, whose mother-daughter relationships have received more attention, sometimes seem by comparison overstuffed with an embarrassment of plots, subplots, and complex themes. In her stories, the disciplined spareness of design compels the reader to confront directly the dramas and difficulties of mother-daughter relationships.

## Richard Eder (review date 20 October 1994)

SOURCE: "Storytelling by Reluctant Extraction," in *Los Angeles Times,* October 20, 1994, p. E8.

[*An American critic, Eder has won the National Book Critics Circle Award and the Pulitzer Prize for Criticism. In the following review, he laments that "Lessing proclaims but does not convey the wretchedness" of her early life in* Under My Skin.]

In the first volume of her autobiography [*Under My Skin*], Doris Lessing writes that in 1947 and 1948 she went through the worst time in her life. Living in Salisbury in what then was Southern Rhodesia, she had left her first husband and two small children and moved into a leftist bohemian circle, where she met and married a German Communist refugee named Gottfried Lessing.

It was an "unhappy though kindly marriage" and it would not last; meanwhile she supported herself by working for a lawyer, sold short stories to South African magazines, and struggled with a first novel.

This could perfectly well add up to wretchedness. The trouble is that Lessing proclaims but does not convey the wretchedness; or just where and how things hurt. Indeed, her tone—detached and grimly buoyant—is no different than the one she uses to recount her childhood and growing up.

None of it was happy in her recollecting; the problem for the reader is not the quality of the unhappiness but of the recollecting.

Asserting the particular horror of 1947-1948, for example, she writes: "I hinted at the dreadfulness in *Going Home* (one of her three dozen previously published works)." Over and over, as she gets to some crucial part of her early life, she refers the reader to one or another of her novels. Lessing is a remarkable novelist; the good stuff is there. It is not here.

"And now, sex," she announces at one point, and proceeds with a few mildly graphic and pleasureless details of a relationship or two. This is autobiography by reluctant extraction. No wonder. There is not much left for it. It is the slurry after the gold is panned; a clothes closet containing hangers, most of the garments having been taken out and worn out. She narrates with frequent elegance and pervading emptiness.

Certainly there is material, and once in a while a phrase or a passage lights it up. Lessing was born in Persia, where her father worked for a British-owned bank. It was a life of some luxury, followed by a far more rigorous struggle homesteading on a Rhodesian farm. Lessing's father was a witty, depressive, restless man; broken in World War I, where he lost a leg and was hospitalized for months. He married his nurse, an expansive woman with a love of books and music.

She abandoned a promising career in the London hospital system to follow her husband's unhappiness abroad, and cultivate her own in the process.

The shadow of her parents' discontent darkens the memoir; even the pleasures are under gray light. Mr. Lessing wore himself out trying to make the farm pay; in a society of hardbitten settlers, his wife missed the gentilities of the English middle class. She had brought engraved calling cards; there was nobody to call on.

Lessing evokes a dismal epiphany at age 12: seeing her parents sitting in the evening, silently smoking and bowed in defeat. Her reaction was not sympathy but a furious determination never to fall into their trap.

Visiting the past is revisiting the trap, one that she found herself so nearly caught by. And she shrinks away from its walls even as she recalls them. Shrinking away is not the best artistic posture; she is much better now and then when she bursts into full-throated rage.

Otherwise, there are a few moments of unclouded evocation—the beauty and freedom of the African back lands, the quiet rhythm of a farm day—but they quickly cloud over. She attempts to portray the neighboring families they knew, but she wards them off by naming them.

Her boarding schools are recounted at a numb distance; so is her marriage to a young and rising civil servant. She played the competent, cheerfully quirky young colonial wife and mother to the point of madness. "Tigger," she recalls with frozen horror, was her nickname—because of the bounciness.

Her husband and children are present but impalpable, as if the scandal and pain of walking out, moving across a stuffy little colonial capital and going to live with artists and leftists were the exchange of matter for anti-matter, with no connection between them, even that of memory.

Only imagination—in her fiction—would make a bridge. Toward the end, before she emigrates to England and her literary career, she, Gottfried Lessing and their baby would occasionally picnic with her first family, but she tells it as if two sets of ghosts were sharing the tea cakes.

## Basil Davidson (review date 22 October 1994)

SOURCE: "She Had a Farm in Africa," in *The Spectator,* Vol. 273, No. 8676, October 22, 1994, p. 48.

[*An English novelist and historian, Davidson is a prominent scholar in the field of African history. In the following review, he remarks favorably on* Under My Skin.]

Does anyone remember Southern Rhodesia? An echo of Cecil Rhodes and the Cape-to-Cairo 'project' must still linger somewhere at the back of the English mind, as relating to unknown places vaguely north of South Africa where such as Selous used to shoot their kudu and various other beasts. Yet the imperial memory, above all in metropolitan terms, is notoriously short and shallow. Even to the English of South Africa, their fellow-settlers in Southern Rhodesia, not to speak of those in lands beyond the Limpopo still more remote, were the dwellers in a deep provincial nowhere. *Fair and fine, fair and fine, 50 farms and a railway line,* was a tolerant response to any stranger from across the seas who might incautiously ask about those hayseed neighbours in their immeasurable acres of high veld 'beyond the end of cultivation'. And for a long time, true enough, there was little else save a scatter of farms along the spider trail to the north. There were of course the natives; but they were not a matter for notice.

This was the improbable country which produced the remarkable writer that is Doris Lessing, who [in *Under My Skin*] gives us, in chapters of characteristic talent and abrasion, the story of her life before, then pushing 30, she emplaned for England and the grand adventure of becoming famous. That was in 1949, and it had to be as difficult an enterprise as one may easily imagine, for she had no reserves of money, no influential friends or even contacts, and no understanding of our war-weary land then trying to set itself to peaceful targets. One thinks at once of a comparison with another 'South African' who had arrived in London 68 years earlier, and rapidly made a name with *The Story of an African Farm*. Olive Schreiner was handicapped with the provincialism of being a South African in our newly-cooked and very self-regarding empire. Her success became memorable. But Lessing's has been much more so. For Lessing had to overleap a double provincialism: from a limping farmer's household somewhere along that northern line of rail to the 'brilliance' of Joh'burg and the 'sophistication' of the Cape, and then from that to the strenuous realities of London in the wake of war.

The proven skills she brought with her were various but no longer useful. She knew how to 'set a hen, look after chickens and rabbits, worm dogs and cats, pan for gold, take samples from reefs', shoot for the pot and other such things, as well as having some insight into the joys of sex and the frailties of man. She soon revealed, however, the onset of a formidable writer's skill, at first with her Martha Quest stories and then aiming further and still more shrewdly, with her unforgettable milestone along routes of modern feminism, *The Golden Notebook*. If anyone does now remember Southern Rhodesia in its human dimensions, this will surely be in large or even total measure thanks to this superbly reckless but entirely determined chronicler of the 50 farms and the railway line.

Her new book is 'volume one of my autobiography', and seems to me a notable success. It covers all the early years and has occasional glimpses into the future. For my taste it is rather too long, being over-generous on ancestral detail, and tedious wherever the author embarks on a wide terrain of political reference: as, for example, with absurdly sarcastic comments on the poor old Atlantic charter of 1941, a political gesture that did some good at the time and surely no harm. There is also much about the dozen or 20 immigrants of those years who, some from South Africa and others from Europe, undertook to advance the cause of communism in Southern Rhodesia, an acutely racist and politically primitive country, without the remotest chance of being heard.

But the hold-ups are brief along the passage of this wonderful kind of *roman fleuve*, and even a competent editor, supposing one had been given the opportunity, must have known better than to mess around with it. For as soon as Lessing steps down from her platform of *Besser-wissen* the lovely flowing talent takes over and there cannot be too many of her pages. Even with the bits of *Besser-wissen*, an

unlovely property, there comes a piercing honesty of self-judgment and perception, with a quality of narrative that almost never falls to excess. Here, repeatedly, is the marvellous immediacy of observation that has marked her best work from the earliest novel of the 1950s, *The Grass Is Singing;* and the 50 farms (and even the railway line, of which we get a little now and then) will never again be so movingly recalled. Various aspects of 'my autobiography' insist on that, as indeed they should, and not least perhaps if surprisingly her rendering of the mind-set miseries that were loaded, even in a remote land, on the returning survivors of the wars of our blood-stained century, and were miseries that could not ever be assuaged. These are true insights, and one can weep in memory over some of these pages; I did myself.

### Michiko Kakutani    (review date 1 November 1994)

SOURCE: "Reality's Chaos, Translated Into Art," in *The New York Times,* November 1, 1994, p. C17.

[*In the following review, Kakutani praises Lessing's evocation of Africa and colonial life but laments that the author's self-portrait is "an incomplete one, filled with rationalizations and evasions."*]

A third of the way through this intriguing memoir [*Under My Skin*], Doris Lessing describes herself as a young girl, watching her parents sitting side by side in front of their house in the Rhodesian countryside, their faces anxious, tense and full of worry: "There they are, together, *stuck together,* held there by poverty and—much worse—secret and inadmissible needs that come from deep in their two so different histories. They seem to me intolerable, pathetic, unbearable, it is their helplessness that I can't bear."

Young Doris tells herself to remember this moment always: "Don't let yourself forget it. *Don't be like them.*"

"Meaning," she adds, "never let yourself be trapped. In other words, I was rejecting the human condition, which is to be trapped by circumstances."

As she recounts it in *Under My Skin,* the first volume of her autobiography, Ms. Lessing would do her best to live up to this imperative, angrily defying all her parents' injunctions of caution. She dropped out of school at 14, left home a year or so later, had a succession of jobs as a nursemaid and a telephone operator, and began dreaming of escape to some glamorous far-off land. To the world, she presented the face of a clever, amusing and highly competent young woman, who was known to her friends as Tigger, after the bouncy tiger in *Winnie-the-Pooh*. It was an image, she says, that belied a troubled, lonely nature: oversensitive, judgmental and defiant.

Although Ms. Lessing's detachment as a writer would aid her in the pursuit of the freedom she so coveted, this liberation would also come at a price. By the time this volume ends and Ms. Lessing is leaving Africa for good, she has not only jettisoned one husband and more or less abandoned a second, but has also left behind two young children. Of this decision, Ms. Lessing writes simply that the unhappiness she felt in her first marriage would have made her "a liability" to her husband and children if she had stayed.

---

**A matter-of-fact tone informs much of *Under My Skin*, leaving us with a vivid, if somewhat chilling picture of the author as a self-absorbed and heedless young woman.**

**—*Michiko Kakutani***

---

"Perhaps it is not possible to abandon one's children without moral and mental contortions," she writes. "But I was not exactly abandoning mine to an early death. Our house was full of concerned and loving people, and the children would be admirably looked after—much better than by me, not because I did not perform this task exactly like every other woman around me, but because of this secret doom that was inside me—and which had brought my parents to their pitiful condition."

This matter-of-fact tone informs much of this volume, leaving us with a vivid, if somewhat chilling picture of the author as a self-absorbed and heedless young woman. Ms. Lessing tells us that she was not in love with her first husband, or her second, and that her maternal instincts temporarily "switched off" after the birth of her second child. Again and again, she describes her actions as a mere reflection of the Zeitgeist, a point of view that may illuminate the social dynamic animating so many of her novels, but that also suggests a certain reluctance to assume responsibility for personal choices.

Of one lover, Ms. Lessing writes, "I was not in love with him nor he with me, but it was the spirit of the times." Of her embrace of Communism, she similarly observes, "I became a Communist because of the spirit of the times, because of the Zeitgeist." Her decision to have a third child (this one with her second husband, Gottfried Lessing) is also explained in terms of larger, impersonal forces, in this case the ravages of World War II: "I believe it was Mother Nature making up for the millions of the dead."

Certainly many of the events recounted in this volume will be familiar to readers of Ms. Lessing's Martha Quest novels: a lonely childhood in the African bush, quarrels with a difficult mother, escape to the big city, an early marriage and immersion in the world of left wing politics. Indeed, this volume not only underscores just how autobiographical the *Children of Violence* novels really were, but also sheds new light on the process whereby Ms. Lessing transmuted the chaotic events of her own life into the hard, bright stillness of art.

One need not be acquainted with any of Ms. Lessing's earlier works, however, to become absorbed in reading this memoir. Set down in quick, fluent prose, *Under My Skin* offers the reader a beautifully observed portrait of the African landscape that's often as sensually resonant as the one Isak Dinesen created in *Out of Africa*. The book gives us a sad, unsentimental portrait of British expatriates like Ms. Lessing's parents, living on daydreams of repatriation and imagined wealth, and a fierce, sometimes very funny portrait of colonial Communists and their hangers-on.

As for the portrait Ms. Lessing draws of herself, it's an incomplete one, filled with rationalizations and evasions, and at the same time is energized by the author's groping efforts to come to terms with her past. Perhaps the next volume of her autobiography, which is to take up the story of her move to London and her determination to become a writer, will more fully address the emotional consequences of her actions and the legacy of her willful youth.

### Caroline Moorehead (review date 4 November 1994)

SOURCE: "Memoirs of a Survivor," in *New Statesman & Society,* Vol. 7, No. 327, November 4, 1994, pp. 38-9.

[*Moorehead is an English journalist and nonfiction writer. In the following review, she praises* Under My Skin *for its vivid and evocative depiction of Rhodesia and for the insights the book offers into the relationship between Lessing's life and fiction.*]

Neither Bertrand Russell nor John Cheever emerged well from their children's portraits of them; one was Olympian and cruelly exacting, the other alcoholic and homosexual. Maude McVeagh was not successful or well-known, but as Doris Lessing's mother she has come to prominence in the first volume of her daughter's autobiography as a desperate manipulative woman with a limitless urge for control. It is a devastating indictment not just of an unhappy woman but of parenthood. The saddest thing is that she tried so hard to get it right.

*Under My Skin* occupies that no-man's land between biography and autobiography, where the characters who play the main parts from time to time take over the narrative and the author is defined more by what is observed than by what is said. In this first volume, which takes her up until her departure from Rhodesia for London in 1949, Doris Lessing also does for herself what biographers traditionally do for literary subjects: she traces the links between the real people and places of her past and the ones in her fiction. Those who enjoyed the sequence of novels about embattled Martha Quest when they appeared in the 1950s will recognise her heroine constantly in these pages.

Few recent writers have brought to their earliest years quite the clarity and definition with which Doris Lessing recalls her childhood. Like Patrick Leigh Fermor minutely describing the central Europe he walked through at the age of 20, at a distance of nearly 50 years, Doris Lessing retrieves texture, smells and sounds most of us have, if not lost, certainly allowed to fade. Alienation, not simply from parents but from most of the human species, began early; few of these recollections are pleasant. Adults, to the watchful three-year-old girl, were smelly and unsavoury, with their "enormous pale bodies, like milk-puddings . . . flailing large pale arms". They have "loose bulging breasts" with "whiskers of hair under arms" and "snot on a face that is grinning and shouting with pleasure".

> *Under My Skin* occupies that no-man's land between biography and autobiography, where the characters who play the main parts from time to time take over the narrative and the author is defined more by what is observed than by what is said.
>
> —*Caroline Moorehead*

It is a terrifying world, in which being tickled is a nightmare, more bullying than fun, and yet "a necessary preparation for life". For Doris Lessing, childhood was a major war, played out across several battlegrounds with vastly inferior weapons, her only defence disguise into another persona, with the name of "Tigger": a cheeky little girl who could make everyone laugh. But even Tigger was no match for Maude McVeagh, a "vibrating column of efficiency and ruthless energy" whose over-attentiveness yet lack of proper love grinds bitterly through the years. The hatred is chilling. No surprise, perhaps that many of the adults took more to Harry, her younger brother, a gentle, responsive child who does not seem to have viewed the world with quite such unremitting hostility.

*Under My Skin* falls into two distinct parts: the years of childhood—a short spell in Persia, then to a farm in Rhodesia and a life of poverty and claustrophobia, clinging to the values of home with liberty bodices and steamed syrup puddings, redeemed only by the magic of the surrounding bush—and ten years of young adulthood before the longed-for departure for England. In these years came two marriages, both precipitate, and a steady output of writing she makes little of.

There was also absorption into the new Communist Party of Rhodesia, a moment of political awakening explored in the Martha Quest books and told at some length here, with incredulity at the misplaced belief in Stalin and nostalgia for a time when "our map of the world was still innocent". From the first marriage came a son and a daughter, both left with her husband; from the second, another son, who went with her to London. What the loss of the first two children cost her is not dwelt on; nor is the cost of her loss to them.

Not that Doris Lessing is easy on herself. She is as tough about her own frantic desire to break away as she is about the hypocrisy and evasions she found so contemptible in her parents. She takes the business of writing autobiography very seriously, and has thought out her position with care. *Under My Skin* was conceived, at least in part, as an act of self-defence, as five biographies of her are currently being written in America.

Had her memoirs been written in her thirties, they would have been, she says, overly combative; in her forties, full of despair and guilt. In her seventies, a far more detached curiosity is possible, though she is strict on the subject of

truth, condemning as absurd the notion that it is the duty of friends, lovers and comrades to tell all, and admiring those who, as they grow older and are told more secrets, learn to keep their mouths shut. At least, by 70, the tricky landscape of memory has become more stable.

*Under My Skin* is a stern book. Wonderfully evocative of both people and places—especially the Rhodesian countryside seen through the eyes of a child—it is sometimes a little thin on humour. There is not much affection or comfort to be found in its pages. The inability ever to remember the good times, but always the bad, is a refrain that she turns to again and again, attributing this pessimism in part to having been born in 1919, "when half of Europe was a graveyard".

The "dark grey cloud, like poison", that settled over her early childhood, fanned by the bitterness of her father who had lost a leg in the war, filled her with this endless "struggling panicky need to escape". It is with a cold eye, and at times an accusatory glare, that Doris Lessing looks out from the "defended observation post" that was her childhood self.

## J. M. Coetzee   (review date 22 December 1994)

SOURCE: "The Heart of Me," in *The New York Review of Books,* Vol. 41, No. 21, December 22, 1994, pp. 51-4.

[*Coetzee is a South African novelist, critic, essayist, and translator. In the review below, he offers a summary of Lessing's life and career, remarking on Lessing's thoughts concerning feminism, politics, sexuality, and her mother.*]

Presented with snapshots of the Tayler family and asked to pick out the artist or artist-to-be among them, one might at a pinch settle on the father, rather stiff and military but clearly not unintelligent; certainly not on the daughter, pleasant enough but ordinary as a loaf of bread. Yet the daughter had it in her not only to escape a future that one can almost read in her face—marriage to a decent young chap and life on a farm in Rhodesia managing servants and having babies—but also to become one of the great visionary novelists of our time.

Alfred Cook Tayler, Doris's sad-eyed father, having lost a leg in the trenches of World War I, married the nurse tending him and quit a native country he could no longer bear. His wife, already in her mid-thirties, had to sacrifice a career in order to have a family. Their daughter Doris—later Doris Wisdom, then Doris Lessing—was born in Persia in 1919.

Following ideas about child-rearing fashionable at the time, Emily Maude Tayler imposed on her two children a rigid schedule of feeding times and bowel movements, reproducing upon them by new means her own upbringing by a cold stepmother. Doris responded with deep anger against a mother who on principle refused to feed her when she cried and who later made it clear that she preferred her son to her daughter. "For years I lived in a state of accusation against [her], at first hot, then cold and hard." There is no need to seek out instances of " 'abuse,' cruelty and the rest" when memories persist of how her mother "chatted on and on in her social voice" about "how the little girl in particular (she was so difficult, so naughty!) made her life a total misery." No child could have stood up to such an "assault on [her] very existence."

Since her mother would not love her, she turned to her father. "The smell of maleness, tobacco, sweat, the smell of father, enveloped her in safety." But there was a darker side to his love. The "scarred pitiful shrunken stump" of his amputated leg poked out at her from his dressing gown, an obscenity "with a life of its own." There was also the tickling game, "when Daddy captures his little daughter and her face is forced down into his lap or crotch, into the unwashed smell. . . . His great hands go to work on my ribs. My screams, helpless, hysterical, desperate." For years afterward she had dreams in which she screamed and struggled while brutal male faces loomed over her. "I wonder how many women who submit to physical suffering at the hands of their men were taught by 'games,' by 'tickling.' "

After Persia the Taylers moved to Rhodesia—a colony then only thirty-five years old—drawn by the lure of quick fortunes to be made in maize farming. But their thousand-acre farm ("It would not have occurred to [my parents] that the land belonged to the blacks") was not large enough to be economically viable. Though her mother adapted well, her father lacked the doggedness needed for farming; they were always in debt.

For the children, however, growing up in the bush was a wonderful, formative experience. From their parents they learned about geology and natural history; bedtime stories fed their imagination (Lessing acknowledges that her mother had a genius for teaching). Books were ordered from London, and devoured. (Books were cheap enough in the 1920s for a struggling colonial family to buy them in quantities; no Zimbabwean child of today, and certainly no rural child, can afford the wealth of reading matter that Lessing had available to her.) By the age of twelve Doris knew

> how to set a hen, look after chickens and rabbits, worm dogs and cats, pan for gold, take samples from reefs, cook, sew, use the milk separator and churn butter, go down a mine shaft in a bucket, make cream cheese and ginger beer, paint stencilled patterns on materials, make papier mâché, walk on stilts . . . , drive the car, shoot pigeons and guineafowl for the pot, preserve eggs—and a lot else. . . .
>
> That is real happiness, a child's happiness: being enabled to do and to make, above all to know you are contributing to the family, you are valuable and valued.

Later Lessing would indict settler society for its "coldness [and] stinginess of the heart" toward blacks; the charge would be fleshed out in *The Grass is Singing* (1950), an astonishingly accomplished debut, though perhaps too wedded to romantic stereotypes of the African for present-day tastes, as well as in *African Stories* (1964). Yet Rhodesia was not a wholly bad environment in which to grow up. Aside from the restorative power of the natural world (about which Lessing is unabashedly Wordsworthian), there reigned among the children of the settlers a strongly egalitarian spirit that helped her escape the class obsessions of her parents. And among the 10,000 whites in Salisbury, the capital, she would discover a sizable contingent of refugees from Europe, most of them left-leaning, many of them Jewish, who would exert a decisive intellectual and political influence on her.

Meanwhile, to the confusing signals that her parents sent out, Doris responded with behavior typical of the unloved child calling for love. She stole, lied, cut up her mother's clothes, set fires; she had fantasies that the Taylers were not her real parents.

At the age of seven, "a frightened and miserable little girl," she was packed off to a convent boarding school where the nuns—themselves the unwanted daughters of German peasants—frightened their charges with hellfire stories. Here she spent four wretched years. After a further stretch in an all-girls high school in Salisbury, with weekly letters from her mother blaming her for the money she was costing them, she dropped out of the education system definitively. She was thirteen.

Yet she had never been a poor student. On the contrary, if only to please her mother, she made sure she always came first in class. She was popular with the other girls, inhabiting a false self she calls "Tigger" (after the A. A. Milne character), "fat and bouncy, . . . brash, jokey, clumsy, and always ready to be a good sport, that is, to laugh at myself, apologize, clown, confess inability." When later she gravitated into Communist circles, she was known as "Comrade Tigger." She repudiated the nickname once she left Rhodesia in 1949; but, refusing to go away, the Tigger self mutated into what Lessing calls the Hostess self, "bright, helpful, attentive, receptive," and disturbingly reminiscent of her mother.

Is this a clue to the title of the first volume of her autobiography: *Under My Skin*? In isolation the title makes a fairly conventional self-revelatory promise. But an epigraph reminds us of its context in Cole Porter: "I've got you under my skin / I've got you deep in the heart of me / So deep in my heart you're really a part of me, / I've got you under my skin. / I've tried so not to give in . . ." The hidden addressee of the book, the "you" deep in Lessing's heart, under her skin, emerges all too plausibly as her long-dead mother.

Averse to any display of emotion, her mother had expressed tenderness by persuading her children they were ill and then nursing them to health. Doris played along, using illness as an excuse to spend days in bed reading. But at home she could not find the privacy she craved. When she began to menstruate, her mother trumpeted the news to the males of the household. When she tried to diet, her mother piled her plate. Her fourteenth year was spent "fighting for my life" against a mother who, as she had tried to control her infant bowel movements, now seemed to be asserting ownership over her body.

To escape an unendurable situation, she took a job as a nursemaid. Guided by her employer, she began to read books on politics and sociology, while nightly the same employer's brother-in-law crept into her bed and ineptly toyed with her. Characteristically, Lessing does not pretend she was a passive victim. She "[fought] the virginity of [her] placid suitor . . . in a fever of erotic longing." "It is my belief," she writes, that some girls—among whom she clearly includes herself—"ought to be put to bed, at the age of fourteen" with an older man as a form of "apprentice love."

Lessing's precocious preschool reading had included Scott, Stevenson, Kipling, the Lambs' versions of Shakespeare, Dickens. (In her time, she notes tartly, "children were not patronized" but on the contrary encouraged to try things that were beyond them.) Now she began to read contemporary fiction, D. H. Lawrence in particular, as well as the great Russians. By the age of eighteen she had written two apprentice novels herself. She was also selling stories to South African magazines. She had, in fact, slipped into being a writer.

Of the three best-known writers southern Africa has produced—Olive Schreiner, Nadine Gordimer, and Lessing (who, though reluctant to accept the label "African writer," freely acknowledges that her sensibility was formed in and by Africa)—none completed high school. All were substantially self-educated, all became formidable intellectuals. This says something about the fierceness with which isolated adolescents on the margins of empire hungered for a life they felt cut off from, the life of the mind—far more fiercely, it turned out, than most of their metropolitan cousins. It also says something about how desultory the pressure was on girls to proceed all the way through the educational mill, domesticity being their ultimate lot.

Intermittent visits home only confirmed to Lessing that she had done well to escape when she did. Her mother was beginning to conform to the worst of colonial stereotypes, complaining about the servants in a "scolding, insistent, nagging voice full of dislike," while her father slowly wasted away from diabetes, a "self-pitying, peevish, dream-sodden old man, talking about his war." When he eventually died, she had an urge to scratch out the words "heart failure" under Cause of Death on the death certificate and write instead "First World War."

Becalmed in what felt more and more like a backwater (the period is evoked in *Landlocked,* 1965), she wrote and rewrote *The Grass is Singing,* the novel that would bring her recognition and, more importantly, a precarious financial independence. "I was waiting for my future, my real life, to begin." Rhodesians still spoke of England as "Home." As for her, "I was not going home . . . I was fleeing from it."

Lessing's first marriage, at the age of nineteen, had been to a man much older than herself—a marriage involving not the real woman but the Tigger self, the "jolly young matron." Not yet ready for motherhood, she gave birth to a son, then neglected him. He responded with anger and bewilderment uncannily like that of the young Doris.

A second child followed. She was drinking more and more, having affairs, treating her husband badly (much of this experience went into *A Proper Marriage,* 1954, the second of the Martha Quest novels and the most directly autobiographical). The situation was clearly untenable. Vowing that her children would one day inherit "a beauti-

ful and perfect world where there would be no race hatred, injustice, and so forth," she gave them into the care of relatives and began to make plans to leave the country without them. She bore within her, she felt, the same "secret doom" that had ruined her parents' lives and would ruin her children's too if she stayed with them. "I was absolutely sincere," she records dryly. "There isn't much to be said for sincerity, in itself."

In the wake of the battle of Stalingrad, with the glory it brought to Russian arms, Lessing was converted to communism. In her account of her Communist years a certain defensiveness is still detectable. In truth, she writes, "I was never committed with all of myself to Communism." By the time the cold war broke out and she and her comrades suddenly become "pariahs" to white Rhodesian society, she was already beginning to have doubts. By 1954 she was no longer a Communist, though for years she felt "residual tugs of loyalty."

The activities of the Salisbury Communists, their loves and hates, take up much of the first three Martha Quest novels. Lessing justifies the extended treatment she gives—in both autobiography and these early novels—to this politically insignificant clique on the grounds that it exhibited "the same group dynamics, that made and unmade the Communist Party of the Soviet Union."

Recruits, as her books suggest, tended to be people with unhappy childhoods behind them, looking for a substitute family; their own children they shrugged off as unwanted nuisances. As an enthusiastic newcomer (and as a woman), Lessing was assigned the task of peddling *The Guardian,* organ of the South African Communist Party, in the poorer districts of Salisbury. Of all her Party activities, this may in fact have been the most useful to her as a writer: it enabled her to meet working-class people and see something of working-class life (*A Ripple from the Storm,* 1958, gives a fuller and livelier account than we get [in *Under My Skin*]).

One consequence of joining the Communists was that Doris met Gottfried Lessing, whom she married in 1943. Gottfried came from a prosperous Russian family of assimilated German Jewish descent, turned back into Germans by the 1917 revolution and then back into Jews by the Nuremberg laws. He was also, in his wife's words, "the embodiment of cold, cutting, Marxist logic," a "cold, silent man" of whom everyone was afraid.

Gottfried does not figure directly in the Martha Quest novels because he was still alive when she wrote them (he ended his life as East German ambassador to Uganda, where he was shot during the coup against Idi Amin). Lessing does her best to explain and portray sympathetically this unappealing man, with whom she describes her sexual life as "sad." What he really needed, she writes, was a woman kind enough to "treat her man as a baby, even for a few hours of the dark."

Gottfried encouraged her writing, though he did not approve of what she wrote. "What I liked best about myself, what I held fast to, he liked least." She had married him to save him from internment as an enemy alien; to strengthen his application for British citizenship she remained in an "unhappy but kindly marriage" long after it should have ended. Only in 1948, when his application was approved (and she, as his wife, could regain her original citizenship), did they feel free to divorce.

Lessing has never been a great stylist—she writes too fast and prunes too lightly for that. The first three Martha Quest novels, or at least long stretches of them, are bent under the burden not only of prosaic language but of an uninventive conception of novelistic form. The problem is compounded by Lessing's passive heroine, dissatisfied with life but unable to take control of her destiny in any meaningful way. But if these novels have not lasted well, they at least attest to ambition on a large scale: the ambition of writing a *Bildungsroman* in which individual development will be traced within an entire social and historical context.

Lessing was not blind to her basic problem, namely that her nineteenth-century models were exhausted. After the third volume she interrupted the series, breaking entirely new ground with the formally adventurous *Golden Notebook,* in which entries from the main character's notebooks are intermingled in a conventional narrative. *Landlocked,* with which the series resumes after a seven-year gap, reflects in its stylistic experiments not only Martha's impatience with a life without a future but Lessing's own impatience with her medium; while *The Four-Gated City,* 1969, with which the series closes, points forward toward *Briefing for a Descent into Hell,* 1971 (which Lessing called "inner-space fiction"), *Memoirs of a Survivor,* 1974, and the speculative fiction of the *Canopus in Argos* series rather than backward to the early books. What Lessing was looking for, and to a degree found, was a more inward, more fully modern conception not only of character but of the self and of the self's experience of time (including historical time). Once this had been arrived at, the nineteenth-century trappings fell away of themselves.

Since the publication of *The Golden Notebook* in 1962, Lessing has had an uneasy relationship with the women's movement—which claimed the book as a founding document—and a positively hostile relationship with academic commentators, who claimed it as a prototypical postmodern novel. Between herself and her most enthusiastic feminist disciples she has maintained a wary distance, while dismissing literary critics as fleas on the backs of writers. She has in turn been criticized by feminists (for example, Adrienne Rich) for failing to imagine an autonomous feminist politics, and by literary critics for trying to control the interpretation of her books rather than allowing them to spin off into textual space.

In her autobiography she does not hesitate to let fly at "correct" political attitudes, which she sees as little different from what in the heyday of the Party was called "the line." Thus—despite her father's tickling game—she labels the present concern with the sexual abuse of children a "hysterical mass movement." She condemns "the avaricious or vindictive divorce terms so often demanded by feminists." Ever since adolescence, she records, she has been more interested in the "amazing possibilities" of the vagina than in the "secondary and inferior pleasure" of the clitoris. "If I had been told that clitoral and vaginal orgasms would within a few decades become ideological enemies . . . I'd have thought it a joke." As for the social construction of gender, she recalls the "ruthlessness" with which she stole her first husband from another woman, a "basic female ruthlessness . . . [that] comes from a much older time than Christianity or any other softener of savage moralities. *It is my right.* When I've seen this creature emerge in myself, or in other women, I have felt awe."

On Western breast-beating about the colonial past, she comments: "[It cannot] be said too often that it is a mistake to exclaim over past wrong-thinking before at least wondering how our present thinking will seem to posterity." A Nigerian writer found one of her stories about African life good enough to plagiarize and publish under his own name, she recalls: so much for the politically correct line that whites should not write about black experience. Her own fiction explores male experience, including male sexual experience, without reserve.

As someone whose life has been substantially involved with public and political matters, Lessing confesses a certain respect for people who don't write memoirs, who "have chosen to keep their mouths shut." Why then her own autobiography? Her answer is candid: "Self-defense." At least five biographers are already at work on her. "You try and claim your own life by writing an autobiography."

But one suspects larger reasons too. Besides the epigraph from Cole Porter, her book bears another from Idries Shah, whose writings on Sufism have been important to her since the 1960s. Shah links individual fate to the fate of society by suggesting that society cannot be reformed until people can individually identify the forces and institutions that have dictated the course of their lives. Self-exploration and social evolution thus go together.

The two epigraphs also cohere in a surprising way. Through the music her generation danced to, such as the music of Cole Porter, says Lessing, pulsed a deep rhythm promising sex and salvation. When this subliminal promise of the Zeitgeist was not fulfilled, the whole generation, including herself, reacted as if cheated of its birthright. "I feel I have been part of some mass illusion or delusion"— the illusion that everyone is entitled to happiness. (In contrast, she suggests, the deep rhythm of today's cacophonous popular music sends people out to torture, kill, and maim.)

As a child born in the aftermath of World War I, Lessing is convinced that she, like her parents, vibrated to the *basso ostinato* of that disastrous epoch. "I wonder now how many of the children brought up in families crippled by war had the same poison running in their veins from before they could even speak."

The idea that the ship of history is guided by currents deeper than consciousness—an idea of which her deep-rhythm hypothesis is a slightly batty example—keeps coming back in Lessing's autobiography. In fact, the turn away from a Marxist, materialist conception of history had already been hinted at in *A Ripple from the Storm,* in which Martha Quest dreams of a huge saurian, fossilized yet still alive, staring dolefully at her from an earth-pit, an archaic power that will not die. One of the problems with the present project—a problem of which she is well aware—is that fiction has better resources for dealing with unconscious forces than discursive autobiography. Her previously most successful explorations of the historically embedded psyche have been in such works as *The Golden Notebook* and the visionary symbolic-allegorical narrative *Memoirs of a Survivor* (in which, incidentally, she attempts to reconceive herself as mother of a daughter rather than daughter of a mother). It is as novelist rather than as memoirist, therefore, that, three quarters of the way through the present project, she pronounces her succinct verdict on it: "There is no doubt fiction makes a better job of the truth."

The best parts of Lessing's autobiography are about her early childhood. To most of us, early experience comes as such a shock that we remember nothing of it—an amnesia, Lessing suggests, that may be a necessary protective mechanism for the species. Her own powerful (and powerfully rendered) first memories revolve with distaste around the ugliness and loudness and smelliness of the world she has been born into—the "loose bulging breasts [and] whiskers of hair under arms" of adults in a swimming pool in Persia, the "cold stuffy metallic stink . . . of lice" in a Russian train.

In their clarity of recall (or of imaginative construction—it makes no difference) and cleanness of articulation, these first five chapters belong among the great pieces of writing about childhood:

> It is as if the thatch is whispering. All at once I understand, my ears fill with the sound of the frogs and toads down in the vlei. It is raining. The sound is the dry thatch filling with water, swelling, and the frogs are exulting with the rain. Because I understand, everything falls into its proper place about me, the thatch of the roof soaking up its wet from the sky, the frogs sounding as loud as if they are down the hill, but they are a couple of miles off, the soft fall of the rain on the earth and the leaves, and the lightning, still far away. And then, confirming the order of the night, there is a sudden bang of thunder. I lie back, content, under the net, listening, and slowly sink back into a sleep full of the sounds of rain.

Passages like this celebrate special moments, Wordsworthian "spots of time," in which the child is intensely open to experience and also aware of heightened openness, aware that the moment is privileged. As Lessing observes, if we give time its due phenomenological weight, then most of our life is over by the time we are ten.

There are also fine passages later in the book where Lessing candidly reinhabits her youthful narcissism. She pedals her bicycle "with long brown smooth legs she is conscious of as if a lover were stroking them." "I pulled up my dress and looked at myself as far up as my panties and was filled with pride of body. There is no exultation like it, the moment when a girl knows that *this* is her body, *these* her fine smooth shapely limbs."

There are also leisurely recollections of pregnancy, childbirth (trouble-free), and nursing, including reports on her babies' feeding habits and stools, written from one of the personae she has now embraced: that of wise mother or grandmother instructing younger women.

It is clear that more effort went into the early chapters than into the rest of the book, in which Lessing all too often slips into the mode of casual reminiscence. Too many of the personages in the later chapters will matter little even to Lessing's more dedicated readers, despite halfhearted attempts to claim relevance for them.

In the end, the book is dominated by the figure of Lessing's mother, who has been present either openly or in disguised form in much of what she has written during a career now into its fifth decade. In this latest round, Lessing does her best to be fair to her opponent. For a page or two she goes so far as to hand over the narration to her—an experiment soon abandoned. "There was never a woman who enjoyed parties and good times more than she did, enjoyed being popular and a hostess and a good sort, the mother of two pretty, well-behaved, well-brought up, clean children." (The hidden barb here, the barb Lessing cannot resist, is the code-word "clean," which in the Tayler household referred to potty-training.) The trunks that accompanied them from Tehran to their mud-walled home in Rhodesia held silver tea trays, watercolors, Persian carpets, scarves, hats, evening dresses—finery that her mother would never have a chance to show off. On the farm this "handsome, well-dressed, dryly humorous woman, efficient, practical, and full of energy," found no outlet adequate to her ambitions. Her affections were transferred from her husband to her son as soon as he was born; he remained bound to her till he went off to boarding school, where, somehow, he learned to say No. "Now I see her as a tragic figure," Lessing writes; during her lifetime, "I saw her as tragic certainly, but was not able to be kind."

Yet despite a determined attempt to appreciate her parents in their historical setting, [*Under My Skin*] repeats the pattern of blaming the mother, familiar from Lessing's earlier writings, and thus, I fear, dooms us to the return of the mother and a rerun of the mother-daughter quarrel in the next volume. There is something depressing in the spectacle of a woman in her seventies still wrestling with an unsubjugated ghost from the past. On the other hand, there is no denying the grandeur of the spectacle when the protagonist is as mordantly honest and as passionately desirous of salvation as Doris Lessing.

## William H. Pritchard   (review date Summer 1995)

SOURCE: "Looking Back at Lessing," in *The Hudson Review*, Vol. XLVIII, No. 2, Summer, 1995, pp. 317-24.

[*Pritchard is an American educator and critic. In the following review, he remarks on the theme and style of* Under My Skin *and summarizes Lessing's development throughout her literary career.*]

A little over two decades ago when Doris Lessing published her ninth novel, *The Summer Before the Dark* (1973), she could lay claim to consideration as the foremost female writer of fiction then working in English. The women's movement was in full swing and among many of the more literarily inclined Lessing occupied a position of respect second only to Virginia Woolf. And she was contemporary in a way Woolf, thirty and more years dead, couldn't be. *The Golden Notebook* (1962), which met with some puzzlement when first published, had become increasingly cited and talked about (if not always read through) by those aspiring toward being what, in the core section of the book, Lessing titled "Free Women." She had also completed the five-volume series, *Children of Violence* (more familiarly the "Martha Quest" novels) in which a woman who shared much of Lessing's biography was tracked, in her quest, from her days as a young woman in Southern Rhodesia, through marriages, pregnancies, divorces, to her eventual death in London. By 1973, Lessing had also published—in addition to many volumes of short fiction—a novel (her first) of Africa, *The Grass is Singing;* two autobiographical prose works; and *Briefing for a Descent into Hell,* a dark, dystopian vision of the future. In *The Summer Before the Dark,* a woman approaching middle age, married and with children, embarks on an affair with a man significantly younger than herself. The novel was given a front-page review by Elizabeth Hardwick in the *New York Times Book Review,* and in the course of her interesting account of it Hardwick identified the "rather flat, puzzling, aching anguish" that she found characteristic of Lessing's fiction, including her latest. "Enormous sadness and depression," was the particular tone Hardwick heard, and she thought it not wholly to the advantage of *The Summer Before the Dark* as a novel.

At present, Lessing's work is a good deal further away from the central concerns of most serious readers of fiction. Nothing in the writing she has published in the last two decades comes even close to challenging these readers, whether female or male, the way *The Golden Notebook* and the Martha Quest novels—especially the concluding, most disturbing one, *The Four-Gated City*—challenged them. She has become a respected and respectable figure to be surveyed in accounts of post-Second War novelists, viewed dispassionately along with Iris Murdoch and Margaret Drabble. So it is a good time for her to weigh in with this enlivening and substantial first volume of autobiography [*Under My Skin*], taking her from childhood up to her move from Africa to London in 1949. Lessing says early in the book that she admires certain people who have chosen to keep their mouths shut; but with rumors of five American biographers at work in one way or another on her life, the motive of self-defense came to the fore. Few people are left who can be hurt by what she has to say, at least in writing about her first thirty years. She can tell the truth, as she sees it, "without snags and blocks of conscience." Thus she prepares us for the leisurely, extremely detailed narrative that unfolds in the effort to tell us exactly what it is she's "got" under her skin.

The easiest answer, and the one Lessing more than hints at in the book, is her mother, Emily Maude McVeagh, a nurse who cared for Lessing's father, Alfred Tayler, in London's Royal Free Hospital where he was suffering from shell shock, depression, and an amputated leg. After the First World War the Taylers went out to Kermanshah, in Persia, where Alfred worked in the Imperial Bank

and where Doris and her brother were born; later, after a sojourn in England, the family settled on a farm in Southern Rhodesia, the country in which Lessing spent her young life. She tells us that she now sees her mother as a "tragic figure, living out her disappointing years with courage and with dignity," but there's not much of this sympathetic figure in the book. Rather we're given the woman who, conforming to procedures back then, refused to feed the infant Doris when she cried; the woman who toilet trained her, who was "a vibrating column of efficiency and ruthless energy," who while Doris leaned against her father's knee (the real one, not the metal-and-wood replacement) went on and on to some visitor about how her children were sapping her strength, how her talents were withering, "how the little girl in particular (she was so difficult, so naughty!) made her life a total misery." When the family traveled home to England from Persia in 1924, Lessing's mother decided they should go via Moscow so as not to expose the children to the heat of the Red Sea. The horrendous journey that ensued, across the Caspian Sea in an oil tanker full of lice, then on a foodless train to Moscow where they subsisted on hard-boiled eggs and bread, bought by the mother at stations from peasant women (with typhoid and typhus everywhere, swarms of beggars and homeless children)—all this formed the substance of stories her mother would tell in future years. Lessing says she doesn't remember these events, nor does she remember how, at the Russian frontier, her mother browbeat a Russian official to let them in even though their passports were imperfectly stamped. Since Doris was only five at the time, one can't blame her for remembering things other than what her mother emphasized afterwards. But the "nervous flight" from her mother Lessing says she was engaged in as far back as she could remember, may have been in play here; at any rate by age fourteen she was "obdurately against" everything that Emily Tayler represented.

This "state of accusation" Lessing identifies is painful to read about, since next to blaming the father, blaming the mother is always something a daughter can indulge in. Of course Lessing doesn't want to indulge herself—she's too severely moral for that—and at certain moments in the book she speaks of herself as marked out for trouble in a way more powerful than can be blamed on her luckless mother or father. For example, later on when she decides to abandon not only her first husband, Frank Wisdom, but also the two children she bore him, it is a delicate moment for the autobiographer to handle. Lessing rationalizes a bit, saying the children would be looked after by loving people who would do the job more efficiently than she. She knew this, not because she hadn't up to that point performed the task just like the other women she saw around her, "but because of this secret doom that was inside me—and which had brought my parents to their pitiful condition." Near the end of the book she speaks of still not understanding, when she settled in London, the fact that she had been "conditioned for tears." These phrases seem to me attempts at naming what is finally beyond understanding, and what no talk about one's father or mother will explain: namely, the demon that drove this intensely gifted, perennially dissatisfied—sometimes to the point of despair and breakdown—young and older woman. "I've got you under my skin / I've got you deep in the heart of me": Cole Porter's lines furnish the book's title and act as one of its epigraphs. But we're asked to ignore the jaunty tone of the song and perhaps not to think of its concluding advice: "Use your mentality, / Wake up to reality," the sort of advice you give only when you've determined that you "never can win"—advice Lessing has never been about to take to heart. [In a footnote, the critic adds: "For someone who makes as much, in the autobiography, of popular lyrics, Lessing time and again gets their words wrong. She does okay with Porter's 'Under My Skin,' but messes up 'Night and Day' ('Night and day / I think of you'). 'It's a Sin to Tell a Lie' doesn't begin 'I love you, yes I do, I love you,' and 'Swinging on a Star' doesn't say 'Do you want to be better off than you are / Carry moonbeams home in a jar . . .' Yeats's little poem 'The Scholars' does not end 'O God, what would they say, if their Catullus came their way.' This probably doesn't matter but if she likes them enough to quote them, why not get the words right?"]

It must be said that the young, extremely attractive girl featured in the excellent photographs in this book, seems unaware that her "secret doom" has already conditioned her to tears. Aware of this odd disparity, Lessing names this healthy resilient animal—proud of her body, able to make others laugh—"Tigger," and the nickname survived through two marriages. (When she became a Communist she was called "Comrade Tigger.") It's Tigger who has pillow-fights with her mother or undergoes her father's tickling so as to play the game.

It's Tigger, the "healthy bouncing beast," who manages to survive the four years in a convent school to which she was sent. It's Tigger who marries Frank Wisdom, a young civil servant, who drinks and dances with the other young marrieds, has children without disaster, says at one point that she could have made a good veterinarian, or a doctor, or a matron, or a farmer. The vitality of Lessing's prose, especially in the first half of the book, testifies to Tigger's claim. What a wonderful place to grow up, her writing convinces us, as she and her brother sit under the telephone lines stretching from the Mandor Mine across a grass field to the Taylers' farm:

> Our ears to the metal pole we listened to the thrumming, drumming, deep-singing of the wind in the wires where we watched, as we listened, the birds, hundreds of birds, alighting, balancing, taking off again, big birds and little birds and plain birds and birds coloured like rainbows or sunsets, the most glamorous of them, the rollers, mauve and grey and pink, like large kingfishers.

As with *The Grass is Singing,* this writing has some of the delicate sensuous life of early D. H. Lawrence. Speaking at one point of the "intense physicality" of Lawrence's prose, she admits that he "must have influenced me." No doubt about it: a memorable Lawrentian passage describes her looking after a brood of hatching chicks when her mother has taken her father to the hospital in Salisbury. As Doris sits up in a cold room and watches the eggs, there appears in one of them a "little rough place" that meant birth was imminent:

> I held the egg to my ear, and heard the tap tap tap of the hidden chick, and wept with excitement and relief. Out flopped that hideous chick, dried at once into adorableness, out flopped another . . . soon all over the cracking eggs lay and sprawled the wet monstrous creatures, and between the eggs trembled the pretty dried-out chicks. I ran out, found the oldest and most experienced hen, and put her into a pen where the nest box was already lined with straw and feathers, and when I brought out a couple of dozen little chicks and put them one by one into the nest she seemed not to know her own mind. Then, her brain switched gear, she clucked, and delicately trod her way among them and became their mother.

This is beyond praise, an example of moments when her writings gets under the alert reader's skin.

In fact I found myself appreciating and admiring passages where the grim spirit in the heart of Lessing isn't wholly allowed to upstage superficial Tigger. Something like an older version of the latter can be heard when, from time to time in the book, Lessing addresses contemporary women out of the wisdom of age seventy-five. Gynecologically speaking she compares herself to the fabled peasant woman who never had anything wrong with her—no "pre-menstrual tension," three normal births, easy periods which ended in her early forties, no unpleasant menopause. So she wants to hold out some hope for young women who are prepared only for "womb troubles":

> When I—my generation—looked forward to our lives as females, we were not full of fear and foreboding. We felt confident, we felt in control. We were not bombarded with bleak information from television, radio, newspapers, women's magazines. If girls were told, from very young, that they can expect bad times of every sort from pre-menstrual tension to menopausal miseries, is it not possible they are attracting bad times?

"I became a Communist because of the spirit of the times, because of the *Zeitgeist*"—so Lessing explains her being recruited into the dissident "progressive" band of believers she discovered in Rhodesia. Typically, she makes her decision an accession to the inevitable, rather than a moral action (she writes in a similar vein about abandoning her husband and children). Whether or not one is convinced by such rationalizations, the latter stages of this autobiography, filled with the names of a great many people we have never heard of and are given no reason to have interest in, are rather heavy going. Never one to have second thoughts about a paragraph or a page she's written, Lessing exercises little stylistic shaping of her outpouring of anecdote, character, and situation. Her hope may be that it's enough merely for her to recount them, but this seems to me very much not the case. Certainly she's right to give as a reason for writing the book the fact that she was part of "an extraordinary time, the end of the British Empire in Africa." It may take a more than ordinary care with sentences and paragraphs to make that time come strongly alive to us.

Critical accounts of Lessing's contribution and stature as a writer of fiction mainly bypass her style by acting as if she didn't have one, or at least that it is of not much account, since the substance of what she says is so important. I do not think she would be pleased by this form of condescension, and there is no reason to avoid the question of what difference style makes in her work, since *The Grass is Singing* and the early "African" stories are written in a direct, unadorned, intelligently observant prose to be admired. D. H. Lawrence's presence is felt, but in a less fevered and rhetorical way. It's with the Martha Quest novels that questions of style and compositional procedure arise. The first four novels of *Children of Violence,* three of which were published before *The Golden Notebook,* are written in the leisurely, extremely conventional novelese Lessing inherited from her realist predecessors; the narrative terms are basically those within which Arnold Bennett, say, worked in *The Old Wives' Tale* and the Clayhanger trilogy. It is expected that we will care about the "story" of this young woman as she deals with her parents and her marriages, and though it's easy enough to caution that Martha Quest is not Doris Lessing, I would guess nobody reads these books without having some interest in Lessing's biography and how it felt to be acting out one's life in the late days of the British Empire in Africa. Yet readers with an appetite for interesting happenings in fiction may be slightly disappointed as they move through the many pages of these novels. Reviewing the second of them, the ironically titled *A Proper Marriage,* Kingsley Amis—whom one wouldn't suspect of being a devoted reader of Lessing—praised various excellent things in it and confided that "Mrs. Lessing is a whole network of streets ahead of the 'average' novelist." But in trying to summarize the story he apologized for implying that almost nothing happens, "especially when, as here, almost nothing happens." Amis doesn't point out what seems to me the case, that these novels also lack a density of psychological speculation that might fill in for the absence of "action." Lessing pretty much stays inside her heroine—unlike, say, the George Eliot of *Middlemarch*—and takes on a neutral tone of presentation that can, cumulatively, provoke exasperation. [In a footnote, the critic adds: "As it evidently did in a reader who scrawled in the margin of our library's copy of *A Proper Marriage,* apropos of Martha Quest's troubles, 'Bitch, bitch, bitch. Why doesn't she *do* something? I don't feel sorry for her.' "]

As for *The Golden Notebook* the consensus seems to be that after writing the first three Martha Quest novels, Lessing felt dissatisfied with her conventional narrative and proceeded to deconstruct, interrogate and elaborately play around with the novel form. Ten years after *Notebook* was published she wrote a rather tendentious preface to a revised edition, claiming that most of the criticism the novel received on its appearance has been "too silly to be true." Perhaps so (I haven't made a comparative study), but Irving Howe's review of it in *The New Republic* was anything but silly. He called it "a work of high seriousness," "the most absorbing and exciting piece of new fiction I have read in a decade." Howe, back there thirty-four years ago, was bowled over by the fact that the center of the novel's action was concerned with Anna Wulf, "a mature intellectual woman." This, Howe said, was a rarity in modern fiction, as was Lessing's ability to insist upon connections between the mind of her heroine and the larger

social and political events of the 1950s. But there were of course other attractions of the book, especially to those women who made and still make up the bulk of its readership (900,000 hardcover copies sold). Here was a book in which a man is described as looking at every woman by "imagining her as she would be when he had fucked her into insensibility." A novel in which a character goes to bat for the vaginal ("real") as opposed to the clitoral orgasm and in which the "free women," Molly and Anna, ruthlessly satirize Molly's ex-husband, the successful businessman Richard. All strong stuff for 1962, though it seems doubtful whether the book can now be read by either sex with the fresh excitement it once provoked. At any rate, it's canonized, the subject of many articles, dissertations, published books, and is certainly the most highly structured of Lessing's books, probably for better rather than worse.

But as the sixties wore on and the world in general became (even) more violent, fragmented and unhappy, so did Lessing's fiction. Her engagement with the irrational, with drugs, with the Sufi mystics and the unsavory psychology of R. D. Laing, made the monstrously overlong novel that concludes *Children of Violence* (*The Four-Gated City,* 1969) a book that at least for this reader provided no pleasure, to put it mildly. And things did not improve with the toneless solemn inner journeys in *Briefing for a Descent into Hell* (1971) and *Memoirs of a Survivor* (1974). Even the more available, previously mentioned, *Summer Before the Dark,* turns at its end into a tale of woe, unrelieved by any humor or irony. As for *Canopus in Argos,* the four-volume science-fiction series that followed (1979-82), there must be those who read it with some interest, though no one I know of did.

After this prolonged stretch of disenchantment with the novel as "bright book of life" (D. H. Lawrence), Lessing published, under the name of Jane Somers, two novels about a woman writer: written in diary form, easy to read, unencumbered by much "thought," they were published pseudonymously, so Lessing said afterwards, to see whether the public that would buy books signed Doris Lessing would do the same for Jane Somers. (They sold only modestly, and were later republished under Lessing's name.) What exactly this little experiment demonstrated I don't really see. Maybe the public and the critics were right not to rave about these books, even though they were "really" authentic products. Maybe the real test would have been, as Jonathan Yardley astutely suggested, for Lessing to have kept on publishing novels under the pseudonym—that would have been a bold experiment. But she didn't, and followed them instead in 1985 with *The Good Terrorist,* about a group of young people in a London "squat," whose animating figure is Alice, the "good" girl of the title. Reviewing it, Alison Lurie unfathomably called it the most interesting political novel since Conrad's *The Secret Agent.* In fact *The Good Terrorist* (unlike Conrad) is shapeless, to the extent of having no chapter breaks in its nearly 400 pages. In *Under My Skin* Lessing refers to her monomaniacal heroine as "quite mad," but evidently still thought it worthwhile to trace her and her dismal companions' fortunes in a detached voice of narrative reportage. Finally, more or less winding up the eighties, appeared *The Fifth Child,* a short and shocking account of what happens to a family when a mother's fifth child turns out to be a "wild" child, more incorrigible animal than human.

I would trade the last twenty years' worth of Lessing's novels for the stories and sketches she published three years ago—in an appropriately named book—*The Real Thing.* The focus here is no more nor less than London, from its restaurants, to Regent's Park and Hampstead Heath, to (in an especially attractive sketch) the London Underground as observed by the author riding on the Jubilee Line:

> Charing Cross and everyone gets out. At the exit machine a girl appears running up from the deeper levels, and she is chirping like a fire alarm. Now she has drawn our attention to it, in fact a steady bleeping is going on, and for all we know, it is a fire alarm. These days there are so many electronic bleeps, cheeps, buzzes, blurps, that we don't hear them. The girl is a fey creature, blonde locks flying around a flushed face. She is laughing dizzily, and racing a flight or flock of young things coming into the West End for an evening's adventure, all of them already crazed with pleasure, and in another dimension of speed and lightness, like sparks speeding up and out.

Who knows, maybe one of these girls was nicknamed Tigger. At any rate Lessing's prose here has the kind of relaxed power and delicacy, making it all look easy and casual, that is evident in many of the pages of *Under My Skin* and that has been so absent from the anguished, hard-driving, monumentally solemn world of her longer fictions. Cole Porter would not have wanted to live there, but he might have found a spot just under the skin of a writer discovering new things about herself and the world as she moves through her eighth decade.

### Carol Franko  (essay date Summer 1995)

SOURCE: "Authority, Truthtelling, and Parody: Doris Lessing and 'the Book,' " in *Papers on Language and Literature,* Vol. 31, No. 3, Summer, 1995, pp. 255-85.

[*In the following essay, Franko examines "Lessing's ambivalent attitude toward canonical authorities" by focusing on the ways in which the narrators of her novels and short stories—including* The Golden Notebook, Briefing for a Descent into Hell, *and* "The Sun Between Their Feet"—*use and view language.*]

> It's O.K. to hate your mom, it's in the book.
> (Lessing, *The Golden Notebook*)

> What is the function of the story-teller? [Heide Ziegler and Christopher Bigsby, "Doris Lessing," *The Radical Imagination and the Literary Tradition: Interviews with English and American Novelists,* 1982]

Photographs or sketches of Doris Lessing (her hair pulled back in a no-nonsense bun) adorn the covers of her books and perhaps are intended to support her image as wise woman and stern prophet. Description of Lessing's prose

as "magisterial" and "confident" function like these bookjackets, presenting a consolidated essence true to the source but missing what I find most interesting about Lessing's fiction. Lessing's narrative voices are often confident—sometimes intrusively so, sometimes snootily so. However, such voices also betray their struggle to assert this author-ity. The parodic moments in her fiction intensify the preoccupation of her narrators with the "contested, and contesting" nature of their words in relation to those of others [the quoted words come from Mikhail Bakhtin, "Discourse in the Novel," in *The Dialogic Imagination: Four Essays,* edited by Michael Holquist, translated by Caryl Emerson and Holquist, 1981]. Gary Saul Morson has remarked pithily that "Parody is the etiology of utterance" [*The Boundaries of Genre: Dostoevsky's "Diary of a Writer" and the Traditions of Literary Utopia,* 1981]. Lessing uses parody in various ways to give her own etiology of the origins and contexts of discourse and to tell with authority her truths about life and language.

The phrase "Doris Lessing and the Book" stands for Lessing's ambivalent attitude toward canonical authorities. By "the Book" I mean first of all the written word, with all of its associations with religious, legal, and other institutional authorities, and the intertextuality that Lessing, like all writers, must negotiate. But with Lessing, meanings of "the Book" must extend to language itself because she continually thematizes language in her fiction, a fact that is sometimes overlooked in the ongoing debate over whether Lessing has always been or has never been a "realist" writer.

The following quotations suggest what Lessing shares with one great realist: a desire to writer truthfully because such writing is an authoritative as well as a responsible social act:

> I aspire to give . . . a faithful account of men and things as they have mirrored themselves in my mind. The mirror is doubtless defective . . . the reflection faint or confused; but I feel as much bound to tell you . . . what that reflection is, as if I were in the witness-box narrating my experience on oath. . . . dreading nothing . . . but falsity. . . . Falsehood is so easy, truth so difficult. (George Eliot, *Adam Bede,* Ch. 17)

> I wouldn't say that . . . now [wouldn't say that "it is not merely a question of preventing an evil but strengthening a vision of good that will defeat evil," from **"A Small Personal Voice,"** Lessing's oft-quoted essay from 1956] because I don't know what good and evil is. But the way I think now is that if writers . . . write really truthfully (it is very hard you know to be truthful, actually) you will find that you are expressing other people. (Ziegler and Bigsby)

The contemplations in chapter 17 of *Adam Bede* are a relatively rare occurrence in George Eliot's fiction, and her narrator does not doubt language so much as her own powers to use it truthfully. In contrast, in (to list some examples) the Children of Violence series, *The Golden Notebook,* and the *Canopus in Argos* novels, Lessing's narrators continually remark on language, continually suggest that language and the discourses that construct identity have great power, but that they do not tell the truth. Lessing never relinquishes the goal of truthtelling, and to approach it she takes up two worldviews: a Marxist and a mystical orientation.

Lessing's narrators often view language from a Marxist perspective, one that unmasks language as the partner of oppressive and lying ideologies. *Martha Quest,* for example, details the heroine's subjectivity as a battleground of discourses, both the ones written down in the books and newspapers she's always reading and the ones inscribed in her "blood." Lessing also critiques language from a mystical perspective that asserts an extra-linguistic knowledge and experience. Thus Anna Wulf comes to believe that

> real experience can't be described. . . . A row of asterisks, like an old-fashioned novel, might be better. Or a symbol of some kind, a circle perhaps, or a square. Anything . . . but not words. The people who have been . . . in the place in themselves where words, patterns, order, dissolve, will know what I mean and the others won't. [*The Golden Notebook*]

As far as her personal beliefs can be gauged, Lessing has moved from an interest in a Marxist metanarrative to an involvement with sufism. However, both the Marxist and mystical critiques of discourse have been evident in her fiction all along.

Lessing, then, wants to write truthfully about the power of language to construct experience and its inadequacy to convey "real" experience. This puts her narrators in a position Bakhtin would relish: the main way they establish their authority in relation to "the Book" is by calling attention to the contextual nature of discourse, thereby disarming potential criticism and implying that *their* utterances transcend dialogism. Lessing's strategies for giving authority to her narrators develop toward this all-purpose double-voicedness that Bakhtin describes as a dialogic relationship with "one's own utterance as a whole":

> Dialogic relationships are also possible toward one's own utterance as a whole, toward its separate parts and toward an individual word within it, if we . . . speak with an inner reservation . . . as if limiting our own authorship or dividing it in two. [*Problems in Dostoevsky's Poetics,* 1984]

This double-voiced stance toward one's utterance extends the activity of parody. Parody reminds us that the words with which we strive to shape our own intentions are "always half someone else's" (Bakhtin, "Discourse"). In **"The Sun Between Their Feet,"** Lessing uses parody in a traditional "realistic" exposure of the falseness of official discourse. *The Golden Notebook* contains a more ambivalent, even duplicitous use of parody both as theme and technique. Anna Wulf, the writer-protagonist, is drawn to parody, yet deplores its complicity in what she terms the "wrong tone"; meanwhile parody makes possible her progress as a writer and a social being. Like **"The Sun Between Their Feet"** and *The Golden Notebook, Briefing for a Descent into Hell* suggests that we must take responsibility for coauthoring the discourses that shape social and private reality. *Briefing,* however, displays neither the "innocent" narrative authority of the African story nor the

ambivalence toward parody of [*The Golden Notebook*]. Its narrator garners authority by emphasizing the paradox that there is no escape from "the Book," no human reality that isn't shaped by narratives, and that the words we use in stories can only point imperfectly to reality. The parodist is thus the only truthteller, since she reminds us that "parody" is the only way to talk or write—this being Lessing's version of the authority that comes from having a dialogic relationship with one's utterance as utterance.

Nothing much happens in Lessing's African story, **"The Sun Between Their Feet."** In this story about watching and telling, an anonymous narrator watches some beetles and describes their efforts to form a ball of dung, presumably around their eggs, and roll it up and down a hill. The narrator watches for a long time in the hot African sun, from midmorning until late afternoon brings a thunderstorm. Her attitude toward the beetles combines amusement and sympathy. Early in her vigil, she moves from sitting above the beetles to crouching behind them on the grass. Later, the sun beating down on her head, she attempts to hurry their progress by scooping up beetles and ball and placing them on a smaller hill. But the beetles return to their steeper choice, demonstrating the narrator's dry remark that "it is not for us to criticise the processes of nature."

This account of **"The Sun Between Their Feet"** leaves out two crucial elements: the opening paragraph that situates the setting in relation to colonial history, and the narrator's references to and quotations from a text she calls "the book," which comments on the behavior of dung beetles. From the opening paragraph we learn that the narrator is exploring some wild land behind a train station. There is a road leading from the train station to a deserted Roman Catholic Mission. Beyond the church, this land of granite boulders, which is a Native Reserve (because useless to white farmers, one presumes) appears impassable. But the narrator finds a way in and remarks that

> people had made use of this wilderness. For one thing there were the remains of earth and rock defences built by the Mashona against the Matabele when they came raiding after cattle and women before Rhodes put an end to all that. For another, the undersurfaces of the great boulders were covered with Bushman paintings.

In a few sentences the narrator sums up the history of *Homo sapiens* in this landscape, and then moves to the dung beetles, whose "history" of ball-rolling reaches back to the Egyptians (who named them sacred) and beyond. **"The Sun Between Their Feet"** is not just a story about watching and telling; it is also about narrative authority and about reading. Aligning herself with the African landscape, with its nonhuman inhabitants, and with "the processes of nature," the narrator detaches herself from mere human concerns (even while conveying her anger at British imperialism in southern Africa). She further develops her authority by her parody of "the book" that purports to explain the beetles; in this way she asserts her independence of the printed page.

The narrator's language becomes exuberant when she describes the dung beetles. Here two beetles are making their ball:

> One had set his back legs over a bit of dung and was heaving and levering at it. The other, with a fast rolling movement, the same that a hen makes settling roused feathers over eggs, was using his body to form the ball. . . . Both beetles assaulted it . . . , frantic with creation, seizing it between their back legs, spinning it, rolling it under them. . . . [When it got away from them, they] start[ed] again on the mother-pile of muck.

The amused tone and maternal imagery meshed with mock-heroic diction are typical of the narrator's descriptions of the beetles, which contrast dramatically with that of the written authority that she first mentions after the above description:

> The book says that dung beetles form a ball of dung, lay their eggs in it, search for a gentle slope, roll the ball up it, and then allow it to roll down again so that in the process of rolling 'the pellet becomes compacted.'

The more the narrator describes what she sees, the more ludicrous such formulations become. The beetles she watches never "allow" their ball to roll down a slope; rather, they keep losing the ball and "plunging" after it. When the narrator positions herself on the grass so that she can "view the ascent through their eyes," she sees that the beetles are *not* "search[ing] for a gentle slope" (the book's phrase) but have selected "a savage mountain." When she tries to transfer them to a little hill, they "mother" their ball "patiently back to the mountain's foot." The narrator then quotes the book again: "The slope is chosen,' says the book, 'by a beautiful instinct.' " Maybe so, but the book is too removed from its subject to convey this truth. When read alongside the narrator's vivid reporting of what she sees, the book's account loses credibility. It falsifies the reality of the dung beetles (the *Scarabaeus,* or *Aleuchus sacer,* as the book informs), these beetles who were sacred to the Egyptians because they hold "the symbol of the sun between their busy stupid feet."

Nature's storyteller (my facetious epithet for Lessing's narrator) thus confidently performs "the dual role of the parodist as reader and author of another's work" [Margaret A. Rose, *Parody//Meta-Fiction: An Analysis of Parody as a Critical Mirror to the Writing and Reception of Fiction,* 1979]. She reveals the inadequacy of "the book" by quoting it "in too much context" (Morson). She does something similar in the terse opening paragraph when she notes that this land once witnessed the warfare of the Mashona and Matabele peoples "before Rhodes put an end to all that"—this phrase both a mocking echo of any knowing British colonialist and a grim statement of fact, since the whites did "put an end" to indigenous cultures in southern Africa. The narrator thus establishes herself as a skeptical truthteller, no respecter of imperialists like Rhodes nor of written authorities like the unnamed book that tamely misses the energy of the dung beetles. What follows is speculation about a third way that Lessing's storyteller usurps the authority of "the Book," now represented by Albert Camus's "The Myth of Sisyphus" [in *The*

*Myth of Sisyphus and Other Essays,* translated by Justin O'Brien, 1961].

Rather like the State of Nature in social contract theory that apparently harbors only adult male humans, there are no bugs, no sun, and no mothers in "The Myth of Sisyphus," although there is earth (on the "earth-clotted hands" of Sisyphus). The setting (nominally the Greek underworld) is an existential paring down of life to one man, one rock, one mountain, and one sympathetic viewer/teller. Camus's narrator imagines that Sisyphus takes his punishment of "futile and hopeless labor" and turns it into a triumph, by claiming it as his own, and thus elevating his story to tragedy: "If this myth is tragic, [it] is because its hero is conscious." The narrator further explains that like the old, blind Oedipus, Sisyphus discovers the intimate connection between absurdity, tragedy, and joy. The stubborn hopefulness of Camus's story ("The struggle itself toward the heights is enough to fill a man's heart" ["Myth of Sisyphus"]) combined with its insistence on the absurdity of existence is a frequent theme in Lessing's fiction. In *The Golden Notebook,* a novel that unbuilds so many certainties, allusions to "The Myth of Sisyphus" function in a rather strained manner to assert the value of "small painful . . . courage" [*The Golden Notebook*], of social consciousness, and of "find[ing] the means to proceed beyond nihilism" (Camus, "Preface").

While it is never mentioned in **"The Sun Between Their Feet,"** it is impossible not to think of "The Myth of Sisyphus," and not to notice the contrast between Camus's tragic hero, always dignified in his labor, and Lessing's comic ones, always ridiculous as they "bundle" themselves after their ball:

> I see that man going back down with a heavy yet measured step toward the torment of which he will never know the end. (Camus, "Myth")

> "The slope is chosen," says the book, "by a beautiful instinct, so that the ball of dung comes to rest in a spot suitable for the hatching of the new generation of sacred insect." (Lessing, **"Sun"**)

> They clung on to . . . their treasure with the desperation of stupidity . . . It was difficult to imagine the perfect shining globe the ball had been— . . . now . . . a bit of refuse . . . Tomorrow . . . [when] the sun had come out, they would again labour and heave a fresh ball of dung. (**"Sun"**)

Lessing's narrator, battling rival voices who have written of "her" subject matter, reveals the text that treats the beetles as too piously abstract, and "The Myth of Sisyphus" as too human-centered, valuing only tragic consciousness and not comic vitality. She writes the myth of an absurd universe as the account of creatures at once earthy and sacred, as the story of life going on in its "stupid" way.

Despite their difference of genre, setting, etc., **"The Sun Between Their Feet"** and *The Golden Notebook* are both about narrative authority and truthtelling in conflict with "the Book(s)" of powerful discourses. The narrator of **"Sun"** positions her discourse in opposition to inadequacies of "the printed page" and in conjunction with the authority of fact and presence, as if her story were not also a text; parody is simply the tool she uses to discover the partial vision of other narrators. In her "Introduction" to **The Golden Notebook** (published in 1971, nine years after the novel first appeared) Lessing takes a similar stance toward textuality, asserting that truth exists as much in oral traditions as in books and criticizing the authority of literary critics, themselves molded by educations that overvalue whatever "Book" represents current dogma. Like the narrator of **"Sun"** presenting her account as somehow separate from textuality, Lessing defines her novel through its independence of novelistic discourse and even of language—it is "new"; it contains "rawer material" than other works she has written, material that she has managed to convey before it "shaped itself into thought and pattern"; and its structure speaks a "wordless statement."

This last oft-quoted phrase provokes skepticism in me. How can "wordless statement" sum up a fiction that features a writer-protagonist who defines herself through her preoccupation with words, texts, and the problem of representation? One of the paradoxes of [**The Golden Notebook**] is that while so much of what we read is supposedly a *private* discourse—that of Anna Wulf's notebooks—Anna's comments to herself become, for readers other than Anna, authorial and authoritative voices that shape our responses to her texts. Anna is author, reader, reviewer, parodist, and critic of her own texts. Early in [**The Golden Notebook**] Lessing gives a vivid image of this authority: Anna is pictured sitting at her desk "looking down at the four notebooks as if she were a general on the top of a mountain, watching her armies deploy in the valley below."

Here is a sketch of "Anna Wulf" in relation to the macro text of **The Golden Notebook**: Anna is a character in the novel *Free Women,* which is divided into five sections; section one opens the macro text, section 5 closes it. Anna also appears in the "first person," as the author of four autobiographical notebooks (the Black one is about her experiences in Africa during WWII and in London with the filmmakers who want to use the commercially successful novel she wrote about the African years, the Red records her history with the British Communist party, the Yellow includes the draft of a novel, and the Blue is an experimental diary), each divided into four sections. She also authors "The Golden Notebook" after she has closed down her other journals; this document is the penultimate section of the macro text. The inner Golden Notebook reveals that the Anna of the notebooks is apparently the author of *Free Women* (which now appears as her semi-autobiographical fiction). The character Saul Green (who appears in the Yellow and Blue notebooks as well as the Golden one) gives her the subject matter and first sentence of *Free Women* (she reciprocates, giving Saul the first sentence of a novel that he completes). The last section of *Free Women* thus follows the revelation that it is not the encompassing text it seems; despite the fact that it "physically" frames the macro text, it is "really" an embedded text.

This "Mobius-strip" structure, with its multiple inscription of Anna-Wulf, resists finalizing interpretations that would make a false whole of Lessing's novel [see Molly Hite, *The Other Side of The Story: Structures and Strategies of Contemporary Feminist Narrative,* 1989]. Yet criticism on **The Golden Notebook** demonstrates that it is hard to avoid discussing Anna as though she were a single, coherent character. The earnest tone of Lessing's novel adds to this difficulty; Anna's painfully honest introspection, for example, makes it hard to keep "her" fragmented fictionality in mind. The Anna Wulf explored here, then, is one of several. This Anna desires a "wordless statement," in a different sense (I think) than Lessing uses it in the "Introduction." This Anna is the voice of a negative narrative authority, the writer who is also the master reader, she who prefaces, interrupts, concludes, and/or later remarks on her texts by explaining their aesthetic and moral failings. This Anna comments that language is "thinning" in the face of modern reality. However, the way she describes her distrust of her medium suggests that language is really too *thick* for her liking—too thick with the poisoned intentions of others, too thick with old, outworn definitions, and just too thick, that is, not a transparent medium for the "real thing."

This Anna is leery of parody, by definition a thick discourse. At first she welcomes "angry parody" for its critical, unmasking function, and uses it not only against the "enemy" without—the commodifiers of art, for example—but also the enemy within her own texts. In Black 1, Anna's parodic film synopsis of her novel *Frontiers of War* uncovers what she judges to be the "immoral" emotion that generated it, a "lying nostalgia" that promotes war and that sells books and movies. This early episode exemplifies Anna's ambivalent relations with parodic discourse. Parody marks her distance from others, a distance that is a mixed blessing: no one else finds her novel immoral, so Anna's self-judgment ironically results in moral isolation. At the same time, parody makes vivid her complicity with the desires and intentions of others, reminding her that she does not have complete control over her meanings; nostalgia, for example, creeps in.

Parody, soon mutates from critical tool to a term Anna uses to condemn her writing when it exhibits symptoms of the two moral and intellectual diseases of Cold War society: nostalgia and its "first cousin," the cynicism she calls the wrong tone:

> I am again falling into the wrong tone—and yet I hate that tone, and yet we all lived inside it for . . . years. . . . It was self-punishing, a locking of feeling, an inability or a refusal to fit conflicting things together to make a whole; so that one can live inside it, no matter how terrible. The refusal means one can neither change nor destroy.

Throughout Black 1, Anna breaks the flow of her narrative to comment that she is falling into the wrong tones of nostalgia or cynicism; she makes similar commentaries in her Yellow and Blue notebooks (on the falseness of fiction and her failure to "just record" daily truths). This self-critique enhances her credibility and makes us self-conscious about our responses to her text: why haven't we noticed the false or blocked feeling? But we may also start thinking about how strict Anna is with her writing, and about how difficult it is to achieve a tone that is not contaminated by unwanted influences—indeed, perhaps it is impossible. Furthermore, if Anna, as model reader, presents reading as a process of looking back and discovering what is wrong with a previously written text, what is to prevent her (or Lessing's readers) from applying the same logic to her passages of self-critique? This question becomes more urgent when we consider that parody, which Anna comes to label "false art," and which (in Yellow 4) she makes quite a point of excluding from her writing, is what finally enables her to enact her vocation as writer/representative of her time and to affirm the agency of responsible, reflective, empathic people like herself—the "boulder-pushers," as she comes to call them.

Anna is torn between individualist and interdependent ideals of the writer's self, between being an "owner" of her words and intentions, a self who takes responsibility but who is vulnerable to isolation, cynicism and/or self-hatred; and an interdependent sharer of selves, experiences, meanings, a self who can say "we" in an uncomfortably literal way but who may fail to distinguish between "real" feeling and nostalgia and whose capacity for empathy could become psychosis. Although I am keenly aware of the simplification involved, I think it is the individualist Anna, the owner/purifier/unmasker of meanings, who "speaks" narrative authority. The second, interdependent version of the writer's self is a theme and a presence—sometimes threatening, sometimes idealized—in Anna's notebooks. This "we-Anna" who shares selves and experiences literally *represents* "her" time. Furthermore, although "she" does not speak except through the critical, self-conscious Anna, the utopic potential "she" represents is the main reason for Anna's clinging to sometimes simplistic notions of truth and reality and for her desire to expel alien voices from her discourse.

"There is something new in the world." This statement, part of an eloquent speech Anna makes to her psychiatrist, declares that she does not want to contain all of her experiences in timeless archetypes, and that she thinks the modern world must be understood as possessing new powers, both of destruction (the H-bomb and the mind control practiced by the modern media are her two examples) and construction, a golden-age building of "a life that isn't full of hatred and fear and envy and competition every minute of the night and the day." Anna's developing mystical attitude that "real experience can't be described" in language is both something Lessing believes and Anna's most drastic effort to protect this utopic potential that she senses, for example, in the new lives many women are leading, despite the pains and dangers of these lives. By arguing that these new truths cannot be described in existing terms, Anna prevents them from being contained and falsified. However, since Anna still regards herself as a representative, she is not content with just sensing these truths herself. The "new" must be communicated.

"If I could say we, really meaning it, I wouldn't be here, would I?" Anna's pithy question, directed to her psychoanalyst [*The Golden Notebook*], evokes several aspects of Anna's alienation: her disillusionment with communism, which like the capitalism she also despises is by its dishonesty vitiating a sense of "we"; her growing belief that fiction writing does not represent but rather evades and deforms reality, thus further severing her connections with a "we"; and, finally, her sense that words themselves are losing their meaning by becoming divorced from intention—she cannot tell, for example, when other writers are using parody, and similarly, her parodies are read "straight." Anna's resulting double bind—her need to communicate new communal truths versus her need to rid her discourse of a diseased dialogism—leads to a dramatic self-censorship: Anna uses her negative narrative authority to reject one mode of writing after another and thus to close down her four notebooks. The following is her closing down of the Yellow notebook, the one she uses for drafts of novels and stories:

> 'Jeez, Mike,' [Dave] said, you'll write it someday, for us all.' . . . 'You'll write . . . how our souls were ruined here on the snow-white Manhattan pavement, the capitalist-money-mammon hound-of-hell hot on our heels?' 'Gee, Dave, I love you,' I said . . . [and] hit him . . . square to the jaw-bone, stammering with love-for-the-world, love-for-my-friends, for the Daves and the Mikes and the Buddies. . . .

> If I've gone back to pastiche, then it's time to stop. [The yellow notebook ended here with a double black line.] ([*The Golden Notebook*]; final brackets are Lessing's)

Anna's dismissal of her parody of "buddy-love" ignores how thick it is with her preoccupations, with her fear and hatred of the commodification of art and her need as an artist to speak for her peers, an act that is a kind of "love-for-the-world." In this sense, Mike and his pals speak for her, even though the parody also expresses her impatience with a view of the artist as (American) macho male whose closest relations are with other guys. Finally, with its cartoon embodiment of cool parodist aping self-indulgent confessor, Anna's "pastiche" arguably signals a transformation of her obsession with nostalgia and cynicism, those twin components of the "wrong tone." How could anything be more sentimental and cynical than this? Yet what language *should* be used to convey the desire for an unalienated, meaningful existence, one that contains occasional explosions of positive feeling ("I hit him then, square to the jaw-bone")? What discourse would pass Anna's test? Anna of the negative narrative authority teaches me to be skeptical of her passages of self-critique; thus, I read her buddy-love parody not as evidence of her moral and artistic exhaustion but as an exaggerated preview of her strategies in the inner Golden Notebook.

In her "Introduction," Lessing takes special pains to discuss the inner Golden Notebook, offended that early treatments of the novel ignored its importance. She claims that in this section readers "can no longer distinguish between what is Saul and what is Anna, and between them and the other people in the book." Lessing's statement implies that we could identify a choral voice in the inner Golden Notebook, maybe something like the symphonic voice in Woolf's *The Waves*. It's more accurate to say that in the inner Golden Notebook (and in the fourth section of the Blue notebook that precedes it) Anna Wulf creates a dialogue between her individualistic self who strives to purge language of poisonous contexts and her communal, perhaps extra-linguistic self who experiences reality without the boundaries drawn by her critical intelligence. This intersubjective sharing of experience seems to be what Lessing has in mind when she claims paradoxically that the reification of characters into types (according to class, gender, politics) throughout the novel co-exists with a salutary mingling of identities: "They [the types] have also reflected each other, been aspects of each other, given birth to each other's thoughts and behavior—*are* each other, form wholes" ("Intro"). The two sections that detail Anna Wulf's and Saul Green's relationship (Blue 4 and the inner Golden Notebook) bring this intersubjective reality to a climax. Anna and Saul (an American writer and disillusioned leftist currently having a breakdown) here embody both the collective madness of their time—bent on war and annihilation—and the utopic potential of transformed personal/political relations; specifically, Anna seems to "catch" Saul's sickness. In these sections Anna is "invaded" by soldiers, peasants, people from her African past, and she realizes that Saul is continually experiencing analogous invasions. We learn that in their constant fighting, she and Saul are speaking the words of others; they are "possessed," forced to be representatives: of men versus women, left versus right, working class versus middle class. When they agree to part, a separation Anna is convinced is necessary to her sanity, they believe that they will always be connected to each other—like brother and sister (Anna's view), or like being on the same team (Saul's expression).

The necessary but dangerous intersubjectivity conveyed in the inner Golden Notebook "unlocks" feeling, enabling Anna and Saul "to fit conflicting things together to make a whole." This denouement is achieved through a parodic revisiting of the sentimental and cynical "wrong tone" that has haunted Anna's notebooks. Anna transcends the false, blocked feeling of the wrong tone not by producing a merging of voices (in which her readers "can no longer distinguish between . . . Saul and . . . Anna, [or] between them and the other people in the book" ["Intro"]) but by living and writing with a heightened, parodic self-consciousness. Saul participates in the process whereby Anna both parodies and reaffirms her moral and aesthetic concern to be truthful to reality, and he is going through an analogous process; however, we are always aware that Anna is the recorder/translator of their adventures in breakdown/breakthrough.

As they experience the feelings of each other and of people around the world, Anna and Saul are aware that they are living out "parodies": Anna, for example enacts a "boo-hoo" parody of the tragically jealous, scorned woman, while Saul is alternately the heartless rake and the good American boy. This self-conscious parodying is radically different from other places in the novel where characters unwittingly ossify into grotesque parodies of various modern "types." Anna's narrative highlights one consequence of hers and Saul's self-awareness; they act out the parodies, and thus finish them, "butto[n] them up." However, parody does not just help Anna and Saul discard outworn patterns; it also enables them to "earn" an affirmation of

values that have come to seem naive or old-fashioned in the complications and disillusionments of Cold War modernity—values like empathy, courage, endurance.

Anna's progress toward reaffirming these values is furthered by her mental encounters with a "disinterested" yet "controlling personality," a part of herself whom she calls "the projectionist," and who appears in a male persona, a version of Saul. Anna sees the projectionist as a destructively cynical figure. This is odd because she also describes him as the part of herself who refuses to let her give into madness and who forces her to re-view the texts that make up her past, thus at once allowing her to affirm that her life is "still there" and asking her to re-write the emphases that she has placed on various events. In a sequence thick with Anna's characteristic dilemmas, the projectionist asks her "And what makes you think that the emphasis you have put on it [on a series of scenes from her past] is the correct emphasis?" Anna hears a "parodic twang" in the word "correct," a parody of both "the Marxist jargon-word *correct*" and of "a primness, like that of a schoolteacher." Although the projectionist is thus parodying what I have been calling Anna's negative narrative authority over her texts, he apparently does want her to scrutinize the correctness of her emphases. He shows her a series of films, *"Directed by Anna Wulf "* that parody the "convention[al], well-made, . . . glossy" quality of her narratives. This episode leaves Anna with a "feeling of nausea" which she interprets as "the strain of trying to expand one's limits beyond what has been possible." I would add that much of the strain is due to the complex use of parody she is asking herself to make: she is to continue to doubt the truth of her writing while at the same time recognizing the conventional, limited form of her self-critique.

Anna's further adventures with the projectionist come after a crucial passage in which she anticipates (i.e., recognizes that she already knows) what he will teach her next. These moments of "knowing" things have characterized her encounters with "craziness and timelessness," and they have convinced her that "the place in [oneself] where words, patterns, order, dissolve" is a more primary reality than any truth that words can convey. However, in a reversal of logic, Anna muses that "the conditions of [this reality] existing at all" may depend on people "preserv[ing] the forms, creat[ing] the patterns," which suggests that language may help produce the reality it fails to represent truthfully. Armed with this paradox and with the exhortation to parody both her writing and her self-critique, Anna re-views the film of her life, which reveals a new emphasis. It now rushes past previous high points and lingers over secondary characters who are captured in moments of sad or stubborn endurance. Anna sees she is redefining heroism as the "small, painful sort of courage which is at the root of every life, because injustice and cruelty is at the root of life."

These new "films" are truer than the previous ones, but they are still conventional—still thick constructions, not mere windows for truth—and thus can be historicized and parodied: Anna notes that they have "a rough, crude, rather jerky quality" that she names "realistic" and that reminds her of "early Russian or German" films. Anna's reaffirmation of basic values in these films is echoed by Saul, who comes back from one of his walks determined to articulate a utopian blueprint for him and Anna to follow. Like Anna's recognition that her efforts to capture reality are at best necessary rituals, Saul admits the absurdity of his assuming the role of "pedagogue," but he still insists that he and Anna and others "around in the world" are "part of the team" ("I hate teams," says Anna), that they need to "rely on each other" and "believe in our beautiful, impossible blueprints." His speech is a return to humanist faith via absurdity and despair, but also via parody, something Anna indirectly acknowledges: she compares his "moral axioms" to "mottoes out of Christmas crackers," but she also notes that he is now performing his rake's persona as a "gallant parody."

Thus parody as discourse and attitude becomes crucial for giving utopic possibility a voice and a "book" in *The Golden Notebook*. Parody allows Anna to say "we" and "really mean it" without losing the critical "I" who still uses under protest a language always steeped in others' intentions and always inadequate to the "truth." Parody also allows Anna and Saul to be friends, sister and brother, part of a team—quite an achievement in a novel that explores the modern war between the sexes. Finally, this utopic use of parody results in Lessing revisioning the "book" as artifact. The materiality or object-ness of the inner Golden Notebook is emphasized: we are told how Anna spots it in a shop, how Saul covets it and tries to appropriate it by writing a verse/curse in it, how it records the topics and first sentences that Anna and Saul give to one another for their future projects, and finally, how, after Anna gives Saul the notebook, her handwriting gives way to his. This portrayal of an "embodied" intertextuality suggests that the team Anna and Saul are on is engaged in literally remaking the books of culture.

If we try to ride the mobius strip of *The Golden Notebook* to some kind of closure, it appears that the Anna Wulf who has the extraordinary experiences recorded in the inner Golden Notebook goes on to write *Free Women,* a flat, "realistic" novel, whose parodic section titles are quietly funny—for example, the heading for *Free Women 2* reads "Two visits, some telephone calls and a tragedy," and the one for *Free Women 4* includes the phrase, "Anna does not feel herself." Of course, in a realist gesture toward narrative authority, one of the points Lessing was making with her structure was how the mess and complexity of the notebooks (real life) gets translated/confined into the "absolutely whole conventional novel" of *Free Women,* a conventionality that Lessing says is "always a lie" ["**A Talk with Doris Lessing,**" in *A Small Personal Voice: Essays, Reviews, Interviews,* edited by Paul Schlueter, 1974]. *Briefing for a Descent Into Hell* expands Anna Wulf 's/Doris Lessing's skepticism of language and literary form, suggesting that the conviction that all language use is a necessary but inadequate ritual fosters a "Maryrose attitude" toward genre. Maryrose, the lovable but inaccessible woman featured in Anna's Black notebooks, typically cuts through the intellectualizing of Anna's circle with the question "What's wrong with that?" [*The Golden Notebook*]. With its pastiche of real-

ism, fantasy, myth, and science fiction, the hybrid structure of *Briefing for a Descent Into Hell* implies a "what's wrong with it" attitude: if all language is inadequate, this amalgam that Lessing terms "inner space fiction" is no more and no less ridiculous than the parodic realism of *Free Women.* Indeed, perhaps its more explicit novelizing of language's inadequacy makes it more truthful and hence more authoritative.

The plot of *Briefing for a Descent into Hell* draws on a contemporary trope: the conflict between institutional mental health and the individual psyche. Protagonist Charles Watkins (Professor of Classics, Cambridge), has amnesia and has been admitted as John Doe into a London psychiatric hospital. As we learn through his fragmented first-person narrative, Charles is experiencing himself as the archetypal quester. He fears "sleep," meaning normal consciousness. His dreams take him on a journey around the southern Atlantic in pursuit of a crystal space ship. When this crystal picks him up, he has visions about a web of being; he sees the earth from the vastness of space and watches the history of the crust of life on it. These visions bring Charles to the brink of recovering an alien memory of his identity and purpose. His narrative becomes increasingly ambiguous as he, or someone, relates two parodic versions of how the "gods" worry about humanity and so periodically send envoys to hell (earth). Meanwhile two psychiatrists debate Charles's case in terse memos. The sinister "Dr. X" uses an experimental drug which puts Charles in a coma and then insists on electric shock treatment, which the nice "Dr. Y" delays as long as possible. However, Y's humaneness leaves him no more open than X to Charles's efforts to explain the reality of his dreams. Letters from Charles's wife, friends, and a former lover further complicate our knowledge of him. Charles decides to have the shock therapy so that X and Y will let him leave the hospital. He also hopes it will allow him to recover the tantalizing remainder of his dream-answers. Not surprisingly, though, the electric shock instead returns him to his Charles Watkins identity, his socially acceptable self that finds all the visionary concerns distasteful and embarrassing.

My reading focuses on a paradigmatic section of this complex structure, one that modulates from a meditation on language and myth through two versions of how the gods attempt to intervene in human life. The conference-of-the-gods opens with an acknowledgment that is also an indictment of the Book—*"I gotta use words when I talk to you,"* a line from T. S. Eliot's "Sweeney Agonistes"—followed by an interpretation: "Probably that sequence of words, I've got to use words, is a definition of all literature, seen from a different perspective." It's not clear whether Charles or a new voice makes this authoritative gloss on Eliot's line. If we assume that Charles is the narrator, we must acknowledge that his tone and function have shifted, from breathless voyager to confident explainer.

The indeterminacy of the narrator enacts the main theme of the novel: interdependence. In the passage preceding the conference Charles/Odysseus reaches a climax of insight:

A divorce there has been . . . between the "I"

and the "We," . . . and I (who am not I, but part of a whole composed of other human beings as they are of me) . . . am . . . spinning back . . . towards a catastrophe . . . when the microbes . . . [were] knocked out of their true understanding, so that ever since most have said, I, I, I . . . and cannot . . . say, We.

With his acceptance of the catastrophic myth that explains Earth's atomized individuality Charles has achieved a new, nonhuman coherence. No longer "I" but "we," he has shed earthly perspectives of time and space:

> I'm on the other side of the Catastrophe . . . before it. Though I'm free . . . to say "after," since like "up and down" it is . . . entirely how you look at it. . . . But man-wise . . . I am before the crash . . . in . . . air that rings with harmony. . . . I, voyager, Odysseus bound for home at last.

Charles expresses his "we" identity in a hybrid myth combining Odysseus's trip home with the visionary claim of interdependence and both with the science-fictional Castastrophe. He speaks in a moment of complete faith, from "within" the hybrid vision. We can choose to read the conference-of-the-gods as told by Charles, who is now "we," and who, with his account of the Descent Team, may be remembering his "real" identity. But we can also read it as an authorial voice (that I will refer to as an androgynous s/he) that has fused with Charles's but is distinct from his in a crucial way: this voice does not speak from "within" vision and myth; rather s/he engages readers in the task of reconstructing myths, rendering her discourse authoritative by openly participating in storytelling as version-making.

The conference-on-the-gods section contains two versions of one story: Near the end of the twentieth century Earth is going through a catastrophic period, and the gods must once more "descend" to Earth with the by-now-hackneyed message: "That there is a Harmony and that if they wish to prosper they must keep in step and, obey its Laws. Quite so." The narrator prefaces this story with a discussion of the Greco-Roman pantheon, modeling how to use stories and myths. S/he advocates at once taking them literally and regarding them skeptically and enacts this double transaction in self-consciously dialogic prose:

> Enmeshed like a chord in Bach, part of a disc as exquisitely coloured as a jelly fish . . . made up of sun and planets and baby planets[,] . . . looking at the thing from any point of view but Earth Time, it is possible a change of emphasis from Saturn to Jupiter involving a change in all conditions on Earth and taking centuries (our time) may perhaps have had to find its message thus: That Jupiter fought Saturn (or Zeus, Chronos) [and] . . . defeated him, and thereafter Jupiter was God to Earth. But here is a thought . . . not for the first time—of course not, there is no thought for the first time—why God? The . . . most kingly and, so they say, most benign of planets whose rays envelop Earth in justice . . . and [touch] . . . humanity, that grey mould struggling for survival in its struggling green

scum. . . . And on Mount Olympus bearded Jove, or Jupiter, lorded it over the subsidiary Gods—not without a certain magnificent tetchiness. But why Father? . . . Who is our Father? . . . None other than the sun, whose name is the deep chord underlying all others, Father, Sun, Amen . . . as the Christians still pray. Why not Father sun, as Lord on Olympus . . . ? . . . Of course, man cannot look directly at his Sun. Gods go in disguise, even now, as then they were, or might be, Pillars of fire—Forcefields, Wavelengths, Presences. It is possible that the Sun, like other monarchs, needs deputies, and who more suitable than Jupiter. . . . After all, Sun is . . . on an equal basis with the other stars, chiming in key with them, and having its chief business with them—for this is nothing if not a hierarchical universe, like it or not, fellow democrats.

This passage "explains" the pantheon, thus setting the stage for the conferences that follow, but it also evokes Lessing's ongoing debates on language and reality. Several strategies are evident: merging of sensory imagery (music and color); frequent use of the subjunctive; skeptical asides; juxtaposition of mythical and scientific diction; and punctuation of lofty subject matter with lowly diction. These dialogic strategies embody the narrator's suggestion that the definition of literature is inseparable from the riddle that there is a reality "beyond" language that nonetheless must be conveyed "through" language ("I gotta use words"). Indeed, the narrator's protracted unfolding of how "Sun" has been represented by lesser deities is probably intended as a little allegory, or another version, of this riddle. This passage and the entire conference-of-the-gods section demonstrate that the authoritative storyteller can offset the tendency of language to deprive reality of its complexity by bringing into play the dialogic *and* myth-making potentials of language. The narrator's techniques—especially the subjunctive ("it is possible," "may perhaps") and the skeptical asides ("so they say")—make readers a partner in the process of reconstructing myths. Our participation in this ambivalent stance toward language affects our response to the two versions of the gods' conference and "descent." We recognize that both are parodic, but because they are set in the context of the search for ways to communicate ineffable reality, we take a double attitude toward them: they are ridiculous; they are true.

The first version of the gods' conference contains several elements that imply a deliberate awkwardness: (1) the didactic message is spelled out in a dialogue (between Mercury and Minerva); (2) the allegorical characters are "fleshed out" with descriptions that are stilted translations of homeric epithets (e.g., Minerva admits to Mercury, "Only an idiot gets into an argument with the Master of Words"); (3) with several references to evolution and progress, the tone is vaguely and bombastically "Victorian." This version emphasizes how Minerva (like her Greek counterpart Athena in *The Odyssey*) wants to help humanity. She scolds Mercury that it is time to descend to Earth again. They banter, alluding to such myths of origin as the theft of fire and the eating of forbidden fruit. Mercury, god of thieves, curiosity, communication and progress, accuses Minerva, pegged as austere Justice, of wanting to trade roles with him. Mercury then descends, "and the Battalions of Progress are strengthened for the fight." The narrator breaks in, dismissing this "whimsical" version for one in the "contemporary mode," which

> is much to be preferred, thus: that Earth is due to receive a pattern of impulses from the planet nearest the Sun. . . . As a result, the Permanent Staff on Earth are reinforced and

### THE CONFERENCE

> was convened on Venus, and had delegates from as far away as Pluto and Neptune. . . . The Sun Himself was represented. . . . Minna Erve was in the Chair.

This excerpt again suggests that the narrator is trying to be awkward, the "modern" names Minna Erve and Merk only the most obvious instances. The parodied sources are more apparent here: science fiction, crudely construed, with some James Bond elements. Exposition comes awkwardly through a film: the Descent Team is shown one called *Forecast,* which details Earth's catastrophic condition. As in the first version, there are attempts to make comedy from the traditional traits of the gods. The humor is strained, the message of Earth's danger and need by now familiar: why then this second version of the gods' council?

In some ways this "contemporary" account of the gods' interest in human affairs, which comes halfway through the novel, is the heart of *Briefing for a Descent into Hell*. It offers a heroic explanation and cure to Charles's insanity: he is a member of a Descent Team, and his amnesia and visions represent his effort to shed his Charles Watkins identity and remember his "true" purpose as messenger of the gods. Merk's descriptions of what the Descent Team will suffer in the "Poisonous Hell" of Earth echo Charles's condition: amnesia, feelings of loss and disorientation, experiencing "waking up" as illness. Moreover, Merk's references to "the Briefing" of the Descent Team echoes the title of the novel (as do references to hell and descent in this section) and may seem to offer a "key" to *Briefing for a Descent into Hell* as an intelligible, aesthetic, and thematic whole: "Which brings me to the final point. . . . There is to be no Briefing. . . . You'd be bound to forget every word. . . . No, you will carry Sealed Orders. . . . brainprints." However, Merk's insistence that "There is to be no Briefing" contradicts Lessing's title in a parodic gesture that reminds us of the ubiquitousness of versions and of an intrusive narrator who wants us to participate in the making and unmaking of stories and myths, all the while keeping in mind the inadequacy of language to convey reality.

Lessing here offers what might be termed a "quixotic" parody of language. Marthe Robert has used the term "quixotic" to describe an attitude toward literary conventions or social ideals that replaces the "categorical *either/or* of satire with a distressing *and* carried to the limits of the absurd"—hence the quixotic writer inscribes genres or ideals with "piety *and* irony, respect *and* humor, admiration *and* criticism, compassion *and* rigor" [*The Old and*

*The New: From "Don Quixote" to Kafka,* translated by Carol Cosman, 1977]. These quixotic "ands" apply equally well to **"The Sun Between their Feet"** and to the inner Golden Notebook, to Nature's Storyteller's amused reverence for the dung beetles and to Anna's and Saul's serious joking about their faith in utopic possibility. The narrator of the conference-of-the gods section is more radically quixotic, however. This section is the "heart" of *Briefing for a Descent into Hell* not just because it may reveal the "true" biography of Charles but also because it represents most dramatically the novel's quixotic "both/and" approach toward language and narrative *in general*. Language and narrative are used parodically *and* seriously— hence the awkward versions of the gods' conference (parodies of parodies) that draw attention to their status as "pastiche" even while they reiterate the serious theme of interdependence and the human failure to perceive it. Just as the novel as a whole ends with Charles recovering his conventional, limited memory, the conference-of-the-gods section ends by fading into an obstetrics ward where a crying newborn is being told to sleep, "like a *good* baby." The "I" here, who experiences itself as a baby "knock[ed] over the head with sleepers, soothers, syrups, drugs and medicines," could be Charles, or any one of the Descent Team, or just anyone. Charles's parodic/heroic alternative biography thus ends with a reminder of the Sisyphean "againness" of failure in any quest.

The maternal reporter of **"The Sun Between their Feet"** affirms *her* revision of the Sisyphean myth without acknowledging that her utterance has any other "etiology" than her detached yet empathic participation in the grand materiality of the beetles, laboring up and tumbling down their mountain under the African sun. The printed word is not to be trusted, but neither does it represent much of a threat to the truth. Simply by quoting "the Book" parodically, in the context of the dung beetles' real activity, Nature's Storyteller reveals it as pathetically removed from their "stupid" yet "shining" participation in creation, energy, life (**"Sun"**). The Anna Wulf who reads her texts with an eye for their envelopment in the "wrong tone" cannot assume authority so easily nor affirm her similar values so emphatically: she does not trust hers or anyone's discourse, and she cannot use iconoclastic parody without thinking of how it is tainted with the Book that it mocks. And yet, caught in the absurd dilemma of laboring to extricate her discourse from a poisonous dialogism so that she can convey the utopic potential of intersubjectivity, Anna makes her Sisyphean progress only via the dialogic, quixotic medium of parody. Parody allows her to inscribe for herself the empathic detachment that comes "naturally" to Nature's Storyteller; it allows the "golden intertextuality" of hers and Saul's notebook, an artifact that suggests that the Book can be made anew.

There is nothing new under "bearded Jove, or Jupiter . . . [or] Father sun" for the narrator of the conference-of-the-gods section of *Briefing for a Descent into Hell,* no escape from the Book for this version-making storyteller who speaks as an anonymous, androgynous "we," and whose originality/authority resides in a tolerant but persistent thematizing of the inadequacy of language and the slipperiness of myth (*Briefing*). "There was a general brightening and steadying of their individual atmosphere, forcefields or auras." This multiple-choice description of how his majesty **"Sun"** affects Merk and others exemplifies the quixotic use of language as parody *and* reporting. The mix of "science" and "mysticism" in such passages has a mixed effect on the credibility of the narrator's "contemporary" rendering of the conference: if it is like a B movie, it also exemplifies how storytelling can undermine exclusionary world views. Thus we can trust this narrator not because s/he is superior to the printed word, nor because s/he feels guilty for contributing to the distortions of reality in the Book, but because s/he is always reminding us that if "parody" is the only way to use language, then the parodist is the only truthteller. And if there is "no thought," or story, "for the first time" (**Briefing**), there is also no end to the author-parodist's creative dung-hauling/boulder-pushing of old stories that still need to be told.

## FURTHER READING

### Criticism

Brightman, Carol. "Doris Lessing: Notes of a Novelist." *Book World—The Washington Post* (16 October 1994): 1, 14.
  Favorably reviews *Under My Skin.*

Burroway, Janet. "An Unfashionable Woman." *The New York Times Book Review* (6 November 1994): 1, 42.
  Argues that the two major themes shaping *Under My Skin* are "the twin workings of memory and projection."

Innes, Charlotte. "A Life of Doing It Her Way." *Los Angeles Times* (8 December 1994): E1, E8.
  Essay based on an interview in which Lessing discusses *Under My Skin.*

Leonard, John. "The African Queen." *The Nation* 259, No. 15 (7 November 1994): 528-36.
  Reviews *Under My Skin,* noting relationships between Lessing's autobiographical account and her fiction.

Rose, Ellen Cronan. "Somebody—but Who?" *Women's Review of Books* 12, No. 6 (March 1995): 11-12.
  Describes *Under My Skin* as a revelation of Lessing's current interpretation of such longstanding issues as her relationship with her mother, her sexuality, and her "fear of becoming . . . mired in the past."

Rubenstein, Roberta. "Life and Doris Lessing." *Chicago Tribune* (23 October 1994): section 14, pp. 1, 12.
  Praises *Under My Skin* for its "vivid reconstructions of decisive experiences and significant people of [Lessing's] childhood."

Rubin, Merle. "Author Doris Lessing Turns a Writer's Spotlight on Herself." *The Christian Science Monitor* 86, No. 248 (17 November 1994): 14.
  Argues that although "*Under My Skin* is sprinkled with provocative, often contradictory, sides on topics from abortion, sexual attraction, and parent-child bonding, to race relations, left-wing zealots, and the colonial legacy," few of these questions are resolved.

Schemo, Diana Jean. "A Portrait Unwinds, as in Life." *New York Times* (2 November 1994): C1, C10.
  Discusses *Under My Skin,* modern art, and biography. The essay is based on an interview with Lessing.

# Robert Pinsky

## 1940-

American poet, nonfiction writer, and translator.

The following entry provides an overview of Pinsky's career through 1995. For further information on his life and works, see *CLC*, Volumes 9, 19, and 38.

## INTRODUCTION

Pinsky's poetry is noted for its combination of vivid imagery and clear, discursive language that explores such themes as truth, the history of nations and individuals, and the transcendent aspects of seemingly simple acts. Pinsky strives to create an organized view of the world, often confronting and trying to explain the past so as to bring order to the present. Recurring subjects in his work include the Holocaust, religion, and childhood. Pinsky's moral tone and mastery of poetic meter are often compared to eighteenth- and nineteenth-century English poets, and the insights conveyed in his analytical works on poetry have caused critics to place him in the tradition of such other poet-critics as Samuel Taylor Coleridge, Matthew Arnold, T. S. Eliot, and W. H. Auden. Pinsky is also an accomplished translator, and his version of the first part of Dante Alighieri's *Commedia* (c.1307-c.1314), *The Inferno of Dante* (1994), has earned high praise and numerous awards.

### Biographical Information

Pinsky was born in Long Branch, New Jersey, a once-famous ocean resort that was decaying by the time of Pinsky's birth. The ethnic makeup of Long Branch was Jewish and Italian, with the resort serving as a summer home for several Mafia families. Pinsky's grandfather had been a bootlegger during Prohibition and owned the local tavern; his father had an established optometric practice. The family, as a result, enjoyed a measure of local prestige and Pinsky was known to many in town; he had, he has said, a kind of "aristocratic upbringing." Although he was not an accomplished student in school, Pinsky attended Rutgers University, where he formed friendships with a group of budding young writers and poets who published work in the school's journal, *The Anthologist*. Shunning creative writing programs, these students considered their apprenticeships as artists to be outside the domain of school and teachers' judgements. After graduating from Rutgers, Pinsky entered Stanford University, where he studied with the noted poet, critic, and teacher Yvor Winters and earned a Ph.D in 1966. The publication of *Sadness and Happiness* (1975), Pinsky's first volume of poetry, was followed by *The Situation of Poetry* (1976), an exploration of poetic language in the works of several of Pinsky's contemporaries. Pinsky has also collaborated on translations of Czesław Miłosz's poetry and on a computerized novel called *Mindwheel* (1985). He has held a variety of teaching

posts, and has been the poetry editor of *The New Republic* since 1978.

### Major Works

Pinsky's two volumes of critical poetic theory—*The Situation of Poetry* and *Poetry and the World* (1988)—articulate his belief in linguistic clarity as the means to expanding the boundaries of poetic expression. *Sadness and Happiness* contains both long and short poems but is noted in particular for the seventeen-page "Essay on Psychiatrists." Offering a variety of literary and cultural references, the poem is said to typify Pinsky's use of discursive poetic forms. Similarly, in the book length poem *An Explanation of America* (1979), one of Pinsky's most ambitious and admired works, the poet teaches his daughter about the past so that she may shape her future. The title poem in *History of My Heart* (1984) is an autobiographical narrative on memory and desire which draws on many of Pinsky's childhood, adolescent, and adult experiences. In *The Want Bone* (1990) he employs a pastiche technique characterized by overt word play in order to symbolize and examine the lust for life and the desire for sensual experience. The volume includes mock Biblical stories on the childhood of Jesus and an extended prose section in which Jesus, in disguise, enters the story of Tristan and Isolde in order to learn about love. *The Inferno of Dante* is an English translation of the first part of Dante's three-part poetic work *Commedia.* The *Inferno* follows Dante and the Roman poet Virgil as they descend and explore the nine levels of Hell, where sinners eternally suffer torments that reflect their sins in life; for example, as Edward Hirsch noted, in *Inferno* "sin is literalized: those who succumbed to anger tear perpetually at one another's naked bodies; gluttons wallow in putrid soil and get chewed by Cerberus; murderers boil in a river of blood." To give the narrative a nearly physical sense of spiraling descent, Dante created the *terza rima* rhyme scheme. *Terza rima* is made up of tercets, three-line stanzas linked by the rhyming pattern *a b a / b c b / d c d* etc. Because *terza rima* is integral to the poetic character of *Inferno,* Pinsky's translation simulates the pattern by using "slant-rhymes," a scheme based on like-sounding consonants at the ends of lines in each tercet. Pinsky also attempts to preserve Dante's intended meanings by expanding on or compressing what a literal translation of the Italian would render.

## Critical Reception

Pinsky is often praised for his grasp of traditional metrical forms and his ability to evoke timeless meaning within the strictures of contemporary idioms. Critics applaud Pinsky's ability to imbue simple images—a Brownie troop square dance, cold weather, the music of Fats Waller—with underlying meaning to create order out of the accidental events people encounter in their lives. Critics admire Pinsky's ambitiousness, his juxtaposition of the personal with the universal, the present with the past, the simple with the complex. Critics note that his intellectual style presents challenges to readers, obliging them to unravel the complexity behind the clarity of language and imagery. Regarding his translation of Dante, while most critics applaud the readability of Pinsky's version and praise his evocation of Dante's "vulgar eloquence," a few commentators suggest that the phrasing in places remains stilted and that his slant-rhymes do not convey the "momentum" of the original *terza rima.* Nevertheless, most critics agree with Hirsch that *The Inferno of Dante* maintains "the original's episodic and narrative velocity while mirroring its formal shape and character," and that "Pinsky succeeds in creating a supple American equivalent for Dante's vernacular music where many others have failed."

---

## PRINCIPAL WORKS

*Landor's Poetry* (essays) 1968
*Sadness and Happiness* (poetry) 1975
*The Situation of Poetry: Contemporary Poetry and Its Traditions* (essays) 1976
*An Explanation of America* (poetry) 1979
*History of My Heart* (poetry) 1984
*Poetry and the World* (poetry and essays) 1988
*The Want Bone* (poetry) 1990

*The Inferno of Dante* [translator] (poetry) 1994

---

## CRITICISM

### Stephen Corey (review date Spring 1985)

SOURCE: A review of *History of My Heart,* in *The Georgia Review,* Vol. XXXIX, No. 1, Spring, 1985, pp. 213-14.

[*Corey is an American poet, critic, and educator. In the following review, a portion of which appeared in CLC-38, he praises Pinsky for the depth of his insights and for not succumbing to sentimentality as he offers hopeful "assertions" about the human condition.*]

The rhythms of Robert Pinsky's work are characterized by a graceful sheen and ease that some readers have taken as an indication of a moral naïveté or indifference or even flippancy; he has been thought too decorous, too much the aesthete, for our difficult age. But his caring and wisdom run deep, and the quiet tones of his poems only lay a delicate skin over the abyss he has seen too well. Apparently, he finds the lullings and liftings of music to be among the only stays sufficiently strong for our bleak confusions: "The world, random, / Is so real, it is as if our own / Good or bad luck were here only / As a kind of filler, holding together / Just that much of the adjacent / Splendor and terror."

One way to bend the luck, to try to steer the random for a moment, is by making memory work hard enough—driving it down to the specific places and names in our histories. Sometimes the drive leads to terror, as in **"The Unseen"** [from *History of My Heart*], a poem about visiting the "monument" of a concentration camp. While there, Pinsky recalls that he has daydreamed about achieving a Lear-like vengeance upon the Nazis by roaming the camps invisibly: "At first I savor my mastery / Slowly by creating small phantom diversions, / Then kill kill kill kill, a detailed and strangely / Passionless inward movie."

Other times, terror softens to profound sadness, as in **"The Questions"**: with a sympathy reminiscent of Philip Levine's in *The Names of the Lost,* Pinsky returns to the stream of adults who moved through his childhood in his father's office: "I want for them not to have died in awful pain, friendless. / Though many of the living are starving, I still pray for these, / Dead, mostly anonymous (but Mr. Monk, Mrs. Rose Vogel) / And barely remembered: that they had a little extra, something / For pleasure, a good meal, a book. . . ."

And for Pinsky, there are even times when splendor wins out—really wins, except for that tinge of sadness whose emergence from all things is the only certainty we have. In the long title poem, Pinsky offers a believable hope and innocence almost extinct in serious American poetry of this century. Across some two hundred lines, he confronts and defeats constant threats of sentimentality as he explores the minutiae of autobiography, searching for what can only be called a theory of desire. Early in **"History of**

**My Heart,"** Pinsky says that "happiness needs a setting," and nearly all of the poem is devoted to providing this—from his mother's early stories of life before his birth, on up through his own memories of infancy, childhood, and adolescence.

The poem culminates with a dozen lines of assertion, just the kind of proselytizing that poets often try to shun. But on the strength and beauty of what he has already said, and of these closing lines themselves, Pinsky carries his poem beyond fashion and proscription. With a dazzling mixture of images and dictions, he recalls his teenage days as a saxophonist, thinking how sometimes "I felt / My heart following after a capacious form, / Sexual and abstract, in the thunk, thrum, / Thrum, come-wallow and then a little screen / Of quicker notes goosing to a fifth higher, winging / To clang-whomp of a major seventh: listen to *me* / Listen to *me,* the heart says in reprise until sometimes / In the course of giving itself it flows out of itself / All the way across the air, in a music piercing / As the kids at the beach calling from the water *Look, / Look at me,* to their mothers, but out of itself, into / The listener the way feeling pretty or full of erotic revery / Makes the one who feels seem beautiful to the beholder / Witnessing the idea of the giving of desire—nothing more wanted / Than the little singing notes of wanting—the heart / Yearning further into giving itself into the air, breath / Strained into song emptying the golden bell it comes from, / The pure source poured altogether out and away."

**Roger Mitchell    (review date January 1986)**

SOURCE: A review of *History of My Heart,* in *Poetry,* Vol. CXLVII, No. 4, January, 1986, pp. 236-38.

[*Mitchell is an American poet, critic, and educator. In the following review, he praises Pinsky's poetic ambitions and the combination of "boldness" and "restraint" in the poems in* History of My Heart.]

Three short poems in *History of My Heart,* called "Three on Luck," are written so convincingly in the rhythms and phrases of contemporary speech that, next to the others in the book, they sound like poems in dialect. Beside them the rest seem formal and ornate. They are also the only poems in the book spoken by someone other than Pinsky, or the person we take to be Pinsky. The older poet in "Three on Luck" says, " 'Don't squander the success of your first book; / Now that you have a little reputation, / Be patient until you've written one as good.' " By contrast, **"The Unseen"** ends with a passage of old-fashioned rhetoric which does what I imagine rhetoric has always done, i.e., compress thought and feeling in an expansion of syntax and locution:

> . . . we have
> No shape, we are poured out like water, but still
>
> We try to take in what won't be turned from in
>     despair:
> As if, just as we turned toward the fumbled
>     drama
> Of the religious art shop window to accuse you
> [God]

Yet again, you were to slit open your red heart
To show us at last the secret of your day and
    also,
Because it also is yours, of your night.

I swore I would not use Pinsky's excellent book of criticism, *The Situation of Poetry,* in reviewing his poetry, but the first thing I want to say about it is said there too well: "There is a temptation to see much of modern poetry's history as a series of strategies for retaining or recovering the elevation of Victorian diction." Pinsky's strategy for doing this seems to be his own. He mixes rhetoric with a quiet, uninflected, undramatic language, one that I associate with Ashbery, as though ordinary language and experience had to be present in the poem in all their ordinariness to make the poem legitimate. Pinsky is not photographing mental experience, as Ashbery often seems to be, but rendering carefully conceived poems, indeed statements on life, in a surreptitious manner.

This is not to say that he lacks ambition for his poems. The person who titles his books *An Explanation of America, Sadness and Happiness,* and *History of My Heart* is aiming high. The poems often have a similar grandiosity, a need to summarize and signify experience, which makes the interest in Victorian diction understandable. The deflated, almost boring, contemporary speech with which it is mixed anchors the poem and keeps it from drifting too far out to sea. In **"The Street,"** for example, we have patches of prose like this:

> Once a stranger drove off in a car
> With somebody's wife,
>
> And he ran after them in his undershirt
> And threw his shoe at the car.

**"The Street"** begins, however, with a self-conscious, elaborated image written in an elevated diction:

> Streaked and fretted with effort, the thick
> Vine of the world, red nervelets
> Coiled at its tips.
>
> All roads lead from it.

The verbless first sentence is almost stagey, but it indicates Pinsky's grand design. As the poem says at the end, in another flourish of rhetoric:

> Nothing was too ugly or petty or terrible
> To be weighed in the immense
>
> Silver scales of the dead: the looming
> Balances set right onto the live, dangerous
> Gray bark of the street.

Pinsky's aim in this book, as I've indicated, is not slight. He wishes to find and, if not find, to give point to the pointless sprawl of existence. The book opens with **"The Figured Wheel,"** a poem that rolls all of creation up, as it were, into one ball, where everything is "figured and prefigured in the nothing-transfiguring wheel." **"The Living"** tries the impossible, namely, to find "glory" in the randomness of existence: " . . . the most miserable // Find in the mere daylight and air / A miraculous daily bread." If that seems too wilful or banal, the poem ends with a more measured, but no less comprehensive, statement in its final image: "this impenetrable haze, this prolonged / But not infinite surfeit of glory."

I like the boldness of the best of these poems, as well as the attempt to praise. The restraint in the praise seems justified, too, considering the atrocities we commit daily. Today, poets are apt to look for what matters in what comes their way. Poems of overt will and design are viewed sceptically. Pinsky may have found a way to hold these incompatible things together, just as he holds "the boredom and the glory" together.

## Anthony Libby   (review date Spring 1989)

SOURCE: "Rat-Rhymers, Shit-Burners, Transformation, and Grandpa Dave," in *The Kenyon Review,* Vol. XI, No. 2, Spring, 1989, pp. 140-45.

[*Libby is an American educator and critic. In the following excerpt from a review in which he examines Pinsky's* Poetry and the World *and Terrence Des Pres's* Praises and Dispraises, Politics and Poetry, the 20th Century *(1988), he discusses the ways in which Pinsky addresses political matters in the reviews and essays collected in the volume.*]

> There is evidence of a measure of [American poetic] self-censorship in the cyclical uproar about the question of the relationship between poetry and politics, which wouldn't even be taken seriously in any other country.
>
> Carolyn Forché, *American Poetry Review* Interview, (November/December 1988)

If poets are really the unacknowledged legislators of the world, they have a lot to answer for. In America we would rather believe, with Auden, that poetry makes nothing happen. Even when we write about politics and poetry, and write out of evident anguish and conviction, we tend to create analyses of negation. Both of these books [*Poetry and the World* and *Praises and Dispraises, Poetry and Politics, the 20th Century* by Terrence Des Pres], which approach the problem of politics and poetry from opposed angles, mix deep intelligence about art and history with a pervasive resistance to ideological thinking, a desire for escape from the burdens of history into the haven of poetry. Neither focuses very much on what we usually think of when we think of political poetry—that is, poetry designed, if not to legislate, to make something happen: for instance the antiwar or ecological poetry of the American sixties and seventies. But the reason for this swerving from the troubling questions may not be self-censorship, even unconscious. In Des Pres's case it may be the despair created by the inevitable darkness of the modern radical vision; in Pinsky's, traditionalist longings perhaps caused by the present failure of liberalism. . . .

Pinsky's book is far more miscellaneous and uneven than *Praise,* essentially consisting of brief reviews, memoirs, and a few extended theoretical pieces. Like his influential *The Situation of Poetry,* which, in the poetry wars of the sixties and seventies, attacked deep image romanticism and campaigned for discursive poetry and "reason" (defined in Enlightenment terms), this is a neo-Wintersian work. There is still the habitual deference to the old curmudgeon Yvor Winters, the emphasis on the morality of forms, the religious longing under the insistent rationalism. There is also an oddly ahistorical tendency to look to seventeenth- or eighteenth-century poems for comparison with works of modern social commentary, and a faintly elitist or traditionalist tendency to define poetry as an activity of "the court." Pinsky speaks for the fathers. But his tone in this collection is softer, more open and engaged than in his earlier book. Somehow Grandpa Dave is a more benevolent presiding spirit than Father Yvor.

Most of the reviews here are a sharp pleasure to read. It is great fun to watch Pinsky being judgmental but strenuously fair to Philip Larkin while Larkin is being judgmental and atrociously unfair to practically everyone, especially blacks and Jews. And Pinsky consistently demonstrates a remarkable ability to define the movements and strategies of particular poems—especially in his Elizabeth Bishop and Marianne Moore pieces. But the most interesting sections of the book are first the most abstract, then the most personal—the excursions into theory, then the memoirs. These occasional pieces are by no means a systematic attempt to deal with the relation of politics and poetry, but partly because they are casual and frank, they reveal much that is distressing about American approaches to the problem.

Pinsky seems to live in a slightly safer world than Des Pres does, one more protected by the traditional absolutes. But his thinking about poetry's place in that world comes to a similar end, if anything even more removed from the optimistic imagination of activism. Part of the reason for this removal is brilliantly analyzed by Pinsky's **"Responsibilities of the Poet."** The difficulty he delineates there convincingly explains the contemporary American problem with political poetry as an aspect of a broader problem, the necessity of transformation. "Before an artist can see a subject—foreign policy, or any other subject—the artist must transform it: answer the received cultural imagination of the subject with something utterly different." So the failure of political poetry (or "poetry of witness"—Pinsky quotes Forché's term) is not a failure of will or conviction but of the capacity for transformation, especially for poets conditioned by a country where politics usually consists of the suppression of ideological thought. Here Pinsky makes an interesting leap: because traditional ideas of "the poetic" can blunt the power of poetry to comprehend the world, the real responsibility of the poet is especially to the "unpoetic," for reasons of craft as well as social morality. "In the most uncompromising sense, this means that whatever important experience seems least poetic to me is likely to be my job."

Having come this far, Pinsky then abruptly swerves away from the political. He ends the lecture with an analysis of the transformations necessary in poems about, respectively, God and love. These are social subjects, yes, but they are also the subjects that most routinely allow escape from political concerns. Here and in later essays we keep expecting Pinsky's clear analytic eye actually to confront contemporary poetry of engagement. Yes, all poetry is political, but what about *political* poetry? The closest we get, among the poems of this century, is a discussion of William Carlos Williams's "To Elsie," which is undeniably social commentary, but understandable more in religious terms—a fall from grace—than directly social ones. Uncharacteristically elitist for Williams, it seems full of horror at the mob, at what Pinsky calls "the terror of the darkness of American freedom." Like *The Waste Land* it describes social collapse in terms of bad sex among the peasants. And it presents us, again, with the familiar excremental vision: "as if the earth under our feet / were / an excrement of some sky / and we degraded prisoners / destined / to hunger until we eat filth." Des Pres might assent.

This highly intelligent poet's analysis of poetry in the world continues to go indicatively askew as Pinsky writes about American backgrounds, and his own. Partly the problem is excessive formalism. A discussion of the social implications of the opposition between high and low vocabularies simply goes too far, dragging down Pinsky's own usually clear style as it goes. More important, there emerge questionable assumptions about poetry and culture, the thrust of which is usually to suggest that poetry exists in some absolute realm beyond cultural conditioning. Pinsky claims that art is by definition liberating, for instance, and that "the appetite for poetry" achieves the status of the other "human appetites; the desire for cuisine, beyond nutrition; for eroticism, beyond sexuality." Well, maybe, but this and other vaguely absolutist statements about the nature of things militate against the historical/political understanding of how cultures change.

This problem emerges most clearly in the autobiographical essays that end this collection, because they are both more open and more careless than the critical theorizing. The scope of those essays makes it clear what "the world" finally comes down to, in Pinsky's typically American experience. This sense of the world is conditioned by the sense of the past, the collective past, but also the memory of childhood. This world consists most strongly of family, small hometown, religion, and European roots, all lovingly rendered with a sort of glow that suggests a civics class definition of the American tradition. This close to the heart, politics is not allowed.

As he makes himself vulnerable to such a description, Pinsky also shows some understanding of the limits of this conception of things. In fact this is more or less the subject of a piece about a trip to Poland during the 1981 Solidarity struggles. It's here that Pinsky presents himself as the stereotypically American "hick," who "underestimated history," the innocent who amuses the Poles burdened by the shit of politics by explaining that in America anti-Semitism is insignificant. They don't believe his protestations of American innocence. Neither do I, not because of anti-Semitism, especially, but because of history, because of what is omitted from Pinsky's essays on America and his past, which end not in a meditation about justice or injustice, but about the religion of his father.

Even as Pinsky admits he exaggerated America's "pure freedom from bloody European mania" he conversely demonstrates his will to believe in it, in what Forché calls "the lie of our own moral superiority." Exploring the territory of our confusion about politics, he becomes an ex-

ample of that confusion. This is the inevitable problem of someone writing, as Des Pres put it, "at the center of empire, a malady now widespread in American letters." But the malady is compounded by the tendency to perceive empire through the reducing mirror of childhood, as a series of small towns steeped in innocence and opportunity.

Pinsky's good cheer is finally more apolitical than Des Pres's modern gloom. Again nostalgia replaces history. Perhaps our truest political text is still Fitzgerald's novel about the will to restore the past, and the deaths that result when a powerful and loving man falls into nostalgia for the world. So we beat on.

### John L. Brown    (review date Autumn 1989)

SOURCE: A review of *Poetry and the World*, in *World Literature Today*, Vol. 63, No. 4, Autumn, 1989, pp. 751-52.

[*In the following favorable review of* Poetry and the World, *Brown summarizes Pinsky's main critical points and contends that the book's most interesting pieces are the ones which relate memories of Pinsky's childhood and family.*]

[*Poetry and the World* is a] mixed salad indeed, but one which is deftly tossed and agreeably seasoned. Robert Pinsky flings into the bowl the most varied ingredients: recollections of his youth in Long Branch, New Jersey; a commentary on some passages of Isaiah memorized for his Bar Mitzvah; an account of his trip to Poland on a cultural mission for the State Department; a section, "Poetry and the World," with essays such as **"Poetry and Pleasure"** and **"The Responsibilities of the Poet"** as well as brief pieces on Marianne Moore, Elizabeth Bishop, George Oppen, Seamus Heaney, and Philip Larkin; a treatment of "American Poetry and American Life" composed of two parts, **"Freneau, Whitman, and Williams"** and **"American Poetry and American Life."** In his foreword he claims that these various elements all concern "the relation of poetry to its great, shadowy social context, the world." They are also linked by a common tone, a tone of relaxed, unpretentious conversation comprehensible to the common reader.

Pinsky's criticism is far removed from that of his deconstructionist academic colleagues. He proclaims his respect for literary tradition. He did a doctoral dissertation on W. S. Landor and has translated Horace. He has none of the urge to destroy the past which fired the avant-garde movements of this century. He writes: "We must feel ready to answer, as if asked by the dead if we have handed on what they gave us or asked by the unborn what we have for them. This is one answer, the great conservative answer, to the question of what responsibility the poet bears in society." It is clear why certain fellow critics regard Pinsky as "deliberately old fashioned." In **"American Poetry and American Life"** he extols P. Freneau and gives an extended analysis of "The Indian Burial Ground," although Freneau is usually dismissed as a versifier whose passionate devotion to Jeffersonian democracy far outweighed his literary gifts. Whitman, of course, is praised for having successfully confronted "the gulf between ideals of liberty, art, democracy and the actual confusion, provinciality and economic struggles of American citizens and slaves." Pinsky observes that at the present time "the Whitmanian vision" has been most vividly expressed "by makers of movies and television and of American songs." He hails W. C. Williams for his success in relating American poetry to American life.

The second part of this section comments on Frank O'Hara, James Wright, Wallace Stevens, Jean Toomer, and Anne Winters as practitioners of what Pinsky styles "formal heteroglossia," a procedure which is "a special American version of the old contest between established rhetoric on one side and the fresh growths of culture and personal experience on the other." Such critical passages may seem pedestrian, however, in comparison with the freshness and zest of boyhood memories of family and friends in Long Branch, with characters as picturesque as Pinsky's grandfather "with his big hands and his ape face," a successful bootlegger and a professional boxer; Izzy Ash, the owner of the town's largest junkyard, who gave him good counsel about graduate studies; and Norman Mailer's aunt, who ran a dress shop called "Estelle's."

## Paul Breslin   (review date August 1990)

SOURCE: "Poetry, Criticism, and the World," in *Poetry,* Vol. CLVI, No. 5, August, 1990, pp. 297-308.

[*Breslin is an American poet, critic, and educator. In the following excerpt from a review of Pinsky's* Poetry and the World *and J. D. McClatchy's* White Paper: On Contemporary American Poetry *(1989), he describes the former as "essential," even though "it promises more 'world' than it delivers."*]

In *Poetry and the World* and *White Paper: On Contemporary American Poetry,* two well-known poets present selections of their essays. Robert Pinsky has already written two prose books, one of which, *The Situation of Poetry,* has been widely and justly praised. (The other, a short study of Walter Savage Landor [*Landor's Poetry*], is less celebrated but well worth reading.) *Poetry and the World,* as its capacious title suggests, is less formal than its predecessors, ranging from critical essays through reflections on the "responsibilities of the poet" to autobiographical pieces such as **"Salt Water."** Nonetheless, Pinsky tells us in his **"Foreword,"** the "parts have been selected and recast, and most of them were written, with the idea in mind of poetry's relation to its great, shadowy social context: 'the world.'" McClatchy's title is less free-wheeling: only contemporary American poetry will be addressed, and although McClatchy has written on many contemporary poets, he has selected those who, despite their diversity, "seem to [his] mind to form a group" in offering "a difficult and exemplary challenge to the middlebrow expectations brought to poetry over the past thirty years by critics and poets alike." One meaning of *White Paper,* McClatchy reminds us, "is 'position paper'"; he has chosen essays that take a "consistent and at times combative" stance against what he regards as "middlebrow" taste.

In **"Responsibilities of the Poet,"** Pinsky suggests that poets respond to a difficult but productive tension between tradition and what he calls, following Carolyn Forché, the need to "witness." Tradition holds us responsible for "the keeping of an art that we did not invent, but were given, so that others who come after us can have it if they want it"; it asks, on behalf of the dead, "if we have handed on what they gave us," and on behalf of the unborn "what we have for them." But the responsibility of bearing witness requires that we "notice" and "include the evidence," and our capacity to do so "can be confused and blunted by the other, conserving responsibility of mediation between the dead and the unborn." Bearing witness troubles the received art into changing and renewing itself: "only the challenge of what may seem unpoetic, that which has not already been made poetic by the tradition, can keep the art truly pure and alive." Pinsky has a keen sense of the relationships of poems to other poems, but he insists on the need for an encounter between poetry and that which is not itself, a "world" that is not always already text. . . .

The passage that leapt out at me most in *Poetry and the World,* perhaps because I was reading it in conjunction with *White Paper* (and certainly because I have been working on West Indian poetry lately), occurs in **"American Poetry and American Life,"** which, along with its companion piece on Freneau, Whitman, and Williams, is my favorite among the critical essays in Pinsky's volume. It concerns the implications of cultural pluralism for poetic style and poetic value—the issue that McClatchy raises and then neglects. Pinsky, winding up a discussion of Jean Toomer's "Georgia Dusk" in which he notes the "multiple fracturing and reblending of linguistic elements— Arabic and Latin, African and English, *juju-man* and *king, swamp* and *caravan, pine* and *guitar, strummings* and *vespers* of the *cane,*" observes that

> This American version of 'The Solitary Reaper' . . . expresses its action partly through a kind of formal inclusion of many actual and potential voices. The somewhat cumbersome technical term might be formal heteroglossia. Each moment of idiom and rhythm asks what tongue should speak next—what language, what person, in what cadence? (From this perspective, the Black poets of the nineteenth and early twentieth century are not fringe elements in the record of our poetry, but characteristic, even quintessential, insofar as the clash between means and experience may require an American to forge imaginatively his own place in what he sees.)

The description of Toomer's poem as an "American version of 'The Solitary Reaper'" presupposes an audience familiar with Wordsworth, but also with Afro-American poetry, and with the history of cultural and linguistic mingling (and conflict) that makes the "formal heteroglossia" of "Georgia Dusk" possible. Pinsky argues that the heterogeneity of American life requires "a formal resourcefulness in defining one's behavior on shifting ground." It must be said that while Pinsky offers a fine commentary on the shifting voices in Anne Winters's "Night Wash," and remarks on the linguistic juxtapositions in Philip Levine, James McMichael, Marianne Moore, and Elizabeth Bishop (along with Freneau, Whitman, and Williams), Toomer is the only Black poet discussed in the entire book. If the Black poets are "characteristic, even quintessential" in the development of an American poetics, one would expect to read more about them. (Please note that it's not some demand on my part for an Equal Opportunity criticism, but Pinsky's own argument that raises this expectation.) No dates are given for the essays in *Poetry and the World,* but I suspect that the reflections on American "heteroglossia" are among the most recent, and that Pinsky will explore their implications further.

Pinsky also has thought about the strained relations between the American audience and the poet, who has never quite been able to compete with the novelist, let alone the film-maker, for the representative role that Whitman sought to fill. Accordingly, some American poems indulge in imagining an audience that could never be addressed on any conceivable occasion—as when Frank O'Hara, in "Ave Maria," tries to convince the "Mothers of America" that it's just as well if their pubescent sons are seduced at the movies by some O'Hara-like stranger, or Williams, in "Tract," harangues his "townspeople" on "how to perform a funeral." In such poems,

> the point is less the advice than the preposterous quality of the advice, the vacuum that flexes when the poem assumes not only a relation with a communal audience, but the perhaps equally unlikely existence of that audience—as if 'my townspeople' or 'Mothers of America' had an objective existence as a group, like a feudal manor or the Kiwanis International. Both poems are slight within their authors' canons because of this similar, perhaps too self-permissive comedy, the license of a voice that does not matter too much, addressing a phantom gathering.

The problem, as Pinsky frames it in **"The Responsibilities of the Poet,"** is to feel "responsible" in "the root sense" of the word, answerable: "we want our answers to be craved," and "An artist needs not so much an audience, as to feel a need to answer, a promise to respond." This way of putting the matter is suggestive but somewhat evasive too: if one has no audience, one's answers are not "craved," and the need to answer is its own reward.

In **"Freneau, Whitman, Williams,"** Pinsky asks: "What is, or what would be, a democratic poetry? What is the relation of an art reborn in European courts to vernacular culture?" For Williams, Whitman's "charge to bring together poetry and democracy" means "to bring together the heritage of royal courts and the reality of American manners. . . ." Both Whitman and Williams took a "double view," in which "the poet celebrating the idea of democracy and liberty" is also "the poet angry and despairing at the place, in the actual United States, of democracy, liberty and poetry. . . ." And "under that dual feeling is an irritable, restlessly energetic passion to sort out the provinciality, rawness, and vulgarity that are the opposite of poetry from the defiant provinciality, the vital rawness and the saving vulgarity that are the sources of an American art." Pinsky stops short of asking outright whether the aristocratic history of poetry is a source of positive value, part of what we must pass on to the unborn, or merely a vestigial survival, like the appendix in the digestive system, that can be removed without harm to the body. If I'm

not mistaken, Pinsky thinks that the aristocratic origins of poetry are what place it in its antithetical relation to American provinciality, rawness, and vulgarity. If so, the critical power of poetry derives partly from those origins, from the conviction that standards of urbanity, polish, and refinement ought not to be levelled entirely. At the same time, if poetry is to become democratic, it must find "saving" graces even where the aristocratic ones are lacking.

Philip Freneau, the first poet to confront this problem, combined "loyalties to the metric of Alexander Pope and to the ideals of the French Revolution," so that his poem "To Sir Toby" inveighs against slavery in balanced syntax and heroic couplets, and succeeds only in spoiling the aristocratic grace of the form by the bluntness of its outrage. Both Pope and Freneau use catalogues containing one "ironically out-of-place element," but whereas in Pope, the incongruity "is like a knowing social joke between reader and writer . . . there is no place in Freneau's poem for the implied social understanding between him and his reader." Though "skillful in execution and truly admirable in feeling," the poem "falls short because it fails to imagine a society—which is to say, an American society—in which the poem itself can take place." In contrast, Williams's "To Elsie" begins by "fitting Elsie into her historical and geographical process," but then "strains to fit itself, 'the imagination,' into the context of her life." "American poetry," Pinsky argues, "includes American life by striving to discover poetry's place in American life."

These essays seem to me the best of those that treat poetry in its political relation to "the world." The others, with one powerful exception, concern "the social world in its alternate glamour and squalor," which poetry falls in and out of love with, torn between fascination and withdrawal to "a distinct world which is other, a spiritual world." The fascination, when it is that, has to do with "the linked pleasures of art and sexual attraction," the "sensuousness" of giving "elegance and significance to the sounds that breath makes vibrating in the mouth and throat," and the desire, whether by writing a poem or by telling a joke, "to give the gift of pleasure and interest." Sometimes, as in **"Poetry and Pleasure,"** worldliness is presented in its relation to poetry; elsewhere, as in **"Salt Water,"** the focus is autobiographical. I don't know whether it's a sour streak in my own temperament or something in the manner of these essays themselves, but I take less pleasure and interest in these pieces than in the wonderful **"Some Passages of Isaiah,"** which is antithetical to them. Isaiah is the poet as prophet, not as courtier; he knows, at the moment of his call to prophecy, that he must address a people who will neither understand nor believe him; indeed, that his prophecy must cause them "to see and to hear in the wrong way" until they deserve the destruction God plans for them. Only at the end of secular time can the world and the prophet's word be reconciled. That, no doubt, is a conception of the poet's task both too bleak and too grandiose for the late twentieth century. But Pinsky, having praised Campion's "Now Winter Nights Enlarge" because it "celebrates with the utmost relish the scenes and diversions [of the court] which it puts in their proper place," nonetheless risks a trivialization of the social by thinking of it as essentially an affair of manners, of pleasing and being pleased. Not that one wishes always to dwell on atrocity stories, but the social world, whether in life or in poetry, includes the battlefield and the prison as well as the court, and Pinsky's account of it, except in his discussion of "witness" in **"Responsibilities of the Poet,"** tends to forget its harshness. Even Pinsky's two essays about a visit to Poland during the heady first triumphs of Solidarity don't quite encompass this larger sense of "world," since the Poles he meets are almost all fellow poets, whose conversation about politics tends to emphasize its implications for the writer.

My main reservation, then, about Pinsky's book—smaller than the one about McClatchy's—concerns its incomplete break with a 'pure' conception of poetry. For all his emphasis on relations between poetry and "the world," he usually presents the world as already transformed into the language of a poem; his account of the transformation itself is often sketchy, even perfunctory. The typography of the cover might be taken as an allegory: "Poetry" is blazoned in large red letters, and beneath it, in slightly smaller type, "The World." The two terms are separated by a thin line, broken to accommodate—in much smaller and razor-thin lettering—the humble connective, "and." On one side of that line are the essays of anecdote and autobiography, offering a concrete but local knowledge; on the other are the attentive, often brilliant analyses of how cultural history registers in the diction, syntax, and tone of poems. But the discussion of culture-in-poetry seems sealed off, to some degree, from any contact with other disciplines, such as history and anthropology, that also concern "the world" and its representation in language. For his discussion of Freneau, Pinsky does cite some historical work on the early National Period, and one misses a similar specificity of context elsewhere. It's perhaps churlish to complain, since within their own chosen limits Pinsky's essays on poetry are arguably the best now being written. Yet I can't help feeling that some interdisciplinary fresh air would invigorate them for a more tenacious engagement with "the world." Such books, for instance, as James Clifford's *The Predicament of Culture* or *The Invention of Tradition*, edited by Eric Hobsbawm and Terence Ranger, have obvious bearing on his argument. Clifford's discussion of "To Elsie" as a poem about the disappearance of "pure products" in the "cultural connections and dissolutions" of modernity supplements and enriches Pinsky's; the Hobsbawm and Ranger volume, with its inquiry into the way the destruction of traditional societies paradoxically results in the fabrication of "largely factitious" continuities, retroactive fantasies of traditions that never were, could usefully complicate his reflections on tradition and witness, or on the relations between democracy and the literary past.

In a talk given at the Modern Language Association and printed in the summer 1981 issue of *Critical Inquiry*, Pinsky remarked on the current gulf between poet and academic critic. Poets, especially those sequestered in M.F.A. programs, tend to combine facility in contemporary techniques of composition with "a fatal ignorance of the past." On the other side of the pale is "the occasional graduate student in English who read Derrida when a sophomore,

and who writes with a fist of ham and an ear of zinc, talking about 'poetics' in a way that every poet I know greets with an incredulous smirk." Many of those graduate students, without improving their prose, have gone on to win fame and tenure. But after looking into theory over the past few years, I am convinced that what Marianne Moore famously said of poetry may be said of it as well: "Reading it . . . with a perfect contempt for it, one discovers in / it after all, a place for the genuine." Like it or not, among the mountebanks and poseurs are a number of people engaged in serious thought about the relationship between literature and "the world."

I would like to see a conversation opened between our best poet-critics, such as Pinsky—or McClatchy, whose book is also quite distinguished, whatever one's misgivings about its *donnée*—and the literary and cultural theorists. (One might guess, from Pinsky's remarks about "heteroglossia," that he is aware of Bakhtin, but if so, he doesn't admit to it; McClatchy refers in passing to Barthes without any apparent inkling of the trouble that an engagement with Barthes would make for his assumptions about self, voice, and allusion.) The dialogue I hope for might challenge the theorists to become less tone-deaf, whether to their own prose or the language of the texts they study, and the poet-critics to become less impressionistic, less inclined to rest on pronouncements of taste or suggestive but undeveloped sketches of an argument. But I'm not holding my breath. In the meanwhile, McClatchy's book has a great deal to offer anyone interested in contemporary poetry, and Pinsky's, though it promises more "world" than it delivers, is essential.

### J. D. McClatchy   (review date 24 September 1990)

SOURCE: "Shapes of Desire," in *The New Republic,* Vol. 203, No. 13, September 24, 1990, pp. 46-8.

[*McClatchy is an American poet, critic, and educator whose books of poetry include* The Rest of the Way *(1990). In the following review of* The Want Bone, *he concludes that Pinsky writes "poems as spirited and weighty, eloquent and startling, as any poet of his generation."*]

Two years ago Robert Pinsky published a vigorous and engaging collection of essays called *Poetry and the World.* Harvested from a decade's work, it was a miscellaneous group: autobiographical sketches, meditations on the Bible and on political attitudes, reviews of recent books, a pair of public lectures on the origins of an American poetry. But underneath the variety of his subjects, Pinsky's preoccupation throughout the book was to clarify, if not to explain, poetry's function as "a bridge between the worldly and the spiritual." By maintaining a "decorum, a limiting boundary" between its voluptuous surfaces and the rigor of its ideas, between the dragging anchor of memory and its flights of imagination, poetry enacts the tension that any reader feels, caught between the communal world of his living and the isolate self of his life. The poets whom Pinsky most admires draw both into their work. "The qualities of physical grace, lively social texture, and inward revelation" that he finds in Whitman and Williams mark the strongest American poetry. They are, not coincidentally, qualities Pinsky strives for in his own poems, and wants us to admire there.

The larger question these matters of style address is one Pinsky also touches on, though never plumbs. How does, how should, a poem situate itself in relation to American life, to the heterogeneity of a democratic society? Has poetry any place in a culture that, decade by decade, pushes it further to the side? If it does, and if our poets are to be mythographers rather than merely reporters, how are they to capture and to inspirit the terms of our shape-shifting national life, its abundance of compassion and cruelty, its exhilarating and disturbing freedoms?

Pinsky looks to the style of American poems less to analyze than to praise their fluidity of idiom and tone, their rhetorical restlessness and dramatic resources, their capacity to include so many actual and imagined voices. Pinsky's view is not unlike Tocqueville's when he first arrived in New York. Sailing into the city by way of the East River, he was "surprised to perceive along the shore, at some distance from the city, a number of little palaces of white marble, several of which were of ancient architecture." The next morning, when he went ashore to inspect them, he discovered their walls were of whitewashed brick, their columns of painted wood. Our grandest gestures seem put up overnight, improvised, makeshift, fool-the-eye.

Pinsky's relish for these gestures is apparent in several poems in his new book [*The Want Bone*], poems about language itself. In one, called **"Window,"** our link to the past is defined by language: "We took their language in our mouth and chewed." It fed us, nourished us; and while it formed us—into the Irish or Chinese or Spanish or Yiddish of our words—we helped to remake its own "bright confusion." In another poem, **"The Refinery"** (a new name for the old melting pot), the gods return to drink at that bright confusion, which the poet imagines processed in the great glittering refinery of language:

> The muttering gods
> Greedily penetrate those bright
>         pavilions—
> Libation of Benzene, Naphthalene,
>         Asphalt,
> Gasoline, Tar: syllables
> Fractioned and cracked from
>         unarticulated
>
> Crude, the smeared keep of life that fed
> On itself in pitchy darkness when the gods
> Were new—inedible, volatile
> And sublimated afresh to sting
> Our tongues who use it, refined from oil
>         of stone.

It was Tocqueville who predicted a hybrid American poetry. On his travels around the fledgling nation he found no worthy art, but expected great things. Americans had "the freedom and the knowledge acquired by their forefathers and the passions which are their own." There was, he discovered, no pioneer's hut without its copy of Shakespeare. (Tocqueville himself first read *Henry V* in a log cabin.) But Americans had not yet learned—they would not learn

until Whitman—how to write of their own passions. As for an eventual American style, he predicted it would be

> fantastic, incorrect, overburdened, and loose, almost always vehement and bold . . . with more wit than erudition, more imagination than profundity. The object of authors will be to astonish rather than to please, and to stir the passions more than to charm the taste.

He also predicted that the subject of an American poetry would be not history (Americans have none), not nature (only a mirror that we hold up to ourselves), but the self. Americans, wrote Tocqueville, are "excited in reality only by a survey of themselves," and "each man instantly sees all his fellows when he surveys himself." "I have only to look at myself," he said on their behalf, fifteen years before the publication of *Leaves of Grass,* in order to "enlarge and to throw light on some of the obscurer recesses of the human heart," in order to touch what he called "the hidden nerve."

Each poet will have his own phrase for "the hidden nerve." At the start of his career, Pinsky's was "the dark wind." In **"Poems About People,"** the very first poem in his first book, he tells us of his concern for "the dark wind crossing / The wide spaces between us." If we take that wind as an early image for what he refers to, in *Poetry and the World,* as "the bridge between the worldly and the spiritual," then it must be said that his early work lingered on the worldly side of things. Even so, I wince when, in his essays, he confesses his desire to be "interesting," to please the reader of his poems. Those are worthy goals in themselves, but they so underestimate Pinsky's own ambition—at least as it has emerged over the course of his four collections.

For a poet who has cultivated a somewhat broad discursive manner in stately pentameters, the sort of style that can too easily substitute the communal "we" for the solitary "I," that is shy of metaphor and more eager to summarize than dramatize, Pinsky has at the same time never lost sight of the dark forces between, behind, and beyond us. The best sections of his splendid long poem from 1979, *An Explanation of America,* still his most capacious and aspiring work, remain those haunted by the violence of American history. But his first two collections, however intelligently they played over the contours of the shared or public life, kept their distance from "the hidden nerve."

*History of My Heart,* which appeared in 1984, was Pinsky's breakthrough, and my guess is that it will come to be seen as one of the best books of the past decade. The change was not radical, but it was decisive. He did not altogether abandon the imperatives of making sense of things, or his controlled tone and subdued metrics. But he pitched his voice higher. He let images do the work of argument; and an appositional momentum of phrases gave the new poems a hurtling, sometimes unnerving brilliance. Even more important, the poet's imaginative sympathies broadened. He might still use poetry as (in Emerson's phrase) "a platform whence we may command a view of our present life, a purchase by which we may move it," but he took his stand on the contradictions and desires of the self.

His new collection, *The Want Bone,* includes many poems as good as, or better than, anything in *History of My Heart,* but the impact of the whole book is not so forceful. The previous book casts its long shadow over the later one: what Pinsky has in part done now is to separate a single theme from the earlier book and to concentrate his considerable powers on it. The title calls it *want.* Desire, sexual appetite, romantic love, religious longing, nostalgia, imaginative poverty: it takes many forms.

At the center of this book is a peculiar fable in prose called **"Jesus and Isolt,"** which fancies Jesus returned to earth in the shape of a heraldic beast, the ciclogriff who rests his head on Isolt's lap as she tells him stories of Tristan. Pinsky has brought together the two most potent myths of Western civilization—the ecstatic, doomed romantic lovers, and the merciless master of suppression; Tintagel and Gethsemane; id and superego—in order to explore the terms of desire. The initial poem in the book, **"From the Childhood of Jesus,"** is a similar fable about the Law and about the Spirit that both giveth life and killeth. The young Jesus—magical, resentful, bored—fashions clay into images of sparrows. When scolded about profaning the Sabbath, he cripples another boy and makes the clay birds come to life. Like his latter-day disciples, "The twelve new sparrows flew aimlessly through the night, / Not blinking or resting, as if never to alight."

Both of these fables should alert the reader to Pinsky's strong interest in narrative—not just as a means to tell a story, but as a method to devise parables about the emotional life. What is less convincing is the new voice. It has always seemed to me that Pinsky has had prose models in his mind's ear. For his first two books, the models were essayists of the seventeenth and early nineteenth century—Bacon, say, or Hazlitt, authors with subtlety and gusto. Now his voice has some of the fireside abstraction of the old storytellers, but even more of the cadences and tropes of the Bible.

He seems drawn to the stern tone, and at times he indulges in deliberate parody: "You shall tell him of the slaying / Of the firstborn of man and of beast / In Egypt when my father came out of Egypt," and so on. At its cleverest, the biblical accent allows him to make poignant or witty qualifications in the talmudic manner. More often, at least to my ear, it sounds merely eccentric. His deeper purpose may be to explore the possibilities of a Jewish-American poetry: How would it be inflected? Do its fictive energies derive from the plaint of exile, the platting of interpretation? Certainly the lore of assimilation fascinates him, and in a poem like **"The Night Game,"** in which he dreams up a Jewish left-hander ("Even more gifted / Than Whitey Ford") who refuses to pitch on Yom Kippur, he wittily adds the Sandy Koufax story to the tribal legends.

The best poems in the book, though, are more personal. They do not wrestle with religious angels or intellectual demons, the myths imposed on us by tradition. Instead, they address the self, those autobiographical myths we make out of memories. Presiding over these poems is Shiva, lord of creation and destruction. **"Shiva and Parvati Hiding in the Rain"** is not a characteristic poem, but it announces—as **"The Figured Wheel"** announced in *His-*

*tory of My Heart*—the relentless round of desire that the poet will track:

> The rosecolored mother-father
>
> Flushed, full, penetrated and
> Also penetrated, entering
> And entering, endowing
> And also devouring, necklace
> Of skulls and also ecstasy
> Of hiding in raindrops . . .

The book's title poem is another urgent litany of desires, this time evoked by the dried jaw of a shark, which in life had ruthlessly gorged on anything and in death—its "welded-open shape kept mouthing O"—has become an emblem of human appetites no less engulfing:

> But O I love you it sings, my little my
>     country
> My food my parent my child I want you
>     my own
> My flower my fin my life my lightness
>     my O.

Several of the book's longer poems stay close to this want bone, this Adam's rib or skull or hard-on. These poems offer vivid accounts of desire by overlapping memories in the particular way Pinsky has made his own, a virtuosic montage. **"The Hearts,"** for instance, studies the "legendary muscle that wants and grieves . . . the pump of thrills / And troubles" by splicing together a heroin addict and Enobarbus, the Buddha and a doo-wop group called Lee Andrews and The Hearts, the Banaras marketplace and the second Temple. Nothing is contrived or forced; instead, each image excites and extends, and all are masterfully controlled by Pinsky even as he writes of abandon. Our desires may be fictions, as empty as a song lyric, yet we believe:

> As the record ends, a coda in retard:
> The Hearts in a shifting velvety *ah,* and
>     *ah*
> Prolonged again, and again as Lee
>     Andrews
>
> Reaches *ah* high for *I have to gain Faith,*
>     *Hope*
> *And Charity, God only knows the girl*
> *Who will love me—Oh! if we only could*
>
> *Start over again*! Then The Hearts chant
>     the chords
> Again a final time, *ah* and the record
>     turns
> Through all the music, and on into silence
>     again.

The most ordinary object of desire has a complex history behind it. In a wonderful set piece called **"Shirt,"** Pinsky broods over his purchase of a shirt. The technical terms for shirt-making in their turn evoke Korean sweatshops, the Triangle Factory fire, Scottish mills, and a black South Carolina shirt "inspector" named Irma, along with planters and pickers and sorters, weavers, carders and loaders. By the end of the poem, the plain sportshirt has become a mythological shirt of flame, a history laid on the poet's back.

History suffuses the book's final poem, too. **"Pleasure Bay"** is set in the poet's native Long Branch, New Jersey. Pinsky has written about Long Branch—his Paterson—all through his career, and this new poem looks back to a series of poems grouped under the title **"The Street of Furthest Memory"** in his first book. **"Pleasure Bay"** is both a real place (where "In 1927 the Chief of Police / And Mrs. W. killed themselves together, / Sitting in a roadster") and an Arcadian scene for reverie and instruction:

> The river pulling and coursing between
>     the piers.
> Never the same phrase twice, the catbird
>     filling
> The humid August evening near the inlet
> With borrowed music that he melds and
>     changes.
> Dragonflies and sandflies, frogs in the
>     rushes, two bodies
> Not moving in the open car among the
>     pines,
> A sliver of story.

Pinsky's catbird, like Keats's nightingale, here pours forth his soul above the world's weariness and fever; he is a figure of art's own transforming power. The tenor at Price's Hotel, the old German piano teacher, the night the theater on the water burned down—local ghosts and legends all wear the patina of memory now. At last the reader is brought into the poem, imagined as a ghost as well. Or it may be the poet himself. In any case, the *you* now is the new life. Having died, "you hover near the ceiling above your body / And watch the mourners awhile." Soon after you float off to the river, then to the far side of the river, and choose from the bodies sleeping there one to whom you make love:

> You lie down and embrace one body, the
>     limbs
> Heavy with sleep reach eagerly up around
>     you
> And you make love until your soul brims
>     up
> And burns free out of you and shifts and
>     spills
> Down over into that other body, and you
> Forget the life you had and begin again
> On the same crossing—maybe as a child
>     who passes
> Through the same place. But never the
>     same way twice.
> Here in the daylight, the catbird in the
>     willows,
> The new cafe, with a terrace and a
>     landing,
> Frogs in the cattails where the swing-
>     bridge was—
> Here's where you might have slipped
>     across the water
> When you were only a presence, at
>     Pleasure Bay.

In a passage like this, Pinsky cashes in the debts to Eastern philosophy and Whitman that he had been accumulating throughout **The Want Bone.** The final desire, underlying and shaping all others, is this soul-hunger for life itself. Here is the book's hidden nerve, throbbing, thrilling. Pinsky touches it, touches us, with a delicacy and an accuracy too rare in contemporary poetry. He may not ultimately want to follow every lead he has opened up in this book, but I admire the way he continues to experiment. He will undoubtedly be writing, as he has written here, poems as spirited and weighty, eloquent and startling, as any poet of his generation can summon.

## Alfred Corn    (review date October 1990)

SOURCE: A review of *The Want Bone,* in *Poetry,* Vol. CLVII, No. 1, October, 1990, pp. 39-41.

[*Corn is an American poet, critic, translator, and educator. In the following highly positive review of* The Want Bone, *he lauds Pinsky for his "wonderful ear for poetic line" and the ways in which he examines the theme of "human wishes and the obstacles to them."*]

Readers of Robert Pinsky's first two books hailed him as a new W. C. Williams, gifted at transforming the dailiness of life into a significant poetry. Realism and narrative characterized those books and continued even into the third, at least in the long title poem, **"The History of My Heart."** With the shorter poems in that book, though, a new approach became evident. Realism gave way to a fabular imagination, to organization by montage and association rather than by narrative or logical exposition. This is the method of almost every poem in **The Want Bone** as well. Realistic detail, even snippets of history appear in the poems, but only as fleeting moments in larger meditations, where they take their place among other details from quite different contexts. Unity isn't achieved through clenched teeth but makes itself felt in recurring key words, themes and contexts. As with cinematic montage, or painterly collage, we're asked to discover the synaptic connection between disparate psychological states and material phenomena. The resulting room for speculation gives the poems an oracular feel; there's nothing pat about them. The actual substantive content is made up of wildly different realia, everything from pop culture to Arthurian legend, industrial history, cabbages, kings, whatever has caught the omnivorous attention of this wide-ranging poet. In a recently published essay in David Rosenberg's *Testimony* (a collection of meditations on the Holocaust), Pinsky says, "The idea of civilization, at each level of intensity, is the capacity to incorporate historical forces into personal gestures." Gestures here are understood to include not only salty shrugs and winces, I think, but also those choices where a whole identity is defined. Growing up in an ethnically mixed shore town in New Jersey, Pinsky was led at an early age to reflect on the forces behind differences in speech and customs, to see how various "walks of life" were at once arbitrary and historically determined. Pinsky's Jewish identity would also have been attached at some early stage to a sense of historical injustice and tragedy, so that the habit of annotating cultural difference could never simply be a pleasant pastime.

One more effort at giving this new book a context and then a look at actual poems. **The Want Bone** focuses on specifically religious themes drawn from several traditions. The least convincing of these are the treatments of Christianity, for example in the poem called **"From the Childhood of Jesus"** and the long prose romance (for lack of a better word) titled **"Jesus and Isolt."** The first poem is based on the apocryphal Gospel of Thomas, which even in the original form is a bit hard to take—unless one is schooled at deciphering Gnostic spiritual metaphors. As for the prose poem, Pinsky has concocted a wildly inventive blend of Christian iconography and medieval romance, sending out centrifugal thrusts of meaning in several directions; but it is long, and it is prose. Pinsky seems more confident when he composes **"Memoir,"** a moving account of an upbringing in Orthodox Judaism (which he, not brought up that way, is nevertheless able convincingly to imagine.) Actually, Pinsky seems most at home in the Hindu tradition, which was first hinted at in a poem called **"The Figured Wheel"** in his previous book. It is a view of existence intently focused on multiplicity and transformation, of destruction and recreation, yesterday's ashes become new growth on the apple tree. Hence the ecstatic and frightening **"Shiva and Parvati Hiding in the Rain,"** or the darkly imagined **"The Ghost Hammer."** Several of the poems stir the various traditions together, not so as to reach a syncretic amalgam but to show how they are also grist in the vast mill of mutability, spiritual conventions braided together and unraveled again through time.

Pinsky has a wonderful ear for poetic line. More than anything else that would seem to be his teacher Yvor Winters's legacy to him. Reading poems like **"What Why When How Who,"** I found myself almost ignoring the content, so subtly overriding was the music of the lines. To pick one at random: "Improvisation framelessly from tires." Notice how the number of syllables decreases in successive words, ending with the monosyllables of the concluding iamb of the pentameter; the play of consonants *m, r,* and *f,* the long *a*'s balanced by a concluding long *i.* This instance is by no means a rare exception. Over and again I stopped to admire the perfect tooling of lines and stanzas, a constantly varying sonic texture, usually iambic with the variety of living speech—proof (if we need it) that "free verse" need not occasion slack or arbitrary composition.

The title of the book and the poem with that title point to the most persistent theme: human wishes and the obstacles to them. Pinsky returns to this theme in a thousand variations it would be lame to summarize. I prefer in any case to recommend the book than put it in a nutshell. And, apart from the poems already praised, here are a few favorites: **"Lament for the Makers," "Icicles," "Pilgrimage," "Shirt," "The Night Game," "The Refinery," "At Pleasure Bay,"** and **"Immortal Longings,"** with its beautiful conclusion:

> Under him, a thirsty brilliance.
> Pulsing or steady,
> The fixed lights of the city
>
> And the flood of carlights coursing
> Through the grid: Delivery,
> Arrival, Departure. Whim. Entering
>
> And entered. Touching
> And touched: down
> The lit boulevards, over the bridges

> And the river like an arm of night.
> Book, cigarette. Bathroom.
> Thirst. Some of us are asleep.
>
> We tilt roaring
> Over the glittering
> Zodiac of intentions.

### Don Bogen    (review date 17 December 1990)

SOURCE: "Running with the Ball," in *The Nation,* New York, Vol. 251, No. 21, December 17, 1990, pp. 780-82.

[*In the following positive review of* The Want Bone, *Bogen hails Pinsky's ability to incorporate a multitude of images, motifs, and styles into his poetry without dissipating his main thematic concerns.*]

With its blunt rhythm, clumsy double "n"s and "aw" sound followed by long "o," the title of Robert Pinsky's new book [***The Want Bone***] is a mouthful. Say it aloud and you can hear the echo of baby talk. Want-bone, want-bone—when the image is defined a few pages into the volume, the infantile overtones seem grimly appropriate. What could be more primal than a shark's jaw?

> The bone tasted of nothing and smelled
>     of nothing,
> A scalded, toothless harp, uncrushed,
>     unstrung.
> The joined arcs made the shape of
>     birth and craving
> And the welded-open shape kept
>     mouthing O.

This is not only strong but very smart poetry. The music in the quatrain shows Pinsky's command of formal technique: a fluent iambic pentameter with alternate unstressed and stressed line endings; a pattern of half-rhymes interrupted perfectly by the final "O"; and well-placed internal echoes stressing important words like "harp" and "arcs," "open" and "O," and the repeated term "shape." The image itself both alludes to and goes beyond its famous predecessors. This is no Romantic aeolian harp set into natural music by a breeze. It's not the charmed lyre of Orpheus or the harp of instant, inexhaustible beauty that Jack got when he climbed up the beanstalk. The want bone is more blunt than these. It sings because even in death it can't stop desiring.

***The Want Bone*** presents an extreme vision—but then Pinsky's work has never been known for its caution. From the beginning of his career he has taken on large subjects. His incisive book of criticism, ***The Situation of Poetry*** (1977), is, among other things, an argument for a kind of poetry that moves beyond the image-oriented personal lyric with the logic and discursive range of the essay. He obviously delights in the liberation of tone and subject this implies. His first volume of poetry, ***Sadness and Happiness*** (1975), included witty verse essays on tennis strategy and psychiatrists, and the title of his second, ***An Explanation of America*** (1979), showed both the breadth and the chutzpah of his enterprise. Though Pinsky's claims are brash, as he examines everything from the Brownies to *Deep Throat,* there is an underlying geniality in these two books that continues in the long title poem of his third collection,

*History of My Heart* (1984). The writing is fluid and measured, much of it in loose blank verse, and the poet renders his own experience—as a child in the decaying beach town of Long Branch, New Jersey; as a teenage sax player and quasi delinquent; as a parent in the Boston suburbs—with grace, human sympathy and a keen eye for detail. Though the poems are never merely narrations of the past—even **"History of My Heart"** becomes a discourse on power and gift giving—Pinsky's memories provide a familiar, comforting base for his analysis.

There is little of Long Branch in the new book. With the want bone, Pinsky has hit on a powerful and disturbing image for his concerns of recent years. This desiccated mouth is both rapacious and life giving, a source of beauty and a death mask. The picture of the world Pinsky develops in *The Want Bone* turns on these merged dualities, in which creation and destruction are part of the same process. It is a cyclic vision, but broader and bleaker than most. If many poets like to remind us that daffodils come back after the winter, Pinsky is concerned with more fundamental losses and gains, with the "necklace / Of skulls and also ecstasy" underlying our condition (**"Shiva and Parvati Hiding in the Rain"**). The Judeo-Christian idea of time as a linear process capped by deliverance is too rosy and too otherworldly. Pinsky's apocalypse is followed not by redemption but dispersal:

> But after the flood the bland Immortals
>       will come
> As holy tourists to our sunken world,
>
> To slide like sunbeams down shimmer-
>       ing layers of blue:
> Artemis, Gog, Priapus, Jehovah and
>       Baal,
> With faces calmer than when we gave
>       them names,
>
> Walking our underwater streets where
>       bones
> And houses bloom fantastic spurts of
>       coral,
> Until they find our books. The pages
>       softened
>
> To a dense immobile pulp between the
>       covers
> Will rise at their touch in swelling
>       plumes like smoke,
> With a faint black gas of ink among
>       the swirls,
>
> And the golden beings shaping their
>       mouths like bells
> Will impel their breath against the
>       weight of ocean
> To sing us into the cold regard of
>       water.
>
>                    (**"The Uncreation"**)

So much for Saint Peter at the Holy Gate and sonnets that will make their subject live forever. The consistent, faintly humorous tone and sustained development of the scene here are typical of Pinsky's achievement. This poet not only has imagination, he knows how to run with the ball.

With the exception of the title poem and the exquisitely rendered **"Icicles,"** the strongest pieces in *The Want Bone* are the longer ones. Several of these are in blank verse, with the poet weaving complex, varied sentences over twenty or thirty three-line stanzas. Pinsky first began to make use of this particular balance of syntactic variety and stanzaic regularity in a few poems from *History of My Heart,* but the new work is less anchored to one scene, hence more open and exploratory. **"Voyage to the Moon,"** for instance, starts and ends inside a child's fantasy based on playing cards but passes along the way through Isaiah, piecework sewing, ecodisaster and the demise of a dictator. What's impressive here is not only the breadth of material but Pinsky's ability to engage it all without losing sight of his central concerns. There are, of course, repeating motifs, and the diverse images are not random. But the structure rarely feels manipulative or forced. As he shifts gears in these poems, Pinsky keeps turning up scenes that are both surprising and apt—you never know where the poem will go, but each new move seems like the right one at the time. His adroit sense of pace within the accumulating swirl of meaning keeps the longer poems from chaos on the one hand or corpulence on the other.

While the pulse of iambic pentameter and the repeating three-line stanza provide a framework for the poet's wild imaginings in pieces like **"Voyage to the Moon"** or **"The Uncreation,"** other poems dispense with this scaffolding. Pinsky's free verse can be hampered at times by a tendency to rely on clipped phrases: **"Visions of Daniel"** and parts of **"Hut"** have a truncated feel to them, like sketches that haven't been fleshed out yet. But when he loosens his grip to allow longer and more varied units, he can do amazing things. There's a jumpy intricacy to the music here that blank verse could never achieve. In **"The Refinery"** the bizarre extended metaphor of human speech as refined crude oil culminates in a swamp of polysyllabic names, awkward line-breaks and alliteration as dense and grotesque as the image itself:

> Libation of Benzene, Napthalene,
>       Asphalt,
> Gasoline, Tar: syllables
> Fractioned and cracked from un-
>       articulated
>
> Crude, the smeared keep of life that fed
> On itself in pitchy darkness when the
>       gods
> Were new—inedible, volatile
> And sublimated afresh to sting
> Our tongues who use it, refined from
>       oil of stone.

*The Want Bone* has a definite cosmological flavor. There are gods everywhere—Judeo-Christian, Greek, Norse, Hindu—and they take an active role in human affairs, drinking up our language, thumbing through our soggy books, sending down rules and visions. With their temper tantrums, hot lovemaking and group expeditions, they function partially as a kind of fun-house mirror of our own dreams and failings. Thus Jehovah seems petty in his obsession with proper procedures, his son can be naïve and petulant, and Shiva and Parvati are too wrapped up in themselves to pay much attention to anyone else. But Pinsky is not interested in humanizing the gods—they may be quirky but they're still supernatural. His perspective is apocalyptic, and he achieves it largely through tone. Over the years he has developed a distinct poetic voice—distanced yet personal, reasonable yet imaginative, and always curious—that allows him to blend fabulous evocation with down-to-earth analysis. His version of Genesis, for example, places the myth in the context of basic human economics:

> In the beginning God drenched
>
> The Emptiness with images: the potter
> Crosslegged at his wheel in Benares
>         market
> Making mud cups, another cup each
>         second
>
> Tapering up between his fingers, one
>         more
> To sell the tea-seller at a penny a
>         dozen,
> And tea a penny a cup. The customers
>         smash
>
> The empties, and waves of traffic
>         grind the shards
> To mud for new cups, in turn; and I
>         keep one here
> Next to me

                                   **("The Hearts")**

Pinsky has always been concerned with origins—of identity, a role in a family, a sense of place. In **The Want Bone** his inquiry goes further to look at the source and value of art—not just at his own but at everything we make. While the catalogues, perorations and sheer abundance of sensory detail in his work show that he is anything but ascetic, **The Want Bone** reflects a certain unease with the relentlessness of the creative impulse. This comes out in what is clearly the strangest piece in the book, the allegorical narrative **"Jesus and Isolt."** Pinsky's prose fable is not entirely successful—its tone waffles between the realistic and the fantastic, and the ending seems a bit pat—but he certainly has a new angle on Tristram. Here the heroic lover and poet is a "bull-necked and scar-covered killer and harper," his craft the obsessive transformation of slaughter into chivalric ballads. It's not the aesthetic distortion that disturbs here as much as the vision of the poet as an automaton who will keep on doing this even in hell. Tristram's harp, it turns out, is another want bone.

With that stream of mud cups and the poetry flowing from the killer's harp, Pinsky has homed in on the basic tension that animates his work. One of our most energetic poets, he wants to get everything into his art: fifties pop groups, Buddha, heroin, barnacles clinging to a pier (this all in one poem). Yet he is also far more aware than most of the final insignificance of human endeavor. In his struggle to reconcile the void and the abundance of this world, he has produced a book that is both unrelenting and rich.

### James McCorkle   (review date Winter 1992)

SOURCE: "Contemporary Poetics and History: Pinsky, Klepfisz, and Rothenberg," in *The Kenyon Review,* Vol. XIV, No. 1, Winter, 1992, pp. 171-88.

*[In the following excerpt from a review in which he examines Pinsky's* The Want Bone, *Irena Klepfisz's* A Few Words in the Mother Tongue *(1990), and Jerome Rothenberg's* Khurbn, and Other Poems *(1989), McCorkle discusses the ways in which Pinsky engages public and political issues in his poetry.]*

Typical of discussions of poetry and politics, and the larger domain of history, is a sense of the necessity or decorum to maintain a division between poetry and the other two areas. The popularization of Adorno's question—can there be poetry after Auschwitz—has further mediated the reception of contemporary poetry, if not the very moment of poesis. Equally prevalent is the argument, generous in some ways, that all poetry is political. Carolyn Forché, in her essay, "El Salvador: An Aide Memoire," writes:

> In those days I kept my work as a poet and journalist separate, of two distinct *mentalités,* but I could not keep El Salvador from my poems because it had become so much a part of my life. I was cautioned to avoid mixing art and politics, that one damages the other, and it was some time before I realized that "political poetry" often means the poetry of protest, accused of polemical didacticism, and not the poetry which implicitly celebrates politically acceptable values. [*American Poetry Review* 10, No. 4 (1981)]

Forché recognizes this deep-seated impulse to separate and maintain only what is acceptable or decorous as poetry, which in turn maintains the values acceptable to the society as a whole. She also points to the implicit politics of acceptable poetry. Restricting poetry to the decorous—or claiming the opposite, that all poetry is political—denies poetry any efficacy. It certainly limits the poem's imagination by limiting the poem to the rhetoric of decorum or the period's style. In fact, such limitations shift poetry's prospects from the realm of authenticity to that of style. Forché's statement points to the silencing of the poet, a censure of what the writer has noticed within experience or what the writer has experienced within the space of writing.

The poet's work, as Adrienne Rich has often stated, is the critique and revisioning of representation [see her *On Lies, Secrets, and Silences: Selected Prose 1966-1978,* 1979]. The space of writing is a shared, social space, yet it does not deny the individual act of creating that space. Such an act is profoundly difficult and one that requires an ethical responsibility or responsiveness, if it is to be authentic in its space and its outward *regard.* To not view poetry as an ethical process, is to initiate a disturbing leveling that extinguishes the very possibility of a responsive writing. The poem is always in the realm of betweenness or dialogue, neither wholly internal nor external; its space is autonomous yet can only be existent as a shared space. By its presence, this festive or autonomous time and space is a critique of the accumulations of history that have opposed and appropriated the imagination.

Wallace Stevens often articulates both the recourse to an autonomous space and a poetics of resistance. His vocabulary in the essay "The Noble Rider and the Sound of Words" [from *The Necessary Angel: Essays on Reality and the Imagination,* 1951] is one of opposition that asks of the artist responsibility and claims that art is of necessity the imagination's resistance to the world and its impoverishing realities:

> It is a violence from within that protects us from a violence without. It is the imagination pressing back against the pressure of reality. It seems, in the last analysis, to have something to do with our self-preservation; and that, no doubt, is why the expression of it, the sound of its words, helps us live our lives.

This violence from within is not identical to "a violence without"—the external violence, that of reality, is "without." External and empty, the world shapes *us* if it is not confronted. Furthermore, the imagination is a collaborator, its creation is the history we are caught in.

Robert Pinsky has understood both Forché's and Stevens's positions and offers important elaborations upon them both in his poems and essays. For Pinsky, the tension between public and private is re-visioned by the poet as necessitating transformation. He argues [in *Poetry and the World*] that one of the poet's responsibilities "is to mediate between the dead and the unborn: we must feel ready to answer, as if asked by the dead if we have handed on what they gave us, or asked by the unborn what we have for them"; furthermore, we, as poets, "must answer for what we see." Pinsky, I sense, implicitly rebukes the rhetorical posturing of Adorno or Auden's oft-quoted and misconstrued phrase "poetry makes nothing happen" that has led to critical disclaimers about poetry which is political, social, or historical. Pinsky argues that the poet is the place of transmission and therefore transformation.

Although this description of the poet's responsibility is conservative by Pinsky's own admission, it is moreover one of conservation—or resourcefulness, in that old sources are maintained and new ones uncovered or pointed to. Turning to the poems in his collection *The Want Bone,* we find that Pinsky offers a vision of the demands of the imagination when bound or pressed by power, that is, pushed to the extreme, hence a vatic imagination:

> For three weeks after this night vision
> I Daniel, he wrote, ate no pleasant
> Bread nor wine, my comeliness
> Turned to corruption, I retained
> No strength, my own countenance
> Changed in me. But I kept the
> Matter in my heart, I was mute
> And set my face toward the earth.
> And afterward I rose up
> And did the king's business.
>
> Appalled initiate. Intimate of power.
> Scorner of golden images, governor.
> In the drinking places they said
> He had wished himself unborn,
> That he had no navel.
>
> So tawny Belteshazzar or Daniel
> With his unclean smell of lion
> And his night visions,

> Who took the thoughts of the King
> Into his mind O Jews, prospered
> In the reign of Nebuchadnezzar
> And of his son Belshazzar
> And in the reign of Darius
> And in the reign of Cyrus the Persian.

In these concluding stanzas of **"Visions of Daniel,"** Pinsky critiques Daniel's political cohabitation, while also understanding that it was necessary for his survival. The poem, furthermore, describes Daniel's ability to reverse the relation of power: his knowledge gives him power the king lacks. He is both prophet and interpreter; hence he occupies a privileged position since only he could unfold the secrets of Nebuchadnezzar's dream or the meaningless writing that appeared on Belshazzar's walls. Moreover, Daniel is challenged to interpret—that is to see clearly what is secret—"a vision / Of the world's entire future / Couched in images." Disliked by the Jews and subjected to the gossip of the pious, Daniel was no collaborator although he was an "appointed officer / Of the crown." Instead, Daniel becomes an emblem of survival through the intercession of the imagination. Daniel's survival, in fact, allows for the survival and emancipation of the Jews under Cyrus.

Pinsky has selected Daniel as the emblem of the vatic poet in that this position and the story of Daniel reveal the complex relationship of power and the imagination. The imagination literally preserves Daniel's youth while the kings age. Daniel is a subject of generations of kings, yet he is able to subject them to terror. Daniel, through his casting of images, compels Nebuchadnezzar "on all fours, driven / To eat grass like the oxen. / His body wet by the dews of heaven, / Hair matted like feathers, fingers / Hooked like the claw of the raven." Pinsky does not suggest that Daniel merely interprets the king's dreams; instead, Daniel's casting of images transforms the king and renders him senseless. Daniel is the traditional bard, for his words become curses that are made literal or made flesh. The catalog and the fortuitous rhymes emphasizes this transformation initiated by language. Daniel serves not only as the prophet of history but also as the maker of history, albeit as an intermediary: "God has weighed you and found you / Wanting, your power will be given / To the Medes and the Persians." History then is seen as a series of transformations—makings and unmakings—produced by a single agency. Pinsky does not intend to critique such a proposition nor does he necessarily accept it. His interest is in the position of the individual voice who witnesses, enacts, and records such conditions.

Pinsky's terse lines of this poem, unlike the long essaying lines of *An Explanation of America,* register immediacy and urgency that is requisite for the challenge God presents to Daniel. As an emblem of the poet, Daniel offers a complex and problematic figure. Daniel, as poet, is presented with the vision of the "world's entire future / Couched in images." a vision of incalculable burdens, a vision that is to remain unuttered, secret but exposed to Daniel. He sees the images or rebuses but is told, "Go thy way O Daniel, for the words / Are closed up and sealed till the end." Revelation also inscribes exclusion and limitation. Daniel will not be allowed the sealed words; hence he can only be mute. Furthermore, Daniel is given a vision of prefiguration; what Daniel thus sees is the literal figuring of the division of Jew and Christian. Inscribed in that figure "Who stood upon the waters" is the cataclysmic history of the Jews. And not only is Daniel forbidden the words, he is also condemned. Pinsky has created a terrifying drama of one ensnared in the webs of historical knowledge masked as prophecy. Daniel's challenge—for it is a challenge to survive the vision and to emerge human again—is that of twentieth-century poets who have been given profoundly disturbing images of their histories, which in turn become our histories. The vision ultimately assures Daniel of his task, his ironic task, of doing "the king's business." Pinsky understands the terror inscribed in both history and imagination as a form of power that interlocks the processes of making and unmaking.

**"Visions of Daniel"** is a public poem for it is a reenactment of Daniel's visions or the re-presenting of a literary and mythic figure. It assumes the very position of the narrative of Daniel without any reflexive commentary or distancing. History hammers out images of its processes and the poet must confront those images. How does Daniel respond to Pinsky's argument in the essay **"Responsibilities of the Poet"** that

> there is a dialectic between the poet and culture: the culture presents us with poetry, and with implicit definitions of what materials and means are poetic. The answer we must promise to give is "no." Real works revise the received idea of what poetry is; by mysterious cultural means the revisions are assimilated and then presented as the next definition to be resisted, violated and renewed. What poets must answer for is the unpoetic. [*Poetry and the World*]

Pinsky's argument recalls Stevens's position that the poem's imagination must have a violence within that resists the violence without in order for the imagination to protect itself. The imagination must defamiliarize; otherwise it meshes with the reality it has made for itself and hence fails to notice.

The truth Pinsky reveals is the complicity of the violence within and the violence without. What Pinsky teaches us in his essays and poems is that we must constantly critique or resist in order to renew. The closing stanza of **"The Ghost Hammer,"** the penultimate poem of *The Want Bone,* reveals our complicity:

> Mattock of want, sickle of Kali, bare hand
> Of hunger—you too have lifted it and let it fall,
> You have committed images, the tool
> Is warm from your hand.

Daniel has "committed images" as have we—no one can avoid judgment. Pinsky shows such complicity more intimately in **"Shirt."** The attention to the details of the making of the shirt—"The back, the yoke, the yardage. Lapped seams, / The nearly invisible stitches along the collar"—at first links the observer to the object and his appreciation of its construction.

The poem quickly acknowledges the Korean and Malaysian workers in sweatshops and the history of the notori-

ous 1911 first in the Triangle Shirt Factory; it shifts then to the Scottish workers controlled by mill owners who, "inspired by the hoax of Ossian," invented clan tartans. The interwined genealogies of oppression and production are relentless:

> The docker, the navvy. The planter, the picker,
>     the sorter
> Sweating at her machine in a litter of cotton
> As slaves in calico headrags sweated in fields:
>
> George Herbert, your descendant is a Black
> Lady in South Carolina, her name is Irma
> And she inspected my shirt. Its color and fit
>
> And feel and clean smell have satisfied
> Both her and me. We have culled its cost and
>     quality
> Down to the buttons of simulated bone

The poem is startlingly explicit about the relationship between the consumer and the worker. The shirt serves as an emblematic article of transaction and as an artifact of our obliviousness of the history of the toil that describes how and who made an object. Pinsky notices the history within the intimate and the daily, which becomes the necessary record of the poet. Pinsky's careful attentiveness—we can see his hand moving across the cloth—recalls Elizabeth Bishop's intimate eye and hand tracing over maps, fish, the clutter of filling stations.

In the daily events, historical forces of transformation reveal themselves. In the stunning poem, **"From the Childhood of Jesus,"** the miraculous occurs when "[o]ne Saturday morning," after Jesus modeled "twelve sparrows out of river clay" and "set the birds he had made, // Evenly as the hours," he

> . . . clapped his hands and shouted to the birds
> To go away. They raised their beaks at his words
>
> And breathed and stirred their feathers and flew
>     away.
> The people were frightened.

The power that allows such a transformation, however, was rooted in anger. Both Joseph's rebuke, "Child, you have offended the Word," and the tattletale, who reports the transgressions to Joseph, "Come see how your child has profaned the Sabbath, // Making images at the river on the Day of Rest," invoke the law and the word against which is set playfulness. Whether out of further play or play as magic or anger, the response to these rebukes is the transformation of clay into flesh by the invocation of words. Here, the words uttered by Jesus have power, while those claiming the word as law are rendered powerless.

The poem, however, depicts the world as possibility through transforming play as a doomed world: the clay-to-flesh sparrows only frighten; the child who disrupts the world created by play is himself destroyed by Jesus' proclamation:

> "Unrighteous, impious, ignorant, what did the
>     water
> Do to harm you? Now you are going to wither
>
> The way a tree does, you shall bear no fruit

And no leaves, you shall wither down to the
   root."

If images can be made into flesh, then the powers of transformation can also destroy, curse, or unmake creation's
flesh. From this curse, Jesus' anger turns to prophecy that
defines ultimate judgment, of which the transformation of
a child into a withered trunk is only a prefiguration. History is seen as a perpetual conflict, where "an endless night
// Endlessly [is] fleeing a Torah written in flame." Although language is the agency of transformation, it marks
limits and absolute ends and thus is complicitous with unmaking. What is created remains marginal or lost when
the imagination turns to wrath:

   And high in the dark, where unknown even to
     Jesus
   The twelve new sparrows flew aimlessly through
     the night,
   Not blinking or resting, as if never to alight.

The poem suggests that we are defined by violent collisions
and all-consuming desires, as the bleached shark's jaw of
the title poem signs: "My food my parent my child I want
you my own / My flower my fin my life my lightness my
O." The whole cosmos is swept into the gaping "O" of the
shark's jaw, into its one annihilating letter.

### Robert Pinsky   (essay date Summer 1994)

SOURCE: "Dante's Canto XXV: Among the Thieves, A
Note and a Translation," in *Raritan: A Quarterly Review,*
Vol. 14, No. 1, Summer, 1994, pp. 18-25.

[*In the following essay, Pinsky discusses the theme of horror
in Canto XXV of* The Inferno. *Pinsky also presents his
translation of the Canto, demonstrating how he handles
Dante's* terza rima *rhyme scheme.*]

The remarkable physical details of *Inferno* XXV suggest
the idea that Dante invented horror.

The notion of horror as we know it from fiction or the
movies involves detailed, uncanny transformation of the
human body, with erotic and moral overtones: the overwhelmed stare of the zombie; the flickering eyes of the
aroused mummy; the elegant neck-bite that changes the
virginal heroine forever; Jekyll or the werewolf helplessly
becoming stronger, hairier, more animal; the hunger of
George Romero's living dead, relentless and contagious.
The body may be snatched or bitten, invaded or inverted
or duplicated, obscenely revived or horribly distorted, but
above all it changes. The human takes on qualities of the
animal or of inert matter. In this sense of the word, horror
at the least has one of its earliest manifestations in Canto
XXV.

The body does change in Ovid and Lucan—as Dante acknowledges here in his audacious challenge to the two
Latin poets, his models here. But it could be argued that
in the *Metamorphoses,* mutation is presented as a fact rather than a moral process: it is magical and objective rather
than psychological. Dante implies something like this
when he says that Ovid "never transformed two individual
/ Front-to-front natures so each form as they met / Was
ready to exchange their substance." That is, Dante sug-

gests that his image of transformation will present not
only the external account of an emotional or erotic
change, as when a man becomes a snake or a woman becomes a fountain: he will give an account of moral inter-
penetration, and of psychological complicity. The idea of
*contrapasso,* in which the suffering in Hell extends or re-
produces the sin, does seem to give this mutual transformation a dimension absent from Dante's pre-Christian
models, as he claims.

The living dead of the *Inferno*—denied eternal life, yet full
of a vigorous otherlife—anticipate the Romantic creation
of horror as a literary and cinematic form, the nineteenth-
century vampires and monsters conceived by Mary Shelley, Robert Louis Stevenson, and others. Dante's attentive
descriptions—in XXV, the way the lizard's hind legs twist
together to form a penis, while from the man's penis a pair
of feet grow; or the way the man's pierced navel emits a
stream of smoke; or the description of the reptile's snout
receding to form a human face—bring dark colors to
Ovidian immediacy.

But this fleshly imagery writhes from the crannies of an
exacting architecture. These thieves who ignored the
boundary of *thine* and *mine* in life now merge as shades,
their shells of personal identity made horribly permeable.
Amid this blending "like melting wax," the eye of the poet
identifies and delineates, carefully distinguishing such details as the uncanny yawn of the victim gazing down at the
reptile who has stung him. And a tough scholastic vocabulary of precise abstractions resists all the merging and
shape-shifting: "With both not what they were, / Yet neither"—a phrase, on the other hand, possibly borrowed
from Ovid's account of Hermaphroditus in Book IV of
*Metamorphoses.*

Canto XXV opens with one character gesturing obscenely
at God with both hands, then proceeds from a snake-
ridden centaur through a series of spectacular transformation scenes, each with a sexual energy counterweighted by
a nausea or confusion of the rational intelligence: the witnessing intelligence that partly carries the day and partly,
in the blur of the canto's closing lines, acknowledges its
bewilderment, infected by the shifting forms in this region
of Hell.

Dante originated *terza rima* (interlocking rhymes in the
pattern *aba bcb cdc ded,* etc.) for his *Commedia.* The
form, conclusive yet propulsive, gives the poem a muscu-
lar quality, moving through narrative, dialogue, cosmology, meditation, and scholastic musing with tremendous
conviction, carrying the reader along as the sentences
cross rhymes and tercets.

Rather than abandoning the form or trying to reproduce
it, this translation tries to achieve a reasonable English
equivalent, by running the sentence freely across the ends
of lines and tercets and by defining rhyme in such a way
as to let English approximate the richness in like sounds
of Italian. That is, I have defined rhyme by like terminal
consonants, no matter how much the vowel may vary.
Thus, in the opening lines of this canto, there are such tri-
ads as *both / forth / mouth* and *neck / snake / alack.* The

goal is to create an audible *terza rima,* within the idiom
of English sentences that can be read with pleasure.

### Canto XXV: Among the Thieves

The thief held up his hands when he was
    through,
      And "God," he cried, making the fig with
    both—
      "Take these: I aim them squarely up at
    you!"

The serpents were my friends from that time
    forth,
      For then one coiled itself about his neck
      As if to say, "That's all then, from your
    mouth,"

And another went around his arms to snake
      Them tight and cinch itself in front, so tied
      They couldn't budge enough to gesture.
    Alack,

Pistoia, Pistoia!—Why haven't you decreed
      Your own incineration, so that you dwell
      On earth no more, since you surpass your
    seed

In evil-doing? In all the circles of Hell
      I saw no spirit so arrogant to God,
      Not even him who fell from the Theban
    wall.
Speaking no more then, Vanni Fucci fled,
      And next I saw a centaur full of rage:
      "Where is he? Where is the bitter one?" he
    cried

As he charged up. I think more snakes than
    lodge
      In Maremma's swamp were riding on his
    croup,
      Swarming along his back up to the edge

Of our human form. He bore behind his nape,
      Along the shoulders, a dragon with wings
    spread wide:
      If any blocked the path, it burnt them up.

"This centaur's name is Cacus," my master said,
      "Who underneath the stones of Aventine
    Many a time has made a lake of blood.

He doesn't walk the same road as his clan
      Because by theft and fraud he tried to get
      The splendid herd that lay near him—a sin

That ended his crooked habits: he died for it.
      When Hercules' club rained onto his head
      Some hundred blows, he lived to feel ten
    hit."

While he was saying this, the centaur sped
      Beyond us, and three new spirits appeared
    below;
      They went unnoticed by me or by my guide

Until they shouted to us, "Who are you?"
      At which we ceased our talk and turned to
    them.
      I did not know them, but as people do

When chance disposes, one had some cause to
    name

Another—"Where have we left Cianfa?" he
    said.
      To be sure my leader heard, I signaled him

To stay alert, with a finger that I laid
      From chin to nose. Reader, if you are slow
      To credit what I tell you next, it should

Be little wonder, for I who saw it know
      That I myself can hardly acknowledge it:
      While I was staring at the sinners below

A serpent darted forward that had six feet,
      And facing one of the three it fastened on
    him
      All over—with the middle feet it got

A grip upon the belly, with each forelimb
      It clasped an arm; its fangs gripped both his
    cheeks;
      It spread its hind feet out to do the same

To both his thighs, extending its tail to flex
      Between them upwards through to the loins
    behind.
      No ivy growing in a tree's bark sticks

As firmly as the horrid beast entwined
      Its limbs around the other. Then, as if made
      Out of hot wax, they clung and made a
    bond

And mixed their colors; and neither could be
    construed
      As what it was at first—so, as the track
      Of flame moves over paper, there is a shade

That moves before it that is not yet black,
      And the white dies away. The other two
      Were looking on, and cried, "Ah me, now
    look

At how you change, Agnello!—already you
      Are neither two nor one." Now the two
    heads
      Had become one; we watched the two
    shapes grow

Into one face, where both were lost. The sides
      Grew two arms, fused from lengths that
    had been four;
      Thighs, legs, chest, belly merged; and in
    their steads

Grew members that were never seen before.
      All of the former features were blotted out.
      A perverse shape, with both not what they
    were,

Yet neither—such, its pace deliberate,
      It moved away. The way a lizard can dash
      Under the dog day's scourge, darting out

Between the hedges so that it seems a flash
      Of lightning if it spurts across the road,
      So did a fiery little serpent rush

Toward the bellies of the two who stayed;
      Peppercorn black and livid, it struck out,
      Transfixing one in the place where we are
    fed

When life begins—then fell before his feet,

Outstretched. The pierced one gazed at it
and stood
    Not speaking, only yawning as if a fit

Of sleep or fever had taken him. He eyed
    The serpent, the serpent him. From this
one's wound
    And that one's mouth smoke violently
flowed,

And their smoke met. Let Lucan now attend
    In silence, who has told the wretched fates
    Of Nasidius and Sabellus—till he has
learned

What I will let fly next. And Ovid, who writes
    Of Cadmus and Arethusa, let him be still—
    For though he in his poet-craft transmutes

One to a serpent, and makes the other spill
    Transformed into a fountain, I envy him
not:
    He never transformed two individual

Front-to-front natures so both forms as they met
    Were ready to exchange their substance.
The twain
    Reacted mutually: the reptile split

Its tail to make a fork; the wounded one
    Conjoined his feet. The legs and thighs were
pressed
    So tight no mark of juncture could be seen;

The split tail took the shape the other lost,
    Its skin grew softer, and the other's hard.
    I saw the arms draw inward to be encased

Inside the armpits; the animal's feet appeared
    To lengthen as the other's arms grew less.
    The hind paws, twisting together like a
cord,

Became the member man conceals. From his,
    The wretch had grown two feet. While the
smoke veils
    Each one with colors that are new, and
grows

Hair here and strips it there, the one shape falls
    And one comes upright. But neither turned
aside
    The unholy lights that stared above the
muzzles

That each was changing: the one who newly
stood
    Drew his in toward his temples, and from
the spare
    Matter from that, ears issued from the
head,

Behind smooth cheeks; what didn't course to an
ear
    But was retained became the face's nose,
    And fleshed the lips to the thickness they
should bear.

He that lay prone propelled his nose and face
    Forward, and shrunk his ears back into the
head
    As a snail does its horns. The tongue that
was

Whole and prepared for speech was split instead—
    And in the other the forked tongue formed
one piece:
    And the smoke ceased. The soul that had
been made

A beast fled down the valley with a hiss;
    The other, speaking now, spat after it,
    Turned his new shoulders on it to address

The third, and said: "I'll have Buoso trot
    On all fours down this road, as I have
done!"
    And so I saw that seventh deadweight
transmute

And mutate—and may its strangeness excuse
my pen,
    If it has tangled things. And though my
eyes
    Were somewhat in confusion at the scene,

My mind somewhat bewildered, yet none of
these
    Could flee to hide himself so secretly
    That I could not distinguish well the face

Of Puccio Sciancato, who of the three
    Companions that we first took notice of,
    Alone was not transformed; the other was
he

Whose death, Gaville, you have good cause to
grieve.

### John Ahern   (review date 1 January 1995)

SOURCE: A review of *The Inferno of Dante,* in *The New York Times Book Review,* January 1, 1995, pp. 3, 21.

[*Ahern is an American educator and noted Dante scholar. In the following favorable review of* The Inferno of Dante, *he discusses the difficulties of rendering into English Dante's "vulgar eloquence" and his polyphony of narrative voices.*]

Ralph Waldo Emerson recommended Dante's *Commedia* as *the* textbook to teach the young the art of writing well: "Dante knew how to throw the weight of his body into each act. . . . I find him full of the *nobil volgare eloquenza;* that he knows 'God damn,' and can be rowdy if he please, and he does please." Neither Emerson nor his young admirer Walt Whitman gave us a rowdy American "Comedy." Henry Wadsworth Longfellow's translation appeared in 1865, a decade after *Leaves of Grass.* As a professor of Romance languages and the author of *Evangeline,* Longfellow seemed an ideal translator, but as one critic quipped, he had translated the *Comedy* into the English dictionary, not the English language. His inert rendering never engaged the living American language. Since then, on both sides of the Atlantic, more than a hundred Englishings of the *Comedy* have appeared, but none has achieved rowdiness or vulgar eloquence.

Dante wrote his epic not in Latin but in ordinary language (Italian) in which, he archly observed, "even little women communicate." The offended cultural elite griped that illiterates croaked out the *Comedy* on the crossroads and sang it in taverns. When blacksmiths and donkey drivers sang it at work, they butchered it. After tradesmen requested public explanation of the hard parts, the city of Florence hired Giovanni Boccaccio, who gave up the task at Canto 19 under attack from alarmed literati. Great poems should not be opened up to the masses, they said.

An entire society speaks in the *Comedy,* in endless regional, city and class accents: haughty Ghibelline warlords from Florence, suave Bolognese pimps, testy Roman popes, mild abducted nuns, oversexed Lombard noblewomen—each with an utterly personal voice. Dante's people stutter, sob, moan, whine, whisper, cajole, screech, ramble and mumble. They talk baby talk, gibberish and Old Provençal. They also execute breath-taking rhetorical performances. The total effect is symphonic. A translator's impossible task is to reinvent all those unique voices. Some translations sound like Mahler transcribed for the piano—not a note is lost, but if you don't know the original, the transcription leaves you clueless. Some American long poems offer an analogous polyphony: *Leaves of Grass,* Edgar Lee Masters's *Spoon River Anthology,* Ezra Pound's *Cantos,* William Carlos Williams's *Paterson.*

Robert Pinsky brings superb credentials to *The Inferno of Dante,* his new translation of the first part of the *"Comedy."* A premier citizen of "American Poetry and American Life" (to borrow one of his titles), he has participated in and chronicled "American poetry's argument with itself." His America is a "many-voiced place" where "dreamy aspiration and saving vulgarity mix," as he observed in *Poetry and the World* (1988). He also collaborated in translating Czeslaw Milosz's notebooks. His skill and power as a poet inform every line of this splendid translation. He shapes sinewy lines whose edges you can actually hear. This is true verse, not the typographical arrangement of poetic prose. Rejecting both blank verse and a clanging triple rhyme that would have reproduced the scheme of the original, he translates into an effective half-strength terza rima. Unlike some translators, he does not match every Italian line with a line in English. Without missing a jot or a title, he makes cantos as much as 20 lines shorter than the originals and so attains a truly Dantean velocity. Epic similes come out clean, not clunky. The following passage from Canto 3 gives his basic music and thrust:

> Teeth chattering in their skulls,
> They called curses on the seed, the place, the hour
> Of their own begetting and their birth. With wails
>
> And tears they gathered on the evil shore
> That waits for all who don't fear God. There demon
> Charon beckons them, with his eyes of fire;
>
> Crowded in a herd, they obey if he should summon,
> And he strikes at any laggards with his oar.
> As leaves in quick succession sail down in autumn
>
> Until the bough beholds its entire store

> Fallen to the earth, so Adam's evil seed
> Swoop from the bank when each is called, as sure
>
> As a trained falcon, to cross to the other side
> Of the dark water; and before one throng can land
> On the far shore, on this side new souls crowd.

Mr. Pinsky opts for savvy paraphrase, not obtuse literalness, occasionally sneaking in a quick footnote. Even so, at times Dante's concision is lost. For example, "I believed that he believed that I believed" comes out as "I believe my guide believed that in my belief. . . ." At times, one wishes his version a bit rowdier. But if "Ovid . . . let him be still" seems too polite, "Shut up, Ovid!" as a possible alternative is undoubtedly *too* rowdy.

Very rarely, he undertranslates. At hell's bottom on a glassy lake of ice a traitor whose head is frozen looking downward into the ice asks Dante (literally translated), "Why do you reflect [or mirror] yourself so much in us?" The literal meaning is clear: unable to look at each other, the two must scrutinize each other's reflection. But the rude query also obliquely conveys unwelcome self-knowledge. Starting at the traitors' reflections, Dante sees a mirror image of himself. Since he kicks one traitor (accidentally?) in the face and double-crosses another, he is, in fact, a traitor. Mr. Pinsky's free but accurate rendering—"Why stare at us so long?" —loses the crucial idea that the traitors' lake is a reflection of Dante himself.

But given the distinction of Mr. Pinsky's achievement, this is nit-picking. From the beginning his translation propels us through a gripping narrative whose drama is always in sharp focus and whose characters speak in distinctive voices. There is far less padding and translationese than in most competitors. If he does not quite attain Dante's full symphonic range, no one has come closer.

Substantial, useful notes by Nicole Pinsky, a daughter of Mr. Pinsky, provide some of "the literary and historical information Dante's original audience might have had" but are not intended as an interpretive guide. She draws on commentaries in English translations of Dante from Longfellow to Allen Mandelbaum but not—surprisingly—the many excellent 20th-century commentaries in Italian. At times, one wishes for greater detail. It is good to be told that Galeotto is the name of the messenger between Lancelot and Guinevere and that the French version of his name became a synonym for "pander," but we also need to know that "Galeotto" is the actual title of the book that Paolo and Francesca were reading before committing adultery.

Readers seeking interpretive guidance will welcome the excellent introduction and micro-commentaries to a half-dozen or so cantos by a leading Dante scholar, John Freccero; they distill a lifetime of scholarship and reflection on Dante. Robert Pinsky himself provides another half-dozen interpretive notes, including a bravura excursus on the horror of human-to-animal and animal-to-human metamorphoses for Canto 25. The artist Michael Mazur provides extensive black-and-white illustrations as well as observations about maps of Dante's hell and his own aerial view of hell in a note to Canto 11.

**Edward Hirsch** (review date 23 January 1995)

SOURCE: "A Fresh Hell," in *The New Yorker,* Vol. LXX, No. 46, January 23, 1995, pp. 87-90.

[*Hirsch is an American poet, critic, and educator. In the following review, he favorably assesses* The Inferno of Dante, *contending that Pinsky's translation is "fast-paced, idiomatic, and accurate."*]

The journey into the underworld is one of the most obsessively recurring stories of the Western imagination. Something in us thrills to the metaphor of a hero descending into the bowels of the earth, into the region of demons and lost souls, and escaping to tell the tale. Greek mythology is filled with such fabulous descents: a Thracian minstrel (Orpheus) sings so poignantly that he charms his way into the netherworld to reclaim his lost bride; a man of murderous physical prowess (Heracles) sets off for Hades to retrieve a hellhound with three heads and a snake's tail in order to fulfill the last of twelve labors. In Book XI of Homer's *Odyssey*, Odysseus sails his ship into a country where the sun never shines, and there, pouring libations to the dead, he summons a swarm of ghosts, among them an unburied friend, his aged mother, and the seer Tiresias. This is echoed in Book VI of Virgil's *Aeneid*, when Aeneas persuades the Sibyl of Cumae to guide him into Hades, so he can speak with his dead father about the future. As Homer's scene informed Virgil's, so Virgil's account served as a prototype for Dante's *Inferno*—the most entrancing, detailed, and audacious treatment of a human being's journey into Hell ever written.

*The Divine Comedy* consists of a hundred cantos, divided into three parts: *Inferno, Purgatorio,* and *Paradiso.* It is at once a metaphysical adventure story (a pilgrim goes forth to discover the fate of souls after death), a personal odyssey understood in allegorical terms ("Midway on our life's journey," the poem famously begins, "I found myself / In dark woods"), an encyclopedic guide to the schematics of the otherworld (from the doomed in Hell, through the atoning sinners in Purgatory, to the blessed souls in Heaven), and a quest beyond the grave for a visionary beauty (Beatrice, who is at different times compared to divine grace in the Church, to the Virgin Mary, and even to Christ himself). The poem is a kind of Augustinian confession: a search for the Absolute written under the sign of eternity, a conversion narrative about losing one's way and turning toward God's light. The *Inferno is* the first installment of the pilgrim's three-part spiritual journey, but it seems to have held a nearly exclusive claim on the majority of modern readers. James Merrill has pointed out that "to most twentieth-century readers the *Inferno* is Dante." Apparently, the siren song of damnation calls to us in ways that atonement and salvation do not—perhaps because we recognize ourselves in the lost, unhappy sinners who emanate from the shadows.

In guiding us through a permanently apocalyptic landscape, Dante was also representing his idea of life on earth. In the Foreword to Robert Pinsky's splendid new transla-

tion, *The Inferno of Dante,* John Freccero, the dean of American Dante scholars, notes, "Hell is the state of the soul after death, but it is also the state of the world as seen by an exile whose experience has taught him no longer to trust the world's values." Dante was exiled in perpetuity from his beloved city of Florence on false political charges in 1302, and by the time he wrote the *Inferno*—the poem is set in 1300 but was composed sometime between 1307 and 1314—he had come to view his birthplace with the skeptical, unforgiving eye of a disabused lover. Here is the opening salvo of Canto XXVI:

> Rejoice, O Florence, since you are so great,
> Beating your wings on land and on the sea,
> That in Hell too your name is spread about!
>
> I found among those there for their thievery
> Five of your citizens . . .

So the *Inferno* is, among other things, a fantastic dream of retribution, "a pawnshop in which all the countries and cities known to Dante were left unredeemed" (Osip Mandelstam), and a treatise on the corrupt and degraded state of society. We don't share Dante's medieval cosmology or politics, but twentieth-century readers have had no trouble recognizing his portrait of Hell as a stand-in for a secular human city.

*The Inferno of Dante* is an informative bilingual edition, with the Italian printed *en face.* It has Freccero's excellent Foreword; useful notes; a detailed plan of Dante's journey through Hell; and thirty-five black-and-white monotypes by the artist Michael Mazur. These are beautifully eerie and restrained—a visual backdrop to the dark night of the soul that constitutes Dante's voyage. Most important, Robert Pinsky's verse translation is fast-paced, idiomatic, and accurate. It moves with the concentrated gait of a lyric poem—the *Inferno* is, after all, an account of two poets, Dante and his guide, Virgil, walking through the nine descending circles of Hell—and the grand sweep of a nineteenth-century novel: Hell is filled with Dostoyevskian sufferers, disenfranchised crowds, Sadean torments. The primary strength of this translation is the way it maintains the original's episodic and narrative velocity while mirroring its formal shape and character. It is no small achievement to reproduce Dante's rhyme scheme and at the same time sound fresh and natural in English, and Pinsky succeeds in creating a supple American equivalent for Dante's vernacular music where many others have failed. This translator is first and foremost a poet.

Dante wrote the *Commedia* in Italian, which in his day was still a nebulous national language, rather than in the customary literary language of Latin, in order to be accessible to a wider audience. He compares himself to David, the "humble psalmist," and, in a sense, his poem sets itself up as a colloquial rival to Scripture. It claims enormous truths for itself in a fresh style. The language is by turns stately, demotic, and mercurial. It can be scholastically dense or intimately conversational. Neologisms, regional dialects, and Latin borrowings abound. Didactic stretches accelerate into passages of dizzying verbal majesty as souls become corporeal and words metamorphose into things. There is no replicating this linguistic richness in another language. As the Italian axiom has it, *"Traduttore tradi-*

*tore"* ("The translator is a traitor"), and in truth the back stacks of our libraries are littered with treacheries, but Pinsky takes his place in a line of estimable poetic predecessors—among them Henry Wadsworth Longfellow (1867) and Laurence Binyon (1933)—who have not only wrestled with Dante's content but also found adventurous formal equivalents for his style and music.

Dante's use of terza rima, a marvellous instrument that he devised specifically for the *Commedia,* is the greatest obstacle to translating the poem into English. He composed his poem in interlocking three-line stanzas called *terzine,* or tercets, which rhyme in the pattern aba, bcb, cdc, etc. Rhyming the first and third lines gives each tercet a sense of temporary closure; rhyming the second line with the first and last lines of the next stanza generates a strong feeling of propulsion. The effect is both open-ended and conclusive, like moving through a series of interpenetrating rooms (indeed, the Italian word *stanza* means "room") or going down a set of winding stairs: you are always travelling forward while looking backward. The movement is reinforced by Dante's skillful use of the hendecasyllabic (eleven-syllable) line common to Italian poetry. Its rhythm incarnates the spiralling action of the form; in fact, many scholars have pointed to the spiral as the closest geometric equivalent to terza rima. (One has even compared it to the helixes of DNA.) The momentum of each canto—an urgency slowed by retrospection—mirrors the larger voyage of the pilgrim through the poem.

It has been estimated that translating the entire *Divine Comedy* into terza rima requires more than forty-five hundred triple rhymes in English. This is a staggering number; whereas Italian is abundantly rich in rhyme, English is relatively poor. English rhymes are also more emphatic than Italian ones, more ringing and noticeable. No wonder that Byron labelled Dante "the most untranslatable of poets." Previous translations have often buckled under the nearly intolerable weight of trying to reproduce Dante's form in credible English. Even such ambitious formal versions of the *Inferno* as those by Dorothy Sayers (1949) and John Ciardi (1954)—who uses a "dummy," or defective, terza rima, leaving out the linking middle rhyme—contort English syntax and strain English diction in order to match the Italian rhyme scheme. It's easy for the imitator of terza rima to feel, in the English poet C. H. Sisson's phrase, "like a clown following a ballet dancer," and in recent decades the most accurate translations have tended to shun rhyme altogether.

The student of the *Inferno* can turn with confidence to the prose version of the Dante scholar Charles Singleton (1970), the most comprehensive annotated edition in our language, and to the blankverse versions of Mark Musa (1971), Sisson himself (1980), Allen Mandelbaum (1980), and Tom Phillips (1985), whose jaunty carriage makes his blank verse especially pleasurable. These versions gesture toward the poem's form—its body—without trying to approximate its true shape. Even Longfellow, whose translation is a magnificent work in its own right, eschews rhyme in favor of a Miltonic blank verse. Every translator knows that terza rima isn't extraneous to Dante's work (T. S. Eliot once said that "Dante *thought* in terza rima"), but

that doesn't make it any less difficult to transport. As if to make the point, Shelley's "Triumph of Life," the finest English poem ever written in the form, was unfinished at his death.

There have been at least fifty renderings of the *Inferno* into English in our century, but Pinsky's is the first rhyming translation unmarred by antiquarianism. He consistently employs slant or half rhymes (pain/sin/down; night/thought/it) as well as full rhymes (dwell/Hell/well), in order to re-create Dante's form while remaining true to his meaning. Consonantal rhyming, based on similar rather than identical internal vowel sounds, allows for a more flexible, more complex, and even dissonant sense of rhythm and harmony. This tactic is crucial when it comes to rhyming disyllabic words, since triple half rhymes (quiet/spirit/merit) don't stop with the dull thud that triple full rhymes do (quailing/railing/wailing) at the ends of English lines. It is precisely these disyllabic, or "feminine," rhymes that have undone so many previous translators. Pinsky's use of Dickinson's or Yeats's method of slant rhyme—to name only two of the poets who fully mastered its effects—supplied him with, in his words, "an audible scaffold of English terza rima, a scaffold that does not distort the English sentence, or draw excessively on the reaches of the English lexicon."

Pinsky also makes accommodations and compromises. He readily admits that he doesn't follow the original line by line, or even stanza by stanza, and that at times he foreshortens cantos in order to mimic Dante's epigrammatic compression. Occasionally, Pinsky, too, wrenches rhymes into place; it's hard to imagine anyone actually saying "Although their burden held them in retard" (XXIII) or "Which wins all battles if it does not despond" (XXIV). While Pinsky uses enjambment—the carrying of phrases across lines—as one of his most successful strategies, he moves sentences across both lines and stanzas more aggressively than Dante, and so runs the risk of emphasizing the poem's forward momentum at the expense of its retrospective vistas. Yet this tactic also enables him to capture the poem's swirling downward rhythm—what Dante calls "the hurricane of Hell in perpetual motion."

Dante's verse has a depth and gravity—at times whirling and tumultuous, at times stately and processional—that Pinsky captures exceedingly well. Here is how he translates the traditional epic invocation that begins Canto II:

> Day was departing, and the darkening air
> Called all earth's creatures to their evening quiet
> While I alone was preparing as though for war
>
> To struggle with my journey and with the spirit
> Of pity, which flawless memory will redraw:
> O Muses, O genius of art, O memory whose
> merit
>
> Has inscribed inwardly those things I saw—
> Help me fulfill the perfection of your nature.

These well-modulated lines evoke Dante's dark misgivings at the beginning of his project, his sense of foreboding as he battles exhaustion and despair. The pilgrim is about to descend into the underworld—"I am no Aeneas or Paul," he will soon declare—and wonders whether he is capable of sustaining a journey beyond death. He knows he will struggle with misplaced sympathy for the damned. And he questions whether he is worthy enough to write the epic (a contemporary Bible? a new Aeneid?) that we are about to read. Thus the triple invocation to the Muses, to the presiding spirit of art, and to the interior god of memory.

To appreciate the cadenced grandeur and Virgilian echoes of Pinsky's flexible iambic pentameter, one has only to compare it to a stilted rendering such as that by Dorothy Sayers: "Day was departing and the dusk drew on, / Loosing from labour every living thing / Save me, in all the world; I—I alone— / Must gird me to the wars—rough travelling." Sayers is actually a stricter translator than Pinsky. She follows Dante's lines and line endings more closely than he does, but one practically has to translate her translation ("I—I alone— / Must gird me to the wars"?) in order to figure out what the poet is saying. She distorts the syntax to maintain the rhymes, in the process making Dante sound like a weak Victorian poet.

A prose crib such as Charles Singleton's, which is nothing if not literal, seems to stand at the opposite extreme from Sayers' high-sounding verse. Here is his rendering of the same passage:

> Day was departing, and the dark air was taking the creatures on earth from their labors; and I alone was making ready to sustain the strife, both of the journey and of the pity, which unerring memory shall retrace. O Muses, O high genius, help me now! O memory that wrote down what I saw, here shall your worthiness appear!

This is preferable to Sayers, because, if nothing else, it's more accurate, and yet poetic models have to come from somewhere, even if they are outmoded or absorbed and expressed unconsciously. Singleton's intentionally flat version starts off agreeably enough, but soon he, too, imitates an archaic diction—"and I alone was making ready to sustain the strife"—that is alien to contemporary speech. And the phrase "both of the journey and of the pity," while it is an exact translation from the Italian, doesn't say much in English. What does it mean to "sustain the strife . . . of the pity"? The translator who is too much a literalist—even such a great Dantista as Singleton—runs the risk of transposing the words but sacrificing their meaning.

Pinsky steers a sure course between the Scylla and Charybdis of dogged literalism and high-flown lyricism, and as a result the contemporary reader experiences the startling seriousness of a pilgrimage that begins in dark woods, falters in the vestibule of Hell, and then proceeds according to an exact route from Limbo and the upper regions toward the center point of the earth. Dante takes pains to describe the journey with geometric and astrological precision, and Mazur has provided an "aerial view" with a schematic overlay at the beginning of Canto XI.

The protagonist of Dante's poem is bewildered by both what he sees and what he doesn't see in the shadowy nether regions, and he repeatedly turns to Virgil for explanations. Here, in Pinsky's strong mimetic rendering, is his initial encounter with the abyss:

> The sighs, groans and laments at first were so loud,
> Resounding through starless air, I began to weep:
> Strange languages, horrible screams, words imbued
>
> With rage or despair, cries as of troubled sleep
> Or of a tortured shrillness—they rose in a coil
> Of tumult, along with noises like the slap
>
> Of beating hands, all fused in a ceaseless flail
> That churns and frenzies that dark and timeless air
> Like sand in a whirlwind. And I, my head in a swirl
>
> Of error, cried: "Master, what is this I hear?"

In a spirited tale of mentorship, Virgil glosses the sights and sounds of Hell, and leads Dante through its physical and spiritual geography. The pilgrim is overwhelmed by the number of wretched souls passing before his eyes. One inevitably thinks of *The Waste Land* at the lines "I would not have thought / Death had undone so many," and, in fact, Eliot's work captures better than most the Dantesque world of living ghosts—the terrifying isolation of souls unmoored from community, alienated even from themselves. At every stage, Dante encounters individuals who want to tell him their heartbreaking stories: Francesca of Rimini, Ulysses, Count Ugolino, and a host of others. This is a key social aspect of the poem, which makes it feel both contemporary and historically rich.

In Dante's underworld, every figure stands for his own transgression. Dante borrowed from Aquinas the Aristotelian term *contrapasso,* or law of retribution, to designate a system in which the punishment distills and matches the crime. Sin is literalized: those who succumbed to anger tear perpetually at one another's naked bodies; gluttons wallow in putrid soil and get chewed by Cerberus; murderers boil in a river of blood. In an insightful note Pinsky suggests that Dante's portrayal of the living dead anticipates the Romantic creation of horror as a literary—and, later, cinematic—genre. The uncanny metamorphosis of human beings continues to intensify throughout the poem, since the farther down Dante and Virgil go the more heinous are the crimes they encounter, until finally, in the darkness of point zero, they crawl across the body of Lucifer himself.

At the conclusion of the poem, the pilgrim (and, by extension, the reader) feels a liberating sense of release at escaping Hell and glimpsing the heavens again:

> To get back up to the shining world from there
> My guide and I went into that hidden tunnel;
>
> And following its path, we took no care
> To rest, but climbed: he first, then I—so far,
> Through a round aperture I saw appear
>
> Some of the beautiful things that Heaven bears,
> Where we came forth, and once more saw the stars.

In recent times, it has been argued, by Erich Auerbach, among others, that Dante's characters are so sympathetically drawn and so realistically portrayed that they subvert the rigid categories in which the allegorist has ensnared them. Dante's medieval typology (the progression from Sins of Incontinence to Sins of Fraud) doesn't mean much to us anymore. It is not the "allegory of theologians" but the flawed humanity of Dante's characters that excites and touches readers. In Auerbach's words, "the beyond becomes a stage for human beings and human passions." This is a tempting argument. It's not particularly troubling to think of schismatics being divided from themselves, but it's another matter to encounter the Provençal poet Bertran de Born, who was beheaded, and whose trunk is forever carrying around his severed head, "gripping its hair like a lantern, letting it swing." And while it's one thing to learn of political treachery that sends traitors to Antenora, in the ninth circle, it's quite another to witness Ugolino, who died of starvation, gnawing his enemy's skull and reliving the story of his gruesome last days. The suffering of individuals writhing in the torture cell of eternity calls out to us from beyond the grave.

Yet in any full reading of the *Inferno,* it is crucial to distinguish between two Dantes: the pilgrim passing through the divisions and subdivisions of Hell, and the poet "remembering" the journey and writing an epic poem about it. Readers identify with the pilgrim, whose heart goes out to "the disconsolate and mutilated shades," but that pilgrim can be readily distinguished from the author, who is unwavering in his judgments. For example, as Freccero notes, the pilgrim Dante seems truly anguished to discover his mentor Brunetto Latini among the sodomites in the seventh circle, but it must be remembered that the poet Dante placed him there. God didn't write the *Inferno,* or decide that there would be no reprieves in the City of Woes, or inscribe over the portals the infamous words "ABANDON ALL HOPE, YOU WHO ENTER HERE." Freccero puts the matter succinctly: "In spite of Dante's reputation as the greatest of Christian poets, there is no sign of Christian forgiveness in the *Inferno.* The dominant theme is not mercy but justice, dispensed with the severity of the ancient law of retribution." Readers will always find that the humane perspective of the pilgrim clashes with the viewpoint of the icy administrator of justice, but that's precisely the point. The tension between the temporal and the transcendental orders—between guilty individuals crying out and an anonymous system of justice relentlessly dispensing with them—is what gives the poem so much of its terrifying force, and the poet his complex, judicial grandeur.

Pinsky's translation is well suited to our time. He has created an idiom that brilliantly suggests the work of both a medieval allegorist and a proto-modern thinker, and, above all, of a writer—one who dramatizes the desperate vulnerability of human beings caught up in an implacable world. At our own apocalyptic moment in history, the reader can scarcely forget that the *Inferno* is a book in which the earth opens and the historical world is suspended outside time. The progress of the soul through the underworld is a theme that cannot date, but it does seem to have special relevance to the modern dilemma. Perhaps that's why the *Inferno,* as opposed to the *Purgatorio* and the *Paradiso,* has inspired so many devastating modern

works, which burn with a true infernal flame—from Gogol's *Dead Souls* and Conrad's *Heart of Darkness* to Eliot's *Waste Land,* Camus's *The Fall,* and Malcolm Lowry's *Under the Volcano.* Dante seems to have anticipated the nervous, unholy epoch in which we find ourselves. Purgatory and Paradise belong to the ages, but Hell is recognizably ours.

**Diane Jean Schemo   (essay date 31 January 1995)**

SOURCE: "Bringing Dante Into the Realm of Contemporary English," in *The New York Times,* January 31, 1995, pp. C13-C14.

[*In the following essay, Schemo discusses the strengths and weaknesses of Pinsky's translation. She also reports on Pinsky's reaction to the attention* The Inferno of Dante *has received.*]

It was not a late-born obsession with evil or the ways of damnation that drove Robert Pinsky to translate Dante's *Inferno,* the 14th-century poet's odyssey through hell. Rather, it was the challenge of tackling the first slice of the *Divine Comedy,* perhaps the greatest poem ever written. The *Inferno* had been rendered into English a hundred times by scholars and writers, and yet remained elusive, unmastered, poetry's Everest of the underworld.

Some, like Dorothy L. Sayers in the late 1940's, had gone for a strict line-by-line translation of the *Divine Comedy,* and ended up with a work that sounded stilted to the English ear, lacking the momentum of the Italian original. The poet Allen Mandelbaum, whose paperback version is widely used in university courses, worked 20 years to preserve the line-by-line sequence and diction of Dante, but did not attempt to match rhymes. Charles S. Singleton's 1970 edition—considered perhaps the most scholarly, with separate volumes for notes—eschewed the poetic form altogether for a painstakingly literal prose translation.

"It just gripped me, like a child with a new video game," said Mr. Pinsky, an American poet whose published work until *The Inferno of Dante* included four books of poetry and three about poetry. "I literally couldn't stop working on it."

Since its release several weeks ago, Mr. Pinsky's translation has been hailed for rendering the tricky terza rima, the interlocking triple rhyme scheme that Dante invented for the *Divine Comedy,* into idiomatic English that preserves both the rowdiness and the dignity of the original. Writing in *The New York Times Book Review,* John Ahern, a professor of Italian letters at Vassar College and a specialist on Dante, called Mr. Pinsky's translation "splendid," and said, "His skill and power as a poet inform every line." The poet Edward Hirsch, in *The New Yorker,* said, "Pinsky succeeds in creating a supple American equivalent for Dante's vernacular music where many others have failed."

Mr. Pinsky, who teaches in the graduate writing program at Boston University, began working on the *Inferno* for a reading of the 34 cantos at the 92d Street Y in Manhattan by 19 of the country's most prominent poets, each of whom was asked to translate a canto or two.

"No one has ever licked it," said James V. Mirollo, a professor of English and comparative literature at Columbia University, "and so many famous poets have tried." He added that a perfect translation of the *Inferno,* which he does not believe Mr. Pinsky has achieved, would represent a substantial earthly prize for its author in the form of academic royalties. "To come up with a successful paperback version," he said, "would guarantee you a comfortable income for the rest of your life."

Mr. Pinsky aimed for near rhymes, or slant rhymes, to reflect the tension of the terza rima's structure—*a-b-a, b-c-b, c-d-c,* etc.—which, like the pilgrim of the poem, looks back and around as it moves ever forward. Direct rhymes, Mr. Pinsky said, would have sounded too harsh and clanging; he opted for more subtle rhymes, like . . .*died* / . . . *vowed* / . . . *lewd* and . . . *rolls* / . . . *antiquity* / . . . *coils.*

Comparing his verses with those by some of his friends, poets like Robert Hass and Seamus Heaney, Mr. Pinsky grew intrigued by the results. The *Inferno* has a way of doing that, of luring artists in, hypnotizing them. T. S. Eliot learned Italian to read Dante, and the *Four Quartets,* which quote liberally from the *Inferno,* have been called the Italian classic's closest equivalent in English. Michelangelo, according to his biographers, listened to the *Inferno* as he painted "The Last Judgment."

And so, Mr. Pinsky said, it was probably inevitable that 1 of the 19 poets at the 92d Street Y would get hooked. Michael Mazur, a friend and artist who had once lived in Florence and visited Dante's haunts, had been hungering to illustrate the *Inferno.* He created austere, dreamlike monotypes to go with each of the cantos. By the time Hell Night, as one article described the nightlong reading session at the 92d Street Y, rolled around in May 1993, Mr. Pinsky had completed his first draft of all 34 cantos. For the moment, he has no plans to continue on to *Purgatory* or *Paradise.*

"I wanted to make it as accurate as I could, but after working on a very little bit of it, I got a strong notion that I could make it sound like a poem in English," he said in a recent interview, stirring a mint tea at a Greenwich Village cafe. Like many other poets who have translated verse—and as Mr. Pinsky told the skeptics at his weekly poker game—his expertise was not so much in a foreign language as in English. He said he relied heavily on the translations of the *Inferno* by Singleton and Henry Wadsworth Longfellow.

As he toiled, Mr. Pinsky was not consumed by the hidden meanings bubbling beneath Dante's vision of hell. He was far more preoccupied with questions of rhyme and meter, and with discovering the closest English word for the Italian "zavorro," which Mr. Pinsky translated as "deadweight," in Canto 25.

"To write triple rhyme in English is not easy," the poet said. "English has an immense vocabulary, larger than Italian. And one of the classic mistakes you can make is to draw on that huge wealth of synonyms to supply rhymes. If you do that, you have an extremely unnatural, unidiomatic language; you end up with phrases that no one would ever say."

Dante, who died in exile from his beloved Florence, was not entirely concerned with the matter of divine retribution either. In part, he enjoyed the disingenuous game of consigning his rivals and erstwhile friends to hell, even as he portrayed the poem's kindly pilgrim pitying the sinners he discovered there. Dante was also upsetting the intellectual conventions of his day from the bottom up, using common Italian. But mostly, Mr. Pinsky believes, Dante was creating a work of art.

"He was an artist, not a theologian," Mr. Pinsky said, adding that he believed Dante used his categories of sin as a scaffold "that would support detailed, powerful, very articulated accounts of souls contorting themselves."

It is only now, after Mr. Pinsky has gained some distance with the project's completion, that he wonders about the conflicting currents of "attraction-repulsion" that drew him, son of a modern Orthodox Jewish home, to take on the quintessential Christian poem of Western civilization. The attraction he said, was obvious, an alluring cultural "cookie jar" of "Bach, Mozart, Christmas trees and church architecture, the language in my mouth—Jackie Robinson and Italian girls."

The 54-year-old poet also remembered adoring *Ivanhoe* as a boy, until the Jew Isaac of York appears. Mimicking the character—"craven, ugly, at best helpless"—Mr. Pinsky suddenly leered up at a grotesque angle in the half-light of late afternoon, his fingers turned into claws stabbing the air over a plate of biscotti. A moment later, his hands dropped, as if lifeless, to the marble table. "I felt wounded and angry—hurt," he recalled.

In the *Inferno,* Mr. Pinsky mused, he perhaps sought an early work questioning the underpinnings of Christian civilization. "We have bad popes piled up," he said. "It's part of a drama of saying, 'What does all this Christian belief in classical mythology, in Virgil, the Church Fathers, Aristotle—what does it mean for people's actual behavior?' "

And he sees a certain poetic truth to the Augustinian notion of sin as killing part of a person's soul, which Dante dramatized to its literal extreme. Thus, those seduced by the idea of romantic love wander through eternity in a tempest; the wrathful tear at one another, and magicians and clairvoyants who would see the future march forever looking backward.

But if to each his own *Inferno,* so also with translations. Professor Mirollo, who is among 50 or so people at Columbia teaching Dante's epic in the university's mandatory course on Western civilization, said he prefers Mr. Mandelbaum's line-by-line version, which he found more faithful to the original and more colloquial than the Pinsky volume. Mr. Mandelbaum's translation corresponds line for line to verses as Dante wrote them, making it easier for students to grasp the relation between the Italian and English; Mr. Pinsky's compresses lines with translations of whole sentences, so the cantos have fewer lines in English than in Italian.

"I think the slant rhymes in some cases are so slant or slight, that you don't get the benefit of the rhyming," Professor Mirollo said, adding that in his opinion "this is not the translation of choice for all eternity."

Not that Mr. Pinsky ever expected to write the translation for all eternity. He walked toward his hotel at Washington Square, where he would have a few hours' rest before reading at Poets House in SoHo that night. He seemed overwhelmed by the sudden attention his *Inferno* has drawn, but shook his head quickly and smiled when asked if he was. "Not overwhelmed," he said. "Just whelmed."

## Larry Kart (review date 12 February 1995)

SOURCE: "When Pinsky Met Dante: A Modern Poet Enters the *Inferno*," in *Chicago Tribune-Books,* February 12, 1995, pp. 5, 8.

[*In the following review of* The Inferno of Dante, *Kart compares Pinsky's translation with that of C. H. Sisson, finding Pinsky's inferior.*]

Robert Pinsky (*The Want Bone, History of My Heart, An Explanation of America,* etc.) is a major American poet and a nearly unique one. Casting about through the literary past, the sole English-language poet who bears much resemblance to him is the too-little-known Elizabethan master Fulke Greville, whose verse, like Pinsky's, can be at once urgently plainspoken and remarkably virtuosic, especially in the sphere of rhythm. It's a paradoxical blend of virtues, arising, I think, because the impulses that drive their work are more public than private. And because they need to speak to, argue with and convince an actual or imagined "us," their verse tends to become elaborate only when what they have to say demands that.

Now Pinsky has given us a translation of Dante's *Inferno*—a poem that, whatever else it might be, is also a starling act of public speech. But Pinsky's *Inferno* [*The Inferno of Dante*] is not a success—an opinion that needs to be amplified, given the acclaim with which this translation has been greeted.

Making Dante "sound like a poem in English" is Pinsky's stated and worthy goal—as it was of British poet C.H. Sisson, whose translation of the entire *Divine Comedy* is arguably the best verse Dante in English. Here, in Pinsky's and Sisson's versions, is the conclusion of Canto V of the *Inferno*—the passage in which Francesca of Rimini tells Dante how she and her brother-in-law Paolo were led to commit adultery as they read about Lancelot and Guinevere. (Galeotto, or Galahalt, was Lancelot and Guinevere's go-between.):

Pinsky:

> "'. . . One day, for pleasure,
> We read of Lancelot, by love constrained:
> Alone, suspecting nothing, at our leisure.
> Sometimes at what we read our glances joined,
> Looking from the book each to the other's eyes,
> And then the color in our faces drained.

> But one particular moment alone it was
> Defeated us: *the longed for smile,* it said,
> *Was kissed by that most noble lover,* at this
> This one, who now will never leave my side,
> Kissed my mouth, trembling. A Galeotto, that
> book!
> And so was he who wrote it; that day we read
> No further.' All the while the one shade spoke,
> The other at her side was weeping; my pity
> Overwhelmed me and I felt myself go slack:
> Swooning as in death, I fell like a dying body."

Sisson:

> "'One day when we were reading for distraction,
> How Lancelot was overcome by love—
> We were alone, without any suspicion;
> Several times, what we were reading forced
> Our eyes to meet, and then we changed color:
> But one page only was more than we could bear.
> When we read how that smile, so much desired,
> Was kissed by such a lover, in the book,
> He, who will never be divided from me,
> Kissed my mouth, he was trembling as he did so;
> The book, the writer played the part of Galahalt:
> That day we got no further with our reading.'
> While one of the spirits was speaking in this
> manner,
> The other shed such tears that, out of pity,
> I felt myself diminish, as if I were dying
> And fell down, as a dead body falls."

It may not be clear right away, because of his use of "slant rhymes" (eyes/was/this, book/spoke/slack), but Pinsky has tried to approximate Dante's self-invented *terza rima* (the rhyming pattern aba, bcb, cdc, etc.). Now *terza rima* is not impossible in English, even though Italian is rich in rhymes and English is relatively poor. At least one major poet (Shelley) wrote major poems ("Mont Blanc" and "Hymn to Intellectual Beauty") in *terza rima*-inspired but even more elaborate patterns. But *terza rima,* for Dante, is a sinuous verbal lope that furthers the flow of his verse, while Pinsky's approximate *terza rima* seems to inhibit the flow of his. Certainly the implacable forward drive of Pinsky's **"What Why When How Who"** (from *The Want Bone*) is nowhere apparent in his version of Canto V—and why should we settle for anything less?

To be fair, a second comparison. Here is the beginning of Pinsky's version of Canto VIII:

> "Continuing, I tell how for some time
> Before we reached the tower's base
> Our eyes were following two points of flame
> Visible at the top; and answering these
> Another returned the signal, so far away
> The eye could barely catch it. I turned to face
> My sea of knowledge and said,'O Master, say:
> What does this beacon mean? And the other
> fire—
> What answer does it signal? And who are they
> Who set it there?' He said: 'It should be clear:
> Over these fetid waves, you can perceive
> What is expected—if this atmosphere
> Of marsh fumes doesn't hide it.' Bow never
> drove
> Arrow through air so quickly as then came
> Skimming across the water a little skiff

Guided by a single boatman at the helm:
'Now, evil soul,' he cried out, you are caught!' "

And here is Sisson's version of that passage:

"To go on with my story, long before
We actually reached the foot of the high tower.
Our eyes were drawn toward the top of it
By two little flames which suddenly appeared
  there,
And by another which answered from far away,
So far indeed that the eye could hardly see it.
I turned toward the ocean of intelligence,
And said: 'What does that say? And what reply
Comes from that other fire? And who are signal-
  ling?'
He answered me: 'Already on the filthy water
Can be seen what it is they are waiting for,
If the mist from the swamp does not conceal it
  from you.'
No bowstring ever sent an arrow off
To run through air with such precipitation
As the little boat which at that moment I saw
Advancing over the water in our direction,
Under the guidance of a crew of one
Who shouted out: 'Now you are for it wretched
  spirit!' "

Robert Pinsky, one feels sure, will write more remarkable verse of his own, while the praise given to his *Inferno* will be considered an anomaly in the history of taste. Whatever, don't deny yourself the experience of C.H. Sisson's Dante.

Additional coverage of Pinsky's life and career is contained in the following sources published by Gale Research: *Contemporary Authors,* Vols. 29-32, rev. ed.; *Contemporary Authors Autobiography Series,* Vol. 4; *Contemporary Literary Criticism,* Vols. 9, 19, 38; *Dictionary of Literary Biography Yearbook, 1982.*

# The Prime of Miss Jean Brodie
## Muriel Spark

The following entry presents criticism on Spark's novel *The Prime of Miss Jean Brodie* (1961). For further information on her life and works, see *CLC*, Volumes 2, 3, 5, 8, 13, 18, and 40.

## INTRODUCTION

One of Spark's best-known and most critically acclaimed works, *The Prime of Miss Jean Brodie* (1961) centers on morality, manipulation, and betrayal at a school for girls in Edinburgh, Scotland, during the 1930s. Praised for its structural complexity, the novel juxtaposes past, present, and future events as well as fantasies as it documents the decline of the title character—the teacher Jean Brodie—and her effect on her students. As Mary Schneider has stated: "*The Prime of Miss Jean Brodie* has long been recognized as a brilliantly woven novel, complex in its narrative techniques and themes."

**Plot and Major Characters**

The primary action of the novel takes place at the Marcia Blaine School for Girls in Edinburgh, Scotland, during the 1930s and focuses on a small group of students, known as "the Brodie set," and their schoolmistress, Miss Jean Brodie. The story begins in 1936, when the girls are sixteen, but quickly flashes back to 1930, when the girls—then in the junior level—began their two year course of study under Brodie's tutelage. Spark utilizes flashbacks and flash-forwards throughout the novel. A domineering eccentric who admires the fascism of Benito Mussolini, Brodie attempts to exert control over her students' lives and fantasies and to mold their beliefs and aesthetic tastes. Although Brodie's affect on each of the girls varies, they remain a distinct clique at the school after they leave the junior level and move up through the senior level. Sandy Stranger and Rose Stanley are the principal figures among the girls, and it is through them that Brodie attempts to carry on a vicarious romance with Teddy Lloyd, the school's art master. Although Brodie is in love with Lloyd, she renounces him because he is married. Brodie instead carries on an affair with Gordon Lowther, the school's singing master, but refuses to marry him. At this point in the story—when the flashbacks have caught up to the time when the novel formally began, in 1936—a new girl, Joyce Emily Hammond, arrives at the school and manages to befriend Brodie. At the same time, the Headmistress, Miss Mackay, is attempting and failing to have Brodie removed. Joyce eventually disappears; it is later learned that she was killed in Spain, where her brother is fighting the fascists in the Spanish Civil War. During the summer of 1938, Brodie tours Germany, where her admiration for fascism increases. At the same time, Sandy has an affair with Lloyd—Brodie had intended for Rose to

sleep with him. Lloyd, who is Catholic, introduces Sandy to Catholicism. She later converts, becomes a nun, and writes a famous psychological treatise, "The Transfiguration of the Commonplace." After returning from Germany, Brodie tells Sandy that she encouraged Joyce to go to Spain and convinced her to switch her allegiance to the fascists. Horrified at Brodie's disregard for human life and individuality, Sandy relates the information to Miss Mackay, who forces Brodie's resignation. Brodie, who dies of cancer seven years later, spends the remainder of her life trying to figure out who betrayed her.

**Major Themes**

Major themes in *The Prime of Miss Jean Brodie* include control and omniscience, Sandy's psychological development, and religion. The first theme centers on Brodie's attempts to influence the girl's actions and beliefs. Brodie tells the girls that they are an elite group—the "crème de la crème"—and she takes them into her confidence and tries to imbue them with her views on culture and life. As Dorothea Walker has stated, Brodie's "determination to broaden [the girls' knowledge] with her distorted version of reality suggests both her authoritarian nature and her desire to control. Her greatest wish is really to reproduce clones of herself." Miss Brodie's admiration for fascism reinforces this theme, and Sandy, in her recollections of "the Brodie Set" and its emphasis on conformity, likens the girls to Mussolini's soldiers. This theme is also reflected in Spark's narrative style—a number of critics have compared her authorial control over the characters with Miss Brodie's totalitarian personality and fascist impulses. Margaret Moan Rowe has stated that "Spark deftly counterpoints authorial omniscience with Brodie's attempts at omniscience; all the author plans works, not so with the plans of the character in the novel." The novel's second theme shows Sandy's development from a young girl who hesitantly accepts Brodie's declarations, to a teenager who questions the limits of her loyalty to Brodie, to a cloistered nun. As a young girl Sandy is obsessed with understanding Brodie's psychology. However, as Sandy matures, her fascination with Brodie gives way to the realization of her moral obligation to the welfare of others and compels her to put an end to Brodie's tenure at the school, thus preventing her from influencing another set of impressionable girls. Spark's characters rarely, however, act from a single motive, and the author suggests that Sandy's impulse to act against Brodie is also tinged with jealousy. The novel's third theme centers on Roman Catholicism. Brodie abhors Catholicism and tells her students that it is a religion for those who do not wish to think for themselves. In authorial commentary, Spark notes that this is an odd view for someone such as Brodie and suggests that Brodie was best suited to the Roman Catholic church, which might have refined her excesses. Sandy's conversion to Catholicism owes to her affair with Lloyd and the influence of Brodie. Commenting on Sandy's conversion and Brodie's role in it, Walker has stated that "Spark appears to be saying that out of evil may come good, in that evil might be refined and tempered into good. To a believer like Spark, the tempering agent is Roman Catholicism."

## Critical Reception

Most critics consider *The Prime of Miss Jean Brodie* to be Spark's finest novel. Commentators have noted its thematic richness as well as its technical achievements, particularly Spark's handling of time through flashbacks and flash-forwards. Others have remarked on Spark's writing and narrative organization, praising it as concise and economical. Rowe has written that "Nothing is wasted in [*The Prime of Miss Jean Brodie*], which is so much about a waste of human energy." Although many scholars consider the novel to be primarily a character study centered on Sandy and Miss Brodie, others have argued that the novel's focus is metafictional. Gerry S. Laffin, for instance, has suggested that "*The Prime of Miss Jean Brodie* is a parable, and a highly autobiographical one, of the artist as a young girl. Further, it seems that in this novel at least, Mrs. Spark believes that any creator of fiction who claims to be a truth-teller is being absurdly, even dangerously, pretentious."

## PRINCIPAL WORKS

*Child of Light: A Reassessment of Mary Wollstonecraft Shelley* (criticism) 1951; also published as *Mary Shelley* [revised edition], 1987
*The Fanfarlo, and Other Verse* (poetry) 1952
*John Masefield* (criticism) 1953; revised edition, 1992
*The Comforters* (novel) 1957
*The Go-Away Bird, with Other Stories* (short stories) 1958; also published as *The Go-Away Bird, and Other Stories,* 1960
*Robinson* (novel) 1958
*Memento Mori* (novel) 1959
*The Bachelors* (novel) 1960
*The Ballad of Peckham Rye* (novel) 1960
*The Prime of Miss Jean Brodie* (novel) 1961
*Voices at Play: Stories and Ear-pieces* (short stories and radio plays) 1961
*Doctors of Philosophy* (play) 1962
*The Girls of Slender Means* (novel) 1963
*The Mandelbaum Gate* (novel) 1965
*Collected Poems I* (poetry) 1967; also published as *Going Up to Sotheby's, and Other Poems,* 1982
*Collected Stories I* (short stories) 1967
*The Public Image* (novel) 1968
*The Very Fine Clock* (juvenilia) 1968
*The Driver's Seat* (novel) 1970
*The French Window* (juvenilia) 1970
*Not to Disturb* (novel) 1971
*The Hothouse by the East River* (novel) 1973
*The Abbess of Crewe* (novel) 1974
*The Takeover* (novel) 1976
*Territorial Rights* (novel) 1979
*Loitering with Intent* (novel) 1981
*Bang-Bang You're Dead, and Other Stories* (short stories) 1982
*The Only Problem* (novel) 1984
*The Stories of Muriel Spark* (short stories) 1985
*A Far Cry from Kensington* (novel) 1988
*Symposium* (novel) 1990
*Curriculum Vitae: Autobiography* (autobiography) 1993

---

## CRITICISM

### Samuel Hynes (review date 23 February 1962)

SOURCE: "In the Great Tradition: The Prime of Muriel Spark," in *The Commonweal,* Vol. 75, No. 22, February 23, 1962, pp. 562-63, 567-68.

[*Hynes is an American educator and critic. In the review below, he comments on Spark's previous novels and argues that, like her earlier works,* The Prime of Miss Jean Brodie *is "intricately designed, and concerned with religious ideas."*]

In this age of book clubs and television interviews and full-page advertisements, it is comforting (and perhaps snobbishly satisfying as well) to find now and then a writer who has made a reputation simply by being read and admired. Only five years have passed since Muriel Spark published her first novel, *The Comforters,* but that book, and the five she has written since then, have given her a status among younger British novelists as secure as anyone's.

No one who claims to be informed on the current state of fiction can afford to overlook her work. Her position in America is somewhat less established—two of her books are in paperbacks, but as far as I know she has not yet penetrated that innermost sanctum, the college curriculum— but her word-of-mouth reputation has already spread in a way that happens only to truly original, and pleasurable, writers.

Certainly *original* and *pleasurable* are the first things to say about Mrs. Spark's novels. Each is in its way unique—a new set of fictional problems, a new kind of plot-invention. She has that evident pleasure in the manipulation of her medium which distinguishes the master novelists from the journeymen. Yet in all of her books, for all their individual uniqueness, there is a uniformity of comic tone, of pace, and of attitude which defines an extraordinary personality and intelligence behind the work. The joy that she takes in the making of fictions, and the attractiveness of her creating mind, are two prime sources of the pleasure that her novels give; for it is a special kind of pleasure that we get from observing a finely creative imagination in the act of invention.

In a biographical note Mrs. Spark once listed her favorite recreations as "Chess and Disguise." There is something of both visible in her novels: a pleasure in intricately patterned plots, and a pleasure in the concealment of motives and meanings. Her novels are both mannered and mysterious, and this combination, along with her comic gifts and her rapid, economical style, makes her work what it is— examples of a new kind of novel.

Mrs. Spark is a Catholic convert, and this is a point of more than parochial interest. For one thing, her life as a novelist began with her conversion. Religion and creation are, by her own testimony, intimately related: she has found Catholicism "conducive to individuality, to finding one's own individual personal point of view." The theme of her first novel she described as "really a convert and a kind of psychic upheaval"; most of her subsequent work involves Catholic characters, and the problems which their Catholicism poses in a non-religious world.

But her writing is also religious in a more pervasive, less specific way; her reality includes the unseen, and her novels are peopled with diabolic characters (she has wisely avoided trafficking in her comedies with saints) and inscrutable forces which exercise mysterious powers over human activities. In *The Comforters,* for example, the heroine hears voices and clacking typewriters which seem to be composing a novel about her life as she lives it, and a demonic old servant vanishes and reappears before our eyes; in *Memento Mori* a number of old people receive inexplicable telephone calls reminding them that they must die; in *The Ballad of Peckham Rye* a devil called Dougal Douglas disrupts a working-class community for the sheer

deviltry of it; in *The Bachelors* a dubious medium clearly communicates with the dead.

Mrs. Spark offers no comfortably secular explanation for any of these events; her stories are more likely to create mystery than to explicate it, and she is content to leave the supernatural that way—Mysterious. The world of human experience is complex, and not ultimately explicable; evil, her demons remind us, is as actual as nasty servants and telephone calls, and reality is odder than you think.

But evil may not be quite the right word to indicate the pervasive metaphysical presences that haunt Mrs. Spark's novels. She is not, like that other distinguished convert, Graham Greene, devil-ridden; the diabolic creatures who turn up in her books are more grotesque than terrifying, and their deeds are rather annoying than destroying. They are eccentrics, liars, meddlers, and bores—the kind of people who bring out the pettiness and uncharitableness in us, not the kind who lead us to damnation. The true metaphysical force is less precise than this, not clearly either evil or benign, but simply there, the author of the human story, the Comforter. To say that Mrs. Spark has chosen to write Catholic comedies does not explain her vision, but perhaps in a way it describes it.

It may strike a reader coming to these remarks without prior knowledge of Mrs. Spark's work that she must be not so much a comic writer as a clownish one. Certainly a summary of her plots would not be the best way to convince a sceptic of her essential seriousness. How, one might ask, *can* a novelist write seriously about religious experience in a plot like that of *The Comforters?* Voices? Typewriters? How ridiculous! Not at all. The theme of the book is the discovery, by an intelligent, sophisticated, slightly neurotic young woman, of the reality of the nonmaterial; this discovery finds spiritual expression in her conversion, and psychological expression in her breakdown. In the end we don't *know* who has operated the typewriter which Caroline Rose heard; the mystery has not been dissipated, but Caroline accepts and is comforted by the existence of an operator, and the book we read is the final evidence that what she heard was real.

"Fiction," Mrs. Spark has observed, "to me is a kind of parable." That is to say, it is beliefs shaped by the imagination. Her parables come from a Catholic imagination, but the truly creative imagination is a transforming one, and in Mrs. Spark's case, a comic one; her curiously conceited plots embody serious matters, but they are imaginative, not doctrinal, and her books are not likely to convert anyone (though they may well make a secular view of things seem rather bare and boring).

To say that fiction is "a kind of parable" is to suggest that one's interest should be on the design and meaning of the fable rather than on the customary objects of our attention in fiction—the empathetic character and the credible, detailed situation. In Mrs. Spark's novels this is so; her gift for intricate design is superb, her detachment from her characters absolute. The effect of this is a reduction in scale of individual characters (only one novel, *Robinson,* is a first-person narration, and this is the one novel that is clearly inferior to the others); her customary habit is to establish a number of more or less equally important characters, and then to compose a pattern around them, relating each to all the others. Individuals are likely to be treated more as "cases" (sometimes specifically medical or legal cases) than as personalities.

The character in **Memento Mori** who observes his fellow septuagenarians (virtually everyone in this remarkable novel is over 70) and records their reactions to old age in a card file is a kind of model of the way Mrs. Spark's mind works: "What were they sick, what did they die of ?" this card-filer thinks. "Lettie Colston . . . comminuted fractures of the skull; Godfrey Colston, hypostatic pneumonia; Charmian Colston, uremia; Jean Taylor, myocardial degeneration . . ." And on through the list of his friends and coevals, coldly ticking them off. But Mrs. Spark adds: "Jean Taylor lingered for a time, employing her pain to magnify the Lord, and meditating sometimes confidingly upon Death, the first of the Four Last Things to be ever remembered."

Compassion is there, but Mrs. Spark's religion protects her from that too-easy compassion which we call sentimentality. She is neither cold nor soft-hearted; on the whole she is amiably disposed toward her characters, finds materials for comedy in them, and records their nastier qualities without rancor. She is not, as has been suggested, a satirist; her writing has neither the motive nor the tone of satire. If she is detached in her attitude toward her characters, this is understandable in a novelist who sees people in terms of the designs into which they fit (including the design of the Four Last Things).

One finds the same quality of detachment in Mrs. Spark's treatment of the physical world that her characters live in. There is about her novels a striking spareness in the description of sensory experience; people occasionally have sex lives, but none of them enjoy themselves—sex is at best a distracting temptation, at worst an abrasive emotional complication. The same is true of other pleasures of the flesh—food, drink, the natural world may compose the physical circumstances of a scene, but they are not dwelt on, and nobody savors them much. That this spareness is intended rather than a limitation of literary gifts the novels everywhere demonstrate; Mrs. Spark can make the physical world as concrete and emotive as she likes, on those occasions she likes.

Consider this passage, the last sentences of **The Ballad of Peckham Rye:** "But it was a sunny day for November, and, as he drove swiftly past the Rye, he saw the children playing there and the women coming home from work with their shopping-bags, the Rye for an instant looking like a cloud of green and gold, the people seeming to ride it, as you might say there was another world than this."

And so Mrs. Spark *does* say. Conversion seems to have seized her, as it sometimes does imaginative persons, with a kind of impatience with the material. The world of children and shopping-bags is all right for those who like it, but there is another world than this, a world of minds and souls, in which the really important human experiences take place.

Her episodes are therefore people talking, rather than people acting, or touching, or feeling, or even seeing. For this reason critics have quite rightly compared her work to that of Henry Green and Ivy Compton-Burnett; she is in the tradition of the intellectual novel, in which what matters is the play of ideas and experiences upon the mind, and the interplay of minds upon each other.

**The Prime of Miss Jean Brodie,** Mrs. Spark's new novel, is very much in this tradition. Like each of her previous novels, it is both a new departure and a continuation. It is different from the others in that it does without manifestations of the supernatural; it is similar in being intricately designed, and concerned with religious ideas.

Miss Brodie is a Scottish schoolmistress who dedicates her prime (for her, the years after 40) to the molding of her students' lives and wills. They will be, she tells them, the crème (Miss Brodie is addicted to resounding clichés); and in the splendid, romantic lives that Miss Brodie plans for her disciples she will live vicariously a life more splendid than her own. She is a romantic idealist, of the authoritarian kind—one of her girls later remarks, "She's a born Fascist"—and the Brodie set under her powerful influence becomes a collective extension of her ego, "a body," one of them thinks, "with Miss Brodie for the head . . . in unified compliance to the destiny of Miss Brodie, as if God had willed them to birth for this purpose."

---

**The Prime of Miss Jean Brodie** is intelligent, witty, and beautifully constructed, and it is *new*—like her previous novels it is a fresh assault upon the limits of the novel form.

**—Samuel Hynes**

---

So long as Miss Brodie's plans for her girls are only fantasies, the girls are willing enough to be the "Brodie set." But when it becomes clear that she seriously intends that the prettiest girl in the set shall become a surrogate mistress of the man Miss Brodie loves, in order that Miss Brodie may vicariously enjoy him, then one of the girls "betrays" her ("betrays" in quotes because the meaning of personal loyalty and betrayal is one of the themes of the book), and the collective, willed destiny of the whole becomes the separate destinies of the individuals.

The novel is religious in two ways. As in many of Mrs. Spark's books, the principal observer and commentator, a girl called Sandy Stranger, is a Catholic convert; the theme of her own story is the theme of authority found and rejected, of Miss Brodie's power versus the power of the Church, and her education through the novel is an education in the meaning of authority. But it is also religious in its treatment of Miss Brodie. The setting of the novel is Edinburgh, and the spirit of Calvin broods over the action. Miss Brodie is an inverted expression of that spirit: "just as an excessive sense of guilt can drive to excessive action, so was Miss Brodie driven to it by an excessive lack of guilt."

The authority that Miss Brodie wields is a warped and egocentric predestinarianism, Calvinism without the religion: "She thinks she is Providence," Sandy observes, "she thinks she is the God of Calvin, she sees the beginning and the end." Out of this delusion arises the principal conflict of the novel, the conflict between Miss Brodie's notion of the girls as the instruments of her personal destiny, and the girls' natural, individual drives toward individual fulfillment.

Her attempt at playing Providence fails, as it must, and her girls desert her for the more attractive business of being themselves, but the force of her effort has had its effects, however ironically unlike her intentions. In the end a visitor asks Sandy, now a nun, "What were the main influences of your school days?" and she answers: "There was a Miss Jean Brodie in her prime."

There seems little left to say about the book by way of peroration. It is as good as anything Mrs. Spark has done and, as should be clear by now, that means to me that it is very good indeed. It is intelligent, witty, and beautifully constructed, and it is *new*—like her previous novels it is a fresh assault upon the limits of the novel form. Mrs. Spark's powers of invention are apparently inexhaustible, and these unique and impressive powers make her a novelist worth taking very seriously.

### Ann B. Dobie (essay date 1969)

SOURCE: "*The Prime of Miss Jean Brodie:* Muriel Spark Bridges the Credibility Gap," in *Arizona Quarterly,* Vol. 25, No. 3, 1969, pp. 217-28.

[*Dobie is an American educator and critic. In the following essay, she discusses the novel's point of view and the development of its major characters.*]

Muriel Spark is certainly one of the most productive novelists writing today. Since 1957 she has published eight novels in addition to verse and short stories. Though all have received critical attention, amounting sometimes to little more than critical puzzlement, most interest has been paid neither to her first nor her latest fiction, but one of the central novels: *The Prime of Miss Jean Brodie* (1962). For example, a few seasons ago it was adapted for the London stage, where it was a popular success, and it was subsequently made available to American audiences in New York City. It has most recently been made into a motion picture which has received approving critical notice.

Critics have not acclaimed *The Prime of Miss Jean Brodie* as Muriel Spark's "masterpiece"; neither does the novel contain sensational depictions of sex or violence which would explain the attention it has been given. Indeed, the reasons for the notice received by this novel rather than Muriel Spark's other fiction are not immediately apparent. Reasons there are, however. And though they satisfy the curiosity of those who ponder such questions, they also enlighten more serious readers who seek answers to the puzzles posed by the author's imaginative, but sometimes thematically baffling, work. *The Prime of Miss*

*Jean Brodie,* occupying a central position in her novels to date, is the answer book to the earlier novels and a guidebook to those that follow. Dealing with the same questions (themes) as *The Comforters* (1957), *Robinson* (1958), *Memento Mori* (1958), *The Ballad of Peckham Rye* (1960), and *The Bachelors* (1961), *The Prime of Miss Jean Brodie* moves away from the depiction of unbelievable supernatural forces and towards the embodiment of out-of-the-ordinary characteristics in quite credible characters. Bizarre, surprising, and imaginative her novels remain. But with *The Prime of Miss Jean Brodie* Muriel Spark leaves the incredible world of invisible, chanting voices and untraceable telephone callers. Though she continues to sketch a world which is filled with demons and to imply that there is a vast reality which is not perceived by the ordinary man, the supernatural is no longer found outside the individual but within man himself. *The Prime of Miss Jean Brodie* retains both the fun and seriousness which were so entertaining and confusing in the early novels, but it presents them in what is to most readers, more acceptable, believable, "realistic" form.

Muriel Spark's movement towards credibility is most apparent in the main character: Miss Jean Brodie. Though it is not difficult to imagine her walking the streets of Edinburgh or conducting a class in history, she does the same sort of things as the demoniac Dougal Douglas in *The Ballad of Peckham Rye*. Everyone who knows her recognizes her difference, yet she is undoubtedly real in an ordinary sense: "there was nothing outwardly odd about Miss Brodie. Inwardly was a different matter, and it remained to be seen, towards what extremities her nature worked her."

If Jean Taylor of *Memento Mori* meditates on the Four Last Things to be ever remembered, Miss Jean Brodie is concerned with those first things to be considered, for she is dealing with the young, those who are just beginning life. And she affects them in much the same, if less mysterious, way as the phone calls affect the aged in the author's earlier novel.

Miss Jean Brodie is set apart from ordinary people because she, in her prime, has come to realize the unity between the physical and spiritual sides of man's nature. As she says, "I ought to know, because my prime has brought me instinct and insight, both." Instinct and insight apparently give one an extraordinary vision of the world, which would undoubtedly please Dougal Douglas of *The Ballad of Peckham Rye*. In fact, Miss Brodie seems to echo him when she says, "Where there is no vision, the people perish." Caroline Rose of *The Comforters* would certainly see the similarity between instinct and insight and the natural and supernatural orders which she comes to know. Miss Brodie, like other Muriel Spark characters who precede her, unifies the ordinary and extraordinary levels of reality, and demoniacally influences the lives of those around her. She is an ordinary school teacher in a quite ordinary school for girls, the Marcia Blaine School in Edinburgh, Scotland. But when she renounces the world and dedicates her prime to her girls, she manages, by most unusual and extraordinary means, to transfigure the commonplace. And indeed, *The Transfiguration of the Commonplace* is the title of the book eventually written by Sandy Stranger, Miss Brodie's favorite pupil.

---

**Though it deals with the same questions as Spark's earlier novels, *The Prime of Miss Jean Brodie* moves away from the depiction of unbelievable supernatural forces and towards the embodiment of out-of-the-ordinary characteristics in quite credible characters.**

**—Ann B. Dobie**

---

Most of the novel is concerned with Miss Brodie's molding of the girls as she gives them the benefit of her prime. By her unorthodox teaching methods she attempts to develop in each of them vision, a rich awareness of the enormity of the world and its possibilities. For instance, she teaches the history of World War I by telling the girls the story of Hugh, her lover, who was a soldier in that war. She teaches geography and history by describing her own vacations in Italy where she has seen Mussolini's troops marching through the streets. She presents the subject matter, but she surrounds the facts with an atmosphere of adventure. By combining historical fact with personal reminiscence a sense of a multileveled reality existing and operating simultaneously is given by Miss Brodie to the girls. She urges them to define themselves not only in terms of the ordinary world but also in terms of the romance which accompanies it.

Miss Brodie's relation to her students and to her peers, therefore, is perhaps best understood as a relation of the "whole" person in whom instinct and insight are united, to the "fragmented" person, who is deficient either in instinct or insight or both. She conceives of her purpose as a teacher to be that of leading her students toward their "prime," when instinct and insight might be united in a total life-gesture, and the personality might attain fulfillment. Miss Brodie's explanation of her job is properly, if curiously, pedantic. She explains:

> The word "education" comes from the root *e* from *ex,* out, and *duco,* I lead. It means a leading out. To me education is a leading out of what is already there in the pupil's soul. . . . [My job] is a leading out of knowledge, and that is true education as is proved by the root meaning.

Miss Brodie deals with the inside of a person by cultivating his nature as a human being. She does not "thrust a lot of information into the pupil's head" like other teachers. She deals with knowledge which is a part of the human makeup but which often lies unawakened and undisturbed. However, because she understands insight and instinct only in terms of her own experience, her girls tend to turn into images of her. And Teddy Lloyd, art teacher at the Marcia Blaine School, can only paint likenesses of her after coming into contact with her vision.

The measure of her success, then, is to be found in the effect she has on her students, the degree to which she energizes the components of instinct and insight, and the response which the students make to this educative process.

The means are as daring as her vision, as is seen, for instance, in her plans for Sandy Stranger and Rose Stanley, her "creme de la creme." Acting as dictator, Miss Brodie has educated each girl for a particular role. Faithful to her philosophy of education, she has not thrust these roles upon the girls, but has led out from them their particular ability. And when her plans are fulfilled, she, the representation of total vision, will stand back watching the various expressions of her vision acting and interacting in a visible re-creation of the whole. Miss Brodie is vision in its abstract (supernatural) form; Sandy, Rose, and Teddy Lloyd are vision in a physical (ordinary) form. As Sandy understands, they are "as a body with Miss Brodie for the head." Rose, who early in life is famous for sex, is to become the lover of Teddy Lloyd, the art master. Though Miss Brodie herself was once involved with him, she renounces him and leaves Rose, who in Miss Brodie's mind represents "instinct," to sleep with him. Sandy, on the other hand, is famous for her small, almost non-existent eyes. To Miss Brodie she represents "insight." Therefore, she is chosen by Miss Brodie to act as informant on the affair between Teddy Lloyd and Rose.

When the plan is made, Sandy is intrigued by it. "There was a whiff of sulphur about the idea which fascinated Sandy in her present mind." The sulphurous atmosphere and Miss Brodie's ethereal beauty at this time remind one that she is one of Muriel Spark's demons: forces, sometimes in human form and sometimes not, which exist simply to disrupt the ordinary and habitual, to confuse the traditional and acceptable, to blend the commonplace and the supernatural so that a person is forced to redefine himself in the context of an environment, or reality, filled with more possibilities than he had heretofore imagined. Their purpose is not to destroy or harm, though sometimes they do so. Neither is their purpose to please or to help, though they do that too. In short, their purpose is to "transfigure the commonplace." Miss Brodie's actions are particularly reminiscent of a Dougal Douglas. Ronald Bridges of *The Bachelors* might have described her as he did others, as little more than a creature of the air. She has made her exit from the stage of action and is simply directing the drama from the wings.

Eventually, however, Sandy rejects Miss Brodie. The irony lies in the fact that in rejecting her, Sandy re-creates her. In an attempt to destroy her, she becomes her. Sandy first tries to destroy Miss Brodie's plan for Rose and Teddy Lloyd to become lovers. She does so by sleeping with Teddy Lloyd herself, thus coming to represent, like Miss Brodie, the union of insight and instinct. Rose happily relinquishes her role, for without insight she has not understood Miss Brodie's plan. The author tells us that she "made a good marriage soon after she left school. She shook off Miss Brodie's influence as a dog shakes pond-water from its coat."

But Sandy has understood toward what extremities Miss Brodie's nature worked; and her understanding that Miss

Brodie stands outside of ordinary reality and attempts to direct the lives of others causes Sandy to rebel. " 'She thinks she is Providence,' thought Sandy, 'she thinks she is the God of Calvin, she sees the beginning and the end.' " Sandy, unlike Caroline Rose in *The Comforters,* finds no comfort in being simultaneously freed from ordinary restraints and controlled by extraordinary forces. She does recognize that Miss Brodie's influence is a liberating one, however. She later realizes that the "creeping vision of disorder" that she received from Miss Brodie "had not been without its beneficient and enlarging effects." Unlike Caroline, who accepts, Sandy rejects—or tries to. In a second effort to reject Miss Brodie Sandy goes to Miss Mackay and accuses Miss Brodie of being a fascist, which is her way of saying that Miss Brodie has tried to control and dictate the lives of all her set. Miss Brodie, who has been an admirer of Mussolini, is removed from her position at Marcia Blaine School.

The third step in Sandy's rebellion is her renunciation of the world by becoming a nun. Miss Brodie is horrified by the act, since she is no admirer of Roman Catholics, though "she was by temperament suited only to the Roman Catholic Church." She does not realize that Sandy has closely followed her own course. Both Miss Brodie and Sandy withdraw from the world and give of their experience and knowledge, their vision, to others. Miss Brodie devotes her prime to her set; Sandy gives to the world her widely acclaimed book, *The Transfiguration of the Commonplace,* a treatise on the nature of moral perception. Sister Helena of the Transfiguration, as Sandy comes to be known, seems eventually to realize that she has become another Miss Brodie, for she says that the main influence in her life was "Miss Jean Brodie in her prime."

Sister Helena is not a nun at peace with the world, for the knowledge that by her betrayal she simply replaced Miss Brodie rather than destroyed her does not bring tranquillity. Even the book, which visitors often come to discuss, she finds difficult to talk about, for it is, apparently, a study of Miss Brodie's "vision." Miss Brodie was right when she said, "Give me a girl at an impressionable age, and she is mine for life."

Miss Brodie's success with Sandy and the other girls is demonstrated when in retrospect they come to understand what she was teaching them. Sandy, for example, realizes that the world she was introduced to as a child was not the one others saw. "And many times throughout her life Sandy knew with a shock, when speaking to people whose childhood had been in Edinburgh, that there were other people's Edinburghs which were quite different from hers, and with which she held only the names of districts and streets and monuments in common." One of her visitors at the convent describes the Edinburgh he knew as a child as cold and gray and his teachers as "supercilious Englishmen, or near-Englishmen, . . . with third-rate degrees." Sandy could not remember ever having questioned the quality of her teachers' degrees, and the school had always been "lit with the sun or, in winter, with a pearly north light." That city, so dreary and so ordinary to many, was not so to Sandy as a child. She remembers later how "dark heavy Edinburgh itself could suddenly be changed into a floating city when the light was a special pearly white and fell upon one of the gracefully fashioned streets." For Sandy the commonplace was transfigured.

Eunice Gardner, to whom Miss Brodie once said, "You are an Ariel," describes Miss Brodie to Sister Helena as "marvelous fun . . . when she was in her prime." When her stories about Miss Brodie cause her doctor husband to remark that her upbringing had been rather peculiar, Eunice protests, "But she wasn't mad. She was as sane as anything. She knew exactly what she was doing." And if Dougal Douglas is right that "vision is the first requisite of sanity," then Miss Brodie is quite sane.

Jenny Gray, Sandy's best friend, is suddenly reminded of her days as one of the Brodie set when years later she is standing outside a famous building in Rome and is "surprised by a reawakening of that same buoyant and airy discovery of sex, a total sensation which it was impossible to say was physical or mental, only that it contained the lost and guileless delight of her eleventh year." The significance of the remembrance is not primarily sexual; it is that she recalls the unified vision of physical and spiritual worlds which she found with Miss Brodie, a vision which made life vibrant and rich and exciting.

But vision is not always possible. Monica Douglas, for example, is famous in the Brodie set for being able to do mathematics in her head. Also, she is easily angered. Miss Brodie objects to Monica's lack of spiritual insight and never makes her one of her favorites. Miss Brodie explains, "that's why she has a bad temper, she understands nothing but signs and symbols and calculations. Nothing infuriates people more than their own lack of spiritual insight. . . ." Miss Brodie's assumption is borne out by Monica's later difficulties with her scientist husband. In a fit of anger she throws a live coal at his sister, and the scientist demands a separation.

Unfortunately, Miss Brodie's opinion of Mary Macgregor also proves to be accurate. Miss Brodie describes her as a silent lump, for she is stupid and unfeeling. She lacks both insight and instinct. Mary never comprehends the world she faces and is totally unequipped to deal with it. For example, when graduated to the Senior school, she does surprisingly well at reading Caesar's *Gallic Wars* until someone explains to her that Latin is not a form of shorthand. She meets death in the same kind of baffled way. Caught in a hallway into which fire is advancing from either end, Mary is unable to find an exit and runs from one fire to the other, distraught and confused. Mary is the epitome of the person who has no vision at all and is, therefore, totally controlled by the forces around her. Due to her lack of insight and instinct, she can never sense the richness of life nor deal with its complexities, for she perceives such a small bit of it.

One of Miss Brodie's fellow teachers at the Marcia Blaine School represents another form of the visionless life. Miss Gaunt, as her name implies, is a sharp, strict, practical, cold, and altogether horrifying person. She has intelligence, which Mary Macgregor has not, but she has long since renounced anything which has to do with the physical side of life. Muriel Spark states that "Her head was very large and bony. Her chest was a slight bulge flattened by a bust bodice, and her jersey was a dark forbidding green." She is a strict Calvinist, and the reader feels that the heavy and forbidding image of Edinburgh always looms menacingly in Miss Gaunt's background, in contrast to the lovely floating city it becomes with the presence of Miss Brodie. Miss Gaunt deals effectively, industriously, and unimaginatively with reality. She faces life grimly and determinedly. She has some degree of insight, but she does not recognize the breadth of life which Miss Brodie does, for she has no instinct whatsoever. Consequently, her life is like her name: gaunt.

Teddy Lloyd, on the other hand, has a great deal of instinct but insufficient insight to become the painter and the man that he would like to be. His instinct is evident in his sensuality, the basis of his art and perhaps of his life. His affair with Sandy fulfills her personality, for afterwards she represents not only insight but also instinct. In reverse, Sandy tries to give him the insight he lacks, but she fails. When more and more of his portraits begin to look like Miss Brodie, she tells him, "Why are you obsessed with that woman? Can't you see she's ridiculous?" He refuses to listen, and his vision is incomplete, just as his body is incomplete (he has only one arm). As a half-personality he cannot rebel as Sandy eventually does. He can only go on painting Miss Brodies, never doing the painting which would make a statement comparable to Sandy's *Transfiguration of the Commonplace.*

The design of *The Prime of Miss Jean Brodie* differs somewhat from that of Muriel Spark's previous novels. Once again she creates a group of diverse individuals who are presented with the same problem, but who react to it in different ways. But in contrast to the preceding novels, *The Prime of Miss Jean Brodie* does not show the characters developing in an uninterrupted line from a point where their lives are dull and ordinary, to an encounter with an extraordinary, sometimes incredible, event, to an existence either characterized by a heightened awareness of oneself and the world or a shocking diminution of life. Instead, early in the novel the girls of the Brodie set are shown to the reader as they eventually come to be. By a complex handling of time the author simultaneously creates two images of the girls. We see them in their prime and we see them creating it.

The point of view is, in effect, a double perspective. Miss Brodie, in her prime, tells the set about her past in order to give them vision. The girls in their prime look back at their past associations with Miss Brodie. By drawing an analogy between the girls and Miss Brodie, the author's theme is "vision" itself. She offers the reader a statement about the nature of reality by depicting a commonplace situation as it is transfigured by a supernatural figure. Miss Brodie offers her set vision by coloring the ordinary facts she teaches by the force of her own extraordinary personality.

The parallel between teacher and student resembles the relationship between the voices and typewriter of *The Comforters* and Caroline, about whom they are writing. The voices give her vision by putting her into a novel. Later she too writes a book in which she records what she has

learned—i.e., her vision. Similarly, Muriel Spark's theme in *The Prime of Miss Jean Brodie* is Miss Brodie's vision. In turn, Miss Brodie is shown relating her somewhat limited vision by teaching her set, and finally Sandy incorporates her broader vision in *The Transfiguration of the Commonplace.*

In two earlier novels Muriel Spark has jumped ahead in time to show the final result of certain bizarre events. In *Robinson* January Marlow is shown safely returned to Chelsea before the reader knows what she has experienced. In *The Ballad of Peckham Rye* the interrupted wedding of Humphrey Place and Dixie Morse begins the novel, and the reader is told that the cancellation is due to Dougal Douglas, though he has not yet entered the narrative. The structural device of disordering the chronology of events becomes far more complex in *The Prime of Miss Jean Brodie*. By choosing to treat the plot in such a manner, the author seems to suggest that the influence of the supernatural does not spend itself in one incredible event, but that it surrounds an individual throughout his lifetime. In *The Prime of Miss Jean Brodie* the reader sees what the girls become as well as how they began. In the design of the novel, one observes the gap between the two states-of-being lessen and, ultimately, close. The unremitting influence of the supernatural, in this case Miss Jean Brodie, is underscored by the inexorable movement of the plot to an already announced end, "towards what extremities her nature worked her," and the ambiguities of Sandy's response to the demoniac teacher.

Just as Caroline struggles against the pre-determination of her life by the mysterious voices in *The Comforters,* so Sandy Stranger rebels against a quite visible Miss Brodie and her effort to dominate Sandy's future as well as her present. She refers to Miss Brodie as a fascist, meaning that the latter insists upon being a dictator. Finally it occurs to Sandy that Miss Brodie has made the mistake of seeing herself not just as another Mussolini, but as God himself. She sets herself up as Providence, directing, controlling, shaping the girls. Ultimately she assumes the power of life and death over them, and she sends Joyce Emily to Spain to fight in the Civil War. Sandy realizes that when Miss Brodie places herself in such a position, she limits what is possible. She limits potential reality. She narrows the world of her girls when she makes herself the most complete expression of that world. Indeed, Sandy eventually realizes that Miss Brodie is not Providence; she is not the God of Calvin; she does not see the beginning and the end. And she recognizes Miss Brodie's "defective sense of self-criticism," which can be called an "excessive lack of guilt," as Samuel Hynes refers to it in "The Prime of Muriel Spark," *Commonweal,* February 16, 1962. Thus, Sandy must reject Miss Brodie, for it becomes evident that even Miss Brodie is incomplete. Sandy's own insight and instinct, plus the benefit of Miss Brodie's prime, ironically give her a perception of a reality far more extensive than Miss Brodie's, broad as it is. Therefore, Sandy removes her allegiance from Miss Brodie and gives it to God by becoming a nun.

But Sandy's new allegiance fails to bring peace and tranquillity as the reader might expect it to.

> She clutched the bars of the grille as if she wanted to escape from the dim parlour beyond, for she was not composed like the other nuns who sat, when they received their rare visitors, well back in the darkness with folded hands. But Sandy always leaned forward and peered, clutching the bars with both hands, and the other sisters remarked it and said that Sister Helena had too much to bear from the world since she had published her psychological book which was so unexpectedly famed.

Indeed, she does have much to bear from the world, but it is not fame that disturbs her. It is vision itself. Just as Ronald Bridges suffers intensely as his understanding of the nature of the world grows, so Sandy the nun realizes with a measure of distress the extent of the goodness and evil in this world and other worlds. Her insight and her instinct, given to her from birth, but nourished and developed either by Miss Brodie or in reaction against her, combine in Sandy to give her vision, which simultaneously disturbs and consoles. Certainly it transfigures for her the commonplace. Thus Sandy Stranger, who was a stranger in this world until she grew in understanding of reality, becomes Sister Helena of the Transfiguration.

### Gerry S. Laffin (essay date Summer 1972)

SOURCE: "Muriel Spark's Portrait of the Artist as a Young Girl," in *Renascence*, Vol. XXIV, No. 4, Summer, 1972, pp. 213-23.

[*In the essay below, Laffin analyzes the religious, Freudian, and novelistic aspects of* The Prime of Miss Jean Brodie *by examining the various motivations of the character Sandy.*]

It was with a sense of relief that Muriel Spark enthusiasts greeted *The Prime of Miss Jean Brodie,* for here at last was the concretely real uncluttered by the mysteriously occult, the supernatural, the fantastic. *The Comforters* had been one of the most puzzling of first novels; one was not altogether sure what to make of it. *Robinson* was almost equally puzzling, though not as complex. *Memento Mori* with its social and psychological realism was absolutely lucid by comparison, notwithstanding the identity of its mysterious caller. But with *The Ballad of Peckham Rye* and *The Bachelors* readers were once again confronted with Mrs. Spark playing fast and loose with the empirical world. It was easy enough to believe with Humphry Place in *The Ballad of Peckham Rye* that "there was another world than this." But how could that other world be reconciled with this concrete one within the form of a single novel? It was as if Mrs. Spark were asking the reader to assent to the literalness of inexplicable supernatural events, while at the same time the novels' purely naturalistic levels seemed to make such an assent impossible. The result was an uneasy feeling that Mrs. Spark's two worlds kept cancelling each other out. Among other novels, *The Bachelors* offers a good example of this phenomenon. While the reader is apparently being asked to believe that a benign God, a "vigilant manipulator" as he is called in the novel, is instrumental in the punishment of Patrick Seton, the agonized existential meditations of Ronald Bridges have such an authentic ring to them that the read-er finds it very difficult to resist them or deny their validity.

It was with some sense of relief, then, that *The Prime of Miss Jean Brodie* was greeted, for here was not the impossible demand of assimilating the supernatural in a realistic context. Moreover, in the title of Sister Helena's famous treatise on the nature of "moral perception," many critics seemed to find the key to Muriel Spark's past performances—"The Transformation of the Commonplace." However, as neat as that phrase may be, it does not clarify Mrs. Spark's fictional practices. At most it indicates that her protagonists acquire a growing awareness of themselves in relation to the world around them. But the notion of the "developing character" is certainly nothing new in fiction, certainly nothing unique with Mrs. Spark. Nor does the transformation-of-the-commonplace approach to her fiction even help to explain the novel in which the phrase appeared. Some years ago, Josephine Jacobsen, in "A Catholic Quartet," *Christian Scholar,* 67 (1964), attempted to do just that in an appraisal that seems strangely out of keeping with the tone of the novel itself: "After the maiming exposure to Miss Brodie's ego, which, under the banner of Truth, Freedom and Beauty, has disclosed itself in cruelty, stupidity and ravaging egotism, Sandy comes to feel that what is essential is to see the commonplace in light of grace. The commonplace unilluminated is stifling; the fabrications of the ego are cruel and basically stupid; but by transfiguration, the materials of the commonplace come into their proper radiance." Transfiguring in the light of grace the materials of the commonplace into their "proper radiance" does not seem a conclusion that one can come to about *The Prime of Miss Jean Brodie,* especially when one considers that in the Church Sandy Stranger found "facists" far worse than Jean Brodie, and especially when one considers that at novel's conclusion Sister Helena is left clutching the bars of her grille "more desperately than ever."

This essentially religious, transformation-of-the-commonplace explanation does not explain, for the novel leaves totally undeveloped the nature of Sandy Stranger's conversion. Moreover, when one attempts to supply the novel with the ostensible religious significance that in fact is lacking, one must conclude that while Jean Brodie is a free-wheeling Justified Sinner in the tradition of Calvinist mythology, Sandy Stranger is, ironically, a child after John Calvin's own heart. Karl Miller, himself a native of Edinburgh, made this point in his review of the novel in *The New Statesman,* November 3, 1961. In seeming to credit Sandy "with exactly 'the sense of joy and salvation' the dangers of which have already been expounded," says Miller, the reader is confronted with a "nasty surprise which makes the author seem to slide back before our eyes into antinomian Calvinism, a justified sinner with the sourness and solipsism of her kind." Mr. Miller consequently concludes: "Catholicism is queer in Edinburgh, but it can't be as queer as that." More recently, in the most extensive article to date on *The Prime of Miss Jean Brodie* ["The Uses and Abuses of Omniscience: Method and Meaning in Muriel Spark's *The Prime of Miss Jean Brodie,*" *Critical Quarterly* (Autumn 1970)], David Lodge offers another religious explanation (though also partly "novelistic") in an attempt to explain Sandy Stranger's enigmatic motives. He says that the novel's "assessment of Miss Brodie is, in the last analysis, an ethical and theological matter." Professor Lodge says, in effect, that Miss Brodie is punished for playing God, for creating myths out of all her fictions, in contrast to Sandy, who, in her growing moral awareness has learned the difference between "fiction" and "truth." Though Professor Lodge's conclusions are questionable, for reasons which I will develop in due course, he is the only critic I can recall who has noted that Sandy Stranger's "moral perceptiveness" was intended by Mrs. Spark to be ironic. This is a very important point, one that helps considerably to clear up some of the puzzles of *The Prime of Miss Jean Brodie*. If Professor Lodge had followed through on this point, one thinks that he might have come to different conclusions.

Another recent commentator, Ann Dobie, says [in *"The Prime of Miss Jean Brodie:* Muriel Spark Bridges the Credibility Gap," *Arizona Quarterly* (1969)] that the theme of the novel is "vision itself," a vision that serves to "transfigure the commonplace" by providing Sandy Stranger with a knowledge of the inextricable mixture in this world of good and evil. According to Miss Dobie, Sandy has acquired this vision, "which simultaneously disturbs and consoles," from Jean Brodie. As far as it goes, this idea is true, of course, provided one insists that the principle of evil is no less active in Sandy Stranger than it is in Jean Brodie; for if as a result of a growing moral awareness Sandy determined to punish Miss Brodie for playing God, it is obvious that Sandy herself is guilty of the same transgression. Indeed, Sandy Stranger is in the long line of moral blackmailers to be found in Muriel Spark's novels, whose motives on close examination turn out to be very private and essentially malicious, not as moral or religious as they pretend to be. The evidence in *The Prime of Miss Jean Brodie* indicates that Mrs. Spark was fully aware of Sandy's duplicity.

The attempt to assign "real" motives in the novel is a game of almost endless speculation, and serves mainly to point up the novel's central "failure." I put the word in quotes because I suggest that to read *The Prime of Miss Jean Brodie* as if it were a work of psychological realism is to necessarily miss its real significance. True enough, in its realistic technique the novel seems to demand such a reading; but every attempt in this direction requires a great deal of explaining in order to accommodate the novel's apparent gaps and obvious ambiguities. I suggest that readers were misled primarily because Mrs. Spark's usual occult and supernatural paraphernalia were missing from *The Prime of Miss Jean Brodie*. Readers failed to notice, it seems, that in this novel Mrs. Spark was employing an even more characteristic technique: namely the novel as parable and allegory. She was also indulging her sense of humor to such subtle effect, it seems, that few saw Sandy Stranger as a comic figure. The movie version of *The Prime of Miss Jean Brodie* may attest to the fact that the novel was taken far too seriously. In fact, the novel was an extended joke, a joke directed at Muriel Spark herself. Its final effect is ambivalent, no doubt, but not ambiguous once its point is seen.

In an *Atlantic Monthly* review of *The Mandelbaum Gate* Frank Kermode wrote: "The suggestion is, in Mrs. Spark's novels, that a genuine relation exists between the forms of fiction and the forms of the world, between the novelist's creation and God's." Consequently, he says that all of her novels "are in a sense novels about the novel, inquiries into the relation between fiction and truth." If there were no other evidence available (and there happens to be considerable), Mrs. Spark's first novel, *The Comforters,* amply attests to the fact that she was extremely interested in the question of how a work of fiction, which is essentially a "lie," can be a vehicle for the truth. The answer is relatively simple, though no doubt philosophically profound: a fiction is true in the same way that the parables of Christ were true. Mrs. Spark wrote in *Twentieth Century,* 170 (1961) "Fiction to me is a kind of parable. You have got to make up your mind it's not true. Some kind of truth emerges from it, but it's not fact." In other words, as Aristotle responded to Plato, a universal truth is no less true because it is not particular. As for allegories, Mrs. Spark had already written a blatant one, *Robinson,* as well as the partially allegorical *The Ballad of Peckham Rye*. Indeed, from one perspective the whole of *The Comforters* itself was an allegory of free will versus determinism. Up to and including the writing of *The Prime of Miss Jean Brodie,* therefore, there is sufficient evidence to believe that Mrs. Spark seldom conceived of characters and events as "real"; they are instead, for the most part, emblematic of the abstract ideas, the universal truths, that are the occasion of her novels. She once said in an interview: "I keep in my mind specifically that what I am writing is fiction because I am interested in truth—absolute truth." One of the major purposes of *The Comforters* was to illustrate how fictional forms could express absolute truths. The evidence from several novels, including *The Prime of Miss Jean Brodie,* seems clearly to suggest that Mrs. Spark was never convinced that she was the truthteller as novelist that she wanted to be. To simplify for the moment, it can be said that *The Prime of Miss Jean Brodie* was written to examine once again the relation between fiction and truth, though not as profoundly as it had been examined in *The Comforters* or even in *The Ballad of Peckham Rye,* for that matter.

It is more complicated than this, however, for a remarkable thing about Mrs. Spark is that whenever she deals with this particular question, she almost inevitably considers the problems of Catholic belief and Freudian myths. There is a sense in which nearly all of her novels are "about" these three subjects in greater or lesser degree. But they are seldom treated separately; instead they are inseparably linked and interrelated in a single intellectual-aesthetic construct. Consider *The Comforters,* for example: clearly the novel is about the relation between fiction and truth; it is just as clearly a novel about coming to terms with the problems of Catholic beliefs; and though the nature of Caroline Rose's neurosis is not made very clear (it would be explicit in *Robinson*), there are sufficient clues in the novel to suggest that it is primarily sexual, the most singular one being the necessity of Caroline's physically touching the loathsome carnality of Mrs. Hogg in the climatic drowning episode. Mrs. Spark's three "subjects," as it were (novelistic, religious, Freudian), are almost perfectly balanced in *The Prime of Miss Jean Brodie*. It is no wonder, then, that many readers have thought of it primarily as a religious novel, while others have considered it essentially a realistic character study. But no one as yet has fully noticed that its major perspective is "novelistic." Professor Lodge has come the closest to this understanding, but he was unfortunately waylaid by asking the wrong question: namely, what is supposed to be the reader's final judgment of Jean Brodie's character? Such a question assumes that the novel is a realistic character study. I suggest instead that *The Prime of Miss Jean Brodie* is a parable, and a highly autobiographical one, of the artist as a young girl. Further, it seems that in this novel at least, Mrs. Spark believes that any creator of fiction who claims to be a truth-teller is being absurdly even dangerously, pretentious.

In the combined characters of Jean Brodie and Sandy Stranger, Mrs. Spark made what is perhaps her most public confession, so to speak, of herself both as person and as novelist. I think that Charles Hoyt was correct [in "Muriel Spark: The Surrealist Jane Austen," in *Contemporary British Novelist,* edited by Charles Shapiro, 1965] when he wrote of this novel: "Surely, the conflict which gives the book its special character, so enigmatic, so wryly amusing and yet profound, is that of Mrs. Spark's own life." He concludes: "Miss Jean Brodie is Muriel Spark's clearest conception of herself to the present and Sandy Stranger her best insight into her most dangerous and self-destructive tendencies." Jean Brodie and Sandy Stranger are not "real" characters in a realistic novel, then; they are allegorical figures in Mrs. Spark's self-portrait, a portrait of the artist as a young girl.

In *The Prime of Miss Jean Brodie* there are three "artists," none of whom ever tells the truth, but each of whom is deluded into believing that he does so. Each of them practices an artistic "economy" (one of Mrs. Spark's most cherished practices) that serves only to distort reality, to make it impossible to ever perceive the truth. The most obvious example of such distortion is to be seen in the portraits of Teddy Lloyd, the one-armed painter (a Freudian joke?). No matter whom he paints, the finished product always looks like Jean Brodie:

> Sandy was fascinated by the economy of Teddy Lloyd's method, as she had been four years earlier by Miss Brodie's variation of her love story, when she had attached to her first war-time lover the attributes of the art master and the singing master who had then newly entered her orbit. Teddy Lloyd's method of presentation was similar, it was economical, and it always seemed afterwards to Sandy that where there was a choice of various courses, the most economical was the best, and that the course to be taken was the most expedient and most suitable at the time for all the objects in hand. She acted on this principle when the time came for her to betray Miss Brodie.

Four years earlier, when Miss Brodie had begun to fictionalize the great love of her life by enlarging it with real incidents out of her present experience, "Sandy was fascinated by this method of making patterns with facts, and was di-

vided between her admiration for the technique and the personal need to prove Miss Brodie guilty of misconduct." (It may be interesting to note that Dougal Douglas employed the same technique in his fictionalized biography of Maria Cheeseman, but with an important difference: all of Dougal's fictions turn out to be surprisingly true in principle if not in fact.) Years later when Miss Brodie tells Sandy about her affair with Gordon Lowther, the singing master, she concludes by saying, "Well, as I say, that is the whole story." But "Sandy was thinking of something else. She was thinking that it was not the whole story." Nor was it, of course, for Jean Brodie was such an inveterate fictionalizer and so solipsistic in the extremity of her supreme egotism that she was simply out of touch with reality. One of the consistent ironies of the novel is that while Miss Brodie sets great store by "vision," she herself is totally lacking in that attribute. Not only does she fail to discover who betrayed her, she fails miserably to assess the moral implication of Facism. Even after the horrors of World War II, the most she can say is that "Hitler was a naughty boy." Moreover, her carefully laid plan to live vicariously in the adulterous relationship between Rose Stanley and Teddy Lloyd goes awry because she fails to perceive the true characters of both Rose and Sandy. In Jean Brodie's self-assured knowingness, one is reminded of Muriel Spark's narrative persona; as Richard Mayne once called it, "a mother-knows-best dead certainty" (*Encounter,* 25 [1965]). But there is considerable difference between fictionalizing by making patterns with facts, as a novelist must, and believing those fictions to be true, as Miss Brodie does.

---

> **Spark's three "subjects" (novelistic, religious, Freudian) are almost perfectly balanced in *The Prime of Miss Jean Brodie*. It is no wonder, then, that many readers have thought of it primarily as a religious novel, while others have considered it essentially a realistic character study. But no one as yet has fully noticed that its major perspective is "novelistic."**
>
> **—*Gerry S. Laffin***

---

Like a novelist, then, Jean Brodie is a story-teller who tells lies. She does not lie deliberately; indeed, she is unconscious of lying, because she fails to understand that to arrange facts into patterns is to necessarily distort the truth. Mrs. Spark herself was aware of this problem, from the time of *The Comforters* at least. In that novel it will be recalled that Caroline Rose objects mightily to being a "character" who is being written into a "novel." At one point she tells Father Jerome: "It's as if the person was waiting to pounce on some insignificant thought or action, in order to make it signify in a strange distorted way." But Jean Brodie is unaware of the existence of such an epistemological problem. And so too Sandy Stranger, the other lying "novelist" in *The Prime of Miss Jean Brodie*. Sandy's case is a more subtle one, however, and for that reason, possibly, has been largely misunderstood.

Besides constantly fantasizing about love, Sandy actually commits her fictions to paper, in particular "The Mountain Eyrie: The True Love Story of Miss Jean Brodie." In addition to its thematic significance, the word "true" in the title of Sandy's story is ironic in the extreme when one considers her story to be a brilliant mixture of rhetorical modes—romantic clichés, vulgar journalese, adolescent slang. The result is, of course, a hilarious distortion of the truth, whatever it may be. Throughout the novel, in fact, Sandy never seems capable of reconciling "reality" (the evidence of her senses) with her innate sense of how things are or ought to be. In this respect, she differs not at all from Miss Brodie. She cannot believe for example that Miss Brodie and Hugh Carruthers ever had sexual intercourse because "their love was above all that." She cannot believe Monica's story of discovering Miss Brodie and Teddy Lloyd embracing in the art room. The only way that this incident can become "real" for Sandy is to have Monica tell the story over and over.

Two incidents especially, however, illustrate the gap between the empirical world and Sandy's subjective understanding. In the first, during a rather traumatic field trip to the Old Town section of Edinburgh, Sandy witnesses a drunken brawl between a man and a woman. Another woman comes up, takes the man by the arm, and says, " 'I'll be your man.' From time to time throughout her life Sandy pondered this, for she was certain that the little woman's words were 'I'll be your man,' not 'I'll be your woman,' and it was never explained." The second incident concerns Sandy's friend Jenny, who one day "out walking alone, was accosted by a man joyfully exposing himself beside the Water of Leith." Sandy is fascinated by this occurrence, especially Jenny's interrogation by a policewoman, and asks Jenny to tell of it again and again. What disturbs Sandy most is to learn that in her talks with Jenny the policewoman had pronounced it properly. The result was that Sandy had to invent a new feeling in Sandy and it put her off the idea of sex for months. All the more as she disapproved of the pronunciation of the word, it made her flesh creep, and she plagued Jenny to change her mind and agree that the policewoman had pronounced the word "nasty" as "nesty." "This gave rise to an extremely nasty speaking-image for the policewoman." In a word, then, only rhetoric is "real" to Sandy, a rhetoric that is rooted in a unique, abstracted, solipsistic vision. By means of such rhetoric is the commonplace "transformed." And by such means as this do novelists tell lies by distorting reality. It is certainly not coincidental that several times Mrs. Spark describes Sandy as having "little pig eyes," almost non-existent eyes. Professor Lodge is probably correct, therefore, in saying that as an "inside narrator" Sandy Stranger is unreliable. This being so, it seems safe to assume that Sister Helena's famous treatise on moral perception was intended by Mrs. Spark to be a joke. Whether one arranges facts into patterns according to abstracted rhetorical, aesthetic, or moral principles, one necessarily distorts the truth.

I have already noted David Lodge's assertion that Sandy's judgment of Jean Brodie, and consequently the reader's own judgment, is ethical and religious, that Miss Brodie is punished for playing God, for creating fictions she literally believes in. Sandy comes to understand this, says Professor Lodge, because unlike Jean Brodie, Sandy has learned the difference between fiction and the real world. In evidence, Professor Lodge notes the symbolic significance of Sandy's literally burying forever in a little cave her fictionalized romance of Miss Brodie's love life. I suggest, however, that it is Muriel Spark, not Sandy Stranger, who perceives the difference between fiction and truth, and that the novel judges Sandy for precisely the same reasons that Sandy judges Miss Brodie. Professor Lodge quotes Christopher Ricks, who complains that Muriel Spark "commits as novelist the sins she condemns in her characters." Readers of Muriel Spark will feel that the charge is not unjustified; but in *The Prime of Miss Jean Brodie* Mrs. Spark clearly has her wits about her, for if Miss Brodie becomes the hapless victim of her own fictional illusions, so too does Sandy Stranger. It might appear that in burying the manuscript of Miss Brodie's love life Sandy abandons her preadolescent fantasies; in fact, however, she substitutes for them another fiction, a fiction that she subsequently acts upon. Having heard all of the delicious details of Jenny's great sexual adventure, Sandy "had quite deserted Alan Breck and Mr. Rochester and all of the heroes of fiction for the summer term, and fell in love with the unseen policewoman who had questioned Jenny." Subsequently, Sandy imagines herself Sergeant Anne Grey's "right-hand woman in the Force, and they were dedicated to eliminate sex from Edinburgh and environs." It is Miss Brodie's "excessive lack of guilt" about her own sexuality that Sandy must put a stop to. When Sandy finally provides Miss Mackay with the handle she needs by revealing Jean Brodie's admiration for Facism, Miss Mackay says, "I had no idea you felt so serious about the state of world affairs." To this Sandy replies, "I'm not really interested in world affairs, only in putting a stop to Miss Brodie." Indeed, politics is not a part of Sandy's consciousness. Her chief preoccupation, almost obsessively so, is with sex.

The point here, however, is not to assign "real" psychological motives for Sandy's puzzling betrayal of Miss Brodie. The point is "novelistic," for in betraying Miss Brodie Sandy acts out the role of her fictional creation, Sergeant Anne Grey's right-hand woman. Miss Brodie, too, behaves like a fictional character. It is evident, for example, that she has been corrupted by romantic fiction. Professor Lodge notes that *Jane Eyre* is Miss Brodie's favorite novel; more importantly and to the point he notes that her own love life "bears a parodic resemblance" to that novel. Whatever the nature of the real relationship between the sexes, an inhabitant of the Twentieth Century would be sorely deluded, as Miss Brodie was, to be guided by Nineteenth Century fictions. But if Miss Brodie was corrupted by the rhetoric of romance, Sandy Stranger was equally corrupted by the sleazy rhetoric of post-Victorian journalese, for all of her adolescent attitudes about sex are informed by this rhetoric: "In the Sunday newspapers, to which Sandy had free access, the correct technical phrases were to be found, such as 'intimacy took place' and 'plaintiff was in a certain condition.' Females who were up for sex were not called 'Miss' or 'Mrs.,' they were referred to by their surnames: 'Willis was remanded in custody . . .' 'Roebuck, said Counsel, was discovered to be in a certain condition.' " At one extreme, then, in Jean Brodie's case, sexuality is corrupted by the transcendent innocence of romantic rhetoric; at the other extreme, in Sandy's case, it is corrupted by an implicitly dirty-minded newspaper rhetoric. Both, of course, are distortions of the truth, whatever complex thing it may be. Sandy's burial, then, of her romantic manuscript in that (Freudian) cave is certainly symbolic: it symbolizes the repression of a youthful innocent, spontaneous sexuality, a repression that is perfectly in keeping with her ultimate vows of chastity as Sister Helena of the Transfiguration. There is a great irony here, for it seems clear that Sandy has not been liberated by her conversion. She has not escaped the Calvinism that she desired to reject; indeed, she became its victim, guilt-ridden and trapped, behind the bars of her grille, in its harsh moral imperatives.

Not only is truth hidden from Sandy behind a veil of false rhetoric, as it is for Miss Brodie, but also both behave as if the real world itself is based upon novelistic techniques. We have already seen, thanks to Professor Lodge, that in many ways Miss Brodie recreates in her own love life the story of *Jane Eyre,* her favorite novel. As for Sandy, besides acting out her fantasy as Sergeant Anne Grey's right-hand woman on the Force, when the time comes for her to betray Miss Brodie she acts upon the principles of aesthetic "economy" which she had learned from both Miss Brodie and Teddy Lloyd. The question is, of course, can moral judgments, which are rooted in the transcendent absolute, be arrived at by means of such strictly aesthetic principles? Assuming that both novels and the world itself have "meanings" which are "true," does one "read" the world as one reads novels to discover that truth? The suggestion is, in *The Prime of Miss Jean Brodie,* that the answer to these questions is no, that it is dangerous to assume that God's real world is created on the same aesthetic principles that an author employs in creating a fictional world. In making such a false assumption, Sandy Stranger failed to see that art and life are radically different. Mrs. Spark makes this same point in *Memento Mori* when Guy Leets is talking to Charmian Colston about her novels. Charmian says:

> "And yet, when I was halfway through writing a novel I always got into a muddle and didn't know where it was leading me."

> Guy thought: She is going to say—dear Chairman—she is going to say, "The characters seemed to take on a life of their own."

> "The characters," said Charmian, "seemed to take control of my pen after awhile. But at first I always got into a tangle . . . because the art of fiction is very like the practice of deception."

> "And in life," he said, "is the practice of deception in life an art too?"

> "In life," she said, "everything is different. Everything is in the Providence of God."

Ironically, of course, Charmian's whole life has been based on deceptions. Even though she knows that art and life are different, she behaves as if they were the same. But poor Sandy Stranger is not even aware of the difference. And at novel's end, now Sister Helena of the Transfiguration, something has gone wrong; somehow she has been trapped, somehow made a victim. She has been victimized by acting upon her unconscious assumption that art and life make the same kind of sense and for the same reasons.

Some years ago Charles Hoyt wrote of Mrs. Spark's novels: "The excitement infused into all her best fiction, that quality which I attempted to define at the outset, derives from some formidable positive charge of Edinburgh Calvinism against its opposite, the negative of mystical Catholicism." It seems clear that embodied in the very structure of many of Mrs. Spark's novels is this unresolved Calvinist-Catholic duality—the Calvinist vision of the world as predestined and damned, on the one hand, versus a liberated Catholic vision of the world as possibilities. And though this would seem to be a strictly theological problem, more often than not Mrs. Spark conceptualizes it in Freudian terms, so that the theological and the Freudian seem irrevocably linked in any given novel. Whether this is done consciously or whether it is instead unconsciously "mythic," so to speak, it is clear from *Robinson,* among other works, that Mrs. Spark was thoroughly familiar with popular Freudian theories. As in *Robinson,* we find once again in *The Prime of Miss Jean Brodie* this characteristic Freudian-theological configuration; and whereas *Robinson* was a blatant Freudian allegory, one might therefore have reason to believe that Sandy Stranger and Jean Brodie are emblematic of the Alter-ego and the Id, respectively. They are elements in the personality of the artist as a young girl, as well as being common coin, it seems, in the patterns of Mrs. Spark's novels. We find, then, a classic Freudian conflict that in *The Comforters* and in *Robinson* finds its resolution in Catholic belief. Only when Caroline Rose forces herself to touch Mrs. Hogg's carnality is her liberation complete. Significantly, of course, this act occurs in a religious context, for in that manner and at that point the novel proves its contention that Caroline is a free-willing agent in God's providential design. Similarly, January Marlow faced the same problem, and resolved it by rejecting Miles Robinson's cold rationality and accepting mystical Mariology, weighted as it is, in the novel, towards the feminine, the irrational, the creative. Barbara Vaughan, too, made a similar choice, finally liberated in her adventures on the irrational side of the Mandelbaum Gate, finally accepting the fact of her sexuality, for "the whole of life is unified under God."

But Sandy Stranger, the artist as a young girl, had not yet been liberated from the conflict between her Id, Jean Brodie, and her Alter-ego, Sergeant Anne Grey and the forbidding religion of Calvin. She had not yet discovered, as the artist as a middle-aged woman obviously had, the syncretic possibilities of mystical Catholicism. True to her instincts as an artist, however, she nevertheless realized that here at the deeper levels of the lawless Id was the probable source of creative energy; and thus its "beneficent and enlarging effects." In Catholicism Mrs. Spark seems to have found her identity, both as a novelist and as an individual.

But in spite of the self-assured tone of her narrative persona, her novels indicate that hers was not an easy faith. It required living with paradoxes and impossible contradictions. What better way to communicate the impossibilities of faith than in the symbol of a convert nun with imperfect "vision," desperately clutching the bars of her grille?

## J. H. Dorenkamp (essay date Autumn 1980)

SOURCE: "Moral Vision in Muriel Spark's *The Prime of Miss Jean Brodie*," in *Renascence,* Vol. XXXIII, No. 1, Autumn, 1980, pp. 3-9.

[*In the following essay, Dorenkamp discusses the theme of morality in* The Prime of Miss Jean Brodie, *focusing on the main characters, Jean Brodie and Sandy Stranger.*]

Muriel Spark's novel, **The Prime of Miss Jean Brodie,** is an economical treatise on moral perception which exemplifies not only the necessity of such perception, but also the terrible responsibility accompanying its acquisition. This relationship, arising from the close association between knowledge and action, is central to the conflict of the book and is reflected in its very structure. To understand how the novel itself becomes a treatise on moral perception, I shall examine three discernible points of view: that of Jean Brodie herself, that of Sandy Stranger, and that of the narrator (or point of view, properly speaking). Finally, I will move from the work itself to examine the relationship between the author and the novel.

From the beginning of Muriel Spark's novel, the reader is invited to view Jean Brodie as a God-like character, a teacher-savior surrounded by her faithful disciples whom she has chosen as the recipients of her saving message and one of whom will eventually betray her. Sandy Stranger says: "She thinks she is Providence, . . . she thinks she is the God of Calvin, she sees the beginning and end." Whether Jean perceives herself in this way or not is uncertain, but she acts as if she were a kind of God: the God of Providence in her attempts to shape, direct, and control the lives of her charges even after they are no longer officially hers and God the Creator, who, in a sense, fashions a world for herself and populates it with creatures of her own imagining.

Within the real world in which Jean lives and moves, she has created another world, a world as it should be as opposed to the world which is. Consequently, Miss Brodie's girls are as much a product of her fancy and imagination as they are real flesh-and-blood students at Marcia Blaine's Academy. They seem to have been chosen not for any particular, common characteristics, but according to a principle of plenitude: one is good at math; one is noted for her voice and her ability to recite; one for her eyes; one is famous for sex; one provides comic relief. Other characters, such as Miss Mackay, Gordon Lowther, Teddy Lloyd, and the Gaunt sisters, are also transformed and recreated by Jean Brodie's fancy. The more removed from present reality they actually are, as is Hugh, Jean's lover killed in the war, the more protean they become in adopting the shapes necessary for Jean Brodie's current vision.

This vision is at once Jean's strength and weakness. It allows her to transcend the mundane, to see values beyond the merely practical. At the same time, however, it is confused, and she fails to distinguish between life and art; that is to say, what ought to be prudential judgments become for her aesthetic judgments. Thus the vision which leads her to regard Giotto as the greatest painter (and to prescribe that view for others) is the same vision that prompts her to admire the order which Fascism imposes upon its subjects. She is blind to the essential evils of Fascism and comes to no stronger conclusion than that Hitler was a bit naughty.

Because she confuses aesthetic judgments with moral ones, it is not surprising that how far a window should be opened or how one should comport oneself are just as important to Jean as are larger political questions. Just as her own affair with Gordon Lowther seems to have no moral dimension, her plan that Rose Stanley should become Teddy Lloyd's lover and that Sandy Stranger should be the one to bring Jean the news is devised without any consideration of the moral rightness or wrongness of the act. Such questions are irrelevant to Jean: "Just as an excessive sense of guilt can drive people to excessive action, so was Miss Brodie driven to it by an excessive lack of guilt." Right and wrong are the concerns of the Miss Mackays of the world, and Jean is careful not to let their world impinge on hers. Unfortunately, she does not see the implications of her own vision in the lives of others who, no matter how she conceives of them, live in the real world as well. Despite her betrayal and final abandonment, Jean never gains any insight into what has really happened to her. Without the requisite moral vision, she remains obsessed with the unimportant question of *who* betrayed her, rather than with the significant one of *why* she was betrayed.

In contrast to Jean Brodie, Sandy Stranger acquires a broader vision of the world. Sandy had shared her teacher's romantic view of life, as is evidenced by her collaboration with Jenny Gray on "The Mountain Eyrie," a romantic story peopled with characters drawn from fiction and from real life and transmogrified by the girls' young imaginations and speculations about Jean Brodie's life and loves. Like Jean, Sandy and Jenny create an unreal, romantic, fictional world, but as Sandy matures, her perception of the world changes. By making a distinction between the world of her own devising and the real world, she develops a moral vision which Jean never achieves. Included in the development of that vision is the ability to separate fiction from fact, romance from reality, the prudential from the aesthetic, good from evil. Sandy's vision reaches its fullest formulation in her psychological treatise on moral perception, "The Transfiguration of the Commonplace," which she writes after she becomes Sister Helena, a member of a cloistered, contemplative religious order.

The title of Sandy's treatise, which has spiritual and scriptural significance, illustrates her change in vision. The scriptural account of the transfiguration occurs in Matthew xvii. 1-8:

> Now after six days Jesus took Peter, James and his brother John, and led them up a high moun-

tain by themselves, and was transfigured before them. And his face shone as the sun, and his garments became white as snow. And behold, there appeared to them Moses and Elias talking together with him. Then Peter addressed Jesus saying, "Lord, it is good for us to be here. If thou wilt, let us set up three tents here, one for thee, one for Moses, and one for Elias." As he was still speaking, behold a bright cloud overshadowed them, and behold, a voice out of the cloud said, "This is my beloved Son, in whom I am well pleased; hear him." And on hearing it the disciples fell on their faces and were exceedingly afraid. And Jesus came near and touched them, and said to them, "Arise and do not be afraid." But lifting up their eyes, they saw no one but Jesus only.

This vision of the glorified Christ afforded Peter, James and John was a kind of beatific vision, a view of eternity. When the everyday is transfigured, the temporal is transcended, and the commonplace, seen in relation to eternal things, takes on eternal significance. The person who has been granted such a vision no longer sees the world from only a temporal point of view, but rather *sub specie aeternitatis*. From that aspect, the world takes on a spiritual and moral dimension which it otherwise does not have; it is this vision, this transfiguration, which Sandy perceives.

Although the full formulation of that vision presented in her treatise does not occur until some years later, Sandy is aware of its essential elements during her time at Marcia Blaine's Academy, and it is this awareness which leads her to betray Jean Brodie. Sandy comes to see not only the divine stance which Jean has assumed, but to recognize also that Jean's manipulation—or attempted manipulation—of people is dangerous. She realizes the potential for evil which Jean possesses and unwittingly exercises because of her narrow vision—not only the foolish pronouncements about art, music, and politics, but the tragedy of Joyce Emily Hammond killed in Spain. Sandy realizes, ultimately, that knowledge is intimately connected with action. Since she sees little hope that anyone else will effectively end Jean's sway, she decides that she must do it herself.

Although she must try to see things *sub specie aeternitatis,* from God's point of view, Sandy does not identify herself with God as she suggests Jean does. Sandy's God is not the God of Calvin, the creator who has "planned for practically everybody before they were born a nasty surprise when they died" and to whom human actions were not meritorious; rather, he is the God of Roman Catholicism, the creator of beings responsible for their own acts, which can merit reward and punishment. This concept of God demands that the person who would act prudently must first adopt God's point of view and then conform his own actions to that view.

Consequently, Sandy's growth in perception, which compels her to view human actions *sub specie aeternitatis,* not only leads her to take action against her teacher but compels her to view her own act from this higher perspective. She does not see her action as a betrayal since there is, she says, no question of betrayal where no loyalty is due. But she is deeply disturbed by having to have acted, and her conversion to Catholicism and subsequent entry into a

convent are results of that action. By choosing to enter a contemplative order, she rejects the life of action and the responsibility for judging and acting on that judgment again. Clutching the bars of the grille separating her from the world and the active life, she is like a caged animal, locked up so that she will do no more harm. By stopping Jean Brodie, Sandy has in effect stopped herself. She is being precise when she replies to the question, "What were the main influences of your school days?" with "There was a Miss Jean Brodie in her prime."

In spite of Sandy's wider vision, she is not a particularly likeable character. Some of our reservations about her spring, I believe, from her striking similarity to Jean Brodie. It is perhaps this similarity which accounts for the fact that Sandy seems to be the only Brodie girl upon whom Jean has had a marked and lasting effect. Most are like Eunice, who remembers Jean fondly as being a bit eccentric, but whose life shows no lasting mark of Jean's training. Both Sandy and Jean are passionate, zealous people. If Jean implicitly thinks herself to be like God, seeing both beginning and end, shaping people and situations for her own purposes, so does Sandy in her decision to judge and sentence Jean. If Jean sees her students not as individuals but as embodiments of abstractions—instinct, insight, comic relief (indicated by the epithets or tags often associated with them)—so does Sandy see Jean as an abstraction: "It was twenty-five years before Sandy had so far recovered from a creeping vision of disorder that she could look back and recognize that Miss Brodie's defective sense of self-criticism had not been without its beneficent and enlarging effects."

Jean, who regarded highly the economy of Teddy Lloyd's painting style and technique, employs a certain economy in her own arrangement of people and events, adapting her plans quickly and efficiently to conform to situations over which she has no control. Sandy, when the time comes to stop Jean, acts upon the principle that "where there was a choice of various courses, the most economical was the best. . . ." Jean's and Sandy's concern with "economy" suggests the theological dimension of the term, in the sense of the divine plan for man. Jean, acting as the God of Calvin, is Providence, her plan similar to the "divine plan hidden in the intellect of God from all eternity . . . and revealed in the divine acts of salvation through His prophets, through Jesus Christ, and through His Holy Spirit." The meaning of Sandy's economy goes a step further: "Divine economy likewise embraces the mystery of the execution of the divine plan of salvation. Creatures to whom God communicates a participation in His causality are secondary agents through whom He acts in applying the fruits of His redemptive act" [M.R.E. Masterman, "Divine Economy," in *New Catholic Encyclopedia, 1967*]. Although she does not think consciously in these terms, Sandy becomes, in effect, a "secondary agent" when she acts to stop Jean.

Sandy herself recognizes her similarity to Jean. The potential for destruction which she herself possesses is impressed upon her when she encounters Jean in a hotel dining room after the war. It is not too fanciful to suggest that the title of the book, *The Prime of Miss Jean Brodie,* refers not only to that time of life when Jean was most flourishing, but also to Sandy. The word *prime* is also used for the mark used to distinguish designations of similar quantities, as in *a* and *á,* and Sandy is certainly "Jean Brodie Prime."

Just as Sandy's vision is wider than that of Jean Brodie, so the narrator's point of view—omniscient—is a term used to identify one of the attributes of God, and the method of narration underscores this quality. Although working within a time frame, 1936 to the time of narration, the narrator prescinds from time, jumping freely back and forth from one time to another, spanning years in one sentence. The technique is not, of course, unusual, nor among Spark's works is it peculiar to this novel. In a review of **The Mandelbaum Gate** ["The Novel as Jerusalem: Muriel Spark's *Mandelbaum Gate,"* *Atlantic Monthly* (October 1965)], for instance, Frank Kermode observes that Spark deliberately gives away the end of the story, and "in a narrative which could have regular climactic moments she fudges them, simply because the design of her world, like God's, has more interesting aspects than mere chronological progress and the satisfaction of naive expectations in the reader." But this technique is particularly appropriate to **The Prime of Miss Jean Brodie**. There, the narrator not only assumes an omniscient, Godlike position in relation to the material and in the method of narration, but creates and shapes the characters themselves in a way not unlike that in which Jean Brodie and Sandy Stranger shape their world and its inhabitants. In addition, the narrator's vision, like Jean's and Sandy's, results in action—that of telling the story. In this sense, what is narrated is a world in itself, a creation based on the narrator's point of view or perception.

There are, then, three visions in Muriel Spark's novel: Jean's, Sandy's, and the narrator's, each one wider and more comprehensive than the preceding and representing a higher degree of knowledge or perception. All three characters, in their roles as knowers and shapers, act according to a principle of order discernible in their actions thereby exemplifying what Ann Dobie says about Muriel Spark [in "Muriel Spark's Definition of Reality," *Critique* (1970)]: "She demonstrates that man is inherently limited in his complete perception of [reality], but that with each additional degree of understanding he experiences a kind of rebirth. She describes understanding as vision, a new concept of oneself and the world which is based upon the individual's acceptance of a basic order in both." The very structure of this particular novel reflects and underscores its message.

There is, of course, another vision implicit in the book, that of Muriel Spark herself. I make here a distinction between the narrator and the author to stress the fact that the novel and everything in it, including the narrator's voice, is an artifact, a creation. Spark herself has said [as quoted by Dobie]: "Fiction to me is a kind of parable," and Kermode points out that in Spark's novels "a genuine relation exists between the forms of fiction and the forms of the world, between the novelist's creation and God's" so that all her novels "are in a sense novels about the

novel, inquiries into the relation between fictions and truth."

By depicting three incremental degrees of understanding, **The Prime of Miss Jean Brodie** reflects yet another degree, another vision and "rebirth," to use Dobie's word. The novel itself becomes a kind of transfiguration of the commonplace, revealing the author's point of view and inviting the reader to share it. It is a point of view applicable to the author's complete *oeuvre.* Furthermore, the novel represents another relationship between knowledge and action. Given the artist's vision, the appropriate action for the artist is to produce a work of art. The appropriate action for Miss Spark is to write a book, an action which is, in its fullest sense, human and moral.


### Velma Bourgeois Richmond    (essay date 1984)

SOURCE: "The Prime of Miss Jean Brodie," in *Muriel Spark,* Frederick Ungar Publishing Co., 1984, pp. 16-28.

[*Richmond is an American educator and critic. In the following excerpt, she discusses theme and technique in* The Prime of Miss Jean Brodie, *arguing that the novel "is concerned to define the nature of the human condition."*]

With **The Prime of Miss Jean Brodie,** Muriel Spark became famous and rich, a celebrated novelist with a wide audience. The title character of the novel fascinated readers and also became known through theater and cinema. Vanessa Redgrave first performed the role of the Scottish schoolteacher in Jay Presson Allen's play version in London in 1966, and Zoe Caldwell played Jean Brodie in New York. Maggie Smith won an Oscar for her creation of the role in the 1969 film, and Geraldine McEwan interpreted Miss Brodie for television audiences in the series shown on PBS in 1979. Jean Brodie and her "set" of girls became widely known, and a common response to the main character was, "I had a Jean Brodie in my life."

The novel has also elicited complex analyses from literary critics, many of whom judge it Spark's most distinctive and effective work. Such diversity of response—from popular media presentations with theatrical flair, to individual empathy, to arguments about theological and moral implications—is most appropriate to a writer noted for her wry wit, satirical view of human behavior, and examination of the nature of truth and art. Her audience's bafflement mirrors Spark's own view that, though everything is possible, no one individual can know reality. Thus personal assertions appear comically grotesque.

**The Prime of Miss Jean Brodie** is more a novella than a novel. Short, compact, and economical, it provides a useful introduction to Spark, who wrote it in eight weeks, calling on memories of her girlhood in Edinburgh. She has described the novel, which most explicitly uses her Scottish heritage, as the work of "an exile in heart and mind—cautious, affectionate, critical" ["What Images Return," in *Memoirs of a Modern Scotland,* edited by Karl Miller, 1970]. The play and film versions provided excellent vehicles for their stars; the charismatic schoolteacher compelled admiration, though Jean Brodie remained sufficiently ambiguous to complicate responses even with the simplification of dramatic presentation. Spark's fiction is more elusive and needs repeated careful and thoughtful readings to understand what lies below the surface appeal.

The main line of the narrative is not easy to discern, for there are many time shifts. Actually, these are crucial to the reader's understanding, for they force greater attention. The manipulation of time leads to something more than the amused delight that might be derived from a straightforward chronology that realistically tells the story of a dazzling eccentric and her impressionable students. Spark deliberately tells the reader early in the novel what the outcome of events will be, that Miss Brodie will be betrayed by her trusted pupil Sandy Stranger. With suspense eschewed, the interest lies in understanding why things happen rather than what happened.

This is further emphasized by the absence of explanations from Jean Brodie of why she behaves as she does. She is seen largely through the eyes of the girls, who speculate about their teacher. Although the novel includes events from a period of twenty years, the time when the "Brodie set" changed from pupils to adults, the concentration is on their girlhood experiences. And the major focus is on one girl, Sandy Stranger.

*The Prime of Miss Jean Brodie* begins in 1936, when the girls are sixteen and have moved out of the junior division of the Marcia Blaine School for Girls in Edinburgh and Miss Brodie's class. Although they remain "the Brodie set," proving the accuracy of their teacher's maxim "Give me a girl at an impressionable age, and she is mine for life," each now wears her hat "with a definite difference." But the story soon shifts back to those formative years, 1930 and 1931, when six schoolgirls receive a remarkable education from a "progressive spinster" who teaches in a school of traditional character, serving as "a leaven in the lump" at "this educational factory." Monica Douglas ("famous for mathematics and anger"), Jenny Gray ("who was going to be an actress"), Eunice Gardner ("famous for gymnastics and swimming"), Rose Stanley ("famous for sex"), Mary Macgregor ("a silent lump, a nobody whom everybody could blame"), and Sandy Stranger ("merely notorious for her small, almost nonexistent eyes" and "famous for her vowel sounds"), are selected at age ten to be the *crème de la crème*. Their formidable teacher epitomizes each as "famous" for something and introduces all to her romantic aesthetic vision. They adopt her taste for Giotto, Pavlova, Sybil Thorndike, and the belief that art comes before science. They have no "team spirit" in the school and are a group set apart. Miss Brodie declares that she is in her *prime,* which she defines as "the moment one was born for," and she dedicates her life to forming her girls, giving them "the fruits of her prime."

The headmistress Miss Mackay, who believes in the slogan "Safety First" and favors practical flowers like chrysanthemums, schemes to rid the Marcia Blaine School of Miss Brodie by discrediting her. However, this is quite difficult, since all the girls in the set (except Mary Macgregor, who is a kind of scapegoat) are clever and capable, and they admire their teacher. Furthermore, Miss Brodie is vigilant and careful about appearances, however outrageously she behaves.

The obvious possibility for discreditation is sex, particularly since in 1931, the year that the girls turn eleven and twelve and first become aware, "sex is everything." Both of the men teachers at the school are certainly interested in "a magnificent woman in her prime," and the girls increasingly recognize that "she was really an exciting woman as a woman." Teddy Lloyd, the art master, is the more dashing, for he lost an arm in World War I. But he is married and a Roman Catholic, and Jean Brodie finds a romantic renunciation of love far more exciting than an actual experience. She begins telling the girls of her lost lover Hugh, who died on Flanders Field, and gradually Teddy Lloyd's characteristics are fused into her fantasies. She also plans a surrogate affair using Rose, who is Lloyd's model (for pictures that all look like Jean Brodie). The other man is Gordon Lowther, the singing master, who is not married and an elder of the Church of Scotland. With him, Jean Brodie does have an affair, often staying at his home in Cramond. But she refuses to marry him, lest she be deterred from her dedication to her girls. Finally he marries the science teacher, Miss Lockhart, because he cannot tolerate Jean Brodie's distorted romanticism. Early in the novel, Sandy and Jenny presciently compare their teacher with their parents: she never got married, and they do not have primes, but they do have sexual intercourse.

The way to trap Miss Brodie is, then, politics, according to Sandy. This "beady eyed" girl, who is most like Miss Brodie in temperament and whose point of view dominates the story, becomes Teddy Lloyd's mistress in the summer of 1938, while Miss Brodie is touring in Germany to see what Hitler's brownshirts are like. In Nazi Germany the domineering Miss Brodie enlarges her earlier admiration for the Italian fascisti, the marching troops of blackshirts, seen in the previous summer's holidays, "with their hands raised at the same angle, while Mussolini stood on platform like a gym teacher or Guides mistress and watched them." The comparison is a deliberate authorial comment, for Sandy Stranger views Miss Brodie as "a born Fascist." Sandy is not interested in politics, but she is obsessed with Miss Brodie. She tells Miss Mackay that Jean Brodie was responsible for sending Joyce Emily Hammond off to Spain, ironically not to join her brother's fight against Franco but to support the Fascist cause. This wretched girl, a latecomer and wouldbe member of the set, is killed in a train en route. Sandy gives the information to Miss Mackay, who then forces Miss Brodie to resign in 1939. Because Sandy recognizes that her teacher's manipulation of the set ignores their individuality and that she has no sense of the importance of another's life, Sandy decides that Jean Brodie's fascist control must be stopped.

By this time Sandy Stranger is no longer Teddy Lloyd's mistress, but she continues to admire his economical method of presentation and uses it in her betrayal of Miss Brodie. In less than a year, the man ceases to interest Sandy, though she was fascinated by his mind. The most important thing that she extracts from Lloyd's mind is his religion, and Sandy enters the Catholic Church. In this, she is in sharp contrast to Miss Brodie, who is contemptuous about Lloyd's religion. Sandy not only converts to the

Church of Rome; she also enters an order of enclosed nuns.

As Sister Helena of the Transfiguration she writes "an odd psychological treatise on the nature of moral perception, called 'The Transfiguration of the Commonplace.' " In her middle age in the late 1950s, she is forced, because of this achievement, to have choice visitors even though her order is enclosed. She explains to an enquiring interviewer that the biggest influence on her was neither politics nor Calvinism, but "a Miss Jean Brodie in her prime." Some of her friends from schooldays also visit, and they talk of their teacher. Always Sister Helena "clutches the bars of her grille," but "more desperately than ever" when she admits what most influenced her.

Miss Brodie spends her last years in the Braid Hills Hotel, trying to learn who "betrayed" her. She dies of cancer in 1946 when she is fifty-six years old. In one way, the novella is an account of this woman's rise and fall, but it also chronicles responses to her "prime." Muriel Spark has explained that she always begins with a title and then works out the story. Both as word and idea, "prime" resonates through the story. In no other work does she so relentlessly repeat a phrase, and the reader is led to a rich contemplation of the meanings of "prime of life" far beyond the narrative itself. The style of this short work, so evocative in its economy and simple language, reflected the experience of Spark's early poetic career. In an interview [with Ian Gillham published as "Keeping It Short," *The Listener* (24 September 1970)], Muriel Spark said that "Jean Brodie represents completely unrealized potentialities." This broad statement of the theme provides a useful way of approaching the story's meaning.

The realistic details of *The Prime of Miss Jean Brodie* are unobtrusive, but so exactly introduced that they establish an immediate sense of time and place. The Edinburgh of the 1930s is vividly evoked in Chapter Two when Miss Brodie takes the girls on a walking excursion "into the reeking network of slums which the Old Town constituted in those years." This is a first direct experience for them away from the security of their middle-class homes. The poverty and desperation, the devastating loss of human possibility, are indicated in a single line: "A man sat on the icy-cold pavement, he just sat." They are stunned by the terrible smell of the area; they see men and women quarreling and a long queue of shabby men waiting for the Dole. Sandy is frightened by the squalor of the Unemployed, and she is aware of the discrepancy between these people and herself, though when she is older she perceives a common misery that has nothing to do with economics. Before World War II, she is more concerned about relief in Edinburgh than events on the Continent.

Spark is not a political novelist, but she is trying to define the context in which she lived. *The Prime of Miss Jean Brodie* corresponds to her own girlhood in Edinburgh, and the historical significance is very important. The Idle Unemployed are most obviously the casualties of the economic depression that shattered the Western world, as the last shudder of the Great War and the wild extravagances of the 1920s that followed it. The emerging Fascists are one answer to the defeat and loss of spirit. Other casualties

of World War I are personally shown—the lost lover Hugh Carruthers, the maimed art master, and Jean herself.

Only one of "the legions of her kind during the nineteen-thirties, women from the age of thirty and upward, who crowded their war-bereaved spinsterhood with voyages of discovery into new ideas and energetic practices in art or social welfare, education, or religion," Jean Brodie epitomizes the plight of the Lost Generation, those who lived in a world where traditional values and expectations had been displaced. The romantic tales with which the teacher regales her girls are an evasion of the realities of human experience. The importance of fantasy in the forming of the child is an accepted tenet of sophisticated psychology, but the fantasy should result in an increasingly mature understanding and coping with human experience.

It is one thing for Sandy and Jenny to write romantic tales modeled on their favorite nineteenth-century narratives, *Kidnapped, The Lady of Shalott,* and *Jane Eyre.* This allows a relatively safe youthful exploration of experience—and an opportunity for Muriel Spark to write hilarious parodies of much-loved English classics and sentimental love letters. But it is quite another thing for forty-year-old Jean Brodie to substitute fantasies of lost and renounced lovers for recognition of her own sexuality, particularly when she wants the fantasy to turn into reality by having one of the girls take her place in Lloyd's bed. A reading of *The Prime of Miss Jean Brodie* as a menopausal crisis or unconscious lesbianism is far too simplistic, but the text provides enough evidence to suggest these possibilities. There is a fervid urgency about her creation of the "set" that argues a desperate lack of fulfillment, "the unrealized potentialities" that are salient.

Nevertheless, the novel can be described as a consideration of excessive self-indulgence, an exposition of the dangers and evil of a life that is concentrated solely in self. For, although Jean Brodie asserts that she is giving her prime to the schoolgirls, she is actually using them to avoid having to act herself, and her constant reiteration of her self-sacrifice limits the worth of whatever she does. Sandy early notes how Miss Brodie has "elected herself to grace." "She thinks she is Providence, thought Sandy, she thinks she is the God of Calvin, she sees the beginning and the end." Miss Brodie believes that God is on her side and has no idea of her own sinful nature. Hers is a very personal and secularized Calvinism.

The term "Calvinism" is used, of course, in many ways. [In an endnote, Richmond explains: "The French Protestant theologian John Calvin (1509-1564) completed the *Institutes of the Christian Religion* in 1536 in Geneva, where austere reforms were later implemented. Civic authorities were responsible for enforcing religious teaching, and all areas of life were regulated. In Scotland John Knox was the advocate of this theology, and in the colonial United States Jonathan Edwards introduced a modified version. Intense biblicism and resolute theocentricity, magnifying the sovereignty and providence of God, are fundamental in Calvinism, which is thus strongly related to the theology of St. Augustine (354-430), the most influential writer in the early period of the Catholic Church. A distinction of Calvinism is that it bridges the gulf between the luxury of the world and the life of the spirit by dedicating them to the service of God. This quality was strongly appealing in an age of expanding capitalism."] In *The Prime of Miss Jean Brodie,* Spark shows this view of humanity as a focal point of Edinburgh, and the characteristics that she emphasizes are a belief in the Elect and the Damned, the idea that man's salvation is predestined by God, and the idea of a community that is righteously and rigorously controlled. Nominally, Jean Brodie has rejected Edinburgh's Calvinism through her flamboyance, but in practice her *crème de la crème* are a secularized elect, the chosen elite selected from the larger group. Sandy deliberately contemplates the architectural landmarks of St. Giles Cathedral and the Tolbooth in an attempt to include the Calvinist theology that is lacking from her English experience. She also recognizes that Catholicism might have been what Miss Brodie lacked. But Sandy's own entry into the Roman Church is not a simplistic triumph of Catholic values. Her betrayal, her book, her spiritual condition—all lack certainty, as indeed is inevitable in this life, even for those who act decisively.

A manipulator of lives, Jean Brodie admires absolutist domination, as her attraction to Fascist leaders most clearly illustrates. Further, she is not capable of recognizing her own failures; even after World War II, she goes no farther than an admission that "Hitler *was* rather naughty." This grotesquely inadequate judgment is like her utter failure to recognize her culpability in treating Mary Macgregor with wanton unkindness, or in precipitating the death of the new girl Joyce Emily Hammond. And obviously she has not the slightest idea of how she influences Sandy Stranger, who betrays her precisely because she judges that no one should be allowed to exercise such unremitting control over the lives of others. (Paradoxically, of course, Sandy is behaving in the same controlling way; and her "small beady eyes" symbolize her limited, narrow vision.) Perhaps nothing so richly illustrates Jean Brodie's self-absorption as her incredulity that anyone could betray her—even Christ was betrayed, and He is God.

The novella, then, is concerned to define the nature of the human condition. The two principals, Jean Brodie and her near double Sandy Stranger (she actually assumes her teacher's role as Lloyd's mistress), know very little about it. Both fail to recognize its essentially mundane quality. The teacher refuses to admit the ordinary; she spins romantic fantasies to evade the limitations of life in this world—both those that come from political and social conditions and those that derive from personal blindness and pride. The pupil becomes renowned for her psychological understanding of "The Transfiguration of the Commonplace." There is an undeniable appeal about escaping from the limits of mundane experience. This is the appeal of nineteenth-century romanticism, with its exaltation of the artist as one who is apart from society, a being more sensitive and suffering than others, who does not live by common standards. Muriel Spark repeatedly explored romanticism—and expressed antipathy to it.

Most members of the Brodie set—Eunice, Monica, Jenny, and Rose—grow beyond its narrow range into adults who are far less exotic and flamboyant than their mentor, but who live quietly and responsibly, able to resist impulses that would lead to the self-indulgences that destroy a perspective about human limitations. But Sandy, who is most like Jean Brodie, lacks such repose. In schoolgirl narratives, she casts herself as the heroine addressed by Alan Breck or Mr. Rochester or as the Lady of Shalott; she fantasizes about Pavlova's depending on her for the future of dance; she imagines herself as the right-hand woman of a mythical policewoman, in another fantasy that is a response to the ugly experience of Jenny's encounter with an exhibitionist. Even as a reclusive nun, she writes on the theme that has defined Jean Brodie's life and her own.

There are, of course, subtle differences. Sandy knows exactly what she is doing, while Jean Brodie is described as a kind of innocent. David Lodge has argued [in "The Uses and Abuses of Omniscience: Method and Meaning in Muriel Spark's *The Prime of Miss Jean Brodie,*" in *The Novelist at the Crossroads,* 1971] that the loss of primal innocence, the fallen world, is the subject of *The Prime of Miss Jean Brodie,* and that Sandy must betray Miss Brodie because she has so many bad qualities mixed with the good traits of enthusiasm, inspiration, and individuality. But Sandy is not to be viewed without uneasiness; her hands "clutch the bars of her grille." She has withdrawn from the world; nevertheless, she has created a "set." Sister Helena's book has more ardent admirers than the selected schoolgirls at Marcia Blaine's School for Girls. Her reclusive life may be viewed as a renunciation of the world to parallel her teacher's renunciation of a lover, or as a penance for the betrayal. But even this does not work out according to plan, for she lacks the repose of the other nuns in the community. They notice her nervous tension and say that "Sister Helena had too much to bear from the world since she had published her psychological book which was so unexpectedly famed." Nevertheless, the dispensation that results in this exposure "was forced" upon her. Once again, Spark shows how separated human expectations are from the realities of experience.

The "prime" of life is supposed to be a time of realization, when the years of preparation and apprenticeship are turned into effective action, but the novella shows how far Jean Brodie is from such realization. The choice of the name "Brodie" is significant: Deacon William Brodie was an eighteenth-century man whose reality was very different from appearances; he was the historical source for Robert Louis Stevenson, another native of Edinburgh, whose classic creation of the "double life," is *Dr. Jekyll and Mr. Hyde.* Publicly very respectable in civic and commercial enterprises, Deacon Brodie kept mistresses and conducted night burglaries. He died cheerfully on the gibbet, and his presence in Edinburgh remains very visible today. At the corner of the Royal Mile and Bank Street—in the Old Town that the Brodie set visit—stands Deacon Brodie's Tavern, an imposing institution that was founded in 1806. This is precisely the curious mixture of human experience that so fascinated Muriel Spark. Thus the name "Sandy Stranger" is also indicative, for it suggests both shifting uncertainties and the fundamental apartness of all people. Sandy is not simply the only English girl in the set, the exile in Scotland, and the favorite who becomes a betrayer. She is also the essential human being who may act, but with unanticipated results.

The unexpected is what should be expected. The most trusted girl, the confidante, is the betrayer. But Sandy insists that "It's only possible to betray where loyalty is due." And loyalty was due to Miss Brodie "only up to a point," so that "the word [betrayal] does not apply." Just after Miss Brodie asserts that Lowther would marry her, she reads of his engagement. Mary Macgregor was not kindly treated, but she remembers her days in Miss Brodie's class as the happiest of her life. One must retain "a sense of the hidden possibilities in all things," for there are always startling revelations. This view of the world can be frightening, for it shows the limits of man's control, his woeful inadequacy and the absurdity of pretensions. Many in the modern world find this a despairing view, but Muriel Spark's faith prevents that conclusion.

Her vision is not limited to this world, for her fiction has both a literal and an allegorical level. The realistic narrative of life in Edinburgh in the 1930s is cogent, but it is only a small part of a much larger scheme. Spark amuses by writing a story about schooldays; she invigorates a strong literary tradition of boys' stories (like Thomas Hughes' *Tom Brown's Schooldays* [1857] and William Golding's *The Lord of the Flies* [1955]) by making her subjects girls—and very sophisticated ones, too. She updates the classic nineteenth-century feminist heroine Jane Eyre—a shy, earnest, plain governess living in an isolated house—into a dynamic twentieth-century woman—an exotic, good-looking, assured, witty teacher who moves freely about a large city and holidays alone on the Continent. The characteristics of the male lovers are exactly paralleled to underscore the analogy with Charlotte Bronte's novel, which the girls also rewrite in their own style. Nevertheless, the literary exactness, like the realistic account, is not the essential concern.

The shifting time sequence serves not only as an effective device to encompass events occurring over twenty years and to keep the reader alert to many possibilities. It also functions significantly to throw human actions into a larger perspective. The events in the girls' lives appear quite different from one time to another. As Miss Brodie's students, the girls are fascinated and absorbed by her fantasies and those that they create in imitation. As adults they perceive these events as relatively unimportant. So all events of this life, even its prime, are recognized as very small when placed in the context of a universe that is God's complex creation. The incidental details may not always be understood, but for the person of faith there is a belief in a design that is not contingent upon merely human actions. Thus the resort to self-indulgent power is a grotesque distortion, important and yet trivial and absurdly laughable.

Muriel Spark's comic vision, then, is not only a dazzling exploitation of witty language and outrageous circumstances in the present world. It is also an extended view of how inconsequential are human assumptions of knowledge and power when viewed in the light of eternity. This is a wisdom not shared by Jean Brodie and Sandy Strang-er; the beady eyes do not see so far, but the novelist's view is much deeper, and it is her own point of view that Muriel Spark offers her readers.

### Isobel Murray and Bob Tait    (essay date 1984)

SOURCE: "Muriel Spark: *The Prime of Miss Jean Brodie,*" in *Ten Modern Scottish Novels,* Aberdeen University Press, 1984, pp. 100-22.

[*In the excerpt below, Murray and Tait focus on Spark's handling of character development, the theme of religion, and literary technique in* The Prime of Miss Jean Brodie.]

Three very different novelists . . . have one thing in common; an adult conversion to Roman Catholicism. They are Fionn MacColla, Muriel Spark and George Mackay Brown. Brown we must meantime leave to one side: his religious beliefs form an integral part of a personal vision of natural harmony in *Greenvoe*. Can anything useful be said in comparing such disparate novelists as MacColla and Spark? Well, both are concerned with Scottish Calvinism in their novels. MacColla reacted vigorously against an extreme Calvinist upbringing, and makes his critique of Calvinism central to all his novels. Spark, on the other hand, was raised in Edinburgh, with an English mother, a Jewish father and a conventionally Presbyterian schooling: perhaps like Stranger she missed having Calvinism to react against. But *The Prime of Miss Jean Brodie* also centres on a critique of the impact of Calvinist thinking, and a magnificent reincarnation of the concept of the Justified Sinner.

Both novelists manage to raise an exceptionally wide range of issues in the apparently narrow contexts of their novels, and to view them in some sense *sub specie aeternitatis*. In both *And the Cock Crew* and *The Prime of Miss Jean Brodie* there is treatment of religion, politics, history, sexuality and art—and the idea of betrayal is central to both. The betrayals in *And the Cock Crew . . .* are multiple, while the obvious case in *The Prime of Miss Jean Brodie* is the betrayal of Jean Brodie by Sandy Stranger—with a clearly arguable prior betrayal of the set by Miss Brodie. MacColla and Spark both choose a central character who is in some sense 'of' the Calvinist enemy, and each treats this central character with sympathy and understanding, so that the character is eventually seen as both attractive and misguided: we remember Sandy and Jenny completing their literary rendition of the love letters of Miss Brodie and Gordon Lowther, finding it 'a delicate question how to present Miss Brodie in both a favourable and an unfavourable light, for now . . . nothing less than this was demanded.' MacColla's instinct is to go for the jugular, and so in his denunciation of the naysaying qualities of Scottish Calvinism he chooses as his central character a minister of the kirk: Spark also goes for a traditionally central element, education. But the differences are clearly much more striking. MacColla expresses his central interests by writing a historical novel which demonstrates to his satisfaction the historical ill effects of the naysaying of Calvinism on Scotland, while Spark expresses hers vitally in relation to her own century—indeed, to the city in which she spent her own school days—and the most important political movements of the time. Where MacColla is making a case, fairly clearly preaching, she is very 'laid back', and refuses to intrude judgements in her novel. And of course, most crucially, she transforms the traditional figure of the dominie into an unusual woman schoolteacher at a privileged girls' school.

All the same, perhaps these two novels have more to say than the others about the nature and character of the Calvinist tradition underlying Scottish life.

Spark refuses to intrude judgements, we say, but the matter is more complex than that. Can we find Muriel Spark anywhere in her fiction? *Miss Jean Brodie* seems to have two narrative centres, the developing consciousness of Sandy Stranger, and a third person narrator who is apparently uncommitted and factual. But we should not over-readily accept this appearance: Mrs Spark has commented on this problem, in a piece called **'My Conversion'**, published in 1961, the year of the novel:

> With a novel, you know the dialogue. It belongs
> to each character. But the narrative part—first
> or third person—belongs to a character as well.
> I have to decide what the author of the narrative
> is like. It's not me, it's a character.

The narrator in this novel has a splendid sense of comedy, and is no respecter of persons; and the wit usually economically serves some satiric purpose or undermines a mood or attitude. Irony is pervasive. We can look at our first experience of the tale of Miss Brodie's lost lover, Hugh. We are nowhere told that Miss Brodie is being wildly romantic and self-indulgent, with apparently no awareness of the realities of the war in which her lover died. Her own prose tells us this, as she starts with an unacknowledged quotation from Keats, 'Season of mists and mellow fruitfulness', and latches onto that alliterated 'f' sound to make Hugh's death insubstantial, melancholy and beautiful: 'He fell on Flanders' Field. . . . He fell. . . . He fell like an autumn leaf.' The narrator effectively punctures the mood while reinforcing the alliteration by referring to 'the story of Miss Brodie's felled fiancé', while Miss Brodie, unheeding, goes on to describe Hugh, inevitably, as 'one of the Flowers of the Forest'.

The witty comment can be lightly satirical in a religious dimension, as when gaunt mistresses say 'good morning' to Miss Brodie 'with predestination in their smiles,' or it can accumulate in gentle mockery of Miss Brodie's behaviour and attitudes, as she declaims 'The Lady of Shalott' with a dedication worthy of Sybil Thorndike, and perhaps too many decibels: 'Miss Brodie's voice soared up to the ceiling, and curled round the feet of the Senior girls upstairs.' Miss Brodie enjoins composure in the full flow of her peculiar declamatory speech—'It is one of the best assets of a woman, an expression of composure, come foul, come fair. Regard the Mona Lisa over yonder!' The narrator punctures the mood again:

> Mona Lisa in her prime smiled in steady compo-
> sure even though she had just come from the
> dentist and her lower jaw was swollen.

The actual narration in the novel is sometimes direct from

this ironic, witty but non-aggressive narrator, and often a rendition of Sandy's thoughts by the narrator. Apart from the ubiquitous witty phrases, the narrator is usually careful not to comment. She (it is surely a woman?) stands back, never judging, and only occasionally offering analysis. We come to recognise these occasions as particularly important, from their very rarity, whether it be the context offered for Miss Brodie by the description of the 'war-bereaved spinsterhood' of Edinburgh, or the passages where the narrator looks closely at Miss Brodie and religion, or at Miss Brodie looking for a confidante, or at Sandy's attempts to come to terms with religion.

Sandy emerges as a central consciousness in chapter two, and we gradually come to accept her as a fairly reliable guide, as we outgrow our distaste for her little piggy eyes—or indeed become irritated with the narrator for such insistence on them. Although we learn fairly early that it was Sandy who betrayed Miss Brodie, we do tend to trust her reactions to people, events, churches, only remaining slightly uneasy about her clutching the bars of the grille—from nervous tension? a false vocation? fear? guilt?

There are other specific narrative techniques which Spark utilises to help us in our understanding of the action: Muriel Spark's refusal to judge for us does not remove the necessity for judgement, but transfers it to the reader as part of the required response. The novel can be seen as a complex problem requiring solution, arranged in both a helpful and a challenging way to facilitate the reader's exercise of judgement.

The chief and most obtrusive of these techniques is to do with chronology. Conventional chronology is continually interrupted with glimpses of future occasions, and future assessments of present issues. Thus we find terrible ironies, for example in the case of Mary Macgregor. Mary is appallingly treated throughout the novel: the description 'the nagged child' is a gross understatement. But we know from the end of the first chapter that Mary will die in a fire at the age of twenty-three, and from the beginning of the next that she will look back on these days of bullying and victimisation as the happiest days of her life. This dismal irony is kept firmly in our awareness, just as Vonnegut keeps the doom of 'poor old Edgar Derby', shot for stealing a teapot in the ruins of Dresden, in the forefront of our consciousness from beginning to end of *Slaughterhouse Five*.

The departure from simple conventional chronology offers a picture of a developing scene: in the first chapter we meet the Brodie set at sixteen—and at ten. We gradually develop a double awareness, not particularly conscious or clear cut at the first reading, of the attractions of Miss Brodie to the ten-year-olds of 1930, and the dangers inherent in her and apparent to Sandy by 1938. In all this we get a lively sense of the whole of Jean Brodie's 'prime', and all sorts of ironies and insights are implicit in our early learning that Miss Brodie was betrayed, and that Sandy betrayed her, and in the retrospective conversations different members of the set have with Sandy in her convent throughout, given in 'flash-forward', as it were.

In fact, the departures from conventional chronology are

fewer than at first appears, and almost always brief: the narrator employs the economy of method Sandy admires in the methods of Teddy Lloyd and Miss Brodie and employs herself in the betrayal. With the exceptions noted above, the novel progresses straightforwardly enough. After the introduction to the sixteen-year-olds, chapter one gives us the beginnings of the Brodie set and our introduction to this amazing teacher and her unconventional methods, and chapter two concentrates on the first year with Miss Brodie, especially the walk through old Edinburgh. Chapter three covers the second year with Miss Brodie, in more senses than one 'the sexual year', as the little girls are preoccupied with sexuality and Miss Brodie falls in love with one master and embarks on an affair with another. This emotional situation for Miss Brodie continues in chapter four, when the Brodie set moves up into the Senior school for session 1932-3. After this, things are telescoped: three years are virtually omitted, and chapter five deals with the girls in fourth year, 1935-36, while in chapter six at age eighteen Sandy leaves school, has her affair with Teddy Lloyd and betrays Miss Brodie.

Another very effective narrative device is juxtaposition of scenes or characters so that a vivid effect of comparison or ironic contrast can be created without overt comment. Early in the novel, the introduction of Miss Brodie is interrupted by a terse little paragraph about Marcia Blaine, founder of the school, like and unlike Miss Brodie. Widow to Miss Brodie's spinster, admirer of Italian patriot Garibaldi and his 'red shirts' to Miss Brodie's celebrator of Mussolini and his 'black shirts', Marcia Blaine is economically described by reference to her 'manly portrait'—Miss Brodie is the eternal feminine. The ethos of Marcia Blaine's school, with which Miss Brodie is so much at odds, is implicit in the Founder's Day bunch 'of hardwearing flowers,' as well as the Bible text underlining a traditional notion of female virtue. (Incidentally, Mrs Spark has a little joke at our expense here: Blaine is an unusual surname, but a biographical dictionary may offer us a nineteenth-century American journalist and statesman called Blain, whose first names were James Gillespie. Spark herself attended James Gillespie's Girls' School in Edinburgh, and Marcia Blaine's is very clearly based on it.)

Again, in the walk in chapter two, Sandy's understanding of the set as 'a body with Miss Brodie for the head' is balanced by her vision of the queue of unemployed men as 'one dragon's body . . . the snaky creature,' and through her meditation we see the Brodie girls, the Girl Guides and Mussolini's fascisti as oddly similar. A final telling instance where juxtaposition lends resonance is in chapter three, everybody's 'sexual year'. After Jenny's experience with the 'terrible beast' who exposed himself, Sandy falls in love with her imagined image of Jenny's policewoman, whom she interestingly decides to call Sergeant Anne Grey, and in Sandy's fantasy the two set out, 'dedicated' (Sandy is not Miss Brodie's pupil for nothing) 'to eliminate sex from Edinburgh and environs.' This immediately precedes the scene where Miss Brodie and Teddy Lloyd have an implicitly charged conversation about Cramond, the home village of Gordon Lowther, and Miss Brodie puts her arm round Rose's shoulder and thanks Teddy

Lloyd, 'as if she and Rose were one.' Thus early, and however unconsciously, while Sandy is reacting against sexuality, Miss Brodie is beginning to manipulate Rose into her own sexual fantasies. The comment through Sandy can apply to the juxtaposing technique as well as the developing relationship between teacher and pupil: it is both intriguing and forward-pointing:

> Sandy was fascinated by this method of making patterns with facts, and was divided between her admiration for the technique and the pressing need to prove Miss Brodie guilty of misconduct.

The final specific technique we will point to here is the effect of introducing parallel situations. One central example should suffice. It is clear to most people reading the book that both Jean Brodie and Sandy Stranger to some extent lead fantasy lives, or double lives, It is made most clear in Sandy's case, where her imaginary life is a preventive for boredom, and is nourished for the most part by her reading—which is directed to a considerable extent by Miss Brodie. Apart from the joint literary compositions with Jenny, we are introduced to Sandy's double life in a bizarre conversation she holds with the Lady of Shalott, who bears, here, a certain resemblance to Miss Brodie (chanting in the classroom the while). Miss Brodie's choice of poem is significant, dealing as it does with a Lady who is destroyed by turning from shadow to reality. Sandy holds a series of romantic conversations with Alan Breck from Stevenson's *Kidnapped,* involved in quest and cause and chivalry, quite transfiguring the commonplace sections of the famous walk through old Edinburgh when she would otherwise have to attend to the tiresome Mary: the 'real life' fantasy here, of a married lady and her husband, is brief and comparatively very unsatisfactory. Later Sandy moves on to Mr Rochester: Miss Brodie has been reading out *Jane Eyre* during sewing lessons. And later still, after Miss Brodie's inspired teaching and a trip to the theatre, she moves on to Pavlova, and has a delicious conversation, one diva to another, soulful, melancholy, and irresistibly funny. Again Pavlova smacks of Miss Brodie, and much of the comic effect rises from that one extravagant detail, the claw:

> 'Sandy,' said Anna Pavlova, 'you are the only truly dedicated dancer, next to me. Your dying Swan is perfect, such a sensitive, final tap of the claw upon the floor of the stage. . . .'

The last example of Sandy's fantasy life is her invention of Sergeant Anne Grey. The interesting things to notice are that Sandy seems always quite conscious of the difference between fantasy and reality, and that we see no more such fancies after she leaves the Junior school.

Miss Brodie's double life is less easy to chart, because we see her only from outside and from her speech, and it is harder to know when she is fantasising completely and when embroidering fact (as in the new picture of Hugh after her greater awareness of both Teddy Lloyd and Gordon Lowther). It does seem clear that she gradually drifts further into fantasy, and determines to make it into reality, when she determines to use Rose to sleep with Teddy Lloyd by proxy. And of course she leads a very conventional kind of 'double life' when she combines the roles of correct Edinburgh spinster schoolmistress and weekend lover to Gordon Lowther: this seems to cause her no trouble. She lays claim to the long tradition of double life or split personality in the Scottish Calvinist consciousness (e.g. Hogg's *Justified Sinner,* Stevenson's *Dr Jekyll and Mr Hyde*) when she claims to be descended from one of the archetypes, Deacon Brodie. As she relates, Deacon Brodie was a pious and respected Edinburgh householder who had a conventional double life, keeping mistresses and indulging in cock-fighting, and he became a burglar by night for the sake of the excitement and danger involved, and died at last for these crimes on a gibbet he designed himself as justicer: 'it is the stuff I am made of ', declares Miss Brodie. The character of Deacon Brodie for many years fascinated Robert Louis Stevenson, like Mrs Spark another notable exile from Edinburgh. He collaborated with Henley to write a play on Deacon Brodie, and this historical character lies behind his most famous novella of double life, *The Strange Case of Dr Jekyll and Mr Hyde.* Miss Brodie's double life is more subtle and much more alarming than Sandy's, and instead of growing out of it, like the little girl, she gets imperceptibly more enmeshed in a complex web of fact and fantasy, and a gradual determination to flesh out her fantasies.

But the notion of a double life does not finish with Sandy and Miss Brodie. Oscar Wilde wrote an essay called 'Pen, Pencil and Poison', about a poet and painter, Thomas Wainewright, who was also a forger and a secret poisoner. Teddy Lloyd's double life is by no means as sensational as this, but it lasts over years and bears some little resemblance to Wainewright's. Wilde quotes a Zola murderer who paints respectable people so that they all bear a curious resemblance to his victim; and he says that Wainewright put the expression of his own wickedness into the portrait of a nice young girl. Teddy Lloyd surely owes something to Wainewright and Zola, as he turns out portrait after portrait of the Brodie set, each bearing an uncanny resemblance to Miss Brodie, each secretly confessing his fascination with her. Sandy precipitates her affair with him when she shocks him by claiming that 'all his portraits, even that of the littlest Lloyd baby, were now turning out to be likenesses of Miss Brodie,' suggesting that Miss Brodie has completely taken over life and art; and it is Sandy's curiosity about Teddy Lloyd's secret love for Miss Brodie that is central to her interest in him, before she is infected by his Catholicism. If we begin to see double lives everywhere, it is not necessarily just our imagination: in an interview with Frank Kermode Mrs Spark acknowledges this tendency:

> When I become interested in a subject, say old age, then the world is peopled for me—just peopled with them. . . . They're the centre of the world, and everyone else is on the periphery. It is an obsession. . . . And that's how I see things. I wrote a book about bachelors, and it seemed to me that 'everyone was a bachelor.

And so we find poor Gordon Lowther attempting to sustain the same relatively mundane double life as Miss Brodie, on the one hand teacher, church elder and choirmaster, on the other hand Miss Brodie's secret lover. But there is no hint of the stuff of Deacon Brodie in Gordon

Lowther: he does not relish his secret life, and would always have preferred to marry Miss Brodie. At last his melancholy outweighs 'her bed-fellowship and her catering,' and he settles for a straightforward married life with Miss Lockhart. Retrospectively, even Mary Macgregor can be seen to have lived a double life at school: her life has been fairly intolerable throughout, but as a young adult she remembers Miss Brodie's class, and its magic for her lay in 'all those stories and opinions which had nothing to do with the ordinary world': Miss Brodie herself was Mary's brief double life. And everything comes to have at least two aspects, not only Miss Brodie but the city of Edinburgh itself. This is summed up in a telling description of Sandy's different attitudes over years to images of Miss Brodie:

> Sandy felt warmly towards Miss Brodie at those times when she saw how she was misled in her idea of Rose. It was then that Miss Brodie looked beautiful and fragile, just as dark heavy Edinburgh itself could suddenly be changed into a floating city when the light was a special pearly white and fell upon one of the gracefully fashioned streets. In the same way Miss Brodie's masterful features became clear and sweet to Sandy when viewed in the curious light of the woman's folly, and she never felt more affection for her in her later years than when she thought upon Miss Brodie as silly.

This profound ambiguity is central to the effect of the book: no simple attitude toward Miss Brodie can last with any justice.

And no simple picture of Miss Brodie emerges from the brief novel: however briefly, she is supplied with suggested and suggestive contexts in culture, art and history, in religion, in matters particularly Scottish or typically Edinburgh, in the politics and life of her time. Perhaps the outstanding of these suggested dimensions is the one which typifies her notions of virtue and dedication and heroism and goes far to explain her devotion to Mussolini and his fascisti, her ideal of Italy throughout history, stemming from ancient Rome.

Her first appearance in the novel is when she interrupts the set, aged sixteen, talking to boys at the school gates, and informs them of 'a new plot' to force her to resign. The understanding girls, who have clearly heard such things before, react to her appearance and their notion of her character in terms she has no doubt taught them:

> She looked a mighty woman with her dark Roman profile in the sun. The Brodie set did not for a moment doubt that she would prevail. As soon expect Julius Caesar to apply for a job at a crank school as Miss Brodie. She would never resign. If the authorities wanted to get rid of her she would have to be assassinated.

The image is unexpected, forceful, and a shade ominous— and Caesar was betrayed by a set including his most trusted friend.

There are a few other memorable ancient Roman moments. Miss Brodie tells her class about an Italian holiday, reliving her scorn of the vulgar American tourists and her own excitement at seeing 'the Colosseum where the gladiators died and the slaves were thrown to the lions.' Recreating that memory, she again appears in ancient Roman guise to the girls, until she herself destroys the mood:

> Miss Brodie stood in her brown dress like a gladiator with raised arm and eyes flashing like a sword. 'Hail Caesar!' she cried again, turning radiantly to the window light, as if Caesar sat there. 'Who opened the window?' said Miss Brodie dropping her arm.
>
> Nobody answered.
>
> 'Whoever has opened the window has opened it too wide,' said Miss Brodie. 'Six inches is perfectly adequate.'

Here the ancient Roman Miss Brodie and the archetypally Edinburgh Miss Brodie uneasily co-exist. She has a 'fine dark Roman head': 'her dead Hugh had admired her head for its Roman appearance,' and there is another splendid image of Miss Brodie in Teddy Lloyd's presence: she 'seated herself nobly like Britannia with her legs apart under her loose brown skirt which came well over her knees.' A few pages later, as Miss Brodie encounters unpleasant colleagues, the image of patrician Roman heroine and warrior is still about her:

> 'Good mawning,' she replied, in the corridors, flattening their scorn beneath the chariot wheels of her superiority, and deviating her head towards them no more than an insulting half-inch.

Till the end of the set's schooldays, 'Miss Brodie as a Roman matron' remains an important image.

Her ardent admiration for the antique Roman past is complemented by Miss Brodie's devotion, shared by Teddy Lloyd, to Italian art through the ages. So the girls are offered Italian paintings as well as pictures of Mussolini's fascisti as holiday trove. They are made familiar with the Italian Renaissance and the Mona Lisa, and instructed that the greatest Italian painter is not Leonardo but Giotto, because he is Miss Brodie's favourite. For Miss Brodie, Mussolini is a natural and admirable part of her Italian ideal. She admires what he seems to stand for, dedication and discipline, efficiency, elimination of unemployment, and his charisma, and she apparently remains blissfully unaware of the bullying tactics he and his henchmen ruthlessly employed. It is easy for us, of course, with benefit of hindsight, to blame an Edinburgh school-teacher for admiring Mussolini and his followers in 1930: a great many better informed people than Jean Brodie shared her admiration at the time. During the walk through Edinburgh we are made particularly conscious of the impact Mussolini has made on both Sandy and Miss Brodie: the event is mainly seen from Sandy's viewpoint, but we can distinguish clearly what she has been and is being taught by Miss Brodie from her new reflections on it.

We begin with Sandy's understanding of the corporate unity of teacher and girls, 'a body with Miss Brodie for the head', the girls as if created to fulfil Miss Brodie's purpose. Miss Brodie's clear dislike of Girl Guides 'with their regimented vigorous look' prompts Sandy to remember her paradoxical admiration for Mussolini's marching troops.

Sandy ponders on juxtaposed set, Guides and fascisti: and she sees

> that the Brodie set was Miss Brodie's fascisti, not to the naked eye, marching along, but all knit together for her need and in another way, marching along.

At this stage Sandy obviously understands even less than Miss Brodie what Mussolini is up to: he 'had put an end to unemployment with his fascisti and there was no litter in the streets'. The resemblance is in the discipline, the perfect way in which the troops are bent to the will of the leader. And so it *does* seem paradoxical that the marching Guides are disapproved, until Sandy begins to suspect jealousy: the Guides are 'too much of a rival fascisti, and Miss Brodie could not bear it'. On the walk Sandy experiences two early temptations to 'betray' Miss Brodie, one by being nice to Mary Macgregor and one here by joining the Brownies, but she recoils from them quickly. Her basic reason is interesting, because this is the only time it is ever put in terms as strong as love: 'Then the group-fright seized her again, and it was necessary to put the idea aside, because she loved Miss Brodie.'

---

**Profound ambiguity is central to the effect of the novel: no simple attitude toward Miss Brodie can last with any justice.**

**—*Isobel Murray and Bob Tait***

---

Now her reactions are to be further tested, by the walk through the previously unvisited slums, 'Sandy's first experience of a foreign country': she is to have her first intimation of the real meaning of unemployment, as she shrinks fearfully from the 'snaky creature', the queue of unemployed. They are first glimpsed, talking, spitting and smoking, and Miss Brodie enjoins the set to pray for the Unemployed, repeating the conventional wisdom that, 'In Italy the unemployment problem has been solved.' It is a powerful argument, faced with Edinburgh reality. Again the men talk and spit a great deal, reinforcing negatively the famous dictum of Lord Howard of Penrith in 1923, as blinkered as Miss Brodie: 'Under Fascism, Italians no longer spit in public.' Sandy's discomfort and fear are acute here: when she betrays Miss Brodie she disclaims interest in 'world affairs', but she remains concerned about Edinburgh's poor and unemployed: 'It did not seem necessary that the world should be saved, only that the poor people in the streets and slums of Edinburgh should be relieved.' Again now she experiences the impulse to desert the set and this time she acts on it, home being the necessary warm notion to oppose to her shivering cold and fear—but she rather repents her self-exile from tea at Miss Brodie's shortly after.

It is of course possible that the reader knows a little more about Fascism than Miss Brodie and Sandy, and Spark gives oblique hints for such readers. Mussolini preached the superficially attractive idea of a corporate state, in which unions, employers and all worked and collaborated together: it is not wholly unlike Miss Brodie's benign dictatorship over her girls, and is lightly referred to here when Sandy finds 'the corporate Brodie set' insufficiently warm.

But Miss Brodie's Fascism is basically very simple-minded and straightforward. After her next summer holiday in Italy she tells the girls; 'Mussolini has performed feats of magnitude and unemployment is even farther abolished under him than it was last year.' Her devotion persists until she transfers it, in 1933, to Hitler:

> a prophet-figure like Thomas Carlyle, and more reliable than Mussolini; the German brownshirts, she said, were exactly the same as the Italian black, only more reliable.

Notice that she seems unaware of the racial persecution in Hitler's Nazism which was not inherent in Mussolini's Fascism. Hitler's methods again resemble her own, arguably, in that some historians say that his singling out and persecution of the Jews helped unite and cement the relieved majority of the Germans thereby passed over: Miss Brodie's outrageous picking on Mary Macgregor and making her a scapegoat has something of the same effect. In chapter three when the class gets sex-conscious giggles, Miss Brodie ejects Mary, one of the last to laugh, and shuts her out:

> returning as one who had solved the whole problem. As indeed she had, for the violent action sobered the girls and made them feel that, in the official sense, an unwanted ring-leader had been apprehended and they were no longer in the wrong.

Nazi or not, this is acutely unpleasant behaviour. Miss Brodie may be a born Fascist, as Sandy claims, but she is an instinctive and a relatively uncomprehending one: before the war she is sure Hitler will save the world, and afterwards she innocently admits: 'Hitler *was* rather naughty,' surely one of the great understatements!

The Italy that has become home to Mrs Spark attracts Jean Brodie almost totally: she is under the spell of its art, history, tradition and contemporary politics—all but the church: she rejects Roman Catholicism, and the narrator suggests that that was the one church which might have 'normalized' her. Miss Brodie is not averse to meeting the Pope. That was part of her Italian holiday, and her Presbyterian soul was satisfied by her bending over the Pope's ring but not kissing it. This was part of her visit to Rome, as her London stay was marked by a visit to A A Milne, the creator of Pooh and Piglet. But the narrator pauses on her rejection of Roman Catholicism. The long paragraph begins by detailing the rota of different denominations she did accept and patronise, indicating at the least an indifference to sectarian strictness. Her rejection of Roman Catholicism is arguably as simple-minded and ignorant as her approval of Mussolini: it is a middle-class Edinburgh belief that the Church of Rome was a church of superstition, 'and that only people who did not want to think for themselves were Roman Catholics'. The narrator suggests that only the Roman Catholic Church truly suited her

temperament: 'Possibly it could have embraced, even while it disciplined, her soaring and diving spirit, it might even have normalized her.' The implication seems to be that the Roman Church provides norms, provides in its rituals and regularities, doctrines and hierarchies a stable framework for the extreme individual to respond to: Calvinist ideas, in part born from a reaction against the notion of a priesthood coming between the individual and God, can help the extremist toward her extremity.

MacColla's critique of Calvinism . . . concentrated on the doctrine of the total depravity of man and human society, and his belief in the life-denying consequences of such a doctrine. Spark in contrast concentrates on the doctrine of election and subsequent dangers of antinomianism, as Hogg did in the *Justified Sinner,* and Burns in *Holy Willie's Prayer.* The problem about predestination to grace, about election, is that, as the Justified Sinner found, it is difficult to be sure one *is* of the Elect. The temptation, as he also found, is that once convinced of his or her election to salvation, the individual can see him- or herself as above the law thereafter, bound for Heaven irrespective of behaviour in this world. This is antinomianism (i.e. flouting the principle of law, —*anti* plus Greek *nomos,* law). We seem to recognise this syndrome, for example, when Miss Brodie sees Rose as Venus incarnate, and above the moral laws.

Here we are told that Miss Brodie persists in her non-Roman rota of church visits with a sublime confidence in her own status:

> She was not in any doubt, she let everyone know she was in no doubt, that God was on her side whatever her course, and so she experienced no difficulty or sense of hypocrisy in worship while at the same time she went to bed with the singing master.

Not only that, but she assumes the election of all her girls also:

> The side-effects of this condition were exhilarating to her special girls in that they in some way partook of the general absolution she had assumed to herself. . . . All the time they were under her influence she and her actions were outside the context of right and wrong.

From the beginning she has promised to make her girls members of 'life's élite, or, as one might say, the crème de la crème'. And as time goes on by her special attentions and confidences she makes them 'feel chosen'. So Miss Brodie elects herself and her girls—as Sandy at last perceives, she has a God-complex:

> She thinks she is Providence, thought Sandy, she thinks she is the God of Calvin, she sees the beginning and the end.

It is all of course a million miles away from orthodox Calvinism, where the election is from God, and the part of the individual is to wait humbly and fearfully. Mrs Spark is criticising the effects of Calvinism, but by no means suggesting that Miss Brodie is a representative Calvinist. She does not know God through the Scriptures as the Reformers insisted, but by the wrong and dangerous means of un-assisted reason and private revelation.

Miss Brodie's religion is not in the end Christian at all. It is in the end personal and perverse, a monstrosity of ego-tism. Early on she applies Calvinist ideas to artists and outstanding personages: Florence Nightingale, Cleopatra, Helen of Troy, Sybil Thorndyke the great actress, Pavlo-va—these are above the despised 'team spirit', which is only for lesser mortals: effectively, they are above the law. So Miss Brodie takes all the furniture of Calvinism, so to speak, all the formulations and habits of mind, and applies it to her blurred perception of reality and fantasy. She never shows any sign of seriously believing that God exists or that she herself could be so lowly a thing as a creature. Is she 'quite an innocent in her way', as Sandy later on sug-gests, or is this outlandish pride, the sin whereby the an-gels fell?

Italy, Fascism, the Christian churches; these are perhaps the main contexts outside the school in which Miss Brodie is presented, but there are others. There are the women she most admires, those just listed, plus the Queen of England, Joan of Arc and Britannia. There is her favourite reading, and the authors she quotes without acknowledgement: they show no bias toward religion, unless a religion of art, including chiefly Keats, Tennyson, Pater, Rossetti, Swin-burne, the early Yeats and Charlotte Brontë. There is her contempt for contemporary British politics, whether of right or left, in comparison with Mussolini. Miss Mackay admires Stanley Baldwin, the Conservative Prime Minis-ter who presided over the General Strike of 1926, and was premier of a coalition government when the Brodie set was in the Junior school, but Miss Brodie does not—and posterity admits that Baldwin was no match for the ruth-less challenge of Fascist dictatorships abroad. Miss Brodie also prefers Mussolini to the Scottish Labour politician Ramsay MacDonald, who formed a National Govern-ment with mainly Conservative support in opposition to most of his own party in 1931, when the girls were eleven.

What we get is a real flavour of the 'thirties, the more ef-fective in that we are repeatedly reminded that it is the pe-riod between two wars, with reference to the 'felled fiancé' and 'war-bereaved spinsters', and flashes forward to the aftermath of the Second World War. And we see Miss Brodie in the context of her fellow spinsters, and of the fads and trivia of the time, and of her own idiosyncrasies. We (and the Brodie set) hear of the Buchmanites, follow-ers of an American evangelist, and we hear of Marie Stopes, the great pioneer of birth control. Marie Stopes was another remarkable woman: at thirty-eight, virgin and with a divorce behind her, she wrote her classic manu-al *Married Love* from books—and like Miss Brodie, she was Edinburgh-born.

The endearing nature of Miss Brodie's Edinburgh-based mentality is seen when her notion of the near-unrefusable proposer of marriage is 'the Lord Lyon King-of-Arms': the Lord Lyon King-of-Arms is king in a Scottish context only, and in the most limited of ways: he is chief heraldic royal officer-of-arms, *for ceremonial purposes*. This can [be] seen as a harmless little limitation, linking Miss Bro-die back to her Edinburgh context. There are several other

instances of this: Eunice may not do cart-wheels at Sunday tea-parties, 'for in many ways Miss Brodie was an Edin-burgh spinster of the deepest dye,' and we have quoted above her anticlimactic interruption of her gladiatorial fantasy to complain that the window has been opened to a 'vulgar' extent. Another such instance interrupts even the affecting story of the felled fiancé; and the comic effect is considerable:

> . . . he fell on Flanders' Field,' said Miss Bro-die. 'Are you thinking, Sandy, of doing a day's washing?'
>
> 'No, Miss Brodie.'
>
> 'Because you have got your sleeves rolled up. I won't have to do with girls who roll up the sleeves of their blouses, however fine the weath-er. Roll them down at once, we are civilized be-ings. He fell the week before Armistice. . . .

The city of Edinburgh is also very important in the novel, and the old churches and the castle are omnipresent. And this is in no way surprising: Mrs Spark [as quoted by Alan Bold in *Modern Scottish Literature,* 1983] admits to a more pervasive influence:

> But Edinburgh where I was born and my father was born has had an effect on my mind, my prose style and my ways of thought.

So, unobtrusively, Mrs Spark supplies a vivid context of the time and the character of her main protagonist. The novel may centre on the influence of one spinster school-teacher on six little girls, in a middle-class, all-female school in a city some have suggested is hardly part of Scot-land at all, but the subject matter turns out to be wide-ranging, and the issues universal.

But the school is also and always credible, and with great economy as ever the narrator informs us right at the start about the general knowledge of the Brodie set when it moved up into the Senior school. The headmistress de-scribes them as 'vastly informed on a lot of subjects irrele-vant to the authorized curriculum, and useless to the school as a school'. The list includes elements of very dif-ferent importance, world affairs, skin care and puberty, as well as Einstein and 'the arguments of those who consider the Bible to be untrue'. It is implied what Miss Mackay would rather have them know, and the authorised curricu-lum sounds on the dull side: 'They knew the rudiments of astrology but not the date of the Battle of Flodden or the capital of Finland.'

We get several glimpses of Miss Brodie teaching, and by no means all are in the classroom: if she is not settled under the elm tree with the English grammers open as a cover, making the little girls weep at the sad fate of her war-slain Hugh, she is likely to be taking them to the the-atre, or an art gallery, or on that most significant land-mark in Sandy's education, the walk through the old Edinburgh of the castle, the cathedral and the slums. Her teaching is certainly unorthodox, and the girls are un-aware how unusual the relaxed atmosphere of her class is until her disappearance with Mr Lowther for a fortnight precipitates them into the untender mercies of Miss Gaunt. Miss Brodie's class is remarkable for absolutes and large understandings which most of us may not associate with school at all, as when Miss Brodie declares: 'Art is greater than science. Art comes first, and then science.' She turns back to the geography map, but turns again to the girls to amplify: 'Art and religion first; then philosophy; lastly science. That is the order of the great subjects of life, that's their order of importance.' And in spite of her dictatorial ways, the class is at ease:

> 'We do a lot of what we like in Miss Brodie's class,' Jenny said. 'My mummy says Miss Brodie gives us too much freedom.'

> 'She's not supposed to give us freedom, she's supposed to give us lessons,' said Sandy.

Our last set-piece of Miss Brodie's teaching is on her return from an Italian holiday in 1931, when she brings them a Cimabue and a new picture of Mussolini's fascisti, and details of all her summer experiences and a reiteration of her famous belief in education as a leading out, 'from *e*, out and *duco*, I lead': nonetheless, she immediately continues: 'Qualifying examination or no qualifying examination, you will have the benefit of my experiences in Italy.' She gets carried away as a gladiator, and returned to Edinburgh spinsterhood by an unduly open window, and back to the romantic subject of Rossetti and Swinburne: no wonder the two new girls stand up 'with wide eyes!'

Is there any harm in all this? One is tempted to say no, or to argue that any harm is well compensated for by the interest and liveliness of it all: Eunice later describes Miss Brodie as 'an Edinburgh Festival all on her own.' The girls *do* scrape through the momentous qualifying examination, with a great deal of extra knowledge, some very bizarre, and an inevitably blurred notion of where truth ends and Miss Brodie's opinion begins. They are enthralled by her personality: in term time she seems the centre of their lives. Being a member of Miss Brodie's set seems the most entertaining possibility by a long way, in the Junior school at Marcia Blaine. Arguably, no harm would have come to the girls if Miss Brodie had let them go when they moved up to Senior school, but her hanging on to the girls, keeping and building on her influence with them—this was where the whole thing began to be out of hand. The evidence of the book indicates that all the Brodie set except Sandy shook off her influence in the end without much trouble: but the example of Joyce Emily Hammond shows in a very dramatic way how dangerous that influence could be.

So we come at last to consider the most enigmatic character in the book, Sandy Stranger, the girl who loved Miss Brodie, fantasised about her, wrote of her love life, and deduced its real life character; who was Miss Brodie's confidante, her proxy lover of Teddy Lloyd and her betrayer, who became a Roman Catholic to Miss Brodie's bafflement and a nun to her hurt despair. Although we see a great deal of her thought processes, Sandy remains for us ultimately, as her name suggests, a stranger. We do not see *all* of her thought processes, and as she grows up we seldom learn of her emotional state, and so her character is very much open to different interpretation by the individual reader—so that Maurice Lindsay in his *History of Scottish Literature* can describe her betrayal of Miss Brodie as

motivated by 'bitchy jealousy', while Peter Kemp attributes it to 'a strong moral sense'. In part it depends what emotional life the reader supplies for Sandy. 'She loved Miss Brodie' during the walk in chapter two, when this love is sufficient to quash temptations to join the Brownies or be nice to Mary—but it is a ten-year-old's understanding of love, which we can hardly rely on completely. Much later we see her bored and afflicted by the betrayed Miss Brodie, nostalgically remembering 'the first and unbetrayable Miss Brodie,' and one general passage indicates warmth and affection toward Miss Brodie whenever she was seen as fallible. But it is not a lot to go on. In general, we are unclear as to her feelings for Miss Brodie, and her feelings for Teddy Lloyd, and her feelings about her conversion to Roman Catholicism and her vocation to the convent: all we have is that repeated image of her hands clutching at the grille: the enigma persists.

Sandy's conversion is something we sense as crucially important to the book, but we are told very little about it, and what we know is cerebral or psychological; that she was interested in Teddy Lloyd's mind because he was so obsessed with the ridiculous Miss Brodie, that when she lost interest in him as a man, she retained interest in the mind, and eventually extracted his faith. But this submerged conversion matters, as does Caroline's conversion in *The Comforters* (1957), or the bizarre conversion and eventual martyrdom of Nicholas Farringdon in *The Girls of Slender Means* (1963), the novel after *The Prime of Miss Jean Brodie*. Sandy's situation is after all a little like what we know of Spark's: both were born and raised in Edinburgh but not entirely of it, within a couple of years of each other, and both had an English mother. Spark's father was Jewish, which helped separate her from a conventional middle-class Edinburgh situation: we hear nothing about Sandy's father, but home is a very warm and comforting notion. Both were educated in the same Presbyterian school, and neither exactly had Scottish Calvinism sternly presented to her, to react against: instead, Sandy had Miss Brodie. Both eventually became converts to Roman Catholicism. All sorts of intriguing questions about Sandy's young adulthood and conversion remain tantalisingly unanswerable—how important was Miss Brodie's adamant opposition to Catholicism to Sandy's eventual acceptance of it? How important was the notion of rivalry with Miss Brodie in her love affair with Teddy Lloyd? Or was it important, mainly, just to frustrate Miss Brodie's plans and roles for Rose and Sandy, to thwart her?

Sandy emerges as a central consciousness in chapter two, with her birthday party *à deux* with Jenny and her insights during the walk. But from the beginning her too-often-insisted-on tiny eyes are on Miss Brodie, scrutinising her chest and noting its different appearances. The collaborative writings with Jenny inevitably centre on Miss Brodie, and they mirror very accurately the changes in the set generally indicated by the narrator. In the first year with Miss Brodie they are essentially little girls, with only the beginnings of the following year's sexual obsession, so *The Mountain Eyrie*, the continuing story of Miss Brodie and Hugh, rings hollow with melodramatic romance. But in the 'sexual year' the set senses the onset of sexual awareness between Miss Brodie and Teddy Lloyd and Gordon

Lowther before any of the teachers do, and when Miss Brodie and Gordon Lowther disappear from school for the same fortnight, it is Sandy who casually suggests an affair, 'merely in order to break up the sexless gloom that surrounded them,' and then she suspects that the affair exists in fact. She is of course only eleven, and subject to the onset of adolescence like any other little girl, so it would be dangerous to make too much of her ambiguous attitude towards sexuality at this time. While in fantasy with Sergeant Anne Grey she was dedicated to eliminate sex from Edinburgh and environs, she was very excited and interested in Monica Douglas's story that she has witnessed a kiss between Miss Brodie and Teddy Lloyd, 'excited and desperately trying to prove the report true by eliminating the doubts'. Sandy is only typical of the set in her interest in Miss Brodie's changed appearance, and fantasies about the possibility of her engaging in sexual activity, and she is still sharing them with Jenny, but her thoughts gradually become more private. It is Sandy alone who looks at Miss Brodie as she looks at Rose 'in a special way' when Teddy Lloyd has remarked on her profile, though she and Jenny continue to speculate on whether Miss Brodie can be desirable to men. And it is Sandy alone who attempts to detect 'any element of surrender about her' in the affair with Gordon Lowther, although Sandy and Jenny collaborate on the outspoken and highly comic fictional correspondence.

Sandy was only eighteen when she finally betrayed Miss Brodie, but the seeds were sown long before. In a sense they were sown by Miss Brodie herself, in her constant raising of the possibility—or impossibility: 'I do not think ever to be betrayed.' But it is when the girls are fifteen that Sandy begins to feel that 'the Brodie set, not to mention Miss Brodie herself, was getting out of hand.' She has discovered the weird phenomenon of Teddy Lloyd's paintings, that all portraits of Brodie girls come to resemble Miss Brodie herself. It is when her little eyes meet his 'with the near-blackmailing insolence of her knowledge' that he kisses her, an important moment, balancing the solitary kiss Monica Douglas witnessed between Lloyd and Miss Brodie. Not surprisingly this, and Lloyd's cruel comment that Sandy is 'just about the ugliest little thing I've ever seen in my life', leave her in some confusion. At about this time, Miss Brodie has begun to look for a confidante: she

> was in fact now on the look-out for a girl amongst her set in whom she could confide entirely, whose curiosity was greater than her desire to make a sensation outside, and who, in the need to gain further confidences from Miss Brodie, would never betray what had been gained. . . . Almost shrewdly, Miss Brodie fixed on Sandy, . . . .

A round of golf full of bunkers and power images is the setting for the first confidences, and they seem harmless enough, reasons why Miss Brodie has no great ambitions for the set, except Sandy and Rose. Obliquely and then directly, Sandy begins to understand:

> It was plain that Miss Brodie wanted Rose with her instinct to start preparing to be Teddy Lloyd's lover, and Sandy with her insight to act as informant on the affair. It was to this end that Rose and Sandy had been chosen as the crème de la crème. There was a whiff of sulphur about the idea which fascinated Sandy in her present mind. After all, it was only an idea.

The Sandy who feels deprived of Calvinism, 'something definite to reject', is tempted by the whiff of sulphur here, and 'for over a year Sandy entered into the spirit of this plan.' She enjoys the long temptation shared. But Sandy was always more a realist than Miss Brodie, could always more clearly discriminate between fantasy and reality. So one day in her sixth year Sandy fully realises the extent and nature of Miss Brodie's manipulative plan:

> All at once Sandy realised that this was not all theory and a kind of Brodie game. . . . But this was not theory; Miss Brodie meant it. Sandy looked at her, and perceived that the woman was obsessed by the need for Rose to sleep with the man she herself was in love with; there was nothing new in the idea, it was the reality that was new.

Miss Brodie's plan is serious, and Sandy has connived at it, feeding her unreality: 'She had told Miss Brodie how peculiarly all his portraits reflected her. She had said so time and again, for Miss Brodie loved to hear it.'

That summer Sandy leaves school, and while Miss Brodie is in Germany and Austria and Deirdre Lloyd and the children are in the country, Sandy seduces Teddy Lloyd by a repetition of her 'insolent blackmailing stare' and her knowledge of Lloyd's obsession with Miss Brodie. We have little detail, but both Sandy and Teddy Lloyd seem more interested in Miss Brodie than in each other. That curiosity which Miss Brodie required in a confidante is Sandy's main spur: 'The more she discovered him to be still in love with Jean Brodie, the more she was curious about the mind that loved the woman.' And when she loses interest in Lloyd in due course she retains her fascination with his religion: 'She left the man and took his religion and became a nun in the course of time.' Arguably, Sandy has already twice betrayed Miss Brodie, in embracing the art master, contrary to the terms of the plan, and in embracing his religion, which Miss Brodie so despises. But it is doubtful if she would ever have betrayed her to Miss Mackay had it not been for Miss Brodie's utterly casual throwaway remark about Joyce Emily.

The much expelled Joyce Emily has been present from chapter one, anxious to join the sixteen-year-old Brodie set, who are too preoccupied to bother with her. So, perhaps a little through their faults, Joyce Emily is taken up by Miss Brodie. For the most part the reader, like the set, knows little about Joyce Emily and cares less. We do know that she has a brother fighting in the Spanish Civil War and wants to go too: we know that she is anti-Franco. We learn that she ran away to Spain and was killed in an accident. And in Miss Brodie's throwaway remark we learn a little more:

> sometimes I regretted urging young Joyce Emily to go to Spain to fight for Franco, she would have done admirably. . . .

Sandy checks that Joyce Emily went to fight for the Fascist Franco, and Miss Brodie agrees: 'I made her see sense.' It is difficult to know which outrages our expectations of a schoolteacher more, talking the girl into changing sides in the war, or 'urging' her to go and fight at all. Both betray a terrifying unconscious egotism which sees Joyce Emily as a pawn rather than a human being, fulfilling a minor ambition of Miss Brodie's, as Rose was intended to fulfil a major one. The juxtaposition of this conversation with Sandy's betrayal clearly indicates that this discovery about Joyce Emily finally triggered the betrayal, Sandy's determination to 'put a stop to Miss Brodie.'

The betrayal itself was a sordid affair which Sandy clearly did not enjoy. Miss Mackay was ready with questions about Miss Brodie's sex life. It is a nice irony that Sandy impeaches Miss Brodie for teaching Fascism although it is 'a side interest': it *was* a side interest in Sandy's experience of Miss Brodie, but a very central and final one for Joyce Emily.

It is easy to understand why Sandy felt is necessary to 'put a stop to Miss Brodie', and the narrator adds an implication of the 'strong moral sense' pointed to by Peter Kemp: 'She was more fuming, now, with Christian morals, than John Knox.' The question that is never directly answered is whether Sandy continued to feel justified in the betrayal. References to her later life in the convent and visits from various members of the set are sprinkled through the novel, and the conversations always centre on Miss Brodie and the betrayal. We would suggest that Sandy attains some wisdom, some detachment in the years in the convent when she writes her psychological treatise on 'The Transfiguration of the Commonplace'—although how much *that* owed to Miss Brodie it is impossible to say. There is no evidence that she regretted the betrayal, ever felt it had been unnecessary, though the cumulative evidence suggests that retrospectively she began to revalue Miss Brodie's positive side. She has accumulated a lot of information. Monica visits Sandy in the late 1950s, and asserts that she really did witness the Brodie/Lloyd kiss; and we learn that Sandy knew this 'even before Miss Brodie had told her so one day after the end of the war': presumably Sandy had been confided in by Teddy Lloyd as well.

These convent interviews years after Miss Brodie's death show us also the continuing naïveté of the other members of the set. It is of all people Rose who innocently asks 'Why did she get the push? Was it sex?' And it is Monica who asks Sandy if Rose ever *did* sleep with Teddy Lloyd, and who ruminates that if Miss Brodie and Teddy Lloyd were in love, 'it was a real renunciation in a way'—although in the past they saw the renunciation claims as comic. Eunice recalls Miss Brodie as marvellous fun, and Jenny wishes she could tell Miss Brodie about her sudden falling in love: 'Miss Brodie would have liked to know about it, sinner as she was.' And that is the point at which Sandy famously replies: 'Oh, she was quite an innocent in her way.' Perhaps the best way to understand this is that Sandy has become able to separate the evil Miss Brodie was undoubtedly doing in the 'extremities' of her late prime from her inability to realise this evil or to will it as such. But it is also another of her enigmatic utterances, for 'an innocent' can mean many things, from 'an innocent or guiltless person' through 'a young child' and 'a guileless,

simple or unsuspecting person' to 'one wanting in ordinary knowledge or intelligence; a simpleton, a silly fellow'.

At her worst, Miss Brodie *is* simple-minded: if she can see no harm in changing Joyce Emily's politics and packing her off to war, to fulfil by proxy her own aim of dedication, she is seriously lacking in the insight on which she prides herself. Her ambitions for her girls were always alarming, if one took them seriously, because her imagination fed her ideal of dedication with a highly coloured extremism—so, when Eunice had a religious phase Miss Brodie 'tried to inspire Eunice to become at least a pioneer missionary in some deadly and dangerous zone of the earth' rather than a Girl Guide leader in the respectable Edinburgh suburb of Corstorphine. The only moment at which Miss Brodie has enough insight to suspect Sandy is when she is angry at the news that Sandy has entered the convent. She has hardly learned from the betrayal if a few weeks before she dies she can respond to such news thus:

> What a waste. That is not the sort of dedication
> I meant. Do you think she has done this to
> annoy me? I begin to wonder if it was not Sandy
> who betrayed me.

Any woman who can seriously think another may have entered a convent to 'annoy' her has perhaps a lopsided view of the universe: perhaps Sandy was right: 'She thinks she is Providence. She thinks she is the God of Calvin.'

The book ends with Sandy in the convent, now for at least a dozen years Sister Helena of the Transfiguration. The Roman Empress Dowager Helena, mother of Constantine, was reputedly British—said indeed to be the daughter of 'Old King Cole'. She transformed a conventional life by departing for the Holy Land in her old age to search for and find the True Cross on which Christ was crucified. The 'Transfiguration' element in Sandy's convent name recalls the occasion when Jesus was transfigured, appeared in his full glory, to a few of the disciples: it recalls of course as well the title of Sandy's treatise, and perhaps records a debt to the woman who first indicated to Sandy the possibility of transfiguring the commonplace.

Sandy is described as 'in her middle age, when she was at last allowed all those visitors to the convent': in fact she is approaching forty, the age at which Miss Brodie entered her prime. Sandy will not have a prime. The visitors are 'a special dispensation . . . enforced on Sandy': dispensations are usually granted, not enforced, and she does not seem very happy in her interviews, but very evidently ill at ease:

> She clutched the bars of the grille as if she want-
> ed to escape from the dim parlour beyond, for
> she was not composed like the other nuns who
> sat, when they received their rare visitors, well
> back in the darkness with folded hands. But
> Sandy always leaned forward and peered,
> clutching the bars with both hands.

That is our lasting image of the unquiet nun.

## Alan Bold (essay date 1986)

SOURCE: "Jean Brodie, the Girls, the Gate," in *Muriel Spark,* Methuen, 1986, pp. 63-86.

*[A Scottish poet and critic, Bold has written extensively on Scottish literature. In the following excerpt, he remarks on language and character in* The Prime of Miss Jean Brodie.*]*

Several of Muriel Spark's novels place characters in insulated areas, contain them in tightly knit communities: the pilgrim centre in *The Comforters* (1957), the island in *Robinson* (1958), the geriatric ward in *Memento Mori* (1959), the hostel in *The Girls of Slender Means* (1963), the big house in *Not to Disturb* (1971), the apartment in *The Hothouse by the East River* (1973), the convent in *The Abbess of Crewe* (1974). Nowhere in Spark's output is the microcosmic world-within-a-world scenario more skilfully realized than in *The Prime of Miss Jean Brodie* (1961), arguably her masterpiece. Rapidly written in eight weeks, the novel is set in and around an Edinburgh girls' school—Marcia Blaine, modelled on James Gillespie's, where Spark was educated—and has for its heroine a woman physically vibrant with vitality, assuredly in her prime.

Jean Brodie is one of the great character-creations of modern fiction, a contradictory soul who distrusts the Roman Catholic Church while spending summer holidays in Rome in search of culture; who admires the Church of Scotland but detests John Knox, its founder; who deplores the team spirit yet idolizes Mussolini's fascisti; who articulates a doctrine of romantic love yet sleeps with the dreary Mr Lowther and denies herself to one-armed Mr Lloyd because he is a married man with children. Though the central part of an accomplished fiction, Jean Brodie seems undeniably real, and Spark's friend Derek Stanford claims [in his *Inside the Forties: Literary Memoirs 1937-1957,* 1977] to have been 'introduced to the original of that audacious teacher by Muriel at the Poetry Society'. Spark herself has stated 'there was no "real" Miss Brodie' [letter to the critic dated 5 October 1982], and 'there was a Christina Kay who died during the '40s, greatly esteemed, but not like Miss Brodie in character' [letter to the critic dated 17 February 1983]. Jean Brodie may be a fact of fiction rather than life (the distinction between the two being blurred by Sparkian metaphysics) but then so are all Spark's characters: the difference between Jean Brodie and the others is that she appears to have an actual existence over and above the pages of a book that operates by implication. This is why she has been successfully transferred to stage, cinema and television. For thousands of readers, Jean Brodie actually exists in the same way that Sherlock Holmes and George Smiley actually exist. Though no saint, Jean Brodie is a literary legend.

The author's affection for Jean Brodie and her native city gives this novel of the 1930s a period charm that is rare in the caustic Spark canon. For *The Prime of Miss Jean Brodie* Spark has reserved some of her most richly lyrical prose. The novel abounds in evocative phrases: 'the haunted November twilight of Edinburgh,' 'The evening paper rattle-snaked its way through the letter box and there was

suddenly a six-o'clock feeling in the house,' 'Miss Brodie's voice soared up to the ceiling, and curled round the feet of the Senior girls upstairs,' 'The bare winter top branches of the trees brushed the windows of this long [science] room, and beyond that was the cold winter sky with a huge red sun,' 'The wind blew from the icy Forth and the sky was loaded with forthcoming snow,' 'Miss Brodie, indifferent to criticism as a crag,' 'Her name and memory, after her death, flitted from mouth to mouth like swallows in summer, and in winter they were gone'. Several of these poetic phrases make the novel, on one level, an elegy for an Edinburgh that has gone, though it lingers in the memory of Muriel Spark. Edinburgh, the home of Jean Brodie, is also identified by Spark as the city where John Knox clashed with Mary Queen of Scots; where Jean Brodie's ancestor Deacon Brodie (the original of Stevenson's dualistic Dr Jekyll) roamed as a burgher by day and a burglar by night; where spinsters such as Jean Brodie 'called themselves Europeans and Edinburgh a European capital, the city of Hume and Boswell.' Haunted by its historic past and pressurized by the 'progressive spinsters of Edinburgh,' the city acquires a magical dimension: 'dark heavy Edinburgh itself could suddenly be changed into a floating city when the light was a special pearly white and fell upon one of the gracefully fashioned streets.'

The contradictions in Jean Brodie's character are partly explained by the contrasts apparent in Edinburgh. On a long winter's walk in 1930, during which Sandy Stranger comes to the conclusion that 'the Brodie set was Miss Brodie's fascisti,' the girls are taken from the classically proportioned New Town to the 'reeking network of slums which the Old Town constituted in those years.' The Old Town is another world-within-a-world (or town-within-a-city), a no-girl's-land that has the alien atmosphere of a foreign country. Miss Brodie leads her privileged girls into the unpromising land of the Grassmarket:

> A man sat on the icy-cold pavement; he just sat. A crowd of children, some without shoes, were playing some fight game, and some boys shouted after Miss Brodie's violet-clad company, with words that the girls had not heard before, but rightly understood to be obscene. Children and women with shawls came in and out of the dark closes. . . . A man and a woman stood in the midst of the crowd which had formed a ring round them. They were shouting at each other and the man hit the woman twice across the head.

In such a city, with its internal and eternal dichotomies, reality has several strata and a woman such as Jean Brodie can be in two minds at once. Like many Scots, Jean Brodie has a divided self.

Theologically, Jean Brodie's Edinburgh—where schoolteachers bid their good mornings 'with predestination in their smiles'—is a place fashioned by John Knox from the philosophy of Calvin. Sandy Stranger, half-English, recognizes that the bleak doctrine of the elect is built into Edinburgh where elegance coexists with squalor. 'In fact,' Spark declares, 'it was the religion of Calvin of which Sandy felt deprived, or rather a specified recognition of it. She desired this birthright; something definite to reject.'

Increasingly, Sandy Stranger makes a connection between Jean Brodie's scholastic élite and John Calvin's elect. The insight causes her to lose faith in her teacher:

> she began to sense what went to the makings of Miss Brodie who had elected herself to grace in so particular a way and with more exotic suicidal enchantment than if she had simply taken to drink like other spinsters who couldn't stand it any more.

If *The Prime of Miss Jean Brodie* is constructed around a microcosmic notion, it is not imaginatively limited by its location: behind the (albeit fictional) reality of Miss Brodie there are the historical figures of Knox, Calvin, Mussolini, Franco and Hitler. Spark's novel is enormously suggestive: the account of a group of schoolgirls and their teacher is also a statement on the nature of faith and fanaticism.

Jean Brodie's prime is officially launched in 1930, when the heroine is 39. A teacher in the Junior department of Marcia Blaine School, she chooses for her disciples (the biblical subtext is evident) six 10-year-old girls: Monica Douglas, who is famous for mathematics and subsequently marries a scientist; Rose Stanley, famous for sex, who marries a businessman; Eunice Gardiner, famous for gymnastics, who becomes a nurse married to a doctor; Mary Macgregor, famous for being 'a silent lump, a nobody,' who dies in a fire at the age of 23; Jenny Gray, famous for being pretty, who becomes an actress; and Sandy Stranger, 'notorious for her small, almost non-existent, eyes,' who becomes a nun famous for her psychological treatise, 'The Transfiguration of the Commonplace'. Sandy, the future Sister Helena of the Transfiguration, Jean Brodie's darling disciple, is the Judas who betrays her teacher to the headmistress, Miss Mackay. As a result Miss Brodie is forced to retire in 1939, the year of a new world war, for teaching fascism—especially to Joyce Emily Hammond, who dies on her way to fight for Franco at Miss Brodie's bidding.

Technically, the novel is told in a series of flashbacks and flashforwards. It opens in 1936, breaks back to 1930 (the first year of Miss Brodie's prime) then uses timeshifts to indicate the rise of the Brodie set and the fall of Miss Brodie. Before the final tale of Miss Brodie's downfall has been told, the reader is given the date of the heroine's death: in 1946, at the age of 55, after 'suffering from an internal growth.' In *The Comforters* Spark queried the concept of authorial omniscience; in *The Prime of Miss Jean Brodie* she makes full use of it, magisterially providing the reader with the information she explores in the novel. She also delivers herself of a personal opinion as if her heroine were an actual rather than a fictional woman:

> In some ways, her attitude [of hostility to Roman Catholicism] was a strange one, because she was by temperament suited only to the Roman Catholic Church; possibly it could have embraced, even while it disciplined, her soaring and diving spirit, it might even have normalized her.

The comment encourages the reader to believe in the reality of Jean Brodie, appropriately so since she is Spark's most forgivable character.

For all her admiration of her heroine, Spark makes fun of her fantasies. There is a reductive, comic quality to Jean Brodie's assumption of the leadership of an élite corps of schoolgirls. An admirer of Il Duce, Mussolini, she defines teaching as 'a leading out, from *e*, out and *duco*, I lead.' Regarding her pupils as the 'crème de la crème' she indoctrinates her élite—her elect—with her own prejudices. Her pupils are 'vastly informed on a lot of subjects irrelevant to the authorized curriculum,' being familiar with the accomplishments of Sybil Thorndike and Anna Pavlova and, above all, with the romantic tale of Jean's lover, Hugh Carruthers, who fell 'like an autumn leaf'—so she informs the girls in autumn under an elm—at Flanders, a tragedy enlarged with frequent retellings. Like her heroes—Mussolini, Franco, Hitler—Miss Brodie is a dogmatist. When she asks her class to name the greatest Italian painter and one pupil names Leonardo da Vinci, she says, revealingly, 'That is incorrect. The answer is Giotto, he is my favourite.' In place of observations, she inflicts on the girls her dogmatic assertions: 'Art is greater than science,' 'Mussolini is one of the greatest men in the world,' and (preposterously) 'unemployment is even farther abolished under [Mussolini] than it was last year.'

Projecting herself as the peer of fascist dictators, Jean Brodie nevertheless remains the victim of her own urban and intellectual environment, 'for in many ways Miss Brodie was an Edinburgh spinster of the deepest dye.' Like other Spark heroines she is inclined to solipsism, unable to understand the wider world except as an extension of herself. If circumstances do not accommodate her expectations she attempts to satisfy her desires deviously. Teddy Lloyd, the art teacher, is a married man, which means that she can only allow herself to kiss him surreptitiously in the art room, a gesture she believes preserves her personal purity. Arrogantly, however, she decides to make love to Teddy vicariously by sacrificing one of her girls, choosing Rose Stanley to be her surrogate. Convinced that the girls only exist to do her will, she feels she can thus have the best of both worlds: the world of the Edinburgh spinster as well as the world of the romantic heroine. In the event, it is Sandy Stranger, not Rose Stanley, who sleeps with Teddy Lloyd. The art teacher accepts the substitute physically but remains besotted by Jean: all his portraits of the Brodie set reproduce her features on their faces. Miss Brodie's physical affair with Mr Lowther, the music teacher, is also rationalized, for she sleeps with this bachelor 'in a spirit of definite duty, if not exactly martyrdom.' Tragically, Jean's hypocrisy leads to the loss of everything that is precious to her: the friendship of Mr Lowther (who marries the science teacher), the devotion of Teddy Lloyd, the position she holds at Marcia Blaine, the adoration of her girls.

---

**Thematically, *The Prime of Miss Jean Brodie* is a persuasive study of the élitist mentality that powers the body of the heroine.**

**—*Alan Bold***

---

Surely no girls in adult fiction have ever been portrayed so unsentimentally as the Brodie set. Sandy Stranger and Jenny Gray are obsessed with sex from the age of 10. Thinking of Miss Brodie's prime, they see her belonging to a different species from their parents. 'They don't have primes,' says Sandy. 'They have sexual intercourse,' adds Jenny. Sandy, who has fantasies about the heroes of *Kidnapped* and *Jane Eyre,* is reduced to giggles when Mr Lloyd shows lantern slides of Italian paintings and points at the curves on Botticelli's female figures. Sandy and Jenny giggle together over the lewd mechanics of sewing machines. Between them Sandy and Jenny concoct a romantic fiction around Jean Brodie's supposed sexual adventures with Hugh of Flanders Field and Mr Lowther. This subplot allows Spark to parody romantic pulp-fiction with glorious comic results, culminating in a letter the girls imagine Miss Brodie writing to Gordon Lowther:

> Your letter has moved me deeply as you may imagine [but] there is another in my life whose mutual love reaches out to me beyond the bounds of Time and Space. He is Teddy Lloyd! Intimacy has never taken place with him. He is married to another. One day in the art room we melted into each other's arms and knew the truth. But I was proud of giving myself to you when you came and took me in the bracken on Arthur's Seat while the storm raged about us. . . . I may permit misconduct to occur again from time to time as an outlet because I am in my Prime. . . . Allow me, in conclusion, to congratulate you warmly upon your sexual intercourse, as well as your singing.

When Jenny sees a man exposing himself beside the Water of Leith, Sandy is transported into a Walter Mitty world in which she befriends the policewoman (suitably romanticized) who had questioned Jenny. By the time they are 12 the two girls feel they have, imaginatively, done it all:

> The world of pure sex seemed years away. Jenny had turned twelve. Her mother had recently given birth to a baby boy, and the event had not moved them even to speculate upon its origin.
>
> 'There's not much time for sex research in the Senior school,' Sandy said.
>
> 'I feel I'm past it,' said Jenny.

Linguistically **The Prime of Miss Jean Brodie** is a treat. Spark's use of cross-references, for example, creates irony. Eunice Gardiner is reprimanded by Miss Brodie for using the adjective 'social' as a noun. The incident connects with a flashforward, early in the novel, when Eunice, a married woman, tells her husband she wishes to go and visit Miss Brodie's grave:

> 'Who was Miss Brodie?'
>
> 'A teacher of mine, she was full of culture. She was an Edinburgh Festival all on her own. She used to give us teas at her flat and tell us about her prime.'

'Prime what?'

Elsewhere Spark's dialogue provides exquisite comic exchanges. Monica Douglas's claim that she has seen Teddy Lloyd kissing Miss Brodie in the art room is queried by Sandy Stranger:

> 'What part of the art room were they standing in?' Sandy said.
>
> 'The far side,' Monica said. 'I know he had his arm round her and was kissing her. They jumped apart when I opened the door.'
>
> 'Which arm?' Sandy snapped.
>
> 'The right of course, he hasn't got a left.'

The interrogation continues:

> 'Was it a long and lingering kiss?' Sandy demanded, while Jenny came close to hear the answer.
>
> Monica cast the corner of her eye up to the ceiling as if doing mental arithmetic. Then when her calculation was finished she said, 'Yes it was.'
>
> 'How do you know if you didn't stop to see how long it was?'
>
> 'I know,' said Monica, getting angry, 'by the bit that I did see. It was a small bit of a good long kiss that I saw, I could tell it by his arm being round her.'

Using a descriptive device, Spark attaches to the principal characters a set of words that stick to them throughout the novel. Jean Brodie is forever proclaiming her prime, Sandy Stranger is constantly condemned by her eyes—her 'small, almost non-existent eyes,' 'her little eyes screwed on Miss Brodie,' 'a hypocritical blinking of her eyes,' 'her little pig-like eyes,' her 'abnormally small eyes.' Teddy Lloyd first kisses Sandy because of her eyes, telling her 'That'll teach you to look at an artist like that.' Mary Macgregor's presence in the novel is verbally linked to death by fire. The manner of her death is described at the beginning of the second chapter of the novel:

> [After the outbreak of the Second World War, Mary] died while on leave in Cumberland in a fire in the hotel. Back and forth along the corridors ran Mary Macgregor, through the thickening smoke. She ran one way; then, turning, the other way; and at either end the blast furnace of the fire met her.

Shortly after this flashforward there is an allusion to Mary 'who later, in that hotel fire, ran hither and thither till she died.' Armed with this foreknowledge, the reader is then alerted to the significance of Mary's panic as a schoolgirl during an experiment in the science room when magnesium flares shoot out of test-tubes:

> Mary Macgregor took fright and ran along a single lane between two benches, met with a white flame, and ran back to meet another brilliant tongue of fire. Hither and thither she ran in panic between the benches until she was caught and induced to calm down.

The prose here has the poetic force of a refrain and in such ways Spark conditions the reader's responses to various situations in the novel.

Thematically, **The Prime of Miss Jean Brodie** is a persuasive study of the élitist mentality that powers the body of the heroine. 'Give me a girl at an impressionable age, and she is mine for life,' says Miss Brodie, but Sandy Stranger, the most reflective of the disciples, realizes that her leader is flawed by fanaticism. Ironically, Sandy's own fantasies are flattened by the sexual facts of life and she retreats from Miss Brodie, who is suddenly seen as ridiculous rather than sublime. After ruining Miss Brodie's teaching career, Sandy retreats further from everyday reality, not into a school but into the Catholic Church, 'in whose ranks she had found quite a number of Facists much less agreeable than Miss Brodie.' It is Sandy Stranger, alias Sister Helena of the Transfiguration, who delivers the last words in the book, from the isolation of her nunnery. Asked about the main influences in her life Sandy says 'there was a Miss Jean Brodie in her prime.' The commonplace has been transfigured: Sandy's life, like the reader's, has been enriched by the charismatic personality of Jean Brodie, who, for all her faults, has a poetic panache.

### Anne L. Bower (essay date Summer 1990)

SOURCE: "The Narrative Structure of Muriel Spark's *The Prime of Miss Jean Brodie*," in *The Midwest Quarterly,* Vol. 31, No. 4, Summer, 1990, pp. 488-98.

[*In the following essay, Bower analyzes Spark's use of flashforwards and fantasies, concluding that they "dramatize the unexpected ways in which a seemingly dedicated teacher can affect her pupils."*]

Because the narrative line of Muriel Spark's **The Prime of Miss Jean Brodie** is often interrupted and time seems to be just a plaything of the author, a first reading may leave one feeling dislocated. Further investigation, however, proves that Spark regularly introduces flashforwards and fantasies into the novel's present time in order to demonstrate the unforeseen ways in which the teacher, Jean Brodie, influences her students, especially Sandy Stranger.

The novel depicts "the Brodie set," a group of six middle-class schoolgirls who are variously influenced by one teacher—Jean Brodie. It follows these girls from the time they are ten years old until a few years after they leave school. The story is centered on one student, Sandy Stranger, whose actions finally lead to the firing of Miss Brodie, and who later becomes a nun. The novel's chronology runs from 1930 into the 1950s. This time line is punctuated by two kinds of out-of-time-sequence events: the flashforward, in which future events are actually depicted; and the fantasy, in which a character imagines or describes events that do not take place in her "real" world. While there are a few brief flashbacks, and some occasional references to past events, it is primarily the use of flashforwards and fantasies that distort the forward motion of time or disrupt the reader's sense of the novel's "reality."

Since the novel's publication in 1961, critics have found many ways to explain Spark's particular way of sequencing the events of this novel. David Lodge concludes [in "The Uses and Abuses of Omniscience: Method and Meaning in Muriel Spark's *The Prime of Miss Jean Brodie*," in *The Novelist at the Crossroads,* 1971] that

> . . . the jumps forwards and backwards in time, the pointed interventions of the authorial voice —constantly check any inclination we may have to 'lose ourselves' in the story or to sink into emotional identification with any of the characters; it detaches us from the experience presented and makes us think about its meaning, or meanings.

In addition, Lodge finds that the flashforwards are useful because they "present the extension of Miss Brodie's influence on the girls in their adult life simultaneously with their relationship as teacher and pupils." The movement between present and future creates a view of reality termed "Godlike" by Anthony Burgess [in *The Novel Now,* 1967], and "disorderly order" by Alan Kennedy [in "Cannibals, Okapis and Self-Slaughter in the Fiction of Muriel Spark," in *The Protean Self,* 1974]. Adding the time shifts, fantasies, and authorial interventions to the depiction of events in the "real world" does create "a series of dislocations, each of which disturbs one's former conception of the novel and transforms it into something new" [Bernard Harrison, "Muriel Spark and Jane Austen," in *The Modern English Novel,* edited by Gabriel Josipovici, 1976].

While these and other critical explanations all add to our understanding of the novel, I do not think enough detailed attention has yet been given to Spark's technique, a technique which economically allows her to show how an individual is formed by a unique combination of internal and external forces. Neither the individual nor those around her will necessarily understand all these forces or their relative value (which are most significant, which least, etc.); the creation of an individual is marvelously complex. As we watch the evolution of Sandy Stranger, we are privy to the influences of people, places, and information, to the plans of Sandy's teacher, and privy also to Sandy's fantasies and future. Spark forces us to see that no individual could have predicted the adult Sandy would become; no one around her could have seen how the pieces of her individual puzzle would fit together. Ann Dobie concludes [in "Muriel Spark's Definition of Reality," *Critique* (1970)] that in **The Prime of Miss Jean Brodie** "experiences of human beings are seen often to be precarious, inconclusive, and transitory though they are considered by the characters to be of great moment." At the same time, events which are not presumed to be of great importance may turn out to have great significance.

Let us turn now to these events. I will look first at time present, and then move on to the flashforwards, followed by the fantasies. I believe it is necessary to pause here, however, and define flashforward.

A flashforward is more than a reference to the future (these are common in novels of all periods) because it includes description, action and/or dialogue, not just summary of what will occur: it is an actual scene in future time. In many parts of this novel there are also brief references to the future. Rose Stanley's future reputation for sex, Monica Douglas's later fame "for mathematics and anger," and mention that the six girls will all feel differently about their studies in the Senior School a few months later, are three such references. However, these do not contain descriptions of place, narration of action, or dialogue. What I am calling flashforwards contain one or more of such dramatizing elements.

Time present in this novel runs from 1930 into the 1950s. It begins with the six girls of the "Brodie set" at age ten, takes them through Junior and then Senior school, and then moves on to the betrayal, retirement, and death of Miss Brodie. It includes Sandy's entry into a convent and conversations about Miss Brodie among Sandy, Eunice, Rose, Monica, and Jenny, and then ends with a conversation between Sandy and a young man who has come to the convent to interview her.

Although time present in the novel begins with 1930, the novel opens in 1936, when the six girls who make up the "Brodie set" are all sixteen. In eight pages we become acquainted with the girls' current qualities and with Miss Brodie's endangered status as a teacher at the Marcia Blaine School. There are two brief references to the past: one indicating that when the girls moved from the Junior to the Senior school they were already a distinctive group, and the other noting that these girls have had a "secret life" for six years. At the end of this introductory scene, Stark reminds us of the date and, simultaneously, lets us see that Miss Brodie, a teacher in the prime of her powers who espouses an eccentric set of nontraditional educational objectives, mourns the loss of certain traditional values: "These years are still the years of my prime. . . . Here is my tram car. I daresay I'll not get a seat. This is nineteen-thirty-six. The age of chivalry is past." This scene has sometimes mistakenly been seen as taking place in present time, with the rest of the novel an "extended flashback from the point . . . when the girls are aged sixteen" [Lodge].

When the next paragraph opens with "Six years previously . . ." we, as readers, might think that we have moved to a flashback. Only later do we realize that the first eight pages were a flashforward and that the time present of the novel begins on page 16, in 1930. Throughout the novel, Spark is very careful to keep the reader oriented in time. There are constant references to the season, school term, actual year, or to the age of the girls. All of these pinpoint where the reader is and root the novel in a particular historic time period. They also allow us to return, in an orderly fashion, from the fantasies and flashforwards that are such striking features of the novel.

Altogether, eleven flashforwards interrupt the present time of the novel. The first, as mentioned above, shows the six girls of the "Brodie set" in 1936; the second depicts the death of Mary, the set's scapegoat; the third shows Eunice, in the year 1959, having a conversation with her husband about the possibility of putting flowers on Miss Brodie's grave; and the seventh, in 1946, describes Monica talking to Miss Brodie, now in a nursing home. Miss Brodie wonders if it might be Sandy who "betrayed" her to the school's headmistress so that she lost her teaching position. The ninth flashforward focuses on Jenny, now a married forty-year-old, who is overwhelmed by a sexual fantasy as powerful as her youthful sexual imaginings. The remaining six flashforwards all emanate from Sandy and show her talking with or about Miss Brodie. Sandy's flashforwards most strongly highlight the influence that Miss Brodie actually had, as opposed to the one described in present time—the one she intended to have.

Flashforward four shows Sandy, now a nun—Sister Helena of the Transfiguration, in conversation with a young man from Edinburgh. They contrast their memories of the city, and the man describes the forces that influenced him in his teens: "Auden and Eliot[;] . . . the Spanish Civil War." He then asks Sandy about the greatest influence upon her: "Was it political, personal? Was it Calvinism?" "Oh no," said Sandy. "But there was a Miss Jean Brodie in her prime." And since Sandy has said that influences in teen-age years are often important "even if they provide something to react against," we suspect that such was Miss Brodie's role for her. Jean Brodie wished to have a positive influence on her students, but for Sandy, the teacher's most important function may have been a negative one.

Flashforward five begins with Monica, in the late 1950s affirming to Sandy that she really did see Miss Brodie kissing the art teacher, Teddy Lloyd, back when she and Sandy were in the Junior school together. It then moves to a conversation between Miss Brodie and Sandy, in 1946—Miss Brodie's last year of life and Sandy's last year outside the convent. Miss Brodie confirms the love she and Mr. Lloyd shared and states that they never did become lovers. She admits she is now past her prime, and she tries to make Sandy her confidante. Sandy is fairly unresponsive, but she does give Miss Brodie one bit of emotional support by telling her ex-teacher that her "prime" was a "good prime." This scene reveals a cool Sandy, withholding herself from her teacher, who finally has to ask "are you listening, Sandy?" The flashforward here confirms that Sandy, once so wrapped up in her teacher's every idea and activity, no longer desires intimacy with Brodie.

Flashforward six continues the conversation between Sandy and Jean Brodie in 1946. It is here that we discover that it was Sandy who betrayed Miss Brodie and discover too that the teacher who once fascinated her is now "tiresome."

Flashforward eight begins with Rose and Sandy as adults, talking about Mary. Sandy wishes she had been nicer to the unfortunate Mary, given the sad end to which she came. And Rose asks "How were we to know?" making the question of influences, foresight, and the unstable nature of reality stand out boldly. The flashforward then jumps back to the time and setting of flashforwards five and six, with Miss Brodie wondering if it were Mary who acted against her. Spark's flashforward technique makes it clear that Miss Brodie is blind to the actual way she affected her students. She cannot tell which of the girls were "loyal" to her and which particular one betrayed her.

In flashforward ten we observe Sandy telling Rose that Miss Brodie lost her job because of her political views, not because of her sexual activities. The scene shift and we observe Sandy and Monica discussing Miss Brodie's love for the art teacher, Teddy Lloyd. The two women agree that Miss Brodie's "renunciation" of Lloyd had some meaning, since she "was a woman in her prime." These scenes, taken together, confirm that Sister Helena has transformed her earlier relationship to and ideas about Miss Brodie in ways her teacher could never imagine.

The last flashforward is very brief; it merely inserts a note to show the frivolity of Miss Brodie's politics, for she admits to Sandy, after the war, that Hitler was "rather naughty." Sandy has no line or look, but she is the silent recipient of this odd assessment of Hitler, and we know it is stored in her mind.

All eleven flashforwards are interwoven into the time line of 1930 through 1938, the years the Brodie set is in school. The fantasies, however, occur only during the time the girls are in the junior division—1930-1932.

In the fantasies, as in the flashforwards, proprietorship belongs mostly to Sandy. Of the eleven fantasies, two are shared between Sandy and Jenny, who together are writing "The Mountain Eyrie," the love story of Jean Brodie and Hugh Carruthers (Miss Brodie's first love, who died in World War One). Of the remaining nine fantasies, one is Sandy's solo writing of this love story, while the other eight are Sandy's vivid imaginings of conversations with romanticized characters.

In five of her conversational fantasies, Sandy speaks with figures from books that are favorites of Miss Brodie: the Lady of Shalott; Alan Breck, the hero of *Kidnapped;* and Rochester, from *Jane Eyre.* In another fantasy, Sandy is a dancer with the skill and status of Pavlova. The two discuss the difficulties of the misunderstood artist. Spark uses these fantasies to demonstrate the effect of Miss Brodie's romanticism on young Sandy.

In two fantasies Sandy is a colleague of Sergeant Anne Grey, the female inspector who questioned Jenny after Jenny was surprised by a man exposing himself. In these two fantasies Sandy and Anne Grey discuss the "intimacy" that has been occurring between Jean Brodie and the music teacher, Gordon Lowther; Sandy's youthful sexuality is expressed here more explicitly than in her earlier fantasies, for as she and Anne Grey gaze at each other "their mutual understanding [is] too deep for words," and Sandy finds her imagined colleague "thrilling." Spark seems to point here to the natural sexuality of the young Sandy, which forms part of her real life attachment to her teacher. Perhaps because of the teacher's actual sexual activity with Gordon Lowther, Sandy seeks a fantasy outlet to redirect her girlish feelings. The confused sexuality that will surround Sandy's ongoing relationship to her teacher is forecast in this fantasy.

The remaining fantasy is a fleeting argument with an imagined husband. The conflict fantasized seems to echo the conflict which Sandy (in time present) is experiencing concerning how to treat her classmate Mary. It is an odd insight into a life Sandy never consciously considers—the life of the mundane, married woman. One knows that Sandy will become a nun, marrying an institution rather than a person. This fantasy therefore seems to encapsulate unresolved sexual tensions of the young girl—tensions that will be exacerbated by her affair with Teddy Lloyd, Miss Brodie's rejected lover, and which may form part of her motive for religious conversion.

In *Prime,* Spark's juxtaposition of fantasies and flashforwards with time present adds to our knowledge of Miss Brodie's effect on Sandy, and, to a lesser extent, her effect on the other girls. In her fantasies, we see the young Sandy attempting to play the role of a romantic heroine—trying to become the equal of models Miss Brodie has placed before her. As a young girl, Sandy longs to live up to her admired teacher's ideals. We also see, via flashforwards (which are not fantasies, but realities) the actual consequences of Sandy's interaction with Miss Brodie. Meanwhile, in the present time of the novel, we watch the egocentric and idiosyncratic Miss Brodie attempt to shape Sandy and the other girls in the set. She tries to give them what she thinks is a valuable education, one that will allow them to become extraordinary—dedicated to work or love. She attempts to attract their love and loyalty, assuming that if given a student "at an impressionable age" she will make that girl hers "for life."

The education and influence offered by Miss Brodie do not last for life, except in negative or distorted ways. In her discussion of *Prime* [in "A World at War: One Big Miss Brodie," in *Communities of Women,* 1978], Nina Auerbach focuses on the power of Miss Brodie to serve as a "primary" source of development upon all the girls but Rose. However, none of the girls become famous and dedicated artists, fulfilling the hopes of their old teacher. Jenny becomes a minor actress, Eunice a nurse, Mary a shorthand typist, and Monica an undistinguished science worker. Rose, who marries well, casts off "Miss Brodie's influence as a dog shakes pond-water from its coat." Joyce Emily, a temporary member of the group, dies in Spain, on her way to fight on the Loyalist side, having been influenced by Miss Brodie to attempt a heroic destiny. In Joyce Emily's case, Miss Brodie's influence was completely detrimental, although Miss Brodie herself insists on seeing the girl as a heroine. The remaining student, Sandy, converts to Catholicism and becomes Sister Helena. She is dedicated to her religious life, but Miss Brodie tells Monica, "that is not the sort of dedication I meant."

In a way, one could view this novel as a comedy of errors. Miss Brodie acts erroneously, although she thinks she is acting in the best interests of her pupils to lift them above the run of ordinary life. Sandy also acts erroneously for, although she becomes a nun, she is lacking in the peace and serenity that a religious conversion ought to allow. She "clutches the bars of the grille" when she talks with visitors; her dedication to a religious life seems to be based more on need than on transcendent peace or joy. In fact, no mention is made of any religious rewards Sandy has received from her life as a nun. The lives of both women have gone comically awry. As Judy Little points out [in *Comedy and the Woman Writer: Woolf, Spark, and Feminism,* 1983], this is the kind of comedy which questions the way the world is ordered and which presents "a relentless mocking of truths otherwise taken to be self-evident or even sacred." The method Spark employs to achieve this comic effect largely depends on shifts into future time and into the imaginative world of Sandy Stranger's mind.

In *The Prime of Miss Jean Brodie,* Muriel Spark sets up a careful counterpoint of flashforwards and fantasies which work against the actual 1930s setting of the novel most effectively. This historical period, in which European fascism developed, is a perfect backdrop against which to display Jean Brodie's eccentric authoritarianism. Brodie's hopes to influence her star pupils to fulfill her own romantic dreams of heroism, artistic fulfillment, dedication to discipline, and elitism are detailed in the time present narration of the story. However, as Spark demonstrates, through the use of out-of-time-sequence events, Brodie's actual influence does not match her conscious intentions. Spark uses eleven flashforwards to present future events, showing the true consequences of Miss Brodie's actions and, particularly, the effects of these actions upon Sandy. Spark interjects eleven fantasies which exhibit otherwise hidden aspects of Sandy's youthful mind, aspects which will later be sublimated into Sandy's betrayal of Miss Brodie and her uneasy conversion to the life of a nun. Together, the fantasies and flashforwards dramatize the unexpected ways in which a seemingly dedicated teacher can affect her pupils.

---

## FURTHER READING

### Criticism

Auerbach, Nina. "A World at War: One Big Miss Brodie." In *Communities of Women: An Idea in Fiction,* pp. 159-91. Cambridge, Mass.: Harvard University Press, 1978.

> Analyzes "the Brodie set" as a community of women, arguing that "the very seclusion of Spark's communities of women assures us that they are not pastoral alternatives to a world at war but symbols of it."

Hicks, Granville. "Treachery and the Teacher." *Saturday Review,* New York, XLV, No. 3 (20 January 1962): 18.

> Favorably reviews *The Prime of Miss Jean Brodie,* concluding that the novel "is admirably written, beautifully constructed, extremely amusing, and deeply serious."

Holloway, John. "Narrative Structure and Text Structure: Isherwood's *A Meeting by the River* and Muriel Spark's *The Prime of Miss Jean Brodie.*" In *Narrative and Structure: Ex-*

*ploratory Essays,* pp. 74-99. Cambridge, England: Cambridge University Press, 1979.

> Theoretical essay on how sets of events in a narrative are interrelated.

Kemp, Peter. "Times Past." In *Muriel Spark,* pp. 71-112. New York: Barnes & Noble, 1975.

> Discusses *The Prime of Miss Jean Brodie, The Girls of Slender Means,* and *The Mandelbaum Gate,* as constituting a "self-contained and tightly knit . . . unit." Kemp argues that central to all three novels is "the idea of group-pressure, chauvinistic membership of some community and what this can entail."

Keyser, Barbara. "The Transfiguration of Edinburgh in *The Prime of Miss Jean Brodie.*" *Studies in Scottish Literature* XII, No. 3 (January 1973): 181-89.

> Examines religion and betrayal in Spark's novel and argues that "the Edinburgh of *Jean Brodie* is no commonplace city . . . but a city transfigured by Spark's imagination into a richly symbolic correlative for the major themes of her fiction."

Lodge, David. "The Uses and Abuses of Omniscience: Method and Meaning in Muriel Spark's *The Prime of Miss Jean Brodie.*" *Critical Quarterly* 12, No. 3 (1970): 235-57.

> Discusses religion, education, and narrative method in Spark's novel.

Paul, Anthony. "Muriel Spark and *The Prime of Miss Jean Brodie.*" *Dutch Quarterly Review* 7, No. 3 (1977): 170-83.

> Discusses style, theme, and technique in Spark's novel and praises her economic use of detail.

Ray, Philip E. "Jean Brodie and Edinburgh: Personality and Place in Muriel Spark's *The Prime of Miss Jean Brodie.*" *Studies in Scottish Literature* XIII (1978): 24-31.

> Argues that Spark's novel is "at its deepest level, 'about Edinburgh' " and that the title character personifies religious and theological attitudes common to the city's citizens.

Walker, Dorothea. "*The Prime of Miss Jean Brodie.*" In *Muriel Spark,* pp. 38-50. Boston: Twayne Publishers, 1988.

> Presents an overview of the novel, noting its depiction of the student-teacher relationship and God-like manipulation. Walker concludes that "on a very real level, *The Prime of Miss Jean Brodie,* in its plot and counterplot, depicts the anatomy of a betrayal."

> **Additional coverage of Spark's life and career is contained in the following sources published by Gale Research:** *Concise Dictionary of British Literary Biography, 1945-1960; Contemporary Authors,* Vols. 5-8, rev. ed.; *Contemporary Authors New Revision Series,* Vols. 12, 36; *Contemporary Literary Criticism,* Vols. 2, 3, 5, 8, 13, 18, 40; *Dictionary of Literary Biography,* Vols. 15, 139; *DISCovering Authors: British Edition; DISCovering Authors Modules: Most-studied Authors* and *Novelists; Major 20th-Century Writers;* **and** *Short Story Criticism,* **Vol. 10.**

# Ray Young Bear

## 19??-

American poet and novelist.

The following entry presents an overview of Young Bear's career.

## INTRODUCTION

One of the best known contemporary Native American writers, Young Bear is highly regarded for verse and prose in which he explores the conflicts arising between his Mesquakie heritage and his identity as a writer. Noting his attempts to recreate the Native American oral tradition, reviewers have praised Young Bear's emphasis on dreams, visions, and traditional Mesquakie songs in his poems. While Young Bear's principle theme is the contemporary Indian's search for identity, he deliberately addresses both Indian and non-Indian readers by writing on two levels—one allows the non-Indian reader to appreciate the imagery and traditions of the Mesquakie people without necessarily understanding their sacred tribal significance; the other level speaks to the Indian reader who recognizes the underlying meaning and can thus identify with Young Bear's thematic project. Young Bear is also one of the few tribal-affiliated writers who speaks and writes in his native language. His two best known and critically acclaimed works are *Winter of the Salamander* (1980) and *Black Eagle Child* (1992).

### Biographical Information

Young Bear was born and raised on the Tama Indian Reservation in Iowa, where his grandmother instructed him in the stories and traditions of his people. In the 1960s he attended college and began his writing career. With his wife Stella Young Bear, he co-founded the Woodland Song and Dance Troupe of Arts Midwest and became an instructor of Native American literature at the University of Iowa.

### Major Works

In *Winter of the Salamander* Young Bear utilizes various Indian songs, myths, and stories to address the plight of the Native American in contemporary American society. For example, in the poem, "i can still picture the caribou," Young Bear examines how Indians and whites have forgotten their origins, thus rendering meaningless the celebration of their ancient festivals and rites. The poetry of *The Invisible Musician* (1990) focuses on the present cultural, ethnic, artistic, and racial "invisibility" of Native Americans in American society, as seen in the poem "Wa ta se Na ka mo ni, Viet Nam Memorial." Because of the numerous references to tribal customs and culture, this work includes notes explaining many of Young Bear's allusions. In 1992 Young Bear published *Black Eagle Child,*

an autobiographical novel that took him twenty years to complete. The plot follows the life of Edgar Bearchild and his coming of age. Bearchild leaves the Black Eagle Child Settlement and his best friend, Ted Facepaint, in order to become a poet. After achieving some literary notoriety, Bearchild decides to come back to Black Eagle Child Settlement to continue his writing career. Upon his return, he realizes how becoming a poet has saved him from some of the dehumanizing effects that reservation life has had on his boyhood friend and his people.

### Critical Reception

Critical reaction to Young Bear's works has generally been favorable. Most critics applaud his imagery as colorful and provocative and praise his ability to effectively incorporate Mesquakie oral tradition into his poetry and prose. Several critics also comment on the unique literary character of *Black Eagle Child,* which employs autobiography, poetry, prose, letter-writing, and Native American oral tradition to tell the story of Edgar Bearchild's coming of age. While some critics suggest that the tone of much of his prose and poetry is too angry, and that some of his dream imagery is too self-centered, obscure, and lacking in general appeal, the majority of critics agree that Young Bear's writings offer valuable insights into the cultural heritage and struggle of contemporary Native Americans. Robert F. Gish has noted that Young Bear "is generally acknowledged by poets, critics, and students of American Indian literature as the nation's foremost contemporary Native American poet."

# PRINCIPAL WORKS

*Waiting to Be Fed*   (poetry)   1975
*Winter of the Salamander: The Keeper of Importance*
      (poetry)   1980
*The Invisible Musician*   (poetry)   1990
*Black Eagle Child: The Facepaint Narratives*   (novel)
      1992

# CRITICISM

### James Ruppert   (essay date 1980)

SOURCE: "The Uses of Oral Tradition in Six Contemporary Native American Poets," in *American Indian Culture and Research Journal*, Vol. 4, No. 4, 1980, pp. 87-110.

[*Former president of the Association for the Study of Native American Literatures, Ruppert is an educator and critic who specializes in English and Native studies. In the following excerpt, he analyzes Young Bear's attempts to recreate the Native American "story world" in his poetry, discussing his focus on song and dreams.*]

[Ray Young Bear's poems] do not speak of the old days, of a story world of "a long time ago" or "in the beginning"; rather, they bring that world into our reality. The old story world is a place and time when humans were finding out the power that other beings held—how they acted, and how that power and those unique creatures created the world as we know it today. Beings with power could transform themselves, separate parts of themselves, dominate time and space, create and destroy on a grand scale. While [Peter] Blue Cloud tries to put us in the *persona* of those story beings, Young Bear tries to have us experience that world—the powers, the perceptions and amazing occurrences germane to it. The time and world of the oral tradition is now, if we will just realize it. Not that the reader defeats monsters, but the powers and perceptions of that story world, those things that define it and give it meaning, are alive and rediscovered in the world today. This is the goal of many Native American poets, but Young Bear's uniqueness lies in his evocative use of composition and elements of the oral story as a form for his work. His poems use the fantastic events and perceptions of the story world to make new stories, rather than using these elements solely as subject.

In poems like **"The Cook,"** the woman has supernatural

powers and is instructed by her contact with those powers. She seems to have a direct power over the weather and an indirect power over any human that may come in contact with her. The poem **"The Way the Bird Sat"** presents a wind that is jealous, a bird that keeps watch and divides the season with song, and blue hearts in the form of a deer. In the animated universe of this poem, an unidentified narrator is guided by animal spirit power into visualizing and thus participating in a ceremony that transforms him into a hummingbird, the originator of his personal power. These occurrences are not unusual in oral tradition, nor are they unusual in Young Bear's work. Dogs climbing down from the sky on a cord of sunlight, a sun growing on someone's back, a face existing in a mouth and rocks with mouths are occurrences typical to Young Bear's poetry. Through these we feel that spirit, the power that accomplishes these miraculous occurrences and incredible transformations, is still here. It lies under the surface of our daily lives. We can touch that world and experience the story reality if we look hard enough, seek visions and believe. Young Bear's poems seem aimed toward changing those who he says [in **"For the Rain in March: The Blackened Hearts of Herons"**], "think that all they see is all they will ever see."

Many of Young Bear's images occur and recur in several poems as if they were resonant oral material trying to find an appropriate niche in the cultural mind. Many of these are hauntingly surreal images. However, the images come more from the story reality, the dream and the vision—peyote and otherwise—than from a European art form. Through this imagery, his poetry becomes vivid because the power of the story and the dream is present, an active force in the events and processes of the poem and the world. The visionary quality of the poetry is as haunting as the ghosts that seem to linger around his verbal campfires. The world of his poems is active, in the process of making itself. [He writes in **"Through Lifetime"**]:

> She combed my hair with wings of the seeking
>       owl
> she sang of spring birds and how brown running
>            waters
> would be a signal to begin family deaths by
>            witchcraft,
> she showed me a handful of ribs shining a land
>       dry

These actions are not so much metaphors as magical occurrences.

As the world is being created in poetry, there are two clear paths that help us achieve that old story world: (1) old traditional songs; since these songs have links to the old ways that are historically strong, they guide and train the listener, complete this world and tie us to the older oral one, (2) even more importantly for Young Bear's poetry, dreams and visions. Dreams put us in the experiential framework of the old culture and are an important part of the imaginative life of the oral. Dreams are life, or at least life on a special level. Visions are messages from the story reality and those who inhabit. They always imply implementation in the present, so they form an important link for us. Underneath it all lies spirit and the possibilities of transformation and power as real as in any story world.

---

**Young Bear's uniqueness lies in his evocative use of composition and elements of the oral story as a form for his work.**

*—James Ruppert*

---

While the stability of the songs in oral tradition is of vital importance, the songs of spirits, animals and winds remain incomplete, having never been completely translated into human language because they belong to those beings. The songs are their experience and their expression; they contain the essence of the story being. The poet speaks of these songs of the non-human, defining their domain and indicating the power these have through their songs. While Young Bear's central aim is to recreate the story world here, to guide us through new and sometimes inexplicable worlds, he is concerned with the songs of animal spirits, but not to the point where he will sing their songs. It is human song that is more central to Young Bear's poetry. In **"4 songs of life"** we explore the place of the old songs in life. For those who have them, they are sources of strength and pride; for those who don't, they are a teacher, the guide they need. Through them, they will grow strong. As one grows strong, his words will be released into various parts of the world. In this manner, the songs, the words carry on and are imbedded in new people. The word, as [N. Scott] Momaday sees it, is then carried on and spread; it becomes the life of the people and quenches their thirst. Literally, in **"Rushing"** the mother's words are associated with the rushing spring she finds; both gush forth and fulfill.

While the songs and words guide life, they also have the ability to guide the dead. In **"The Last Dream"** the old man, who spends his time singing the old songs and learning the ones he does not know, uses his talent to speak to the relatives of the dead, helping them understand and direct their lives. However, his real role is to direct the dead, to give them the "last dream" as they start on the ghost road. He must touch spirit, and in touching that, touch the other world. [In **"The Last Dream"** he writes]:

> . . .he knew it was wrong
> to ask them to go on, but he
> couldn't refuse lives that were already lost.
> Everybody
> counted on him. Each knew that
> if they died within his time,
> he would be the one to give away
> the last dream,
> the grandfather of all
> dream.

While Young Bear is interested in the dream and vision as an experience of the spirit world, he also sees it as a link between various levels of existence.

In the oral tradition, the dream or vision is often a message or precognition of events significant either to the individual or a people. Young Bear develops this in his poem **"From His Dream"** where the events of a man's dream are fulfilled in the subsequent death of his son. However, for Young Bear, the dream or vision isn't just one-way communication; we get the sense that each level of life is a dream and that they can communicate with other [in **"The Place of O"**]:

> at the funeral,
> the dead sorts you out
> from the rest and knows
> you are only pretending,
> tells you it is no
> longer important
> and sends you on
> to another dream
> of lesser importance.

The poem ends with the dream triumphing over death, since the dream is existence on whatever level you happen to have found yourself. For the woman with child in **"Waiting To Be Fed"** the dream is so real that she is seduced into the river's dream and passes that dream on to her daughter; however, her existence in the normal human level becomes an impossibility. The ability of the dream to create transformations makes a world of all possibilities for those in it and a confusion as to identity for those not in it. It is difficult to tell the creature one confronts in Young Bear's poems; it changes.

Moreover, there is a recurrent question of identity for the poet, as well as about the nature of things. Since transformations and movement between dreams seems possible, since we can enter and participate in the older story reality and recreate it here, who are we? Story or Reality? Where are our roots? Which world is our home, our place? There are so many possibilities, or as he says [in **"For the Rain in March"**], "I am always surprised at how many different minds drift across each other." In many of his poems it is difficult to know who the narrator is because the "I" transforms into various characters from everyday reality to dream and vision. [**"In Dream: the Privacy of Sequence"**] is a poem that begins and ends with dream. The poem almost reads like an origin story, yet the focus on the narrator shifts in and out, as if he were transforming. A Young Bear-like narrator admits to a certain confusion:

> I found myself between the airs
> of changing weather
> unable to distinguish what to kill, layers of
> wind over my eyes.

The poem exists somewhere between reality and dream/vision. The question of identity is more directly stated in another poem [**"For the Rain in March"**], "I will never know who I actually am."

Young Bear's total dedication to the form and substance of the old story reality is a distinguishing characteristic of his poetry. His poems are dreams and visions. They ask us to experience a spiritual reality in the manner of the oral tradition, yet if the transformation of our reality is complete, we lose the boundaries of self. Often it is hard to tell the visionary from the vision.

## Norma Wilson   (review date Summer 1981)

SOURCE: A review of *Winter of the Salamander: The Keeper of Importance,* in *World Literature Today,* Vol. 65, No. 3, Summer, 1981, pp. 515-16.

[*In the review below, Wilson praises* Winter of the Salamander, *stating that Young Bear's poetry "is best when he looks both inside himself and out at the world."*]

Ray Young Bear's first book [*Winter of the Salamander*] is impressive, his imagery precise. In **"grandmother"** the woman with "the purple scarf / and the plastic / shopping bag" is hardly the stereotypical Indian grandmother. At the same time she has a symbolic connection to the oldest part of the earth—"a voice / coming from / a rock."

While Young Bear's own people, the Mesquaki, have an ancestral bond with the earth, their present condition is fragmented, and despair permeates the poems. Young Bear's voice, alienated even from his own people, is poignant; in **"morning-water train woman"** the result of loving one's brother is attempted suicide. The title poem of the collection is about his people dying: "we'd like to understand . . . / . . . why the dead grow / in number, the role i play in speaking / to mouths that darken with swollen / gunpowder burns, chapped lips and alcohol."

Young Bear's honesty is commendable. However, while he recognizes some of the causes of the destruction of the earth and his people, he proposes no solutions.

> i tell the students
>
> . . . . .
>
> of the poison produced and distributed
> by their white fathers
> through the rivers
> and waters
> of the poison their babies
> will suck through the breasts
> of their mothers
> no one cares to know.
>                    **("three reasons for transgression")**

His poetry is best when he looks both inside himself and out at the world. In **"march eight/1979,"** the last poem in the collection, he offers some momentary peace, if not hope, in a family "bonded permanently by a child." The narrator wishes "to explain . . . my incredible joy / how my mixed depression was momentarily quelled" by seeing the eagles. Perhaps inadvertently Young Bear offers in this last poem some elucidation of the unity that is necessary if the healing process is to begin.

## Michael Sheridan   (review date Autumn 1981)

SOURCE: A review of *Winter of the Salamander,* in *Southwest Review,* Vol. 66, No. 4, Autumn, 1981, pp. 427-30.

[*In the following excerpt, Sheridan applauds* Winter of the Salamander *for its imagery and "ambition," but faults Young Bear for his political and social commentary and his emphasis on dreams.*]

Young Bear's book [*Winter of the Salamander*] is, I am sorry to say, seriously flawed. Too often Young Bear lapses into stilted or bloated language: "faraway trains ring the existence of time"; "i relinquished that i had been correct / in not going out to the night"; "we stood like lonely eagles / huddled against each other . . ." When Young Bear's poems make political or social commentary, they sometimes sound like letters-to-the-editor:

> . . . they're no different except for the side
> of railroad tracks they were born on
> and whatever small town social
> prominence they were born into.
> it is the same attitude shared by lesser
> intelligent animals who can't adapt
> and get along with their environmental
> surroundings.
>        [from **"in viewpoint: poem for 14 catfish and
>                     the town of tama, iowa"**]

Finally, many of Young Bear's poems are concerned with dreams, or contain dream passages; and while everyone is fascinated by his own dreams, it is awfully tedious having to listen to someone else's. Perhaps this is the reason psychoanalysts demand such handsome fees.

Despite these flaws, and after considerable wading, I still find a great deal to admire in Young Bear's book. He is capable, for example, of creating marvelous imagery:

> . . . old white wolves lying on their bellies
> gathered into a circle and eating the ground
> that bled as if it had been torn
> from an enemy's shoulder during battle
> or a child's heart
> suddenly coughed up without reason . . .
>        [from **"the crow children walking circles in
>                     the snow"**]

I admire, further, the range and ambition of this book. Young Bear can write convincingly about his family, his land, his culture—the spirit of his life. He does so in whole poems such as **"the woman's vision," "this house,"** and the title poem. There are also many poems with brilliant passages: **"before leaving me, the poem: eagle butte and black river falls"; "for the rain in march: the blackened hearts of herons";** and **"memories for no one,"** from which I quote the following stanza:

> it is morning and i have just
> closed the windows, the birds
> crowd on the branch and they signal
> each other: all of them sing directly
> into the one window that's open,
> simultaneously.
> my wife is still beading.
> the television voices remind me
> of the way people speak when death
> is present. it's soft and you can barely
> hear anything but you know it's
> important.

Ray Young Bear seems to me a gifted poet in search of a good editor.

## Paul N. Pavich   (review date February 1982)

SOURCE: A review of *Winter of the Salamander,* in *West-*

*ern American Literature,* Vol. XVI, No. 4, February, 1982, pp. 330-31.

[*In the following positive review, Pavich provides a thematic overview of* Winter of the Salamander.]

Ray Young Bear's volume of poetry, **Winter of the Salamander,** is the tenth in Harper and Row's Native American Publishing Program. The themes are those of much contemporary Native American literature: confusion, violence and death, despair and loss, anger. However, Young Bear exhibits a beautiful command of the language and an ability to elicit strong emotional responses. At times the impact of the imagery is itself like a blast from a shotgun. His landscape is filled with charred trees, half-dead animals, peeling faces, violated humans.

Much of the horror in these poems is a result of the inability of the white and Indian cultures to achieve any understanding at all. Young Bear's handling of the conflict of views ranges from the ironic to the bitter. In **"the character of our addiction"** he wryly notes that white culture has separated itself from the natural cycles and needs a machine to dictate the changing of the seasons:

> . . .the lawn mower speaks
> for everyone. to the majority
> of whites on this block
> it represents the spring.

In a number of other poems he depicts a white culture which has lost itself and its gods and seems bent on the destruction of life on this planet.

At the same time that he berates the whites, Young Bear shows his understanding of some of the contradictions of modern Indian culture. In **"i can still picture the caribou"** he reflects upon a tribal gathering:

> Seventy-five years ago, our places
> were probably filled with dance
> and constant prayer.
> breath made of the day's
> offering instead of alcohol.

The poetry reveals a painful awareness that for some individuals the festivals and dances have become empty forms which have lost their significance. In the Indian as well as the white world there are those who have forgotten their origins.

Despite the eschatological mood of many of the poems there is still a sense of reverence for the ancient traditions and for the land which sustains them. **"Four songs of life"** celebrates the continuance of life and the power of the ancient songs to create a sense of beauty, comfort and meaning. The first two songs are a contrast between a young man who is unsure of things and an old man who understands "the old hard tests of living." The last two songs are reflections on the strength of traditions to guide one through life.

While much of the poetry is concerned with the values of the Indian and white cultures there are also those which are considerations of the contemporary situation in general. There are poems on Vietnam, love, nature and dreams. Some are surrealistic visions loaded with startling meta-phors and bizarre scenes. Others seem to be stretchings of the language in an attempt to see what new effects might be achieved. Young Bear prepares the reader for all this from the very beginning. On the opening page of the book he states, "There are no elucidations or foresights / merely / experiments with words."

**Winter of the Salamander** is certainly not an easy night's reading of lyrical reflections on the romantic ways of native America. It is both an unsettling commentary on the problems of modern America and a vivid demonstration of Ray Young Bear's poetic talent.

### James Ruppert (essay date 1984)

SOURCE: "The Poetic Languages of Ray Young Bear," in *Coyote Was Here: Essays on Contemporary Native American Literary and Political Mobilization,* edited by Bo Schöler, Seklos, 1984, pp. 124-33.

[*In the following essay, Ruppert discusses Young Bear's poetic language, contending that it is "mediative," that it includes "a fusion of public and private voice," and that it "creates a persona in the process."*]

Contemporary American Indian writers are mediators. By that I do not mean that they are spokesmen or apologists for a cultural sphere, but rather that they are participants in two cultural and literary traditions. Through their work, they express amazing potential for synthesis and creation. They address two audiences—white and Indian, or maybe three—a local one, a pan-Indian one and a white one. This multiplicity of background and audience forces the work into a complex texture. In this complexity, the writer may utilize the epistemological structures of one culture to illuminate the other, stay within one code or change every other line. This incredible ability to move from one epistemological code to another is what I call mediation. It is the axis which generates the text producing a text which is a record of mediative discourse.

Ray Young Bear's poetic languages illustrate a range of response possible in mediation. While uniquely exploring the functions and processes of oral tradition as they emerge into print, Young Bear uses traditional Indian values and traditional Western ways of knowledge to express his insights. The contemporary Indian writer, especially the poet, must find a way to speak successfully to all the audiences and still hold his/her vision intact. That act and vision are not static reinterpretations of one's cultural traditions, but rather a dynamic constantly informing the text. American Indian writer Paula Allen [in 'Answering the Deer,' in *American Indian Culture and Research Journal,* Vol. 6, 1982] puts it this way:

> A contemporary American Indian is always
> faced with a dual perception of the world: that
> which is particular to American Indian life and
> that which exists ignorant of that life. Each is
> largely irrelevant to the other except where they
> meet—in the experience and consciousness of
> the Indian. Because the divergent realities must
> meet and form comprehensible patterns within
> Indian life, an Indian poet must develop meta-
> phors that will not only reflect the dual percep-

tions of Indian/non-Indian but that will reconcile them. The ideal metaphor will harmonize the contradictions and balance them so that internal equilibrium can be achieved, so that each perspective is meaningful and in their joining, psychic unity rather than fragmentation occurs.

The image must be completed in a mediation of language. A balancing metaphor must harmonize the divergent oral and written realities. While stressing oral form and content, one of Young Bear's special strengths is his consistent introduction of the function of oral tradition into mediation. His poetic languages are pulled toward various oral functions. A writer with a political motivation must create those balancing images, and yet speak to all his/her audiences. Young Bear's most powerful poetic language is built on a mediatory base which fuses oral functions with contemporary poetry.

For the purpose of analysis, one could isolate two discourse poles on the spectrum of oral tradition—ceremonial language and oratorical language. In a well-known piece, Allen has commented that 'the purpose of ceremony is to integrate: to fuse the individual with his or her fellows, the community of people with that of the other kingdoms and this larger communal group with the worlds beyond this one' ["The Sacred Hoop: A Contemporary Perspective," in *Studies in American Indian Literature,* edited by Paula Allen, 1983]. The individual's vision is expanded and he is restored to harmony. This general purpose is, of course, modified by the more specific purposes of individual ceremonies, but the bedrock function is to create and support the expanded community of beings. An essential element of this oral function is the individual's experience in the ceremony and the way in which that individual's experience is harmonized with the context of interrelated spirit. 'The person sheds the isolated, individual personality and is restored to conscious harmony with the universe' ['The Sacred Hoop']. The voice behind the Kachina mask speaks for all, not just himself. The experience of the ceremony guides the language and not the individual's expression. Ideally they should unite, but experience is the predominant element. It would be unthinkable for the voice behind the mask to complain about car payments. The purpose would be destroyed. Clearly, the experience of the speech act structures the language and meaning.

On the other hand, oratorical language is concerned with the singular expression of an individual. The function of the speech act is to define the individual as thinking and feeling in a way different from those around him. Any harmony or unified thinking that results must be built on the individual's message. The discourse is intended to influence the listener, and the language is one where expression dominates experience.

Two writers have addressed similar concerns provocatively. Writer-essayist Simon Ortiz discusses song in the oral tradition. He insists that rightly understood song is a fusion of expression and experience. Song should be appreciated as a whole. The experience of singing brings one into a position to perceive the essence of song as act as well as personal expression. We learn what we can express by ex-

---

**Young Bear uses traditional Indian values and traditional Western ways of knowledge to express his insights.**

*—James Ruppert*

---

periencing the context of the song. 'Language as expression and perception—that is at the core of what a song is. . . . Song at the beginning was experience. There was no division between experience and expression. . . . I express myself as well as realize the experience' [*Song, Poetry, and Language: Expression and Perception,* 1977]. He explains how one must learn to sing the song properly so as to realize the physical, mental, cultural and spiritual context that gives the song meaning. Viewed as prayer, then, song and, perhaps by extension, ceremonial language are ideally a unity of experience and expression. Yet, it is important to learn the song right, to follow the process by which the learner realizes the 'original meaning' of the song and thus situates himself in the context which makes the song meaningful and substantial. The function of song and of ceremonial language seems similar, and experience determines expression at some initial point. But perhaps it is inappropriate to make the extension from song to ceremonial language. Perhaps one should consider it as a mid-point between ceremonial and oratorical language with ramifications for written texts because of its ideal mediatory position.

In looking at a few old texts which straddle an oral and written tradition, Tzvetan Todorov identifies two modes of speech which seem to structure such intermediary texts—Speech-as-Action and Speech-as-Narrative. These ideas complement the terms of experience and expression because they attempt to place the discourse in an interactive context. He is concerned with the effect produced and how the words are uttered.

> First, in the case of speech-as-action, we react to the referential aspect of what is said [It is concerned with the act performed which is not simply the utterance of the words.] . . . Speech-as-action is perceived as information, speech-as-narrative as a discourse. Second, and this seems contradictory, speech-as-narratives derives from the constative mode of discourse, whereas speech-as-action is always performative. It is in the case of speech-as-action that the whole process of speaking assumes a primordial importance and becomes the essential factor of the message; speech-as-narrative deals with something else and evokes the presence of an action other than that of speech itself. [*The Poetics of Prose,* translated by Richard Howard, 1977]

For the purpose of discussion, one could see the two modes of speech as functioning similarly to the two poles of oral tradition, ceremonial language and oratorical language. Ceremonial language like speech-as-action centers on the primary importance of the act of speaking. The act of uttering, chanting and praying carries the meaning as much if not more than the words. It creates its own referential frame and seeks harmony with all-that-is by the very act. Experience leads and molds expression until they are one. On the other hand, oratorical language like speech-as-narrative points to something outside the speech act itself and calls for action on another plane. Its referential frame is fixed and somewhat expected since the speech act is seen in the context of a larger set of interactive discourse. The message is strongly conditioned by the speaker's intention and expression. This is not to say that oratorical language does not have prescribed rules of discourse, nor that either could ignore their common cultural and philosophical contexts, but that the speech act itself has varying goals and differing determinants within that context.

Young Bear's poetic languages are pulled toward these two poles. They dot the spectrum from discourse oriented oratorical language to the non-discourse story language that leans toward the ceremonial pole. In a previous essay, I tried to identify a group of poems that placed the reader in the epistemological frame of the old story reality [James Ruppert, "The Uses of Oral Tradition in Six Contemporary Native American Poets," in *American Indian Culture and Research Journal,* Vol. 4, 1980]. These story reality poems incorporate many of the elements of speech-as-action. Not that these poems are ceremonies, or that he of necessity uses traditional ceremonial words, but viewed from the function of the speech act, these poems come closest to the ceremonial pole of oral tradition. Poems such as **'the way the bird sat', 'the cook', 'in dream: the privacy of sequence'** and **'waiting to be fed',** to name a few, constitute a pole of poetic language which becomes intensely internal, metaphorical, surreal. The language and the images turn in upon themselves creating their own frame of reference. The poem may participate in larger mythical structures, but the reader must experience the immediacy of the poem first. It calls for a creative response on the part of the reader. In that experience of the poem and finding significance in it, the reader finds harmony in the many worlds of all-that-is. Of course, the nature of the response may vary with the different audiences addressed in the text, but the reader is placed perceptually in the middle of a story/myth in the making, and the reader must let the mythic logic take over. A reader may sense the power of the piece, but remain uncertain of its exact significance until he allows his mythic imagination to grasp the story. The reader must experience the story and the experience of it determines the meaning of the reader. The poem is performative, it is speech-as-action.

In poems like **'in viewpoint: poem for 14 catfish and the town of tama, iowa',** Young Bear is attracted toward the oratorical pole and discourse begins to dominate the text. The poetic voice attempts to overtly influence the reader. The poetic language surges through expression. The language points outward to a frame of reference easily identifiable, one that exists before the speech act enclosed in the text of the poem. Here is a section of that poem:

> but the farmers and the local whites
> from the nearby town of tama and surrounding
> towns, with their usual characteristic
> ignorance and disregard, have driven noisily

> over the ice and across our lands
> on their pickups and snowmobiles
> disturbing the dwindling fish
> and wildlife—
> and due to their
> own personal greed and self-
> displeasure in avoiding the holes
> made by tribal fishermen in
> search of food (which would die
> anyway because of the abnormal weather),
> the snowmobilers ran and complained
> like a bunch of spoiled and obnoxious children
> to the conservation officer, who, with
> nothing better to do along with a deputy
> sheriff and a highway patrolman, rode out
> to tribal land and arrested the fishermen
> and their catfish.

The sense of injury, indictment and violation call out clearly to the reader. The poem goes on to develop a political point about racism and society in a public and political language. The oratorical functions are fulfilled as the poem strives to reinforce cultural and social cohesiveness. Yet, expression predominates experience. The reader's mythic imagination is not engaged, and he is not brought to a new experience in the text. He integrates the discourse into his own defined frame of reference, at once common and public.

However, much of his poetry, perhaps most, falls somewhere between the two poles of attraction. At these points, the texts become records of mediative discourse, not only between the two oral language poles, but also between the epistemological positions and contemporary American poetry. I would like to refer to this position of the text as mediatory language, and I think this is what Allen refers to when she speaks of the image unifying world-views, or Ortiz' Acoma ideal of perception and expression merging. These poems construct their own frames of reference while pursuing expression through linkage with existing frames. They encourage the reader's experience while they express. As an example of these poems, I would like to look at the poem **'all day i have seen you'.**

> it would have to be a very good reason.
> i would see you off and then the next thing
> i'd know you'd be gone, permanently.
> everything that is us is represented
> by secondhand furniture.
> i keep thinking i can withstand it.
> it's easy to sit towards the east
> on a summer evening, erasing the memory
> of your absence with a cold beer.
> all thoughts centered on the bird's airway.
> the small dish of food which i placed
> by the stream last summer was the closest
> and only thing i did to remind the dead
> and the sacred of my presence.
>
> once, a one-eyed rabbit came right up
> to me and i greeted it. another time,
> a ground squirrel ate its way through
> the plastic garbage bag. it dragged out
> a photograph of us holding each other
> both of our eyes lost in miscarriage
>
> it would have to happen on a dull grey day
> like this. i like to make myself believe

that i will have things planned long before
you have notions of leaving me.

you walk towards me from the west
with your head bowed down. the sound
of a bicycle leaves behind you. all day
i have seen you hanging clothes.
as you walk toward me you lose your
footing and i catch you by your wrists.

i ask how you see me. i always thought
you were kind. you know that one boy who
everybody thinks is a pervert? he's going
to wait for me until i finish school.

a tall and lone figure comes out
from the house and we hide behind
the station wagon, swatting mosquitoes
with the one towel which i eventually
give to you, i don't trust him. he is
good friends with the fly now
in sioux city.
how do you see me?

There are many aspects of the poem which mark it as contemporary American poetry. The notes of alienation and searching for identity are clear and characteristic. The audience is presented with a direct, personal voice which tends to transform the public voice into the personal. The poem presents a struggle with what in Western psychological tradition we would call the ego. The voice of the poems seeks identity outside itself as the voice questions an ego definition. On a personal level, the poem strives to unify the subjective (how one is perceived by others and oneself) with the objective (one's true identity).

The voice in the poem ties identity with a sense of its own control and capacity to dominate events. Clearly, as it does so, it reveals a fear that the attempt to control events such as the other person's leaving, will be in vain much as the attempt to define identity. This fear could, of course, have roots in man's existential fear of letting things outside himself define and dominate him. Subsequently, much of the poem seems to be the ego defending itself from destruction. The breaking point of the fear comes when the 'you' approaches the speaker, stumbles and is caught by the wrist. The definition of identity linked to ego-control gives way to one of inter-relatedness, of tentative connections, of a fall checked in mid-air, of two together with the loss of a miscarriage. With its emphasis on ego and identity, the poem encourages the audience to read it in terms of Western psychological thought and contemporary poetic practice.

---

**For Young Bear, the world of values is in harmonious existence, and it is the individual who has momentarily separated himself from the Web that connects the Sacred to human relations.**

**—James Ruppert**

---

Yet, when contemporary American poets meet this question, they tend to adopt a schizophrenic approach. They feel that the non-ego parts of self have value because of their more natural connection with immanent values in the world around us. Consequently, they often pursue ways to merge the unconscious or personally mythic with nature. These poets of pre-sense seek the experience of immanent values in the world, unsure of where to find them. Yet they must retain ego to create poems, and poems have value. Their solution is to create a poetry whose purpose is to put the reader and poet in a position to find value himself.

For Young Bear, the existence of those immanent values is an unstated assumption. The world of values is in harmonious existence, and it is the individual who has momentarily separated himself from the web that connects the sacred to human relations such as those with the person who may be leaving and the tall person who is not trusted. He questions to reestablish connections, not to create new ones. It is not the psychological state of the poet that is important, but the act of the poem. He questions to allow for some tentative unity. In Western terms he asks the people around him for self-definition while in keeping with the Indian code assuming that identity extends from the web of inter-relatedness. Thus, the poem encompasses the function of ceremony as Allen has described it—to bring the individual into harmony with all-that-is, reaffirming a place the individual always had. The assumption of an Indian epistemological stance predominates the poem while contemporary poetic codes are utilized to create mediation.

Also the poem emphasizes the multiple significance of event as much Indian tradition does. The animal references in the second stanza take on personal and mythical significance after the poet mentions centering his thoughts on the natural medium between birds and nature. This realm is traditionally associated with spirit, and the poet's sense of separation from the sacred deepens the context in which to see his interaction with animals. They seem full of message, of tentative painful connections which the poet still holds. The animal, human and spirit realms all conspire to encourage the questioning of the poet. Only through the questioning can the separation be eliminated.

With this in mind, the tentative union in the last stanza takes on added significance. While feeling a certain alienation from the natural, spiritual and communal worlds, the 'you' and 'I' of the poem meet, united by fear, perhaps outside the communal web as represented by the tall man and his friend. This tentative union is paralleled by the potential union of the outcast boy and the 'you', or by the picture of the two together 'lost in miscarriage'. The last stanza reminds us that appearances are not always true as the boy is not a pervert, but really kind and patient. The merely social definition of identity is discredited. Another untrusted character *the fly* is mentioned. His name is written in italics perhaps to emphasize his mystery or mythical connections. This character's apparent spiritual and animal definition of identity is not to be trusted. However, the tenuous union at the end does give rise to some hope, some connectedness beyond the value of mere questioning. With this balance of union and doubt, the final question increases in resonance.

Viewed psychologically, the moment of union provokes a renewal of the internal questioning 'How do you see me?' aimed at the 'you' of the poem. Viewed from a mediatory angle, the reader must see that the definition of identity is not only existential. Traditional American Indian thought encourages the individual to participate in identity defined more through social and cultural terms than through personal terms. While the final question seems ostensibly aimed at one person, the poem explores a satisfactory sense of identity on a larger plane. As the union at the end of the poem carries a wider significance than the merely personal, so does the question. A good case could be made that it is addressed to the reader, but that again locks a definition of identity into a narrow, Western sense. Since it follows after some tentative connections to the web of interrelations from which the poet has felt alienated, we could see it as a non-restrictive question, one addressed to the powers of interrelation, the harmony, the sacred, the community—all at once. This stance would be very much in keeping with traditional Native American assumptions about harmony and identity.

The final image of the two hiding behind the station wagon and the final question express the characteristics of mediation—cross-illumination of epistemological codes. The image also functions to harmonize the contradictions between two perspectives as described by Allen. The questioning psychological code is fulfilled while the holistic a-psychological code is implied and satisfied.

Also the poet's expression of his feelings, his attitude fuses with his perception of his relation to the universe around him. One determines and complements the other. The situation is much as Ortiz's father thinks of song: 'My father teaches that a song is part of the way you're supposed to recognize everything, that the singing of it is a way of recognizing this all-inclusiveness because it is a way of expressing yourself and perceiving. It is basically a way to understand and appreciate your relationship to all things [*Songs, Poetry, and Language*]. The more he expresses himself, the more he perceives his relationship to all things. The question at the end has grown in meaning until it expresses the poet's tentative connection to the all-inclusive, and ultimately the poet seeks to define himself in its terms.

---

**Young Bear and many other Indian writers write what has been called "protest poetry." In this poetic language, expression dominates. The voice is strongly public.**

—*James Ruppert*

---

In the mediation of the poem, the distinction Todorov makes between speech-as-action and speech-as-narrative

becomes modified by the two poles of oral tradition functions. While the poem may lean toward the ceremonial function and an identification with speech-as-action, it does break out of its referential frame. The message being communicated is as important as the act of speaking. Yet this apparent speech-as-narrative aspect is mediated by the fact that the speaking of the poem is an integral part of its message. The poem has successfully harmonized traditional functions. The process of questioning in the poem and the act of writing the poem are essential in helping the individual understand his place in the universe. The Indian frame of reference which supplies context for speech-as-action gives meaning to the message of the speech-as-narrative discourse. In Ortiz's words, perception is expression. The poem and its images harmonize the various perceptual worlds, and a mediation has occurred.

One may rightly ask how all this fits into the topic of this volume—political mobilization. I hope to make that clear shortly. It is certain from the foregoing discussion that Young Bear is a man of many talents, many languages. His poetry is pulled between two poles by the demands and functions of an oral tradition and conditioned by contemporary poetry. At one end, Young Bear and many other Indian writers write what has been called 'protest poetry'. In this poetic language, expression dominates. The voice is strongly public, and the statement while powerful, is expected. The reader has a ready frame of reference in which to place the semantic message, and he recognizes the text as discourse, or the speaker's visible attempt to influence the reader. The presentation of the message is less important than the expression of the message. The reader then accepts the discourse or not. This speech-as-narrative invokes the presence of political and social problems to indite and confront. Those readers, Indian or white, that agree with the expression and have had similar experiences previous to the poem, may be ready to mobilize for action.

At the other end of the spectrum, Young Bear's story reality poems exist as speech-as-action. They contain an unidentifiable narrator. The expression merges with perception and the ceremonial functions of oral tradition are fulfilled as the poem sets the reader into the story reality. The poems create their own referential frame, and the reader must develop his mythic imagination to participate in meaning. In this poetic language, oral tradition may be more completely reproduced. Indian and white readers may be mobilized to value oral tradition more as they participate in it on a wider and more conscious level. Political mobilization on the basis of an increased appreciation and dedication to Indian cultures may result. Yet, the referential frame created by these poems may be too restricted and subjective to motivate a wide readership into any immediate or effective political action.

I would argue that those poems that express the poetic language of mediation effectively and convincingly encourage political mobilization. Political poetry must recognize foremost the tremendous gulf between the ideals of one's position and the grimy reality which does not admit those ideals, or perhaps only in a debased form. Political poetry must profoundly engage the reader's sympathies, if not his political allegiance. It must move from within the reader's social and epistemological code and transform it. Ideals make dualists of us all, but the most effective position that Young Bear and other Indian writers can take is a mediatory position which does not let social conflict remain abstract and predictable, nor invites self-righteous judgements. Equally ineffective for political purposes is a poetry that circles around ideals, creating a world with a narrow referential frame. One solution might be to acknowledge that differing poetic languages may be useful for reaching different audiences, matching language and political goal, but a lasting and powerful poetic ethic that unites audiences must be built on a broad mediatory base.

Young Bear's poems of mediative discourse build on a fusion of public and private voice. They create a persona in the process of defining self. The projected results of political mobilization in the social world find ready parallel in the remaking of the self imaginatively. His struggle gives meaning and authority to any pursuit of a new alignment of the social order. The reader is brought into a new frame of reference and his perception is educated while mediated. As with **'all day i have seen you'**, the reader is encouraged to epistemologically grow with the poet to realize the harmony Allen speaks of and in it to value American Indian experience more fully. Such a poetic language is conditioned by a sense of drama and conflict. Such a poetic persona can speak to society, not just lament the impersonal fiendish forces of society, nor dwell purely in idealized mythic worlds. When a poet desires political mobilization, he must speak with two tongues, see with two sets of eyes.

## Ray A. Young Bear with Joseph Bruchac (interview date 1987)

SOURCE: "Connected to the Past," in *Survival This Way: Interviews with Native American Poets,* Sun Tracks and The University of Arizona Press, 1987, pp. 337-48.

[*Bruchac is an Abenaki poet, short story writer, novelist, author of children's books, editor, educator, and critic. In the following excerpt, Young Bear discusses the development of his literary style and his use of Indian heritage and oral traditions in the composition of his works.*]

[*Bruchac*]: *Ray, I'd like to ask you a couple of very simple questions. First, when did you start writing?*

[Young Bear]: I think in 1964, to be exact. I was in seventh grade then, and we were given an assignment by the English teacher to compose an essay on our family lives or something to that effect. So, I went home and wrote my paper—or what I thought was a paper—and the next day I went back to class and handed it in to the teacher. I then found out that my essay wasn't among those to be read that day. It came back with a lot of red marks on it, and I got discouraged because this was my first year out from the Bureau of Indian Affairs day school. At that moment I realized just how far I had to go as far as trying to write the English language and write it well. From that day on in the seventh grade I tried to make it a point to learn the English language, write it, and think in it, while at the same time trying to present some aspects of Mesquakie culture—without dealing with sensitive material. . . .

*The Statement was made on the dust jacket of your book of poems,* **Winter of the Salamander,** *that you think your poems in Mesquakie and then translate them into English. Is it true that you use or used that method of composition?*

I think that in the beginning when I was trying to write I started out first in the Mesquakie language. I found out that most of our language translated almost . . . backward. So I used that method for a while and found it to be very successful, especially when I compared my translated poems with those which were being written then, around 1969, the period of Robert Bly—who has been a great influence on my poems. I liked the type of poems being written in the late '60s. I thought that some of my translations had, in some form or another, a connection to what they were writing. So, I did think some of my poems out in Mesquakie in the beginning. Lately, though, I think they all come out in English. Which reminds me of something that happened recently, and I would like to share it since it has reference to translating. An interesting example, anyway. Not too long ago, I submitted what I thought was a very good poem, **"The Language of Weather"** to *Another Chicago Magazine.* It came back with small notations on it to the effect that it was "abstract." I forget the editor's name. I was a bit let down by this because this was the fifth or sixth time this poem had been sent out. I keep a very good record of where my poems go and I keep more or less a collage of rejections to keep myself aware of how literary-minded people look upon *real* Native American poetry: poetic/cultural injustice and so forth. Anyway, once I got this rejection sheet I sat down and said "What will they publish?" I thought *ACM* had once published Ortiz and Harjo, so I whimsically asked myself, "What am I doing wrong?" So I sat down one day and thought, "Well, I'm going to write a poem out in Mesquakie and see what happens." I started talking to myself and seeing how best a poem could be translated from Mesquakie. I wrote four little poems, probably about ten lines each, typed them out—I think I did this in an hour—sent them and in two weeks I got an acceptance from *Another Chicago Magazine.* But, I am wondering whether one has to do this all the time, whether one has to revert to what I read recently in *The American Book Review* called "Ugh talk."

*Robert Penn Warren did that in his Chief Joseph book, a book which I don't particularly like.*

To me it is kind of a negative term, but it does make a little bit of sense because I just wrote it from the basics. Whatever—the point is, I didn't touch it up, use hard words, or surrealistic images. Just realistic images, simple ideas of how facets of tribal life are. But that really surprised the hell out of me when the poem got accepted so quickly.

*That makes me think of a number of things. One of them is my original second question. Where do you get the ideas for your poems? Where do your poems come from, both in the idea sense and the other sense of where poems come from?*

I think that poems come from a series of complex and intertwining graphic images which, in one form or another, somehow resembles what is for me the poetic, free verse form. Let's take the most recent poem that I've had published, **"The King Cobra as Political Assassin,"** written on May 30th, 1981, and published by *Triquarterly* this year. It was a poem written mostly out of frustration because that year I was having some difficulty trying to come up with ideas of how I should write a poem and where the inspiration was going to come from. I had this dream the day before Ronald Reagan was shot by Hinckley, so I started this poem called **"The King Cobra as Political Assassin"** based upon that dream. I think it wasn't necessarily the idea that I was prescient. I wasn't thinking I was that. I was just trying to find a subject to write about. So I connected that dream to the attempted assassination. What came out of it was something I really liked because in it I discussed the fact that in the dream I was somewhere else apart from the Mesquakie Settlement and in the dream these two serpents were fighting in land which I had assumed to be land purchased by my Ukimau (Sacred Chief) grandfather. So I valued this dream a lot, but as far as trying to connect it to the Reagan deal, the poem was in reality just a statement on real estate and the need for investments in land. (chuckles)

---

**I sort of tie in dreams, some of my own imagery and my thoughts and, on rare occasions, something I heard which my Grandmother said—how we are connected to the past.**

**—*Ray Young Bear***

---

*I love that! You know, the story of the Mesquakie people regaining that part of their land where the settlement now is—having it taken away and then purchasing it back—is a great inspiration. They sold their horse herd, didn't they, to buy back their own land?*

Yes, land was purchased but the "horse herd" story has been stretched out a bit; it was a cash transaction. Anyway, that's how that particular **"King Cobra"** poem came about. But I sort of tie in dreams, some of my own imagery and my thoughts and, on rare occasions, something I heard which my Grandmother said—how we are connected to the past. Once in a great while, whether I am socializing in a university or an Indian tavern with my friends, I sometimes find out that some of my friends are great bearers of poetic images, even though they don't realize it. So I listen with keen interest and, in a sense, I can see that everyone in an Indian community is a poet of sorts. That's where I get my images, my poems, from—from just about anything.

*Can I ask you a few questions about who your primary influences were, as far as poets go?*

I think my primary influences developed in the summer of 1968, when I was in an Upward Bound program at Luther College in Decorah, Iowa, and at Bemidji, Minnesota, where they were having a midwestern poets' and writers'

conference. There I met Robert Bly, David Ignatow, David Ray, and John Milton, and several other very important people. They were there and why I decided to go I don't know. The Upward Bound people and English Department people at Luther College decided that perhaps going to a writers' conference and being around literary people would be a good influence.

I was impressed by the talk about poetry, the reading of poetry, and the teaching of poetry, mostly through Robert Bly. At that time I think I was more involved with just trying to make proclamations as to who I was, trying to get my identity lined. I had a manuscript of some sorts—at about eighteen years of age I had about a twenty-page manuscript—and one night Robert Bly along with David Ray invited me to their room and I took my poems. They started looking at my poems and started crossing lines off and editing it on the spot. I had no idea what they were doing until they started telling me word for word exactly what was going on, saying things like "Don't use i-n-g all the time!" I said, "Okay." "Don't use hard words!" I said, "Okay." They told me a bunch of other things which I still use to this day.

*Yes. They did it to me, too! (laughter) The same two people!*

So I left the conference with great enthusiasm for poetry. That fall I went out to college in California and, even though I didn't know many of the poets then, since I was very new to the field, I started going to various poetry readings sponsored by the school. Among those reading there whose works I looked upon with great interest and respect were Diane Wakoski, Seamus Heaney, and Galway Kinnell. They had quite an array of these people coming in—oh, and Charles Bukowski. I went to all their readings and tried to absorb some of what they were saying. But I discovered that they had limitations, such as the absence of one's roots—which Native Americans have. So I said, "Well, maybe I can say something else a little better than what they're trying to do," which was this aboriginal, primal sort of poetry. Those people were probably the first influence, but since 1969 or '70 I don't read too many people any more. I'm not trying in desperation to keep up with who won the Pulitzer Prize this year and so forth, even though I did go into a poetry class—for one day—with Donald Justice and found out that I didn't belong in workshops. Or vice versa. On that same level, with no offense to anyone, I don't read the work of my tribal contemporaries. Because of my cultural and geographic isolation, my access to anyone's work is limited to what comes in free via the U.S. mail.

*I'd like to ask you about your first real book of poetry* **Winter of the Salamanders.** *I believe that you signed a contract for it at least four or five years before it was actually published. Is that correct?*

Yes.

*It was published by Harper & Row in 1980. How was it that it took such a considerable amount of time from the signing of the contract to the actual publication?*

Well, let's see. I called Douglas Lattimer in New York and asked him what my chances would be of signing on with the Native American Publishing Program at Harper & Row. He responded by saying that, since he liked by work, admired it, the chances would be very good that they would accept. So I told him that I would send him a manuscript that I had, which was only about fifty pages long. I sent it and told him that I had some more poems forthcoming. He accepted it and sent a contract and a small advance. So, at a time when a writer should be enthusiastic and celebrating the fact that they had just gotten a contract, I thought that I had just taken on a heavy load. I began to see my inadequacies with the English language and in terms of how poems should be written correctly. It was, more or less, a sense of underestimation which is, I think, a congenital thing. So I kept writing and pushed myself to get this manuscript off to him. Six months went by and I was still working on the first sixty pages I had sent him and another year went by and I was still working on them. Then another year went by . . . and another year went by . . . and I was still communicating with him and he was glad, at least, that I was still working on it. Finally, when the time came to send the whole manuscript, I found he was no longer involved with Harper & Row. He told me the program was being transferred to San Francisco and he gave me a new address. Then I started communicating with a whole series of new people who, I must say, were very, very patient with my work and still are. Finally, in the winter of 1979, I looked at the third or fourth galleys and thought, "I can no longer be a poet at this point, I can no longer be a critic from a tribal or a literary point of view." As an old English professor by the name of Loren Taylor at the University of Northern Iowa used to tell me, "Just get the stuff out. To hell with it." Meaning to hell with my insecurities. It took me five years, but that's how I actually felt in the last leg. A painful gestation for an ordinary, lackluster birth.

*How do you feel about the book now?*

That's a good question because I was going over it the past few days before this reading at Iowa State University and trying to pick out some poems I thought would be appropriate. I only read one poem, **"Grandmother,"** which I take great pride in, and as for the rest, somehow, I consider the rest of the poems experimentation. I'm not too satisfied with my work. As I said, there's a sense of underestimation that prevails in each stage of my writing. I know that within the course of time I'll develop some sort of aim and I think **Winter of the Salamander** is merely a stepping-stone toward higher things and better experience.

*One of the poems in the book, **"For the Rain in March,"** is a response to the poem "Pow-wow" by W. D. Snodgrass. An African writer named Chinua Achebe once said that he wrote his first novel* Things Fall Apart *because he read a book about his native Nigeria* Mr. Johnson, *by the English writer Joyce Cary, Cary's book was such a terrible representation of his people and his culture that Achebe felt he had to set the record straight. It strikes me that **"For the Rain in March"** comes from a similar feeling on your part.*

Iowa State University Press published one of my poems in an anthology of poets that have been around the Iowa region at one time or another and this poem by Snodgrass was, appropriately or inappropriately, placed right next to

me. I took great offense to this poem. I believe, at least, that is where I first read it.

*It's also included in his second book* After Experience. *It's a pretty well-known poem.*

Perhaps, then, it is in there. I think that is the motivation which started me writing the short segment on him. After reading the poem, I was just amazed at how someone could go to a powwow, pay the standard admission fee, and think that the whole world of the Mesquakie people was going to be revealed to him in one program, when the fact of the matter is that these dances performed by the Mesquakie people are just tribal celebration dances. Snodgrass thought he saw a lot more than he did—especially when he thought he could make it a poetic commentary about the singers, some of the children, the songs. To degrade a form of tribal entertainment was, to me, a great slap in the face to the Mesquakies. I knew that a lot of the Mesquakie people who were the subjects of this poem were not going to read it at all. So I thought I would do an "eye for an eye" sort of thing and write some negative commentary back to him and hopefully he would see it somewhere along the line and know that we weren't as simple-minded and savage, I guess, as he put it in his poem.

### Robert F. Gish    (review date May-June 1990)

SOURCE: "Retrieving the Melodies of the Heart," in *The Bloomsbury Review,* Vol. 10, No. 3, May-June, 1990, p. 9.

[*Gish is an American educator and critic of Choctaw and Cherokee descent. In the following review, he favorably assesses* The Invisible Musician.]

Mesquakie poet Ray A. Young Bear is generally acknowledged by poets, critics, and students of American Indian literature as the nation's foremost contemporary Native American poet. His first book, **Winter of the Salamander,** brought together a powerful grouping of Young Bear's poetry which had appeared first in relatively obscure literary journals and then, with more and more frequency, in leading national publications.

Soon after the appearance of **Salamander,** academic organizations and their annual conferences scheduled sessions on Young Bear and his startlingly atavistic yet modern word way. Courses in American Indian literature soon adopted his book, and, in the wake of such national accolades and attention, Young Bear was invited to teach in southwestern and far western schools and universities. Closer to home, he was invited to teach a course in American Indian literature as part of the American Studies program at the University of Iowa.

Now, with the publication of his second book of poems, **The Invisible Musician,** Young Bear is destined for even wider and more fulsome recognition (and I say this quite matter of factly) as a national treasure. Certainly Iowans must hail him with their own special exclamations of admiration, their own cheers of "Hurray! Hot damn! and Holy Cow!" —for here is a true native son who has already brought much honor to his Mesquakie settlement, his Red Earth family, and his fellow Iowans. As he hits his maturity, he promises to become even more widely known during the 1990s, especially among general readers, promises to become more visible to those who—through no fault or volition of their own—have not given Young Bear the notice he and his poetry so much merit.

It is imperative to mention this ironic discrepancy between Young Bear's esteemed national status in poetry circles and his relative invisibility in Iowa and the American popular mind. For "invisibility" (dare we tag it "insensitivity" or "ignorance") of various kinds—artistic, cultural, racial, ethnic, ecological, etc.—is a major theme, a tonic chord in the forty-odd poems which comprise *The Invisible Musician.*

Anyone who lives in our media-enhanced world, who at least partially subsists on the national diet of consumerism and materialism, athletic icons, and mall rituals of seasonal sales, knows that beyond the jingles and slogans of advertising and the crashing cacophonies of rock music, poetry is a hard sell. And yet—part of Young Bear's beautiful concern in *Musician*—poetry is as close to our heartbeat, as profound and eternal as the migrations of waterfowl, as moving as the mysterious chants of pond frogs or crickets on a summer's eve, as portentous and invigorating as an approaching storm.

And if, in today's Yuppie-driven acquisitiveness, the essences of more primal, aboriginal connections and rhythms are drowned out by automotive and industrial machinery, no wonder that the Native American way, its earth-rooted reverences, myths, dreams, ceremonies, and songs, are relegated to stereotype and stylization. All the more reason to listen to, to tune in to, to hear Young Bear and his anguished longing to simultaneously relearn the old songs and perpetuate them among his own Sac and Fox people, and—a true occasion for thanksgiving—share them with those of us more removed from primal doings by canned language and through Americanized (dare we say trivialized?) "stuff."

---

**Young Bear's gift is to sing—at times in celebration, often in lament—of assimilations accepted and thwarted. He is at once of this country, its citizen and before it—standing beside his grandfathers.**

**—*Robert F. Gish***

---

Young Bear's own attempts to relocate and recenter the invisible melodies and words, the voicings and intonations, of his ancestral Mesquakie music have not been without struggle. The marginality of contemporary Indian life is much documented by sociologists whose case studies of the alleged vanishing American undergird much contemporary social scientific description and explanation.

Young Bear's gift is to sing—at times in celebration, often in lament—of assimilations accepted and thwarted. He is

at once of this country, its citizen, and before it—there, standing beside his grandfathers, letting their hopes and dreams, their superstitions and songs of wisdom and prophecy guide him back to "memories" of his past and extrapolated future. Less completely, and inevitably so, Young Bear's music and his role as musician reaffirm the more general, Anglo-European American myth which is, remember it or not, appropriate it or not, inseparable from and inextricably linked to the aboriginal voice, to what William Carlos Williams, whose own modern verse owed much to American Indian oral traditions, called the "satyric dance."

The late Richard Hugo, who knew modern poetry and modern poets, once observed about Young Bear that he spoke with a voice thousands of years old. In part, this is due to Young Bear's conceiving the world poetically—imagistically, rhythmically. In part it is due to Young Bear's bilingualism, his ability to think of his poetry in his ancient Algonquin tongue and speak it or translate it into the accessibilities of English.

In doing so, in *Salamander* and now in *Musician,* the effect is a transportation which allows modern non-Indian readers to catch a glimmering of pure WORD, pure language, in a kind of atemporal, projected, eternalized moment. There is a feeling, when reading Young Bear's poetry, when listening to him listen to his ancient and primal urgings and melodies, of transcendence—of, in a word (and again I use this particular word intending no overstatement), of sacrality. It is a feeling of and for the sacredness of WORD—of inherent music, of poetry. In this special sense, *Musician* is not just another book of poetry, it is an awe-inspiring event in honor of the human mind and soul and heart to comprehend and exceed itself through WORD.

Such profundity in Young Bear's verse is often itself invisible. Many of his poems are five and six pages long—and divided into intriguingly complex parts; some poems, especially his Mesquakie love songs, are quite short—and disarmingly simple. Here is one such song:

> Ne to bwa ka na,
> bya te na ma wi ko;
> ne to bwa ka na,
> bya te na ma wi ko;
> ne to bwa ka na,
> bya te na ma wi ko.
>
> Ne a ta be swa
> a ta ma
> sha ske si a.
>
> Ne to bwa ka na,
> bya te na ma wi ko.
>
> My pipe
> hand it over to me
> my pipe,
> hand it over to me,
> my pipe,
> hand it over to me.
>
> I shall light and inhale
> tobacco
> for the single woman.

My pipe,
hand it over to me.

In the beauty of its tribal sound and rhythms, **"Mesquakie Love Song,"** as in numerous other traditional translations and renderings in *Musician,* Young Bear's voice as leader of his own Woodland Song & Dance Troupe of Arts Midwest (co-founded with his wife Stella), sings out strong and vibrantly, as if from a settlement powwow or some other ancient, now encoded and repeated love yearning and resolve.

Such ancient updatings are complemented throughout *Musician* by contemporary dirges apropos of the angst of modern America—Indian and non-Indian. In **"Wa ta se Na ka mo ni, Viet Nam Memorial,"** a poem which reflexively reiterates the volume's title, Young Bear bridges the ancient and the modern as only his atavistically contemporary vision and voice can do:

> Last night when the yellow moon
> of November broke through the last line
> of turbulent Midwestern clouds,
> a lone frog, the same one
> who probably announced the premature spring
>    floods,
> attempted to sing,
> Veterans' Day, and it was
> sore throat weather.
> In reality the invisible musician
> reminded me of my own doubt.
> The knowledge that my grandfathers
> were singers as well as composers—
> one of whom felt the simple utterance
> of a vowel made for the start
> of a melody—did not produce
> the necessary memory or feeling
> to make a Wa ta se Na ka mo ni,
> Veterans' Song.
> All I could think of
> was the absence of my name
> on a distant black rock.
> Without this monument
> I felt I would not be here.
> For a moment I questioned why I had to im-
>    merse
> myself
> in country, controversy, and guilt;
> but I wanted to honor them.
> Surely, the song they presently
> listened to along with my grandfathers
> was the ethereal kind which did not stop.

So too is the music, the poetry of the Mesquakie Settlement's own, of Iowa's, of the nation's own—Ray A. Young Bear: the "ethereal kind" which links us all to the old verities recognized by Young Bear's colleague across time, John Keats. Keats sensed (not all that many years ago as poesy goes) the shadow of the magnitude behind the phenomenon of perceiving the Elgin Marbles; or, as a first-time reader of Chapman's Homer, aligned himself with the men of "stout Cortez," struck to silence on a peak in Darien by their first sight of the Pacific. Keats shared Young Bear's own remembered, prescient revelations when listening to the silence of a Grecian Urn, another "invisible musician": The truth, the beauty, the "ethereal music" of poetry is united and eternal.

## Douglas Glover    (review date 12 April 1992)

SOURCE: "A Dancer at the World's Rim," in *Los Angeles Times Book Review,* April 12, 1992, p. 10.

[*Glover is a Canadian writer, educator, and critic whose short story collection* A Guide to Animal Behavior *was nominated for the Governor General's Literary Award in 1991. In the following favorable review of* Black Eagle Child, *he praises Young Bear's ability to discuss Mesquakie culture without betraying tribal secrets.*]

Albert E. Stone, in his foreword to [**Black Eagle Child: The Facepaint Narratives**], calls this book an experimental autobiography. But the reader quickly discovers two things: This tale is not factual—it is full of composite characters and fictionalized events—and it is only tangentially about its author, the Mesquakie Indian poet Ray A. Young Bear, who eventually disappears behind a series of changed names, false leads, alter egos, digressions, epistories and myths.

Young Bear is a poet who makes his aesthetic home between two worlds, the native and the non-native. He is a dancer at the world's rim—a fan dancer, for he conceals as much as he reveals of himself and his people. Concealment is a key aesthetic principle, for as Young Bear constantly reiterates, there is a price to be paid for telling tribal secrets to outsiders. In his afterword to **Black Eagle Child,** he recollects how his grandmother taught him that "there were things I could not write about."

As an Indian who sets himself up as an author in the white sense, Young Bear is freighted with a terrible dual responsibility: to satisfy his readers that he is being truthful and informative, and to satisfy his personal and tribal need for secrecy. He must invent a new form, the nature of which is duality, a form that is never straightforward, yet full of implication. It will be poetic, but it will not fulfill every demand of traditional poetic genre. It will always be surprising; it may not end. A code, in other words, that only the right people can break.

In his first book of poems. *Winter of the Salamander* (1980), a much younger Ray Young Bear gave a hint of forms to come:

> What do you do when
>       there is a man
> who represents your dreams
> who goes talking and appraising
> his deeds
> and for no reason he stops
> and says something new
> there is a chance
> for those who want to learn
> but not for those who feel it
> hard and difficult

For "those who want to learn," **Black Eagle Child** is a kind of non-autobiographical Zen treasure trove of non-information about Mesquakie Indians and Young Bear. It is ostensibly a poetic *Bildungsroman* centered around Edgar Bearchild, a Mesquakie boy from the Black Eagle Child Settlement in central Iowa (Young Bear is from the Mesquakie settlement near Tama, Iowa). It begins with Edgar in grade eight in 1965 and follows him through his career as the community's youngest treatable alcoholic. There's a brief stint at a prestigious liberal-arts college in California, then back to Iowa, where he becomes a successful poet haunted by UFOs. He lives off grants from the fictional Maecenas Foundation (Young Bear received grants from the National Endowment for the Arts in the 1970s).

This process of becoming a writer fascinates Edgar, who sees himself wrapped in a paper cocoon, changing, altering, saving himself from the usual fates of a reservation Indian. Learning to translate between worlds redeems him, though with redemption comes alienation and survivor's guilt, since he must separate himself from the normal communal life of his people.

Twinned with Edgar (like the twin boys of Indian legend) is the more adventurous and traditional Ted Facepaint, who follows the tenets of the Well-Off Man Church, a fictional Mesquakie affiliate of the mushroom-eating, pan-Indian Native American Church. (This, by the way, is Young Bear being highly elusive. Rather than reveal traditional Mesquakie rites and legends, he describes a modern cultural intrusion in which he has no stake. Here he seems to reveal without revealing anything.)

Like Edgar, Facepaint also heads west to college. He drops out and hitchhikes across America, trying to reach some romanticized accommodation with this alien white country, only to be beaten and robbed along the way. Back in Iowa, he continues his frenetic drinking and eventually dies—metaphorically, at least—stabbed repeatedly with a screwdriver by rogue Mesquakies nicknamed the Hyenas. He is then mystically transported to Orion, the sacred constellation of the Well-Off Man Church. *Black Eagle Child* closes, however, with Facepaint's resurrection at the hands of Rosie Grassleggings, an immensely obese native healer.

Young Bear knits together these two narrative lines with a complex pattern of imagery. Red-haired and red-hatted people relate to the red-capped hallucinogenic mushrooms, and also to the red-haired man of some native legends. White rabbits recall the Great Hare, Nanebojo, an Algonquin culture hero, who is often paired with Jesus Christ in modern native myth.

This is the bare skeleton of Young Bear's code, the vastly complex and engaging system the reader has to learn to read. Only superficially chaotic, his narrative bears all the indications of a sophisticated and cunning literary intelligence. Young Bear has a novelist's eye for precise social and atmospheric detail.

In his afterword, the author himself calls his book a collage, but whatever you call it, *Black Eagle Child* is an example of the new blood flowing back into the hardened arteries of Anglo-American literature from the margins— from the formerly colonized, enslaved and defeated peoples who must, inevitably, change us as we have changed them.

**Carl L. Bankston III   (review date September 1992)**

SOURCE: "Weaving the Line of the Spirit," in *The*

*Bloomsbury Review,* Vol. 12, No. 6, September, 1992, p. 7.

[*In the following excerpt, Bankston remarks on the storyline of* Black Eagle Child, *noting Young Bear's focus on the importance of "bearing tribal heritage and personal experience through a despoiled cultural and physical environment."*]

At the opening of *The Aeneid,* the hero makes his appearance fleeing from the burning city of Troy, carrying his lame father and household goods on his back and leading his small son by the hand. Contemporary American Indian writers find themselves in a situation similar to that of Aeneas: Around them lies an occupied homeland being destroyed by foreign invaders. As the voices of their people, they carry the salvaged traditions of the past into an uncertain future. As modern writers they move toward this future grasping the materials used by other contemporary artists—mainstream literary techniques, formal and pop culture, and Euro-American conventions of individual personality and identity.

Ray A. Young Bear and Sherman Alexie are highly acclaimed young American Indian poets. Young Bear is a Mesquakie of Iowa and Alexie a Spokane Indian of Washington. In their latest books they show two different ways of bearing tribal heritage and personal experience through a despoiled cultural and physical environment.

Young Bear's *Black Eagle Child* takes the form of autobiographical fiction. In style, the book presents itself as both a prose novel and an epic poem, mirroring the fact that it is a fictional version of the author's life and a tribal memory finding expression in the author's voice. In content it is a series of narratives of events in the life of Edgar Bearchild, who grows to manhood on the Black Eagle Child Settlement, goes off to college to avoid the draft, and becomes a poet and storyteller.

The interweaving of autobiography and tribal memory begins with the two narratives that open the story. In the first, Bearchild and his friend, Ted Facepaint, move from a Thanksgiving Day party at an elementary school to a peyote ceremony conducted by Facepaint's grandfather. The party at the school is an empty event:

> Poor planning and late hand-delivered
> newsletters by the Limelighters contributed
> to a disappointing evening for the few families
> of the Black Eagle Child Settlement who had ar-
> rived
> early with lawn chairs, blankets, and children
> predressed in ornate dance costumes.

In contrast, the peyote ceremony is a genuine encounter with the sacred past:

> In a low voice
> Ted told me his grandfather and two cousins
> represented the Three-Stars-in-a-Row,
> the Orion constellation, "Stars symbolize our re-
> ligious beginnings."

The second narrative recounts young Bearchild's participation in the rite. Through the "Gift of the Star-Medicine" (the peyote), the beginning of the protagonist's own story intersects with the story of the beginning of the Star-Medicine religion in, as the elder Facepaint tells, "a past which is holy and more / close to us than ourselves." The seamless union of tribal myth with the often comic events of Bearchild's own life begins with this scene.

The Facepaints, we learn later, "were Painters of Magic / and Protective Symbols for the soldier / clans and their subdivisions." Ted Facepaint, the boyhood friend who has introduced Bearchild to the Star-Medicine magic, reappears at critical points in the story. Together, Ted and Edgar, accompanied by an Ontario Indian girl named Charlotte, best the "Hyena" family in a memorable fight three years after the Star-Medicine episode.

---

**The interweaving of autobiography and tribal memory begins with the two narratives that open *Black Eagle Child.***

**—Carl L. Bankston III**

---

Two years later, in 1970, "The Year of the Jefferson Airplane," Facepaint visits the nineteen-year-old Bearchild at Pomona College in California, and the friends swallow a synthetic psychedelic that provides a distorted, unsatisfying echo of the earlier ritual. Finally, as the tale ends in 1989, Ted appears in a hospital, having been assaulted by the vengeful "Hyenas." Here it becomes clear that he and Bearchild have been one another's alter egos: "the Star-Medicine changed Bearchild's / twisted perceptions, but they had somehow / remained with Ted over the years." Facepaint is the person Edgar Bearchild would have been had the latter not set out on his "Journey of Words" through writing. But Facepaint, also, ultimately finds some peace through the old ways. Mrs. Grassleggings, a traditional healer, comes to his bed to fan him with an eagle-wing fan and "he knew that the fan had been blessed / with the Ancient Fire of his Grandfathers. / There would be tranquility."

Young Bear writes with a sharp eye for detail, and the intensity of his spiritual concerns is balanced by a picaresque sense of humor. He is capable of speaking with a confessional voice as unrelenting and intimate as that of Rousseau. At the same time, the book avoids self-absorption; the characters are varied and lifelike. He shows us the young Ontario Indian Junior Pipestar who travels to Indian communities around the U.S. and Canada trying to achieve some understanding of his own heritage. Claude Youthman, a barely literate woodsman, is unjustly sent to prison where he acquires a college degree in art history and becomes a celebrity as a writer and artist, only to return to a life of frustration at Black Eagle Child Settlement. Others, such as the hermaphrodite Brook Grassleggings, Bearchild's wife Selene Buffalo Husband, or the boyhood friend Pat "Dirty" Red Hat, are equally vivid.

This is a magnificent piece of literature. Its multileveled design and the richness of its language enable it to bear continual rereading, and each reading offers new rewards. The reader will find poetry, fiction, political statement, social criticism, ethnography, legend, and a unique voice.

**James Ruppert    (review date December 1992-January 1993)**

SOURCE: "Events Remain Contradictory," in *The American Book Review,* Vol. 14, No. 5, December, 1992-January, 1993, p. 9.

[*In the review below, Ruppert discusses Young Bear's focus on identity, voice, self-definition, and the process of becoming a writer in* Black Eagle Child.]

With this experimental autobiography, [***Black Eagle Child: The Facepaint Narratives***] Ray Young Bear steps confidently into an area of literary endeavor new to him, yet with some familiar touches. The free verse (almost blank verse) format is periodically juxtaposed to prose sections, verse with differing typefaces, and a variety of speaking voices. Through these competing elements emerge narratives from the lives of Edgar Bearchild and Ted Facepaint that poetically suggest the process of becoming a writer and finding a place in the world. While the author does allow other voices to speak, the text is not intended to be a portrait of a community; indeed, looked at from one angle, the book is not even a portrait of Young Bear, for much of its concern is to explore the mix of experience, perception, identity, background, social responsibility, and accident that produces an individual who can find self-definition and even salvation in writing. I get the feeling at times that Young Bear even wants to point out how odd that compilation is. There is no great cracking open of the intimate heart here; rather, there are some stories about Edgar Bearchild, his friend Ted Facepaint, and a few others, told with humor, great dramatic sense, a skeptical, even critical outlook, and surreal imagery all working to create the text and the writer of the text.

The writer's identity is never a simple matter. We often spend great energy trying to explain what we do and why to those around us. Young Bear tries to explore this self-explanation in one individual with one unique background. Rather than psychological analysis, we read the narratives of people striving toward self-definition and direction. The reader will not find paragraphs of abstract vague generalizations about inspiration and process. This is not a craft talk, or if it is, it starts with the craft of living in a difficult situation. Young Bear observes, "From any perspective it was complicated to be anybody here." Yet writing as revelation is the hidden force behind all the stories. The reader catches glimpses of some of the sources of the literary impulse in a note-writing girlfriend who inspires Bearchild. We also learn of an uncle who clears the girlfriend's notes out of a dresser to make room for his *Mad* magazine collection. In its place, the uncle inspires Bearchild when he lets him read passages from a powerful diary. However, the strongest influence is the storytelling of Bearchild's grandmother, "During the winters whenever my grandmother would lean over the table and delicately cup her hand over the lamp to blow out the flame, I knew beforehand I would be taken in mind and spirit to another world." During that childhood, though con-strained by family limitations and poverty, the young Bearchild is not mauled by experience into questioning his essence. "I never questioned who I was or where I came from. That issue didn't become important until later." That ontological probing is taken up in some of Young Bear's poetry and now implicitly addressed in *Black Eagle Child,* where writing becomes a salvation, but also separates Bearchild. In the words of Ted Facepaint, Edgar's Journey of Words becomes "a paper wall from tribal responsibilities—and our friendship." Thus a tension evolves, a distance grows.

The question of distance is always present in Young Bear's work. As a poet noted for his dense imagery and intricate poetic structures, Young Bear seems to invite the reader into his vision and yet hold him off in the same motion. Personal images and transforming actions strive to reso-nate from myth and dream to deep common experience and yet maintain mystery. In *Black Eagle Child,* the writ-ing is remarkably narrative, though that is not to say rigid-ly chronological. The distance at first appears to close, but the communication of symbols overpowers the plots. To accomplish this, Young Bear feels free to juxtapose memo-ries, speculations, history, myth, social comment, and the images of popular culture when it suits his purpose. While most of the shifts from poetry to prose are clear in their intention, there are a few switches that are not. And some of the later sections develop the narratives of characters like Rose, the healer acquainted with the terrible costs of her power; Junior, the outsider who turns disaster into in-spiration; Claude Youthman, the cantaloupe terrorist who went to prison because he did not understand English well enough. These narratives may imply something about the pain and power of a writer or of the particular forms of creative transformation that take place on the Black Eagle Child settlement, but they push artistic detachment to its autobiographical limits. If "circumspection is the para-digm of harmony" for close-knit societies, then *Black Eagle Child* is an engagingly harmonious book that mostly walks the stage performing what Vizenor calls the "cultur-al striptease." Only infrequently does it end up in the or-chestra pit.

Mostly the events in the narratives are drawn from specif-ic events in Bearchild's life during the 1960s, 1970s, and 1980s. Some of the incidents Young Bear chooses are ones that have appeared in his poems, like his experience of an earthquake in California. Presented in a narrative form here, they help the reader of his poems tease out more of their implications. Other experiences, like his introduction into a peyote meeting, may not be too familiar to some readers, but still other events, like the night of riding, drinking, and snagging referred to as "going out," will strike many familiar chords. To this mix of the common and the exotic, add a car that becomes animate, a young girl with male sex organs, a medicine man's curse that in-fluences the lives of some of Edgar's friends, and a scene where the comatose Facepaint becomes a bird and takes to flight and the text becomes something like "imminent celestial revelation" ready to awaken the reader into the tumultuous perception of both Bearchild and the Black Eagle Child settlement.

In an afterword addressing the book and his writing, Young Bear expressed the fear that sometimes the mix "turns out to be a minute and insignificant fraction of one's perpetual metamorphosis." While one could point to previously published poems where the charge is justi-fied, *Black Eagle Child* never slips into the insignificant. One central concern in Young Bear's work has been an "artistic interlacing of ethereality, past and present" that blurs the distinction between myth and dream, and what we might call objective reality. What *Black Eagle Child* gives the reader is a way to see how that effort grows out of personal metamorphosis and how it informs the making of one specific writer. Ideally, one should read this book while looking at Young Bear's two published books of poems, *The Winter of the Salamander* and *The Invisible Musician.*

---

**Young Bear allows the events he presents to retain their own mystery. He is not quick to limit their meanings, though he is always ready with a comment on how they contribute to the geometry of pain and despair of some contemporary Native American experience.**

**—James Ruppert**

---

In all his work, Young Bear allows the events he presents to retain their own mystery. He is not quick to limit their meanings, though he is always ready with a comment on how they contribute to the geometry of pain and despair of some contemporary Native American experience. The Black Eagle Child Settlement serves as the backdrop for Bearchild and Facepaint's coming of age. The community emerges as a place where the old formulas of names and ceremonies have only a circumscribed power to guide the youth to find their places. The realities of poverty and de-spair abound, and in this turmoil, Young Bear clearly sees the flaws of human actors on all sides. In one section that changes typeface and explores the local atrocities, he writes

> . . ."What's next?"
> said the people. There was a firm belief
> in tribalhood, equality and fairness,
> but in truth we were such a burden
> to each other, an encumbrance, that
> our chances of advancing into a reasonable
> state of cultural acquiescence diminished
> with each novel prejudice acquired.
> There were instances of how we went
> to extraordinary measures to impede
> understanding, humanity, and the overwhelm-
>    ing future.

There is much internalized agony in the stories, but there is also much externalized surreal expression of individual perception in a world gone astray. Peyote visions vie with a medicine man's curse to produce a climate where events are never simple, never without cognitive and mythic resonance. This connection closes the distance between the individual and his world and provides a silent central source of identity and, in this case, writing. All the actors in this book seem to feel by cultural instinct that "an invisible, life-affecting element hovering around us, instilled respect and understanding of our tenuous existence." Is this the shadow of destiny?

While there is a *Love Medicine* quality to some of the bizarre, symbolic occurrences, Young Bear is much keener, much more postmodern in his ability to let events remain contradictory, perpetually in resolution. Bearchild "discovers concrete answers, like windfish, are elusive" and so does the reader. Ted Facepaint, speaking with the insight of the author, sees self-deception on the part of the Settlement and stereotyping on the part of white society. He penetratingly speculates on the psychological causes in both realms. His classifications and analysis of residents of the settlements and of the nearby white towns are "a reality check for reservation dwellers," a native writer friend of mine says.

But ultimately the book acquaints us with the faces of transformation, with the unseen powers and their interface with our perceptions. Youthman realizes that few of those around him "possessed the voracity to follow through / with their own ideas," but Young Bear has. In doing so he has enriched contemporary literature immensely. This book is not the last word on becoming a writer and an individual; the reality of both is constant evolution. It is a visitation by mysterious lights that illuminate and frighten us. We are left with the haunting image of the writer as human parchment:

> The long arduous task of pasting paper to every inch of my body had already begun, and all that remained was the wait for it to set like a cocoon. I figured a metamorphosis was my only salvation.
>
> Once sunlight entered the bedroom, Selene had agreed to spin me as I hung from the ceiling like a giant pinata. Otherwise, in her own words, I'd be another "preserved face on the shelf of depression, on permanent exhibit at some carnival sideshow, a wrinkled face with blue lips for all the world to see."

### Bruce Murphy    (review date March 1993)

SOURCE: "Spirit and Substance," in *Poetry,* Vol. CLXI, No. 6, March, 1993, pp. 339-55.

[*In the following excerpt, Murphy discusses various themes in* Black Eagle Child, *notably the search for self-identity and "the story of humanity."*]

Ray A. Young Bear describes **Black Eagle Child** as a "poetic journey" which began in 1970 when he started outlining this autobiographical work. Subtitled "The Facepaint Narratives," the book is a collection of stories in verse, prose narratives, and letters tracing the growth of Edgar Bearchild, a member of the Black Eagle Child Settlement, a "fictitious counterpart" of the Mesquakie community

where Young Bear lives in central Iowa. Parts of the narrative are written in his native language, but translations are skillfully woven into the text. Perhaps because the process of writing the narratives was such a long journey, **Black Eagle Child** does not read like a heterogeneous compilation, but "a collage done over a lifetime via the tedious layering upon layering of images by an artist who didn't believe in endings."

The story begins with the participation of Bearchild and his friend, Ted Facepaint, in a traditional tribal ceremony in the Well-Off Man Church, presided over by Ted's grandfather. Bearchild is introduced to the "Star Medicine," a natural hallucinogen which leads to visions with sacred meanings. It is typical of **Black Eagle Child** that this episode is solemn, fascinating, deeply religious, and absolutely hilarious. The foul-tasting medicine, a "green golf ball" he must eat, reminds Bearchild of the One-A-Day vitamins he could never digest. As they stumble around in the dark looking for the outhouse and high as kites, Ted says, "isn't this better than Lone Ranger?" The boys' lives are uncompartmentalized (as are the narratives), a swirl of identifications—ancient ritual, Ozzie and Harriet's America, tribal factions, global politics—in which they try to find some solid ground. Ted places his hopes in the medicine, vision, and faith. Edgar, whom Ted calls "a waverer" who avoids "compacts with God," becomes a writer, hoping to reach the same place through a journey of words. For a moment, they share one vision:

> In his father's station wagon we quietly sat
> and witnessed a birch tree give intimate birth
> to snowflakes. Up through the birch tree's crys-
>   tal
> veins, we followed the snowflakes before they
>   shot
> out from the branch-tips like fireworks.
> Rockets telling us the vitality of this
> Woman-Tree. Children fell from her branches
> in tiny slivers of light. Icicles splintered into
> a thousand pieces on gravel. We were enthralled
> as they massed together at the tree's base
> and started over. Each waited politely
> to ride and flourish on one of the veins.
> Life renewing life. Oxygen. The spell
> was broken by the windshield wipers
> Ted had turned on. "The scene can be
> changed by simple adjustments." He then
> rolled down the car window for fresh air.

Young Bear skillfully shows the scene through several lenses at once. We witness Edgar's awakening through his vision of the tree of life, and also stand at a distance to see two zonked adolescent boys, changing channels with the windshield wipers.

The post-*Dances with Wolves* era has renewed both interest in Native Americans and the trite image of them as natives of the Happy Valley, living in perfect harmony with each other and nature. It is easy to idealize the past; however, Young Bear's narrative, though chronological, is also longitudinal. He exposes the settlement's caste-like divisions, dividing full members of the tribe from EBNOS (Enrolled But in Name Only), BRYPUS (Blood-Related Yet Paternally Unclaimed), and other less pure members. Edgar's friend Junior comes from another branch of the tribe and does not know the tribal language, and "not knowing your people's / language, in the harshest consequence, meant / excommunication from God." Bearchild sees him as "a speechless stump / beside a road with no one near to remove him, / no one willing to carry him home." Lyric beauty, like humor, is a piece which can suddenly appear again at any point in Young Bear's collage. Here it expresses both the cruelty and oppression tradition can inflict on an individual, while reminding us of the healing powers of language. Though living without endings also means living without answers.

However, it does not mean living without stories. **Black Eagle Child** is about modern life, but reminds one of the origins of poetry in naming and the preservation of collective memory. The life of the community came first, as the elder, Carson Two Red Foot, tells Edgar: "Survival before self." Singers derive their individuality not from the attention given to their performance per se, but from the enactment, or re-enactment, of stories that structure the world which gives them an identity:

> In retrospect it is clear now where my interest in storytelling began. During the winters whenever my grandmother would lean over the table and delicately cup her hand over the lamp to blow out the flame, I knew beforehand I would be taken in mind and spirit to another world.

> In a room lit only by the snow's paleness coming through the frosted windows, I would lie still on the floor and patiently wait for awe-inspiring tales of the supernatural past when the forces of good and evil fought a battle which eventually led to the very Creation of our lives.

---

**Black Eagle Child is a collection of stories in verse, prose narratives, and letters tracing the growth of Edgar Bearchild, a member of the Black Eagle Child Settlement, a fictitious counterpart of the Mesquakie community where Young Bear lives.**

*—Bruce Murphy*

---

But, like Carson Two Red Foot, Edgar has to undergo "a long uncomfortable adjustment to being an Indian, *E ne no te wi ya ni,* in the world of the white man." How does one preserve a world of vision in a society which ignores or opposes it? Edgar recollects how "during the first spring thunderstorms, we were handed tobacco and told to stand outside in the pounding rain and release it for the passing Grandfathers." And in the winter, because "the

snow-covered ground symbolized his return," and "his very body covered the earth," the children were "strictly forbidden to roll and shape snow into a figure resembling a human":

> As much as we wanted to, we did not make snowmen. The idea of creating something from snow was a nonhuman endeavor. . . . At day's end, when large, decorated snowmen stood in the neighboring yards, our yard was desolate.

> This acknowledgement of an invisible, life-affecting element, hovering around us, instilled respect and understanding of our tenuous existence.

I do not want to idealize the Mesquakie sense of an invisible unity of man and nature, because this would imply that it belongs to the past. **Black Eagle Child** shows that there is more than one way to tell a story, including the story of humanity, and also that there is more than one way to live that story. Our "selves" stray across borders more often than we'd like them to, but we can learn to follow these leads. Edgar, Ted, and Junior search for identity in what is larger than themselves, but the whole, like the narratives, consists of many strands, pieces of different cultures, collages of people present and past. Spiritual wisdom is to be faithful to the task, which as a process is both never finished but also never "incomplete." It is not values, which may be nothing more than labels and bumper stickers, but valuing, that will cure what ails us.

---

# FURTHER READING

## Criticism

Highwater, Jamake. Review of *Winter of the Salamander: The Keeper of Importance,* by Ray Young Bear. *American Book Review* 4, No. 2 (January-February 1982): 16-7.

> Comparative review in which Highwater discusses Peter Michelson's *Pacific Plainsong,* Wendy Rose's *Lost Copper,* and Young Bear's *Winter of the Salamander.*

Kallet, Marilyn. "The Arrow's Own Language." *American Book Review* 13, No. 1 (April-May 1992): 10-11.

> Comparative review of Young Bear's *The Invisible Musician* and Joy Harjo's *In Mad Love and War.*

Saucerman, James R. "A Critical Approach to Plains Poetry." *Western American Literature* XV, No. 2 (Summer 1980): 93-102.

> Examines the poetic writings of Young Bear and several other Native American authors, focusing on the themes of self-identity and the "relationship between the actual and the spiritual."

Additional coverage of Young Bear's life and career is contained in the following sources published by Gale Research: *Contemporary Authors,* Vol. 146; and *Native North American Literature.*

# ☐ Contemporary Literary Criticism

## Indexes

Literary Criticism Series
Cumulative Author Index
Cumulative Topic Index
Cumulative Nationality Index

# How to Use This Index

## The main references

## list all author entries in the following Gale Literary Criticism series:

*BLC* = *Black Literature Criticism*
*CLC* = *Contemporary Literary Criticism*
*CLR* = *Children's Literature Review*
*CMLC* = *Classical and Medieval Literature Criticism*
*DA* = *DISCovering Authors*
*DAB* = *DISCovering Authors: British*
*DAC* = *DISCovering Authors: Canadian*
*DC* = *Drama Criticism*
*HLC* = *Hispanic Literature Criticism*
*LC* = *Literature Criticism from 1400 to 1800*
*NCLC* = *Nineteenth-Century Literature Criticism*
*PC* = *Poetry Criticism*
*SSC* = *Short Story Criticism*
*TCLC* = *Twentieth-Century Literary Criticism*
*WLC* = *World Literature Criticism, 1500 to the Present*

## The cross-references

## list all author entries in the following Gale biographical and literary sources:

*AAYA* = *Authors & Artists for Young Adults*
*AITN* = *Authors in the News*
*BEST* = *Bestsellers*
*BW* = *Black Writers*
*CA* = *Contemporary Authors*
*CAAS* = *Contemporary Authors Autobiography Series*
*CABS* = *Contemporary Authors Bibliographical Series*
*CANR* = *Contemporary Authors New Revision Series*
*CAP* = *Contemporary Authors Permanent Series*
*CDALB* = *Concise Dictionary of American Literary Biography*
*CDBLB* = *Concise Dictionary of British Literary Biography*
*DAM* = *DISCovering Authors Modules*
  *DRAM* = *dramatists; MST* = *most-studied*

authors; *MULT* = *multicultural authors; NOV* = *novelists; POET* = *poets; POP* = *popular/genre writers*
*DLB* = *Dictionary of Literary Biography*
*DLBD* = *Dictionary of Literary Biography Documentary Series*
*DLBY* = *Dictionary of Literary Biography Yearbook*
*HW* = *Hispanic Writers*
*JRDA* = *Junior DISCovering Authors*
*MAICYA* = *Major Authors and Illustrators for Children and Young Adults*
*MTCW* = *Major 20th-Century Writers*
*NNAL* = *Native North American Literature*
*SAAS* = *Something about the Author Autobiography Series*
*SATA* = *Something about the Author*
*YABC* = *Yesterday's Authors of Books for Children*

# Literary Criticism Series
# Cumulative Author Index

A. E. . . . . . . . . . . . . . . . . . . . . . . . TCLC 3, 10
See also Russell, George William

Abasiyanik, Sait Faik   1906-1954
See Sait Faik
See also CA 123

Abbey, Edward   1927-1989 . . . . . . CLC 36, 59
See also CA 45-48; 128; CANR 2, 41

Abbott, Lee K(ittredge)   1947- . . . . . . CLC 48
See also CA 124; CANR 51; DLB 130

Abe, Kobo   1924-1993 . . . . . CLC 8, 22, 53, 81
See also CA 65-68; 140; CANR 24;
DAM NOV; MTCW

Abelard, Peter   c. 1079-c. 1142 . . . CMLC 11
See also DLB 115

Abell, Kjeld   1901-1961. . . . . . . . . . . CLC 15
See also CA 111

Abish, Walter   1931- . . . . . . . . . . . . . CLC 22
See also CA 101; CANR 37; DLB 130

Abrahams, Peter (Henry)   1919- . . . . . CLC 4
See also BW 1; CA 57-60; CANR 26;
DLB 117; MTCW

Abrams, M(eyer) H(oward)   1912-. . . CLC 24
See also CA 57-60; CANR 13, 33; DLB 67

Abse, Dannie   1923-. . . . . . CLC 7, 29; DAB
See also CA 53-56; CAAS 1; CANR 4, 46;
DAM POET; DLB 27

Achebe, (Albert) Chinua(lumogu)
1930- . . . . . CLC 1, 3, 5, 7, 11, 26, 51, 75;
BLC; DA; DAB; DAC; WLC
See also AAYA 15; BW 2; CA 1-4R;
CANR 6, 26, 47; CLR 20; DAM MST,
MULT, NOV; DLB 117; MAICYA;
MTCW; SATA 40; SATA-Brief 38

Acker, Kathy   1948- . . . . . . . . . . . . . CLC 45
See also CA 117; 122

Ackroyd, Peter   1949-. . . . . . . . . CLC 34, 52
See also CA 123; 127; CANR 51; DLB 155;
INT 127

Acorn, Milton   1923-. . . . . . . . . CLC 15; DAC
See also CA 103; DLB 53; INT 103

Adamov, Arthur   1908-1970 . . . . . CLC 4, 25
See also CA 17-18; 25-28R; CAP 2;
DAM DRAM; MTCW

Adams, Alice (Boyd)
1926- . . . . . . . . . CLC 6, 13, 46; SSC 23
See also CA 81-84; CANR 26; DLBY 86;
INT CANR-26; MTCW

Adams, Andy   1859-1935. . . . . . . . . TCLC 56
See also YABC 1

Adams, Douglas (Noel)   1952- . . . CLC 27, 60
See also AAYA 4; BEST 89:3; CA 106;
CANR 34; DAM POP; DLBY 83; JRDA

Adams, Francis   1862-1893 . . . . . . NCLC 33

Adams, Henry (Brooks)
1838-1918 . . . . . . TCLC 4, 52; DA; DAB;
DAC
See also CA 104; 133; DAM MST; DLB 12,
47

Adams, Richard (George)
1920- . . . . . . . . . . . . . . . . . CLC 4, 5, 18
See also AAYA 16; AITN 1, 2; CA 49-52;
CANR 3, 35; CLR 20; DAM NOV;
JRDA; MAICYA; MTCW; SATA 7, 69

Adamson, Joy(-Friederike Victoria)
1910-1980 . . . . . . . . . . . . . . . . . . CLC 17
See also CA 69-72; 93-96; CANR 22;
MTCW; SATA 11; SATA-Obit 22

Adcock, Fleur   1934-. . . . . . . . . . . . . CLC 41
See also CA 25-28R; CAAS 23; CANR 11,
34; DLB 40

Addams, Charles (Samuel)
1912-1988 . . . . . . . . . . . . . . . . . CLC 30
See also CA 61-64; 126; CANR 12

Addison, Joseph   1672-1719 . . . . . . . . LC 18
See also CDBLB 1660-1789; DLB 101

Adler, Alfred (F.)   1870-1937 . . . . . . TCLC 61
See also CA 119

Adler, C(arole) S(chwerdtfeger)
1932- . . . . . . . . . . . . . . . . . . . . . CLC 35
See also AAYA 4; CA 89-92; CANR 19,
40; JRDA; MAICYA; SAAS 15;
SATA 26, 63

Adler, Renata   1938-. . . . . . . . . . . CLC 8, 31
See also CA 49-52; CANR 5, 22; MTCW

Ady, Endre   1877-1919 . . . . . . . . . . TCLC 11
See also CA 107

Aeschylus
525B.C.-456B.C. . . . . . . . CMLC 11; DA;
DAB; DAC
See also DAM DRAM, MST

Afton, Effie
See Harper, Frances Ellen Watkins

Agapida, Fray Antonio
See Irving, Washington

Agee, James (Rufus)
1909-1955 . . . . . . . . . . . . . . TCLC 1, 19
See also AITN 1; CA 108; 148;
CDALB 1941-1968; DAM NOV; DLB 2,
26, 152

Aghill, Gordon
See Silverberg, Robert

Agnon, S(hmuel) Y(osef Halevi)
1888-1970 . . . . . . . . . . . . . . CLC 4, 8, 14
See also CA 17-18; 25-28R; CAP 2; MTCW

Agrippa von Nettesheim, Henry Cornelius
1486-1535 . . . . . . . . . . . . . . . . . . LC 27

Aherne, Owen
See Cassill, R(onald) V(erlin)

Ai   1947-. . . . . . . . . . . . . . . . . . . CLC 4, 14, 69
See also CA 85-88; CAAS 13; DLB 120

Aickman, Robert (Fordyce)
1914-1981 . . . . . . . . . . . . . . . . . CLC 57
See also CA 5-8R; CANR 3

Aiken, Conrad (Potter)
1889-1973 . . . CLC 1, 3, 5, 10, 52; SSC 9
See also CA 5-8R; 45-48; CANR 4;
CDALB 1929-1941; DAM NOV, POET;
DLB 9, 45, 102; MTCW; SATA 3, 30

Aiken, Joan (Delano)   1924-. . . . . . . . CLC 35
See also AAYA 1; CA 9-12R; CANR 4, 23,
34; CLR 1, 19; DLB 161; JRDA;
MAICYA; MTCW; SAAS 1; SATA 2,
30, 73

Ainsworth, William Harrison
1805-1882 . . . . . . . . . . . . . . . . . NCLC 13
See also DLB 21; SATA 24

Aitmatov, Chingiz (Torekulovich)
1928- . . . . . . . . . . . . . . . . . . . . . CLC 71
See also CA 103; CANR 38; MTCW;
SATA 56

Akers, Floyd
See Baum, L(yman) Frank

Akhmadulina, Bella Akhatovna
1937- . . . . . . . . . . . . . . . . . . . . . CLC 53
See also CA 65-68; DAM POET

Akhmatova, Anna
1888-1966 . . . . . . . CLC 11, 25, 64; PC 2
See also CA 19-20; 25-28R; CANR 35;
CAP 1; DAM POET; MTCW

Aksakov, Sergei Timofeyvich
1791-1859 . . . . . . . . . . . . . . . . . NCLC 2

Aksenov, Vassily
See Aksyonov, Vassily (Pavlovich)

Aksyonov, Vassily (Pavlovich)
1932-. . . . . . . . . . . . . . . . . . . . CLC 22, 37
See also CA 53-56; CANR 12, 48

Akutagawa Ryunosuke
1892-1927 . . . . . . . . . . . . . . . . . TCLC 16
See also CA 117

Alain   1868-1951 . . . . . . . . . . . . . . . TCLC 41

Alain-Fournier. . . . . . . . . . . . . . . . . . . TCLC 6
See also Fournier, Henri Alban
See also DLB 65

Alarcon, Pedro Antonio de
1833-1891 . . . . . . . . . . . . . . . . . NCLC 1

Alas (y Urena), Leopoldo (Enrique Garcia)
1852-1901 . . . . . . . . . . . . . . . . . TCLC 29
See also CA 113; 131; HW

Albee, Edward (Franklin III)
1928- . . . . . . CLC 1, 2, 3, 5, 9, 11, 13, 25,
53, 86; DA; DAB; DAC; WLC
See also AITN 1; CA 5-8R; CABS 3;
CANR 8; CDALB 1941-1968;
DAM DRAM, MST; DLB 7;
INT CANR-8; MTCW

Alberti, Rafael   1902- . . . . . . . . . . . . . CLC 7
See also CA 85-88; DLB 108

Andreae, Johann V(alentin)
1586-1654 .................... LC 32
See also DLB 164

Andreas-Salome, Lou   1861-1937... TCLC 56
See also DLB 66

Andrewes, Lancelot   1555-1626 ....... LC 5
See also DLB 151

Andrews, Cicily Fairfield
See West, Rebecca

Andrews, Elton V.
See Pohl, Frederik

Andreyev, Leonid (Nikolaevich)
1871-1919 .................. TCLC 3
See also CA 104

Andric, Ivo   1892-1975 ............. CLC 8
See also CA 81-84; 57-60; CANR 43;
DLB 147; MTCW

Angelique, Pierre
See Bataille, Georges

Angell, Roger   1920- .............. CLC 26
See also CA 57-60; CANR 13, 44

Angelou, Maya
1928- .... CLC 12, 35, 64, 77; BLC; DA;
DAB; DAC
See also AAYA 7; BW 2; CA 65-68;
CANR 19, 42; DAM MST, MULT,
POET, POP; DLB 38; MTCW; SATA 49

Annensky, Innokenty Fyodorovich
1856-1909 .................. TCLC 14
See also CA 110

Anon, Charles Robert
See Pessoa, Fernando (Antonio Nogueira)

Anouilh, Jean (Marie Lucien Pierre)
1910-1987 ...... CLC 1, 3, 8, 13, 40, 50
See also CA 17-20R; 123; CANR 32;
DAM DRAM; MTCW

Anthony, Florence
See Ai

Anthony, John
See Ciardi, John (Anthony)

Anthony, Peter
See Shaffer, Anthony (Joshua); Shaffer,
Peter (Levin)

Anthony, Piers   1934- ............. CLC 35
See also AAYA 11; CA 21-24R; CANR 28;
DAM POP; DLB 8; MTCW; SAAS 22;
SATA 84

Antoine, Marc
See Proust, (Valentin-Louis-George-Eugene-)
Marcel

Antoninus, Brother
See Everson, William (Oliver)

Antonioni, Michelangelo   1912- ..... CLC 20
See also CA 73-76; CANR 45

Antschel, Paul   1920-1970
See Celan, Paul
See also CA 85-88; CANR 33; MTCW

Anwar, Chairil   1922-1949 ....... TCLC 22
See also CA 121

Apollinaire, Guillaume .. TCLC 3, 8, 51; PC 7
See also Kostrowitzki, Wilhelm Apollinaris
de
See also DAM POET

Appelfeld, Aharon   1932- ....... CLC 23, 47
See also CA 112; 133

Apple, Max (Isaac)   1941-......... CLC 9, 33
See also CA 81-84; CANR 19; DLB 130

Appleman, Philip (Dean)   1926- ..... CLC 51
See also CA 13-16R; CAAS 18; CANR 6,
29

Appleton, Lawrence
See Lovecraft, H(oward) P(hillips)

Apteryx
See Eliot, T(homas) S(tearns)

Apuleius, (Lucius Madaurensis)
125(?)-175(?) .............. CMLC 1

Aquin, Hubert   1929-1977......... CLC 15
See also CA 105; DLB 53

Aragon, Louis   1897-1982....... CLC 3, 22
See also CA 69-72; 108; CANR 28;
DAM NOV, POET; DLB 72; MTCW

Arany, Janos   1817-1882........ NCLC 34

Arbuthnot, John   1667-1735 ......... LC 1
See also DLB 101

Archer, Herbert Winslow
See Mencken, H(enry) L(ouis)

Archer, Jeffrey (Howard)   1940- .... CLC 28
See also AAYA 16; BEST 89:3; CA 77-80;
CANR 22; DAM POP; INT CANR-22

Archer, Jules   1915- ............. CLC 12
See also CA 9-12R; CANR 6; SAAS 5;
SATA 4, 85

Archer, Lee
See Ellison, Harlan (Jay)

Arden, John   1930- ......... CLC 6, 13, 15
See also CA 13-16R; CAAS 4; CANR 31;
DAM DRAM; DLB 13; MTCW

Arenas, Reinaldo
1943-1990 ............. CLC 41; HLC
See also CA 124; 128; 133; DAM MULT;
DLB 145; HW

Arendt, Hannah   1906-1975 ....... CLC 66
See also CA 17-20R; 61-64; CANR 26;
MTCW

Aretino, Pietro   1492-1556 ......... LC 12

Arghezi, Tudor.................. CLC 80
See also Theodorescu, Ion N.

Arguedas, Jose Maria
1911-1969 ............... CLC 10, 18
See also CA 89-92; DLB 113; HW

Argueta, Manlio   1936-............ CLC 31
See also CA 131; DLB 145; HW

Ariosto, Ludovico   1474-1533........ LC 6

Aristides
See Epstein, Joseph

Aristophanes
450B.C.-385B.C......... CMLC 4; DA;
DAB; DAC; DC 2
See also DAM DRAM, MST

Arlt, Roberto (Godofredo Christophersen)
1900-1942 ............ TCLC 29; HLC
See also CA 123; 131; DAM MULT; HW

Armah, Ayi Kwei   1939-.... CLC 5, 33; BLC
See also BW 1; CA 61-64; CANR 21;
DAM MULT, POET; DLB 117; MTCW

Armatrading, Joan   1950-......... CLC 17
See also CA 114

Arnette, Robert
See Silverberg, Robert

Arnim, Achim von (Ludwig Joachim von
Arnim)   1781-1831 ......... NCLC 5
See also DLB 90

Arnim, Bettina von   1785-1859.... NCLC 38
See also DLB 90

Arnold, Matthew
1822-1888 ..... NCLC 6, 29; DA; DAB;
DAC; PC 5; WLC
See also CDBLB 1832-1890; DAM MST,
POET; DLB 32, 57

Arnold, Thomas   1795-1842 ...... NCLC 18
See also DLB 55

Arnow, Harriette (Louisa) Simpson
1908-1986 ............... CLC 2, 7, 18
See also CA 9-12R; 118; CANR 14; DLB 6;
MTCW; SATA 42; SATA-Obit 47

Arp, Hans
See Arp, Jean

Arp, Jean   1887-1966............... CLC 5
See also CA 81-84; 25-28R; CANR 42

Arrabal
See Arrabal, Fernando

Arrabal, Fernando   1932- ... CLC 2, 9, 18, 58
See also CA 9-12R; CANR 15

Arrick, Fran..................... CLC 30
See also Gaberman, Judie Angell

Artaud, Antonin (Marie Joseph)
1896-1948 ................. TCLC 3, 36
See also CA 104; 149; DAM DRAM

Arthur, Ruth M(abel)   1905-1979.... CLC 12
See also CA 9-12R; 85-88; CANR 4;
SATA 7, 26

Artsybashev, Mikhail (Petrovich)
1878-1927 ................. TCLC 31

Arundel, Honor (Morfydd)
1919-1973 ................... CLC 17
See also CA 21-22; 41-44R; CAP 2;
CLR 35; SATA 4; SATA-Obit 24

Asch, Sholem   1880-1957 .......... TCLC 3
See also CA 105

Ash, Shalom
See Asch, Sholem

Ashbery, John (Lawrence)
1927- ...... CLC 2, 3, 4, 6, 9, 13, 15, 25,
41, 77
See also CA 5-8R; CANR 9, 37;
DAM POET; DLB 5, 165; DLBY 81;
INT CANR-9; MTCW

Ashdown, Clifford
See Freeman, R(ichard) Austin

Ashe, Gordon
See Creasey, John

Ashton-Warner, Sylvia (Constance)
1908-1984 ................... CLC 19
See also CA 69-72; 112; CANR 29; MTCW

Asimov, Isaac
1920-1992 ... CLC 1, 3, 9, 19, 26, 76, 92
See also AAYA 13; BEST 90:2; CA 1-4R;
137; CANR 2, 19, 36; CLR 12;
DAM POP; DLB 8; DLBY 92;
INT CANR-19; JRDA; MAICYA;
MTCW; SATA 1, 26, 74

Astley, Thea (Beatrice May)
1925- ....................... CLC 41
See also CA 65-68; CANR 11, 43

**Aston, James**
See White, T(erence) H(anbury)

**Asturias, Miguel Angel**
1899-1974 . . . . . . . . **CLC 3, 8, 13; HLC**
See also CA 25-28; 49-52; CANR 32;
CAP 2; DAM MULT, NOV; DLB 113;
HW; MTCW

**Atares, Carlos Saura**
See Saura (Atares), Carlos

**Atheling, William**
See Pound, Ezra (Weston Loomis)

**Atheling, William, Jr.**
See Blish, James (Benjamin)

**Atherton, Gertrude (Franklin Horn)**
1857-1948 . . . . . . . . . . . . . . . . . . . **TCLC 2**
See also CA 104; DLB 9, 78

**Atherton, Lucius**
See Masters, Edgar Lee

**Atkins, Jack**
See Harris, Mark

**Attaway, William (Alexander)**
1911-1986 . . . . . . . . . . . . . . **CLC 92; BLC**
See also BW 2; CA 143; DAM MULT;
DLB 76

**Atticus**
See Fleming, Ian (Lancaster)

**Atwood, Margaret (Eleanor)**
1939- . . . . . **CLC 2, 3, 4, 8, 13, 15, 25, 44,
84; DA; DAB; DAC; PC 8; SSC 2; WLC**
See also AAYA 12; BEST 89:2; CA 49-52;
CANR 3, 24, 33; DAM MST, NOV,
POET; DLB 53; INT CANR-24; MTCW;
SATA 50

**Aubigny, Pierre d'**
See Mencken, H(enry) L(ouis)

**Aubin, Penelope** 1685-1731(?) . . . . . . . . **LC 9**
See also DLB 39

**Auchincloss, Louis (Stanton)**
1917- . . . . . . **CLC 4, 6, 9, 18, 45; SSC 22**
See also CA 1-4R; CANR 6, 29;
DAM NOV; DLB 2; DLBY 80;
INT CANR-29; MTCW

**Auden, W(ystan) H(ugh)**
1907-1973 . . . . . . **CLC 1, 2, 3, 4, 6, 9, 11,
14, 43; DA; DAB; DAC; PC 1; WLC**
See also CA 9-12R; 45-48; CANR 5;
CDBLB 1914-1945; DAM DRAM, MST,
POET; DLB 10, 20; MTCW

**Audiberti, Jacques** 1900-1965 . . . . . . **CLC 38**
See also CA 25-28R; DAM DRAM

**Audubon, John James**
1785-1851 . . . . . . . . . . . . . . . . . **NCLC 47**

**Auel, Jean M(arie)** 1936- . . . . . . . . . . **CLC 31**
See also AAYA 7; BEST 90:4; CA 103;
CANR 21; DAM POP; INT CANR-21

**Auerbach, Erich** 1892-1957 . . . . . . **TCLC 43**
See also CA 118

**Augier, Emile** 1820-1889 . . . . . . . . **NCLC 31**

**August, John**
See De Voto, Bernard (Augustine)

**Augustine, St.** 354-430 . . . . . . **CMLC 6; DAB**

**Aurelius**
See Bourne, Randolph S(illiman)

**Aurobindo, Sri** 1872-1950 . . . . . . . **TCLC 63**

**Austen, Jane**
1775-1817 . . . . . **NCLC 1, 13, 19, 33, 51;
DA; DAB; DAC; WLC**
See also CDBLB 1789-1832; DAM MST,
NOV; DLB 116

**Auster, Paul** 1947- . . . . . . . . . . . . . . **CLC 47**
See also CA 69-72; CANR 23, 51

**Austin, Frank**
See Faust, Frederick (Schiller)

**Austin, Mary (Hunter)**
1868-1934 . . . . . . . . . . . . . . . . . . **TCLC 25**
See also CA 109; DLB 9, 78

**Autran Dourado, Waldomiro**
See Dourado, (Waldomiro Freitas) Autran

**Averroes** 1126-1198 . . . . . . . . . . . . **CMLC 7**
See also DLB 115

**Avicenna** 980-1037 . . . . . . . . . . . . . **CMLC 16**
See also DLB 115

**Avison, Margaret** 1918- . . . . **CLC 2, 4; DAC**
See also CA 17-20R; DAM POET; DLB 53;
MTCW

**Axton, David**
See Koontz, Dean R(ay)

**Ayckbourn, Alan**
1939- . . . . . . . **CLC 5, 8, 18, 33, 74; DAB**
See also CA 21-24R; CANR 31;
DAM DRAM; DLB 13; MTCW

**Aydy, Catherine**
See Tennant, Emma (Christina)

**Ayme, Marcel (Andre)** 1902-1967 . . . **CLC 11**
See also CA 89-92; CLR 25; DLB 72

**Ayrton, Michael** 1921-1975 . . . . . . . . **CLC 7**
See also CA 5-8R; 61-64; CANR 9, 21

**Azorin** . . . . . . . . . . . . . . . . . . . . . . . . **CLC 11**
See also Martinez Ruiz, Jose

**Azuela, Mariano**
1873-1952 . . . . . . . . . . . . . **TCLC 3; HLC**
See also CA 104; 131; DAM MULT; HW;
MTCW

**Baastad, Babbis Friis**
See Friis-Baastad, Babbis Ellinor

**Bab**
See Gilbert, W(illiam) S(chwenck)

**Babbis, Eleanor**
See Friis-Baastad, Babbis Ellinor

**Babel, Isaak (Emmanuilovich)**
1894-1941(?) . . . . . . **TCLC 2, 13; SSC 16**
See also CA 104

**Babits, Mihaly** 1883-1941 . . . . . . . . **TCLC 14**
See also CA 114

**Babur** 1483-1530 . . . . . . . . . . . . . . . . . **LC 18**

**Bacchelli, Riccardo** 1891-1985 . . . . . **CLC 19**
See also CA 29-32R; 117

**Bach, Richard (David)** 1936- . . . . . . . **CLC 14**
See also AITN 1; BEST 89:2; CA 9-12R;
CANR 18; DAM NOV, POP; MTCW;
SATA 13

**Bachman, Richard**
See King, Stephen (Edwin)

**Bachmann, Ingeborg** 1926-1973 . . . . . **CLC 69**
See also CA 93-96; 45-48; DLB 85

**Bacon, Francis** 1561-1626 . . . . . . . **LC 18, 32**
See also CDBLB Before 1660; DLB 151

**Bacon, Roger** 1214(?)-1292 . . . . . . **CMLC 14**
See also DLB 115

**Bacovia, George** . . . . . . . . . . . . . . . . **TCLC 24**
See also Vasiliu, Gheorghe

**Badanes, Jerome** 1937- . . . . . . . . . . . **CLC 59**

**Bagehot, Walter** 1826-1877 . . . . . . **NCLC 10**
See also DLB 55

**Bagnold, Enid** 1889-1981 . . . . . . . . . **CLC 25**
See also CA 5-8R; 103; CANR 5, 40;
DAM DRAM; DLB 13, 160; MAICYA;
SATA 1, 25

**Bagritsky, Eduard** 1895-1934 . . . . . **TCLC 60**

**Bagrjana, Elisaveta**
See Belcheva, Elisaveta

**Bagryana, Elisaveta** . . . . . . . . . . . . . . **CLC 10**
See also Belcheva, Elisaveta
See also DLB 147

**Bailey, Paul** 1937- . . . . . . . . . . . . . . . **CLC 45**
See also CA 21-24R; CANR 16; DLB 14

**Baillie, Joanna** 1762-1851 . . . . . . . . **NCLC 2**
See also DLB 93

**Bainbridge, Beryl (Margaret)**
1933- . . . . **CLC 4, 5, 8, 10, 14, 18, 22, 62**
See also CA 21-24R; CANR 24;
DAM NOV; DLB 14; MTCW

**Baker, Elliott** 1922- . . . . . . . . . . . . . . . **CLC 8**
See also CA 45-48; CANR 2

**Baker, Nicholson** 1957- . . . . . . . . . . . **CLC 61**
See also CA 135; DAM POP

**Baker, Ray Stannard** 1870-1946 . . . **TCLC 47**
See also CA 118

**Baker, Russell (Wayne)** 1925- . . . . . . **CLC 31**
See also BEST 89:4; CA 57-60; CANR 11,
41; MTCW

**Bakhtin, M.**
See Bakhtin, Mikhail Mikhailovich

**Bakhtin, M. M.**
See Bakhtin, Mikhail Mikhailovich

**Bakhtin, Mikhail**
See Bakhtin, Mikhail Mikhailovich

**Bakhtin, Mikhail Mikhailovich**
1895-1975 . . . . . . . . . . . . . . . . . . **CLC 83**
See also CA 128; 113

**Bakshi, Ralph** 1938(?)- . . . . . . . . . . . **CLC 26**
See also CA 112; 138

**Bakunin, Mikhail (Alexandrovich)**
1814-1876 . . . . . . . . . . . . . . . . **NCLC 25**

**Baldwin, James (Arthur)**
1924-1987 . . . . . . **CLC 1, 2, 3, 4, 5, 8, 13,
15, 17, 42, 50, 67, 90; BLC; DA; DAB;
DAC; DC 1; SSC 10; WLC**
See also AAYA 4; BW 1; CA 1-4R; 124;
CABS 1; CANR 3, 24;
CDALB 1941-1968; DAM MST, MULT,
NOV, POP; DLB 2, 7, 33; DLBY 87;
MTCW; SATA 9; SATA-Obit 54

**Ballard, J(ames) G(raham)**
1930- . . . . . . . . . **CLC 3, 6, 14, 36; SSC 1**
See also AAYA 3; CA 5-8R; CANR 15, 39;
DAM NOV, POP; DLB 14; MTCW

**Balmont, Konstantin (Dmitriyevich)**
1867-1943 . . . . . . . . . . . . . . . . . **TCLC 11**
See also CA 109

**Balzac, Honore de**
1799-1850 . . . . . . . NCLC 5, 35, 53; DA;
DAB; DAC; SSC 5; WLC
See also DAM MST, NOV; DLB 119

**Bambara, Toni Cade**
1939-1995 . . . . . . CLC 19, 88; BLC; DA;
DAC
See also AAYA 5; BW 2; CA 29-32R; 150;
CANR 24, 49; DAM MST, MULT;
DLB 38; MTCW

**Bamdad, A.**
See Shamlu, Ahmad

**Banat, D. R.**
See Bradbury, Ray (Douglas)

**Bancroft, Laura**
See Baum, L(yman) Frank

**Banim, John** 1798-1842 . . . . . . . . NCLC 13
See also DLB 116, 158, 159

**Banim, Michael** 1796-1874 . . . . . . NCLC 13
See also DLB 158, 159

**Banks, Iain**
See Banks, Iain M(enzies)

**Banks, Iain M(enzies)** 1954- . . . . . . . CLC 34
See also CA 123; 128; INT 128

**Banks, Lynne Reid** . . . . . . . . . . . . . CLC 23
See also Reid Banks, Lynne
See also AAYA 6

**Banks, Russell** 1940- . . . . . . . . . CLC 37, 72
See also CA 65-68; CAAS 15; CANR 19;
DLB 130

**Banville, John** 1945- . . . . . . . . . . . . . CLC 46
See also CA 117; 128; DLB 14; INT 128

**Banville, Theodore (Faullain) de**
1832-1891 . . . . . . . . . . . . . . . . . NCLC 9

**Baraka, Amiri**
1934- . . . . . . . . CLC 1, 2, 3, 5, 10, 14, 33;
BLC; DA; DAC; DC 6; PC 4
See also Jones, LeRoi
See also BW 2; CA 21-24R; CABS 3;
CANR 27, 38; CDALB 1941-1968;
DAM MST, MULT, POET, POP;
DLB 5, 7, 16, 38; DLBD 8; MTCW

**Barbauld, Anna Laetitia**
1743-1825 . . . . . . . . . . . . . . . . NCLC 50
See also DLB 107, 109, 142, 158

**Barbellion, W. N. P.** . . . . . . . . . . . . TCLC 24
See also Cummings, Bruce F(rederick)

**Barbera, Jack (Vincent)** 1945- . . . . . . CLC 44
See also CA 110; CANR 45

**Barbey d'Aurevilly, Jules Amedee**
1808-1889 . . . . . . . . . . NCLC 1; SSC 17
See also DLB 119

**Barbusse, Henri** 1873-1935 . . . . . . . . TCLC 5
See also CA 105; DLB 65

**Barclay, Bill**
See Moorcock, Michael (John)

**Barclay, William Ewert**
See Moorcock, Michael (John)

**Barea, Arturo** 1897-1957 . . . . . . . . TCLC 14
See also CA 111

**Barfoot, Joan** 1946- . . . . . . . . . . . . . CLC 18
See also CA 105

**Baring, Maurice** 1874-1945 . . . . . . . . TCLC 8
See also CA 105; DLB 34

**Barker, Clive** 1952- . . . . . . . . . . . . . CLC 52
See also AAYA 10; BEST 90:3; CA 121;
129; DAM POP; INT 129; MTCW

**Barker, George Granville**
1913-1991 . . . . . . . . . . . . . . . CLC 8, 48
See also CA 9-12R; 135; CANR 7, 38;
DAM POET; DLB 20; MTCW

**Barker, Harley Granville**
See Granville-Barker, Harley
See also DLB 10

**Barker, Howard** 1946- . . . . . . . . . . . . CLC 37
See also CA 102; DLB 13

**Barker, Pat(ricia)** 1943- . . . . . . . . CLC 32, 94
See also CA 117; 122; CANR 50; INT 122

**Barlow, Joel** 1754-1812 . . . . . . . . . NCLC 23
See also DLB 37

**Barnard, Mary (Ethel)** 1909- . . . . . . . CLC 48
See also CA 21-22; CAP 2

**Barnes, Djuna**
1892-1982 . . . CLC 3, 4, 8, 11, 29; SSC 3
See also CA 9-12R; 107; CANR 16; DLB 4,
9, 45; MTCW

**Barnes, Julian** 1946- . . . . . . . . CLC 42; DAB
See also CA 102; CANR 19; DLBY 93

**Barnes, Peter** 1931- . . . . . . . . . . . CLC 5, 56
See also CA 65-68; CAAS 12; CANR 33,
34; DLB 13; MTCW

**Baroja (y Nessi), Pio**
1872-1956 . . . . . . . . . . . . TCLC 8; HLC
See also CA 104

**Baron, David**
See Pinter, Harold

**Baron Corvo**
See Rolfe, Frederick (William Serafino
Austin Lewis Mary)

**Barondess, Sue K(aufman)**
1926-1977 . . . . . . . . . . . . . . . . . . CLC 8
See also Kaufman, Sue
See also CA 1-4R; 69-72; CANR 1

**Baron de Teive**
See Pessoa, Fernando (Antonio Nogueira)

**Barres, Maurice** 1862-1923 . . . . . . . TCLC 47
See also DLB 123

**Barreto, Afonso Henrique de Lima**
See Lima Barreto, Afonso Henrique de

**Barrett, (Roger) Syd** 1946- . . . . . . . . CLC 35

**Barrett, William (Christopher)**
1913-1992 . . . . . . . . . . . . . . . . . CLC 27
See also CA 13-16R; 139; CANR 11;
INT CANR-11

**Barrie, J(ames) M(atthew)**
1860-1937 . . . . . . . . . . . . TCLC 2; DAB
See also CA 104; 136; CDBLB 1890-1914;
CLR 16; DAM DRAM, DLB 10, 141,
156; MAICYA; YABC 1

**Barrington, Michael**
See Moorcock, Michael (John)

**Barrol, Grady**
See Bograd, Larry

**Barry, Mike**
See Malzberg, Barry N(athaniel)

**Barry, Philip** 1896-1949 . . . . . . . . . TCLC 11
See also CA 109; DLB 7

**Bart, Andre Schwarz**
See Schwarz-Bart, Andre

**Barth, John (Simmons)**
1930- . . . . . . CLC 1, 2, 3, 5, 7, 9, 10, 14,
27, 51, 89; SSC 10
See also AITN 1, 2; CA 1-4R; CABS 1;
CANR 5, 23, 49; DAM NOV; DLB 2;
MTCW

**Barthelme, Donald**
1931-1989 . . . . . . CLC 1, 2, 3, 5, 6, 8, 13,
23, 46, 59; SSC 2
See also CA 21-24R; 129; CANR 20;
DAM NOV; DLB 2; DLBY 80, 89;
MTCW; SATA 7; SATA-Obit 62

**Barthelme, Frederick** 1943- . . . . . . . . CLC 36
See also CA 114; 122; DLBY 85; INT 122

**Barthes, Roland (Gerard)**
1915-1980 . . . . . . . . . . . . . . CLC 24, 83
See also CA 130; 97-100; MTCW

**Barzun, Jacques (Martin)** 1907- . . . . CLC 51
See also CA 61-64; CANR 22

**Bashevis, Isaac**
See Singer, Isaac Bashevis

**Bashkirtseff, Marie** 1859-1884 . . . NCLC 27

**Basho**
See Matsuo Basho

**Bass, Kingsley B., Jr.**
See Bullins, Ed

**Bass, Rick** 1958- . . . . . . . . . . . . . . . . CLC 79
See also CA 126

**Bassani, Giorgio** 1916- . . . . . . . . . . . . CLC 9
See also CA 65-68; CANR 33; DLB 128;
MTCW

**Bastos, Augusto (Antonio) Roa**
See Roa Bastos, Augusto (Antonio)

**Bataille, Georges** 1897-1962 . . . . . . . CLC 29
See also CA 101; 89-92

**Bates, H(erbert) E(rnest)**
1905-1974 . . . . . . CLC 46; DAB; SSC 10
See also CA 93-96; 45-48; CANR 34;
DAM POP; DLB 162; MTCW

**Bauchart**
See Camus, Albert

**Baudelaire, Charles**
1821-1867 . . . . . . . . NCLC 6, 29, 55; DA;
DAB; DAC; PC 1; SSC 18; WLC
See also DAM MST, POET

**Baudrillard, Jean** 1929- . . . . . . . . . . . CLC 60

**Baum, L(yman) Frank** 1856-1919 . . . TCLC 7
See also CA 108; 133; CLR 15; DLB 22;
JRDA; MAICYA; MTCW; SATA 18

**Baum, Louis F.**
See Baum, L(yman) Frank

**Baumbach, Jonathan** 1933- . . . . . . CLC 6, 23
See also CA 13-16R; CAAS 5; CANR 12;
DLBY 80; INT CANR-12; MTCW

**Bausch, Richard (Carl)** 1945- . . . . . . CLC 51
See also CA 101; CAAS 14; CANR 43;
DLB 130

**Baxter, Charles** 1947- . . . . . . . . . CLC 45, 78
See also CA 57-60; CANR 40; DAM POP;
DLB 130

**Baxter, George Owen**
See Faust, Frederick (Schiller)

Bennett, (Enoch) Arnold
    1867-1931 . . . . . . . . . . . . . . . **TCLC 5, 20**
    See also CA 106; CDBLB 1890-1914;
    DLB 10, 34, 98, 135

Bennett, Elizabeth
    See Mitchell, Margaret (Munnerlyn)

Bennett, George Harold    1930-
    See Bennett, Hal
    See also BW 1; CA 97-100

Bennett, Hal . . . . . . . . . . . . . . . . . . . **CLC 5**
    See also Bennett, George Harold
    See also DLB 33

Bennett, Jay    1912- . . . . . . . . . . . . . . **CLC 35**
    See also AAYA 10; CA 69-72; CANR 11,
    42; JRDA; SAAS 4; SATA 41, 87;
    SATA-Brief 27

Bennett, Louise (Simone)
    1919- . . . . . . . . . . . . . . . . **CLC 28; BLC**
    See also BW 2; DAM MULT; DLB 117

Benson, E(dward) F(rederic)
    1867-1940 . . . . . . . . . . . . . . . . **TCLC 27**
    See also CA 114; DLB 135, 153

Benson, Jackson J.    1930- . . . . . . . . . **CLC 34**
    See also CA 25-28R; DLB 111

Benson, Sally    1900-1972 . . . . . . . . . . **CLC 17**
    See also CA 19-20; 37-40R; CAP 1;
    SATA 1, 35; SATA-Obit 27

Benson, Stella    1892-1933 . . . . . . . . **TCLC 17**
    See also CA 117; DLB 36, 162

Bentham, Jeremy    1748-1832 . . . . . **NCLC 38**
    See also DLB 107, 158

Bentley, E(dmund) C(lerihew)
    1875-1956 . . . . . . . . . . . . . . . . **TCLC 12**
    See also CA 108; DLB 70

Bentley, Eric (Russell)    1916- . . . . . . . **CLC 24**
    See also CA 5-8R; CANR 6; INT CANR-6

Beranger, Pierre Jean de
    1780-1857 . . . . . . . . . . . . . . . . **NCLC 34**

Berendt, John (Lawrence)    1939- . . . . **CLC 86**
    See also CA 146

Berger, Colonel
    See Malraux, (Georges-)Andre

Berger, John (Peter)    1926- . . . . . . **CLC 2, 19**
    See also CA 81-84; CANR 51; DLB 14

Berger, Melvin H.    1927- . . . . . . . . . . **CLC 12**
    See also CA 5-8R; CANR 4; CLR 32;
    SAAS 2; SATA 5

Berger, Thomas (Louis)
    1924- . . . . . . . . . **CLC 3, 5, 8, 11, 18, 38**
    See also CA 1-4R; CANR 5, 28, 51;
    DAM NOV; DLB 2; DLBY 80;
    INT CANR-28; MTCW

Bergman, (Ernst) Ingmar
    1918- . . . . . . . . . . . . . . . . . . . **CLC 16, 72**
    See also CA 81-84; CANR 33

Bergson, Henri    1859-1941 . . . . . . . **TCLC 32**

Bergstein, Eleanor    1938- . . . . . . . . . . **CLC 4**
    See also CA 53-56; CANR 5

Berkoff, Steven    1937- . . . . . . . . . . . **CLC 56**
    See also CA 104

Bermant, Chaim (Icyk)    1929- . . . . . . **CLC 40**
    See also CA 57-60; CANR 6, 31

Bern, Victoria
    See Fisher, M(ary) F(rances) K(ennedy)

Bernanos, (Paul Louis) Georges
    1888-1948 . . . . . . . . . . . . . . . . . . **TCLC 3**
    See also CA 104; 130; DLB 72

Bernard, April    1956- . . . . . . . . . . . . **CLC 59**
    See also CA 131

Berne, Victoria
    See Fisher, M(ary) F(rances) K(ennedy)

Bernhard, Thomas
    1931-1989 . . . . . . . . . . . . . **CLC 3, 32, 61**
    See also CA 85-88; 127; CANR 32;
    DLB 85, 124; MTCW

Berriault, Gina    1926- . . . . . . . . . . . . **CLC 54**
    See also CA 116; 129; DLB 130

Berrigan, Daniel    1921- . . . . . . . . . . . . **CLC 4**
    See also CA 33-36R; CAAS 1; CANR 11,
    43; DLB 5

Berrigan, Edmund Joseph Michael, Jr.
    1934-1983
    See Berrigan, Ted
    See also CA 61-64; 110; CANR 14

Berrigan, Ted. . . . . . . . . . . . . . . . . . . **CLC 37**
    See also Berrigan, Edmund Joseph Michael,
    Jr.
    See also DLB 5

Berry, Charles Edward Anderson    1931-
    See Berry, Chuck
    See also CA 115

Berry, Chuck . . . . . . . . . . . . . . . . . . . **CLC 17**
    See also Berry, Charles Edward Anderson

Berry, Jonas
    See Ashbery, John (Lawrence)

Berry, Wendell (Erdman)
    1934- . . . . . . . . . . . . . **CLC 4, 6, 8, 27, 46**
    See also AITN 1; CA 73-76; CANR 50;
    DAM POET; DLB 5, 6

Berryman, John
    1914-1972 . . . . . . **CLC 1, 2, 3, 4, 6, 8, 10,
    13, 25, 62**
    See also CA 13-16; 33-36R; CABS 2;
    CANR 35; CAP 1; CDALB 1941-1968;
    DAM POET; DLB 48; MTCW

Bertolucci, Bernardo    1940- . . . . . . . . **CLC 16**
    See also CA 106

Bertrand, Aloysius    1807-1841 . . . . **NCLC 31**

Bertran de Born    c. 1140-1215 . . . . . **CMLC 5**

Besant, Annie (Wood)    1847-1933 . . . **TCLC 9**
    See also CA 105

Bessie, Alvah    1904-1985. . . . . . . . . . **CLC 23**
    See also CA 5-8R; 116; CANR 2; DLB 26

Bethlen, T. D.
    See Silverberg, Robert

Beti, Mongo. . . . . . . . . . . . . . . . **CLC 27; BLC**
    See also Biyidi, Alexandre
    See also DAM MULT

Betjeman, John
    1906-1984 . . . **CLC 2, 6, 10, 34, 43; DAB**
    See also CA 9-12R; 112; CANR 33;
    CDBLB 1945-1960; DAM MST, POET;
    DLB 20; DLBY 84; MTCW

Bettelheim, Bruno    1903-1990 . . . . . . **CLC 79**
    See also CA 81-84; 131; CANR 23; MTCW

Betti, Ugo    1892-1953 . . . . . . . . . . . . **TCLC 5**
    See also CA 104

Betts, Doris (Waugh)    1932- . . . . **CLC 3, 6, 28**
    See also CA 13-16R; CANR 9; DLBY 82;
    INT CANR-9

Bevan, Alistair
    See Roberts, Keith (John Kingston)

Bialik, Chaim Nachman
    1873-1934 . . . . . . . . . . . . . . . . **TCLC 25**

Bickerstaff, Isaac
    See Swift, Jonathan

Bidart, Frank    1939- . . . . . . . . . . . . . **CLC 33**
    See also CA 140

Bienek, Horst    1930- . . . . . . . . . . . . **CLC 7, 11**
    See also CA 73-76; DLB 75

Bierce, Ambrose (Gwinett)
    1842-1914(?) . . . . . . . **TCLC 1, 7, 44; DA;
    DAC; SSC 9; WLC**
    See also CA 104; 139; CDALB 1865-1917;
    DAM MST; DLB 11, 12, 23, 71, 74

Billings, Josh
    See Shaw, Henry Wheeler

Billington, (Lady) Rachel (Mary)
    1942- . . . . . . . . . . . . . . . . . . . . . . **CLC 43**
    See also AITN 2; CA 33-36R; CANR 44

Binyon, T(imothy) J(ohn)    1936- . . . . **CLC 34**
    See also CA 111; CANR 28

Bioy Casares, Adolfo
    1914- . . . **CLC 4, 8, 13, 88; HLC; SSC 17**
    See also CA 29-32R; CANR 19, 43;
    DAM MULT; DLB 113; HW; MTCW

Bird, Cordwainer
    See Ellison, Harlan (Jay)

Bird, Robert Montgomery
    1806-1854 . . . . . . . . . . . . . . . . . **NCLC 1**

Birney, (Alfred) Earle
    1904- . . . . . . . . . . **CLC 1, 4, 6, 11; DAC**
    See also CA 1-4R; CANR 5, 20;
    DAM MST, POET; DLB 88; MTCW

Bishop, Elizabeth
    1911-1979 . . . . . . **CLC 1, 4, 9, 13, 15, 32;
    DA; DAC; PC 3**
    See also CA 5-8R; 89-92; CABS 2;
    CANR 26; CDALB 1968-1988;
    DAM MST, POET; DLB 5; MTCW;
    SATA-Obit 24

Bishop, John    1935- . . . . . . . . . . . . . . **CLC 10**
    See also CA 105

Bissett, Bill    1939- . . . . . . . . . . **CLC 18; PC 14**
    See also CA 69-72; CAAS 19; CANR 15;
    DLB 53; MTCW

Bitov, Andrei (Georgievich)    1937- . . . **CLC 57**
    See also CA 142

Biyidi, Alexandre    1932-
    See Beti, Mongo
    See also BW 1; CA 114; 124; MTCW

Bjarme, Brynjolf
    See Ibsen, Henrik (Johan)

Bjornson, Bjornstjerne (Martinius)
    1832-1910 . . . . . . . . . . . . . . **TCLC 7, 37**
    See also CA 104

Black, Robert
    See Holdstock, Robert P.

Blackburn, Paul    1926-1971 . . . . . . **CLC 9, 43**
    See also CA 81-84; 33-36R; CANR 34;
    DLB 16; DLBY 81

**Boswell, James**
1740-1795 ...... LC 4; DA; DAB; DAC;
WLC
See also CDBLB 1660-1789; DAM MST;
DLB 104, 142

**Bottoms, David** 1949- ........... CLC 53
See also CA 105; CANR 22; DLB 120;
DLBY 83

**Boucicault, Dion** 1820-1890 ...... NCLC 41

**Boucolon, Maryse** 1937-
See Conde, Maryse
See also CA 110; CANR 30

**Bourget, Paul (Charles Joseph)**
1852-1935 ............... TCLC 12
See also CA 107; DLB 123

**Bourjaily, Vance (Nye)** 1922- .... CLC 8, 62
See also CA 1-4R; CAAS 1; CANR 2;
DLB 2, 143

**Bourne, Randolph S(illiman)**
1886-1918 ................. TCLC 16
See also CA 117; DLB 63

**Bova, Ben(jamin William)** 1932- .... CLC 45
See also AAYA 16; CA 5-8R; CAAS 18;
CANR 11; CLR 3; DLBY 81;
INT CANR-11; MAICYA; MTCW;
SATA 6, 68

**Bowen, Elizabeth (Dorothea Cole)**
1899-1973 ...... CLC 1, 3, 6, 11, 15, 22;
SSC 3
See also CA 17-18; 41-44R; CANR 35;
CAP 2; CDBLB 1945-1960; DAM NOV;
DLB 15, 162; MTCW

**Bowering, George** 1935- ........ CLC 15, 47
See also CA 21-24R; CAAS 16; CANR 10;
DLB 53

**Bowering, Marilyn R(uthe)** 1949- ... CLC 32
See also CA 101; CANR 49

**Bowers, Edgar** 1924- .............. CLC 9
See also CA 5-8R; CANR 24; DLB 5

**Bowie, David** .................... CLC 17
See also Jones, David Robert

**Bowles, Jane (Sydney)**
1917-1973 ................. CLC 3, 68
See also CA 19-20; 41-44R; CAP 2

**Bowles, Paul (Frederick)**
1910- ........ CLC 1, 2, 19, 53; SSC 3
See also CA 1-4R; CAAS 1; CANR 1, 19,
50; DLB 5, 6; MTCW

**Box, Edgar**
See Vidal, Gore

**Boyd, Nancy**
See Millay, Edna St. Vincent

**Boyd, William** 1952- ....... CLC 28, 53, 70
See also CA 114; 120; CANR 51

**Boyle, Kay**
1902-1992 ..... CLC 1, 5, 19, 58; SSC 5
See also CA 13-16R; 140; CAAS 1;
CANR 29; DLB 4, 9, 48, 86; DLBY 93;
MTCW

**Boyle, Mark**
See Kienzle, William X(avier)

**Boyle, Patrick** 1905-1982 ......... CLC 19
See also CA 127

**Boyle, T. C.** 1948-
See Boyle, T(homas) Coraghessan

**Boyle, T(homas) Coraghessan**
1948- ......... CLC 36, 55, 90; SSC 16
See also BEST 90:4; CA 120; CANR 44;
DAM POP; DLBY 86

**Boz**
See Dickens, Charles (John Huffam)

**Brackenridge, Hugh Henry**
1748-1816 .................. NCLC 7
See also DLB 11, 37

**Bradbury, Edward P.**
See Moorcock, Michael (John)

**Bradbury, Malcolm (Stanley)**
1932- .................... CLC 32, 61
See also CA 1-4R; CANR 1, 33;
DAM NOV; DLB 14; MTCW

**Bradbury, Ray (Douglas)**
1920- ........ CLC 1, 3, 10, 15, 42; DA;
DAB; DAC; WLC
See also AAYA 15; AITN 1, 2; CA 1-4R;
CANR 2, 30; CDALB 1968-1988;
DAM MST, NOV, POP; DLB 2, 8;
INT CANR-30; MTCW; SATA 11, 64

**Bradford, Gamaliel** 1863-1932 ..... TCLC 36
See also DLB 17

**Bradley, David (Henry, Jr.)**
1950- .................... CLC 23; BLC
See also BW 1; CA 104; CANR 26;
DAM MULT; DLB 33

**Bradley, John Ed(mund, Jr.)**
1958- .................... CLC 55
See also CA 139

**Bradley, Marion Zimmer** 1930- .... CLC 30
See also AAYA 9; CA 57-60; CAAS 10;
CANR 7, 31, 51; DAM POP; DLB 8;
MTCW

**Bradstreet, Anne**
1612(?)-1672 ...... LC 4, 30; DA; DAC;
PC 10
See also CDALB 1640-1865; DAM MST,
POET; DLB 24

**Brady, Joan** 1939- .............. CLC 86
See also CA 141

**Bragg, Melvyn** 1939- ............. CLC 10
See also BEST 89:3; CA 57-60; CANR 10,
48; DLB 14

**Braine, John (Gerard)**
1922-1986 .............. CLC 1, 3, 41
See also CA 1-4R; 120; CANR 1, 33;
CDBLB 1945-1960; DLB 15; DLBY 86;
MTCW

**Brammer, William** 1930(?)-1978 .... CLC 31
See also CA 77-80

**Brancati, Vitaliano** 1907-1954 ..... TCLC 12
See also CA 109

**Brancato, Robin F(idler)** 1936- ..... CLC 35
See also AAYA 9; CA 69-72; CANR 11,
45; CLR 32; JRDA; SAAS 9; SATA 23

**Brand, Max**
See Faust, Frederick (Schiller)

**Brand, Millen** 1906-1980 .......... CLC 7
See also CA 21-24R; 97-100

**Branden, Barbara** ................. CLC 44
See also CA 148

**Brandes, Georg (Morris Cohen)**
1842-1927 ................. TCLC 10
See also CA 105

**Brandys, Kazimierz** 1916- ........ CLC 62

**Branley, Franklyn M(ansfield)**
1915- ...................... CLC 21
See also CA 33-36R; CANR 14, 39;
CLR 13; MAICYA; SAAS 16; SATA 4,
68

**Brathwaite, Edward Kamau** 1930- ... CLC 11
See also BW 2; CA 25-28R; CANR 11, 26,
47; DAM POET; DLB 125

**Brautigan, Richard (Gary)**
1935-1984 .... CLC 1, 3, 5, 9, 12, 34, 42
See also CA 53-56; 113; CANR 34;
DAM NOV; DLB 2, 5; DLBY 80, 84;
MTCW; SATA 56

**Brave Bird, Mary** 1953-
See Crow Dog, Mary
See also NNAL

**Braverman, Kate** 1950- ........... CLC 67
See also CA 89-92

**Brecht, Bertolt**
1898-1956 ...... TCLC 1, 6, 13, 35; DA;
DAB; DAC; DC 3; WLC
See also CA 104; 133; DAM DRAM, MST;
DLB 56, 124; MTCW

**Brecht, Eugen Berthold Friedrich**
See Brecht, Bertolt

**Bremer, Fredrika** 1801-1865 ..... NCLC 11

**Brennan, Christopher John**
1870-1932 ................. TCLC 17
See also CA 117

**Brennan, Maeve** 1917- ............ CLC 5
See also CA 81-84

**Brentano, Clemens (Maria)**
1778-1842 ................. NCLC 1
See also DLB 90

**Brent of Bin Bin**
See Franklin, (Stella Maraia Sarah) Miles

**Brenton, Howard** 1942- ........... CLC 31
See also CA 69-72; CANR 33; DLB 13;
MTCW

**Breslin, James** 1930-
See Breslin, Jimmy
See also CA 73-76; CANR 31; DAM NOV;
MTCW

**Breslin, Jimmy** ................. CLC 4, 43
See also Breslin, James
See also AITN 1

**Bresson, Robert** 1901- ........... CLC 16
See also CA 110; CANR 49

**Breton, Andre**
1896-1966 ..... CLC 2, 9, 15, 54; PC 15
See also CA 19-20; 25-28R; CANR 40;
CAP 2; DLB 65; MTCW

**Breytenbach, Breyten** 1939(?)- ... CLC 23, 37
See also CA 113; 129; DAM POET

**Bridgers, Sue Ellen** 1942- ......... CLC 26
See also AAYA 8; CA 65-68; CANR 11,
36; CLR 18; DLB 52; JRDA; MAICYA;
SAAS 1; SATA 22

**Bridges, Robert (Seymour)**
1844-1930 ................. TCLC 1
See also CA 104; CDBLB 1890-1914;
DAM POET; DLB 19, 98

Bridie, James................TCLC 3
See also Mavor, Osborne Henry
See also DLB 10

Brin, David 1950-...............CLC 34
See also CA 102; CANR 24;
INT CANR-24; SATA 65

Brink, Andre (Philippus)
1935-...............CLC 18, 36
See also CA 104; CANR 39; INT 103;
MTCW

Brinsmead, H(esba) F(ay) 1922-....CLC 21
See also CA 21-24R; CANR 10; MAICYA;
SAAS 5; SATA 18, 78

Brittain, Vera (Mary)
1893(?)-1970.................CLC 23
See also CA 13-16; 25-28R; CAP 1; MTCW

Broch, Hermann 1886-1951......TCLC 20
See also CA 117; DLB 85, 124

Brock, Rose
See Hansen, Joseph

Brodkey, Harold (Roy) 1930-1996..CLC 56
See also CA 111; 151; DLB 130

Brodsky, Iosif Alexandrovich 1940-1996
See Brodsky, Joseph
See also AITN 1; CA 41-44R; 151;
CANR 37; DAM POET; MTCW

Brodsky, Joseph..CLC 4, 6, 13, 36, 50; PC 9
See also Brodsky, Iosif Alexandrovich

Brodsky, Michael Mark 1948-.....CLC 19
See also CA 102; CANR 18, 41

Bromell, Henry 1947-.............CLC 5
See also CA 53-56; CANR 9

Bromfield, Louis (Brucker)
1896-1956.................TCLC 11
See also CA 107; DLB 4, 9, 86

Broner, E(sther) M(asserman)
1930-......................CLC 19
See also CA 17-20R; CANR 8, 25; DLB 28

Bronk, William 1918-............CLC 10
See also CA 89-92; CANR 23; DLB 165

Bronstein, Lev Davidovich
See Trotsky, Leon

Bronte, Anne 1820-1849..........NCLC 4
See also DLB 21

Bronte, Charlotte
1816-1855.........NCLC 3, 8, 33; DA;
DAB; DAC; WLC
See also AAYA 17; CDBLB 1832-1890;
DAM MST, NOV; DLB 21, 159

Bronte, Emily (Jane)
1818-1848....NCLC 16, 35; DA; DAB;
DAC; PC 8; WLC
See also AAYA 17; CDBLB 1832-1890;
DAM MST, NOV, POET; DLB 21, 32

Brooke, Frances 1724-1789.........LC 6
See also DLB 39, 99

Brooke, Henry 1703(?)-1783.........LC 1
See also DLB 39

Brooke, Rupert (Chawner)
1887-1915.......TCLC 2, 7; DA; DAB;
DAC; WLC
See also CA 104; 132; CDBLB 1914-1945;
DAM MST, POET; DLB 19; MTCW

Brooke-Haven, P.
See Wodehouse, P(elham) G(renville)

Brooke-Rose, Christine 1926-......CLC 40
See also CA 13-16R; DLB 14

Brookner, Anita
1928-...........CLC 32, 34, 51; DAB
See also CA 114; 120; CANR 37;
DAM POP; DLBY 87; MTCW

Brooks, Cleanth 1906-1994.....CLC 24, 86
See also CA 17-20R; 145; CANR 33, 35;
DLB 63; DLBY 94; INT CANR-35;
MTCW

Brooks, George
See Baum, L(yman) Frank

Brooks, Gwendolyn
1917-......CLC 1, 2, 4, 5, 15, 49; BLC;
DA; DAC; PC 7; WLC
See also AITN 1; BW 2; CA 1-4R;
CANR 1, 27; CDALB 1941-1968;
CLR 27; DAM MST, MULT, POET;
DLB 5, 76, 165; MTCW; SATA 6

Brooks, Mel.....................CLC 12
See also Kaminsky, Melvin
See also AAYA 13; DLB 26

Brooks, Peter 1938-..............CLC 34
See also CA 45-48; CANR 1

Brooks, Van Wyck 1886-1963......CLC 29
See also CA 1-4R; CANR 6; DLB 45, 63,
103

Brophy, Brigid (Antonia)
1929-1995.............CLC 6, 11, 29
See also CA 5-8R; 149; CAAS 4; CANR 25;
DLB 14; MTCW

Brosman, Catharine Savage 1934-....CLC 9
See also CA 61-64; CANR 21, 46

Brother Antoninus
See Everson, William (Oliver)

Broughton, T(homas) Alan 1936-...CLC 19
See also CA 45-48; CANR 2, 23, 48

Broumas, Olga 1949-..........CLC 10, 73
See also CA 85-88; CANR 20

Brown, Charles Brockden
1771-1810.................NCLC 22
See also CDALB 1640-1865; DLB 37, 59,
73

Brown, Christy 1932-1981.........CLC 63
See also CA 105; 104; DLB 14

Brown, Claude 1937-........CLC 30; BLC
See also AAYA 7; BW 1; CA 73-76;
DAM MULT

Brown, Dee (Alexander) 1908-..CLC 18, 47
See also CA 13-16R; CAAS 6; CANR 11,
45; DAM POP; DLBY 80; MTCW;
SATA 5

Brown, George
See Wertmueller, Lina

Brown, George Douglas
1869-1902.................TCLC 28

Brown, George Mackay
1921-1996................CLC 5, 48
See also CA 21-24R; 151; CAAS 6;
CANR 12, 37; DLB 14, 27, 139; MTCW;
SATA 35

Brown, (William) Larry 1951-......CLC 73
See also CA 130; 134; INT 133

Brown, Moses
See Barrett, William (Christopher)

Brown, Rita Mae 1944-.....CLC 18, 43, 79
See also CA 45-48; CANR 2, 11, 35;
DAM NOV, POP; INT CANR-11;
MTCW

Brown, Roderick (Langmere) Haig-
See Haig-Brown, Roderick (Langmere)

Brown, Rosellen 1939-............CLC 32
See also CA 77-80; CAAS 10; CANR 14, 44

Brown, Sterling Allen
1901-1989.........CLC 1, 23, 59; BLC
See also BW 1; CA 85-88; 127; CANR 26;
DAM MULT, POET; DLB 48, 51, 63;
MTCW

Brown, Will
See Ainsworth, William Harrison

Brown, William Wells
1813-1884........NCLC 2; BLC; DC 1
See also DAM MULT; DLB 3, 50

Browne, (Clyde) Jackson 1948(?)-...CLC 21
See also CA 120

Browning, Elizabeth Barrett
1806-1861.....NCLC 1, 16; DA; DAB;
DAC; PC 6; WLC
See also CDBLB 1832-1890; DAM MST,
POET; DLB 32

Browning, Robert
1812-1889.......NCLC 19; DA; DAB;
DAC; PC 2
See also CDBLB 1832-1890; DAM MST,
POET; DLB 32, 163; YABC 1

Browning, Tod 1882-1962.........CLC 16
See also CA 141; 117

Brownson, Orestes (Augustus)
1803-1876.................NCLC 50

Bruccoli, Matthew J(oseph) 1931-..CLC 34
See also CA 9-12R; CANR 7; DLB 103

Bruce, Lenny....................CLC 21
See also Schneider, Leonard Alfred

Bruin, John
See Brutus, Dennis

Brulard, Henri
See Stendhal

Brulls, Christian
See Simenon, Georges (Jacques Christian)

Brunner, John (Kilian Houston)
1934-1995.................CLC 8, 10
See also CA 1-4R; 149; CAAS 8; CANR 2,
37; DAM POP; MTCW

Bruno, Giordano 1548-1600........LC 27

Brutus, Dennis 1924-........CLC 43; BLC
See also BW 2; CA 49-52; CAAS 14;
CANR 2, 27, 42; DAM MULT, POET;
DLB 117

Bryan, C(ourtlandt) D(ixon) B(arnes)
1936-......................CLC 29
See also CA 73-76; CANR 13;
INT CANR-13

Bryan, Michael
See Moore, Brian

Bryant, William Cullen
1794-1878.....NCLC 6, 46; DA; DAB;
DAC
See also CDALB 1640-1865; DAM MST,
POET; DLB 3, 43, 59

Bryusov, Valery Yakovlevich
    1873-1924 .................. TCLC 10
    See also CA 107

Buchan, John 1875-1940 ... TCLC 41; DAB
    See also CA 108; 145; DAM POP; DLB 34,
    70, 156; YABC 2

Buchanan, George 1506-1582 ........ LC 4

Buchheim, Lothar-Guenther 1918- ... CLC 6
    See also CA 85-88

Buchner, (Karl) Georg
    1813-1837 ................. NCLC 26

Buchwald, Art(hur) 1925-.......... CLC 33
    See also AITN 1; CA 5-8R; CANR 21;
    MTCW; SATA 10

Buck, Pearl S(ydenstricker)
    1892-1973 .... CLC 7, 11, 18; DA; DAB;
                                              DAC
    See also AITN 1; CA 1-4R; 41-44R;
    CANR 1, 34; DAM MST, NOV; DLB 9,
    102; MTCW; SATA 1, 25

Buckler, Ernest 1908-1984.... CLC 13; DAC
    See also CA 11-12; 114; CAP 1;
    DAM MST; DLB 68; SATA 47

Buckley, Vincent (Thomas)
    1925-1988 ................... CLC 57
    See also CA 101

Buckley, William F(rank), Jr.
    1925- ................. CLC 7, 18, 37
    See also AITN 1; CA 1-4R; CANR 1, 24;
    DAM POP; DLB 137; DLBY 80;
    INT CANR-24; MTCW

Buechner, (Carl) Frederick
    1926-................. CLC 2, 4, 6, 9
    See also CA 13-16R; CANR 11, 39;
    DAM NOV; DLBY 80; INT CANR-11;
    MTCW

Buell, John (Edward) 1927-........ CLC 10
    See also CA 1-4R; DLB 53

Buero Vallejo, Antonio 1916- ... CLC 15, 46
    See also CA 106; CANR 24, 49; HW;
    MTCW

Bufalino, Gesualdo 1920(?)-........ CLC 74

Bugayev, Boris Nikolayevich 1880-1934
    See Bely, Andrey
    See also CA 104

Bukowski, Charles
    1920-1994 ......... CLC 2, 5, 9, 41, 82
    See also CA 17-20R; 144; CANR 40;
    DAM NOV, POET; DLB 5, 130; MTCW

Bulgakov, Mikhail (Afanas'evich)
    1891-1940 ........ TCLC 2, 16; SSC 18
    See also CA 105; DAM DRAM, NOV

Bulgya, Alexander Alexandrovich
    1901-1956 ................. TCLC 53
    See also Fadeyev, Alexander
    See also CA 117

Bullins, Ed 1935- .. CLC 1, 5, 7; BLC; DC 6
    See also BW 2; CA 49-52; CAAS 16;
    CANR 24, 46; DAM DRAM, MULT;
    DLB 7, 38; MTCW

Bulwer-Lytton, Edward (George Earle Lytton)
    1803-1873 .............. NCLC 1, 45
    See also DLB 21

Bunin, Ivan Alexeyevich
    1870-1953 ........... TCLC 6; SSC 5
    See also CA 104

Bunting, Basil 1900-1985.... CLC 10, 39, 47
    See also CA 53-56; 115; CANR 7;
    DAM POET; DLB 20

Bunuel, Luis 1900-1983 .. CLC 16, 80; HLC
    See also CA 101; 110; CANR 32;
    DAM MULT; HW

Bunyan, John
    1628-1688 ...... LC 4; DA; DAB; DAC;
                                              WLC
    See also CDBLB 1660-1789; DAM MST;
    DLB 39

Burckhardt, Jacob (Christoph)
    1818-1897 ................. NCLC 49

Burford, Eleanor
    See Hibbert, Eleanor Alice Burford

Burgess, Anthony
    CLC 1, 2, 4, 5, 8, 10, 13, 15, 22, 40, 62,
                                              81, 94; DAB
    See also Wilson, John (Anthony) Burgess
    See also AITN 1; CDBLB 1960 to Present;
    DLB 14

Burke, Edmund
    1729(?)-1797 .... LC 7; DA; DAB; DAC;
                                              WLC
    See also DAM MST; DLB 104

Burke, Kenneth (Duva)
    1897-1993 ................. CLC 2, 24
    See also CA 5-8R; 143; CANR 39; DLB 45,
    63; MTCW

Burke, Leda
    See Garnett, David

Burke, Ralph
    See Silverberg, Robert

Burke, Thomas 1886-1945 ....... TCLC 63
    See also CA 113

Burney, Fanny 1752-1840 .... NCLC 12, 54
    See also DLB 39

Burns, Robert 1759-1796............ PC 6
    See also CDBLB 1789-1832; DA; DAB;
    DAC; DAM MST, POET; DLB 109;
    WLC

Burns, Tex
    See L'Amour, Louis (Dearborn)

Burnshaw, Stanley 1906-..... CLC 3, 13, 44
    See also CA 9-12R; DLB 48

Burr, Anne 1937- ................. CLC 6
    See also CA 25-28R

Burroughs, Edgar Rice
    1875-1950 ................. TCLC 2, 32
    See also AAYA 11; CA 104; 132;
    DAM NOV; DLB 8; MTCW; SATA 41

Burroughs, William S(eward)
    1914- ....... CLC 1, 2, 5, 15, 22, 42, 75;
                                              DA; DAB; DAC; WLC
    See also AITN 2; CA 9-12R; CANR 20;
    DAM MST, NOV, POP; DLB 2, 8, 16,
    152; DLBY 81; MTCW

Burton, Richard F. 1821-1890.... NCLC 42
    See also DLB 55

Busch, Frederick 1941- ... CLC 7, 10, 18, 47
    See also CA 33-36R; CAAS 1; CANR 45;
    DLB 6

Bush, Ronald 1946- .............. CLC 34
    See also CA 136

Bustos, F(rancisco)
    See Borges, Jorge Luis

Bustos Domecq, H(onorio)
    See Bioy Casares, Adolfo; Borges, Jorge
    Luis

Butler, Octavia E(stelle) 1947- ..... CLC 38
    See also BW 2; CA 73-76; CANR 12, 24,
    38; DAM MULT, POP; DLB 33;
    MTCW; SATA 84

Butler, Robert Olen (Jr.) 1945-..... CLC 81
    See also CA 112; DAM POP; INT 112

Butler, Samuel 1612-1680 .......... LC 16
    See also DLB 101, 126

Butler, Samuel
    1835-1902 ...... TCLC 1, 33; DA; DAB;
                                              DAC; WLC
    See also CA 143; CDBLB 1890-1914;
    DAM MST, NOV; DLB 18, 57

Butler, Walter C.
    See Faust, Frederick (Schiller)

Butor, Michel (Marie Francois)
    1926-............. CLC 1, 3, 8, 11, 15
    See also CA 9-12R; CANR 33; DLB 83;
    MTCW

Buzo, Alexander (John) 1944-...... CLC 61
    See also CA 97-100; CANR 17, 39

Buzzati, Dino 1906-1972 .......... CLC 36
    See also CA 33-36R

Byars, Betsy (Cromer) 1928-....... CLC 35
    See also CA 33-36R; CANR 18, 36; CLR 1,
    16; DLB 52; INT CANR-18; JRDA;
    MAICYA; MTCW; SAAS 1; SATA 4,
    46, 80

Byatt, A(ntonia) S(usan Drabble)
    1936- ................... CLC 19, 65
    See also CA 13-16R; CANR 13, 33, 50;
    DAM NOV, POP; DLB 14; MTCW

Byrne, David 1952-............... CLC 26
    See also CA 127

Byrne, John Keyes 1926-
    See Leonard, Hugh
    See also CA 102; INT 102

Byron, George Gordon (Noel)
    1788-1824 ..... NCLC 2, 12; DA; DAB;
                                              DAC; WLC
    See also CDBLB 1789-1832; DAM MST,
    POET; DLB 96, 110

C. 3. 3.
    See Wilde, Oscar (Fingal O'Flahertie Wills)

Caballero, Fernan 1796-1877..... NCLC 10

Cabell, James Branch 1879-1958 ... TCLC 6
    See also CA 105; DLB 9, 78

Cable, George Washington
    1844-1925 ............ TCLC 4; SSC 4
    See also CA 104; DLB 12, 74; DLBD 13

Cabral de Melo Neto, Joao 1920-... CLC 76
    See also DAM MULT

Cabrera Infante, G(uillermo)
    1929- ............ CLC 5, 25, 45; HLC
    See also CA 85-88; CANR 29;
    DAM MULT; DLB 113; HW; MTCW

Cade, Toni
    See Bambara, Toni Cade

Cadmus and Harmonia
    See Buchan, John

**Carter, Nick**
  See Smith, Martin Cruz

**Carver, Raymond**
  1938-1988 ... **CLC 22, 36, 53, 55; SSC 8**
  See also CA 33-36R; 126; CANR 17, 34;
  DAM NOV; DLB 130; DLBY 84, 88;
  MTCW

**Cary, Elizabeth, Lady Falkland**
  1585-1639 ..................... **LC 30**

**Cary, (Arthur) Joyce (Lunel)**
  1888-1957 ............... **TCLC 1, 29**
  See also CA 104; CDBLB 1914-1945;
  DLB 15, 100

**Casanova de Seingalt, Giovanni Jacopo**
  1725-1798 ..................... **LC 13**

**Casares, Adolfo Bioy**
  See Bioy Casares, Adolfo

**Casely-Hayford, J(oseph) E(phraim)**
  1866-1930 .............. **TCLC 24; BLC**
  See also BW 2; CA 123; DAM MULT

**Casey, John (Dudley)** 1939-........ **CLC 59**
  See also BEST 90:2; CA 69-72; CANR 23

**Casey, Michael** 1947-............. **CLC 2**
  See also CA 65-68; DLB 5

**Casey, Patrick**
  See Thurman, Wallace (Henry)

**Casey, Warren (Peter)** 1935-1988 ... **CLC 12**
  See also CA 101; 127; INT 101

**Casona, Alejandro**................. **CLC 49**
  See also Alvarez, Alejandro Rodriguez

**Cassavetes, John** 1929-1989........ **CLC 20**
  See also CA 85-88; 127

**Cassill, R(onald) V(erlin)** 1919-... **CLC 4, 23**
  See also CA 9-12R; CAAS 1; CANR 7, 45;
  DLB 6

**Cassirer, Ernst** 1874-1945 ........ **TCLC 61**

**Cassity, (Allen) Turner** 1929- .... **CLC 6, 42**
  See also CA 17-20R; CAAS 8; CANR 11;
  DLB 105

**Castaneda, Carlos** 1931(?)-......... **CLC 12**
  See also CA 25-28R; CANR 32; HW;
  MTCW

**Castedo, Elena** 1937- ............. **CLC 65**
  See also CA 132

**Castedo-Ellerman, Elena**
  See Castedo, Elena

**Castellanos, Rosario**
  1925-1974 ............. **CLC 66; HLC**
  See also CA 131; 53-56; DAM MULT;
  DLB 113; HW

**Castelvetro, Lodovico** 1505-1571..... **LC 12**

**Castiglione, Baldassare** 1478-1529 ... **LC 12**

**Castle, Robert**
  See Hamilton, Edmond

**Castro, Guillen de** 1569-1631........ **LC 19**

**Castro, Rosalia de** 1837-1885 ..... **NCLC 3**
  See also DAM MULT

**Cather, Willa**
  See Cather, Willa Sibert

**Cather, Willa Sibert**
  1873-1947 ....... **TCLC 1, 11, 31; DA;**
             **DAB; DAC; SSC 2; WLC**
  See also CA 104; 128; CDALB 1865-1917;
  DAM MST, NOV; DLB 9, 54, 78;
  DLBD 1; MTCW; SATA 30

**Catton, (Charles) Bruce**
  1899-1978 ................... **CLC 35**
  See also AITN 1; CA 5-8R; 81-84;
  CANR 7; DLB 17; SATA 2;
  SATA-Obit 24

**Catullus** c. 84B.C.-c. 54B.C. ..... **CMLC 18**

**Cauldwell, Frank**
  See King, Francis (Henry)

**Caunitz, William J.** 1933- ......... **CLC 34**
  See also BEST 89:3; CA 125; 130; INT 130

**Causley, Charles (Stanley)** 1917-..... **CLC 7**
  See also CA 9-12R; CANR 5, 35; CLR 30;
  DLB 27; MTCW; SATA 3, 66

**Caute, David** 1936-............... **CLC 29**
  See also CA 1-4R; CAAS 4; CANR 1, 33;
  DAM NOV; DLB 14

**Cavafy, C(onstantine) P(eter)**
  1863-1933 ................. **TCLC 2, 7**
  See also Kavafis, Konstantinos Petrou
  See also CA 148; DAM POET

**Cavallo, Evelyn**
  See Spark, Muriel (Sarah)

**Cavanna, Betty** ................... **CLC 12**
  See also Harrison, Elizabeth Cavanna
  See also JRDA; MAICYA; SAAS 4;
  SATA 1, 30

**Cavendish, Margaret Lucas**
  1623-1673 ................... **LC 30**
  See also DLB 131

**Caxton, William** 1421(?)-1491(?)..... **LC 17**

**Cayrol, Jean** 1911-............... **CLC 11**
  See also CA 89-92; DLB 83

**Cela, Camilo Jose**
  1916-............ **CLC 4, 13, 59; HLC**
  See also BEST 90:2; CA 21-24R; CAAS 10;
  CANR 21, 32; DAM MULT; DLBY 89;
  HW; MTCW

**Celan, Paul** ...... **CLC 10, 19, 53, 82; PC 10**
  See also Antschel, Paul
  See also DLB 69

**Celine, Louis-Ferdinand**
  ............. **CLC 1, 3, 4, 7, 9, 15, 47**
  See also Destouches, Louis-Ferdinand
  See also DLB 72

**Cellini, Benvenuto** 1500-1571 ........ **LC 7**

**Cendrars, Blaise** ................. **CLC 18**
  See also Sauser-Hall, Frederic

**Cernuda (y Bidon), Luis**
  1902-1963 ................... **CLC 54**
  See also CA 131; 89-92; DAM POET;
  DLB 134; HW

**Cervantes (Saavedra), Miguel de**
  1547-1616 ....... **LC 6, 23; DA; DAB;**
            **DAC; SSC 12; WLC**
  See also DAM MST, NOV

**Cesaire, Aime (Fernand)**
  1913- ............... **CLC 19, 32; BLC**
  See also BW 2; CA 65-68; CANR 24, 43;
  DAM MULT, POET; MTCW

**Chabon, Michael** 1965(?)- ......... **CLC 55**
  See also CA 139

**Chabrol, Claude** 1930- ............ **CLC 16**
  See also CA 110

**Challans, Mary** 1905-1983
  See Renault, Mary
  See also CA 81-84; 111; SATA 23;
  SATA-Obit 36

**Challis, George**
  See Faust, Frederick (Schiller)

**Chambers, Aidan** 1934- ........... **CLC 35**
  See also CA 25-28R; CANR 12, 31; JRDA;
  MAICYA; SAAS 12; SATA 1, 69

**Chambers, James** 1948-
  See Cliff, Jimmy
  See also CA 124

**Chambers, Jessie**
  See Lawrence, D(avid) H(erbert Richards)

**Chambers, Robert W.** 1865-1933... **TCLC 41**

**Chandler, Raymond (Thornton)**
  1888-1959 ........ **TCLC 1, 7; SSC 23**
  See also CA 104; 129; CDALB 1929-1941;
  DLBD 6; MTCW

**Chang, Jung** 1952- ............... **CLC 71**
  See also CA 142

**Channing, William Ellery**
  1780-1842 ................. **NCLC 17**
  See also DLB 1, 59

**Chaplin, Charles Spencer**
  1889-1977 ................... **CLC 16**
  See also Chaplin, Charlie
  See also CA 81-84; 73-76

**Chaplin, Charlie**
  See Chaplin, Charles Spencer
  See also DLB 44

**Chapman, George** 1559(?)-1634...... **LC 22**
  See also DAM DRAM; DLB 62, 121

**Chapman, Graham** 1941-1989 ...... **CLC 21**
  See also Monty Python
  See also CA 116; 129; CANR 35

**Chapman, John Jay** 1862-1933 ..... **TCLC 7**
  See also CA 104

**Chapman, Walker**
  See Silverberg, Robert

**Chappell, Fred (Davis)** 1936-.... **CLC 40, 78**
  See also CA 5-8R; CAAS 4; CANR 8, 33;
  DLB 6, 105

**Char, Rene(-Emile)**
  1907-1988 ........... **CLC 9, 11, 14, 55**
  See also CA 13-16R; 124; CANR 32;
  DAM POET; MTCW

**Charby, Jay**
  See Ellison, Harlan (Jay)

**Chardin, Pierre Teilhard de**
  See Teilhard de Chardin, (Marie Joseph)
  Pierre

**Charles I** 1600-1649 ............... **LC 13**

**Charyn, Jerome** 1937- ........ **CLC 5, 8, 18**
  See also CA 5-8R; CAAS 1; CANR 7;
  DLBY 83; MTCW

**Chase, Mary (Coyle)** 1907-1981 ...... **DC 1**
  See also CA 77-80; 105; SATA 17;
  SATA-Obit 29

Clark, Walter Van Tilburg
1909-1971 .................. **CLC 28**
See also CA 9-12R; 33-36R; DLB 9;
SATA 8

Clarke, Arthur C(harles)
1917- ...... **CLC 1, 4, 13, 18, 35; SSC 3**
See also AAYA 4; CA 1-4R; CANR 2, 28;
DAM POP; JRDA; MAICYA; MTCW;
SATA 13, 70

Clarke, Austin 1896-1974........ **CLC 6, 9**
See also CA 29-32; 49-52; CAP 2;
DAM POET; DLB 10, 20

Clarke, Austin C(hesterfield)
1934- .......... **CLC 8, 53; BLC; DAC**
See also BW 1; CA 25-28R; CAAS 16;
CANR 14, 32; DAM MULT; DLB 53,
125

Clarke, Gillian 1937- ............. **CLC 61**
See also CA 106; DLB 40

Clarke, Marcus (Andrew Hislop)
1846-1881 ................. **NCLC 19**

Clarke, Shirley 1925-............. **CLC 16**

Clash, The
See Headon, (Nicky) Topper; Jones, Mick;
Simonon, Paul; Strummer, Joe

Claudel, Paul (Louis Charles Marie)
1868-1955 ............... **TCLC 2, 10**
See also CA 104

Clavell, James (duMaresq)
1925-1994 ............ **CLC 6, 25, 87**
See also CA 25-28R; 146; CANR 26, 48;
DAM NOV, POP; MTCW

Cleaver, (Leroy) Eldridge
1935- .................. **CLC 30; BLC**
See also BW 1; CA 21-24R; CANR 16;
DAM MULT

Cleese, John (Marwood) 1939- ..... **CLC 21**
See also Monty Python
See also CA 112; 116; CANR 35; MTCW

Cleishbotham, Jebediah
See Scott, Walter

Cleland, John 1710-1789 ............ **LC 2**
See also DLB 39

Clemens, Samuel Langhorne 1835-1910
See Twain, Mark
See also CA 104; 135; CDALB 1865-1917;
DA; DAB; DAC; DAM MST, NOV;
DLB 11, 12, 23, 64, 74; JRDA;
MAICYA; YABC 2

Cleophil
See Congreve, William

Clerihew, E.
See Bentley, E(dmund) C(lerihew)

Clerk, N. W.
See Lewis, C(live) S(taples)

Cliff, Jimmy...................... **CLC 21**
See also Chambers, James

Clifton, (Thelma) Lucille
1936- ............... **CLC 19, 66; BLC**
See also BW 2; CA 49-52; CANR 2, 24, 42;
CLR 5; DAM MULT, POET; DLB 5, 41;
MAICYA; MTCW; SATA 20, 69

Clinton, Dirk
See Silverberg, Robert

Clough, Arthur Hugh 1819-1861.. **NCLC 27**
See also DLB 32

Clutha, Janet Paterson Frame 1924-
See Frame, Janet
See also CA 1-4R; CANR 2, 36; MTCW

Clyne, Terence
See Blatty, William Peter

Cobalt, Martin
See Mayne, William (James Carter)

Cobbett, William 1763-1835 ..... **NCLC 49**
See also DLB 43, 107, 158

Coburn, D(onald) L(ee) 1938- ...... **CLC 10**
See also CA 89-92

Cocteau, Jean (Maurice Eugene Clement)
1889-1963 .... **CLC 1, 8, 15, 16, 43; DA;
DAB; DAC; WLC**
See also CA 25-28; CANR 40; CAP 2;
DAM DRAM, MST, NOV; DLB 65;
MTCW

Codrescu, Andrei 1946- .......... **CLC 46**
See also CA 33-36R; CAAS 19; CANR 13,
34; DAM POET

Coe, Max
See Bourne, Randolph S(illiman)

Coe, Tucker
See Westlake, Donald E(dwin)

Coetzee, J(ohn) M(ichael)
1940- ................. **CLC 23, 33, 66**
See also CA 77-80; CANR 41; DAM NOV;
MTCW

Coffey, Brian
See Koontz, Dean R(ay)

Cohan, George M. 1878-1942 ..... **TCLC 60**

Cohen, Arthur A(llen)
1928-1986 ............... **CLC 7, 31**
See also CA 1-4R; 120; CANR 1, 17, 42;
DLB 28

Cohen, Leonard (Norman)
1934- ................ **CLC 3, 38; DAC**
See also CA 21-24R; CANR 14;
DAM MST; DLB 53; MTCW

Cohen, Matt 1942-.......... **CLC 19; DAC**
See also CA 61-64; CAAS 18; CANR 40;
DLB 53

Cohen-Solal, Annie 19(?)- ........... **CLC 50**

Colegate, Isabel 1931- ............ **CLC 36**
See also CA 17-20R; CANR 8, 22; DLB 14;
INT CANR-22; MTCW

Coleman, Emmett
See Reed, Ishmael

Coleridge, Samuel Taylor
1772-1834 ..... **NCLC 9, 54; DA; DAB;
DAC; PC 11; WLC**
See also CDBLB 1789-1832; DAM MST,
POET; DLB 93, 107

Coleridge, Sara 1802-1852....... **NCLC 31**

Coles, Don 1928- ................. **CLC 46**
See also CA 115; CANR 38

Colette, (Sidonie-Gabrielle)
1873-1954 ...... **TCLC 1, 5, 16; SSC 10**
See also CA 104; 131; DAM NOV; DLB 65;
MTCW

Collett, (Jacobine) Camilla (Wergeland)
1813-1895 ................ **NCLC 22**

Collier, Christopher 1930- ......... **CLC 30**
See also AAYA 13; CA 33-36R; CANR 13,
33; JRDA; MAICYA; SATA 16, 70

Collier, James L(incoln) 1928- ..... **CLC 30**
See also AAYA 13; CA 9-12R; CANR 4,
33; CLR 3; DAM POP; JRDA;
MAICYA; SAAS 21; SATA 8, 70

Collier, Jeremy 1650-1726.......... **LC 6**

Collier, John 1901-1980.......... **SSC 19**
See also CA 65-68; 97-100; CANR 10;
DLB 77

Collins, Hunt
See Hunter, Evan

Collins, Linda 1931-.............. **CLC 44**
See also CA 125

Collins, (William) Wilkie
1824-1889 .............. **NCLC 1, 18**
See also CDBLB 1832-1890; DLB 18, 70,
159

Collins, William 1721-1759 .......... **LC 4**
See also DAM POET; DLB 109

Collodi, Carlo 1826-1890........ **NCLC 54**
See also Lorenzini, Carlo
See also CLR 5

Colman, George
See Glassco, John

Colt, Winchester Remington
See Hubbard, L(afayette) Ron(ald)

Colter, Cyrus 1910- .............. **CLC 58**
See also BW 1; CA 65-68; CANR 10;
DLB 33

Colton, James
See Hansen, Joseph

Colum, Padraic 1881-1972........ **CLC 28**
See also CA 73-76; 33-36R; CANR 35;
CLR 36; MAICYA; MTCW; SATA 15

Colvin, James
See Moorcock, Michael (John)

Colwin, Laurie (E.)
1944-1992 .......... **CLC 5, 13, 23, 84**
See also CA 89-92; 139; CANR 20, 46;
DLBY 80; MTCW

Comfort, Alex(ander) 1920-........ **CLC 7**
See also CA 1-4R; CANR 1, 45; DAM POP

Comfort, Montgomery
See Campbell, (John) Ramsey

Compton-Burnett, I(vy)
1884(?)-1969 ...... **CLC 1, 3, 10, 15, 34**
See also CA 1-4R; 25-28R; CANR 4;
DAM NOV; DLB 36; MTCW

Comstock, Anthony 1844-1915 .... **TCLC 13**
See also CA 110

Comte, Auguste 1798-1857....... **NCLC 54**

Conan Doyle, Arthur
See Doyle, Arthur Conan

Conde, Maryse 1937-.......... **CLC 52, 92**
See also Boucolon, Maryse
See also BW 2; DAM MULT

Condillac, Etienne Bonnot de
1714-1780 ................... **LC 26**

Crane, R(onald) S(almon)
   1886-1967 . . . . . . . . . . . . . . . . . . CLC 27
   See also CA 85-88; DLB 63

Crane, Stephen (Townley)
   1871-1900 . . . . . . TCLC 11, 17, 32; DA;
                              DAB; DAC; SSC 7; WLC
   See also CA 109; 140; CDALB 1865-1917;
   DAM MST, NOV, POET; DLB 12, 54,
   78; YABC 2

Crase, Douglas   1944- . . . . . . . . . . . . CLC 58
   See also CA 106

Crashaw, Richard   1612(?)-1649 . . . . . . LC 24
   See also DLB 126

Craven, Margaret
   1901-1980 . . . . . . . . . . . . . CLC 17; DAC
   See also CA 103

Crawford, F(rancis) Marion
   1854-1909 . . . . . . . . . . . . . . . . TCLC 10
   See also CA 107; DLB 71

Crawford, Isabella Valancy
   1850-1887 . . . . . . . . . . . . . . . . NCLC 12
   See also DLB 92

Crayon, Geoffrey
   See Irving, Washington

Creasey, John   1908-1973 . . . . . . . . . . CLC 11
   See also CA 5-8R; 41-44R; CANR 8;
   DLB 77; MTCW

Crebillon, Claude Prosper Jolyot de (fils)
   1707-1777 . . . . . . . . . . . . . . . . . . LC 28

Credo
   See Creasey, John

Creeley, Robert (White)
   1926- . . . . . CLC 1, 2, 4, 8, 11, 15, 36, 78
   See also CA 1-4R; CAAS 10; CANR 23, 43;
   DAM POET; DLB 5, 16; MTCW

Crews, Harry (Eugene)
   1935- . . . . . . . . . . . . . . . . CLC 6, 23, 49
   See also AITN 1; CA 25-28R; CANR 20;
   DLB 6, 143; MTCW

Crichton, (John) Michael
   1942- . . . . . . . . . . . . . . CLC 2, 6, 54, 90
   See also AAYA 10; AITN 2; CA 25-28R;
   CANR 13, 40; DAM NOV, POP;
   DLBY 81; INT CANR-13; JRDA;
   MTCW; SATA 9

Crispin, Edmund . . . . . . . . . . . . . . . . CLC 22
   See also Montgomery, (Robert) Bruce
   See also DLB 87

Cristofer, Michael   1945(?)- . . . . . . . . CLC 28
   See also CA 110; DAM DRAM; DLB 7

Croce, Benedetto   1866-1952 . . . . . . TCLC 37
   See also CA 120

Crockett, David   1786-1836 . . . . . . . NCLC 8
   See also DLB 3, 11

Crockett, Davy
   See Crockett, David

Crofts, Freeman Wills
   1879-1957 . . . . . . . . . . . . . . . . TCLC 55
   See also CA 115; DLB 77

Croker, John Wilson   1780-1857 . . NCLC 10
   See also DLB 110

Crommelynck, Fernand   1885-1970 . . CLC 75
   See also CA 89-92

Cronin, A(rchibald) J(oseph)
   1896-1981 . . . . . . . . . . . . . . . . . CLC 32
   See also CA 1-4R; 102; CANR 5; SATA 47;
   SATA-Obit 25

Cross, Amanda
   See Heilbrun, Carolyn G(old)

Crothers, Rachel   1878(?)-1958 . . . . . TCLC 19
   See also CA 113; DLB 7

Croves, Hal
   See Traven, B.

Crow Dog, Mary . . . . . . . . . . . . . . . . CLC 93
   See also Brave Bird, Mary

Crowfield, Christopher
   See Stowe, Harriet (Elizabeth) Beecher

Crowley, Aleister . . . . . . . . . . . . . . . . TCLC 7
   See also Crowley, Edward Alexander

Crowley, Edward Alexander   1875-1947
   See Crowley, Aleister
   See also CA 104

Crowley, John   1942- . . . . . . . . . . . . . CLC 57
   See also CA 61-64; CANR 43; DLBY 82;
   SATA 65

Crud
   See Crumb, R(obert)

Crumarums
   See Crumb, R(obert)

Crumb, R(obert)   1943- . . . . . . . . . . . CLC 17
   See also CA 106

Crumbum
   See Crumb, R(obert)

Crumski
   See Crumb, R(obert)

Crum the Bum
   See Crumb, R(obert)

Crunk
   See Crumb, R(obert)

Crustt
   See Crumb, R(obert)

Cryer, Gretchen (Kiger)   1935- . . . . . . CLC 21
   See also CA 114; 123

Csath, Geza   1887-1919 . . . . . . . . . . TCLC 13
   See also CA 111

Cudlip, David   1933- . . . . . . . . . . . . . CLC 34

Cullen, Countee
   1903-1946 . . . . . . TCLC 4, 37; BLC; DA;
                                                          DAC
   See also BW 1; CA 108; 124;
   CDALB 1917-1929; DAM MST, MULT,
   POET; DLB 4, 48, 51; MTCW; SATA 18

Cum, R.
   See Crumb, R(obert)

Cummings, Bruce F(rederick)   1889-1919
   See Barbellion, W. N. P.
   See also CA 123

Cummings, E(dward) E(stlin)
   1894-1962 . . . . . . CLC 1, 3, 8, 12, 15, 68;
                              DA; DAB; DAC; PC 5; WLC 2
   See also CA 73-76; CANR 31;
   CDALB 1929-1941; DAM MST, POET;
   DLB 4, 48; MTCW

Cunha, Euclides (Rodrigues Pimenta) da
   1866-1909 . . . . . . . . . . . . . . . . TCLC 24
   See also CA 123

Cunningham, E. V.
   See Fast, Howard (Melvin)

Cunningham, J(ames) V(incent)
   1911-1985 . . . . . . . . . . . . . . CLC 3, 31
   See also CA 1-4R; 115; CANR 1; DLB 5

Cunningham, Julia (Woolfolk)
   1916- . . . . . . . . . . . . . . . . . . . . CLC 12
   See also CA 9-12R; CANR 4, 19, 36;
   JRDA; MAICYA; SAAS 2; SATA 1, 26

Cunningham, Michael   1952- . . . . . . . CLC 34
   See also CA 136

Cunninghame Graham, R(obert) B(ontine)
   1852-1936 . . . . . . . . . . . . . . . . TCLC 19
   See also Graham, R(obert) B(ontine)
   Cunninghame
   See also CA 119; DLB 98

Currie, Ellen   19(?)- . . . . . . . . . . . . . . CLC 44

Curtin, Philip
   See Lowndes, Marie Adelaide (Belloc)

Curtis, Price
   See Ellison, Harlan (Jay)

Cutrate, Joe
   See Spiegelman, Art

Czaczkes, Shmuel Yosef
   See Agnon, S(hmuel) Y(osef Halevi)

Dabrowska, Maria (Szumska)
   1889-1965 . . . . . . . . . . . . . . . . . CLC 15
   See also CA 106

Dabydeen, David   1955- . . . . . . . . . . . CLC 34
   See also BW 1; CA 125

Dacey, Philip   1939- . . . . . . . . . . . . . . CLC 51
   See also CA 37-40R; CAAS 17; CANR 14,
   32; DLB 105

Dagerman, Stig (Halvard)
   1923-1954 . . . . . . . . . . . . . . . . TCLC 17
   See also CA 117

Dahl, Roald
   1916-1990 . . . . . . CLC 1, 6, 18, 79; DAB;
                                                          DAC
   See also AAYA 15; CA 1-4R; 133;
   CANR 6, 32, 37; CLR 1, 7; DAM MST,
   NOV, POP; DLB 139; JRDA; MAICYA;
   MTCW; SATA 1, 26, 73; SATA-Obit 65

Dahlberg, Edward   1900-1977 . . . CLC 1, 7, 14
   See also CA 9-12R; 69-72; CANR 31;
   DLB 48; MTCW

Dale, Colin . . . . . . . . . . . . . . . . . . . . TCLC 18
   See also Lawrence, T(homas) E(dward)

Dale, George E.
   See Asimov, Isaac

Daly, Elizabeth   1878-1967 . . . . . . . . CLC 52
   See also CA 23-24; 25-28R; CAP 2

Daly, Maureen   1921- . . . . . . . . . . . . . CLC 17
   See also AAYA 5; CANR 37; JRDA;
   MAICYA; SAAS 1; SATA 2

Damas, Leon-Gontran   1912-1978 . . . CLC 84
   See also BW 1; CA 125; 73-76

Dana, Richard Henry Sr.
   1787-1879 . . . . . . . . . . . . . . . . NCLC 53

Daniel, Samuel   1562(?)-1619 . . . . . . . . LC 24
   See also DLB 62

Daniels, Brett
   See Adler, Renata

**Deledda, Grazia (Cosima)**
1875(?)-1936 ............... **TCLC 23**
See also CA 123

**Delibes, Miguel** ............... **CLC 8, 18**
See also Delibes Setien, Miguel

**Delibes Setien, Miguel** 1920-
See Delibes, Miguel
See also CA 45-48; CANR 1, 32; HW;
MTCW

**DeLillo, Don**
1936- ..... **CLC 8, 10, 13, 27, 39, 54, 76**
See also BEST 89:1; CA 81-84; CANR 21;
DAM NOV, POP; DLB 6; MTCW

**de Lisser, H. G.**
See De Lisser, Herbert George
See also DLB 117

**De Lisser, Herbert George**
1878-1944 ................. **TCLC 12**
See also de Lisser, H. G.
See also BW 2; CA 109

**Deloria, Vine (Victor), Jr.** 1933- .... **CLC 21**
See also CA 53-56; CANR 5, 20, 48;
DAM MULT; MTCW; NNAL; SATA 21

**Del Vecchio, John M(ichael)**
1947- ...................... **CLC 29**
See also CA 110; DLBD 9

**de Man, Paul (Adolph Michel)**
1919-1983 ................. **CLC 55**
See also CA 128; 111; DLB 67; MTCW

**De Marinis, Rick** 1934- ........... **CLC 54**
See also CA 57-60; CANR 9, 25, 50

**Dembry, R. Emmet**
See Murfree, Mary Noailles

**Demby, William** 1922- ....... **CLC 53; BLC**
See also BW 1; CA 81-84; DAM MULT;
DLB 33

**Demijohn, Thom**
See Disch, Thomas M(ichael)

**de Montherlant, Henry (Milon)**
See Montherlant, Henry (Milon) de

**Demosthenes** 384B.C.-322B.C. ... **CMLC 13**

**de Natale, Francine**
See Malzberg, Barry N(athaniel)

**Denby, Edwin (Orr)** 1903-1983 ..... **CLC 48**
See also CA 138; 110

**Denis, Julio**
See Cortazar, Julio

**Denmark, Harrison**
See Zelazny, Roger (Joseph)

**Dennis, John** 1658-1734 ........... **LC 11**
See also DLB 101

**Dennis, Nigel (Forbes)** 1912-1989 .... **CLC 8**
See also CA 25-28R; 129; DLB 13, 15;
MTCW

**De Palma, Brian (Russell)** 1940- .... **CLC 20**
See also CA 109

**De Quincey, Thomas** 1785-1859 ... **NCLC 4**
See also CDBLB 1789-1832; DLB 110; 144

**Deren, Eleanora** 1908(?)-1961
See Deren, Maya
See also CA 111

**Deren, Maya** .................... **CLC 16**
See also Deren, Eleanora

**Derleth, August (William)**
1909-1971 ................... **CLC 31**
See also CA 1-4R; 29-32R; CANR 4;
DLB 9; SATA 5

**Der Nister** 1884-1950 ........... **TCLC 56**

**de Routisie, Albert**
See Aragon, Louis

**Derrida, Jacques** 1930- ........ **CLC 24, 87**
See also CA 124; 127

**Derry Down Derry**
See Lear, Edward

**Dersonnes, Jacques**
See Simenon, Georges (Jacques Christian)

**Desai, Anita** 1937- ...... **CLC 19, 37; DAB**
See also CA 81-84; CANR 33; DAM NOV;
MTCW; SATA 63

**de Saint-Luc, Jean**
See Glassco, John

**de Saint Roman, Arnaud**
See Aragon, Louis

**Descartes, Rene** 1596-1650 ......... **LC 20**

**De Sica, Vittorio** 1901(?)-1974 ..... **CLC 20**
See also CA 117

**Desnos, Robert** 1900-1945 ....... **TCLC 22**
See also CA 121

**Destouches, Louis-Ferdinand**
1894-1961 ................. **CLC 9, 15**
See also Celine, Louis-Ferdinand
See also CA 85-88; CANR 28; MTCW

**Deutsch, Babette** 1895-1982 ....... **CLC 18**
See also CA 1-4R; 108; CANR 4; DLB 45;
SATA 1; SATA-Obit 33

**Devenant, William** 1606-1649 ....... **LC 13**

**Devkota, Laxmiprasad**
1909-1959 ................. **TCLC 23**
See also CA 123

**De Voto, Bernard (Augustine)**
1897-1955 ................. **TCLC 29**
See also CA 113; DLB 9

**De Vries, Peter**
1910-1993 .... **CLC 1, 2, 3, 7, 10, 28, 46**
See also CA 17-20R; 142; CANR 41;
DAM NOV; DLB 6; DLBY 82; MTCW

**Dexter, Martin**
See Faust, Frederick (Schiller)

**Dexter, Pete** 1943- ........... **CLC 34, 55**
See also BEST 89:2; CA 127; 131;
DAM POP; INT 131; MTCW

**Diamano, Silmang**
See Senghor, Leopold Sedar

**Diamond, Neil** 1941- ............. **CLC 30**
See also CA 108

**Diaz del Castillo, Bernal** 1496-1584 .. **LC 31**

**di Bassetto, Corno**
See Shaw, George Bernard

**Dick, Philip K(indred)**
1928-1982 ............. **CLC 10, 30, 72**
See also CA 49-52; 106; CANR 2, 16;
DAM NOV, POP; DLB 8; MTCW

**Dickens, Charles (John Huffam)**
1812-1870 ...... **NCLC 3, 8, 18, 26, 37,**
**50; DA; DAB; DAC; SSC 17; WLC**
See also CDBLB 1832-1890; DAM MST,
NOV; DLB 21, 55, 70, 159; JRDA;
MAICYA; SATA 15

**Dickey, James (Lafayette)**
1923- ........ **CLC 1, 2, 4, 7, 10, 15, 47**
See also AITN 1, 2; CA 9-12R; CABS 2;
CANR 10, 48; CDALB 1968-1988;
DAM NOV, POET, POP; DLB 5;
DLBD 7; DLBY 82, 93; INT CANR-10;
MTCW

**Dickey, William** 1928-1994 ...... **CLC 3, 28**
See also CA 9-12R; 145; CANR 24; DLB 5

**Dickinson, Charles** 1951- .......... **CLC 49**
See also CA 128

**Dickinson, Emily (Elizabeth)**
1830-1886 ....... **NCLC 21; DA; DAB;**
**DAC; PC 1; WLC**
See also CDALB 1865-1917; DAM MST,
POET; DLB 1; SATA 29

**Dickinson, Peter (Malcolm)**
1927- .................... **CLC 12, 35**
See also AAYA 9; CA 41-44R; CANR 31;
CLR 29; DLB 87, 161; JRDA; MAICYA;
SATA 5, 62

**Dickson, Carr**
See Carr, John Dickson

**Dickson, Carter**
See Carr, John Dickson

**Diderot, Denis** 1713-1784 .......... **LC 26**

**Didion, Joan** 1934- ..... **CLC 1, 3, 8, 14, 32**
See also AITN 1; CA 5-8R; CANR 14;
CDALB 1968-1988; DAM NOV; DLB 2;
DLBY 81, 86; MTCW

**Dietrich, Robert**
See Hunt, E(verette) Howard, (Jr.)

**Dillard, Annie** 1945- ............ **CLC 9, 60**
See also AAYA 6; CA 49-52; CANR 3, 43;
DAM NOV; DLBY 80; MTCW;
SATA 10

**Dillard, R(ichard) H(enry) W(ilde)**
1937- ...................... **CLC 5**
See also CA 21-24R; CAAS 7; CANR 10;
DLB 5

**Dillon, Eilis** 1920-1994 ............ **CLC 17**
See also CA 9-12R; 147; CAAS 3; CANR 4,
38; CLR 26; MAICYA; SATA 2, 74;
SATA-Obit 83

**Dimont, Penelope**
See Mortimer, Penelope (Ruth)

**Dinesen, Isak** .......... **CLC 10, 29; SSC 7**
See also Blixen, Karen (Christentze
Dinesen)

**Ding Ling** ...................... **CLC 68**
See also Chiang Pin-chin

**Disch, Thomas M(ichael)** 1940- ... **CLC 7, 36**
See also AAYA 17; CA 21-24R; CAAS 4;
CANR 17, 36; CLR 18; DLB 8;
MAICYA; MTCW; SAAS 15; SATA 54

**Disch, Tom**
See Disch, Thomas M(ichael)

**d'Isly, Georges**
See Simenon, Georges (Jacques Christian)

**Drummond de Andrade, Carlos**
    1902-1987 .................. **CLC 18**
    See also Andrade, Carlos Drummond de
    See also CA 132; 123

**Drury, Allen (Stuart)** 1918-........ **CLC 37**
    See also CA 57-60; CANR 18;
    INT CANR-18

**Dryden, John**
    1631-1700 ........ **LC 3, 21; DA; DAB;**
                        **DAC; DC 3; WLC**
    See also CDBLB 1660-1789; DAM DRAM,
    MST, POET; DLB 80, 101, 131

**Duberman, Martin** 1930-........... **CLC 8**
    See also CA 1-4R; CANR 2

**Dubie, Norman (Evans)** 1945-...... **CLC 36**
    See also CA 69-72; CANR 12; DLB 120

**Du Bois, W(illiam) E(dward) B(urghardt)**
    1868-1963 ...... **CLC 1, 2, 13, 64; BLC;**
                        **DA; DAC; WLC**
    See also BW 1; CA 85-88; CANR 34;
    CDALB 1865-1917; DAM MST, MULT,
    NOV; DLB 47, 50, 91; MTCW; SATA 42

**Dubus, Andre** 1936-... **CLC 13, 36; SSC 15**
    See also CA 21-24R; CANR 17; DLB 130;
    INT CANR-17

**Duca Minimo**
    See D'Annunzio, Gabriele

**Ducharme, Rejean** 1941-.......... **CLC 74**
    See also DLB 60

**Duclos, Charles Pinot** 1704-1772 ..... **LC 1**

**Dudek, Louis** 1918- ........... **CLC 11, 19**
    See also CA 45-48; CAAS 14; CANR 1;
    DLB 88

**Duerrenmatt, Friedrich**
    1921-1990 ...... **CLC 1, 4, 8, 11, 15, 43**
    See also CA 17-20R; CANR 33;
    DAM DRAM; DLB 69, 124; MTCW

**Duffy, Bruce** (?)-................ **CLC 50**

**Duffy, Maureen** 1933- ............ **CLC 37**
    See also CA 25-28R; CANR 33; DLB 14;
    MTCW

**Dugan, Alan** 1923- .............. **CLC 2, 6**
    See also CA 81-84; DLB 5

**du Gard, Roger Martin**
    See Martin du Gard, Roger

**Duhamel, Georges** 1884-1966 ....... **CLC 8**
    See also CA 81-84; 25-28R; CANR 35;
    DLB 65; MTCW

**Dujardin, Edouard (Emile Louis)**
    1861-1949 .................. **TCLC 13**
    See also CA 109; DLB 123

**Dumas, Alexandre (Davy de la Pailleterie)**
    1802-1870 ...... **NCLC 11; DA; DAB;**
                        **DAC; WLC**
    See also DAM MST, NOV; DLB 119;
    SATA 18

**Dumas, Alexandre**
    1824-1895 ............. **NCLC 9; DC 1**

**Dumas, Claudine**
    See Malzberg, Barry N(athaniel)

**Dumas, Henry L.** 1934-1968 ..... **CLC 6, 62**
    See also BW 1; CA 85-88; DLB 41

**du Maurier, Daphne**
    1907-1989 ....... **CLC 6, 11, 59; DAB;**
                        **DAC; SSC 18**
    See also CA 5-8R; 128; CANR 6;
    DAM MST, POP; MTCW; SATA 27;
    SATA-Obit 60

**Dunbar, Paul Laurence**
    1872-1906 ...... **TCLC 2, 12; BLC; DA;**
                        **DAC; PC 5; SSC 8; WLC**
    See also BW 1; CA 104; 124;
    CDALB 1865-1917; DAM MST, MULT,
    POET; DLB 50, 54, 78; SATA 34

**Dunbar, William** 1460(?)-1530(?) .... **LC 20**
    See also DLB 132, 146

**Duncan, Lois** 1934-............... **CLC 26**
    See also AAYA 4; CA 1-4R; CANR 2, 23,
    36; CLR 29; JRDA; MAICYA; SAAS 2;
    SATA 1, 36, 75

**Duncan, Robert (Edward)**
    1919-1988 .... **CLC 1, 2, 4, 7, 15, 41, 55;**
                        **PC 2**
    See also CA 9-12R; 124; CANR 28;
    DAM POET; DLB 5, 16; MTCW

**Duncan, Sara Jeannette**
    1861-1922 .................. **TCLC 60**
    See also DLB 92

**Dunlap, William** 1766-1839 ....... **NCLC 2**
    See also DLB 30, 37, 59

**Dunn, Douglas (Eaglesham)**
    1942-.................... **CLC 6, 40**
    See also CA 45-48; CANR 2, 33; DLB 40;
    MTCW

**Dunn, Katherine (Karen)** 1945-..... **CLC 71**
    See also CA 33-36R

**Dunn, Stephen** 1939- .............. **CLC 36**
    See also CA 33-36R; CANR 12, 48;
    DLB 105

**Dunne, Finley Peter** 1867-1936.... **TCLC 28**
    See also CA 108; DLB 11, 23

**Dunne, John Gregory** 1932-........ **CLC 28**
    See also CA 25-28R; CANR 14, 50;
    DLBY 80

**Dunsany, Edward John Moreton Drax**
    **Plunkett** 1878-1957
    See Dunsany, Lord
    See also CA 104; 148; DLB 10

**Dunsany, Lord**................. **TCLC 2, 59**
    See also Dunsany, Edward John Moreton
    Drax Plunkett
    See also DLB 77, 153, 156

**du Perry, Jean**
    See Simenon, Georges (Jacques Christian)

**Durang, Christopher (Ferdinand)**
    1949-.................... **CLC 27, 38**
    See also CA 105; CANR 50

**Duras, Marguerite**
    1914-1996 .. **CLC 3, 6, 11, 20, 34, 40, 68**
    See also CA 25-28R; 151; CANR 50;
    DLB 83; MTCW

**Durban, (Rosa) Pam** 1947-........ **CLC 39**
    See also CA 123

**Durcan, Paul** 1944-............ **CLC 43, 70**
    See also CA 134; DAM POET

**Durkheim, Emile** 1858-1917 ...... **TCLC 55**

**Durrell, Lawrence (George)**
    1912-1990 .... **CLC 1, 4, 6, 8, 13, 27, 41**
    See also CA 9-12R; 132; CANR 40;
    CDBLB 1945-1960; DAM NOV; DLB 15,
    27; DLBY 90; MTCW

**Durrenmatt, Friedrich**
    See Duerrenmatt, Friedrich

**Dutt, Toru** 1856-1877........... **NCLC 29**

**Dwight, Timothy** 1752-1817...... **NCLC 13**
    See also DLB 37

**Dworkin, Andrea** 1946-........... **CLC 43**
    See also CA 77-80; CAAS 21; CANR 16,
    39; INT CANR-16; MTCW

**Dwyer, Deanna**
    See Koontz, Dean R(ay)

**Dwyer, K. R.**
    See Koontz, Dean R(ay)

**Dylan, Bob** 1941-...... **CLC 3, 4, 6, 12, 77**
    See also CA 41-44R; DLB 16

**Eagleton, Terence (Francis)** 1943-
    See Eagleton, Terry
    See also CA 57-60; CANR 7, 23; MTCW

**Eagleton, Terry**................... **CLC 63**
    See also Eagleton, Terence (Francis)

**Early, Jack**
    See Scoppettone, Sandra

**East, Michael**
    See West, Morris L(anglo)

**Eastaway, Edward**
    See Thomas, (Philip) Edward

**Eastlake, William (Derry)** 1917-..... **CLC 8**
    See also CA 5-8R; CAAS 1; CANR 5;
    DLB 6; INT CANR-5

**Eastman, Charles A(lexander)**
    1858-1939 .................. **TCLC 55**
    See also DAM MULT; NNAL; YABC 1

**Eberhart, Richard (Ghormley)**
    1904-................ **CLC 3, 11, 19, 56**
    See also CA 1-4R; CANR 2;
    CDALB 1941-1968; DAM POET;
    DLB 48; MTCW

**Eberstadt, Fernanda** 1960-........ **CLC 39**
    See also CA 136

**Echegaray (y Eizaguirre), Jose (Maria Waldo)**
    1832-1916 .................. **TCLC 4**
    See also CA 104; CANR 32; HW; MTCW

**Echeverria, (Jose) Esteban (Antonino)**
    1805-1851 .................. **NCLC 18**

**Echo**
    See Proust, (Valentin-Louis-George-Eugene-)
    Marcel

**Eckert, Allan W.** 1931- ........... **CLC 17**
    See also CA 13-16R; CANR 14, 45;
    INT CANR-14; SAAS 21; SATA 29;
    SATA-Brief 27

**Eckhart, Meister** 1260(?)-1328(?) .. **CMLC 9**
    See also DLB 115

**Eckmar, F. R.**
    See de Hartog, Jan

**Eco, Umberto** 1932-........... **CLC 28, 60**
    See also BEST 90:1; CA 77-80; CANR 12,
    33; DAM NOV, POP; MTCW

**Engelhardt, Frederick**
See Hubbard, L(afayette) Ron(ald)

**Enright, D(ennis) J(oseph)**
1920- . . . . . . . . . . . . . . . . . . CLC **4, 8, 31**
See also CA 1-4R; CANR 1, 42; DLB 27;
SATA 25

**Enzensberger, Hans Magnus**
1929- . . . . . . . . . . . . . . . . . . . . . . CLC **43**
See also CA 116; 119

**Ephron, Nora** 1941- . . . . . . . . . . . CLC **17, 31**
See also AITN 2; CA 65-68; CANR 12, 39

**Epsilon**
See Betjeman, John

**Epstein, Daniel Mark** 1948- . . . . . . . . CLC **7**
See also CA 49-52; CANR 2

**Epstein, Jacob** 1956- . . . . . . . . . . . . CLC **19**
See also CA 114

**Epstein, Joseph** 1937- . . . . . . . . . . . . . CLC **39**
See also CA 112; 119; CANR 50

**Epstein, Leslie** 1938- . . . . . . . . . . . . . CLC **27**
See also CA 73-76; CAAS 12; CANR 23

**Equiano, Olaudah**
1745(?)-1797 . . . . . . . . . . . . . LC **16; BLC**
See also DAM MULT; DLB 37, 50

**Erasmus, Desiderius** 1469(?)-1536. . . . LC **16**

**Erdman, Paul E(mil)** 1932- . . . . . . . . CLC **25**
See also AITN 1; CA 61-64; CANR 13, 43

**Erdrich, Louise** 1954- . . . . . . . . . . CLC **39, 54**
See also AAYA 10; BEST 89:1; CA 114;
CANR 41; DAM MULT, NOV, POP;
DLB 152; MTCW; NNAL

**Erenburg, Ilya (Grigoryevich)**
See Ehrenburg, Ilya (Grigoryevich)

**Erickson, Stephen Michael** 1950-
See Erickson, Steve
See also CA 129

**Erickson, Steve** . . . . . . . . . . . . . . . . CLC **64**
See also Erickson, Stephen Michael

**Ericson, Walter**
See Fast, Howard (Melvin)

**Eriksson, Buntel**
See Bergman, (Ernst) Ingmar

**Ernaux, Annie** 1940- . . . . . . . . . . . . . CLC **88**
See also CA 147

**Eschenbach, Wolfram von**
See Wolfram von Eschenbach

**Eseki, Bruno**
See Mphahlele, Ezekiel

**Esenin, Sergei (Alexandrovich)**
1895-1925 . . . . . . . . . . . . . . . . . TCLC **4**
See also CA 104

**Eshleman, Clayton** 1935- . . . . . . . . . . CLC **7**
See also CA 33-36R; CAAS 6; DLB 5

**Espriella, Don Manuel Alvarez**
See Southey, Robert

**Espriu, Salvador** 1913-1985 . . . . . . . . CLC **9**
See also CA 115; DLB 134

**Espronceda, Jose de** 1808-1842 . . . NCLC **39**

**Esse, James**
See Stephens, James

**Esterbrook, Tom**
See Hubbard, L(afayette) Ron(ald)

**Estleman, Loren D.** 1952- . . . . . . . . CLC **48**
See also CA 85-88; CANR 27; DAM NOV,
POP; INT CANR-27; MTCW

**Eugenides, Jeffrey** 1960(?)- . . . . . . . CLC **81**
See also CA 144

**Euripides** c. 485B.C.-406B.C. . . . . . . . . DC **4**
See also DA; DAB; DAC; DAM DRAM,
MST

**Evan, Evin**
See Faust, Frederick (Schiller)

**Evans, Evan**
See Faust, Frederick (Schiller)

**Evans, Marian**
See Eliot, George

**Evans, Mary Ann**
See Eliot, George

**Evarts, Esther**
See Benson, Sally

**Everett, Percival L.** 1956- . . . . . . . . . CLC **57**
See also BW 2; CA 129

**Everson, R(onald) G(ilmour)**
1903- . . . . . . . . . . . . . . . . . . . . . . CLC **27**
See also CA 17-20R; DLB 88

**Everson, William (Oliver)**
1912-1994 . . . . . . . . . . . . . . CLC **1, 5, 14**
See also CA 9-12R; 145; CANR 20; DLB 5,
16; MTCW

**Evtushenko, Evgenii Aleksandrovich**
See Yevtushenko, Yevgeny (Alexandrovich)

**Ewart, Gavin (Buchanan)**
1916-1995 . . . . . . . . . . . . . . . CLC **13, 46**
See also CA 89-92; 150; CANR 17, 46;
DLB 40; MTCW

**Ewers, Hanns Heinz** 1871-1943 . . . TCLC **12**
See also CA 109; 149

**Ewing, Frederick R.**
See Sturgeon, Theodore (Hamilton)

**Exley, Frederick (Earl)**
1929-1992 . . . . . . . . . . . . . . . . CLC **6, 11**
See also AITN 2; CA 81-84; 138; DLB 143;
DLBY 81

**Eynhardt, Guillermo**
See Quiroga, Horacio (Sylvestre)

**Ezekiel, Nissim** 1924- . . . . . . . . . . . . . CLC **61**
See also CA 61-64

**Ezekiel, Tish O'Dowd** 1943- . . . . . . . CLC **34**
See also CA 129

**Fadeyev, A.**
See Bulgya, Alexander Alexandrovich

**Fadeyev, Alexander** . . . . . . . . . . . . . . TCLC **53**
See also Bulgya, Alexander Alexandrovich

**Fagen, Donald** 1948- . . . . . . . . . . . . . CLC **26**

**Fainzilberg, Ilya Arnoldovich** 1897-1937
See Ilf, Ilya
See also CA 120

**Fair, Ronald L.** 1932- . . . . . . . . . . . . . CLC **18**
See also BW 1; CA 69-72; CANR 25;
DLB 33

**Fairbairns, Zoe (Ann)** 1948- . . . . . . . CLC **32**
See also CA 103; CANR 21

**Falco, Gian**
See Papini, Giovanni

**Falconer, James**
See Kirkup, James

**Falconer, Kenneth**
See Kornbluth, C(yril) M.

**Falkland, Samuel**
See Heijermans, Herman

**Fallaci, Oriana** 1930- . . . . . . . . . . . . . CLC **11**
See also CA 77-80; CANR 15; MTCW

**Faludy, George** 1913- . . . . . . . . . . . . . CLC **42**
See also CA 21-24R

**Faludy, Gyoergy**
See Faludy, George

**Fanon, Frantz** 1925-1961 . . . . . CLC **74; BLC**
See also BW 1; CA 116; 89-92;
DAM MULT

**Fanshawe, Ann** 1625-1680 . . . . . . . . . LC **11**

**Fante, John (Thomas)** 1911-1983 . . . CLC **60**
See also CA 69-72; 109; CANR 23;
DLB 130; DLBY 83

**Farah, Nuruddin** 1945- . . . . . . . CLC **53; BLC**
See also BW 2; CA 106; DAM MULT;
DLB 125

**Fargue, Leon-Paul** 1876(?)-1947 . . . TCLC **11**
See also CA 109

**Farigoule, Louis**
See Romains, Jules

**Farina, Richard** 1936(?)-1966 . . . . . . . CLC **9**
See also CA 81-84; 25-28R

**Farley, Walter (Lorimer)**
1915-1989 . . . . . . . . . . . . . . . . . . CLC **17**
See also CA 17-20R; CANR 8, 29; DLB 22;
JRDA; MAICYA; SATA 2, 43

**Farmer, Philip Jose** 1918- . . . . . . . CLC **1, 19**
See also CA 1-4R; CANR 4, 35; DLB 8;
MTCW

**Farquhar, George** 1677-1707 . . . . . . . . LC **21**
See also DAM DRAM; DLB 84

**Farrell, J(ames) G(ordon)**
1935-1979 . . . . . . . . . . . . . . . . . . . CLC **6**
See also CA 73-76; 89-92; CANR 36;
DLB 14; MTCW

**Farrell, James T(homas)**
1904-1979 . . . . . . . . . CLC **1, 4, 8, 11, 66**
See also CA 5-8R; 89-92; CANR 9; DLB 4,
9, 86; DLBD 2; MTCW

**Farren, Richard J.**
See Betjeman, John

**Farren, Richard M.**
See Betjeman, John

**Fassbinder, Rainer Werner**
1946-1982 . . . . . . . . . . . . . . . . . . CLC **20**
See also CA 93-96; 106; CANR 31

**Fast, Howard (Melvin)** 1914- . . . . . . CLC **23**
See also AAYA 16; CA 1-4R; CAAS 18;
CANR 1, 33; DAM NOV; DLB 9;
INT CANR-33; SATA 7

**Faulcon, Robert**
See Holdstock, Robert P.

**Faulkner, William (Cuthbert)**
1897-1962 . . . . . CLC **1, 3, 6, 8, 9, 11, 14,
18, 28, 52, 68; DA; DAB; DAC; SSC 1;
WLC**
See also AAYA 7; CA 81-84; CANR 33;
CDALB 1929-1941; DAM MST, NOV;
DLB 9, 11, 44, 102; DLBD 2; DLBY 86;
MTCW

**Fauset, Jessie Redmon**
1884(?)-1961 . . . . . . . . **CLC 19, 54; BLC**
See also BW 1; CA 109; DAM MULT;
DLB 51

**Faust, Frederick (Schiller)**
1892-1944(?) . . . . . . . . . . . . . . **TCLC 49**
See also CA 108; DAM POP

**Faust, Irvin** 1924- . . . . . . . . . . . . . . . **CLC 8**
See also CA 33-36R; CANR 28; DLB 2, 28;
DLBY 80

**Fawkes, Guy**
See Benchley, Robert (Charles)

**Fearing, Kenneth (Flexner)**
1902-1961 . . . . . . . . . . . . . . . . . **CLC 51**
See also CA 93-96; DLB 9

**Fecamps, Elise**
See Creasey, John

**Federman, Raymond** 1928- . . . . . . **CLC 6, 47**
See also CA 17-20R; CAAS 8; CANR 10,
43; DLBY 80

**Federspiel, J(uerg) F.** 1931- . . . . . . . . **CLC 42**
See also CA 146

**Feiffer, Jules (Ralph)** 1929- . . . . **CLC 2, 8, 64**
See also AAYA 3; CA 17-20R; CANR 30;
DAM DRAM; DLB 7, 44;
INT CANR-30; MTCW; SATA 8, 61

**Feige, Hermann Albert Otto Maximilian**
See Traven, B.

**Feinberg, David B.** 1956-1994 . . . . . . **CLC 59**
See also CA 135; 147

**Feinstein, Elaine** 1930- . . . . . . . . . . . . **CLC 36**
See also CA 69-72; CAAS 1; CANR 31;
DLB 14, 40; MTCW

**Feldman, Irving (Mordecai)** 1928- . . . . **CLC 7**
See also CA 1-4R; CANR 1

**Fellini, Federico** 1920-1993 . . . . . **CLC 16, 85**
See also CA 65-68; 143; CANR 33

**Felsen, Henry Gregor** 1916- . . . . . . . **CLC 17**
See also CA 1-4R; CANR 1; SAAS 2;
SATA 1

**Fenton, James Martin** 1949- . . . . . . . **CLC 32**
See also CA 102; DLB 40

**Ferber, Edna** 1887-1968 . . . . . . . **CLC 18, 93**
See also AITN 1; CA 5-8R; 25-28R; DLB 9,
28, 86; MTCW; SATA 7

**Ferguson, Helen**
See Kavan, Anna

**Ferguson, Samuel** 1810-1886 . . . . . **NCLC 33**
See also DLB 32

**Fergusson, Robert** 1750-1774 . . . . . . . **LC 29**
See also DLB 109

**Ferling, Lawrence**
See Ferlinghetti, Lawrence (Monsanto)

**Ferlinghetti, Lawrence (Monsanto)**
1919(?)- . . . . . . . . **CLC 2, 6, 10, 27; PC 1**
See also CA 5-8R; CANR 3, 41;
CDALB 1941-1968; DAM POET; DLB 5,
16; MTCW

**Fernandez, Vicente Garcia Huidobro**
See Huidobro Fernandez, Vicente Garcia

**Ferrer, Gabriel (Francisco Victor) Miro**
See Miro (Ferrer), Gabriel (Francisco
Victor)

**Ferrier, Susan (Edmonstone)**
1782-1854 . . . . . . . . . . . . . . . . . **NCLC 8**
See also DLB 116

**Ferrigno, Robert** 1948(?)- . . . . . . . . . **CLC 65**
See also CA 140

**Ferron, Jacques** 1921-1985 . . . **CLC 94; DAC**
See also CA 117; 129; DLB 60

**Feuchtwanger, Lion** 1884-1958 . . . . . **TCLC 3**
See also CA 104; DLB 66

**Feuillet, Octave** 1821-1890 . . . . . . **NCLC 45**

**Feydeau, Georges (Leon Jules Marie)**
1862-1921 . . . . . . . . . . . . . . . . . **TCLC 22**
See also CA 113; DAM DRAM

**Ficino, Marsilio** 1433-1499 . . . . . . . . **LC 12**

**Fiedeler, Hans**
See Doeblin, Alfred

**Fiedler, Leslie A(aron)**
1917- . . . . . . . . . . . . . . . . **CLC 4, 13, 24**
See also CA 9-12R; CANR 7; DLB 28, 67;
MTCW

**Field, Andrew** 1938- . . . . . . . . . . . . . **CLC 44**
See also CA 97-100; CANR 25

**Field, Eugene** 1850-1895 . . . . . . . . . **NCLC 3**
See also DLB 23, 42, 140; DLBD 13;
MAICYA; SATA 16

**Field, Gans T.**
See Wellman, Manly Wade

**Field, Michael** . . . . . . . . . . . . . . . . . **TCLC 43**

**Field, Peter**
See Hobson, Laura Z(ametkin)

**Fielding, Henry**
1707-1754 . . . . . . **LC 1; DA; DAB; DAC;
WLC**
See also CDBLB 1660-1789; DAM DRAM,
MST, NOV; DLB 39, 84, 101

**Fielding, Sarah** 1710-1768 . . . . . . . . . . **LC 1**
See also DLB 39

**Fierstein, Harvey (Forbes)** 1954- . . . **CLC 33**
See also CA 123; 129; DAM DRAM, POP

**Figes, Eva** 1932- . . . . . . . . . . . . . . . . **CLC 31**
See also CA 53-56; CANR 4, 44; DLB 14

**Finch, Robert (Duer Claydon)**
1900- . . . . . . . . . . . . . . . . . . . . . **CLC 18**
See also CA 57-60; CANR 9, 24, 49;
DLB 88

**Findley, Timothy** 1930- . . . . . . **CLC 27; DAC**
See also CA 25-28R; CANR 12, 42;
DAM MST; DLB 53

**Fink, William**
See Mencken, H(enry) L(ouis)

**Firbank, Louis** 1942-
See Reed, Lou
See also CA 117

**Firbank, (Arthur Annesley) Ronald**
1886-1926 . . . . . . . . . . . . . . . . . **TCLC 1**
See also CA 104; DLB 36

**Fisher, M(ary) F(rances) K(ennedy)**
1908-1992 . . . . . . . . . . . . . . **CLC 76, 87**
See also CA 77-80; 138; CANR 44

**Fisher, Roy** 1930- . . . . . . . . . . . . . . . **CLC 25**
See also CA 81-84; CAAS 10; CANR 16;
DLB 40

**Fisher, Rudolph**
1897-1934 . . . . . . . . . . . . **TCLC 11; BLC**
See also BW 1; CA 107; 124; DAM MULT;
DLB 51, 102

**Fisher, Vardis (Alvero)** 1895-1968 . . . . **CLC 7**
See also CA 5-8R; 25-28R; DLB 9

**Fiske, Tarleton**
See Bloch, Robert (Albert)

**Fitch, Clarke**
See Sinclair, Upton (Beall)

**Fitch, John IV**
See Cormier, Robert (Edmund)

**Fitzgerald, Captain Hugh**
See Baum, L(yman) Frank

**FitzGerald, Edward** 1809-1883 . . . . **NCLC 9**
See also DLB 32

**Fitzgerald, F(rancis) Scott (Key)**
1896-1940 . . . . . . . **TCLC 1, 6, 14, 28, 55;
DA; DAB; DAC; SSC 6; WLC**
See also AITN 1; CA 110; 123;
CDALB 1917-1929; DAM MST, NOV;
DLB 4, 9, 86; DLBD 1; DLBY 81;
MTCW

**Fitzgerald, Penelope** 1916- . . . **CLC 19, 51, 61**
See also CA 85-88; CAAS 10; DLB 14

**Fitzgerald, Robert (Stuart)**
1910-1985 . . . . . . . . . . . . . . . . . **CLC 39**
See also CA 1-4R; 114; CANR 1; DLBY 80

**FitzGerald, Robert D(avid)**
1902-1987 . . . . . . . . . . . . . . . . . **CLC 19**
See also CA 17-20R

**Fitzgerald, Zelda (Sayre)**
1900-1948 . . . . . . . . . . . . . . . . . **TCLC 52**
See also CA 117; 126; DLBY 84

**Flanagan, Thomas (James Bonner)**
1923- . . . . . . . . . . . . . . . . . . **CLC 25, 52**
See also CA 108; DLBY 80; INT 108;
MTCW

**Flaubert, Gustave**
1821-1880 . . . . . . . . **NCLC 2, 10, 19; DA;
DAB; DAC; SSC 11; WLC**
See also DAM MST, NOV; DLB 119

**Flecker, Herman Elroy**
See Flecker, (Herman) James Elroy

**Flecker, (Herman) James Elroy**
1884-1915 . . . . . . . . . . . . . . . . . **TCLC 43**
See also CA 109; 150; DLB 10, 19

**Fleming, Ian (Lancaster)**
1908-1964 . . . . . . . . . . . . . . . . **CLC 3, 30**
See also CA 5-8R; CDBLB 1945-1960;
DAM POP; DLB 87; MTCW; SATA 9

**Fleming, Thomas (James)** 1927- . . . . **CLC 37**
See also CA 5-8R; CANR 10;
INT CANR-10; SATA 8

**Fletcher, John** 1579-1625 . . . . . . **LC 33; DC 6**
See also CDBLB Before 1660; DLB 58

**Fletcher, John Gould** 1886-1950 . . . **TCLC 35**
See also CA 107; DLB 4, 45

**Fleur, Paul**
See Pohl, Frederik

**Flooglebuckle, Al**
See Spiegelman, Art

**Flying Officer X**
See Bates, H(erbert) E(rnest)

**Fo, Dario** 1926-.................. CLC 32
See also CA 116; 128; DAM DRAM;
MTCW

**Fogarty, Jonathan Titulescu Esq.**
See Farrell, James T(homas)

**Folke, Will**
See Bloch, Robert (Albert)

**Follett, Ken(neth Martin)** 1949- .... CLC 18
See also AAYA 6; BEST 89:4; CA 81-84;
CANR 13, 33; DAM NOV, POP;
DLB 87; DLBY 81; INT CANR-33;
MTCW

**Fontane, Theodor** 1819-1898 ..... NCLC 26
See also DLB 129

**Foote, Horton** 1916-........... CLC 51, 91
See also CA 73-76; CANR 34, 51;
DAM DRAM; DLB 26; INT CANR-34

**Foote, Shelby** 1916- ............... CLC 75
See also CA 5-8R; CANR 3, 45;
DAM NOV, POP; DLB 2, 17

**Forbes, Esther** 1891-1967.......... CLC 12
See also AAYA 17; CA 13-14; 25-28R;
CAP 1; CLR 27; DLB 22; JRDA;
MAICYA; SATA 2

**Forche, Carolyn (Louise)**
1950- .......... CLC 25, 83, 86; PC 10
See also CA 109; 117; CANR 50;
DAM POET; DLB 5; INT 117

**Ford, Elbur**
See Hibbert, Eleanor Alice Burford

**Ford, Ford Madox**
1873-1939 ......... TCLC 1, 15, 39, 57
See also CA 104; 132; CDBLB 1914-1945;
DAM NOV; DLB 162; MTCW

**Ford, John** 1895-1973............. CLC 16
See also CA 45-48

**Ford, Richard** 1944-.............. CLC 46
See also CA 69-72; CANR 11, 47

**Ford, Webster**
See Masters, Edgar Lee

**Foreman, Richard** 1937-........... CLC 50
See also CA 65-68; CANR 32

**Forester, C(ecil) S(cott)**
1899-1966 ..................... CLC 35
See also CA 73-76; 25-28R; SATA 13

**Forez**
See Mauriac, Francois (Charles)

**Forman, James Douglas** 1932-...... CLC 21
See also AAYA 17; CA 9-12R; CANR 4,
19, 42; JRDA; MAICYA; SATA 8, 70

**Fornes, Maria Irene** 1930-...... CLC 39, 61
See also CA 25-28R; CANR 28; DLB 7;
HW; INT CANR-28; MTCW

**Forrest, Leon** 1937- ............... CLC 4
See also BW 2; CA 89-92; CAAS 7;
CANR 25; DLB 33

**Forster, E(dward) M(organ)**
1879-1970 ..... CLC 1, 2, 3, 4, 9, 10, 13,
15, 22, 45, 77; DA; DAB; DAC; WLC
See also AAYA 2; CA 13-14; 25-28R;
CANR 45; CAP 1; CDBLB 1914-1945;
DAM MST, NOV; DLB 34, 98, 162;
DLBD 10; MTCW; SATA 57

**Forster, John** 1812-1876 ........ NCLC 11
See also DLB 144

**Forsyth, Frederick** 1938-...... CLC 2, 5, 36
See also BEST 89:4; CA 85-88; CANR 38;
DAM NOV, POP; DLB 87; MTCW

**Forten, Charlotte L.** ......... TCLC 16; BLC
See also Grimke, Charlotte L(ottie) Forten
See also DLB 50

**Foscolo, Ugo** 1778-1827.......... NCLC 8

**Fosse, Bob** ....................... CLC 20
See also Fosse, Robert Louis

**Fosse, Robert Louis** 1927-1987
See Fosse, Bob
See also CA 110; 123

**Foster, Stephen Collins**
1826-1864 ................. NCLC 26

**Foucault, Michel**
1926-1984 ............. CLC 31, 34, 69
See also CA 105; 113; CANR 34; MTCW

**Fouque, Friedrich (Heinrich Karl) de la Motte**
1777-1843 .................. NCLC 2
See also DLB 90

**Fourier, Charles** 1772-1837 ...... NCLC 51

**Fournier, Henri Alban** 1886-1914
See Alain-Fournier
See also CA 104

**Fournier, Pierre** 1916-............. CLC 11
See also Gascar, Pierre
See also CA 89-92; CANR 16, 40

**Fowles, John**
1926- ...... CLC 1, 2, 3, 4, 6, 9, 10, 15,
33, 87; DAB; DAC
See also CA 5-8R; CANR 25; CDBLB 1960
to Present; DAM MST; DLB 14, 139;
MTCW; SATA 22

**Fox, Paula** 1923-................ CLC 2, 8
See also AAYA 3; CA 73-76; CANR 20,
36; CLR 1; DLB 52; JRDA; MAICYA;
MTCW; SATA 17, 60

**Fox, William Price (Jr.)** 1926- ..... CLC 22
See also CA 17-20R; CAAS 19; CANR 11;
DLB 2; DLBY 81

**Foxe, John** 1516(?)-1587 ........... LC 14

**Frame, Janet** ........... CLC 2, 3, 6, 22, 66
See also Clutha, Janet Paterson Frame

**France, Anatole**................... TCLC 9
See also Thibault, Jacques Anatole Francois
See also DLB 123

**Francis, Claude** 19(?)- ............. CLC 50

**Francis, Dick** 1920- ......... CLC 2, 22, 42
See also AAYA 5; BEST 89:3; CA 5-8R;
CANR 9, 42; CDBLB 1960 to Present;
DAM POP; DLB 87; INT CANR-9;
MTCW

**Francis, Robert (Churchill)**
1901-1987 ................... CLC 15
See also CA 1-4R; 123; CANR 1

**Frank, Anne(lies Marie)**
1929-1945 ........ TCLC 17; DA; DAB;
DAC; WLC
See also AAYA 12; CA 113; 133;
DAM MST; MTCW; SATA 87;
SATA-Brief 42

**Frank, Elizabeth** 1945-............ CLC 39
See also CA 121; 126; INT 126

**Frankl, Viktor E(mil)** 1905-........ CLC 93
See also CA 65-68

**Franklin, Benjamin**
See Hasek, Jaroslav (Matej Frantisek)

**Franklin, Benjamin**
1706-1790 ..... LC 25; DA; DAB; DAC
See also CDALB 1640-1865; DAM MST;
DLB 24, 43, 73

**Franklin, (Stella Maraia Sarah) Miles**
1879-1954 ................... TCLC 7
See also CA 104

**Fraser, (Lady) Antonia (Pakenham)**
1932- ....................... CLC 32
See also CA 85-88; CANR 44; MTCW;
SATA-Brief 32

**Fraser, George MacDonald** 1925-.... CLC 7
See also CA 45-48; CANR 2, 48

**Fraser, Sylvia** 1935-............... CLC 64
See also CA 45-48; CANR 1, 16

**Frayn, Michael** 1933-...... CLC 3, 7, 31, 47
See also CA 5-8R; CANR 30;
DAM DRAM, NOV; DLB 13, 14;
MTCW

**Fraze, Candida (Merrill)** 1945-..... CLC 50
See also CA 126

**Frazer, J(ames) G(eorge)**
1854-1941 ................. TCLC 32
See also CA 118

**Frazer, Robert Caine**
See Creasey, John

**Frazer, Sir James George**
See Frazer, J(ames) G(eorge)

**Frazier, Ian** 1951-................ CLC 46
See also CA 130

**Frederic, Harold** 1856-1898...... NCLC 10
See also DLB 12, 23; DLBD 13

**Frederick, John**
See Faust, Frederick (Schiller)

**Frederick the Great** 1712-1786 ...... LC 14

**Fredro, Aleksander** 1793-1876..... NCLC 8

**Freeling, Nicolas** 1927- ........... CLC 38
See also CA 49-52; CAAS 12; CANR 1, 17,
50; DLB 87

**Freeman, Douglas Southall**
1886-1953 ................. TCLC 11
See also CA 109; DLB 17

**Freeman, Judith** 1946-............ CLC 55
See also CA 148

**Freeman, Mary Eleanor Wilkins**
1852-1930 ............ TCLC 9; SSC 1
See also CA 106; DLB 12, 78

**Freeman, R(ichard) Austin**
1862-1943 ................. TCLC 21
See also CA 113; DLB 70

**French, Albert** 1943- ............. CLC 86

**French, Marilyn** 1929-...... CLC 10, 18, 60
See also CA 69-72; CANR 3, 31;
DAM DRAM, NOV, POP;
INT CANR-31; MTCW

**French, Paul**
See Asimov, Isaac

**Freneau, Philip Morin** 1752-1832 .. NCLC 1
See also DLB 37, 43

**Freud, Sigmund** 1856-1939 ....... TCLC 52
See also CA 115; 133; MTCW

**Garland, (Hannibal) Hamlin**
1860-1940 . . . . . . . . . . **TCLC 3; SSC 18**
See also CA 104; DLB 12, 71, 78

**Garneau, (Hector de) Saint-Denys**
1912-1943 . . . . . . . . . . . . . . . . . **TCLC 13**
See also CA 111; DLB 88

**Garner, Alan**  1934- . . . . . . . . . **CLC 17; DAB**
See also CA 73-76; CANR 15; CLR 20;
DAM POP; DLB 161; MAICYA;
MTCW; SATA 18, 69

**Garner, Hugh**  1913-1979 . . . . . . . . . **CLC 13**
See also CA 69-72; CANR 31; DLB 68

**Garnett, David**  1892-1981 . . . . . . . . . **CLC 3**
See also CA 5-8R; 103; CANR 17; DLB 34

**Garos, Stephanie**
See Katz, Steve

**Garrett, George (Palmer)**
1929- . . . . . . . . . . . . . . . . **CLC 3, 11, 51**
See also CA 1-4R; CAAS 5; CANR 1, 42;
DLB 2, 5, 130, 152; DLBY 83

**Garrick, David**  1717-1779 . . . . . . . . . **LC 15**
See also DAM DRAM; DLB 84

**Garrigue, Jean**  1914-1972 . . . . . . . . **CLC 2, 8**
See also CA 5-8R; 37-40R; CANR 20

**Garrison, Frederick**
See Sinclair, Upton (Beall)

**Garth, Will**
See Hamilton, Edmond; Kuttner, Henry

**Garvey, Marcus (Moziah, Jr.)**
1887-1940 . . . . . . . . . . . . **TCLC 41; BLC**
See also BW 1; CA 120; 124; DAM MULT

**Gary, Romain** . . . . . . . . . . . . . . . . . **CLC 25**
See also Kacew, Romain
See also DLB 83

**Gascar, Pierre** . . . . . . . . . . . . . . . . . **CLC 11**
See also Fournier, Pierre

**Gascoyne, David (Emery)**  1916- . . . . **CLC 45**
See also CA 65-68; CANR 10, 28; DLB 20;
MTCW

**Gaskell, Elizabeth Cleghorn**
1810-1865 . . . . . . . . . . . . . **NCLC 5; DAB**
See also CDBLB 1832-1890; DAM MST;
DLB 21, 144, 159

**Gass, William H(oward)**
1924- . . . **CLC 1, 2, 8, 11, 15, 39; SSC 12**
See also CA 17-20R; CANR 30; DLB 2;
MTCW

**Gasset, Jose Ortega y**
See Ortega y Gasset, Jose

**Gates, Henry Louis, Jr.**  1950- . . . . . . **CLC 65**
See also BW 2; CA 109; CANR 25;
DAM MULT; DLB 67

**Gautier, Theophile**
1811-1872 . . . . . . . . . . **NCLC 1; SSC 20**
See also DAM POET; DLB 119

**Gawsworth, John**
See Bates, H(erbert) E(rnest)

**Gay, Oliver**
See Gogarty, Oliver St. John

**Gaye, Marvin (Penze)**  1939-1984 . . . **CLC 26**
See also CA 112

**Gebler, Carlo (Ernest)**  1954- . . . . . . . **CLC 39**
See also CA 119; 133

**Gee, Maggie (Mary)**  1948- . . . . . . . . **CLC 57**
See also CA 130

**Gee, Maurice (Gough)**  1931- . . . . . . . **CLC 29**
See also CA 97-100; SATA 46

**Gelbart, Larry (Simon)**  1923- . . . **CLC 21, 61**
See also CA 73-76; CANR 45

**Gelber, Jack**  1932- . . . . . . . . **CLC 1, 6, 14, 79**
See also CA 1-4R; CANR 2; DLB 7

**Gellhorn, Martha (Ellis)**  1908- . . **CLC 14, 60**
See also CA 77-80; CANR 44; DLBY 82

**Genet, Jean**
1910-1986 . . . **CLC 1, 2, 5, 10, 14, 44, 46**
See also CA 13-16R; CANR 18;
DAM DRAM; DLB 72; DLBY 86;
MTCW

**Gent, Peter**  1942- . . . . . . . . . . . . . . . **CLC 29**
See also AITN 1; CA 89-92; DLBY 82

**Gentlewoman in New England, A**
See Bradstreet, Anne

**Gentlewoman in Those Parts, A**
See Bradstreet, Anne

**George, Jean Craighead**  1919- . . . . . . **CLC 35**
See also AAYA 8; CA 5-8R; CANR 25;
CLR 1; DLB 52; JRDA; MAICYA;
SATA 2, 68

**George, Stefan (Anton)**
1868-1933 . . . . . . . . . . . . . . . **TCLC 2, 14**
See also CA 104

**Georges, Georges Martin**
See Simenon, Georges (Jacques Christian)

**Gerhardi, William Alexander**
See Gerhardie, William Alexander

**Gerhardie, William Alexander**
1895-1977 . . . . . . . . . . . . . . . . . . **CLC 5**
See also CA 25-28R; 73-76; CANR 18;
DLB 36

**Gerstler, Amy**  1956- . . . . . . . . . . . . . . **CLC 70**
See also CA 146

**Gertler, T.** . . . . . . . . . . . . . . . . . . . . **CLC 34**
See also CA 116; 121; INT 121

**Ghalib** . . . . . . . . . . . . . . . . . . . . . . **NCLC 39**
See also Ghalib, Hsadullah Khan

**Ghalib, Hsadullah Khan**  1797-1869
See Ghalib
See also DAM POET

**Ghelderode, Michel de**
1898-1962 . . . . . . . . . . . . . . . . **CLC 6, 11**
See also CA 85-88; CANR 40;
DAM DRAM

**Ghiselin, Brewster**  1903- . . . . . . . . . . **CLC 23**
See also CA 13-16R; CAAS 10; CANR 13

**Ghose, Zulfikar**  1935- . . . . . . . . . . . . **CLC 42**
See also CA 65-68

**Ghosh, Amitav**  1956- . . . . . . . . . . . . . **CLC 44**
See also CA 147

**Giacosa, Giuseppe**  1847-1906 . . . . . . **TCLC 7**
See also CA 104

**Gibb, Lee**
See Waterhouse, Keith (Spencer)

**Gibbon, Lewis Grassic** . . . . . . . . . . . **TCLC 4**
See also Mitchell, James Leslie

**Gibbons, Kaye**  1960- . . . . . . . . . **CLC 50, 88**
See also DAM POP

**Gibran, Kahlil**
1883-1931 . . . . . . . . . . **TCLC 1, 9; PC 9**
See also CA 104; 150; DAM POET, POP

**Gibran, Khalil**
See Gibran, Kahlil

**Gibson, William**
1914- . . . . . . . . **CLC 23; DA; DAB; DAC**
See also CA 9-12R; CANR 9, 42;
DAM DRAM, MST; DLB 7; SATA 66

**Gibson, William (Ford)**  1948- . . . **CLC 39, 63**
See also AAYA 12; CA 126; 133;
DAM POP

**Gide, Andre (Paul Guillaume)**
1869-1951 . . . . . . . . **TCLC 5, 12, 36; DA;
DAB; DAC; SSC 13; WLC**
See also CA 104; 124; DAM MST, NOV;
DLB 65; MTCW

**Gifford, Barry (Colby)**  1946- . . . . . . . **CLC 34**
See also CA 65-68; CANR 9, 30, 40

**Gilbert, W(illiam) S(chwenck)**
1836-1911 . . . . . . . . . . . . . . . . . . **TCLC 3**
See also CA 104; DAM DRAM, POET;
SATA 36

**Gilbreth, Frank B., Jr.**  1911- . . . . . . . **CLC 17**
See also CA 9-12R; SATA 2

**Gilchrist, Ellen**  1935- . . **CLC 34, 48; SSC 14**
See also CA 113; 116; CANR 41;
DAM POP; DLB 130; MTCW

**Giles, Molly**  1942- . . . . . . . . . . . . . . . **CLC 39**
See also CA 126

**Gill, Patrick**
See Creasey, John

**Gilliam, Terry (Vance)**  1940- . . . . . . . **CLC 21**
See also Monty Python
See also CA 108; 113; CANR 35; INT 113

**Gillian, Jerry**
See Gilliam, Terry (Vance)

**Gilliatt, Penelope (Ann Douglass)**
1932-1993 . . . . . . . . . . **CLC 2, 10, 13, 53**
See also AITN 2; CA 13-16R; 141;
CANR 49; DLB 14

**Gilman, Charlotte (Anna) Perkins (Stetson)**
1860-1935 . . . . . . . . **TCLC 9, 37; SSC 13**
See also CA 106; 150

**Gilmour, David**  1949- . . . . . . . . . . . . . **CLC 35**
See also CA 138, 147

**Gilpin, William**  1724-1804 . . . . . . . **NCLC 30**

**Gilray, J. D.**
See Mencken, H(enry) L(ouis)

**Gilroy, Frank D(aniel)**  1925- . . . . . . . . **CLC 2**
See also CA 81-84; CANR 32; DLB 7

**Ginsberg, Allen**
1926- . . . . . . **CLC 1, 2, 3, 4, 6, 13, 36, 69;
DA; DAB; DAC; PC 4; WLC 3**
See also AITN 1; CA 1-4R; CANR 2, 41;
CDALB 1941-1968; DAM MST, POET;
DLB 5, 16; MTCW

**Ginzburg, Natalia**
1916-1991 . . . . . . . . . . **CLC 5, 11, 54, 70**
See also CA 85-88; 135; CANR 33; MTCW

**Giono, Jean**  1895-1970 . . . . . . . . . **CLC 4, 11**
See also CA 45-48; 29-32R; CANR 2, 35;
DLB 72; MTCW

Giovanni, Nikki
1943- ...... **CLC 2, 4, 19, 64; BLC; DA; DAB; DAC**
See also AITN 1; BW 2; CA 29-32R; CAAS 6; CANR 18, 41; CLR 6; DAM MST, MULT, POET; DLB 5, 41; INT CANR-18; MAICYA; MTCW; SATA 24

Giovene, Andrea 1904- ............. **CLC 7**
See also CA 85-88

Gippius, Zinaida (Nikolayevna) 1869-1945
See Hippius, Zinaida
See also CA 106

Giraudoux, (Hippolyte) Jean
1882-1944 ................. **TCLC 2, 7**
See also CA 104; DAM DRAM; DLB 65

Gironella, Jose Maria 1917- ....... **CLC 11**
See also CA 101

Gissing, George (Robert)
1857-1903 ............. **TCLC 3, 24, 47**
See also CA 105; DLB 18, 135

Giurlani, Aldo
See Palazzeschi, Aldo

Gladkov, Fyodor (Vasilyevich)
1883-1958 .................. **TCLC 27**

Glanville, Brian (Lester) 1931- ...... **CLC 6**
See also CA 5-8R; CAAS 9; CANR 3; DLB 15, 139; SATA 42

Glasgow, Ellen (Anderson Gholson)
1873(?)-1945 ............... **TCLC 2, 7**
See also CA 104; DLB 9, 12

Glaspell, Susan (Keating)
1882(?)-1948 ................. **TCLC 55**
See also CA 110; DLB 7, 9, 78; YABC 2

Glassco, John 1909-1981 ........... **CLC 9**
See also CA 13-16R; 102; CANR 15; DLB 68

Glasscock, Amnesia
See Steinbeck, John (Ernst)

Glasser, Ronald J. 1940(?)- ........ **CLC 37**

Glassman, Joyce
See Johnson, Joyce

Glendinning, Victoria 1937- ........ **CLC 50**
See also CA 120; 127; DLB 155

Glissant, Edouard 1928- ........ **CLC 10, 68**
See also DAM MULT

Gloag, Julian 1930- .............. **CLC 40**
See also AITN 1; CA 65-68; CANR 10

Glowacki, Aleksander
See Prus, Boleslaw

Glueck, Louise (Elisabeth)
1943- .............. **CLC 7, 22, 44, 81**
See also CA 33-36R; CANR 40; DAM POET; DLB 5

Gobineau, Joseph Arthur (Comte) de
1816-1882 ................. **NCLC 17**
See also DLB 123

Godard, Jean-Luc 1930- ........... **CLC 20**
See also CA 93-96

Godden, (Margaret) Rumer 1907- ... **CLC 53**
See also AAYA 6; CA 5-8R; CANR 4, 27, 36; CLR 20; DLB 161; MAICYA; SAAS 12; SATA 3, 36

Godoy Alcayaga, Lucila 1889-1957
See Mistral, Gabriela
See also BW 2; CA 104; 131; DAM MULT; HW; MTCW

Godwin, Gail (Kathleen)
1937- ............. **CLC 5, 8, 22, 31, 69**
See also CA 29-32R; CANR 15, 43; DAM POP; DLB 6; INT CANR-15; MTCW

Godwin, William 1756-1836...... **NCLC 14**
See also CDBLB 1789-1832; DLB 39, 104, 142, 158, 163

Goethe, Johann Wolfgang von
1749-1832 ........ **NCLC 4, 22, 34; DA; DAB; DAC; PC 5; WLC 3**
See also DAM DRAM, MST, POET; DLB 94

Gogarty, Oliver St. John
1878-1957 .................. **TCLC 15**
See also CA 109; 150; DLB 15, 19

Gogol, Nikolai (Vasilyevich)
1809-1852 ........ **NCLC 5, 15, 31; DA; DAB; DAC; DC 1; SSC 4; WLC**
See also DAM DRAM, MST

Goines, Donald
1937(?)-1974 ............ **CLC 80; BLC**
See also AITN 1; BW 1; CA 124; 114; DAM MULT, POP; DLB 33

Gold, Herbert 1924- ....... **CLC 4, 7, 14, 42**
See also CA 9-12R; CANR 17, 45; DLB 2; DLBY 81

Goldbarth, Albert 1948- ......... **CLC 5, 38**
See also CA 53-56; CANR 6, 40; DLB 120

Goldberg, Anatol 1910-1982 ....... **CLC 34**
See also CA 131; 117

Goldemberg, Isaac 1945- .......... **CLC 52**
See also CA 69-72; CAAS 12; CANR 11, 32; HW

Golding, William (Gerald)
1911-1993 .... **CLC 1, 2, 3, 8, 10, 17, 27, 58, 81; DA; DAB; DAC; WLC**
See also AAYA 5; CA 5-8R; 141; CANR 13, 33; CDBLB 1945-1960; DAM MST, NOV; DLB 15, 100; MTCW

Goldman, Emma 1869-1940...... **TCLC 13**
See also CA 110; 150

Goldman, Francisco 1955- ......... **CLC 76**

Goldman, William (W.) 1931- .... **CLC 1, 48**
See also CA 9-12R; CANR 29; DLB 44

Goldmann, Lucien 1913-1970 ...... **CLC 24**
See also CA 25-28; CAP 2

Goldoni, Carlo 1707-1793 .......... **LC 4**
See also DAM DRAM

Goldsberry, Steven 1949- .......... **CLC 34**
See also CA 131

Goldsmith, Oliver
1728-1774 ...... **LC 2; DA; DAB; DAC; WLC**
See also CDBLB 1660-1789; DAM DRAM, MST, NOV, POET; DLB 39, 89, 104, 109, 142; SATA 26

Goldsmith, Peter
See Priestley, J(ohn) B(oynton)

Gombrowicz, Witold
1904-1969 ........... **CLC 4, 7, 11, 49**
See also CA 19-20; 25-28R; CAP 2; DAM DRAM

Gomez de la Serna, Ramon
1888-1963 ................... **CLC 9**
See also CA 116; HW

Goncharov, Ivan Alexandrovich
1812-1891 ................. **NCLC 1**

Goncourt, Edmond (Louis Antoine Huot) de
1822-1896 ................. **NCLC 7**
See also DLB 123

Goncourt, Jules (Alfred Huot) de
1830-1870 ................. **NCLC 7**
See also DLB 123

Gontier, Fernande 19(?)- .......... **CLC 50**

Goodman, Paul 1911-1972 .... **CLC 1, 2, 4, 7**
See also CA 19-20; 37-40R; CANR 34; CAP 2; DLB 130; MTCW

Gordimer, Nadine
1923- .... **CLC 3, 5, 7, 10, 18, 33, 51, 70; DA; DAB; DAC; SSC 17**
See also CA 5-8R; CANR 3, 28; DAM MST, NOV; INT CANR-28; MTCW

Gordon, Adam Lindsay
1833-1870 ................. **NCLC 21**

Gordon, Caroline
1895-1981 ... **CLC 6, 13, 29, 83; SSC 15**
See also CA 11-12; 103; CANR 36; CAP 1; DLB 4, 9, 102; DLBY 81; MTCW

Gordon, Charles William 1860-1937
See Connor, Ralph
See also CA 109

Gordon, Mary (Catherine)
1949- ................. **CLC 13, 22**
See also CA 102; CANR 44; DLB 6; DLBY 81; INT 102; MTCW

Gordon, Sol 1923-................ **CLC 26**
See also CA 53-56; CANR 4; SATA 11

Gordone, Charles 1925-1995 ...... **CLC 1, 4**
See also BW 1; CA 93-96; 150; DAM DRAM; DLB 7; INT 93-96; MTCW

Gorenko, Anna Andreevna
See Akhmatova, Anna

Gorky, Maxim........ **TCLC 8; DAB; WLC**
See also Peshkov, Alexei Maximovich

Goryan, Sirak
See Saroyan, William

Gosse, Edmund (William)
1849-1928 ................. **TCLC 28**
See also CA 117; DLB 57, 144

Gotlieb, Phyllis Fay (Bloom)
1926- ..................... **CLC 18**
See also CA 13-16R; CANR 7; DLB 88

Gottesman, S. D.
See Kornbluth, C(yril) M.; Pohl, Frederik

Gottfried von Strassburg
fl. c. 1210- ................ **CMLC 10**
See also DLB 138

Gould, Lois ..................... **CLC 4, 10**
See also CA 77-80; CANR 29; MTCW

**Hall, (Marguerite) Radclyffe**
1886-1943 . . . . . . . . . . . . . . . . TCLC 12
See also CA 110; 150

**Hall, Rodney** 1935- . . . . . . . . . . . . CLC 51
See also CA 109

**Halleck, Fitz-Greene** 1790-1867 . . NCLC 47
See also DLB 3

**Halliday, Michael**
See Creasey, John

**Halpern, Daniel** 1945- . . . . . . . . . . . CLC 14
See also CA 33-36R

**Hamburger, Michael (Peter Leopold)**
1924- . . . . . . . . . . . . . . . . . . . . . CLC 5, 14
See also CA 5-8R; CAAS 4; CANR 2, 47;
DLB 27

**Hamill, Pete** 1935- . . . . . . . . . . . . . . . CLC 10
See also CA 25-28R; CANR 18

**Hamilton, Alexander**
1755(?)-1804 . . . . . . . . . . . . . . NCLC 49
See also DLB 37

**Hamilton, Clive**
See Lewis, C(live) S(taples)

**Hamilton, Edmond** 1904-1977 . . . . . . . CLC 1
See also CA 1-4R; CANR 3; DLB 8

**Hamilton, Eugene (Jacob) Lee**
See Lee-Hamilton, Eugene (Jacob)

**Hamilton, Franklin**
See Silverberg, Robert

**Hamilton, Gail**
See Corcoran, Barbara

**Hamilton, Mollie**
See Kaye, M(ary) M(argaret)

**Hamilton, (Anthony Walter) Patrick**
1904-1962 . . . . . . . . . . . . . . . . . CLC 51
See also CA 113; DLB 10

**Hamilton, Virginia** 1936- . . . . . . . . . CLC 26
See also AAYA 2; BW 2; CA 25-28R;
CANR 20, 37; CLR 1, 11, 40;
DAM MULT; DLB 33, 52;
INT CANR-20; JRDA; MAICYA;
MTCW; SATA 4, 56, 79

**Hammett, (Samuel) Dashiell**
1894-1961 . . . . . . . . CLC 3, 5, 10, 19, 47;
SSC 17
See also AITN 1; CA 81-84; CANR 42;
CDALB 1929-1941; DLBD 6; MTCW

**Hammon, Jupiter**
1711(?)-1800(?) . . . . . . . . . NCLC 5; BLC
See also DAM MULT, POET; DLB 31, 50

**Hammond, Keith**
See Kuttner, Henry

**Hamner, Earl (Henry), Jr.** 1923- . . . CLC 12
See also AITN 2; CA 73-76; DLB 6

**Hampton, Christopher (James)**
1946- . . . . . . . . . . . . . . . . . . . . . . CLC 4
See also CA 25-28R; DLB 13; MTCW

**Hamsun, Knut** . . . . . . . . . . . . TCLC 2, 14, 49
See also Pedersen, Knut

**Handke, Peter** 1942- . . CLC 5, 8, 10, 15, 38
See also CA 77-80; CANR 33;
DAM DRAM, NOV; DLB 85, 124;
MTCW

**Hanley, James** 1901-1985 . . . CLC 3, 5, 8, 13
See also CA 73-76; 117; CANR 36; MTCW

**Hannah, Barry** 1942- . . . . . . . CLC 23, 38, 90
See also CA 108; 110; CANR 43; DLB 6;
INT 110; MTCW

**Hannon, Ezra**
See Hunter, Evan

**Hansberry, Lorraine (Vivian)**
1930-1965 . . . . . . CLC 17, 62; BLC; DA;
DAB; DAC; DC 2
See also BW 1; CA 109; 25-28R; CABS 3;
CDALB 1941-1968; DAM DRAM, MST,
MULT; DLB 7, 38; MTCW

**Hansen, Joseph** 1923- . . . . . . . . . . . . CLC 38
See also CA 29-32R; CAAS 17; CANR 16,
44; INT CANR-16

**Hansen, Martin A.** 1909-1955 . . . . . TCLC 32

**Hanson, Kenneth O(stlin)** 1922- . . . . CLC 13
See also CA 53-56; CANR 7

**Hardwick, Elizabeth** 1916- . . . . . . . . CLC 13
See also CA 5-8R; CANR 3, 32;
DAM NOV; DLB 6; MTCW

**Hardy, Thomas**
1840-1928 . . . . . TCLC 4, 10, 18, 32, 48,
53; DA; DAB; DAC; PC 8; SSC 2; WLC
See also CA 104; 123; CDBLB 1890-1914;
DAM MST, NOV, POET; DLB 18, 19,
135; MTCW

**Hare, David** 1947- . . . . . . . . . . . . CLC 29, 58
See also CA 97-100; CANR 39; DLB 13;
MTCW

**Harford, Henry**
See Hudson, W(illiam) H(enry)

**Hargrave, Leonie**
See Disch, Thomas M(ichael)

**Harjo, Joy** 1951- . . . . . . . . . . . . . . . CLC 83
See also CA 114; CANR 35; DAM MULT;
DLB 120; NNAL

**Harlan, Louis R(udolph)** 1922- . . . . . CLC 34
See also CA 21-24R; CANR 25

**Harling, Robert** 1951(?)- . . . . . . . . . . CLC 53
See also CA 147

**Harmon, William (Ruth)** 1938- . . . . . CLC 38
See also CA 33-36R; CANR 14, 32, 35;
SATA 65

**Harper, F. E. W.**
See Harper, Frances Ellen Watkins

**Harper, Frances E. W.**
See Harper, Frances Ellen Watkins

**Harper, Frances E. Watkins**
See Harper, Frances Ellen Watkins

**Harper, Frances Ellen**
See Harper, Frances Ellen Watkins

**Harper, Frances Ellen Watkins**
1825-1911 . . . . . . . . . . . . . TCLC 14; BLC
See also BW 1; CA 111; 125; DAM MULT,
POET; DLB 50

**Harper, Michael S(teven)** 1938- . . CLC 7, 22
See also BW 1; CA 33-36R; CANR 24;
DLB 41

**Harper, Mrs. F. E. W.**
See Harper, Frances Ellen Watkins

**Harris, Christie (Lucy) Irwin**
1907- . . . . . . . . . . . . . . . . . . . . . CLC 12
See also CA 5-8R; CANR 6; DLB 88;
JRDA; MAICYA; SAAS 10; SATA 6, 74

**Harris, Frank** 1856-1931 . . . . . . . . . TCLC 24
See also CA 109; 150; DLB 156

**Harris, George Washington**
1814-1869 . . . . . . . . . . . . . . . . NCLC 23
See also DLB 3, 11

**Harris, Joel Chandler**
1848-1908 . . . . . . . . . . . TCLC 2; SSC 19
See also CA 104; 137; DLB 11, 23, 42, 78,
91; MAICYA; YABC 1

**Harris, John (Wyndham Parkes Lucas)**
**Beynon** 1903-1969
See Wyndham, John
See also CA 102; 89-92

**Harris, MacDonald** . . . . . . . . . . . . . . . CLC 9
See also Heiney, Donald (William)

**Harris, Mark** 1922- . . . . . . . . . . . . . . CLC 19
See also CA 5-8R; CAAS 3; CANR 2;
DLB 2; DLBY 80

**Harris, (Theodore) Wilson** 1921- . . . . CLC 25
See also BW 2; CA 65-68; CAAS 16;
CANR 11, 27; DLB 117; MTCW

**Harrison, Elizabeth Cavanna** 1909-
See Cavanna, Betty
See also CA 9-12R; CANR 6, 27

**Harrison, Harry (Max)** 1925- . . . . . . CLC 42
See also CA 1-4R; CANR 5, 21; DLB 8;
SATA 4

**Harrison, James (Thomas)**
1937- . . . . . . . CLC 6, 14, 33, 66; SSC 19
See also CA 13-16R; CANR 8, 51;
DLBY 82; INT CANR-8

**Harrison, Jim**
See Harrison, James (Thomas)

**Harrison, Kathryn** 1961- . . . . . . . . . . CLC 70
See also CA 144

**Harrison, Tony** 1937- . . . . . . . . . . . . . CLC 43
See also CA 65-68; CANR 44; DLB 40;
MTCW

**Harriss, Will(ard Irvin)** 1922- . . . . . . CLC 34
See also CA 111

**Harson, Sley**
See Ellison, Harlan (Jay)

**Hart, Ellis**
See Ellison, Harlan (Jay)

**Hart, Josephine** 1942(?)- . . . . . . . . . . CLC 70
See also CA 138; DAM POP

**Hart, Moss** 1904-1961 . . . . . . . . . . . . CLC 66
See also CA 109; 89-92; DAM DRAM;
DLB 7

**Harte, (Francis) Bret(t)**
1836(?)-1902 . . . . TCLC 1, 25; DA; DAC;
SSC 8; WLC
See also CA 104; 140; CDALB 1865-1917;
DAM MST; DLB 12, 64, 74, 79;
SATA 26

**Hartley, L(eslie) P(oles)**
1895-1972 . . . . . . . . . . . . . . . CLC 2, 22
See also CA 45-48; 37-40R; CANR 33;
DLB 15, 139; MTCW

**Hartman, Geoffrey H.** 1929- . . . . . . . CLC 27
See also CA 117; 125; DLB 67

**Hartmann von Aue**
c. 1160-c. 1205 . . . . . . . . . . . . CMLC 15
See also DLB 138

**Hartmann von Aue** 1170-1210 . . . . CMLC 15

**Haruf, Kent** 1943- . . . . . . . . . . . . . . **CLC 34**
See also CA 149

**Harwood, Ronald** 1934- . . . . . . . . . . **CLC 32**
See also CA 1-4R; CANR 4; DAM DRAM,
MST; DLB 13

**Hasek, Jaroslav (Matej Frantisek)**
1883-1923 . . . . . . . . . . . . . . . . . . **TCLC 4**
See also CA 104; 129; MTCW

**Hass, Robert** 1941- . . . . . . . . . . **CLC 18, 39**
See also CA 111; CANR 30, 50; DLB 105

**Hastings, Hudson**
See Kuttner, Henry

**Hastings, Selina** . . . . . . . . . . . . . . . . **CLC 44**

**Hatteras, Amelia**
See Mencken, H(enry) L(ouis)

**Hatteras, Owen** . . . . . . . . . . . . . . . . **TCLC 18**
See also Mencken, H(enry) L(ouis); Nathan,
George Jean

**Hauptmann, Gerhart (Johann Robert)**
1862-1946 . . . . . . . . . . . . . . . . . . **TCLC 4**
See also CA 104; DAM DRAM; DLB 66,
118

**Havel, Vaclav**
1936- . . . . . . . . . **CLC 25, 58, 65; DC 6**
See also CA 104; CANR 36; DAM DRAM;
MTCW

**Haviaras, Stratis** . . . . . . . . . . . . . . . . **CLC 33**
See also Chaviaras, Strates

**Hawes, Stephen** 1475(?)-1523(?) . . . . . **LC 17**

**Hawkes, John (Clendennin Burne, Jr.)**
1925- . . . . . . **CLC 1, 2, 3, 4, 7, 9, 14, 15,
27, 49**
See also CA 1-4R; CANR 2, 47; DLB 2, 7;
DLBY 80; MTCW

**Hawking, S. W.**
See Hawking, Stephen W(illiam)

**Hawking, Stephen W(illiam)**
1942- . . . . . . . . . . . . . . . . . . . . . . **CLC 63**
See also AAYA 13; BEST 89:1; CA 126;
129; CANR 48

**Hawthorne, Julian** 1846-1934 . . . . . **TCLC 25**

**Hawthorne, Nathaniel**
1804-1864 . . . . . . . **NCLC 39; DA; DAB;
DAC; SSC 3; WLC**
See also CDALB 1640-1865; DAM MST,
NOV; DLB 1, 74; YABC 2

**Haxton, Josephine Ayres** 1921-
See Douglas, Ellen
See also CA 115; CANR 41

**Hayaseca y Eizaguirre, Jorge**
See Echegaray (y Eizaguirre), Jose (Maria
Waldo)

**Hayashi Fumiko** 1904-1951 . . . . . . **TCLC 27**

**Haycraft, Anna**
See Ellis, Alice Thomas
See also CA 122

**Hayden, Robert E(arl)**
1913-1980 . . . . . . **CLC 5, 9, 14, 37; BLC;
DA; DAC; PC 6**
See also BW 1; CA 69-72; 97-100; CABS 2;
CANR 24; CDALB 1941-1968;
DAM MST, MULT, POET; DLB 5, 76;
MTCW; SATA 19; SATA-Obit 26

**Hayford, J(oseph) E(phraim) Casely**
See Casely-Hayford, J(oseph) E(phraim)

**Hayman, Ronald** 1932- . . . . . . . . . . . **CLC 44**
See also CA 25-28R; CANR 18, 50;
DLB 155

**Haywood, Eliza (Fowler)**
1693(?)-1756 . . . . . . . . . . . . . . . . . . **LC 1**

**Hazlitt, William** 1778-1830 . . . . . **NCLC 29**
See also DLB 110, 158

**Hazzard, Shirley** 1931- . . . . . . . . . . . **CLC 18**
See also CA 9-12R; CANR 4; DLBY 82;
MTCW

**Head, Bessie** 1937-1986 . . . **CLC 25, 67; BLC**
See also BW 2; CA 29-32R; 119; CANR 25;
DAM MULT; DLB 117; MTCW

**Headon, (Nicky) Topper** 1956(?)- . . . **CLC 30**

**Heaney, Seamus (Justin)**
1939- . . . . . . **CLC 5, 7, 14, 25, 37, 74, 91;
DAB**
See also CA 85-88; CANR 25, 48;
CDBLB 1960 to Present; DAM POET;
DLB 40; DLBY 95; MTCW

**Hearn, (Patricio) Lafcadio (Tessima Carlos)**
1850-1904 . . . . . . . . . . . . . . . . . . **TCLC 9**
See also CA 105; DLB 12, 78

**Hearne, Vicki** 1946- . . . . . . . . . . . . . **CLC 56**
See also CA 139

**Hearon, Shelby** 1931- . . . . . . . . . . . . **CLC 63**
See also AITN 2; CA 25-28R; CANR 18,
48

**Heat-Moon, William Least** . . . . . . . . . **CLC 29**
See also Trogdon, William (Lewis)
See also AAYA 9

**Hebbel, Friedrich** 1813-1863 . . . . . **NCLC 43**
See also DAM DRAM; DLB 129

**Hebert, Anne** 1916- . . . **CLC 4, 13, 29; DAC**
See also CA 85-88; DAM MST, POET;
DLB 68; MTCW

**Hecht, Anthony (Evan)**
1923- . . . . . . . . . . . . . . . . . **CLC 8, 13, 19**
See also CA 9-12R; CANR 6; DAM POET;
DLB 5

**Hecht, Ben** 1894-1964 . . . . . . . . . . . . . **CLC 8**
See also CA 85-88; DLB 7, 9, 25, 26, 28, 86

**Hedayat, Sadeq** 1903-1951 . . . . . . . **TCLC 21**
See also CA 120

**Hegel, Georg Wilhelm Friedrich**
1770-1831 . . . . . . . . . . . . . . . . . **NCLC 46**
See also DLB 90

**Heidegger, Martin** 1889-1976 . . . . . . **CLC 24**
See also CA 81-84; 65-68; CANR 34;
MTCW

**Heidenstam, (Carl Gustaf) Verner von**
1859-1940 . . . . . . . . . . . . . . . . . . **TCLC 5**
See also CA 104

**Heifner, Jack** 1946- . . . . . . . . . . . . . . **CLC 11**
See also CA 105; CANR 47

**Heijermans, Herman** 1864-1924 . . . **TCLC 24**
See also CA 123

**Heilbrun, Carolyn G(old)** 1926- . . . . . **CLC 25**
See also CA 45-48; CANR 1, 28

**Heine, Heinrich** 1797-1856 . . . . **NCLC 4, 54**
See also DLB 90

**Heinemann, Larry (Curtiss)** 1944- . . **CLC 50**
See also CA 110; CAAS 21; CANR 31;
DLBD 9; INT CANR-31

**Heiney, Donald (William)** 1921-1993
See Harris, MacDonald
See also CA 1-4R; 142; CANR 3

**Heinlein, Robert A(nson)**
1907-1988 . . . . . . **CLC 1, 3, 8, 14, 26, 55**
See also AAYA 17; CA 1-4R; 125;
CANR 1, 20; DAM POP; DLB 8; JRDA;
MAICYA; MTCW; SATA 9, 69;
SATA-Obit 56

**Helforth, John**
See Doolittle, Hilda

**Hellenhofferu, Vojtech Kapristian z**
See Hasek, Jaroslav (Matej Frantisek)

**Heller, Joseph**
1923- . . . . **CLC 1, 3, 5, 8, 11, 36, 63; DA;
DAB; DAC; WLC**
See also AITN 1; CA 5-8R; CABS 1;
CANR 8, 42; DAM MST, NOV, POP;
DLB 2, 28; DLBY 80; INT CANR-8;
MTCW

**Hellman, Lillian (Florence)**
1906-1984 . . . . . . **CLC 2, 4, 8, 14, 18, 34,
44, 52; DC 1**
See also AITN 1, 2; CA 13-16R; 112;
CANR 33; DAM DRAM; DLB 7;
DLBY 84; MTCW

**Helprin, Mark** 1947- . . . . . **CLC 7, 10, 22, 32**
See also CA 81-84; CANR 47; DAM NOV,
POP; DLBY 85; MTCW

**Helvetius, Claude-Adrien**
1715-1771 . . . . . . . . . . . . . . . . . . **LC 26**

**Helyar, Jane Penelope Josephine** 1933-
See Poole, Josephine
See also CA 21-24R; CANR 10, 26;
SATA 82

**Hemans, Felicia** 1793-1835 . . . . . . **NCLC 29**
See also DLB 96

**Hemingway, Ernest (Miller)**
1899-1961 . . . . **CLC 1, 3, 6, 8, 10, 13, 19,
30, 34, 39, 41, 44, 50, 61, 80; DA; DAB;
DAC; SSC 1; WLC**
See also CA 77-80; CANR 34;
CDALB 1917-1929; DAM MST, NOV;
DLB 4, 9, 102; DLBD 1; DLBY 81, 87;
MTCW

**Hempel, Amy** 1951- . . . . . . . . . . . . . . **CLC 39**
See also CA 118; 137

**Henderson, F. C.**
See Mencken, H(enry) L(ouis)

**Henderson, Sylvia**
See Ashton-Warner, Sylvia (Constance)

**Henley, Beth** . . . . . . . . . . . . . . **CLC 23; DC 6**
See also Henley, Elizabeth Becker
See also CABS 3; DLBY 86

**Henley, Elizabeth Becker** 1952-
See Henley, Beth
See also CA 107; CANR 32; DAM DRAM,
MST; MTCW

**Henley, William Ernest**
1849-1903 . . . . . . . . . . . . . . . . . . **TCLC 8**
See also CA 105; DLB 19

**Hennissart, Martha**
See Lathen, Emma
See also CA 85-88

**Henry, O.** . . . . . . . . **TCLC 1, 19; SSC 5; WLC**
See also Porter, William Sydney

Henry, Patrick 1736-1799 . . . . . . . . . **LC 25**

Henryson, Robert 1430(?)-1506(?). . . . **LC 20**
See also DLB 146

Henry VIII 1491-1547 . . . . . . . . . . . . **LC 10**

Henschke, Alfred
See Klabund

Hentoff, Nat(han Irving) 1925- . . . . . **CLC 26**
See also AAYA 4; CA 1-4R; CAAS 6;
CANR 5, 25; CLR 1; INT CANR-25;
JRDA; MAICYA; SATA 42, 69;
SATA-Brief 27

Heppenstall, (John) Rayner
1911-1981 . . . . . . . . . . . . . . . . . . **CLC 10**
See also CA 1-4R; 103; CANR 29

Herbert, Frank (Patrick)
1920-1986 . . . . . . **CLC 12, 23, 35, 44, 85**
See also CA 53-56; 118; CANR 5, 43;
DAM POP; DLB 8; INT CANR-5;
MTCW; SATA 9, 37; SATA-Obit 47

Herbert, George
1593-1633 . . . . . . . . . **LC 24; DAB; PC 4**
See also CDBLB Before 1660; DAM POET;
DLB 126

Herbert, Zbigniew 1924- . . . . . . . . **CLC 9, 43**
See also CA 89-92; CANR 36;
DAM POET; MTCW

Herbst, Josephine (Frey)
1897-1969 . . . . . . . . . . . . . . . . . . **CLC 34**
See also CA 5-8R; 25-28R; DLB 9

Hergesheimer, Joseph
1880-1954 . . . . . . . . . . . . . . . . . **TCLC 11**
See also CA 109; DLB 102, 9

Herlihy, James Leo 1927-1993 . . . . . . **CLC 6**
See also CA 1-4R; 143; CANR 2

Hermogenes fl. c. 175- . . . . . . . . . . **CMLC 6**

Hernandez, Jose 1834-1886 . . . . . . **NCLC 17**

Herodotus c. 484B.C.-429B.C. . . . . **CMLC 17**

Herrick, Robert
1591-1674 . . . . . **LC 13; DA; DAB; DAC;
                                                    PC 9**
See also DAM MST, POP; DLB 126

Herring, Guilles
See Somerville, Edith

Herriot, James 1916-1995 . . . . . . . . . **CLC 12**
See also Wight, James Alfred
See also AAYA 1; CA 148; CANR 40;
DAM POP; SATA 86

Herrmann, Dorothy 1941- . . . . . . . . **CLC 44**
See also CA 107

Herrmann, Taffy
See Herrmann, Dorothy

Hersey, John (Richard)
1914-1993 . . . . . . . **CLC 1, 2, 7, 9, 40, 81**
See also CA 17-20R; 140; CANR 33;
DAM POP; DLB 6; MTCW; SATA 25;
SATA-Obit 76

Herzen, Aleksandr Ivanovich
1812-1870 . . . . . . . . . . . . . . . . . **NCLC 10**

Herzl, Theodor 1860-1904 . . . . . . . **TCLC 36**

Herzog, Werner 1942- . . . . . . . . . . . **CLC 16**
See also CA 89-92

Hesiod c. 8th cent. B.C.- . . . . . . . . **CMLC 5**

Hesse, Hermann
1877-1962 . . . . **CLC 1, 2, 3, 6, 11, 17, 25,
                                  69; DA; DAB; DAC; SSC 9; WLC**
See also CA 17-18; CAP 2; DAM MST,
NOV; DLB 66; MTCW; SATA 50

Hewes, Cady
See De Voto, Bernard (Augustine)

Heyen, William 1940- . . . . . . . . . **CLC 13, 18**
See also CA 33-36R; CAAS 9; DLB 5

Heyerdahl, Thor 1914- . . . . . . . . . . . **CLC 26**
See also CA 5-8R; CANR 5, 22; MTCW;
SATA 2, 52

Heym, Georg (Theodor Franz Arthur)
1887-1912 . . . . . . . . . . . . . . . . . . **TCLC 9**
See also CA 106

Heym, Stefan 1913- . . . . . . . . . . . . . **CLC 41**
See also CA 9-12R; CANR 4; DLB 69

Heyse, Paul (Johann Ludwig von)
1830-1914 . . . . . . . . . . . . . . . . . . **TCLC 8**
See also CA 104; DLB 129

Heyward, (Edwin) DuBose
1885-1940 . . . . . . . . . . . . . . . . . **TCLC 59**
See also CA 108; DLB 7, 9, 45; SATA 21

Hibbert, Eleanor Alice Burford
1906-1993 . . . . . . . . . . . . . . . . . . . **CLC 7**
See also BEST 90:4; CA 17-20R; 140;
CANR 9, 28; DAM POP; SATA 2;
SATA-Obit 74

Hichens, Robert S. 1864-1950 . . . . . **TCLC 64**
See also DLB 153

Higgins, George V(incent)
1939- . . . . . . . . . . . . . . . **CLC 4, 7, 10, 18**
See also CA 77-80; CAAS 5; CANR 17, 51;
DLB 2; DLBY 81; INT CANR-17;
MTCW

Higginson, Thomas Wentworth
1823-1911 . . . . . . . . . . . . . . . . . **TCLC 36**
See also DLB 1, 64

Highet, Helen
See MacInnes, Helen (Clark)

Highsmith, (Mary) Patricia
1921-1995 . . . . . . . . . . . **CLC 2, 4, 14, 42**
See also CA 1-4R; 147; CANR 1, 20, 48;
DAM NOV, POP; MTCW

Highwater, Jamake (Mamake)
1942(?)- . . . . . . . . . . . . . . . . . . . . **CLC 12**
See also AAYA 7; CA 65-68; CAAS 7;
CANR 10, 34; CLR 17; DLB 52;
DLBY 85; JRDA; MAICYA; SATA 32,
69; SATA-Brief 30

Highway, Tomson 1951- . . . . . . **CLC 92; DAC**
See also DAM MULT; NNAL

Higuchi, Ichiyo 1872-1896 . . . . . . . **NCLC 49**

Hijuelos, Oscar 1951- . . . . . . **CLC 65; HLC**
See also BEST 90:1; CA 123; CANR 50;
DAM MULT, POP; DLB 145; HW

Hikmet, Nazim 1902(?)-1963 . . . . . . **CLC 40**
See also CA 141; 93-96

Hildesheimer, Wolfgang
1916-1991 . . . . . . . . . . . . . . . . . . **CLC 49**
See also CA 101; 135; DLB 69, 124

Hill, Geoffrey (William)
1932- . . . . . . . . . . . . . . . **CLC 5, 8, 18, 45**
See also CA 81-84; CANR 21;
CDBLB 1960 to Present; DAM POET;
DLB 40; MTCW

Hill, George Roy 1921- . . . . . . . . . . . **CLC 26**
See also CA 110; 122

Hill, John
See Koontz, Dean R(ay)

Hill, Susan (Elizabeth)
1942- . . . . . . . . . . . . . . . . . **CLC 4; DAB**
See also CA 33-36R; CANR 29;
DAM MST, NOV; DLB 14, 139; MTCW

Hillerman, Tony 1925- . . . . . . . . . . . **CLC 62**
See also AAYA 6; BEST 89:1; CA 29-32R;
CANR 21, 42; DAM POP; SATA 6

Hillesum, Etty 1914-1943 . . . . . . . . **TCLC 49**
See also CA 137

Hilliard, Noel (Harvey) 1929- . . . . . . **CLC 15**
See also CA 9-12R; CANR 7

Hillis, Rick 1956- . . . . . . . . . . . . . . . **CLC 66**
See also CA 134

Hilton, James 1900-1954 . . . . . . . . **TCLC 21**
See also CA 108; DLB 34, 77; SATA 34

Himes, Chester (Bomar)
1909-1984 . . . . **CLC 2, 4, 7, 18, 58; BLC**
See also BW 2; CA 25-28R; 114; CANR 22;
DAM MULT; DLB 2, 76, 143; MTCW

Hinde, Thomas . . . . . . . . . . . . . . . **CLC 6, 11**
See also Chitty, Thomas Willes

Hindin, Nathan
See Bloch, Robert (Albert)

Hine, (William) Daryl 1936- . . . . . . . **CLC 15**
See also CA 1-4R; CAAS 15; CANR 1, 20;
DLB 60

Hinkson, Katharine Tynan
See Tynan, Katharine

Hinton, S(usan) E(loise)
1950- . . . . . . . . **CLC 30; DA; DAB; DAC**
See also AAYA 2; CA 81-84; CANR 32;
CLR 3, 23; DAM MST, NOV; JRDA;
MAICYA; MTCW; SATA 19, 58

Hippius, Zinaida . . . . . . . . . . . . . . . . **TCLC 9**
See also Gippius, Zinaida (Nikolayevna)

Hiraoka, Kimitake 1925-1970
See Mishima, Yukio
See also CA 97-100; 29-32R; DAM DRAM;
MTCW

Hirsch, E(ric) D(onald), Jr. 1928- . . . **CLC 79**
See also CA 25-28R; CANR 27, 51;
DLB 67; INT CANR-27; MTCW

Hirsch, Edward 1950- . . . . . . . . . **CLC 31, 50**
See also CA 104; CANR 20, 42; DLB 120

Hitchcock, Alfred (Joseph)
1899-1980 . . . . . . . . . . . . . . . . . . **CLC 16**
See also CA 97-100; SATA 27;
SATA-Obit 24

Hitler, Adolf 1889-1945 . . . . . . . . . . **TCLC 53**
See also CA 117; 147

Hoagland, Edward 1932- . . . . . . . . . . **CLC 28**
See also CA 1-4R; CANR 2, 31; DLB 6;
SATA 51

Hoban, Russell (Conwell) 1925- . . **CLC 7, 25**
See also CA 5-8R; CANR 23, 37; CLR 3;
DAM NOV; DLB 52; MAICYA;
MTCW; SATA 1, 40, 78

Hobbs, Perry
See Blackmur, R(ichard) P(almer)

**Hobson, Laura Z(ametkin)**
1900-1986 . . . . . . . . . . . . . . . . CLC 7, 25
See also CA 17-20R; 118; DLB 28;
SATA 52

**Hochhuth, Rolf** 1931- . . . . . . . . CLC 4, 11, 18
See also CA 5-8R; CANR 33;
DAM DRAM; DLB 124; MTCW

**Hochman, Sandra** 1936- . . . . . . . . . CLC 3, 8
See also CA 5-8R; DLB 5

**Hochwaelder, Fritz** 1911-1986 . . . . . . CLC 36
See also CA 29-32R; 120; CANR 42;
DAM DRAM; MTCW

**Hochwalder, Fritz**
See Hochwaelder, Fritz

**Hocking, Mary (Eunice)** 1921- . . . . . CLC 13
See also CA 101; CANR 18, 40

**Hodgins, Jack** 1938- . . . . . . . . . . . . . CLC 23
See also CA 93-96; DLB 60

**Hodgson, William Hope**
1877(?)-1918 . . . . . . . . . . . . . . TCLC 13
See also CA 111; DLB 70, 153, 156

**Hoffman, Alice** 1952- . . . . . . . . . . . CLC 51
See also CA 77-80; CANR 34; DAM NOV;
MTCW

**Hoffman, Daniel (Gerard)**
1923- . . . . . . . . . . . . . . . . . CLC 6, 13, 23
See also CA 1-4R; CANR 4; DLB 5

**Hoffman, Stanley** 1944- . . . . . . . . . . . CLC 5
See also CA 77-80

**Hoffman, William M(oses)** 1939- . . . CLC 40
See also CA 57-60; CANR 11

**Hoffmann, E(rnst) T(heodor) A(madeus)**
1776-1822 . . . . . . . . . . . NCLC 2; SSC 13
See also DLB 90; SATA 27

**Hofmann, Gert** 1931- . . . . . . . . . . . . CLC 54
See also CA 128

**Hofmannsthal, Hugo von**
1874-1929 . . . . . . . . . . . TCLC 11; DC 4
See also CA 106; DAM DRAM; DLB 81,
118

**Hogan, Linda** 1947- . . . . . . . . . . . . . CLC 73
See also CA 120; CANR 45; DAM MULT;
NNAL

**Hogarth, Charles**
See Creasey, John

**Hogarth, Emmett**
See Polonsky, Abraham (Lincoln)

**Hogg, James** 1770-1835 . . . . . . . . . . NCLC 4
See also DLB 93, 116, 159

**Holbach, Paul Henri Thiry Baron**
1723-1789 . . . . . . . . . . . . . . . . . . LC 14

**Holberg, Ludvig** 1684-1754 . . . . . . . . . LC 6

**Holden, Ursula** 1921- . . . . . . . . . . . . CLC 18
See also CA 101; CAAS 8; CANR 22

**Holderlin, (Johann Christian) Friedrich**
1770-1843 . . . . . . . . . . . . NCLC 16; PC 4

**Holdstock, Robert**
See Holdstock, Robert P.

**Holdstock, Robert P.** 1948- . . . . . . . . CLC 39
See also CA 131

**Holland, Isabelle** 1920- . . . . . . . . . . CLC 21
See also AAYA 11; CA 21-24R; CANR 10,
25, 47; JRDA; MAICYA; SATA 8, 70

**Holland, Marcus**
See Caldwell, (Janet Miriam) Taylor
(Holland)

**Hollander, John** 1929- . . . . . . CLC 2, 5, 8, 14
See also CA 1-4R; CANR 1; DLB 5;
SATA 13

**Hollander, Paul**
See Silverberg, Robert

**Holleran, Andrew** 1943(?)- . . . . . . . . . CLC 38
See also CA 144

**Hollinghurst, Alan** 1954- . . . . . . . CLC 55, 91
See also CA 114

**Hollis, Jim**
See Summers, Hollis (Spurgeon, Jr.)

**Holmes, John**
See Souster, (Holmes) Raymond

**Holmes, John Clellon** 1926-1988 . . . . CLC 56
See also CA 9-12R; 125; CANR 4; DLB 16

**Holmes, Oliver Wendell**
1809-1894 . . . . . . . . . . . . . . . NCLC 14
See also CDALB 1640-1865; DLB 1;
SATA 34

**Holmes, Raymond**
See Souster, (Holmes) Raymond

**Holt, Victoria**
See Hibbert, Eleanor Alice Burford

**Holub, Miroslav** 1923- . . . . . . . . . . . . CLC 4
See also CA 21-24R; CANR 10

**Homer**
c. 8th cent. B.C.- . . . . . CMLC 1, 16; DA;
DAB; DAC
See also DAM MST, POET

**Honig, Edwin** 1919- . . . . . . . . . . . . . CLC 33
See also CA 5-8R; CAAS 8; CANR 4, 45;
DLB 5

**Hood, Hugh (John Blagdon)**
1928- . . . . . . . . . . . . . . . . . . CLC 15, 28
See also CA 49-52; CAAS 17; CANR 1, 33;
DLB 53

**Hood, Thomas** 1799-1845 . . . . . . . . NCLC 16
See also DLB 96

**Hooker, (Peter) Jeremy** 1941- . . . . . . CLC 43
See also CA 77-80; CANR 22; DLB 40

**hooks, bell** . . . . . . . . . . . . . . . . . . . CLC 94
See also Watkins, Gloria

**Hope, A(lec) D(erwent)** 1907- . . . . CLC 3, 51
See also CA 21-24R; CANR 33; MTCW

**Hope, Brian**
See Creasey, John

**Hope, Christopher (David Tully)**
1944- . . . . . . . . . . . . . . . . . . . . CLC 52
See also CA 106; CANR 47; SATA 62

**Hopkins, Gerard Manley**
1844-1889 . . . . . . . NCLC 17; DA; DAB;
DAC; PC 15; WLC
See also CDBLB 1890-1914; DAM MST,
POET; DLB 35, 57

**Hopkins, John (Richard)** 1931- . . . . . . CLC 4
See also CA 85-88

**Hopkins, Pauline Elizabeth**
1859-1930 . . . . . . . . . . . . . TCLC 28; BLC
See also BW 2; CA 141; DAM MULT;
DLB 50

**Hopkinson, Francis** 1737-1791 . . . . . . LC 25
See also DLB 31

**Hopley-Woolrich, Cornell George** 1903-1968
See Woolrich, Cornell
See also CA 13-14; CAP 1

**Horatio**
See Proust, (Valentin-Louis-George-Eugene-)
Marcel

**Horgan, Paul (George Vincent O'Shaughnessy)**
1903-1995 . . . . . . . . . . . . . . . CLC 9, 53
See also CA 13-16R; 147; CANR 9, 35;
DAM NOV; DLB 102; DLBY 85;
INT CANR-9; MTCW; SATA 13;
SATA-Obit 84

**Horn, Peter**
See Kuttner, Henry

**Hornem, Horace Esq.**
See Byron, George Gordon (Noel)

**Hornung, E(rnest) W(illiam)**
1866-1921 . . . . . . . . . . . . . . . TCLC 59
See also CA 108; DLB 70

**Horovitz, Israel (Arthur)** 1939- . . . . . CLC 56
See also CA 33-36R; CANR 46;
DAM DRAM; DLB 7

**Horvath, Odon von**
See Horvath, Oedoen von
See also DLB 85, 124

**Horvath, Oedoen von** 1901-1938 . . . TCLC 45
See also Horvath, Odon von
See also CA 118

**Horwitz, Julius** 1920-1986 . . . . . . . . CLC 14
See also CA 9-12R; 119; CANR 12

**Hospital, Janette Turner** 1942- . . . . . CLC 42
See also CA 108; CANR 48

**Hostos, E. M. de**
See Hostos (y Bonilla), Eugenio Maria de

**Hostos, Eugenio M. de**
See Hostos (y Bonilla), Eugenio Maria de

**Hostos, Eugenio Maria**
See Hostos (y Bonilla), Eugenio Maria de

**Hostos (y Bonilla), Eugenio Maria de**
1839-1903 . . . . . . . . . . . . . . . TCLC 24
See also CA 123; 131; HW

**Houdini**
See Lovecraft, H(oward) P(hillips)

**Hougan, Carolyn** 1943- . . . . . . . . . . . CLC 34
See also CA 139

**Household, Geoffrey (Edward West)**
1900-1988 . . . . . . . . . . . . . . . . . CLC 11
See also CA 77-80; 126; DLB 87; SATA 14;
SATA-Obit 59

**Housman, A(lfred) E(dward)**
1859-1936 . . . . . . TCLC 1, 10; DA; DAB;
DAC; PC 2
See also CA 104; 125; DAM MST, POET;
DLB 19; MTCW

**Housman, Laurence** 1865-1959 . . . . . TCLC 7
See also CA 106; DLB 10; SATA 25

**Howard, Elizabeth Jane** 1923- . . . CLC 7, 29
See also CA 5-8R; CANR 8

**Howard, Maureen** 1930- . . . . . CLC 5, 14, 46
See also CA 53-56; CANR 31; DLBY 83;
INT CANR-31; MTCW

**Howard, Richard**  1929-  . . . . . . **CLC 7, 10, 47**
See also AITN 1; CA 85-88; CANR 25;
DLB 5; INT CANR-25

**Howard, Robert Ervin**  1906-1936 . . . **TCLC 8**
See also CA 105

**Howard, Warren F.**
See Pohl, Frederik

**Howe, Fanny**  1940-  . . . . . . . . . . . . . **CLC 47**
See also CA 117; SATA-Brief 52

**Howe, Irving**  1920-1993 . . . . . . . . . . **CLC 85**
See also CA 9-12R; 141; CANR 21, 50;
DLB 67; MTCW

**Howe, Julia Ward**  1819-1910 . . . . . **TCLC 21**
See also CA 117; DLB 1

**Howe, Susan**  1937- . . . . . . . . . . . . . . **CLC 72**
See also DLB 120

**Howe, Tina**  1937- . . . . . . . . . . . . . . . **CLC 48**
See also CA 109

**Howell, James**  1594(?)-1666 . . . . . . . **LC 13**
See also DLB 151

**Howells, W. D.**
See Howells, William Dean

**Howells, William D.**
See Howells, William Dean

**Howells, William Dean**
1837-1920 . . . . . . . . . . . **TCLC 7, 17, 41**
See also CA 104; 134; CDALB 1865-1917;
DLB 12, 64, 74, 79

**Howes, Barbara**  1914- . . . . . . . . . . . . **CLC 15**
See also CA 9-12R; CAAS 3; SATA 5

**Hrabal, Bohumil**  1914- . . . . . . . . **CLC 13, 67**
See also CA 106; CAAS 12

**Hsun, Lu**
See Lu Hsun

**Hubbard, L(afayette) Ron(ald)**
1911-1986 . . . . . . . . . . . . . . . . . **CLC 43**
See also CA 77-80; 118; CANR 22;
DAM POP

**Huch, Ricarda (Octavia)**
1864-1947 . . . . . . . . . . . . . . . . . **TCLC 13**
See also CA 111; DLB 66

**Huddle, David**  1942- . . . . . . . . . . . . . **CLC 49**
See also CA 57-60; CAAS 20; DLB 130

**Hudson, Jeffrey**
See Crichton, (John) Michael

**Hudson, W(illiam) H(enry)**
1841-1922 . . . . . . . . . . . . . . . . . **TCLC 29**
See also CA 115; DLB 98, 153; SATA 35

**Hueffer, Ford Madox**
See Ford, Ford Madox

**Hughart, Barry**  1934- . . . . . . . . . . . . . **CLC 39**
See also CA 137

**Hughes, Colin**
See Creasey, John

**Hughes, David (John)**  1930- . . . . . . . **CLC 48**
See also CA 116; 129; DLB 14

**Hughes, Edward James**
See Hughes, Ted
See also DAM MST, POET

**Hughes, (James) Langston**
1902-1967 . . . . . **CLC 1, 5, 10, 15, 35, 44;**
**BLC; DA; DAB; DAC; DC 3; PC 1;**
**SSC 6; WLC**
See also AAYA 12; BW 1; CA 1-4R;
25-28R; CANR 1, 34; CDALB 1929-1941;
CLR 17; DAM DRAM, MST, MULT,
POET; DLB 4, 7, 48, 51, 86; JRDA;
MAICYA; MTCW; SATA 4, 33

**Hughes, Richard (Arthur Warren)**
1900-1976 . . . . . . . . . . . . . . . . . **CLC 1, 11**
See also CA 5-8R; 65-68; CANR 4;
DAM NOV; DLB 15, 161; MTCW;
SATA 8; SATA-Obit 25

**Hughes, Ted**
1930- . . . . . . . **CLC 2, 4, 9, 14, 37; DAB;**
**DAC; PC 7**
See also Hughes, Edward James
See also CA 1-4R; CANR 1, 33; CLR 3;
DLB 40, 161; MAICYA; MTCW;
SATA 49; SATA-Brief 27

**Hugo, Richard F(ranklin)**
1923-1982 . . . . . . . . . . . . . . **CLC 6, 18, 32**
See also CA 49-52; 108; CANR 3;
DAM POET; DLB 5

**Hugo, Victor (Marie)**
1802-1885 . . . . . . . . **NCLC 3, 10, 21; DA;**
**DAB; DAC; WLC**
See also DAM DRAM, MST, NOV, POET;
DLB 119; SATA 47

**Huidobro, Vicente**
See Huidobro Fernandez, Vicente Garcia

**Huidobro Fernandez, Vicente Garcia**
1893-1948 . . . . . . . . . . . . . . . . . **TCLC 31**
See also CA 131; HW

**Hulme, Keri**  1947- . . . . . . . . . . . . . . . **CLC 39**
See also CA 125; INT 125

**Hulme, T(homas) E(rnest)**
1883-1917 . . . . . . . . . . . . . . . . . **TCLC 21**
See also CA 117; DLB 19

**Hume, David**  1711-1776 . . . . . . . . . . . . **LC 7**
See also DLB 104

**Humphrey, William**  1924- . . . . . . . . . **CLC 45**
See also CA 77-80; DLB 6

**Humphreys, Emyr Owen**  1919- . . . . . **CLC 47**
See also CA 5-8R; CANR 3, 24; DLB 15

**Humphreys, Josephine**  1945- . . . . **CLC 34, 57**
See also CA 121; 127; INT 127

**Hungerford, Pixie**
See Brinsmead, H(esba) F(ay)

**Hunt, E(verette) Howard, (Jr.)**
1918- . . . . . . . . . . . . . . . . . . . . . . **CLC 3**
See also AITN 1; CA 45-48; CANR 2, 47

**Hunt, Kyle**
See Creasey, John

**Hunt, (James Henry) Leigh**
1784-1859 . . . . . . . . . . . . . . . . . . **NCLC 1**
See also DAM POET

**Hunt, Marsha**  1946- . . . . . . . . . . . . . . **CLC 70**
See also BW 2; CA 143

**Hunt, Violet**  1866-1942 . . . . . . . . . **TCLC 53**
See also DLB 162

**Hunter, E. Waldo**
See Sturgeon, Theodore (Hamilton)

**Hunter, Evan**  1926- . . . . . . . . . . . **CLC 11, 31**
See also CA 5-8R; CANR 5, 38;
DAM POP; DLBY 82; INT CANR-5;
MTCW; SATA 25

**Hunter, Kristin (Eggleston)**  1931- . . . **CLC 35**
See also AITN 1; BW 1; CA 13-16R;
CANR 13; CLR 3; DLB 33;
INT CANR-13; MAICYA; SAAS 10;
SATA 12

**Hunter, Mollie**  1922- . . . . . . . . . . . . . **CLC 21**
See also McIlwraith, Maureen Mollie
Hunter
See also AAYA 13; CANR 37; CLR 25;
DLB 161; JRDA; MAICYA; SAAS 7;
SATA 54

**Hunter, Robert**  (?)-1734 . . . . . . . . . . . . **LC 7**

**Hurston, Zora Neale**
1903-1960 . . . . **CLC 7, 30, 61; BLC; DA;**
**DAC; SSC 4**
See also AAYA 15; BW 1; CA 85-88;
DAM MST, MULT, NOV; DLB 51, 86;
MTCW

**Huston, John (Marcellus)**
1906-1987 . . . . . . . . . . . . . . . . . . **CLC 20**
See also CA 73-76; 123; CANR 34; DLB 26

**Hustvedt, Siri**  1955- . . . . . . . . . . . . . . **CLC 76**
See also CA 137

**Hutten, Ulrich von**  1488-1523 . . . . . . . **LC 16**

**Huxley, Aldous (Leonard)**
1894-1963 . . . . . **CLC 1, 3, 4, 5, 8, 11, 18,**
**35, 79; DA; DAB; DAC; WLC**
See also AAYA 11; CA 85-88; CANR 44;
CDBLB 1914-1945; DAM MST, NOV;
DLB 36, 100, 162; MTCW; SATA 63

**Huysmans, Charles Marie Georges**
1848-1907
See Huysmans, Joris-Karl
See also CA 104

**Huysmans, Joris-Karl** . . . . . . . . . . . . . **TCLC 7**
See also Huysmans, Charles Marie Georges
See also DLB 123

**Hwang, David Henry**
1957- . . . . . . . . . . . . . . . . . **CLC 55; DC 4**
See also CA 127; 132; DAM DRAM;
INT 132

**Hyde, Anthony**  1946- . . . . . . . . . . . . . **CLC 42**
See also CA 136

**Hyde, Margaret O(ldroyd)**  1917- . . . **CLC 21**
See also CA 1-4R; CANR 1, 36; CLR 23;
JRDA; MAICYA; SAAS 8; SATA 1, 42,
76

**Hynes, James**  1956(?)- . . . . . . . . . . . . **CLC 65**

**Ian, Janis**  1951- . . . . . . . . . . . . . . . . . **CLC 21**
See also CA 105

**Ibanez, Vicente Blasco**
See Blasco Ibanez, Vicente

**Ibarguengoitia, Jorge**  1928-1983 . . . . **CLC 37**
See also CA 124; 113; HW

**Ibsen, Henrik (Johan)**
1828-1906 . . . . . . . **TCLC 2, 8, 16, 37, 52;**
**DA; DAB; DAC; DC 2; WLC**
See also CA 104; 141; DAM DRAM, MST

**Ibuse Masuji**  1898-1993 . . . . . . . . . . **CLC 22**
See also CA 127; 141

**Ichikawa, Kon**  1915- . . . . . . . . . . . . . **CLC 20**
See also CA 121

**Kuprin, Aleksandr Ivanovich**
 1870-1938 . . . . . . . . . . . . . . . . . . TCLC 5
 See also CA 104

**Kureishi, Hanif** 1954(?)-. . . . . . . . . . CLC 64
 See also CA 139

**Kurosawa, Akira** 1910-. . . . . . . . . . . CLC 16
 See also AAYA 11; CA 101; CANR 46;
 DAM MULT

**Kushner, Tony** 1957(?)- . . . . . . . . . . . CLC 81
 See also CA 144; DAM DRAM

**Kuttner, Henry** 1915-1958. . . . . . . TCLC 10
 See also CA 107; DLB 8

**Kuzma, Greg** 1944-. . . . . . . . . . . . . . . CLC 7
 See also CA 33-36R

**Kuzmin, Mikhail** 1872(?)-1936 . . . . TCLC 40

**Kyd, Thomas** 1558-1594. . . . . . . LC 22; DC 3
 See also DAM DRAM; DLB 62

**Kyprianos, Iossif**
 See Samarakis, Antonis

**La Bruyere, Jean de** 1645-1696. . . . . . LC 17

**Lacan, Jacques (Marie Emile)**
 1901-1981 . . . . . . . . . . . . . . . . . . CLC 75
 See also CA 121; 104

**Laclos, Pierre Ambroise Francois Choderlos**
 **de** 1741-1803 . . . . . . . . . . . . . . NCLC 4

**Lacolere, Francois**
 See Aragon, Louis

**La Colere, Francois**
 See Aragon, Louis

**La Deshabilleuse**
 See Simenon, Georges (Jacques Christian)

**Lady Gregory**
 See Gregory, Isabella Augusta (Persse)

**Lady of Quality, A**
 See Bagnold, Enid

**La Fayette, Marie (Madelaine Pioche de la**
 **Vergne Comtes** 1634-1693. . . . . . LC 2

**Lafayette, Rene**
 See Hubbard, L(afayette) Ron(ald)

**Laforgue, Jules**
 1860-1887 . . . . . . . NCLC 5, 53; PC 14;
                                                    SSC 20

**Lagerkvist, Paer (Fabian)**
 1891-1974 . . . . . . . . . . . CLC 7, 10, 13, 54
 See also Lagerkvist, Par
 See also CA 85-88; 49-52; DAM DRAM,
 NOV; MTCW

**Lagerkvist, Par** . . . . . . . . . . . . . . . . . SSC 12
 See also Lagerkvist, Paer (Fabian)

**Lagerloef, Selma (Ottiliana Lovisa)**
 1858-1940 . . . . . . . . . . . . . . . TCLC 4, 36
 See also Lagerlof, Selma (Ottiliana Lovisa)
 See also CA 108; SATA 15

**Lagerlof, Selma (Ottiliana Lovisa)**
 See Lagerloef, Selma (Ottiliana Lovisa)
 See also CLR 7; SATA 15

**La Guma, (Justin) Alex(ander)**
 1925-1985 . . . . . . . . . . . . . . . . . . CLC 19
 See also BW 1; CA 49-52; 118; CANR 25;
 DAM NOV; DLB 117; MTCW

**Laidlaw, A. K.**
 See Grieve, C(hristopher) M(urray)

**Lainez, Manuel Mujica**
 See Mujica Lainez, Manuel
 See also HW

**Lamartine, Alphonse (Marie Louis Prat) de**
 1790-1869 . . . . . . . . . . . . . . . . . NCLC 11
 See also DAM POET

**Lamb, Charles**
 1775-1834 . . . . . . . NCLC 10; DA; DAB;
                                                    DAC; WLC
 See also CDBLB 1789-1832; DAM MST;
 DLB 93, 107, 163; SATA 17

**Lamb, Lady Caroline** 1785-1828. . NCLC 38
 See also DLB 116

**Lamming, George (William)**
 1927- . . . . . . . . . . . . . . CLC 2, 4, 66; BLC
 See also BW 2; CA 85-88; CANR 26;
 DAM MULT; DLB 125; MTCW

**L'Amour, Louis (Dearborn)**
 1908-1988 . . . . . . . . . . . . . . . CLC 25, 55
 See also AAYA 16; AITN 2; BEST 89:2;
 CA 1-4R; 125; CANR 3, 25, 40;
 DAM NOV, POP; DLBY 80; MTCW

**Lampedusa, Giuseppe (Tomasi) di** . . . TCLC 13
 See also Tomasi di Lampedusa, Giuseppe

**Lampman, Archibald** 1861-1899 . . NCLC 25
 See also DLB 92

**Lancaster, Bruce** 1896-1963. . . . . . . CLC 36
 See also CA 9-10; CAP 1; SATA 9

**Landau, Mark Alexandrovich**
 See Aldanov, Mark (Alexandrovich)

**Landau-Aldanov, Mark Alexandrovich**
 See Aldanov, Mark (Alexandrovich)

**Landis, John** 1950-. . . . . . . . . . . . . . CLC 26
 See also CA 112; 122

**Landolfi, Tommaso** 1908-1979. . . CLC 11, 49
 See also CA 127; 117

**Landon, Letitia Elizabeth**
 1802-1838 . . . . . . . . . . . . . . . . . NCLC 15
 See also DLB 96

**Landor, Walter Savage**
 1775-1864 . . . . . . . . . . . . . . . . . NCLC 14
 See also DLB 93, 107

**Landwirth, Heinz** 1927-
 See Lind, Jakov
 See also CA 9-12R; CANR 7

**Lane, Patrick** 1939- . . . . . . . . . . . . . CLC 25
 See also CA 97-100; DAM POET; DLB 53;
 INT 97-100

**Lang, Andrew** 1844-1912. . . . . . . . . TCLC 16
 See also CA 114; 137; DLB 98, 141;
 MAICYA; SATA 16

**Lang, Fritz** 1890-1976 . . . . . . . . . . . CLC 20
 See also CA 77-80; 69-72; CANR 30

**Lange, John**
 See Crichton, (John) Michael

**Langer, Elinor** 1939- . . . . . . . . . . . . CLC 34
 See also CA 121

**Langland, William**
 1330(?)-1400(?) . . . . . . LC 19; DA; DAB;
                                                    DAC
 See also DAM MST, POET; DLB 146

**Langstaff, Launcelot**
 See Irving, Washington

**Lanier, Sidney** 1842-1881 . . . . . . . . NCLC 6
 See also DAM POET; DLB 64; DLBD 13;
 MAICYA; SATA 18

**Lanyer, Aemilia** 1569-1645 . . . . . . LC 10, 30
 See also DLB 121

**Lao Tzu** . . . . . . . . . . . . . . . . . . . . . . CMLC 7

**Lapine, James (Elliot)** 1949-. . . . . . CLC 39
 See also CA 123; 130; INT 130

**Larbaud, Valery (Nicolas)**
 1881-1957 . . . . . . . . . . . . . . . . . . TCLC 9
 See also CA 106

**Lardner, Ring**
 See Lardner, Ring(gold) W(ilmer)

**Lardner, Ring W., Jr.**
 See Lardner, Ring(gold) W(ilmer)

**Lardner, Ring(gold) W(ilmer)**
 1885-1933 . . . . . . . . . . . . . . . TCLC 2, 14
 See also CA 104; 131; CDALB 1917-1929;
 DLB 11, 25, 86; MTCW

**Laredo, Betty**
 See Codrescu, Andrei

**Larkin, Maia**
 See Wojciechowska, Maia (Teresa)

**Larkin, Philip (Arthur)**
 1922-1985 . . . . CLC 3, 5, 8, 9, 13, 18, 33,
                                                    39, 64; DAB
 See also CA 5-8R; 117; CANR 24;
 CDBLB 1960 to Present; DAM MST,
 POET; DLB 27; MTCW

**Larra (y Sanchez de Castro), Mariano Jose de**
 1809-1837 . . . . . . . . . . . . . . . . . NCLC 17

**Larsen, Eric** 1941- . . . . . . . . . . . . . . CLC 55
 See also CA 132

**Larsen, Nella** 1891-1964 . . . . . CLC 37; BLC
 See also BW 1; CA 125; DAM MULT;
 DLB 51

**Larson, Charles R(aymond)** 1938-. . . CLC 31
 See also CA 53-56; CANR 4

**Las Casas, Bartolome de** 1474-1566. . LC 31

**Lasker-Schueler, Else** 1869-1945 . . TCLC 57
 See also DLB 66, 124

**Latham, Jean Lee** 1902-. . . . . . . . . . CLC 12
 See also AITN 1; CA 5-8R; CANR 7;
 MAICYA; SATA 2, 68

**Latham, Mavis**
 See Clark, Mavis Thorpe

**Lathen, Emma** . . . . . . . . . . . . . . . . . . CLC 2
 See also Hennissart, Martha; Latsis, Mary
 J(ane)

**Lathrop, Francis**
 See Leiber, Fritz (Reuter, Jr.)

**Latsis, Mary J(ane)**
 See Lathen, Emma
 See also CA 85-88

**Lattimore, Richmond (Alexander)**
 1906-1984 . . . . . . . . . . . . . . . . . . CLC 3
 See also CA 1-4R; 112; CANR 1

**Laughlin, James** 1914-. . . . . . . . . . . CLC 49
 See also CA 21-24R; CAAS 22; CANR 9,
 47; DLB 48

**Laurence, (Jean) Margaret (Wemyss)**
  1926-1987 ....... **CLC 3, 6, 13, 50, 62;**
                              **DAC; SSC 7**
  See also CA 5-8R; 121; CANR 33;
  DAM MST; DLB 53; MTCW;
  SATA-Obit 50

**Laurent, Antoine** 1952- ........... **CLC 50**

**Lauscher, Hermann**
  See Hesse, Hermann

**Lautreamont, Comte de**
  1846-1870 ......... **NCLC 12; SSC 14**

**Laverty, Donald**
  See Blish, James (Benjamin)

**Lavin, Mary** 1912- ...... **CLC 4, 18; SSC 4**
  See also CA 9-12R; CANR 33; DLB 15;
  MTCW

**Lavond, Paul Dennis**
  See Kornbluth, C(yril) M.; Pohl, Frederik

**Lawler, Raymond Evenor** 1922- .... **CLC 58**
  See also CA 103

**Lawrence, D(avid) H(erbert Richards)**
  1885-1930 .... **TCLC 2, 9, 16, 33, 48, 61;**
  **DA; DAB; DAC; SSC 4, 19; WLC**
  See also CA 104; 121; CDBLB 1914-1945;
  DAM MST, NOV, POET; DLB 10, 19,
  36, 98, 162; MTCW

**Lawrence, T(homas) E(dward)**
  1888-1935 .................. **TCLC 18**
  See also Dale, Colin
  See also CA 115

**Lawrence of Arabia**
  See Lawrence, T(homas) E(dward)

**Lawson, Henry (Archibald Hertzberg)**
  1867-1922 .......... **TCLC 27; SSC 18**
  See also CA 120

**Lawton, Dennis**
  See Faust, Frederick (Schiller)

**Laxness, Halldor** .................. **CLC 25**
  See also Gudjonsson, Halldor Kiljan

**Layamon** fl. c. 1200- ............. **CMLC 10**
  See also DLB 146

**Laye, Camara** 1928-1980 ... **CLC 4, 38; BLC**
  See also BW 1; CA 85-88; 97-100;
  CANR 25; DAM MULT; MTCW

**Layton, Irving (Peter)**
  1912- ............... **CLC 2, 15; DAC**
  See also CA 1-4R; CANR 2, 33, 43;
  DAM MST, POET; DLB 88; MTCW

**Lazarus, Emma** 1849-1887 ....... **NCLC 8**

**Lazarus, Felix**
  See Cable, George Washington

**Lazarus, Henry**
  See Slavitt, David R(ytman)

**Lea, Joan**
  See Neufeld, John (Arthur)

**Leacock, Stephen (Butler)**
  1869-1944 ............. **TCLC 2; DAC**
  See also CA 104; 141; DAM MST; DLB 92

**Lear, Edward** 1812-1888 ........ **NCLC 3**
  See also CLR 1; DLB 32, 163; MAICYA;
  SATA 18

**Lear, Norman (Milton)** 1922- ...... **CLC 12**
  See also CA 73-76

**Leavis, F(rank) R(aymond)**
  1895-1978 .................. **CLC 24**
  See also CA 21-24R; 77-80; CANR 44;
  MTCW

**Leavitt, David** 1961- ............. **CLC 34**
  See also CA 116; 122; CANR 50;
  DAM POP; DLB 130; INT 122

**Leblanc, Maurice (Marie Emile)**
  1864-1941 .................. **TCLC 49**
  See also CA 110

**Lebowitz, Fran(ces Ann)**
  1951(?)- .................. **CLC 11, 36**
  See also CA 81-84; CANR 14;
  INT CANR-14; MTCW

**Lebrecht, Peter**
  See Tieck, (Johann) Ludwig

**le Carre, John** .......... **CLC 3, 5, 9, 15, 28**
  See also Cornwell, David (John Moore)
  See also BEST 89:4; CDBLB 1960 to
  Present; DLB 87

**Le Clezio, J(ean) M(arie) G(ustave)**
  1940- ...................... **CLC 31**
  See also CA 116; 128; DLB 83

**Leconte de Lisle, Charles-Marie-Rene**
  1818-1894 .................. **NCLC 29**

**Le Coq, Monsieur**
  See Simenon, Georges (Jacques Christian)

**Leduc, Violette** 1907-1972 ......... **CLC 22**
  See also CA 13-14; 33-36R; CAP 1

**Ledwidge, Francis** 1887(?)-1917 ... **TCLC 23**
  See also CA 123; DLB 20

**Lee, Andrea** 1953- .......... **CLC 36; BLC**
  See also BW 1; CA 125; DAM MULT

**Lee, Andrew**
  See Auchincloss, Louis (Stanton)

**Lee, Chang-rae** 1965- ............. **CLC 91**
  See also CA 148

**Lee, Don L.** ....................... **CLC 2**
  See also Madhubuti, Haki R.

**Lee, George W(ashington)**
  1894-1976 .............. **CLC 52; BLC**
  See also BW 1; CA 125; DAM MULT;
  DLB 51

**Lee, (Nelle) Harper**
  1926- .... **CLC 12, 60; DA; DAB; DAC;**
                                     **WLC**
  See also AAYA 13; CA 13-16R; CANR 51;
  CDALB 1941-1968; DAM MST, NOV;
  DLB 6; MTCW; SATA 11

**Lee, Helen Elaine** 1959(?)- ........ **CLC 86**
  See also CA 148

**Lee, Julian**
  See Latham, Jean Lee

**Lee, Larry**
  See Lee, Lawrence

**Lee, Laurie** 1914- ........... **CLC 90; DAB**
  See also CA 77-80; CANR 33; DAM POP;
  DLB 27; MTCW

**Lee, Lawrence** 1941-1990 ......... **CLC 34**
  See also CA 131; CANR 43

**Lee, Manfred B(ennington)**
  1905-1971 .................. **CLC 11**
  See also Queen, Ellery
  See also CA 1-4R; 29-32R; CANR 2;
  DLB 137

**Lee, Stan** 1922- ................. **CLC 17**
  See also AAYA 5; CA 108; 111; INT 111

**Lee, Tanith** 1947- ................ **CLC 46**
  See also AAYA 15; CA 37-40R; SATA 8

**Lee, Vernon** ...................... **TCLC 5**
  See also Paget, Violet
  See also DLB 57, 153, 156

**Lee, William**
  See Burroughs, William S(eward)

**Lee, Willy**
  See Burroughs, William S(eward)

**Lee-Hamilton, Eugene (Jacob)**
  1845-1907 .................. **TCLC 22**
  See also CA 117

**Leet, Judith** 1935- ............... **CLC 11**

**Le Fanu, Joseph Sheridan**
  1814-1873 ........... **NCLC 9; SSC 14**
  See also DAM POP; DLB 21, 70, 159

**Leffland, Ella** 1931- .............. **CLC 19**
  See also CA 29-32R; CANR 35; DLBY 84;
  INT CANR-35; SATA 65

**Leger, Alexis**
  See Leger, (Marie-Rene Auguste) Alexis
  Saint-Leger

**Leger, (Marie-Rene Auguste) Alexis**
  **Saint-Leger** 1887-1975 ........ **CLC 11**
  See also Perse, St.-John
  See also CA 13-16R; 61-64; CANR 43;
  DAM POET; MTCW

**Leger, Saintleger**
  See Leger, (Marie-Rene Auguste) Alexis
  Saint-Leger

**Le Guin, Ursula K(roeber)**
  1929- ...... **CLC 8, 13, 22, 45, 71; DAB;**
                                   **DAC; SSC 12**
  See also AAYA 9; AITN 1; CA 21-24R;
  CANR 9, 32; CDALB 1968-1988; CLR 3,
  28; DAM MST, POP; DLB 8, 52;
  INT CANR-32; JRDA; MAICYA;
  MTCW; SATA 4, 52

**Lehmann, Rosamond (Nina)**
  1901-1990 .................. **CLC 5**
  See also CA 77-80; 131; CANR 8; DLB 15

**Leiber, Fritz (Reuter, Jr.)**
  1910-1992 .................. **CLC 25**
  See also CA 45-48; 139; CANR 2, 40;
  DLB 8; MTCW; SATA 45;
  SATA-Obit 73

**Leimbach, Martha** 1963-
  See Leimbach, Marti
  See also CA 130

**Leimbach, Marti** .................. **CLC 65**
  See also Leimbach, Martha

**Leino, Eino** ...................... **TCLC 24**
  See also Loennbohm, Armas Eino Leopold

**Leiris, Michel (Julien)** 1901-1990 ... **CLC 61**
  See also CA 119; 128; 132

**Leithauser, Brad** 1953- ............ **CLC 27**
  See also CA 107; CANR 27; DLB 120

**Lelchuk, Alan** 1938- ............... **CLC 5**
  See also CA 45-48; CAAS 20; CANR 1

**Lem, Stanislaw** 1921- ........ **CLC 8, 15, 40**
  See also CA 105; CAAS 1; CANR 32;
  MTCW

**Loxsmith, John**
See Brunner, John (Kilian Houston)

**Loy, Mina** ....................... **CLC 28**
See also Lowry, Mina Gertrude
See also DAM POET; DLB 4, 54

**Loyson-Bridet**
See Schwob, (Mayer Andre) Marcel

**Lucas, Craig** 1951- ............... **CLC 64**
See also CA 137

**Lucas, George** 1944- .............. **CLC 16**
See also AAYA 1; CA 77-80; CANR 30;
SATA 56

**Lucas, Hans**
See Godard, Jean-Luc

**Lucas, Victoria**
See Plath, Sylvia

**Ludlam, Charles** 1943-1987 ..... **CLC 46, 50**
See also CA 85-88; 122

**Ludlum, Robert** 1927- ......... **CLC 22, 43**
See also AAYA 10; BEST 89:1, 90:3;
CA 33-36R; CANR 25, 41; DAM NOV,
POP; DLBY 82; MTCW

**Ludwig, Ken** ..................... **CLC 60**

**Ludwig, Otto** 1813-1865 .......... **NCLC 4**
See also DLB 129

**Lugones, Leopoldo** 1874-1938 ..... **TCLC 15**
See also CA 116; 131; HW

**Lu Hsun** 1881-1936 ...... **TCLC 3; SSC 20**
See also Shu-Jen, Chou

**Lukacs, George** ................... **CLC 24**
See also Lukacs, Gyorgy (Szegeny von)

**Lukacs, Gyorgy (Szegeny von)** 1885-1971
See Lukacs, George
See also CA 101; 29-32R

**Luke, Peter (Ambrose Cyprian)**
1919-1995 ................... **CLC 38**
See also CA 81-84; 147; DLB 13

**Lunar, Dennis**
See Mungo, Raymond

**Lurie, Alison** 1926- ....... **CLC 4, 5, 18, 39**
See also CA 1-4R; CANR 2, 17, 50; DLB 2;
MTCW; SATA 46

**Lustig, Arnost** 1926- ............. **CLC 56**
See also AAYA 3; CA 69-72; CANR 47;
SATA 56

**Luther, Martin** 1483-1546 .......... **LC 9**

**Luxemburg, Rosa** 1870(?)-1919 .... **TCLC 63**
See also CA 118

**Luzi, Mario** 1914- ................. **CLC 13**
See also CA 61-64; CANR 9; DLB 128

**L'Ymagier**
See Gourmont, Remy (-Marie-Charles) de

**Lynch, B. Suarez**
See Bioy Casares, Adolfo; Borges, Jorge
Luis

**Lynch, David (K.)** 1946- ........... **CLC 66**
See also CA 124; 129

**Lynch, James**
See Andreyev, Leonid (Nikolaevich)

**Lynch Davis, B.**
See Bioy Casares, Adolfo; Borges, Jorge
Luis

**Lyndsay, Sir David** 1490-1555 ...... **LC 20**

**Lynn, Kenneth S(chuyler)** 1923- .... **CLC 50**
See also CA 1-4R; CANR 3, 27

**Lynx**
See West, Rebecca

**Lyons, Marcus**
See Blish, James (Benjamin)

**Lyre, Pinchbeck**
See Sassoon, Siegfried (Lorraine)

**Lytle, Andrew (Nelson)** 1902-1995 .. **CLC 22**
See also CA 9-12R; 150; DLB 6; DLBY 95

**Lyttelton, George** 1709-1773 ....... **LC 10**

**Maas, Peter** 1929- .............. **CLC 29**
See also CA 93-96; INT 93-96

**Macaulay, Rose** 1881-1958 ..... **TCLC 7, 44**
See also CA 104; DLB 36

**Macaulay, Thomas Babington**
1800-1859 ................ **NCLC 42**
See also CDBLB 1832-1890; DLB 32, 55

**MacBeth, George (Mann)**
1932-1992 ............... **CLC 2, 5, 9**
See also CA 25-28R; 136; DLB 40; MTCW;
SATA 4; SATA-Obit 70

**MacCaig, Norman (Alexander)**
1910- ................... **CLC 36; DAB**
See also CA 9-12R; CANR 3, 34;
DAM POET; DLB 27

**MacCarthy, (Sir Charles Otto) Desmond**
1877-1952 ................. **TCLC 36**

**MacDiarmid, Hugh**
............ **CLC 2, 4, 11, 19, 63; PC 9**
See also Grieve, C(hristopher) M(urray)
See also CDBLB 1945-1960; DLB 20

**MacDonald, Anson**
See Heinlein, Robert A(nson)

**Macdonald, Cynthia** 1928- ...... **CLC 13, 19**
See also CA 49-52; CANR 4, 44; DLB 105

**MacDonald, George** 1824-1905 ..... **TCLC 9**
See also CA 106; 137; DLB 18, 163;
MAICYA; SATA 33

**Macdonald, John**
See Millar, Kenneth

**MacDonald, John D(ann)**
1916-1986 .............. **CLC 3, 27, 44**
See also CA 1-4R; 121; CANR 1, 19;
DAM NOV, POP; DLB 8; DLBY 86;
MTCW

**Macdonald, John Ross**
See Millar, Kenneth

**Macdonald, Ross** ..... **CLC 1, 2, 3, 14, 34, 41**
See also Millar, Kenneth
See also DLBD 6

**MacDougal, John**
See Blish, James (Benjamin)

**MacEwen, Gwendolyn (Margaret)**
1941-1987 ................ **CLC 13, 55**
See also CA 9-12R; 124; CANR 7, 22;
DLB 53; SATA 50; SATA-Obit 55

**Macha, Karel Hynek** 1810-1846 .. **NCLC 46**

**Machado (y Ruiz), Antonio**
1875-1939 .................. **TCLC 3**
See also CA 104; DLB 108

**Machado de Assis, Joaquim Maria**
1839-1908 ............. **TCLC 10; BLC**
See also CA 107

**Machen, Arthur** .......... **TCLC 4; SSC 20**
See also Jones, Arthur Llewellyn
See also DLB 36, 156

**Machiavelli, Niccolo**
1469-1527 ...... **LC 8; DA; DAB; DAC**
See also DAM MST

**MacInnes, Colin** 1914-1976 ...... **CLC 4, 23**
See also CA 69-72; 65-68; CANR 21;
DLB 14; MTCW

**MacInnes, Helen (Clark)**
1907-1985 ................ **CLC 27, 39**
See also CA 1-4R; 117; CANR 1, 28;
DAM POP; DLB 87; MTCW; SATA 22;
SATA-Obit 44

**Mackay, Mary** 1855-1924
See Corelli, Marie
See also CA 118

**Mackenzie, Compton (Edward Montague)**
1883-1972 ................... **CLC 18**
See also CA 21-22; 37-40R; CAP 2;
DLB 34, 100

**Mackenzie, Henry** 1745-1831 .... **NCLC 41**
See also DLB 39

**Mackintosh, Elizabeth** 1896(?)-1952
See Tey, Josephine
See also CA 110

**MacLaren, James**
See Grieve, C(hristopher) M(urray)

**Mac Laverty, Bernard** 1942- ....... **CLC 31**
See also CA 116; 118; CANR 43; INT 118

**MacLean, Alistair (Stuart)**
1922-1987 ........... **CLC 3, 13, 50, 63**
See also CA 57-60; 121; CANR 28;
DAM POP; MTCW; SATA 23;
SATA-Obit 50

**Maclean, Norman (Fitzroy)**
1902-1990 ........... **CLC 78; SSC 13**
See also CA 102; 132; CANR 49;
DAM POP

**MacLeish, Archibald**
1892-1982 ............. **CLC 3, 8, 14, 68**
See also CA 9-12R; 106; CANR 33;
DAM POET; DLB 4, 7, 45; DLBY 82;
MTCW

**MacLennan, (John) Hugh**
1907-1990 ........ **CLC 2, 14, 92; DAC**
See also CA 5-8R; 142; CANR 33;
DAM MST; DLB 68; MTCW

**MacLeod, Alistair** 1936- ..... **CLC 56; DAC**
See also CA 123; DAM MST; DLB 60

**MacNeice, (Frederick) Louis**
1907-1963 ..... **CLC 1, 4, 10, 53; DAB**
See also CA 85-88; DAM POET; DLB 10,
20; MTCW

**MacNeill, Dand**
See Fraser, George MacDonald

**Macpherson, James** 1736-1796 ...... **LC 29**
See also DLB 109

**Macpherson, (Jean) Jay** 1931- ...... **CLC 14**
See also CA 5-8R; DLB 53

**MacShane, Frank** 1927- ............ **CLC 39**
See also CA 9-12R; CANR 3, 33; DLB 111

**Macumber, Mari**
See Sandoz, Mari(e Susette)

**Madach, Imre** 1823-1864 ........ **NCLC 19**

**Markham, Edwin** 1852-1940 . . . . . . **TCLC 47**
See also DLB 54

**Markham, Robert**
See Amis, Kingsley (William)

**Marks, J**
See Highwater, Jamake (Mamake)

**Marks-Highwater, J**
See Highwater, Jamake (Mamake)

**Markson, David M(errill)** 1927- . . . . **CLC 67**
See also CA 49-52; CANR 1

**Marley, Bob** . . . . . . . . . . . . . . . . . . . . **CLC 17**
See also Marley, Robert Nesta

**Marley, Robert Nesta** 1945-1981
See Marley, Bob
See also CA 107; 103

**Marlowe, Christopher**
1564-1593 . . . . . **LC 22; DA; DAB; DAC;**
**DC 1; WLC**
See also CDBLB Before 1660;
DAM DRAM, MST; DLB 62

**Marmontel, Jean-Francois**
1723-1799 . . . . . . . . . . . . . . . . . . . . **LC 2**

**Marquand, John P(hillips)**
1893-1960 . . . . . . . . . . . . . . . . **CLC 2, 10**
See also CA 85-88; DLB 9, 102

**Marquez, Gabriel (Jose) Garcia**
See Garcia Marquez, Gabriel (Jose)

**Marquis, Don(ald Robert Perry)**
1878-1937 . . . . . . . . . . . . . . . . . . **TCLC 7**
See also CA 104; DLB 11, 25

**Marric, J. J.**
See Creasey, John

**Marrow, Bernard**
See Moore, Brian

**Marryat, Frederick** 1792-1848 . . . . **NCLC 3**
See also DLB 21, 163

**Marsden, James**
See Creasey, John

**Marsh, (Edith) Ngaio**
1899-1982 . . . . . . . . . . . . . . . **CLC 7, 53**
See also CA 9-12R; CANR 6; DAM POP;
DLB 77; MTCW

**Marshall, Garry** 1934- . . . . . . . . . . . . **CLC 17**
See also AAYA 3; CA 111; SATA 60

**Marshall, Paule**
1929- . . . . . . . . **CLC 27, 72; BLC; SSC 3**
See also BW 2; CA 77-80; CANR 25;
DAM MULT; DLB 157; MTCW

**Marsten, Richard**
See Hunter, Evan

**Marston, John** 1576-1634 . . . . . . . . . **LC 33**
See also DAM DRAM; DLB 58

**Martha, Henry**
See Harris, Mark

**Martial** c. 40-c. 104 . . . . . . . . . . . . . . **PC 10**

**Martin, Ken**
See Hubbard, L(afayette) Ron(ald)

**Martin, Richard**
See Creasey, John

**Martin, Steve** 1945- . . . . . . . . . . . . . **CLC 30**
See also CA 97-100; CANR 30; MTCW

**Martin, Valerie** 1948- . . . . . . . . . . . . **CLC 89**
See also BEST 90:2; CA 85-88; CANR 49

**Martin, Violet Florence**
1862-1915 . . . . . . . . . . . . . . . . . . **TCLC 51**

**Martin, Webber**
See Silverberg, Robert

**Martindale, Patrick Victor**
See White, Patrick (Victor Martindale)

**Martin du Gard, Roger**
1881-1958 . . . . . . . . . . . . . . . . . **TCLC 24**
See also CA 118; DLB 65

**Martineau, Harriet** 1802-1876 . . . . **NCLC 26**
See also DLB 21, 55, 159, 163; YABC 2

**Martines, Julia**
See O'Faolain, Julia

**Martinez, Jacinto Benavente y**
See Benavente (y Martinez), Jacinto

**Martinez Ruiz, Jose** 1873-1967
See Azorin; Ruiz, Jose Martinez
See also CA 93-96; HW

**Martinez Sierra, Gregorio**
1881-1947 . . . . . . . . . . . . . . . . . . **TCLC 6**
See also CA 115

**Martinez Sierra, Maria (de la O'LeJarraga)**
1874-1974 . . . . . . . . . . . . . . . . . . **TCLC 6**
See also CA 115

**Martinsen, Martin**
See Follett, Ken(neth Martin)

**Martinson, Harry (Edmund)**
1904-1978 . . . . . . . . . . . . . . . . . . **CLC 14**
See also CA 77-80; CANR 34

**Marut, Ret**
See Traven, B.

**Marut, Robert**
See Traven, B.

**Marvell, Andrew**
1621-1678 . . . . . . **LC 4; DA; DAB; DAC;**
**PC 10; WLC**
See also CDBLB 1660-1789; DAM MST,
POET; DLB 131

**Marx, Karl (Heinrich)**
1818-1883 . . . . . . . . . . . . . . . . **NCLC 17**
See also DLB 129

**Masaoka Shiki** . . . . . . . . . . . . . . . . . . **TCLC 18**
See also Masaoka Tsunenori

**Masaoka Tsunenori** 1867-1902
See Masaoka Shiki
See also CA 117

**Masefield, John (Edward)**
1878-1967 . . . . . . . . . . . . . . . **CLC 11, 47**
See also CA 19-20; 25-28R; CANR 33;
CAP 2; CDBLB 1890-1914; DAM POET;
DLB 10, 19, 153, 160; MTCW; SATA 19

**Maso, Carole** 19(?)- . . . . . . . . . . . . . **CLC 44**

**Mason, Bobbie Ann**
1940- . . . . . . . . . **CLC 28, 43, 82; SSC 4**
See also AAYA 5; CA 53-56; CANR 11,
31; DLBY 87; INT CANR-31; MTCW

**Mason, Ernst**
See Pohl, Frederik

**Mason, Lee W.**
See Malzberg, Barry N(athaniel)

**Mason, Nick** 1945- . . . . . . . . . . . . . . **CLC 35**

**Mason, Tally**
See Derleth, August (William)

**Mass, William**
See Gibson, William

**Masters, Edgar Lee**
1868-1950 . . . . . . **TCLC 2, 25; DA; DAC;**
**PC 1**
See also CA 104; 133; CDALB 1865-1917;
DAM MST, POET; DLB 54; MTCW

**Masters, Hilary** 1928- . . . . . . . . . . . . **CLC 48**
See also CA 25-28R; CANR 13, 47

**Mastrosimone, William** 19(?)- . . . . . . **CLC 36**

**Mathe, Albert**
See Camus, Albert

**Matheson, Richard Burton** 1926- . . . **CLC 37**
See also CA 97-100; DLB 8, 44; INT 97-100

**Mathews, Harry** 1930- . . . . . . . . . **CLC 6, 52**
See also CA 21-24R; CAAS 6; CANR 18,
40

**Mathews, John Joseph** 1894-1979 . . . **CLC 84**
See also CA 19-20; 142; CANR 45; CAP 2;
DAM MULT; NNAL

**Mathias, Roland (Glyn)** 1915- . . . . . . **CLC 45**
See also CA 97-100; CANR 19, 41; DLB 27

**Matsuo Basho** 1644-1694 . . . . . . . . . . . . **PC 3**
See also DAM POET

**Mattheson, Rodney**
See Creasey, John

**Matthews, Greg** 1949- . . . . . . . . . . . . **CLC 45**
See also CA 135

**Matthews, William** 1942- . . . . . . . . . **CLC 40**
See also CA 29-32R; CAAS 18; CANR 12;
DLB 5

**Matthias, John (Edward)** 1941- . . . . . . **CLC 9**
See also CA 33-36R

**Matthiessen, Peter**
1927- . . . . . . . . . . . **CLC 5, 7, 11, 32, 64**
See also AAYA 6; BEST 90:4; CA 9-12R;
CANR 21, 50; DAM NOV; DLB 6;
MTCW; SATA 27

**Maturin, Charles Robert**
1780(?)-1824 . . . . . . . . . . . . . . . **NCLC 6**

**Matute (Ausejo), Ana Maria**
1925- . . . . . . . . . . . . . . . . . . . . . . **CLC 11**
See also CA 89-92; MTCW

**Maugham, W. S.**
See Maugham, W(illiam) Somerset

**Maugham, W(illiam) Somerset**
1874-1965 . . . . . . . **CLC 1, 11, 15, 67, 93;**
**DA; DAB; DAC; SSC 8; WLC**
See also CA 5-8R; 25-28R; CANR 40;
CDBLB 1914-1945; DAM DRAM, MST,
NOV; DLB 10, 36, 77, 100, 162; MTCW;
SATA 54

**Maugham, William Somerset**
See Maugham, W(illiam) Somerset

**Maupassant, (Henri Rene Albert) Guy de**
1850-1893 . . . . . **NCLC 1, 42; DA; DAB;**
**DAC; SSC 1; WLC**
See also DAM MST; DLB 123

**Maurhut, Richard**
See Traven, B.

**Mauriac, Claude** 1914- . . . . . . . . . . . . **CLC 9**
See also CA 89-92; DLB 83

Mauriac, Francois (Charles)
1885-1970 .............. CLC 4, 9, 56
See also CA 25-28; CAP 2; DLB 65;
MTCW

Mavor, Osborne Henry  1888-1951
See Bridie, James
See also CA 104

Maxwell, William (Keepers, Jr.)
1908- ...................... CLC 19
See also CA 93-96; DLBY 80; INT 93-96

May, Elaine  1932- .............. CLC 16
See also CA 124; 142; DLB 44

Mayakovski, Vladimir (Vladimirovich)
1893-1930 ............... TCLC 4, 18
See also CA 104

Mayhew, Henry  1812-1887 ...... NCLC 31
See also DLB 18, 55

Mayle, Peter  1939(?)-............. CLC 89
See also CA 139

Maynard, Joyce  1953-............ CLC 23
See also CA 111; 129

Mayne, William (James Carter)
1928- ...................... CLC 12
See also CA 9-12R; CANR 37; CLR 25;
JRDA; MAICYA; SAAS 11; SATA 6, 68

Mayo, Jim
See L'Amour, Louis (Dearborn)

Maysles, Albert  1926- ............ CLC 16
See also CA 29-32R

Maysles, David  1932-............. CLC 16

Mazer, Norma Fox  1931- ......... CLC 26
See also AAYA 5; CA 69-72; CANR 12,
32; CLR 23; JRDA; MAICYA; SAAS 1;
SATA 24, 67

Mazzini, Guiseppe  1805-1872 .... NCLC 34

McAuley, James Phillip
1917-1976 .................. CLC 45
See also CA 97-100

McBain, Ed
See Hunter, Evan

McBrien, William Augustine
1930- ...................... CLC 44
See also CA 107

McCaffrey, Anne (Inez)  1926-...... CLC 17
See also AAYA 6; AITN 2; BEST 89:2;
CA 25-28R; CANR 15, 35; DAM NOV,
POP; DLB 8; JRDA; MAICYA; MTCW;
SAAS 11; SATA 8, 70

McCall, Nathan  1955(?)- .......... CLC 86
See also CA 146

McCann, Arthur
See Campbell, John W(ood, Jr.)

McCann, Edson
See Pohl, Frederik

McCarthy, Charles, Jr.  1933-
See McCarthy, Cormac
See also CANR 42; DAM POP

McCarthy, Cormac  1933-..... CLC 4, 57, 59
See also McCarthy, Charles, Jr.
See also DLB 6, 143

McCarthy, Mary (Therese)
1912-1989 ... CLC 1, 3, 5, 14, 24, 39, 59
See also CA 5-8R; 129; CANR 16, 50;
DLB 2; DLBY 81; INT CANR-16;
MTCW

McCartney, (James) Paul
1942- ................... CLC 12, 35
See also CA 146

McCauley, Stephen (D.)  1955- ..... CLC 50
See also CA 141

McClure, Michael (Thomas)
1932- .................... CLC 6, 10
See also CA 21-24R; CANR 17, 46;
DLB 16

McCorkle, Jill (Collins)  1958-...... CLC 51
See also CA 121; DLBY 87

McCourt, James  1941-............. CLC 5
See also CA 57-60

McCoy, Horace (Stanley)
1897-1955 ................. TCLC 28
See also CA 108; DLB 9

McCrae, John  1872-1918........ TCLC 12
See also CA 109; DLB 92

McCreigh, James
See Pohl, Frederik

McCullers, (Lula) Carson (Smith)
1917-1967 .... CLC 1, 4, 10, 12, 48; DA;
DAB; DAC; SSC 9; WLC
See also CA 5-8R; 25-28R; CABS 1, 3;
CANR 18; CDALB 1941-1968;
DAM MST, NOV; DLB 2, 7; MTCW;
SATA 27

McCulloch, John Tyler
See Burroughs, Edgar Rice

McCullough, Colleen  1938(?)-...... CLC 27
See also CA 81-84; CANR 17, 46;
DAM NOV, POP; MTCW

McDermott, Alice  1953- .......... CLC 90
See also CA 109; CANR 40

McElroy, Joseph  1930- ......... CLC 5, 47
See also CA 17-20R

McEwan, Ian (Russell)  1948- ... CLC 13, 66
See also BEST 90:4; CA 61-64; CANR 14,
41; DAM NOV; DLB 14; MTCW

McFadden, David  1940-........... CLC 48
See also CA 104; DLB 60; INT 104

McFarland, Dennis  1950- ......... CLC 65

McGahern, John
1934- .......... CLC 5, 9, 48; SSC 17
See also CA 17-20R; CANR 29; DLB 14;
MTCW

McGinley, Patrick (Anthony)
1937- ...................... CLC 41
See also CA 120; 127; INT 127

McGinley, Phyllis  1905-1978 ...... CLC 14
See also CA 9-12R; 77-80; CANR 19;
DLB 11, 48; SATA 2, 44; SATA-Obit 24

McGinniss, Joe  1942-............. CLC 32
See also AITN 2; BEST 89:2; CA 25-28R;
CANR 26; INT CANR-26

McGivern, Maureen Daly
See Daly, Maureen

McGrath, Patrick  1950-........... CLC 55
See also CA 136

McGrath, Thomas (Matthew)
1916-1990 ................ CLC 28, 59
See also CA 9-12R; 132; CANR 6, 33;
DAM POET; MTCW; SATA 41;
SATA-Obit 66

McGuane, Thomas (Francis III)
1939- ................ CLC 3, 7, 18, 45
See also AITN 2; CA 49-52; CANR 5, 24,
49; DLB 2; DLBY 80; INT CANR-24;
MTCW

McGuckian, Medbh  1950-......... CLC 48
See also CA 143; DAM POET; DLB 40

McHale, Tom  1942(?)-1982....... CLC 3, 5
See also AITN 1; CA 77-80; 106

McIlvanney, William  1936-........ CLC 42
See also CA 25-28R; DLB 14

McIlwraith, Maureen Mollie Hunter
See Hunter, Mollie
See also SATA 2

McInerney, Jay  1955- ............ CLC 34
See also CA 116; 123; CANR 45;
DAM POP; INT 123

McIntyre, Vonda N(eel)  1948- ..... CLC 18
See also CA 81-84; CANR 17, 34; MTCW

McKay, Claude
........ TCLC 7, 41; BLC; DAB; PC 2
See also McKay, Festus Claudius
See also DLB 4, 45, 51, 117

McKay, Festus Claudius  1889-1948
See McKay, Claude
See also BW 1; CA 104; 124; DA; DAC;
DAM MST, MULT, NOV, POET;
MTCW; WLC

McKuen, Rod  1933-............. CLC 1, 3
See also AITN 1; CA 41-44R; CANR 40

McLoughlin, R. B.
See Mencken, H(enry) L(ouis)

McLuhan, (Herbert) Marshall
1911-1980 ............... CLC 37, 83
See also CA 9-12R; 102; CANR 12, 34;
DLB 88; INT CANR-12; MTCW

McMillan, Terry (L.)  1951-..... CLC 50, 61
See also BW 2; CA 140; DAM MULT,
NOV, POP

McMurtry, Larry (Jeff)
1936- .......... CLC 2, 3, 7, 11, 27, 44
See also AAYA 15; AITN 2; BEST 89:2;
CA 5-8R; CANR 19, 43;
CDALB 1968-1988; DAM NOV, POP;
DLB 2, 143; DLBY 80, 87; MTCW

McNally, T. M.  1961- ............ CLC 82

McNally, Terrence  1939-... CLC 4, 7, 41, 91
See also CA 45-48; CANR 2;
DAM DRAM; DLB 7

McNamer, Deirdre  1950-.......... CLC 70

McNeile, Herman Cyril  1888-1937
See Sapper
See also DLB 77

McNickle, (William) D'Arcy
1904-1977 .................. CLC 89
See also CA 9-12R; 85-88; CANR 5, 45;
DAM MULT; NNAL; SATA-Obit 22

McPhee, John (Angus)  1931- ...... CLC 36
See also BEST 90:1; CA 65-68; CANR 20,
46; MTCW

McPherson, James Alan
1943- .................... CLC 19, 77
See also BW 1; CA 25-28R; CAAS 17;
CANR 24; DLB 38; MTCW

**McPherson, William (Alexander)**
1933-...................... **CLC 34**
See also CA 69-72; CANR 28;
INT CANR-28

**Mead, Margaret** 1901-1978........ **CLC 37**
See also AITN 1; CA 1-4R; 81-84;
CANR 4; MTCW; SATA-Obit 20

**Meaker, Marijane (Agnes)** 1927-
See Kerr, M. E.
See also CA 107; CANR 37; INT 107;
JRDA; MAICYA; MTCW; SATA 20, 61

**Medoff, Mark (Howard)** 1940-... **CLC 6, 23**
See also AITN 1; CA 53-56; CANR 5;
DAM DRAM; DLB 7; INT CANR-5

**Medvedev, P. N.**
See Bakhtin, Mikhail Mikhailovich

**Meged, Aharon**
See Megged, Aharon

**Meged, Aron**
See Megged, Aharon

**Megged, Aharon** 1920-............ **CLC 9**
See also CA 49-52; CAAS 13; CANR 1

**Mehta, Ved (Parkash)** 1934-....... **CLC 37**
See also CA 1-4R; CANR 2, 23; MTCW

**Melanter**
See Blackmore, R(ichard) D(oddridge)

**Melikow, Loris**
See Hofmannsthal, Hugo von

**Melmoth, Sebastian**
See Wilde, Oscar (Fingal O'Flahertie Wills)

**Meltzer, Milton** 1915-............ **CLC 26**
See also AAYA 8; CA 13-16R; CANR 38;
CLR 13; DLB 61; JRDA; MAICYA;
SAAS 1; SATA 1, 50, 80

**Melville, Herman**
1819-1891..... **NCLC 3, 12, 29, 45, 49;**
**DA; DAB; DAC; SSC 1, 17; WLC**
See also CDALB 1640-1865; DAM MST,
NOV; DLB 3, 74; SATA 59

**Menander**
c. 342B.C.-c. 292B.C.... **CMLC 9; DC 3**
See also DAM DRAM

**Mencken, H(enry) L(ouis)**
1880-1956 ................... **TCLC 13**
See also CA 105; 125; CDALB 1917-1929;
DLB 11, 29, 63, 137; MTCW

**Mercer, David** 1928-1980.......... **CLC 5**
See also CA 9-12R; 102; CANR 23;
DAM DRAM; DLB 13; MTCW

**Merchant, Paul**
See Ellison, Harlan (Jay)

**Meredith, George** 1828-1909... **TCLC 17, 43**
See also CA 117; CDBLB 1832-1890;
DAM POET; DLB 18, 35, 57, 159

**Meredith, William (Morris)**
1919-.............. **CLC 4, 13, 22, 55**
See also CA 9-12R; CAAS 14; CANR 6, 40;
DAM POET; DLB 5

**Merezhkovsky, Dmitry Sergeyevich**
1865-1941 ................. **TCLC 29**

**Merimee, Prosper**
1803-1870 ........... **NCLC 6; SSC 7**
See also DLB 119

**Merkin, Daphne** 1954-............ **CLC 44**
See also CA 123

**Merlin, Arthur**
See Blish, James (Benjamin)

**Merrill, James (Ingram)**
1926-1995 .... **CLC 2, 3, 6, 8, 13, 18, 34,**
**91**
See also CA 13-16R; 147; CANR 10, 49;
DAM POET; DLB 5, 165; DLBY 85;
INT CANR-10; MTCW

**Merriman, Alex**
See Silverberg, Robert

**Merritt, E. B.**
See Waddington, Miriam

**Merton, Thomas**
1915-1968 .. **CLC 1, 3, 11, 34, 83; PC 10**
See also CA 5-8R; 25-28R; CANR 22;
DLB 48; DLBY 81; MTCW

**Merwin, W(illiam) S(tanley)**
1927-... **CLC 1, 2, 3, 5, 8, 13, 18, 45, 88**
See also CA 13-16R; CANR 15, 51;
DAM POET; DLB 5; INT CANR-15;
MTCW

**Metcalf, John** 1938-.............. **CLC 37**
See also CA 113; DLB 60

**Metcalf, Suzanne**
See Baum, L(yman) Frank

**Mew, Charlotte (Mary)**
1870-1928 .................. **TCLC 8**
See also CA 105; DLB 19, 135

**Mewshaw, Michael** 1943-.......... **CLC 9**
See also CA 53-56; CANR 7, 47; DLBY 80

**Meyer, June**
See Jordan, June

**Meyer, Lynn**
See Slavitt, David R(ytman)

**Meyer-Meyrink, Gustav** 1868-1932
See Meyrink, Gustav
See also CA 117

**Meyers, Jeffrey** 1939-............ **CLC 39**
See also CA 73-76; DLB 111

**Meynell, Alice (Christina Gertrude Thompson)**
1847-1922 .................. **TCLC 6**
See also CA 104; DLB 19, 98

**Meyrink, Gustav** ............... **TCLC 21**
See also Meyer-Meyrink, Gustav
See also DLB 81

**Michaels, Leonard**
1933-............. **CLC 6, 25; SSC 16**
See also CA 61-64; CANR 21; DLB 130;
MTCW

**Michaux, Henri** 1899-1984 ...... **CLC 8, 19**
See also CA 85-88; 114

**Michelangelo** 1475-1564........... **LC 12**

**Michelet, Jules** 1798-1874....... **NCLC 31**

**Michener, James A(lbert)**
1907(?)-.......... **CLC 1, 5, 11, 29, 60**
See also AITN 1; BEST 90:1; CA 5-8R;
CANR 21, 45; DAM NOV, POP; DLB 6;
MTCW

**Mickiewicz, Adam** 1798-1855 ..... **NCLC 3**

**Middleton, Christopher** 1926-...... **CLC 13**
See also CA 13-16R; CANR 29; DLB 40

**Middleton, Richard (Barham)**
1882-1911 .................. **TCLC 56**
See also DLB 156

**Middleton, Stanley** 1919-........ **CLC 7, 38**
See also CA 25-28R; CAAS 23; CANR 21,
46; DLB 14

**Middleton, Thomas**
1580-1627 .............. **LC 33; DC 5**
See also DAM DRAM, MST; DLB 58

**Migueis, Jose Rodrigues** 1901-..... **CLC 10**

**Mikszath, Kalman** 1847-1910 ..... **TCLC 31**

**Miles, Josephine**
1911-1985 ........ **CLC 1, 2, 14, 34, 39**
See also CA 1-4R; 116; CANR 2;
DAM POET; DLB 48

**Militant**
See Sandburg, Carl (August)

**Mill, John Stuart** 1806-1873..... **NCLC 11**
See also CDBLB 1832-1890; DLB 55

**Millar, Kenneth** 1915-1983 ........ **CLC 14**
See also Macdonald, Ross
See also CA 9-12R; 110; CANR 16;
DAM POP; DLB 2; DLBD 6; DLBY 83;
MTCW

**Millay, E. Vincent**
See Millay, Edna St. Vincent

**Millay, Edna St. Vincent**
1892-1950 ...... **TCLC 4, 49; DA; DAB;**
**DAC; PC 6**
See also CA 104; 130; CDALB 1917-1929;
DAM MST, POET; DLB 45; MTCW

**Miller, Arthur**
1915-.... **CLC 1, 2, 6, 10, 15, 26, 47, 78;**
**DA; DAB; DAC; DC 1; WLC**
See also AAYA 15; AITN 1; CA 1-4R;
CABS 3; CANR 2, 30;
CDALB 1941-1968; DAM DRAM, MST;
DLB 7; MTCW

**Miller, Henry (Valentine)**
1891-1980 .... **CLC 1, 2, 4, 9, 14, 43, 84;**
**DA; DAB; DAC; WLC**
See also CA 9-12R; 97-100; CANR 33;
CDALB 1929-1941; DAM MST, NOV;
DLB 4, 9; DLBY 80; MTCW

**Miller, Jason** 1939(?)- ............ **CLC 2**
See also AITN 1; CA 73-76; DLB 7

**Miller, Sue** 1943- ................. **CLC 44**
See also BEST 90:3; CA 139; DAM POP;
DLB 143

**Miller, Walter M(ichael, Jr.)**
1923- ..................... **CLC 4, 30**
See also CA 85-88; DLB 8

**Millett, Kate** 1934-................. **CLC 67**
See also AITN 1; CA 73-76; CANR 32;
MTCW

**Millhauser, Steven** 1943-........ **CLC 21, 54**
See also CA 110; 111; DLB 2; INT 111

**Millin, Sarah Gertrude** 1889-1968 .. **CLC 49**
See also CA 102; 93-96

**Milne, A(lan) A(lexander)**
1882-1956 .......... **TCLC 6; DAB; DAC**
See also CA 104; 133; CLR 1, 26;
DAM MST; DLB 10, 77, 100, 160;
MAICYA; MTCW; YABC 1

**Milner, Ron(ald)** 1938-........ **CLC 56; BLC**
See also AITN 1; BW 1; CA 73-76;
CANR 24; DAM MULT; DLB 38;
MTCW

**Milosz, Czeslaw**
1911- . . . CLC 5, 11, 22, 31, 56, 82; PC 8
See also CA 81-84; CANR 23, 51;
DAM MST, POET; MTCW

**Milton, John**
1608-1674 . . . . . . LC 9; DA; DAB; DAC;
WLC
See also CDBLB 1660-1789; DAM MST,
POET; DLB 131, 151

**Min, Anchee** 1957- . . . . . . . . . . . . . . CLC 86
See also CA 146

**Minehaha, Cornelius**
See Wedekind, (Benjamin) Frank(lin)

**Miner, Valerie** 1947- . . . . . . . . . . . . . CLC 40
See also CA 97-100

**Minimo, Duca**
See D'Annunzio, Gabriele

**Minot, Susan** 1956- . . . . . . . . . . . . . . CLC 44
See also CA 134

**Minus, Ed** 1938- . . . . . . . . . . . . . . . . CLC 39

**Miranda, Javier**
See Bioy Casares, Adolfo

**Mirbeau, Octave** 1848-1917 . . . . . . TCLC 55
See also DLB 123

**Miro (Ferrer), Gabriel (Francisco Victor)**
1879-1930 . . . . . . . . . . . . . . . . . . TCLC 5
See also CA 104

**Mishima, Yukio**
. . . . . . . CLC 2, 4, 6, 9, 27; DC 1; SSC 4
See also Hiraoka, Kimitake

**Mistral, Frederic** 1830-1914 . . . . . . TCLC 51
See also CA 122

**Mistral, Gabriela** . . . . . . . . . . . . TCLC 2; HLC
See also Godoy Alcayaga, Lucila

**Mistry, Rohinton** 1952- . . . . . . CLC 71; DAC
See also CA 141

**Mitchell, Clyde**
See Ellison, Harlan (Jay); Silverberg, Robert

**Mitchell, James Leslie** 1901-1935
See Gibbon, Lewis Grassic
See also CA 104; DLB 15

**Mitchell, Joni** 1943- . . . . . . . . . . . . . . CLC 12
See also CA 112

**Mitchell, Margaret (Munnerlyn)**
1900-1949 . . . . . . . . . . . . . . . . . . TCLC 11
See also CA 109; 125; DAM NOV, POP;
DLB 9; MTCW

**Mitchell, Peggy**
See Mitchell, Margaret (Munnerlyn)

**Mitchell, S(ilas) Weir** 1829-1914 . . TCLC 36

**Mitchell, W(illiam) O(rmond)**
1914- . . . . . . . . . . . . . . . . . CLC 25; DAC
See also CA 77-80; CANR 15, 43;
DAM MST; DLB 88

**Mitford, Mary Russell** 1787-1855 . . NCLC 4
See also DLB 110, 116

**Mitford, Nancy** 1904-1973 . . . . . . . . CLC 44
See also CA 9-12R

**Miyamoto, Yuriko** 1899-1951 . . . . . TCLC 37

**Mo, Timothy (Peter)** 1950(?)- . . . . . . CLC 46
See also CA 117; MTCW

**Modarressi, Taghi (M.)** 1931- . . . . . . CLC 44
See also CA 121; 134; INT 134

**Modiano, Patrick (Jean)** 1945- . . . . . CLC 18
See also CA 85-88; CANR 17, 40; DLB 83

**Moerck, Paal**
See Roelvaag, O(le) E(dvart)

**Mofolo, Thomas (Mokopu)**
1875(?)-1948 . . . . . . . . . . . TCLC 22; BLC
See also CA 121; DAM MULT

**Mohr, Nicholasa** 1935- . . . . . . CLC 12; HLC
See also AAYA 8; CA 49-52; CANR 1, 32;
CLR 22; DAM MULT; DLB 145; HW;
JRDA; SAAS 8; SATA 8

**Mojtabai, A(nn) G(race)**
1938- . . . . . . . . . . . . . . . CLC 5, 9, 15, 29
See also CA 85-88

**Moliere**
1622-1673 . . . . . LC 28; DA; DAB; DAC;
WLC
See also DAM DRAM, MST

**Molin, Charles**
See Mayne, William (James Carter)

**Molnar, Ferenc** 1878-1952 . . . . . . . TCLC 20
See also CA 109; DAM DRAM

**Momaday, N(avarre) Scott**
1934- . . . CLC 2, 19, 85; DA; DAB; DAC
See also AAYA 11; CA 25-28R; CANR 14,
34; DAM MST, MULT, NOV, POP;
DLB 143; INT CANR-14; MTCW;
NNAL; SATA 48; SATA-Brief 30

**Monette, Paul** 1945-1995 . . . . . . . . . CLC 82
See also CA 139; 147

**Monroe, Harriet** 1860-1936 . . . . . . . TCLC 12
See also CA 109; DLB 54, 91

**Monroe, Lyle**
See Heinlein, Robert A(nson)

**Montagu, Elizabeth** 1917- . . . . . . . . NCLC 7
See also CA 9-12R

**Montagu, Mary (Pierrepont) Wortley**
1689-1762 . . . . . . . . . . . . . . . . . . . . LC 9
See also DLB 95, 101

**Montagu, W. H.**
See Coleridge, Samuel Taylor

**Montague, John (Patrick)**
1929- . . . . . . . . . . . . . . . . . . CLC 13, 46
See also CA 9-12R; CANR 9; DLB 40;
MTCW

**Montaigne, Michel (Eyquem) de**
1533-1592 . . . . . . LC 8; DA; DAB; DAC;
WLC
See also DAM MST

**Montale, Eugenio**
1896-1981 . . . . . . . CLC 7, 9, 18; PC 13
See also CA 17-20R; 104; CANR 30;
DLB 114; MTCW

**Montesquieu, Charles-Louis de Secondat**
1689-1755 . . . . . . . . . . . . . . . . . . . . LC 7

**Montgomery, (Robert) Bruce** 1921-1978
See Crispin, Edmund
See also CA 104

**Montgomery, L(ucy) M(aud)**
1874-1942 . . . . . . . . . . . TCLC 51; DAC
See also AAYA 12; CA 108; 137; CLR 8;
DAM MST; DLB 92; JRDA; MAICYA;
YABC 1

**Montgomery, Marion H., Jr.** 1925- . . CLC 7
See also AITN 1; CA 1-4R; CANR 3, 48;
DLB 6

**Montgomery, Max**
See Davenport, Guy (Mattison, Jr.)

**Montherlant, Henry (Milon) de**
1896-1972 . . . . . . . . . . . . . . . . CLC 8, 19
See also CA 85-88; 37-40R; DAM DRAM;
DLB 72; MTCW

**Monty Python**
See Chapman, Graham; Cleese, John
(Marwood); Gilliam, Terry (Vance); Idle,
Eric; Jones, Terence Graham Parry; Palin,
Michael (Edward)
See also AAYA 7

**Moodie, Susanna (Strickland)**
1803-1885 . . . . . . . . . . . . . . . . . NCLC 14
See also DLB 99

**Mooney, Edward** 1951-
See Mooney, Ted
See also CA 130

**Mooney, Ted** . . . . . . . . . . . . . . . . . . . CLC 25
See also Mooney, Edward

**Moorcock, Michael (John)**
1939- . . . . . . . . . . . . . . . . CLC 5, 27, 58
See also CA 45-48; CAAS 5; CANR 2, 17,
38; DLB 14; MTCW

**Moore, Brian**
1921- . . . . . . CLC 1, 3, 5, 7, 8, 19, 32, 90;
DAB; DAC
See also CA 1-4R; CANR 1, 25, 42;
DAM MST; MTCW

**Moore, Edward**
See Muir, Edwin

**Moore, George Augustus**
1852-1933 . . . . . . . . . . . TCLC 7; SSC 19
See also CA 104; DLB 10, 18, 57, 135

**Moore, Lorrie** . . . . . . . . . . . . . CLC 39, 45, 68
See also Moore, Marie Lorena

**Moore, Marianne (Craig)**
1887-1972 . . . . CLC 1, 2, 4, 8, 10, 13, 19,
47; DA; DAB; DAC; PC 4
See also CA 1-4R; 33-36R; CANR 3;
CDALB 1929-1941; DAM MST, POET;
DLB 45; DLBD 7; MTCW; SATA 20

**Moore, Marie Lorena** 1957-
See Moore, Lorrie
See also CA 116; CANR 39

**Moore, Thomas** 1779-1852 . . . . . . . NCLC 6
See also DLB 96, 144

**Morand, Paul** 1888-1976 . . CLC 41; SSC 22
See also CA 69-72; DLB 65

**Morante, Elsa** 1918-1985 . . . . . . . . CLC 8, 47
See also CA 85-88; 117; CANR 35; MTCW

**Moravia, Alberto** . . . . . . . CLC 2, 7, 11, 27, 46
See also Pincherle, Alberto

**More, Hannah** 1745-1833 . . . . . . . NCLC 27
See also DLB 107, 109, 116, 158

**More, Henry** 1614-1687 . . . . . . . . . . . . LC 9
See also DLB 126

**More, Sir Thomas** 1478-1535 . . . . LC 10, 32

**Moreas, Jean** . . . . . . . . . . . . . . . . . . TCLC 18
See also Papadiamantopoulos, Johannes

**Morgan, Berry** 1919- . . . . . . . . . . . . . . CLC 6
See also CA 49-52; DLB 6

**Morgan, Claire**
See Highsmith, (Mary) Patricia

**Morgan, Edwin (George)** 1920- ..... **CLC 31**
See also CA 5-8R; CANR 3, 43; DLB 27

**Morgan, (George) Frederick**
1922- ....................... **CLC 23**
See also CA 17-20R; CANR 21

**Morgan, Harriet**
See Mencken, H(enry) L(ouis)

**Morgan, Jane**
See Cooper, James Fenimore

**Morgan, Janet** 1945- ............. **CLC 39**
See also CA 65-68

**Morgan, Lady** 1776(?)-1859...... **NCLC 29**
See also DLB 116, 158

**Morgan, Robin** 1941- .............. **CLC 2**
See also CA 69-72; CANR 29; MTCW;
SATA 80

**Morgan, Scott**
See Kuttner, Henry

**Morgan, Seth** 1949(?)-1990 ........ **CLC 65**
See also CA 132

**Morgenstern, Christian**
1871-1914 ................... **TCLC 8**
See also CA 105

**Morgenstern, S.**
See Goldman, William (W.)

**Moricz, Zsigmond** 1879-1942 ..... **TCLC 33**

**Morike, Eduard (Friedrich)**
1804-1875 ................. **NCLC 10**
See also DLB 133

**Mori Ogai** ..................... **TCLC 14**
See also Mori Rintaro

**Mori Rintaro** 1862-1922
See Mori Ogai
See also CA 110

**Moritz, Karl Philipp** 1756-1793 ...... **LC 2**
See also DLB 94

**Morland, Peter Henry**
See Faust, Frederick (Schiller)

**Morren, Theophil**
See Hofmannsthal, Hugo von

**Morris, Bill** 1952-............... **CLC 76**

**Morris, Julian**
See West, Morris L(anglo)

**Morris, Steveland Judkins** 1950(?)-
See Wonder, Stevie
See also CA 111

**Morris, William** 1834-1896 ....... **NCLC 4**
See also CDBLB 1832-1890; DLB 18, 35,
57, 156

**Morris, Wright** 1910-... **CLC 1, 3, 7, 18, 37**
See also CA 9-12R; CANR 21; DLB 2;
DLBY 81, MTCW

**Morrison, Chloe Anthony Wofford**
See Morrison, Toni

**Morrison, James Douglas** 1943-1971
See Morrison, Jim
See also CA 73-76; CANR 40

**Morrison, Jim** ................... **CLC 17**
See also Morrison, James Douglas

**Morrison, Toni**
1931- ........ **CLC 4, 10, 22, 55, 81, 87;**
**BLC; DA; DAB; DAC**
See also AAYA 1; BW 2; CA 29-32R;
CANR 27, 42; CDALB 1968-1988;
DAM MST, MULT, NOV, POP; DLB 6,
33, 143; DLBY 81; MTCW; SATA 57

**Morrison, Van** 1945- ............. **CLC 21**
See also CA 116

**Mortimer, John (Clifford)**
1923- ................... **CLC 28, 43**
See also CA 13-16R; CANR 21;
CDBLB 1960 to Present; DAM DRAM,
POP; DLB 13; INT CANR-21; MTCW

**Mortimer, Penelope (Ruth)** 1918-.... **CLC 5**
See also CA 57-60; CANR 45

**Morton, Anthony**
See Creasey, John

**Mosher, Howard Frank** 1943-...... **CLC 62**
See also CA 139

**Mosley, Nicholas** 1923- ........ **CLC 43, 70**
See also CA 69-72; CANR 41; DLB 14

**Moss, Howard**
1922-1987 .......... **CLC 7, 14, 45, 50**
See also CA 1-4R; 123; CANR 1, 44;
DAM POET; DLB 5

**Mossgiel, Rab**
See Burns, Robert

**Motion, Andrew (Peter)** 1952-...... **CLC 47**
See also CA 146; DLB 40

**Motley, Willard (Francis)**
1909-1965 ................... **CLC 18**
See also BW 1; CA 117; 106; DLB 76, 143

**Motoori, Norinaga** 1730-1801 .... **NCLC 45**

**Mott, Michael (Charles Alston)**
1930- ................... **CLC 15, 34**
See also CA 5-8R; CAAS 7; CANR 7, 29

**Mountain Wolf Woman**
1884-1960 ................... **CLC 92**
See also CA 144; NNAL

**Moure, Erin** 1955- ............... **CLC 88**
See also CA 113; DLB 60

**Mowat, Farley (McGill)**
1921- ................... **CLC 26; DAC**
See also AAYA 1; CA 1-4R; CANR 4, 24,
42; CLR 20; DAM MST; DLB 68;
INT CANAR-24; JRDA; MAICYA;
MTCW; SATA 3, 55

**Moyers, Bill** 1934- .............. **CLC 74**
See also AITN 2; CA 61-64; CANR 31

**Mphahlele, Es'kia**
See Mphahlele, Ezekiel
See also DLB 125

**Mphahlele, Ezekiel** 1919-..... **CLC 25; BLC**
See also Mphahlele, Es'kia
See also BW 2; CA 81-84; CANR 26;
DAM MULT

**Mqhayi, S(amuel) E(dward) K(rune Loliwe)**
1875-1945 ............. **TCLC 25; BLC**
See also DAM MULT

**Mr. Martin**
See Burroughs, William S(eward)

**Mrozek, Slawomir** 1930- ........ **CLC 3, 13**
See also CA 13-16R; CAAS 10; CANR 29;
MTCW

**Mrs. Belloc-Lowndes**
See Lowndes, Marie Adelaide (Belloc)

**Mtwa, Percy** (?)-................. **CLC 47**

**Mueller, Lisel** 1924-........... **CLC 13, 51**
See also CA 93-96; DLB 105

**Muir, Edwin** 1887-1959 .......... **TCLC 2**
See also CA 104; DLB 20, 100

**Muir, John** 1838-1914 .......... **TCLC 28**

**Mujica Lainez, Manuel**
1910-1984 ................... **CLC 31**
See also Lainez, Manuel Mujica
See also CA 81-84; 112; CANR 32; HW

**Mukherjee, Bharati** 1940- ........ **CLC 53**
See also BEST 89:2; CA 107; CANR 45;
DAM NOV; DLB 60; MTCW

**Muldoon, Paul** 1951- .......... **CLC 32, 72**
See also CA 113; 129; DAM POET;
DLB 40; INT 129

**Mulisch, Harry** 1927-............. **CLC 42**
See also CA 9-12R; CANR 6, 26

**Mull, Martin** 1943-............... **CLC 17**
See also CA 105

**Mulock, Dinah Maria**
See Craik, Dinah Maria (Mulock)

**Munford, Robert** 1737(?)-1783 ....... **LC 5**
See also DLB 31

**Mungo, Raymond** 1946-........... **CLC 72**
See also CA 49-52; CANR 2

**Munro, Alice**
1931- ... **CLC 6, 10, 19, 50; DAC; SSC 3**
See also AITN 2; CA 33-36R; CANR 33;
DAM MST, NOV; DLB 53; MTCW;
SATA 29

**Munro, H(ector) H(ugh)** 1870-1916
See Saki
See also CA 104; 130; CDBLB 1890-1914;
DA; DAB; DAC; DAM MST, NOV;
DLB 34, 162; MTCW; WLC

**Murasaki, Lady** ................. **CMLC 1**

**Murdoch, (Jean) Iris**
1919- ...... **CLC 1, 2, 3, 4, 6, 8, 11, 15,**
**22, 31, 51; DAB; DAC**
See also CA 13-16R; CANR 8, 43;
CDBLB 1960 to Present; DAM MST,
NOV; DLB 14; INT CANR-8; MTCW

**Murfree, Mary Noailles**
1850-1922 ................... **SSC 22**
See also CA 122; DLB 12, 74

**Murnau, Friedrich Wilhelm**
See Plumpe, Friedrich Wilhelm

**Murphy, Richard** 1927-........... **CLC 41**
See also CA 29-32R; DLB 40

**Murphy, Sylvia** 1937-............. **CLC 34**
See also CA 121

**Murphy, Thomas (Bernard)** 1935-... **CLC 51**
See also CA 101

**Murray, Albert L.** 1916- .......... **CLC 73**
See also BW 2; CA 49-52; CANR 26;
DLB 38

**Murray, Les(lie) A(llan)** 1938- ..... **CLC 40**
See also CA 21-24R; CANR 11, 27;
DAM POET

**Murry, J. Middleton**
See Murry, John Middleton

Murry, John Middleton
1889-1957 . . . . . . . . . . . . . . . . TCLC 16
See also CA 118; DLB 149

Musgrave, Susan   1951- . . . . . . . . CLC 13, 54
See also CA 69-72; CANR 45

Musil, Robert (Edler von)
1880-1942 . . . . . . . . . . TCLC 12; SSC 18
See also CA 109; DLB 81, 124

Muske, Carol   1945- . . . . . . . . . . . . . . CLC 90
See also Muske-Dukes, Carol (Anne)

Muske-Dukes, Carol (Anne)   1945-
See Muske, Carol
See also CA 65-68; CANR 32

Musset, (Louis Charles) Alfred de
1810-1857 . . . . . . . . . . . . . . . . . NCLC 7

My Brother's Brother
See Chekhov, Anton (Pavlovich)

Myers, L. H.   1881-1944 . . . . . . . . . TCLC 59
See also DLB 15

Myers, Walter Dean   1937- . . . CLC 35; BLC
See also AAYA 4; BW 2; CA 33-36R;
CANR 20, 42; CLR 4, 16, 35;
DAM MULT, NOV; DLB 33;
INT CANR-20; JRDA; MAICYA;
SAAS 2; SATA 41, 71; SATA-Brief 27

Myers, Walter M.
See Myers, Walter Dean

Myles, Symon
See Follett, Ken(neth Martin)

Nabokov, Vladimir (Vladimirovich)
1899-1977 . . . . . CLC 1, 2, 3, 6, 8, 11, 15,
23, 44, 46, 64; DA; DAB; DAC; SSC 11;
WLC
See also CA 5-8R; 69-72; CANR 20;
CDALB 1941-1968; DAM MST, NOV;
DLB 2; DLBD 3; DLBY 80, 91; MTCW

Nagai Kafu . . . . . . . . . . . . . . . . . . . . . . TCLC 51
See also Nagai Sokichi

Nagai Sokichi   1879-1959
See Nagai Kafu
See also CA 117

Nagy, Laszlo   1925-1978 . . . . . . . . . . . CLC 7
See also CA 129; 112

Naipaul, Shiva(dhar Srinivasa)
1945-1985 . . . . . . . . . . . . . . . . CLC 32, 39
See also CA 110; 112; 116; CANR 33;
DAM NOV; DLB 157; DLBY 85;
MTCW

Naipaul, V(idiadhar) S(urajprasad)
1932- . . . . CLC 4, 7, 9, 13, 18, 37; DAB;
DAC
See also CA 1-4R; CANR 1, 33, 51;
CDBLB 1960 to Present; DAM MST,
NOV; DLB 125; DLBY 85; MTCW

Nakos, Lilika   1899(?)- . . . . . . . . . . . . CLC 29

Narayan, R(asipuram) K(rishnaswami)
1906- . . . . . . . . . . . . . . . . CLC 7, 28, 47
See also CA 81-84; CANR 33; DAM NOV;
MTCW; SATA 62

Nash, (Frediric) Ogden   1902-1971 . . CLC 23
See also CA 13-14; 29-32R; CANR 34;
CAP 1; DAM POET; DLB 11;
MAICYA; MTCW; SATA 2, 46

Nathan, Daniel
See Dannay, Frederic

Nathan, George Jean   1882-1958 . . . TCLC 18
See also Hatteras, Owen
See also CA 114; DLB 137

Natsume, Kinnosuke   1867-1916
See Natsume, Soseki
See also CA 104

Natsume, Soseki . . . . . . . . . . . . . . TCLC 2, 10
See also Natsume, Kinnosuke

Natti, (Mary) Lee   1919-
See Kingman, Lee
See also CA 5-8R; CANR 2

Naylor, Gloria
1950- . . . . . CLC 28, 52; BLC; DA; DAC
See also AAYA 6; BW 2; CA 107;
CANR 27, 51; DAM MST, MULT,
NOV, POP; MTCW

Neihardt, John Gneisenau
1881-1973 . . . . . . . . . . . . . . . . . . CLC 32
See also CA 13-14; CAP 1; DLB 9, 54

Nekrasov, Nikolai Alekseevich
1821-1878 . . . . . . . . . . . . . . . . NCLC 11

Nelligan, Emile   1879-1941 . . . . . . . TCLC 14
See also CA 114; DLB 92

Nelson, Willie   1933- . . . . . . . . . . . . . CLC 17
See also CA 107

Nemerov, Howard (Stanley)
1920-1991 . . . . . . . . . . . . CLC 2, 6, 9, 36
See also CA 1-4R; 134; CABS 2; CANR 1,
27; DAM POET; DLB 5, 6; DLBY 83;
INT CANR-27; MTCW

Neruda, Pablo
1904-1973 . . . . . CLC 1, 2, 5, 7, 9, 28, 62;
DA; DAB; DAC; HLC; PC 4; WLC
See also CA 19-20; 45-48; CAP 2;
DAM MST, MULT, POET; HW; MTCW

Nerval, Gerard de
1808-1855 . . . . . NCLC 1; PC 13; SSC 18

Nervo, (Jose) Amado (Ruiz de)
1870-1919 . . . . . . . . . . . . . . . . TCLC 11
See also CA 109; 131; HW

Nessi, Pio Baroja y
See Baroja (y Nessi), Pio

Nestroy, Johann   1801-1862 . . . . . . NCLC 42
See also DLB 133

Neufeld, John (Arthur)   1938- . . . . . . CLC 17
See also AAYA 11; CA 25-28R; CANR 11,
37; MAICYA; SAAS 3; SATA 6, 81

Neville, Emily Cheney   1919- . . . . . . . CLC 12
See also CA 5-8R; CANR 3, 37; JRDA;
MAICYA; SAAS 2; SATA 1

Newbound, Bernard Slade   1930-
See Slade, Bernard
See also CA 81-84; CANR 49;
DAM DRAM

Newby, P(ercy) H(oward)
1918- . . . . . . . . . . . . . . . . . . . CLC 2, 13
See also CA 5-8R; CANR 32; DAM NOV;
DLB 15; MTCW

Newlove, Donald   1928- . . . . . . . . . . . . CLC 6
See also CA 29-32R; CANR 25

Newlove, John (Herbert)   1938- . . . . . CLC 14
See also CA 21-24R; CANR 9, 25

Newman, Charles   1938- . . . . . . . . . CLC 2, 8
See also CA 21-24R

Newman, Edwin (Harold)   1919- . . . . CLC 14
See also AITN 1; CA 69-72; CANR 5

Newman, John Henry
1801-1890 . . . . . . . . . . . . . . . . NCLC 38
See also DLB 18, 32, 55

Newton, Suzanne   1936- . . . . . . . . . . CLC 35
See also CA 41-44R; CANR 14; JRDA;
SATA 5, 77

Nexo, Martin Andersen
1869-1954 . . . . . . . . . . . . . . . . TCLC 43

Nezval, Vitezslav   1900-1958 . . . . . . TCLC 44
See also CA 123

Ng, Fae Myenne   1957(?)- . . . . . . . . . CLC 81
See also CA 146

Ngema, Mbongeni   1955- . . . . . . . . . . CLC 57
See also BW 2; CA 143

Ngugi, James T(hiong'o) . . . . . . . . CLC 3, 7, 13
See also Ngugi wa Thiong'o

Ngugi wa Thiong'o   1938- . . . . . CLC 36; BLC
See also Ngugi, James T(hiong'o)
See also BW 2; CA 81-84; CANR 27;
DAM MULT, NOV; DLB 125; MTCW

Nichol, B(arrie) P(hillip)
1944-1988 . . . . . . . . . . . . . . . . . CLC 18
See also CA 53-56; DLB 53; SATA 66

Nichols, John (Treadwell)   1940- . . . . CLC 38
See also CA 9-12R; CAAS 2; CANR 6;
DLBY 82

Nichols, Leigh
See Koontz, Dean R(ay)

Nichols, Peter (Richard)
1927- . . . . . . . . . . . . . . . . CLC 5, 36, 65
See also CA 104; CANR 33; DLB 13;
MTCW

Nicolas, F. R. E.
See Freeling, Nicolas

Niedecker, Lorine   1903-1970 . . . . CLC 10, 42
See also CA 25-28; CAP 2; DAM POET;
DLB 48

Nietzsche, Friedrich (Wilhelm)
1844-1900 . . . . . . . . . . TCLC 10, 18, 55
See also CA 107; 121; DLB 129

Nievo, Ippolito   1831-1861 . . . . . . . NCLC 22

Nightingale, Anne Redmon   1943-
See Redmon, Anne
See also CA 103

Nik. T. O.
See Annensky, Innokenty Fyodorovich

Nin, Anais
1903-1977 . . . . . . CLC 1, 4, 8, 11, 14, 60;
SSC 10
See also AITN 2; CA 13-16R; 69-72;
CANR 22; DAM NOV, POP; DLB 2, 4,
152; MTCW

Nishiwaki, Junzaburo   1894-1982 . . . . PC 15
See also CA 107

Nissenson, Hugh   1933- . . . . . . . . . . CLC 4, 9
See also CA 17-20R; CANR 27; DLB 28

Niven, Larry . . . . . . . . . . . . . . . . . . . . . CLC 8
See also Niven, Laurence Van Cott
See also DLB 8

Niven, Laurence Van Cott   1938-
See Niven, Larry
See also CA 21-24R; CAAS 12; CANR 14,
44; DAM POP; MTCW

Nixon, Agnes Eckhardt  1927-...... **CLC 21**
    See also CA 110

Nizan, Paul  1905-1940.......... **TCLC 40**
    See also DLB 72

Nkosi, Lewis  1936-......... **CLC 45; BLC**
    See also BW 1; CA 65-68; CANR 27;
    DAM MULT; DLB 157

Nodier, (Jean) Charles (Emmanuel)
    1780-1844 ................ **NCLC 19**
    See also DLB 119

Nolan, Christopher  1965-......... **CLC 58**
    See also CA 111

Noon, Jeff  1957-................. **CLC 91**
    See also CA 148

Norden, Charles
    See Durrell, Lawrence (George)

Nordhoff, Charles (Bernard)
    1887-1947 ................. **TCLC 23**
    See also CA 108; DLB 9; SATA 23

Norfolk, Lawrence  1963-......... **CLC 76**
    See also CA 144

Norman, Marsha  1947- .......... **CLC 28**
    See also CA 105; CABS 3; CANR 41;
    DAM DRAM; DLBY 84

Norris, Benjamin Franklin, Jr.
    1870-1902 ................. **TCLC 24**
    See also Norris, Frank
    See also CA 110

Norris, Frank
    See Norris, Benjamin Franklin, Jr.
    See also CDALB 1865-1917; DLB 12, 71

Norris, Leslie  1921- ............. **CLC 14**
    See also CA 11-12; CANR 14; CAP 1;
    DLB 27

North, Andrew
    See Norton, Andre

North, Anthony
    See Koontz, Dean R(ay)

North, Captain George
    See Stevenson, Robert Louis (Balfour)

North, Milou
    See Erdrich, Louise

Northrup, B. A.
    See Hubbard, L(afayette) Ron(ald)

North Staffs
    See Hulme, T(homas) E(rnest)

Norton, Alice Mary
    See Norton, Andre
    See also MAICYA; SATA 1, 43

Norton, Andre  1912- ............. **CLC 12**
    See also Norton, Alice Mary
    See also AAYA 14; CA 1-4R; CANR 2, 31;
    DLB 8, 52; JRDA; MTCW

Norton, Caroline  1808-1877...... **NCLC 47**
    See also DLB 21, 159

Norway, Nevil Shute  1899-1960
    See Shute, Nevil
    See also CA 102; 93-96

Norwid, Cyprian Kamil
    1821-1883 ................ **NCLC 17**

Nosille, Nabrah
    See Ellison, Harlan (Jay)

Nossack, Hans Erich  1901-1978 ..... **CLC 6**
    See also CA 93-96; 85-88; DLB 69

Nostradamus  1503-1566............ **LC 27**

Nosu, Chuji
    See Ozu, Yasujiro

Notenburg, Eleanora (Genrikhovna) von
    See Guro, Elena

Nova, Craig  1945-.............. **CLC 7, 31**
    See also CA 45-48; CANR 2

Novak, Joseph
    See Kosinski, Jerzy (Nikodem)

Novalis  1772-1801 ............. **NCLC 13**
    See also DLB 90

Nowlan, Alden (Albert)
    1933-1983 .............. **CLC 15; DAC**
    See also CA 9-12R; CANR 5; DAM MST;
    DLB 53

Noyes, Alfred  1880-1958 .......... **TCLC 7**
    See also CA 104; DLB 20

Nunn, Kem  19(?)-................ **CLC 34**

Nye, Robert  1939- ........... **CLC 13, 42**
    See also CA 33-36R; CANR 29;
    DAM NOV; DLB 14; MTCW; SATA 6

Nyro, Laura  1947- .............. **CLC 17**

Oates, Joyce Carol
    1938-...... **CLC 1, 2, 3, 6, 9, 11, 15, 19,**
    **33, 52; DA; DAB; DAC; SSC 6; WLC**
    See also AAYA 15; AITN 1; BEST 89:2;
    CA 5-8R; CANR 25, 45;
    CDALB 1968-1988; DAM MST, NOV,
    POP; DLB 2, 5, 130; DLBY 81;
    INT CANR-25; MTCW

O'Brien, Darcy  1939-............ **CLC 11**
    See also CA 21-24R; CANR 8

O'Brien, E. G.
    See Clarke, Arthur C(harles)

O'Brien, Edna
    1936-... **CLC 3, 5, 8, 13, 36, 65; SSC 10**
    See also CA 1-4R; CANR 6, 41;
    CDBLB 1960 to Present; DAM NOV;
    DLB 14; MTCW

O'Brien, Fitz-James  1828-1862... **NCLC 21**
    See also DLB 74

O'Brien, Flann....... **CLC 1, 4, 5, 7, 10, 47**
    See also O Nuallain, Brian

O'Brien, Richard  1942- ........... **CLC 17**
    See also CA 124

O'Brien, Tim  1946-.......... **CLC 7, 19, 40**
    See also AAYA 16; CA 85-88; CANR 40;
    DAM POP; DLB 152; DLBD 9;
    DLBY 80

Obstfelder, Sigbjoern  1866-1900... **TCLC 23**
    See also CA 123

O'Casey, Sean
    1880-1964 ...... **CLC 1, 5, 9, 11, 15, 88;**
    **DAB; DAC**
    See also CA 89-92; CDBLB 1914-1945;
    DAM DRAM, MST, DLB 10; MTCW

O'Cathasaigh, Sean
    See O'Casey, Sean

Ochs, Phil  1940-1976............. **CLC 17**
    See also CA 65-68

O'Connor, Edwin (Greene)
    1918-1968 ................. **CLC 14**
    See also CA 93-96; 25-28R

O'Connor, (Mary) Flannery
    1925-1964 .... **CLC 1, 2, 3, 6, 10, 13, 15,**
    **21, 66; DA; DAB; DAC; SSC 1, 23; WLC**
    See also AAYA 7; CA 1-4R; CANR 3, 41;
    CDALB 1941-1968; DAM MST, NOV;
    DLB 2, 152; DLBD 12; DLBY 80;
    MTCW

O'Connor, Frank........... **CLC 23; SSC 5**
    See also O'Donovan, Michael John
    See also DLB 162

O'Dell, Scott  1898-1989........... **CLC 30**
    See also AAYA 3; CA 61-64; 129;
    CANR 12, 30; CLR 1, 16; DLB 52;
    JRDA; MAICYA; SATA 12, 60

Odets, Clifford
    1906-1963 ........... **CLC 2, 28; DC 6**
    See also CA 85-88; DAM DRAM; DLB 7,
    26; MTCW

O'Doherty, Brian  1934-.......... **CLC 76**
    See also CA 105

O'Donnell, K. M.
    See Malzberg, Barry N(athaniel)

O'Donnell, Lawrence
    See Kuttner, Henry

O'Donovan, Michael John
    1903-1966 ................. **CLC 14**
    See also O'Connor, Frank
    See also CA 93-96

Oe, Kenzaburo
    1935-......... **CLC 10, 36, 86; SSC 20**
    See also CA 97-100; CANR 36, 50;
    DAM NOV; DLBY 94; MTCW

O'Faolain, Julia  1932-....... **CLC 6, 19, 47**
    See also CA 81-84; CAAS 2; CANR 12;
    DLB 14; MTCW

O'Faolain, Sean
    1900-1991 ........ **CLC 1, 7, 14, 32, 70;**
    **SSC 13**
    See also CA 61-64; 134; CANR 12;
    DLB 15, 162; MTCW

O'Flaherty, Liam
    1896-1984 .......... **CLC 5, 34; SSC 6**
    See also CA 101; 113; CANR 35; DLB 36,
    162; DLBY 84; MTCW

Ogilvy, Gavin
    See Barrie, J(ames) M(atthew)

O'Grady, Standish James
    1846-1928 .................. **TCLC 5**
    See also CA 104

O'Grady, Timothy  1951-.......... **CLC 59**
    See also CA 138

O'Hara, Frank
    1926-1966 ............ **CLC 2, 5, 13, 78**
    See also CA 9-12R; 25-28R; CANR 33;
    DAM POET; DLB 5, 16; MTCW

O'Hara, John (Henry)
    1905-1970 ....... **CLC 1, 2, 3, 6, 11, 42;**
    **SSC 15**
    See also CA 5-8R; 25-28R; CANR 31;
    CDALB 1929-1941; DAM NOV; DLB 9,
    86; DLBD 2; MTCW

O Hehir, Diana  1922- ............. **CLC 41**
    See also CA 93-96

**Pancake, Breece D'J.** . . . . . . . . . . . . . . CLC 29
  See also Pancake, Breece Dexter
  See also DLB 130

**Panko, Rudy**
  See Gogol, Nikolai (Vasilyevich)

**Papadiamantis, Alexandros**
  1851-1911 . . . . . . . . . . . . . . . . . TCLC 29

**Papadiamantopoulos, Johannes** 1856-1910
  See Moreas, Jean
  See also CA 117

**Papini, Giovanni** 1881-1956 . . . . . . TCLC 22
  See also CA 121

**Paracelsus** 1493-1541 . . . . . . . . . . . . . . LC 14

**Parasol, Peter**
  See Stevens, Wallace

**Parfenie, Maria**
  See Codrescu, Andrei

**Parini, Jay (Lee)** 1948- . . . . . . . . . . . CLC 54
  See also CA 97-100; CAAS 16; CANR 32

**Park, Jordan**
  See Kornbluth, C(yril) M.; Pohl, Frederik

**Parker, Bert**
  See Ellison, Harlan (Jay)

**Parker, Dorothy (Rothschild)**
  1893-1967 . . . . . . . . CLC 15, 68; SSC 2
  See also CA 19-20; 25-28R; CAP 2;
  DAM POET; DLB 11, 45, 86; MTCW

**Parker, Robert B(rown)** 1932- . . . . . . CLC 27
  See also BEST 89:4; CA 49-52; CANR 1,
  26; DAM NOV, POP; INT CANR-26;
  MTCW

**Parkin, Frank** 1940- . . . . . . . . . . . . . . CLC 43
  See also CA 147

**Parkman, Francis, Jr.**
  1823-1893 . . . . . . . . . . . . . . . NCLC 12
  See also DLB 1, 30

**Parks, Gordon (Alexander Buchanan)**
  1912- . . . . . . . . . . . . . . . . CLC 1, 16; BLC
  See also AITN 2; BW 2; CA 41-44R;
  CANR 26; DAM MULT; DLB 33;
  SATA 8

**Parnell, Thomas** 1679-1718 . . . . . . . . . LC 3
  See also DLB 94

**Parra, Nicanor** 1914- . . . . . . . . CLC 2; HLC
  See also CA 85-88; CANR 32;
  DAM MULT; HW; MTCW

**Parrish, Mary Frances**
  See Fisher, M(ary) F(rances) K(ennedy)

**Parson**
  See Coleridge, Samuel Taylor

**Parson Lot**
  See Kingsley, Charles

**Partridge, Anthony**
  See Oppenheim, E(dward) Phillips

**Pascoli, Giovanni** 1855-1912 . . . . . . TCLC 45

**Pasolini, Pier Paolo**
  1922-1975 . . . . . . . . . . . . . . CLC 20, 37
  See also CA 93-96; 61-64; DLB 128;
  MTCW

**Pasquini**
  See Silone, Ignazio

**Pastan, Linda (Olenik)** 1932- . . . . . . CLC 27
  See also CA 61-64; CANR 18, 40;
  DAM POET; DLB 5

**Pasternak, Boris (Leonidovich)**
  1890-1960 . . . . . CLC 7, 10, 18, 63; DA;
              DAB; DAC; PC 6; WLC
  See also CA 127; 116; DAM MST, NOV,
  POET; MTCW

**Patchen, Kenneth** 1911-1972 . . . CLC 1, 2, 18
  See also CA 1-4R; 33-36R; CANR 3, 35;
  DAM POET; DLB 16, 48; MTCW

**Pater, Walter (Horatio)**
  1839-1894 . . . . . . . . . . . . . . . . NCLC 7
  See also CDBLB 1832-1890; DLB 57, 156

**Paterson, A(ndrew) B(arton)**
  1864-1941 . . . . . . . . . . . . . . . TCLC 32

**Paterson, Katherine (Womeldorf)**
  1932- . . . . . . . . . . . . . . . . . CLC 12, 30
  See also AAYA 1; CA 21-24R; CANR 28;
  CLR 7; DLB 52; JRDA; MAICYA;
  MTCW; SATA 13, 53

**Patmore, Coventry Kersey Dighton**
  1823-1896 . . . . . . . . . . . . . . . . NCLC 9
  See also DLB 35, 98

**Paton, Alan (Stewart)**
  1903-1988 . . . . . . CLC 4, 10, 25, 55; DA;
               DAB; DAC; WLC
  See also CA 13-16; 125; CANR 22; CAP 1;
  DAM MST, NOV; MTCW; SATA 11;
  SATA-Obit 56

**Paton Walsh, Gillian** 1937-
  See Walsh, Jill Paton
  See also CANR 38; JRDA; MAICYA;
  SAAS 3; SATA 4, 72

**Paulding, James Kirke** 1778-1860 . . NCLC 2
  See also DLB 3, 59, 74

**Paulin, Thomas Neilson** 1949-
  See Paulin, Tom
  See also CA 123; 128

**Paulin, Tom** . . . . . . . . . . . . . . . . . . . . CLC 37
  See also Paulin, Thomas Neilson
  See also DLB 40

**Paustovsky, Konstantin (Georgievich)**
  1892-1968 . . . . . . . . . . . . . . . . CLC 40
  See also CA 93-96; 25-28R

**Pavese, Cesare**
  1908-1950 . . . . . TCLC 3; PC 13; SSC 19
  See also CA 104; DLB 128

**Pavic, Milorad** 1929- . . . . . . . . . . . . . CLC 60
  See also CA 136

**Payne, Alan**
  See Jakes, John (William)

**Paz, Gil**
  See Lugones, Leopoldo

**Paz, Octavio**
  1914- . . . . . . . CLC 3, 4, 6, 10, 19, 51, 65;
           DA; DAB; DAC; HLC; PC 1; WLC
  See also CA 73-76; CANR 32; DAM MST,
  MULT, POET; DLBY 90; HW; MTCW

**Peacock, Molly** 1947- . . . . . . . . . . . . . CLC 60
  See also CA 103; CAAS 21; DLB 120

**Peacock, Thomas Love**
  1785-1866 . . . . . . . . . . . . . . . NCLC 22
  See also DLB 96, 116

**Peake, Mervyn** 1911-1968 . . . . . . . CLC 7, 54
  See also CA 5-8R; 25-28R; CANR 3;
  DLB 15, 160; MTCW; SATA 23

**Pearce, Philippa** . . . . . . . . . . . . . . . . CLC 21
  See also Christie, (Ann) Philippa
  See also CLR 9; DLB 161; MAICYA;
  SATA 1, 67

**Pearl, Eric**
  See Elman, Richard

**Pearson, T(homas) R(eid)** 1956- . . . . CLC 39
  See also CA 120; 130; INT 130

**Peck, Dale** 1967- . . . . . . . . . . . . . . . . CLC 81
  See also CA 146

**Peck, John** 1941- . . . . . . . . . . . . . . . . . CLC 3
  See also CA 49-52; CANR 3

**Peck, Richard (Wayne)** 1934- . . . . . . CLC 21
  See also AAYA 1; CA 85-88; CANR 19,
  38; CLR 15; INT CANR-19; JRDA;
  MAICYA; SAAS 2; SATA 18, 55

**Peck, Robert Newton**
  1928- . . . . . . . . . . . . . CLC 17; DA; DAC
  See also AAYA 3; CA 81-84; CANR 31;
  DAM MST; JRDA; MAICYA; SAAS 1;
  SATA 21, 62

**Peckinpah, (David) Sam(uel)**
  1925-1984 . . . . . . . . . . . . . . . . CLC 20
  See also CA 109; 114

**Pedersen, Knut** 1859-1952
  See Hamsun, Knut
  See also CA 104; 119; MTCW

**Peeslake, Gaffer**
  See Durrell, Lawrence (George)

**Peguy, Charles Pierre**
  1873-1914 . . . . . . . . . . . . . . . TCLC 10
  See also CA 107

**Pena, Ramon del Valle y**
  See Valle-Inclan, Ramon (Maria) del

**Pendennis, Arthur Esquir**
  See Thackeray, William Makepeace

**Penn, William** 1644-1718 . . . . . . . . . . LC 25
  See also DLB 24

**Pepys, Samuel**
  1633-1703 . . . . . LC 11; DA; DAB; DAC;
                    WLC
  See also CDBLB 1660-1789; DAM MST;
  DLB 101

**Percy, Walker**
  1916-1990 . . . . CLC 2, 3, 6, 8, 14, 18, 47,
                       65
  See also CA 1-4R; 131; CANR 1, 23;
  DAM NOV, POP; DLB 2; DLBY 80, 90;
  MTCW

**Perec, Georges** 1936-1982 . . . . . . . . CLC 56
  See also CA 141; DLB 83

**Pereda (y Sanchez de Porrua), Jose Maria de**
  1833-1906 . . . . . . . . . . . . . . . TCLC 16
  See also CA 117

**Pereda y Porrua, Jose Maria de**
  See Pereda (y Sanchez de Porrua), Jose
  Maria de

**Peregoy, George Weems**
  See Mencken, H(enry) L(ouis)

**Perelman, S(idney) J(oseph)**
  1904-1979 . . . CLC 3, 5, 9, 15, 23, 44, 49
  See also AITN 1, 2; CA 73-76; 89-92;
  CANR 18; DAM DRAM; DLB 11, 44;
  MTCW

**Poet of Titchfield Street, The**
See Pound, Ezra (Weston Loomis)

**Pohl, Frederik** 1919- . . . . . . . . . . . . **CLC 18**
See also CA 61-64; CAAS 1; CANR 11, 37;
DLB 8; INT CANR-11; MTCW;
SATA 24

**Poirier, Louis** 1910-
See Gracq, Julien
See also CA 122; 126

**Poitier, Sidney** 1927- . . . . . . . . . . . . **CLC 26**
See also BW 1; CA 117

**Polanski, Roman** 1933- . . . . . . . . . . **CLC 16**
See also CA 77-80

**Poliakoff, Stephen** 1952- . . . . . . . . . . **CLC 38**
See also CA 106; DLB 13

**Police, The**
See Copeland, Stewart (Armstrong);
Summers, Andrew James; Sumner,
Gordon Matthew

**Polidori, John William**
1795-1821 . . . . . . . . . . . . . . . **NCLC 51**
See also DLB 116

**Pollitt, Katha** 1949- . . . . . . . . . . . . **CLC 28**
See also CA 120; 122; MTCW

**Pollock, (Mary) Sharon**
1936- . . . . . . . . . . . . . . . . . . **CLC 50; DAC**
See also CA 141; DAM DRAM, MST;
DLB 60

**Polo, Marco** 1254-1324 . . . . . . . . **CMLC 15**

**Polonsky, Abraham (Lincoln)**
1910- . . . . . . . . . . . . . . . . . . . . . **CLC 92**
See also CA 104; DLB 26; INT 104

**Polybius** c. 200B.C.-c. 118B.C. . . . . **CMLC 17**

**Pomerance, Bernard** 1940- . . . . . . . . **CLC 13**
See also CA 101; CANR 49; DAM DRAM

**Ponge, Francis (Jean Gaston Alfred)**
1899-1988 . . . . . . . . . . . . . . . . . **CLC 6, 18**
See also CA 85-88; 126; CANR 40;
DAM POET

**Pontoppidan, Henrik** 1857-1943 . . . **TCLC 29**

**Poole, Josephine** . . . . . . . . . . . . . . . . **CLC 17**
See also Helyar, Jane Penelope Josephine
See also SAAS 2; SATA 5

**Popa, Vasko** 1922-1991 . . . . . . . . . . . **CLC 19**
See also CA 112; 148

**Pope, Alexander**
1688-1744 . . . . . . **LC 3; DA; DAB; DAC;**
WLC
See also CDBLB 1660-1789; DAM MST,
POET; DLB 95, 101

**Porter, Connie (Rose)** 1959(?)- . . . . . **CLC 70**
See also BW 2; CA 142; SATA 81

**Porter, Gene(va Grace) Stratton**
1863(?)-1924 . . . . . . . . . . . . . . . **TCLC 21**
See also CA 112

**Porter, Katherine Anne**
1890-1980 . . . . . . **CLC 1, 3, 7, 10, 13, 15,**
**27; DA; DAB; DAC; SSC 4**
See also AITN 2; CA 1-4R; 101; CANR 1;
DAM MST, NOV; DLB 4, 9, 102;
DLBD 12; DLBY 80; MTCW; SATA 39;
SATA-Obit 23

**Porter, Peter (Neville Frederick)**
1929- . . . . . . . . . . . . . . . . . . **CLC 5, 13, 33**
See also CA 85-88; DLB 40

**Porter, William Sydney** 1862-1910
See Henry, O.
See also CA 104; 131; CDALB 1865-1917;
DA; DAB; DAC; DAM MST; DLB 12,
78, 79; MTCW; YABC 2

**Portillo (y Pacheco), Jose Lopez**
See Lopez Portillo (y Pacheco), Jose

**Post, Melville Davisson**
1869-1930 . . . . . . . . . . . . . . . . . **TCLC 39**
See also CA 110

**Potok, Chaim** 1929- . . . . . . . **CLC 2, 7, 14, 26**
See also AAYA 15; AITN 1, 2; CA 17-20R;
CANR 19, 35; DAM NOV; DLB 28, 152;
INT CANR-19; MTCW; SATA 33

**Potter, Beatrice**
See Webb, (Martha) Beatrice (Potter)
See also MAICYA

**Potter, Dennis (Christopher George)**
1935-1994 . . . . . . . . . . . . . . . **CLC 58, 86**
See also CA 107; 145; CANR 33; MTCW

**Pound, Ezra (Weston Loomis)**
1885-1972 . . . . . . **CLC 1, 2, 3, 4, 5, 7, 10,**
**13, 18, 34, 48, 50; DA; DAB; DAC; PC 4;**
WLC
See also CA 5-8R; 37-40R; CANR 40;
CDALB 1917-1929; DAM MST, POET;
DLB 4, 45, 63; MTCW

**Povod, Reinaldo** 1959-1994 . . . . . . . . **CLC 44**
See also CA 136; 146

**Powell, Adam Clayton, Jr.**
1908-1972 . . . . . . . . . . . . . . **CLC 89; BLC**
See also BW 1; CA 102; 33-36R;
DAM MULT

**Powell, Anthony (Dymoke)**
1905- . . . . . . . . . . **CLC 1, 3, 7, 9, 10, 31**
See also CA 1-4R; CANR 1, 32;
CDBLB 1945-1960; DLB 15; MTCW

**Powell, Dawn** 1897-1965 . . . . . . . . . **CLC 66**
See also CA 5-8R

**Powell, Padgett** 1952- . . . . . . . . . . . **CLC 34**
See also CA 126

**Power, Susan** . . . . . . . . . . . . . . . . . . . **CLC 91**

**Powers, J(ames) F(arl)**
1917- . . . . . . . . . . **CLC 1, 4, 8, 57; SSC 4**
See also CA 1-4R; CANR 2; DLB 130;
MTCW

**Powers, John J(ames)** 1945-
See Powers, John R.
See also CA 69-72

**Powers, John R.** . . . . . . . . . . . . . . . . . **CLC 66**
See also Powers, John J(ames)

**Powers, Richard (S.)** 1957- . . . . . . . . **CLC 93**
See also CA 148

**Pownall, David** 1938- . . . . . . . . . . . . **CLC 10**
See also CA 89-92; CAAS 18; CANR 49;
DLB 14

**Powys, John Cowper**
1872-1963 . . . . . . . . . . . **CLC 7, 9, 15, 46**
See also CA 85-88; DLB 15; MTCW

**Powys, T(heodore) F(rancis)**
1875-1953 . . . . . . . . . . . . . . . . . . **TCLC 9**
See also CA 106; DLB 36, 162

**Prager, Emily** 1952- . . . . . . . . . . . . . **CLC 56**

**Pratt, E(dwin) J(ohn)**
1883(?)-1964 . . . . . . . . . . . **CLC 19; DAC**
See also CA 141; 93-96; DAM POET;
DLB 92

**Premchand** . . . . . . . . . . . . . . . . . . . . **TCLC 21**
See also Srivastava, Dhanpat Rai

**Preussler, Otfried** 1923- . . . . . . . . . . **CLC 17**
See also CA 77-80; SATA 24

**Prevert, Jacques (Henri Marie)**
1900-1977 . . . . . . . . . . . . . . . . . **CLC 15**
See also CA 77-80; 69-72; CANR 29;
MTCW; SATA-Obit 30

**Prevost, Abbe (Antoine Francois)**
1697-1763 . . . . . . . . . . . . . . . . . . . . **LC 1**

**Price, (Edward) Reynolds**
1933- . . **CLC 3, 6, 13, 43, 50, 63; SSC 22**
See also CA 1-4R; CANR 1, 37;
DAM NOV; DLB 2; INT CANR-37

**Price, Richard** 1949- . . . . . . . . . . . **CLC 6, 12**
See also CA 49-52; CANR 3; DLBY 81

**Prichard, Katharine Susannah**
1883-1969 . . . . . . . . . . . . . . . . . **CLC 46**
See also CA 11-12; CANR 33; CAP 1;
MTCW; SATA 66

**Priestley, J(ohn) B(oynton)**
1894-1984 . . . . . . . . . . **CLC 2, 5, 9, 34**
See also CA 9-12R; 113; CANR 33;
CDBLB 1914-1945; DAM DRAM, NOV;
DLB 10, 34, 77, 100, 139; DLBY 84;
MTCW

**Prince** 1958(?)- . . . . . . . . . . . . . . . . . **CLC 35**

**Prince, F(rank) T(empleton)** 1912- . . **CLC 22**
See also CA 101; CANR 43; DLB 20

**Prince Kropotkin**
See Kropotkin, Peter (Aleksieevich)

**Prior, Matthew** 1664-1721 . . . . . . . . . . **LC 4**
See also DLB 95

**Pritchard, William H(arrison)**
1932- . . . . . . . . . . . . . . . . . . . . . **CLC 34**
See also CA 65-68; CANR 23; DLB 111

**Pritchett, V(ictor) S(awdon)**
1900- . . . . . . **CLC 5, 13, 15, 41; SSC 14**
See also CA 61-64; CANR 31; DAM NOV;
DLB 15, 139; MTCW

**Private 19022**
See Manning, Frederic

**Probst, Mark** 1925- . . . . . . . . . . . . . **CLC 59**
See also CA 130

**Prokosch, Frederic** 1908-1989 . . . . **CLC 4, 48**
See also CA 73-76; 128; DLB 48

**Prophet, The**
See Dreiser, Theodore (Herman Albert)

**Prose, Francine** 1947- . . . . . . . . . . . . **CLC 45**
See also CA 109; 112; CANR 46

**Proudhon**
See Cunha, Euclides (Rodrigues Pimenta) da

**Proulx, E. Annie** 1935- . . . . . . . . . . **CLC 81**

**Proust, (Valentin-Louis-George-Eugene-)**
**Marcel**
1871-1922 . . . . . . . . **TCLC 7, 13, 33; DA;**
**DAB; DAC; WLC**
See also CA 104; 120; DAM MST, NOV;
DLB 65; MTCW

**Prowler, Harley**
See Masters, Edgar Lee

**Prus, Boleslaw** 1845-1912 ....... **TCLC 48**

**Pryor, Richard (Franklin Lenox Thomas)**
   1940- ....................... **CLC 26**
   See also CA 122

**Przybyszewski, Stanislaw**
   1868-1927 .................. **TCLC 36**
   See also DLB 66

**Pteleon**
   See Grieve, C(hristopher) M(urray)
   See also DAM POET

**Puckett, Lute**
   See Masters, Edgar Lee

**Puig, Manuel**
   1932-1990 ... **CLC 3, 5, 10, 28, 65; HLC**
   See also CA 45-48; CANR 2, 32;
   DAM MULT; DLB 113; HW; MTCW

**Purdy, Al(fred Wellington)**
   1918- .......... **CLC 3, 6, 14, 50; DAC**
   See also CA 81-84; CAAS 17; CANR 42;
   DAM MST, POET; DLB 88

**Purdy, James (Amos)**
   1923- ............ **CLC 2, 4, 10, 28, 52**
   See also CA 33-36R; CAAS 1; CANR 19,
   51; DLB 2; INT CANR-19; MTCW

**Pure, Simon**
   See Swinnerton, Frank Arthur

**Pushkin, Alexander (Sergeyevich)**
   1799-1837 ..... **NCLC 3, 27; DA; DAB;**
   **DAC; PC 10; WLC**
   See also DAM DRAM, MST, POET;
   SATA 61

**P'u Sung-ling** 1640-1715 ............ **LC 3**

**Putnam, Arthur Lee**
   See Alger, Horatio, Jr.

**Puzo, Mario** 1920- ......... **CLC 1, 2, 6, 36**
   See also CA 65-68; CANR 4, 42;
   DAM NOV, POP; DLB 6; MTCW

**Pym, Barbara (Mary Crampton)**
   1913-1980 ............. **CLC 13, 19, 37**
   See also CA 13-14; 97-100; CANR 13, 34;
   CAP 1; DLB 14; DLBY 87; MTCW

**Pynchon, Thomas (Ruggles, Jr.)**
   1937- ..... **CLC 2, 3, 6, 9, 11, 18, 33, 62,**
   **72; DA; DAB; DAC; SSC 14; WLC**
   See also BEST 90:2; CA 17-20R; CANR 22,
   46; DAM MST, NOV, POP; DLB 2;
   MTCW

**Qian Zhongshu**
   See Ch'ien Chung-shu

**Qroll**
   See Dagerman, Stig (Halvard)

**Quarrington, Paul (Lewis)** 1953- .... **CLC 65**
   See also CA 129

**Quasimodo, Salvatore** 1901-1968 ... **CLC 10**
   See also CA 13-16; 25-28R; CAP 1;
   DLB 114; MTCW

**Queen, Ellery** .................. **CLC 3, 11**
   See also Dannay, Frederic; Davidson,
   Avram; Lee, Manfred B(ennington);
   Sturgeon, Theodore (Hamilton); Vance,
   John Holbrook

**Queen, Ellery, Jr.**
   See Dannay, Frederic; Lee, Manfred
   B(ennington)

**Queneau, Raymond**
   1903-1976 ........... **CLC 2, 5, 10, 42**
   See also CA 77-80; 69-72; CANR 32;
   DLB 72; MTCW

**Quevedo, Francisco de** 1580-1645 .... **LC 23**

**Quiller-Couch, Arthur Thomas**
   1863-1944 .................. **TCLC 53**
   See also CA 118; DLB 135, 153

**Quin, Ann (Marie)** 1936-1973 ....... **CLC 6**
   See also CA 9-12R; 45-48; DLB 14

**Quinn, Martin**
   See Smith, Martin Cruz

**Quinn, Peter** 1947- ............... **CLC 91**

**Quinn, Simon**
   See Smith, Martin Cruz

**Quiroga, Horacio (Sylvestre)**
   1878-1937 ............ **TCLC 20; HLC**
   See also CA 117; 131; DAM MULT; HW;
   MTCW

**Quoirez, Francoise** 1935- ........... **CLC 9**
   See also Sagan, Francoise
   See also CA 49-52; CANR 6, 39; MTCW

**Raabe, Wilhelm** 1831-1910 ....... **TCLC 45**
   See also DLB 129

**Rabe, David (William)** 1940- ... **CLC 4, 8, 33**
   See also CA 85-88; CABS 3; DAM DRAM;
   DLB 7

**Rabelais, Francois**
   1483-1553 ...... **LC 5; DA; DAB; DAC;**
   **WLC**
   See also DAM MST

**Rabinovitch, Sholem** 1859-1916
   See Aleichem, Sholom
   See also CA 104

**Racine, Jean** 1639-1699 ....... **LC 28; DAB**
   See also DAM MST

**Radcliffe, Ann (Ward)**
   1764-1823 .............. **NCLC 6, 55**
   See also DLB 39

**Radiguet, Raymond** 1903-1923 .... **TCLC 29**
   See also DLB 65

**Radnoti, Miklos** 1909-1944 ....... **TCLC 16**
   See also CA 118

**Rado, James** 1939- ............... **CLC 17**
   See also CA 105

**Radvanyi, Netty** 1900-1983
   See Seghers, Anna
   See also CA 85-88; 110

**Rae, Ben**
   See Griffiths, Trevor

**Raeburn, John (Hay)** 1941- ........ **CLC 34**
   See also CA 57-60

**Ragni, Gerome** 1942-1991 ........ **CLC 17**
   See also CA 105; 134

**Rahv, Philip** 1908-1973 ........... **CLC 24**
   See also Greenberg, Ivan
   See also DLB 137

**Raine, Craig** 1944- .............. **CLC 32**
   See also CA 108; CANR 29, 51; DLB 40

**Raine, Kathleen (Jessie)** 1908- ... **CLC 7, 45**
   See also CA 85-88; CANR 46; DLB 20;
   MTCW

**Rainis, Janis** 1865-1929 ......... **TCLC 29**

**Rakosi, Carl** ..................... **CLC 47**
   See also Rawley, Callman
   See also CAAS 5

**Raleigh, Richard**
   See Lovecraft, H(oward) P(hillips)

**Raleigh, Sir Walter** 1554(?)-1618 .... **LC 31**
   See also CDBLB Before 1660

**Rallentando, H. P.**
   See Sayers, Dorothy L(eigh)

**Ramal, Walter**
   See de la Mare, Walter (John)

**Ramon, Juan**
   See Jimenez (Mantecon), Juan Ramon

**Ramos, Graciliano** 1892-1953 ..... **TCLC 32**

**Rampersad, Arnold** 1941- ......... **CLC 44**
   See also BW 2; CA 127; 133; DLB 111;
   INT 133

**Rampling, Anne**
   See Rice, Anne

**Ramsay, Allan** 1684(?)-1758 ........ **LC 29**
   See also DLB 95

**Ramuz, Charles-Ferdinand**
   1878-1947 .................. **TCLC 33**

**Rand, Ayn**
   1905-1982 ...... **CLC 3, 30, 44, 79; DA;**
   **DAC; WLC**
   See also AAYA 10; CA 13-16R; 105;
   CANR 27; DAM MST, NOV, POP;
   MTCW

**Randall, Dudley (Felker)**
   1914- ................... **CLC 1; BLC**
   See also BW 1; CA 25-28R; CANR 23;
   DAM MULT; DLB 41

**Randall, Robert**
   See Silverberg, Robert

**Ranger, Ken**
   See Creasey, John

**Ransom, John Crowe**
   1888-1974 ........ **CLC 2, 4, 5, 11, 24**
   See also CA 5-8R; 49-52; CANR 6, 34;
   DAM POET; DLB 45, 63; MTCW

**Rao, Raja** 1909- .............. **CLC 25, 56**
   See also CA 73-76; CANR 51; DAM NOV;
   MTCW

**Raphael, Frederic (Michael)**
   1931- ..................... **CLC 2, 14**
   See also CA 1-4R; CANR 1; DLB 14

**Ratcliffe, James P.**
   See Mencken, H(enry) L(ouis)

**Rathbone, Julian** 1935- ........... **CLC 41**
   See also CA 101; CANR 34

**Rattigan, Terence (Mervyn)**
   1911-1977 ................... **CLC 7**
   See also CA 85-88; 73-76;
   CDBLB 1945-1960; DAM DRAM;
   DLB 13; MTCW

**Ratushinskaya, Irina** 1954- ........ **CLC 54**
   See also CA 129

**Raven, Simon (Arthur Noel)**
   1927- ...................... **CLC 14**
   See also CA 81-84

**Rawley, Callman** 1903-
   See Rakosi, Carl
   See also CA 21-24R; CANR 12, 32

**Rawlings, Marjorie Kinnan**
1896-1953 . . . . . . . . . . . . . . . . . **TCLC 4**
See also CA 104; 137; DLB 9, 22, 102;
JRDA; MAICYA; YABC 1

**Ray, Satyajit** 1921-1992. . . . . . . **CLC 16, 76**
See also CA 114; 137; DAM MULT

**Read, Herbert Edward** 1893-1968. . . . **CLC 4**
See also CA 85-88; 25-28R; DLB 20, 149

**Read, Piers Paul** 1941- . . . . . . **CLC 4, 10, 25**
See also CA 21-24R; CANR 38; DLB 14;
SATA 21

**Reade, Charles** 1814-1884 . . . . . . . . **NCLC 2**
See also DLB 21

**Reade, Hamish**
See Gray, Simon (James Holliday)

**Reading, Peter** 1946- . . . . . . . . . . . . . **CLC 47**
See also CA 103; CANR 46; DLB 40

**Reaney, James** 1926- . . . . . . . . **CLC 13; DAC**
See also CA 41-44R; CAAS 15; CANR 42;
DAM MST; DLB 68; SATA 43

**Rebreanu, Liviu** 1885-1944 . . . . . . . **TCLC 28**

**Rechy, John (Francisco)**
1934- . . . . . . . . . . **CLC 1, 7, 14, 18; HLC**
See also CA 5-8R; CAAS 4; CANR 6, 32;
DAM MULT; DLB 122; DLBY 82; HW;
INT CANR-6

**Redcam, Tom** 1870-1933 . . . . . . . . . **TCLC 25**

**Reddin, Keith**. . . . . . . . . . . . . . . . . . . **CLC 67**

**Redgrove, Peter (William)**
1932- . . . . . . . . . . . . . . . . . . . . . **CLC 6, 41**
See also CA 1-4R; CANR 3, 39; DLB 40

**Redmon, Anne**. . . . . . . . . . . . . . . . . . **CLC 22**
See also Nightingale, Anne Redmon
See also DLBY 86

**Reed, Eliot**
See Ambler, Eric

**Reed, Ishmael**
1938- . . . **CLC 2, 3, 5, 6, 13, 32, 60; BLC**
See also BW 2; CA 21-24R; CANR 25, 48;
DAM MULT; DLB 2, 5, 33; DLBD 8;
MTCW

**Reed, John (Silas)** 1887-1920 . . . . . . **TCLC 9**
See also CA 106

**Reed, Lou**. . . . . . . . . . . . . . . . . . . . . . **CLC 21**
See also Firbank, Louis

**Reeve, Clara** 1729-1807 . . . . . . . . . **NCLC 19**
See also DLB 39

**Reich, Wilhelm** 1897-1957. . . . . . . **TCLC 57**

**Reid, Christopher (John)** 1949- . . . . . **CLC 33**
See also CA 140; DLB 40

**Reid, Desmond**
See Moorcock, Michael (John)

**Reid Banks, Lynne** 1929-
See Banks, Lynne Reid
See also CA 1-4R; CANR 6, 22, 38;
CLR 24; JRDA; MAICYA; SATA 22, 75

**Reilly, William K.**
See Creasey, John

**Reiner, Max**
See Caldwell, (Janet Miriam) Taylor
(Holland)

**Reis, Ricardo**
See Pessoa, Fernando (Antonio Nogueira)

**Remarque, Erich Maria**
1898-1970 . . . . **CLC 21; DA; DAB; DAC**
See also CA 77-80; 29-32R; DAM MST,
NOV; DLB 56; MTCW

**Remizov, A.**
See Remizov, Aleksei (Mikhailovich)

**Remizov, A. M.**
See Remizov, Aleksei (Mikhailovich)

**Remizov, Aleksei (Mikhailovich)**
1877-1957 . . . . . . . . . . . . . . . . . **TCLC 27**
See also CA 125; 133

**Renan, Joseph Ernest**
1823-1892 . . . . . . . . . . . . . . . . **NCLC 26**

**Renard, Jules** 1864-1910 . . . . . . . . . **TCLC 17**
See also CA 117

**Renault, Mary**. . . . . . . . . . . . . . **CLC 3, 11, 17**
See also Challans, Mary
See also DLBY 83

**Rendell, Ruth (Barbara)** 1930- . . **CLC 28, 48**
See also Vine, Barbara
See also CA 109; CANR 32; DAM POP;
DLB 87; INT CANR-32; MTCW

**Renoir, Jean** 1894-1979 . . . . . . . . . . **CLC 20**
See also CA 129; 85-88

**Resnais, Alain** 1922-. . . . . . . . . . . . . **CLC 16**

**Reverdy, Pierre** 1889-1960 . . . . . . . . **CLC 53**
See also CA 97-100; 89-92

**Rexroth, Kenneth**
1905-1982 . . . . . . **CLC 1, 2, 6, 11, 22, 49**
See also CA 5-8R; 107; CANR 14, 34;
CDALB 1941-1968; DAM POET;
DLB 16, 48, 165; DLBY 82;
INT CANR-14; MTCW

**Reyes, Alfonso** 1889-1959 . . . . . . . **TCLC 33**
See also CA 131; HW

**Reyes y Basoalto, Ricardo Eliecer Neftali**
See Neruda, Pablo

**Reymont, Wladyslaw (Stanislaw)**
1868(?)-1925 . . . . . . . . . . . . . . . . . **TCLC 5**
See also CA 104

**Reynolds, Jonathan** 1942- . . . . . . . **CLC 6, 38**
See also CA 65-68; CANR 28

**Reynolds, Joshua** 1723-1792 . . . . . . . **LC 15**
See also DLB 104

**Reynolds, Michael Shane** 1937- . . . . **CLC 44**
See also CA 65-68; CANR 9

**Reznikoff, Charles** 1894-1976 . . . . . . . **CLC 9**
See also CA 33-36; 61-64; CAP 2; DLB 28,
45

**Rezzori (d'Arezzo), Gregor von**
1914- . . . . . . . . . . . . . . . . . . . . . . **CLC 25**
See also CA 122; 136

**Rhine, Richard**
See Silverstein, Alvin

**Rhodes, Eugene Manlove**
1869-1934 . . . . . . . . . . . . . . . . . **TCLC 53**

**R'hoone**
See Balzac, Honore de

**Rhys, Jean**
1890(?)-1979 . . . . **CLC 2, 4, 6, 14, 19, 51;
SSC 21**
See also CA 25-28R; 85-88; CANR 35;
CDBLB 1945-1960; DAM NOV; DLB 36,
117, 162; MTCW

**Ribeiro, Darcy** 1922- . . . . . . . . . . . . **CLC 34**
See also CA 33-36R

**Ribeiro, Joao Ubaldo (Osorio Pimentel)**
1941- . . . . . . . . . . . . . . . . . . . **CLC 10, 67**
See also CA 81-84

**Ribman, Ronald (Burt)** 1932- . . . . . . . **CLC 7**
See also CA 21-24R; CANR 46

**Ricci, Nino** 1959- . . . . . . . . . . . . . . . **CLC 70**
See also CA 137

**Rice, Anne** 1941- . . . . . . . . . . . . . . . **CLC 41**
See also AAYA 9; BEST 89:2; CA 65-68;
CANR 12, 36; DAM POP

**Rice, Elmer (Leopold)**
1892-1967 . . . . . . . . . . . . . . . . . **CLC 7, 49**
See also CA 21-22; 25-28R; CAP 2;
DAM DRAM; DLB 4, 7; MTCW

**Rice, Tim(othy Miles Bindon)**
1944- . . . . . . . . . . . . . . . . . . . . . . **CLC 21**
See also CA 103; CANR 46

**Rich, Adrienne (Cecile)**
1929- . . . . **CLC 3, 6, 7, 11, 18, 36, 73, 76;
PC 5**
See also CA 9-12R; CANR 20;
DAM POET; DLB 5, 67; MTCW

**Rich, Barbara**
See Graves, Robert (von Ranke)

**Rich, Robert**
See Trumbo, Dalton

**Richard, Keith**. . . . . . . . . . . . . . . . . . **CLC 17**
See also Richards, Keith

**Richards, David Adams**
1950- . . . . . . . . . . . . . . . . . . **CLC 59; DAC**
See also CA 93-96; DLB 53

**Richards, I(vor) A(rmstrong)**
1893-1979 . . . . . . . . . . . . . . . . **CLC 14, 24**
See also CA 41-44R; 89-92; CANR 34;
DLB 27

**Richards, Keith** 1943-
See Richard, Keith
See also CA 107

**Richardson, Anne**
See Roiphe, Anne (Richardson)

**Richardson, Dorothy Miller**
1873-1957 . . . . . . . . . . . . . . . . . . **TCLC 3**
See also CA 104; DLB 36

**Richardson, Ethel Florence (Lindesay)**
1870-1946
See Richardson, Henry Handel
See also CA 105

**Richardson, Henry Handel**. . . . . . . . . **TCLC 4**
See also Richardson, Ethel Florence
(Lindesay)

**Richardson, John**
1796-1852 . . . . . . . . . . . . **NCLC 55; DAC**
See also CA 140; DLB 99

**Richardson, Samuel**
1689-1761 . . . . . . **LC 1; DA; DAB; DAC;
WLC**
See also CDBLB 1660-1789; DAM MST,
NOV; DLB 39

**Ronsard, Pierre de**
1524-1585 .............. **LC 6; PC 11**

**Rooke, Leon** 1934- ............ **CLC 25, 34**
See also CA 25-28R; CANR 23; DAM POP

**Roper, William** 1498-1578 ......... **LC 10**

**Roquelaure, A. N.**
See Rice, Anne

**Rosa, Joao Guimaraes** 1908-1967 ... **CLC 23**
See also CA 89-92; DLB 113

**Rose, Wendy** 1948- ......... **CLC 85; PC 13**
See also CA 53-56; CANR 5, 51;
DAM MULT; NNAL; SATA 12

**Rosen, Richard (Dean)** 1949- ....... **CLC 39**
See also CA 77-80; INT CANR-30

**Rosenberg, Isaac** 1890-1918 ...... **TCLC 12**
See also CA 107; DLB 20

**Rosenblatt, Joe** .................. **CLC 15**
See also Rosenblatt, Joseph

**Rosenblatt, Joseph** 1933-
See Rosenblatt, Joe
See also CA 89-92; INT 89-92

**Rosenfeld, Samuel** 1896-1963
See Tzara, Tristan
See also CA 89-92

**Rosenthal, M(acha) L(ouis)** 1917- ... **CLC 28**
See also CA 1-4R; CAAS 6; CANR 4, 51;
DLB 5; SATA 59

**Ross, Barnaby**
See Dannay, Frederic

**Ross, Bernard L.**
See Follett, Ken(neth Martin)

**Ross, J. H.**
See Lawrence, T(homas) E(dward)

**Ross, Martin**
See Martin, Violet Florence
See also DLB 135

**Ross, (James) Sinclair**
1908- .............. **CLC 13; DAC**
See also CA 73-76; DAM MST; DLB 88

**Rossetti, Christina (Georgina)**
1830-1894 ..... **NCLC 2, 50; DA; DAB;
DAC; PC 7; WLC**
See also DAM MST, POET; DLB 35, 163;
MAICYA; SATA 20

**Rossetti, Dante Gabriel**
1828-1882 ........ **NCLC 4; DA; DAB;
DAC; WLC**
See also CDBLB 1832-1890; DAM MST,
POET; DLB 35

**Rossner, Judith (Perelman)**
1935- ................... **CLC 6, 9, 29**
See also AITN 2; BEST 90:3; CA 17-20R;
CANR 18, 51; DLB 6; INT CANR-18;
MTCW

**Rostand, Edmond (Eugene Alexis)**
1868-1918 ...... **TCLC 6, 37; DA; DAB;
DAC**
See also CA 104; 126; DAM DRAM, MST;
MTCW

**Roth, Henry** 1906-1995 ...... **CLC 2, 6, 11**
See also CA 11-12; 149; CANR 38; CAP 1;
DLB 28; MTCW

**Roth, Joseph** 1894-1939 ......... **TCLC 33**
See also DLB 85

**Roth, Philip (Milton)**
1933- ...... **CLC 1, 2, 3, 4, 6, 9, 15, 22,
31, 47, 66, 86; DA; DAB; DAC; WLC**
See also BEST 90:3; CA 1-4R; CANR 1, 22,
36; CDALB 1968-1988; DAM MST,
NOV, POP; DLB 2, 28; DLBY 82;
MTCW

**Rothenberg, Jerome** 1931- ...... **CLC 6, 57**
See also CA 45-48; CANR 1; DLB 5

**Roumain, Jacques (Jean Baptiste)**
1907-1944 ............. **TCLC 19; BLC**
See also BW 1; CA 117; 125; DAM MULT

**Rourke, Constance (Mayfield)**
1885-1941 .................. **TCLC 12**
See also CA 107; YABC 1

**Rousseau, Jean-Baptiste** 1671-1741 ... **LC 9**

**Rousseau, Jean-Jacques**
1712-1778 ..... **LC 14; DA; DAB; DAC;
WLC**
See also DAM MST

**Roussel, Raymond** 1877-1933 ..... **TCLC 20**
See also CA 117

**Rovit, Earl (Herbert)** 1927- ......... **CLC 7**
See also CA 5-8R; CANR 12

**Rowe, Nicholas** 1674-1718 .......... **LC 8**
See also DLB 84

**Rowley, Ames Dorrance**
See Lovecraft, H(oward) P(hillips)

**Rowson, Susanna Haswell**
1762(?)-1824 ............... **NCLC 5**
See also DLB 37

**Roy, Gabrielle**
1909-1983 ..... **CLC 10, 14; DAB; DAC**
See also CA 53-56; 110; CANR 5;
DAM MST; DLB 68; MTCW

**Rozewicz, Tadeusz** 1921- ........ **CLC 9, 23**
See also CA 108; CANR 36; DAM POET;
MTCW

**Ruark, Gibbons** 1941- .............. **CLC 3**
See also CA 33-36R; CAAS 23; CANR 14,
31; DLB 120

**Rubens, Bernice (Ruth)** 1923- ... **CLC 19, 31**
See also CA 25-28R; CANR 33; DLB 14;
MTCW

**Rudkin, (James) David** 1936- ...... **CLC 14**
See also CA 89-92; DLB 13

**Rudnik, Raphael** 1933- .............. **CLC 7**
See also CA 29-32R

**Ruffian, M.**
See Hasek, Jaroslav (Matej Frantisek)

**Ruiz, Jose Martinez** ............... **CLC 11**
See also Martinez Ruiz, Jose

**Rukeyser, Muriel**
1913-1980 .... **CLC 6, 10, 15, 27; PC 12**
See also CA 5-8R; 93-96; CANR 26;
DAM POET; DLB 48; MTCW;
SATA-Obit 22

**Rule, Jane (Vance)** 1931- ......... **CLC 27**
See also CA 25-28R; CAAS 18; CANR 12;
DLB 60

**Rulfo, Juan** 1918-1986 .... **CLC 8, 80; HLC**
See also CA 85-88; 118; CANR 26;
DAM MULT; DLB 113; HW; MTCW

**Runeberg, Johan** 1804-1877 ...... **NCLC 41**

**Runyon, (Alfred) Damon**
1884(?)-1946 ............... **TCLC 10**
See also CA 107; DLB 11, 86

**Rush, Norman** 1933- .............. **CLC 44**
See also CA 121; 126; INT 126

**Rushdie, (Ahmed) Salman**
1947- ...... **CLC 23, 31, 55; DAB; DAC**
See also BEST 89:3; CA 108; 111;
CANR 33; DAM MST, NOV, POP;
INT 111; MTCW

**Rushforth, Peter (Scott)** 1945- ..... **CLC 19**
See also CA 101

**Ruskin, John** 1819-1900 .......... **TCLC 63**
See also CA 114; 129; CDBLB 1832-1890;
DLB 55, 163; SATA 24

**Russ, Joanna** 1937- ............... **CLC 15**
See also CA 25-28R; CANR 11, 31; DLB 8;
MTCW

**Russell, George William** 1867-1935
See A. E.
See also CA 104; CDBLB 1890-1914;
DAM POET

**Russell, (Henry) Ken(neth Alfred)**
1927- ....................... **CLC 16**
See also CA 105

**Russell, Willy** 1947- .............. **CLC 60**

**Rutherford, Mark** ................. **TCLC 25**
See also White, William Hale
See also DLB 18

**Ruyslinck, Ward** 1929- ............ **CLC 14**
See also Belser, Reimond Karel Maria de

**Ryan, Cornelius (John)** 1920-1974 ... **CLC 7**
See also CA 69-72; 53-56; CANR 38

**Ryan, Michael** 1946- ............. **CLC 65**
See also CA 49-52; DLBY 82

**Rybakov, Anatoli (Naumovich)**
1911- ................... **CLC 23, 53**
See also CA 126; 135; SATA 79

**Ryder, Jonathan**
See Ludlum, Robert

**Ryga, George** 1932-1987 ..... **CLC 14; DAC**
See also CA 101; 124; CANR 43;
DAM MST; DLB 60

**S. S.**
See Sassoon, Siegfried (Lorraine)

**Saba, Umberto** 1883-1957 ........ **TCLC 33**
See also CA 144; DLB 114

**Sabatini, Rafael** 1875-1950 ....... **TCLC 47**

**Sabato, Ernesto (R.)**
1911- .............. **CLC 10, 23; HLC**
See also CA 97-100; CANR 32;
DAM MULT; DLB 145; HW; MTCW

**Sacastru, Martin**
See Bioy Casares, Adolfo

**Sacher-Masoch, Leopold von**
1836(?)-1895 ............... **NCLC 31**

**Sachs, Marilyn (Stickle)** 1927- ..... **CLC 35**
See also AAYA 2; CA 17-20R; CANR 13,
47; CLR 2; JRDA; MAICYA; SAAS 2;
SATA 3, 68

**Sachs, Nelly** 1891-1970 ........... **CLC 14**
See also CA 17-18; 25-28R; CAP 2

Savan, Glenn   19(?)- . . . . . . . . . . . . . CLC 50

Sayers, Dorothy L(eigh)
    1893-1957 . . . . . . . . . . . . . . . TCLC 2, 15
    See also CA 104; 119; CDBLB 1914-1945;
    DAM POP; DLB 10, 36, 77, 100; MTCW

Sayers, Valerie   1952- . . . . . . . . . . . . CLC 50
    See also CA 134

Sayles, John (Thomas)
    1950- . . . . . . . . . . . . . . . . . CLC 7, 10, 14
    See also CA 57-60; CANR 41; DLB 44

Scammell, Michael . . . . . . . . . . . . . . . CLC 34

Scannell, Vernon   1922- . . . . . . . . . . CLC 49
    See also CA 5-8R; CANR 8, 24; DLB 27;
    SATA 59

Scarlett, Susan
    See Streatfeild, (Mary) Noel

Schaeffer, Susan Fromberg
    1941- . . . . . . . . . . . . . . . CLC 6, 11, 22
    See also CA 49-52; CANR 18; DLB 28;
    MTCW; SATA 22

Schary, Jill
    See Robinson, Jill

Schell, Jonathan   1943- . . . . . . . . . . . CLC 35
    See also CA 73-76; CANR 12

Schelling, Friedrich Wilhelm Joseph von
    1775-1854 . . . . . . . . . . . . . . . . NCLC 30
    See also DLB 90

Schendel, Arthur van   1874-1946 . . . TCLC 56

Scherer, Jean-Marie Maurice   1920-
    See Rohmer, Eric
    See also CA 110

Schevill, James (Erwin)   1920- . . . . . . . CLC 7
    See also CA 5-8R; CAAS 12

Schiller, Friedrich   1759-1805 . . . . NCLC 39
    See also DAM DRAM; DLB 94

Schisgal, Murray (Joseph)   1926- . . . . . CLC 6
    See also CA 21-24R; CANR 48

Schlee, Ann   1934- . . . . . . . . . . . . . . . CLC 35
    See also CA 101; CANR 29; SATA 44;
    SATA-Brief 36

Schlegel, August Wilhelm von
    1767-1845 . . . . . . . . . . . . . . . NCLC 15
    See also DLB 94

Schlegel, Friedrich   1772-1829 . . . . NCLC 45
    See also DLB 90

Schlegel, Johann Elias (von)
    1719(?)-1749 . . . . . . . . . . . . . . . . . LC 5

Schlesinger, Arthur M(eier), Jr.
    1917- . . . . . . . . . . . . . . . . . . . . CLC 84
    See also AITN 1; CA 1-4R; CANR 1, 28;
    DLB 17; INT CANR-28; MTCW;
    SATA 61

Schmidt, Arno (Otto)   1914-1979 . . . . CLC 56
    See also CA 128; 109; DLB 69

Schmitz, Aron Hector   1861-1928
    See Svevo, Italo
    See also CA 104; 122; MTCW

Schnackenberg, Gjertrud   1953- . . . . . CLC 40
    See also CA 116; DLB 120

Schneider, Leonard Alfred   1925-1966
    See Bruce, Lenny
    See also CA 89-92

Schnitzler, Arthur
    1862-1931 . . . . . . . . . . TCLC 4; SSC 15
    See also CA 104; DLB 81, 118

Schopenhauer, Arthur
    1788-1860 . . . . . . . . . . . . . . . NCLC 51
    See also DLB 90

Schor, Sandra (M.)   1932(?)-1990 . . . CLC 65
    See also CA 132

Schorer, Mark   1908-1977 . . . . . . . . . . CLC 9
    See also CA 5-8R; 73-76; CANR 7;
    DLB 103

Schrader, Paul (Joseph)   1946- . . . . . . CLC 26
    See also CA 37-40R; CANR 41; DLB 44

Schreiner, Olive (Emilie Albertina)
    1855-1920 . . . . . . . . . . . . . . . . . TCLC 9
    See also CA 105; DLB 18, 156

Schulberg, Budd (Wilson)
    1914- . . . . . . . . . . . . . . . . . . . CLC 7, 48
    See also CA 25-28R; CANR 19; DLB 6, 26,
    28; DLBY 81

Schulz, Bruno
    1892-1942 . . . . . . . . TCLC 5, 51; SSC 13
    See also CA 115; 123

Schulz, Charles M(onroe)   1922- . . . . CLC 12
    See also CA 9-12R; CANR 6;
    INT CANR-6; SATA 10

Schumacher, E(rnst) F(riedrich)
    1911-1977 . . . . . . . . . . . . . . . . . CLC 80
    See also CA 81-84; 73-76; CANR 34

Schuyler, James Marcus
    1923-1991 . . . . . . . . . . . . . . . CLC 5, 23
    See also CA 101; 134; DAM POET; DLB 5;
    INT 101

Schwartz, Delmore (David)
    1913-1966 . . . CLC 2, 4, 10, 45, 87; PC 8
    See also CA 17-18; 25-28R; CANR 35;
    CAP 2; DLB 28, 48; MTCW

Schwartz, Ernst
    See Ozu, Yasujiro

Schwartz, John Burnham   1965- . . . . CLC 59
    See also CA 132

Schwartz, Lynne Sharon   1939- . . . . . CLC 31
    See also CA 103; CANR 44

Schwartz, Muriel A.
    See Eliot, T(homas) S(tearns)

Schwarz-Bart, Andre   1928- . . . . . . . CLC 2, 4
    See also CA 89-92

Schwarz-Bart, Simone   1938- . . . . . . . . CLC 7
    See also BW 2; CA 97-100

Schwob, (Mayer Andre) Marcel
    1867-1905 . . . . . . . . . . . . . . . . . TCLC 20
    See also CA 117; DLB 123

Sciascia, Leonardo
    1921-1989 . . . . . . . . . . . . . CLC 8, 9, 41
    See also CA 85-88; 130; CANR 35; MTCW

Scoppettone, Sandra   1936- . . . . . . . . CLC 26
    See also AAYA 11; CA 5-8R; CANR 41;
    SATA 9

Scorsese, Martin   1942- . . . . . . . . CLC 20, 89
    See also CA 110; 114; CANR 46

Scotland, Jay
    See Jakes, John (William)

Scott, Duncan Campbell
    1862-1947 . . . . . . . . . . . TCLC 6; DAC
    See also CA 104; DLB 92

Scott, Evelyn   1893-1963. . . . . . . . . . CLC 43
    See also CA 104; 112; DLB 9, 48

Scott, F(rancis) R(eginald)
    1899-1985 . . . . . . . . . . . . . . . . . CLC 22
    See also CA 101; 114; DLB 88; INT 101

Scott, Frank
    See Scott, F(rancis) R(eginald)

Scott, Joanna   1960- . . . . . . . . . . . . . CLC 50
    See also CA 126

Scott, Paul (Mark)   1920-1978 . . . . CLC 9, 60
    See also CA 81-84; 77-80; CANR 33;
    DLB 14; MTCW

Scott, Walter
    1771-1832 . . . . . . . NCLC 15; DA; DAB;
                        DAC; PC 13; WLC
    See also CDBLB 1789-1832; DAM MST,
    NOV, POET; DLB 93, 107, 116, 144, 159;
    YABC 2

Scribe, (Augustin) Eugene
    1791-1861 . . . . . . . . . . . NCLC 16; DC 5
    See also DAM DRAM

Scrum, R.
    See Crumb, R(obert)

Scudery, Madeleine de   1607-1701 . . . . . LC 2

Scum
    See Crumb, R(obert)

Scumbag, Little Bobby
    See Crumb, R(obert)

Seabrook, John
    See Hubbard, L(afayette) Ron(ald)

Sealy, I. Allan   1951- . . . . . . . . . . . . . CLC 55

Search, Alexander
    See Pessoa, Fernando (Antonio Nogueira)

Sebastian, Lee
    See Silverberg, Robert

Sebastian Owl
    See Thompson, Hunter S(tockton)

Sebestyen, Ouida   1924- . . . . . . . . . . . CLC 30
    See also AAYA 8; CA 107; CANR 40;
    CLR 17; JRDA; MAICYA; SAAS 10;
    SATA 39

Secundus, H. Scriblerus
    See Fielding, Henry

Sedges, John
    See Buck, Pearl S(ydenstricker)

Sedgwick, Catharine Maria
    1789-1867 . . . . . . . . . . . . . . . . NCLC 19
    See also DLB 1, 74

Seelye, John   1931- . . . . . . . . . . . . . . . CLC 7

Seferiades, Giorgos Stylianou   1900-1971
    See Seferis, George
    See also CA 5-8R; 33-36R; CANR 5, 36;
    MTCW

Seferis, George . . . . . . . . . . . . . . . . CLC 5, 11
    See also Seferiades, Giorgos Stylianou

Segal, Erich (Wolf)   1937- . . . . . . . CLC 3, 10
    See also BEST 89:1; CA 25-28R; CANR 20,
    36; DAM POP; DLBY 86;
    INT CANR-20; MTCW

Seger, Bob   1945-. . . . . . . . . . . . . . . . CLC 35

Seghers, Anna . . . . . . . . . . . . . . . . . . . CLC 7
    See also Radvanyi, Netty
    See also DLB 69

Sherman, Jonathan Marc.......... **CLC 55**

Sherman, Martin 1941(?)-........ **CLC 19**
See also CA 116; 123

Sherwin, Judith Johnson 1936-... **CLC 7, 15**
See also CA 25-28R; CANR 34

Sherwood, Frances 1940-.......... **CLC 81**
See also CA 146

Sherwood, Robert E(mmet)
1896-1955 ................... **TCLC 3**
See also CA 104; DAM DRAM; DLB 7, 26

Shestov, Lev 1866-1938 ......... **TCLC 56**

Shevchenko, Taras 1814-1861 .... **NCLC 54**

Shiel, M(atthew) P(hipps)
1865-1947 .................. **TCLC 8**
See also CA 106; DLB 153

Shields, Carol 1935-......... **CLC 91; DAC**
See also CA 81-84; CANR 51

Shiga, Naoya 1883-1971... **CLC 33; SSC 23**
See also CA 101; 33-36R

Shilts, Randy 1951-1994 .......... **CLC 85**
See also CA 115; 127; 144; CANR 45;
INT 127

Shimazaki Haruki 1872-1943
See Shimazaki Toson
See also CA 105; 134

Shimazaki Toson................. **TCLC 5**
See also Shimazaki Haruki

Sholokhov, Mikhail (Aleksandrovich)
1905-1984 ................. **CLC 7, 15**
See also CA 101; 112; MTCW;
SATA-Obit 36

Shone, Patric
See Hanley, James

Shreve, Susan Richards 1939-...... **CLC 23**
See also CA 49-52; CAAS 5; CANR 5, 38;
MAICYA; SATA 46; SATA-Brief 41

Shue, Larry 1946-1985............ **CLC 52**
See also CA 145; 117; DAM DRAM

Shu-Jen, Chou 1881-1936
See Lu Hsun
See also CA 104

Shulman, Alix Kates 1932-...... **CLC 2, 10**
See also CA 29-32R; CANR 43; SATA 7

Shuster, Joe 1914-............... **CLC 21**

Shute, Nevil..................... **CLC 30**
See also Norway, Nevil Shute

Shuttle, Penelope (Diane) 1947-..... **CLC 7**
See also CA 93-96; CANR 39; DLB 14, 40

Sidney, Mary 1561-1621 .......... **LC 19**

Sidney, Sir Philip
1554-1586 ..... **LC 19; DA; DAB; DAC**
See also CDBLB Before 1660; DAM MST,
POET

Siegel, Jerome 1914-............. **CLC 21**
See also CA 116

Siegel, Jerry
See Siegel, Jerome

Sienkiewicz, Henryk (Adam Alexander Pius)
1846-1916 .................. **TCLC 3**
See also CA 104; 134

Sierra, Gregorio Martinez
See Martinez Sierra, Gregorio

Sierra, Maria (de la O'LeJarraga) Martinez
See Martinez Sierra, Maria (de la
O'LeJarraga)

Sigal, Clancy 1926-............... **CLC 7**
See also CA 1-4R

Sigourney, Lydia Howard (Huntley)
1791-1865 ................. **NCLC 21**
See also DLB 1, 42, 73

Siguenza y Gongora, Carlos de
1645-1700 ................... **LC 8**

Sigurjonsson, Johann 1880-1919... **TCLC 27**

Sikelianos, Angelos 1884-1951 .... **TCLC 39**

Silkin, Jon 1930- ............ **CLC 2, 6, 43**
See also CA 5-8R; CAAS 5; DLB 27

Silko, Leslie (Marmon)
1948- .......... **CLC 23, 74; DA; DAC**
See also AAYA 14; CA 115; 122;
CANR 45; DAM MST, MULT, POP;
DLB 143; NNAL

Sillanpaa, Frans Eemil 1888-1964... **CLC 19**
See also CA 129; 93-96; MTCW

Sillitoe, Alan
1928- .......... **CLC 1, 3, 6, 10, 19, 57**
See also AITN 1; CA 9-12R; CAAS 2;
CANR 8, 26; CDBLB 1960 to Present;
DLB 14, 139; MTCW; SATA 61

Silone, Ignazio 1900-1978 .......... **CLC 4**
See also CA 25-28; 81-84; CANR 34;
CAP 2; MTCW

Silver, Joan Micklin 1935- ........ **CLC 20**
See also CA 114; 121; INT 121

Silver, Nicholas
See Faust, Frederick (Schiller)

Silverberg, Robert 1935- ........... **CLC 7**
See also CA 1-4R; CAAS 3; CANR 1, 20,
36; DAM POP; DLB 8; INT CANR-20;
MAICYA; MTCW; SATA 13

Silverstein, Alvin 1933- ........... **CLC 17**
See also CA 49-52; CANR 2; CLR 25;
JRDA; MAICYA; SATA 8, 69

Silverstein, Virginia B(arbara Opshelor)
1937- ...................... **CLC 17**
See also CA 49-52; CANR 2; CLR 25;
JRDA; MAICYA; SATA 8, 69

Sim, Georges
See Simenon, Georges (Jacques Christian)

Simak, Clifford D(onald)
1904-1988 ................. **CLC 1, 55**
See also CA 1-4R; 125; CANR 1, 35;
DLB 8; MTCW; SATA-Obit 56

Simenon, Georges (Jacques Christian)
1903-1989 ....... **CLC 1, 2, 3, 8, 18, 47**
See also CA 85-88; 129; CANR 35;
DAM POP; DLB 72; DLBY 89; MTCW

Simic, Charles 1938-... **CLC 6, 9, 22, 49, 68**
See also CA 29-32R; CAAS 4; CANR 12,
33; DAM POET; DLB 105

Simmel, Georg 1858-1918 ........ **TCLC 64**

Simmons, Charles (Paul) 1924-..... **CLC 57**
See also CA 89-92; INT 89-92

Simmons, Dan 1948-.............. **CLC 44**
See also AAYA 16; CA 138; DAM POP

Simmons, James (Stewart Alexander)
1933- ...................... **CLC 43**
See also CA 105; CAAS 21; DLB 40

Simms, William Gilmore
1806-1870 ................. **NCLC 3**
See also DLB 3, 30, 59, 73

Simon, Carly 1945-............... **CLC 26**
See also CA 105

Simon, Claude 1913-...... **CLC 4, 9, 15, 39**
See also CA 89-92; CANR 33; DAM NOV;
DLB 83; MTCW

Simon, (Marvin) Neil
1927- .......... **CLC 6, 11, 31, 39, 70**
See also AITN 1; CA 21-24R; CANR 26;
DAM DRAM; DLB 7; MTCW

Simon, Paul 1942(?)- .............. **CLC 17**
See also CA 116

Simonon, Paul 1956(?)- ........... **CLC 30**

Simpson, Harriette
See Arnow, Harriette (Louisa) Simpson

Simpson, Louis (Aston Marantz)
1923- .................. **CLC 4, 7, 9, 32**
See also CA 1-4R; CAAS 4; CANR 1;
DAM POET; DLB 5; MTCW

Simpson, Mona (Elizabeth) 1957-... **CLC 44**
See also CA 122; 135

Simpson, N(orman) F(rederick)
1919- ...................... **CLC 29**
See also CA 13-16R; DLB 13

Sinclair, Andrew (Annandale)
1935- ..................... **CLC 2, 14**
See also CA 9-12R; CAAS 5; CANR 14, 38;
DLB 14; MTCW

Sinclair, Emil
See Hesse, Hermann

Sinclair, Iain 1943-............... **CLC 76**
See also CA 132

Sinclair, Iain MacGregor
See Sinclair, Iain

Sinclair, Mary Amelia St. Clair 1865(?)-1946
See Sinclair, May
See also CA 104

Sinclair, May.................. **TCLC 3, 11**
See also Sinclair, Mary Amelia St. Clair
See also DLB 36, 135

Sinclair, Upton (Beall)
1878-1968 ...... **CLC 1, 11, 15, 63; DA;
DAB; DAC; WLC**
See also CA 5-8R; 25-28R; CANR 7;
CDALB 1929-1941; DAM MST, NOV;
DLB 9; INT CANR-7; MTCW; SATA 9

Singer, Isaac
See Singer, Isaac Bashevis

Singer, Isaac Bashevis
1904-1991 .... **CLC 1, 3, 6, 9, 11, 15, 23,
38, 69; DA; DAB; DAC; SSC 3; WLC**
See also AITN 1, 2; CA 1-4R; 134;
CANR 1, 39; CDALB 1941-1968; CLR 1;
DAM MST, NOV; DLB 6, 28, 52;
DLBY 91; JRDA; MAICYA; MTCW;
SATA 3, 27; SATA-Obit 68

Singer, Israel Joshua 1893-1944... **TCLC 33**

Singh, Khushwant 1915-........... **CLC 11**
See also CA 9-12R; CAAS 9; CANR 6

Sinjohn, John
See Galsworthy, John

**Sorrentino, Gilbert**
    1929- ............ **CLC 3, 7, 14, 22, 40**
    See also CA 77-80; CANR 14, 33; DLB 5;
    DLBY 80; INT CANR-14

**Soto, Gary**  1952-........ **CLC 32, 80; HLC**
    See also AAYA 10; CA 119; 125;
    CANR 50; CLR 38; DAM MULT;
    DLB 82; HW; INT 125; JRDA; SATA 80

**Soupault, Philippe**  1897-1990 ...... **CLC 68**
    See also CA 116; 147; 131

**Souster, (Holmes) Raymond**
    1921- ............... **CLC 5, 14; DAC**
    See also CA 13-16R; CAAS 14; CANR 13,
    29; DAM POET; DLB 88; SATA 63

**Southern, Terry**  1924(?)-1995 ....... **CLC 7**
    See also CA 1-4R; 150; CANR 1; DLB 2

**Southey, Robert**  1774-1843 ....... **NCLC 8**
    See also DLB 93, 107, 142; SATA 54

**Southworth, Emma Dorothy Eliza Nevitte**
    1819-1899 ................ **NCLC 26**

**Souza, Ernest**
    See Scott, Evelyn

**Soyinka, Wole**
    1934- ....... **CLC 3, 5, 14, 36, 44; BLC;**
                **DA; DAB; DAC; DC 2; WLC**
    See also BW 2; CA 13-16R; CANR 27, 39;
    DAM DRAM, MST, MULT; DLB 125;
    MTCW

**Spackman, W(illiam) M(ode)**
    1905-1990 .................. **CLC 46**
    See also CA 81-84; 132

**Spacks, Barry**  1931-.............. **CLC 14**
    See also CA 29-32R; CANR 33; DLB 105

**Spanidou, Irini**  1946- ............. **CLC 44**

**Spark, Muriel (Sarah)**
    1918- ..... **CLC 2, 3, 5, 8, 13, 18, 40, 94;**
                **DAB; DAC; SSC 10**
    See also CA 5-8R; CANR 12, 36;
    CDBLB 1945-1960; DAM MST, NOV;
    DLB 15, 139; INT CANR-12; MTCW

**Spaulding, Douglas**
    See Bradbury, Ray (Douglas)

**Spaulding, Leonard**
    See Bradbury, Ray (Douglas)

**Spence, J. A. D.**
    See Eliot, T(homas) S(tearns)

**Spencer, Elizabeth**  1921-.......... **CLC 22**
    See also CA 13-16R; CANR 32; DLB 6;
    MTCW; SATA 14

**Spencer, Leonard G.**
    See Silverberg, Robert

**Spencer, Scott**  1945-.............. **CLC 30**
    See also CA 113; CANR 51; DLBY 86

**Spender, Stephen (Harold)**
    1909-1995 ...... **CLC 1, 2, 5, 10, 41, 91**
    See also CA 9-12R; 149; CANR 31;
    CDBLB 1945-1960; DAM POET;
    DLB 20; MTCW

**Spengler, Oswald (Arnold Gottfried)**
    1880-1936 ................ **TCLC 25**
    See also CA 118

**Spenser, Edmund**
    1552(?)-1599 .... **LC 5; DA; DAB; DAC;**
                            **PC 8; WLC**
    See also CDBLB Before 1660; DAM MST,
    POET

**Spicer, Jack**  1925-1965 ...... **CLC 8, 18, 72**
    See also CA 85-88; DAM POET; DLB 5, 16

**Spiegelman, Art**  1948- ............ **CLC 76**
    See also AAYA 10; CA 125; CANR 41

**Spielberg, Peter**  1929- ............. **CLC 6**
    See also CA 5-8R; CANR 4, 48; DLBY 81

**Spielberg, Steven**  1947- ........... **CLC 20**
    See also AAYA 8; CA 77-80; CANR 32;
    SATA 32

**Spillane, Frank Morrison**  1918-
    See Spillane, Mickey
    See also CA 25-28R; CANR 28; MTCW;
    SATA 66

**Spillane, Mickey** ................ **CLC 3, 13**
    See also Spillane, Frank Morrison

**Spinoza, Benedictus de**  1632-1677 .... **LC 9**

**Spinrad, Norman (Richard)**  1940-... **CLC 46**
    See also CA 37-40R; CAAS 19; CANR 20;
    DLB 8; INT CANR-20

**Spitteler, Carl (Friedrich Georg)**
    1845-1924 .................. **TCLC 12**
    See also CA 109; DLB 129

**Spivack, Kathleen (Romola Drucker)**
    1938- ..................... **CLC 6**
    See also CA 49-52

**Spoto, Donald**  1941-.............. **CLC 39**
    See also CA 65-68; CANR 11

**Springsteen, Bruce (F.)**  1949- ...... **CLC 17**
    See also CA 111

**Spurling, Hilary**  1940-............ **CLC 34**
    See also CA 104; CANR 25

**Spyker, John Howland**
    See Elman, Richard

**Squires, (James) Radcliffe**
    1917-1993 ................... **CLC 51**
    See also CA 1-4R; 140; CANR 6, 21

**Srivastava, Dhanpat Rai**  1880(?)-1936
    See Premchand
    See also CA 118

**Stacy, Donald**
    See Pohl, Frederik

**Stael, Germaine de**
    See Stael-Holstein, Anne Louise Germaine
    Necker Baronn
    See also DLB 119

**Stael-Holstein, Anne Louise Germaine Necker**
    **Baronn**  1766-1817 ......... **NCLC 3**
    See also Stael, Germaine de

**Stafford, Jean**  1915-1979 ... **CLC 4, 7, 19, 68**
    See also CA 1-4R; 85-88; CANR 3; DLB 2;
    MTCW; SATA-Obit 22

**Stafford, William (Edgar)**
    1914-1993 ................ **CLC 4, 7, 29**
    See also CA 5-8R; 142; CAAS 3; CANR 5,
    22; DAM POET; DLB 5; INT CANR-22

**Staines, Trevor**
    See Brunner, John (Kilian Houston)

**Stairs, Gordon**
    See Austin, Mary (Hunter)

**Stannard, Martin**  1947-........... **CLC 44**
    See also CA 142; DLB 155

**Stanton, Maura**  1946- ............. **CLC 9**
    See also CA 89-92; CANR 15; DLB 120

**Stanton, Schuyler**
    See Baum, L(yman) Frank

**Stapledon, (William) Olaf**
    1886-1950 ................ **TCLC 22**
    See also CA 111; DLB 15

**Starbuck, George (Edwin)**  1931-.... **CLC 53**
    See also CA 21-24R; CANR 23;
    DAM POET

**Stark, Richard**
    See Westlake, Donald E(dwin)

**Staunton, Schuyler**
    See Baum, L(yman) Frank

**Stead, Christina (Ellen)**
    1902-1983 ......... **CLC 2, 5, 8, 32, 80**
    See also CA 13-16R; 109; CANR 33, 40;
    MTCW

**Stead, William Thomas**
    1849-1912 ................ **TCLC 48**

**Steele, Richard**  1672-1729.......... **LC 18**
    See also CDBLB 1660-1789; DLB 84, 101

**Steele, Timothy (Reid)**  1948-....... **CLC 45**
    See also CA 93-96; CANR 16, 50; DLB 120

**Steffens, (Joseph) Lincoln**
    1866-1936 ................ **TCLC 20**
    See also CA 117

**Stegner, Wallace (Earle)**
    1909-1993 .............. **CLC 9, 49, 81**
    See also AITN 1; BEST 90:3; CA 1-4R;
    141; CAAS 9; CANR 1, 21, 46;
    DAM NOV; DLB 9; DLBY 93; MTCW

**Stein, Gertrude**
    1874-1946 ...... **TCLC 1, 6, 28, 48; DA;**
                            **DAB; DAC; WLC**
    See also CA 104; 132; CDALB 1917-1929;
    DAM MST, NOV, POET; DLB 4, 54, 86;
    MTCW

**Steinbeck, John (Ernst)**
    1902-1968 ...... **CLC 1, 5, 9, 13, 21, 34,**
                **45, 75; DA; DAB; DAC; SSC 11; WLC**
    See also AAYA 12; CA 1-4R; 25-28R;
    CANR 1, 35; CDALB 1929-1941;
    DAM DRAM, MST, NOV; DLB 7, 9;
    DLBD 2; MTCW; SATA 9

**Steinem, Gloria**  1934-............. **CLC 63**
    See also CA 53-56; CANR 28, 51; MTCW

**Steiner, George**  1929-............. **CLC 24**
    See also CA 73-76; CANR 31; DAM NOV;
    DLB 67; MTCW; SATA 62

**Steiner, K. Leslie**
    See Delany, Samuel R(ay, Jr.)

**Steiner, Rudolf**  1861-1925........ **TCLC 13**
    See also CA 107

**Stendhal**
    1783-1842 .... **NCLC 23, 46; DA; DAB;**
                                    **DAC; WLC**
    See also DAM MST, NOV; DLB 119

**Stephen, Leslie**  1832-1904 ........ **TCLC 23**
    See also CA 123; DLB 57, 144

**Stephen, Sir Leslie**
    See Stephen, Leslie

**Su Chien** 1884-1918
See Su Man-shu
See also CA 123

**Suckow, Ruth** 1892-1960 . . . . . . . . . **SSC 18**
See also CA 113; DLB 9, 102

**Sudermann, Hermann** 1857-1928 . . **TCLC 15**
See also CA 107; DLB 118

**Sue, Eugene** 1804-1857 . . . . . . . . . . **NCLC 1**
See also DLB 119

**Sueskind, Patrick** 1949- . . . . . . . . . . **CLC 44**
See also Suskind, Patrick

**Sukenick, Ronald** 1932- . . . . . **CLC 3, 4, 6, 48**
See also CA 25-28R; CAAS 8; CANR 32;
DLBY 81

**Suknaski, Andrew** 1942- . . . . . . . . . **CLC 19**
See also CA 101; DLB 53

**Sullivan, Vernon**
See Vian, Boris

**Sully Prudhomme** 1839-1907 . . . . . . **TCLC 31**

**Su Man-shu** . . . . . . . . . . . . . . . . . . . **TCLC 24**
See also Su Chien

**Summerforest, Ivy B.**
See Kirkup, James

**Summers, Andrew James** 1942- . . . . . **CLC 26**

**Summers, Andy**
See Summers, Andrew James

**Summers, Hollis (Spurgeon, Jr.)**
1916- . . . . . . . . . . . . . . . . . . . . . . **CLC 10**
See also CA 5-8R; CANR 3; DLB 6

**Summers, (Alphonsus Joseph-Mary Augustus)**
**Montague** 1880-1948 . . . . . . . . **TCLC 16**
See also CA 118

**Sumner, Gordon Matthew** 1951- . . . . **CLC 26**

**Surtees, Robert Smith**
1803-1864 . . . . . . . . . . . . . . . . . . **NCLC 14**
See also DLB 21

**Susann, Jacqueline** 1921-1974 . . . . . . **CLC 3**
See also AITN 1; CA 65-68; 53-56; MTCW

**Su Shih** 1036-1101 . . . . . . . . . . . . . **CMLC 15**

**Suskind, Patrick**
See Sueskind, Patrick
See also CA 145

**Sutcliff, Rosemary**
1920-1992 . . . . . . . **CLC 26; DAB; DAC**
See also AAYA 10; CA 5-8R; 139;
CANR 37; CLR 1, 37; DAM MST, POP;
JRDA; MAICYA; SATA 6, 44, 78;
SATA-Obit 73

**Sutro, Alfred** 1863-1933 . . . . . . . . . . **TCLC 6**
See also CA 105; DLB 10

**Sutton, Henry**
See Slavitt, David R(ytman)

**Svevo, Italo** . . . . . . . . . . . . . . . **TCLC 2, 35**
See also Schmitz, Aron Hector

**Swados, Elizabeth (A.)** 1951- . . . . . . . **CLC 12**
See also CA 97-100; CANR 49; INT 97-100

**Swados, Harvey** 1920-1972 . . . . . . . . **CLC 5**
See also CA 5-8R; 37-40R; CANR 6;
DLB 2

**Swan, Gladys** 1934- . . . . . . . . . . . . . **CLC 69**
See also CA 101; CANR 17, 39

**Swarthout, Glendon (Fred)**
1918-1992 . . . . . . . . . . . . . . . . . . **CLC 35**
See also CA 1-4R; 139; CANR 1, 47;
SATA 26

**Sweet, Sarah C.**
See Jewett, (Theodora) Sarah Orne

**Swenson, May**
1919-1989 . . . . **CLC 4, 14, 61; DA; DAB;**
**DAC; PC 14**
See also CA 5-8R; 130; CANR 36;
DAM MST, POET; DLB 5; MTCW;
SATA 15

**Swift, Augustus**
See Lovecraft, H(oward) P(hillips)

**Swift, Graham (Colin)** 1949- . . . . **CLC 41, 88**
See also CA 117; 122; CANR 46

**Swift, Jonathan**
1667-1745 . . . . . . **LC 1; DA; DAB; DAC;**
**PC 9; WLC**
See also CDBLB 1660-1789; DAM MST,
NOV, POET; DLB 39, 95, 101; SATA 19

**Swinburne, Algernon Charles**
1837-1909 . . . . . . **TCLC 8, 36; DA; DAB;**
**DAC; WLC**
See also CA 105; 140; CDBLB 1832-1890;
DAM MST, POET; DLB 35, 57

**Swinfen, Ann** . . . . . . . . . . . . . . . . . . **CLC 34**

**Swinnerton, Frank Arthur**
1884-1982 . . . . . . . . . . . . . . . . . . **CLC 31**
See also CA 108; DLB 34

**Swithen, John**
See King, Stephen (Edwin)

**Sylvia**
See Ashton-Warner, Sylvia (Constance)

**Symmes, Robert Edward**
See Duncan, Robert (Edward)

**Symonds, John Addington**
1840-1893 . . . . . . . . . . . . . . . . . . **NCLC 34**
See also DLB 57, 144

**Symons, Arthur** 1865-1945 . . . . . . . **TCLC 11**
See also CA 107; DLB 19, 57, 149

**Symons, Julian (Gustave)**
1912-1994 . . . . . . . . . . . . . **CLC 2, 14, 32**
See also CA 49-52; 147; CAAS 3; CANR 3,
33; DLB 87, 155; DLBY 92; MTCW

**Synge, (Edmund) J(ohn) M(illington)**
1871-1909 . . . . . . . . . . **TCLC 6, 37; DC 2**
See also CA 104; 141; CDBLB 1890-1914;
DAM DRAM; DLB 10, 19

**Syruc, J.**
See Milosz, Czeslaw

**Szirtes, George** 1948- . . . . . . . . . . . . **CLC 46**
See also CA 109; CANR 27

**Tabori, George** 1914- . . . . . . . . . . . . **CLC 19**
See also CA 49-52; CANR 4

**Tagore, Rabindranath**
1861-1941 . . . . . . . . . **TCLC 3, 53; PC 8**
See also CA 104; 120; DAM DRAM,
POET; MTCW

**Taine, Hippolyte Adolphe**
1828-1893 . . . . . . . . . . . . . . . . . . **NCLC 15**

**Talese, Gay** 1932- . . . . . . . . . . . . . . . **CLC 37**
See also AITN 1; CA 1-4R; CANR 9;
INT CANR-9; MTCW

**Tallent, Elizabeth (Ann)** 1954- . . . . . **CLC 45**
See also CA 117; DLB 130

**Tally, Ted** 1952- . . . . . . . . . . . . . . . . **CLC 42**
See also CA 120; 124; INT 124

**Tamayo y Baus, Manuel**
1829-1898 . . . . . . . . . . . . . . . . . . **NCLC 1**

**Tammsaare, A(nton) H(ansen)**
1878-1940 . . . . . . . . . . . . . . . . . . **TCLC 27**

**Tan, Amy** 1952- . . . . . . . . . . . . . . . . **CLC 59**
See also AAYA 9; BEST 89:3; CA 136;
DAM MULT, NOV, POP; SATA 75

**Tandem, Felix**
See Spitteler, Carl (Friedrich Georg)

**Tanizaki, Jun'ichiro**
1886-1965 . . . . . . **CLC 8, 14, 28; SSC 21**
See also CA 93-96; 25-28R

**Tanner, William**
See Amis, Kingsley (William)

**Tao Lao**
See Storni, Alfonsina

**Tarassoff, Lev**
See Troyat, Henri

**Tarbell, Ida M(inerva)**
1857-1944 . . . . . . . . . . . . . . . . . . **TCLC 40**
See also CA 122; DLB 47

**Tarkington, (Newton) Booth**
1869-1946 . . . . . . . . . . . . . . . . . . **TCLC 9**
See also CA 110; 143; DLB 9, 102;
SATA 17

**Tarkovsky, Andrei (Arsenyevich)**
1932-1986 . . . . . . . . . . . . . . . . . . **CLC 75**
See also CA 127

**Tartt, Donna** 1964(?)- . . . . . . . . . . . . **CLC 76**
See also CA 142

**Tasso, Torquato** 1544-1595 . . . . . . . . . **LC 5**

**Tate, (John Orley) Allen**
1899-1979 . . . . **CLC 2, 4, 6, 9, 11, 14, 24**
See also CA 5-8R; 85-88; CANR 32;
DLB 4, 45, 63; MTCW

**Tate, Ellalice**
See Hibbert, Eleanor Alice Burford

**Tate, James (Vincent)** 1943- . . **CLC 2, 6, 25**
See also CA 21-24R; CANR 29; DLB 5

**Tavel, Ronald** 1940- . . . . . . . . . . . . . . **CLC 6**
See also CA 21-24R; CANR 33

**Taylor, C(ecil) P(hilip)** 1929-1981 . . . **CLC 27**
See also CA 25-28R; 105; CANR 47

**Taylor, Edward**
1642(?)-1729 . . . **LC 11; DA; DAB; DAC**
See also DAM MST, POET; DLB 24

**Taylor, Eleanor Ross** 1920- . . . . . . . . . **CLC 5**
See also CA 81-84

**Taylor, Elizabeth** 1912-1975 . . . **CLC 2, 4, 29**
See also CA 13-16R; CANR 9; DLB 139;
MTCW; SATA 13

**Taylor, Henry (Splawn)** 1942- . . . . . . **CLC 44**
See also CA 33-36R; CAAS 7; CANR 31;
DLB 5

**Taylor, Kamala (Purnaiya)** 1924-
See Markandaya, Kamala
See also CA 77-80

Taylor, Mildred D. . . . . . . . . . . . . . . . CLC 21
See also AAYA 10; BW 1; CA 85-88;
CANR 25; CLR 9; DLB 52; JRDA;
MAICYA; SAAS 5; SATA 15, 70

Taylor, Peter (Hillsman)
1917-1994 . . . . . CLC 1, 4, 18, 37, 44, 50,
71; SSC 10
See also CA 13-16R; 147; CANR 9, 50;
DLBY 81, 94; INT CANR-9; MTCW

Taylor, Robert Lewis 1912- . . . . . . . . CLC 14
See also CA 1-4R; CANR 3; SATA 10

Tchekhov, Anton
See Chekhov, Anton (Pavlovich)

Teasdale, Sara 1884-1933. . . . . . . . . . TCLC 4
See also CA 104; DLB 45; SATA 32

Tegner, Esaias 1782-1846. . . . . . . . . NCLC 2

Teilhard de Chardin, (Marie Joseph) Pierre
1881-1955 . . . . . . . . . . . . . . . . . . TCLC 9
See also CA 105

Temple, Ann
See Mortimer, Penelope (Ruth)

Tennant, Emma (Christina)
1937- . . . . . . . . . . . . . . . . . . . . CLC 13, 52
See also CA 65-68; CAAS 9; CANR 10, 38;
DLB 14

Tenneshaw, S. M.
See Silverberg, Robert

Tennyson, Alfred
1809-1892 . . . . . . . NCLC 30; DA; DAB;
DAC; PC 6; WLC
See also CDBLB 1832-1890; DAM MST,
POET; DLB 32

Teran, Lisa St. Aubin de . . . . . . . . . . CLC 36
See also St. Aubin de Teran, Lisa

Terence 195(?)B.C.-159B.C. . . . . . . CMLC 14

Teresa de Jesus, St. 1515-1582 . . . . . . LC 18

Terkel, Louis 1912-
See Terkel, Studs
See also CA 57-60; CANR 18, 45; MTCW

Terkel, Studs . . . . . . . . . . . . . . . . . . . . CLC 38
See also Terkel, Louis
See also AITN 1

Terry, C. V.
See Slaughter, Frank G(ill)

Terry, Megan 1932- . . . . . . . . . . . . . . CLC 19
See also CA 77-80; CABS 3; CANR 43;
DLB 7

Tertz, Abram
See Sinyavsky, Andrei (Donatevich)

Tesich, Steve 1943(?)- . . . . . . . . . . CLC 40, 69
See also CA 105; DLBY 83

Teternikov, Fyodor Kuzmich 1863-1927
See Sologub, Fyodor
See also CA 104

Tevis, Walter 1928-1984 . . . . . . . . . . CLC 42
See also CA 113

Tey, Josephine. . . . . . . . . . . . . . . . . . TCLC 14
See also Mackintosh, Elizabeth
See also DLB 77

Thackeray, William Makepeace
1811-1863 . . . . NCLC 5, 14, 22, 43; DA;
DAB; DAC; WLC
See also CDBLB 1832-1890; DAM MST,
NOV; DLB 21, 55, 159, 163; SATA 23

Thakura, Ravindranatha
See Tagore, Rabindranath

Tharoor, Shashi 1956- . . . . . . . . . . . CLC 70
See also CA 141

Thelwell, Michael Miles 1939- . . . . . CLC 22
See also BW 2; CA 101

Theobald, Lewis, Jr.
See Lovecraft, H(oward) P(hillips)

Theodorescu, Ion N. 1880-1967
See Arghezi, Tudor
See also CA 116

Theriault, Yves 1915-1983 . . . . CLC 79; DAC
See also CA 102; DAM MST; DLB 88

Theroux, Alexander (Louis)
1939- . . . . . . . . . . . . . . . . . . . . CLC 2, 25
See also CA 85-88; CANR 20

Theroux, Paul (Edward)
1941- . . . . . . . . CLC 5, 8, 11, 15, 28, 46
See also BEST 89:4; CA 33-36R; CANR 20,
45; DAM POP; DLB 2; MTCW;
SATA 44

Thesen, Sharon 1946- . . . . . . . . . . . . CLC 56

Thevenin, Denis
See Duhamel, Georges

Thibault, Jacques Anatole Francois
1844-1924
See France, Anatole
See also CA 106; 127; DAM NOV; MTCW

Thiele, Colin (Milton) 1920- . . . . . . . CLC 17
See also CA 29-32R; CANR 12, 28;
CLR 27; MAICYA; SAAS 2; SATA 14,
72

Thomas, Audrey (Callahan)
1935- . . . . . . . . . . CLC 7, 13, 37; SSC 20
See also AITN 2; CA 21-24R; CAAS 19;
CANR 36; DLB 60; MTCW

Thomas, D(onald) M(ichael)
1935- . . . . . . . . . . . . . . . . CLC 13, 22, 31
See also CA 61-64; CAAS 11; CANR 17,
45; CDBLB 1960 to Present; DLB 40;
INT CANR-17; MTCW

Thomas, Dylan (Marlais)
1914-1953 . . . TCLC 1, 8, 45; DA; DAB;
DAC; PC 2; SSC 3; WLC
See also CA 104; 120; CDBLB 1945-1960;
DAM DRAM, MST, POET; DLB 13, 20,
139; MTCW; SATA 60

Thomas, (Philip) Edward
1878-1917 . . . . . . . . . . . . . . . . . TCLC 10
See also CA 106; DAM POET; DLB 19

Thomas, Joyce Carol 1938- . . . . . . . . CLC 35
See also AAYA 12; BW 2; CA 113; 116;
CANR 48; CLR 19; DLB 33; INT 116;
JRDA; MAICYA; MTCW; SAAS 7;
SATA 40, 78

Thomas, Lewis 1913-1993 . . . . . . . . . CLC 35
See also CA 85-88; 143; CANR 38; MTCW

Thomas, Paul
See Mann, (Paul) Thomas

Thomas, Piri 1928- . . . . . . . . . . . . . . CLC 17
See also CA 73-76; HW

Thomas, R(onald) S(tuart)
1913- . . . . . . . . . . . . CLC 6, 13, 48; DAB
See also CA 89-92; CAAS 4; CANR 30;
CDBLB 1960 to Present; DAM POET;
DLB 27; MTCW

Thomas, Ross (Elmore) 1926-1995 . . CLC 39
See also CA 33-36R; 150; CANR 22

Thompson, Francis Clegg
See Mencken, H(enry) L(ouis)

Thompson, Francis Joseph
1859-1907 . . . . . . . . . . . . . . . . . . TCLC 4
See also CA 104; CDBLB 1890-1914;
DLB 19

Thompson, Hunter S(tockton)
1939- . . . . . . . . . . . . . . . . . CLC 9, 17, 40
See also BEST 89:1; CA 17-20R; CANR 23,
46; DAM POP; MTCW

Thompson, James Myers
See Thompson, Jim (Myers)

Thompson, Jim (Myers)
1906-1977(?) . . . . . . . . . . . . . . . . CLC 69
See also CA 140

Thompson, Judith . . . . . . . . . . . . . . . . CLC 39

Thomson, James 1700-1748 . . . . . . LC 16, 29
See also DAM POET; DLB 95

Thomson, James 1834-1882 . . . . . . NCLC 18
See also DAM POET; DLB 35

Thoreau, Henry David
1817-1862 . . . . . NCLC 7, 21; DA; DAB;
DAC; WLC
See also CDALB 1640-1865; DAM MST;
DLB 1

Thornton, Hall
See Silverberg, Robert

Thucydides c. 455B.C.-399B.C. . . . CMLC 17

Thurber, James (Grover)
1894-1961 . . . . CLC 5, 11, 25; DA; DAB;
DAC; SSC 1
See also CA 73-76; CANR 17, 39;
CDALB 1929-1941; DAM DRAM, MST,
NOV; DLB 4, 11, 22, 102; MAICYA;
MTCW; SATA 13

Thurman, Wallace (Henry)
1902-1934 . . . . . . . . . . . . . . TCLC 6; BLC
See also BW 1; CA 104; 124; DAM MULT;
DLB 51

Ticheburn, Cheviot
See Ainsworth, William Harrison

Tieck, (Johann) Ludwig
1773-1853 . . . . . . . . . . . . . . NCLC 5, 46
See also DLB 90

Tiger, Derry
See Ellison, Harlan (Jay)

Tilghman, Christopher 1948(?)- . . . . . CLC 65

Tillinghast, Richard (Williford)
1940- . . . . . . . . . . . . . . . . . . . . . . CLC 29
See also CA 29-32R; CAAS 23; CANR 26,
51

Timrod, Henry 1828-1867 . . . . . . . NCLC 25
See also DLB 3

Tindall, Gillian 1938- . . . . . . . . . . . . . CLC 7
See also CA 21-24R; CANR 11

Tiptree, James, Jr. . . . . . . . . . . . . . CLC 48, 50
See also Sheldon, Alice Hastings Bradley
See also DLB 8

Titmarsh, Michael Angelo
See Thackeray, William Makepeace

Tocqueville, Alexis (Charles Henri Maurice
Clerel Comte) 1805-1859 . . . . . NCLC 7

**Tolkien, J(ohn) R(onald) R(euel)**
    1892-1973 . . . . . . CLC 1, 2, 3, 8, 12, 38;
                DA; DAB; DAC; WLC
    See also AAYA 10; AITN 1; CA 17-18;
        45-48; CANR 36; CAP 2;
        CDBLB 1914-1945; DAM MST, NOV,
        POP; DLB 15, 160; JRDA; MAICYA;
        MTCW; SATA 2, 32; SATA-Obit 24

**Toller, Ernst**   1893-1939 . . . . . . . . . TCLC 10
    See also CA 107; DLB 124

**Tolson, M. B.**
    See Tolson, Melvin B(eaunorus)

**Tolson, Melvin B(eaunorus)**
    1898(?)-1966 . . . . . . . . . . . CLC 36; BLC
    See also BW 1; CA 124; 89-92;
        DAM MULT, POET; DLB 48, 76

**Tolstoi, Aleksei Nikolaevich**
    See Tolstoy, Alexey Nikolaevich

**Tolstoy, Alexey Nikolaevich**
    1882-1945 . . . . . . . . . . . . . . TCLC 18
    See also CA 107

**Tolstoy, Count Leo**
    See Tolstoy, Leo (Nikolaevich)

**Tolstoy, Leo (Nikolaevich)**
    1828-1910 . . . . . . TCLC 4, 11, 17, 28, 44;
                DA; DAB; DAC; SSC 9; WLC
    See also CA 104; 123; DAM MST, NOV;
        SATA 26

**Tomasi di Lampedusa, Giuseppe**   1896-1957
    See Lampedusa, Giuseppe (Tomasi) di
    See also CA 111

**Tomlin, Lily** . . . . . . . . . . . . . . . . . CLC 17
    See also Tomlin, Mary Jean

**Tomlin, Mary Jean**   1939(?)-
    See Tomlin, Lily
    See also CA 117

**Tomlinson, (Alfred) Charles**
    1927- . . . . . . . . . . . . . CLC 2, 4, 6, 13, 45
    See also CA 5-8R; CANR 33; DAM POET;
        DLB 40

**Tonson, Jacob**
    See Bennett, (Enoch) Arnold

**Toole, John Kennedy**
    1937-1969 . . . . . . . . . . . . . . . CLC 19, 64
    See also CA 104; DLBY 81

**Toomer, Jean**
    1894-1967 . . . . . . CLC 1, 4, 13, 22; BLC;
                    PC 7; SSC 1
    See also BW 1; CA 85-88;
        CDALB 1917-1929; DAM MULT;
        DLB 45, 51; MTCW

**Torley, Luke**
    See Blish, James (Benjamin)

**Tornimparte, Alessandra**
    See Ginzburg, Natalia

**Torre, Raoul della**
    See Mencken, H(enry) L(ouis)

**Torrey, E(dwin) Fuller**   1937- . . . . . . . CLC 34
    See also CA 119

**Torsvan, Ben Traven**
    See Traven, B.

**Torsvan, Benno Traven**
    See Traven, B.

**Torsvan, Berick Traven**
    See Traven, B.

**Torsvan, Berwick Traven**
    See Traven, B.

**Torsvan, Bruno Traven**
    See Traven, B.

**Torsvan, Traven**
    See Traven, B.

**Tournier, Michel (Edouard)**
    1924- . . . . . . . . . . . . . . . . . CLC 6, 23, 36
    See also CA 49-52; CANR 3, 36; DLB 83;
        MTCW; SATA 23

**Tournimparte, Alessandra**
    See Ginzburg, Natalia

**Towers, Ivar**
    See Kornbluth, C(yril) M.

**Towne, Robert (Burton)**   1936(?)- . . . . CLC 87
    See also CA 108; DLB 44

**Townsend, Sue**   1946- . . CLC 61; DAB; DAC
    See also CA 119; 127; INT 127; MTCW;
        SATA 55; SATA-Brief 48

**Townshend, Peter (Dennis Blandford)**
    1945- . . . . . . . . . . . . . . . . . . CLC 17, 42
    See also CA 107

**Tozzi, Federigo**   1883-1920 . . . . . . . TCLC 31

**Traill, Catharine Parr**
    1802-1899 . . . . . . . . . . . . . . . NCLC 31
    See also DLB 99

**Trakl, Georg**   1887-1914 . . . . . . . . . . TCLC 5
    See also CA 104

**Transtroemer, Tomas (Goesta)**
    1931- . . . . . . . . . . . . . . . . . CLC 52, 65
    See also CA 117; 129; CAAS 17;
        DAM POET

**Transtromer, Tomas Gosta**
    See Transtroemer, Tomas (Goesta)

**Traven, B.**   (?)-1969 . . . . . . . . . . . . . CLC 8, 11
    See also CA 19-20; 25-28R; CAP 2; DLB 9,
        56; MTCW

**Treitel, Jonathan**   1959- . . . . . . . . . . . CLC 70

**Tremain, Rose**   1943- . . . . . . . . . . . . . CLC 42
    See also CA 97-100; CANR 44; DLB 14

**Tremblay, Michel**   1942- . . . . . . CLC 29; DAC
    See also CA 116; 128; DAM MST; DLB 60;
        MTCW

**Trevanian** . . . . . . . . . . . . . . . . . . . . CLC 29
    See also Whitaker, Rod(ney)

**Trevor, Glen**
    See Hilton, James

**Trevor, William**
    1928- . . . . . CLC 7, 9, 14, 25, 71; SSC 21
    See also Cox, William Trevor
    See also DLB 14, 139

**Trifonov, Yuri (Valentinovich)**
    1925-1981 . . . . . . . . . . . . . . . . . CLC 45
    See also CA 126; 103; MTCW

**Trilling, Lionel**   1905-1975 . . . . CLC 9, 11, 24
    See also CA 9-12R; 61-64; CANR 10;
        DLB 28, 63; INT CANR-10; MTCW

**Trimball, W. H.**
    See Mencken, H(enry) L(ouis)

**Tristan**
    See Gomez de la Serna, Ramon

**Tristram**
    See Housman, A(lfred) E(dward)

**Trogdon, William (Lewis)**   1939-
    See Heat-Moon, William Least
    See also CA 115; 119; CANR 47; INT 119

**Trollope, Anthony**
    1815-1882 . . . . . NCLC 6, 33; DA; DAB;
                    DAC; WLC
    See also CDBLB 1832-1890; DAM MST,
        NOV; DLB 21, 57, 159; SATA 22

**Trollope, Frances**   1779-1863 . . . . . NCLC 30
    See also DLB 21

**Trotsky, Leon**   1879-1940 . . . . . . . . TCLC 22
    See also CA 118

**Trotter (Cockburn), Catharine**
    1679-1749 . . . . . . . . . . . . . . . . . LC 8
    See also DLB 84

**Trout, Kilgore**
    See Farmer, Philip Jose

**Trow, George W. S.**   1943- . . . . . . . . CLC 52
    See also CA 126

**Troyat, Henri**   1911- . . . . . . . . . . . . . CLC 23
    See also CA 45-48; CANR 2, 33; MTCW

**Trudeau, G(arretson) B(eekman)**   1948-
    See Trudeau, Garry B.
    See also CA 81-84; CANR 31; SATA 35

**Trudeau, Garry B.** . . . . . . . . . . . . . . . CLC 12
    See also Trudeau, G(arretson) B(eekman)
    See also AAYA 10; AITN 2

**Truffaut, Francois**   1932-1984 . . . . . . . CLC 20
    See also CA 81-84; 113; CANR 34

**Trumbo, Dalton**   1905-1976 . . . . . . . . CLC 19
    See also CA 21-24R; 69-72; CANR 10;
        DLB 26

**Trumbull, John**   1750-1831 . . . . . . . NCLC 30
    See also DLB 31

**Trundlett, Helen B.**
    See Eliot, T(homas) S(tearns)

**Tryon, Thomas**   1926-1991 . . . . . . . CLC 3, 11
    See also AITN 1; CA 29-32R; 135;
        CANR 32; DAM POP; MTCW

**Tryon, Tom**
    See Tryon, Thomas

**Ts'ao Hsueh-ch'in**   1715(?)-1763 . . . . . . . LC 1

**Tsushima, Shuji**   1909-1948
    See Dazai, Osamu
    See also CA 107

**Tsvetaeva (Efron), Marina (Ivanovna)**
    1892-1941 . . . . . . . . . TCLC 7, 35; PC 14
    See also CA 104; 128; MTCW

**Tuck, Lily**   1938- . . . . . . . . . . . . . . . CLC 70
    See also CA 139

**Tu Fu**   712-770 . . . . . . . . . . . . . . . . . . PC 9
    See also DAM MULT

**Tunis, John R(oberts)**   1889-1975 . . . CLC 12
    See also CA 61-64; DLB 22; JRDA;
        MAICYA; SATA 37; SATA-Brief 30

**Tuohy, Frank** . . . . . . . . . . . . . . . . . . CLC 37
    See also Tuohy, John Francis
    See also DLB 14, 139

**Tuohy, John Francis**   1925-
    See Tuohy, Frank
    See also CA 5-8R; CANR 3, 47

**Turco, Lewis (Putnam)**   1934- . . . CLC 11, 63
    See also CA 13-16R; CAAS 22; CANR 24,
        51; DLBY 84

Turgenev, Ivan
    1818-1883 ....... NCLC 21; DA; DAB;
                      DAC; SSC 7; WLC
    See also DAM MST, NOV

Turgot, Anne-Robert-Jacques
    1727-1781 ................... LC 26

Turner, Frederick 1943-........... CLC 48
    See also CA 73-76; CAAS 10; CANR 12,
    30; DLB 40

Tutu, Desmond M(pilo)
    1931- ................. CLC 80; BLC
    See also BW 1; CA 125; DAM MULT

Tutuola, Amos 1920- ... CLC 5, 14, 29; BLC
    See also BW 2; CA 9-12R; CANR 27;
    DAM MULT; DLB 125; MTCW

Twain, Mark
    ..... TCLC 6, 12, 19, 36, 48, 59; SSC 6;
                                          WLC
    See also Clemens, Samuel Langhorne
    See also DLB 11, 12, 23, 64, 74

Tyler, Anne
    1941- ........ CLC 7, 11, 18, 28, 44, 59
    See also BEST 89:1; CA 9-12R; CANR 11,
    33; DAM NOV, POP; DLB 6, 143;
    DLBY 82; MTCW; SATA 7

Tyler, Royall 1757-1826.......... NCLC 3
    See also DLB 37

Tynan, Katharine 1861-1931 ....... TCLC 3
    See also CA 104; DLB 153

Tyutchev, Fyodor 1803-1873..... NCLC 34

Tzara, Tristan .................... CLC 47
    See also Rosenfeld, Samuel
    See also DAM POET

Uhry, Alfred 1936-............... CLC 55
    See also CA 127; 133; DAM DRAM, POP;
    INT 133

Ulf, Haerved
    See Strindberg, (Johan) August

Ulf, Harved
    See Strindberg, (Johan) August

Ulibarri, Sabine R(eyes) 1919- ..... CLC 83
    See also CA 131; DAM MULT; DLB 82;
    HW

Unamuno (y Jugo), Miguel de
    1864-1936 .... TCLC 2, 9; HLC; SSC 11
    See also CA 104; 131; DAM MULT, NOV;
    DLB 108; HW; MTCW

Undercliffe, Errol
    See Campbell, (John) Ramsey

Underwood, Miles
    See Glassco, John

Undset, Sigrid
    1882-1949 ........ TCLC 3; DA; DAB;
                      DAC; WLC
    See also CA 104; 129; DAM MST, NOV;
    MTCW

Ungaretti, Giuseppe
    1888-1970 .............. CLC 7, 11, 15
    See also CA 19-20; 25-28R; CAP 2;
    DLB 114

Unger, Douglas 1952-............. CLC 34
    See also CA 130

Unsworth, Barry (Forster) 1930-.... CLC 76
    See also CA 25-28R; CANR 30

Updike, John (Hoyer)
    1932- ...... CLC 1, 2, 3, 5, 7, 9, 13, 15,
    23, 34, 43, 70; DA; DAB; DAC; SSC 13;
                                          WLC
    See also CA 1-4R; CABS 1; CANR 4, 33,
    51; CDALB 1968-1988; DAM MST,
    NOV, POET, POP; DLB 2, 5, 143;
    DLBD 3; DLBY 80, 82; MTCW

Upshaw, Margaret Mitchell
    See Mitchell, Margaret (Munnerlyn)

Upton, Mark
    See Sanders, Lawrence

Urdang, Constance (Henriette)
    1922-...................... CLC 47
    See also CA 21-24R; CANR 9, 24

Uriel, Henry
    See Faust, Frederick (Schiller)

Uris, Leon (Marcus) 1924-....... CLC 7, 32
    See also AITN 1, 2; BEST 89:2; CA 1-4R;
    CANR 1, 40; DAM NOV, POP; MTCW;
    SATA 49

Urmuz
    See Codrescu, Andrei

Urquhart, Jane 1949-........ CLC 90; DAC
    See also CA 113; CANR 32

Ustinov, Peter (Alexander) 1921-.... CLC 1
    See also AITN 1; CA 13-16R; CANR 25,
    51; DLB 13

Vaculik, Ludvik 1926-............. CLC 7
    See also CA 53-56

Valdez, Luis (Miguel)
    1940-................. CLC 84; HLC
    See also CA 101; CANR 32; DAM MULT;
    DLB 122; HW

Valenzuela, Luisa 1938-... CLC 31; SSC 14
    See also CA 101; CANR 32; DAM MULT;
    DLB 113; HW

Valera y Alcala-Galiano, Juan
    1824-1905 ................. TCLC 10
    See also CA 106

Valery, (Ambroise) Paul (Toussaint Jules)
    1871-1945 .......... TCLC 4, 15; PC 9
    See also CA 104; 122; DAM POET; MTCW

Valle-Inclan, Ramon (Maria) del
    1866-1936 ............. TCLC 5; HLC
    See also CA 106; DAM MULT; DLB 134

Vallejo, Antonio Buero
    See Buero Vallejo, Antonio

Vallejo, Cesar (Abraham)
    1892-1938 .......... TCLC 3, 56; HLC
    See also CA 105; DAM MULT; HW

Valle Y Pena, Ramon del
    See Valle-Inclan, Ramon (Maria) del

Van Ash, Cay 1918-.............. CLC 34

Vanbrugh, Sir John 1664-1726 ...... LC 21
    See also DAM DRAM; DLB 80

Van Campen, Karl
    See Campbell, John W(ood, Jr.)

Vance, Gerald
    See Silverberg, Robert

Vance, Jack ..................... CLC 35
    See also Vance, John Holbrook
    See also DLB 8

Vance, John Holbrook 1916-
    See Queen, Ellery; Vance, Jack
    See also CA 29-32R; CANR 17; MTCW

Van Den Bogarde, Derek Jules Gaspard Ulric
    Niven 1921-
    See Bogarde, Dirk
    See also CA 77-80

Vandenburgh, Jane ................ CLC 59

Vanderhaeghe, Guy 1951- ......... CLC 41
    See also CA 113

van der Post, Laurens (Jan) 1906- ... CLC 5
    See also CA 5-8R; CANR 35

van de Wetering, Janwillem 1931- .. CLC 47
    See also CA 49-52; CANR 4

Van Dine, S. S. ................. TCLC 23
    See also Wright, Willard Huntington

Van Doren, Carl (Clinton)
    1885-1950 ................. TCLC 18
    See also CA 111

Van Doren, Mark 1894-1972..... CLC 6, 10
    See also CA 1-4R; 37-40R; CANR 3;
    DLB 45; MTCW

Van Druten, John (William)
    1901-1957 .................. TCLC 2
    See also CA 104; DLB 10

Van Duyn, Mona (Jane)
    1921-................... CLC 3, 7, 63
    See also CA 9-12R; CANR 7, 38;
    DAM POET; DLB 5

Van Dyne, Edith
    See Baum, L(yman) Frank

van Itallie, Jean-Claude 1936-....... CLC 3
    See also CA 45-48; CAAS 2; CANR 1, 48;
    DLB 7

van Ostaijen, Paul 1896-1928 ..... TCLC 33

Van Peebles, Melvin 1932- ...... CLC 2, 20
    See also BW 2; CA 85-88; CANR 27;
    DAM MULT

Vansittart, Peter 1920-............ CLC 42
    See also CA 1-4R; CANR 3, 49

Van Vechten, Carl 1880-1964 ...... CLC 33
    See also CA 89-92; DLB 4, 9, 51

Van Vogt, A(lfred) E(lton) 1912-..... CLC 1
    See also CA 21-24R; CANR 28; DLB 8;
    SATA 14

Varda, Agnes 1928- .............. CLC 16
    See also CA 116; 122

Vargas Llosa, (Jorge) Mario (Pedro)
    1936- .... CLC 3, 6, 9, 10, 15, 31, 42, 85;
                      DA; DAB; DAC; HLC
    See also CA 73-76; CANR 18, 32, 42;
    DAM MST, MULT, NOV; DLB 145;
    HW; MTCW

Vasiliu, Gheorghe 1881-1957
    See Bacovia, George
    See also CA 123

Vassa, Gustavus
    See Equiano, Olaudah

Vassilikos, Vassilis 1933-........ CLC 4, 8
    See also CA 81-84

Vaughan, Henry 1621-1695........ LC 27
    See also DLB 131

Vaughn, Stephanie................. CLC 62

**Vazov, Ivan (Minchov)**
1850-1921 ................. **TCLC 25**
See also CA 121; DLB 147

**Veblen, Thorstein (Bunde)**
1857-1929 ................. **TCLC 31**
See also CA 115

**Vega, Lope de** 1562-1635 .......... **LC 23**

**Venison, Alfred**
See Pound, Ezra (Weston Loomis)

**Verdi, Marie de**
See Mencken, H(enry) L(ouis)

**Verdu, Matilde**
See Cela, Camilo Jose

**Verga, Giovanni (Carmelo)**
1840-1922 .......... **TCLC 3; SSC 21**
See also CA 104; 123

**Vergil**
70B.C.-19B.C. ..... **CMLC 9; DA; DAB;
DAC; PC 12**
See also DAM MST, POET

**Verhaeren, Emile (Adolphe Gustave)**
1855-1916 ................. **TCLC 12**
See also CA 109

**Verlaine, Paul (Marie)**
1844-1896 ..... **NCLC 2, 51; PC 2**
See also DAM POET

**Verne, Jules (Gabriel)**
1828-1905 ............. **TCLC 6, 52**
See also AAYA 16; CA 110; 131; DLB 123;
JRDA; MAICYA; SATA 21

**Very, Jones** 1813-1880 .......... **NCLC 9**
See also DLB 1

**Vesaas, Tarjei** 1897-1970 ......... **CLC 48**
See also CA 29-32R

**Vialis, Gaston**
See Simenon, Georges (Jacques Christian)

**Vian, Boris** 1920-1959 ............ **TCLC 9**
See also CA 106; DLB 72

**Viaud, (Louis Marie) Julien** 1850-1923
See Loti, Pierre
See also CA 107

**Vicar, Henry**
See Felsen, Henry Gregor

**Vicker, Angus**
See Felsen, Henry Gregor

**Vidal, Gore**
1925- ..... **CLC 2, 4, 6, 8, 10, 22, 33, 72**
See also AITN 1; BEST 90:2; CA 5-8R;
CANR 13, 45; DAM NOV, POP; DLB 6,
152; INT CANR-13; MTCW

**Viereck, Peter (Robert Edwin)**
1916- ....................... **CLC 4**
See also CA 1-4R; CANR 1, 47; DLB 5

**Vigny, Alfred (Victor) de**
1797-1863 ................. **NCLC 7**
See also DAM POET; DLB 119

**Vilakazi, Benedict Wallet**
1906-1947 ................. **TCLC 37**

**Villiers de l'Isle Adam, Jean Marie Mathias
Philippe Auguste Comte**
1838-1889 .......... **NCLC 3; SSC 14**
See also DLB 123

**Villon, Francois** 1431-1463(?) ....... **PC 13**

**Vinci, Leonardo da** 1452-1519 ...... **LC 12**

**Vine, Barbara** ................... **CLC 50**
See also Rendell, Ruth (Barbara)
See also BEST 90:4

**Vinge, Joan D(ennison)** 1948- ...... **CLC 30**
See also CA 93-96; SATA 36

**Violis, G.**
See Simenon, Georges (Jacques Christian)

**Visconti, Luchino** 1906-1976 ...... **CLC 16**
See also CA 81-84; 65-68; CANR 39

**Vittorini, Elio** 1908-1966 ..... **CLC 6, 9, 14**
See also CA 133; 25-28R

**Vizinczey, Stephen** 1933- .......... **CLC 40**
See also CA 128; INT 128

**Vliet, R(ussell) G(ordon)**
1929-1984 ................. **CLC 22**
See also CA 37-40R; 112; CANR 18

**Vogau, Boris Andreyevich** 1894-1937(?)
See Pilnyak, Boris
See also CA 123

**Vogel, Paula A(nne)** 1951- ........ **CLC 76**
See also CA 108

**Voight, Ellen Bryant** 1943- ........ **CLC 54**
See also CA 69-72; CANR 11, 29; DLB 120

**Voigt, Cynthia** 1942- ............. **CLC 30**
See also AAYA 3; CA 106; CANR 18, 37,
40; CLR 13; INT CANR-18; JRDA;
MAICYA; SATA 48, 79; SATA-Brief 33

**Voinovich, Vladimir (Nikolaevich)**
1932- ................... **CLC 10, 49**
See also CA 81-84; CAAS 12; CANR 33;
MTCW

**Vollmann, William T.** 1959- ....... **CLC 89**
See also CA 134; DAM NOV, POP

**Voloshinov, V. N.**
See Bakhtin, Mikhail Mikhailovich

**Voltaire**
1694-1778 ..... **LC 14; DA; DAB; DAC;
SSC 12; WLC**
See also DAM DRAM, MST

**von Daeniken, Erich** 1935- ........ **CLC 30**
See also AITN 1; CA 37-40R; CANR 17,
44

**von Daniken, Erich**
See von Daeniken, Erich

**von Heidenstam, (Carl Gustaf) Verner**
See Heidenstam, (Carl Gustaf) Verner von

**von Heyse, Paul (Johann Ludwig)**
See Heyse, Paul (Johann Ludwig von)

**von Hofmannsthal, Hugo**
See Hofmannsthal, Hugo von

**von Horvath, Odon**
See Horvath, Oedoen von

**von Horvath, Oedoen**
See Horvath, Oedoen von

**von Liliencron, (Friedrich Adolf Axel) Detlev**
See Liliencron, (Friedrich Adolf Axel)
Detlev von

**Vonnegut, Kurt, Jr.**
1922- ...... **CLC 1, 2, 3, 4, 5, 8, 12, 22,
40, 60; DA; DAB; DAC; SSC 8; WLC**
See also AAYA 6; AITN 1; BEST 90:4;
CA 1-4R; CANR 1, 25, 49;
CDALB 1968-1988; DAM MST, NOV,
POP; DLB 2, 8, 152; DLBD 3; DLBY 80;
MTCW

**Von Rachen, Kurt**
See Hubbard, L(afayette) Ron(ald)

**von Rezzori (d'Arezzo), Gregor**
See Rezzori (d'Arezzo), Gregor von

**von Sternberg, Josef**
See Sternberg, Josef von

**Vorster, Gordon** 1924- ............ **CLC 34**
See also CA 133

**Vosce, Trudie**
See Ozick, Cynthia

**Voznesensky, Andrei (Andreievich)**
1933- ................. **CLC 1, 15, 57**
See also CA 89-92; CANR 37;
DAM POET; MTCW

**Waddington, Miriam** 1917- ........ **CLC 28**
See also CA 21-24R; CANR 12, 30;
DLB 68

**Wagman, Fredrica** 1937- .......... **CLC 7**
See also CA 97-100; INT 97-100

**Wagner, Richard** 1813-1883 ....... **NCLC 9**
See also DLB 129

**Wagner-Martin, Linda** 1936- ...... **CLC 50**

**Wagoner, David (Russell)**
1926- ................... **CLC 3, 5, 15**
See also CA 1-4R; CAAS 3; CANR 2;
DLB 5; SATA 14

**Wah, Fred(erick James)** 1939- ...... **CLC 44**
See also CA 107; 141; DLB 60

**Wahloo, Per** 1926-1975 ............ **CLC 7**
See also CA 61-64

**Wahloo, Peter**
See Wahloo, Per

**Wain, John (Barrington)**
1925-1994 ........... **CLC 2, 11, 15, 46**
See also CA 5-8R; 145; CAAS 4; CANR 23;
CDBLB 1960 to Present; DLB 15, 27,
139, 155; MTCW

**Wajda, Andrzej** 1926- ............. **CLC 16**
See also CA 102

**Wakefield, Dan** 1932- .............. **CLC 7**
See also CA 21-24R; CAAS 7

**Wakoski, Diane**
1937- .... **CLC 2, 4, 7, 9, 11, 40; PC 15**
See also CA 13-16R; CAAS 1; CANR 9;
DAM POET; DLB 5; INT CANR-9

**Wakoski-Sherbell, Diane**
See Wakoski, Diane

**Walcott, Derek (Alton)**
1930- .... **CLC 2, 4, 9, 14, 25, 42, 67, 76;
BLC; DAB; DAC**
See also BW 2; CA 89-92; CANR 26, 47;
DAM MST, MULT, POET; DLB 117;
DLBY 81; MTCW

**Waldman, Anne** 1945- ............. **CLC 7**
See also CA 37-40R; CAAS 17; CANR 34;
DLB 16

**Waldo, E. Hunter**
See Sturgeon, Theodore (Hamilton)

**Waldo, Edward Hamilton**
See Sturgeon, Theodore (Hamilton)

Walker, Alice (Malsenior)
1944- ....... CLC 5, 6, 9, 19, 27, 46, 58;
BLC; DA; DAB; DAC; SSC 5
See also AAYA 3; BEST 89:4; BW 2;
CA 37-40R; CANR 9, 27, 49;
CDALB 1968-1988; DAM MST, MULT,
NOV, POET, POP; DLB 6, 33, 143;
INT CANR-27; MTCW; SATA 31

Walker, David Harry 1911-1992.... CLC 14
See also CA 1-4R; 137; CANR 1; SATA 8;
SATA-Obit 71

Walker, Edward Joseph 1934-
See Walker, Ted
See also CA 21-24R; CANR 12, 28

Walker, George F.
1947- ........ CLC 44, 61; DAB; DAC
See also CA 103; CANR 21, 43;
DAM MST; DLB 60

Walker, Joseph A. 1935- ......... CLC 19
See also BW 1; CA 89-92; CANR 26;
DAM DRAM, MST; DLB 38

Walker, Margaret (Abigail)
1915- ................ CLC 1, 6; BLC
See also BW 2; CA 73-76; CANR 26;
DAM MULT; DLB 76, 152; MTCW

Walker, Ted...................... CLC 13
See also Walker, Edward Joseph
See also DLB 40

Wallace, David Foster 1962-....... CLC 50
See also CA 132

Wallace, Dexter
See Masters, Edgar Lee

Wallace, (Richard Horatio) Edgar
1875-1932 .................. TCLC 57
See also CA 115; DLB 70

Wallace, Irving 1916-1990...... CLC 7, 13
See also AITN 1; CA 1-4R; 132; CAAS 1;
CANR 1, 27; DAM NOV, POP;
INT CANR-27; MTCW

Wallant, Edward Lewis
1926-1962 ................. CLC 5, 10
See also CA 1-4R; CANR 22; DLB 2, 28,
143; MTCW

Walley, Byron
See Card, Orson Scott

Walpole, Horace 1717-1797......... LC 2
See also DLB 39, 104

Walpole, Hugh (Seymour)
1884-1941 .................. TCLC 5
See also CA 104; DLB 34

Walser, Martin 1927-............ CLC 27
See also CA 57-60; CANR 8, 46; DLB 75,
124

Walser, Robert
1878-1956 .......... TCLC 18; SSC 20
See also CA 118; DLB 66

Walsh, Jill Paton................. CLC 35
See also Paton Walsh, Gillian
See also AAYA 11; CLR 2; DLB 161;
SAAS 3

Walter, Villiam Christian
See Andersen, Hans Christian

Wambaugh, Joseph (Aloysius, Jr.)
1937- .................... CLC 3, 18
See also AITN 1; BEST 89:3; CA 33-36R;
CANR 42; DAM NOV, POP; DLB 6;
DLBY 83; MTCW

Ward, Arthur Henry Sarsfield 1883-1959
See Rohmer, Sax
See also CA 108

Ward, Douglas Turner 1930-....... CLC 19
See also BW 1; CA 81-84; CANR 27;
DLB 7, 38

Ward, Mary Augusta
See Ward, Mrs. Humphry

Ward, Mrs. Humphry
1851-1920 ................. TCLC 55
See also DLB 18

Ward, Peter
See Faust, Frederick (Schiller)

Warhol, Andy 1928(?)-1987........ CLC 20
See also AAYA 12; BEST 89:4; CA 89-92;
121; CANR 34

Warner, Francis (Robert le Plastrier)
1937- ..................... CLC 14
See also CA 53-56; CANR 11

Warner, Marina 1946-........... CLC 59
See also CA 65-68; CANR 21

Warner, Rex (Ernest) 1905-1986.... CLC 45
See also CA 89-92; 119; DLB 15

Warner, Susan (Bogert)
1819-1885 ................. NCLC 31
See also DLB 3, 42

Warner, Sylvia (Constance) Ashton
See Ashton-Warner, Sylvia (Constance)

Warner, Sylvia Townsend
1893-1978 ........ CLC 7, 19; SSC 23
See also CA 61-64; 77-80; CANR 16;
DLB 34, 139; MTCW

Warren, Mercy Otis 1728-1814... NCLC 13
See also DLB 31

Warren, Robert Penn
1905-1989 .... CLC 1, 4, 6, 8, 10, 13, 18,
39, 53, 59; DA; DAB; DAC; SSC 4; WLC
See also AITN 1; CA 13-16R; 129;
CANR 10, 47; CDALB 1968-1988;
DAM MST, NOV, POET; DLB 2, 48,
152; DLBY 80, 89; INT CANR-10;
MTCW; SATA 46; SATA-Obit 63

Warshofsky, Isaac
See Singer, Isaac Bashevis

Warton, Thomas 1728-1790........ LC 15
See also DAM POET; DLB 104, 109

Waruk, Kona
See Harris, (Theodore) Wilson

Warung, Price 1855-1911........ TCLC 45

Warwick, Jarvis
See Garner, Hugh

Washington, Alex
See Harris, Mark

Washington, Booker T(aliaferro)
1856-1915 ............. TCLC 10; BLC
See also BW 1; CA 114; 125; DAM MULT;
SATA 28

Washington, George 1732-1799...... LC 25
See also DLB 31

Wassermann, (Karl) Jakob
1873-1934 .................. TCLC 6
See also CA 104; DLB 66

Wasserstein, Wendy
1950- ........... CLC 32, 59, 90; DC 4
See also CA 121; 129; CABS 3;
DAM DRAM; INT 129

Waterhouse, Keith (Spencer)
1929- ...................... CLC 47
See also CA 5-8R; CANR 38; DLB 13, 15;
MTCW

Waters, Frank (Joseph)
1902-1995 .................. CLC 88
See also CA 5-8R; 149; CAAS 13; CANR 3,
18; DLBY 86

Waters, Roger 1944-.............. CLC 35

Watkins, Frances Ellen
See Harper, Frances Ellen Watkins

Watkins, Gerrold
See Malzberg, Barry N(athaniel)

Watkins, Gloria 1955(?)-
See hooks, bell
See also BW 2; CA 143

Watkins, Paul 1964-.............. CLC 55
See also CA 132

Watkins, Vernon Phillips
1906-1967 .................. CLC 43
See also CA 9-10; 25-28R; CAP 1; DLB 20

Watson, Irving S.
See Mencken, H(enry) L(ouis)

Watson, John H.
See Farmer, Philip Jose

Watson, Richard F.
See Silverberg, Robert

Waugh, Auberon (Alexander) 1939- .. CLC 7
See also CA 45-48; CANR 6, 22; DLB 14

Waugh, Evelyn (Arthur St. John)
1903-1966 ...... CLC 1, 3, 8, 13, 19, 27,
44; DA; DAB; DAC; WLC
See also CA 85-88; 25-28R; CANR 22;
CDBLB 1914-1945; DAM MST, NOV,
POP; DLB 15, 162; MTCW

Waugh, Harriet 1944- ............. CLC 6
See also CA 85-88; CANR 22

Ways, C. R.
See Blount, Roy (Alton), Jr.

Waystaff, Simon
See Swift, Jonathan

Webb, (Martha) Beatrice (Potter)
1858-1943 .................. TCLC 22
See also Potter, Beatrice
See also CA 117

Webb, Charles (Richard) 1939-...... CLC 7
See also CA 25-28R

Webb, James H(enry), Jr. 1946-.... CLC 22
See also CA 81-84

Webb, Mary (Gladys Meredith)
1881-1927 .................. TCLC 24
See also CA 123; DLB 34

Webb, Mrs. Sidney
See Webb, (Martha) Beatrice (Potter)

Webb, Phyllis 1927-.............. CLC 18
See also CA 104; CANR 23; DLB 53

White, Terence de Vere
    1912-1994 . . . . . . . . . . . . . . . . . CLC 49
    See also CA 49-52; 145; CANR 3

White, Walter F(rancis)
    1893-1955 . . . . . . . . . . . . . . . TCLC 15
    See also White, Walter
    See also BW 1; CA 115; 124; DLB 51

White, William Hale    1831-1913
    See Rutherford, Mark
    See also CA 121

Whitehead, E(dward) A(nthony)
    1933- . . . . . . . . . . . . . . . . . . . . . . CLC 5
    See also CA 65-68

Whitemore, Hugh (John)    1936- . . . . . CLC 37
    See also CA 132; INT 132

Whitman, Sarah Helen (Power)
    1803-1878 . . . . . . . . . . . . . . . . NCLC 19
    See also DLB 1

Whitman, Walt(er)
    1819-1892 . . . . . NCLC 4, 31; DA; DAB;
                                    DAC; PC 3; WLC
    See also CDALB 1640-1865; DAM MST,
    POET; DLB 3, 64; SATA 20

Whitney, Phyllis A(yame)    1903- . . . . CLC 42
    See also AITN 2; BEST 90:3; CA 1-4R;
    CANR 3, 25, 38; DAM POP; JRDA;
    MAICYA; SATA 1, 30

Whittemore, (Edward) Reed (Jr.)
    1919- . . . . . . . . . . . . . . . . . . . . . . CLC 4
    See also CA 9-12R; CAAS 8; CANR 4;
    DLB 5

Whittier, John Greenleaf
    1807-1892 . . . . . . . . . . . . . . NCLC 8, 57
    See also CDALB 1640-1865; DAM POET;
    DLB 1

Whittlebot, Hernia
    See Coward, Noel (Peirce)

Wicker, Thomas Grey    1926-
    See Wicker, Tom
    See also CA 65-68; CANR 21, 46

Wicker, Tom . . . . . . . . . . . . . . . . . . . . . CLC 7
    See also Wicker, Thomas Grey

Wideman, John Edgar
    1941- . . . . . . . . . CLC 5, 34, 36, 67; BLC
    See also BW 2; CA 85-88; CANR 14, 42;
    DAM MULT; DLB 33, 143

Wiebe, Rudy (Henry)
    1934- . . . . . . . . . . . . CLC 6, 11, 14; DAC
    See also CA 37-40R; CANR 42;
    DAM MST; DLB 60

Wieland, Christoph Martin
    1733-1813 . . . . . . . . . . . . . . . NCLC 17
    See also DLB 97

Wiene, Robert    1881-1938 . . . . . . . . TCLC 56

Wieners, John    1934- . . . . . . . . . . . . . . CLC 7
    See also CA 13-16R; DLB 16

Wiesel, Elie(zer)
    1928- . . . . . . CLC 3, 5, 11, 37; DA; DAB;
                                                    DAC
    See also AAYA 7; AITN 1; CA 5-8R;
    CAAS 4; CANR 8, 40; DAM MST,
    NOV; DLB 83; DLBY 87; INT CANR-8;
    MTCW; SATA 56

Wiggins, Marianne    1947- . . . . . . . . . CLC 57
    See also BEST 89:3; CA 130

Wight, James Alfred    1916-
    See Herriot, James
    See also CA 77-80; SATA 55;
    SATA-Brief 44

Wilbur, Richard (Purdy)
    1921- . . . CLC 3, 6, 9, 14, 53; DA; DAB;
                                                    DAC
    See also CA 1-4R; CABS 2; CANR 2, 29;
    DAM MST, POET; DLB 5;
    INT CANR-29; MTCW; SATA 9

Wild, Peter    1940- . . . . . . . . . . . . . . . CLC 14
    See also CA 37-40R; DLB 5

Wilde, Oscar (Fingal O'Flahertie Wills)
    1854(?)-1900 . . . . TCLC 1, 8, 23, 41; DA;
                        DAB; DAC; SSC 11; WLC
    See also CA 104; 119; CDBLB 1890-1914;
    DAM DRAM, MST, NOV; DLB 10, 19,
    34, 57, 141, 156; SATA 24

Wilder, Billy . . . . . . . . . . . . . . . . . . . . CLC 20
    See also Wilder, Samuel
    See also DLB 26

Wilder, Samuel    1906-
    See Wilder, Billy
    See also CA 89-92

Wilder, Thornton (Niven)
    1897-1975 . . . . . . CLC 1, 5, 6, 10, 15, 35,
                82; DA; DAB; DAC; DC 1; WLC
    See also AITN 2; CA 13-16R; 61-64;
    CANR 40; DAM DRAM, MST, NOV;
    DLB 4, 7, 9; MTCW

Wilding, Michael    1942- . . . . . . . . . . . CLC 73
    See also CA 104; CANR 24, 49

Wiley, Richard    1944- . . . . . . . . . . . . . CLC 44
    See also CA 121; 129

Wilhelm, Kate . . . . . . . . . . . . . . . . . . . . CLC 7
    See also Wilhelm, Katie Gertrude
    See also CAAS 5; DLB 8; INT CANR-17

Wilhelm, Katie Gertrude    1928-
    See Wilhelm, Kate
    See also CA 37-40R; CANR 17, 36; MTCW

Wilkins, Mary
    See Freeman, Mary Eleanor Wilkins

Willard, Nancy    1936- . . . . . . . . . . . CLC 7, 37
    See also CA 89-92; CANR 10, 39; CLR 5;
    DLB 5, 52; MAICYA; MTCW;
    SATA 37, 71; SATA-Brief 30

Williams, C(harles) K(enneth)
    1936- . . . . . . . . . . . . . . . . . . . CLC 33, 56
    See also CA 37-40R; DAM POET; DLB 5

Williams, Charles
    See Collier, James L(incoln)

Williams, Charles (Walter Stansby)
    1886-1945 . . . . . . . . . . . . . . . TCLC 1, 11
    See also CA 104; DLB 100, 153

Williams, (George) Emlyn
    1905-1987 . . . . . . . . . . . . . . . . . . CLC 15
    See also CA 104; 123; CANR 36;
    DAM DRAM; DLB 10, 77; MTCW

Williams, Hugo    1942- . . . . . . . . . . . . . CLC 42
    See also CA 17-20R; CANR 45; DLB 40

Williams, J. Walker
    See Wodehouse, P(elham) G(renville)

Williams, John A(lfred)
    1925- . . . . . . . . . . . . . . CLC 5, 13; BLC
    See also BW 2; CA 53-56; CAAS 3;
    CANR 6, 26, 51; DAM MULT; DLB 2,
    33; INT CANR-6

Williams, Jonathan (Chamberlain)
    1929- . . . . . . . . . . . . . . . . . . . . . . CLC 13
    See also CA 9-12R; CAAS 12; CANR 8;
    DLB 5

Williams, Joy    1944- . . . . . . . . . . . . . . CLC 31
    See also CA 41-44R; CANR 22, 48

Williams, Norman    1952- . . . . . . . . . . CLC 39
    See also CA 118

Williams, Sherley Anne
    1944- . . . . . . . . . . . . . . . . . CLC 89; BLC
    See also BW 2; CA 73-76; CANR 25;
    DAM MULT, POET; DLB 41;
    INT CANR-25; SATA 78

Williams, Shirley
    See Williams, Sherley Anne

Williams, Tennessee
    1911-1983 . . . . . CLC 1, 2, 5, 7, 8, 11, 15,
            19, 30, 39, 45, 71; DA; DAB; DAC;
                                            DC 4; WLC
    See also AITN 1, 2; CA 5-8R; 108;
    CABS 3; CANR 31; CDALB 1941-1968;
    DAM DRAM, MST; DLB 7; DLBD 4;
    DLBY 83; MTCW

Williams, Thomas (Alonzo)
    1926-1990 . . . . . . . . . . . . . . . . . CLC 14
    See also CA 1-4R; 132; CANR 2

Williams, William C.
    See Williams, William Carlos

Williams, William Carlos
    1883-1963 . . . . CLC 1, 2, 5, 9, 13, 22, 42,
                            67; DA; DAB; DAC; PC 7
    See also CA 89-92; CANR 34;
    CDALB 1917-1929; DAM MST, POET;
    DLB 4, 16, 54, 86; MTCW

Williamson, David (Keith)    1942- . . . . CLC 56
    See also CA 103; CANR 41

Williamson, Ellen Douglas    1905-1984
    See Douglas, Ellen
    See also CA 17-20R; 114; CANR 39

Williamson, Jack . . . . . . . . . . . . . . . . . CLC 29
    See also Williamson, John Stewart
    See also CAAS 8; DLB 8

Williamson, John Stewart    1908-
    See Williamson, Jack
    See also CA 17-20R; CANR 23

Willie, Frederick
    See Lovecraft, H(oward) P(hillips)

Willingham, Calder (Baynard, Jr.)
    1922-1995 . . . . . . . . . . . . . . . . CLC 5, 51
    See also CA 5-8R; 147; CANR 3; DLB 2,
    44; MTCW

Willis, Charles
    See Clarke, Arthur C(harles)

Willy
    See Colette, (Sidonie-Gabrielle)

Willy, Colette
    See Colette, (Sidonie-Gabrielle)

Wilson, A(ndrew) N(orman)    1950- . . CLC 33
    See also CA 112; 122; DLB 14, 155

Wilson, Angus (Frank Johnstone)
1913-1991 . . CLC 2, 3, 5, 25, 34; SSC 21
See also CA 5-8R; 134; CANR 21; DLB 15,
139, 155; MTCW

Wilson, August
1945- . . . . . . . CLC 39, 50, 63; BLC; DA;
DAB; DAC; DC 2
See also AAYA 16; BW 2; CA 115; 122;
CANR 42; DAM DRAM, MST, MULT;
MTCW

Wilson, Brian 1942- . . . . . . . . . . . . . CLC 12

Wilson, Colin 1931- . . . . . . . . . . . CLC 3, 14
See also CA 1-4R; CAAS 5; CANR 1, 22,
33; DLB 14; MTCW

Wilson, Dirk
See Pohl, Frederik

Wilson, Edmund
1895-1972 . . . . . . . . . CLC 1, 2, 3, 8, 24
See also CA 1-4R; 37-40R; CANR 1, 46;
DLB 63; MTCW

Wilson, Ethel Davis (Bryant)
1888(?)-1980 . . . . . . . . . . . CLC 13; DAC
See also CA 102; DAM POET; DLB 68;
MTCW

Wilson, John 1785-1854 . . . . . . . . . NCLC 5

Wilson, John (Anthony) Burgess 1917-1993
See Burgess, Anthony
See also CA 1-4R; 143; CANR 2, 46; DAC;
DAM NOV; MTCW

Wilson, Lanford 1937- . . . . . . . CLC 7, 14, 36
See also CA 17-20R; CABS 3; CANR 45;
DAM DRAM; DLB 7

Wilson, Robert M. 1944- . . . . . . . . CLC 7, 9
See also CA 49-52; CANR 2, 41; MTCW

Wilson, Robert McLiam 1964- . . . . . CLC 59
See also CA 132

Wilson, Sloan 1920- . . . . . . . . . . . . . CLC 32
See also CA 1-4R; CANR 1, 44

Wilson, Snoo 1948- . . . . . . . . . . . . . CLC 33
See also CA 69-72

Wilson, William S(mith) 1932- . . . . . CLC 49
See also CA 81-84

Winchilsea, Anne (Kingsmill) Finch Counte
1661-1720 . . . . . . . . . . . . . . . . . . . . LC 3

Windham, Basil
See Wodehouse, P(elham) G(renville)

Wingrove, David (John) 1954- . . . . . . CLC 68
See also CA 133

Winters, Janet Lewis . . . . . . . . . . . . . CLC 41
See also Lewis, Janet
See also DLBY 87

Winters, (Arthur) Yvor
1900-1968 . . . . . . . . . . . . CLC 4, 8, 32
See also CA 11-12; 25-28R; CAP 1;
DLB 48; MTCW

Winterson, Jeanette 1959- . . . . . . . . CLC 64
See also CA 136; DAM POP

Winthrop, John 1588-1649 . . . . . . . . . LC 31
See also DLB 24, 30

Wiseman, Frederick 1930- . . . . . . . . CLC 20

Wister, Owen 1860-1938 . . . . . . . TCLC 21
See also CA 108; DLB 9, 78; SATA 62

Witkacy
See Witkiewicz, Stanislaw Ignacy

Witkiewicz, Stanislaw Ignacy
1885-1939 . . . . . . . . . . . . . . . . . . TCLC 8
See also CA 105

Wittgenstein, Ludwig (Josef Johann)
1889-1951 . . . . . . . . . . . . . . . . TCLC 59
See also CA 113

Wittig, Monique 1935(?)- . . . . . . . . . CLC 22
See also CA 116; 135; DLB 83

Wittlin, Jozef 1896-1976 . . . . . . . . . . CLC 25
See also CA 49-52; 65-68; CANR 3

Wodehouse, P(elham) G(renville)
1881-1975 . . . CLC 1, 2, 5, 10, 22; DAB;
DAC; SSC 2
See also AITN 2; CA 45-48; 57-60;
CANR 3, 33; CDBLB 1914-1945;
DAM NOV; DLB 34, 162; MTCW;
SATA 22

Woiwode, L.
See Woiwode, Larry (Alfred)

Woiwode, Larry (Alfred) 1941- . . . CLC 6, 10
See also CA 73-76; CANR 16; DLB 6;
INT CANR-16

Wojciechowska, Maia (Teresa)
1927- . . . . . . . . . . . . . . . . . . . . . CLC 26
See also AAYA 8; CA 9-12R; CANR 4, 41;
CLR 1; JRDA; MAICYA; SAAS 1;
SATA 1, 28, 83

Wolf, Christa 1929- . . . . . . . . CLC 14, 29, 58
See also CA 85-88; CANR 45; DLB 75;
MTCW

Wolfe, Gene (Rodman) 1931- . . . . . . CLC 25
See also CA 57-60; CAAS 9; CANR 6, 32;
DAM POP; DLB 8

Wolfe, George C. 1954- . . . . . . . . . . CLC 49
See also CA 149

Wolfe, Thomas (Clayton)
1900-1938 . . . . . TCLC 4, 13, 29, 61; DA;
DAB; DAC; WLC
See also CA 104; 132; CDALB 1929-1941;
DAM MST, NOV; DLB 9, 102; DLBD 2;
DLBY 85; MTCW

Wolfe, Thomas Kennerly, Jr. 1931-
See Wolfe, Tom
See also CA 13-16R; CANR 9, 33;
DAM POP; INT CANR-9; MTCW

Wolfe, Tom . . . . . . . . CLC 1, 2, 9, 15, 35, 51
See also Wolfe, Thomas Kennerly, Jr.
See also AAYA 8; AITN 2; BEST 89:1;
DLB 152

Wolff, Geoffrey (Ansell) 1937- . . . . . CLC 41
See also CA 29-32R; CANR 29, 43

Wolff, Sonia
See Levitin, Sonia (Wolff)

Wolff, Tobias (Jonathan Ansell)
1945- . . . . . . . . . . . . . . . . . CLC 39, 64
See also AAYA 16; BEST 90:2; CA 114;
117; CAAS 22; DLB 130; INT 117

Wolfram von Eschenbach
c. 1170-c. 1220 . . . . . . . . . . . . . CMLC 5
See also DLB 138

Wolitzer, Hilma 1930- . . . . . . . . . . . CLC 17
See also CA 65-68; CANR 18, 40;
INT CANR-18; SATA 31

Wollstonecraft, Mary 1759-1797 . . . . . . LC 5
See also CDBLB 1789-1832; DLB 39, 104,
158

Wonder, Stevie . . . . . . . . . . . . . . . . . CLC 12
See also Morris, Steveland Judkins

Wong, Jade Snow 1922- . . . . . . . . . . CLC 17
See also CA 109

Woodcott, Keith
See Brunner, John (Kilian Houston)

Woodruff, Robert W.
See Mencken, H(enry) L(ouis)

Woolf, (Adeline) Virginia
1882-1941 . . . . . . . TCLC 1, 5, 20, 43, 56;
DA; DAB; DAC; SSC 7; WLC
See also CA 104; 130; CDBLB 1914-1945;
DAM MST, NOV; DLB 36, 100, 162;
DLBD 10; MTCW

Woollcott, Alexander (Humphreys)
1887-1943 . . . . . . . . . . . . . . . . . TCLC 5
See also CA 105; DLB 29

Woolrich, Cornell 1903-1968 . . . . . . . CLC 77
See also Hopley-Woolrich, Cornell George

Wordsworth, Dorothy
1771-1855 . . . . . . . . . . . . . . . . NCLC 25
See also DLB 107

Wordsworth, William
1770-1850 . . . . NCLC 12, 38; DA; DAB;
DAC; PC 4; WLC
See also CDBLB 1789-1832; DAM MST,
POET; DLB 93, 107

Wouk, Herman 1915- . . . . . . . . . CLC 1, 9, 38
See also CA 5-8R; CANR 6, 33;
DAM NOV, POP; DLBY 82;
INT CANR-6; MTCW

Wright, Charles (Penzel, Jr.)
1935- . . . . . . . . . . . . . . . . CLC 6, 13, 28
See also CA 29-32R; CAAS 7; CANR 23,
36; DLB 165; DLBY 82; MTCW

Wright, Charles Stevenson
1932- . . . . . . . . . . . . . . . CLC 49; BLC 3
See also BW 1; CA 9-12R; CANR 26;
DAM MULT, POET; DLB 33

Wright, Jack R.
See Harris, Mark

Wright, James (Arlington)
1927-1980 . . . . . . . . . . . CLC 3, 5, 10, 28
See also AITN 2; CA 49-52; 97-100;
CANR 4, 34; DAM POET; DLB 5;
MTCW

Wright, Judith (Arandell)
1915- . . . . . . . . . . . . . CLC 11, 53; PC 14
See also CA 13-16R; CANR 31; MTCW;
SATA 14

Wright, L(aurali) R. 1939- . . . . . . . . CLC 44
See also CA 138

Wright, Richard (Nathaniel)
1908-1960 . . . . CLC 1, 3, 4, 9, 14, 21, 48,
74; BLC; DA; DAB; DAC; SSC 2; WLC
See also AAYA 5; BW 1; CA 108;
CDALB 1929-1941; DAM MST, MULT,
NOV; DLB 76, 102; DLBD 2; MTCW

Wright, Richard B(ruce) 1937- . . . . . . CLC 6
See also CA 85-88; DLB 53

Wright, Rick 1945- . . . . . . . . . . . . . . CLC 35

Wright, Rowland
See Wells, Carolyn

Wright, Stephen Caldwell 1946- . . . . CLC 33
See also BW 2

Wright, Willard Huntington  1888-1939
See Van Dine, S. S.
See also CA 115

Wright, William  1930- . . . . . . . . . . . CLC 44
See also CA 53-56; CANR 7, 23

Wroth, LadyMary  1587-1653(?) . . . . . LC 30
See also DLB 121

Wu Ch'eng-en  1500(?)-1582(?). . . . . . . LC 7

Wu Ching-tzu  1701-1754 . . . . . . . . . . . LC 2

Wurlitzer, Rudolph  1938(?)- . . . CLC 2, 4, 15
See also CA 85-88

Wycherley, William  1641-1715 . . . . LC 8, 21
See also CDBLB 1660-1789; DAM DRAM;
DLB 80

Wylie, Elinor (Morton Hoyt)
1885-1928 . . . . . . . . . . . . . . . . . . TCLC 8
See also CA 105; DLB 9, 45

Wylie, Philip (Gordon)  1902-1971. . . CLC 43
See also CA 21-22; 33-36R; CAP 2; DLB 9

Wyndham, John. . . . . . . . . . . . . . . . CLC 19
See also Harris, John (Wyndham Parkes
Lucas) Beynon

Wyss, Johann David Von
1743-1818 . . . . . . . . . . . . . . . . NCLC 10
See also JRDA; MAICYA; SATA 29;
SATA-Brief 27

Xenophon
c. 430B.C.-c. 354B.C. . . . . . . . . CMLC 17

Yakumo Koizumi
See Hearn, (Patricio) Lafcadio (Tessima
Carlos)

Yanez, Jose Donoso
See Donoso (Yanez), Jose

Yanovsky, Basile S.
See Yanovsky, V(assily) S(emenovich)

Yanovsky, V(assily) S(emenovich)
1906-1989 . . . . . . . . . . . . . . . CLC 2, 18
See also CA 97-100; 129

Yates, Richard  1926-1992 . . . . . CLC 7, 8, 23
See also CA 5-8R; 139; CANR 10, 43;
DLB 2; DLBY 81, 92; INT CANR-10

Yeats, W. B.
See Yeats, William Butler

Yeats, William Butler
1865-1939 . . . . . TCLC 1, 11, 18, 31; DA;
DAB; DAC; WLC
See also CA 104; 127; CANR 45;
CDBLB 1890-1914; DAM DRAM, MST,
POET; DLB 10, 19, 98, 156; MTCW

Yehoshua, A(braham) B.
1936- . . . . . . . . . . . . . . . . . . . CLC 13, 31
See also CA 33-36R; CANR 43

Yep, Laurence Michael  1948- . . . . . . CLC 35
See also AAYA 5; CA 49-52; CANR 1, 46;
CLR 3, 17; DLB 52; JRDA; MAICYA;
SATA 7, 69

Yerby, Frank G(arvin)
1916-1991 . . . . . . . . . . CLC 1, 7, 22; BLC
See also BW 1; CA 9-12R; 136; CANR 16;
DAM MULT; DLB 76; INT CANR-16;
MTCW

Yesenin, Sergei Alexandrovich
See Esenin, Sergei (Alexandrovich)

Yevtushenko, Yevgeny (Alexandrovich)
1933- . . . . . . . . . . . . CLC 1, 3, 13, 26, 51
See also CA 81-84; CANR 33;
DAM POET; MTCW

Yezierska, Anzia  1885(?)-1970 . . . . . CLC 46
See also CA 126; 89-92; DLB 28; MTCW

Yglesias, Helen  1915- . . . . . . . . . . . CLC 7, 22
See also CA 37-40R; CAAS 20; CANR 15;
INT CANR-15; MTCW

Yokomitsu Riichi  1898-1947 . . . . . TCLC 47

Yonge, Charlotte (Mary)
1823-1901 . . . . . . . . . . . . . . . . TCLC 48
See also CA 109; DLB 18, 163; SATA 17

York, Jeremy
See Creasey, John

York, Simon
See Heinlein, Robert A(nson)

Yorke, Henry Vincent  1905-1974 . . . CLC 13
See also Green, Henry
See also CA 85-88; 49-52

Yosano Akiko  1878-1942 . . TCLC 59; PC 11

Yoshimoto, Banana . . . . . . . . . . . . . . CLC 84
See also Yoshimoto, Mahoko

Yoshimoto, Mahoko  1964-
See Yoshimoto, Banana
See also CA 144

Young, Al(bert James)
1939- . . . . . . . . . . . . . . . . . CLC 19; BLC
See also BW 2; CA 29-32R; CANR 26;
DAM MULT; DLB 33

Young, Andrew (John)  1885-1971. . . . CLC 5
See also CA 5-8R; CANR 7, 29

Young, Collier
See Bloch, Robert (Albert)

Young, Edward  1683-1765. . . . . . . . . . LC 3
See also DLB 95

Young, Marguerite (Vivian)
1909-1995 . . . . . . . . . . . . . . . . . CLC 82
See also CA 13-16; 150; CAP 1

Young, Neil  1945- . . . . . . . . . . . . . . CLC 17
See also CA 110

Young Bear, Ray A.  1950- . . . . . . . . CLC 94
See also CA 146; DAM MULT; NNAL

Yourcenar, Marguerite
1903-1987 . . . . . . . . . CLC 19, 38, 50, 87
See also CA 69-72; CANR 23; DAM NOV;
DLB 72; DLBY 88; MTCW

Yurick, Sol  1925- . . . . . . . . . . . . . . . CLC 6
See also CA 13-16R; CANR 25

Zabolotskii, Nikolai Alekseevich
1903-1958 . . . . . . . . . . . . . . . . TCLC 52
See also CA 116

Zamiatin, Yevgenii
See Zamyatin, Evgeny Ivanovich

Zamora, Bernice (B. Ortiz)
1938- . . . . . . . . . . . . . . . CLC 89; HLC
See also DAM MULT; DLB 82; HW

Zamyatin, Evgeny Ivanovich
1884-1937 . . . . . . . . . . . . . . TCLC 8, 37
See also CA 105

Zangwill, Israel  1864-1926. . . . . . . TCLC 16
See also CA 109; DLB 10, 135

Zappa, Francis Vincent, Jr.  1940-1993
See Zappa, Frank
See also CA 108; 143

Zappa, Frank . . . . . . . . . . . . . . . . . . . CLC 17
See also Zappa, Francis Vincent, Jr.

Zaturenska, Marya  1902-1982. . . . CLC 6, 11
See also CA 13-16R; 105; CANR 22

Zelazny, Roger (Joseph)
1937-1995 . . . . . . . . . . . . . . . . . CLC 21
See also AAYA 7; CA 21-24R; 148;
CANR 26; DLB 8; MTCW; SATA 57;
SATA-Brief 39

Zhdanov, Andrei A(lexandrovich)
1896-1948 . . . . . . . . . . . . . . . . TCLC 18
See also CA 117

Zhukovsky, Vasily  1783-1852 . . . . NCLC 35

Ziegenhagen, Eric . . . . . . . . . . . . . . . CLC 55

Zimmer, Jill Schary
See Robinson, Jill

Zimmerman, Robert
See Dylan, Bob

Zindel, Paul
1936- . . . . . CLC 6, 26; DA; DAB; DAC;
DC 5
See also AAYA 2; CA 73-76; CANR 31;
CLR 3; DAM DRAM, MST, NOV;
DLB 7, 52; JRDA; MAICYA; MTCW;
SATA 16, 58

Zinov'Ev, A. A.
See Zinoviev, Alexander (Aleksandrovich)

Zinoviev, Alexander (Aleksandrovich)
1922- . . . . . . . . . . . . . . . . . . . . . CLC 19
See also CA 116; 133; CAAS 10

Zoilus
See Lovecraft, H(oward) P(hillips)

Zola, Emile (Edouard Charles Antoine)
1840-1902 . . . . . . TCLC 1, 6, 21, 41; DA;
DAB; DAC; WLC
See also CA 104; 138; DAM MST, NOV;
DLB 123

Zoline, Pamela  1941- . . . . . . . . . . . . CLC 62

Zorrilla y Moral, Jose  1817-1893 . . NCLC 6

Zoshchenko, Mikhail (Mikhailovich)
1895-1958 . . . . . . . . . . TCLC 15; SSC 15
See also CA 115

Zuckmayer, Carl  1896-1977. . . . . . . CLC 18
See also CA 69-72; DLB 56, 124

Zuk, Georges
See Skelton, Robin

Zukofsky, Louis
1904-1978 . . . . . . . CLC 1, 2, 4, 7, 11, 18;
PC 11
See also CA 9-12R; 77-80; CANR 39;
DAM POET; DLB 5, 165; MTCW

Zweig, Paul  1935-1984. . . . . . . . CLC 34, 42
See also CA 85-88; 113

Zweig, Stefan  1881-1942 . . . . . . . . TCLC 17
See also CA 112; DLB 81, 118

# Literary Criticism Series
# Cumulative Topic Index

This index lists all topic entries in Gale's *Classical and Medieval Literature Criticism, Contemporary Literary Criticism, Literature Criticism from 1400 to 1800, Nineteenth-Century Literature Criticism,* and *Twentieth-Century Literary Criticism.*

Topic Index

**Topic Index**

# *CLC* Cumulative Nationality Index

**Nationality Index**

Nationality Index

Nationality Index

Nationality Index

Nationality Index

ISBN 0-7876-0768-1

90000